Financial Aid
for African Americans
2012-2014

RSP FINANCIAL AID DIRECTORIES
OF INTEREST TO MINORITIES

College Student's Guide to Merit and Other No-Need Funding
Selected as one of the "Outstanding Titles of the Year" by *Choice,* this directory describes 1,300 no-need funding opportunities for college students. 490 pages. ISBN 1588412121. $32.50, plus $7 shipping.

Directory of Financial Aids for Women
There are 1,400+ funding programs set aside for women described in this biennial directory, which has been called "the cream of the crop" by *School Library Journal* and the "best available reference source" by *Guide to Reference.* 552 pages. ISBN 1588412164. $45, plus $7 shipping.

Financial Aid for African Americans
Nearly 1,300 funding opportunities open to African American college students, professionals, and postdoctorates are described in this award-winning directory. 490 pages. ISBN 1588412172. $42.50, plus $7 shipping.

Financial Aid for Asian Americans
This is the source to use if you are looking for funding for Asian Americans, from college-bound high school seniors to professionals and postdoctorates; more than 1,000 sources of free money are described here. 350 pages. ISBN 1588412180. $40, plus $7 shipping.

Financial Aid for Hispanic Americans
The 1,100 biggest and best sources of free money available to undergraduates, graduates students, professionals, and postdoctorates of Mexican, Puerto Rican, Central American, or other Latin American heritage are described here. 446 pages. ISBN 1588412199. $42.50, plus $7 shipping.

Financial Aid for Native Americans
Detailed information is provided on nearly 1,400 funding opportunities open to American Indians, Native Alaskans, and Native Pacific Islanders for college, graduate school, or professional activities. 506 pages. ISBN 1588412202. $45, plus $7 shipping.

Financial Aid for Research and Creative Activities Abroad
Described here are more than 1,000 scholarships, fellowships, grants, etc. available to support research, professional, or creative activities abroad. 422 pages. ISBN 1588412067. $45, plus $7 shipping.

Financial Aid for Study and Training Abroad
This directory, which the reviewers call "invaluable," describes nearly 1,000 financial aid opportunities available to support study abroad. 362 pages. ISBN 1588412059. $40, plus $7 shipping.

Financial Aid for Veterans, Military Personnel, & Their Families
According to *Reference Book Review,* this directory (with its 1,100 entries) is "the most comprehensive guide available on the subject." 436 pages. ISBN 1588412091. $40, plus $7 shipping.

High School Senior's Guide to Merit and Other No-Need Funding
Here's your guide to 1,100 funding programs that *never* look at income level when making awards to college-bound high school seniors. 416 pages. ISBN 1588412105. $29.95, plus $7 shipping.

Money for Graduate Students in the Arts & Humanities
Use this directory to identify 1,000 funding opportunities available to support graduate study and research in the arts/humanities. 292 pages. ISBN 1588411974. $42.50, plus $7 shipping

Money for Graduate Students in the Biological Sciences
This unique directory focuses solely on funding for graduate study/research in the biological sciences (800+ funding opportunities). 248 pages. ISBN 1588411982. $37.50, plus $7 shipping.

Money for Graduate Students in the Health Sciences
Described here are 1,000+ funding opportunities just for students interested in a graduate degree in dentistry, medicine, nursing, nutrition, pharmacology, etc. 304 pages. ISBN 1588411990. $42.50, plus $7 shipping.

Money for Graduate Students in the Physical & Earth Sciences
Nearly 900 funding opportunities for graduate students in the physical and earth sciences are described in detail here. 276 pages. ISBN 1588412008. $40, plus $7 shipping.

Money for Graduate Students in the Social & Behavioral Sciences
Looking for money for a graduate degree in the social/behavioral sciences? Here are 1,100 funding programs for you. 316 pages. ISBN 1588412016. $42.50, plus $7 shipping.

Financial Aid for African Americans 2012-2014

Gail Ann Schlachter
R. David Weber

A Listing of Scholarships, Fellowships, Grants, Awards, Internships, and Other Sources of Free Money Available Primarily or Exclusively to African Americans, Plus a Set of Six Indexes (Program Title, Sponsoring Organization, Residency, Tenability, Subject, and Deadline Date)

Reference Service Press
El Dorado Hills, California

ISBN 10: 1588412172
ISBN 13: 9781588412171

10 9 8 7 6 5 4 3 2 1

Reference Service Press (RSP) began in 1977 with a single financial aid publication (*The Directory of Financial Aids for Women*) and now specializes in the development of financial aid resources in multiple formats, including books, large print books, print-on-demand reports, eBooks, and online sources. Long recognized as a leader in the field, RSP has been called by the *Simba Report on Directory Publishing* "a true success in the world of independent directory publishers." Both Kaplan Educational Centers and Military.com have hailed RSP as "the leading authority on scholarships."

Reference Service Press
El Dorado Hills Business Park
5000 Windplay Drive, Suite 4
El Dorado Hills, CA 95762-9319
       (916) 939-9620
       Fax: (916) 939-9626
       E-mail: info@rspfunding.com
Visit our web site: www.rspfunding.com

Manufactured in the United States of America
Price: $42.50, plus $7 shipping.

ACADEMIC INSTITUTIONS, LIBRARIES, ORGANIZATIONS AND OTHER QUANTITY BUYERS:
Discounts on this book are available for bulk purchases. Write or call for information on our discount programs.

Contents

Introduction

WHY THIS DIRECTORY IS NEEDED

Despite our country's ongoing economic problems and increased college costs, the financial aid picture for minorities has never looked brighter. Currently, billions of dollars are set aside each year specifically for African Americans, Asian Americans, Hispanic Americans, and Native Americans. This funding is open to minorities at any level (high school through postdoctoral and professional) for a variety of activities, including study, research, travel, training, career development, and creative projects.

While numerous print or online listings have been prepared to identify and describe general financial aid opportunities (those open to all segments of society), those resources have never covered more than a small portion of the programs designed primarily or exclusively for minorities. As a result, many advisors, librarians, scholars, researchers, and students are often unaware of the extensive funding available to African Americans and other minorities. But, with the ongoing publication of *Financial Aid for African Americans,* that has all changed. Here, in just one place, African American students, professionals, and postdoctorates now have current and detailed information about the special resources set aside specifically for them.

Financial Aid for African Americans is prepared biennially as part of Reference Service Press' four-volume *Minority Funding Set* (the other volumes in the set cover funding for Asian Americans, Hispanic Americans, and Native Americans). Each of the volumes in this set is sold separately, or the complete set can be purchased at a discounted price. For more information, contact Reference Service Press's marketing department or visit www.rspfunding.com/prod_prodalpha.html.

No other source, in print or online, offers the extensive coverage provided by these titles. That's why the Grantsmanship Center labeled the set "a must for every organization serving minorities," *Reference Sources for Small and Medium-Sized Libraries* called the titles "the absolute best guides for finding funding," and *Reference Books Bulletin* selected each of the volumes in the *Minority Funding Set* as their "Editor's Choice." *Financial Aid for African Americans,* itself, has also received rave reviews. *Off to College* rated it as "the top of all books of this sort," About.com selected it as one of the seven "Top Financial Aid and Scholarship Guides," and *EMIE Bulletin* called it "the only comprehensive and current listing of programs for this group." Perhaps *Multicultural Review* sums up the critical reaction best: "nothing short of superb."

WHAT'S UPDATED?

The preparation of each new edition of *Financial Aid for African Americans* involves extensive updating and revision. To make sure that the information included here is both reliable and current, the editors at Reference Service Press 1) reviewed and updated all relevant programs covered in the previous edition of the directory, 2) collected information on all programs open to African Americans that were added to Reference Service Press' funding database since the last edition of the directory, and then 3) searched extensively for new program leads in a variety of sources, including printed directories, news reports, journals, newsletters, house organs, annual reports, and sites on the Internet. We only include program descriptions that are written directly from information supplied by the sponsoring organization in print or online (no information is ever taken from secondary sources). When that information could not be found, we sent up to four collection letters (followed by up to three telephone or email inquiries, if necessary) to those sponsors. Despite our best efforts, however, some sponsoring organizations still failed to respond and, as a result, their programs are not included in this edition of the directory.

The 2012-2014 edition of *Financial Aid for African Americans* completely revises and updates the previous (sixth) edition. Programs that have ceased operations have been dropped from the listing. Similarly, programs that have broadened their scope and no longer focus on African Americans have also been removed from the listing. Profiles of continuing programs have been rewritten to reflect current requirements; more than 80 percent of the continuing programs reported substantive changes in their locations, requirements (particularly application deadline), benefits, or eligibility requirements since the 2009-2011 edition. In addition, more than 380 new entries have been added to the program section of the directory. The resulting listing describes the nearly 1,300 biggest and best sources of free money available to African Americans, including scholarships, fellowships, grants, awards, and internships.

WHAT MAKES THIS DIRECTORY UNIQUE?

The 2012-2014 edition of *Financial Aid for African Americans* identifies billions of dollars available for study, research, creative activities, past accomplishments, future projects, professional development, work experience, and many other activities. The listings cover every major subject area, are sponsored by more than 900 different private and public agencies and organizations, and are open to African Americans at any level, from college-bound high school students through professionals and postdoctorates.

Not only does *Financial Aid for African Americans* provide the most comprehensive coverage of available funding (1,292 entries), but it also displays the most informative program descriptions (on the average, more than twice the detail found in any other listing). In addition to this extensive and focused coverage, *Financial Aid for African Americans* also offers several other unique features. First of all, hundreds of funding opportunities listed here have never been covered in any other source. So, even if you have checked elsewhere, you will want to look at *Financial Aid for African Americans* for additional leads. And, here's another plus: all of the funding programs in this edition of the directory offer "free" money; not one of the programs will ever require you to pay anything back (provided, of course, that you meet the program requirements).

Further, unlike other funding directories, which generally follow a straight alphabetical arrangement, *Financial Aid for African Americans* groups entries by intended recipients (undergraduates, graduate students, or professionals/postdoctorates), to make it easy for you to search for appropriate programs. This same convenience is offered in the indexes, where title, sponsoring organization, geographic, subject, and deadline date entries are each subdivided by recipient group.

Finally, we have tried to anticipate all the ways you might wish to search for funding. The volume is organized so you can identify programs not only by intended recipient, but by subject focus, sponsoring organization, program title, residency requirements, where the money can be spent, and even deadline date. Plus, we've included all the information you'll need to decide if a program is right for you: purpose, eligibility requirements, financial data, duration, special features, limitations, number awarded, and application date. You even get fax numbers, toll-free numbers, e-mail addresses, and web sites (when available), along with complete contact information.

WHAT'S EXCLUDED?

While this book is intended to be the most comprehensive source of information on funding available to African Americans, there are some programs we've specifically excluded from the directory:

- *Programs that do not accept applications from U.S. citizens or residents.* If a program is open only to foreign nationals or excludes Americans from applying, it is not covered.

- *Programs that are open equally to all segments of the population.* Only funding opportunities set aside primarily or exclusively for African Americans are included here.

SAMPLE ENTRY

(1) **[390]**

(2) **NATIONAL ACHIEVEMENT
SCHOLARSHIP PROGRAM**

(3) National Merit Scholarship Corporation
Attn: National Achievement Scholarship
1560 Sherman Avenue, Suite 200
Evanston, IL 60201-4897
(847) 866-5100
Web: www.nationalmerit.org/nasp.php

(4) **Summary** To provide financial assistance for college to Black American high school seniors with exceptional scores on the SAT and/or PSAT/NMSQT.

(5) **Eligibility** This program is open to Black American seniors who are enrolled full time in a secondary school and progressing normally toward graduation or completion of high school requirements. Applicants must be U.S. citizens (or intend to become a citizen as soon as qualified) and be planning to attend an accredited college or university in the United States. They must take the PSAT/NMSQT at the proper time in high school (no later than the 11th grade) and mark section 14 on the PSAT/NMSQT answer sheet, which identifies them as a Black American who is requesting consideration in the Achievement Program. Final selection is based on the student's academic record, a self-description, PSAT/NMSQT and SAT scores, and a recommendation written by the principal or another official. Financial information is not considered, nor are college choice, course of study, or career plans.

(6) **Financial data** The stipend is $2,500.

(7) **Duration** 1 year.

(8) **Additional information** A sizeable group of each year's Achievement Program's nonwinners are brought to the attention of U.S. institutions of higher education for the College-Sponsored Achievement Program or for the Corporate-Sponsored Achievement Program. Each winner must enroll as a full-time day student in a course of study leading to 1 of the traditional baccalaureate degrees.

(9) **Number awarded** Approximately 700 each year.

(10) **Deadline** Applicants must take the PSAT/NMSQT no later than October of their junior year.

DEFINITION

(1) **Entry number:** The consecutive number that is given to each entry and used to identify the entry in the index.

(2) **Program title:** Title of scholarship, fellowship, grant, award, internship or other source of free money described in the directory.

(3) **Sponsoring organization:** Name, address, and telephone number, toll-free number, fax number, e-mail address, and/or web site (when information was available) for organization sponsoring the program.

(4) **Summary:** Identifies the major program requirements; read the rest of the entry for additional detail.

(5) **Eligibility:** Qualifications required of applicants, plus information on application procedure and selection process.

(6) **Financial data:** Financial details of the program, including fixed sum, average amount, or range of funds offered, expenses for which funds may and may not be applied, and cash-related benefits supplied (e.g., room and board).

(7) **Duration:** Period for which support is provided; renewal prospects.

(8) **Additional information:** Any unusual (generally nonmonetary) benefits, features, restrictions, or limitations associated with the program.

(9) **Number awarded:** Total number of recipients each year or other specified period.

(10) **Deadline:** The month by which applications must be submitted.

- *Money for study or research outside the United States.* Since there are comprehensive and up-to-date directories that describe the available funding for study, research, and other activities abroad (see the list of Reference Service Press titles opposite the directory's title page), only programs that fund activities in the United States are covered here.

- *Very restrictive programs.* In general, programs are excluded if they are open only to a limited geographic area (less than a state) or offer limited financial support (less than $1,000). Note, however, that the vast majority of programs included here go way beyond that, paying up to full tuition or stipends that exceed $25,000 a year!

- *Programs administered by individual academic institutions solely for their own students.* The directory identifies "portable" programs—ones that can be used at any number of schools. Financial aid administered by individual schools specifically for their own students is not covered. Write directly to the schools you are considering to get information on their offerings.

- *Money that must be repaid.* Only "free money" is identified here. If a program requires repayment or charges interest, it's not listed. Now you can find out about billions of dollars in aid and know (if you meet the program requirements) that not one dollar of that will ever need to be repaid.

HOW THE DIRECTORY IS ORGANIZED

Financial Aid for African Americans is divided into two sections: 1) a detailed list of funding opportunities open to African Americans and 2) a set of six indexes to help you pinpoint appropriate funding programs.

Financial Aid Programs Open to African Americans. The first section of the directory describes 1,292 sources of free money available to African Americans. The focus is on financial aid aimed at American citizens or residents to support study, research, or other activities in the United States. The programs listed here are sponsored by more than 900 different government agencies, professional organizations, corporations, sororities and fraternities, foundations, religious groups, educational associations, and military/veterans organizations. All areas of the sciences, social sciences, and humanities are covered.

To help you focus your search, the entries in this section are grouped into the following three chapters:

- **Undergraduates:** Included here are nearly 600 scholarships, grants, awards, internships, and other sources of free money that support undergraduate study, training, research, or creative activities. These programs are open to high school seniors, high school graduates, currently-enrolled college students, and students returning to college after an absence. Money is available to support these students in any type of public or private postsecondary institution, ranging from technical schools and community colleges to major universities in the United States.

- **Graduate Students:** Described here are nearly 500 fellowships, grants, awards, internships, and other sources of free money that support post-baccalaureate study, training, research, and creative activities. These programs are open to students applying to, currently enrolled in, or returning to a master's, doctoral, professional, or specialist program in public or private graduate schools in the United States.

- **Professionals/Postdoctorates:** Included here are more than 200 funding programs for U.S. citizens or residents who 1) are in professional positions (e.g., artists, writers), whether or not they have an advanced degree; 2) are master's or professional degree recipients; 3) have earned a doctoral degree or its equivalent (e.g., Ph.D., Ed.D., M.D.); or 4) have recognized stature as established scientists, scholars, academicians, or researchers.

Within each of these three chapters, entries appear alphabetically by program title. Since some of the programs supply assistance to more than one specific group, those are listed in all relevant chapters. For example, the Agnes Jones Jackson Scholarships support both undergraduate or graduate study, so the program is described in both the Undergraduates *and* Graduate Students chapters.

Each program entry has been designed to give you a concise profile that, as the sample on page 7 illustrates, includes information (when available) on organization address and telephone numbers (including toll-free and fax numbers), e-mail addresses and web site, purpose, eligibility, money awarded, duration, special features, limitations, number of awards, and application deadline.

The information reported for each of the programs in this section was gathered from research conducted through the beginning of 2012. While the listing is intended to cover as comprehensively as possible the biggest and best sources of free money available to African Americans, some sponsoring organizations did not post information online or respond to our research inquiries and, consequently, are not included in this edition of the directory.

Indexes. To help you find the aid you need, we have constructed six indexes; these will let you access the listings by program title, sponsoring organization, residency, tenability, subject focus, and deadline date. These indexes use a word-by-word alphabetical arrangement. Note: numbers in the index refer to entry numbers, not to page numbers in the book.

Program Title Index. If you know the name of a particular funding program and want to find out where it is covered in the directory, use the Program Title Index. To assist you in your search, every program is listed by all its known names, former names, and abbreviations. Since one program can be included in more than one place (e.g., a program providing assistance to both undergraduate and graduate students is described in both the first and second chapter), each entry number in the index has been coded to indicate the intended recipient group (for example, "U" = Undergraduates; "G" = Graduate Students). By using this coding system, you can avoid duplicate entries and turn directly to the programs that match your eligibility characteristics.

Sponsoring Organization Index. This index makes it easy to identify agencies that offer funding primarily or exclusively to African Americans. More than 900 organizations are indexed here. As in the Program Title Index, we've used a code to help you determine which organizations sponsor programs that match your educational level.

Residency Index. Some programs listed in this book are restricted to African Americans in a particular state or region. Others are open to African Americans wherever they live. This index helps you identify programs available only to residents in your area as well as programs that have no residency requirements. Further, to assist you in your search, we've also indicated the recipient level for the funding offered to residents in each of the areas listed in the index.

Tenability Index. This index identifies the geographic locations where the funding described in *Financial Aid for African Americans* may be used. Index entries (city, county, state, region) are arranged alphabetically (word by word) and subdivided by recipient group. Use this index when you are looking for money to support your activities in a particular geographic area.

Subject Index. This index allows you to identify the subject focus of each of the financial aid opportunities described in *Financial Aid for African Americans.* More than 250 different subject terms are listed. Extensive "see" and "see also" references, as well as recipient group subdivisions, will help you locate appropriate funding opportunities.

Calendar Index. Since most financial aid programs have specific deadline dates, some may have closed by the time you begin to look for funding. You can use the Calendar Index to determine which programs are still open. This index is arranged by recipient group (Undergraduates, Graduate Students, and Professionals/Postdoctorates) and subdivided by month during which the deadline falls. Filing dates can and quite often do vary from year to year; consequently, this index should be used only as a guide for deadlines beyond 2014.

HOW TO USE THE DIRECTORY

Here are some tips to help you get the most out of the funding opportunities listed in *Financial Aid for African Americans.*

To Locate Funding by Recipient Group.   To bring together programs with a similar educational focus, this directory is divided into three chapters: Undergraduates, Graduate Students, and Professionals/Postdoctorates. If you want to get an overall picture of the sources of free money available to African Americans in any of these categories, turn to the appropriate chapter and then review the entries there. Since each of these chapters functions as a self-contained entity, you can browse through any of them without having to first consulting an index.

To Find Information on a Particular Financial Aid Program.   If you know the name of a particular financial aid program, and the group eligible for that award, then go directly to the appropriate chapter in the directory (e.g., Undergraduates, Graduate Students), where you will find the program profiles arranged alphabetically by title. To save time, though, you should always check the Program Title Index first if you know the name of a specific award but are not sure in which chapter it has been listed. Plus, since we index each program by all its known names and abbreviations, you'll also be able to track down a program there when you only know the popular rather than official name.

To Locate Programs Sponsored by a Particular Organization.   The Sponsoring Organization Index makes it easy to identify agencies that provide financial assistance to African Americans or to identify specific financial aid programs offered by a particular organization. Each entry number in the index is coded to identify recipient group (Undergraduates, Graduate Students, Professionals/Postdoctorates), so that you can easily target appropriate entries.

To Browse Quickly Through the Listings.   Look at the listings in the chapter that relates to you (Undergraduates, Graduate Students, or Professionals/Postdoctorates) and read the "Summary" paragraph in each entry. In seconds, you'll know if this is an opportunity that you might want to pursue. If it is, be sure to read the rest of the information in the entry, to make sure you meet all of the program requirements before writing or going online for an application form. Please, save your time and energy. Don't apply if you don't qualify!

To Locate Funding Available to African Americans from or Tenable in a Particular City, County, or State.   The Residency Index identifies financial aid programs open to African Americans in a specific state, region, etc. The Tenability Index shows where the money can be spent. In both indexes, "see" and "see also" references are used liberally, and index entries for a particular geographic area are subdivided by recipient group (Undergraduates, Graduate Students, and Professional/Postdoctorates) to help you identify the funding that's right for you. When using these indexes, always check the listings under the term "United States," since the programs indexed there have no geographic restrictions and can be used in any area.

To Locate Financial Aid Programs Open to African Americans in a Particular Subject Area.   Turn to the Subject Index first if you are interested in identifying funding programs for African Americans that are focused on a particular subject area. To make your search easier, the intended recipient groups (Undergraduates, Graduate Students, Professionals/Postdoctorates) are clearly labeled in the more than 250 subject listings. Extensive cross-references are also provided. Since a large number of programs are not restricted by subject, be sure to check the references listed under the "General programs" heading in the index, in addition to the specific terms that directly relate to your interest areas. The listings under "General programs" can be used to fund activities in any subject area (although the programs may be restricted in other ways).

To Locate Financial Aid Programs for African Americans by Deadline Date.   If you are working with specific time constraints and want to weed out the financial aid programs whose filing dates you won't be able to meet, turn first to the Calendar Index and check the program references listed under the appropriate recipient group and month. Note: not all sponsoring organizations supplied deadline information; those programs are listed under the "Deadline not specified" entries in the index. To identify every relevant financial aid program, regardless of filing date, go the appropriate chapter and read through all the entries there that match your educational level.

To Locate Financial Aid Programs Open to All Segments of the Population. Only programs available to African Americans are listed in this publication. However, there are thousands of other programs that are open equally to all segments of the population. To identify these programs, talk to your local librarian, check with your financial aid office on campus, look at the list of RSP print resources on the page opposite the title page in this directory, or see if your library subscribes to Reference Service Press' interactive online funding database (for more information on that resource, go online to: www.rspfunding.com/esubscriptions.html).

PLANS TO UPDATE THE DIRECTORY

This volume, covering 2012-2014, is the seventh edition of *Financial Aid for African Americans.* The next biennial edition will cover the years 2014-2016 and will be issued in mid-2014.

OTHER RELATED PUBLICATIONS

In addition to *Financial Aid for African Americans,* Reference Service Press publishes several other titles dealing with fundseeking, including the award-winning *Directory of Financial Aids for Women; Financial Aid for the Disabled and Their Families;* and *Financial Aid for Veterans, Military Personnel, and Their Families.* Since each of these titles focuses on a separate population group, there is very little duplication in the listings. For more information on Reference Service Press' award-winning publications, write to the company at 5000 Windplay Drive, Suite 4, El Dorado Hills, CA 95762, give us a call at (916) 939-9620, fax us at (916) 939-9626, send us an e-mail at info@rspfunding.com, or visit our expanded web site: www.rspfunding.com.

ACKNOWLEDGEMENTS

A debt of gratitude is owed all the organizations that contributed information to the 2012-2014 edition of *Financial Aid for African Americans.* Their generous cooperation has helped to make this publication a current and comprehensive survey of awards.

ABOUT THE AUTHORS

Dr. Gail Ann Schlachter has worked for more than three decades as a library manager, a library educator, and an administrator of library-related publishing companies. Among the reference books to her credit are the biennially-issued *Directory of Financial Aids for Women* and two award-winning bibliographic guides: *Minorities and Women: A Guide to Reference Literature in the Social Sciences* (which was chosen as an "outstanding reference book of the year" by *Choice)* and *Reference Sources in Library and Information Services* (which won the first Knowledge Industry Publications "Award for Library Literature"). She was the reference book review editor for *RQ* (now *Reference and User Services Quarterly)* for 10 years, is a past president of the American Library Association's Reference and User Services Association, is the former editor-in-chief of the *Reference and User Services Association Quarterly,* and is currently serving her fifth term on the American Library Association's governing council. In recognition of her outstanding contributions to reference service, Dr. Schlachter has been named the University of Wisconsin School of Library and Information Studies "Alumna of the Year" and has been awarded both the Isadore Gilbert Mudge Citation and the Louis Shores/Oryx Press Award.

Dr. R. David Weber taught history and economics at Los Angeles Harbor College (in Wilmington, California) for many years and continues to teach history as an emeritus professor. During his years of full-time teaching there, and at East Los Angeles College, he directed the Honors Program and was frequently chosen the "Teacher of the Year." He has written a number of critically-acclaimed reference works, including *Dissertations in Urban History* and the three-volume *Energy Information Guide.* With Gail Schlachter, he is the author of Reference Service Press' *Financial Aid for the Disabled and Their Families,* which was selected by *Library Journal* as one of the "best reference books of the year," and a number of other financial aid titles, including the *College Student's Guide to Merit and Other No-Need Funding,* which was chosen as one of the "outstanding reference books of the year" by *Choice.*

Financial Aid Programs
Open to African Americans

Undergraduates ●

Graduate Students ●

Professionals/Postdoctorates ●

Undergraduates

Listed alphabetically by program title and described in detail here are 599 scholarships, scholarship/loans, grants, awards, internships, and other sources of "free money" set aside for African Americans who are college-bound high school seniors or continuing and returning undergraduate students. This funding is available to support study, training, research, and/or creative activities in the United States.

[1]
100 BLACK MEN OF AMERICA NATIONAL SCHOLARSHIP PROGRAM

100 Black Men of America, Inc.
Attn: Scholarship Administrator
141 Auburn Avenue
Atlanta, GA 30303
(404) 688-5100   Toll Free: (800) 598-3411
Fax: (404) 688-1028   E-mail: info@100bmoa.org
Web: www.100blackmen.org

Summary To provide financial assistance for college to African American males and other high school seniors or current undergraduates who submit essays on topics related to African Americans.

Eligibility This program is a to high school seniors and undergraduates who are attending or planning to attend an accredited postsecondary institution as a full-time student. Applicants must have a GPA of 2.5 or higher and have completed at least 50 hours of active community service within the past 12 months. Along with their application, they must submit a 600-word essay on their choice of a topic that changes annually; recently, students were invited to write on 1 of the following: 1) Black male suicide; 2) the war in Iraq; 3) bailout for whom; 4) role of the Black church; or 5) the first African American president. Financial need is not considered in the selection process.

Financial data Stipends range from $1,000 to $3,000 and are paid directly to the institution.

Duration 1 year.

Number awarded Varies each year.

Deadline February of each year.

[2]
ABSALOM JONES SCHOLARSHIP FUND

St. Philip's Episcopal Church
Attn: Absalom Jones Scholarship Selection Committee
522 Main Street
Laurel, MD 20707
(301) 776-5151   Fax: (301) 776-6337
E-mail: absalomjonesfund@stphilipslaurel.org
Web: www.stphilipslaurel.org

Summary To provide financial assistance to African American and other undergraduate and graduate students at schools in any state who have a tie to the Episcopal Diocese of Washington, D.C.

Eligibility This program is open to students who reside, work, attend school, or are members of a parish in the Episcopal Diocese of Washington. Applicants must be attending or planning to attend a college, seminary, or vocational/technical institute in any state as an undergraduate or graduate student. They must be able to demonstrate the qualities for which Absalom Jones, the first African American priest in the Episcopal Church, was noted: compassion, service, leadership, and an emphasis on education. Financial need is considered in the selection process.

Financial data The stipend is $1,000.

Duration 1 year.

Additional information The Episcopal Diocese of Washington serves the District of Columbia and the Maryland counties of Charles, St. Mary's, Prince George's, and Montgomery.

Number awarded 2 each year.

Deadline March of each year.

[3]
ACADEMIC MAJOR-BASED SCHOLARSHIPS OF THE UNITED NEGRO COLLEGE FUND

United Negro College Fund
Attn: Scholarships and Grants Department
8260 Willow Oaks Corporate Drive
P.O. Box 10444
Fairfax, VA 22031-8044
(703) 205-3466   Toll Free: (800) 331-2244
Fax: (703) 205-3574
Web: www.uncf.org/forstudents/scholarship.asp

Summary To provide financial assistance to students who are interested in majoring in specified fields at academic institutions affiliated with the United Negro College Fund (UNCF).

Eligibility These programs are open to students planning to pursue designated majors at UNCF-member institutions. Applicants must be high school graduates with strong academic backgrounds (minimum GPA of 2.5). Students who have completed their junior year in high school with a record of distinction may also be considered. Financial need must be demonstrated. Applications should be submitted directly to the UNCF-member institution the student plans to attend.

Financial data The awards are intended to cover tuition and range from a minimum of $500 to a maximum of $7,500 per year.

Duration 1 year; may be renewed.

Additional information Recipients must attend a UNCF-member institution of higher learning. These are: Miles College, Oakwood College, Stillman College, Talladega College, and Tuskegee University in Alabama; Philander Smith College in Arkansas; Bethune-Cookman College, Edward Waters College, and Florida Memorial College in Florida; Clark Atlanta University, Interdenominational Theological Center, Morehouse College, Paine College, and Spelman College in Georgia; Dillard University and Xavier University in Louisiana; Rust College and Tougaloo College in Mississippi; Bennett College, Johnson C. Smith University, Livingstone College, Saint Augustine's College, and Shaw University in North Carolina; Wilberforce University in Ohio; Allen University, Benedict College, Claflin University, Morris College, and Voorhees College in South Carolina; Fisk University, Lane College, and LeMoyne-Owen College in Tennessee; Huston-Tillotson College, Jarvis Christian College, Paul Quinn College, Texas College, and Wiley College in Texas; and Saint Paul's College and Virginia Union University in Virginia.

Number awarded A total of nearly 1,200 UNCF scholarships are awarded each year.

Deadline Deadline dates vary, depending upon the individual institution's requirements.

[4]
ACCOUNTANCY BOARD OF OHIO EDUCATION ASSISTANCE PROGRAM

Accountancy Board of Ohio
77 South High Street, 18th Floor
Columbus, OH 43215-6128
(614) 466-4135   Fax: (614) 466-2628
Web: acc.ohio.gov/educasst.htm

Summary To provide financial assistance to African American or other minority/financially disadvantaged students enrolled in an accounting education program at Ohio academic institutions approved by the Accountancy Board of Ohio.

Eligibility This program is open to minority and financially disadvantaged Ohio residents who apply as full-time sophomores, juniors, or seniors in an accounting program at an accredited college or university in the state. Students who remain in good standing at their institutions and who enter a qualified fifth-year program are then eligible to receive these funds. Minority is defined as people with significant ancestry from Africa (excluding the Middle East), Asia (excluding the Middle East), Central America and the Caribbean islands, South America, and the islands of the Pacific Ocean; in addition, persons with significant ancestry from the original peoples of North America who are of non-European descent. Financial disadvantage is defined according to information provided on the Free Application for Federal Student Aid (FAFSA). U.S. citizenship or permanent resident status is required.

Financial data The amount of the stipend is determined annually but does not exceed the in-state tuition at Ohio public universities (currently, $10,426).

Duration 1 year (the fifth year of an accounting program). Funds committed to students who apply as sophomores must be used within 5 calendar years of the date of the award; funds committed to students who apply as juniors must be used within 4 years; and funds committed to students who apply as seniors must be used within 3 years. The award is nonrenewable and may only be used when the student enrolls in the fifth year of a program.

Number awarded Several each year.

Deadline Applications may be submitted at any time.

[5]
ACT SIX SCHOLARSHIPS

Act Six
c/o Northwest Leadership Foundation
717 Tacoma Avenue South, Suite A
Tacoma, WA 98402
(253) 272-0771   Fax: (253) 272-0719
E-mail: info@actsix.org
Web: www.actsix.org

Summary To provide financial assistance to African Americans and other residents of Washington and Oregon who come from diverse backgrounds and are interested in attending designated private faith-based universities in those states.

Eligibility This program is open to residents of Washington and Oregon who are high school seniors or recent graduates and planning to enter college as freshmen. Applicants must come from diverse, multicultural backgrounds. They must be planning to attend 1 of the following institutions: George Fox University (Newberg, Oregon), Gonzaga University (Spokane, Washington), Heritage University (Yakima, Washington), Northwest University (Kirkland, Washington), Pacific Lutheran University (Tacoma, Washington), Trinity Lutheran College (Everett, Washington), Warner Pacific College (Portland, Oregon), or Whitworth University (Spokane, Washington). Students are not required to identify as Christians, but they must be interested in engaging in a year-long exploration and discussion of Christian perspectives on leadership, diversity, and reconciliation. Ethnicity and family income are considered as factors in selecting an intentionally diverse group of scholars, but there are no income restrictions and students from all ethnic backgrounds are encouraged to apply.

Financial data The program makes up the difference between any other assistance the student receives and full tuition. For recipients who demonstrate financial need in excess of tuition, awards cover some or all of the cost of room and board, books, travel, and personal expenses.

Duration 1 year; may be renewed.

Number awarded Varies each year; recently, 48 scholarships were awarded to the Washington schools and 21 to the Oregon schools.

Deadline October of each year.

[6]
AFRICAN AMERICAN COMMUNITY COLLEGE SCHOLARSHIP

Scholarship Administrative Services, Inc.
Attn: MEFUSA Program
457 Ives Terrace
Sunnyvale, CA 94087

Summary To provide financial assistance to African American high school seniors who are interested in attending a community college.

Eligibility This program is open to African Americans graduating from high schools anywhere in the United States. Applicants must be planning to attend a community college on a full-time basis. Along with their application, they must submit a 1,000-word essay on their educational and career goals, how a community college education will help them to achieve those goals, and how they plan to serve the African American community after completing their education. Selection is based on the essay, high school GPA (2.5 or higher), SAT or ACT scores, involvement in the African American community, and financial need.

Financial data The stipend is $5,000 per year.

Duration 1 year; may be renewed 1 additional year if the recipient maintains full-time enrollment and a GPA of 2.5 or higher.

Additional information This program is sponsored by the Minority Educational Foundation of the United States of America (MEFUSA) and administered by Scholarship Administrative Services, Inc. MEFUSA was established in 2001 to meet the needs of minority students who "show a determination to get a college degree," but who, for financial or other personal reasons, are not able to attend a 4-year college or university. Requests for applications should be accompanied by a self-addressed stamped envelope, the student's e-mail address, and the name of the source where they found the scholarship information.

Number awarded Up to 100 each year.

Deadline April of each year.

[7]
AFRICAN AMERICAN FUTURE ACHIEVERS SCHOLARSHIP PROGRAM

Ronald McDonald House Charities
Attn: U.S. Scholarship Program
One Kroc Drive
Oak Brook, IL 60523
(630) 623-7048   Fax: (630) 623-7488
E-mail: info@rmhc.org
Web: rmhc.org/what-we-do/rmhc-u-s-scholarships

Summary To provide financial assistance for college to African American high school seniors in specified geographic areas.

Eligibility This program is open to high school seniors in designated McDonald's market areas who are legal residents of the United States and have at least 1 parent of African American or Black Caribbean heritage. Applicants must be planning to enroll full time at an accredited 2- or 4-year college, university, or vocational/technical school. They must have a GPA of 2.7 or higher. Along with their application, they must submit a personal statement, up to 2 pages in length, on their African American or Black Caribbean background, career goals, and desire to contribute to their community; information about unique, personal, or financial circumstances may be added. Selection is based on that statement, high school transcripts, a letter of recommendation, and financial need.

Financial data Most awards are $1,000 per year. Funds are paid directly to the recipient's school.

Duration 1 year; nonrenewable.

Additional information This program is a component of the Ronald McDonald House Charities U.S. Scholarship Program, which began in 1985. It is administered by International Scholarship and Tuition Services, Inc., 200 Crutchfield Avenue, Nashville, TN 37210, (615) 320-3149, Fax: (615) 320-3151, E-mail: info@applyists.com. For a list of participating McDonald's market areas, contact Ronald McDonald House Charities (RMHC).

Number awarded Varies each year; since RMHC began this program, it has awarded more than $37 million in scholarships.

Deadline February of each year.

[8]
AFRO-ACADEMIC, CULTURAL, TECHNOLOGICAL AND SCIENTIFIC OLYMPICS (ACT-SO)

National Association for the Advancement of Colored People
Attn: ACT-SO Director
4805 Mt. Hope Drive
Baltimore, MD 21215
(410) 580-5650   Toll Free: (877) NAACP-98
E-mail: ACTSO@naacpnet.org
Web: www.naacp.org/programs/entry/act-so

Summary To recognize and reward (with college scholarships) outstanding African American high school students who distinguish themselves in the Afro-Academic, Cultural, Technological and Scientific Olympics (ACT-SO) program.

Eligibility This competition is open to high school students (grades 9-12) of African descent who are U.S. citizens and amateurs in the category in which they wish to participate. Competitions are held in 26 categories in 5 general areas: humanities (music composition, original essay, playwriting, and poetry), sciences (biology and microbiology, biochemistry, computer science, earth and space science, engineering, mathematics, medicine and health, and physics), performing arts (dance, dramatics, music instrumental/classical, music instrumental/contemporary, music vocal/classical, music vocal/contemporary, and oratory), visual arts (architecture, drawing, filmmaking, painting, photography, and sculpture), and business (entrepreneurship). Competition is first conducted by local chapters of the NAACP; winners in each event at the local level then compete at the national level.

Financial data In each category, the first-prize winner receives a gold medal and a $1,000 scholarship, the second-prize winner receives a silver medal and a $750 scholarship, and the third-prize winner receives a bronze medal and a $500 scholarship.

Duration The competition is held annually.

Additional information This competition began in 1977.

Number awarded 78 each year: 3 in each of 26 categories.

Deadline Local competitions usually take place between February and April. The national finals are held each year in July.

[9]
AGNES JONES JACKSON SCHOLARSHIPS

National Association for the Advancement of Colored People
Attn: Education Department
4805 Mt. Hope Drive
Baltimore, MD 21215-3297
(410) 580-5760   Toll Free: (877) NAACP-98
E-mail: youth@naacpnet.org
Web: www.naacp.org/pages/naacp-scholarships

Summary To provide financial assistance to members of the National Association for the Advancement of Colored People (NAACP) who are attending or planning to attend college or graduate school.

Eligibility This program is open to members of the NAACP who are younger than 25 years of age and full-time undergraduates or full- or part-time graduate students. The minimum GPA is 2.5 for graduating high school seniors and undergraduate students or 3.0 for graduate students. All applicants must be able to demonstrate financial need (family income must be less than $16,245 for a family of 1, ranging up to $49,905 for a family of 7) and U.S. citizenship. Along with their application, they must submit a 1-page essay on their interest in their major and a career, their life's ambition, what they hope to accomplish in their lifetime, and what position they hope to attain.

Financial data The stipend is $1,500 per year for undergraduate students or $2,500 per year for graduate students.

Duration 1 year; recipients may apply for renewal.

Number awarded Varies each year; recently, 5 of these scholarships were awarded.

Deadline March of each year.

[10]
AHIMA FOUNDATION DIVERSITY SCHOLARSHIPS

American Health Information Management Association
Attn: AHIMA Foundation
233 North Michigan Avenue, 21st Floor
Chicago, IL 60601-5809
(312) 233-1175   Fax: (312) 233-1475
E-mail: info@ahimafoundation.org
Web: www.ahimafoundation.org

Summary To provide financial assistance to African Americans and other members of the American Health Information Management Association (AHIMA) who are interested in working on an undergraduate degree in health information administration or technology and will contribute to diversity in the profession.

Eligibility This program is open to AHIMA members who are enrolled at least half time in a program accredited by the Commission on Accreditation of Allied Health Education Programs. Applicants must be working on an associate degree in health information technology or a bachelor's degree in health information administration. They must have a GPA of 3.0 or higher and at least 1 full semester remaining after the date of the award. To qualify for this support, applicants must demonstrate how they will contribute to diversity in the health information management profession; diversity is defined as differences in race, ethnicity, nationality, gender, sexual orientation, socioeconomic status, age, physical capabilities, and religious beliefs. Financial need is not considered in the selection process.

Financial data Stipends are $1,000 for students working on an associate degree or $1,200 for students working on a bachelor's degree.

Duration 1 year.

Number awarded Varies each year; recently, 8 of these scholarships were awarded.

Deadline April or October of each year.

[11]
AIR FORCE ENHANCED ROTC HISTORICALLY BLACK COLLEGES AND UNIVERSITIES SCHOLARSHIP PROGRAM

U.S. Air Force
Attn: Headquarters AFROTC/RRUC
551 East Maxwell Boulevard
Maxwell AFB, AL 36112-5917
(334) 953-2091   Toll Free: (866) 4-AFROTC
Fax: (334) 953-6167   E-mail: afrotc1@maxwell.af.mil
Web: afrotc.com

Summary To provide financial assistance to students at designated Historically Black Colleges and Universities (HBCUs) who are willing to join Air Force ROTC and serve as Air Force officers following completion of their bachelor's degree.

Eligibility This program is open to U.S. citizens at least 17 years of age who are currently enrolled as freshmen at 1 of the 7 HBCUs that have an Air Force ROTC unit on campus. Applicants must have a cumulative GPA of 2.5 or higher. At the time of commissioning, they may be no more than 31 years of age. They must be able to pass the Air Force Officer Qualifying Test (AFOQT) and the Air Force ROTC Physical

Fitness Test. Currently, the program is accepting applications from students with any major.

Financial data Awards are type 2 AFROTC scholarships that provide for payment of tuition and fees, to a maximum of $18,000 per year, plus an annual book allowance of $900. Recipients are also awarded a tax-free subsistence allowance for 10 months of each year that is $350 per month during the sophomore year, $450 during the junior year, and $500 during the senior year.

Duration Up to 3 and a half years (beginning as early as the spring semester of the freshman year).

Additional information The participating HBCUs are Tuskegee University (Tuskegee, Alabama), Alabama State University (Montgomery, Alabama), Howard University (Washington, D.C.), North Carolina A&T State University (Greensboro, North Carolina), Fayetteville State University (Fayetteville, North Carolina), Tennessee State University (Nashville, Tennessee), and Jackson State University (Jackson, Mississippi). While scholarship recipients can major in any subject, they must complete 4 years of aerospace courses at 1 of the HBCUs that have an Air Force ROTC unit on campus. Recipients must also attend a 4-week summer training camp at an Air Force base, usually between their sophomore and junior years; 2-year scholarship awardees attend in the summer after their junior year. Current military personnel are eligible for early release from active duty in order to enter the Air Force ROTC program. Following completion of their bachelor's degree, scholarship recipients earn a commission as a second lieutenant in the Air Force and serve at least 4 years.

Number awarded Up to 105 each year: 15 at each of the participating AFROTC units.

Deadline Applications may be submitted at any time.

[12]
AIR FORCE REGULAR ROTC HISTORICALLY BLACK COLLEGES AND UNIVERSITIES SCHOLARSHIP PROGRAM

U.S. Air Force
Attn: Headquarters AFROTC/RRUC
551 East Maxwell Boulevard
Maxwell AFB, AL 36112-5917
(334) 953-2091   Toll Free: (866) 4-AFROTC
Fax: (334) 953-6167   E-mail: afrotc1@maxwell.af.mil
Web: afrotc.com

Summary To provide financial assistance to students at Historically Black Colleges and Universities (HBCUs) who are willing to serve as Air Force officers following completion of their bachelor's degree.

Eligibility This program is open to U.S. citizens at least 17 years of age who are currently enrolled at an HBCU that has an Air Force ROTC unit on campus or that has a cross-enrollment agreement with another school that hosts a unit. Applicants do not need to be African American, as long as they are attending an HBCU and have a cumulative GPA of 2.5 or higher. At the time of commissioning, they may be no more than 31 years of age. They must be able to pass the Air Force Officer Qualifying Test (AFOQT) and the Air Force ROTC Physical Fitness Test. Currently, the program is accepting applications from students with any major.

Financial data Awards are type 2 AFROTC scholarships that provide for payment of tuition and fees, to a maximum of

$18,000 per year, plus an annual book allowance of $900. Recipients are also awarded a tax-free subsistence allowance for 10 months of each year that is $350 per month during the sophomore year, $450 during the junior year, and $500 during the senior year.

Duration 2 to 3 years, beginning during the current term.

Additional information While scholarship recipients can major in any subject, they must complete 4 years of aerospace courses at 1 of the HBCUs that have an Air Force ROTC unit on campus. Recipients must also attend a 4-week summer training camp at an Air Force base, usually between their sophomore and junior years; 2-year scholarship awardees attend in the summer after their junior year. Current military personnel are eligible for early release from active duty in order to enter the Air Force ROTC program. Following completion of their bachelor's degree, scholarship recipients earn a commission as a second lieutenant in the Air Force and serve at least 4 years.

Number awarded Varies each year; AFROTC units at every HBCU may nominate an unlimited number of cadets to receive these scholarships.

Deadline Applications may be submitted at any time.

[13]
ALAN COMPTON AND BOB STANLEY MINORITY AND INTERNATIONAL SCHOLARSHIP

Baptist Communicators Association
Attn: Scholarship Committee
1715-K South Rutherford Boulevard, Suite 295
Murfreesboro, TN 37130
(615) 904-0152   E-mail: bca.office@comcast.net
Web: www.baptistcommunicators.org/about/scholarship.cfm

Summary To provide financial assistance to African American and other minority or international students who are working on an undergraduate degree to prepare for a career in Baptist communications.

Eligibility This program is open to undergraduate students of minority or international origin. Applicants must be majoring in communications, English, journalism, or public relations with a GPA of 2.5 or higher. Their vocational objective must be in Baptist communications. Along with their application, they must submit a statement explaining why they want to receive this scholarship.

Financial data The stipend is $1,000.

Duration 1 year; recipients may reapply.

Additional information This program was established in 1996.

Number awarded 1 each year.

Deadline December of each year.

[14]
ALLISON E. FISHER SCHOLARSHIP

National Association of Black Journalists
Attn: Program Coordinator
8701-A Adelphi Road
Adelphi, MD 20783-1716
(301) 445-7100, ext. 108   Toll Free: (866) 479-NABJ
Fax: (301) 445-7101   E-mail: nabj@nabj.org
Web: www.nabj.org

Summary To provide financial assistance to undergraduate or graduate student members of the National Association of Black Journalists (NABJ) who are majoring in journalism.

Eligibility This program is open to African American undergraduate or graduate students who are currently attending an accredited 4-year college or university. Applicants must be majoring in print or broadcast journalism, have a GPA of 3.0 or higher, and be able to demonstrate community service. They must be NABJ members. Along with their application, they must submit samples of their work, an official college transcript, 2 letters of recommendation, a resume, and a 500- to 800-word essay describing their accomplishments as a student journalist, their career goals, and their financial need.

Financial data The stipend is $2,500. Funds are paid directly to the recipient's college or university.

Duration 1 year; nonrenewable.

Number awarded 1 each year.

Deadline April of each year.

[15]
ALMA EXLEY SCHOLARSHIP

Community Foundation of Greater New Britain
Attn: Scholarship Manager
74A Vine Street
New Britain, CT 06052-1431
(860) 229-6018, ext. 305   Fax: (860) 225-2666
E-mail: cfarmer@cfgnb.org
Web: www.cfgnb.org

Summary To provide financial assistance to African American and other minority college students in Connecticut who are interested in preparing for a teaching career.

Eligibility This program is open to students of color (African Americans, Asian Americans, Hispanic Americans, and Native Americans) enrolled in a teacher preparation program in Connecticut. Applicant must 1) have been admitted to a traditional teacher preparation program at an accredited 4-year college or university in the state; or 2) be participating in the Alternate Route to Certification (ARC) program sponsored by the Connecticut Department of Higher Education.

Financial data The stipend is $1,500 per year for students at a 4-year college or university or $500 for a student in the ARC program.

Duration 2 years for students at 4-year colleges or universities; 1 year for students in the ARC program.

Number awarded 2 each year: 1 to a 4-year student and 1 to an ARC student.

Deadline October of each year.

[16]
ALPHA KAPPA ALPHA ENDOWMENT AWARDS

Alpha Kappa Alpha Sorority, Inc.
Attn: Educational Advancement Foundation
5656 South Stony Island Avenue
Chicago, IL 60637
(773) 947-0026   Toll Free: (800) 653-6528
Fax: (773) 947-0277   E-mail: akaeaf@akaeaf.net
Web: www.akaeaf.org/fellowships_endowments.htm

Summary To provide financial assistance to undergraduate and graduate students (especially African American women) who meet designated requirements.

Eligibility This program is open to undergraduate and graduate students who are enrolled full time as sophomores or higher in an accredited degree-granting institution and are planning to continue their program of education. Applicants may apply for scholarships that include specific requirements established by the donor of the endowment that supports it. Along with their application, they must submit 1) a list of honors, awards, and scholarships received; 2) a list of organizations in which they have memberships, especially minority organizations; and 3) a statement of their personal and career goals, including how this scholarship will enhance their ability to attain those goals. The sponsor is a traditionally African American women's sorority.

Financial data Award amounts are determined by the availability of funds from the particular endowment. Recently, stipends averaged more than $1,700 per year.

Duration 1 year or longer.

Additional information Each endowment establishes its own requirements. Examples of requirements include residence of the applicant, major field of study, minimum GPA, attendance at an Historically Black College or University (HBCU) or member institution of the United Negro College Fund (UNCF), or other personal feature. For further information on all endowments, contact the sponsor.

Number awarded Varies each year; recently, 30 of these scholarships, with a total value of $52,082, were awarded.

Deadline April of each year.

[17]
ALPHA KAPPA ALPHA UNDERGRADUATE SCHOLARSHIPS

Alpha Kappa Alpha Sorority, Inc.
Attn: Educational Advancement Foundation
5656 South Stony Island Avenue
Chicago, IL 60637
(773) 947-0026   Toll Free: (800) 653-6528
Fax: (773) 947-0277   E-mail: akaeaf@akaeaf.net
Web: www.akaeaf.org/undergraduate_scholarships.htm

Summary To provide financial assistance to students (especially African American women) who are working on an undergraduate degree in any field.

Eligibility This program is open to undergraduate students who are enrolled full time as sophomores or higher in an accredited degree-granting institution and are planning to continue their program of education. Applicants may apply either for a scholarship based on merit (requires a GPA of 3.0 or higher) or on financial need (requires a GPA of 2.5 or higher). Along with their application, they must submit 1) a list of honors, awards, and scholarships received; 2) a list of organizations in which they have memberships, especially minority organizations; and 3) a statement of their personal and career goals, including how this scholarship will enhance their ability to attain those goals. The sponsor is a traditionally African American women's sorority.

Financial data Stipends range from $750 to $2,500.

Duration 1 year; nonrenewable.

Number awarded Varies each year; recently, 69 of these scholarships, with a total value of $74,700 were awarded.

Deadline April of each year.

[18]
ALPHA PHI ALPHA FRATERNITY SCHOLARSHIPS

Alpha Phi Alpha Fraternity, Inc.
Attn: Director of Educational Activities
2313 St. Paul Street
Baltimore, MD 21218-5234
(410) 554-0040   Fax: (410) 554-0054
E-mail: jjames@apa1906.net
Web: www.alpha-phi-alpha.com/Page.php?id=102

Summary To provide financial assistance for college or graduate school to brothers of Alpha Phi Alpha Fraternity.

Eligibility This program is open to brothers of the fraternity who either 1) are working full time on an undergraduate degree, or 2) have been admitted to a graduate or professional program. Applicants must have a GPA of 3.5 or higher. Along with their application, they must submit a resume, a list of their involvement in the fraternity's national programs and special projects, an official transcript, 3 letters of recommendation, and an essay on their career ambitions, goals, and why they should be awarded the scholarship.

Financial data The stipend is $1,500.

Duration 1 year.

Additional information Alpha Phi Alpha is the first collegiate fraternity established primarily for African American men.

Number awarded 15 each year: 3 in each of the fraternity's 5 geographic regions.

Deadline April of each year.

[19]
ALPHONSO DEAL SCHOLARSHIP AWARD

National Black Police Association
1409 South Lamar, Suite 211
Dallas, TX 75215
(214) 421-7644   Fax: (214) 421-8408
E-mail: nationaloffice@blackpolice.org
Web: www.blackpolice.org/scholarships.html

Summary To provide financial assistance to African American high school seniors interested in preparing for a career in criminal justice.

Eligibility This program is open to high school seniors who are planning to attend an accredited 2- or 4-year college or university to prepare for a career in criminal justice. Applicants must be U.S. citizens and of good character. Along with their application, they must submit a brief statement describing the course of study they plan to pursue and their general outlook as to future endeavors. Selection is based on academic record, extracurricular activities, and recommendations; financial need is not considered.

Financial data A stipend is awarded (amount not specified).

Duration 1 year.

Deadline May of each year.

[20]
ALTRIA SCHOLARSHIPS OF THE THURGOOD MARSHALL COLLEGE FUND

Thurgood Marshall College Fund
Attn: Scholarship Manager
80 Maiden Lane, Suite 2204
New York, NY 10038
(212) 573-8487   Toll Free: (877) 690-8673
Fax: (212) 573-8497   E-mail: srogers@tmcfund.org
Web: www.thurgoodmarshallfund.net

Summary To provide financial assistance to African American upper-division students working on a degree in designated fields at selected universities.

Eligibility This program is open to full-time students currently enrolled as sophomores at Florida A&M University, Harris-Stowe State University, Howard University, North Carolina A&T State University, Virginia State University, or Winston-Salem State University. Applicants must be majoring in accounting, business, finance, engineering, or technology. They must have a GPA of 3.5 or higher and be able to demonstrate financial need.

Financial data The stipend is $2,200 per semester ($4,400 per year).

Duration 1 year.

Additional information This program is sponsored by Altria Group (parent company of Philip Morris USA). Recipients also have a opportunity to apply for paid summer internships at the company between their junior and senior year.

Number awarded 17 each year.

Deadline Deadline not specified.

[21]
AME CHURCH PREACHER'S KID SCHOLARSHIP

African Methodist Episcopal Church
Connectional Ministers' Spouses, Widows and Widowers
  Organization
c/o Jennifer Green, Scholarship Committee Chair
2386 S.W. 102nd Avenue
Miramar, FL 33025-6509
E-mail: ConnMSWAWOPk@aol.com
Web: www.amemswwpk.org/pr01.htm

Summary To provide financial assistance for college to children of ministers in the African Methodist Episcopal (AME) Church.

Eligibility This program is open to dependent children under 21 years of age whose parent or legal guardian is an AME minister. Applicants must be a member of the AME Church, have a satisfactory score on the SAT or ACT, rank in the top 50% of their high school class, and have a cumulative GPA of 2.5 or higher. Along with their application, they must submit a 300-word essay on how the AME Church has made a difference in their life and what they will do to support their church. Their minister parent must be a member of the Connectional AME Ministers' Spouses, Widows and Widowers Organization.

Financial data The scholarship stipend is $2,500. Book awards are $500.

Duration 1 year.

Number awarded Varies each year; recently, the program awarded 1 scholarship for districts 14-20 (which serve Africa and the Caribbean) and 4 book awards for districts 1-20 (which includes districts 1-13 that serve the United States).

Deadline April of each year.

[22]
AMERICAN ASSOCIATION OF BLACKS IN ENERGY NATIONAL SCHOLARSHIPS

American Association of Blacks in Energy
Attn: Scholarship Committee
1625 K Street, N.W., Suite 405
Washington, DC 20006
(202) 371-9530   Fax: (202) 371-9218
E-mail: info@aabe.org
Web: aabe.org/index.php?component=pages&id=4

Summary To provide financial assistance to African Americans and other underrepresented minority high school seniors who are interested in majoring in business, engineering, mathematics, or physical science in college.

Eligibility This program is open to members of minority groups underrepresented in energy-related fields (African Americans, Hispanics, and Native Americans) who are graduating high school seniors. Applicants must have a "B" academic average overall and a "B" average in mathematics and science courses. They must be planning to attend an accredited college or university to major in business, engineering, mathematics, technology, or the physical sciences. Along with their application, they must submit a transcript, 2 letters of reference, and documentation of financial need. The applicant who demonstrates the most outstanding achievement and promise is presented with the Premier Award. All applications must be submitted to the local office of the sponsoring organization in the student's state. For a list of local offices, contact the scholarship committee at the national office.

Financial data The stipends are $3,000. The Premier Award is an additional $5,000. All funds are paid directly to the students upon proof of enrollment at an accredited college or university.

Duration 1 year; nonrenewable.

Number awarded 6 each year (1 in each of the organization's regions); of those 6 winners, 1 is chosen to receive the Premier Award.

Deadline March of each year.

[23]
AMERICAN CHEMICAL SOCIETY SCHOLARS PROGRAM

American Chemical Society
Attn: Department of Diversity Programs
1155 16th Street, N.W.
Washington, DC 20036
(202) 872-6250   Toll Free: (800) 227-5558, ext. 6250
Fax: (202) 872-4361   E-mail: scholars@acs.org
Web: portal.acs.org

Summary To provide financial assistance to African Americans and other underrepresented minority students who have a strong interest in chemistry and a desire to prepare for a career in a chemically-related science.

Eligibility This program is open to 1) college-bound high school seniors; 2) freshmen, sophomores, and juniors enrolled full time at an accredited college or university; 3) community college graduates and transfer students who plan to study for a bachelor's degree; and 4) community college freshmen. Applicants must be African American, Hispanic/Latino, or American Indian. They must be majoring or planning to major in chemistry, biochemistry, chemical engineering, or other chemically-related fields, such as environmental science, materials science, or toxicology, in preparation for a career in the chemical sciences or chemical technology. Students planning careers in medicine or pharmacy are not eligible. U.S. citizenship or permanent resident status is required. Selection is based on academic record (GPA of 3.0 or higher), career objective, leadership ability, participation in school activities, community service, and financial need.

Financial data Stipends range up to $5,000 per year. Funds are sent directly to the recipient's college or university.

Duration 1 year; may be renewed.

Additional information This program was established in 1994.

Number awarded Approximately 135 new awards are granted each year.

Deadline February of each year.

[24]
AMERICAN METEOROLOGICAL SOCIETY UNDERGRADUATE NAMED SCHOLARSHIPS

American Meteorological Society
Attn: Fellowship/Scholarship Program
45 Beacon Street
Boston, MA 02108-3693
(617) 227-2426, ext. 246   Fax: (617) 742-8718
E-mail: scholar@ametsoc.org
Web: www.ametsoc.org

Summary To provide financial assistance to undergraduates (especially African Americans or other minorities and women) who are majoring in meteorology or an aspect of atmospheric sciences.

Eligibility This program is open to full-time students entering their final year of undergraduate study and majoring in meteorology or an aspect of the atmospheric or related oceanic and hydrologic sciences. Applicants must intend to make atmospheric or related sciences their career. They must be U.S. citizens or permanent residents enrolled at a U.S. institution and have a cumulative GPA of 3.25 or higher. Along with their application, they must submit 200-word essays on 1) their most important attributes and achievements that qualify them for this scholarship, and 2) their career goals in the atmospheric or related sciences. Financial need is considered in the selection process. The sponsor specifically encourages applications from women, minorities, and students with disabilities who are traditionally underrepresented in the atmospheric and related oceanic sciences.

Financial data Stipend amounts vary each year.

Duration 1 year.

Additional information All scholarships awarded through this program are named after individuals who have assisted the sponsor in various ways.

Number awarded Varies each year; recently, 20 of these scholarships were awarded.

Deadline February of each year.

[25]
ANA MULTICULTURAL EXCELLENCE SCHOLARSHIP

American Association of Advertising Agencies
Attn: AAAA Foundation
405 Lexington Avenue, 18th Floor
New York, NY 10174-1801
(212) 682-2500   Toll Free: (800) 676-9333
Fax: (212) 682-2028   E-mail: ameadows@aaaa.org
Web: www2.aaaa.org

Summary To provide financial assistance to African Americans and other multicultural students who are working on an undergraduate degree in advertising.

Eligibility This program is open to undergraduate students who are U.S. citizens of proven multicultural heritage and have at least 1 grandparent of multicultural heritage. Applicants must be participating in the Multicultural Advertising Intern Program (MAIP). They must be entering their senior year at an accredited college or university in the United States and have a GPA of 3.0 or higher. Selection is based on academic ability.

Financial data The stipend is $2,000.

Duration 1 year.

Additional information This program was established by the Association of National Advertisers (ANA) in 2001. The American Association of Advertising Agencies (AAAA) assumed administration in 2003.

Number awarded 3 each year.

Deadline Deadline not specified.

[26]
ANNA M. WINSTON AWARD

National Association of Black Accountants
Attn: National Scholarship Program
7474 Greenway Center Drive, Suite 1120
Greenbelt, MD 20770
(301) 474-NABA, ext. 114   Fax: (301) 474-3114
E-mail: customerservice@nabainc.org
Web: www.nabainc.org

Summary To provide financial assistance to student members of the National Association of Black Accountants (NABA) who are attending an Historically Black College or University (HBCU) to work on an undergraduate or graduate degree in a field related to accounting.

Eligibility This program is open to NABA members enrolled full time as 1) an undergraduate freshman, sophomore, junior, or first-semester senior majoring in accounting, business, or finance at an HBCU; or 2) a graduate student working on a master's degree in accounting at an HBCU. High school seniors are not eligible. Applicants must have a GPA of 2.0 or higher in their major and 2.5 or higher overall. Selection is based on grades, financial need, and a 500-word autobiography that discusses career objectives, leadership abilities, community activities, and involvement in NABA.

Financial data The stipend ranges from $500 to $1,000.

Duration 1 year.

Additional information Applicants for this scholarship are required to sign a pledge form with a promise to fund it within 5 years of graduation from college.

Number awarded 1 each year.

Deadline January of each year.

[27]
ANNIE B. AND L. ESSEX MOSELEY SCHOLARSHIP FUND

Synod of the Mid-Atlantic
Attn: Finance and Scholarship Committee
3218 Chamberlayne Avenue
P.O. Box 27026
Richmond, VA 23261-7026
(804) 342-0016   Toll Free: (800) 743-7670
Fax: (804) 355-8535
Web: www.synatlantic.org/scholarships/right.html

Summary To provide financial assistance to African Americans who are members of Presbyterian churches within designated presbyteries throughout Virginia and interested in attending college in any state.

Eligibility This program is open to members of racial ethnic groups, preferably African Americans, who are active members of churches within the presbyteries of Eastern Virginia, James, and Peaks. Applicants must be a graduate or a graduating senior of a public school who are accepted or enrolled at an accredited college, university, or presbytery technical institute program in any state. Selection is based on academic achievement and financial need.

Financial data A stipend is awarded (amount not specified).

Duration 1 year; nonrenewable.

Additional information This fund was established in 1988.

Number awarded 1 or more each year.

Deadline February of each year.

[28]
ANS ACCELERATOR APPLICATIONS DIVISION SCHOLARSHIP

American Nuclear Society
Attn: Scholarship Coordinator
555 North Kensington Avenue
La Grange Park, IL 60526-5592
(708) 352-6611   Toll Free: (800) 323-3044
Fax: (708) 352-0499   E-mail: outreach@ans.org
Web: www.ans.org/honors/scholarships/aad.html

Summary To provide financial assistance to undergraduate students (particularly African Americans or other minorities and women) who are interested in preparing for a career dealing with accelerator applications aspects of nuclear science or nuclear engineering.

Eligibility This program is open to students entering their junior year in physics, engineering, or materials science at an accredited institution in the United States. Applicants must submit a description of their long- and short-term professional objectives, including their research interests related to accelerator aspects of nuclear science and engineering. Selection is based on that statement, faculty recommendations, and academic performance. Special consideration is given to members of underrepresented groups (women and minorities), students who can demonstrate financial need, and applicants who have a record of service to the American Nuclear Society (ANS).

Financial data The stipend is $1,000 per year.

Duration 1 year (the junior year); may be renewed for the senior year.

Additional information This program is offered by the Accelerator Applications Division (AAD) of the ANS.

Number awarded 1 each year.

Deadline January of each year.

[29]
ANSP RESEARCH EXPERIENCES FOR UNDERGRADUATES FELLOWSHIPS

Academy of Natural Sciences of Philadelphia
Attn: REU Coordinator
1900 Benjamin Franklin Parkway
Philadelphia, PA 19103-1195
(215) 299-1000   Fax: (215) 299-1028
E-mail: reucoordinator@ansp.org
Web: www.ansp.org/research/opportunities/reu.php

Summary To provide an opportunity to participate in a research internship during the summer at the Academy of Natural Sciences of Philadelphia to undergraduate students from any state, especially African Americans and other minorities, women, and students with disabilities.

Eligibility This program is open to U.S. citizens and permanent residents who are entering their sophomore, junior, or senior year at a college or university. Applicants must be interested in working on a research project under the mentorship of an academy scientist in biogeochemistry, botany, database programming, entomology, evolutionary systematics (molecular studies), fisheries, ichthyology, malacology, natural history and museum studies, paleontology, phycology, science library research, or stream ecology. Applications are encouraged from women, minorities, and students with disabilities.

Financial data The program covers travel to and from Philadelphia, housing, supplies, field trips, and research, and provides a stipend of $350 per week.

Duration 10 weeks, beginning in June.

Additional information This program is funded by the National Science Foundation as part of its Research Experiences for Undergraduates (REU) Program.

Number awarded Varies each year.

Deadline February of each year.

[30]
ARKANSAS CONFERENCE ETHNIC LOCAL CHURCH CONCERNS SCHOLARSHIPS

United Methodist Church-Arkansas Conference
Attn: Committee on Ethnic Local Church Concerns
800 Daisy Bates Drive
Little Rock, AR 72202
(501) 324-8045   Toll Free: (877) 646-1816
Fax: (501) 324-8018   E-mail: mallen@arumc.org
Web: www.arumc.org

Summary To provide financial assistance to African American and other minority Methodist students from Arkansas who are interested in attending college or graduate school in any state.

Eligibility This program is open to ethnic minority undergraduate and graduate students who are active members of local congregations affiliated with the Arkansas Conference of the United Methodist Church (UMC). Applicants must be currently enrolled in an accredited institution of higher education in any state. Along with their application, they must submit a transcript (GPA of 2.0 or higher) and documentation of participation in local church activities. Preference is given to students attending a UMC-affiliated college or university.

Financial data The stipend is $500 per semester ($1,000 per year) for undergraduates or $1,000 per semester ($2,000 per year) for graduate students.

Duration 1 year; may be renewed.

Number awarded 1 or more each year.

Deadline September of each year.

[31]
ARKANSAS MINORITY TEACHERS SCHOLARSHIPS

Arkansas Department of Higher Education
Attn: Financial Aid Division
114 East Capitol Avenue
Little Rock, AR 72201-3818
(501) 371-2050
Fax: (501) 371-2001
Web: www.adhe.edu

Toll Free: (800) 54-STUDY
E-mail: finaid@adhe.edu

Summary To provide funding to African American and other minority undergraduates in Arkansas who want to become teachers in the state.

Eligibility This program is open to minority (African American, Native American, Hispanic, or Asian American) residents of Arkansas who are U.S. citizens or permanent residents and enrolled full time as juniors or seniors in an approved teacher certification program at an Arkansas public or independent 4-year institution. Applicants must have a cumulative GPA of 2.5 or higher and be willing to teach in an Arkansas public school for at least 5 years after completion of their teaching certificate (3 years if the teaching is in 1 of the 42 counties of Arkansas designated as the Delta Region, or if the teaching is in a critical subject shortage area, or if the recipient is an African American male teaching at the elementary level).

Financial data Loans up to $5,000 per year are available. The loan will be forgiven at the rate of 20% for each year the recipient teaches full time in an Arkansas public school (or 33% per year if the obligation is fulfilled in 3 years). If the loan is not forgiven by service, it must be repaid with interest at 10%.

Duration 1 year; may be renewed for 1 additional year if the recipient remains enrolled full time with a GPA of 2.5 or higher.

Additional information Recently, the critical subject shortage areas included art (K-12), foreign language (French, German, Spanish), mathematics (secondary), middle childhood (4-8 mathematics and science, 4-8 English language arts or social studies), science (secondary life or physical), or special education (deaf education, visually impaired, instructional specialist).

Number awarded Varies each year; recently, 97 of these forgivable loans were approved.

Deadline May of each year.

[32]
ARMY MINORITY COLLEGE RELATIONS PROGRAM INTERNSHIPS

Vista Sciences Corporation
Attn: Intern Program Manager
7700 Alabama Street, Suite E
El Paso, TX 79904
(915) 757-3331
E-mail: romy.ledesma@vistasciences.com
Web: www.vistasciences.com/services.asp?service=19

Fax: (915) 757-3371

Summary To provide work experience at facilities of the U.S. Army to upper-division and graduate students at Historically Black Colleges and Universities and other minority institutions.

Eligibility This program is open to students working on an undergraduate or graduate degree at Historically Black Colleges and Universities (HBCUs), Hispanic Serving Institutions (HSIs), or Tribal Colleges and Universities (TCUs). Applicants must be U.S. citizens currently enrolled as a junior or above and have a GPA of 2.5 or higher; recent (within 6 months) graduates are also eligible. They must be interested in an internship at an Army facility in such fields as engineering (civil, computer, construction, electrical, environmental), sciences (agronomy, biology, environmental, natural resources, safety), business (accounting, finance, legal, management, marketing, operations), computer science and engineering (data management, information systems, information technology, languages, programming, trouble shooting, website/webpage design and management), or other (communications, English, history, human resources, journalism, library sciences, mathematics, public administration, public relations, quality control, risk management, statistics, training development and management). Along with their application, they must submit a resume and a transcript.

Financial data Interns are paid a stipend of $500 per week and are reimbursed for housing and transportation costs.

Duration 10 weeks in the summer or 15 weeks in spring.

Additional information This program, which began in 1997, is currently administered by Vista Sciences Corporation under a contract with the Army. Recently, assignments were available at the Crane Army Ammunition Activity (Crane, Indiana), Sierra Army Depot (Herlong, California), McAlester Army Ammunition Plant (McAlester, Oklahoma), Blue Grass Army Depot (Richmond, Kentucky), Rock Island Arsenal (Rock Island, Illinois), Anniston Defense Munitions Center (Anniston, Alabama), Pine Bluff Arsenal (Pine Bluff, Arkansas), and Tooele Army Depot (Tooele, Utah).

Number awarded Varies each year.

Deadline May of each year for summer; November of each year for spring.

[33]
ARTHUR B.C. WALKER SCHOLARSHIP

National Society of Black Physicists
Attn: Scholarship Committee Chair
1100 North Glebe Road, Suite 1010
Arlington, VA 22201
(703) 536-4207
E-mail: scholarship@nsbp.org
Web: www.nsbp.org/scholarships

Fax: (703) 536-4203

Summary To provide financial assistance to African American students majoring in physics in college.

Eligibility This program is open to African American students who are entering their junior or senior year of college and majoring in physics. Applicants must submit an essay on their academic and career objectives, information on their participation in extracurricular activities, a description of any awards and honors they have received, and 3 letters of recommendation. Financial need is not considered.

Financial data The stipend is $1,000.

Duration 1 year; nonrenewable.

Number awarded 1 each year.

Deadline January of each year.

[34]
ASLA COUNCIL OF FELLOWS SCHOLARSHIPS

Landscape Architecture Foundation
Attn: Scholarship Program
818 18th Street, N.W., Suite 810
Washington, DC 20006-3520
(202) 331-7070   Fax: (202) 331-7079
E-mail: scholarships@lafoundation.org
Web: www.laprofession.org/financial/scholarships.htm

Summary To provide financial assistance to upper-division students, especially African Americans and those from other disadvantaged or underrepresented groups, working on a degree in landscape architecture.

Eligibility This program is open to landscape architecture students in the third, fourth, or fifth year of undergraduate work. Preference is given to, and 1 scholarship is reserved for, members of underrepresented ethnic or cultural groups. Applicants must submit a 300-word essay on how they envision themselves contributing to the profession of landscape architecture, 2 letters of recommendation, documentation of financial need, and (for students applying for the scholarship reserved for underrepresented groups) a statement identifying their association with a specific ethnic or cultural group. U.S. citizenship or permanent resident status is required.

Financial data The stipend is $4,000. Students also receive a 1-year membership in the American Society of Landscape Architecture (ASLA), general registration fees for the ASLA annual meeting, and a travel stipend to attend the meeting.

Duration 1 year.

Additional information This program is sponsored by ASLA and administered by the Landscape Architecture Foundation.

Number awarded 2 each year.

Deadline February of each year.

[35]
ASSE UPS DIVERSITY SCHOLARSHIPS

American Society of Safety Engineers
Attn: ASSE Foundation
1800 East Oakton Street
Des Plaines, IL 60018
(847) 768-3435   Fax: (847) 768-3434
E-mail: agabanski@asse.org
Web: www.asse.org

Summary To provide financial assistance to African Americans and other minority upper-division student members of the American Society of Safety Engineers (ASSE).

Eligibility This program is open to ASSE student members who are U.S. citizens and members of minority ethnic or racial groups. Applicants must be majoring in occupational safety, health, and environment or a closely-related field (e.g., industrial or environmental engineering, environmental science, industrial hygiene, occupational health nursing). They must be full-time students who have completed at least 60 semester hours with a GPA of 3.0 or higher. Along with their application, they must submit 2 essays of 300 words or less: 1) why they are seeking a degree in occupational safety and health or a closely-related field, a brief description of their current activities, and how those relate to their career goals and objectives; and 2) why they should be awarded this scholarship (including career goals and financial need).

Financial data The stipend is $5,250 per year.

Duration 1 year; recipients may reapply.

Additional information Funding for this program is provided by the UPS Foundation.

Number awarded 2 each year.

Deadline November of each year.

[36]
ASSOCIATED FOOD AND PETROLEUM DEALERS MINORITY SCHOLARSHIPS

Associated Food and Petroleum Dealers
Attn: AFPD Foundation
30415 West 13 Mile Road
Farmington Hills, MI 48334
(248) 671-9600   Toll Free: (800) 666-6233
Fax: (248) 671-9610   E-mail: info@afdom.org
Web: www.afpdonline.org

Summary To provide financial assistance to African American and other minority high school seniors or current college students from Michigan who are enrolled or planning to enroll at a college in any state.

Eligibility This program is open to Michigan residents who are high school seniors or college freshmen, sophomores, or juniors. Applicants must be members of 1 of the following minority groups: African American, Hispanic, Asian, Native American, or Arab/Chaldean. They must be enrolled or planning to enroll full time at a college or university in any state. Preferential consideration is given to applicants with a membership affiliation in the Associated Food and Petroleum Dealers (AFPD), although membership is not required. Selection is based on academic performance, leadership, and participation in school and community activities; college grades are considered if the applicant is already enrolled in college.

Financial data The stipend is $1,500.

Duration 1 year; nonrenewable.

Additional information This program is administered by International Scholarship and Tuition Services, Inc. The AFPD was formed in 2006 by a merger of the Associated Food Dealers of Michigan and the Great Lakes Petroleum Retailers and Allied Trades Association.

Number awarded At least 10 each year, of which at least 3 must be awarded to member customers.

Deadline March of each year.

[37]
AWARD FOR EXCELLENCE IN BUSINESS COMMENTARY

Executive Leadership Council
Attn: Executive Leadership Foundation
1001 North Fairfax Street, Suite 300
Alexandria, VA 22314
(703) 706-5200   E-mail: cmghee@elcinfo.com
Web: www.elcinfo.com/higher_education.php

Summary To recognize and reward outstanding essays written by African American students on selected business topics.

Eligibility This program is open to African American undergraduate students in good academic standing enrolled in an accredited college or university. They must write an essay between 2,000 and 3,000 words on a topic that changes each year; recently, applicants were invited to write on the topic, "Corporate America: Leading Passionately. Thinking Globally."

Financial data The first-place winner receives a $7,000 award, second $6,000, third $5,000, fourth $4,000, fifth $3,000, and each sixth place $1,000. All contest winners receive a trip to New York City and Washington D.C. to participate in the foundation's Student Honors Symposium.

Duration The competition is held annually.

Additional information The Executive Leadership Foundation was founded in 1989 as an affiliate of the Executive Leadership Council, the association of African American senior executives of Fortune 500 companies. This competition is sponsored by the Coca-Cola Company.

Number awarded 10 each year: 1 for each of the first 5 places and 5 sixth-place winners.

Deadline May of each year.

[38]
AWG MINORITY SCHOLARSHIP

Association for Women Geoscientists
Attn: AWG Foundation
12000 North Washington Street, Suite 285
Thornton, CO 80241
(303) 412-6219   Fax: (303) 253-9220
E-mail: minorityscholarship@awg.org
Web: www.awg.org/EAS/scholarships.html

Summary To provide financial assistance to African American or other minority women who are interested in working on an undergraduate degree in the geosciences.

Eligibility This program is open to women who are African American, Hispanic, or Native American (including Eskimo, Hawaiian, Samoan, or American Indian). Applicants must be full-time students working on, or planning to work on, an undergraduate degree in the geosciences (including geology, geophysics, geochemistry, hydrology, meteorology, physical oceanography, planetary geology, or earth science education). They must submit a 500-word essay on their academic and career goals, 2 letters of recommendation, high school and/or college transcripts, and SAT or ACT scores. Financial need is not considered in the selection process.

Financial data A total of $6,000 is available for this program each year.

Duration 1 year; may be renewed.

Additional information This program, first offered in 2004, is supported by ExxonMobil Foundation.

Number awarded 1 or more each year.

Deadline June of each year.

[39]
AWIS INTERNSHIPS

Association for Women in Science
Attn: Internship Coordinator
1442 Duke Street
Alexandria, VA 22314
(703) 372-4380   Toll Free: (800) 886-AWIS
Fax: (703) 778-7807   E-mail: awis@awis.org
Web: www.awis.org/careers/internship.html

Summary To provide an opportunity for African American and other underrepresented minority female undergraduates to gain summer work experience at the offices of the Association for Women in Science (AWIS) in the Washington, D.C. area.

Eligibility This program is open to women who are working on an undergraduate degree in a field of science, technology, engineering, or mathematics (STEM) and interested in a summer internship at AWIS. Applicants must be members of a group currently underrepresented in STEM fields (African Americans, Latinas/Hispanics, Native Americans, and Pacific Islanders). Along with their application, they must submit a resume, cover letter, writing sample, and letter of recommendation.

Financial data The stipend is $3,500.

Duration 10 weeks during the summer.

Additional information Interns may be assigned to publish the Washington Wire, contribute to the *AWIS Magazine,* develop content for the AWIS web site, advocate at Capitol Hill briefings, conduct research grants, perform special projects affiliated with AWIS committees, and interact with board members and top STEM professionals.

Number awarded Varies each year.

Deadline March of each year.

[40]
BAKER HUGHES SCHOLARSHIPS

Society of Women Engineers
Attn: Scholarship Selection Committee
120 South LaSalle Street, Suite 1515
Chicago, IL 60603-3572
(312) 596-5223   Toll Free: (877) SWE-INFO
Fax: (312) 644-8557
E-mail: scholarshipapplication@swe.org
Web: societyofwomenengineers.swe.org

Summary To provide financial assistance to African Americans and other minorities or women who are working on an undergraduate or graduate degree in designated engineering specialties.

Eligibility This program is open to women who are sophomores, juniors, seniors, or graduate students at 4-year ABET-accredited colleges and universities. Applicants must be working on a degree in computer science or chemical, electrical, mechanical, or petroleum engineering and have a GPA of 3.0 or higher. Preference is given to members of groups underrepresented in engineering or computer science. Selection is based on merit.

Financial data The stipend is $5,000 per year.

Duration 1 year; may be renewed up to 2 additional years.

Additional information This program is sponsored by Baker Hughes Incorporated.

Number awarded 3 each year.

Deadline February of each year.

[41]
BARBARA JORDAN HISTORICAL ESSAY COMPETITION

University of Texas at Austin
Attn: Division of Diversity and Community Engagement
100 West Dean Keaton Street, Suite 4.400
1 University Station A5700
Austin, TX 78712
(512) 232-4660   Fax: (512) 232-3963
E-mail: abumphus@mail.utexas.edu
Web: www.utexas.edu/world/barbarajordan

Summary To recognize and reward, with college scholarships, high school students in Texas who submit outstanding essays on topics related to African Americans in the state.

Eligibility This competition is open to high school students in grades 9-12 in Texas. Applicants must submit an essay, from 1,500 to 2,500 words in length, on the topic "The African American in Texas: Past and Present." Competitions are first held in 10 regions in the state, with 3 regional winners advancing to the state finals. Papers are judged on historical quality (60%), clarity of presentation (20%), and relation to theme (20%).

Financial data In the state finals, first prize is $2,500, second $1,500, and third $1,000. Prizes are scholarships that may be used at any institution of the winner's choice.

Duration The competition is held annually.

Additional information The winning essays are submitted to the Texas State Historical Association for possible publication in its student journal, *Texas Historian.*

Number awarded 3 prizes are awarded each year.

Deadline January of each year.

[42]
BARBARA JORDAN MEMORIAL SCHOLARSHIPS

Association of Texas Professional Educators
Attn: ATPE Foundation
305 East Huntland Drive, Suite 300
Austin, TX 78752-3792
(512) 467-0071   Toll Free: (800) 777-ATPE
Fax: (512) 467-2203   E-mail: admin@atpefoundation.org
Web: www.atpefoundation.org/scholarships.asp

Summary To provide financial assistance to upper-division and graduate students from any state who are enrolled in educator preparation programs at Historically Black Colleges and Universities or other predominantly ethnic minority institutions in Texas.

Eligibility This program is open to juniors, seniors, and graduate students from any state who are enrolled in educator preparation programs at predominantly ethnic minority institutions in Texas. Applicants must submit a 2-page essay on their personal educational philosophy, why they want to become an educator, who influenced them the most in making their career decision, and why they are applying for the

scholarship. Financial need is not considered in the selection process.

Financial data The stipend is $1,500.

Duration 1 year.

Additional information The qualifying institutions are Huston-Tillotson College, Jarvis Christian College, Our Lady of the Lake University, Paul Quinn College, Prairie View A&M University, St. Mary's University of San Antonio, Sul Ross State University, Sul Ross State University Rio Grande College, Texas A&M International University, Texas A&M University at Kingsville, Texas Southern University, University of Houston, University of Houston-Downtown, University of Texas at Brownsville and Texas Southmost College, University of Texas at El Paso, University of Texas at San Antonio, University of Texas-Pan American, University of the Incarnate Word, and Wiley College.

Number awarded Up to 6 each year.

Deadline May of each year.

[43]
BATTELLE COLLEGIATE SCHOLARSHIPS

National Society of Black Engineers
Attn: Programs Department
205 Daingerfield Road
Alexandria, VA 22314
(703) 549-2207   Fax: (703) 683-5312
E-mail: scholarships@nsbe.org
Web: www.nsbe.org

Summary To provide financial assistance and summer work experience to undergraduate student members of the National Society of Black Engineers (NSBE) who are working on a degree in designated fields of science or engineering.

Eligibility This program is open to members of the society who are entering their junior or senior year of college. Applicants must be working on a degree in chemistry, computer science, materials science, mathematics, statistics, applied or engineering physics, or the following engineering specialties: chemical, civil, electrical, materials, mechanical, or software. They must be interested in a summer internship at Battelle or designated national laboratories.

Financial data The scholarship stipend is $5,000. A stipend (amount not specified) is paid for the internships.

Duration 1 year.

Additional information This program was established in 2008 by Battelle Memorial Institute of Columbus, Ohio. Internships are provided at Brookhaven National Laboratory (BNL) in Upton, New York, Idaho National Laboratory (INL) in Idaho Falls, Idaho, Oak Ridge National Laboratory (ORNL) in Oak Ridge, Tennessee, and Pacific Northwest National Laboratory (PNNL) in Richland, Washington.

Number awarded 14 each year, including 6 with internships at Battelle and 2 each with internships at BNL, INL, ORNL, and PNNL.

Deadline January of each year.

[44]
BATTELLE HIGH SCHOOL SCHOLARSHIP PROGRAM

National Society of Black Engineers
Attn: Pre-College Initiative Program
205 Daingerfield Road
Alexandria, VA 22314
(703) 549-2207   Fax: (703) 683-5312
E-mail: pci@nsbe.org
Web: www.nsbe.org/Programs/Scholarships/PCI.aspx

Summary To provide financial assistance to high school seniors who are junior members of the National Society of Black Engineers (NSBE) in Ohio and planning to major in science, technology, engineering, or mathematics (STEM) at a college in any state.

Eligibility This program is open to seniors graduating from high schools in Ohio who are junior members of the society. Applicants must be planning to attend college in any state and major in a STEM-related field.

Financial data The stipend is $5,000.

Duration 1 year.

Additional information This program was established in 2008 as the result of a major gift from Battelle Memorial Institute to NSBE.

Number awarded 6 each year.

Deadline January of each year.

[45]
BB&T CHARITABLE FOUNDATION SCHOLARSHIP PROGRAM OF THE HISPANIC SCHOLARSHIP FUND

Hispanic Scholarship Fund
Attn: Selection Committee
55 Second Street, Suite 1500
San Francisco, CA 94105
(415) 808-2365   Toll Free: (877) HSF-INFO
Fax: (415) 808-2302   E-mail: scholar1@hsf.net
Web: www.hsf.net/BBT.aspx

Summary To provide financial assistance to African and Hispanic American upper-division students from selected states who are working on a degree related to business or law.

Eligibility This program is open to U.S. citizens and permanent residents (must have a permanent resident card or a passport stamped I-551) who are African American or of Hispanic heritage. Applicants must be residents of or attending school in Alabama, Florida, Georgia, Indiana, Kentucky, Maryland, North Carolina, Puerto Rico, South Carolina, Tennessee, Virginia, Washington, D.C., or West Virginia. They must be full-time juniors with a major in a business, legal, or liberal arts discipline and a GPA of 3.0 or higher. Selection is based on academic achievement, personal strengths, leadership, and financial need.

Financial data A stipend is awarded (amount not specified).

Duration 1 year (the junior year of college).

Additional information This program is funded by the BB&T Charitable Foundation. Students may have an opportunity to participate in an internship at its corporate sponsor, Branch Banking and Trust Company.

Number awarded 1 or more each year.

Deadline December of each year.

[46]
BDPA ORACLE SCHOLARSHIP

Black Data Processing Associates
Attn: Scholarship
9500 Arena Drive, Suite 350
Largo, MD 20774
(301) 584-3135   Fax: (301) 560-8300
E-mail: scholarships@bdpa.org
Web: www.bdpa.org/?page=Scholarships

Summary To provide financial assistance to members of Black Data Processing Associates (BDPA) who are working on an undergraduate degree in a field related to computer technology.

Eligibility This program is open to graduating high school seniors and current undergraduates who are BDPA members. Applicants must be enrolled or planning to enroll full time at an accredited college or university and major in engineering, computer and information science, computer engineering, or mathematics. They must have a GPA of 3.0 or higher. Along with their application, they must submit a 300-word essay that covers 1 or more of the following topics: the role that computer technology has played in their life, their dream and goal for technology in their future, how they will use their talent to give back or enrich their community, and/or how this scholarship will be used to help them with their education study and career. Financial need is not considered in the selection process.

Financial data A stipend is awarded (amount not specified).

Duration 1 year.

Additional information This scholarship, first awarded in 2009, is sponsored by Oracle.

Number awarded 1 each year.

Deadline November of each year.

[47]
BECHTEL UNDERGRADUATE FELLOWSHIP AWARD

National Action Council for Minorities in Engineering
Attn: University Programs
440 Hamilton Avenue, Suite 302
White Plains, NY 10601-1813
(914) 539-4010   Fax: (914) 539-4032
E-mail: scholarships@nacme.org
Web: www.nacme.org/NACME_D.aspx?pageid=105

Summary To provide financial assistance to African American and other underrepresented minority college juniors majoring in construction engineering.

Eligibility This program is open to African American, Latino, and American Indian college juniors who have a GPA of 3.0 or higher and have demonstrated academic excellence, leadership skills, and a commitment to science and engineering as a career. Applicants must be enrolled full time at an ABET-accredited engineering program and preparing for a career in a construction-related engineering discipline.

Financial data The stipend is $2,500 per year. Funds are sent directly to the recipient's university.

Duration Up to 2 years.

Additional information This program was established by the Bechtel Group Foundation.

Number awarded 2 each year.

Deadline April of each year.

[48]
BEHAVIORAL SCIENCES STUDENT FELLOWSHIPS IN EPILEPSY

Epilepsy Foundation
Attn: Research Department
8301 Professional Place
Landover, MD 20785-2237
(301) 459-3700   Toll Free: (800) EFA-1000
Fax: (301) 577-2684   TDD: (800) 332-2070
E-mail: grants@efa.org
Web: www.epilepsyfoundation.org

Summary To provide funding to undergraduate and graduate students (particularly African Americans or other minorities, women, and students with disabilities) who are interested in working on a summer research training project in a behavioral science field relevant to epilepsy.

Eligibility This program is open to undergraduate and graduate students in a behavioral science program relevant to epilepsy research or clinical care, including, but not limited to, sociology, social work, psychology, anthropology, nursing, economics, vocational rehabilitation, counseling, or political science. Applicants must be interested in working on an epilepsy research project under the supervision of a qualified mentor. Because the program is designed as a training opportunity, the quality of the training plans and environment are considered in the selection process. Other selection criteria include the quality of the proposed project, the relevance of the proposed work to epilepsy, the applicant's interest in the field of epilepsy, the applicant's qualifications, and the mentor's qualifications (including his or her commitment to the student and the project), and the quality of the training environment for research related to epilepsy. U.S. citizenship is not required, but the project must be conducted in the United States. Applications from women, members of minority groups, and people with disabilities are especially encouraged. The program is not intended for students working on a dissertation research project.

Financial data The grant is $3,000.

Duration 3 months during the summer.

Additional information This program is supported by the American Epilepsy Society, Abbott Laboratories, Ortho-McNeil Pharmaceutical Corporation, and Pfizer Inc.

Number awarded Varies each year.

Deadline March of each year.

[49]
BENJAMIN BANNEKER CHAPTER SCHOLARSHIP

Blacks in Government-Benjamin Banneker Chapter
Attn: Scholarship Awards Committee
P.O. Box 15652
Arlington, VA 22215-5652
Web: bbcgsa.org/Educational_Scholarships.aspx

Summary To provide financial assistance to African American and other high school seniors and GED recipients in the

Washington, D.C. metropolitan area who plan to attend college in any state.

Eligibility This program is open to residents of the Washington, D.C. metropolitan area who either are graduating high school seniors or have a GED diploma. Applicants must have a GPA of 2.5 higher and be planning to attend an accredited institution of higher learning in any state. Along with their application, they must submit an essay on applying the teaching of Benjamin Banneker to today's life issues. Selection is based on that essay, academic achievement, extracurricular activities, community and public service, SAT scores, and a statement of educational and career goals.

Financial data A stipend is awarded (amount not specified).

Duration 1 year.

Additional information The Benjamin Banneker Chapter of Blacks in Government serves African American employees of the General Services Administration in the Washington, D.C. metropolitan area.

Number awarded 1 or more each year.

Deadline January of each year.

[50]
BERNARD HARRIS MATH AND SCIENCE SCHOLARSHIPS

Council of the Great City Schools
1301 Pennsylvania Avenue, N.W., Suite 702
Washington, DC 20004
(202) 393-2427   Fax: (202) 393-2400
Web: www.cgcs.org/about/award_programs.aspx

Summary To provide financial assistance to African American and Hispanic high school seniors interested in studying science, technology, engineering, or mathematics (STEM) in college.

Eligibility This program is open to African American and Hispanic seniors graduating from high schools in a district that is a member of the Council of the Great City Schools, a coalition of 65 of the nation's largest urban public school systems. Applicants must be planning to enroll full time at a 4-year college or university and major in a STEM field of study. They must have a GPA of 3.0 or higher. Along with their application, they must submit 1-page essays on 1) how mathematics and science education has impacted their lives so far; and 2) why they have chosen to prepare for a career in a STEM field. Selection is based on those essays; academic achievement; extracurricular activities, community service, or other experiences that demonstrate commitment to a career in a STEM field; and 3 letters of recommendation. Financial need is not considered. Males and females are judged separately.

Financial data The stipend is $5,000.

Duration 1 year; nonrenewable.

Additional information This program, which began in 2010, is sponsored by the ExxonMobil Corporation and The Harris Foundation.

Number awarded 4 each year: an African American male and female and an Hispanic male and female.

Deadline May of each year.

[51]
BERTHA PITTS CAMPBELL SCHOLARSHIP PROGRAM

Delta Sigma Theta Sorority, Inc.
Attn: Scholarship and Standards Committee Chair
1707 New Hampshire Avenue, N.W.
Washington, DC 20009
(202) 986-2400   Fax: (202) 986-2513
E-mail: dstemail@deltasigmatheta.org
Web: www.deltasigmatheta.org

Summary To provide financial assistance to members of Delta Sigma Theta who are working on an undergraduate degree in education.

Eligibility This program is open to current undergraduate students who are working on a degree in education. Applicants must be active, dues-paying members of Delta Sigma Theta. Selection is based on meritorious achievement.

Financial data The stipends range from $1,000 to $2,000. The funds may be used to cover tuition, fees, and living expenses.

Duration 1 year; may be renewed for 1 additional year.

Additional information This sponsor is a traditionally African American social sorority. The application fee is $20.

Deadline April of each year.

[52]
BIOMEDICAL RESEARCH TRAINING PROGRAM FOR UNDERREPRESENTED GROUPS

National Heart, Lung, and Blood Institute
Attn: Office of Training and Minority Health
6701 Rockledge Drive, Suite 9180
Bethesda, MD 20892-7913
(301) 451-5081   Toll Free: (301) 451-0088
Fax: (301) 480-0862   E-mail: mishoeh@nhlbi.nih.gov
Web: www.nhlbi.nih.gov

Summary To provide training in fundamental biomedical sciences and clinical research disciplines to African Americans and other undergraduates, graduate students, and post-baccalaureates from underrepresented groups.

Eligibility This program is open to underrepresented undergraduate and graduate students (and postbaccalaureate individuals) interested in receiving training in fundamental biomedical sciences and clinical research disciplines of interest to the National Heart, Lung, and Blood Institute (NHLBI) of the National Institutes of Health (NIH). Underrepresented individuals include African Americans, Hispanic Americans, Native Americans, Alaskan Natives, Native Hawaiians and Pacific Islanders, individuals with disabilities, and individuals from disadvantaged backgrounds. Applicants must be U.S. citizens or permanent residents; have completed academic course work relevant to biomedical, behavioral, or statistical research; be enrolled full time or have recently completed baccalaureate work; and have a GPA of 3.3 or higher. Research experiences are available in the NHLBI Division of Intramural Research (in its cardiology, hematology, vascular medicine, or pulmonary critical care medicine branches) and its Division of Cardiovascular Sciences (which provides training in the basic principles of design, implementation, and analysis of epidemiology studies and clinical trials).

Financial data Stipends are paid at the annual rate of $24,000 for sophomores, $25,200 for juniors, $26,400 for seniors, $27,200 for postbaccalaureate individuals, $27,600 for first-year graduate students, $31,200 for second-year graduate students, or $34,900 for third-year graduate students.

Duration 6 to 24 months over a 2-year period; training must be completed in increments during consecutive academic years.

Additional information Training is conducted in the laboratories of the NHLBI in Bethesda, Maryland.

Number awarded Varies each year.

Deadline January of each year for placements beginning in June; March of each year for post-baccalaureate research internships beginning from June through September.

[53]
BIRMINGHAM CHAPTER AABE SCHOLARSHIPS

American Association of Blacks in Energy-Birmingham
  Chapter
Attn: Scholarship Committee
P.O. Box 3035
Birmingham, AL 35202
(205) 325-7500   E-mail: apjuett@southernco.com
Web: www.aabe.org/index.php?component=pages&id=740

Summary To provide financial assistance to African Americans and members of other underrepresented minority groups who are high school seniors in Alabama and planning to major in an energy-related field at a college in any state.

Eligibility This program is open to seniors graduating from high schools in Alabama and planning to attend a college or university in any state. Applicants must be African Americans, Hispanics, or Native Americans who have a GPA of 3.0 or higher and who can demonstrate financial need. Their intended major must be business, engineering, technology, mathematics, the physical sciences, or other energy-related field. Along with their application, they must submit a 350-word statement on why they should receive this scholarship, how their professional career objectives relate to energy, and any other relevant information.

Financial data The stipend is $5,000.

Duration 1 year.

Additional information The winner is eligible to compete for regional and national scholarships.

Number awarded 1 each year.

Deadline March of each year.

[54]
BISHOP JOSEPH B. BETHEA SCHOLARSHIPS

United Methodist Church
Attn: General Board of Higher Education and Ministry
Office of Loans and Scholarships
1001 19th Avenue South
P.O. Box 340007
Nashville, TN 37203-0007
(615) 340-7344   Fax: (615) 340-7367
E-mail: umscholar@gbhem.org
Web: www.gbhem.org/loansandscholarships

Summary To provide financial assistance for college to African American Methodist students from the southeastern states.

Eligibility This program is open to full-time undergraduate students at accredited colleges and universities who have been active, full members of a United Methodist Church for at least 1 year prior to applying. Applicants must be African Americans and members of Black Methodists for Church Renewal in the Southeastern Jurisdiction (which covers Alabama, Florida, Georgia, Kentucky, Mississippi, North Carolina, South Carolina, Tennessee, and Virginia). They must have a GPA of 2.8 or higher and be able to demonstrate financial need. U.S. citizenship or permanent resident status is required.

Financial data A stipend is awarded (amount not specified).

Duration 1 year; recipients may reapply.

Number awarded 1 or more each year.

Deadline March of each year.

[55]
BISHOP T. LARRY KIRKLAND SCHOLARSHIP OF EXCELLENCE

African Methodist Episcopal Church
Fifth Episcopal District Lay Organization
400 Corporate Pointe, Suite 300
Culver City, CA 90230
(424) 750-3065   Fax: (424) 750-3067
E-mail: AmecEpiscopal5@aol.com
Web: www.amec5th.net/scholarship_of_excellence.aspx

Summary To provide financial assistance to members of African Methodist Episcopal (AME) churches in its Fifth Episcopal District who are attending college in any state.

Eligibility This program is open to residents of the AME Fifth Episcopal District (Alaska, Arizona, California, Colorado, Idaho, Kansas, Missouri, Montana, Nebraska, Nevada, New Mexico, North Dakota, Oregon, South Dakota, Utah, Washington, and Wyoming) who are currently enrolled at an accredited institution of higher learning in any state. Applicants must have been a member of an AME church for at least 12 months and have been an active member of its Lay Organization, another lay-sponsored program, the Young People's Department (YPD), the Missionary Society, or a missionary-sponsored program. They must have a GPA of 2.5 or higher. Along with their application, they must submit a 500-word personal essay that describes their long-range plans, community and church involvement, accomplishments or special awards, challenges they have faced, and how they responded. Selection is based on that essay, academic record, letters of recommendation, accomplishments, and level of participation in church activities.

Financial data The stipend is $1,500.

Duration 1 year.

Number awarded 1 each year.

Deadline May of each year.

[56]
BLACKS AT MICROSOFT SCHOLARSHIPS

Blacks at Microsoft
Attn: BAM Scholarship
One Microsoft Way
Redmond, WA 98052
E-mail: bamship@microsoft.com
Web: www.microsoft.com

Summary To provide financial assistance to African American high school seniors who plan to major in engineering, computer science, or a business-related field in college.

Eligibility This program is open to seniors of African descent graduating from high school and planning to attend a 4-year college or university. Applicants must be planning to work on a bachelor's degree in engineering, computer science, computer information systems, or selected business fields (such as finance, business administration, or marketing). They must be able to demonstrate a "passion for technology," leadership at school or in the community, a need for financial assistance to attend college, and a GPA of 3.3 or higher. Along with their application, they must submit a 500-word essay on how they plan to engage in the technology industry in their future career and a 250-word essay on their financial need for this scholarship.

Financial data The stipend is $5,000 per year.

Duration 1 year; may be renewed up to 3 additional years.

Additional information Blacks at Microsoft is an organization of African American employees of Microsoft.

Number awarded 2 each year.

Deadline March of each year.

[57]
BLACKS IN SAFETY ENGINEERING SCHOLARSHIP

American Society of Safety Engineers
Attn: ASSE Foundation
1800 East Oakton Street
Des Plaines, IL 60018
(847) 768-3435   Fax: (847) 768-3434
E-mail: agabanski@asse.org
Web: www.asse.org

Summary To provide financial assistance to African American and other upper-division student members of the American Society of Safety Engineers (ASSE).

Eligibility This program is open to ASSE student members who are majoring in occupational safety, health, and environment or a closely-related field (e.g., industrial or environmental engineering, environmental science, industrial hygiene, occupational health nursing). Priority is given to students who are Black. Applicants must be full-time students who have completed at least 60 semester hours with a GPA of 3.0 or higher. Along with their application, they must submit 2 essays of 300 words or less: 1) why they are seeking a degree in occupational safety and health or a closely-related field, a brief description of their current activities, and how those relate to their career goals and objectives; and 2) why they should be awarded this scholarship (including career goals and financial need). U.S. citizenship is not required.

Financial data The stipend is $1,000 per year.

Duration 1 year; recipients may reapply.

Number awarded 1 each year.

Deadline November of each year.

[58]
BOARD OF CORPORATE AFFILIATES SCHOLARS AWARDS

National Society of Black Engineers
Attn: Programs Department
205 Daingerfield Road
Alexandria, VA 22314
(703) 549-2207   Fax: (703) 683-5312
E-mail: scholarships@nsbe.org
Web: www.nsbe.org

Summary To provide financial assistance to members of the National Society of Black Engineers (NSBE) who are working on a degree in engineering.

Eligibility This program is open to members of the society who are undergraduate or graduate engineering students. Applicants must have a GPA of 3.0 or higher. Selection is based on an essay; academic achievement; service to the society at the chapter, regional, and/or national level; and other professional, campus, and community activities. Applicants for the National Society of Black Engineers Fellows Scholarship Program who rank in the highest of 3 tiers receive these awards.

Financial data The stipend is $3,000. Travel, hotel accommodations, and registration to the national convention are also provided.

Duration 1 year.

Number awarded Varies each year; recently, 37 of these scholarships were awarded.

Deadline January of each year.

[59]
BOB GLAHN SCHOLARSHIP IN STATISTICAL METEOROLOGY

American Meteorological Society
Attn: Fellowship/Scholarship Program
45 Beacon Street
Boston, MA 02108-3693
(617) 227-2426, ext. 246   Fax: (617) 742-8718
E-mail: scholar@ametsoc.org
Web: www.ametsoc.org

Summary To provide financial assistance to undergraduates (especially African Americans or other minorities, women, and students with disabilities) who are majoring in meteorology or an aspect of atmospheric sciences with an interest in statistical meteorology.

Eligibility This program is open to full-time students entering their final year of undergraduate study and majoring in meteorology or an aspect of the atmospheric or related oceanic and hydrologic sciences. Applicants must intend to make atmospheric or related sciences their career, with preference given to students who have demonstrated a strong interest in statistical meteorology. They must be U.S. citizens or permanent residents enrolled at a U.S. institution and have a cumulative GPA of 3.25 or higher. Along with their application, they must submit 200-word essays on 1) their studies in statistics and their career plans for the future, and 2) their career plans in the statistical meteorology field. Financial need is considered in the selection process. The sponsor specifically encourages applications from women, minorities, and students with disabilities who are traditionally underrepresented in the atmospheric and related oceanic sciences.

Financial data The stipend is $2,500.

Duration 1 year.

Number awarded 1 each year.

Deadline February of each year.

[60]
BOOKER T. WASHINGTON SCHOLARSHIPS

National FFA Organization
Attn: Scholarship Office
6060 FFA Drive
P.O. Box 68960
Indianapolis, IN 46268-0960
(317) 802-4419   Fax: (317) 802-5419
E-mail: scholarships@ffa.org
Web: www.ffa.org

Summary To provide financial assistance to African American and other minority FFA members who are interested in studying agriculture in college.

Eligibility This program is open to members who are graduating high school seniors planning to enroll full time in college. Applicants must be members of a minority ethnic group (African American, Asian American, Pacific Islander, Hispanic, Alaska Native, or American Indian) planning to work on a 4-year degree in agriculture. Selection is based on academic achievement (10 points for GPA, 10 points for SAT or ACT score, 10 points for class rank), leadership in FFA activities (30 points), leadership in community activities (10 points), and participation in the Supervised Agricultural Experience (SAE) program (30 points). U.S. citizenship is required.

Financial data Scholarships are either $10,000 or $5,000. Funds are paid directly to the recipient.

Duration 1 year; nonrenewable.

Number awarded 4 each year: 1 at $10,000 and 3 at $5,000.

Deadline February of each year.

[61]
BOSTON ALUMNAE CHAPTER SCHOLARSHIPS

Delta Sigma Theta Sorority, Inc.-Boston Alumnae Chapter
Attn: Scholarship Committee
P.O. Box 51424
Boston, MA 02205
(617) 548-3642   E-mail: scholarship@bostondst.org
Web: www.bostondst.org

Summary To provide financial assistance to African American and other high school seniors in Massachusetts interested in attending a 4-year college or university in any state.

Eligibility This program is open to seniors graduating from high schools in Massachusetts. Applicants must be planning to attend a 4-year college or university in any state. They must be able to demonstrate academic achievement and commitment to community service. Along with their application, they must submit a 500-word essay on a topic that changes annually but relates to young people in our society. Financial need is not considered in the selection process.

Financial data Stipends range from $250 to $1,000.

Duration 1 year.

Additional information The sponsor is the local alumnae chapter of a traditionally African American social sorority.

Number awarded 1 or more each year.
Deadline April of each year.

[62]
BOSTON UNIVERSITY RESEARCH EXPERIENCE FOR UNDERGRADUATES IN BIOPHOTONICS

Boston University
Attn: College of Engineering
44 Cummington Street, Room 107
Boston, MA 02215
(617) 353-6447   Toll Free: (800) 578-1223
E-mail: reu@bu.edu
Web: www.bu.edu/eng/reu/ece

Summary To provide an opportunity for undergraduates (particularly African Americans, other minorities, and women) to work on a summer research project related to biophotonics at Boston University.

Eligibility This program is open to undergraduates entering their sophomore, junior, or senior year and majoring in engineering, mathematics, or the natural sciences. Applicants must be interested in participating in a summer research program at Boston University in which they will work under the mentorship of faculty on the science and engineering of light and its applications to engineering, chemistry, biology, and medicine. Women and underrepresented minorities are especially encouraged to apply. U.S. citizenship or permanent resident status is required.

Financial data Participants receive a stipend of $5,000, free on-campus housing, and limited travel support.

Duration 10 weeks during the summer.

Additional information Support for this program is provided by the National Science Foundation (NSF) through its Research Experiences for Undergraduates (REU) program.

Number awarded Approximately 10 each year.

Deadline February of each year.

[63]
BP NSBE CORPORATE SCHOLARSHIP PROGRAM

National Society of Black Engineers
Attn: Programs Department
205 Daingerfield Road
Alexandria, VA 22314
(703) 549-2207   Fax: (703) 683-5312
E-mail: scholarships@nsbe.org
Web: www.nsbe.org

Summary To provide financial assistance to members of the National Society of Black Engineers (NSBE) who are majoring in designated engineering fields.

Eligibility This program is open to members of the society who are enrolled as college sophomores, juniors, or seniors and majoring in chemical, mechanical, or petroleum engineering. Applicants must have a GPA of 3.0 or higher and a demonstrated interest in employment with British Petroleum (BP). Along with their application, they must submit a 250-word essay describing how they will use their education to make a positive impact on the world, including the African American community, and how this scholarship will advance their career goals and benefit BP.

Financial data The stipend is $2,500.

Duration 1 year.

Additional information This program is sponsored by BP.

Number awarded Varies each year; recently, 4 of these scholarships were awarded.

Deadline January of each year.

[64]
BREAKTHROUGH TO NURSING SCHOLARSHIPS

National Student Nurses' Association
Attn: Foundation
45 Main Street, Suite 606
Brooklyn, NY 11201
(718) 210-0705   Fax: (718) 797-1186
E-mail: nsna@nsna.org
Web: www.nsna.org

Summary To provide financial assistance to African Americans and other minority undergraduate and graduate students who wish to prepare for careers in nursing.

Eligibility This program is open to students currently enrolled in state-approved schools of nursing or pre-nursing associate degree, baccalaureate, diploma, generic master's, generic doctoral, R.N. to B.S.N., R.N. to M.S.N., or L.P.N./L.V.N. to R.N. programs. Graduating high school seniors are not eligible. Support for graduate education is provided only for a first degree in nursing. Applicants must be members of a racial or ethnic minority underrepresented among registered nurses (American Indian or Alaska Native, Hispanic or Latino, Native Hawaiian or other Pacific Islander, Black or African American, or Asian). They must be committed to providing quality health care services to underserved populations. Along with their application, they must submit a 200-word description of their professional and educational goals and how this scholarship will help them achieve those goals. Selection is based on academic achievement, financial need, and involvement in student nursing organizations and community health activities. U.S. citizenship or permanent resident status is required.

Financial data Stipends range from $1,000 to $2,500. A total of approximately $155,000 is awarded each year by the foundation for all its scholarship programs.

Duration 1 year.

Additional information Applications must be accompanied by a $10 processing fee.

Number awarded Varies each year; recently, 5 of these scholarships were awarded: 2 sponsored by the American Association of Critical-Care Nurses and 3 sponsored by the Mayo Clinic.

Deadline January of each year.

[65]
BRO. DR. FRANK T. SIMPSON SCHOLARSHIPS

Alpha Phi Alpha Fraternity, Inc.-Beta Sigma Lambda Chapter
Attn: BSL Education Foundation, Inc.
P.O. Box 335
Hartford, CT 06141-0335
(203) 982-4956   E-mail: president@hartfordalphas.com
Web: www.hartfordalphas.com/page.php?page_id=112674

Summary To provide financial assistance to high school seniors in Connecticut, especially African American males, who plan to attend college in any state.

Eligibility This program is open to seniors graduating from public and private high schools in Connecticut and planning to enroll at a 2- or 4-year college or university in any state. Preference is given to African American males. Applicants must have a GPA of 3.0 or higher and a record of community service and extracurricular activities. Along with their application, they must submit a 500-word personal essay that covers how they perceive their life 10 years after high school graduation, their personal interests, and their goals for the future. Financial need is not considered in the selection process.

Financial data The stipend is $1,500.

Duration 1 year; nonrenewable.

Additional information This program is offered through the Hartford Foundation for Public Giving.

Number awarded Up to 4 each year.

Deadline March of each year.

[66]
BROOKHAVEN NATIONAL LABORATORY SCIENCE AND ENGINEERING PROGRAMS FOR WOMEN AND MINORITIES

Brookhaven National Laboratory
Attn: Diversity Office, Human Resources Division
Building 400B
P.O. Box 5000
Upton, New York 11973-5000
(631) 344-2703   Fax: (631) 344-5305
E-mail: palmore@bnl.gov
Web: www.bnl.gov/diversity/programs.asp

Summary To provide on-the-job training in scientific areas at Brookhaven National Laboratory (BNL) during the summer to African American, other underrepresented minorities. and women college students.

Eligibility This program at BNL is open to women and underrepresented minority (African American/Black, Hispanic, Native American, or Pacific Islander) students who have completed their freshman, sophomore, or junior year of college. Applicants must be U.S. citizens or permanent residents, at least 18 years of age, and majoring in applied mathematics, biology, chemistry, computer science, engineering, high and low energy particle accelerators, nuclear medicine, physics, or scientific writing. Since no transportation or housing allowance is provided, preference is given to students who reside in the BNL area.

Financial data Participants receive a competitive stipend.

Duration 10 to 12 weeks during the summer.

Additional information Students work with members of the scientific, technical, and professional staff of BNL in an educational training program developed to give research experience.

Deadline April of each year.

[67]
BROWN AND CALDWELL MINORITY SCHOLARSHIP

Brown and Caldwell
Attn: Scholarship Program
201 North Civic Drive, Suite 115
P.O. Box 8045
Walnut Creek, CA 94596
(925) 937-9010   Fax: (925) 937-9026
E-mail: scholarships@brwncald.com
Web: www.brownandcaldwell.com/_Index_scholarships.htm

Summary To provide financial assistance and work experience to African American and other minority students working on an undergraduate degree in an environmental or engineering field.

Eligibility This program is open to members of minority groups (African Americans, Hispanics, Asians, Pacific Islanders, Native Americans, and Alaska Natives) who are full-time students in their junior year at an accredited 4-year college or university. Applicants must have a GPA of 3.0 or higher and a declared major in civil, chemical, or environmental engineering or an environmental science (e.g., ecology, geology, hydrogeology). Along with their application, they must submit an essay (up to 250 words) on their future career goals in environmental science. They must be U.S. citizens or permanent residents and available to participate in a summer internship at a Brown and Caldwell office. Financial need is not considered in the selection process.

Financial data The stipend is $5,000.

Duration 1 year.

Additional information As part of the paid summer internship at a Brown and Caldwell office at 1 of more than 45 cities in the country, the program provides a mentor to guide the intern through the company's information and communications resources.

Number awarded 1 each year.

Deadline February of each year.

[68]
BUICK ACHIEVERS SCHOLARSHIP PROGRAM

Scholarship America
Attn: Scholarship Management Services
One Scholarship Way
P.O. Box 297
St. Peter, MN 56082
(507) 931-1682   Toll Free: (866) 243-4644
Fax: (507) 931-9168
E-mail: buickachievers@scholarshipamerica.org
Web: www.buickachievers.com

Summary To provide financial assistance to minority and other students entering college for the first time and planning to major in specified fields related to engineering, design, or business.

Eligibility This program is open to high school seniors and graduates who are planning to enroll full time at an accredited 4-year college or university as first-time freshmen. Applicants must be planning to major in accounting, business administration, engineering (chemical, controls, electrical, environmental, industrial, manufacturing, mechanical, plastic/polymers, or engineering technology), design (graphic, industrial, product, or transportation), ergonomics, finance, industrial hygiene, labor and industrial relations, management (logistics, manufacturing, operations, or supply chain), marketing, mathematics, occupational health and safety, or statistics. U.S. citizenship or permanent resident status is required. Selection is based on academic achievement, financial need, participation and leadership in community and school activities, work experience, educational and career goals, and other unusual circumstances. Special consideration is given to first-generation college students, women, minorities, military veterans, and dependents of military personnel.

Financial data Stipends are $25,000 or $2,000 per year.

Duration 1 year; may be renewed up to 3 additional years (or 4 years for students entering a 5-year engineering program).

Additional information This program is funded by the General Motors Foundation.

Number awarded 1,100 each year: 100 at $25,000 and 1,000 at $2,000.

Deadline March of each year.

[69]
BYRON K. ARMSTRONG SCHOLARS AWARD

Kappa Alpha Psi Fraternity
2322-24 North Broad Street
Philadelphia, PA 19132-4590
(215) 228-7184   Fax: (215) 228-7181
Web: www.kappaalphapsi1911.com

Summary To recognize and reward members of Kappa Alpha Psi Fraternity, a traditionally African American men's organization, who demonstrate outstanding achievement.

Eligibility This program is open to undergraduate members of the fraternity who are eligible for graduation in the term immediately preceding or during the period that the Province Council is being held. Candidates must have a GPA of 3.0 or higher. Selection is based on involvement in fraternity, college or university, and community activities.

Financial data Awards are $1,000 for first place, $750 for second place, and $500 for third place.

Duration Awards are presented annually.

Number awarded 3 each year.

Deadline Applications must be received within 14 days following the candidate's Province Council.

[70]
CABJ COLLEGE JOURNALISM SCHOLARSHIP

Colorado Association of Black Journalists
Attn: Scholarship Committee
P.O. Box 48192
Denver, CO 80204
(303) 929-7299   E-mail: info@cabj-denver.org
Web: www.cabj-denver.org/awards.html

Summary To provide financial assistance to African American residents of Colorado who are majoring in a field related to journalism at a college in any state.

Eligibility This program is open to African American residents of Colorado who are majoring in journalism, communications, news editorial, photojournalism, broadcast journalism, advertising, public relations, or related fields at an accredited institution of higher learning in any state. Applicants must submit a 2-page essay that covers why they chose to seek a degree in their particular field of study; their

career goals; their involvement in campus, community, or school activities that demonstrates their commitment to journalism or a related field; how they imagine making a contribution to the African American community through a career in journalism or a related field; any circumstances that have affected their GPA or decreased campus involvement (if any); and why they feel they should receive this scholarship.

Financial data A stipend is awarded (amount not specified).

Duration 1 year.

Number awarded 1 or more each year.

Deadline June of each year.

[71]
CALIFORNIA PLANNING FOUNDATION OUTSTANDING DIVERSITY AWARD

American Planning Association-California Chapter
Attn: California Planning Foundation
c/o Paul Wack
P.O. Box 1086
Morro Bay, CA 93443-1086
(805) 756-6331   Fax: (805) 756-1340
E-mail: pwack@calpoly.edu
Web: www.californiaplanningfoundation.org

Summary To provide financial assistance to African Americans and other undergraduate and graduate students in accredited planning programs at California universities who will increase diversity in the profession.

Eligibility This program is open to students entering their final year for an undergraduate or master's degree in an accredited planning program at a university in California. Applicants must be students who will increase diversity in the planning profession. Selection is based on academic performance, professional promise, and financial need.

Financial data The stipend is $3,000. The award includes a 1-year student membership in the American Planning Association (APA) and payment of registration for the APA California Conference.

Duration 1 year.

Additional information The accredited planning programs are at 3 campuses of the California State University system (California State Polytechnic University at Pomona, California Polytechnic State University at San Luis Obispo, and San Jose State University), 3 campuses of the University of California (Berkeley, Irvine, and Los Angeles), and the University of Southern California.

Number awarded 1 each year.

Deadline March of each year.

[72]
CALL ME MISTER PROGRAM

Clemson University
Attn: Call Me MISTER Program
203 Holtzendorff
Clemson, SC 29634
(864) 656-4646   Toll Free: (800) 640-2657
E-mail: MISTER@clemson.edu
Web: www.callmemister.clemson.edu/index.htm

Summary To provide financial assistance to students, especially African American males, who are attending selected colleges and universities in South Carolina to become teachers.

Eligibility This program is open to students who are attending or planning to attend a participating college or university in South Carolina to prepare for a career as an elementary school teacher. Applicants must submit an essay on why they want to teach, including their motivation for entering the teaching profession and the contributions they hope to make to the profession and to the community as a teacher. A goal of the program has been to increase the number of African American males teaching in South Carolina. An interview is required.

Financial data The program provides tuition assistance at participating colleges and universities.

Duration 1 year; may be renewed.

Additional information The participating institutions include Anderson University, Benedict College, Claflin University, Clemson University, College of Charleston, Coastal Carolina University, Morris College, South Carolina State University and University of South Carolina at Beaufort. In addition, students can enroll at a 2-year partner college (Greenville Technical College, Midlands Technical College, Tri-County Technical College, or Trident Technical College) and then transfer to 1 of the 4-year institutions.

Number awarded Varies each year.

Deadline Deadline not specified.

[73]
CANFIT PROGRAM CULINARY ARTS SCHOLARSHIPS

California Adolescent Nutrition and Fitness Program
Attn: Scholarship Program
2140 Shattuck Avenue, Suite 610
Berkeley, CA 94704
(510) 644-1533   Toll Free: (800) 200-3131
Fax: (510) 644-1535   E-mail: info@canfit.org
Web: canfit.org/scholarships

Summary To provide financial assistance to African American and other minority culinary arts students in California.

Eligibility This program is open to American Indians, Alaska Natives, African Americans, Asian Americans, Pacific Islanders, and Latinos/Hispanics from California who are enrolled at a culinary arts college in the state. Applicants are not required to have completed any college units. Along with their application, they must submit 1) documentation of financial need; 2) letters of recommendation from 2 individuals; 3) a 1-to 2-page letter describing their academic goals and involvement in community nutrition and/or physical education activities; and 4) an essay of 500 to 1,000 words on a topic related to healthy foods for youth from low-income communities of color.

Financial data A stipend is awarded (amount not specified).

Number awarded 1 or more each year.

Deadline March of each year.

[74]
CANFIT PROGRAM UNDERGRADUATE SCHOLARSHIPS

California Adolescent Nutrition and Fitness Program
Attn: Scholarship Program
2140 Shattuck Avenue, Suite 610
Berkeley, CA 94704
(510) 644-1533   Toll Free: (800) 200-3131
Fax: (510) 644-1535   E-mail: info@canfit.org
Web: canfit.org/scholarships

Summary To provide financial assistance to African American and other minority undergraduate students who are working on a degree in nutrition or physical education in California.

Eligibility This program is open to American Indians, Alaska Natives, African Americans, Asian Americans, Pacific Islanders, and Latinos/Hispanics from California who are enrolled in an approved bachelor's degree program in nutrition or physical education in the state. Applicants must have completed at least 50 semester units and have a GPA of 2.5 or higher. Along with their application, they must submit 1) documentation of financial need; 2) letters of recommendation from 2 individuals; 3) a 1-to 2-page letter describing their academic goals and involvement in community nutrition and/or physical education activities; and 4) an essay of 500 to 1,000 words on a topic related to healthy foods for youth from low-income communities of color.

Financial data A stipend is awarded (amount not specified).

Number awarded 1 or more each year.

Deadline March of each year.

[75]
CAREER DEVELOPMENT GRANTS

American Association of University Women
Attn: AAUW Educational Foundation
301 ACT Drive, Department 60
P.O. Box 4030
Iowa City, IA 52243-4030
(319) 337-1716, ext. 60   Fax: (319) 337-1204
E-mail: aauw@act.org
Web: www.aauw.org

Summary To provide financial assistance to African American and other women who are seeking career advancement, career change, or reentry into the workforce.

Eligibility This program is open to women who are U.S. citizens or permanent residents, have earned a bachelor's degree, received their most recent degree more than 4 years ago, and are making career changes, seeking to advance in current careers, or reentering the work force. Applicants must be interested in working toward a master's degree, second bachelor's or associate degree, professional degree (e.g., M.D., J.D.), certification program, or technical school certificate. They must be planning to undertake course work at an accredited 2- or 4-year college or university (or a technical school that is licensed, accredited, or approved by the U.S. Department of Education). Special consideration is given to women of color and women pursuing credentials in nontraditional fields. Support is not provided for prerequisite course work or for Ph.D. course work or dissertations. Selection is based on demonstrated commitment to education and equity for women and girls, reason for seeking higher education or technical training, degree to which study plan is consistent with career objectives, potential for success in chosen field, documentation of opportunities in chosen field, feasibility of study plans and proposed time schedule, validity of proposed budget and budget narrative (including sufficient outside support), and quality of written proposal.

Financial data Grants range from $2,000 to $12,000. Funds may be used for tuition, fees, books, supplies, local transportation, dependent child care, or purchase of a computer required for the study program.

Duration 1 year, beginning in July; nonrenewable.

Additional information The filing fee is $35.

Number awarded Varies each year; recently, 47 of these grants, with a value of $500,000, were awarded.

Deadline December of each year.

[76]
CAREERS IN TRANSPORTATION FOR YOUTH (CITY) INTERNSHIP PROGRAM

Conference of Minority Transportation Officials
Attn: Internship Program
818 18th Street, N.W., Suite 850
Washington, DC 20006
(202) 530-0551   Fax: (202) 530-0617
Web: www.comto.org/news-city.php

Summary To provide summer work experience in transportation-related fields to African American and other underrepresented upper-division students.

Eligibility This program is open to full-time underrepresented students entering their junior or senior year with a GPA of 2.5 or higher. Applicants must be working on a degree related to public transportation. They must be interested in a summer internship with transit firms or agencies in Atlanta, Austin, San Francisco, or Washington, D.C. Along with their application, they must submit a 1-page essay on their transportation interests, including how participation in this internship will enhance their educational plan, their mid- and long-term professional goals, their specific transportation-related goal, the issues of interest to them, their plans to further their education and assist in making future contributions to their field of study, and their expectations for this internship experience. U.S. citizenship is required.

Financial data The stipend recently was $4,000.

Duration 10 weeks during the summer.

Additional information This program is managed by the Conference of Minority Transportation Officials (COMTO), with funding provided by the Federal Transit Administration. Interns work at transit agencies, private transit-related consulting firms, transportation service providers, manufacturers, and suppliers.

Number awarded 12 each year.

Deadline April of each year.

[77]
CARMEN E. TURNER SCHOLARSHIPS

Conference of Minority Transportation Officials
Attn: National Scholarship Program
818 18th Street, N.W., Suite 850
Washington, DC 20006
(202) 530-0551   Fax: (202) 530-0617
Web: www.comto.org/news-youth.php

Summary To provide financial assistance for college or graduate school to African American and other members of the Conference of Minority Transportation Officials (COMTO).

Eligibility This program is open to undergraduate and graduate students who have been members of COMTO for at least 1 year. Applicants must be working on a degree in a field related to transportation with a GPA of 2.5 or higher. Along with their application, they must submit a cover letter with a 500-word statement of career goals. Financial need is not considered in the selection process. U.S. citizenship is required.

Financial data The stipend is $3,500. Funds are paid directly to the recipient's college or university.

Duration 1 year.

Additional information COMTO was established in 1971 to promote, strengthen, and expand the roles of minorities in all aspects of transportation. Recipients are expected to attend the COMTO National Scholarship Luncheon.

Number awarded 2 each year.

Deadline April of each year.

[78]
CARMEN MERCER SCHOLARSHIP

National Sorority of Phi Delta Kappa, Inc.-Delta Beta Chapter
c/o Nancy Thompson, Chapter Scholarship Chair
4703 Broadhill Drive
Austin, TX 78723
(512) 926-6309

Summary To provide financial assistance to African American high school seniors who plan to study education in college.

Eligibility This program is open to African American graduating high school seniors who are planning to attend a 4-year college and major in the field of education. Along with their application, they must submit documentation of financial need, high school transcripts, 2 letters of recommendation, SAT and/or ACT scores, a list of honors and awards received in high school, and a list of extracurricular, community, and volunteer activities.

Financial data The stipend is $2,000.

Duration 1 year.

Number awarded 1 each year.

Deadline January of each year.

[79]
CAROL HAYES TORIO MEMORIAL UNDERGRADUATE SCHOLARSHIP

California Dietetic Association
Attn: CDA Foundation
7740 Manchester Avenue, Suite 102
Playa del Rey, CA 90293-8499
(310) 822-0177   Fax: (310) 823-0264
E-mail: patsmith@dietitian.org
Web: www.dietitian.org/cdaf_scholarships.htm

Summary To provide financial assistance to residents of California (especially African Americans and other minorities, males, and residents with disabilities) who are members of the American Dietetic Association (ADA) and interested in working on an undergraduate degree at a school in any state.

Eligibility This program is open to California residents who are ADA members and 1) entering at least the second year of an accredited Coordinated Program (CP) or Didactic Program in Dietetics (DPD) in any state; or 2) accepted to an accredited Supervised Practice Program in any state to begin within 6 months. Along with their application, they must submit a letter of application that includes a discussion of their career goals. Selection is based on that letter (15%), academic ability (25%), work or volunteer experience (15%), letters of recommendation (15%), extracurricular activities (5%), and financial need (25%). Applications are especially encouraged from ethnic minorities, men, and people with physical disabilities.

Financial data The stipend is normally $1,000.

Duration 1 year.

Number awarded 1 each year.

Deadline February of each year.

[80]
CAROLE SIMPSON NABJ SCHOLARSHIP

National Association of Black Journalists
Attn: Program Coordinator
8701-A Adelphi Road
Adelphi, MD 20783-1716
(301) 445-7100, ext. 108   Toll Free: (866) 479-NABJ
Fax: (301) 445-7101   E-mail: nabj@nabj.org
Web: www.nabj.org

Summary To provide financial assistance to undergraduate or graduate student members of the National Association of Black Journalists (NABJ) who are majoring in broadcast journalism.

Eligibility This program is open to African American undergraduate or graduate students who are currently attending an accredited 4-year college or university. Applicants must be majoring in broadcast journalism and have a GPA of 2.5 or higher. They must be NABJ members. Along with their application, they must submit samples of their work, an official college transcript, 2 letters of recommendation, a resume, and a 500- to 800-word essay describing their accomplishments as a student journalist, their career goals, and their financial need.

Financial data The stipend is $2,500. Funds are paid directly to the recipient's college or university.

Duration 1 year; nonrenewable.

Number awarded 1 each year.

Deadline April of each year.

[81]
CAROLE SIMPSON RTDNF SCHOLARSHIP

Radio Television Digital News Foundation
Attn: RTDNF Fellowship Program
4121 Plank Road, Suite 512
Fredericksburg, VA 22407
(202) 467-5214   Fax: (202) 223-4007
E-mail: staceys@rtdna.org
Web: www.rtdna.org/pages/education/undergraduates.php

Summary To provide financial assistance to African American and other minority undergraduate students who are interested in preparing for a career in electronic journalism.

Eligibility This program is open to sophomore or more advanced minority undergraduate students enrolled in an electronic journalism sequence at an accredited or nationally-recognized college or university. Applicants must submit 1 to 3 examples of their journalistic skills on audio CD or DVD (no more than 15 minutes total, accompanied by scripts); a description of their role on each story and a list of who worked on each story and what they did; a 1-page statement explaining why they are preparing for a career in electronic journalism with reference to their specific career preference (radio, television, online, reporting, producing, or newsroom management); a resume; and a letter of reference from their dean or faculty sponsor explaining why they are a good candidate for the award and certifying that they have at least 1 year of school remaining.

Financial data The stipend is $2,000, paid in semiannual installments of $1,000 each.

Duration 1 year.

Additional information The Radio Television Digital News Foundation (RTDNF) also provides an all-expense paid trip to the Radio Television Digital News Association (RTDNA) annual international conference. The RTDNF was formerly the Radio and Television News Directors Foundation (RTNDF). Previous winners of any RTDNF scholarship or internship are not eligible.

Number awarded 1 each year.

Deadline May of each year.

[82]
CARROLL R. GIBSON SCHOLARSHIP AWARD

National Association of Black Narcotic Agents
Attn: Scholarship Award Committee
P.O. Box 6467
Fredericksburg, VA 22403
E-mail: nabna1@verizon.net
Web: www.nabna.org/scholarship.htm

Summary To provide financial assistance to undergraduates working on a degree in criminal justice at an Historically Black College or University (HBCU).

Eligibility This program is open to full-time students currently enrolled at an HBCU and working on a degree in criminal justice. Applicants must have a GPA of 2.5 or higher and a record of school and community involvement. A personal interview is required. Selection is based on merit; financial need is not considered.

Financial data Stipends range from $500 to $5,000.

Duration 1 year.

Number awarded 1 or more each year.

Deadline Deadline not specified.

[83]
CATERPILLAR NSBE CORPORATE SCHOLARSHIPS

National Society of Black Engineers
Attn: Programs Department
205 Daingerfield Road
Alexandria, VA 22314
(703) 549-2207   Fax: (703) 683-5312
E-mail: scholarships@nsbe.org
Web: www.nsbe.org

Summary To provide financial assistance to members of the National Society of Black Engineers (NSBE) who are majoring in designated science and engineering fields.

Eligibility This program is open to members of the society who are enrolled as college sophomores, juniors, or seniors. Applicants must be majoring in computer science, computer information technology, materials science, applied or engineering physics, or the following fields of engineering: agricultural, chemical, civil, computer, electrical, industrial, materials, mechanical, or metallurgical. They must have a GPA of 2.8 or higher.

Financial data The stipend is $2,000.

Duration 1 year.

Additional information This program is sponsored by Caterpillar, Inc.

Number awarded 5 each year.

Deadline January of each year.

[84]
CATERPILLAR SCHOLARS AWARD

Society of Manufacturing Engineers
Attn: SME Education Foundation
One SME Drive
P.O. Box 930
Dearborn, MI 48121-0930
(313) 425-3300   Toll Free: (800) 733-4763, ext. 3300
Fax: (313) 425-3411   E-mail: foundation@sme.org
Web: www.smeef.org

Summary To provide financial assistance to African Americans and other undergraduates enrolled in a degree program in manufacturing engineering or manufacturing engineering technology.

Eligibility Applicants must be full-time students attending a degree-granting institution in North America and preparing for a career in manufacturing engineering. They must have completed at least 30 units in a manufacturing engineering or manufacturing engineering technology curriculum with a minimum GPA of 3.0. Minority applicants may apply as incoming freshmen. Along with their application, they must submit a 300-word essay that covers their career and educational objectives, how this scholarship will help them attain those objectives, and why they want to enter this field. Financial need is not considered in the selection process. Preference is given to applicants who have participated in a Science, Technology, and Engineering Preview Summer (STEPS) camp sponsored by the foundation.

Financial data Stipend amounts vary; recently, the value of all scholarships provided by this foundation averaged approximately $2,728.

Duration 1 year; may be renewed.

Additional information This program is sponsored by Caterpillar, Inc.

Number awarded Varies each year; recently, 10 of these scholarships were awarded.

Deadline January of each year.

[85]
CATHERYN SMITH MEMORIAL SCHOLARSHIP

Delta Sigma Theta Detroit Foundation, Inc.
24760 West Seven Mile Road
P.O. Box 441921
Detroit, MI 48244-1921
(313) 537-7137   E-mail: President@dstdfi.org
Web: www.dstdfi.org/scholarship-application.html

Summary To provide financial assistance to members of Delta Sigma Theta (a traditionally African American social sorority) who are majoring in education at a college in Michigan.

Eligibility This program is open to members of the sorority who are currently enrolled at an accredited 4-year college or university in Michigan. Applicants must be majoring in education and have a GPA of 3.0 or higher. Along with their application, they must submit 1) an essay up to 150 words on why they chose education as a major and how they plan to impact positively the field of education after graduating; 2) an essay up to 75 words describing their community service activities and involvement; and 3) an essay up to 75 words providing any other information that might be relevant to their application. Financial need is not considered in the selection process.

Financial data The stipend is $2,500.

Duration 1 year.

Number awarded 2 each year.

Deadline October of each year.

[86]
CBC SPOUSES VISUAL ARTS SCHOLARSHIP

Congressional Black Caucus Foundation, Inc.
Attn: Director, Educational Programs
1720 Massachusetts Avenue, N.W.
Washington, DC 20036
(202) 263-2800   Toll Free: (800) 784-2577
Fax: (202) 775-0773   E-mail: info@cbcfinc.org
Web: www.cbcfinc.org/scholarships.html

Summary To provide financial assistance to Black Americans and other undergraduate and graduate students who are interested in studying the visual arts.

Eligibility This program is open to 1) minority and other graduating high school seniors planning to attend an accredited institution of higher education; and 2) currently-enrolled full-time undergraduate, graduate, and doctoral students in good academic standing with a GPA of 2.5 or higher. Applicants must be interested in preparing for a career in the visual arts. Along with their application, they must submit a CD of 5 original pieces of their artwork and a personal statement of 500 to 1,000 words on 1) their future goals, major field of study, and how that field of study will help them to achieve their future career goals; 2) involvement in school activities, community and public service, hobbies, and sports; 3) how receiving this award will affect their current and future plans; and 4) other experiences, skills, or qualifications. They must also be able to demonstrate financial need, leadership ability, and participation in community service activities.

Financial data The stipend is $3,000.

Duration 1 year.

Additional information This program was established in 2006.

Number awarded 5 each year.

Deadline April of each year.

[87]
CDM SCHOLARSHIP

National Forum for Black Public Administrators
Attn: Scholarship Program
777 North Capitol Street, N.E., Suite 807
Washington, DC 20002
(202) 408-9300, ext. 112   Fax: (202) 408-8558
E-mail: vreed@nfbpa.org
Web: www.nfbpa.org/i4a/pages/index.cfm?pageid=3630

Summary   To provide financial assistance to African Americans working on a undergraduate or graduate degree in public administration or a related field.

Eligibility   This program is open to African American undergraduate and graduate students preparing for a career in public service. Applicants must be working full time on a degree in public administration, political science, urban affairs, public policy, or a related field. They must have a GPA of 3.0 or higher, excellent interpersonal and analytical abilities, and strong oral and written communication skills. Along with their application, they must submit a 3-page autobiographical essay that includes their academic and career goals and objectives. Although this is not a need-based program, first consideration is given to applicants who are not currently receiving other financial aid.

Financial data   The stipend is $5,000.

Duration   1 year.

Additional information   This program is sponsored by the consulting, engineering, construction, and operations firm CDM. Recipients are required to attend the sponsor's annual conference to receive their scholarship; limited hotel and air accommodations are arranged and provided.

Number awarded   1 each year.

Deadline   February of each year.

[88]
CENIE JOMO WILLIAMS TUITION SCHOLARSHIP

National Association of Black Social Workers
Attn: Office of Student Affairs
2305 Martin Luther King Avenue, S.E.
Washington, DC 20020
(202) 678-4570   Fax: (202) 678-4572
E-mail: nabsw.Harambee@verizon.net
Web: www.nabsw.org/mserver/StudentAffairs.aspx

Summary   To provide financial assistance for college or graduate school to members of the National Association of Black Social Workers (NABSW).

Eligibility   This program is open to African American members of NABSW who are enrolled full time in an accredited social work or social welfare program and have a GPA of 2.5 or higher. Applicants must be able to demonstrate community service and a research interest in the Black community. Along with their application, they must submit an essay of 2 to 3 pages on their professional interests, future social work aspirations, previous social work experiences (volunteer and professional), honors and achievements (academic and community service), and research interests within the Black community (for master's and doctoral students). Financial need is considered in the selection process.

Financial data   The stipend is $2,000. Funds are sent directly to the recipient's school.

Duration   1 year.

Number awarded   2 each year.

Deadline   December of each year.

[89]
CENTER FOR STUDENT OPPORTUNITY SCHOLARSHIP

Center for Student Opportunity
Attn: Opportunity Scholarship
4903 Auburn Avenue
P.O. Box 30370
Bethesda, MD 20824
(301) 951-7101, ext. 214   Fax: (301) 951-7104
E-mail: scholarship@csopportunity.org
Web: www.csopportunity.org/ss/oppscholarship.aspx

Summary   To provide financial assistance to first-generation, low-income, and/or minority high school seniors who have participated in activities of the sponsoring organization and plan to attend selected universities.

Eligibility   This program is open to graduating high school (or home-schooled) seniors who have participated in high school activities of the sponsoring organization. Applicants must be planning to attend a 4-year college or university that has a partnership arrangement with the sponsoring organization. They must be students whose parents did not go to or graduate from college, and/or students who need financial aid or scholarships to go to college, and/or students who identify as African American/Black, American Indian/Alaska Native, Hispanic/Latino, or Asian/Pacific Islander. Along with their application, they must submit 500-word essays on 1) the challenges they have faced in their college preparation, search, and application process; and 2) why they are deserving of this scholarship. There are no minimum academic requirements.

Financial data   The stipend is $2,000 per year.

Duration   1 year; may be renewed up to 3 additional years.

Additional information   The sponsor has partnership arrangements with more than 250 universities in nearly every state; most of them are private institutions, although some public universities are included. For a list, contact the sponsor. Recipients are invited to serve as monthly guest bloggers on the sponsor's web blog to share insight and perspective about their transition to college with high school participants in the sponsor's activities.

Number awarded   1 or more each year.

Deadline   May of each year.

[90]
CENTER ON BUDGET AND POLICY PRIORITIES INTERNSHIPS

Center on Budget and Policy Priorities
Attn: Internship Coordinator
820 First Street, N.E., Suite 510
Washington, DC 20002
(202) 408-1080   Fax: (202) 408-1056
E-mail: internship@cbpp.org
Web: www.cbpp.org/jobs/index.cfm?fa=internships

Summary   To provide work experience at the Center on Budget and Policy Priorities (CBPP) in Washington, D.C. to African Americans and other undergraduates, graduate students, and recent college graduates.

Eligibility This program is open to undergraduates, graduate students, and recent college graduates who are interested in public policy issues affecting low-income families and individuals. Applicants must be interested in working at CBPP in the following areas: media, federal legislation, health policy, housing policy, international budget project, Food Stamps, national budget and tax policy, outreach campaigns, state budget and tax policy, welfare reform, and income support. They should have research, fact-gathering, writing, analytic, and computer skills and a willingness to do administrative as well as substantive tasks. Women, international students, and minorities are encouraged to apply.

Financial data Hourly stipends are $8.50 for undergraduates, $9.50 for interns with a bachelor's degree, $10.50 for graduate students, $12.50 for interns with a master's or law degree, and $12.50 to $15.50 for doctoral students (depending on progress towards completion of degree requirements, relevant course work, and research).

Duration 1 semester; may be renewed.

Additional information The center specializes in research and analysis oriented toward practical policy decisions and produces analytic reports that are accessible to public officials at national, state, and local levels, to nonprofit organizations, and to the media.

Number awarded Varies each semester; recently, 5 interns were appointed for a fall semester.

Deadline February of each year for summer internships; June of each year for fall internships; October of each year for spring internships.

[91]
CESDA DIVERSITY SCHOLARSHIPS

Colorado Educational Services and Development Association
P.O. Box 40214
Denver, CO 80204
Web: www.cesda.org/664.html

Summary To provide financial assistance to high school seniors in Colorado who are planning to attend college in the state and are either first-generation college students or members of underrepresented ethnic or racial minorities.

Eligibility This program is open to seniors graduating from high schools in Colorado who are 1) the first member of their family to attend college; 2) a member of an underrepresented ethnic or racial minority (African American, Asian/Pacific Islander, American Indian, Hispanic/Chicano/Latino); and/or 3) able to demonstrate financial need. Applicants must have a GPA of 2.8 or higher and be planning to enroll at a 2- or 4-year college or university in Colorado. U.S. citizenship or permanent resident status is required. Selection is based on leadership and community service (particularly within minority communities), past academic performance, personal and professional accomplishments, personal attributes, special abilities, academic goals, and financial need.

Financial data The stipend is $1,000.

Duration 1 year; nonrenewable.

Number awarded Varies each year.

Deadline March of each year.

[92]
CHARLES L. GITTENS SCHOLARSHIP AWARD

National Organization of Black Law Enforcement Executives
Attn: NOBLE Scholarships
4609 Pinecrest Office Park Drive, Suite F
Alexandria, VA 22312-1442
(703) 658-1529   Fax: (703) 658-9479
E-mail: noble@noblenatl.org
Web: www.noblenational.org

Summary To provide financial assistance for college to African American and other high school seniors who are interested in preparing for a criminal justice career.

Eligibility This program is open to high school seniors who have a GPA of 2.5 or higher and are interested in preparing for a career in criminal justice. Applicants must be planning to attend an accredited academic institution in the United States to major in a social science (e.g. technology, forensic investigations, or other criminal investigative studies) related to a career in law enforcement or criminal justice. They must be able to demonstrate financial need. Along with their application, they must submit a 1-page essay on their career goals and interests and why they feel they should receive this scholarship. The sponsor is an organization of African American law enforcement officers.

Financial data The stipend is $1,500.

Duration 1 year; nonrenewable.

Number awarded 1 each year.

Deadline March of each year.

[93]
CHARLES S. BROWN SCHOLARSHIP IN PHYSICS

National Society of Black Physicists
Attn: Scholarship Committee Chair
1100 North Glebe Road, Suite 1010
Arlington, VA 22201
(703) 536-4207   Fax: (703) 536-4203
E-mail: scholarship@nsbp.org
Web: www.nsbp.org/scholarships

Summary To provide financial assistance to African American students working on an undergraduate or graduate degree in physics.

Eligibility This program is open to African American students who are working on an undergraduate or graduate degree in physics. Applicants must submit an essay on their academic and career objectives, information on their participation in extracurricular activities, a description of any awards and honors they have received, and 3 letters of recommendation. Financial need is not considered.

Financial data A stipend is awarded (amount not specified).

Duration 1 year; nonrenewable.

Number awarded 1 each year.

Deadline January of each year.

[94]
CHARLOTTE CHAPTER NBMBAA UNDERGRADUATE SCHOLARSHIP

National Black MBA Association-Charlotte Chapter
Attn: Scholarship Program
P.O. Box 34613
Charlotte, NC 28234
Toll Free: (877) 732-0314
E-mail: info@nbmbaacharlotte.org
Web: nbmbaacharlotte.org/Education.aspx

Summary   To provide financial assistance to African American and other minority residents of North and South Carolina who are working on a bachelor's degree at a business school in any state.

Eligibility   This program is open to minority residents of North and South Carolina who are currently enrolled full time at a college or university in any state. Applicants must be working on a bachelor's degree in business or management and have a GPA of 3.0 or higher. Selection is based primarily on a 2-page essay on a topic that changes annually but relates to African Americans and business.

Financial data   Stipends are $1,000 or $500.

Duration   1 year.

Number awarded   Varies each year; recently, 6 of these scholarships were awarded: 5 at $1,000 and 1 at $500.

Deadline   August of each year.

[95]
CHEERIOS BRAND HEALTH INITIATIVE SCHOLARSHIP

Congressional Black Caucus Foundation, Inc.
Attn: Director, Educational Programs
1720 Massachusetts Avenue, N.W.
Washington, DC 20036
(202) 263-2800   Toll Free: (800) 784-2577
Fax: (202) 775-0773   E-mail: info@cbcfinc.org
Web: www.cbcfinc.org/scholarships.html

Summary   To provide financial assistance to minority and other undergraduate students who reside in a Congressional district represented by an African American and are interested in preparing for a health-related career.

Eligibility   This program is open to 1) minority and other graduating high school seniors planning to attend an accredited institution of higher education; and 2) currently-enrolled full-time undergraduate students in good academic standing with a GPA of 2.5 or higher. Applicants must reside or attend school in a Congressional district represented by a member of the Congressional Black Caucus. They must be interested in preparing for a career in a medical or other health-related field, including medicine, nursing, technology, nutrition, or engineering. Along with their application, they must submit a personal statement of 500 to 1,000 words on 1) their future goals, major field of study, and how that field of study will help them to achieve their future career goals; 2) involvement in school activities, community and public service, hobbies, and sports; 3) how receiving this award will affect their current and future plans; and 4) other experiences, skills, or qualifications. They must also be able to demonstrate financial need, leadership ability, and participation in community service activities.

Financial data   A stipend is awarded (amount not specified).

Duration   1 year.

Additional information   The program was established in 1998 with support from General Mills, Inc.

Number awarded   Varies each year.

Deadline   May of each year.

[96]
CHEVRON SWE SCHOLARSHIPS

Society of Women Engineers
Attn: Scholarship Selection Committee
120 South LaSalle Street, Suite 1515
Chicago, IL 60603-3572
(312) 596-5223   Toll Free: (877) SWE-INFO
Fax: (312) 644-8557
E-mail: scholarshipapplication@swe.org
Web: societyofwomenengineers.swe.org

Summary   To provide financial assistance to African American and other members of the Society of Women Engineers (SWE) who are attending specified colleges and universities and majoring in designated engineering specialties.

Eligibility   This program is open to members of the society who are sophomores at specified ABET-accredited 4-year colleges or universities. Applicants must be majoring in computer science or chemical, computer, electrical, environmental, mechanical, or petroleum engineering and have a GPA of 3.0 or higher. Preference is given to members of groups underrepresented in computer science and engineering. Selection is based on merit. U.S. citizenship is required.

Financial data   The stipend is $2,000. The award includes a travel grant for the recipient to attend the SWE national conference.

Duration   1 year.

Additional information   This program, established in 1991, is sponsored by Chevron Corporation. For a list of the specified schools, contact SWE.

Number awarded   5 each year.

Deadline   February of each year.

[97]
CHIPS QUINN SCHOLARS PROGRAM

Freedom Forum
Attn: Chips Quinn Scholars Program
555 Pennsylvania Avenue, N.W.
Washington, DC 20001
(202) 292-6271   Fax: (202) 292-6275
E-mail: kcatone@freedomforum.org
Web: www.chipsquinn.org

Summary   To provide work experience to African American and other minority college students or recent graduates who are majoring in journalism.

Eligibility   This program is open to students of color who are college juniors, seniors, or recent graduates with journalism majors or career goals in newspapers. Candidates must be nominated or endorsed by journalism faculty, campus media advisers, editors of newspapers, or leaders of minority journalism associations. Along with their application, they must submit a resume, transcripts, 2 letters of recommendation, and an essay of 200 to 500 words on why they want to be a Chips Quinn Scholar. Reporters must also submit 6 samples of published articles they have written; photographers must submit 10 to 20 photographs on a CD. Applicants must have a car and be available to work as a full-time intern during the spring or summer. U.S. citizenship or permanent resident status is required. Campus newspaper experience is strongly encouraged.

Financial data Students chosen for this program receive a travel stipend to attend a Multimedia training program in Nashville, Tennessee prior to reporting for their internship, a $500 housing allowance from the Freedom Forum, and a competitive salary during their internship.

Duration Internships are for 10 to 12 weeks, in spring or summer.

Additional information This program was established in 1991 in memory of the late John D. Quinn Jr., managing editor of the *Poughkeepsie Journal.* Funding is provided by the Freedom Forum, formerly the Gannett Foundation. After graduating from college and obtaining employment with a newspaper, alumni of this program are eligible to apply for fellowship support to attend professional journalism development activities.

Number awarded Approximately 70 each year. Since the program began, more than 1,200 scholars have been selected.

Deadline October of each year.

[98]
CHRISTIAN COLLEGE LEADERS SCHOLARSHIPS

Foundation for College Christian Leaders
2658 Del Mar Heights Road
PMB 266
Del Mar, CA 92014
(858) 481-0848   E-mail: LMHays@aol.com
Web: www.collegechristianleader.com

Summary To provide financial assistance for college to Christian students (especially African Americans and other minorities) from California, Oregon, and Washington.

Eligibility This program is open to entering or continuing undergraduate students who reside or attend college in California, Oregon, or Washington. Applicants must have a GPA of 3.0 or higher, be able to document financial need (parents must have a combined income of less than $60,000), and be able to demonstrate Christian testimony and Christian leadership. Selection is based on identified leadership history, academic achievement, financial need, and demonstrated academic, vocational, and ministry training to further the Kingdom of Jesus Christ. Special consideration is given to minority students.

Financial data A stipend is awarded (amount not specified).

Duration 1 year; may be renewed.

Additional information The foundation, formerly known as the Eckmann Foundation, was founded in 1988.

Deadline May of each year.

[99]
CIGNA HEALTHCARE UNDERGRADUATE SCHOLARSHIP

National Forum for Black Public Administrators
Attn: Scholarship Program
777 North Capitol Street, N.E., Suite 807
Washington, DC 20002
(202) 408-9300, ext. 112   Fax: (202) 408-8558
E-mail: vreed@nfbpa.org
Web: www.nfbpa.org/i4a/pages/index.cfm?pageid=3630

Summary To provide financial assistance to African Americans working on an undergraduate degree in public administration at an Historically Black College or University (HBCU).

Eligibility This program is open to African American undergraduate students preparing for a career in public administration. Applicants must be working on a degree in public administration, political science, urban affairs, public policy, or a related field at an HBCU. They must have a GPA of 3.5 or higher, excellent interpersonal and analytical abilities, and strong oral and written communication skills. Along with their application, they must submit a 3-page autobiographical essay that includes their academic and career goals and objectives and a 3-page essay giving their opinion on the 5 most critical skills public administrators ought to possess and why. Financial need must be demonstrated.

Financial data The stipend is $10,000.

Duration 1 year.

Additional information This program is sponsored by CIGNA Healthcare. Recipients are required to attend the sponsor's annual conference to receive their scholarship; limited hotel and air accommodations are arranged and provided.

Number awarded 1 each year.

Deadline February of each year.

[100]
CIND M. TRESER MEMORIAL SCHOLARSHIP

Washington State Environmental Health Association
Attn: Executive Secretary
103 Sea Pine Lane
Bellingham, WA 98229-9363
(360) 738-8946   Fax: (360) 738-8949
E-mail: Kerri@wseha.org
Web: www.wseha.org

Summary To provide financial assistance to undergraduate students (particularly African Americans and other minorities) who are majoring in environmental health or other life sciences and are interested in preparing for a career in environmental health in the state of Washington.

Eligibility This program is open to undergraduates who 1) intend to become employed in the field of environmental health in Washington following graduation and 2) are enrolled in a program either accredited by the National Accreditation Council for Environmental Health Curricula or with a curriculum comparable to the model curriculum recommended by that Council (i.e., the program must include substantial course work in biology and microbiology, organic and inorganic chemistry, epidemiology, biostatistics, and environmental health sciences). Applicants must be members of the Washington State Environmental Health Association

(WSEHA). Students of color and specially challenged students are especially encouraged to apply.

Financial data The stipend is $1,000.

Duration 1 year.

Additional information This program was formerly known as the Ed Pickett Memorial Student Scholarship. The first scholarship was awarded in 1985. Recipients must attend the association's annual educational conference to accept the scholarship award.

Number awarded 1 each year.

Deadline August of each year.

[101]
CITE NON-TRADITIONAL SCHOLARSHIPS

Consortium of Information and Telecommunications
  Executives, Inc.
c/o Marvelle H. Martin, Scholarship Committee Chair
1342 Bailing Drive
Lawrenceville, GA 30043-5299
E-mail: m.martin@citese.org
Web: www.forcite.org/forcite/scholarships.asp

Summary To provide financial assistance to nontraditional African American students who plan to major in selected engineering- or business-related fields in college.

Eligibility This program is open to African Americans who have been out of high school for a period of time but who have now been accepted by an accredited college or vocational/technical school as a full-time student. Applicants must have a family income of $75,000 per year or less. They must be planning to major in 1 of the following fields: accounting, advertising, business, computer science, electrical engineering, finance, industrial engineering, information technology, marketing, or mathematics. Along with their application, they must submit 1) a 500-word essay on their educational and career goals; 2) a 500-word essay on how they got to this point in their life; and 3) a recommendation from their local chapter of the Consortium of Information and Telecommunications Executives (CITE) or an Historically Black College or University (HBCU). Employees of Verizon Communications or affiliated subsidiaries and their family members are ineligible. U.S. citizenship is required.

Financial data The stipend is $3,000.

Duration 1 year; nonrenewable.

Additional information CITE is an organization of African American employees of Verizon, founded in 1984 after the dissolution of the former Bell systems. Recipients must attend the CITE annual conference. Travel, conference, lodging, and other expenses are paid by CITE.

Number awarded 1 each year.

Deadline March of each year.

[102]
CITE TRADITIONAL SCHOLARSHIPS

Consortium of Information and Telecommunications
  Executives, Inc.
c/o Marvelle H. Martin, Scholarship Committee Chair
1342 Bailing Drive
Lawrenceville, GA 30043-5299
E-mail: m.martin@citese.org
Web: www.forcite.org/forcite/scholarships.asp

Summary To provide financial assistance to African American high school seniors who plan to major in selected business-related fields in college.

Eligibility This program is open to African American high school seniors who have been accepted by an accredited 4-year college or university as a full-time student. Applicants must have a GPA of 3.0 or higher and a family income of $75,000 per year or less. They must be planning to major in 1 of the following fields: accounting, advertising, business, computer science, electrical engineering, finance, industrial engineering, information technology, marketing, or mathematics. Along with their application, they must submit a 1-page essay on their educational and career goals. Employees of Verizon Communications or affiliated subsidiaries and their family members are ineligible. U.S. citizenship is required.

Financial data The stipend is $3,000.

Duration 1 year; nonrenewable.

Additional information The Consortium of Information and Telecommunications Executives (CITE) is an organization of African American employees of Verizon, founded in 1984 after the dissolution of the former Bell systems. Recipients must attend the CITE annual conference. Travel, conference, lodging, and other expenses are paid by CITE.

Number awarded 1 each year.

Deadline March of each year.

[103]
CLANSEER AND ANNA JOHNSON SCHOLARSHIPS

Community Foundation of New Jersey
Attn: Donor Services
35 Knox Hill Road
P.O. Box 338
Morristown, NJ 07963-0338
(973) 267-5533, ext. 221   Toll Free: (800) 659-5533
Fax: (973) 267-2903   E-mail: mrivera@cfnj.org
Web: www.cfnj.org/funds/scholarship/index.php

Summary To provide financial assistance to African American high school seniors in New Jersey who plan to attend college in any state.

Eligibility This program is open to African American seniors graduating from high schools in New Jersey who will be attending an educational institution in the United States. Applicants must have earned a grade of "A' or "B" in classes related to the sciences or mathematics and have maintained above average grades in all course work. They must have been born in the United States. Selection is based primarily on financial need, but academic performance, extracurricular activities, and work experience are also considered.

Financial data Recently, the stipend was $1,550 per year. Funds are made payable jointly to the recipients and their educational institution.

Duration 4 years, provided the recipient maintains a GPA of 2.5 or higher.

Additional information Recipients must agree to donate at least 10 hours of community service per week within New Jersey for 1 year following graduation.

Number awarded 6 each year.

Deadline March of each year.

[104]
CLARKE WATSON SCHOLARSHIPS

American Association of Blacks in Energy-Denver Area
  Chapter
Attn: Scholarship Committee
14405 West Colfax Avenue, Suite 264
Lakewood, CO 80401-3206
E-mail: haynes_carter@comcast.net
Web: www.aabe.org/index.php?component=pages&id=270

Summary To provide financial assistance to African Americans and members of other underrepresented minority groups who are high school seniors in Colorado and planning to major in an energy-related field at a college in any state.

Eligibility This program is open to seniors graduating from high schools in Colorado who are planning to work on a bachelor's degree at a college or university in any state. Applicants must be African Americans, Hispanics, or Native Americans who have a GPA of 3.5 or higher and who can demonstrate financial need. They must have a combined critical reading and mathematics SAT score of at least 900 or an ACT composite score of at least 19. Their intended major must be a science or mathematics field related to energy. Along with their application, they must submit a 350-word statement on why they should receive this scholarship, how their professional career objectives relate to energy, and any other relevant information. U.S. citizenship is required.

Financial data The stipend is $2,000. Funds are disbursed directly to the recipient's college or university.

Duration 1 year; may be renewed.

Additional information Winners are eligible to compete for regional and national scholarships.

Number awarded 2 each year.

Deadline March of each year.

[105]
COAST GUARD HEADQUARTERS BLACKS IN GOVERNMENT SCHOLARSHIP

Blacks in Government-Coast Guard Headquarters
  Chapter
Attn: Scholarship Program
3005 Georgia Avenue, N.W.
Washington, DC 20001-5015
(202) 475-5057   E-mail: Gail.M.McGee@uscg.mil
Web: www.bignet.org/regional/CGHC/whatsnew.htm

Summary To provide financial assistance for college to African American and other high school seniors in the Washington, D.C. metropolitan area.

Eligibility This program is open to seniors graduating from high schools in the Washington, D.C. metropolitan area who have a GPA of 2.0 or higher. Applicants must be planning to attend an accredited institution of higher learning. Along with their application, they must submit an essay of 350 to 500 words on 1 of the following topics: their chosen field of study and why; how their community, church, or family has influenced them; or why it is important for them to attend college. Finalists are interviewed.

Financial data A stipend is awarded (amount not specified).

Duration 1 year.

Additional information This program was established in 2004.

Number awarded Up to 3 each year.

Deadline March of each year.

[106]
COCHRAN/GREENE SCHOLARSHIP

National Naval Officers Association-Washington, D.C.
  Chapter
Attn: Scholarship Program
2701 Park Center Drive, A1108
Alexandria, VA 22302
(703) 566-3840   Fax: (703) 566-3813
E-mail: Stephen.Williams@Navy.mil
Web: dcnnoa.memberlodge.com

Summary To provide financial assistance to African American and other minority female high school seniors from the Washington, D.C. area who are interested in attending college in any state.

Eligibility This program is open to female minority seniors graduating from high schools in the Washington, D.C. metropolitan area who plan to enroll full time at an accredited 2- or 4-year college or university in any state. Applicants must have a GPA of 2.5 or higher. Selection is based on academic achievement, community involvement, and financial need.

Financial data The stipend is $1,500.

Duration 1 year; nonrenewable.

Additional information Recipients are not required to join or affiliate with the military in any way.

Number awarded 1 each year.

Deadline March of each year.

[107]
COKER/DAVIS SCHOLARSHIP

National Naval Officers Association-Washington, D.C.
  Chapter
Attn: Scholarship Program
2701 Park Center Drive, A1108
Alexandria, VA 22302
(703) 566-3840   Fax: (703) 566-3813
E-mail: Stephen.Williams@Navy.mil
Web: dcnnoa.memberlodge.com

Summary To provide financial assistance to male African American high school seniors from the Washington, D.C. area who are interested in attending college in any state.

Eligibility This program is open to male African American seniors graduating from high schools in the Washington, D.C. metropolitan area who plan to enroll full time at an accredited 2- or 4-year college or university in any state. Applicants must have a GPA of 2.5 or higher and be U.S. citizens or permanent residents. Selection is based on academic achievement, community involvement, and financial need.

Financial data The stipend is $1,000.

Duration 1 year; nonrenewable.

Additional information Recipients are not required to join or affiliate with the military in any way.

Number awarded 1 each year.

Deadline March of each year.

[108]
COLGATE "BRIGHT SMILES, BRIGHT FUTURES" MINORITY SCHOLARSHIPS

American Dental Hygienists' Association
Attn: Institute for Oral Health
444 North Michigan Avenue, Suite 3400
Chicago, IL 60611-3980
(312) 440-8944   Toll Free: (800) 735-4916
Fax: (312) 467-1806   E-mail: institute@adha.net
Web: www.adha.org/ioh/programs/scholarships.htm

Summary To provide financial assistance to African Americans, other minority students, and males of any race who are members of the Student American Dental Hygienists' Association (SADHA) or the American Dental Hygienists' Association (ADHA) and enrolled in certificate programs in dental hygiene.

Eligibility This program is open to members of groups currently underrepresented in the dental hygiene profession (Native Americans, African Americans, Hispanics, Asians, and males) who are active members of the SADHA or the ADHA. Applicants must have a GPA of 3.0 or higher, be able to document financial need of at least $1,500, and have completed at least 1 year of full-time enrollment in an accredited dental hygiene certificate program in the United States. Along with their application, they must submit a statement that covers their long-term career goals, their intended contribution to the dental hygiene profession, their professional interests, and how their extracurricular activities and their degree enhance the attainment of their goals.

Financial data The stipend ranges from $1,000 to $2,000.

Duration 1 year; nonrenewable.

Additional information These scholarships are sponsored by the Colgate-Palmolive Company.

Number awarded 2 each year.

Deadline January of each year.

[109]
COLGATE PALMOLIVE-LUBRIZOL UNDERGRADUATE RESEARCH AWARD

National Organization for the Professional Advancement
    of Black Chemists and Chemical Engineers
Attn: Awards Committee Chair
P.O. Box 77040
Washington, DC 20013
Toll Free: (800) 776-1419   Fax: (202) 667-1705
E-mail: nobccheawards@gmail.com
Web: www.nobcche.org

Summary To recognize and reward African American undergraduates who have conducted outstanding research in chemistry or related fields.

Eligibility This competition is open to African American students who have completed at least 2 years of full-time work on a bachelor's degree in chemistry, materials science, polymer science, materials engineering, or chemical engineering. Applicants must be planning to continue on to work on a graduate degree in those fields. They must submit an abstract for a 15-minute oral presentation of their original research at the annual conference of the National Organization for the Professional Advancement of Black Chemists and Chemical Engineers (NOBCChE).

Financial data The award is $1,000. The winners also receive reimbursement of travel and lodging for the NOBCChE annual conference and an offer of a paid summer internship with Lubrizol Corporation or Colgate-Palmolive Company, the program's sponsors.

Duration 1 year; nonrenewable.

Number awarded 1 each year.

Deadline October of each year.

[110]
COLLEGE SCHOLARSHIPS FOUNDATION MINORITY STUDENT SCHOLARSHIP

College Scholarships Foundation
5506 Red Robin Road
Raleigh, NC 27613
(919) 630-4895   Toll Free: (888) 501-9050
E-mail: info@collegescholarships.org
Web: www.collegescholarships.org

Summary To provide financial assistance to African Americans and other minority undergraduate and graduate students.

Eligibility This program is open to full-time undergraduate and graduate students who are Black, Hispanic, Native American, or Pacific Islander. Applicants must have a GPA of 3.0 or higher. Along with their application, they must submit a 300-word essay on how being a minority affected their pre-college education, how being a minority has positively affected their character, and where they see themselves in 10 years. U.S. citizenship is required.

Financial data The stipend is $1,000.

Duration 1 year.

Additional information This scholarship was first awarded in 2006. The sponsor was formerly known as the Daniel Kovach Scholarship Foundation.

Number awarded 1 each year.

Deadline December of each year.

[111]
COLLEGE STUDENT PRE-COMMISSIONING INITIATIVE

U.S. Coast Guard
Attn: Recruiting Command
2300 Wilson Boulevard, Suite 500
Arlington, VA 22201
(703) 235-1775   Toll Free: (877) NOW-USCG
Fax: (703) 235-1881
E-mail: Margaret.A.Jackson@uscg.mil
Web: www.gocoastguard.com

Summary To provide financial assistance to college students at Historically Black Colleges and Universities or other minority institutions who are willing to serve in the Coast Guard following graduation.

Eligibility This program is open to students entering their junior or senior year at a college or university designated as an Historically Black College or University (HBCU), Hispanic Serving Institution (HSI), Tribal College or University (TCU), or an institution located in Guam, Puerto Rico, or the U.S. Virgin Islands. Applicants must be U.S. citizens; have a GPA of 2.5 or higher; have scores of 1100 or higher on the critical reading and mathematics SAT, 23 or higher on the ACT, or 109 or higher on the ASVAB GT; be between 19 and 27 years of age; have no more than 2 dependents; and meet all physical requirements for a Coast Guard commission. They must agree to attend the Coast Guard Officer Candidate School following graduation and serve on active duty as an officer for at least 3 years.

Financial data Those selected to participate receive full payment of tuition, books, and fees; monthly housing and food allowances; medical and life insurance; special training in leadership, management, law enforcement, navigation, and marine science; 30 days of paid vacation per year; and a monthly salary of up to $2,200.

Duration Up to 2 years.

Number awarded Varies each year.

Deadline February of each year.

[112]
COLLEGE-SPONSORED ACHIEVEMENT SCHOLARSHIP AWARDS

National Merit Scholarship Corporation
Attn: National Achievement Scholarship Program
1560 Sherman Avenue, Suite 200
Evanston, IL 60201-4897
(847) 866-5100   Fax: (847) 866-5113
Web: www.nationalmerit.org/nasp.php

Summary To provide financial assistance from participating colleges to African American high school seniors who achieve high scores on the National Achievement Scholarship Program but who are not named as semifinalists.

Eligibility This program is open to African American high school seniors who apply for the National Achievement Scholarship Program and are among the top scorers but are not named semifinalists. Their names are circulated to about 1,500 4-year colleges and universities in the United States. College officials select the award winners.

Financial data College officials calculate each winner's stipend (based on financial information reported directly to the college), which ranges from $500 to $2,000 per year. Some colleges use a method known as "packaging aid" to meet the financial need of their award winners; in such instances, a College-Sponsored Achievement Scholarship may be supplemented with loans, employment, and grants. However, unless all of the winner's need is met with gift aid, the stipend must represent at least half of the student's need, up to a maximum annual stipend of $2,000.

Duration 1 year; renewable for up to 3 additional years.

Additional information Recently, 28 colleges and universities in the United States offered scholarships as part of this program. Every scholarship offered through this program is awarded with the condition that it can be used only at the institution funding it; therefore, an offer is canceled if a winner changes college choice.

Number awarded Approximately 200 each year.

Deadline Applicants must take the PSAT/NMSQT no later than October of their junior year.

[113]
COLORADO EDUCATION ASSOCIATION ETHNIC MINORITY SCHOLARSHIPS

Colorado Education Association
Attn: Ethnic Minority Advisory Council
1500 Grant Street
Denver, CO 80203
(303) 837-1500   Toll Free: (800) 332-5939
Web: coloradoea.org/education/grants.aspx

Summary To provide financial assistance to African American and other minority high school seniors in Colorado who are children of members of the Colorado Education Association (CEA) and planning to attend college in any state.

Eligibility This program is open to seniors graduating from high schools in Colorado who are members of a minority ethnic group, defined to include American Indians/Alaska Natives, Asians, Blacks, Hispanics, Native Hawaiians/Pacific Islanders, and multi-ethnic. Applicants must be the dependent child of an active, retired, or deceased CEA member. They must be planning to attend an accredited institution of higher education in any state. Along with their application, they must submit brief statements on 1) their need for this scholarship; and 2) why they plan to pursue a college education.

Financial data The stipend is $1,000.

Duration 1 year; nonrenewable.

Number awarded 4 each year.

Deadline March of each year.

[114]
COMMUNICATIONS INTERNSHIP AWARD FOR STUDENTS OF COLOR

College and University Public Relations Association of Pennsylvania
Calder Square
P.O. Box 10034
State College, PA 16805-0034
Fax: (814) 863-3428   E-mail: kathyettinger@psu.edu
Web: www.cuprap.org/default.aspx?pageid=16

Summary To provide an opportunity for African Americans and other students of color at institutions that are members of the College and University Public Relations Association of Pennsylvania (CUPRAP) to complete an internship in communications.

Eligibility This program is open to students of color (i.e., African Americans, Asian/Pacific Islanders, Hispanics/Latinos, and Native Americans) who have completed the first year of college and are enrolled as a degree candidate in the second year or higher. Applicants must obtain and complete a verifiable internship of at least 150 hours in a communications-related field (e.g., print media, radio, television, public relations, advertising, graphic/web design). They must be enrolled full time at an accredited 2- or 4-year college or university that is a member of CUPRAP, but they are not required to be residents of Pennsylvania. Selection is based on financial need, academic ability, communication skills, and creativity as demonstrated through work samples.

Financial data The stipend is $1,500, paid upon confirmation of employment in an internship position.

Duration The internship award is presented annually; recipients may reapply.

Additional information   This internship award was first presented in 1983.

Number awarded   1 each year.

Deadline   January.

[115]
COMTO ROSA L. PARKS SCHOLARSHIPS

Conference of Minority Transportation Officials
Attn: National Scholarship Program
818 18th Street, N.W., Suite 850
Washington, DC 20006
(202) 530-0551   Fax: (202) 530-0617
Web: www.comto.org/news-youth.php

Summary   To provide financial assistance for college to 1) children of African American and other members of the Conference of Minority Transportation Officials (COMTO) and 2) other students working on a bachelor's or master's degree in transportation.

Eligibility   This program is open to 1) college-bound high school seniors whose parent has been a COMTO member for at least 1 year; 2) undergraduates who have completed at least 60 semester credit hours in a transportation discipline; and 3) students working on a master's degree in transportation who have completed at least 15 credits. Applicants must have a GPA of 3.0 or higher. Along with their application, they must submit a cover letter with a 500-word statement of career goals. Financial need is not considered in the selection process. U.S. citizenship is required.

Financial data   The stipend is $4,500. Funds are paid directly to the recipient's college or university.

Duration   1 year.

Additional information   COMTO was established in 1971 to promote, strengthen, and expand the roles of minorities in all aspects of transportation. Recipients are expected to attend the COMTO National Scholarship Luncheon.

Number awarded   2 each year.

Deadline   April of each year.

[116]
CONGRESSIONAL BLACK CAUCUS FOUNDATION CONGRESSIONAL INTERNSHIP PROGRAM

Congressional Black Caucus Foundation, Inc.
Attn: Internship Coordinator
1720 Massachusetts Avenue, N.W.
Washington, DC 20036
(202) 263-2800   Toll Free: (800) 784-2577
Fax: (202) 775-0773   E-mail: internships@cbcfinc.org
Web: www.cbcfinc.org

Summary   To provide African American and other undergraduate students with an opportunity to work during the summer in a Congressional office and to participate in the legislative process.

Eligibility   This program is open to African Americans and other full-time undergraduate students in good academic standing. Applicants must be interested in a legislative internship on the staff of an African American member of Congress. They should have a demonstrated interest in public service, governance, and the policy-making process. Selection is based on scholastic achievement, evidence of leadership skills, writing skills, and community service contributions.

Financial data   Interns receive housing accommodations and a stipend of $3,000 to cover expenses related to travel, meals, and personal expenses.

Duration   9 weeks during the summer.

Additional information   This program was established in 1986.

Number awarded   Varies each year; recently, 42 interns served in this program.

Deadline   February of each year.

[117]
CONGRESSIONAL BLACK CAUCUS FOUNDATION ENVIRONMENTAL STUDIES SCHOLARSHIPS

Congressional Black Caucus Foundation, Inc.
Attn: Director, Educational Programs
1720 Massachusetts Avenue, N.W.
Washington, DC 20036
(202) 263-2800   Toll Free: (800) 784-2577
Fax: (202) 775-0773   E-mail: info@cbcfinc.org
Web: www.cbcfinc.org/scholarships.html

Summary   To provide financial assistance to African American and female upper-division students who are working on a degree in environmental science.

Eligibility   This program is open to African Americans and women who are currently enrolled as full-time juniors at a 4-year college or university. Applicants must be working on a degree in environmental science and have a GPA of 2.5 or higher. They must be able to demonstrate understanding and acceptance of ServiceMaster's core values. Along with their application, they must submit a personal statement of 500 to 1,000 words on 1) their future goals, major field of study, and how that field of study will help them to achieve their future career goals; 2) involvement in school activities, community and public service, hobbies, and sports; 3) how receiving this award will affect their current and future plans; and 4) other experiences, skills, or qualifications. They must also be able to demonstrate financial need, leadership ability, and participation in community service activities. Preference is given to students who plan to complete a 4-year degree and work in an underserved community. U.S. citizenship or permanent resident status is required.

Financial data   The stipend is $10,000. Funds are paid directly to the student's institution.

Duration   1 year.

Additional information   This program is sponsored by ServiceMaster.

Number awarded   2 each year.

Deadline   March of each year.

[118]
CONGRESSIONAL BLACK CAUCUS SPOUSES EDUCATION SCHOLARSHIP

Congressional Black Caucus Foundation, Inc.
Attn: Director, Educational Programs
1720 Massachusetts Avenue, N.W.
Washington, DC 20036
(202) 263-2800   Toll Free: (800) 784-2577
Fax: (202) 775-0773   E-mail: info@cbcfinc.org
Web: www.cbcfinc.org/scholarships.html

Summary To provide financial assistance to African American and other undergraduate and graduate students who reside in a Congressional district represented by an African American.

Eligibility This program is open to 1) African American and other graduating high school seniors planning to attend an accredited institution of higher education; and 2) currently-enrolled full-time undergraduate, graduate, and doctoral students in good academic standing with a GPA of 2.5 or higher. Applicants must reside or attend school in a Congressional district represented by a member of the Congressional Black Caucus. Along with their application, they must a personal statement of 500 to 1,000 words on 1) their future goals, major field of study, and how that field of study will help them to achieve their future career goals; 2) involvement in school activities, community and public service, hobbies, and sports; 3) how receiving this award will affect their current and future plans; and 4) other experiences, skills, or qualifications. They must also be able to demonstrate financial need, leadership ability, and participation in community service activities.

Financial data A stipend is awarded (amount not specified).

Duration 1 year.

Additional information The program was established in 1988.

Number awarded Varies each year.

Deadline May of each year.

[119]
CONNECTICUT CHAPTER AABE SCHOLARSHIPS

American Association of Blacks in Energy-Connecticut
Chapter
Attn: Scholarship Committee
P.O. Box 1898
Hartford, CT 06144
E-mail: lawandaa.leslie@uinet.com
Web: www.aabe.org/index.php?component=pages&id=787

Summary To provide financial assistance to African Americans and members of other underrepresented minority groups who are high school seniors in Connecticut and western Massachusetts and planning to major in an energy-related field at a college in any state.

Eligibility This program is open to seniors graduating from high schools in Connecticut or western Massachusetts and planning to work on a bachelor's degree at a college or university in any state. Applicants must be African Americans, Hispanics, or Native Americans who have a GPA of 3.0 or higher and who can demonstrate financial need. Their intended major must be a field of business, engineering, science, or mathematics related to energy. Along with their application, they must submit a 350-word statement on why they should receive this scholarship, their professional career objectives, and any other relevant information.

Financial data The stipend is $2,500. Funds are disbursed directly to the students.

Duration 1 year; nonrenewable.

Additional information Winners are eligible to compete for regional and national scholarships.

Number awarded 1 or more each year.

Deadline April of each year.

[120]
CONNECTICUT MINORITY TEACHER INCENTIVE PROGRAM

Connecticut Department of Higher Education
Attn: Office of Student Financial Aid
61 Woodland Street
Hartford, CT 06105-2326
(860) 947-1857   Fax: (860) 947-1838
E-mail: mtip@ctdhe.org
Web: www.ctdhe.org/SFA/default.htm

Summary To provide financial assistance and loan repayment to African Americans and other minority upper-division college students in Connecticut who are interested in teaching at public schools in the state.

Eligibility This program is open to juniors and seniors enrolled full time in Connecticut college and university teacher preparation programs. Applicants must be members of a minority group, defined as African American, Hispanic/Latino, Asian American, or Native American. They must be nominated by the education dean at their institution.

Financial data The maximum stipend is $5,000 per year. In addition, if recipients complete a credential and begin teaching at a public school in Connecticut within 16 months of graduation, they may receive up to $2,500 per year, for up to 4 years, to help pay off college loans.

Duration Up to 2 years.

Number awarded Varies each year.

Deadline September of each year.

[121]
CONSORTIUM FOR ENTERPRISE SYSTEMS MANAGEMENT SCHOLARSHIP FOR BDPA STUDENTS

Black Data Processing Associates
Attn: BDPA Education Technology Foundation
4423 Lehigh Road, Number 277
College Park, MD 20740
(513) 284-4968   Fax: (202) 318-2194
E-mail: scholarships@betf.org
Web: www.betf.org/scholarships/cesm.shtml

Summary To provide financial assistance to high school seniors in North or South Carolina who are members of the Black Data Processing Associates (BDPA) and interested in studying information technology at a college in those states.

Eligibility This program is open to seniors graduating from high schools in North or South Carolina and planning to enroll at an accredited 4-year college or university in their state. Applicants must be planning to work on a degree in information technology. They must have a GPA of 3.0 or higher. Along with their application, they must submit a 500-word essay on why information technology is important. Selection is based on that essay, academic achievement, leadership ability through academic or civic involvement, and participation in community service activities. U.S. citizenship or permanent resident status is required.

Financial data The stipend is $2,000. Funds may be used to pay for tuition, fees, books, room and board, or other college-related expenses.

Duration 1 year; nonrenewable.

Additional information The BDPA established its Education and Technology Foundation (BETF) in 1992 to advance the skill sets needed by African American and other minority adults and young people to compete in the information technology industry. This program is sponsored by the Consortium for Enterprise Systems Management.

Number awarded 1 or more each year.

Deadline December of each year.

[122]
CORPORATE PARTNER SCHOLARSHIPS

National Association of Black Accountants
Attn: National Scholarship Program
7474 Greenway Center Drive, Suite 1120
Greenbelt, MD 20770
(301) 474-NABA, ext. 114   Fax: (301) 474-3114
E-mail: customerservice@nabainc.org
Web: www.nabainc.org

Summary To provide financial assistance to student members of the National Association of Black Accountants (NABA) who are working on an undergraduate or graduate degree in a field related to accounting.

Eligibility This program is open to NABA members who are enrolled full time as 1) an undergraduate freshman, sophomore, junior, or first-semester senior majoring in accounting, business, or finance at a 4-year college or university; or 2) a graduate student working on a master's degree in accounting. High school seniors are not eligible. Applicants must have a GPA of 3.5 or higher in their major and 3.3 or higher overall. Selection is based on grades, financial need, and a 500-word autobiography that discusses career objectives, leadership abilities, community activities, and involvement in NABA.

Financial data Stipends range from $1,000 to $10,000.

Duration 1 year.

Number awarded Varies each year.

Deadline January of each year.

[123]
CORPORATE-SPONSORED ACHIEVEMENT SCHOLARSHIPS

National Merit Scholarship Corporation
Attn: National Achievement Scholarship Program
1560 Sherman Avenue, Suite 200
Evanston, IL 60201-4897
(847) 866-5100   Fax: (847) 866-5113
Web: www.nationalmerit.org/nasp.php

Summary To provide financial assistance from corporate sponsors to African American finalists for the National Achievement Scholarship Program who are not awarded Achievement Scholarships.

Eligibility African American high school seniors who are high scorers in the National Achievement Scholarship Program but who are not awarded scholarships are considered for this program. Because winners of these scholarships must meet preferential criteria specified by sponsors, not all finalists for the National Achievement Scholarship Program are considered for this award, and the awards are not subject to regional allocation. Further, corporate sponsors frequently offer their awards to finalists who are children of their employees or residents of an area where a plant or office is located. Some companies offer scholarships to students who plan to pursue particular college majors or careers. Finalists who have qualifications that especially interest a sponsor are identified and winners are selected from among eligible candidates. Financial need is considered for some of the awards.

Financial data Most of these scholarships provide stipends that are individually determined, taking into account college costs and family financial circumstances. Variable stipend awards of this type range from at least $500 to $2,000 per year, although some have a higher annual minimum and a few range as high as $10,000 per year. Some renewable awards provide a fixed annual stipend (between $1,000 and $5,000) that is the same for every recipient of the sponsor's awards. Other corporate-sponsored scholarships are nonrenewable and provide a single payment (from $2,500 to $5,000) for the recipient's first year of college study.

Duration 1 year; most awards are renewable up to 3 additional years.

Additional information Recently, these awards were sponsored by 42 corporations, company foundations, and professional organizations.

Number awarded Approximately 100 each year.

Deadline Applicants must take the PSAT/NMSQT no later than October of their junior year.

[124]
COSTCO WHOLESALE SCHOLARSHIPS

Independent Colleges of Washington
600 Stewart Street, Suite 600
Seattle, WA 98101
(206) 623-4494   Fax: (206) 625-9621
E-mail: info@icwashington.org
Web: www.icwashington.org/scholarships/index.html

Summary To provide financial assistance to African Americans and other underrepresented minority students who are enrolled at participating academic institutions that are members of the Independent Colleges of Washington (ICW).

Eligibility This program is open to students enrolled at ICW-member colleges and universities. Applicants must be members of underrepresented minority populations and able to demonstrate financial need. No application is required; each ICW institution makes a selection from all of its students.

Financial data The stipend varies at each institution.

Duration 1 year; nonrenewable.

Additional information The participating ICW-member institutions are Pacific Lutheran University, Saint Martin's College, Seattle Pacific University, University of Puget Sound, Walla Walla University, Whitman College, and Whitworth University. This program is sponsored by Costco Wholesale.

Number awarded Varies each year; recently, 18 of these scholarships were awarded.

Deadline Each institution sets its own deadline.

[125]
CRACKER BARREL-MINORITY TEACHER EDUCATION SCHOLARSHIPS

Florida Fund for Minority Teachers, Inc.
Attn: Executive Director
G415 Norman Hall
P.O. Box 117045
Gainesville, FL 32611-7045
(352) 392-9196, ext. 21   Fax: (352) 846-3011
E-mail: info@ffmt.org
Web: www.ffmt.org

Summary To provide funding to African Americans and other minorities who are Florida residents preparing for a career as a teacher.

Eligibility This program is open to Florida residents who are African American/Black, Hispanic/Latino, Asian American/Pacific Islander, or American Indian/Alaskan Native. Applicants must be entering their junior year in a teacher education program at a participating college or university in Florida. Special consideration is given to community college graduates. Selection is based on writing ability, communication skills, overall academic performance, and evidence of commitment to the youth of America (preferably demonstrated through volunteer activities).

Financial data The stipend is $2,000 per year. Recipients are required to teach 1 year in a Florida public school for each year they receive the scholarship. If they fail to teach in a public school, they are required to repay the total amount of support received at an annual interest rate of 8%.

Duration Up to 2 consecutive years, provided the recipient remains enrolled full time with a GPA of 2.5 or higher.

Additional information For a list of the 16 participating public institutions and the 18 participating private institutions, contact the Florida Fund for Minority Teachers (FFMT). Recipients are also required to attend the annual FFMT recruitment and retention conference.

Number awarded Varies each year.

Deadline July of each year for fall semester; November of each year for spring semester.

[126]
CSLA LEADERSHIP FOR DIVERSITY SCHOLARSHIP

California School Library Association
Attn: Executive Director
950 Glenn Drive, Suite 150
Folsom, CA 95630
(916) 447-2684   Fax: (916) 447-2695
E-mail: info@csla.net
Web: www.csla.net/awa/scholarships.htm

Summary To provide financial assistance to African Americans and other students who reflect the diversity of California's population and are interested in earning a credential as a library media teacher in the state.

Eligibility This program is open to students who are members of a traditionally underrepresented group enrolled in a college or university library media teacher credential program in California. Applicants must intend to work as a library media teacher in a California school library media center for a minimum of 3 years. Along with their application, they must submit a 250-word statement on their school library media

career interests and goals, why they should be considered, what they can contribute, their commitment to serving the needs of multicultural and multilingual students, and their financial situation.

Financial data The stipend is $1,500.

Duration 1 year.

Number awarded 1 each year.

Deadline April of each year.

[127]
CSPI PUBLIC INTEREST INTERNSHIP PROGRAM

Center for Science in the Public Interest
Attn: Internships
1875 Connecticut Avenue, N.W., Suite 300
Washington, DC 20009-5728
(202) 332-9110   Fax: (202) 265-4954
E-mail: hr@cspinet.org
Web: www.cspinet.org/about/jobs/200801042.html

Summary To provide summer work experience to minority and other students who are interested in working on health and nutritional issues at the Center for Science in the Public Interest (CSPI).

Eligibility This program is open to undergraduate, graduate, law, and medical students who are interested in working at the center, which is concerned with evaluating the effects of science and technology on society and promoting national policies responsive to consumers' interests. CSPI focuses primarily on health and nutritional issues, disclosing deceptive marketing practices, dangerous food additives or contaminants, and flawed science propagated by profits. Applicants must submit a cover letter indicating issues of interest, future plans, and dates of availability; a resume; writing samples; 2 letters of recommendation from instructors or employers; and an official transcript of courses and grades. Minorities, women, and persons with disabilities are especially encouraged to apply.

Financial data Undergraduate interns earn $8.25 per hour; graduate student interns earn $9.25 per hour.

Duration 10 weeks during the summer.

Number awarded A small number each year.

Deadline January of each year.

[128]
CULTURAL RESOURCES DIVERSITY INTERNSHIP PROGRAM

Student Conservation Association, Inc.
Attn: Diversity Internships
1800 North Kent Street, Suite 102
Arlington, VA 22209
(703) 524-2441   Fax: (703) 524-2451
E-mail: jchow@thesca.org
Web: www.thesca.org/partners/special-initiatives

Summary To provide summer work experience to African Americans, other ethnically diverse undergraduate and graduate students, and students with disabilities at facilities of the U.S. National Park Service (NPS).

Eligibility This program is open to currently-enrolled students at the sophomore or higher level. Applicants must be U.S. citizens or permanent residents with a GPA of 3.0 or higher. Although all students may apply, the program is designed to give ethnically diverse students and students with disabilities the opportunity to experience the diversity of careers in the federal sector. Applicants are assigned to a position within the NPS. Possible projects include editing publications, planning exhibits, participating in archaeological excavations, preparing research reports, cataloguing park and museum collections, providing interpretive programs on historical topics, developing community outreach, and writing lesson plans based on historical themes.

Financial data Interns receive a salary of $225 per week, basic medical insurance coverage, a housing stipend of up to $800 per month, a $100 uniform allowance, travel expenses up to $630, and eligibility for an Americorps Educational Award of $1,000.

Duration 10 weeks in the summer (beginning in June).

Additional information While participating in the internship, students engage in tri-weekly evening career and professional development events, ongoing career counseling, mentoring, and personal and career development services.

Number awarded Approximately 15 each year.

Deadline February of each year.

[129]
CUMMINS NSBE CORPORATE SCHOLARSHIP PROGRAM

National Society of Black Engineers
Attn: Programs Department
205 Daingerfield Road
Alexandria, VA 22314
(703) 549-2207　　　　　　　　Fax: (703) 683-5312
E-mail: scholarships@nsbe.org
Web: www.nsbe.org

Summary To provide financial assistance to undergraduate members of the National Society of Black Engineers (NSBE) who are majoring in engineering.

Eligibility This program is open to members of the society who are currently sophomores or juniors. Applicants may be studying any field of engineering, but the target majors are electrical and mechanical. They must have a GPA of 3.0 or higher and an interest in employment with Cummins, Inc., including an internship if offered. Along with their application, they must submit a 250-word essay describing how they will use their education to make a positive impact on the community, how they will contribute toward a more sustainable world in a personal or business manner, and how this scholarship opportunity will advance their career goals and benefit Cummins.

Financial data The stipend is $5,000 per year.

Duration 1 year; may be renewed until graduation.

Additional information This program is sponsored by Cummins, Inc. If a paid summer internship is offered, students must accept it to continue receiving scholarship funds.

Number awarded 4 each year.

Deadline January of each year.

[130]
CUMMINS SCHOLARSHIPS

Society of Women Engineers
Attn: Scholarship Selection Committee
120 South LaSalle Street, Suite 1515
Chicago, IL 60603-3572
(312) 596-5223　　　　　　Toll Free: (877) SWE-INFO
Fax: (312) 644-8557
E-mail: scholarshipapplication@swe.org
Web: societyofwomenengineers.swe.org

Summary To provide financial assistance to minority and other women working on an undergraduate or graduate degree in designated engineering specialties.

Eligibility This program is open to women who are sophomores, juniors, seniors, or graduate students at 4-year ABET-accredited colleges and universities. Applicants must be working on a degree in computer science or automotive, chemical, computer, electrical, industrial, manufacturing, materials, or mechanical engineering and have a GPA of 3.5 or higher. Preference is given to members of groups underrepresented in engineering or computer science. Selection is based on merit. U.S. citizenship is required.

Financial data The stipend is $1,000.

Duration 1 year.

Additional information This program is sponsored by Cummins, Inc.

Number awarded 2 each year.

Deadline February of each year.

[131]
DAMON P. MOORE SCHOLARSHIP

Indiana State Teachers Association
Attn: Scholarships
150 West Market Street, Suite 900
Indianapolis, IN 46204-2875
(317) 263-3400　　　　　　Toll Free: (800) 382-4037
Fax: (317) 655-3700　　　　E-mail: mshoup@ista-in.org
Web: www.ista-in.org/dynamic.aspx?id=1212

Summary To provide financial assistance to African American and other minority high school seniors in Indiana who are interested in studying education in college.

Eligibility This program is open to ethnic minority public high school seniors in Indiana who are interested in studying education in college. Selection is based on academic achievement, leadership ability as expressed through co-curricular activities and community involvement, recommendations, and a 300-word essay on their educational goals and how they plan to use this scholarship.

Financial data The stipend is $1,000.

Duration 1 year; may be renewed for 2 additional years if the recipient maintains at least a "C+" GPA.

Additional information This program was established in 1987.

Number awarded 1 each year.

Deadline February of each year.

[132]
DAVID AND SHEILA GARNETT LEADERSHIP SCHOLARSHIP

National Naval Officers Association-Washington, D.C.
  Chapter
Attn: Scholarship Program
2701 Park Center Drive, A1108
Alexandria, VA 22302
(703) 566-3840   Fax: (703) 566-3813
E-mail: Stephen.Williams@Navy.mil
Web: dcnnoa.memberlodge.com

Summary To provide financial assistance to African American high school seniors from the Washington, D.C. area who are interested in attending college in any state.

Eligibility This program is open to African American seniors graduating from high schools in the Washington, D.C. metropolitan area who plan to enroll full time at an accredited 2- or 4-year college or university in any state. Applicants must have a GPA of 2.5 or higher. Selection is based on academic achievement, community involvement, and financial need.

Financial data The stipend is $1,000.

Duration 1 year; nonrenewable.

Additional information Recipients are not required to join or affiliate with the military in any way.

Number awarded 1 each year.

Deadline March of each year.

[133]
DAVID SANKEY MINORITY SCHOLARSHIP IN METEOROLOGY

National Weather Association
Attn: Executive Director
228 West Millbrook Road
Raleigh, NC 27609-4304
(919) 845-1546   Fax: (919) 845-2956
E-mail: exdir@nwas.org
Web: www.nwas.org

Summary To provide financial assistance to African Americans and other minorities working on an undergraduate or graduate degree in meteorology.

Eligibility This program is open to members of minority groups who are either entering their sophomore or higher year of undergraduate study or enrolled as graduate students. Applicants must be working on a degree in meteorology. Along with their application, they must submit a 1-page statement explaining why they are applying for this scholarship. Selection is based on that statement, academic achievement, and 2 letters of recommendation.

Financial data The stipend is $1,000.

Duration 1 year.

Additional information This program was established in 2002.

Number awarded 1 each year.

Deadline April of each year.

[134]
DAVIS & DAVIS SCHOLARSHIP

National Naval Officers Association-Washington, D.C.
  Chapter
Attn: Scholarship Program
2701 Park Center Drive, A1108
Alexandria, VA 22302
(703) 566-3840   Fax: (703) 566-3813
E-mail: Stephen.Williams@Navy.mil
Web: dcnnoa.memberlodge.com

Summary To provide financial assistance to female African American high school seniors from the Washington, D.C. area who are interested in attending college in any state.

Eligibility This program is open to female African American seniors graduating from high schools in the Washington, D.C. metropolitan area who plan to enroll full time at an accredited 2- or 4-year college or university in any state. Applicants must have a GPA of 2.5 or higher and be U.S. citizens or permanent residents. Selection is based on academic achievement, community involvement, and financial need.

Financial data The stipend is $1,000.

Duration 1 year; nonrenewable.

Additional information Recipients are not required to join or affiliate with the military in any way.

Number awarded 1 each year.

Deadline March of each year.

[135]
DCBMBAA CHAPTER UNDERGRADUATE SCHOLARSHIP PROGRAM

National Black MBA Association-Washington, DC Chapter
Attn: Scholarship Program
P.O. Box 14042
Washington, DC 20044
(202) 628-0138   E-mail: info@dcbmbaa.org
Web: www.dcbmbaa.org/scholarships.htm

Summary To provide financial assistance to African Americans and other minority students from Washington, D.C., Maryland, or Virginia who are working on an undergraduate degree in business or management at a school in any state.

Eligibility This program is open to minority students who are enrolled full time in an undergraduate business or management program in any state and working on a bachelor's degree. Applicants must currently reside in Washington, D.C., Maryland, or Virginia, either permanently or as a student. Along with their application, they must submit an essay (from 2 to 5 pages) on 1 of 2 assigned topics that change annually but focus on minorities in business. Selection is based on the essay, transcripts, and a list of extracurricular activities and awards.

Financial data The stipend is $1,000.

Duration 1 year.

Additional information This program began in 2000.

Number awarded 1 each year.

Deadline June of each year.

[136]
DCNNOA/GENERAL DYNAMICS SCHOLARSHIP

National Naval Officers Association-Washington, D.C.
  Chapter
Attn: Scholarship Program
2701 Park Center Drive, A1108
Alexandria, VA 22302
(703) 566-3840   Fax: (703) 566-3813
E-mail: Stephen.Williams@Navy.mil
Web: dcnnoa.memberlodge.com

Summary   To provide financial assistance to African American high school seniors from the Washington, D.C. area who are interested in majoring in engineering at a college in any state.

Eligibility   This program is open to African American seniors graduating from high schools in the Washington, D.C. metropolitan area who plan to enroll full time in an engineering program at an accredited 2- or 4-year college or university in any state. Applicants must have a GPA of 3.0 or higher and be U.S. citizens or permanent residents. Selection is based on academic achievement, community involvement, and financial need.

Financial data   The stipend is $10,000.

Duration   1 year; nonrenewable.

Additional information   Recipients are not required to join or affiliate with the military in any way. This program is sponsored by General Dynamics.

Number awarded   1 each year.

Deadline   March of each year.

[137]
DEFENSE INTELLIGENCE AGENCY UNDERGRADUATE TRAINING ASSISTANCE PROGRAM

Defense Intelligence Agency
Attn: Human Resources, HCH-4
200 MacDill Boulevard, Building 6000
Bolling AFB, DC 20340-5100
(202) 231-8228   Fax: (202) 231-4889
TDD: (202) 231-5002   E-mail: staffing@dia.mil
Web: www.dia.mil/employment/student/index.htm

Summary   To provide funding and work experience to high school seniors and lower-division students (particularly African Americans, other minorities, females, and students with disabilities) who are interested in majoring in specified fields and working for the U.S. Defense Intelligence Agency (DIA).

Eligibility   This program is open to graduating high school seniors and college freshmen and sophomores interested in working full time on a baccalaureate degree in 1 of the following fields in college: biology, chemistry, computer science, engineering, foreign area studies, intelligence analysis, international relations, microbiology, pharmacology, physics, political science, or toxicology. High school seniors must have a GPA of 2.75 or higher and either 1) an SAT combined critical reading and mathematics score of 1000 or higher plus 500 or higher on the writing portion or 2) an ACT score of 21 or higher. College freshmen and sophomores must have a GPA of 3.0 or higher. All applicants must be able to demonstrate financial need (household income ceiling of $70,000 for a family of 4 or $80,000 for a family of 5 or more) and leadership abilities through extracurricular activities, civic involvement,

volunteer work, or part-time employment. Students and all members of their immediate family must be U.S. citizens. Minorities, women, and persons with disabilities are strongly encouraged to apply.

Financial data   Students accepted into this program receive tuition (up to $18,000 per year) at an accredited college or university selected by the student and endorsed by the sponsor; reimbursement for books and needed supplies; an annual salary to cover college room and board expenses and for summer employment; and a position at the sponsoring agency after graduation. Recipients must work for DIA after college graduation for at least 1 and a half times the length of study. For participants who leave DIA earlier than scheduled, the agency arranges for payments to reimburse DIA for the total cost of education (including the employee's pay and allowances).

Duration   4 years, provided the recipient maintains a GPA of 2.75 during the freshman year and 3.0 or higher in subsequent semesters.

Additional information   Recipients are provided a challenging summer internship and guaranteed a job at the agency in their field of study upon graduation.

Number awarded   Only a few are awarded each year.

Deadline   November of each year.

[138]
DELL THURMOND WOODARD FELLOWSHIP

The Fund for American Studies
Attn: Fellowships
1706 New Hampshire Avenue, N.W.
Washington, DC 20009
(202) 986-0384   Toll Free: (800) 741-6964
Fax: (202) 986-8930   E-mail: jtilley@tfas.org
Web: www.tfas.org/Page.aspx?pid=1511

Summary   To provide an opportunity for upper-division and graduate students (especially African Americans and others with an interest in diversity and ethics issues) to learn about high technology public policy issues during a summer internship in Washington, D.C.

Eligibility   This program is open to juniors, seniors, and graduate students who have an interest and background in issues regarding diversity and ethics and are currently enrolled at a 4-year college or university in the United States. Applicants must be interested in working in the government relations office of a high technology company or association in Washington while they also attend weekly seminar lunches hosted by the program's sponsors. They must have an interest in public policy and the high technology industry; a background in computer science or other high technology fields is helpful but not required. International students are eligible. Selection is based on evidence of a strong interest in a career in high technology public policy, civic mindedness and participation in community activities or organizations, academic achievements, and recommendations.

Financial data   Fellows receive a grant of $5,000.

Duration   8 weeks during the summer.

Additional information   This program was established in 2007 with support from the Congressional Black Caucus Foundation (CBCF), the Congressional Hispanic Caucus Institute (CHCI), and the Asian Pacific Institute for Congressional Studies (APAICS). Those 3 sponsors select the fellow on a rotational basis.

Number awarded 1 each year.

Deadline February of each year.

[139]
DELPHI NSBE CORPORATE SCHOLARSHIPS

National Society of Black Engineers
Attn: Programs Department
205 Daingerfield Road
Alexandria, VA 22314
(703) 549-2207   Fax: (703) 683-5312
E-mail: scholarships@nsbe.org
Web: www.nsbe.org

Summary To provide financial assistance to undergraduate and graduate student members of the National Society of Black Engineers (NSBE) who are working on a degree in designated fields of engineering.

Eligibility This program is open to members of the society who are enrolled as college sophomores, juniors, or seniors or as full-time graduate students, Applicants must be working on a degree in electrical, industrial, or mechanical engineering. They must have a GPA of 3.0 or higher and a demonstrated interest in employment (summer or full time) with Delphi. Along with their application, they must submit a 250-word essay on how they, Delphi, and their community will benefit from this support.

Financial data The stipend is $2,500.

Duration 1 year.

Additional information This program is sponsored by Delphi Corporation.

Number awarded 1 each year.

Deadline January of each year.

[140]
DELTA SIGMA THETA SORORITY GENERAL SCHOLARSHIPS

Delta Sigma Theta Sorority, Inc.
Attn: Scholarship and Standards Committee Chair
1707 New Hampshire Avenue, N.W.
Washington, DC 20009
(202) 986-2400   Fax: (202) 986-2513
E-mail: dstemail@deltasigmatheta.org
Web: www.deltasigmatheta.org

Summary To provide financial assistance to members of Delta Sigma Theta who are working on an undergraduate or graduate degree in any field.

Eligibility This program is open to active, dues-paying members of Delta Sigma Theta who are currently enrolled in college or graduate school. Applicants must submit an essay on their major goals and educational objectives, including realistic steps they foresee as necessary for the fulfillment of their plans. Financial need is considered in the selection process.

Financial data The stipends range from $1,000 to $2,000. The funds may be used to cover tuition, fees, and living expenses.

Duration 1 year; may be renewed for 1 additional year.

Additional information This sponsor is a traditionally African American social sorority. The application fee is $20.

Deadline April of each year.

[141]
DEPARTMENT OF ENERGY THURGOOD MARSHALL COLLEGE FUND SCHOLARSHIPS

Thurgood Marshall College Fund
Attn: Scholarship Manager
80 Maiden Lane, Suite 2204
New York, NY 10038
(212) 573-8487   Toll Free: (877) 690-8673
Fax: (212) 573-8497   E-mail: srogers@tmcfund.org
Web: www.thurgoodmarshallfund.net

Summary To provide financial assistance and work experience to students majoring in science, technology, engineering, or mathematics (STEM) at colleges and universities that are members of the Thurgood Marshall College Fund (TMCF).

Eligibility This program is open to full-time students majoring in STEM disciplines at 1 of the 47 colleges and universities that are TMCF members. Applicants must be available for an internship at a facility of the U.S. Department of Energy. They must have a GPA of 3.0 or higher and be able to demonstrate financial need. U.S. citizenship is required.

Financial data The stipend is $2,200 per semester ($4,400 per year).

Duration 1 year.

Additional information This program is sponsored by the U.S. Department of Energy. The 47 participating TMCF institutions are Alabama A&M University, Alabama State University, Albany State University, Alcorn State University, Bluefield State College, Bowie State University, Central State University (Ohio), Charles R. Drew University of Medicine (California), Cheyney University of Pennsylvania, Chicago State University, Coppin State College, Delaware State University, Elizabeth City State University, Fayetteville State University, Florida A&M University, Fort Valley State University, Grambling State University, Harris-Stowe State College, Howard University, Jackson State University, Kentucky State University, Langston University, Lincoln University (Missouri), Lincoln University (Pennsylvania), Medgar Evers College (New York), Mississippi Valley State University, Morgan State University, Norfolk State University, North Carolina A&T State University, North Carolina Central University, Prairie View A&M University, Savannah State University, South Carolina State University, Southern University and A&M College, Southern University at New Orleans, Southern University at Shreveport-Bossier City, Tennessee State University, Texas Southern University, Tuskegee University, University of Arkansas at Pine Bluff, University of the District of Columbia, University of Maryland-Eastern Shore, University of the Virgin Islands, Virginia State University, West Virginia State College, Winston-Salem State University, and York College.

Number awarded 10 each year.

Deadline July of each year.

[142]
DEPARTMENT OF HOMELAND SECURITY SUMMER FACULTY AND STUDENT RESEARCH TEAM PROGRAM

Oak Ridge Institute for Science and Education
Attn: Science and Engineering Education
P.O. Box 117
Oak Ridge, TN 37831-0117
(865) 574-1447   Fax: (865) 241-5219
E-mail: Patti.Obenour@orau.gov
Web: see.orau.org

Summary To provide an opportunity for teams of students and faculty from Historically Black Colleges and Universities (HBCUs) and other minority serving educational institutions to conduct summer research in areas of interest to the Department of Homeland Security (DHS).

Eligibility This program is open to teams of up to 2 students (undergraduate and/or graduate) and 1 faculty from Historically Black Colleges and Universities (HBCUs), Hispanic Serving Institutions (HSIs), Tribal Colleges and Universities (TCUs), Alaska Native Serving Institutions (ANSIs), and Native Hawaiian Serving Institutions (NHSIs). Applicants must be interested in conducting research at designated DHS Centers of Excellence in science, technology, engineering, or mathematics related to homeland security (HS-STEM), including explosives detection, mitigation, and response; social, behavioral, and economic sciences; risk and decision sciences; human factors aspects of technology; chemical threats and countermeasures; biological threats and countermeasures; community, commerce, and infrastructure resilience; food and agricultural security; transportation security; border security; immigration studies; maritime and port security; infrastructure protection; natural disasters and related geophysical studies; emergency preparedness and response; communications and interoperability; or advanced data analysis and visualization. Faculty must have a full-time appointment at an eligible institution and have received a Ph.D. in an HS-STEM discipline no more than 7 years previously; at least 2 years of full-time research and/or teaching experience is preferred. Students must have a GPA of 3.0 or higher and be enrolled full time. Undergraduates must be entering their junior or senior year. U.S. citizenship is required. Selection is based on relevance and intrinsic merit of the research (40%), faculty applicant qualifications (30%), academic benefit to the faculty applicant and his/her institution (10%), and student applicant qualifications (20%).

Financial data Stipends are $1,200 per week for faculty, $600 per week for graduate students, and $500 per week for undergraduates. Faculty members who live more than 50 miles from their assigned site may receive a relocation allowance of $1,500 and travel expenses up to an additional $500. Limited travel expenses for 1 round trip are reimbursed for undergraduate and graduate students living more than 50 miles from their assigned site.

Duration 12 weeks during the summer.

Additional information This program is funded by DHS and administered by Oak Ridge Institute for Science and Education (ORISE). Recently, the available DHS Centers of Excellence were the Center for Advancing Microbial Risk Assessment (led by Michigan State University and Drexel University); the Center for Risk and Economic Analysis of Terrorism Events (led by University of Southern California); the National Center for Food Protection and Defense (led by University of Minnesota); the Center of Excellence for Foreign Animal and Zoonotic Disease Defense (led by Texas A&M University and Kansas State University); the National Center for the Study of Preparedness and Catastrophic Event Response (led by Johns Hopkins University); the National Consortium for the Study of Terrorism and Responses to Terrorism (led by University of Maryland); the Center of Excellence for Awareness and Location of Explosives-Related Threats (led by Northeastern University and University of Rhode Island); the National Center for Border Security and Immigration (led by the University of Arizona and the University of Texas at El Paso); the Center for Maritime, Island and Remote and Extreme Environment Security (led by the University of Hawaii and Stevens Institute of Technology); the Center for Natural Disasters, Coastal Infrastructure, and Emergency Management (led by the University of North Carolina at Chapel Hill and Jackson State University); the National Transportation Security Center of Excellence (consisting of 7 institutions); and the Center of Excellence in Command, Control, and Interoperability (led by Purdue University and Rutgers University).

Number awarded Approximately 12 teams are selected each year.

Deadline January of each year.

[143]
DEPARTMENT OF STATE STUDENT INTERN PROGRAM

Department of State
Attn: HR/REE
2401 E Street, N.W., Suite 518 H
Washington, DC 20522-0108
(202) 261-8888   Toll Free: (800) JOB-OVERSEAS
Fax: (301) 562-8968   E-mail: Careers@state.gov
Web: www.careers.state.gov/students/programs

Summary To provide a work/study opportunity to undergraduate and graduate students (especially African Americans, other minorities, and women) who are interested in foreign service.

Eligibility This program is open to full- and part-time continuing college and university juniors, seniors, and graduate students. Applications are encouraged from students with a broad range of majors, such as business or public administration, social work, economics, information management, journalism, and the biological, engineering, and physical sciences, as well as those majors more traditionally identified with international affairs. U.S. citizenship is required. The State Department particularly encourages eligible women and minority students with an interest in foreign affairs to apply.

Financial data Most internships are unpaid. A few paid internships are granted to applicants who can demonstrate financial need. If they qualify for a paid internship, they are placed at the GS-4 step 5 level (currently with an annual rate of $27,786). Interns placed abroad may also receive housing, medical insurance, a travel allowance, and a dependents' allowance.

Duration Paid internships are available only for 10 weeks during the summer. Unpaid internships are available for 1 semester or quarter during the academic year, or for 10 weeks during the summer.

Additional information About half of all internships are in Washington, D.C., or occasionally in other large cities in the United States. The remaining internships are at embassies and consulates abroad. Depending upon the needs of the department, interns are assigned junior-level professional duties, which may include research, preparing reports, drafting replies to correspondence, working in computer science, analyzing international issues, financial management, intelligence, security, or assisting in cases related to domestic and international law. Interns must agree to return to their schooling immediately upon completion of their internship.

Number awarded Approximately 800 internships are offered each year, but only about 5% of those are paid positions.

Deadline February of each year for fall internships; June of each year for spring internships; October of each year for summer internships.

[144]
DEPARTMENT OF THE INTERIOR DIVERSITY INTERN PROGRAM

Department of the Interior
Attn: Office of Educational Partnerships
1849 C Street, N.W., MS 5221 MIB
Washington, DC 20240
(202) 208-6403   Toll Free: (888) 447-4392
Fax: (202) 208-3620   TDD: (202) 208-5069
E-mail: ed_partners@ios.doi.gov
Web: www.doi.gov/hrm/dipfact.html

Summary To provide work experience to 1) African American and other minority college and graduate students and 2) students with disabilities at federal agencies involved with natural and cultural resources.

Eligibility This program is open to currently-enrolled students at the sophomore or higher level at Historically Black Colleges and Universities (HBCUs), Hispanic-Serving Institutions (HSIs), Tribal Colleges and Universities (TCUs), and some other major institutions. Applicants must be U.S. citizens or permanent residents with a GPA of 3.0 or higher. Although all students may apply, the program is designed to give ethnically diverse students and students with disabilities the opportunity to experience the diversity of careers in the federal sector. Applicants are assigned to a position within the U.S. Department of the Interior (DOI). Possible placements include archaeology and anthropology; wildlife and fisheries biology; business administration, accounting, and finance; civil and environmental engineering; computer science, especially GIS applications; human resources; mining and petroleum engineering; communications and public relations; web site and database design; environmental and realty law; geology, hydrology, and geography; Native American studies; interpretation and environmental education; natural resource and range management; public policy and administration; and surveying and mapping.

Financial data The weekly stipend is $420 for sophomores and juniors, $450 for seniors, or $520 for law and graduate students. Other benefits include a pre-term orientation, transportation to the orientation and the work site, worker's compensation, and accident insurance.

Duration 10 weeks in the summer (beginning in June) or 15 weeks in the fall (beginning in September) or spring (beginning in January).

Additional information This program, which began in 1994, is administered through 5 nonprofit organizations: Hispanic Association of Colleges and Universities, Minority Access, Inc., Student Conservation Association, and National Association for Equal Opportunity in Higher Education. While participating in the internship, students engage in tri-weekly evening career and professional development events, ongoing career counseling, mentoring, and personal and career development services.

Number awarded Varies each year; since the program began, more than 700 interns have participated.

Deadline February of each year for summer; June of each year for fall; November of each year for spring.

[145]
DETROIT CHAPTER NBMBAA UNDERGRADUATE SCHOLARSHIP

National Black MBA Association-Detroit Chapter
Attn: Scholarship Awards
P.O. Box 02398
Detroit, MI 48202
(313) 237-0089   Fax: (313) 237-0093
Web: www.nbmbaa.org

Summary To provide financial assistance to African American and other minority undergraduates from any state working on an undergraduate degree in business at a college or university in the Detroit area of Michigan.

Eligibility This program is open to African American and other minority residents of any state enrolled as full-time sophomores, juniors, or seniors at a college or university in the Detroit area. Applicants must be working on an undergraduate degree in business or management. Along with their application, they must submit a 2-page essay on a topic that changes annually but relates to African Americans and business. Selection is based on that essay, transcripts, and extracurricular activities.

Financial data The stipend is $1,500.

Duration 1 year.

Number awarded 1 each year.

Deadline April of each year.

[146]
DEVERNE CALLOWAY SCHOLARSHIP

Missouri Legislative Black Caucus Foundation
c/o Senator Yvonne Wilson
4609 Paseo Boulevard, Suite 102
Kansas City, MO 64110
Toll Free: (877) 63-MLBCF   E-mail: mlbcf@aol.com
Web: www.mlbcf.com

Summary To provide financial assistance to African American and other disadvantaged residents of Missouri who are interested in working on an undergraduate degree in any field at a school in any state.

Eligibility This program is open to African American and other undergraduate students from Missouri who come from a disadvantaged background. Applicants may be attending or planning to attend a college or university in any state. They must have a GPA of 2.5 or higher. Along with their application, they must submit a 250-word personal statement on how their education will assist them in achieving their goals. Selection is based on academic excellence, community service, leadership skills, and financial need.

Financial data A stipend is awarded (amount not specified).

Duration 1 year; recipients may reapply for up to 5 years of support.

Number awarded 1 or more each year.

Deadline April of each year.

[147]
DIETETIC TECHNICIAN PROGRAM SCHOLARSHIPS

American Dietetic Association
Attn: Commission on Accreditation for Dietetics Education
120 South Riverside Plaza, Suite 2000
Chicago, IL 60606-6995
(312) 899-0040   Toll Free: (800) 877-1600, ext. 5400
Fax: (312) 899-4817   E-mail: education@eatright.org
Web: www.eatright.org/CADE/content.aspx?id=7934

Summary To provide financial assistance to underrepresented minorities and other student members of the American Dietetic Association (ADA) who are in the first year of a dietetic technician program.

Eligibility This program is open to ADA student members in the first year of study in a CADE-approved or accredited dietetic technician program. Applicants must be U.S. citizens or permanent residents and show promise of being a valuable, contributing member of the profession. Some scholarships require membership in a specific dietetic practice group, residency in a specific state, or underrepresented minority group status. The same application form can be used for all categories.

Financial data Stipends range from $500 to $3,000; most are for $1,000.

Duration 1 year.

Additional information Funds must be used for the second year of study.

Number awarded Varies each year, depending upon the funds available; recently, the sponsoring organization awarded 222 scholarships for all its programs.

Deadline February of each year.

[148]
DISTRICT AND INTERNATIONAL SCHOLAR OF THE YEAR AWARDS

Omega Psi Phi Fraternity
Attn: Charles R. Drew Memorial Scholarship Commission
3951 Snapfinger Parkway
Decatur, GA 30035-3203
(404) 284-5533   Fax: (404) 284-0333
E-mail: scholarshipchairman@oppf.org
Web: oppf.org/scholarship

Summary To recognize and reward members of Omega Psi Phi fraternity who demonstrate outstanding academic achievement and involvement in extracurricular and community activities.

Eligibility This program is open to members of the fraternity who are enrolled as a full-time sophomore or higher at a 4-year college or university. Applicants must have a GPA of 3.3 or higher. Chapters nominate their most outstanding member to the district. Each of the 12 districts selects a District Scholar of the Year winner. Those winners become candidates for the International Scholar of the Year Award. Candidates must submit a statement of 200 to 250 words on their purpose for applying for this scholarship, how they believe funds from the fraternity can assist them in achieving their career goals, and other circumstances (including financial need) that make it important for them to receive financial assistance. Selection is based on academic excellence, participation in extracurricular activities, and campus and community involvement.

Financial data District Scholars win a certificate and $6,500. The International Scholar of the Year wins an additional $10,000.

Duration The awards are presented annually.

Number awarded 12 district winners are selected each year; 1 of those is designated International Scholar of the Year.

Deadline Applications must be submitted to the district scholarship committee chair by January of each year.

[149]
DISTRICT OF COLUMBIA CHAPTER AABE SCHOLARSHIPS

American Association of Blacks in Energy-District of
  Columbia Chapter
Attn: Scholarship Committee
P.O. Box 333
Washington, DC 20044
E-mail: lbeal@ingaa.org
Web: www.aabe.org/index.php?component=pages&id=533

Summary To provide financial assistance to African American and other underrepresented minority high school seniors in the Washington, D.C. metropolitan area who are planning to major in an energy-related field at a college in any state.

Eligibility This program is open to seniors graduating from high schools in the Washington, D.C. metropolitan area who are planning to work on a bachelor's degree at a college or university in any state. Applicants must be African Americans, Hispanics, or Native Americans who have a GPA of 3.0 or higher and who can demonstrate financial need. Their intended major must be a field of business, engineering, physical science, mathematics, or technology related to energy. Along with their application, they must submit a 350-word statement on why they should receive this scholarship, their professional career objectives, and any other relevant information.

Financial data A total of $5,000 is available for this program each year.

Duration 1 year; nonrenewable.

Additional information Winners are eligible to compete for regional and national scholarships.

Number awarded 1 or more each year.

Deadline February of each year.

[150]
DIVERSITY COMMITTEE SCHOLARSHIP

American Society of Safety Engineers
Attn: ASSE Foundation
1800 East Oakton Street
Des Plaines, IL 60018
(847) 768-3435   Fax: (847) 768-3434
E-mail: agabanski@asse.org
Web: www.asse.org

Summary To provide financial assistance to upper-division and graduate student members of the American Society of Safety Engineers (ASSE) who are African American or come from other diverse groups.

Eligibility This program is open to ASSE student members who are working on an undergraduate or graduate degree in occupational safety, health, and environment or a closely-related field (e.g., industrial or environmental engineering, environmental science, industrial hygiene, occupational health nursing). Applicants must be full-time students who have completed at least 60 semester hours with a GPA of 3.0 or higher as undergraduates or at least 9 semester hours with a GPA of 3.5 or higher as graduate students. Along with their application, they must submit 2 essays of 300 words or less: 1) why they are seeking a degree in occupational safety and health or a closely-related field, a brief description of their current activities, and how those relate to their career goals and objectives; and 2) why they should be awarded this scholarship (including career goals and financial need). A goal of this program is to support individuals regardless of race, ethnicity, gender, religion, personal beliefs, age, sexual orientation, physical challenges, geographic location, university, or specific area of study. U.S. citizenship is not required.

Financial data The stipend is $1,000 per year.

Duration 1 year; recipients may reapply.

Number awarded 1 each year.

Deadline November of each year.

[151]
DIVERSITY SUMMER HEALTH-RELATED RESEARCH EDUCATION PROGRAM

Medical College of Wisconsin
Attn: Student Affairs/Diversity Program Coordinator
8701 Watertown Plank Road
Milwaukee, WI 53226
(414) 955-8735   Fax: (414) 955-0129
Web: www.mcw.edu/display/router.asp?docid=619

Summary To provide an opportunity for African Americans and other undergraduate residents of any state who come from diverse backgrounds to participate in a summer research training experience at the Medical College of Wisconsin.

Eligibility This program is open to U.S. citizens and permanent residents who come from diverse and economically and/or educationally disadvantaged backgrounds. Applicants must be interested in participating in a summer research training program at the Medical College of Wisconsin. They must have completed at least 1 year of undergraduate study at an accredited college or university (or be a community college student enrolled in at least 3 courses per academic term) and have a GPA of 3.0 or higher.

Financial data The stipend is $10 per hour for a 40-hour week. Housing is provided for students who live outside the Milwaukee area and travel expenses are paid for those who live outside Wisconsin.

Duration 10 weeks during the summer.

Additional information Students are "matched" with a full-time faculty investigator to participate in a research project addressing the causes, prevention, and treatment of cardiovascular, pulmonary, or hematological diseases. This program is funded by the National Heart, Lung, and Blood Institute (NHLBI) of the National Institutes of Health (NIH). Participants are required to prepare an abstract of their research and make a brief oral presentation of their project at the conclusion of the summer.

Number awarded Approximately 12 each year.

Deadline February of each year.

[152]
DON SAHLI–KATHY WOODALL MINORITY STUDENT SCHOLARSHIP

Tennessee Education Association
801 Second Avenue North
Nashville, TN 37201-1099
(615) 242-8392   Toll Free: (800) 342-8367
Fax: (615) 259-4581   E-mail: wdickens@tea.nea.org
Web: www.teateachers.org

Summary To provide financial assistance to African Americans and other minority high school seniors in Tennessee who are interested in majoring in education at a college or university in the state.

Eligibility This program is open to minority high school seniors in Tennessee who are planning to attend a college or university in the state and major in education. Application must be made either by a Future Teachers of America chapter affiliated with the Tennessee Education Association (TEA) or by the student with the recommendation of an active TEA member. Selection is based on academic record, leadership ability, financial need, and demonstrated interest in becoming a teacher.

Financial data The stipend is $1,000.

Duration 1 year.

Number awarded 1 each year.

Deadline February of each year.

[153]
DOROTHY E. GENERAL SCHOLARSHIP

Seattle Foundation
Attn: African American Scholarship Program
1200 Fifth Avenue, Suite 1300
Seattle, WA 98101-3151
(206) 622-2294   Fax: (206) 622-7673
E-mail: scholarships@seattlefoundation.org
Web: www.seattlefoundation.org

Summary To provide financial assistance to African Americans from any state working on an undergraduate or graduate degree in a field related to health care.

Eligibility This program is open to African American undergraduate and graduate students who are preparing for a career in a health care profession, including public health, medicine, nursing, or dentistry; pre-professional school students are also eligible. Applicants must be able to demonstrate financial need, academic competence, and leadership of African American students. They may be residents of any state attending school in any state. Along with their application, they must submit a 2-page essay describing their future aspirations, including their career goals and how their study of health care will help them achieve those goals and contribute to the African American community.

Financial data The stipend is $1,000 per year. Payments are made directly to the recipient's educational institution.

Duration 1 year; may be renewed.

Number awarded 1 or more each year.

Deadline February of each year.

[154]
DR. BLANCA MOORE-VELEZ WOMAN OF SUBSTANCE SCHOLARSHIP

National Association of Negro Business and Professional
   Women's Clubs
Attn: Scholarship Committee
1806 New Hampshire Avenue, N.W.
Washington, DC 20009-3206
(202) 483-4206   Fax: (202) 462-7253
E-mail: education@nanbpwc.org
Web: www.nanbpwc.org/ScholarshipApplications.asp

Summary To provide financial assistance to mature African American women from North Carolina who are interested in working on an undergraduate degree at a college in any state.

Eligibility This program is open to African American women over 35 years of age who are residents of North Carolina. Applicants must be working on an undergraduate degree at an accredited college or university in any state. They must have a GPA of 3.0 or higher. Along with their application, they must submit a 500-word essay on "Challenges to the Mature Student and How I Overcame Them." Financial need is not considered in the selection process.

Financial data A stipend is awarded (amount not specified).

Duration 1 year.

Number awarded 1 each year.

Deadline February of each year.

[155]
DR. JESSE BEMLEY SCHOLARSHIP

Black Data Processing Associates
Attn: BDPA Education Technology Foundation
4423 Lehigh Road, Number 277
College Park, MD 20740
(513) 284-4968   Fax: (202) 318-2194
E-mail: scholarships@betf.org
Web: www.betf.org/scholarships/jesse-bemley.shtml

Summary To recognize and reward, with college scholarships, high school students who participate in the annual national computer competition of the Black Data Processing Associates (BDPA).

Eligibility This competition is open to students who are members of a team that participates in the High School Computer Competition at the BDPA annual conference. Each team consists of 5 students. At the end of the competition, the sponsor sends award letters to all of the eligible team members who have graduated from high school, have been

accepted to a 4-year degree program, and plan to major in an information technology field. Letter recipients are invited to apply for these scholarships. Selection is based on performance at the computer competition.

Financial data Awards for each member of the top teams are $2,500 for first place, $2,000 for second place, $1,500 for third place, $1,000 for fourth place, and $500 for fifth place. Funds are paid directly to the student's college or university to be used for tuition or other school expenses.

Duration The competition is held annually.

Additional information The BDPA established its Education and Technology Foundation (BETF) in 1992 to advance the skill sets needed by African American and other minority adults and young people to compete in the information technology industry. Previously, this program was known as the Student Information Technology Education & Scholarship.

Number awarded 25 each year: 5 members of each of the top 5 teams win awards.

Deadline Deadline not specified.

[156]
DR. JO ANN OTA FUJIOKA SCHOLARSHIP

Phi Delta Kappa International
Attn: PDK Educational Foundation
408 North Union Street
P.O. Box 7888
Bloomington, IN 47407-7888
(812) 339-1156   Toll Free: (800) 766-1156
Fax: (812) 339-0018   E-mail: scholarships@pdkintl.org
Web: www.pdkintl.org/awards/prospective.htm

Summary To provide financial assistance to African American and other high school seniors of color who plan to study education at a college in any state and have a connection to Phi Delta Kappa (PDK).

Eligibility This program is open to high school seniors of color who are planning to major in education and can meet 1 of the following criteria: 1) is a member of a Future Educators Association (FEA) chapter; 2) is the child or grandchild of a PDK member; 3) has a reference letter written by a PDK member; or 4) is selected to represent the local PDK chapter. Applicants must submit a 500-word essay on a topic related to education that changes annually; recently, they were invited to explain what caused them to choose a career in education, what they hope to accomplish during their career as an educator, and how they will measure their success. Selection is based on the essay, academic standing, letters of recommendation, service activities, educational activities, and leadership activities; financial need is not considered.

Financial data The stipend depends on the availability of funds; recently, it was $2,000.

Duration 1 year.

Additional information This program was established in 2006.

Number awarded 1 each year.

Deadline January of each year.

[157]
DR. JULIANNE MALVEAUX SCHOLARSHIP

National Association of Negro Business and Professional Women's Clubs
Attn: Scholarship Committee
1806 New Hampshire Avenue, N.W.
Washington, DC 20009-3206
(202) 483-4206   Fax: (202) 462-7253
E-mail: education@nanbpwc.org
Web: www.nanbpwc.org/ScholarshipApplications.asp

Summary To provide financial assistance to African American women studying journalism, economics, or a related field in college.

Eligibility This program is open to African American women enrolled at an accredited college or university as a sophomore or junior. Applicants must have a GPA of 3.0 or higher and be majoring in journalism, economics, or a related field. Along with their application, they must submit an essay, up to 1,000 words in length, on their career plans and their relevance to the theme of the program: "Black Women's Hands Can Rock the World." U.S. citizenship is required.

Financial data The stipend is $1,000.

Duration 1 year.

Number awarded 1 or more each year.

Deadline February of each year.

[158]
DUANE MOORER SCHOLARSHIP

Organization of Black Aerospace Professionals, Inc.
Attn: Scholarship Coordinator
1 Westbrook Corporate Center, Suite 300
Westchester, IL 60154
(708) 449-7755   Toll Free: (800) JET-OBAP
Fax: (708) 449-7754
E-mail: obapscholarship@gmail.com
Web: www.obap.org/scholarships

Summary To provide financial assistance to African American high school seniors in selected states who plan to work on an aerospace degree at a school in any state.

Eligibility This program is open to African American seniors graduating from high schools within 400 miles of Memphis (includes all of Alabama, Arkansas, Kentucky, Louisiana, Mississippi, and Missouri, plus portions of northwestern Florida, western Georgia, southern Illinois, southern Indiana, eastern Kansas, eastern Oklahoma, and eastern Texas). Applicants must be interested in enrolling in a 2- or 4-year aerospace degree program. They must have a GPA of 2.5 or higher and have participated in a program of the Organization of Black Aerospace Professionals (OBAP) within the past 3 years. Along with their application, they must submit a 250-word essay on the importance of giving back.

Financial data A stipend is awarded (amount not specified).

Duration 1 year.

Additional information The OBAP was originally established in 1976 as the Organization of Black Airline Pilots to make certain Blacks and other minorities had a group that would keep them informed about opportunities for advancement within commercial aviation.

Number awarded 1 each year.

Deadline Applications must be submitted at least 30 days prior to the OBAP convention.

[159]
DUKE UNIVERSITY SUMMER RESEARCH OPPORTUNITY PROGRAM

Duke University
Graduate School
2127 Campus Drive
Box 90070
Durham, NC 27708-0070
(919) 681-3257   Fax: (919) 681-8018
E-mail: SROP@duke.edu
Web: gradschool.duke.edu/gsa/srop

Summary To provide African American and other undergraduate students from underrepresented groups with an opportunity to spend a summer learning research techniques in biomedical research laboratories at Duke University.

Eligibility This program is open to undergraduates who are seriously considering joining a Ph.D. graduate program following completion of their undergraduate degree. Applicants must be interested in participating in a summer program at Duke University, during which they will spend most of their time learning research techniques in a laboratory, mentored by faculty members who are actively engaged in conducting research and who would be particularly adept at training undergraduates from underrepresented groups. Eligible departments of study include biochemistry, biological and biologically inspired materials, biological chemistry, biology, biomedical engineering, cell and molecular biology, cell biology, computational biology and bioinformatics, developmental biology, ecology, environment, evolutionary anthropology, genetics and genomics, immunology, integrated toxicology, molecular cancer biology, molecular genetics and microbiology, neurobiology, pathology, pharmacology, and structural biology and biophysics. Along with their application, they must submit a 250-word essay on why they are interested in participating in this program, a 300-word essay on their career goals and how they plan to accomplish those goals, a 400-word description of past research experiences, and a 200-word description of current research interests. Both U.S. and international students are eligible.

Financial data Students receive an on-campus apartment, travel assistance, a food allowance, and a competitive stipend.

Duration 10 weeks during the summer.

Number awarded Approximately 15 each year.

Deadline February of each year.

[160]
DWIGHT DAVID EISENHOWER HISTORICALLY BLACK COLLEGES AND UNIVERSITIES TRANSPORTATION FELLOWSHIP PROGRAM

Department of Transportation
Federal Highway Administration
Attn: Office of PCD, HPC-32
4600 North Fairfax Drive, Suite 800
Arlington, VA 22203-1553
(703) 235-0538   Toll Free: (877) 558-6873
Fax: (703) 235-0593   E-mail: transportationedu@dot.gov
Web: www.fhwa.dot.gov/ugp/index.htm

Summary   To provide financial assistance to undergraduate and graduate students working on a degree in a transportation-related field at an Historically Black College or University (HBCU).

Eligibility   This program is open to students working on a bachelor's, master's, or doctoral degree at a federally-designated 4-year HBCU. Applicants must be working on a degree in a transportation-related field (i.e., engineering, accounting, business, architecture, environmental sciences). They must be U.S. citizens or have an I-20 (foreign student) or I-551 (permanent resident) identification card. Undergraduates must be entering at least their junior year and have a GPA of 3.0 or higher. Graduate students must have a GPA of at least 3.25. Selection is based on their proposed plan of study, academic achievement (based on class standing, GPA, and transcripts), transportation work experience, and letters of recommendation.

Financial data   Fellows receive payment of full tuition and fees (to a maximum of $10,000) and a monthly stipend of $1,450 for undergraduates, $1,700 for master's students, or $2,000 for doctoral students. They are also provided with a 1-time allowance of up to $1,500 to attend the annual Transportation Research Board (TRB) meeting.

Duration   1 year.

Additional information   This program is administered by the participating HBCUs.

Number awarded   Varies each year.

Deadline   January of each year.

[161]
EARL G. GRAVES SCHOLARSHIP

National Association for the Advancement of Colored People
Attn: Education Department
4805 Mt. Hope Drive
Baltimore, MD 21215-3297
(410) 580-5760   Toll Free: (877) NAACP-98
E-mail: youth@naacpnet.org
Web: www.naacp.org/pages/naacp-scholarships

Summary   To provide financial assistance to African American and other upper-division and graduate students majoring in business.

Eligibility   This program is open to full-time juniors, seniors, and graduate students working on a degree in business. Applicants must be currently in good academic standing, making satisfactory progress toward an undergraduate or graduate degree, and in the top 20% of their class. Along with their application, they must submit a 1-page essay on their interest in their major and a career, their life's ambition, what

they hope to accomplish in their lifetime, and what position they hope to attain. Financial need is not considered in the selection process.

Financial data   The stipend is $5,000.

Duration   1 year.

Number awarded   Varies each year; recently, 12 of these scholarships were awarded.

Deadline   March of each year.

[162]
ED BRADLEY SCHOLARSHIP

Radio Television Digital News Foundation
Attn: RTDNF Fellowship Program
4121 Plank Road, Suite 512
Fredericksburg, VA 22407
(202) 467-5214   Fax: (202) 223-4007
E-mail: staceys@rtdna.org
Web: www.rtdna.org/pages/education/undergraduates.php

Summary   To provide financial assistance to African American and other minority undergraduate students who are preparing for a career in electronic journalism.

Eligibility   This program is open to sophomore or more advanced minority undergraduate students enrolled in an electronic journalism sequence at an accredited or nationally-recognized college or university. Applicants must submit 1 to 3 examples of their journalistic skills on audio CD or DVD (no more than 15 minutes total, accompanied by scripts); a description of their role on each story and a list of who worked on each story and what they did; a 1-page statement explaining why they are preparing for a career in electronic journalism with reference to their specific career preference (radio, television, online, reporting, producing, or newsroom management); a resume; and a letter of reference from their dean or faculty sponsor explaining why they are a good candidate for the award and certifying that they have at least 1 year of school remaining.

Financial data   The stipend is $10,000, paid in semiannual installments of $5,000 each.

Duration   1 year.

Additional information   The Radio Television Digital News Foundation (RTDNF) also provides an all-expense paid trip to the Radio Television Digital News Association (RTDNA) annual international conference. The RTDNF was formerly the Radio and Television News Directors Foundation (RTNDF). Previous winners of any RTDNF scholarship or internship are not eligible.

Number awarded   1 each year.

Deadline   May of each year.

[163]
EDITH M. ALLEN SCHOLARSHIPS

United Methodist Church
Attn: General Board of Higher Education and Ministry
Office of Loans and Scholarships
1001 19th Avenue South
P.O. Box 340007
Nashville, TN 37203-0007
(615) 340-7344   Fax: (615) 340-7367
E-mail: umscholar@gbhem.org
Web: www.gbhem.org/loansandscholarships

Summary To provide financial assistance to Methodist students who are African American and working on an undergraduate or graduate degree in specified fields.

Eligibility This program is open to full-time undergraduate and graduate students at Methodist colleges and universities (preferably Historically Black United Methodist colleges) who have been active, full members of a United Methodist Church for at least 3 years prior to applying. Applicants must be African Americans working on a degree in education, social work, medicine, and/or other health professions. They must have at least a "B+" average and be recognized as a person whose academic and vocational contributions will help improve the quality of life for others.

Financial data A stipend is awarded (amount not specified).

Duration 1 year; recipients may reapply.

Number awarded Varies each year.

Deadline March of each year.

[164]
EDSA MINORITY SCHOLARSHIP

Landscape Architecture Foundation
Attn: Scholarship Program
818 18th Street, N.W., Suite 810
Washington, DC 20006-3520
(202) 331-7070   Fax: (202) 331-7079
E-mail: scholarships@lafoundation.org
Web: www.laprofession.org/financial/scholarships.htm

Summary To provide financial assistance to African American and other minority college students who are interested in studying landscape architecture.

Eligibility This program is open to African American, Hispanic, Native American, and minority college students of other cultural and ethnic backgrounds. Applicants must be entering their final 2 years of undergraduate study in landscape architecture. Along with their application, they must submit a 500-word essay on a design or research effort they plan to pursue (explaining how it will contribute to the advancement of the profession and to their ethnic heritage), work samples, and 2 letters of recommendation. Selection is based on professional experience, community involvement, extracurricular activities, and financial need.

Financial data The stipend is $3,500.

Additional information This scholarship was formerly designated the Edward D. Stone, Jr. and Associates Minority Scholarship.

Number awarded 1 each year.

Deadline February of each year.

[165]
EDWARD S. ROTH MANUFACTURING ENGINEERING SCHOLARSHIP

Society of Manufacturing Engineers
Attn: SME Education Foundation
One SME Drive
P.O. Box 930
Dearborn, MI 48121-0930
(313) 425-3300   Toll Free: (800) 733-4763, ext. 3300
Fax: (313) 425-3411   E-mail: foundation@sme.org
Web: www.smeef.org

Summary To provide financial assistance to students (especially African Americans and other minorities) who are enrolled or planning to work on a bachelor's or master's degree in manufacturing engineering at selected universities.

Eligibility This program is open to U.S. citizens who are graduating high school seniors or currently-enrolled undergraduate or graduate students. Applicants must be enrolled or planning to enroll as a full-time student at 1 of 13 selected 4-year universities to work on a bachelor's or master's degree in manufacturing engineering. They must have a GPA of 3.0 or higher. Preference is given to 1) students demonstrating financial need, 2) minority students, and 3) students participating in a co-op program. Some preference may also be given to graduating high school seniors and graduate students. Along with their application, they must submit a 300-word essay that covers their career and educational objectives, how this scholarship will help them attain those objectives, and why they want to enter this field.

Financial data Stipend amounts vary; recently, the value of all scholarships provided by this foundation annually averages approximately $2,700.

Duration 1 year; may be renewed.

Additional information The eligible institutions are California Polytechnic State University at San Luis Obispo, California State Polytechnic State University at Pomona, University of Miami (Florida), Bradley University (Illinois), Central State University (Ohio), Miami University (Ohio), Boston University, Worcester Polytechnic Institute (Massachusetts), University of Massachusetts, St. Cloud State University (Minnesota), University of Texas-Pan American, Brigham Young University (Utah), and Utah State University.

Number awarded 2 each year.

Deadline January of each year.

[166]
EISENHOWER GRANTS FOR RESEARCH AND INTERN FELLOWSHIPS

Department of Transportation
Federal Highway Administration
Attn: Office of PCD, HPC-32
4600 North Fairfax Drive, Suite 800
Arlington, VA 22203-1553
(703) 235-0538   Toll Free: (877) 558-6873
Fax: (703) 235-0593   E-mail: transportationedu@dot.gov
Web: www.fhwa.dot.gov/ugp/grf_ann.htm

Summary To offer students (particularly African Americans and other minorities) an opportunity to participate in transportation-related research activities either at facilities of the U.S. Department of Transportation (DOT) Federal Highway Administration in the Washington, D.C. area or private organizations.

Eligibility This program is open to 1) students in their junior year of a baccalaureate program who will complete their junior year before being awarded a fellowship; 2) students in their senior year of a baccalaureate program; and 3) students who have completed their baccalaureate degree and are enrolled in a program leading to a master's, Ph.D., or equivalent degree. Applicants must be enrolled full time at an accredited U.S institution of higher education and planning to enter the transportation profession after completing their higher education. They must be U.S. citizens or have an I-20 (foreign student) or I-551 (permanent resident) identification card. For research fellowships, they select 1 or more projects from a current list of research activities underway at various DOT facilities; the research is conducted with academic supervision provided by a faculty adviser from their home university (which grants academic credit for the research project) and with technical direction provided by the DOT staff. Intern fellowships provide students with opportunities to perform transportation-related research, development, technology transfer, and other activities at public and private sector organizations. Specific requirements for the target projects vary; most require engineering backgrounds, but others involve transportation planning, information management, public administration, physics, materials science, statistical analysis, operations research, chemistry, economics, technology transfer, urban studies, geography, and urban and regional planning. The DOT encourages students at Historically Black Colleges and Universities (HBCUs), Hispanic Serving Institutions (HSIs), and Tribal Colleges and Universities (TCUs) to apply for these grants. Selection is based on match of the student's qualifications with the proposed research project (including the student's ability to accomplish the project in the available time), recommendation letters regarding the nominee's qualifications to conduct the research, academic records (including class standing, GPA, and transcripts), and transportation work experience (if any), including the employer's endorsement.

Financial data Fellows receive full tuition and fees that relate to the academic credits for the approved research project (to a maximum of $10,000) and a monthly stipend of $1,450 for undergraduates, $1,700 for master's students, or $2,000 for doctoral students. An allowance for travel to and from the DOT facility where the research is conducted is also provided, but selectees are responsible for their own housing accommodations. Recipients are also provided with a 1-time allowance of up to $1,500 to attend the annual Transportation Research Board (TRB) meeting.

Duration Projects normally range from 3 to 12 months.

Number awarded Varies each year; recently, 9 students participated in this program.

Deadline Applications remain open until each project is filled.

[167]
ELI LILLY AND COMPANY/BLACK DATA PROCESSING ASSOCIATES SCHOLARSHIP

Black Data Processing Associates
Attn: BDPA Education Technology Foundation
4423 Lehigh Road, Number 277
College Park, MD 20740
(513) 284-4968   Fax: (202) 318-2194
E-mail: scholarships@betf.org
Web: www.betf.org/scholarships/eli-lilly.shtml

Summary To provide financial assistance to African American and other minority high school seniors or current college students who are interested in studying information technology at a college in any state.

Eligibility This program is open to graduating high school seniors and current college undergraduates who are members of minority groups (African American, Hispanic, Asian, or Native American). Applicants must be enrolled or planning to enroll at an accredited 4-year college or university and work on a degree in information technology. They must have a GPA of 3.0 or higher. Along with their application, they must submit a 500-word essay on why information technology is important. Selection is based on that essay, academic achievement, leadership ability through academic or civic involvement, and participation in community service activities. U.S. citizenship or permanent resident status is required.

Financial data The stipend is $2,500. Funds may be used to pay for tuition, fees, books, room and board, or other college-related expenses.

Duration 1 year; nonrenewable.

Additional information The BDPA established its Education and Technology Foundation (BETF) in 1992 to advance the skill sets needed by African American and other minority adults and young people to compete in the information technology industry. This program is sponsored by Eli Lilly and Company.

Number awarded 1 or more each year.

Deadline July of each year.

[168]
ELIZABETH KNIGHT SCHOLARSHIP AWARDS

Consortium of Information and Telecommunications Executives-Maryland Chapter
P.O. Box 1286
Baltimore, MD 21203
(410) 393-2337   E-mail: scholarship@cite-md.org
Web: www.cite-md.org

Summary To provide financial assistance to African American high school seniors in Maryland who plan to attend college in any state.

Eligibility This program is open to African American seniors graduating from high schools in Maryland with a GPA of 3.0 or higher. Applicants must have been accepted by an accredited college or university in any state and be able to document financial need. Employees and immediate family members of employees of the Verizon Corporation or an affiliated subsidiary are ineligible.

Financial data The stipend is $1,000.

Duration 1 year.

Additional information The Consortium of Information and Telecommunications Executives (CITE) is an organization of African American employees of Verizon, founded in 1984 after the dissolution of the former Bell systems.

Number awarded 3 each year.

Deadline March of each year.

[169]
ELLA TACKWOOD FUND

United Methodist Higher Education Foundation
Attn: Scholarships Administrator
1001 19th Avenue South
P.O. Box 340005
Nashville, TN 37203-0005
(615) 340-7385   Toll Free: (800) 811-8110
Fax: (615) 340-7330
E-mail: umhefscholarships@gbhem.org
Web: www.umhef.org/receive.php?id=endowed_funds

Summary To provide financial assistance to Methodist undergraduate and graduate students at Historically Black Colleges and Universities (HBCUs) of the United Methodist Church.

Eligibility This program is open to students enrolling as full-time undergraduate and graduate students at HBCUs of the United Methodist Church. Applicants must have been active, full members of a United Methodist Church for at least 1 year prior to applying. They must have a GPA of 2.5 or higher and be able to demonstrate financial need. Along with their application, they must submit a 200-word essay on their involvement and/or leadership responsibilities in their church, school, and community within the last 3 years. U.S. citizenship or permanent resident status is required.

Financial data The stipend is at least $1,000 per year.

Duration 1 year; nonrenewable.

Additional information This program was established in 1985. The qualifying schools are Bennett College for Women, Bethune-Cookman College, Claflin University, Clark Atlanta University, Dillard University, Huston-Tillotson College, Meharry Medical College, Paine College, Philander Smith College, Rust College, and Wiley College.

Number awarded Varies each year; recently, 3 of these scholarships were awarded.

Deadline May of each year.

[170]
ELLIS/CORLEY COMMUNITY ACTIVISM SCHOLARSHIP

National Naval Officers Association-Washington, D.C.
    Chapter
Attn: Scholarship Program
2701 Park Center Drive, A1108
Alexandria, VA 22302
(703) 566-3840   Fax: (703) 566-3813
E-mail: Stephen.Williams@Navy.mil
Web: dcnnoa.memberlodge.com

Summary To provide financial assistance to African American high school seniors from the Washington, D.C. area who are interested in attending an Historically Black College or University (HBCU) in any state.

Eligibility This program is open to African American seniors graduating from high schools in the Washington, D.C. metropolitan area who plan to enroll full time at an HBCU in any state. Applicants must have a GPA of 2.5 or higher and be U.S. citizens or permanent residents. Selection is based on academic achievement, community involvement, and financial need.

Financial data The stipend is $1,000.

Duration 1 year; nonrenewable.

Additional information Recipients are not required to join or affiliate with the military in any way.

Number awarded 1 each year.

Deadline March of each year.

[171]
ELMER S. IMES SCHOLARSHIP IN PHYSICS

National Society of Black Physicists
Attn: Scholarship Committee Chair
1100 North Glebe Road, Suite 1010
Arlington, VA 22201
(703) 536-4207   Fax: (703) 536-4203
E-mail: scholarship@nsbp.org
Web: www.nsbp.org/scholarships

Summary To provide financial assistance to African American students majoring in physics in college.

Eligibility This program is open to African American students who are entering their junior or senior year of college and majoring in physics. Applicants must submit an essay on their academic and career objectives, information on their participation in extracurricular activities, a description of any awards and honors they have received, and 3 letters of recommendation. Financial need is not considered.

Financial data A stipend is awarded (amount not specified).

Duration 1 year; nonrenewable.

Number awarded 1 each year.

Deadline January of each year.

[172]
EMMA AND MELOID ALGOOD SCHOLARSHIP

National Association of Black Social Workers
Attn: Office of Student Affairs
2305 Martin Luther King Avenue, S.E.
Washington, DC 20020
(202) 678-4570   Fax: (202) 678-4572
E-mail: nabsw.Harambee@verizon.net
Web: www.nabsw.org/mserver/StudentAffairs.aspx

Summary To provide financial assistance to members of the National Association of Black Social Workers (NABSW) who are working on a bachelor's degree.

Eligibility This program is open to African American members of NABSW working full time on a bachelor's degree at an accredited U.S. social work or social welfare program with a GPA of 2.5 or higher. Applicants must be able to demonstrate community service. Along with their application, they must submit an essay of 2 to 3 pages on their professional interests, future social work aspirations, previous social work experiences (volunteer and professional), and honors and achievements (academic and community service). Financial need is considered in the selection process.

Financial data The stipend is $1,000. Funds are sent directly to the recipient's school.

Duration 1 year.

Number awarded 1 each year.

Deadline December of each year.

[173]
EMPOWER SCHOLARSHIP AWARD

Courage Center
Attn: EMPOWER Scholarship Program
3915 Golden Valley Road
Minneapolis, MN 55422
(763) 520-0214   Toll Free: (888) 8-INTAKE
Fax: (763) 520-0562   TDD: (763) 520-0245
E-mail: empower@couragecenter.org
Web: www.couragecenter.org

Summary To provide financial assistance to African Americans and other students of color from Minnesota and western Wisconsin interested in attending college in any state to prepare for a career in the medical rehabilitation field.

Eligibility This program is open to ethnically diverse students accepted at or enrolled in an institution of higher learning in any state. Applicants must be residents of Minnesota or western Wisconsin (Burnett, Pierce, Polk, and St. Croix counties). They must be able to demonstrate a career interest in the medical rehabilitation field by a record of volunteer involvement related to health care and must have a GPA of 2.0 or higher. Along with their application, they must submit a 1-page essay that covers their experiences and interactions to date with the area of volunteering, what they have accomplished and gained from those experiences, how those experiences will assist them in their future endeavors, why education is important to them, how this scholarship will help them with their financial need and their future career goals.

Financial data   The stipend is $1,500.

Duration   1 year.

Additional information   This program, established in 1995, is also identified by its acronym as the EMPOWER Scholarship Award.

Number awarded   2 each year.

Deadline   May of each year.

[174]
ENVIRONMENTAL PROTECTION AGENCY STUDENT DIVERSITY INTERNSHIP PROGRAM

United Negro College Fund Special Programs
  Corporation
Attn: NASA Science and Technology Institute
6402 Arlington Boulevard, Suite 600
Falls Church, VA 22042
(703) 677-3400   Toll Free: (800) 530-6232
Fax: (703) 205-7645   E-mail: portal@uncfsp.org
Web: www.uncfsp.org

Summary   To provide an opportunity for African Americans and other underrepresented undergraduate and graduate students to work on a summer research project at research sites of the U.S. Environmental Protection Agency (EPA).

Eligibility   This program is open to rising college sophomores, juniors, and seniors and to full-time graduate students at accredited institutions who are members of underrepresented groups, including ethnic minorities (African Americans, Hispanic/Latinos, Native Americans, Asians, Alaskan Natives, and Native Hawaiians/Pacific Islanders) and persons with disabilities. Applicants must have a GPA of 2.8 or higher and be working on a degree in business, communications, economics, engineering, environmental science/management, finance, information technology, law, marketing, or science. They must be interested in working on a research project during the summer at their choice of 23 EPA research sites (for a list, contact EPA). U.S. citizenship is required.

Financial data   The stipend is $5,000 for undergraduates or $6,000 for graduate students. Interns also receive a travel and housing allowance, but they are responsible for covering their local transportation, meals, and miscellaneous expenses.

Duration   10 weeks during the summer.

Additional information   This program is funded by EPA and administered by the United Negro College Fund Special Programs Corporation.

Number awarded   Varies each year.

Deadline   May of each year.

[175]
ESTER BOONE MEMORIAL SCHOLARSHIPS

National Naval Officers Association-Washington, D.C.
  Chapter
Attn: Scholarship Program
2701 Park Center Drive, A1108
Alexandria, VA 22302
(703) 566-3840   Fax: (703) 566-3813
E-mail: Stephen.Williams@Navy.mil
Web: dcnnoa.memberlodge.com

Summary   To provide financial assistance to African American and other minority high school seniors from the Washington, D.C. area.

Eligibility   This program is open to minority seniors at high schools in the Washington, D.C. metropolitan area who plan to enroll full time at an accredited 2- or 4-year college or university. Applicants must have a GPA of 2.5 or higher. Selection is based on academic achievement, community involvement, and financial need.

Financial data   The stipend is $1,000.

Duration   1 year; nonrenewable.

Additional information   Recipients are not required to join or affiliate with the military in any way.

Number awarded   1 or more each year.

Deadline   March of each year.

[176]
ETHAN AND ALLAN MURPHY ENDOWED MEMORIAL SCHOLARSHIP

American Meteorological Society
Attn: Fellowship/Scholarship Program
45 Beacon Street
Boston, MA 02108-3693
(617) 227-2426, ext. 246   Fax: (617) 742-8718
E-mail: scholar@ametsoc.org
Web: www.ametsoc.org

Summary   To provide financial assistance to undergraduates (especially African Americans or other minorities, women, and students with disabilities) who are majoring in meteorology or an aspect of atmospheric sciences with an interest in weather forecasting.

Eligibility   This program is open to full-time students entering their final year of undergraduate study and majoring in meteorology or an aspect of the atmospheric or related oceanic and hydrologic sciences. Applicants must intend to make atmospheric or related sciences their career and be able to demonstrate, through curricular or extracurricular activities, an interest in weather forecasting or in the value and utilization of forecasts. They must be U.S. citizens or permanent residents enrolled at a U.S. institution and have a cumulative GPA of 3.25 or higher. Along with their application, they must submit 200-word essays on 1) their most important achievements that qualify them for this scholarship, and 2) their career goals in the atmospheric or related oceanic or hydrologic fields. Financial need is considered in the selection process. The sponsor specifically encourages applications from women, minorities, and students with disabilities who are traditionally underrepresented in the atmospheric and related oceanic sciences.

Financial data   The stipend is $2,000.

Duration   1 year.

Number awarded 1 each year.
Deadline February of each year.

[177]
ETHEL LEE HOOVER ELLIS SCHOLARSHIP

National Association of Negro Business and Professional
  Women's Clubs
Attn: Scholarship Committee
1806 New Hampshire Avenue, N.W.
Washington, DC 20009-3206
(202) 483-4206   Fax: (202) 462-7253
E-mail: education@nanbpwc.org
Web: www.nanbpwc.org/ScholarshipApplications.asp

Summary To provide financial assistance to African American women from designated southern states studying business at a college in any state.

Eligibility This program is open to African Americans
women who are residents of Alabama, Florida, Georgia, Mississippi, North Carolina, South Carolina, Tennessee, or West
Virginia. Applicants must be enrolled at an accredited college
or university in any state as a sophomore or junior. They must
have a GPA of 3.0 or higher and be majoring in business.
Along with their application, they must submit an essay, up to
750 words in length, on the topic, "Business and Community
United: How the Two Can Work Together for Success." U.S.
citizenship is required.

Financial data A stipend is awarded (amount not specified).

Duration 1 year.

Number awarded 1 or more each year.

Deadline February of each year.

[178]
EXCELLENCE IN CARDIOVASCULAR SCIENCES
SUMMER RESEARCH PROGRAM

Wake Forest University School of Medicine
Attn: Hypertension and Vascular Research Center
Medical Center Boulevard
Winston-Salem, NC 27157-1032
(336) 716-1080   Fax: (336) 716-2456
E-mail: nsarver@wfubmc.edu
Web: www.wfubmc.edu

Summary To provide African Americans and other underrepresented students with an opportunity to engage in a summer research project in cardiovascular science at Wake Forest University in Winston-Salem, North Carolina.

Eligibility This program is open to undergraduates and
master's degree students who are members of underrepresented minority groups (African Americans, Alaskan Natives,
Asian Americans, Native Americans, Pacific Islanders, and
Hispanics) or who come from disadvantaged backgrounds
(e.g., rural areas, first generation college students). Applicants must be interested in participating in a program of summer research in the cardiovascular sciences that includes
"hands-on" laboratory research, a lecture series by faculty
and guest speakers, and a research symposium at which students present their research findings. U.S. citizenship or permanent resident status is required.

Financial data The stipend is $1,731 per month, housing
in a university dormitory, and round-trip transportation
expense.

Duration 2 months during the summer.

Additional information This program is sponsored by the
National Heart, Lung, and Blood Institute (NHLBI) of the
National Institutes of Health (NIH).

Number awarded Approximately 10 each year.

Deadline February of each year.

[179]
EXXONMOBIL NSBE CORPORATE
SCHOLARSHIPS

National Society of Black Engineers
Attn: Programs Department
205 Daingerfield Road
Alexandria, VA 22314
(703) 549-2207   Fax: (703) 683-5312
E-mail: scholarships@nsbe.org
Web: www.nsbe.org

Summary To provide financial assistance to members of
the National Society of Black Engineers (NSBE) who are
majoring in designated engineering fields.

Eligibility This program is open to members of the society
who are college freshmen, sophomores, or juniors majoring
in chemical, civil, electrical, or mechanical engineering. Applicants for regional awards must have a GPA of 3.3 or higher;
applicants for the national award must have a GPA of 3.5 or
higher. Along with their application, they must submit an
essay of 150 words on the advice they would offer fellow engineering students to motivate them to make academic excellence a priority in their college career.

Financial data The national stipend is $2,000; the regional
stipends are $1,500.

Duration 1 year.

Additional information This program is sponsored by
ExxonMobil Corporation.

Number awarded 13 each year: 1 national award and 12
regional awards (2 in each NSBE region).

Deadline January of each year.

[180]
FARM CREDIT EAST SCHOLARSHIPS

Farm Credit East
Attn: Scholarship Program
240 South Road
Enfield, CT 06082
(860) 741-4380   Toll Free: (800) 562-2235
Fax: (860) 741-4389
Web: www.farmcrediteast.com

Summary To provide financial assistance to residents of
designated northeastern states (especially African Americans and other minorities) who plan to attend school in any
state to work on an undergraduate or graduate degree in a
field related to agriculture, forestry, or fishing.

Eligibility This program is open to residents of Massachusetts, Connecticut, Rhode Island, New Jersey, and portions of
New York and New Hampshire. Applicants must be working
on or planning to work on an associate, bachelor's, or graduate degree in production agriculture, agribusiness, the forest
products industry, or commercial fishing at a college or university in any state. They must submit a 200-word essay on
why they wish to prepare for a career in agriculture, forestry,
or fishing. Selection is based on the essay, extracurricular

activities (especially farm work experience and activities indicative of an interest in preparing for a career in agriculture or agribusiness), and interest in agriculture. The program includes scholarships reserved for members of minority (Black or African American, American Indian or Alaska Native, Asian, Native Hawaiian or other Pacific Islander, or Hispanic or Latino) groups.

Financial data The stipend is $1,500. Funds are paid directly to the student to be used for tuition, room and board, books, and other academic charges.

Duration 1 year; nonrenewable.

Additional information Recipients are given priority for an internship with the sponsor in the summer following their junior year. Farm Credit East was formerly named First Pioneer Farm Credit.

Number awarded Up to 28 each year, including several reserved for members of minority groups.

Deadline April of each year.

[181]
FAYE AND ROBERT LETT SCHOLARSHIP

American Baptist Churches of Ohio
Attn: Ohio Baptist Education Society
136 Galway Drive North
P.O. Box 288
Granville, OH 43023-0288
(740) 587-0804   Fax: (740) 587-0807
E-mail: pastorchris@neo.rr.com
Web: www.abc-ohio.org

Summary To provide funding to African American upper-division and graduate students from Ohio who are interested in preparing for the Baptist ministry at a college or seminary in any state.

Eligibility This program is open to African American residents of Ohio who have completed at least 2 years of study at an accredited college or university in any state and are interested in continuing their education as an upper-division or seminary student. Applicants must 1) hold active membership in a church affiliated with the American Baptist Churches of Ohio or a church dually-aligned with the American Baptist Churches of Ohio; 2) be in the process of preparing for a professional career in Christian ministry (such as a local church pastor, church education, youth or young adult ministries, church music, specialized ministry, chaplaincy, ministry in higher education, or missionary service); 3) be committed to working professionally within the framework of the American Baptist Churches USA; and 4) acknowledge a personal commitment to the Gospel of Jesus Christ, an understanding of the Christian faith, and a definite call to professional Christian ministry as a life work. Financial need must be demonstrated.

Financial data Stipends generally range from $1,000 to $1,500 a year.

Duration 1 year.

Additional information This program was established in 1990.

Number awarded 1 or more each year.

Deadline March of each year.

[182]
FEDERAL CITY ALUMNAE CHAPTER ACADEMIC EXCELLENCE SCHOLARSHIPS

Delta Sigma Theta Sorority, Inc.-Federal City Alumnae Chapter
Attn: Educational Development Committee
P.O. Box 1605
Washington, DC 20013
(202) 545-1913   E-mail: thefcacdst@yahoo.com
Web: thefcacdst.org

Summary To provide financial assistance to African American and other high school seniors in Washington, D.C. who plan to attend a 4-year college or university in any state.

Eligibility This program is open to seniors graduating from high schools in the District of Columbia and planning to enroll full time at an accredited 4-year college or university in any state. Applicants must have a GPA of 3.3 or higher. Along with their application, they must submit a 500-word essay on either how they plan to use their education to make the world a better place or why they should be selected to receive this scholarship.

Financial data The stipend is $5,000.

Duration 1 year.

Additional information The sponsor is the local alumnae chapter of a traditionally African American social sorority.

Number awarded 2 each year.

Deadline February of each year.

[183]
FEDERAL EMPLOYEE EDUCATION AND ASSISTANCE FUND-BLACKS IN GOVERNMENT SCHOLARSHIP PROGRAM

Blacks in Government
c/o Federal Employee Education and Assistance Fund
Attn: Scholarship Program
3333 South Wadsworth Boulevard, Suite 300
Lakewood, CO 80227
(303) 933-7580   Toll Free: (800) 323-4140
Fax: (303) 933-7587   E-mail: admin@feea.org
Web: www.feea.org

Summary To provide financial assistance for college or graduate school to members of Blacks in Government (BIG) and their dependents.

Eligibility This program is open to BIG members and their children, stepchildren, and grandchildren. Applicants or their sponsoring BIG member must have at least 3 years of federal, state, or local government employment and 2 years of membership in BIG. They must be entering or enrolled full time in an accredited 2- or 4-year postsecondary, graduate, or postgraduate program with a GPA of 3.0 or higher. Along with their application, they must submit a 2-page essay on a topic related to a career in public service with the government, a letter of recommendation, a transcript, a list of extracurricular and community service activities, and verification of government employment; high school seniors must also submit a copy of their ACT, SAT, or other examination scores. Financial need is not considered in the selection process.

Financial data The stipend is $1,000 per year.

Duration 1 year; may be renewed.

Additional information This program, established in 2007, is jointly administered by BIG and the Federal Employee Education and Assistance Fund (FEEA).

Number awarded 22 each year: 2 in each BIG region.

Deadline March of each year.

[184]
FISHER COMMUNICATIONS SCHOLARSHIPS FOR MINORITIES

Fisher Communications
Attn: Minority Scholarship
100 Fourth Avenue North, Suite 510
Seattle, WA 98109
(206) 404-7000   Fax: (206) 404-6037
E-mail: Info@fsci.com
Web: www.fsci.com/scholarship.html

Summary To provide financial assistance to African Americans and other minority college students in selected states who are interested in preparing for a career in broadcasting.

Eligibility This program is open to U.S. citizens of non-white origin who have a GPA of 2.5 or higher and are at least sophomores enrolled in 1) a broadcasting curriculum (radio, television, marketing, or broadcast technology) leading to a bachelor's degree at an accredited 4-year college or university; 2) a broadcast curriculum at an accredited community college, transferable to a 4-year baccalaureate degree program; or 3) a broadcast curriculum at an accredited vocational/technical school. Applicants must be either 1) residents of California, Washington, Oregon, Idaho, or Montana; or 2) attending a school in those states. They must submit an essay that explains their financial need, educational and career goals, any experience or interest they have in broadcast communications that they feel qualifies them for this scholarship, and involvement in school activities. Selection is based on need, academic achievement, and personal qualities.

Financial data A stipend is awarded (amount not specified).

Duration 1 year; recipients may reapply.

Additional information This program began in 1987.

Number awarded Varies; a total of $10,000 is available for this program each year.

Deadline May of each year.

[185]
FLORIDA FUND FOR MINORITY TEACHERS SCHOLARSHIPS

Florida Fund for Minority Teachers, Inc.
Attn: Executive Director
G415 Norman Hall
P.O. Box 117045
Gainesville, FL 32611-7045
(352) 392-9196, ext. 21   Fax: (352) 846-3011
E-mail: info@ffmt.org
Web: www.ffmt.org

Summary To provide funding to African Americans and other minorities residing in Florida who are preparing for a career as a teacher.

Eligibility This program is open to Florida residents who are African American/Black, Hispanic/Latino, Asian American/Pacific Islander, or American Indian/Alaskan Native.

Applicants must be entering their junior year in a teacher education program at a participating college or university in Florida. Special consideration is given to community college graduates. Selection is based on writing ability, communication skills, overall academic performance, and evidence of commitment to the youth of America (preferably demonstrated through volunteer activities).

Financial data The stipend is $4,000 per year. Recipients are required to teach 1 year in a Florida public school for each year they receive the scholarship. If they fail to teach in a public school, they are required to repay the total amount of support received at an annual interest rate of 8%.

Duration Up to 2 consecutive years, provided the recipient remains enrolled full time with a GPA of 2.5 or higher.

Additional information For a list of the 16 participating public institutions and the 18 participating private institutions, contact the Florida Fund for Minority Teachers (FFMT). Recipients are also required to attend the annual FFMT recruitment and retention conference.

Number awarded Varies each year.

Deadline July of each year for fall semester; November of each year for spring semester.

[186]
FLORIDA GOVERNOR'S BLACK HISTORY MONTH ESSAY CONTEST

Office of the Governor
Attn: Black History Month Committee
820 East Park Avenue, Suite E-100
Tallahassee, FL 32301
(850) 410-0501   Fax: (850) 413-0909
E-mail: blackhistoryessay@myflorida.com
Web: www.floridablackhistory.com/essay.cfm

Summary To recognize and reward, with college scholarships, African American and other students in Florida who submit outstanding essays on a topic related to Black History Month.

Eligibility This competition is open to all Florida students in 3 categories: elementary (grades 4-5), middle (grades 6-8), and high school (grades 9-12). Applicants must submit an essay, up to 500 words in length, on a topic that changes annually but relates to Black history. A recent topic was "Celebrating African American Businesses-Past, Present, and Future"

Financial data Winners receive full payment of tuition at the Florida state college or university of their choice.

Duration The competition is held annually. Winners receive payment of tuition for 4 years.

Additional information This competition was first held in 2003.

Number awarded 6 each year: 2 in each of the grade categories.

Deadline February of each year.

[187]
FOURTH DISTRICT MOSAIC SCHOLARSHIP

American Advertising Federation-District 4
c/o Tami L. Grimes, Education Chair
4712 Southwood Lane
Lakeland, FL 33813
(863) 648-5392   E-mail: tamilgrimes@yahoo.com
Web: www.4aaf.com/scholarships.cfm

Summary To provide financial assistance to African American and other minority undergraduate and graduate students from any state who are enrolled at colleges and universities in Florida and interested in entering the field of advertising.

Eligibility This program is open to undergraduate and graduate students from any state enrolled at accredited colleges and universities in Florida who are U.S. citizens or permanent residents of African, African American, Hispanic, Hispanic American, Indian, Native American, Asian, Asian American, or Pacific Islander descent. Applicants must be working on a bachelor's or master's degree in advertising, marketing, communications, public relations, art, graphic arts, or a related field. They must have an overall GPA of 3.0 or higher. Along with their application, they must submit a 250-word essay on why multiculturalism, diversity, and inclusion are important in the advertising, marketing, and communications industry today. Preference is given to members of the American Advertising Federation.

Financial data The stipend is $1,000.

Duration 1 year.

Number awarded 1 or more each year.

Deadline May of each year.

[188]
FRANCES W. HARRIS SCHOLARSHIP

New England Regional Black Nurses Association, Inc.
P.O. Box 190690
Boston, MA 02119
(617) 524-1951
Web: www.nerbna.org/org/scholarships.html

Summary To provide financial assistance to nursing students from New England who have contributed to the African American community.

Eligibility The program is open to residents of the New England states who are enrolled full time in a NLN-accredited generic diploma, associate, or bachelor's nursing program in any state. Applicants must have at least 1 full year of school remaining. Along with their application, they must submit a 3-page essay that covers their career aspirations in the nursing profession; how they have contributed to the African American or other communities of color in such areas as work, volunteering, church, or community outreach; an experience that has enhanced their personal and/or professional growth; and any financial hardships that may hinder them from completing their education.

Financial data A stipend is awarded (amount not specified).

Duration 1 year.

Number awarded 1 or more each year.

Deadline March of each year.

[189]
FRANK WATTS SCHOLARSHIP

Watts Charity Association, Inc.
6245 Bristol Parkway, Suite 224
Culver City, CA 90230
(323) 671-0394   Fax: (323) 778-2613
E-mail: wattscharity@aol.com
Web: 4watts.tripod.com/id5.html

Summary To provide financial assistance to upper-division African Americans interested in preparing for a career as a minister.

Eligibility This program is open to U.S. citizens of African American descent who are enrolled full time as a college or university junior. Applicants must be studying to become a minister. They must have a GPA of 3.0 or higher, be between 17 and 24 years of age, and be able to demonstrate that they intend to continue their education for at least 2 years. Along with their application, they must submit 1) a 1-paragraph statement on why they should be awarded a Watts Foundation scholarship, and 2) a 1- to 2-page essay on a specific type of cancer, based either on how it has impacted their life or on researched information.

Financial data A stipend is awarded (amount not specified).

Duration 1 year.

Additional information Royce R. Watts, Sr. established the Watts Charity Association after he learned he had cancer in 2001.

Number awarded 1 each year.

Deadline May of each year.

[190]
FRANKLIN WILLIAMS INTERNSHIP

Council on Foreign Relations
Attn: Human Resources Office
58 East 68th Street
New York, NY 10021
(212) 434-9489   Fax: (212) 434-9893
E-mail: humanresources@cfr.org
Web: www.cfr.org

Summary To provide undergraduate and graduate students (particularly African Americans and other minorities) with an opportunity to gain work experience in international affairs at the Council on Foreign Relations in New York.

Eligibility Applicants should be currently enrolled in either their senior year of an undergraduate program or in a graduate program in the area of international relations or a related field. They should have a record of high academic achievement, proven leadership ability, and previous related internship or work experience. Minority students are strongly encouraged to apply.

Financial data The stipend is $10 per hour.

Duration 1 academic term (fall, spring, or summer). Fall and spring interns are required to make a commitment of at least 12 hours per week. Summer interns may choose to make a full-time commitment.

Additional information Interns work closely with a program director or fellow in either the studies or meetings program and are involved with program coordination, substantive and business writing, research, and budget management. In addition, they are encouraged to attend the council's programs and participate in informal training designed to enhance management and leadership skills.

Number awarded 3 each year: 1 each academic term.

Deadline Applications may be submitted at any time.

[191]
FRED J. STUART SCHOLARSHIP OF EXCELLENCE

African Methodist Episcopal Church
Fifth Episcopal District Lay Organization
400 Corporate Pointe, Suite 300
Culver City, CA 90230
(424) 750-3065   Fax: (424) 750-3067
E-mail: AmecEpiscopal5@aol.com
Web: www.amec5th.net/scholarship_of_excellence.aspx

Summary To provide financial assistance to members of African Methodist Episcopal (AME) churches in its Fifth Episcopal District who are interested in attending college in any state.

Eligibility This program is open to residents of the AME Fifth Episcopal District (Alaska, Arizona, California, Colorado, Idaho, Kansas, Missouri, Montana, Nebraska, Nevada, New Mexico, North Dakota, Oregon, South Dakota, Utah, Washington, and Wyoming) who are graduating high school seniors or students currently enrolled at an accredited institution of higher learning in any state. Applicants must have been a member of an AME church for at least 12 months and have been an active member of its Lay Organization or other lay-sponsored programs. High school seniors must have a GPA of 3.0 or higher; students already enrolled in college must have a GPA of 2.5 or higher. Along with their application, they must submit a 250-word personal essay that describes their long-range plans, community and church involvement, accomplishments or special awards, challenges they have faced, and how they responded. Selection is based on that essay, academic record, letters of recommendation, accomplishments, and Lay Organization participation.

Financial data The stipend is $1,000.

Duration 1 year.

Number awarded 1 each year.

Deadline May of each year.

[192]
FRED JOHNSON YOUTH SCHOLARSHIP

James B. Morris Scholarship Fund
Attn: Scholarship Selection Committee
525 S.W. Fifth Street, Suite A
Des Moines, IA 50309-4501
(515) 282-8192   Fax: (515) 282-9117
E-mail: morris@assoc-mgmt.com
Web: www.morrisscholarship.org

Summary To provide financial assistance for college to African American high school seniors in Iowa.

Eligibility This program is open to African American seniors graduating from high schools in Iowa. Applicants must be planning to attend a college or university.

Financial data A stipend is awarded (amount not specified).

Duration 1 year.

Number awarded 1 or more each year.

Deadline March of each year.

[193]
FREEPORT-MCMORAN COPPER AND GOLD FOUNDATION NSBE SCHOLARSHIPS

National Society of Black Engineers
Attn: Programs Department
205 Daingerfield Road
Alexandria, VA 22314
(703) 549-2207   Fax: (703) 683-5312
E-mail: scholarships@nsbe.org
Web: www.nsbe.org

Summary To provide financial assistance to members of the National Society of Black Engineers (NSBE) from the United States or designated countries who are majoring in a field related to engineering or mining at an institution in North America.

Eligibility This program is open to members of the society who are entering their junior or senior year in college and have a GPA of 2.7 or higher. Applicants must be enrolled in a field related to the mining industry, especially mining engineering, metallurgical engineering, geology, or geological engineering. They must be citizens of the United States, Australia, Canada, Chile, Democratic Republic of Congo, Indonesia, Mexico, or Peru. Along with their application, they must submit a 200-word essay on how they selected their intended major and their personal goals, including why they have chosen to apply for this scholarship.

Financial data The stipend is $4,500.

Duration 1 year.

Additional information This program is sponsored by Freeport-McMoRan Copper and Gold Foundation.

Number awarded 2 each year.

Deadline February of each year.

[194]
FULFILLING THE LEGACY SCHOLARSHIPS

National Society of Black Engineers
Attn: Programs Department
205 Daingerfield Road
Alexandria, VA 22314
(703) 549-2207   Fax: (703) 683-5312
E-mail: scholarships@nsbe.org
Web: www.nsbe.org

Summary To provide financial assistance to members of the National Society of Black Engineers (NSBE) who are working on an undergraduate or graduate degree in engineering.

Eligibility This program is open to members of the society who are undergraduate or graduate engineering students. High school seniors are also eligible. Applicants must epitomize the society's mission of producing culturally responsible Black engineers who excel academically, succeed professionally, and positively impact the community. Selection is based on an essay; academic achievement; service to the society at the chapter, regional, and/or national level; and other professional, campus, and community activities.

Financial data The stipend is $1,000.

Duration 1 year; may be renewed.

Number awarded Varies each year, depending on the availability of funds; recently, 10 of these scholarships were awarded to undergraduate and graduate students and 5 to high school seniors.

Deadline   January of each year.

[195]
GATES MILLENNIUM SCHOLARS PROGRAM

Bill and Melinda Gates Foundation
P.O. Box 10500
Fairfax, VA 22031-8044
Toll Free: (877) 690-GMSP   Fax: (703) 205-2079
Web: www.gmsp.org

Summary   To provide financial assistance to African Americans and other outstanding low-income minority students, particularly those interested in majoring in specific fields in college.

Eligibility   This program is open to African Americans, Alaska Natives, American Indians, Hispanic Americans, and Asian Pacific Islander Americans who are graduating high school seniors with a GPA of 3.3 or higher. Principals, teachers, guidance counselors, tribal higher education representatives, and other professional educators are invited to nominate students with outstanding academic qualifications, particularly those likely to succeed in the fields of computer science, education, engineering, library science, mathematics, public health, or science. Nominees should have significant financial need and have demonstrated leadership abilities through participation in community service, extracurricular, or other activities. U.S. citizenship, nationality, or permanent resident status is required. Nominees must be planning to enter an accredited college or university as a full-time, degree-seeking freshman in the following fall.

Financial data   The program covers the cost of tuition, fees, books, and living expenses not paid for by grants and scholarships already committed as part of the recipient's financial aid package.

Duration   4 years or the completion of the undergraduate degree, if the recipient maintains at least a 3.0 GPA.

Additional information   This program, established in 1999, is funded by the Bill and Melinda Gates Foundation and administered by the United Negro College Fund with support from the American Indian Graduate Center, the Hispanic Scholarship Fund, and the Asian & Pacific Islander American Scholarship Fund.

Number awarded   1,000 new scholarships are awarded each year.

Deadline   January of each year.

[196]
GATEWAYS TO THE LABORATORY PROGRAM

Cornell University
Attn: Weill Cornell/Rockefeller/Sloan-Kettering Tri-
   Institutional MD-PhD Program
Gateways to the Laboratory Program
1300 York Avenue, Room C-103
New York, NY 10065-4805
(212) 746-6023   Fax: (212) 746-8678
E-mail: mdphd@med.cornell.edu
Web: www.med.cornell.edu/mdphd/summerprogram

Summary   To provide African Americans and other underrepresented minorities or disadvantaged college freshmen and sophomores with an opportunity to participate in a summer research internship in New York City through the Tri-Institutional MD-PhD Program of Weill Cornell Medical College, Rockefeller University, and Sloan-Kettering Institute.

Eligibility   This program is open to college freshmen and sophomores who are defined by the National Institutes of Health (NIH) as in need of special recruitment and retention, i.e., members of racial and ethnic groups underrepresented in health-related sciences (American Indians or Alaska Natives, Blacks or African Americans, Hispanics or Latinos, and Native Hawaiians or Other Pacific Islanders), persons with disabilities, and individuals from disadvantaged backgrounds (low-income or from a rural or inner-city environment). Applicants must be interested in continuing on to a combined M.D./Ph.D. program following completion of their undergraduate degree. Along with their application, they must submit an essay summarizing their laboratory experience, research interests, and goals. U.S. citizenship or permanent resident status is required.

Financial data   Students receive a stipend of $4,300 and reimbursement of travel expenses. At the end of the summer, 1 family member receives airfare and hotel accommodations to come to New York for the final presentations.

Duration   10 weeks, during the summer.

Additional information   Participants work independently on a research project at Weill Cornell Medical College, Rockefeller University, or Memorial Sloan-Kettering Cancer Center, all located across the street from each other on the Upper East Side of New York City.

Number awarded   15 each year.

Deadline   January of each year.

[197]
GE LLOYD TROTTER AFRICAN AMERICAN
FORUM SCHOLARSHIP

National Society of Black Engineers
Attn: Programs Department
205 Daingerfield Road
Alexandria, VA 22314
(703) 549-2207   Fax: (703) 683-5312
E-mail: scholarships@nsbe.org
Web: www.nsbe.org

Summary   To provide financial assistance to members of the National Society of Black Engineers (NSBE) who are working on an undergraduate or graduate degree in engineering.

Eligibility   This program is open to members of the society who are U.S. citizens or authorized to work in the United States and rising sophomores, juniors, seniors, or graduate students. Applicants must be working on a degree in computer science, physics, or the engineering specialties of aeronautical/aerospace, biomechanical, chemical, computer, electrical, industrial, materials, mechanical, nuclear, or systems. They must have a GPA of 3.0 or higher. Selection is based on an essay; academic achievement; service to the society at the chapter, regional, and/or national level; and other professional, campus, and community activities.

Financial data   The stipend is $2,500.

Duration   1 year.

Additional information   This program is supported by General Electric employees with matching contributions from the GE Fund. Recipients must be willing to accept a paid internship at a GE location for 10 weeks during the summer.

Number awarded Varies each year, depending on the availability of funds; recently, 2 of these scholarships were awarded.

Deadline October of each year.

[198]
GEOCORPS AMERICA DIVERSITY INTERNSHIPS

Geological Society of America
Attn: Program Officer, GeoCorps America
3300 Penrose Place
P.O. Box 9140
Boulder, CO 80301-9140
(303) 357-1025   Toll Free: (800) 472-1988, ext. 1025
Fax: (303) 357-1070   E-mail: mdawson@geosociety.org
Web: rock.geosociety.org/g.corps/index

Summary To provide work experience at national parks to student members of the Geological Society of America (GSA) who are African American or come from other underrepresented groups.

Eligibility This program is open to all GSA members, but applications are especially encouraged from groups historically underrepresented in the sciences (African Americans, American Indians, Alaska Natives, Hispanics, Native Hawaiians, other Pacific Islanders, and persons with disabilities). Applicants must be interested in a summer work experience in facilities of the U.S. government, currently limited to the National Park Service but planned for expansion to the Forest Service and the Bureau of Land Management. Geoscience knowledge and skills are a significant requirement for most positions, but students from diverse disciplines (e.g., chemistry, physics, engineering, mathematics, computer science, ecology, hydrology, meteorology, the social sciences, and the humanities) are also invited to apply. Activities involve research; interpretation and education; inventory and monitoring; or mapping, surveying, and GIS. Prior interns are not eligible. U.S. citizenship or possession of a proper visa is required.

Financial data Each internship provides a $2,750 stipend. Also provided are free housing or a housing allowance of $1,500 to $2,000.

Duration 10 to 12 weeks during the summer.

Number awarded Varies each year.

Deadline Deadline not specified.

[199]
GEORGE A. LOTTIER GOLF FOUNDATION INTERNSHIP AND SCHOLARSHIP AWARD

Atlanta Tribune: The Magazine
Attn: Editor
875 Old Roswell Road, Suite C-100
Roswell, GA 30076-1660
(770) 587-0501, ext. 202   Fax: (770) 642-6501
E-mail: scholarships@atlantatribune.com
Web: www.atlantatribune.com

Summary To provide financial assistance and summer work experience at the *Atlanta Tribune: The Magazine* to African American and other minority upper-division and graduate students from any state.

Eligibility This program is open to African American and other minority college students from any state entering their junior or senior year of college or enrolled in a graduate program with a GPA of 3.0 or higher. Applicants must be majoring in a field related to print media, including communications, English, graphic design (with an emphasis on publication layout and design), journalism, marketing, or sales. Along with their application, they must submit a 500-word personal essay.

Financial data The program provides a paid internship and a scholarship stipend of $2,500.

Duration 1 year, including 10 weeks during the summer for the internship.

Number awarded Varies each year; recently, 4 of these scholarships and internships were awarded.

Deadline April of each year.

[200]
GEORGE CAMPBELL, JR. FELLOWSHIP IN ENGINEERING

National Action Council for Minorities in Engineering
Attn: University Programs
440 Hamilton Avenue, Suite 302
White Plains, NY 10601-1813
(914) 539-4010   Fax: (914) 539-4032
E-mail: scholarships@nacme.org
Web: www.nacme.org/NACME_D.aspx?pageid=105

Summary To provide financial assistance to African American and other underrepresented minority college sophomores majoring in engineering or related fields.

Eligibility This program is open to African American, Latino, and American Indian college sophomores who have a GPA of 3.0 or higher and have demonstrated academic excellence, leadership skills, and a commitment to science and engineering as a career. Applicants must be enrolled full time at an ABET-accredited engineering program. Fields of study include all areas of engineering as well as computer science, materials science, mathematics, operations research, or physics.

Financial data The stipend is $5,000 per year. Funds are sent directly to the recipient's university.

Duration Up to 3 years.

Number awarded 1 each year.

Deadline April of each year.

[201]
GEORGE GENG ON LEE MINORITIES IN LEADERSHIP SCHOLARSHIP

Capture the Dream, Inc.
Attn: Scholarship Program
484 Lake Park Avenue, Suite 15
Oakland, CA 94610
(510) 343-3635   E-mail: info@capturethedream.org
Web: www.capturethedream.org/programs/scholarship.php

Summary To provide financial assistance for college to African Americans and other minorities who can demonstrate leadership.

Eligibility This program is open to members of minority groups who are graduating high school seniors or current full-time undergraduates at 4-year colleges and universities. Applicants must submit a 1,000-word essay on why they should be selected to receive this scholarship, using their experiences within school, work, and home to display the challenges they have faced as a minority and how they overcame adversity to assume a leadership role. They should also explain how their career goals and future aspirations will build them as a future minority leader. Financial need is considered in the selection process. U.S. citizenship or permanent resident status is required.

Financial data The stipend is $1,000.

Duration 1 year.

Number awarded 1 or more each year.

Deadline July of each year.

[202]
GERALD BOYD/ROBIN STONE SCHOLARSHIP

National Association of Black Journalists
Attn: Program Coordinator
8701-A Adelphi Road
Adelphi, MD 20783-1716
(301) 445-7100, ext. 108   Toll Free: (866) 479-NABJ
Fax: (301) 445-7101   E-mail: nabj@nabj.org
Web: www.nabj.org

Summary To provide financial assistance to undergraduate or graduate student members of the National Association of Black Journalists (NABJ) who are majoring in print journalism.

Eligibility This program is open to African American undergraduate or graduate students who are currently attending an accredited 4-year college or university. Applicants must be majoring in print journalism and have a GPA of 2.5 or higher. They must be NABJ members. Along with their application, they submit samples of their work, an official college transcript, 2 letters of recommendation, a resume, and a 500- to 800-word essay describing their accomplishments as a student journalist, their career goals, and their financial need.

Financial data The stipend is $2,500. Funds are paid directly to the recipient's college or university.

Duration 1 year; nonrenewable.

Number awarded 1 each year.

Deadline April of each year.

[203]
GERTRUDE ROBERTSON SCHOLARSHIP

National Sorority of Phi Delta Kappa, Inc.-Delta Beta
   Chapter
c/o Nancy Thompson, Chapter Scholarship Chair
4703 Broadhill Drive
Austin, TX 78723
(512) 926-6309

Summary To provide financial assistance to African American high school seniors from selected states who plan to study education in college.

Eligibility This program is open to African Americans graduating from high schools in Alabama, Arkansas, Louisiana, Oklahoma, and Texas. Applicants must be planning to enter college and major in the field of education. They must have a GPA of 2.5 or higher and a minimum ACT score of 12 or comparable SAT score. Along with their application, they must submit documentation of financial need, high school transcripts, 2 letters of recommendation, evidence of leadership

and potential, and a 250-word essay on their interest in the teaching profession and their perception of leadership.

Financial data The stipend is $1,500.

Duration 1 year.

Number awarded 2 each year.

Deadline January of each year.

[204]
GLOBAL CHANGE SUMMER UNDERGRADUATE RESEARCH EXPERIENCE (SURE)

Oak Ridge Institute for Science and Education
Attn: Global Change Education Program
120 Badger Avenue, M.S. 36
P.O. Box 117
Oak Ridge, TN 37831-0117
(865) 576-7009   Fax: (865) 241-9445
E-mail: gcep@orau.gov
Web: www.atmos.anl.gov/GCEP/SURE/index.html

Summary To provide undergraduate students (particularly African American or other minorities and women) with an opportunity to conduct research during the summer on global change.

Eligibility This program is open to undergraduates in their sophomore and junior years, although outstanding freshman and seniors are also considered. Applicants must be proposing to conduct research in a program area within the Department of Energy's Office of Biological and Environmental Research (DOE-BER): the atmospheric science program, the environmental meteorology program, the atmospheric radiation measurement program, the terrestrial carbon processes effort, the program for ecosystem research, and studies carried out under the direction of the National Institute for Global Environmental Change. They must have a GPA of 3.0 or higher overall and in their major. Minority and female students are particularly encouraged to apply. U.S. citizenship is required.

Financial data Participants receive a weekly stipend of $475 and support for travel and housing.

Duration 10 weeks during the summer. Successful participants are expected to reapply for a second year of research with their mentors.

Additional information This program, funded by DOE-BER, began in summer 1999. The first week is spent in an orientation and focus session at a participating university. For the remaining 9 weeks, students conduct mentored research at 1 of the national laboratories or universities conducting BER-supported global change research.

Number awarded Approximately 20 each year.

Deadline December of each year.

[205]
GLOSTER B. CURRENT, SR. SCHOLARSHIP

United Methodist Church-New York Annual Conference
Attn: Gloster B. Current Scholarship Committee
c/o Rev. Dr. John E. Carrington
50 Ralph Road
New Rochelle, NY 10804
(917) 617-4360   Fax: (914) 235-7313
E-mail: johnecarrington@aol.com
Web: www.nyac.com/pages/detail/1725

Summary To provide financial assistance to Methodist undergraduate students of African descent from any state who are preparing for a career in public service.
Eligibility This program is open to members of United Methodist Church (UMC) congregations in any state who are of African descent. Applicants must be enrolled or planning to enroll at an accredited institution of higher education in any state to work on an undergraduate degree in a field of public service (e.g., the ministry, social work, health care, or government service). They must be between 16 and 25 years of age and have a GPA of at least "C" in high school and/or 2.75 or higher in college. Along with their application, they must submit a 1-page essay on their interest in a career of public service. Selection is based on academic record, leadership potential, a letter of recommendation from a UMC local pastor, and financial need.
Financial data The stipend is $1,000.
Duration 1 year; nonrenewable.
Additional information This program was established in 2003.
Number awarded 1 or more each year.
Deadline April of each year.

[206]
GOLDEN TORCH AWARDS
National Society of Black Engineers
Attn: Pre-College Initiative Program
205 Daingerfield Road
Alexandria, VA 22314
(703) 549-2207   Fax: (703) 683-5312
E-mail: pci@nsbe.org
Web: www.nsbe.org/Programs/Scholarships/PCI.aspx

Summary To provide financial assistance to high school seniors who are junior members of the National Society of Black Engineers (NSBE) and planning to major in a field related to engineering in college.
Eligibility This program is open to junior members of the society who are high school seniors. Applicants must have been accepted as a full-time student at a 4-year college or university to major in engineering, computer science, mathematics, or technology. They must have a GPA of 3.0 or higher. Along with their application, they must submit an essay, up to 500 words in length, on how they will continue the legacy of NSBE and how they will serve as role models in their community after college.
Financial data The stipend is $1,000 per year.
Duration 1 year; may be renewed 3 additional years if the recipient maintains a GPA of 2.75 or higher in college.
Number awarded Varies each year; recently, 7 of these awards were presented.
Deadline January of each year.

[207]
GOLDMAN SACHS SCHOLARSHIP FOR EXCELLENCE
Goldman Sachs
Attn: Human Capital Management
30 Hudson Street, 34th Floor
Jersey City, NJ 07302
(212) 902-1000   E-mail: Julie.Mantilla@gs.com
Web: www2.goldmansachs.com

Summary To provide financial assistance and work experience to African American and other underrepresented minority students preparing for a career in the financial services industry.
Eligibility This program is open to undergraduate students of Black, Latino, or Native American heritage. Applicants must be entering their sophomore or junior year with a GPA of 3.4 or higher. Students with all majors and disciplines are encouraged to apply, but they must be able to demonstrate an interest in the financial services industry. Along with their application, they must submit 2 essays of 500 words or fewer on the following topics: 1) why they are interested in the financial services industry; and 2) how they have demonstrated team-oriented leadership through their involvement with a campus-based or community-based organization. Selection is based on academic achievement, interest in the financial services industry, community involvement, and demonstrated leadership and teamwork capabilities.
Financial data Sophomores receive a stipend of $5,000, a summer internship at Goldman Sachs, an opportunity to receive a second award upon successful completion of the internship, and an offer to return for a second summer internship. Juniors receive a stipend of $10,000 and a summer internship at Goldman Sachs.
Duration Up to 2 years.
Additional information This program was initiated in 1994 when it served only students at 4 designated Historically Black Colleges and Universities: Florida A&M University, Howard University, Morehouse College, and Spelman College. It has since been expanded to serve underrepresented minority students in all states.
Number awarded 1 or more each year.
Deadline December of each year.

[208]
GRADY-RAYAM PRIZE IN SACRED MUSIC
"Negro Spiritual" Scholarship Foundation
P.O. Box 547728
Orlando, FL 32854-7728
(407) 841-NSSF
Web: www.negrospiritual.org/competition

Summary To recognize and reward, with college scholarships, African American high school seniors in selected eastern states who excel at singing "Negro spirituals."
Eligibility This competition is open to high school juniors and seniors of Afro-ethnic heritage in 5 districts: 1) Florida; 2) Southeast (Georgia, North Carolina, and South Carolina); 3) Mid-south (Alabama, Arkansas, Louisiana, Mississippi, and Tennessee); 4) New England (Connecticut, Maine, Massachusetts, New Hampshire, Rhode Island, and Vermont); and 5) Capital (Delaware, Maryland, Virginia, Washington, D.C., and West Virginia). Participants must perform 2 "Negro spiritual" songs, 1 assigned and 1 selected. Selection is based on technique (tone quality, intonation, and vocal production), musicianship and artistry (inflection, diction, authenticity, rhythmic energy, and memorization), and stage presence (demeanor, posture, and sincerity of delivery). U.S. citizenship or permanent resident status is required.
Financial data Winners earn tuition assistance grants for college of $3,000 and cash prizes of $300. In Florida, the second-place winners receive tuition assistance grants of $2,000

and cash prizes of $200. Other finalists receive cash prizes of $100.

Duration   The competition is held annually at a site in each of the 5 regions.

Additional information   This program began in Florida in 1997, in the Mid-south district in 2006, in the New England and Capital districts in 2008, and in the Southeast district in 2010. The entry fee is $20.

Number awarded   10 tuition assistance grants and cash prizes (1 to a male and 1 to a female in each of the 5 districts) and 2 second-place tuition grants and cash prizes (1 to a male and 1 to a female in Florida) are awarded each year. The number of other cash prizes awarded to finalists varies each year.

Deadline   December of each year for Florida; January of each year for the Southeast and Mid-south districts; February of each year for the New England and Capital districts.

[209]
HAITIAN AMERICAN NURSES ASSOCIATION SCHOLARSHIPS

Haitian American Nurses Association
Attn: Chair of the Education Committee
P.O. Box 694933
Miami, FL 33269
(305) 609-7498   E-mail: info@hana84.org
Web: www.hana84.org/scholarshipinfo.html

Summary   To provide financial assistance to students who are of Haitian descent and enrolled in an accredited nursing program.

Eligibility   This program is open to nursing students who are of Haitian descent and enrolled at a school in any state. Applicants must have a GPA of 3.0 or higher. Along with their application, they must submit a 1-page essay on why they selected nursing as a career. An interview is required.

Financial data   A stipend is awarded (amount not specified).

Duration   1 year; nonrenewable.

Number awarded   Varies each year; recently, 3 of these scholarships were awarded.

Deadline   March of each year.

[210]
HALLIE Q. BROWN SCHOLARSHIPS

National Association of Colored Women's Clubs
1601 R Street, N.W.
Washington, DC 20009
(202) 667-4080   Fax: (202) 667-2574
E-mail: Drmariewtolliver@aol.com
Web: www.nacwc.org/programs/scholarships.php

Summary   To provide financial assistance for college to students who are nominated by a member of the National Association of Colored Women's Clubs.

Eligibility   This program is open to students who have completed at least 1 semester of postsecondary education. Candidates must be nominated by a member of the National Association of Colored Women's Clubs; the nomination must be endorsed by the member's club and the club's region. Nominees must have a GPA of 2.0 or higher and be able to demonstrate financial need.

Financial data   The amount awarded varies, according to financial need, and has ranged from $1,000 to $2,000 per year.

Duration   The award is presented biennially, in even-numbered years.

Additional information   In the past, recipients were to attend 1 of the United Negro College Fund universities or colleges; now, recipients may enroll in any accredited postsecondary institution of their choice.

Number awarded   Approximately 20 every other year.

Deadline   March of even-numbered years.

[211]
HAMPTON ROADS BLACK MEDIA PROFESSIONALS SCHOLARSHIPS

Hampton Roads Black Media Professionals
P.O. Box 2622
Norfolk, VA 23501-2622
(757) 222-5857   E-mail: hrbmpinc@aim.com
Web: www.hrbmp.us

Summary   To provide financial assistance to outstanding African American undergraduate and graduate students in Virginia who are preparing for a career in journalism.

Eligibility   This program is open to 1) African American undergraduate and graduate students pursuing media-related degrees at a Virginia college or university, and 2) African American students who are residents of Hampton Roads and pursuing media-related degrees at a college or university anywhere in the country. Undergraduates must be freshmen, sophomores, or juniors taking at least 12 credit hours per semester; graduate students must be taking at least 9 credit hours. Applicants must submit an official college transcript, a resume, 2 letters of recommendation, and a 500-word essay that is judged on clarity, presentation, and originality.

Financial data   The stipend is $1,000.

Duration   1 year; may be renewed.

Number awarded   Varies; generally 5 to 6 each year. Since 1989, when the award was initiated, more than $70,000 in scholarships has been awarded.

Deadline   December of each year.

[212]
HANDY SIMMONS SCHOLARSHIP

African Methodist Episcopal Church
Women's Missionary Society
c/o Mrs. Braunwin H. Camp
1250 Heritage Lakes Drive
Mableton, GA 30126
(770) 739-1069   E-mail: bhcamp@yahoo.com
Web: www.wmsscholarships.com

Summary   To provide financial assistance to members of African Methodist Episcopal (AME) churches who are interested in attending college.

Eligibility   This program is open to active members of AME churches and its Young People's Department (YPD). Applicants must be high school seniors or students currently working on an associate, technical, or bachelor's degree in any field. Along with their application, they must submit an essay of 500 to 1,000 words on a topic that changes annually but relates to Christian themes. Selection is based on that essay, academic performance, quality and level of church participation, leadership and extracurricular activities, letters of reference, and financial need.

Financial data Stipends range from $300 to $1,000.

Duration 1 year.

Number awarded 1 or more each year.

Deadline January of each year.

[213]
HAROLD HAYDEN MEMORIAL SCHOLARSHIP

National Organization of Black County Officials
1090 Vermont Avenue, N.W., Suite 1290
Washington, DC 20005
(202) 350-6696   Fax: (202) 350-6699
E-mail: nobco@nocboinc.org
Web: www.nobcoinc.org/scholarship.html

Summary To provide financial assistance for college to high school and currently-enrolled college students nominated by members of the National Association of Black County Officials (NABCO).

Eligibility This program is open to high school seniors and currently-enrolled college students. Applicants must submit an endorsement from a NABCO member and a brief (up to 3 pages) autobiographical essay. Selection is based on academic record, leadership record, character and personality, personal achievement, interest in government and politics, and commitment to human and civil rights. Financial need is not considered in the selection process.

Financial data A stipend is awarded (amount not specified).

Duration 1 year.

Additional information This fund was established in 1984 to honor a co-founder of the NABCO.

Number awarded Varies each year; recently, 5 of these scholarships were awarded.

Deadline June of each year.

[214]
HARRY L. MORRISON SCHOLARSHIP

National Society of Black Physicists
Attn: Scholarship Committee Chair
1100 North Glebe Road, Suite 1010
Arlington, VA 22201
(703) 536-4207   Fax: (703) 536-4203
E-mail: scholarship@nsbp.org
Web: www.nsbp.org/scholarships

Summary To provide financial assistance to African American students majoring in physics in college.

Eligibility This program is open to African American students who are entering their junior or senior year of college and majoring in physics. Applicants must submit an essay on their academic and career objectives, information on their participation in extracurricular activities, a description of any awards and honors they have received, and 3 letters of recommendation. Financial need is not considered.

Financial data The stipend is $1,000.

Duration 1 year; nonrenewable.

Number awarded 1 each year.

Deadline January of each year.

[215]
HARRY R. KENDALL LEADERSHIP DEVELOPMENT SCHOLARSHIPS

United Methodist Church
General Board of Global Ministries
Attn: United Methodist Committee on Relief
475 Riverside Drive, Room 1522
New York, NY 10115
(212) 870-3871   Toll Free: (800) UMC-GBGM
E-mail: jyoung@gbgm-umc.org
Web: new.gbgm-umc.org/umcor/work/health/scholarships

Summary To provide financial assistance to African Americans who are Methodists or other Christians and preparing for a career in a health-related field.

Eligibility This program is open to undergraduate and graduate students who are U.S. citizens or permanent residents of African American descent. Applicants must be professed Christians, preferably United Methodists. They must be planning to enter a health care field or already be a practitioner in such a field. Financial need is considered in the selection process.

Financial data The stipend is $2,000.

Duration 1 year.

Additional information This program was established in 1980.

Number awarded Varies each year.

Deadline June of each year.

[216]
HARVARD MEDICAL SCHOOL SUMMER HONORS UNDERGRADUATE RESEARCH PROGRAM

Harvard Medical School
Attn: Division of Medical Sciences
Diversity Programs Office
260 Longwood Avenue, Room 432
Boston, MA 02115-5720
(617) 432-1342   Toll Free: (800) 367-9019
Fax: (617) 432-2644   E-mail: SHURP@hms.harvard.edu
Web: www.hms.harvard.edu

Summary To provide an opportunity for African American and other underrepresented minority students to engage in research at Harvard Medical School during the summer.

Eligibility This program at Harvard Medical School is open to undergraduate students belonging to minority groups that are underrepresented in the sciences. Applicants must have had at least 1 summer (or equivalent) of experience in a research laboratory and have taken at least 1 upper-level biology course that includes molecular biology. They should be considering a career in biological or biomedical research. U.S. citizenship or permanent resident status is required.

Financial data The program provides a stipend of $420 per week, dormitory housing, travel costs, a meal card, and health insurance if it is needed.

Duration 10 weeks during the summer.

Number awarded Varies each year.

Deadline January of each year.

[217]
HARVARD SCHOOL OF PUBLIC HEALTH SUMMER PROGRAM IN BIOLOGICAL SCIENCES IN PUBLIC HEALTH

Harvard School of Public Health
Attn: Division of Biological Sciences
655 Huntington Avenue, Building 2-113
Boston, MA 02115
(617) 432-4397   Fax: (617) 432-0433
E-mail: aharmon@hsph.harvard.edu
Web: www.hsph.harvard.edu

Summary   To enable African American and other disadvantaged college science students to participate in a summer research internship in biological sciences at Harvard School of Public Health.

Eligibility   This program is open to 1) members of ethnic groups underrepresented in graduate education (African Americans, Hispanics/Latinos, American Indians/Alaskan Natives, Pacific Islanders, and biracial/multiracial); 2) first-generation college students; and 3) low-income students. Applicants must be entering their junior or senior year and interested in preparing for a research career in the biological sciences. They must be interested in participating in a summer research project related to biological science questions that are important to the prevention of disease, especially such public health questions as cancer, infections (malaria, tuberculosis, parasites), lung diseases, common diseases of aging, diabetes, and obesity.

Financial data   The program provides a stipend of at least $3,460, a travel allowance of up to $475, and free dormitory housing.

Duration   9 weeks, beginning in mid-June.

Additional information   Interns conduct research under the mentorship of Harvard faculty members who are specialists in cancer cell biology, immunology and infectious diseases, molecular and cellular toxicology, environmental health sciences, nutrition, and cardiovascular research. Funding for this program is provided by the National Institutes of Health.

Number awarded   Up to 6 each year.

Deadline   January of each year.

[218]
HARVARD-SMITHSONIAN CENTER FOR ASTROPHYSICS SOLAR REU PROGRAM

Harvard-Smithsonian Center for Astrophysics
Attn: Solar REU Program
60 Garden Street, Mail Stop 70
Cambridge, MA 02138
(617) 496-7703   E-mail: dnickerson-at-cfa@harvard.edu
Web: www.cfa.harvard.edu/opportunities/solar_reu

Summary   To enable undergraduates (especially African Americans and other underrepresented students) to participate in a summer research program at the Harvard-Smithsonian Center for Astrophysics (CfA).

Eligibility   This program is open to U.S. citizens who are full-time undergraduates, preferable those entering their junior or senior year. Applicants must be interested in working during the summer on a project in either of 2 CfA divisions: high energy astrophysics (which focuses on X-ray astronomy) or solar, stellar, and planetary sciences (which focuses on

understanding star and planet formation and the physical processes in the Sun, stars, and stellar systems). Applications from members of traditionally underrepresented groups are encouraged.

Financial data   The stipend is $4,500. Housing and travel expenses are also covered.

Duration   10 weeks during the summer.

Additional information   This program is supported by the National Science Foundation as part of its Research Experience for Undergraduates (REU) Program.

Number awarded   8 each year.

Deadline   February of each year.

[219]
HARVEY WASHINGTON BANKS SCHOLARSHIP IN ASTRONOMY

National Society of Black Physicists
Attn: Scholarship Committee Chair
1100 North Glebe Road, Suite 1010
Arlington, VA 22201
(703) 536-4207   Fax: (703) 536-4203
E-mail: scholarship@nsbp.org
Web: www.nsbp.org/scholarships

Summary   To provide financial assistance to African American students majoring in astronomy in college.

Eligibility   This program is open to African American students who are entering their junior or senior year of college and majoring in astronomy. Applicants must submit an essay on their academic and career objectives, information on their participation in extracurricular activities, a description of any awards and honors they have received, and 3 letters of recommendation. Financial need is not considered.

Financial data   The stipend is $1,000.

Duration   1 year; nonrenewable.

Additional information   This program is offered in partnership with the American Astronomical Society.

Number awarded   1 each year.

Deadline   January of each year.

[220]
HAYNES/HETTING AWARD

Philanthrofund Foundation
Attn: Scholarship Committee
1409 Willow Street, Suite 210
Minneapolis, MN 55403-3251
(612) 870-1806   Toll Free: (800) 435-1402
Fax: (612) 871-6587   E-mail: info@PfundOnline.org
Web: www.pfundonline.org/scholarships.html

Summary   To provide funds to African American and Native American Minnesota students who are associated with gay, lesbian, bisexual, and transgender (GLBT) activities.

Eligibility   This program is open to residents of Minnesota and students attending a Minnesota educational institution who are African American or Native American. Applicants must be self-identified as GLBT or from a GLBT family. They may be attending or planning to attend trade school, technical college, college, or university (as an undergraduate or graduate student). Selection is based on the applicant's 1) affirmation of GLBT identity or commitment to GLBT communities; 2) evidence of experience and skills in service and leadership; and 3) evidence of service and leadership in GLBT communities, including serving as a role model, mentor, and/or adviser.

Financial data The stipend ranges up to $2,000. Funds must be used for tuition, books, fees, or dissertation expenses.

Duration 1 year.

Number awarded 1 or more each year.

Deadline January of each year.

[221]
HBCU SCHOLARSHIPS

Delta Sigma Theta Sorority, Inc.-Federal City Alumnae
   Chapter
Attn: Educational Development Committee
P.O. Box 1605
Washington, DC 20013
(202) 545-1913   E-mail: thefcacdst@yahoo.com
Web: thefcacdst.org

Summary To provide financial assistance to high school seniors in Washington, D.C. who plan to attend a 4-year Historically Black College or University (HBCU) in any state.

Eligibility This program is open to seniors graduating from high schools in the District of Columbia and planning to enroll full time at an accredited 4-year HBCU in any state. Applicants must have a GPA of 3.3 or higher. Along with their application, they must submit a 500-word essay on either how they plan to use their education to make the world a better place or why they should be selected to receive this scholarship.

Financial data The stipend is $2,000.

Duration 1 year.

Additional information The sponsor is the local alumnae chapter of a traditionally African American social sorority.

Number awarded 2 each year.

Deadline February of each year.

[222]
HBCUCONNECT MEMBER SCHOLARSHIPS

HBCUConnect.com, LLC.
Attn: Scholarship Administrator
750 Cross Pointe Road, Suite Q
Columbus, OH 43230
Toll Free: (877) 864-4446
E-mail: culpepper@hbcuconnect.com
Web: hbcuconnect.com

Summary To provide financial assistance to underrepresented minority students attending or planning to attend an Historically Black College or University (HBCU).

Eligibility This program is open to high school seniors and current full-time college students who are members of an underrepresented minority group (African American, Hispanic American, Native American). Applicants must be attending or interested in attending an HBCU to work on a 4-year degree. Along with their application, they must submit a 350-word essay on why they chose to attend an HBCU. Selection is based on quality of content in their online registration with HBCUConnect and financial need.

Financial data The stipend is $1,000.

Duration 1 year.

Number awarded Up to 4 each year.

Deadline May of each year.

[223]
HDR ENGINEERING SCHOLARSHIP FOR DIVERSITY IN ENGINEERING

Association of Independent Colleges and Universities of
   Pennsylvania
101 North Front Street
Harrisburg, PA 17101-1405
(717) 232-8649   Fax: (717) 233-8574
E-mail: info@aicup.org
Web: www.aicup.org

Summary To provide financial assistance to African Americans, other minorities, and women from any state who are enrolled at member institutions of the Association of Independent Colleges and Universities of Pennsylvania (AICUP) and majoring in designated fields of engineering.

Eligibility This program is open to undergraduate students from any state enrolled full time at AICUP colleges and universities. Applicants must be women and/or members of the following minority groups: American Indians, Alaska Natives, Asians, Blacks/African Americans, Hispanics/Latinos, Native Hawaiians, or Pacific Islanders. They must be juniors majoring in civil, geotechnical, or structural engineering with a GPA of 3.0 or higher. Along with their application, they must submit a 2-page essay on their characteristics, accomplishments, primary interests, plans, and goals.

Financial data The stipend is $5,000 per year.

Duration 1 year; may be renewed 1 additional year if the recipient maintains appropriate academic standards.

Additional information This program, sponsored by HDR Engineering, Inc., is available at the 83 private colleges and universities in Pennsylvania that comprise the AICUP.

Number awarded 1 each year.

Deadline April of each year.

[224]
HEALTH RESEARCH AND EDUCATIONAL TRUST SCHOLARSHIPS

New Jersey Hospital Association
Attn: Health Research and Educational Trust
760 Alexander Road
P.O. Box 1
Princeton, NJ 08543-0001
(609) 275-4224   Fax: (609) 452-8097
Web: www.njha.com/hret/scholarship.aspx

Summary To provide financial assistance to New Jersey residents (particularly African Americans, other minorities, and women) who are working on an undergraduate or graduate degree in a field related to health care administration at a school in any state.

Eligibility This program is open to residents of New Jersey enrolled in an upper-division or graduate program in hospital or health care administration, public administration, nursing, or other allied health profession at a school in any state. Graduate students working on an advanced degree to prepare to teach nursing are also eligible. Applicants must have a GPA of 3.0 or higher and be able to demonstrate financial need. Along with their application, they must submit a 2-page essay (on which 50% of the selection is based) describing their academic plans for the future. Minorities and women are especially encouraged to apply.

Financial data The stipend is $2,000.

Duration 1 year.

Additional information This program began in 1983.

Number awarded Varies each year; recently, 3 of these scholarships were awarded.

Deadline July of each year.

[225]
HEINEKEN USA PERFORMING ARTS SCHOLARSHIP

Congressional Black Caucus Foundation, Inc.
Attn: Director, Educational Programs
1720 Massachusetts Avenue, N.W.
Washington, DC 20036
(202) 263-2800 Toll Free: (800) 784-2577
Fax: (202) 775-0773 E-mail: info@cbcfinc.org
Web: www.cbcfinc.org/scholarships.html

Summary To provide financial assistance to African American and other undergraduate and graduate students who are interested in studying the performing arts.

Eligibility This program is open to 1) minority and other graduating high school seniors planning to attend an accredited institution of higher education; and 2) currently-enrolled full-time undergraduate, graduate, and doctoral students in good academic standing with a GPA of 2.5 or higher. Applicants be interested in preparing for a career in the performing arts, including theater, motion pictures, drama, comedy, music, dance, opera, marching bands, and other musical ensembles. Along with their application, they must submit a 2-minute CD or DVD of their performance and a personal statement of 500 to 1,000 words on 1) their future goals, major field of study, and how that field of study will help them to achieve their future career goals; 2) involvement in school activities, community and public service, hobbies, and sports; 3) how receiving this award will affect their current and future plans; and 4) other experiences, skills, or qualifications. They must also be able to demonstrate financial need, leadership ability, and participation in community service activities.

Financial data The stipend is $3,000.

Duration 1 year.

Additional information This program, established in 2000, is sponsored by Heineken USA.

Number awarded 10 each year.

Deadline April of each year.

[226]
HENRY ARTHUR CALLIS SCHOLARSHIP FUND

Alpha Phi Alpha Fraternity, Inc.-Mu Lambda Chapter
Attn: Mu Lambda Foundation
P.O. Box 4582
Washington, DC 20017-4582
Web: www.mulambda.org/henry-arthur-callis-scholarship

Summary To provide financial assistance to African American high school seniors from the Washington, D.C. metropolitan area who plan to attend college in any state.

Eligibility This program is open to African American seniors graduating from high schools in Washington, D.C. and neighboring school districts. Applicants must be planning to attend a college or university in any state. Along with their application, they must submit 2 letters of recommendation, a transcript, a copy of their SAT and/or ACT scores, documen-

tation of financial need, and a personal essay describing their involvement in extracurricular and community activities.

Financial data The stipend is $1,000.

Duration 1 year.

Additional information Alpha Phi Alpha is the first collegiate fraternity established primarily for African American men. Mu Lambda is the alumni chapter for Washington, D.C.

Number awarded 1 or more each year.

Deadline February of each year.

[227]
HERBERT LEHMAN EDUCATION FUND

NAACP Legal Defense and Educational Fund
Attn: Director of Scholarship Programs
99 Hudson Street, Suite 1600
New York, NY 10013-2897
(212) 965-2265 Fax: (212) 219-1595
E-mail: scholarships@naacpldf.org
Web: www.naacpldf.org/scholarships

Summary To provide financial assistance for college to high school seniors and recent graduates, especially African Americans.

Eligibility This program is open to high school seniors, high school graduates, and college freshmen attending or planning to attend 4-year colleges and universities. Applicants must be dedicated to advancing the cause of civil rights, excel academically, show exceptional leadership potential, and have made an impact on their communities through service to others. They must also be able to demonstrate financial need.

Financial data The stipend is $2,000 per year.

Duration 1 year; may be renewed for up to 3 additional years if the student remains enrolled full time, maintains good academic standing, and fulfills all program requirements.

Additional information The NAACP Legal Defense and Educational Fund established this program in 1964 so African American students in the South could attend formerly segregated schools.

Number awarded Varies each year; recently, a total of 79 new and renewal scholarships were awarded.

Deadline March of each year.

[228]
HERMAN S. DREER SCHOLARSHIP/ LEADERSHIP AWARD

Omega Psi Phi Fraternity
Attn: Charles R. Drew Memorial Scholarship Commission
3951 Snapfinger Parkway
Decatur, GA 30035-3203
(404) 284-5533 Fax: (404) 284-0333
E-mail: scholarshipchairman@oppf.org
Web: oppf.org/scholarship

Summary To provide financial assistance to undergraduate Omega Psi Phi Fraternity men attending a 4-year college.

Eligibility This program is open to members of Omega Psi Phi at 4-year colleges and universities who are full-time sophomores or higher and have a GPA of 3.0 or higher. Each of the fraternity's 12 district representatives may nominate 1 member. Candidates must submit 1) a statement of 200 to 250 words on their purpose for applying for this scholarship, how they believe funds from the fraternity can assist them in achieving their career goals, and other circumstances (including financial need) that make it important for them to receive financial assistance; and 2) a 500-word essay detailing their leadership and humanitarian accomplishments. The award is given to the undergraduate student best exemplifying the fraternity's principles of manhood, scholarship, perseverance, and uplift.

Financial data The stipend is $5,000.

Duration 1 year.

Number awarded 1 each year.

Deadline May of each year.

[229]
HILTON WORLDWIDE NSBE CORPORATE SCHOLARSHIP PROGRAM

National Society of Black Engineers
Attn: Programs Department
205 Daingerfield Road
Alexandria, VA 22314
(703) 549-2207   Fax: (703) 683-5312
E-mail: scholarships@nsbe.org
Web: www.nsbe.org

Summary To provide financial assistance to undergraduate members of the National Society of Black Engineers (NSBE) who are working on a degree in engineering, science, or technology.

Eligibility This program is open to members of the society who are working on a technical undergraduate degree in engineering, science, or technology. Applicants must have a GPA of 3.0 or higher. Along with their application, they must submit official transcripts and a resume.

Financial data The stipend is $10,000 per year.

Duration 3 years.

Additional information This program is sponsored by Hilton Worldwide.

Number awarded 1 each year.

Deadline January of each year.

[230]
HISTORICALLY BLACK COLLEGE SCHOLARSHIPS

U.S. Navy
Attn: Naval Education and Training Command
NSTC OD2
250 Dallas Street, Suite A
Pensacola, FL 32508-5268
(850) 452-4941, ext. 25166
Toll Free: (800) NAV-ROTC, ext. 25166
Fax: (850) 452-2486
E-mail: PNSC_NROTC.scholarship@navy.mil
Web: www.nrotc.navy.mil/hist_black.aspx

Summary To provide financial assistance to students at specified Historically Black Colleges or Universities (HBCUs) who are interested in joining Navy ROTC.

Eligibility This program is open to students attending or planning to attend 1 of 15 specified HBCUs with a Navy ROTC unit on campus. Applicants must be nominated by the professor of naval science at their institution and meet academic requirements set by each school. They must be U.S. citizens between 17 and 23 years of age who are willing to serve for 4 years as active-duty Navy officers following grad-

uation from college. They must not have reached their 27th birthday by the time of college graduation and commissioning; applicants who have prior active-duty military service may be eligible for age adjustments for the amount of time equal to their prior service, up to a maximum of 36 months. The qualifying scores for the Navy option are 530 critical reading and 520 mathematics on the SAT or 22 on both English and mathematics on the ACT; for the Marine Corps option they are 1000 composite on the SAT or 22 composite on the ACT. Current enlisted and former military personnel are also eligible if they will complete the program by the age of 30.

Financial data These scholarships provide payment of full tuition and required educational fees, as well as a specified amount for textbooks, supplies, and equipment. The program also provides a stipend for 10 months of the year that is $250 per month as a freshman, $300 per month as a sophomore, $350 per month as a junior, and $400 per month as a senior.

Duration Up to 4 years.

Additional information Students may apply for either a Navy or Marine Corps option scholarship, but not for both. Recipients must complete 4 years of study in naval science classes as students at 1 of the following HBCUs: Clark Atlanta University, Dillard University, Florida A&M University, Hampton University, Howard University, Huston-Tillotson University, Morehouse College, Norfolk State University, Prairie View A&M University, Savannah State University, Southern University and A&M College, Spelman College, Tennessee State University, Tuskegee University, or Xavier University. After completing the program, all participants are commissioned as ensigns in the Naval Reserve or second lieutenants in the Marine Corps Reserve with an 8-year service obligation, including 4 years of active duty. Current military personnel who are accepted into this program are released from active duty and are not eligible for active-duty pay and allowances, medical benefits, or other active-duty entitlements.

Number awarded Varies each year.

Deadline January of each year.

[231]
HOLY FAMILY MEMORIAL SCHOLARSHIP PROGRAM

Holy Family Memorial
Attn: Human Resources
2300 Western Avenue
P.O. Box 1450
Manitowoc, WI 54221-1450
(920) 320-4031   Toll Free: (800) 994-3662, ext. 4031
Fax: (920) 320-8522   E-mail: recruiter@hfmhealth.org
Web: www.hfmhealth.org/?id=118&sid=1

Summary To provide funding to students (particularly African Americans and other minorities) who are working on a degree in a health-related area and willing to work at a designated hospital in Wisconsin following completion of their degree.

Eligibility This program is open to students working on a degree in health-related areas that include, but are not limited to, nursing, pharmacy, sonography, occupational therapy, physical therapy, speech/language pathology, respiratory therapy, or radiology. Applicants must have a GPA of 3.0 or higher. Selection is based on a personal interview, likelihood for professional success, customer service orientation, work ethic, enthusiasm, and professionalism. Minorities are especially encouraged to apply.

Financial data Stipends are $800 per semester ($1,600 per year) for students at technical colleges, $2,000 per semester ($4,000 per year) for students at public universities, or $2,500 per semester ($5,000 per year) for students at private universities. Recipients must commit to working 6 months for each semester of support received at Holy Family Memorial in Manitowoc, Wisconsin following completion of their degree.

Duration 1 semester; renewable.

Deadline Deadline not specified.

[232]
HONEYWELL INTERNATIONAL SCHOLARSHIPS

Society of Women Engineers
Attn: Scholarship Selection Committee
120 South LaSalle Street, Suite 1515
Chicago, IL 60603-3572
(312) 596-5223   Toll Free: (877) SWE-INFO
Fax: (312) 644-8557
E-mail: scholarshipapplication@swe.org
Web: societyofwomenengineers.swe.org

Summary To provide financial assistance to African American and other underrepresented women interested in studying specified fields of engineering in college.

Eligibility This program is open to women who are graduating high school seniors or rising college sophomores, juniors, or seniors. Applicants must be enrolled or planning to enroll full time at an ABET-accredited 4-year college or university and major in computer science or aerospace, chemical, computer, electrical, industrial, manufacturing, materials, or mechanical engineering. Preference is given to members of groups underrepresented in computer science and engineering. U.S. citizenship is required. Financial need is considered in the selection process.

Financial data The stipend is $5,000.

Duration 1 year.

Additional information This program is sponsored by Honeywell International Inc.

Number awarded 3 each year.

Deadline February of each year for current college students; May of each year for high school seniors.

[233]
HONORABLE ERNESTINE WASHINGTON LIBRARY SCIENCE/ENGLISH LANGUAGE ARTS SCHOLARSHIP

African-American/Caribbean Education Association, Inc.
P.O. Box 1224
Valley Stream, NY 11582-1224
(718) 949-6733   E-mail: aaceainc@yahoo.com
Web: www.aaceainc.com/Scholarships.html

Summary To provide financial assistance to high school seniors of African American or Caribbean heritage who plan to study a field related to library science or English language arts in college.

Eligibility This program is open to graduating high school seniors who are U.S. citizens of African American or Caribbean heritage. Applicants must be planning to attend a college or university and major in a field related to library science

or English language arts. They must have completed 4 years of specified college preparatory courses with a grade of 90 or higher and have an SAT score of at least 1790. They must also have completed at least 200 hours of community service during their 4 years of high school, preferably in the field that they plan to study in college. Financial need is not considered in the selection process. New York residency is not required, but applicants must be available for an interviews in the Queens, New York area.

Financial data The stipend ranges from $1,000 to $2,500. Funds are paid directly to the recipient.

Duration 1 year.

Number awarded 1 each year.

Deadline April of each year.

[234]
HORACE AND SUSIE REVELS CAYTON SCHOLARSHIP

Public Relations Society of America-Puget Sound
    Chapter
c/o Diane Bevins
1006 Industry Drive
Seattle, WA 98188-4801
(206) 623-8632   E-mail: prsascholarship@asi-seattle.net
Web: www.prsapugetsound.org/scholars.html

Summary To provide financial assistance to African American and other minority upper-classmen from Washington who are interested in preparing for a career in public relations.

Eligibility This program is open to U.S. citizens who are members of minority groups, defined as African Americans, Asian Americans, Hispanic/Latino Americans, Native Americans, and Pacific Islanders. Applicants must be full-time juniors or seniors attending a college in Washington or Washington students (who graduated from a Washington high school or whose parents live in the state year-round) attending college elsewhere. They must be able to demonstrate aptitude in public relations and related courses, activities, and/or internships. Along with their application, they must submit a description of their career goals and the skills that are most important in general to a public relations career (15 points in the selection process); a description of their activities in communications in class, on campus, in the community, or during internships, including 3 samples of their work (15 points); a statement on the value of public relations to an organization (10 points); a description of any barriers, financial or otherwise, they have encountered in pursuing their academic or personal goals and how they have addressed them (15 points); a discussion of their heritage, and how their cultural background and/or the discrimination they may have experienced has impacted them (15 points); a certified transcript (15 points); and 2 or more letters of recommendation (15 points).

Financial data The stipend is $2,500.

Duration 1 year.

Additional information This program was established in 1992.

Number awarded 1 each year.

Deadline April of each year.

[235]
HOUSTON SUN SCHOLARSHIP

National Association of Negro Business and Professional
Women's Clubs
Attn: Scholarship Committee
1806 New Hampshire Avenue, N.W.
Washington, DC 20009-3206
(202) 483-4206   Fax: (202) 462-7253
E-mail: education@nanbpwc.org
Web: www.nanbpwc.org/ScholarshipApplications.asp

Summary   To provide financial assistance to African Americans from designated states studying journalism at a college in any state.

Eligibility   This program is open to African Americans (men or women) who are residents of Arkansas, Kansas, Louisiana, Missouri, New Mexico, Oklahoma, or Texas. Applicants must be enrolled at an accredited college or university in any state as a sophomore or junior. They must have a GPA of 3.0 or higher and be majoring in journalism. Along with their application, they must submit an essay, up to 750 words in length, on the topic, "Credo of the Black Press." U.S. citizenship is required.

Financial data   The stipend is $1,000.

Duration   1 year.

Number awarded   1 or more each year.

Deadline   February of each year.

[236]
HUBERTUS W.V. WILLEMS SCHOLARSHIP FOR MALE STUDENTS

National Association for the Advancement of Colored
People
Attn: Education Department
4805 Mt. Hope Drive
Baltimore, MD 21215-3297
(410) 580-5760   Toll Free: (877) NAACP-98
E-mail: youth@naacpnet.org
Web: www.naacp.org/pages/naacp-scholarships

Summary   To provide funding to males, particularly male members of the National Association for the Advancement of Colored People (NAACP), who are interested in undergraduate or graduate education in selected scientific fields.

Eligibility   This program is open to males who are high school seniors, college students, or graduate students. Applicants must be majoring (or planning to major) in 1 of the following fields: engineering, chemistry, physics, or mathematics. Membership and participation in the NAACP are highly desirable. The required minimum GPA is 2.5 for graduating high school seniors and undergraduate students or 3.0 for graduate students. Applicants must be able to demonstrate financial need, defined as a family income of less than $16,245 for a family of 1 ranging to less than $49,905 for a family of 7. Along with their application, they must submit a 1-page essay on their interest in their major and a career, their life's ambition, what they hope to accomplish in their lifetime, and what position they hope to attain. Full-time enrollment is required for undergraduate students, although graduate students may be enrolled full or part time. U.S. citizenship is required.

Financial data   The stipend is $2,000 per year for undergraduate students or $3,000 per year for graduate students.

Duration   1 year; may be renewed.

Number awarded   Varies each year; recently, 7 of these scholarships were awarded.

Deadline   March of each year.

[237]
HURSTON/WRIGHT AWARD FOR COLLEGE WRITERS

Zora Neale Hurston/Richard Wright Foundation
Attn: Hurston/Wright Awards
12138 Central Avenue, Suite 209
Bowie, MD 20721
(301) 459-2108   E-mail: info@hurstonwright.org
Web: www.hurstonwright.org

Summary   To recognize and reward the best fiction written by undergraduate or graduate students of African descent.

Eligibility   This program is open to students of African descent who are enrolled full time as undergraduate or graduate students at a college or university in the United States. Applicants should submit a manuscript of a short story (up to 25 pages) or novel excerpt (up to 15 pages). They should indicate whether it is a short story or novel excerpt. Only 1 entry may be submitted per applicant. Writers who have already published a book (in any genre) are ineligible.

Financial data   The first-place award is $1,000; finalist awards are $500.

Duration   The prizes are awarded annually.

Additional information   There is a $10 processing fee.

Number awarded   3 awards are presented each year: 1 first-place award and 2 finalist awards.

Deadline   January of each year.

[238]
HYATT HOTELS FUND FOR MINORITY LODGING MANAGEMENT STUDENTS

American Hotel & Lodging Educational Foundation
Attn: Manager of Foundation Programs
1201 New York Avenue, N.W., Suite 600
Washington, DC 20005-3931
(202) 289-3181   Fax: (202) 289-3199
E-mail: ahlef@ahlef.org
Web: www.ahlef.org/content.aspx?id=19828

Summary   To provide financial assistance to African American and other minority college students working on a degree in hotel management.

Eligibility   This program is open to students majoring in hospitality management at a 4-year college or university as at least a sophomore. Applicants must be members of a minority group (African American, Hispanic, American Indian, Alaskan Native, Asian, or Pacific Islander). They must be enrolled full time. Along with their application, they must submit a 500-word essay on their personal background, including when they became interested in the hospitality field, what traits they possess or will need to succeed in the industry, and their plans as related to their educational and career objectives and future goals. Selection is based on industry-related work experience; financial need; academic record and educational qualifications; professional, community, and extracurricular activities; personal attributes, including career goals; the essay; and neatness and completeness of the application. U.S. citizenship or permanent resident status is required.

Financial data   The stipend is $2,000.

Duration   1 year.

Additional information   Funding for this program, established in 1988, is provided by Hyatt Hotels & Resorts.

Number awarded   Varies each year; recently, 10 of these scholarships were awarded. Since this program was established, it has awarded scholarships worth $508,000 to approximately 255 minority students.

Deadline   April of each year.

[239]
IBE/CCC SCHOLARSHIP PROGRAM

Indiana Black Expo, Inc.
Attn: Scholarship Program
3145 North Meridian
Indianapolis, IN 46208
(317) 925-2702   Fax: (317) 925-6624
E-mail: communications@indianablackexpo.com
Web: www.indianablackexpo.com/programs-youth.asp

Summary   To provide financial assistance to high school seniors in Indiana who are planning to enroll at a college or university in any state, especially at an Historically Black College or University (HBCU).

Eligibility   This program is open to seniors graduating from high schools in Indiana and planning to enroll full time at a college or university in any state. Applicants must have a GPA of 2.5 or higher and a family income of $30,000 per year or less. Special consideration is given to students who 1) are the first in their family to attend college, or 2) plan to attend an HBCU. Along with their application, they must submit a 1-page essay on how this scholarship will help them achieve their educational goals and benefit their community. Selection is based on academic achievement, extracurricular activities, and financial need.

Financial data   Stipends are $1,000 per year.

Duration   1 year.

Additional information   Indiana Black Expo (IBE) was established in 1984 to promote the social and economic advancement of African Americans in Indiana. Support for this program is provided by the Coca-Cola Company through its sponsorship of the Circle City Classic (CCC) football game.

Number awarded   Varies each year; recently, 58 of these scholarships were awarded. At least 2 scholarships are reserved for students attending an HBCU. Since its establishment, this program has awarded nearly $2 million in scholarships.

Deadline   April of each year.

[240]
IBM CORPORATION SWE SCHOLARSHIPS

Society of Women Engineers
Attn: Scholarship Selection Committee
120 South LaSalle Street, Suite 1515
Chicago, IL 60603-3572
(312) 596-5223   Toll Free: (877) SWE-INFO
Fax: (312) 644-8557
E-mail: scholarshipapplication@swe.org
Web: societyofwomenengineers.swe.org

Summary   To provide financial assistance to African American or other minority women majoring in designated engineering specialties.

Eligibility   This program is open to women who are entering their sophomore or junior year at a 4-year ABET-accredited college or university. Applicants must be majoring in computer science or electrical or computer engineering and have a GPA of 3.4 or higher. Preference is given to members of groups underrepresented in engineering or computer science. Selection is based on merit. U.S. citizenship is required.

Financial data   The stipend is $1,000.

Duration   1 year.

Additional information   This program is sponsored by the IBM Corporation.

Number awarded   4 each year.

Deadline   February of each year.

[241]
IDAHO MINORITY AND "AT RISK" STUDENT SCHOLARSHIP

Idaho State Board of Education
Len B. Jordan Office Building
650 West State Street, Room 307
P.O. Box 83720
Boise, ID 83720-0037
(208) 332-1574   Fax: (208) 334-2632
E-mail: scholarshiphelp@osbe.idaho.gov
Web: www.boardofed.idaho.gov/scholarships/minority.asp

Summary   To provide financial assistance to African Americans and other "at risk" high school seniors in Idaho who plan to attend college in the state.

Eligibility   This program is open to residents of Idaho who are graduates of high schools in the state. Applicants must meet at least 3 of the following 5 requirements: 1) have a disability; 2) be a member of an ethnic minority group historically underrepresented in higher education in Idaho; 3) have substantial financial need; 4) be a first-generation college student; 5) be a migrant farm worker or a dependent of a farm worker. U.S. citizenship is required.

Financial data   The maximum stipend is $3,000 per year.

Duration   1 year; may be renewed for up to 3 additional years.

Additional information   This program was established in 1991 by the Idaho state legislature. Information is also available from high school counselors and financial aid offices of colleges and universities in Idaho. Recipients must plan to attend or be attending 1 of 11 participating colleges and universities in the state on a full-time basis. For a list of those schools, write to the State of Idaho Board of Education.

Number awarded   Approximately 40 each year.

Deadline   Deadline not specified.

[242]
IDAHO STATE BROADCASTERS ASSOCIATION SCHOLARSHIPS

Idaho State Broadcasters Association
270 North 27th Street, Suite B
Boise, ID 83702-4741
(208) 345-3072　　　　　　　　Fax: (208) 343-8946
E-mail: isba@qwestoffice.net
Web: www.idahobroadcasters.org/scholarships.aspx

Summary To provide financial assistance to students at Idaho colleges and universities (particularly African American and other minority students) who are preparing for a career in the broadcasting field.

Eligibility This program is open to full-time students at Idaho schools who are preparing for a career in broadcasting, including business administration, sales, journalism, or engineering. Applicants must have a GPA of at least 2.0 for the first 2 years of school or 2.5 for the last 2 years. Along with their application, they must submit a letter of recommendation from the general manager of a broadcasting station that is a member of the Idaho State Broadcasters Association and a 1-page essay describing their career plans and why they want the scholarship. Applications are encouraged from a wide and diverse student population. Financial need is not considered in the selection process.

Financial data The stipend is $1,000.

Duration 1 year.

Number awarded 2 each year.

Deadline March of each year.

[243]
I.H. MCLENDON MEMORIAL SCHOLARSHIP

Sickle Cell Disease Association of America-Connecticut
　Chapter
140 Woodland Street, Suite 102
Hartford, CT 06105
(860) 527-0147　　　　　　　　Fax: (860) 548-0220
E-mail: scdaan1@iconn.net

Summary To provide financial assistance to high school seniors in Connecticut who have sickle cell disease and are interested in attending college in any state.

Eligibility This program is open to Connecticut residents who have sickle cell disease. Applicants must be graduating high school seniors, have a GPA of 3.0 or higher, be in the top third of their class, and be interested in attending a 2- or 4-year college or university in any state. Along with their application, they must submit a statement outlining their personal and career goals and how the scholarship will help them achieve those goals, 3 letters of recommendation, and a letter from their physician attesting to existence of sickle cell disease. Finalists are interviewed.

Financial data The stipend is $1,000.

Duration 1 year; nonrenewable.

Additional information This program is offered in collaboration with the Hartford Foundation for Public Giving.

Number awarded 1 each year.

Deadline April of each year.

[244]
ILLINOIS BROADCASTERS ASSOCIATION MULTICULTURAL INTERNSHIPS

Illinois Broadcasters Association
Attn: MIP Coordinator
200 Missouri Avenue
Carterville, IL 62918
(618) 985-5555　　　　　　　　Fax: (618) 985-6070
E-mail: iba@ilba.org
Web: www.ilba.org

Summary To provide funding to African American and other minority college students in Illinois who are majoring in broadcasting and interested in interning at a radio or television station in the state.

Eligibility This program is open to currently-enrolled minority students majoring in broadcasting at a college or university in Illinois. Applicants must be interested in a fall, spring, or summer internship at a radio or television station that is a member of the Illinois Broadcasters Association. Along with their application, they must submit 1) a 250-word essay on how they expect to benefit from a grant through this program, and 2) at least 2 letters of recommendation from a broadcasting faculty member or professional familiar with their career potential and 1 other letter. The president of the sponsoring organization selects those students nominated by their schools who have the best opportunity to make it in the world of broadcasting and matches them with internship opportunities that would otherwise be unpaid.

Financial data This program provides a grant to pay the living expenses for the interns in the Illinois communities where they are assigned. The amount of the grant depends on the length of the internship.

Duration 16 weeks in the fall and spring terms or 12 weeks in the summer.

Number awarded 12 each year: 4 in each of the 3 terms.

Deadline Deadline not specified.

[245]
ILLINOIS FUTURE TEACHER CORPS PROGRAM

Illinois Student Assistance Commission
Attn: Scholarship and Grant Services
1755 Lake Cook Road
Deerfield, IL 60015-5209
(847) 948-8550　　　　　　　　Toll Free: (800) 899-ISAC
Fax: (847) 831-8549　　　　　　TDD: (800) 526-0844
E-mail: collegezone@isac.org
Web: www.collegezone.com/studentzone/407_660.htm

Summary To provide funding to college students in Illinois (especially African American and other minority students) who are interested in training or retraining for a teaching career in academic shortage areas.

Eligibility This program is open to Illinois residents who are enrolled at the junior level or higher at an institution of higher education in the state. Applicants must be planning to prepare for a career as a preschool, elementary, or secondary school teacher. They must have a cumulative GPA of 2.5 or higher. Priority is given to 1) minority students; 2) students with financial need; and 3) applicants working on a degree in designated teacher shortage disciplines or making a commitment to teach at a hard-to-staff school. Recently, the teacher shortage disciplines included early childhood education, special education (speech and language impaired, learning behavior specialist), and regular education (bilingual education, mathematics, physical education (K-8), reading, and science). U.S. citizenship or eligible noncitizen status is required.

Financial data　Stipends are $5,000 per year for students who agree to teach in a teacher shortage discipline, $5,000 per year for students who agree to teach at a hard-to-staff school, or $10,000 for students who agree to teach in a teacher shortage discipline at a hard-to-staff school. Funds are paid directly to the school. This is a scholarship/loan program. Recipients must agree to teach in an Illinois public, private, or parochial preschool, elementary school, or secondary school for 1 year for each full year of assistance received. The teaching obligation must be completed within 5 years of completion of the degree or certificate program for which the scholarship was awarded. That time period may be extended if the recipient serves in the U.S. armed forces, enrolls full time in a graduate program related to teaching, becomes temporarily disabled, is unable to find employment as a teacher, or takes additional courses on at least a half-time basis to teach in a specialized teacher shortage discipline. Recipients who fail to honor this work obligation must repay the award with interest.

Duration　1 year; may be renewed.

Additional information　This program was formerly known as the David A. DeBolt Teacher Shortage Scholarship Program.

Number awarded　Varies each year, depending on the availability of funds.

Deadline　Priority consideration is given to applications submitted by February of each year.

[246]
ILLINOIS NURSES ASSOCIATION CENTENNIAL SCHOLARSHIP

Illinois Nurses Association
Attn: Illinois Nurses Foundation
105 West Adams Street, Suite 2101
Chicago, IL 60603
(312) 419-2900　　　　　　　　Fax: (312) 419-2920
E-mail: info@illinoisnurses.com
Web: www.illinoisnurses.com

Summary　To provide financial assistance to nursing undergraduate and graduate students who are African American or members of other underrepresented groups.

Eligibility　This program is open to students working on an associate, bachelor's, or master's degree at an accredited NLNAC or CCNE school of nursing. Applicants must be members of a group underrepresented in nursing (African Americans, Hispanics, American Indians, Asians, and males). Undergraduates must have earned a passing grade in all nursing courses taken to date and have a GPA of 2.85 or higher. Graduate students must have completed at least 12 semester hours of graduate work and have a GPA of 3.0 or higher. All applicants must be willing to 1) act as a spokesperson to other student groups on the value of the scholarship to continuing their nursing education, and 2) be profiled in any media or marketing materials developed by the Illinois Nurses Foundation. Along with their application, they must submit a narrative of 250 to 500 words on how they, nurses, plan to affect policy at either the state or national level that impacts

on nursing or health care generally, or how they believe they will impact the nursing profession in general.

Financial data　A stipend is awarded (amount not specified).

Duration　1 year.

Number awarded　1 or more each year.

Deadline　March of each year.

[247]
INDIANA CHAPTER AABE SCHOLARSHIPS

American Association of Blacks in Energy-Indiana
　Chapter
Attn: Scholarship Committee
P.O. Box 44531
Indianapolis, IN 46244
(317) 249-5264　　　　　　E-mail: mdknox@midwestiso.com
Web: www.aabe.org/index.php?component=pages&id=338

Summary　To provide financial assistance to African Americans or members of other underrepresented minority groups who are high school seniors in Indiana and planning to major in an energy-related field at a college in any state.

Eligibility　This program is open to seniors graduating from high schools in Indiana and planning to work on a bachelor's degree at a college or university in any state. Applicants must be African Americans, Hispanics, or Native Americans who have a GPA of 3.0 or higher and are able to demonstrate financial need. Their intended major must be a field of business, engineering, physical science, mathematics, or technology related to energy. Along with their application, they must submit a 350-word statement on why they should receive this scholarship, their professional career objectives, and any other relevant information.

Financial data　The stipend is $1,000.

Duration　1 year; nonrenewable.

Additional information　Winners are eligible to compete for regional and national scholarships.

Number awarded　3 each year.

Deadline　March of each year.

[248]
INDIANA INDUSTRY LIAISON GROUP SCHOLARSHIP

Indiana Industry Liaison Group
c/o Tony Pickell, Vice Chair
AAP Precision Planning, LLC
6215 Meridian Street West Drive
Indianapolis, IN 46260
(317) 590-4797
E-mail: tony.pickell@precisionplanningaap.com
Web: www.indianailg.org/scholardetails.html

Summary　To provide financial assistance to African American and other students from any state enrolled at colleges and universities in Indiana who have been involved in activities to promote diversity.

Eligibility　This program is open to residents of any state currently enrolled at an accredited college or university in Indiana. Applicants must either 1) be studying programs or classes related to diversity/Affirmative Action (AA)/Equal Employment Opportunity (EEO), or 2) have work or volunteer experience for diversity/AA/EEO organizations. Along with their application, they must submit an essay of 400 to 500 words on 1 of the following topics: 1) their personal commitment to diversity/AA/EEO within their community or business; 2) a time or situation in which they were able to establish and/or sustain a commitment to diversity; 3) a time when they have taken a position in favor of affirmative action and/or diversity; or 4) activities in which they have participated within their community that demonstrate their personal commitment to moving the community's diversity agenda forward. Financial need is not considered in the selection process.

Financial data The stipend is $1,000.

Duration 1 year.

Number awarded 1 each year.

Deadline March of each year.

[249]
INDIANA MINORITY TEACHER/SPECIAL EDUCATION SERVICES SCHOLARSHIP

State Student Assistance Commission of Indiana
Attn: Director of Special Programs
150 West Market Street, Suite 500
Indianapolis, IN 46204-2811
(317) 232-2350   Toll Free: (888) 528-4719 (within IN)
Fax: (317) 232-3260   E-mail: special@ssaci.state.in.us
Web: www.in.gov/ssaci/2342.htm

Summary To provide funding to Black and Hispanic undergraduate students in Indiana interested in preparing for a teaching career and to other residents of the state preparing for a career in special education, occupational therapy, or physical therapy.

Eligibility This program is open to 1) Black and Hispanic students seeking teacher certification; 2) students seeking special education teaching certification; or 3) students seeking occupational or physical therapy certification. Applicants must be Indiana residents and U.S. citizens who are enrolled or accepted for enrollment as full-time students at an academic institution in Indiana. Students who are already enrolled in college must have a GPA of 2.0 or higher. Applicants must be preparing to teach in an accredited elementary or secondary school in Indiana or to work as an occupational or physical therapist at a school or rehabilitation facility. Financial need may be considered, but it is not a requirement. In the selection process, awards are presented in the following priority order: 1) minority students seeking a renewal scholarship; 2) newly-enrolling minority students; 3) non-minority students seeking a renewal scholarship; and 4) newly-enrolling non-minority students.

Financial data Minority students demonstrating financial need may receive up to $4,000 per year. For non-minority students, the maximum award is $1,000. For 3 out of the 5 years following graduation, recipients must teach full time in an elementary or secondary school in Indiana or practice as an occupational or physical therapist at a school or rehabilitation facility in the state. If they fail to meet that service requirement, they are required to reimburse the state of Indiana for all funds received.

Duration 1 year; may be renewed up to 3 additional years if recipients maintain a 2.0 GPA. They may, however, take up to 6 years to complete the program from the start of receiving the first scholarship.

Additional information This program was established in 1988 to address the critical shortage of Black and Hispanic teachers in Indiana. An amendment in 1990 added the field of

special education, and in 1991 the fields of occupational and physical therapy were added. Participating colleges in Indiana select the recipients. Students must submit their application to the financial aid office of the college they plan to attend (not to the State Student Assistance Commission of Indiana).

Number awarded Varies each year.

Deadline Each participating college or university establishes its own filing deadline for this program.

[250]
INDIANAPOLIS CHAPTER NBMBAA UNDERGRADUATE SCHOLARSHIP PROGRAM

National Black MBA Association-Indianapolis Chapter
Attn: Scholarship Program
P.O. Box 2325
Indianapolis, IN 46206-2325
(317) 308-6447   E-mail: scholarship@nbmbaa-indy.org
Web: www.nbmbaa-indy.org/nbmbaa_education.htm

Summary To provide financial assistance to African American students from any state working on an undergraduate degree in business or management.

Eligibility This program is open to African American students enrolled full time in an undergraduate business or management program and working on a bachelor's degree at a college or university in any state. Applicants must submit a 2-page essay on a current events topic that changes annually; recently, students were invited to write on how social networking has influenced the way companies conduct business in today's market. Selection is based on the essay, transcripts, and a list of extracurricular activities; financial need is not considered.

Financial data The stipend is $1,000.

Duration 1 year.

Number awarded 1 each year.

Deadline October of each year.

[251]
INDUSTRY MINORITY SCHOLARSHIPS

American Meteorological Society
Attn: Fellowship/Scholarship Program
45 Beacon Street
Boston, MA 02108-3693
(617) 227-2426, ext. 246   Fax: (617) 742-8718
E-mail: scholar@ametsoc.org
Web: www.ametsoc.org

Summary To provide financial assistance to African Americans and other underrepresented minority students entering college and planning to major in meteorology or an aspect of atmospheric sciences.

Eligibility This program is open to members of minority groups traditionally underrepresented in the sciences (especially Hispanics, Native Americans, and Blacks/African Americans) who are entering their freshman year at a college or university and planning to work on a degree in the atmospheric or related oceanic and hydrologic sciences. Applicants must submit an official high school transcript showing grades from the past 3 years, a letter of recommendation from a high school teacher or guidance counselor, a copy of scores from an SAT or similar national entrance exam, and a 500-word essay on a topic that changes annually; recently, applicants were invited to write on global change and how they would use their college education in atmospheric science (or a closely-related field) to make their community a better place in which to live. Selection is based on the essay and academic performance in high school.

Financial data The stipend is $3,000 per year.

Duration 1 year; may be renewed for the second year of college study.

Additional information This program is funded by grants from industry and by donations to the American Meteorological Society (AMS) 21st Century Campaign. Requests for an application must be accompanied by a self-addressed stamped envelope.

Number awarded Varies each year; recently, 5 of these scholarships were awarded.

Deadline February of each year.

[252]
INROADS NATIONAL COLLEGE INTERNSHIPS

INROADS, Inc.
10 South Broadway, Suite 300
St. Louis, MO 63102
(314) 241-7488   Fax: (314) 241-9325
E-mail: info@inroads.org
Web: www.inroads.org

Summary To provide an opportunity for African Americans and other young people of color to gain work experience in business or industry.

Eligibility This program is open to African Americans, Hispanics, and Native Americans who reside in the areas served by INROADS. Applicants must be interested in preparing for a career in business, computer and information sciences, engineering, health, marketing, retail store management, or sales. They must be 1) seniors in high school with a GPA of 3.0 or higher; or 2) freshmen or sophomores in 4-year colleges and universities with a GPA of 2.8 or higher. Citizenship is required.

Financial data Salaries vary, depending upon the specific internship assigned; recently, the range was from $170 to $750 per week.

Duration Up to 4 years.

Additional information INROADS places interns in Fortune 1000 companies, where training focuses on preparing them for corporate and community leadership. The INROADS organization offers internship opportunities through 35 local affiliates in 26 states, Canada, and Mexico.

Number awarded Approximately 2,000 high school and college students are currently working for more than 200 corporate sponsors nationwide.

Deadline March of each year.

[253]
INSTITUTE FOR INTERNATIONAL PUBLIC POLICY FELLOWSHIPS

United Negro College Fund Special Programs
   Corporation
Attn: Institute for International Public Policy
6402 Arlington Boulevard, Suite 600
Falls Church, VA 22042
(703) 677-3400   Toll Free: (800) 530-6232
Fax: (703) 205-7645   E-mail: iippl@uncfsp.org
Web: www.uncfsp.org

Summary To provide financial assistance and work experience to African Americans and other minority students who are interested in preparing for a career in international affairs.

Eligibility This program is open to full-time sophomores at 4-year institutions who have a GPA of 3.2 or higher and are nominated by the president of their institution. Applicants must be African American, Hispanic/Latino American, Asian American, American Indian, Alaskan Native, Native Hawaiian, or Pacific Islander. They must be interested in participating in policy institutes, study abroad, language training, internships, and graduate education that will prepare them for a career in international service. U.S. citizenship or permanent resident status is required.

Financial data For the sophomore summer policy institute, fellows receive student housing and meals in a university facility, books and materials, all field trips and excursions, and a $1,050 stipend. For the junior year study abroad component, half the expenses for 1 semester, to a maximum of $8,000, is provided. For the junior summer policy institute, fellows receive student housing and meals in a university facility, books and materials, travel to and from the institute, and a $1,000 stipend. For the summer language institute, fellows receive tuition and fees, books and materials, room and board, travel to and from the institute, and a $1,000 stipend. During the internship, a stipend of up to $3,500 is paid. During the graduate school period, fellowships are funded jointly by this program and the participating graduate school. The program provides $15,000 toward a master's degree in international affairs with the expectation that the graduate school will provide $15,000 in matching funds.

Duration 2 years of undergraduate work and 2 years of graduate work, as well as the intervening summers.

Additional information This program consists of 6 components: 1) a sophomore year summer policy institute based at Howard University that introduces fellows to international policy development, foreign affairs, cultural competence, careers in those fields, and options for graduate study; 2) a junior year study abroad program at an accredited overseas institution; 3) a 7-week junior year summer institute at the University of Maryland's School of Public Policy; 4) for students without established foreign language competency, a summer language institute at Middlebury College Language Schools in Middlebury, Vermont following the senior year; 5) fellows with previously established foreign language competence participate in a post-baccalaureate internship to provide the practical experience needed for successful graduate studies in international affairs; and 6) a master's degree in international affairs (for students who are admitted to such a program). This program is administered by the United Negro College Fund Special Programs Corporation with funding provided by a grant from the U.S. Department of Education.

Number awarded 30 each year.

Deadline February of each year.

[254]
INTERMOUNTAIN SECTION AWWA DIVERSITY SCHOLARSHIP

American Water Works Association-Intermountain
  Section
3430 East Danish Road
Sandy, UT 94093
(801) 712-1619   Fax: (801) 487-6699
E-mail: nicoleb@ims-awwa.org
Web: www.ims-awwa.org

Summary   To provide financial assistance to African American and other underrepresented undergraduate and graduate students working on a degree in the field of water quality, supply, and treatment at a university in Idaho or Utah.

Eligibility   This program is open to women and students who identify as Hispanic or Latino, Black or African American, Native Hawaiian or other Pacific Islander, Asian, or American Indian or Alaska Native. Applicants must be entering or enrolled in an undergraduate or graduate program at a college or university in Idaho or Utah that relates to water quality, supply, or treatment. Along with their application, they must submit a 2-page essay on their academic interests and career goals and how those relate to water quality, supply, or treatment. Selection is based on that essay, letters of recommendation, and potential to contribute to the field of water quality, supply, and treatment in the Intermountain West.

Financial data   The stipend is $1,000. The winner also receives a 1-year student membership in the Intermountain Section of the American Water Works Association (AWWA) and a 1-year subscription to *Journal AWWA*.

Duration   1 year; nonrenewable.

Number awarded   1 each year.

Deadline   October of each year.

[255]
INTERNATIONAL ASSOCIATION OF BLACK ACTUARIES SCHOLARSHIPS

International Association of Black Actuaries
Attn: IABA Foundation Scholarship Committee
P.O. Box 369
Windsor, CT 06095
(860) 219-9534   Fax: (215) 219-9546
E-mail: iaba@blackactuaries.org
Web: www.blackactuaries.org/scholarships

Summary   To provide financial assistance to Black upper-division and graduate students preparing for an actuarial career.

Eligibility   This program is open to full-time juniors, seniors, and graduate students who are of African descent, originating from the United States, Canada, the Caribbean, or African nations. Applicants must have been admitted to a college or university offering either a program in actuarial science or courses that will prepare them for an actuarial career. They must be citizens or permanent residents of the United States or Canada or eligible to study in those countries under a U.S. student visa or Canadian student authorization. Other requirements include a GPA of 3.0 or higher, a mathematics SAT score of at least 600 or a mathematics ACT score of at least 28, completion of probability and calculus courses, attempting or passing an actuarial examination, completion of Validation by Educational Experience (VEE) requirements,

and familiarity with actuarial profession demands. Selection is based on merit and financial need.

Financial data   Stipends range from $500 to $4,000 per year.

Duration   1 year; may be renewed.

Number awarded   1 or more each year.

Deadline   May of each year.

[256]
INTERNATIONAL COMMUNICATIONS INDUSTRIES FOUNDATION AV SCHOLARSHIPS

InfoComm International
International Communications Industries Foundation
11242 Waples Mill Road, Suite 200
Fairfax, VA 22030
(703) 273-7200   Toll Free: (800) 659-7469
Fax: (703) 278-8082   E-mail: srieger@infocomm.org
Web: www.infocomm.org

Summary   To provide financial assistance to high school seniors and college students (especially African Americans, other minorities, and women) who are interested in preparing for a career in the audiovisual (AV) industry.

Eligibility   This program is open to high school seniors, undergraduates, and graduate students already enrolled in college. Applicants must have a GPA of 2.75 or higher and be majoring or planning to major in audiovisual subjects or related fields, including audio, video, electronics, telecommunications, technical aspects of the theater, data networking, software development, or information technology. Students in other programs, such as journalism, may be eligible if they can demonstrate a relationship to career goals in the AV industry. Along with their application, they must submit 1) an essay of 150 to 200 words on the career path they plan to pursue in the audiovisual industry in the next 5 years, and 2) an essay of 250 to 300 words on the experience or person influencing them the most in selecting the audiovisual industry as their career of choice. Minority and women candidates are especially encouraged to apply. Selection is based on the essays, presentation of the application, GPA, AV-related experience, work experience, and letters of recommendation.

Financial data   The stipend is $1,200 per year. Funds are sent directly to the school.

Duration   1 year; recipients may reapply.

Additional information   InfoComm International, formerly the International Communications Industries Association, established the International Communications Industries Foundation (ICIF) to manage its charitable and educational activities.

Number awarded   Varies each year; recently, 29 of these scholarships were awarded.

Deadline   May of each year.

[257]
INTERPUBLIC GROUP SCHOLARSHIP AND INTERNSHIP

New York Women in Communications, Inc.
Attn: NYWICI Foundation
355 Lexington Avenue, 15th Floor
New York, NY 10017-6603
(212) 297-2133   Fax: (212) 370-9047
E-mail: nywicipr@nywici.org
Web: www.nywici.org/foundation/scholarships

Summary   To provide financial assistance and work experience to African American and other minority women who are residents of designated eastern states and enrolled as juniors at a college in any state to prepare for a career in advertising or public relations.

Eligibility   This program is open to female residents of New York, New Jersey, Connecticut, or Pennsylvania who are from ethnically diverse groups and currently enrolled as juniors at a college or university in any state. Also eligible are women who reside outside the 4 states but are currently enrolled at a college or university within 1 of the 5 boroughs of New York City. Applicants must be preparing for a career in advertising or public relations and have a GPA of 3.2 or higher. They must be available for a summer internship with Interpublic Group (IPG) in New York City. Along with their application, they must submit a 2-page resume that includes school and extracurricular activities, significant achievements, academic honors and awards, and community service work; a personal essay of 300 to 500 words on their choice of an assigned topic that changes annually; 2 letters of recommendation; and an official transcript. Selection is based on academic record, need, demonstrated leadership, participation in school and community activities, honors, work experience, goals and aspirations, and unusual personal and/or family circumstances. U.S. citizenship is required.

Financial data   The scholarship stipend ranges up to $10,000; the internship is paid (amount not specified).

Duration   1 year.

Additional information   This program is sponsored by IPG, a holding company for a large number of firms in the advertising industry.

Number awarded   1 each year.

Deadline   January of each year.

[258]
IRA DORSEY SCHOLARSHIP ENDOWMENT FUND

Alpha Phi Alpha Fraternity, Inc.-Xi Alpha Lambda Chapter
Attn: Director of Education
P.O. Box 10371
Alexandria, VA 22310
(240) 463-2529   E-mail: xal_education@gmail.com
Web: apaxal.com/foundation/idsefdescr

Summary   To provide financial assistance to African American and other high school seniors in the Washington, D.C. metropolitan area who plan to attend college in any state.

Eligibility   This program is open to seniors graduating from high schools in the metropolitan Washington area of Virginia, Maryland, and the District of Columbia. Applicants must have a GPA of 2.5 or higher and be planning to attend a 4-year college or university in any state. Along with their application,

they must submit a 500-word essay on a topic that changes annually; recently, they were invited to comment on the challenges facing the President of the United States. Selection is based on the quality of that essay, academic achievement, participation in school and community clubs and organizations, honors and awards, and financial need.

Financial data   The stipend is $1,500.

Duration   1 year; nonrenewable.

Additional information   Alpha Phi Alpha is the first collegiate fraternity established primarily for African American men. Xi Alpha Lambda is the alumni chapter for northern Virginia.

Number awarded   Several each year.

Deadline   April of each year.

[259]
IRLET ANDERSON SCHOLARSHIP AWARD

National Organization of Black Law Enforcement
  Executives
Attn: NOBLE Scholarships
4609 Pinecrest Office Park Drive, Suite F
Alexandria, VA 22312-1442
(703) 658-1529   Fax: (703) 658-9479
E-mail: noble@noblenatl.org
Web: www.noblenational.org

Summary   To provide financial assistance for college to African American and other high school seniors who are interested in preparing for a criminal justice career.

Eligibility   This program is open to high school seniors who have a GPA of 2.5 or higher and are interested in preparing for a career in criminal justice. Applicants must be planning to attend an accredited academic institution in the United States to major in a social science field (e.g. technology, forensic investigations, or other criminal investigative studies) related to law enforcement or criminal justice. They must be able to demonstrate financial need. Along with their application, they must submit a 1-page essay on their career goals and interests and why they feel they should receive this scholarship.

Financial data   The stipend is $5,000.

Duration   1 year; nonrenewable.

Additional information   The sponsor is an organization of African American law enforcement officers.

Number awarded   1 each year.

Deadline   March of each year.

[260]
IRTS SUMMER FELLOWSHIP PROGRAM

International Radio and Television Society Foundation
Attn: Director, Special Projects
420 Lexington Avenue, Suite 1601
New York, NY 10170-0101
(212) 867-6650   Toll Free: (888) 627-1266
Fax: (212) 867-6653   E-mail: apply@irts.org
Web: irts.org/summerfellowshipprogram.html

Summary   To provide summer work experience to upper-division and graduate students (particularly African Americans and other minorities) who are interested in working during the summer in broadcasting and related fields in the New York City area.

Eligibility   This program is open to juniors, seniors, and graduate students at 4-year colleges and universities. Applicants must either be a communications major or have demonstrated a strong interest in the field through extracurricular activities or other practical experience. Minority (Black, Hispanic, Asian/Pacific Islander, American Indian/Alaskan Native) students are especially encouraged to apply.

Financial data Travel, housing, and a living allowance are provided.

Duration 9 weeks during the summer.

Additional information The first week consists of a comprehensive orientation to broadcasting, cable, advertising, and new media. Then, the participants are assigned an 8-week fellowship. This full-time "real world" experience in a New York-based corporation allows them to reinforce or redefine specific career goals before settling into a permanent job. Fellows have worked at all 4 major networks, at local New York City radio and television stations, and at national rep firms, advertising agencies, and cable operations. This program includes fellowships reserved for students at designated universities (Notre Dame, Pennsylvania State University, Boston College, Holy Cross College) and the following named awards: the Thomas S. Murphy Fellowship (sponsored by ABC National Television Sales), the Helen Karas Memorial Fellowship, the Leslie Moonves Fellowship (sponsored by CBS Television Station Sales, and the Sumner Redstone Fellowship (sponsored by CBS Television Station Sales).

Number awarded Varies; recently, 23 of these fellowships were awarded.

Deadline November of each year.

[261]
ITW SCHOLARSHIPS

Society of Women Engineers
Attn: Scholarship Selection Committee
120 South LaSalle Street, Suite 1515
Chicago, IL 60603-3572
(312) 596-5223   Toll Free: (877) SWE-INFO
Fax: (312) 644-8557
E-mail: scholarshipapplication@swe.org
Web: societyofwomenengineers.swe.org

Summary To provide financial assistance to undergraduate women (particularly African Americans and those from other underrepresented minority groups) majoring in designated engineering specialties.

Eligibility This program is open to women who are entering their junior year at a 4-year ABET-accredited college or university. Applicants must be majoring in computer science, electrical or mechanical engineering, or polymer science. They must have a GPA of 3.0 or higher. Preference is given to members of groups underrepresented in engineering or computer science. Selection is based on merit. U.S. citizenship is required.

Financial data The stipend is $2,500.

Duration 1 year.

Additional information This program is sponsored by Illinois Tool Works, Inc.

Number awarded 2 each year.

Deadline February of each year.

[262]
IVY VINE CHARITIES SCHOLARSHIPS

Alpha Kappa Alpha Sorority, Inc.-Theta Omega Omega Chapter
Attn: Ivy Vine Charities, Inc.
43 Randolph Road
PMB 102
Silver Spring, MD 20904
(301) 570-4700   Fax: (301) 774-2910
E-mail: TOOscholarship@yahoo.com
Web: www.thetaomegaomegacharities.org/scholarship.html

Summary To provide financial assistance to high school seniors from the Washington, D.C. metropolitan area who plan to attend college, especially an Historically Black College or University (HBCU), in any state.

Eligibility This program is open to seniors graduating from high schools in Washington, D.C. or the Maryland counties of Montgomery or Prince George's. Students who have participated in the sponsor's debutante cotillion are also eligible. Applicants must have a GPA of 3.0 or higher and a record of participation in school and community activities. They must have been accepted by a college or university in any state; for some of the awards, that must be an HBCU.

Financial data Scholarship stipends are $4,000; book awards are $1,000.

Duration 1 year.

Additional information Alpha Kappa Alpha was founded in 1908 at Howard University and is currently 1 of the largest social sororities whose membership is predominantly African American women. The Theta Omega Omega chapter serves alumnae members in the Washington, D.C. metropolitan area.

Number awarded 3 scholarships (2 for students attending an HBCU and 1 for a student at another college or university) are awarded each year. The number of book awards varies; recently, 4 were presented.

Deadline April of each year.

[263]
J. PARIS MOSLEY SCHOLARSHIP

Cleveland Foundation
Attn: Scholarship Officer
1422 Euclid Avenue, Suite 1300
Cleveland, OH 44115-2001
(216) 861-3810   Fax: (216) 861-1729
E-mail: mbaker@clevefdn.org
Web: www.clevelandfoundation.org/Scholarships

Summary To provide financial assistance for college to African American and other high school seniors in any state who are deaf or whose primary caregivers are deaf.

Eligibility This program is open to high school seniors in any state who are deaf or hard of hearing or the children or grandchildren of deaf or hard of hearing parents or grandparents. Applicants must be planning to attend a college, university, vocational school, or other postsecondary program in any state. They must use some form of sign language, have a GPA of 2.5 or higher, and be able to demonstrate financial need. Preference is given to students of African American, Latino American, or Native American descent.

Financial data A stipend is awarded (amount not specified).

Duration 1 year.
Number awarded 1 or more each year.
Deadline March of each year.

[264]
JACK AND JILL SCHOLARSHIPS

Jack and Jill Foundation of America
1930 17th Street, N.W.
Washington, DC 20009
(202) 232-5290　　　　　　　　Fax: (202) 232-1747
Web: www.jackandjillfoundation.org/scholarships

Summary To provide financial assistance to African American high school seniors who plan to attend college in any state.

Eligibility This program is open to African American seniors graduating from high schools in any state with a GPA of 3.0 or higher. Applicants must be planning to enroll full time at an accredited 4-year college or university. Dependents of members of Jack and Jill of America are not eligible.

Financial data Stipends range from $1,500 to $2,500. Funds may be used for tuition or room and board.

Duration 1 year.

Additional information Jack and Jill of America was established in 1938 as an organization for African American mothers who wished to ensure greater opportunity for their children.

Number awarded Varies each year.
Deadline March of each year.

[265]
JACKIE ROBINSON SCHOLARSHIPS

Jackie Robinson Foundation
Attn: Education and Leadership Development Program
75 Varick Street, Second Floor
New York, NY 10013-1917
(212) 290-8600　　　　　　　　Fax: (212) 290-8081
E-mail: general@jackierobinson.org
Web: www.jackierobinson.org

Summary To provide financial assistance for college to African American and other minority high school seniors.

Eligibility This program is open to members of an ethnic minority group who are high school seniors accepted at a 4-year college or university. Applicants must have a mathematics and critical reading SAT score of 1000 or higher or ACT score of 21 or higher. Selection is based on academic achievement, financial need, dedication towards community service, and leadership potential. U.S. citizenship is required.

Financial data The maximum stipend is $7,500 per year.

Duration 4 years.

Additional information The program also offers personal and career counseling on a year-round basis, a week of interaction with other scholarship students from around the country, and assistance in obtaining summer jobs and permanent employment after graduation. It was established in 1973 by a grant from Chesebrough-Pond.

Number awarded 100 or more each year.
Deadline March of each year.

[266]
JACOBS ENGINEERING SCHOLARSHIP

Conference of Minority Transportation Officials
Attn: National Scholarship Program
818 18th Street, N.W., Suite 850
Washington, DC 20006
(202) 530-0551　　　　　　　　Fax: (202) 530-0617
Web: www.comto.org/news-youth.php

Summary To provide financial assistance to African American and other minority upper-division and graduate students in a field related to transportation.

Eligibility This program is open to minority juniors, seniors, and graduate students in fields related to transportation (e.g., civil engineering, construction engineering, environmental engineering, safety, transportation, urban planning). Undergraduates must have a GPA of 3.0 or higher; graduate students must have a GPA of at least 3.5. Applicants must submit a cover letter with a 500-word statement of career goals. Financial need is not considered in the selection process. U.S. citizenship is required.

Financial data The stipend is $4,000. Funds are paid directly to the recipient's college or university.

Duration 1 year.

Additional information The Conference of Minority Transportation Officials (COMTO) was established in 1971 to promote, strengthen, and expand the roles of minorities in all aspects of transportation. This program is sponsored by Jacobs Engineering Group Inc. Recipients are required to become members of COMTO and attend the COMTO National Scholarship Luncheon.

Number awarded 1 or more each year.
Deadline April of each year.

[267]
JAMES B. MORRIS SCHOLARSHIP

James B. Morris Scholarship Fund
Attn: Scholarship Selection Committee
525 S.W. Fifth Street, Suite A
Des Moines, IA 50309-4501
(515) 282-8192　　　　　　　　Fax: (515) 282-9117
E-mail: morris@assoc-mgmt.com
Web: www.morrisscholarship.org

Summary To provide financial assistance to African American and other minority undergraduate, graduate, and law students in Iowa.

Eligibility This program is open to minority students (African Americans, Asian/Pacific Islanders, Hispanics, or Native Americans) who are interested in studying at a college, graduate school, or law school. Applicants must be either Iowa residents and high school graduates who are attending a college or university anywhere in the United States or non-Iowa residents who are attending a college or university in Iowa; preference is given to native Iowans who are attending an Iowa college or university. Along with their application, they must submit an essay of 250 to 500 words on why they are applying for this scholarship, activities or organizations in which they are involved, and their future plans. Selection is based on the essay, academic achievement (GPA of 2.5 or higher), community service, and financial need. U.S. citizenship is required.

Financial data The stipend is $2,300 per year.

Duration 1 year; may be renewed.

Additional information This fund was established in 1978 in honor of the J.B. Morris family, who founded the Iowa branch of the National Association for the Advancement of Colored People and published the *Iowa Bystander* newspaper.

Number awarded Varies each year; recently, 24 of these scholarships were awarded.

Deadline March of each year.

[268]
JAMES CARLSON MEMORIAL SCHOLARSHIP

Oregon Student Assistance Commission
Attn: Grants and Scholarships Division
1500 Valley River Drive, Suite 100
Eugene, OR 97401-2146
(541) 687-7395   Toll Free: (800) 452-8807, ext. 7395
Fax: (541) 687-7414   TDD: (800) 735-2900
E-mail: awardinfo@osac.state.or.us
Web: www.osac.state.or.us/osac_programs.html

Summary To provide financial assistance to students from diverse environments (including African Americans) and other Oregon residents who are majoring in education on the undergraduate or graduate school level at a school in any state.

Eligibility This program is open to residents of Oregon who are U.S. citizens or permanent residents and enrolled at a college or university in any state. Applicants must be either 1) college seniors or fifth-year students majoring in elementary or secondary education or 2) graduate students working on an elementary or secondary certificate. Full-time enrollment and financial need are required. Priority is given to 1) students who come from diverse environments and submit an essay of 250 to 350 words on their experience living or working in diverse environments; 2) dependents of members of the Oregon Education Association; and 3) applicants committed to teaching autistic children.

Financial data Stipend amounts vary; recently, they were at least $1,300.

Duration 1 year.

Additional information This program is administered by the Oregon Student Assistance Commission (OSAC) with funds provided by the Oregon Community Foundation.

Number awarded Varies each year; recently, 3 of these scholarships were awarded.

Deadline February of each year.

[269]
JAMES E. WEBB INTERNSHIPS

Smithsonian Institution
Attn: Office of Fellowships
470 L'Enfant Plaza, Suite 7102
P.O. Box 37012, MRC 902
Washington, DC 20013-7012
(202) 633-7070   Fax: (202) 633-7069
E-mail: siofg@si.edu
Web: www.si.edu/ofg/Applications/WEBB/WEBBapp.htm

Summary To provide internship opportunities throughout the Smithsonian Institution to African American and other minority upper-division or graduate students in business or public administration.

Eligibility This program is open to minorities who are juniors, seniors, or graduate students majoring in areas of business or public administration (finance, human resource management, accounting, or general business administration). Applicants must have a GPA of 3.0 or higher. They must seek placement in offices, museums, and research institutes within the Smithsonian Institution.

Financial data Interns receive a stipend of $550 per week and a travel allowance.

Duration 10 weeks during the summer, fall, or spring.

Number awarded Varies each year; recently, 8 of these internships were awarded.

Deadline January of each year for summer or fall; September of each year for spring.

[270]
JAMES J. WYCHOR SCHOLARSHIPS

Minnesota Broadcasters Association
Attn: Scholarship Program
3033 Excelsior Boulevard, Suite 440
Minneapolis, MN 55416
(612) 926-8123   Toll Free: (800) 245-5838
Fax: (612) 926-9761
E-mail: llasere@minnesotabroadcasters.com
Web: www.minnesotabroadcasters.com

Summary To provide financial assistance to minorities and other Minnesota residents interested in studying broadcasting at a college in any state.

Eligibility This program is open to residents of Minnesota who are accepted or enrolled at an accredited postsecondary institution in any state offering a broadcast-related curriculum. Applicants must have a high school or college GPA of 3.0 or higher and must submit a 500-word essay on why they wish to prepare for a career in broadcasting or electronic media. Employment in the broadcasting industry is not required, but students who are employed must include a letter from their general manager describing the duties they have performed as a radio or television station employee and evaluating their potential for success in the industry. Financial need is not considered in the selection process. Some of the scholarships are awarded only to minority and women candidates.

Financial data The stipend is $1,500.

Duration 1 year; recipients who are college seniors may reapply for an additional 1-year renewal as a graduate student.

Number awarded 10 each year, distributed as follows: 3 within the 7-county metro area, 5 allocated geographically throughout the state (northeast, northwest, central, southeast, southwest), and 2 reserved specifically for women and minority applicants.

Deadline June of each year.

[271]
JAMYE COLEMAN WILLIAMS AND JOSEPH C. MCKINNEY SCHOLARSHIPS

African Methodist Episcopal Church
Connectional Lay Organization
c/o Evelyn Welch Graham
2910 Fourth Avenue South
St. Petersburg, FL 33712
(727) 327-9927   E-mail: verne764@aol.com
Web: www.connectionallay-amec.org

Summary To provide financial assistance to members of the African Methodist Episcopal (AME) Church who are interested in attending a college or university, especially those interested preparing for leadership in the denomination.

Eligibility This program is open to members of AME churches who are working on or planning to work on a bachelor's degree at a college or university. Applicants must submit a 500-word essay on why they want to attend college. Preference is given to students who desire to serve the AME Church in a leadership capacity. Selection is based on academic record, qualities of leadership, extracurricular activities and accomplishments, reference letters, and financial need.

Financial data The stipend is $1,500. Funds are sent directly to the student's college or university.

Duration 1 year.

Number awarded 2 each year.

Deadline May of each year.

[272]
J.D. WILLIAMS SCHOLARSHIP

African Methodist Episcopal Church
Connectional Lay Organization
c/o Evelyn Welch Graham
2910 Fourth Avenue South
St. Petersburg, FL 33712
(727) 327-9927   E-mail: verne764@aol.com
Web: www.connectionallay-amec.org

Summary To provide financial assistance to members of the African Methodist Episcopal (AME) Church who are interested in attending a college or university affiliated with the denomination.

Eligibility This program is open to members of AME churches who are working on or planning to work on a bachelor's degree in any field at an AME college or university. Applicants must submit a 500-word essay on the importance of a college education in the 21st century. Selection is based on that essay, academic achievement, quality of church involvement, leadership, extracurricular activities, and reference letters.

Financial data The stipend is $2,500. Funds are sent directly to the student.

Duration 1 year.

Number awarded 1 or more each year.

Deadline May of each year.

[273]
JERRY MORRIS AND SUMMER HOUSTON MEMORIAL SCHOLARSHIP

Union Pacific Railroad Black Employee Network
1400 Douglass Street
Mailstop 0780
Omaha, NE 68179
(402) 544-5000   Toll Free: (888) 870-8777
Web: www.uprr.com

Summary To provide financial assistance to African Americans who plan to attend college in any state.

Eligibility This program is open to U.S. citizens who are African American seniors in high school or full-time freshmen or sophomores at a college or university in any state. Applicants must have a GPA of 2.5 or higher, a record of active involvement in school and community activities, and demonstrated social awareness and involvement. Along with their application, they must submit a 300-word essay on the 3 most important issues facing African Americans today and how they feel those events will affect their future. Selection is based on that essay (25 points), GPA (20 points), activities and work experience (20 points), SAT/ACT scores (20 points), composite application (10 points), and financial need (5 points).

Financial data Stipends range from $500 to $1,000.

Duration 1 year; may be renewed 1 additional year.

Number awarded 1 or more each year.

Deadline March of each year.

[274]
JESSICA M. BLANDING MEMORIAL SCHOLARSHIP

New England Regional Black Nurses Association, Inc.
P.O. Box 190690
Boston, MA 02119
(617) 524-1951
Web: www.nerbna.org/org/scholarships.html

Summary To provide financial assistance to licensed practical nurses from New England who are working on a degree and have contributed to the African American community.

Eligibility The program is open to residents of the New England states who are licensed practical nurses working on an associate or bachelor's degree in nursing at a school in any state. Applicants must have at least 1 full year of school remaining. Along with their application, they must submit a 3-page essay that covers their career aspirations in the nursing profession; how they have contributed to the African American or other communities of color in such areas as work, volunteering, church, or community outreach; an experience that has enhanced their personal and/or professional growth; and any financial hardships that may hinder them from completing their education.

Financial data A stipend is awarded (amount not specified).

Duration 1 year.

Number awarded 1 or more each year.

Deadline March of each year.

[275]
JEWEL JOHNSON HOPEFUL TEACHER SCHOLARSHIP

United Negro College Fund
Attn: Scholarships and Grants Department
8260 Willow Oaks Corporate Drive
P.O. Box 10444
Fairfax, VA 22031-8044
(703) 205-3466   Toll Free: (800) 331-2244
Fax: (703) 205-3574
Web: www.uncf.org/forstudents/scholarship.asp

Summary   To provide financial assistance to African American and other students from Louisiana who are college freshmen and interested in majoring in education.

Eligibility   This program is open to freshmen who are either attending a 4-year college or university in Louisiana or residents of the state attending college anywhere in the country. Applicants must have an expressed career objective of becoming a teacher. They must have a cumulative high school GPA of 2.5 or higher and either a score of 900 on the critical reading and mathematics SAT or 16 on the ACT.

Financial data   The stipend is $5,000 per year.

Duration   1 year; may be renewed, provided the recipient agrees to obtain a teacher certification upon graduation.

Additional information   This program is sponsored by the H.O.P.E. Foundation and Fuzion Athlete Management; it is administered by the United Negro College Fund, the country's largest provider of financial aid for African American students.

Number awarded   4 each year.

Deadline   Deadline not specified.

[276]
JOANNE ROBINSON MEMORIAL SCHOLARSHIP

JoAnne Robinson Memorial Scholarship Fund
c/o WEWS
3001 Euclid Avenue
Cleveland, OH 44115
(216) 431-5555

Summary   To provide financial assistance to African American undergraduates who are majoring in broadcast journalism.

Eligibility   This program is open to full-time college students who are African American and majoring in broadcast journalism. Applicants must exemplify the following characteristics: hard working, detail oriented, outstanding communication and interpersonal skills, and dedication to excellence (personally and professionally). Along with their application, they must submit a statement on the goals, values, and characteristics that make them worthy of this scholarship. Financial need is not considered in the selection process.

Financial data   The stipend is $1,000. Funds may be used for tuition, books, and other educational expenses.

Duration   1 year; nonrenewable.

Additional information   This scholarship is administered by the Scripps Howard Foundation, which forwards the stipend to the recipient's institution.

Number awarded   1 each year.

Deadline   February of each year.

[277]
JOHN AND MURIEL LANDIS SCHOLARSHIPS

American Nuclear Society
Attn: Scholarship Coordinator
555 North Kensington Avenue
La Grange Park, IL 60526-5592
(708) 352-6611   Toll Free: (800) 323-3044
Fax: (708) 352-0499   E-mail: outreach@ans.org
Web: www.ans.org/honors/scholarships

Summary   To provide financial assistance to undergraduate or graduate students (especially African Americans, other minorities, and women) who are interested in preparing for a career in nuclear-related fields.

Eligibility   This program is open to undergraduate and graduate students at colleges or universities located in the United States who are preparing for, or planning to prepare for, a career in nuclear science, nuclear engineering, or a nuclear-related field. Qualified high school seniors are also eligible. Applicants must have greater than average financial need and have experienced circumstances that render them disadvantaged. They must be sponsored by an organization (e.g., plant branch, local section, student section) within the American Nuclear Society (ANS). Along with their application, they must submit an essay on their academic and professional goals, experiences that have affected those goals, etc. Selection is based on that essay, academic achievement, letters of recommendation, and financial need. Women and members of minority groups are especially urged to apply. U.S. citizenship is not required.

Financial data   The stipend is $5,000, to be used to cover tuition, books, fees, room, and board.

Duration   1 year; nonrenewable.

Number awarded   Up to 8 each year.

Deadline   January of each year.

[278]
JOHN B. MCLENDON SCHOLARSHIP FUND

North Carolina State Education Assistance Authority
Attn: Grants, Training, and Outreach Department
P.O. Box 13663
Research Triangle Park, NC 27709-3663
(919) 549-8614   Toll Free: (800) 700-1775
Fax: (919) 248-4687   E-mail: information@ncseaa.edu
Web: www.ncseaa.edu/McLendon.htm

Summary   To provide financial assistance to residents of North Carolina who are varsity athletes enrolled at designated Historically Black Colleges and Universities (HBCUs) in the state.

Eligibility   This program is open to residents of North Carolina who have been enrolled for at least 2 semesters at Bennett College for Women, Elizabeth City State University, Fayetteville State University, Johnson C. Smith University, Livingstone College, North Carolina A&T State University, North Carolina Central University, Shaw University, St. Augustine's College, or Winston-Salem State University. Applicants must be varsity athletes at their campus. Selection is made by the institution and based on leadership qualities, academics, and involvement in the institution's community. Men and women are considered separately.

Financial data   The stipend is $1,250.

Duration   1 year; nonrenewable.

Additional information The North Carolina General Assembly established this program in 2007.

Number awarded 20 each year: 2 (1 man and 1 woman) at each participating institution (except Bennett College for Women, which selects 2 women).

Deadline Each institution sets its own deadline.

[279]
JOHN W. WORK III MEMORIAL FOUNDATION SCHOLARSHIP

Community Foundation of Middle Tennessee
Attn: Scholarship Committee
3833 Cleghorn Avenue, Suite 400
Nashville, TN 37215-2519
(615) 321-4939　　　　　Toll Free: (888) 540-5200
Fax: (615) 327-2746　　　E-mail: mail@cfmt.org
Web: www.cfmt.org/scholarships

Summary To provide financial assistance to upper-division and graduate students from Tennessee, especially African Americans who are working on a degree in music at a school in any state.

Eligibility This program is open to residents of Tennessee, especially African Americans, enrolled as juniors, seniors, or graduate students at an accredited college, university, or institute in any state. Applicants must be working on a degree in music and have a GPA of 3.0 or higher. Selection is based on demonstrated potential for excellence in music, academic record, standardized test scores, extracurricular activities, work experience, community involvement, recommendations, and financial need.

Financial data Stipends range from $500 to $2,500 per year. Funds are paid to the recipient's school and must be used for tuition, fees, books, supplies, room, board, or miscellaneous expenses.

Duration 1 year.

Number awarded 1 or more each year.

Deadline March of each year.

[280]
JOHNNIE L. COCHRAN, JR./MWH SCHOLARSHIP

National Forum for Black Public Administrators
Attn: Scholarship Program
777 North Capitol Street, N.E., Suite 807
Washington, DC 20002
(202) 408-9300, ext. 112　　　Fax: (202) 408-8558
E-mail: vreed@nfbpa.org
Web: www.nfbpa.org/i4a/pages/index.cfm?pageid=3630

Summary To provide financial assistance to African Americans working on a undergraduate or graduate degree in public administration.

Eligibility This program is open to African American undergraduate and graduate students preparing for a career in public service. Applicants must be working full time on a degree in public administration, political science, urban affairs, public policy, or a related field. They must have a GPA of 3.0 or higher, excellent interpersonal and analytical abilities, and strong oral and written communication skills. Along with their application, they must submit a 3-page autobiographical essay that includes their academic and career

goals and objectives. First consideration is given to applicants who are not currently receiving other financial aid.

Financial data The stipend is $5,000.

Duration 1 year.

Additional information This program is sponsored by the engineering and financial consulting firm MWH. Recipients are required to attend the sponsor's annual conference to receive their scholarship; limited hotel and air accommodations are arranged and provided.

Number awarded 1 each year.

Deadline February of each year.

[281]
JOSHUA DAVID GARDNER MEMORIAL SCHOLARSHIP

Joshua David Gardner Memorial Scholarship
　Endowment, Inc.
4196 Merchant Plaza, Suite 816
Lake Ridge, VA 22192-5085
(719) 433-8101
E-mail: gardner@joshgardnerendowment.org
Web: www.joshgardnerendowment.org

Summary To provide financial assistance to undergraduates enrolled or planning to enroll at an Historically Black College or University (HBCU).

Eligibility This program is open to U.S. citizens between 17 and 25 years of age who are enrolled or planning to enroll at an accredited 4-year HBCU. Applicants must have a GPA of 3.0 or higher and scores of at least 1000 on the critical reading and mathematics SAT or 19 on the ACT. Along with their application, they must submit a 500-word essay on the importance of personal integrity for leaders. Financial need is considered in the selection process.

Financial data The stipend is $2,000.

Duration 1 year; nonrenewable.

Additional information This program was established in 2007.

Number awarded At least 1 each year.

Deadline April of each year.

[282]
JOSIE K. CLAIBORNE MEMORIAL SCHOLARSHIPS

American Association of Blacks in Energy-South Carolina
　Chapter
Attn: Scholarship Committee
P.O. Box 7696
Columbia, SC 29202
(803) 217-2863　　　　　Fax: (803) 933-7605
E-mail: cbellamy@scana.com
Web: www.aabe.org/index.php?component=pages&id=920

Summary To provide financial assistance to African Americans and members of other underrepresented minority groups who are high school seniors in South Carolina and planning to major in an energy-related field at a college in any state.

Eligibility This program is open to seniors graduating from high schools in South Carolina and planning to work on a bachelor's degree at a college or university in any state. Applicants must be African Americans, Hispanics, or Native Americans who have a GPA of 3.0 or higher and are able to demonstrate financial need. Their intended major must be a field of business, engineering, physical science (e.g., astronomy, chemistry, geology, mineralogy, meteorology, physics), mathematics, or technology related to energy. Along with their application, they must submit a 350-word statement on why they should receive this scholarship, their professional career objectives, and any other relevant information.

Financial data Stipends range from $1,000 to $3,000.

Duration 1 year; nonrenewable.

Additional information Winners are eligible to compete for regional and national scholarships.

Number awarded Varies each year; recently, 5 of these scholarships were awarded.

Deadline February of each year.

[283]
JOYCE WASHINGTON SCHOLARSHIP

Watts Charity Association, Inc.
6245 Bristol Parkway, Suite 224
Culver City, CA 90230
(323) 671-0394   Fax: (323) 778-2613
E-mail: wattscharity@aol.com
Web: 4watts.tripod.com/id5.html

Summary To provide financial assistance to upper-division African Americans majoring in child development, teaching, or social services.

Eligibility This program is open to U.S. citizens of African American descent who are enrolled full time as a college or university junior. Applicants must be majoring in child development, teaching, or the study of social services. They must have a GPA of 3.0 or higher, be between 17 and 24 years of age, and be able to demonstrate that they intend to continue their education for at least 2 years. Along with their application, they must submit 1) a 1-paragraph statement on why they should be awarded a Watts Foundation scholarship, and 2) a 1- to 2-page essay on a specific type of cancer, based either on how it has impacted their life or on researched information.

Financial data A stipend is awarded (amount not specified).

Duration 1 year.

Additional information Royce R. Watts, Sr. established the Watts Charity Association after he learned he had cancer in 2001.

Number awarded 1 each year.

Deadline May of each year.

[284]
JUANITA KIDD STOUT SCHOLARSHIP PROGRAM

Delta Sigma Theta Sorority, Inc.
Attn: Scholarship and Standards Committee Chair
1707 New Hampshire Avenue, N.W.
Washington, DC 20009
(202) 986-2400   Fax: (202) 986-2513
E-mail: dstemail@deltasigmatheta.org
Web: www.deltasigmatheta.org

Summary To provide financial assistance to members of Delta Sigma Theta who are working on an undergraduate degree in criminal justice.

Eligibility This program is open to current undergraduate students who are working on a degree in criminal justice. Applicants must be active, dues-paying members of Delta Sigma Theta. Selection is based on meritorious achievement.

Financial data The stipends range from $1,000 to $2,000. The funds may be used to cover tuition, fees, and living expenses.

Duration 1 year; may be renewed for 1 additional year.

Additional information This sponsor is a traditionally African American social sorority. The application fee is $20.

Deadline April of each year.

[285]
JUDITH MCMANUS PRICE SCHOLARSHIPS

American Planning Association
Attn: Leadership Affairs Associate
205 North Michigan Avenue, Suite 1200
Chicago, IL 60601
(312) 431-9100   Fax: (312) 786-6700
E-mail: fellowship@planning.org
Web: www.planning.org/scholarships/apa

Summary To provide financial assistance to African Americans and other underrepresented students enrolled in undergraduate or graduate degree programs at recognized planning schools.

Eligibility This program is open to undergraduate and graduate students in urban and regional planning who are women or members of the following minority groups: African American, Hispanic American, or Native American. Applicants must be citizens of the United States and able to document financial need. They must intend to work as practicing planners in the public sector. Along with their application, they must submit a 2-page personal and background statement describing how their education will be applied to career goals and why they chose planning as a career path. Selection is based (in order of importance), on: 1) commitment to planning as reflected in their personal statement and on their resume; 2) academic achievement and/or improvement during the past 2 years; 3) letters of recommendation; 4) financial need; and 5) professional presentation.

Financial data Stipends range from $2,000 to $4,000 per year. The money may be applied to tuition and living expenses only. Payment is made to the recipient's university and divided by terms in the school year.

Duration 1 year; recipients may reapply.

Additional information This program was established in 2002.

Number awarded Varies each year; recently, 3 of these scholarships were awarded.

Deadline April of each year.

[286]
JULIUS S., JR. AND IANTHIA H. SCOTT ENDOWED SCHOLARSHIP

United Methodist Higher Education Foundation
Attn: Scholarships Administrator
1001 19th Avenue South
P.O. Box 340005
Nashville, TN 37203-0005
(615) 340-7385　　　　　Toll Free: (800) 811-8110
Fax: (615) 340-7330
E-mail: umhefscholarships@gbhem.org
Web: www.umhef.org/receive.php?id=endowed_funds

Summary　To provide financial assistance to Methodist undergraduate students at designated Historically Black Colleges and Universities of the United Methodist Church.

Eligibility　This program is open to students entering their sophomore year at the following Historically Black Colleges and Universities of the United Methodist Church: Wiley College, Paine College, or Philander Smith College. Applicants must have been active, full members of a United Methodist Church for at least 1 year prior to applying. They must have a GPA of 3.0 or higher and be able to demonstrate financial need. Along with their application, they must submit a 200-word essay on their involvement and/or leadership responsibilities in their church, school, and community within the last 3 years. U.S. citizenship or permanent resident status is required.

Financial data　The stipend is at least $1,000 per year.

Duration　1 year; nonrenewable.

Additional information　This program was established in 1999.

Number awarded　1 scholarship is awarded each year on a rotational basis among the 3 participating institutions.

Deadline　May of each year.

[287]
JUSTINE E. GRANNER MEMORIAL SCHOLARSHIP

Iowa United Methodist Foundation
2301 Rittenhouse Street
Des Moines, IA 50321
(515) 974-8927
Web: www.iumf.org/otherscholarships.html

Summary　To provide financial assistance to African Americans and other ethnic minorities in Iowa interested in majoring in a health-related field.

Eligibility　This program is open to ethnic minority students preparing for a career in nursing, public health, or a related field at a college or school of nursing in Iowa. Applicants must have a GPA of 3.0 or higher. Preference is given to graduates of Iowa high schools. Financial need is considered in the selection process.

Financial data　The stipend is $1,000.

Duration　1 year.

Number awarded　1 each year.

Deadline　March of each year.

[288]
K. LEROY IRVIS UNDERGRADUATE SCHOLARSHIPS

Pennsylvania Black Conference on Higher Education
c/o Judith A.W. Thomas, Scholarship Committee Chair
Lincoln University, School of Social Sciences and
　Behavioral Studies
1570 Old Baltimore Pike
P.O. Box 179
Lincoln University, PA 19352
(484) 365-8159　　　　E-mail: scholarships@pbcohe.org
Web: www.phcohe.org

Summary　To provide financial assistance to African American residents of any state who are enrolled as undergraduates at colleges in Pennsylvania.

Eligibility　This program is open to African Americans from any state who have completed at least the first semester as an undergraduate at a college or university in Pennsylvania. Applicants must have a GPA of 3.0 or higher. Along with their application, they must submit an essay, up to 5 pages in length, on why they should receive this scholarship. Selection is based on that essay, academics, extracurricular activity participation, leadership qualities, and interpersonal qualities.

Financial data　The stipend is $1,000.

Duration　1 year.

Number awarded　6 each year: 2 in each of 3 regions (eastern, central, and western) in Pennsylvania.

Deadline　January of each year.

[289]
KAISER PERMANENTE COLORADO DIVERSITY SCHOLARSHIP PROGRAM

Kaiser Permanente
Attn: Multicultural Associations/Employee Resource
　Groups
P.O. Box 378066
Denver, CO 80247-8066
E-mail: co-diversitydevelopment@kp.org
Web: physiciancareers.kp.org

Summary　To provide financial assistance to Colorado residents who are African American or come from another diverse background and are interested in working on an undergraduate or graduate degree in a health care field at a school in any state.

Eligibility　This program is open to all residents of Colorado, including those who identify as 1 or more of the following: African American, Asian Pacific, Latino, lesbian, gay, bisexual, transgender, intersex, Native American, and/or a person with a disability. Applicants must be 1) a graduating high school senior with a GPA of 2.7 or higher and planning to enroll full time at a college or technical school in any state; 2) a GED recipient with a GED score of 520 or higher and planning to enroll full time at a college or technical school in any state; 3) a full-time undergraduate student at a college or technical school in any state; or 4) a full-time graduate or doctoral student at a school in any state. They must be preparing for a career in health care (e.g., doctor, nurse, surgeon, physician assistant, dentist), mental health, public health, or health policy. Along with their application, they must submit 300-word essays on 1) a personal setback in their life and how they responded and learned from it; 2) how they give back to their community; and 3) why they have chosen health care and/or public health for their educational and career path. Selection is based on academic achievement, character qualities, community outreach and volunteering, and financial need.

Financial data Stipends range from $1,400 to $2,600.

Duration 1 year.

Number awarded Varies each year; recently, 17 of these scholarships were awarded.

Deadline January of each year.

[290]
KANSAS AFRICAN AMERICAN MONUMENTAL LIFE SETTLEMENT SCHOLARSHIPS

Kansas Insurance Department
Attn: Scholarship Fund
420 S.W. Ninth Street
Topeka, KS 66612-1678
(785) 296-3071   Toll Free: (800) 432-2484 (within KS)
Fax: (785) 296-7805
E-mail: commissioner@ksinsurance.org
Web: www.ksinsurance.org/gpa/scholarship.htm

Summary To provide financial assistance to African American upper-division and graduate students who are majoring in business, computer science, or mathematics at a college or university in Kansas.

Eligibility This program is open to African American students enrolled as juniors, seniors, or graduate students at accredited institutions of higher education in Kansas. Applicants must be majoring in business (with an emphasis on accounting, economics, finance, or investments), computer science, or mathematics. They must have a GPA of 3.0 or higher. Along with their application, they must submit a 1-page essay describing their career goals and how this scholarship would help them achieve those goals.

Financial data The stipend is $1,000.

Duration 1 year.

Additional information These scholarships were first awarded in 2005 with funds received in a settlement with Monumental Life as a result of the firm's race-based pricing of life insurance policies.

Number awarded 12 each year.

Deadline April of each year for fall semester; September of each year for spring semester.

[291]
KANSAS ETHNIC MINORITY SCHOLARSHIP PROGRAM

Kansas Board of Regents
Attn: Student Financial Assistance
1000 S.W. Jackson Street, Suite 520
Topeka, KS 66612-1368
(785) 296-3517   Fax: (785) 296-0983
E-mail: dlindeman@ksbor.org
Web: www.kansasregents.org/scholarships_and_grants

Summary To provide financial assistance to African Americans and other minority students in Kansas who are interested in attending college in the state.

Eligibility Eligible to apply are Kansas residents who fall into 1 of these minority groups: American Indian, Alaskan Native, African American, Asian, Pacific Islander, or Hispanic. Applicants may be current college students (enrolled in com-

munity colleges, colleges, or universities in Kansas), but high school seniors graduating in the current year receive priority consideration. Minimum academic requirements include 1 of the following: 1) ACT score of 21 or higher or combined mathematics and critical reading SAT score of 990 or higher; 2) cumulative GPA of 3.0 or higher; 3) high school rank in upper 33%; 4) completion of the Kansas Scholars Curriculum (4 years of English, 3 years of mathematics, 3 years of science, 3 years of social studies, and 2 years of foreign language); 5) selection by the National Merit Corporation in any category; or 6) selection by the College Board as a Hispanic Scholar. Selection is based primarily on financial need.

Financial data A stipend of up to $1,850 is provided, depending on financial need and availability of state funds.

Duration 1 year; may be renewed for up to 3 additional years (4 additional years for designated 5-year programs) if the recipient maintains a 2.0 cumulative GPA and has financial need.

Additional information There is a $10 application fee.

Number awarded Approximately 200 each year.

Deadline April of each year.

[292]
KANSAS SPJ MINORITY STUDENT SCHOLARSHIP

Society of Professional Journalists-Kansas Professional Chapter
c/o Denise Neil, Scholarship Committee
Wichita Eagle
825 East Douglas Avenue
P.O. Box 820
Wichita, KS 67201-0820
(316) 268-6327   E-mail: dneil@wichitaeagle.com
Web: www.spjchapters.org/kansas/gridiron.html

Summary To provide financial assistance to residents of any state enrolled at colleges and universities in Kansas who are African American or members of another ethnic minority group and interested in a career in journalism.

Eligibility This program is open to residents of any state who are members of a racial or ethnic minority group and entering their junior or senior year at colleges and universities in Kansas. Applicants do not have to be journalism or communication majors, but they must demonstrate a strong and sincere interest in print journalism, broadcast journalism, online journalism, or photojournalism. They must have a GPA of 2.5 or higher. Along with their application, they must submit a professional resume, 4 to 6 examples of their best work (clips or stories, copies of photographs, tapes or transcripts of broadcasts, printouts of web pages) and a 1-page cover letter about themselves, how they came to be interested in journalism, their professional goals, and (if appropriate) their financial need for this scholarship.

Financial data The stipend is $1,000.

Duration 1 year.

Number awarded 1 each year.

Deadline April of each year.

[293]
KAPPA SCHOLARSHIP ENDOWMENT FUND AWARDS

Kappa Alpha Psi Fraternity-Washington (DC) Alumni
    Chapter
Attn: Kappa Scholarship Endowment Fund, Inc.
P.O. Box 29331
Washington, DC 20017-0331
(202) 829-8367   Fax: (202) 829-8367
Web: www.ksef-inc.com/students.html

Summary   To provide financial assistance to African Americans and other high school seniors in Washington, D.C. who plan to attend college in any state.

Eligibility   This program is open to seniors graduating from public or charter high schools in Washington, D.C. with a GPA of 2.5 or higher. Applicants must be planning to enroll full time at an accredited 4-year institution of higher learning in any state. They must be able to demonstrate involvement in school and community activities and financial need.

Financial data   Stipend amounts vary; recently, they averaged $4,000.

Duration   1 year.

Additional information   The sponsor is an historically African American social fraternity, but both women and men are eligible for these scholarships.

Number awarded   Varies each year; recently, 29 of these scholarships, with a total value of $116,000, were awarded.

Deadline   March of each year.

[294]
KATU THOMAS R. DARGAN SCHOLARSHIP

KATU-TV
Attn: Human Resources
2153 N.E. Sandy Boulevard
P.O. Box 2
Portland, OR 97207-0002
(503) 231-4222
Web: www.katu.com/about/scholarship

Summary   To provide financial assistance and work experience to African Americans and other minority students from Oregon and Washington who are studying broadcasting or communications in college.

Eligibility   This program is open to minority (Asian, Black/African American, Hispanic or Latino, Native Hawaiian or Pacific Islander, American Indian or Alaska Native) U.S. citizens currently enrolled as a sophomore or higher at a 4-year college or university or an accredited community college in Oregon or Washington. Residents of Oregon or Washington enrolled at a school in any state are also eligible. Applicants must be majoring in broadcasting or communications and have a GPA of 3.0 or higher. Community college students must be enrolled in a broadcast curriculum that is transferable to a 4-year accredited university. Finalists will be interviewed. Selection is based on financial need, academic achievement, and an essay on personal and professional goals.

Financial data   The stipend is $6,000. Funds are sent directly to the recipient's school.

Duration   1 year; recipients may reapply if they have maintained a GPA of 3.0 or higher.

Additional information   Winners are also eligible for a paid internship in selected departments at Fisher Broadcasting/KATU in Portland, Oregon.

Number awarded   1 each year.

Deadline   April of each year.

[295]
KAY LONGCOPE SCHOLARSHIP AWARD

National Lesbian & Gay Journalists Association
2120 L Street, N.W., Suite 850
Washington, DC 20037
(202) 588-9888   Fax: (202) 588-1818
E-mail: info@nlgfa.org
Web: www.nlgja.org/students/longcope.htm

Summary   To provide financial assistance to African American and other lesbian, gay, bisexual, and transgender (LGBT) undergraduate and graduate students of color who are interested in preparing for a career in journalism.

Eligibility   This program is open to LGBT students of color who are 1) high school seniors accepted to a U.S. community college or 4-year university and planning to enroll full time; 2) full-time undergraduate students at U.S. community colleges and 4-year universities; or 3) undergraduate students who have been accepted for their first year at a U.S. graduate school. Applicants must be planning a career in journalism and be committed to furthering the sponsoring organization's mission of fair and accurate coverage of the LGBT community. They must demonstrate an awareness of the issues facing the LGBT community and the importance of fair and accurate news coverage. For undergraduates, a declared major in journalism and/or communications is desirable but not required; non-journalism majors may demonstrate their commitment to a journalism career through work samples, internships, and work on a school news publication, online news service, or broadcast affiliate. Graduate students must be enrolled in a journalism program. Along with their application, they must submit a 1-page resume, 5 work samples, official transcripts, 3 letters of recommendation, and a 1,000-word autobiography written in the third person as a news story, describing the applicant's commitment and passion for journalism and career goals. U.S. citizenship or permanent resident status is required. Selection is based on journalistic and scholastic ability.

Financial data   The stipend is $5,000.

Duration   1 year.

Additional information   This program was established in 2008.

Number awarded   1 each year.

Deadline   January of each year.

[296]
KAY MADRY SULLIVAN FELLOWSHIP

Alpha Kappa Alpha Sorority, Inc.
Attn: Educational Advancement Foundation
5656 South Stony Island Avenue
Chicago, IL 60637
(773) 947-0026   Toll Free: (800) 653-6528
Fax: (773) 947-0277   E-mail: akaeaf@akaeaf.net
Web: www.akaeaf.org/fellowships_endowments.htm

Summary   To provide financial assistance to residents of designated states (especially African American women) who have been involved in foster care and are interested in attending college in any state.

Eligibility This program is open to undergraduate students who are enrolled full time as sophomores or higher at an accredited degree-granting institution in any state. Applicants must have been involved in the foster care system and be residents of Florida; if no residents of Florida apply, the scholarship may be awarded to a resident of Georgia or South Carolina. Along with their application, they must submit 1) a list of honors, awards, and scholarships received; 2) a list of organizations in which they have memberships, especially minority organizations; and 3) a statement of their personal and career goals, including how this scholarship will enhance their ability to attain those goals. The sponsor is a traditionally African American women's sorority.

Financial data A stipend is awarded (amount not specified).

Duration 1 year.

Number awarded 1 or more each even-numbered year.

Deadline April of each even-numbered year.

[297]
KEN KASHIWAHARA SCHOLARSHIP

Radio Television Digital News Foundation
Attn: RTDNF Fellowship Program
4121 Plank Road, Suite 512
Fredericksburg, VA 22407
(202) 467-5214   Fax: (202) 223-4007
E-mail: staceys@rtdna.org
Web: www.rtdna.org/pages/education/undergraduates.php

Summary To provide financial assistance to African Americans and other minority undergraduate students who are interested in preparing for a career in electronic journalism.

Eligibility This program is open to sophomores or more advanced minority undergraduate students enrolled in an electronic journalism sequence at an accredited or nationally-recognized college or university. Applicants must submit 1 to 3 examples of their journalistic skills on audio CD or DVD (no more than 15 minutes total, accompanied by scripts); a description of their role on each story and a list of who worked on each story and what they did; a 1-page statement explaining why they are preparing for a career in electronic journalism with reference to their specific career preference (radio, television, online, reporting, producing, or newsroom management); a resume; and a letter of reference from their dean or faculty sponsor explaining why they are a good candidate for the award and certifying that they have at least 1 year of school remaining.

Financial data The stipend is $2,500, paid in semiannual installments of $1,250 each.

Duration 1 year.

Additional information The Radio Television Digital News Foundation (RTDNF) was formerly the Radio and Television News Directors Foundation (RTNDF). Previous winners of any RTDNF scholarship or internship are not eligible to apply for this program.

Number awarded 1 each year.

Deadline May of each year.

[298]
KERMIT B. NASH ACADEMIC SCHOLARSHIP

Sickle Cell Disease Association of America
Attn: Scholarship Committee
231 East Baltimore Street, Suite 900
Baltimore, MD 21202
(410) 528-1555   Toll Free: (800) 421-8453
Fax: (410) 528-1495
E-mail: scdaa@sicklecelldisease.org
Web: www.sicklecelldisease.org

Summary To provide financial assistance for college to graduating high school seniors who have sickle cell disease.

Eligibility This program is open to graduating high school seniors who have sickle cell disease (not the trait). Applicants must have a GPA of 3.0 or higher and be U.S. citizens or permanent residents planning to attend an accredited 4-year college or university as a full-time student. They must submit a personal essay, up to 1,000 words, on an aspect of the impact of the disease on their lives or on society. Selection is based on GPA, general academic achievement and promise, SAT scores, leadership and community service, severity of academic challenges and obstacles posed by sickle cell disease, and the quality of their essay.

Financial data The stipend is $5,000 per year.

Duration Up to 4 years.

Additional information The Sickle Cell Disease Association of America (SCDAA) was formerly the National Association for Sickle Cell Disease. It established this program in 1999. Requests for applications must be submitted in writing; telephone requests are not honored.

Number awarded 1 each year.

Deadline May of each year.

[299]
KITTRELL-ALLEN-ADAMS SCHOLARSHIP

African Methodist Episcopal Church
Second Episcopal District
c/o Jettie Williams, District Coordinator
905 Lira Drive
Fort Washington, MD 20744
(301) 203-6836

Summary To provide financial assistance to members of the African Methodist Episcopal (AME) Church in its Second Episcopal District who are interested in attending college in any state.

Eligibility This program is open to AME members in the Second Episcopal District, which includes the Conferences of Baltimore, Washington, Virginia, North Carolina, and Western North Carolina. Applicants must be graduating high school seniors or students already working on an undergraduate degree at a college or university in any state. Along with their application, they must submit an autobiographical essay of 1 to 2 pages that includes information about their future goals and family, school, church, and community involvements. Selection is based on that essay, high school grades and SAT scores, letters of recommendation, and financial need.

Financial data A stipend is awarded (amount not specified).

Duration 1 year.

Number awarded   1 or more each year.
Deadline   July of each year.

[300]
KONZA PRAIRIE BIOLOGICAL STATION RESEARCH EXPERIENCE FOR UNDERGRADUATES

Konza Prairie Biological Station
c/o Kansas State University
Division of Biology
Attn: REU Program Coordinator
Manhattan, KS 66506-4901
(785) 532-2430   E-mail: biologyreu@ksu.edu
Web: www.k-state.edu/bsanderc/reu

Summary   To provide an opportunity for minority and other undergraduate students to conduct original research in grasslands biology during the summer at Konza Prairie Biological Station (KPBS) in Manhattan, Kansas.

Eligibility   This program is open to undergraduate students who are U.S. citizens or permanent residents and have a GPA of 3.0 or higher. Applicants must be interested in conducting a summer research project at KPBS that relates to the ecology, evolution, and genomics or grassland organisms. Along with their application, they must submit a 2-page essay that covers their interest in ecology and evolutionary or molecular biology, the specific areas of research interest in genomics or grassland ecology, and current professional goals. The program is committed to promoting diversity in undergraduate research activities and welcomes applications from members of underrepresented groups in the sciences (African Americans, Native Americans, Alaska Natives, Hispanics, and Pacific Islanders), nontraditional students returning to undergraduate studies after a break, and students who are the first member of their family to attend college.

Financial data   The program provides a stipend of $4,500, free housing, a meal allowance of $500, a research budget of $500 for consumable supplies used for the summer research project, and reimbursement of up to $350 for travel expenses.

Duration   10 weeks during the summer.

Additional information   Funding for this program, which began in 1995, is provided by the National Science Foundation. It is jointly administered by KPBS and the Division of Biology at Kansas State University.

Number awarded   10 each year.
Deadline   February of each year.

[301]
LAGRANT FOUNDATION UNDERGRADUATE SCHOLARSHIPS

Lagrant Foundation
Attn: Programs Manager
626 Wilshire Boulevard, Suite 700
Los Angeles, CA 90071-2920
(323) 469-8680   Fax: (323) 469-8683
E-mail: erickaavila@lagrant.com
Web: www.lagrantfoundation.org/site/?page_id=3

Summary   To provide financial assistance to African American and other minority college students who are interested in majoring in advertising, public relations, or marketing.

Eligibility   This program is open to African Americans, Asian Pacific Americans, Hispanics/Latinos, and Native Americans/Alaska Natives who are full-time students at a 4-year accredited institution. Applicants must have a GPA of 2.75 or higher and be either majoring in advertising, marketing, or public relations or minoring in communications with plans to prepare for a career in advertising, marketing, or public relations. Along with their application, they must submit 1) a 1- to 2-page essay outlining their career goals; what steps they will take to increase ethnic representation in the fields of advertising, marketing, and public relations; and the role of an advertising, marketing, or public relations practitioner; 2) a paragraph describing the college and/or community activities in which they are involved; 3) a brief paragraph describing any honors and awards they have received; 4) a letter of reference; 5) a resume; and 6) an official transcript. U.S. citizenship or permanent resident status is required.

Financial data   The stipend is $5,000.
Duration   1 year.
Number awarded   10 each year.
Deadline   February of each year.

[302]
LANDMARK SCHOLARS PROGRAM

Landmark Media Enterprises LLC
c/o Ann Morris, Managing Editor
Greensboro News & Record
200 East Market Street
Greensboro, NC 27401
(540) 981-3211   Toll Free: (800) 346-1234
E-mail: amorris@news-record.com
Web: company.news-record.com/intern.htm

Summary   To provide work experience and financial aid to African American and other minority undergraduates who are interested in preparing for a career in journalism.

Eligibility   This program is open to minority (Asian, Hispanic, African American, Native American) college sophomores, preferably those with ties to the mid-Atlantic states (Delaware, Maryland, North Carolina, South Carolina, Virginia, and Washington, D.C.). Applicants must be full-time students with a GPA of 2.5 or higher in a 4-year degree program. They must be interested in preparing for a career in print journalism and participating in an internship in news, features, sports, copy editing, photography, or graphics/illustration. U.S. citizenship or permanent resident status is required. Selection is based on grades, work samples, recommendations, targeted selection interview skills, and financial need.

Financial data   The stipend is $5,000 per year. During the summers following their sophomore and junior years, recipients are provided with paid internships. Following graduation, they are offered a 1-year internship with full benefits and the possibility of continued employment.

Duration   2 years (the junior and senior years of college).

Additional information   The internships are offered at the *News & Record* in Greensboro, North Carolina, the *Virginian-Pilot* in Norfolk, Virginia, or the *Roanoke Times* in Roanoke, Virginia.

Number awarded   1 or more each year.
Deadline   December of each year.

[303]
LARONA J. MORRIS SCHOLARSHIP

Sigma Gamma Rho Sorority, Inc.
Attn: National Education Fund
1000 Southhill Drive, Suite 200
Cary, NC 27513
(919) 678-9720   Toll Free: (888) SGR-1922
Fax: (919) 678-9721   E-mail: info@sgrho1922.org
Web: www.sgrho1922.org/service.htm

Summary To provide financial assistance to African American and other undergraduate students working on a degree in hotel and restaurant management.

Eligibility This program is open to undergraduates working on a degree in hotel and restaurant management. Applicants must have a GPA of "C" or higher and be able to demonstrate financial need.

Financial data A stipend is awarded (amount not specified).

Duration 1 year.

Additional information The sponsor is a traditionally African American sorority. A processing fee of $20 is required.

Number awarded 1 each year.

Deadline April of each year.

[304]
LARRY W. CARTER SCHOLARSHIP

Greater Des Moines Community Foundation
Finkbine Mansion
1915 Grand Avenue
Des Moines, IA 50309
(515) 883-2626   Fax: (515) 883-2630
E-mail: info@desmoinesfoundation.org
Web: www.desmoinesfoundation.org/page32888.cfm

Summary To provide financial assistance to African American undergraduate and graduate students in Iowa.

Eligibility Eligible to apply are African Americans who reside in Iowa and are enrolled in college or graduate school on a full- or part-time basis. Applicants must submit a personal statement that includes their personal and educational goals, motivations, and reasons for pursuing higher education.

Financial data The stipend is $3,000.

Duration 1 year.

Number awarded Varies each year; recently, 3 of these scholarships were awarded.

Deadline May of each year.

[305]
LARRY W. MCCORMICK COMMUNICATIONS SCHOLARSHIP FOR UNDERREPRESENTED STUDENTS

The Lullaby Guild, Inc.
Attn: Scholarship Committee
6709 La Tijera, Suite 116
Los Angeles, CA 90045
(310) 335-5655   E-mail: mail@lullabyguild.org
Web: www.lullabyguild.org

Summary To provide financial assistance to African American and other underrepresented upper-division students who are working on a degree in a field related to mass communications.

Eligibility This program is open to underrepresented (e.g., African American, Hispanic American, Native American, Alaskan American, Pacific Islander, Asian) students entering their junior or senior year at an accredited college or university. Applicants must be working on a degree in a field related to mass communications, including audiovisual and electronic and print journalism. Along with their application, they must submit a personal statement regarding their volunteer services, official transcripts, 3 letters of recommendation, 3 samples of their journalistic work, and a 500-word personal statement about their interest in journalism or mass communication. Selection is based on academic achievement, letters of recommendation, journalistic experience and/or evidence of journalistic talent, clarity of purpose in plans and goals for a future in journalism or mass communications, and involvement in volunteer community service.

Financial data The stipend is $2,500.

Duration 1 year.

Number awarded 1 each year.

Deadline February of each year.

[306]
LARRY WHITESIDE SCHOLARSHIP

National Association of Black Journalists
Attn: Program Coordinator
8701-A Adelphi Road
Adelphi, MD 20783-1716
(301) 445-7100, ext. 108   Toll Free: (866) 479-NABJ
Fax: (301) 445-7101   E-mail: nabj@nabj.org
Web: www.nabj.org

Summary To provide financial assistance to undergraduate or graduate student members of the National Association of Black Journalists (NABJ) who are preparing for a career in sports journalism.

Eligibility This program is open to African American juniors, seniors, and graduate students who are currently attending an accredited 4-year college or university. Applicants must be majoring in journalism or communications or have a demonstrated commitment to the field (e.g., long-term work on the school paper, internships at professional news gathering organizations). They must have a GPA of 2.5 or higher in their major and 2.0 overall, be NABJ members, and be preparing for a career in sports journalism. Along with their application, they must submit 3 samples of their work, an official college transcript, 3 letters of recommendation, a resume, and a 700- to 800-word profile of a sports journalist.

Financial data The stipend is $2,500. Funds are paid directly to the recipient's college or university.

Duration 1 year; nonrenewable.

Number awarded 1 each year.

Deadline May of each year.

[307]
LAUNCHING LEADERS UNDERGRADUATE SCHOLARSHIP

JPMorgan Chase
Campus Recruiting
Attn: Launching Leaders
277 Park Avenue, Second Floor
New York, NY 10172
(212) 270-6000
E-mail: bronwen.x.baumgardner@jpmorgan.com
Web: www.jpmorgan.com

Summary   To provide financial assistance and work experience to African American and other underrepresented undergraduate students interested in a career in financial services.

Eligibility   This program is open to Black, Hispanic, and Native American students enrolled as sophomores or juniors and interested in financial services. Applicants must have a GPA of 3.5 or higher. Along with their application, they must submit 500-word essays on 1) why they should be considered potential candidates for CEO of the sponsoring bank in 2020; and 2) the special background and attributes they would contribute to the sponsor's diversity agenda. They must be interested in a summer associate position in the sponsor's investment banking, sales and trading, or research divisions.

Financial data   The stipend is $5,000 for recipients accepted as sophomores or $10,000 for recipients accepted as juniors. For students accepted as sophomores and whose scholarship is renewed for a second year, the stipend is $15,000. The summer internship is a paid position.

Duration   1 year; may be renewed 1 additional year if the recipient successfully completes the 10-week summer intern program and maintains a GPA of 3.5 or higher.

Number awarded   Approximately 12 each year.

Deadline   October of each year.

[308]
LAURENCE R. FOSTER MEMORIAL UNDERGRADUATE SCHOLARSHIPS

Oregon Student Assistance Commission
Attn: Grants and Scholarships Division
1500 Valley River Drive, Suite 100
Eugene, OR 97401-2146
(541) 687-7395   Toll Free: (800) 452-8807, ext. 7395
Fax: (541) 687-7414   TDD: (800) 735-2900
E-mail: awardinfo@osac.state.or.us
Web: www.osac.state.or.us/osac_programs.html

Summary   To provide financial assistance to minority and other undergraduate students from Oregon who are interested in enrolling at a school in any state to prepare for a public health career.

Eligibility   This program is open to residents of Oregon who are enrolled at least half time at a 4-year college or university in any state to prepare for a career in public health (not private practice). Applicants must be entering the junior or senior year of a health program, including nursing, medical technology, and physician assistant. Preference is given to applicants from diverse environments. Along with their application, they must submit brief essays on 1) what public health means to them; 2) the public health aspect they intend to practice and the health and population issues impacted by that aspect; and 3) their experience living or working in diverse environments.

Financial data   Stipend amounts vary; recently, they were at least $4,167.

Duration   1 year.

Additional information   This program is administered by the Oregon Student Assistance Commission (OSAC) with funds provided by the Oregon Community Foundation.

Number awarded   Varies each year; recently, 6 undergraduate and graduate scholarships were awarded.

Deadline   February of each year.

[309]
LEONARD M. PERRYMAN COMMUNICATIONS SCHOLARSHIP FOR ETHNIC MINORITY STUDENTS

United Methodist Communications
Attn: Communications Resourcing Team
810 12th Avenue South
P.O. Box 320
Nashville, TN 37202-0320
(615) 742-5481   Toll Free: (888) CRT-4UMC
Fax: (615) 742-5485   E-mail: scholarships@umcom.org
Web: crt.umc.org/interior.asp?ptid=44&mid=10270

Summary   To provide financial assistance to African American and other minority United Methodist college students who are interested in careers in religious communications.

Eligibility   This program is open to United Methodist ethnic minority students enrolled in accredited institutions of higher education as juniors or seniors. Applicants must be interested in preparing for a career in religious communications. For the purposes of this program, "communications" is meant to cover audiovisual, electronic, and print journalism. Selection is based on Christian commitment and involvement in the life of the United Methodist church, academic achievement, journalistic experience, clarity of purpose, and professional potential as a religion communicator.

Financial data   The stipend is $2,500 per year.

Duration   1 year.

Additional information   The scholarship may be used at any accredited institution of higher education.

Number awarded   1 each year.

Deadline   March of each year.

[310]
LEONARDO WATTS SCHOLARSHIP

Watts Charity Association, Inc.
6245 Bristol Parkway, Suite 224
Culver City, CA 90230
(323) 671-0394   Fax: (323) 778-2613
E-mail: wattscharity@aol.com
Web: 4watts.tripod.com/id5.html

Summary   To provide financial assistance to upper-division African Americans working on a degree in classical music.

Eligibility   This program is open to U.S. citizens of African American descent who are enrolled full time as a college or university junior. Applicants must be studying classical music, including voice and/or instrumental. They must have a GPA of 3.0 or higher, be between 17 and 24 years of age, and be able to demonstrate that they intend to continue their education for at least 2 years. Along with their application, they must submit 1) a 1-paragraph statement on why they should be awarded a Watts Foundation scholarship, and 2) a 1- to 2-page essay on a specific type of cancer, based either on how it has impacted their life or on researched information.

Financial data A stipend is awarded (amount not specified).

Duration 1 year.

Additional information Royce R. Watts, Sr. established the Watts Charity Association after he learned he had cancer in 2001.

Number awarded 1 each year.

Deadline May of each year.

[311]
LIBRARY OF CONGRESS JUNIOR FELLOWS PROGRAM

Library of Congress
Library Services
Attn: Junior Fellows Program Coordinator
101 Independence Avenue, S.E., Room LM-642
Washington, DC 20540-4600
(202) 707-0901   Fax: (202) 707-6269
E-mail: jrfell@loc.gov
Web: www.loc.gov/hr/jrfellows/index.html

Summary To provide summer work experience at the Library of Congress (LC) to African American and other 1) upper-division or graduate students and 2) recent graduates.

Eligibility This program is open to U.S. citizens with subject expertise in the following areas: American history, including veterans and military history; American popular culture; area studies (African, Asian, European, Hispanic, Middle Eastern); bibliographic description and access; film, television, and radio; folklife; geography and maps; history of photography; history of popular and applied graphic arts, architecture, and design; manuscript collections processing; music; preservation and conservation; rare books and manuscripts; science, technology, and business; serials and government publications and newspapers; or sound recordings. Applicants must 1) be juniors or seniors at an accredited college or university, 2) be graduate students, or 3) have completed their degree in the past year. Applications from women, minorities, and persons with disabilities are particularly encouraged. Selection is based on academic achievement, letters of recommendation, and an interview.

Financial data Fellows are paid a taxable stipend of $300 per week.

Duration 3 months, beginning in either May or June. Fellows work a 40-hour week.

Additional information Fellows work with primary source materials and assist selected divisions at LC in the organization and documentation of archival collections, production of finding aids and bibliographic records, preparation of materials for preservation and service, completion of bibliographical research, and digitization of LC's historical collections.

Number awarded Varies each year; recently, 6 of these internships were awarded.

Deadline March of each year.

[312]
LILLIAN AND SAMUEL SUTTON EDUCATION SCHOLARSHIPS

National Association for the Advancement of Colored People
Attn: Education Department
4805 Mt. Hope Drive
Baltimore, MD 21215-3297
(410) 580-5760   Toll Free: (877) NAACP-98
E-mail: youth@naacpnet.org
Web: www.naacp.org/pages/naacp-scholarships

Summary To provide financial assistance to members of the National Association for the Advancement of Colored People (NAACP) and others who are working on a degree in education on the undergraduate or graduate level.

Eligibility This program is open to full-time undergraduates and full- and part-time graduate students majoring in the field of education. The required minimum GPA is 2.5 for graduating high school seniors and current undergraduates or 3.0 for graduate students. Membership and participation in the association are highly desirable. Applicants must be able to demonstrate financial need and be U.S. citizens. Along with their application, they must submit a 1-page essay on their interest in their major and a career, their life's ambition, what they hope to accomplish in their lifetime, and what position they hope to attain.

Financial data The stipend is $1,000 per year for undergraduate students or $2,000 per year for graduate students.

Duration 1 year; may be renewed as long as the recipient maintains a GPA of 2.5 or higher as an undergraduate or 3.0 or higher as a graduate student.

Number awarded Varies each year; recently, 9 of these scholarships were awarded.

Deadline March of each year.

[313]
LIN MEDIA MINORITY SCHOLARSHIP AND TRAINING PROGRAM

LIN Television Corporation
Attn: Vice President, Human Resources
One West Exchange Street, Suite 5A
Providence, RI 02903-1064
(401) 454-2880   Fax: (401) 454-6990
Web: www.linmedia.com/contact-us/careers.php

Summary To provide funding to African Americans and other minority undergraduates interested in earning a degree in a field related to broadcast journalism and working at a station owned by LIN Television Corporation.

Eligibility This program is open to U.S. citizens of nonwhite origin who are enrolled as a sophomore or higher at a college or university. Applicants must have a declared major in broadcast journalism, mass communication, television production, or marketing and a GPA of 3.0 or higher. Along with their application, they must submit a list of organizations and activities in which they have held leadership positions, 3 references, a 50-word description of their career goals, a list of personal achievements and honors, and a 500-word essay about themselves. Financial need is not considered in the selection process.

Financial data The program pays for tuition and fees, books, and room and board, to a maximum of $20,000 per year. Recipients must sign an employment agreement that guarantees them part-time employment as an intern during school and a 2-year regular position at a television station owned by LIN Television Corporation following graduation. If they fail to honor the employment agreement, they must repay all scholarship funds received.

Duration 2 years.

Additional information LIN Television Corporation owns 28 television stations in 17 media markets in the United States. Recipients of these scholarships must work at a station selected by LIN management.

Number awarded 1 or more each year.

Deadline March of each year.

[314]
LINCOLN CULTURAL DIVERSITY SCHOLARSHIP

American Advertising Federation-Lincoln
Attn: Scholarship Chair
P.O. Box 80093
Lincoln, NE 68501-0093
Web: www.aaflincoln.org/resources/scholarships.htm

Summary To provide financial assistance to African American and other minority residents of any state preparing for a career in a field related to advertising at a college in Nebraska.

Eligibility This program is open to minority residents of any state currently enrolled full time at an accredited college or university in Nebraska. Applicants must be working on a degree in advertising, marketing, public relations, communications, or commercial art. Along with their application, they must submit an essay describing their interest in receiving this scholarship and why they should be selected. They may also submit up to 3 samples of their work, although this is not required. Finalists are interviewed. Selection is based on ability, commitment and enthusiasm for the advertising profession, academic performance, participation in extracurricular activities, and career goals. U.S. citizenship is required.

Financial data The stipend is $1,000. Awards are provided in the form of a credit at the recipient's institution.

Duration 1 year.

Number awarded 1 each year.

Deadline October of each year.

[315]
LOCKHEED MARTIN NSBE CORPORATE SCHOLARSHIP PROGRAM

National Society of Black Engineers
Attn: Programs Department
205 Daingerfield Road
Alexandria, VA 22314
(703) 549-2207   Fax: (703) 683-5312
E-mail: scholarships@nsbe.org
Web: www.nsbe.org

Summary To provide financial assistance to members of the National Society of Black Engineers (NSBE) who are majoring in fields related to engineering.

Eligibility This program is open to members of the society who are entering their junior or senior year in college and majoring in computer science, mathematics, or the following fields of engineering: aerospace, computer, electrical, mechanical, or systems. Applicants must have a GPA of 3.0

or higher and a demonstrated interest in employment with Lockheed Martin Corporation. Along with their application, they must submit a 250-word essay describing their career goals and how they can make a community and professional impact as a Lockheed Martin employee. Selection is based on that essay; NSBE and university academic achievement; professional development; service to the society at the chapter, regional, and/or national level; and campus and community activities.

Financial data The stipend is $2,000.

Duration 1 year.

Additional information This program is sponsored by Lockheed Martin Corporation.

Number awarded 5 each year.

Deadline January of each year.

[316]
LOREN W. CROW MEMORIAL SCHOLARSHIP

American Meteorological Society
Attn: Fellowship/Scholarship Program
45 Beacon Street
Boston, MA 02108-3693
(617) 227-2426, ext. 246   Fax: (617) 742-8718
E-mail: scholar@ametsoc.org
Web: www.ametsoc.org

Summary To provide financial assistance to underrepresented minorities and other undergraduates majoring in meteorology or an aspect of atmospheric sciences with an interest in applied meteorology.

Eligibility This program is open to full-time students entering their final year of undergraduate study and majoring in meteorology or an aspect of the atmospheric or related oceanic and hydrologic sciences. Applicants must intend to make atmospheric or related sciences their career; preference is given to students who have demonstrated a strong interest in applied meteorology. They must be U.S. citizens or permanent residents enrolled at a U.S. institution and have a cumulative GPA of 3.25 or higher. Along with their application, they must submit 200-word essays on 1) their most important achievements that qualify them for this scholarship, and 2) their career goals in the atmospheric or related oceanic or hydrologic fields. Financial need is considered in the selection process. The sponsor specifically encourages applications from women, minorities, and students with disabilities who are traditionally underrepresented in the atmospheric and related oceanic sciences.

Financial data The stipend is $2,000.

Duration 1 year.

Number awarded 1 each year.

Deadline February of each year.

[317]
LOUIS B. RUSSELL, JR. MEMORIAL SCHOLARSHIP

Indiana State Teachers Association
Attn: Scholarships
150 West Market Street, Suite 900
Indianapolis, IN 46204-2875
(317) 263-3400   Toll Free: (800) 382-4037
Fax: (317) 655-3700   E-mail: mshoup@ista-in.org
Web: www.ista-in.org/dynamic.aspx?id=1038

Summary To provide financial assistance to African American and other minority high school seniors in Indiana who are interested in attending vocational school in any state.

Eligibility This program is open to ethnic minority high school seniors in Indiana who are interested in continuing their education in the area of industrial arts, vocational education, or technical preparation at an accredited postsecondary institution in any state. Selection is based on academic achievement, leadership ability as expressed through co-curricular activities and community involvement, recommendations, and a 300-word essay on their educational goals and how they plan to use this scholarship.

Financial data The stipend is $1,000.

Duration 1 year; may be renewed for 1 additional year, provided the recipient maintains a GPA of "C+" or higher.

Number awarded 1 each year.

Deadline February of each year.

[318]
LOUIS STOKES HEALTH SCHOLARS PROGRAM

Congressional Black Caucus Foundation, Inc.
Attn: Director, Educational Programs
1720 Massachusetts Avenue, N.W.
Washington, DC 20036
(202) 263-2800   Toll Free: (800) 784-2577
Fax: (202) 775-0773   E-mail: info@cbcfinc.org
Web: www.cbcfinc.org/scholarships.html

Summary To provide financial assistance to African Americans and other underrepresented undergraduate students who are interested in preparing for a health-related career.

Eligibility This program is open to 1) underrepresented graduating high school seniors planning to attend an accredited institution of higher education; and 2) currently-enrolled full-time undergraduate students in good academic standing with a GPA of 3.0 or higher. Applicants must be planning to work on a degree in a subject that will lead to a degree in a health field. Along with their application, they must submit a personal statement of 500 to 1,000 words on 1) their future goals, major field of study, and how that field of study will help them to achieve their future career goals; 2) involvement in school activities, community and public service, hobbies, and sports; 3) how receiving this award will affect their current and future plans; and 4) other experiences, skills, or qualifications. They must also be able to demonstrate financial need, leadership ability, and participation in community service activities. Preference is given to students who demonstrate an interest in working with underserved communities. Students currently attending 2-year institutions are strongly encouraged to apply. U.S. citizenship or permanent resident status is required.

Financial data The stipend is $8,000. Funds are paid directly to the student's institution.

Duration 1 year.

Additional information This program is sponsored by UnitedHealth Group.

Number awarded 10 each year.

Deadline March of each year.

[319]
LOUISE JANE MOSES/AGNES DAVIS MEMORIAL SCHOLARSHIP

California Librarians Black Caucus-Greater Los Angeles Chapter
Attn: Scholarship Committee
P.O. Box 882276
Los Angeles, CA 90009
E-mail: scholarship@clbc.org
Web: www.clbc.org/home/scholarship

Summary To provide financial assistance to African Americans in California who are interested in becoming librarians or library paraprofessionals.

Eligibility This program is open to African American residents of California who are working on a degree from an accredited library/information science program or an accredited library/information science paraprofessional program in the state. Applicants must submit an essay of 300 to 500 words on their professional goals and their interest in a library or information-related career. Selection is based on demonstrated financial need, scholastic achievement, and commitment to the goals of encouraging and supporting African American library professionals and improving library service to the African American community. Interviews are required.

Financial data Stipends range from $750 to $1,500.

Duration 1 year.

Number awarded 2 to 3 each year.

Deadline October of each year.

[320]
LOUISIANA WMU SCHOLARSHIP FOR AFRICAN-AMERICAN MISSION PASTORS

Louisiana Baptist Convention
Attn: Woman's Missionary Union
P.O. Box 311
Alexandria, LA 71309
(318) 448-3402   Toll Free: (800) 622-6549
E-mail: wmu@lbc.org
Web: www.lbc.org

Summary To provide financial assistance to African American Southern Baptists from Louisiana who are enrolled at a seminary in any state to prepare for a career as a missions pastor.

Eligibility This program is open to African Americans who are endorsed by the director of missions and the pastor of a sponsoring Southern Baptist church in Louisiana. Applicants must be enrolled full time at a seminary or a satellite campus to prepare for a career as a missions pastor and have a GPA of 2.5 or higher. They must be participating in a missions education organization of the church or on campus and must contribute to offerings of the church and other programs. Along with their application, they must submit a brief summary of their Christian walk in their life, including what they believe the Lord has called them to do in a church-related vocation.

Financial data The stipend is $1,200 per year.

Duration Up to 3 years.

Number awarded 1 or more each year.

Deadline June of each year.

[321]
LOVETTE HOOD JR. SCHOLARSHIP

Sigma Gamma Rho Sorority, Inc.
Attn: National Education Fund
1000 Southhill Drive, Suite 200
Cary, NC 27513
(919) 678-9720   Toll Free: (888) SGR-1922
Fax: (919) 678-9721   E-mail: info@sgrho1922.org
Web: www.sgrho1922.org/service.htm

Summary To provide financial assistance to African American and other undergraduate students working on a degree in theology.

Eligibility This program is open to undergraduates working on a degree in theology. The sponsor is a traditionally African American sorority, but support is available to males and females. Applicants must have a GPA of "C" or higher and be able to demonstrate financial need.

Financial data A stipend is awarded (amount not specified).

Duration 1 year.

Additional information A processing fee of $20 is required.

Number awarded 1 each year.

Deadline April of each year.

[322]
LTK SCHOLARSHIP

Conference of Minority Transportation Officials
Attn: National Scholarship Program
818 18th Street, N.W., Suite 850
Washington, DC 20006
(202) 530-0551   Fax: (202) 530-0617
Web: www.comto.org/news-youth.php

Summary To provide financial assistance to African American and other minority upper-division and graduate students in engineering or other field related to transportation.

Eligibility This program is open to full-time minority juniors, seniors, and graduate students in engineering of other technical transportation-related disciplines. Applicants must have a GPA of 3.0 or higher. Along with their application, they must submit a cover letter with a 500-word statement of career goals. Financial need is not considered in the selection process. U.S. citizenship is required.

Financial data The stipend is $6,000. Funds are paid directly to the recipient's college or university.

Duration 1 year.

Additional information The Conference of Minority Transportation Officials (COMTO) was established in 1971 to promote, strengthen, and expand the roles of minorities in all aspects of transportation. This program is sponsored by LTK Engineering Services. Recipients are required to become members of COMTO if they are not already members and attend the COMTO National Scholarship Luncheon.

Number awarded 1 or more each year.

Deadline April of each year.

[323]
LYNN DEAN FORD/INDIANAPOLIS ASSOCIATION OF BLACK JOURNALISTS SCHOLARSHIP

Indianapolis Association of Black Journalists
Attn: President
P.O. Box 441795
Indianapolis, IN 46244-1795
(317) 432-4469   E-mail: sjefferson@wthr.com
Web: www.iabj.org/contactiabj/scholarshipinformation.html

Summary To provide financial assistance to African Americans from Indiana who are interested in studying journalism in college.

Eligibility This program is open to African Americans who are either 1) graduates of an Indiana high school and enrolled in a school of communications or journalism in any state; or 2) current college students majoring in communications or journalism at a 4-year accredited college or university in Indiana. Applicants must submit 2 letters of recommendation, samples of their work in the media (newspaper or magazine clips, audition tapes), and an essay of 250 to 500 words on what attracted them to a career in journalism and their goals in their area of interest (print or broadcast).

Financial data The stipend is $1,000.

Duration 1 year.

Number awarded 1 each year.

Deadline Deadline not specified.

[324]
MABEL D. RUSSELL BLACK COLLEGE FUND

United Methodist Higher Education Foundation
Attn: Scholarships Administrator
1001 19th Avenue South
P.O. Box 340005
Nashville, TN 37203-0005
(615) 340-7385   Toll Free: (800) 811-8110
Fax: (615) 340-7330
E-mail: umhefscholarships@gbhem.org
Web: www.umhef.org/receive.php?id=endowed_funds

Summary To provide financial assistance to Methodist undergraduate and graduate students at Historically Black Colleges and Universities of the United Methodist Church.

Eligibility This program is open to students enrolling as full-time undergraduate and graduate students at the Historically Black Colleges and Universities of the United Methodist Church. Applicants must have been active, full members of a United Methodist Church for at least 1 year prior to applying. They must have a GPA of 3.0 or higher and be able to demonstrate financial need. Along with their application, they must submit a 200-word essay on their involvement and/or leadership responsibilities in their church, school, and community within the last 3 years. U.S. citizenship or permanent resident status is required.

Financial data The stipend is at least $1,000 per year.

Duration 1 year; nonrenewable.

Additional information This program was established in 1978. The qualifying schools are Bennett College for Women, Bethune-Cookman College, Claflin University, Clark Atlanta University, Dillard University, Huston-Tillotson College, Meharry Medical College, Paine College, Philander Smith College, Rust College, and Wiley College.

Number awarded 1 each year.
Deadline May of each year.

[325]
MABEL G. YOUNG SCHOLARSHIP

National Forum for Black Public Administrators
Attn: Scholarship Program
777 North Capitol Street, N.E., Suite 807
Washington, DC 20002
(202) 408-9300, ext. 112   Fax: (202) 408-8558
E-mail: vreed@nfbpa.org
Web: www.nfbpa.org/i4a/pages/index.cfm?pageid=3630

Summary To provide financial assistance to African Americans working on an undergraduate or graduate degree in public administration with an emphasis on public finance.

Eligibility This program is open to African American undergraduate and graduate students preparing for a career in public service. Applicants must be working full time on a degree in public administration, public finance, accounting, political science, urban affairs, public policy, or a related field. They must have a GPA of 3.0 or higher, a record of involvement in extracurricular activities (excluding athletics), excellent interpersonal and leadership abilities, and strong oral and written communication skills. Along with their application, they must submit a 3-page autobiographical essay that includes their academic and career goals and objectives. First consideration is given to applicants who are not currently receiving other financial aid.

Financial data The stipend is $5,000.

Duration 1 year.

Additional information This program is sponsored by the Grant Capital Management Corporation. Recipients are required to attend the sponsor's annual conference to receive their scholarship; limited hotel and air accommodations are arranged and provided.

Number awarded 1 each year.

Deadline February of each year.

[326]
MABEL SMITH MEMORIAL SCHOLARSHIP

Wisconsin Women of Color Network, Inc.
Attn: MSMS Committee
P.O. Box 2337
Madison, WI 53701-2337
E-mail: contact@womenofcolornetwork-wis.org
Web: www.womenofcolornetwork-wis.org/scholarship.html

Summary To provide financial assistance for vocation/technical school or community college to African Americans and other minority residents of Wisconsin.

Eligibility This program is open to residents of Wisconsin who are high school or GED-equivalent graduating seniors planning to continue their education at a vocational/technical school or community college in any state. Applicants must be a member of 1 of the following groups: African American, Asian, American Indian, Hispanic, or biracial. They must have a GPA of 2.0 or higher and be able to demonstrate financial need. Along with their application, they must submit a 1-page essay on how this scholarship will help them accomplish their educational goal. U.S. citizenship is required.

Financial data A stipend is awarded (amount not specified).

Duration 1 year.

Additional information This program was established in 1990.

Number awarded 1 each year.

Deadline May of each year.

[327]
MADISON/KALATHAS/DAVIS SCHOLARSHIP AWARD

National Naval Officers Association-Washington, D.C. Chapter
Attn: Scholarship Program
2701 Park Center Drive, A1108
Alexandria, VA 22302
(703) 566-3840   Fax: (703) 566-3813
E-mail: Stephen.Williams@Navy.mil
Web: dcnnoa.memberlodge.com

Summary To provide financial assistance to African American and other minority high school seniors from the Washington, D.C. area who plan to attend college in any state.

Eligibility This program is open to minority seniors graduating from high schools in the Washington, D.C. metropolitan area who plan to enroll full time at an accredited 2- or 4-year college or university in any state. Applicants must be U.S. citizens or permanent residents and have a GPA of 3.0 or higher. Selection is based on academic achievement, community involvement, and financial need.

Financial data The stipend is $1,500.

Duration 1 year; nonrenewable.

Additional information Recipients are not required to join or affiliate with the military in any way.

Number awarded 1 each year.

Deadline March of each year.

[328]
MAHLON MARTIN FELLOWSHIPS

Arkansas Department of Higher Education
Attn: Financial Aid Division
114 East Capitol Avenue
Little Rock, AR 72201-3818
(501) 371-2050   Toll Free: (800) 54-STUDY
Fax: (501) 371-2001   E-mail: finaid@adhe.edu
Web: www.adhe.edu

Summary To provide funding to African American undergraduate students in Arkansas interested in conducting a research project.

Eligibility This program is open to African American undergraduate students at Arkansas colleges and universities who are interested in conducting a research project in their field of study under the mentorship of a faculty member. Applicants must have completed at least 30 semester credit hours toward their degree and have a GPA of 3.25 or higher. Their institution may be a public or private institution of higher education in Arkansas that offers 2 or more years of college study. The faculty member must be tenured or tenure-track; temporary instructors and adjunct faculty are not eligible. Students must be U.S. citizens or permanent residents.

Financial data The maximum grant is $1,250. Students are also eligible for a travel grant up to $400 to attend a meeting of experts in their research area. Faculty mentors are eligible for grants up to $1,000.

Duration   Grants are available for academic year only, summer only, or academic year and summer; students may compete for up to 2 years of additional funding.

Number awarded   2 to 4 each year.

Deadline   October of each year.

[329]
MAINE SECTION SCHOLARSHIP

American Society of Civil Engineers-Maine Section
c/o Leslie L. Corrow, Scholarship Chair
Kleinschmidt Associates
75 Main Street
P.O. Box 576
Pittsfield, ME 04967
(207) 487-3328   Fax: (207) 487-3124
E-mail: scholarships@maineasce.org
Web: www.maineasce.org

Summary   To provide financial assistance to minority and other high school seniors in Maine who are interested in studying civil engineering in college.

Eligibility   This program is open to graduating high school seniors who are Maine residents and who intend to study civil engineering in college. Women and minorities are especially encouraged to apply. Applicants must submit a 200-word statement describing why they have chosen civil engineering as a career and what they hope to accomplish by being a civil engineer. Selection is based on the statement, academic performance, extracurricular activities, and letters of recommendation.

Financial data   The stipend is $2,000.

Duration   1 year; nonrenewable.

Number awarded   1 each year.

Deadline   January of each year.

[330]
MAJOR SPONSORS SCHOLARS AWARDS

National Society of Black Engineers
Attn: Programs Department
205 Daingerfield Road
Alexandria, VA 22314
(703) 549-2207   Fax: (703) 683-5312
E-mail: scholarships@nsbe.org
Web: www.nsbe.org

Summary   To provide financial assistance to members of the National Society of Black Engineers (NSBE) who are working on a degree in engineering.

Eligibility   This program is open to members of the society who are undergraduate or graduate engineering students. Applicants must have a GPA of 3.0 or higher. Selection is based on an essay; academic achievement; service to the society at the chapter, regional, and/or national level; and other professional, campus, and community activities. Applicants for the National Society of Black Engineers Fellows Scholarship Program who rank in the second of 3 tiers receive these awards.

Financial data   The stipend is $1,500. Travel, hotel accommodations, and registration to the national convention are also provided.

Duration   1 year.

Number awarded   Varies each year; recently, 10 of these scholarships were awarded.

Deadline   January of each year.

[331]
MARATHON OIL CORPORATION COLLEGE SCHOLARSHIP PROGRAM OF THE HISPANIC SCHOLARSHIP FUND

Hispanic Scholarship Fund
Attn: Selection Committee
55 Second Street, Suite 1500
San Francisco, CA 94105
(415) 808-2365   Toll Free: (877) HSF-INFO
Fax: (415) 808-2302   E-mail: scholar1@hsf.net
Web: www.hsf.net/Scholarships.aspx?id=464

Summary   To provide financial assistance to African American and other minority upper-division and graduate students working on a degree in a field related to the oil and gas industry.

Eligibility   This program is open to U.S. citizens and permanent residents (must have a permanent resident card or a passport stamped I-551) who are of Hispanic American, African American, Asian Pacific Islander American, or American Indian/Alaskan Native heritage. Applicants must be currently enrolled full time at an accredited 4-year college or university in the United States, Puerto Rico, Guam, or the U.S. Virgin Islands with a GPA of 3.0 or higher. They must be 1) sophomores majoring in accounting, chemical engineering, civil engineering, computer engineering, computer science, electrical engineering, energy management or petroleum land management, environmental engineering, environmental health and safety, finance, geology, geophysics, geotechnical engineering, global procurement or supply chain management, information technology/management information systems, marketing, mechanical engineering, petroleum engineering, or transportation and logistics,; or 2) seniors planning to work on a master's degree in geology or geophysics. Selection is based on academic achievement, personal strengths, interest and commitment to a career in the oil and gas industry, leadership, and financial need.

Financial data   The stipend is $15,000 per year.

Duration   2 years (the junior and senior undergraduate years or the first 2 years of a master's degree program).

Additional information   This program is jointly sponsored by Marathon Oil Corporation and the Hispanic Scholarship Fund (HSF). Recipients may be offered a paid 8- to 10-week summer internship at various Marathon Oil Corporation locations.

Number awarded   1 or more each year.

Deadline   November of each year.

[332]
MARCUS GARVEY SCHOLARSHIP

West Indian Foundation, Inc.
Attn: Scholarship Committee
1229 Albany Avenue
P.O. Box 320394
Hartford, CT 06132-0394
(860) 243-8812   Fax: (860) 243-8812
E-mail: Emailwestif@att.net
Web: www.westindianfoundation.org/programs.php

Summary To provide financial assistance to Connecticut high school seniors of West Indian parentage who plan to attend college in any state.

Eligibility This program is open to seniors graduating from high schools in Connecticut who are of West Indian parentage. Applicants must be planning to attend a college or university in any state. Selection is based on an essay on "The Significance of the Life of Marcus Garvey," academic achievement, community service, and financial need.

Financial data The stipend is $1,000.

Duration 1 year.

Number awarded 1 each year.

Deadline June of each year.

[333]
MARK MILLER AWARD

National Association of Black Accountants
Attn: National Scholarship Program
7474 Greenway Center Drive, Suite 1120
Greenbelt, MD 20770
(301) 474-NABA, ext. 114   Fax: (301) 474-3114
E-mail: customerservice@nabainc.org
Web: www.nabainc.org

Summary To provide financial assistance to student members of the National Association of Black Accountants (NABA) who are working on an undergraduate or graduate degree in a field related to accounting.

Eligibility This program is open to NABA members who are ethnic minorities enrolled full time as 1) an undergraduate freshman, sophomore, junior, or first-semester senior majoring in accounting, business, or finance at a 4-year college or university; or 2) a graduate student working on a master's degree in accounting. High school seniors are not eligible. Applicants must have a GPA of 2.0 or higher in their major and 2.5 or higher overall. Along with their application, they must submit 1) a 500-word autobiography that discusses career objectives, leadership abilities, community activities, and involvement in NABA; and 2) a 500-word statement on a personal, family, or financial hardship they have overcome, the circumstances involved, and how the obstacles were overcome.

Financial data The stipend is $2,500.

Duration 1 year.

Number awarded 1 each year.

Deadline January of each year.

[334]
MARTIN LUTHER KING, JR. MEMORIAL SCHOLARSHIP FUND

California Teachers Association
Attn: Human Rights Department
1705 Murchison Drive
P.O. Box 921
Burlingame, CA 94011-0921
(650) 552-5446   Fax: (650) 552-5002
E-mail: scholarships@cta.org
Web: www.cta.org

Summary To provide financial assistance for college or graduate school to African American and other racial and ethnic minorities who are members of the California Teachers

Association (CTA), children of members, or members of the Student CTA.

Eligibility This program is open to members of racial or ethnic minority groups (African Americans, American Indians/ Alaska Natives, Asians/Pacific Islanders, and Hispanics) who are 1) active CTA members; 2) dependent children of active, retired, or deceased CTA members; or 3) members of Student CTA. Applicants must be interested in preparing for a teaching career in public education or already engaged in such a career.

Financial data Stipends vary each year; recently, they ranged from $1,000 to $4,000.

Duration 1 year.

Number awarded Varies each year; recently, 12 of these scholarships were awarded: 4 to CTA members, 6 to children of CTA members, and 2 to Student CTA members.

Deadline March of each year.

[335]
MARTIN LUTHER KING, JR. SCHOLARSHIP

North Carolina Association of Educators, Inc.
Attn: Minority Affairs Commission
700 South Salisbury Street
P.O. Box 27347
Raleigh, NC 27611-7347
(919) 832-3000, ext. 205
Toll Free: (800) 662-7924, ext. 205
Fax: (919) 839-8229
Web: www.ncae.org

Summary To provide financial assistance to minority and other high school seniors in North Carolina who plan to attend college in any state.

Eligibility This program is open to seniors graduating from high schools in North Carolina who plan to attend a college or university in any state. They must have a GPA of 2.5 or higher. Applications are considered and judged by members of the association's Minority Affairs Commission. Selection is based on character, personality, and scholastic achievement.

Financial data A stipend is awarded (amount not specified).

Duration 1 year.

Number awarded 1 or more each year.

Deadline January of each year.

[336]
MARY E. WOOD SCHOLARSHIP

Greater Des Moines Community Foundation
Finkbine Mansion
1915 Grand Avenue
Des Moines, IA 50309
(515) 883-2626   Fax: (515) 883-2630
E-mail: info@desmoinesfoundation.org
Web: www.desmoinesfoundation.org/page32888.cfm

Summary To provide financial assistance to African American residents of Iowa working on an undergraduate degree at a school in any state.

Eligibility Eligible to apply are African Americans who reside in Iowa and have received either a high school diploma or a GED diploma. Applicants must be attending or planning to attend a college, university, or trade school in any state. Along with their application, they must submit a personal statement that includes evidence of strong character or demonstrated ability to overcome obstacles, financial need, community involvement, and reasons for pursuing higher education.

Financial data A stipend is awarded (amount not specified).

Duration 1 year.

Number awarded 1 or more each year.

Deadline May of each year.

[337]
MARY ELIZA MAHONEY SCHOLARSHIP

New England Regional Black Nurses Association, Inc.
P.O. Box 190690
Boston, MA 02119
(617) 524-1951
Web: www.nerbna.org/org/scholarships.html

Summary To provide financial assistance to high school seniors New England who have contributed to the African American community and are interested in studying nursing at a school in any state.

Eligibility The program is open to seniors graduating from high schools in New England who are planning to enroll full time in an NLN-accredited baccalaureate program in nursing in any state. Applicants must have at least 1 full year of school remaining. Along with their application, they must submit a 3-page essay that covers their career aspirations in the nursing profession; how they have contributed to the African American or other communities of color in such areas as work, volunteering, church, or community outreach; an experience that has enhanced their personal and/or professional growth; and any financial hardships that may hinder them from completing their education.

Financial data A stipend is awarded (amount not specified).

Duration 1 year.

Number awarded 1 or more each year.

Deadline March of each year.

[338]
MARY HILL DAVIS ETHNIC/MINORITY STUDENT SCHOLARSHIP PROGRAM

Baptist General Convention of Texas
Attn: Institutional Ministries Department
333 North Washington
Dallas, TX 75246-1798
(214) 828-5252   Toll Free: (888) 244-9400
Fax: (214) 828-5261   E-mail: institutions@bgct.org
Web: texasbaptists.org

Summary To provide financial assistance for college to African Americans and other minority residents of Texas who are members of Texas Baptist congregations.

Eligibility This program is open to members of Texas Baptist congregations who are of African American, Hispanic, Native American, Asian, or other intercultural heritage. Applicants must be attending or planning to attend a university affiliated with the Baptist General Convention of Texas to work on a bachelor's degree as preparation for service as a future lay or vocational ministry leader in a Texas Baptist ethnic/minority church. They must have been active in their respective ethnic/minority community. Along with their appli-

cation, they must submit a letter of recommendation from their pastor and transcripts. Students still in high school must have a GPA of at least 3.0; students previously enrolled in a college must have at least a 2.0 GPA. U.S. citizenship or permanent resident status is required.

Financial data Stipends are $800 per semester ($1,600 per year) for full-time students or $400 per semester ($800 per year) for part-time students.

Duration 1 semester; may be renewed up to 7 additional semesters.

Additional information The scholarships are funded through the Week of Prayer and the Mary Hill Davis Offering for state missions sponsored annually by Women's Missionary Union of Texas. The eligible institutions are Baptist University of The Americas, Baylor University, Dallas Baptist University, East Texas Baptist University, Hardin Simmons University, Houston Baptist University, Howard Payne University, University of Mary Hardin Baylor, and Wayland Baptist University.

Number awarded Varies each year.

Deadline April of each year.

[339]
MARY MCLEOD BETHUNE SCHOLARSHIPS

Florida Department of Education
Attn: Office of Student Financial Assistance
325 West Gaines Street
Tallahassee, FL 32399-0400
(850) 410-5160   Toll Free: (888) 827-2004
Fax: (850) 487-1809   E-mail: osfa@fldoe.org
Web: www.floridastudentfinancialaid.org

Summary To provide financial assistance to high school seniors interested in attending Historically Black Colleges and Universities (HBCUs) in Florida.

Eligibility Eligible are high school seniors who wish to attend Florida A&M University, Bethune-Cookman College, Edward Waters College, or Florida Memorial University for a minimum of 12 credit hours per term. Applicants must be Florida residents, be U.S. citizens or eligible noncitizens, have a GPA of 3.0 or higher, be able to demonstrate financial need, and not be in default or owe repayment on any federal or state grant, scholarship, or loan program. Priority may be given to students with the lowest total family resources.

Financial data The stipend is $3,000 per year.

Duration 1 year; may be renewed up to 3 additional years if the student maintains full-time enrollment and a GPA of 3.0 or higher and continues to demonstrate financial need.

Number awarded Varies each year; recently, this program awarded 154 new and 87 renewal grants.

Deadline Deadlines are established by the participating institutions.

[340]
MARY WOLFSKILL TRUST FUND INTERNSHIP

Library of Congress
Library Services
Attn: Junior Fellows Program Coordinator
101 Independence Avenue, S.E., Room LM-642
Washington, DC 20540-4600
(202) 707-3301   Fax: (202) 707-6269
E-mail: jrfell@loc.gov
Web: www.loc.gov/hr/jrfellows/index.html

Summary To provide summer work experience in the Manuscript Division of the Library of Congress (LC) to upper-division and graduate students (especially African American and other minority students).

Eligibility This program is open to undergraduate and graduate students who have expertise in library science or collections conservation and preservation. Applicants must be interested in gaining an introductory knowledge of the principles, concepts, and techniques of archival management through a summer internship in the LC Manuscript Division. They should be able to demonstrate an ability to communicate effectively in writing and have knowledge of integrated library systems, basic library applications, and other information technologies. Knowledge of American history is beneficial. Applications from minorities and students at smaller and lesser-known schools are particularly encouraged. U.S. citizenship is required.

Financial data The stipend is $3,000.

Duration 10 weeks during the summer. Fellows work a 40-hour week.

Number awarded 1 each year.

Deadline March of each year.

[341]
MARYLAND SEA GRANT RESEARCH EXPERIENCES FOR UNDERGRADUATES

Maryland Sea Grant College
c/o University of Maryland
4321 Hartwick Road, Suite 300
College Park, MD 20740
(301) 405-7500   Fax: (301) 314-5780
E-mail: moser@mdsg.umd.edu
Web: www.mdsg.umd.edu

Summary To provide underrepresented minorities and other undergraduate students with an opportunity to conduct summer research on Chesapeake Bay in fields related to marine biology.

Eligibility This program is open to undergraduate students who have completed at least 2 years of study towards a bachelor's degree. Applicants must be interested in conducting individual research projects (under the mentorship of scientists from the University of Maryland or the Academy of Natural Science Estuarine Research Center) in biology, chemistry, ecology, environmental science, engineering, marine science, mathematics, or physics. U.S. citizenship or permanent resident status is required. Selection is based on a 1-page description of interests, course work and grades, letters of recommendation, and the potential benefits students will gain from the research experience. Preference is given to rising seniors. Students from underrepresented groups and from institutions with limited research opportunities are especially encouraged to apply.

Financial data Fellows receive a stipend of $4,300, payment of dormitory costs, round-trip travel expenses, and funding to assist in publishing or presenting the results of summer research.

Duration 12 weeks during the summer.

Additional information This program is supported by the National Science Foundation as part of the Research Experiences for Undergraduates Program.

Number awarded 14 each year.

Deadline February of each year.

[342]
MAUDE DAVIS/JOSEPH C. MCKINNEY SCHOLARSHIP

African Methodist Episcopal Church
Second Episcopal District Lay Organization
c/o Dr. V. Susie Oliphant, District Coordinator
910 Luray Place
Hyattsville, MD 20783
(301) 559-9488   E-mail: vsfo@verizon.net

Summary To provide financial assistance to members of the African Methodist Episcopal (AME) Church in its Second Episcopal District who are interested in attending college in any state.

Eligibility This program is open to AME members in the Second Episcopal District, which includes the Conferences of Baltimore, Washington, Virginia, North Carolina, and Western North Carolina. Applicants must be graduating high school seniors or college freshmen who are attending or planning to attend a college or university in any state to work on an undergraduate degree or certification. Along with their application, they must submit a high school transcript and SAT scores, 3 letters of recommendation, a 1-page biographical statement that includes career goals, and documentation of financial need.

Financial data A stipend is awarded (amount not specified).

Duration 1 year.

Number awarded Each of the 5 Conferences may award 1 or more of these scholarships each year.

Deadline June of each year.

[343]
MAUREEN L. AND HOWARD N. BLITMAN, P.E. SCHOLARSHIP TO PROMOTE DIVERSITY IN ENGINEERING

National Society of Professional Engineers
Attn: NSPE Educational Foundation
1420 King Street
Alexandria, VA 22314-2794
(703) 684-2833   Toll Free: (888) 285-NSPE
Fax: (703) 836-4875   E-mail: education@nspe.org
Web: www.nspe.org/Students/Scholarships/index.html

Summary To provide financial assistance for college to African American and members of other underrepresented ethnic minority groups interested in preparing for a career in engineering.

Eligibility This program is open to members of underrepresented ethnic minorities (African Americans, Hispanics, or Native Americans) who are high school seniors accepted into an ABET-accredited engineering program at a 4-year college or university. Applicants must have a GPA of 3.5 or higher, verbal SAT score of 600 or higher, and math SAT score of 700 or higher (or English ACT score of 29 or higher and math ACT score of 29 or higher). They must submit brief essays on an experience they consider significant to their interest in engineering, how their study of engineering will contribute to their long-term career plans, how their ethnic background has influenced their personal development and perceptions, and anything special about them that they would like the selection committee to know. Selection is based on those essays, GPA, internship/co-op experience and community involvement, 2 faculty recommendations, and honors/scholarships/awards. U.S. citizenship is required.

Financial data The stipend is $5,000 per year; funds are paid directly to the recipient's institution.

Duration 1 year; nonrenewable.

Number awarded 1 each year.

Deadline February of each year.

[344]
MAX MAYFIELD SCHOLARSHIP IN WEATHER FORECASTING

American Meteorological Society
Attn: Fellowship/Scholarship Program
45 Beacon Street
Boston, MA 02108-3693
(617) 227-2426, ext. 246   Fax: (617) 742-8718
E-mail: scholar@ametsoc.org
Web: www.ametsoc.org

Summary To provide financial assistance to underrepresented minorities and other undergraduates majoring in meteorology or an aspect of atmospheric sciences with an interest in weather forecasting.

Eligibility This program is open to full-time students entering their final year of undergraduate study and majoring in meteorology or an aspect of the atmospheric or related oceanic and hydrologic sciences. Applicants must have demonstrated a strong interest in weather forecasting. They must be U.S. citizens or permanent residents enrolled at a U.S. institution and have a cumulative GPA of 3.25 or higher. Along with their application, they must submit 200-word essays on 1) their most important achievements that qualify them for this scholarship, and 2) their career goals in the atmospheric or related oceanic or hydrologic fields. Financial need is considered in the selection process. The sponsor specifically encourages applications from women, minorities, and students with disabilities who are traditionally underrepresented in the atmospheric and related oceanic sciences.

Financial data The stipend is $2,000.

Duration 1 year.

Additional information Requests for an application must be accompanied by a self-addressed stamped envelope.

Number awarded 1 each year.

Deadline February of each year.

[345]
MAXINE V. FENNELL MEMORIAL SCHOLARSHIP

New England Regional Black Nurses Association, Inc.
P.O. Box 190690
Boston, MA 02119
(617) 524-1951
Web: www.nerbna.org/org/scholarships.html

Summary To provide financial assistance to licensed practical nurses from New England who are studying to become a registered nurse (R.N.) and have contributed to the African American community.

Eligibility The program is open to residents of the New England states who are licensed practical nurses and currently enrolled in an NLN-accredited R.N. program (diploma, associate, baccalaureate) at a school in any state. Applicants must have at least 1 full year of school remaining. Along with their application, they must submit a 3-page essay that covers their career aspirations in the nursing profession; how they have contributed to the African American or other communities of color in such areas as work, volunteering, church, or community outreach; an experience that has enhanced their personal and/or professional growth; and any financial hardships that may hinder them from completing their education.

Financial data A stipend is awarded (amount not specified).

Duration 1 year.

Number awarded 1 or more each year.

Deadline March of each year.

[346]
MCKINLEY FINANCIAL SERVICES SCHOLARSHIP

National Forum for Black Public Administrators
Attn: Scholarship Program
777 North Capitol Street, N.E., Suite 807
Washington, DC 20002
(202) 408-9300, ext. 112   Fax: (202) 408-8558
E-mail: vreed@nfbpa.org
Web: www.nfbpa.org/i4a/pages/index.cfm?pageid=3630

Summary To provide financial assistance to African Americans working on an undergraduate or graduate degree in public administration.

Eligibility This program is open to African American undergraduate and graduate students preparing for a career in public service. Applicants must be working full time on a degree in public administration, political science, urban affairs, public policy, or a related field. They must have a GPA of 3.0 or higher, excellent interpersonal and analytical abilities, and strong oral and written communication skills. Along with their application, they must submit a 3-page autobiographical essay that includes their academic and career goals and objectives. First consideration is given to applicants who are not currently receiving other financial aid.

Financial data The stipend is $1,000.

Duration 1 year.

Additional information This program is sponsored by McKinley Financial Services, Inc. Recipients are required to attend the sponsor's annual conference to receive their scholarship; limited hotel and air accommodations are arranged and provided.

Number awarded 1 each year.

Deadline February of each year.

[347]
MEDICAL SCIENTIST TRAINING PROGRAM

University of California at San Diego
Attn: School of Medicine
Summer Undergraduate Research Fellowship Program
9500 Gilman Drive, MC 0606
La Jolla, CA 92093-0606
(858) 822-5631 Toll Free: (800) 925-8704
Fax: (858) 534-8556 E-mail: mstp@ucsd.edu
Web: meded.ucsd.edu/asa/mstp/surf

Summary To provide an internship opportunity for African Americans and other undergraduate students from underrepresented groups to work during the summer on a research project in the biomedical sciences at the University of California at San Diego (UCSD).

Eligibility This program is open to undergraduate students at colleges in any state who are members of an underrepresented group (racial and ethnic groups that have been shown to be underrepresented in health-related sciences, individuals with disabilities, or individuals from a disadvantaged background). Applicants must be interested in working on a research project in the laboratory of a UCSD faculty member in the biomedical sciences. Along with their application, they must submit brief essays on 1) why they consider themselves an individual from a disadvantaged ethnicity or background or are underrepresented in the biomedical sciences; 2) their past research experiences; 3) the areas of research they wish to pursue in the program; 4) their educational and career plans and how this program will advance them towards their goals; and 5) anything else that might help to evaluate their application.

Financial data The program provides a stipend of $1,600 per month, room (but not board), and a $500 travel allowance.

Duration 8 weeks during the summer.

Additional information This program is sponsored by the National Heart, Lung, and Blood Institute (NHLBI) of the National Institutes of Health (NIH).

Number awarded From 12 to 20 each year.

Deadline February of each year.

[348]
MENTORSHIP FOR ENVIRONMENTAL SCHOLARS

United Negro College Fund Special Programs
 Corporation
6402 Arlington Boulevard, Suite 600
Falls Church, VA 22042
(703) 677-3400 Toll Free: (800) 530-6232
Fax: (703) 205-7645 E-mail: portal@uncfsp.org
Web: www.uncfsp.org

Summary To provide an opportunity for upper-division students at Historically Black Colleges and Universities and other Minority Institutions (MIs) to work on a summer research internship in a field of interest to the U.S. Department of Energy (DOE).

Eligibility This program is open to rising juniors and seniors at MIs (Historically Black Colleges and Universities, Hispanic Serving Institutions, and Tribal Colleges and Univer-

sities) who are members of underrepresented groups, including ethnic minorities and persons with disabilities. Applicants must be working on a degree in a science, technology, engineering, or mathematics (STEM) field of interest to DOE (e.g., biology, chemistry, physics, engineering, environmental science) and have a GPA of 3.0 or higher. They must be interested in working on a research project during the summer at a DOE laboratory or research facility. U.S. citizenship is required.

Financial data A stipend is provided (amount not specified).

Duration 9 weeks during the summer.

Additional information This program is funded by DOE and administered by the United Negro College Fund Special Programs Corporation.

Number awarded Varies each year.

Deadline February of each year.

[349]
MICHAEL BAKER CORPORATION SCHOLARSHIP PROGRAM FOR DIVERSITY IN ENGINEERING

Association of Independent Colleges and Universities of
 Pennsylvania
101 North Front Street
Harrisburg, PA 17101-1405
(717) 232-8649 Fax: (717) 233-8574
E-mail: info@aicup.org
Web: www.aicup.org/fundraising

Summary To provide financial assistance to women and minority students from any state enrolled at member institutions of the Association of Independent Colleges and Universities of Pennsylvania (AICUP) who are majoring in designated fields of engineering.

Eligibility This program is open to full-time undergraduate students from any state enrolled at designated AICUP colleges and universities who are women and/or members of the following minority groups: American Indians, Alaska Natives, Asians, Blacks/African Americans, Hispanics/Latinos, Native Hawaiians, or Pacific Islanders. Applicants must be juniors majoring in architectural, civil, or environmental engineering with a GPA of 3.0 or higher. Along with their application, they must submit a 2-page essay on what they believe will be the greatest challenge facing the engineering profession over the next decade, and why.

Financial data The stipend is $2,500 per year.

Duration 1 year; may be renewed 1 additional year if the recipient maintains appropriate academic standards.

Additional information This program, sponsored by the Michael Baker Corporation, is available at the 83 private colleges and universities in Pennsylvania that comprise the AICUP.

Number awarded 1 each year.

Deadline April of each year.

[350]
MICHAEL P. ANDERSON SCHOLARSHIP IN SPACE SCIENCE

National Society of Black Physicists
Attn: Scholarship Committee Chair
1100 North Glebe Road, Suite 1010
Arlington, VA 22201
(703) 536-4207   Fax: (703) 536-4203
E-mail: scholarship@nsbp.org
Web: www.nsbp.org/scholarships

Summary To provide financial assistance to African American students majoring in space science in college.

Eligibility This program is open to African American students who are entering their junior or senior year of college and majoring in space science. Applicants must submit an essay on their academic and career objectives, information on their participation in extracurricular activities, a description of any awards and honors they have received, and 3 letters of recommendation. Financial need is not considered.

Financial data The stipend is $1,000.

Duration 1 year; nonrenewable.

Additional information This program is offered in partnership with the American Astronomical Society.

Number awarded 1 each year.

Deadline January of each year.

[351]
MICHIGAN CHAPTER AABE SCHOLARSHIPS

American Association of Blacks in Energy-Michigan
  Chapter
Attn: Sheila Patterson
One Energy Plaza 7-253
Jackson, MI 49201
(517) 788-1893   E-mail: sapatterson@cmsenergy.com
Web: www.aabe.org/index.php?component=pages&id=572

Summary To provide financial assistance to African American and members of other underrepresented minority groups who are high school seniors in Michigan and planning to major in an energy-related field at a college in any state.

Eligibility This program is open to seniors graduating from high schools in Michigan and planning to work on a bachelor's degree at a college or university in any state. Applicants must be African Americans, Hispanics, or Native Americans who have a GPA of 3.0 or higher and are able to demonstrate financial need. Their intended major must be a field of business, engineering, physical science, mathematics, or technology related to energy. Along with their application, they must submit a 350-word statement on why they should receive this scholarship, what are their professional career objectives, and any other relevant information.

Financial data The stipend is $1,000.

Duration 1 year; nonrenewable.

Additional information Winners are eligible to compete for regional and national scholarships.

Number awarded At least 1 each year.

Deadline March of each year.

[352]
MICKEY LELAND ENERGY FELLOWSHIPS

Department of Energy
Attn: Office of Fossil Energy
19901 Germantown Road, FE-6
Germantown, MD 20874
(301) 903-4293   E-mail: MLEF@hq.doe.gov
Web: fossil.energy.gov

Summary To provide summer work experience at fossil energy sites of the Department of Energy (DOE) to African American and other underrepresented students.

Eligibility This program is open to U.S. citizens currently enrolled full time at an accredited college or university. Applicants must be undergraduate, graduate, or postdoctoral students in mathematics, physical sciences, technology, or engineering and have a GPA of 3.0 or higher. They must be interested in a summer work experience at a DOE fossil energy research facility. Along with their application, they must submit a 100-word statement on why they want to participate in this program. A goal of the program is to recruit women and underrepresented minorities into careers related to fossil energy.

Financial data Weekly stipends are $500 for undergraduates, $650 for master's degree students, or $750 for doctoral and postdoctoral students. Travel costs for a round trip to and from the site and for a trip to a designated place for technical presentations are also paid.

Duration 10 weeks during the summer.

Additional information This program began as 3 separate activities: the Historically Black Colleges and Universities Internship Program, established in 1995; the Hispanic Internship Program, established in 1998; and the Tribal Colleges and Universities Internship Program, established in 2000. Those 3 programs were merged into the Fossil Energy Minority Education Initiative, renamed the Mickey Leland Energy Fellowship Program in 2000. Sites to which interns may be assigned include the Albany Research Center (Albany, Oregon), the National Energy Technology Laboratory (Morgantown, West Virginia and Pittsburgh, Pennsylvania), Pacific Northwest National Laboratory (Richland, Washington), Rocky Mountain Oilfield Testing Center (Casper, Wyoming), Strategic Petroleum Reserve Project Management Office (New Orleans, Louisiana), or U.S. Department of Energy Headquarters (Washington, D.C.).

Number awarded Varies each year; recently, 30 students participated in this program.

Deadline January of each year.

[353]
MICROBIOLOGY UNDERGRADUATE RESEARCH FELLOWSHIP

American Society for Microbiology
Attn: Education Board
1752 N Street, N.W.
Washington, DC 20036-2904
(202) 942-9283   Fax: (202) 942-9329
E-mail: fellowships@asmusa.org
Web: www.asm.org

Summary To provide African American and other underrepresented minority college students with the opportunity to work on a summer research project in microbiology under the mentorship of a member of the American Society for Microbiology (ASM).

Eligibility This program is open to African Americans, Hispanics, Native Americans, Alaskan Natives, and Pacific Islanders who 1) are enrolled as full-time undergraduate students; 2) have taken introductory courses in biology, chemistry, and (preferably) microbiology prior to applying; 3) have a strong interest in obtaining a Ph.D. or M.D./Ph.D. in the microbiological sciences; 4) have laboratory research experience; and 5) are U.S. citizens or permanent residents. Applicants must be interested in conducting basic science research at a host institution during the summer under an ASM mentor. Selection is based on academic achievement, achievement in previous research experiences or independent projects, career goals as a research scientist, commitment to research, personal motivation to participate in the project, willingness to conduct summer research with an ASM member located at an institution other than their own, leadership skills, and involvement in activities that serve the needs of underrepresented groups.

Financial data Students receive $3,500 as a stipend, up to $1,000 for student lodging, up to $500 for round-trip travel to the host institution, 2-year student membership in the ASM, and travel support up to $1,000 if they present the results of the research project at the ASM general meeting the following year.

Duration 10 to 12 weeks during the summer.

Additional information This program was formerly named the American Society for Microbiology Minority Undergraduate Research Fellowship. In addition to their research activities, fellows participate in a weekly seminar series, journal club, GRE preparatory course, graduate admission counseling, and career counseling.

Number awarded 5 to 8 students are placed at each institution.

Deadline January of each year.

[354]
MIDWEST CONFERENCE WOMEN'S MISSIONARY SOCIETY YOUTH EDUCATION SCHOLARSHIP AWARD

African Methodist Episcopal Church
Midwest Conference
Attn: Women's Missionary Society
YES Scholarship Committee
P.O. Box 171488
Kansas City, KS 66117-0488
Web: www.midwestwms.org/ypd.html

Summary To provide financial assistance to members of African Methodist Episcopal (AME) churches in its Midwest Conference who are interested in attending college in any state.

Eligibility This program is open to high school seniors and students already enrolled at a college, university, junior college, or vocational school in any state. Applicants must be a member of an AME church and its Young People's Department (YPD) in the Midwest Conference (Kansas, Nebraska, and northwest Missouri).

Financial data A stipend is awarded (amount not specified).

Duration 1 year.

Number awarded 1 or more each year.

Deadline June of each year.

[355]
MIKE SHINN DISTINGUISHED MEMBER OF THE YEAR AWARDS

National Society of Black Engineers
Attn: Programs Department
205 Daingerfield Road
Alexandria, VA 22314
(703) 549-2207   Fax: (703) 683-5312
E-mail: scholarships@nsbe.org
Web: www.nsbe.org

Summary To provide financial assistance to male and female members of the National Society of Black Engineers (NSBE) who are working on a degree in engineering.

Eligibility This program is open to members of the society who are undergraduate or graduate engineering students. Applicants must have a GPA of 3.2 or higher. Selection is based on an essay; NSBE and university academic achievement; professional development; service to the society at the chapter, regional, and/or national level; and campus and community activities. The male and female applicants for the NSBE Fellows Scholarship Program who are judged most outstanding receive these awards.

Financial data The stipend is $7,500. Travel, hotel accommodations, and registration to the national convention are also provided.

Duration 1 year.

Number awarded 2 each year: 1 male and 1 female.

Deadline November of each year.

[356]
MILDRED COLLINS NURSING/HEALTH SCIENCE/MEDICINE SCHOLARSHIP

African-American/Caribbean Education Association, Inc.
P.O. Box 1224
Valley Stream, NY 11582-1224
(718) 949-6733   E-mail: aaceainc@yahoo.com
Web: www.aaceainc.com/Scholarships.html

Summary To provide financial assistance to high school seniors of African American or Caribbean heritage who plan to study a field related to nursing, health science, or medicine in college.

Eligibility This program is open to graduating high school seniors who are U.S. citizens of African American or Caribbean heritage. Applicants must be planning to attend a college or university and major in a field related to a career in nursing, health science, or medicine. They must have completed 4 years of specified college preparatory courses with a grade of 90 or higher and have an SAT score of at least 1790. They must also have completed at least 200 hours of community service during their 4 years of high school, preferably in the field that they plan to study in college. Financial need is not considered in the selection process. New York residency is not required, but applicants must be available for an interviews in the Queens, New York area.

Financial data The stipend ranges from $1,000 to $2,500. Funds are paid directly to the recipient.

Duration 1 year.

Number awarded 1 each year.
Deadline April of each year.

[357]
MILDRED TOWLE SCHOLARSHIP FOR AFRICAN AMERICANS

Hawai'i Community Foundation
Attn: Scholarship Department
827 Fort Street Mall
Honolulu, HI 96813
(808) 537-6333   Toll Free: (888) 731-3863
Fax: (808) 521-6286
E-mail: scholarships@hcf-hawaii.org
Web: www.hawaiicommunityfoundation.org/scholarships

Summary To provide financial assistance to African Americans from any state studying at colleges and universities in Hawaii.

Eligibility This program is open to African Americans from any state enrolled full time at a college or university in Hawaii. Applicants are not required to be residents of Hawaii. They must be able to demonstrate academic achievement (GPA of 3.0 or higher), good moral character, and financial need. Along with their application, they must submit a short statement indicating their reasons for attending college, their planned course of study, their career goals, and what community service means to them.

Financial data The amounts of the awards depend on the availability of funds and the need of the recipient. Recently, the average value of each of the scholarships awarded by the foundation was $2,041.

Duration 1 year.

Number awarded Varies each year; recently, 11 of these scholarships were awarded.

Deadline February of each year.

[358]
MILLER/CURRY/JACKSON LEADERSHIP AND EXCELLENCE SCHOLARSHIP

National Naval Officers Association-Washington, D.C. Chapter
Attn: Scholarship Program
2701 Park Center Drive, A1108
Alexandria, VA 22302
(703) 566-3840   Fax: (703) 566-3813
E-mail: Stephen.Williams@Navy.mil
Web: dcnnoa.memberlodge.com

Summary To provide financial assistance to African American and Hispanic high school seniors from the Washington, D.C. area who are interested in attending a college or university in any state and enrolling in the Navy Reserve Officers Training Corps (NROTC) program.

Eligibility This program is open to African American and Hispanic seniors graduating from high schools in the Washington, D.C. metropolitan area who plan to enroll full time at an accredited 2- or 4-year college or university in any state. Applicants must be planning to enroll in the NROTC program. They must have a GPA of 3.0 or higher and be U.S. citizens or permanent residents. Selection is based on academic achievement, community involvement, and financial need.

Financial data The stipend is $1,500.

Duration 1 year; nonrenewable.

Additional information If the recipient fails to enroll in the NROTC unit, all scholarship funds must be returned.

Number awarded 1 each year.

Deadline March of each year.

[359]
MINORITIES IN HOSPITALITY SCHOLARS PROGRAM

International Franchise Association
Attn: IFA Educational Foundation
1501 K Street, N.W., Suite 350
Washington, DC 20005
(202) 662-0784   Fax: (202) 628-0812
E-mail: mbrewer@franchise.org
Web: www.franchise.org/Scholarships.aspx

Summary To provide financial assistance to African American and other minority students working on an undergraduate degree related to hospitality.

Eligibility This program is open to college sophomores, juniors, and seniors who are U.S. citizens and members of a minority group (defined as African Americans, American Indians, Hispanic Americans, and Asian Americans). Applicants must be working on a degree in a field related to the hospitality industry. Along with their application, they must submit a 500-word essay on why they should be selected to receive this scholarship. Financial need is not considered in the selection process.

Financial data The stipend is $2,000.

Duration 1 year.

Additional information This program is cosponsored by the IFA Educational Foundation and Choice Hotels International.

Number awarded 1 or more each year.

Deadline January of each year.

[360]
MINORITIES IN MARINE AND ENVIRONMENTAL SCIENCES INTERNSHIP PROGRAM

South Carolina Department of Natural Resources
Attn: Marine Resources Division
217 Fort Johnson Road
P.O. Box 12559
Charleston, SC 29422-2559
(843) 953-9840   Fax: (843) 953-9820
E-mail: Kingsley-SmithP@dnr.sc.gov
Web: www.dnr.sc.gov/marine/minority/index.htm

Summary To provide African American and other minority undergraduate students with an opportunity to engage in summer research activities in marine and environmental sciences on James Island, South Carolina.

Eligibility This program is open to minority undergraduate students at colleges and universities in any state who have a GPA of 2.5 or higher in their major and 2.0 overall. Applicants must be majoring in a field of marine and environmental sciences, including chemistry, marine biology, fisheries science, toxicology, microbiology, estuarine and wetland ecology, and natural resource management and policy. They must be interested in participating in a summer research experience on James Island, near Charleston, South Carolina, that includes participating in field work, meeting successful minority scientists, taking classes, and conducting an independent research project under the mentorship of scientists from the Marine Resources Center in Charleston. They must submit transcripts, 2 letters of recommendation, and a written statement of interests and goals. U.S. citizenship or permanent resident status is required.

Financial data Interns receive a stipend of $4,500 and support for living and travel costs.

Duration 10 weeks during the summer.

Additional information This program, which began in 1989, receives support from the National Science Foundation (through its Research Experiences for Undergraduates program) and the National Oceanic and Atmospheric Administration.

Number awarded 6 to 8 each year.

Deadline March of each year.

[361]
MINORITY ACCESS INTERNSHIP

Minority Access, Inc.
Attn: Directory of Internship Program
5214 Baltimore Avenue
Hyattsville, MD 20781
(301) 779-7100   Fax: (301) 779-9812
Web: www.minorityaccess.org

Summary To provide work experience to African American and other minority undergraduate and graduate students interested in internships at participating entities in Washington, D.C. and throughout the United States.

Eligibility This program is open to full-time undergraduate and graduate students who have a GPA of 3.0 or higher. Applicants must be U.S. citizens for most positions. All academic majors are eligible. Interns are selected by participating federal government and other agencies. Most of these are located in Washington, D.C., but placements may be made anywhere in the United States.

Financial data The weekly stipend is $450 for sophomores and juniors, $500 for seniors, or $550 for graduate and professional students. In addition, most internships include paid round-trip travel between home and the internship location.

Duration Spring internships are 5 months, starting in January; summer internships are 3 months, starting in August; fall internships are 4 months, starting in September.

Additional information Minority Access, Inc. is committed to the diversification of institutions, federal agencies, and corporations of all kinds and to improving their recruitment, retention, and enhancement of minorities. The majority of interns are placed in the Washington, D.C. metropolitan area. Both full-time and part-time internships are awarded. Students may receive academic credit for full-time internships. Students are expected to pay all housing costs. They are required to attend a pre-employment session in Washington, D.C., all seminars and workshops hosted by Minority Access, and any mandatory activities sponsored by the host agency.

Number awarded Varies each year.

Deadline February of each year for summer internships; June of each year for fall internships; and November of each year for spring internships.

[362]
MINORITY AFFAIRS COMMITTEE AWARD FOR OUTSTANDING SCHOLASTIC ACHIEVEMENT

American Institute of Chemical Engineers
Attn: Minority Affairs Committee
Three Park Avenue
New York, NY 10016-5991
(646) 495-1348   Fax: (646) 495-1504
E-mail: awards@aiche.org
Web: www.aiche.org/About/Awards/MACScholastic.aspx

Summary To recognize and reward African American and other underrepresented minority students majoring in chemical engineering who serve as role models for other minority students.

Eligibility Members of the American Institute of Chemical Engineers (AIChE) may nominate any chemical engineering student who serves as a role model for minority students in that field. Nominees must be members of a minority group that is underrepresented in chemical engineering (i.e., African American, Hispanic, Native American, Alaskan Native). They must have a GPA of 3.0 or higher. Along with their application, they must submit a 300-word essay on their immediate plans after graduation, areas of chemical engineering of most interest, and long-range career plans. Selection is based on that essay, academic record, participation in AIChE student chapter and professional or civic activities, and financial need.

Financial data The award consists of a plaque and a $1,500 honorarium.

Duration The award is presented annually.

Additional information This award was first presented in 1996.

Number awarded 1 each year.

Deadline Nominations must be submitted by May of each year.

[363]
MINORITY ENTREPRENEURS SCHOLARSHIP PROGRAM

International Franchise Association
Attn: IFA Educational Foundation
1501 K Street, N.W., Suite 350
Washington, DC 20005
(202) 662-0784   Fax: (202) 628-0812
E-mail: mbrewer@franchise.org
Web: www.franchise.org/Scholarships.aspx

Summary To provide financial assistance to African Americans, other minority students, and adult entrepreneurs enrolled in academic or professional development programs related to franchising.

Eligibility This program is open to 1) college students enrolled at an accredited college or university, and 2) adult entrepreneurs who have at least 5 years of business ownership or managerial experience. Applicants must be U.S. citizens and members of a minority group (defined as African Americans, American Indians, Hispanic Americans, and Asian Americans). Students should be enrolled in courses or programs relating to business, finance, marketing, hospitality, franchising, or entrepreneurship. Adult entrepreneurs should be enrolled in professional development courses related to franchising, such as those recognized by the Institute of Certified Franchise Executives (ICFE). All applicants must submit a 500-word essay on why they want the scholarship and their career goals. Financial need is not considered in the selection process.

Financial data   The stipend is $3,000.

Duration   1 year.

Additional information   This program is cosponsored by the IFA Educational Foundation and Marriott International.

Number awarded   5 each year.

Deadline   June of each year.

[364]
MINORITY GEOSCIENCE STUDENT SCHOLARSHIPS

American Geological Institute
Attn: Minority Participation Program
4220 King Street
Alexandria, VA 22302-1502
(703) 379-2480, ext. 227   Fax: (703) 379-7563
E-mail: mpp@agiweb.org
Web: www.agiweb.org/mpp/index.html

Summary   To provide financial assistance to African American and other underrepresented minority undergraduate or graduate students interested in working on a degree in the geosciences.

Eligibility   This program is open to members of ethnic minority groups underrepresented in the geosciences (Blacks, Hispanics, American Indians, Eskimos, Hawaiians, and Samoans). U.S. citizenship is required. Applicants must be full-time students enrolled in an accredited institution working on an undergraduate or graduate degree in the geosciences, including geology, geochemistry, geophysics, hydrology, meteorology, physical oceanography, planetary geology, or earth science education; students in other natural sciences, mathematics, or engineering are not eligible. Selection is based on a 250-word essay on career goals and why the applicant has chosen a geoscience as a major, work experience, recommendations, honors and awards, extracurricular activities, and financial need.

Financial data   Stipends range from $500 to $3,000 per year.

Duration   1 academic year; renewable if the recipient maintains satisfactory performance.

Additional information   Funding for this program is provided by ExxonMobil Corporation, ConocoPhillips, ChevronTexaco Corporation, Marathon Corporation, and the Seismological Society of America.

Number awarded   Varies each year; recently, 18 of these scholarships were awarded.

Deadline   March of each year.

[365]
MINORITY SCHOLARSHIP AWARD FOR ACADEMIC EXCELLENCE IN PHYSICAL THERAPY

American Physical Therapy Association
Attn: Honors and Awards Program
1111 North Fairfax Street
Alexandria, VA 22314-1488
(703) 684-APTA   Toll Free: (800) 999-APTA
Fax: (703) 684-7343   TDD: (703) 683-6748
E-mail: executivedept@apta.org
Web: www.apta.org

Summary   To provide financial assistance to African American and other minority students who are interested in becoming a physical therapist or physical therapy assistant.

Eligibility   This program is open to U.S. citizens and permanent residents who are members of the following minority groups: African American or Black, Asian, Native Hawaiian or other Pacific Islander, American Indian or Alaska Native, or Hispanic/Latino. Applicants must be in the final year of a professional physical therapy or physical therapy assistant education program. They must submit a personal essay outlining their professional goals and minority service. U.S. citizenship or permanent resident status is required. Selection is based on 1) demonstrated evidence of contributions in the area of minority affairs and services with an emphasis on contributions made while enrolled in a physical therapy program; 2) potential to contribute to the profession of physical therapy; and 3) scholastic achievement.

Financial data   The stipend varies; recently, minimum awards were $6,000 for physical therapy students or $2,500 for physical therapy assistant students.

Duration   1 year.

Number awarded   Varies each year; recently, 8 of these awards were granted: 7 to professional physical therapy students and 1 to a physical therapy assistant student.

Deadline   November of each year.

[366]
MINORITY SCHOLARSHIP AWARDS FOR COLLEGE STUDENTS IN CHEMICAL ENGINEERING

American Institute of Chemical Engineers
Attn: Minority Affairs Committee
Three Park Avenue
New York, NY 10016-5991
(646) 495-1348   Fax: (646) 495-1504
E-mail: awards@aiche.org
Web: www.aiche.org/Students/Scholarships/index.aspx

Summary   To provide financial assistance for the undergraduate study of chemical engineering to African American and other underrepresented minority college student members of the American Institute of Chemical Engineers (AIChE).

Eligibility   This program is open to undergraduate student AIChE members who are also members of a minority group that is underrepresented in chemical engineering (African Americans, Hispanics, Native Americans, and Alaskan Natives). They must have a GPA of 3.0 or higher. Along with their application, they must submit a 300-word essay on their immediate plans after graduation, areas of chemical engineering of most interest, and long-range career plans. Selection is based on that essay, academic record, participation in AIChE student chapter and professional or civic activities, and financial need.

Financial data The stipend is $1,000.

Duration 1 year; nonrenewable.

Number awarded Approximately 10 each year.

Deadline June of each year.

[367]
MINORITY SCHOLARSHIP AWARDS FOR INCOMING COLLEGE FRESHMEN IN CHEMICAL ENGINEERING

American Institute of Chemical Engineers
Attn: Minority Affairs Committee
Three Park Avenue
New York, NY 10016-5991
(646) 495-1348　　　　Fax: (646) 495-1504
E-mail: awards@aiche.org
Web: www.aiche.org/Students/Scholarships/index.aspx

Summary To provide financial assistance to African American and other incoming minority freshmen who are interested in studying science or engineering in college.

Eligibility Eligible are members of a minority group that is underrepresented in chemical engineering (African Americans, Hispanics, Native Americans, and Alaskan Natives). Applicants must be graduating high school seniors planning to enroll at a 4-year university with a major in science or engineering. They must be nominated by an American Institute of Chemical Engineers (AIChE) local section. Selection is based on academic record (including a GPA of 3.0 or higher), participation in school and work activities, a 300-word letter outlining the reasons for choosing science or engineering, and financial need.

Financial data The stipend is $1,000.

Duration 1 year; nonrenewable.

Number awarded Approximately 10 each year.

Deadline Nominations must be submitted by June of each year.

[368]
MINORITY SCIENCE WRITERS INTERNSHIP

American Association for the Advancement of Science
Directorate for Education and Human Resources
Attn: Minority Science Writers Internship
1200 New York Avenue, N.W., Room 639
Washington, DC 20005-3920
(202) 326-6441　　　　Fax: (202) 371-9849
E-mail: raculver@aaas.org
Web: www.aaas.org

Summary To provide summer work experience at *Science* magazine to African American and other minority undergraduate students.

Eligibility This program is open to minority undergraduates with a serious interest in science writing. Preference is given to students majoring in journalism. Applicants must be interested in a summer internship at *Science* magazine, the journal of the American Association for the Advancement of Science (AAAS). Along with their application, they must submit an 800-word essay on their commitment to journalism, their career goals, their thoughts about science and science writing, and what they hope to get out of this opportunity. A telephone interview is conducted of semifinalists.

Financial data Interns receive a salary and reimbursement of travel expenses to the work site in Washington, D.C.

Duration 10 weeks during the summer.

Number awarded Varies each year.

Deadline February of each year.

[369]
MINORITY TEACHERS OF ILLINOIS SCHOLARSHIP PROGRAM

Illinois Student Assistance Commission
Attn: Scholarship and Grant Services
1755 Lake Cook Road
Deerfield, IL 60015-5209
(847) 948-8550　　　　Toll Free: (800) 899-ISAC
Fax: (847) 831-8549　　　TDD: (800) 526-0844
E-mail: collegezone@isac.org
Web: www.collegezone.com/studentzone/407_655.htm

Summary To provide funding to African Americans and other minority students in Illinois who plan to become teachers at the preschool, elementary, or secondary level.

Eligibility Applicants must be Illinois residents, U.S. citizens or eligible noncitizens, members of a minority group (African American/Black, Hispanic American, Asian American, or Native American), and high school graduates or holders of a General Educational Development (GED) certificate. They must be enrolled in college full time at the sophomore level or above, have a GPA of 2.5 or higher, not be in default on any student loan, and be enrolled or accepted for enrollment in a teacher education program. U.S. citizenship or eligible noncitizenship status is required.

Financial data Grants up to $5,000 per year are awarded. This is a scholarship/loan program. Recipients must agree to teach full time 1 year for each year of support received. The teaching agreement may be fulfilled at a public, private, or parochial preschool, elementary school, or secondary school in Illinois; at least 30% of the student body at those schools must be minority. It must be fulfilled within the 5-year period following the completion of the undergraduate program for which the scholarship was awarded. The time period may be extended if the recipient serves in the U.S. armed forces, enrolls full time in a graduate program related to teaching, becomes temporarily disabled, is unable to find employment as a teacher at a qualifying school, or takes additional courses on at least a half-time basis to obtain certification as a teacher in Illinois. Recipients who fail to honor this work obligation must repay the award with 5% interest.

Duration 1 year; may be renewed for a total of 8 semesters or 12 quarters.

Number awarded Varies each year.

Deadline Priority consideration is given to applications received by February of each year.

[370]
MIRIAM WEINSTEIN PEACE AND JUSTICE EDUCATION AWARD

Philanthrofund Foundation
Attn: Scholarship Committee
1409 Willow Street, Suite 210
Minneapolis, MN 55403-3251
(612) 870-1806   Toll Free: (800) 435-1402
Fax: (612) 871-6587   E-mail: info@PfundOnline.org
Web: www.pfundonline.org/scholarships.html

Summary   To provide financial assistance to African Americans and other minority students from Minnesota who are associated with gay, lesbian, bisexual, and transgender (GLBT) activities and interested in working on a degree in education.

Eligibility   This program is open to residents of Minnesota and students attending a Minnesota educational institution who are members of a religious, racial, or ethnic minority. Applicants must be self-identified as GLBT or from a GLBT family and have demonstrated a commitment to peace and justice issues. They may be attending or planning to attend trade school, technical college, college, or university (as an undergraduate or graduate student). Preference is given to students who have completed at least 2 years of college and are working on a degree in education. Selection is based on the applicant's 1) affirmation of GLBT identity or commitment to GLBT communities; 2) participation and leadership in community and/or GLBT activities; and 3) service as role model, mentor, and/or adviser for the GLBT community.

Financial data   The stipend is $3,000. Funds must be used for tuition, books, fees, or dissertation expenses.

Duration   1 year.

Number awarded   1 each year.

Deadline   January of each year.

[371]
MISS BLACK AMERICA

Miss Black America Pageant
P.O. Box 25668
Philadelphia, PA 19144
(215) 844-8872 E-mail: Contact@MissBlackAmerica.com
Web: www.missblackamerica.com

Summary   To recognize and reward beautiful and talented Black American women.

Eligibility   All African American women between 17 and 29 years of age, including married contestants and contestants with children, are eligible. Finalists who compete in the national pageant are selected after competitions on the local and state levels. The winner at the national pageant is chosen by a panel of judges on the basis of beauty, talent, and personality.

Financial data   Miss Black America receives a cash award and an array of prizes.

Duration   The competition is held annually.

Additional information   This competition began in 1968. There is a $50 application fee and an $800 sponsorship fee.

Number awarded   1 each year.

Deadline   December of each year.

[372]
MISSISSIPPI CHAPTER AABE SCHOLARSHIPS

American Association of Blacks in Energy-Mississippi
  Chapter
Attn: Scholarship Committee Chair
P.O. Box 986
Jackson, MS 39205
E-mail: rkent@entergy.com
Web: www.aabe.org/index.php?component=pages&id=387

Summary   To provide financial assistance to African Americans and members of other underrepresented minority groups who are high school seniors in Mississippi and planning to major in an energy-related field at a college in any state.

Eligibility   This program is open to seniors graduating from high schools in Mississippi and planning to attend a 4-year college or university in any state. Applicants must be African Americans, Hispanics, or Native Americans who have a GPA of 3.0 or higher and are able to demonstrate financial need. Their intended major must be computer technology, engineering, technology, mathematics, the physical sciences (chemistry, geology, meteorology, or physics only), or other energy-related field. Along with their application, they must submit a 350-word statement on why they should receive this scholarship, how their professional career objectives relate to energy, and any other relevant information.

Financial data   Stipends are $2,000 or $1,000.

Duration   1 year.

Additional information   Winners are eligible to compete for regional and national scholarships.

Number awarded   4 or more each year: 1 at $2,000 and 3 or more at $1,000.

Deadline   March of each year.

[373]
MISSOURI MINORITY TEACHER EDUCATION SCHOLARSHIP PROGRAM

Missouri Department of Higher Education
Attn: Student Financial Assistance
3515 Amazonas Drive
Jefferson City, MO 65109-5717
(573) 751-2361   Toll Free: (800) 473-6757
Fax: (573) 751-6635   E-mail: info@dhe.mo.gov
Web: www.dhe.mo.gov/minorityteaching.html

Summary   To provide funding to African American and other minority high school seniors, high school graduates, and college students in Missouri who are interested in preparing for a teaching career in mathematics or science.

Eligibility   This program is open to Missouri residents who are African American, Asian American, Hispanic American, or Native American. Applicants must be 1) high school seniors, college students, or returning adults (without a degree) who rank in the top 25% of their high school class and scored at or above the 75th percentile on the ACT or SAT examination; 2) individuals who have completed 30 college hours and have a cumulative GPA of 3.0 or better; or 3) baccalaureate degree-holders who are returning to an approved mathematics or science teacher education program. They must be a U.S. citizen or permanent resident or otherwise lawfully present in the United States. All applicants must be enrolled full time in an approved teacher education program at a community college, 4-year college, or university in Missouri. Selection is based on academic performance, the quantity and quality of school and community activities, range of interests and activities, leadership abilities, interpersonal skills, and desire to enter the field of education.

Financial data The stipend is $3,000 per year, of which $2,000 is provided by the state as a forgivable loan and $1,000 is provided by the school as a scholarship. Recipients must commit to teaching in a Missouri public elementary or secondary school for 5 years following graduation. If they fail to fulfill that obligation, they must repay the state portion of the scholarship with interest at 9.5%.

Duration Up to 4 years.

Number awarded Up to 100 each year.

Deadline February of each year.

[374]
MR. COLLEGIATE AFRICAN AMERICAN SCHOLARSHIP PROGRAM

Mr. Collegiate African American Scholarship Pageant
P.O. Box 2906
Prairie View, TX 77446
E-mail: mrcollegiateafricanamerican@gmail.com
Web: mrcollegiatepageant.blogspot.com

Summary To recognize and reward, with college scholarships, outstanding African American men who participate in a pageant.

Eligibility This competition is open to African American men between 18 and 30 years of age attending 4-year colleges and universities, especially Historically Black Colleges and Universities. Applicants must be interested in participating in a pageant where they are judged on a personal and private interview (20%), platform expression (25%), talent (35%), evening wear (10%), and on-stage interview (10%).

Financial data A total of $10,000 in scholarships and prizes are awarded.

Duration The pageant is held annually.

Additional information This program was established in 1990. The pageant is held in Prairie View, Texas.

Number awarded Varies each year.

Deadline February of each year.

[375]
MRS. PATRICIA THOMPSON SCHOLARSHIP

National Naval Officers Association-Washington, D.C.
  Chapter
Attn: Scholarship Program
2701 Park Center Drive, A1108
Alexandria, VA 22302
(703) 566-3840   Fax: (703) 566-3813
E-mail: Stephen.Williams@Navy.mil
Web: dcnnoa.memberlodge.com

Summary To provide financial assistance to male African American high school seniors from the Washington, D.C. area who are interested in attending college in any state.

Eligibility This program is open to male African American seniors graduating from high schools in the Washington, D.C. metropolitan area who plan to enroll full time at an accredited 2- or 4-year college or university in any state. Applicants must have a GPA of 2.5 or higher. Selection is based on academic achievement, community involvement, and financial need.

Financial data The stipend is $1,000.

Duration 1 year; nonrenewable.

Additional information Recipients are not required to join or affiliate with the military in any way.

Number awarded 1 each year.

Deadline March of each year.

[376]
MULTICULTURAL ADVERTISING INTERN PROGRAM

American Association of Advertising Agencies
Attn: Manager of Diversity Programs
405 Lexington Avenue, 18th Floor
New York, NY 10174-1801
(212) 850-0732   Toll Free: (800) 676-9333
Fax: (212) 682-2028   E-mail: maip@aaaa.org
Web: www2.aaaa.org

Summary To provide African American and other minority students with summer work experience in advertising agencies and to present them with an overview of the agency business.

Eligibility This program is open to U.S. citizens and permanent residents who are Black/African American, Asian/Asian American, Pacific Islander, Hispanic, North American Indian/Native American, or multiracial and either 1) college juniors, seniors, or graduate students at an accredited college or university, or 2) students at any academic level attending a portfolio school of the sponsor. Applicants may be majoring in any field, but they must be able to demonstrate a serious commitment to preparing for a career in advertising. They must have a GPA of 3.0 or higher. Students with a cumulative GPA of 2.7 to 2.9 are encouraged to apply, but they must complete an additional essay question.

Financial data Interns are paid a salary of at least $70 per day. If they do not live in the area of their host agencies, they may stay in housing arranged by the sponsor. They are responsible for a percentage of the cost of housing and materials.

Duration 10 weeks during the summer.

Additional information Interns may be assigned duties in the following departments: account management, broadcast production, media buying/planning, creative (art direction or copywriting), digital/interactive technologies, print production, strategic/account planning, or traffic. The portfolio schools are the AdCenter at Virginia Commonwealth University, the Creative Circus and the Portfolio Center in Atlanta, the Miami Ad School, the University of Texas at Austin, Pratt Institute, the Minneapolis College of Art and Design, and the Art Center College of Design in Pasadena, California.

Number awarded 70 to 100 each year.

Deadline December of each year.

[377]
MULTICULTURAL UNDERGRADUATE INTERNSHIPS AT THE GETTY CENTER

Getty Foundation
Attn: Multicultural Undergraduate Internships
1200 Getty Center Drive, Suite 800
Los Angeles, CA 90049-1685
(310) 440-7320   Fax: (310) 440-7703
E-mail: summerinterns@getty.edu
Web: www.getty.edu

Summary To provide summer work experience at facilities of the Getty Center to African American and other minority undergraduates with ties to Los Angeles County, California.

Eligibility This program is open to currently-enrolled undergraduates who either reside or attend college in Los Angeles County, California. Applicants must be members of groups currently underrepresented in museum professions and fields related to the visual arts and humanities: individuals of African American, Asian, Latino/Hispanic, Native American, or Pacific Islander descent. They may be majoring in any field, including the sciences and technology, and are not required to have demonstrated a previous commitment to the visual arts. Along with their application, they must submit a personal statement of up to 500 words on why they are interested in this internship, including what they hope to gain from the program, their interest or involvement in issues of multiculturalism, aspects of their past experience that they feel are most relevant to the application, and any specific career or educational avenues they are interested in exploring. U.S. citizenship or permanent resident status is required.

Financial data The stipend is $3,500.

Duration 10 weeks during the summer.

Additional information Internships provide training and work experience in such areas as conservation, curatorship, education, publications, and related programmatic activities.

Number awarded 15 to 20 each year.

Deadline February of each year.

[378]
MUSIC AND CHRISTIAN ARTS MINISTRY SCHOLARSHIP

African Methodist Episcopal Church
Attn: Christian Education Department
Music and Christian Arts Ministry
500 Eighth Avenue South
Nashville, TN 37203
Toll Free: (800) 525-7282   Fax: (615) 726-1866
E-mail: cedoffice@ameced.com
Web: www.ameced.com/music.shtml

Summary To provide financial assistance to members of African Methodist Episcopal (AME) churches who are interested in working on an undergraduate degree in music at a Black-related college in any state.

Eligibility This program is open to graduating high school seniors who are members of an AME congregation. Applicants must be planning to attend an AME-supported college or university or an Historically Black College or University (HBCU) in any state to study music. They must be planning to assume a music leadership position in a local AME church. Along with their application, they must submit a current high school transcript, 3 letters of recommendation (including 1 from their music teacher or director and 1 from their pastor), a 1-page essay on why they should be awarded this scholarship, and a CD or cassette recording of a musical performance. Selection is based on academic achievement, school involvement, music involvement and performance genre, community involvement, and other honors and awards.

Financial data The stipend is $2,000 per year. Funds are sent directly to the student upon proof of enrollment.

Duration 1 year; recipients may apply for 1 additional year if they earn a GPA of 3.3 or higher in their first year.

Number awarded 1 or more each year.

Deadline April of each year.

[379]
MUTUAL OF OMAHA ACTUARIAL SCHOLARSHIP FOR MINORITY STUDENTS

Mutual of Omaha
Attn: Strategic Staffing-Actuarial Recruitment
Mutual of Omaha Plaza
Omaha, NE 68175
(402) 351-3300   E-mail: diversity@mutualofomaha.com
Web: www.mutualofomaha.com

Summary To provide financial assistance and work experience to African American and other minority undergraduate students who are preparing for an actuarial career.

Eligibility This program is open to members of minority groups (African American, Hispanic, Native American, Asian or Pacific Islander, or Alaskan Eskimo) who have completed at least 24 semester hours of full-time study. Applicants must be working on an actuarial or mathematics-related degree with the goal of preparing for an actuarial career. They must have a GPA of 3.0 or higher and have passed at least 1 actuarial examination. Prior to accepting the award, they must be available to complete a summer internship at the sponsor's home office in Omaha, Nebraska. Along with their application, they must submit a 1-page personal statement on why they are interested in becoming an actuary and how they are preparing themselves for an actuarial career. Status as a U.S. citizen, permanent resident, or asylee or refugee must be established.

Financial data The scholarship stipend is $5,000 per year. Funds are paid directly to the student. For the internship, students receive an hourly rate of pay, subsidized housing, and financial incentives for successful examination results received during the internship period.

Duration 1 year. Recipients may reapply if they maintain a cumulative GPA of 3.0 or higher.

Number awarded Varies each year.

Deadline October of each year.

[380]
N. JOYCE PAYNE/MILLER BREWING COMPANY SCHOLARSHIP

Thurgood Marshall College Fund
Attn: Scholarship Manager
80 Maiden Lane, Suite 2204
New York, NY 10038
(212) 573-8487   Toll Free: (877) 690-8673
Fax: (212) 573-8497   E-mail: srogers@tmcfund.org
Web: www.thurgoodmarshallfund.net

Summary To provide financial assistance to African American males enrolled at colleges and universities that are members of the Thurgood Marshall College Fund (TMCF).

Eligibility This program is open to African American males currently enrolled full time at 1 of the 47 colleges and universities that are TMCF members. Applicants must have a GPA of 3.0 or higher and be able to demonstrate financial need. U.S. citizenship is required.

Financial data The stipend is $4,400.

Duration 1 year.

Additional information This program was originally sponsored by Miller Brewing Company (now MillerCoors). The 47 participating TMCF institutions are Alabama A&M University, Alabama State University, Albany State University, Alcorn State University, Bluefield State College, Bowie State University, Central State University (Ohio), Charles R. Drew University of Medicine (California), Cheyney University of Pennsylvania, Chicago State University, Coppin State College, Delaware State University, Elizabeth City State University, Fayetteville State University, Florida A&M University, Fort Valley State University, Grambling State University, Harris-Stowe State College, Howard University, Jackson State University, Kentucky State University, Langston University, Lincoln University (Missouri), Lincoln University (Pennsylvania), Medgar Evers College (New York), Mississippi Valley State University, Morgan State University, Norfolk State University, North Carolina A&T State University, North Carolina Central University, Prairie View A&M University, Savannah State University, South Carolina State University, Southern University and A&M College, Southern University at New Orleans, Southern University at Shreveport-Bossier City, Tennessee State University, Texas Southern University, Tuskegee University, University of Arkansas at Pine Bluff, University of the District of Columbia, University of Maryland-Eastern Shore, University of the Virgin Islands, Virginia State University, West Virginia State College, Winston-Salem State University, and York College.

Number awarded 1 each year.

Deadline July of each year.

[381]
NAACP HBCU SCHOLARSHIPS

National Association for the Advancement of Colored People
Attn: Education Department
4805 Mt. Hope Drive
Baltimore, MD 21215-3297
(410) 580-5760   Toll Free: (877) NAACP-98
E-mail: youth@naacpnet.org
Web: www.naacp.org/youth/scholarships/information

Summary To provide financial assistance to members of the National Association for the Advancement of Colored People (NAACP) who are entering freshmen or enrolled at an Historically Black College or University (HBCU).

Eligibility This program is open to students currently enrolled full time or entering an HBCU with a GPA of 2.5 or higher. Applicants must be able to demonstrate financial need (family income must be less than $16,245 for a family of 1, ranging up to $49,905 for a family of) and U.S. citizens. Along with their application, they must submit a 1-page essay on their interest in their major and a career, their life's ambition, what they hope to accomplish in their lifetime, and what posi-

tion they hope to attain. Membership and participation in the NAACP are highly desirable.

Financial data The stipend is $2,000 per year.

Duration 1 year; recipients may apply for renewal.

Additional information Renewal awards may be reduced or denied based on insufficient NAACP activities.

Number awarded Varies each year.

Deadline March of each year.

[382]
NABA 20 PEARLS SCHOLARSHIP

National Association of Black Accountants
Attn: National Scholarship Program
7474 Greenway Center Drive, Suite 1120
Greenbelt, MD 20770
(301) 474-NABA, ext. 114   Fax: (301) 474-3114
E-mail: customerservice@nabainc.org
Web: www.nabainc.org

Summary To provide financial assistance to student members of the National Association of Black Accountants (NABA) who are also members of Alpha Kappa Alpha sorority and working on an undergraduate or graduate degree in a field related to accounting.

Eligibility This program is open to NABA members who are also Alpha Kappa Alpha members and enrolled full time as 1) an undergraduate freshman, sophomore, junior, or first-semester senior majoring in accounting, business, or finance at a 4-year college or university; or 2) a graduate student working on a master's degree in accounting. High school seniors are not eligible. Applicants must have a GPA of 3.5 or higher in their major and 3.3 or higher overall. Selection is based on grades, financial need, and a 500-word autobiography that discusses career objectives, leadership abilities, community activities, and involvement in NABA.

Financial data The stipend is $1,500.

Duration 1 year.

Number awarded 1 each year.

Deadline January of each year.

[383]
NABJ CNN SCHOLARSHIPS

National Association of Black Journalists
Attn: Program Coordinator
8701-A Adelphi Road
Adelphi, MD 20783-1716
(301) 445-7100, ext. 108   Toll Free: (866) 479-NABJ
Fax: (301) 445-7101   E-mail: nabj@nabj.org
Web: www.nabj.org/programs/scholarships/cnn/index.php

Summary To provide financial assistance to high school senior members of the National Association of Black Journalists (NABJ) who are planning to major in broadcast journalism in college.

Eligibility This program is open to African American graduating high school seniors who are planning to attend an accredited 4-year college or university. Applicants must be NABJ members, be planning to major in broadcast journalism, have a GPA of 3.0 or higher, and have a record of community involvement. Along with their application, they must submit 2 letters of recommendation and an essay of 800 to 1,000 words explaining why they want to be a journalist, what they feel is the biggest obstacle currently facing African

Americans, and why they feel they are deserving of this scholarship.

Financial data   The stipend is $6,250 per year. Funds are paid directly to the recipient's college or university.

Duration   4 years, provided the recipient maintains a GPA of 3.0 or higher.

Additional information   This program was established in 2006 by CNN to celebrate its 25th anniversary.

Number awarded   2 each year.

Deadline   April of each year.

[384]
NABJ SCHOLARSHIPS

National Association of Black Journalists
Attn: Program Coordinator
8701-A Adelphi Road
Adelphi, MD 20783-1716
(301) 445-7100, ext. 108   Toll Free: (866) 479-NABJ
Fax: (301) 445-7101   E-mail: nabj@nabj.org
Web: www.nabj.org

Summary   To provide financial assistance to undergraduate or graduate student members of the National Association of Black Journalists (NABJ) who are majoring in a field related to journalism.

Eligibility   This program is open to African American undergraduate or graduate students who are currently attending an accredited 4-year college or university. Applicants must be majoring in broadcast (radio or television), print, or online journalism and have a GPA of 2.5 or higher. They must be NABJ members. Along with their application, they must submit samples of their work, an official college transcript, 2 letters of recommendation, a resume, and a 500- to 800-word essay describing their accomplishments as a student journalist, their career goals, and their financial need.

Financial data   The stipend is $2,500. Funds are paid directly to the recipient's college or university.

Duration   1 year; nonrenewable.

Number awarded   Varies each year; recently, 10 of these scholarships were awarded.

Deadline   April of each year.

[385]
NABNA-FEEA SCHOLARSHIP PROGRAM

National Association of Black Narcotic Agents
c/o Federal Employee Education and Assistance Fund
Attn: Scholarship Program
3333 South Wadsworth Boulevard, Suite 300
Lakewood, CO 80227
(303) 933-7580   Toll Free: (800) 323-4140
Fax: (303) 933-7587   E-mail: admin@feea.org
Web: www.feea.org

Summary   To provide financial assistance for college or graduate school to members of the National Association of Black Narcotic Agents (NABNA) and their dependents.

Eligibility   This program is open to federal employees who are NABNA members and their dependent spouses and children entering or enrolled in an accredited 2- or 4-year undergraduate, graduate, or postgraduate program. Dependents must be full-time students; federal employees may be part-time students. Applicants or their sponsoring federal employee must have at least 3 years of civilian federal ser-

vice. Along with their application, they must submit a 2-page essay on a topic related to a career in public service with the federal government, a letter of recommendation, a transcript with a GPA of 3.0 or higher, and a copy of their federal "Notice of Personnel Action;" high school seniors must also submit a copy of their ACT, SAT, or other examination scores. Financial need is not considered in the selection process.

Financial data   The stipend is $1,000 per year.

Duration   1 year; may be renewed.

Additional information   This program is jointly administered by NABNA and the Federal Employee Education and Assistance Fund (FEEA).

Number awarded   1 or more each year.

Deadline   March of each year.

[386]
NACME PRE-ENGINEERING STUDENT SCHOLARSHIPS

National Action Council for Minorities in Engineering
Attn: University Programs
440 Hamilton Avenue, Suite 302
White Plains, NY 10601-1813
(914) 539-4010   Fax: (914) 539-4032
E-mail: scholarships@nacme.org
Web: www.nacmebacksme.org/NBM_C.aspx?pageid=153

Summary   To provide financial assistance to African American and other underrepresented minority high school seniors interested in studying engineering or related fields in college.

Eligibility   This program is open to African American, Latino, and American Indian high school seniors who are in the top 10% of their graduating class and have demonstrated academic excellence, leadership skills, and a commitment to science and engineering as a career. Candidates must have been accepted as a full-time student at an ABET-accredited engineering program. They must be nominated by their school (each high school may nominate only 1 student). Fields of study include all areas of engineering as well as computer science, materials science, mathematics, operations research, or physics. Letters of nomination must be accompanied by a transcript, SAT or ACT report form, resume, and 100-word statement of why the student should receive this scholarship.

Financial data   The stipend is $1,500. Funds are sent directly to the recipient's university.

Duration   1 year.

Number awarded   Varies each year; recently, 95 of these scholarships were awarded.

Deadline   April of each year.

[387]
NASA MOTIVATING UNDERGRADUATES IN SCIENCE AND TECHNOLOGY (MUST) SCHOLARSHIP PROGRAM

National Aeronautics and Space Administration
Attn: Vanessa R. Webbs, MUST Project Manager
NASA John H. Glenn Research Center at Lewis Field
2100 Brookpark Road, M.S. 500-107
Cleveland, OH 44135
(216) 433-3768   Fax: (216) 433-3344
E-mail: vanessa.r.webbs@nasa.gov
Web: www.nasa.gov

Summary To provide financial assistance to African Americans and members of other underrepresented groups who are working on an undergraduate degree in a field of science, technology, engineering, or mathematics (STEM).
Eligibility This program is open to U.S. citizens from an underrepresented group, including women, African Americans, Hispanic Americans, Native Americans, and persons with disabilities. Applicants must be entering their sophomore or junior year at an accredited college or university in the 50 states or Puerto Rico as a full-time student. They must have a GPA of 3.0 or higher and a major in a STEM field of study.
Financial data Stipends provide payment of 50% of the tuition and fees at the recipient's institution, to a maximum of $10,000.
Duration 1 year; may be renewed 1 additional year.
Deadline January of each year.

[388]
NASA SCIENCE AND TECHNOLOGY INSTITUTE (NSTI) SUMMER SCHOLARS PROGRAM

United Negro College Fund Special Programs
  Corporation
Attn: NASA Science and Technology Institute
6402 Arlington Boulevard, Suite 600
Falls Church, VA 22042
(703) 677-3400   Toll Free: (800) 530-6232
Fax: (703) 205-7645   E-mail: portal@uncfsp.org
Web: www.uncfsp.org

Summary To provide an internship opportunity for African American and other underrepresented undergraduate students to work on a summer research project at designated research centers of the U.S. National Aeronautics and Space Administration (NASA).
Eligibility This program is open to current college freshmen, sophomores, and juniors at accredited institutions who are members of underrepresented groups, including women, ethnic minorities, and persons with disabilities. Applicants must be working on a degree in a science, technology, engineering, or mathematics (STEM) field and have a GPA of 3.0 or higher. They must be interested in working on a research project during the summer at Ames Research Center (Moffett Field, California), Johnson Space Center (Houston, Texas), or Glenn Research Center (Cleveland, Ohio). U.S. citizenship is required.
Financial data A stipend is provided (amount not specified).
Duration 10 weeks during the summer.
Additional information This program, which began in 2006, is funded by NASA and administered by the United Negro College Fund Special Programs Corporation.
Number awarded Varies each year.
Deadline January of each year.

[389]
NASPA UNDERGRADUATE FELLOWSHIP PROGRAM

National Association of Student Personnel Administrators
Attn: NUFP
111 K Street, N.E., Tenth Floor
Washington, DC 20002
(202) 204-6079   Fax: (202) 893-5737
E-mail: nvictoria@naspa.org
Web: www.naspa.org/programs/nufp/index.cfm

Summary To provide summer work experience and leadership training to African Americans and other minorities, students with disabilities, and persons who identify as lesbian, gay, bisexual, or transgender (LGBT) and are completing their second year in college.
Eligibility Eligible to be nominated for this program are 1) ethnic minority students (Indigenous, African, Asian, or Hispanic Americans), 2) students with disabilities; or 3) students who identify as LGBT. Applicants must be completing their sophomore year in a 4-year institution or their second year in a 2-year transfer program. They must have a GPA of 2.5 or higher and be able to demonstrate academic promise and an interest in a future in higher education.
Financial data Participants are offered a paid summer internship, and all expenses are paid to attend the leadership institutes.
Duration The internship lasts 8 weeks during the summer. Leadership institutes last 4 days.
Additional information The program was initiated in the 1989-90 academic year as the Minority Undergraduate Fellows Program (MUFP). In 2000-01 it was broadened to include students with disabilities and in 2005 was renamed and expanded again to include LGBT students. It offers 3 main components: 1) participation in a 1- or 2-year internship or field experience under the guidance of a mentor; 2) participation in a summer leadership institute designed to enhance skill building and career development; and 3) participation in an 8-week paid summer internship designed to encourage the development of future student affairs and higher education administrators.
Number awarded Varies each year; recently, 65 undergraduates were participating in the program.
Deadline September of each year.

[390]
NATIONAL ACHIEVEMENT SCHOLARSHIP PROGRAM

National Merit Scholarship Corporation
Attn: National Achievement Scholarship Program
1560 Sherman Avenue, Suite 200
Evanston, IL 60201-4897
(847) 866-5100   Fax: (847) 866-5113
Web: www.nationalmerit.org/nasp.php

Summary To provide financial assistance for college to Black American high school seniors with exceptional scores on the SAT and/or PSAT/NMSQT.
Eligibility This program is open to Black American seniors who are enrolled full time in a secondary school and progressing normally toward graduation or completion of high school requirements. Applicants must be U.S. citizens (or intend to become a citizen as soon as qualified) and be plan-

ning to attend an accredited college or university in the United States. They must take the PSAT/NMSQT at the proper time in high school (no later than the 11th grade) and mark section 14 on the PSAT/NMSQT answer sheet, which identifies them as a Black American who is requesting consideration in the Achievement Program. Final selection is based on the student's academic record, a self-description, PSAT/NMSQT and SAT scores, and a recommendation written by the principal or another official. Financial information is not considered, nor are college choice, course of study, or career plans.

Financial data The stipend is $2,500.

Duration 1 year.

Additional information A sizeable group of each year's Achievement Program's nonwinners are brought to the attention of U.S. institutions of higher education for the College-Sponsored Achievement Program or for the Corporate-Sponsored Achievement Program. Each winner must enroll as a full-time day student in a course of study leading to 1 of the traditional baccalaureate degrees. Recipients must meet the standards of performance and terms set forth in their scholarship offer. Students who have completed high school, or who are now enrolled in college or have attended college in the past, are not eligible for consideration.

Number awarded Approximately 700 each year.

Deadline Applicants must take the PSAT/NMSQT no later than October of their junior year.

[391]
NATIONAL ASSOCIATION FOR EQUAL OPPORTUNITY IN HIGHER EDUCATION INCLUSION SCHOLARS PROGRAM

National Association for Equal Opportunity in Higher
  Education
Attn: Inclusion Scholars Program
209 Third Street, S.E.
Washington, DC 20003
(202) 552-3300   Fax: (202) 552-3330
Web: www.nafeo.org/community/index.php

Summary To provide financial assistance to high school seniors who have a disability and plan to attend a designated Historically Black College or University (HBCU).

Eligibility This program is open to high school seniors who have a disability, as defined by the Americans with Disabilities Act (ADA). Applicants must be planning to enroll full time at 1 of 3 designated HBCUs (that rotate annually). Along with their application, they must submit a 500-word essay that includes what they bring that makes them a real asset to the campus, what they hope to gain from their college experience at an HBCU, and the contributions they want to make to the world.

Financial data The stipend is $9,000 per year.

Duration 1 year; may be renewed up to 3 additional years, provided the recipient remains enrolled full time and maintains a GPA of 2.75 or higher.

Additional information This program, which began in 2010, is sponsored by AT&T. In its inaugural year, the designated HBCUs were Bethune-Cookman College (Daytona, Florida), Morgan State University (Baltimore, Maryland), and Tennessee State University (Nashville, Tennessee).

Number awarded 3 each year: 1 at each designated HBCU.

Deadline March of each year.

[392]
NATIONAL ASSOCIATION FOR EQUAL OPPORTUNITY INTERNSHIP PROGRAM

National Association for Equal Opportunity in Higher
  Education
Attn: Internship Program
209 Third Street, S.E.
Washington, DC 20003
(202) 552-3300   Fax: (202) 552-3330
E-mail: internships@nafeo.org
Web: www.nafeointernships.net/home.php

Summary To provide summer work experience in Washington, D.C. to undergraduate and graduate students enrolled at an Historically Black College or University (HBCU) or Predominantly Black Institute (PBI).

Eligibility This program is open undergraduate and graduate students currently enrolled at an HBCU or PBI. Applicants must be interested in a summer internship, mostly with federal agencies, in Washington, D.C. They must have a GPA of 3.0 or higher. Some positions require U.S. citizenship.

Financial data The stipend is $400 per week for undergraduates or $500 per week for graduate students. Other benefits include a housing stipend and a travel allowance of $200.

Duration 10 weeks during the summer.

Number awarded 1 or more each year.

Deadline March of each year.

[393]
NATIONAL ASSOCIATION OF BLACK ACCOUNTANTS MICROSOFT INNOVATION AWARD

National Association of Black Accountants
Attn: National Scholarship Program
7474 Greenway Center Drive, Suite 1120
Greenbelt, MD 20770
(301) 474-NABA, ext. 114   Fax: (301) 474-3114
E-mail: customerservice@nabainc.org
Web: www.nabainc.org

Summary To recognize and reward members of the National Association of Black Accountants (NABA) who submit outstanding essays on topics related to innovation in business.

Eligibility This competition is open to undergraduate student and professional members of NABA who are 18 years of age or older and U.S. citizens or equivalent. Applicants must submit a paper following an online template that addresses their choice from among 3 categories. Recently, those were 1) the recession challenge, on how they would, as CFO of Microsoft, respond to the financial challenges arising from the recession; 2) the green challenge, on how they would, as CFO of Microsoft, propose decreasing the firm's carbon footprint; or 3) the business challenger, in which they assess a change that would enable Microsoft to achieve majority market share. Based on those papers, 2 students and 2 professionals are invited to the NABA national convention, where they make an oral presentation of their ideas. The winner and runner-up are selected at the convention on the basis of quality, clarity, and overall creativity of recommendations; innovative incorporation of technology into the solution; feasibility of the recommendations; and presentation style and persuasiveness.

Financial data   The award is $10,000 for each winner and $2,500 for each runner-up.

Duration   The competition is held annually.

Additional information   This competition, first held in 2009, is sponsored by Microsoft.

Number awarded   2 winners (1 student and 1 professional) and 2 runners-up (1 student and 1 professional) are selected each year.

Deadline   May of each year.

[394]
NATIONAL ASSOCIATION OF BLACK ACCOUNTANTS NATIONAL SCHOLARSHIP

National Association of Black Accountants
Attn: National Scholarship Program
7474 Greenway Center Drive, Suite 1120
Greenbelt, MD 20770
(301) 474-NABA, ext. 114   Fax: (301) 474-3114
E-mail: customerservice@nabainc.org
Web: www.nabainc.org

Summary   To provide financial assistance to student members of the National Association of Black Accountants (NABA) who are working on an undergraduate or graduate degree in a field related to accounting.

Eligibility   This program is open to NABA members enrolled full time as 1) an undergraduate freshman, sophomore, junior, or first-semester senior majoring in accounting, business, or finance at a 4-year college or university; or 2) a graduate student working on a master's degree in accounting. High school seniors are not eligible. Applicants must have a GPA of 3.5 or higher in their major and 3.3 or higher overall. Selection is based on grades, financial need, and a 500-word autobiography that discusses career objectives, leadership abilities, community activities, and involvement in NABA.

Financial data   The stipend is $3,000.

Duration   1 year.

Number awarded   1 each year.

Deadline   January of each year.

[395]
NATIONAL ASSOCIATION OF BLACK JOURNALISTS INTERNSHIP PROGRAM

National Association of Black Journalists
Attn: Program Coordinator
8701-A Adelphi Road
Adelphi, MD 20783-1716
(301) 445-7100, ext. 108   Fax: (301) 445-7101
E-mail: nabj@nabj.org
Web: www.nabj.org/programs/internships/index.php

Summary   To provide newspaper work experience to African American journalism students.

Eligibility   This program is open to African American full-time journalism students who have prior experience at collegiate or professional media that allows them to write basic news stories for publication or to do basic copy editing, graphic design, or photojournalism in print, broadcast, or online media for publication. Applicants must be interested in working in 1 of the following kinds of internships: print (report-

ing, business reporting, copy editing, graphic design), broadcast (radio or television), online, photojournalism, or sports (multicultural program). They must be members of the National Association of Black Journalists (NABJ). Selection is based on samples of published or broadcast work.

Financial data   Stipends range from $400 to $600 per week. Interns are responsible for transportation to the internship city and for their living expenses.

Duration   10 weeks.

Additional information   Broadcast interns are required to attend the NABJ Broadcast Short Course and sports journalism interns are required to attend the annual convention of the Associated Press Sports Editors.

Number awarded   Varies each year; recently, 11 students were provided with internships.

Deadline   December of each year.

[396]
NATIONAL ASSOCIATION OF NEGRO BUSINESS AND PROFESSIONAL WOMEN'S CLUBS NATIONAL SCHOLARSHIPS

National Association of Negro Business and Professional Women's Clubs
Attn: Scholarship Committee
1806 New Hampshire Avenue, N.W.
Washington, DC 20009-3206
(202) 483-4206   Fax: (202) 462-7253
E-mail: education@nanbpwc.org
Web: www.nanbpwc.org/ScholarshipApplications.asp

Summary   To provide financial assistance for college to African American high school seniors.

Eligibility   This program is open to African American high school seniors planning to enroll in an accredited college or university. Applicants must have a GPA of 3.0 or higher. Along with their application, they must submit an essay (at least 300 words) on "Why Education is Important to Me." Financial need is not considered in the selection process.

Financial data   The stipend is $1,000.

Duration   1 year.

Number awarded   10 each year.

Deadline   February of each year.

[397]
NATIONAL BLACK MBA ASSOCIATION COLLEGIATE CHAPTER SCHOLARSHIP PROGRAM

National Black MBA Association
180 North Michigan Avenue, Suite 1400
Chicago, IL 60601
(312) 236-BMBA, ext. 8086   Fax: (312) 236-0390
E-mail: Scholarship@nbmbaa.org
Web: www.nbmbaa.org/index.aspx?pageID=792

Summary   To provide financial assistance to members of collegiate chapters of the National Black MBA Association (NBMBAA).

Eligibility   This program is open to minority students enrolled full time in their first, second, third, or fourth year of a bachelor's or master's business degree program at a college or university that has a collegiate chapter of the NBMBAA. Applicants must be chapter members actively involved in its activities and local communities through service to others.

Along with their application, they must submit a 300-word essay on a topic that changes annually; recently, students were asked to explain how working on a graduate business degree would serve as a catalyst for change for the Black community. Selection is based on that essay, academic excellence, leadership potential, community involvement, and a recommendation from the faculty adviser.

Financial data The stipend is $5,000. Recipients are also provided with complimentary registration, round-trip airfare, and housing to attend the NBMBAA annual conference and exposition.

Duration 1 year.

Number awarded Varies each year; recently, 4 of these scholarships were awarded.

Deadline May of each year.

[398]
NATIONAL BLACK NURSES ASSOCIATION SCHOLARSHIPS

National Black Nurses Association, Inc.
Attn: Scholarship Committee
8630 Fenton Street, Suite 330
Silver Spring, MD 20910-3803
(301) 589-3200   Toll Free: (800) 575-6298
Fax: (301) 589-3223   E-mail: contact@nbna.org
Web: www.nbna.org

Summary To provide financial assistance for undergraduate nursing education to members of the National Black Nurses Association (NBNA).

Eligibility This program is open to members of the association who are currently enrolled in a B.S.N., A.D., diploma, or L.P.N./L.V.N. program with at least 1 full year of school remaining. Along with their application, they must submit a 2-page essay 1) describing their extracurricular activities and community involvement (including local chapter activities, community-based projects, school level projects, organizational efforts, state-level student nurse activities, and other activities impacting on the health and social condition of African Americans and other culturally diverse groups), 2) presenting their ideas of what they can do as an individual nurse to improve the health status and/or social condition of African Americans; and 3) stating their future goals in nursing.

Financial data The stipend ranges from $500 to $2,000 per year.

Duration 1 year; may be renewed.

Additional information This program includes the following named scholarships: the Dr. Hilda Richards Scholarship, the Dr. Lauranne Sams Scholarship, the Kaiser Permanente Scholarship, the Martha R. Dudley LVN/LPN Scholarship, the Mayo Foundation Scholarship, the NBNA Board of Directors Scholarship, the Pepsi Company Scholarship, the Gannett Healthcare Group Scholarship, the Cynthia J. Hickman "Pay It Forward" Scholarship, the Rita E. Miller Scholarship, the Martha A. Dawson Genesis Scholarship, the Le Grande Trottman Scholarship, the Margaret Pemberton Scholarship, and the Nursing Spectrum Scholarship.

Number awarded Varies each year.

Deadline April of each year.

[399]
NATIONAL MARITIME INTELLIGENCE CENTER BLACKS IN GOVERNMENT SCHOLARSHIP

Blacks in Government-National Maritime Intelligence
    Center Chapter
c/o Jeanelle Jones
P.O. Box 1034
Suitland, MD 20752-1034
(301) 669-3693   E-mail: jjones@nmic.navy.mil

Summary To provide financial assistance to African Americans and other high school seniors in the Washington, D.C. metropolitan area who plan to attend college in any state.

Eligibility This program is open to African Americans and other seniors graduating from high schools within a 200-mile radius of Washington, D.C. Applicants must have a GPA of 2.5 higher and be planning to attend an accredited institution of higher learning in any state. Along with their application, they must submit an essay of 450 to 600 words on 1 of the following topics: their intended degree and how it might impact their life and/or community; who has influenced and/or shaped their life and how; how they plan to impact and elevate their community; and what education means to them. Finalists are interviewed. Financial need is not considered in the selection process.

Financial data A stipend is awarded (amount not specified).

Duration 1 year.

Additional information This program was established in 2003.

Number awarded 1 or more each year.

Deadline March of each year.

[400]
NATIONAL ORGANIZATION OF PROFESSIONAL BLACK NATURAL RESOURCES CONSERVATION SERVICE EMPLOYEES SCHOLARSHIPS

National Organization of Professional Black Natural
    Resources Conservation Service Employees
c/o HBCU Scholarship Committee Chair
25 Underwood Street, N.W.
Washington, DC 20012
(202) 720-1088   E-mail: kim.bradford@wdc.usda.gov
Web: www.nopbnrcse.org/scholar-awards/scholarship.htm

Summary To provide financial assistance to students working on a bachelor's degree in agriculture, natural resource sciences, or a related field at an 1890 Historically Black Land-Grant Institution.

Eligibility This program is open to students enrolled or planning to enroll at 1 of the 18 universities designated as an 1890 Historically Black Land-Grant Institution. Applicants must be interested in working on a bachelor's degree in 1 of the following fields: agriculture, agricultural business/management, agricultural economics, agricultural engineering/mechanics, agricultural production and technology, agronomy or crop science, animal science, botany, farm and range management, forestry, horticulture, natural resource management, soil conservation and science, and wildlife management. They must have a GPA of 2.8 or higher. Along with their application, they must submit 250-word essays on 1) the reason they are majoring in their selected field; 2) their short- and long-term career goals and objectives; and 3) why they need financial assistance to continue their education. U.S. citizenship is required.

Financial data The stipend is $1,000.

Duration 1 year; nonrenewable.

Additional information The eligible 1890 Historically Black Land-Grant Institutions are Alabama A&M University, Alcorn State University (Mississippi), Delaware State University, Florida A&M University, Fort Valley State University (Georgia), Kentucky State University, Langston University (Oklahoma), Lincoln University (Missouri), North Carolina A&T State University, Prairie View A&M University (Texas), South Carolina State University, Southern University (Louisiana), Tennessee State University, Tuskegee University (Alabama), University of Arkansas at Pine Bluff, University of Maryland Eastern Shore, Virginia State University, and West Virginia State University.

Number awarded 10 each year.

Deadline January of each year.

[401]
NATIONAL PRESS CLUB SCHOLARSHIP FOR JOURNALISM DIVERSITY

National Press Club
Attn: General Manager's Office
529 14th Street, N.W.
Washington, DC 20045
(202) 662-7599
Web: www.press.org/activities/aboutscholarship.cfm

Summary To provide funding to African Americans and other high school seniors who are planning to major in journalism in college and will bring diversity to the field.

Eligibility This program is open to high school seniors who have been accepted to college and plan to prepare for a career in journalism. Applicants must submit 1) a 500-word essay explaining how they would add diversity to U.S. journalism; 2) up to 5 work samples demonstrating an ongoing interest in journalism through work on a high school newspaper or other media; 3) letters of recommendation from 3 people; 4) a copy of their high school transcript; 5) documentation of financial need; 6) a letter of acceptance from the college or university of their choice; and 7) a brief description of how they have pursued journalism in high school.

Financial data The stipend is $2,000 for the first year and $2,500 for each subsequent year. The program also provides an additional $500 book stipend, designated the Ellen Masin Persina Scholarship, for the first year.

Duration 4 years.

Additional information The program began in 1990.

Number awarded 1 each year.

Deadline February of each year.

[402]
NATIONAL SOCIETY OF BLACK ENGINEERS FELLOWS SCHOLARSHIP PROGRAM

National Society of Black Engineers
Attn: Programs Department
205 Daingerfield Road
Alexandria, VA 22314
(703) 549-2207   Fax: (703) 683-5312
E-mail: scholarships@nsbe.org
Web: www.nsbe.org

Summary To provide financial assistance to members of the National Society of Black Engineers (NSBE) who are working on a degree in engineering.

Eligibility This program is open to members of the society who are undergraduate or graduate engineering students. Applicants must have a GPA of 2.7 or higher. Selection is based on an essay; academic achievement; service to the society at the chapter, regional, and/or national level; and other professional, campus, and community activities.

Financial data The stipend is $1,000.

Duration 1 year.

Number awarded Varies each year; recently, 10 of these scholarships were awarded.

Deadline January of each year.

[403]
NATIONAL SORORITY OF PHI DELTA KAPPA SCHOLARSHIPS

National Sorority of Phi Delta Kappa, Inc.
Attn: Perpetual Scholarship Foundation
8233 South King Drive
Chicago, IL 60619
(773) 783-7379   Fax: (773) 783-7354
E-mail: nspdkhdq@aol.com
Web: www.sororitynpdk.org/scholarships.html

Summary To provide financial assistance to African American high school seniors interested in studying education in college.

Eligibility This program is open to African American high school seniors who are interested in working on a 4-year college degree in education. Men and women compete separately. Financial need is considered in the selection process.

Financial data The stipend is $1,250 per year.

Duration 4 years, provided the recipient maintains a GPA of 3.0 or higher and a major in education.

Additional information The sponsor was founded in 1923 as an organization of female African American educators.

Number awarded 10 each year: 1 male and 1 female in each of the organization's 5 regions.

Deadline Applications must be submitted to a local chapter of the organization by January of each year.

[404]
NATIONAL SPACE GRANT COLLEGE AND FELLOWSHIP PROGRAM

National Aeronautics and Space Administration
Attn: Office of Education
300 E Street, S.W.
Mail Suite 6M35
Washington, DC 20546-0001
(202) 358-1069   Fax: (202) 358-7097
E-mail: Diane.D.DeTroye@nasa.gov
Web: www.nasa.gov

Summary To provide financial assistance to African Americans and other undergraduate and graduate students interested in preparing for a career in a space-related field.

Eligibility This program is open to undergraduate and graduate students at colleges and universities that participate in the National Space Grant program of the U.S. National Aeronautics and Space Administration (NASA) through their state consortium. Applicants must be interested in a program of study and/or research in a field of science, technology, engineering, or mathematics (STEM) related to space. A specific goal of the program is to increase preparation by members of underrepresented groups (minorities, women, and persons with disabilities) for STEM space-related careers. Financial need is not considered in the selection process.

Financial data Each consortium establishes the terms of the fellowship program in its state.

Additional information NASA established the Space Grant program in 1989. It operates through 52 consortia in each state, the District of Columbia, and Puerto Rico. Each consortium includes selected colleges and universities in that state as well as other affiliates from industry, museums, science centers, and state and local agencies.

Number awarded Varies each year.

Deadline Each consortium sets its own deadlines.

[405]
NAVY/MARINE CORPS JROTC SCHOLARSHIP

National Naval Officers Association-Washington, D.C.
  Chapter
Attn: Scholarship Program
2701 Park Center Drive, A1108
Alexandria, VA 22302
(703) 566-3840   Fax: (703) 566-3813
E-mail: Stephen.Williams@Navy.mil
Web: dcnnoa.memberlodge.com

Summary To provide financial assistance to African American and other minority high school seniors from the Washington, D.C. area who have participated in Navy or Marine Corps Junior Reserve Officers Training Corps (JROTC) and are planning to attend college in any state.

Eligibility This program is open to minority seniors graduating from high schools in the Washington, D.C. metropolitan area who have participated in Navy or Marine Corps JROTC. Applicants must be planning to enroll full time at an accredited 2- or 4-year college or university in any state. They must have a GPA of 2.5 or higher. Selection is based on academic achievement, community involvement, and financial need.

Financial data The stipend is $1,000.

Duration 1 year; nonrenewable.

Additional information Recipients are not required to join or affiliate with the military in any way after college.

Number awarded 1 each year.

Deadline March of each year.

[406]
NEW ENGLAND CITE SCHOLARSHIPS

Consortium of Information and Telecommunications
  Executives-New England Chapter
Attn: Scholarship Committee
P.O. Box 960275
Boston, MA 02196
(508) 921-2144   E-mail: Scholar@cite-newengland.org
Web: www.cite-newengland.org

Summary To provide financial assistance to African American residents of New England states who are attending or planning to attend college in any state.

Eligibility This program is open to African American residents of Maine, Massachusetts, New Hampshire, Rhode Island, or Vermont who are graduating high school seniors or current college freshmen, sophomores, or juniors. Applicants must be attending or planning to attend a 4-year college or university in any state and have a GPA of 3.0 or higher. Along with their application, they must submit a 300-word essay on a topic that changes annually but relates to the legacy of the sponsoring organization in serving the African American community of New England. Financial need is not considered in the selection process. U.S. citizenship is required.

Financial data The stipend is $1,000.

Duration 1 year; nonrenewable.

Additional information The Consortium of Information and Telecommunications Executives (CITE) is an organization of African American employees of Verizon, founded in 1984 after the dissolution of the former Bell systems. Recipients are required to attend the sponsor's presentation ceremony.

Number awarded 1 or more each year.

Deadline May of each year.

[407]
NEW JERSEY SCHOLARSHIPS

Consortium of Information and Telecommunications
  Executives-New Jersey Chapter
Attn: Scholarship Committee
P.O. Box 20310
Newark, NJ 07101
(609) 351-4699   E-mail: scholarship@cite-md.org
Web: www.cite-nj.org/Documents.aspx

Summary To provide financial assistance to African American high school seniors in New Jersey who plan to attend college in any state.

Eligibility This program is open to African American seniors graduating from high schools in Maryland with a GPA of 3.0 or higher. Applicants must have been accepted by an accredited college or university in any state and be able to document financial need. Along with their application, they must submit a 1-page essay on their educational and career goals. Employees and immediate family members of employees of the Verizon Corporation or an affiliated subsidiary are ineligible. U.S. citizenship is required.

Financial data A stipend is awarded (amount not specified).

Duration 1 year.

Additional information The Consortium of Information and Telecommunications Executives (CITE) is an organization of African American employees of Verizon, founded in 1984 after the dissolution of the former Bell systems.

Number awarded 1 or more each year.

Deadline March of each year.

[408]
NEW JERSEY UTILITIES ASSOCIATION EQUAL EMPLOYMENT OPPORTUNITY SCHOLARSHIPS

New Jersey Utilities Association
50 West State Street, Suite 1117
Trenton, NJ 08608
(609) 392-1000   Fax: (609) 396-4231
Web: www.njua.org/html/njua_eeo_scholarship.cfm

Summary To provide financial assistance to high school seniors in New Jersey (especially African Americans, other minorities, and women) who are interested in attending college in any state.

Eligibility This program is open to seniors graduating from high schools in New Jersey who are women, minorities (Black or African American, Hispanic or Latino, American Indian or Alaska Native, Asian, Native Hawaiian or Pacific Islander, or 2 or more races), and persons with disabilities. Applicants must be planning to work on a bachelor's degree at a college or university in any state. They must be able to demonstrate financial need. Children of employees of any New Jersey Utilities Association-member company are ineligible. Selection is based on overall academic excellence and demonstrated financial need. U.S. citizenship or permanent resident status is required.

Financial data The stipend is $1,500 per year.

Duration 4 years.

Number awarded 2 each year.

Deadline March of each year.

[409]
NEW YORK CITE TRADITIONAL SCHOLARSHIPS

Consortium of Information and Telecommunications
  Executives-New York Chapter
c/o Debra James-Phillip, Scholarship Committee Chair
Church Street Station
P.O. Box 3452
New York, NY 10008
(212) 962-1730
E-mail: debra.k.james-phillip@verizon.com
Web: www.citeny.org/scholarship.html

Summary To provide financial assistance to African American high school seniors from New York who plan to major in selected business- or engineering-related fields in college.

Eligibility This program is open to African American seniors graduating from high schools in New York who have been accepted by an accredited 4-year college or university in any state as a full-time student. Applicants must have a GPA of 3.0 or higher and a family income of $55,000 per year or less. They must be planning to major in 1 of the following fields: accounting, advertising, business, computer science, electrical engineering, finance, industrial engineering, information technology, marketing, or mathematics. Along with their application, they must submit a 1-page essay on their educational and career goals. Employees of Verizon Communications or affiliated subsidiaries and their family members are ineligible. U.S. citizenship is required.

Financial data The stipend is $1,500.

Duration 1 year; nonrenewable.

Additional information The Consortium of Information and Telecommunications Executives (CITE) is an organization of African American employees of Verizon, founded in 1984 after the dissolution of the former Bell systems.

Number awarded 2 each year.

Deadline March of each year.

[410]
NEWHOUSE FOUNDATION SCHOLARSHIPS

National Association of Black Journalists
Attn: Program Coordinator
8701-A Adelphi Road
Adelphi, MD 20783-1716
(301) 445-7100, ext. 108   Toll Free: (866) 479-NABJ
Fax: (301) 445-7101   E-mail: nabj@nabj.org
Web: www.nabj.org

Summary To provide financial assistance to members of the National Association of Black Journalists (NABJ) who are majoring or planning to major in print journalism.

Eligibility This program is open to African American students who are currently attending an accredited 4-year college or university or high school seniors planning to enroll at such an institution. Applicants must be majoring or planning to major in print journalism, have a GPA of 3.0 or higher, and have experience working on their campus newspaper. They must be NABJ members. Along with their application, they must submit samples of their work, an official college transcript, 2 letters of recommendation, a resume, and a 500- to 800-word essay describing their accomplishments as a student journalist, their career goals, and their financial need.

Financial data The stipend is $5,000 per year.

Duration 1 year; may be renewed up to 3 additional years.

Additional information This program is sponsored by the Samuel I. Newhouse Foundation.

Number awarded Varies each year; recently, 4 of these scholarships were awarded.

Deadline April of each year.

[411]
NFBPA FUTURE COLLEAGUES SCHOLARSHIP

National Forum for Black Public Administrators
Attn: Scholarship Program
777 North Capitol Street, N.E., Suite 807
Washington, DC 20002
(202) 408-9300, ext. 112   Fax: (202) 408-8558
E-mail: vreed@nfbpa.org
Web: www.nfbpa.org/i4a/pages/index.cfm?pageid=3630

Summary To provide financial assistance to African Americans working on an undergraduate degree in public administration.

Eligibility This program is open to African American undergraduate students working full time on a degree in public administration. Applicants must have average academic credentials (GPA of 2.5 to 3.0) and strong written, oral, and analytical skills. Along with their application, they must submit a 500-word essay that provides an example of prior public or community service involvement and how it has influenced their future aspirations in public administration.

Financial data The stipend is $1,000.

Duration 1 year.

Additional information Recipients are required to attend the sponsor's annual conference to receive their scholarship; limited hotel and air accommodations are arranged and provided.

Number awarded 1 each year.

Deadline February of each year.

[412]
NIDDK/OMHRC SUMMER INTERNSHIP PROGRAM FOR UNDERREPRESENTED MINORITIES

National Institute of Diabetes and Digestive and Kidney Diseases
Attn: Office of Minority Health Research Coordination
6707 Democracy Boulevard, Room 906A
Bethesda, MD 20892-5454
(301) 435-2988　　　　　　　　Fax: (301) 594-9358
E-mail: MartinezW@mail.nih.gov
Web: www2.niddk.nih.gov/Funding

Summary　To provide African Americans and other underrepresented minority undergraduate students with an opportunity to conduct research in the laboratory of a National Institute of Diabetes and Digestive and Kidney Diseases (NIDDK) intramural scientist during the summer.

Eligibility　This program is open to undergraduate students who are members of underrepresented minority groups (African Americans, Hispanic Americans, Native Americans, Native Hawaiians, other Pacific Islanders, and Alaska Natives). Applicants must be interested in participating in a research project conducted at an intramural research laboratory of NIDDK in Bethesda, Maryland or Phoenix, Arizona. They must have completed at least 1 year at an accredited institution and have a GPA of 3.0 or higher. Along with their application, they must submit a 2-page personal statement of their research interest, career goals, and reasons for applying to training at NIDDK. U.S. citizenship or permanent resident status is required.

Financial data　Students receive a stipend of $2,500, housing, and (for those who live outside the Washington metropolitan area or the state of Arizona) a travel allowance of $500.

Duration　10 weeks during the summer.

Deadline　February of each year.

[413]
NORTH CAROLINA CHAPTER AABE SCHOLARSHIPS

American Association of Blacks in Energy-North Carolina Chapter
Attn: Scholarship Committee
P.O. Box 207
Raleigh, NC 27602-0207
(919) 334-3092　　　　　　E-mail: carlwilkins@nc.rr.com
Web: www.aabe.org/index.php?component=pages&id=416

Summary　To provide financial assistance to African Americans and members of other underrepresented minority groups who are high school seniors in North Carolina and planning to major in an energy-related field at a college in any state.

Eligibility　This program is open to seniors graduating from high schools in North Carolina and planning to work on a bachelor's degree at a college or university in any state. Applicants must be African Americans, Hispanics, or Native Americans who have a GPA of 3.0 or higher and are able to demonstrate financial need. Their intended major must be a field of business, engineering, physical science, mathematics, or technology related to energy. Along with their application, they must submit a 350-word statement on why they

should receive this scholarship, their professional career objectives, and any other relevant information.

Financial data　The stipend is $1,000.

Duration　1 year; nonrenewable.

Additional information　Winners are eligible to compete for regional and national scholarships.

Number awarded　1 or more each year.

Deadline　March of each year.

[414]
NORTH CAROLINA MILLENNIUM TEACHER SCHOLARSHIP/LOAN PROGRAM

North Carolina State Education Assistance Authority
Attn: Millennium Teacher Scholarship Program
P.O. Box 13663
Research Triangle Park, NC 27709-3663
(919) 549-8614　　　　　　Toll Free: (800) 700-1775
Fax: (919) 248-4687　　　　　E-mail: eew@ncseaa.edu
Web: www.ncseaa.edu/MTSLP.htm

Summary　To provide funding to high school seniors in North Carolina who are interested in attending designated Historically Black Colleges and Universities (HBCUs) in the state to work on a degree in education.

Eligibility　This program is open to seniors graduating from high schools in North Carolina who have been accepted at Elizabeth City State University, Fayetteville State University, or Winston-Salem State University. Applicants must have a combined mathematics and critical reading SAT score of at least 900, have a GPA of at least 2.5, and be able to demonstrate at least $3,000 worth of financial need. They must be interested in teaching at a North Carolina public school after graduation; priority is given to applicants planning to teach in designated critical shortage licensure areas.

Financial data　The stipend is $6,500 per year. This is a loan for service program. Recipients are required to teach 1 year in a North Carolina public school for each year of support they receive. If they fail to fulfill that service obligation, they must repay all funds received with 10% interest. Repayment in service or cash must be completed within 10 years.

Duration　1 year; may be renewed up to 3 additional years.

Additional information　The North Carolina General Assembly established this program in 2004.

Number awarded　Up to 20 students are accepted at each of the 3 participating universities each year; recently, a total of 98 students were receiving $614,750 through this program.

Deadline　Deadline not specified.

[415]
NORTH CAROLINA TEACHING FELLOWS SCHOLARSHIP PROGRAM

North Carolina Teaching Fellows Commission
Koger Center, Cumberland Building
3739 National Drive, Suite 100
Raleigh, NC 27612
(919) 781-6833　　　　　　Fax: (919) 781-6527
E-mail: tfellows@ncforum.org
Web: www.teachingfellows.org

Summary　To provide funding to minority and other high school seniors in North Carolina who wish to prepare for a career in teaching.

Eligibility This program is open to seniors at high schools in North Carolina who are interested in preparing for a career as a teacher and have been accepted for enrollment at a participating school in the state. Applicants must demonstrate superior achievement on the basis of high school grades, class standing, SAT scores, writing samples, community service, extracurricular activities, and references from teachers and members of the community. U.S. citizenship is required. A particular goal of the program is to recruit and retain greater numbers of male and minority teacher education candidates in North Carolina. Financial need is not considered in the selection process.

Financial data The maximum stipend is $6,500 per year. This is a scholarship/loan program; recipients must teach in a North Carolina public school 1 year for each year of support received. If they cannot fulfill the service requirement, they must repay the loan with 10% interest.

Duration 1 year; renewable for up to 3 additional years if the recipient maintains full-time enrollment and a GPA of 2.25 or higher for the freshman year and 2.50 or higher in the sophomore year.

Additional information The participating schools are Appalachian State University, Campbell University, Catawba College, East Carolina University, Elon College, Lenoir-Rhyne College, Meredith College, North Carolina A&T State University, North Carolina Central University, North Carolina State University, Queens University of Charlotte, University of North Carolina at Asheville, University of North Carolina at Chapel Hill, University of North Carolina at Charlotte, University of North Carolina at Greensboro, University of North Carolina at Pembroke, University of North Carolina at Wilmington, and Western Carolina University. This program was established in 1986 and the first fellows were named in 1987.

Number awarded Up to 500 each year. Approximately 20% of the program's recipients are minority and 30% are male.

Deadline October of each year.

[416]
NORTHROP GRUMMAN NSBE CORPORATE SCHOLARSHIPS

National Society of Black Engineers
Attn: Programs Department
205 Daingerfield Road
Alexandria, VA 22314
(703) 549-2207   Fax: (703) 683-5312
E-mail: scholarships@nsbe.org
Web: www.nsbe.org

Summary To provide financial assistance to members of the National Society of Black Engineers (NSBE) who are working on an undergraduate degree in designated science and engineering fields.

Eligibility This program is open to members of the society who are U.S. citizens currently enrolled in college. Applicants must be majoring in computer science, information science, mathematics, naval architecture, physics, or the following engineering fields: aerospace, chemical, civil (structural), computer, electrical, industrial, manufacturing, marine, mechanical, or ocean. They must have a GPA of 3.0 or higher and a demonstrated interest in employment with Northrop Grumman.

Financial data The stipend is $5,000.

Duration 1 year.

Additional information This program is sponsored by Northrop Grumman Corporation.

Number awarded 4 each year.

Deadline January of each year.

[417]
NORTHROP GRUMMAN SCHOLARSHIPS

Advancing Hispanic Excellence in Technology, Engineering, Math and Science, Inc.
c/o University of Texas at Arlington
416 Yates Street, Room 609
Box 19019
Arlington, TX 76019-0019
(817) 272-1116   Fax: (817) 272-2548
E-mail: ahetems@shpe.org
Web: www.ahetems.org

Summary To provide financial assistance to undergraduate students who are working on a degree in engineering or a related field at an Historically Black College or University (HBCU), an Hispanic Service Institution (HSI), or other specified universities.

Eligibility This program is open to entering full-time sophomores, juniors, or seniors at an accredited university in the United States or Puerto Rico that is an HBCU, an HIS, or another designated institution. Applicants must be majoring in computer science, engineering (aerospace, computer, electrical, industrial, mechanical, or systems), mathematics, naval architecture, or physics. They must have a GPA of 3.0 or higher. Along with their application, they must submit a 500-word personal statement covering their community involvement, leadership, academic achievements, research internship and co-op experiences, and short-term and long-term goals and aspirations. Selection is based on merit. U.S. citizenship is required.

Financial data The stipend is $5,000.

Duration 1 year.

Additional information Advancing Hispanic Excellence in Technology, Engineering, Math and Science (AHETEMS) was established in 2004 by the Society of Hispanic Professional Engineers (SHPE) as an independent nonprofit foundation. This program is sponsored by Northrop Grumman. The other designated institutions are California Polytechnic State University at San Luis Obispo, California Institute of Technology, Georgia Institute of Technology, Massachusetts Institute of Technology, North Carolina State University, Ohio State University, Pennsylvania State University, Purdue University, University of California at Los Angeles, University of Illinois at Urbana-Champaign, University of Maryland, University of Southern California, University of Virginia, and Virginia Polytechnic Institute and State University.

Number awarded 1 or more each year.

Deadline March of each year.

[418]
NORTHWEST JOURNALISTS OF COLOR SCHOLARSHIP AWARDS

Northwest Journalists of Color
c/o Caroline Li
14601 Ninth Avenue N.E.
Shoreline, WA 98155
E-mail: editor@earthwalkersmag.com
Web: www.aajaseattle.org

Summary To provide financial assistance to African American and other minority students from Washington state who are interested in careers in journalism.

Eligibility This program is open to members of minority groups (Asian American, African American, Native American, and Latino) who are 1) residents of Washington attending an accredited college or university in any state; 2) residents of any state attending a Washington college or university; or 3) seniors graduating from Washington high schools. Applicants must be planning a career in broadcast, photo, or print journalism. Along with their application, they must submit 1) a brief essay about themselves, including why they want to be a journalist, challenges they foresee, how they think they can contribute to the profession, and the influence their ethnic heritage might have on their perspective as a working journalist; 2) a current resume; 3) up to 3 work samples; 4) reference letters; and 5) documentation of financial need.

Financial data Stipends range up to $2,500 per year.

Duration 1 year; may be renewed.

Additional information This program, established in 1986, is sponsored by the Seattle chapters of the Asian American Journalists Association, the Native American Journalists Association, the National Association of Black Journalists, and the Latino Media Association. It includes the Walt and Milly Woodward Memorial Scholarship donated by the Western Washington Chapter of the Society of Professional Journalists.

Number awarded Varies each year.

Deadline April of each year.

[419]
NUCLEAR REGULATORY COMMISSION HISTORICALLY BLACK COLLEGES AND UNIVERSITIES STUDENT RESEARCH PARTICIPATION PROGRAM

Oak Ridge Institute for Science and Education
Attn: Science and Engineering Education
P.O. Box 117
Oak Ridge, TN 37831-0117
(865) 576-3937   Fax: (865) 241-5220
E-mail: michael.hubbard@orau.gov
Web: see.orau.org

Summary To provide funding to students at Historically Black Colleges and Universities (HBCUs) who wish to participate in research at various facilities of the U.S. Nuclear Regulatory Commission (NRC).

Eligibility This program is open to undergraduate and graduate students at HBCUs who are U.S. citizens or permanent residents. Applicants must be studying computer science, engineering, earth or geosciences, health physics, materials science, mathematics, molecular/radiation biology, performance and risk assessments, physical sciences, or sta-

tistics-related nuclear material control and accounting. They must be interested in participating in a research project at a laboratory where NRC research is being conducted, on an HBCU campus, or at a host university under the guidance of a principal investigator who has an NRC research grants.

Financial data The stipend is $600 per week for graduate students or $500 per week for undergraduates. Also provided is limited travel reimbursement for round-trip transportation between the facility and home or campus.

Duration 10 to 12 weeks during the summer. Some 1-year appointments at participating facilities or on campus are also available.

Additional information This program is funded by the NRC and administered by Oak Ridge Institute for Science and Education (ORISE).

Number awarded Varies each year.

Deadline Applications may be submitted at any time.

[420]
OHIO NEWSPAPERS FOUNDATION MINORITY SCHOLARSHIPS

Ohio Newspapers Foundation
1335 Dublin Road, Suite 216-B
Columbus, OH 43215-7038
(614) 486-6677   Fax: (614) 486-4940
E-mail: ariggs@ohionews.org
Web: www.ohionews.org/students/scholarships

Summary To provide financial assistance to African Americans and other minority high school seniors in Ohio planning to attend college in the state to prepare for a career in journalism.

Eligibility This program is open to high school seniors in Ohio who are members of minority groups (African American, Hispanic, Asian American, or American Indian) and planning to prepare for a career in newspaper journalism. Applicants must have a high school GPA of 2.5 or higher and demonstrate writing ability in an autobiography of 750 to 1,000 words that describes their academic and career interests, awards, extracurricular activities, and journalism-related activities. They must be planning to attend a college or university in Ohio.

Financial data The stipend is $1,500.

Duration 1 year; nonrenewable.

Additional information This program was established in 1990.

Number awarded 1 each year.

Deadline March of each year.

[421]
OMEGA PSI PHI FOUNDERS' MEMORIAL SCHOLARSHIPS

Omega Psi Phi Fraternity
Attn: Charles R. Drew Memorial Scholarship Commission
3951 Snapfinger Parkway
Decatur, GA 30035-3203
(404) 284-5533   Fax: (404) 284-0333
E-mail: scholarshipchairman@oppf.org
Web: oppf.org/scholarship

Summary To provide financial assistance to outstanding undergraduate and graduate members of Omega Psi Phi fraternity.

Eligibility This program is open to members of the fraternity who are enrolled full time as sophomores, juniors, or graduate students and have a GPA of 3.0 or higher. Each chapter may nominate 1 undergraduate and 1 graduate member to the district. Candidates must submit a statement of 200 to 250 words on their purpose for applying for this scholarship, how they believe funds from the fraternity can assist them in achieving their career goals, and other circumstances (including financial need) that make it important for them to receive financial assistance. Selection is based on academic achievement, extracurricular activities, and community and campus involvement.

Financial data The stipend is $5,000.

Duration The scholarships are offered annually.

Number awarded 4 each year: 3 to undergraduates and 1 to a graduate student.

Deadline Applications must be submitted to the district scholarship committee chair by January of each year.

[422]
OMEGA PSI PHI UNDERGRADUATE AND GRADUATE SCHOLARSHIPS

Omega Psi Phi Fraternity
Attn: Charles R. Drew Memorial Scholarship Commission
3951 Snapfinger Parkway
Decatur, GA 30035-3203
(404) 284-5533   Fax: (404) 284-0333
E-mail: scholarshipchairman@oppf.org
Web: oppf.org/scholarship

Summary To provide financial assistance for undergraduate, graduate, or professional education to members of Omega Psi Phi who have an outstanding academic record.

Eligibility This program is open to members of the fraternity who are either 1) a sophomore, junior, or senior planning to continue on to graduate or professional school, or 2) currently attending graduate or professional school. Applicants must be enrolled full time at a 4-year college or university and have a GPA of 3.0 or higher. Along with their application, they must submit a statement of 200 to 250 words on their purpose for applying for this scholarship, how they believe funds from the fraternity can assist them in achieving their career goals, and other circumstances (including financial need) that make it important for them to receive financial assistance.

Financial data The stipend is $5,000.

Duration 1 year.

Number awarded 2 each year: 1 to an undergraduate and 1 to a graduate student.

Deadline May of each year.

[423]
OPERATION JUMP START III SCHOLARSHIPS

American Association of Advertising Agencies
Attn: AAAA Foundation
405 Lexington Avenue, 18th Floor
New York, NY 10174-1801
(212) 682-2500   Toll Free: (800) 676-9333
Fax: (212) 682-2028   E-mail: ameadows@aaaa.org
Web: www2.aaaa.org

Summary To provide financial assistance to African American and other minority art directors and copywriters inter-

ested in working on an undergraduate or graduate degree in advertising.

Eligibility This program is open to African Americans, Asian Americans, Hispanic Americans, and Native Americans who are U.S. citizens or permanent residents. Applicants must be incoming graduate students at 1 of 6 designated portfolio schools or full-time juniors at 1 of 2 designated colleges. They must be able to demonstrate extreme financial need, creative talent, and promise. Along with their application, they must submit 10 samples of creative work in their respective field of expertise.

Financial data The stipend is $5,000 per year.

Duration Most awards are for 2 years.

Additional information Operation Jump Start began in 1997 and was followed by Operation Jump Start II in 2002. The current program began in 2006. The 6 designated portfolio schools are the AdCenter at Virginia Commonwealth University, the Creative Circus in Atlanta, the Portfolio Center in Atlanta, the Miami Ad School, the University of Texas at Austin, and Pratt Institute. The 2 designated colleges are the Minneapolis College of Art and Design and the Art Center College of Design at Pasadena, California.

Number awarded 20 each year.

Deadline Deadline not specified.

[424]
ORACLE AMERICA NSBE CORPORATE SCHOLARSHIP PROGRAM

National Society of Black Engineers
Attn: Programs Department
205 Daingerfield Road
Alexandria, VA 22314
(703) 549-2207   Fax: (703) 683-5312
E-mail: scholarships@nsbe.org
Web: www.nsbe.org

Summary To provide financial assistance to high school seniors and current undergraduates who are members of the National Society of Black Engineers (NSBE) and are interested in studying engineering or a related field.

Eligibility This program is open to members of the society who are either high school seniors or current college freshmen, sophomores, juniors, or seniors. Applicants must be majoring or planning to major in engineering, computer or information science, computer engineering, or mathematics. They must have a GPA of 3.0 or higher. Along with their application, they must submit 3 essays on assigned topics. U.S. citizenship is required.

Financial data The stipend is $4,000.

Duration 1 year.

Additional information This program is sponsored by Oracle America, Inc.

Number awarded 5 each year.

Deadline January of each year.

[425]
OREGON DEPARTMENT OF TRANSPORTATION SCHOLARSHIPS

National Society of Black Engineers
Attn: Programs Department
205 Daingerfield Road
Alexandria, VA 22314
(703) 549-2207   Fax: (703) 683-5312
E-mail: scholarships@nsbe.org
Web: www.nsbe.org

Summary   To provide financial assistance to members of the National Society of Black Engineers (NSBE) in designated regions who are working on an undergraduate or graduate degree in a field related to transportation.

Eligibility   This program is open to members of the society who have completed at least their freshman year at a college or university in its Region 2 (which covers the central Atlantic states), Region 3 (which covers the Southeast), or Region 6 (which covers western states). Applicants must be working on an undergraduate or graduate degree in civil engineering, construction engineering, or other field related to transportation. They must have a GPA of 2.5 or higher. Along with their application, they must submit a 2-page concept paper for a research project on a topic related to the work of the Oregon Department of Transportation (which sponsors the program). U.S. citizenship or permanent resident status is required.

Financial data   Stipends are $1,000 or $500.

Duration   1 year.

Number awarded   2 each year: 1 at $1,000 and 1 at $500.

Deadline   October of each year.

[426]
ORGANIZATION OF BLACK AEROSPACE PROFESSIONALS GENERAL SCHOLARSHIP

Organization of Black Aerospace Professionals, Inc.
Attn: Scholarship Coordinator
1 Westbrook Corporate Center, Suite 300
Westchester, IL 60154
(708) 449-7755   Toll Free: (800) JET-OBAP
Fax: (708) 449-7754
E-mail: obapscholarship@gmail.com
Web: www.obap.org/scholarships

Summary   To provide financial assistance to members of the Organization of Black Aerospace Professionals (OBAP) who are interested in further training to advance their career in the aviation industry.

Eligibility   This program is open to OBAP members who have participated in at least 1 of its events and have at least a private pilot's license. Applicants must be interested in participating in further training that will advance their career in the aviation industry. Along with their application, they must submit an essay on their greatest life challenge and how it has enriched their and/or someone else's life, a current resume, 2 letters of recommendation, a copy of their medical permit, and a 2-page autobiography.

Financial data   The stipend is $7,000.

Duration   1 year.

Additional information   The OBAP was originally established in 1976 as the Organization of Black Airline Pilots to make certain Blacks and other minorities had a group that

would keep them informed about opportunities for advancement within commercial aviation.

Number awarded   1 each year.

Deadline   Applications must be submitted at least 30 days prior to the OBAP convention.

[427]
PAGE EDUCATION FOUNDATION GRANTS

Page Education Foundation
P.O. Box 581254
Minneapolis, MN 55458-1254
(612) 332-0406   E-mail: info@page-ed.org
Web: www.page-ed.org

Summary   To provide funding to African Americans and other high school seniors of color in Minnesota who plan to attend college in the state.

Eligibility   This program is open to students of color who are graduating from high schools in Minnesota and planning to enroll full time at a postsecondary school in the state. Applicants must submit a 500-word essay that deals with why they believe education is important, their plans for the future, and the service-to-children project they would like to complete in the coming school year. Selection is based on the essay, 3 letters of recommendation, and financial need.

Financial data   Stipends range from $1,000 to $2,500 per year.

Duration   1 year; may be renewed up to 3 additional years.

Additional information   This program was founded in 1988 by Alan Page, a former football player for the Minnesota Vikings. While attending college, the Page Scholars fulfill a 50-hour service-to-children contract that brings them into contact with K-8 students of color.

Number awarded   Varies each year; recently, 560 Page Scholars (218 new recipients and 342 renewals) were enrolled, of whom 337 were African American, 114 Asian American, 63 Chicano/Latino, and 16 American Indian.

Deadline   April of each year.

[428]
PARSONS BRINCKERHOFF ENGINEERING SCHOLARSHIP

Conference of Minority Transportation Officials
Attn: National Scholarship Program
818 18th Street, N.W., Suite 850
Washington, DC 20006
(202) 530-0551   Fax: (202) 530-0617
Web: www.comto.org/news-youth.php

Summary   To provide financial assistance to African American and other members of the Conference of Minority Transportation Officials (COMTO) who are working on an undergraduate degree in engineering.

Eligibility   This program is open to undergraduate students who have been members of COMTO for at least 1 year. Applicants must be working on a degree in engineering with a GPA of 3.0 or higher. Along with their application, they must submit a cover letter with a 500-word statement of career goals. Financial need is not considered in the selection process. U.S. citizenship is required.

Financial data   The stipend is $5,000. Funds are paid directly to the recipient's college or university.

Duration   1 year.

Additional information COMTO was established in 1971 to promote, strengthen, and expand the roles of minorities in all aspects of transportation. This program is sponsored by Parsons Brinckerhoff, Inc. Recipients are expected to attend the COMTO National Scholarship Luncheon.

Number awarded 1 or more each year.

Deadline April of each year.

[429]
PARSONS BRINCKERHOFF GOLDEN APPLE SCHOLARSHIP

Conference of Minority Transportation Officials
Attn: National Scholarship Program
818 18th Street, N.W., Suite 850
Washington, DC 20006
(202) 530-0551   Fax: (202) 530-0617
Web: www.comto.org/news-youth.php

Summary To provide financial assistance to African American and other members of the Conference of Minority Transportation Officials (COMTO) who are high school seniors planning to attend college to prepare for a career in the business aspects of the transportation industry.

Eligibility This program is open to graduating high school seniors who have been members of COMTO for at least 1 year. Applicants must be planning to attend an accredited college, university, or vocational/technical institution to prepare for a career in transportation in the fields of communications, finance, or marketing. They must have a GPA of 2.0 or higher. Along with their application, they must submit a cover letter with a 500-word statement of career goals. Financial need is not considered in the selection process. U.S. citizenship is required.

Financial data The stipend is $2,500. Funds are paid directly to the recipient's college or university.

Duration 1 year.

Additional information COMTO was established in 1971 to promote, strengthen, and expand the roles of minorities in all aspects of transportation. This program is sponsored by Parsons Brinckerhoff, Inc. Recipients are expected to attend the COMTO National Scholarship Luncheon.

Number awarded 1 or more each year.

Deadline April of each year.

[430]
PAULA HILL REED STUDENT ENCOURAGEMENT SCHOLARSHIP

National Forum for Black Public Administrators
Attn: Scholarship Program
777 North Capitol Street, N.E., Suite 807
Washington, DC 20002
(202) 408-9300, ext. 112   Fax: (202) 408-8558
E-mail: vreed@nfbpa.org
Web: www.nfbpa.org/i4a/pages/index.cfm?pageid=3630

Summary To provide financial assistance to African Americans working on an undergraduate degree in specified fields of human service at an Historically Black College or University (HBCU).

Eligibility This program is open to African American undergraduate students preparing for a career in social services, public service, or education. Applicants must be enrolled full time at an HBCU. They must have average academic creden-

tials (GPA of 2.8 to 3.2), excellent leadership abilities, and strong written, oral, and analytical skills. Volunteer and community service participation is considered favorably. Along with their application, they must submit a 3-page autobiographical essay that includes their academic and career goals and objectives.

Financial data The stipend is $1,800.

Duration 1 year.

Additional information Recipients are required to attend the sponsor's annual conference to receive their scholarship; limited hotel and air accommodations are arranged and provided.

Number awarded 1 each year.

Deadline February of each year.

[431]
PBS&J ACHIEVEMENT SCHOLARSHIP

Conference of Minority Transportation Officials
Attn: National Scholarship Program
818 18th Street, N.W., Suite 850
Washington, DC 20006
(202) 530-0551   Fax: (202) 530-0617
Web: www.comto.org/news-youth.php

Summary To provide financial assistance to African American and other minority high school seniors, undergraduates, and graduate students interested in studying the field of transportation.

Eligibility This program is open to minority graduating high school seniors, current undergraduates, and graduate students interested in the field of transportation. Applicants must be enrolled or planning to enroll full time at an accredited college, university, or vocational/technical institution. They must have a GPA of 2.0 or higher. Along with their application, they must submit a cover letter with a 500-word statement of career goals. Financial need is not considered in the selection process. U.S. citizenship is required.

Financial data The stipend is $4,000. Funds are paid directly to the recipient's college or university.

Duration 1 year.

Additional information The Conference of Minority Transportation Officials (COMTO) was established in 1971 to promote, strengthen, and expand the roles of minorities in all aspects of transportation. This program is sponsored by the engineering, architecture, and sciences company PBS&J. Recipients are expected to attend the COMTO National Scholarship Luncheon.

Number awarded 1 or more each year.

Deadline April of each year.

[432]
PEGGY VATTER MEMORIAL SCHOLARSHIPS

Washington Science Teachers Association
c/o Patricia MacGowan, Washington MESA
University of Washington
P.O. Box 352181
Seattle, WA 98195-2181
(206) 543-0562   Fax: (206) 685-0666
E-mail: macgowan@engr.washington.edu
Web: www.wsta.net

Summary To provide financial assistance to upper-division students and teachers in Washington (especially African

Americans, other underrepresented minorities, and women)interested in training in science education.

Eligibility   This program is open to 1) juniors and seniors at colleges and universities in Washington who are working on certification in science education or in elementary education with an emphasis on science; and 2) certified teachers in Washington interested in improving their skills in providing equitable science education through professional development. In the student category, preference is given to African Americans, Hispanics, Native Americans, and women. Applicants must submit a 1-page essay on why they are applying for this scholarship.

Financial data   The stipend is $1,500.

Duration   1 year; nonrenewable.

Additional information   This program was established in 2003.

Number awarded   1 or more each year.

Deadline   April of each year.

[433]
PENNSYLVANIA DIETETIC ASSOCIATION FOUNDATION DIVERSITY SCHOLARSHIP

Pennsylvania Dietetic Association
Attn: Foundation
96 Northwoods Boulevard, Suite B2
Columbus, OH 43235
(614) 436-6136
Web: www.eatrightpa.org/scholarships/applications.htm

Summary   To provide financial assistance to African American and other minority members of the Pennsylvania Dietetic Association (PDA) who are working on an associate or bachelor's degree in dietetics.

Eligibility   This program is open to PDA members who are Black, Hispanic, Asian or Pacific Islander, or Native American (Alaskan Native, American Indian, or Hawaiian Native). Applicants must be 1) enrolled in the first year of study in an accredited dietetic technology program; or 2) enrolled in the third year of study in an accredited undergraduate or coordinated program in dietetics. They must have a GPA of 2.5 or higher. Along with their application, they must submit a letter indicating their intent and the reason they are applying for the scholarship, including a description of their personal financial situation. Selection is based on academic achievement (20%), commitment to the dietetic profession (30%), leadership ability (30%), and financial need (20%).

Financial data   The stipend is $1,000.

Duration   1 year.

Number awarded   1 or more each year.

Deadline   March of each year.

[434]
PGA TOUR DIVERSITY INTERNSHIP PROGRAM

PGA Tour, Inc.
Attn: Minority Internship Program
100 PGA Tour Boulevard
Ponte Vedra Beach, FL 32082
(904) 285-3700
Web: www.pgatour.com/company/internships.html

Summary   To provide summer work experience to African American and other undergraduate or graduate students who are interested in learning about the business side of golf and will contribute to diversity in the profession.

Eligibility   This program is open to students who either have completed at least their sophomore year at an accredited 4-year college or university or are enrolled in graduate school. Applicants should be able to enrich the PGA Tour and its partnering organizations through diversity. They must have a GPA of 2.8 or higher. International students are eligible if they are legally permitted to work in the United States. Although all interns work in the business side of golf, the ability to play golf or knowledge of the game is not required for many positions.

Financial data   Interns receive competitive wages and up to $500 for travel expenses to orientation in Ponte Vedra Beach, Florida or their initial work location. Depending on position and location, other benefits include subsidized housing, discounts on company merchandise, access to company training seminars, and possible golf privileges.

Duration   Most assignments are for 10 to 12 weeks during the summer.

Additional information   This program was established in 1992. Positions are available in accounting, corporate marketing, business development, international TV, information systems, event management, tournament services, tournament operations, retail licensing, sales, human resources, new media, and other areas within the PGA Tour. Most assignments are in Ponte Vedra Beach, Florida.

Number awarded   Approximately 30 each year.

Deadline   February of each year.

[435]
PHIL B. CURLS, SR. SCHOLARSHIP

Missouri Legislative Black Caucus Foundation
c/o Senator Yvonne Wilson
4609 Paseo Boulevard, Suite 102
Kansas City, MO 64110
Toll Free: (877) 63-MLBCF   E-mail: mlbcf@aol.com
Web: www.mlbcf.com

Summary   To provide financial assistance to African Americans and other residents of Missouri who come from a disadvantaged background and are interested in working on an undergraduate or graduate degree in a health-related field at a school in any state.

Eligibility   This program is open to undergraduate and graduate students from Missouri who are preparing for a career as a physician, nurse, dentist, health researcher, hospital administrator, or other health-related professional. Applicants must come from a disadvantaged background and have a GPA of 2.5 or higher. They may be attending a college or university in any state. Along with their application, they must submit a 250-word personal statement on how their education will assist them in achieving their goals. Selection is based on academic excellence, community service, leadership skills, and financial need.

Financial data   A stipend is awarded (amount not specified).

Duration   1 year; recipients may reapply for up to 5 years of support.

Additional information   This foundation was established in 1989 to provide scholarships and other assistance to disadvantaged youths in Missouri. Its motto is, "Building a Brighter Future for African American families."

Number awarded 1 or more each year.

Deadline April of each year.

[436]
PHILADELPHIA CHAPTER AABE SCHOLARSHIPS

American Association of Blacks in Energy-Philadelphia Chapter
Attn: Scholarship Committee
P.O. Box 38849
Philadelphia, PA 19104-8849
(610) 943-5614 E-mail: nancy.mifflin@exeloncorp.com
Web: www.aabe.org/index.php?component=pages&id=455

Summary To provide financial assistance to African Americans and members of other underrepresented minority groups who are high school seniors in Delaware and Pennsylvania and planning to major in an energy-related field at a college in any state.

Eligibility This program is open to seniors graduating from high schools in Delaware or Pennsylvania and planning to work on a bachelor's degree at a college or university in any state. Applicants must be African Americans, Hispanics, or Native Americans who have a GPA of 3.0 or higher and are able to demonstrate financial need. Their intended major must be a field of business, engineering, physical science (e.g., chemistry, earth science, meteorology, physics), mathematics, or technology related to energy. Along with their application, they must submit a 350-word statement on why they should receive this scholarship, their professional career objectives, and anything else that is relevant.

Financial data Stipends are $1,000 or $500.

Duration 1 year; nonrenewable.

Additional information Winners are eligible to compete for regional and national scholarships.

Number awarded 2 each year: 1 at $1,000 and 1 at $500.

Deadline March of each year.

[437]
PHILLIP D. REED UNDERGRADUATE ENDOWMENT FELLOWSHIP

National Action Council for Minorities in Engineering
Attn: University Programs
440 Hamilton Avenue, Suite 302
White Plains, NY 10601-1813
(914) 539-4010 Fax: (914) 539-4032
E-mail: scholarships@nacme.org
Web: www.nacme.org/NACME_D.aspx?pageid=105

Summary To provide financial assistance to African Americans and other underrepresented minority college sophomores majoring in engineering or related fields.

Eligibility This program is open to African American, Latino, and American Indian college sophomores who have a GPA of 3.0 or higher and have demonstrated academic excellence, leadership skills, and a commitment to science and engineering as a career. Applicants must be enrolled full time at an ABET-accredited engineering program. Fields of study include all areas of engineering as well as computer science, materials science, mathematics, operations research, or physics.

Financial data The stipend is $5,000 per year. Funds are sent directly to the recipient's university.

Duration Up to 3 years.

Number awarded 1 each year.

Deadline April of each year.

[438]
PHYSICAL AND LIFE SCIENCES DIRECTORATE INTERNSHIPS

Lawrence Livermore National Laboratory
Physical and Life Sciences Directorate
Attn: Education Coordinator
7000 East Avenue, L-418
Livermore, CA 94550
(925) 422-0455 E-mail: hutcheon3@llnl.gov
Web: www-pls.llnl.gov

Summary To provide an opportunity for undergraduate and graduate students (particularly African Americans, other minorities, and women) to work on summer research projects within the Physical and Life Sciences Directorate (PLS) of Lawrence Livermore National Laboratory (LLNL).

Eligibility This program is open to full-time undergraduate and graduate students who are interested in working on research projects within the PLS Directorate of LLNL. Openings are currently available in chemistry (organic, inorganic, synthetic, analytical, computational, nuclear, and environmental) and materials science (theory, simulation and modeling, synthesis and processing, materials under extreme conditions, dynamic materials science, metallurgy, nuclear fuels, optical materials, and surface science). Applicants must have a GPA of 3.0 or higher. Selection is based on academic record, aptitude, research interests, and recommendations of instructors. Women and minorities are encouraged to apply.

Financial data The stipend is $14 to $20 per hour for undergraduates or $4,100 to $4,900 per month for graduate students. Living accommodations and arrangements are the responsibility of the intern.

Duration 2 or 3 months, during the summer.

Number awarded Varies each year.

Deadline February of each year.

[439]
P.O. PISTILLI SCHOLARSHIPS

Design Automation Conference
c/o Cherrice Traver
Union College
Steinmetz Hall, Room 202
Schenectady, NY 12308
(518) 388-6326 Fax: (518) 388-6789
E-mail: traverc@union.edu
Web: doc.union.edu/acsee.html

Summary To provide financial assistance to female, minority, or disabled high school seniors who are interested in preparing for a career in computer science or electrical engineering.

Eligibility This program is open to graduating high school seniors who are members of underrepresented groups: women, African Americans, Hispanics, Native Americans, and persons with disabilities. Applicants must be interested in preparing for a career in electrical engineering, computer engineering, or computer science. They must have at least a

3.0 GPA, have demonstrated high achievements in math and science courses, have demonstrated involvement in activities associated with the underrepresented group they represent, and be able to demonstrate significant financial need. U.S. citizenship is not required, but applicants must be U.S. residents when they apply and must plan to attend an accredited U.S. college or university. Along with their application, they must submit 3 letters of recommendation, official transcripts, ACT/SAT and/or PSAT scores, a personal statement outlining future goals and why they think they should receive this scholarship, and documentation of financial need.

Financial data Stipends are $4,000 per year. Awards are paid each year in 2 equal installments.

Duration 1 year; renewable for up to 4 additional years.

Additional information This program is funded by the Design Automation Conference of the Association for Computing Machinery's Special Interest Group on Design Automation.

Number awarded 2 to 7 each year.

Deadline January of each year.

[440]
PRE-MED ENRICHMENT PROGRAM FOR UNDERREPRESENTED MINORITY UNDERGRADUATES

University of Pennsylvania Health System
Attn: Center of Excellence for Diversity in Health
  Education and Research
3508 Market Street, Suite 234
Philadelphia, PA 19104-3357
(215) 898-3913   Fax: (215) 573-2793
E-mail: taylor2@mail.med.upenn.edu
Web: www.uphs.upenn.edu/coeomh/premed.htm

Summary To provide an opportunity for African American and other underrepresented minority undergraduates to gain research experience in medicine during a summer program at the University of Pennsylvania.

Eligibility This program is open to undergraduate students who are members of ethnic or racial groups underrepresented in medicine. Applicants must have completed at least 60 credits of a premedical program and have a GPA of 2.75 or higher. They must be interested in participating in a program at the University of Pennsylvania that includes research, clinical observations, classroom exercises, and teaching observation designed to stimulate and cultivate their interest in academic medicine. U.S. citizenship or permanent resident status is required.

Financial data The program provides a stipend (amount not specified), housing, and 2 meals per day.

Duration 10 weeks during the summer.

Additional information This program, which began in 1993, is sponsored by the Bureau of Health Professions of the U.S. Health Resources and Services Administration.

Number awarded 10 to 12 each year.

Deadline January of each year.

[441]
PRINCETON SUMMER UNDERGRADUATE RESEARCH EXPERIENCE

Princeton University
Attn: Graduate School
Office of Academic Affairs and Diversity
Clio Hall
Princeton, NJ 08544-0255
(609) 258-2066   E-mail: diverse@princeton.edu
Web: www.princeton.edu

Summary To provide an opportunity for minority and other disadvantaged students to assist Princeton faculty in any area during the summer.

Eligibility This program is open to full-time undergraduate students at all colleges and universities in the United States who have a GPA of 3.5 or higher in their major. Current college freshmen and graduating seniors are not eligible. Applicants must be interested in working during the summer with a Princeton faculty member. They should have a goal of continuing on for a Ph.D. and preparing for a career in college or university teaching and research. Students in the sciences and engineering normally work in a laboratory group on an aspect of the faculty member's current research. Students in the humanities and social sciences might assist a faculty member engaged in a particular research, editing, bibliographical, or course-preparation project; alternatively, they may work on a research paper under faculty supervision. Members of racial and ethnic minority groups underrepresented in doctoral research programs, students from socio-economically disadvantaged backgrounds, and students at small liberal arts colleges are especially encouraged to apply.

Financial data Participants receive a stipend of $3,750, housing in a campus dormitory, a $250 meal card, and up to $500 in reimbursement of travel costs.

Duration 8 weeks during the summer.

Number awarded Up to 20 each year.

Deadline January of each year.

[442]
PRINGLE & PRINGLE HIGHER EDUCATION SCHOLARSHIP

National Naval Officers Association-Washington, D.C.
  Chapter
Attn: Scholarship Program
2701 Park Center Drive, A1108
Alexandria, VA 22302
(703) 566-3840   Fax: (703) 566-3813
E-mail: Stephen.Williams@Navy.mil
Web: dcnnoa.memberlodge.com

Summary To provide financial assistance to African American high school seniors from the Washington, D.C. area who are interested in attending college in any state.

Eligibility This program is open to African American seniors graduating from high schools in the Washington, D.C. metropolitan area who plan to enroll full time at an accredited 2- or 4-year college or university in any state. Applicants must have a GPA of 2.5 or higher and be U.S. citizens. Selection is based on academic achievement, community involvement, and financial need.

Financial data The stipend is $1,000.

Duration 1 year; nonrenewable.

Additional information Recipients are not required to join or affiliate with the military in any way.

Number awarded 1 each year.

Deadline March of each year.

[443]
PROFESSIONAL GOLF MANAGEMENT DIVERSITY SCHOLARSHIP

Professional Golfers' Association of America
Attn: PGA Foundation
100 Avenue of the Champions
Palm Beach Gardens, FL 33418
Toll Free: (888) 532-6661
Web: www.pgafoundation.com

Summary To provide financial assistance to women and minorities interested in attending a designated college or university to prepare for a career as a golf professional.

Eligibility This program is open to women and minorities interested in becoming a licensed PGA Professional. Applicants must be interested in attending 1 of 20 colleges and universities that offer the Professional Golf Management (PGM) curriculum sanctioned by the PGA.

Financial data The stipend is $3,000 per year.

Duration 1 year; may be renewed.

Additional information This program began in 1993. Programs are offered at Arizona State University (Mesa, Arizona), Campbell University (Buies Creek, North Carolina), Clemson University (Clemson, South Carolina), Coastal Carolina University (Conway, South Carolina), Eastern Kentucky University (Richmond, Kentucky), Ferris State University (Big Rapids, Michigan), Florida Gulf Coast University (Fort Myers, Florida), Florida State University (Tallahassee, Florida), Methodist College (Fayetteville, North Carolina), Mississippi State University (Mississippi State, Mississippi), New Mexico State University (Las Cruces, New Mexico), North Carolina State University (Raleigh, North Carolina), Pennsylvania State University (University Park, Pennsylvania), Sam Houston State University (Huntsville, Texas), University of Central Oklahoma (Edmond, Oklahoma), University of Colorado (Colorado Springs, Colorado), University of Idaho (Moscow, Idaho), University of Maryland Eastern Shore (Princess Anne, Maryland), University of Nebraska (Lincoln, Nebraska), and University of Nevada (Las Vegas, Nevada).

Number awarded Varies each year; recently, 20 of these scholarships were awarded.

Deadline Deadline not specified.

[444]
PROJECT SEED SCHOLARSHIPS

American Chemical Society
Attn: Education Division
1155 16th Street, N.W.
Washington, DC 20036
(202) 872-4380   Toll Free: (800) 227-5558, ext. 4380
E-mail: projectseed@acs.org
Web: portal.acs.org

Summary To provide financial assistance for college to underrepresented minorities and other high school students who participated in the American Chemical Society's Project SEED: Summer Education Experience for the Disadvantaged.

Eligibility Applicants for Project SEED must have completed the junior or senior year in high school, live within commuting distance of a sponsoring institution, have completed a course in high school chemistry, and come from an economically disadvantaged family. Preference is given to students whose family income is below $34,340 or does not exceed 200% of the federal poverty guidelines based on family size; family income may be up to $48,260 if the student is a member of an ethnic group underrepresented in the sciences (African American, Hispanic, American Indian), if their parents did not attend college, if they live in a single parent household, or if they are a member of a large family. Participants in the Project SEED program are eligible to apply for these scholarships during their senior year in high school if they plan to major in college in a chemical science or engineering field, such as chemistry, chemical engineering, biochemistry, materials science, or another closely-related field.

Financial data Stipends up to $5,000 per year are available.

Duration 1 year; nonrenewable.

Number awarded Varies each year; recently, 37 of these scholarships were awarded.

Deadline March of each year.

[445]
PROMISING SCHOLARS FUND EDWARD A. BOUCHET SCHOLARSHIPS

Community Foundation for Greater New Haven
Attn: Administrative Assistant
70 Audubon Street
New Haven, CT 06510-9755
(203) 777-7079   Fax: (203) 777-6584
E-mail: gackeifi@cfgnh.org
Web: www.cfgnh.org

Summary To provide financial assistance to African American high school seniors and graduates in Connecticut who plan to attend college in any state.

Eligibility This program is open to African American high school seniors and recent graduates in Connecticut who are planning to enter an accredited 2- or 4-year college or university in any state as a full-time undergraduate. Applicants must be U.S. citizens and have a GPA of 2.5 or higher. Selection is based on academic record, demonstrated leadership, and participation in school and community activities. Some consideration is given to honors, work experience, a statement of goals and aspirations, and unusual personal or family circumstances. Preference is given to males and to residents of New Haven County.

Financial data Stipends range from $1,000 to $4,000 per year.

Duration 1 year; recipients may reapply.

Additional information This program, established in 2007, is funded by the Beta Tau Boulé (the New Haven chapter) of Sigma Pi Phi and administered by the Scholarship Management Services division of Scholarship America.

Number awarded Up to 20 each year.

Deadline March of each year.

[446]
PROVIDENCE ALUMNAE CHAPTER COLLEGE AWARDS

Delta Sigma Theta Sorority, Inc.-Providence Alumnae
  Chapter
Attn: Financial Awards Review Committee
P.O. Box 40175
Providence, RI 02940-0175
E-mail: providencealumnae@hotmail.com
Web: www.dstprovidencealumnae.com

Summary To provide financial assistance to African American female residents of Rhode Island who are attending college in any state.

Eligibility This program is open to African American women who are residents of Rhode Island. Applicants must be attending a 4-year college or university in any state and have a GPA of 3.0 or higher. Along with their application, they must submit a current official transcript, a letter of recommendation, and an essay describing their career goals, community service activities, educational accomplishments, and personal interests and talents.

Financial data A stipend is awarded (amount not specified).

Duration 1 year.

Number awarded 1 or more each year.

Deadline February of each year.

[447]
PROVIDENCE ALUMNAE CHAPTER GENERAL HIGH SCHOOL AWARDS

Delta Sigma Theta Sorority, Inc.-Providence Alumnae
  Chapter
Attn: Financial Awards Review Committee
P.O. Box 40175
Providence, RI 02904-0175
E-mail: providencealumnae@hotmail.com
Web: www.dstprovidencealumnae.com

Summary To provide financial assistance to African American high school seniors from Rhode Island who plan to attend college in any state.

Eligibility This program is open to African American seniors graduating from high schools in Rhode Island. Applicants must be planning to attend a college or university in any state. Along with their application, they must submit a current official transcript, a letter of recommendation, and an essay describing their career goals, community service activities, educational accomplishments, and personal interests and talents.

Financial data A stipend is awarded (amount not specified).

Duration 1 year.

Number awarded 1 or more each year.

Deadline February of each year.

[448]
PROVIDENCE MEMORIAM AWARD

Delta Sigma Theta Sorority, Inc.-Providence Alumnae
  Chapter
Attn: Financial Awards Review Committee
P.O. Box 40175
Providence, RI 02904-0175
E-mail: providencealumnae@hotmail.com
Web: www.dstprovidencealumnae.com

Summary To provide financial assistance to African American female high school seniors from Rhode Island who are planning to attend college in any state.

Eligibility This program is open to African American women who are seniors graduating from high schools in Rhode Island. Applicants must be planning to enroll at a college in any state. Along with their application, they must submit a current official transcript, a letter of recommendation, and an essay describing their career goals, community service activities, educational accomplishments, and personal interests and talents.

Financial data A stipend is awarded (amount not specified).

Duration 1 year.

Number awarded 1 or more each year.

Deadline February of each year.

[449]
PUBLIC RELATIONS SOCIETY OF AMERICA MULTICULTURAL AFFAIRS SCHOLARSHIPS

Public Relations Student Society of America
Attn: Vice President of Member Services
33 Maiden Lane, 11th Floor
New York, NY 10038-5150
(212) 460-1474   Fax: (212) 995-0757
E-mail: prssa@prsa.org
Web: www.prssa.org/awards/awardMulticultural.aspx

Summary To provide financial assistance to African American and other minority college students who are interested in preparing for a career in public relations.

Eligibility This program is open to minority (African American/Black, Hispanic/Latino, Asian, Native American, Alaskan Native, or Pacific Islander) students who are at least juniors at an accredited 4-year college or university. Applicants must be enrolled full time, be able to demonstrate financial need, and have earned a GPA of 3.0 or higher. Membership in the Public Relations Student Society of America is preferred but not required. A major or minor in public relations is preferred; students who attend a school that does not offer a public relations degree or program must be enrolled in a communications degree program (e.g., journalism, mass communications).

Financial data The stipend is $1,500.

Duration 1 year.

Additional information This program was established in 1989.

Number awarded 2 each year.

Deadline April of each year.

[450]
PWC EXCEED SCHOLARSHIP PROGRAM

PricewaterhouseCoopers LLP
Attn: Campus Recruiting Manager
125 High Street
Boston, MA 02110
(617) 530-5349   Fax: (813) 741-8595
Web: www.pwc.com

Summary To provide financial assistance to African Americans and other underrepresented minority undergraduate students interested in preparing for a career in public accounting.

Eligibility This program is open to African American, Native American, and Hispanic American students entering their sophomore, junior, or senior year of college. Applicants must have a GPA of 3.4 or higher, be able to demonstrate interpersonal skills and leadership ability, and be working on a bachelor's degree in accounting, computer information systems, management information systems, finance, economics, or actuarial science. Along with their application, they must submit a 300-word essay on how they have demonstrated the core values of PricewaterhouseCoopers (PwC) of achieving excellence, developing teamwork, and inspiring leadership in their academic and/or professional career.

Financial data The stipend is $3,000.

Duration 1 year; nonrenewable.

Additional information Recipients also participate in the annual Diversity in Business Leadership Conference (held in New York City), are considered for an internship position with PwC, and engage in a mentoring program. This program began in 1990.

Number awarded Varies each year; recently, 81 of these scholarships were awarded.

Deadline December of each year.

[451]
RA CONSULTING SERVICE MARIA RILEY SCHOLARSHIP

National Forum for Black Public Administrators
Attn: Scholarship Program
777 North Capitol Street, N.E., Suite 807
Washington, DC 20002
(202) 408-9300, ext. 112   Fax: (202) 408-8558
E-mail: vreed@nfbpa.org
Web: www.nfbpa.org/i4a/pages/index.cfm?pageid=3630

Summary To provide financial assistance to African Americans working on a undergraduate or graduate degree in engineering technology.

Eligibility This program is open to African American undergraduate and graduate students preparing for a career as a public administrator serving the engineering and information technology fields. Applicants must be working full time on a degree in engineering or information technology. They must have a GPA of 3.0 or higher, excellent interpersonal and analytical abilities, and strong oral and written communication skills. Along with their application, they must submit a 3-page autobiographical essay that includes their academic and career goals and objectives. First consideration is given to applicants who are not currently receiving other financial aid.

Financial data The stipend is $2,500.

Duration 1 year.

Additional information This program is sponsored by RA Consulting Service. Recipients are required to attend the sponsor's annual conference to receive their scholarship; limited hotel and air accommodations are arranged and provided.

Number awarded 1 each year.

Deadline February of each year.

[452]
RACE RELATIONS MULTIRACIAL STUDENT SCHOLARSHIP

Christian Reformed Church
Attn: Office of Race Relations
2850 Kalamazoo Avenue, S.E.
Grand Rapids, MI 49560-0200
(616) 241-1691   Toll Free: (877) 279-9994
Fax: (616) 224-0803   E-mail: crcna@crcna.org
Web: www.crcna.org/pages/racerelations_scholar.cfm

Summary To provide financial assistance to African American and other undergraduate and graduate minority students interested in attending colleges related to the Christian Reformed Church in North America (CRCNA).

Eligibility Students of color in the United States and Canada are eligible to apply. Normally, applicants are expected to be members of CRCNA congregations who plan to pursue their educational goals at Calvin Theological Seminary or any of the colleges affiliated with the CRCNA. Students who have no prior history with the CRCNA must attend a CRCNA-related college or seminary for a full academic year before they are eligible to apply for this program. Students entering their sophomore year must have earned a GPA of 2.0 or higher as freshmen; students entering their junior year must have earned a GPA of 2.3 or higher as sophomores; students entering their senior year must have earned a GPA of 2.6 or higher as juniors.

Financial data First-year students receive $500 per semester. Other levels of students may receive up to $2,000 per academic year.

Duration 1 year.

Additional information This program was first established in 1971 and revised in 1991. Recipients are expected to train to engage actively in the ministry of racial reconciliation in church and in society. They must be able to work in the United States or Canada upon graduating and must consider working for 1 of the agencies of the CRCNA.

Number awarded Varies each year; recently, 31 students received a total of $21,000 in support.

Deadline March of each year.

[453]
RACIAL ETHNIC EDUCATIONAL SCHOLARSHIPS

Synod of the Trinity
Attn: Scholarships
3040 Market Street
Camp Hill, PA 17011-4599
(717) 737-0421, ext. 233
Toll Free: (800) 242-0534, ext. 233
Fax: (717) 737-8211   E-mail: mhumer@syntrinity.org
Web: www.syntrinity.org

Summary To provide financial assistance to African American and other ethnic minority students in Pennsylvania, West

Virginia, and designated counties in Ohio who are interested in attending college in any state.

Eligibility This program is open to members of a racial minority group (African American, Asian, Hispanic, Latino, Middle Eastern, or Native American) who are enrolled or planning to enroll full time at an accredited college or vocational school in any state. Applicants may be of any religious denomination, but they must be residents of the area served by the Presbyterian Church (USA) Synod of the Trinity, which covers all of Pennsylvania; West Virginia except for the counties of Berkeley, Grant, Hampshire, Hardy, Jefferson, Mineral, Morgan, and Pendleton; and the Ohio counties of Belmont, Harrison, Jefferson, Monroe, and the southern sector of Columbiana. They must have total income of less than $85,000 for a family of 4. U.S. citizenship or permanent resident status is required.

Financial data Awards range from $100 to $1,000 per year, depending on the need of the recipient.

Duration 1 year; recipients may reapply.

Number awarded Varies each year.

Deadline April of each year.

[454]
RALEIGH-DURHAM CHAPTER NBMBAA UNDERGRADUATE SCHOLARSHIPS

National Black MBA Association-Raleigh-Durham
  Chapter
Attn: Scholarship Program
P.O. Box 13614
Research Triangle Park, NC 27709
(919) 990-2351   E-mail: rdumba@gmail.com
Web: www.rdumba.org/?page_id=25

Summary To provide financial assistance to African American and other minority students who have ties to North Carolina and are working on an undergraduate degree in business.

Eligibility This program is open to African American and other minority students who are enrolled full time in a business or management bachelor's degree program at a college or university in any state. Applicants must have some ties to North Carolina, either through residence or college attendance there. Along with their application, they must submit a 2-page essay on a topic that changes annually but relates to African Americans and business. Selection is based on that essay, transcripts, a resume, and extracurricular activities.

Financial data The stipend is $1,000.

Duration 1 year.

Additional information Recipients must be available attend the sponsor's scholarship reception in October.

Number awarded 1 or more each year.

Deadline October of each year.

[455]
RALPH AND VALERIE THOMAS SCHOLARSHIP

National Association of Black Accountants
Attn: National Scholarship Program
7474 Greenway Center Drive, Suite 1120
Greenbelt, MD 20770
(301) 474-NABA, ext. 114   Fax: (301) 474-3114
E-mail: customerservice@nabainc.org
Web: www.nabainc.org

Summary To provide financial assistance to student members of the National Association of Black Accountants (NABA) who are working on an undergraduate or graduate degree in a field related to accounting.

Eligibility This program is open to NABA members enrolled full time as 1) an undergraduate freshman, sophomore, junior, or first-semester senior majoring in accounting, business, or finance at a 4-year college or university; or 2) a graduate student working on a master's degree in accounting. High school seniors are not eligible. Applicants must have a GPA of 3.5 or higher in their major and 3.3 or higher overall. Selection is based on grades, financial need, and a 500-word autobiography that discusses career objectives, leadership abilities, community activities, and involvement in NABA.

Financial data The stipend is $1,000.

Duration 1 year.

Number awarded 1 each year.

Deadline January of each year.

[456]
RALPH BUNCHE SUMMER INSTITUTE

American Political Science Association
Attn: Ralph Bunch Summer Institute
1527 New Hampshire Avenue, N.W.
Washington, DC 20036-1206
(202) 483-2512   Fax: (202) 483-2657
E-mail: minority@apsanet.org
Web: www.apsanet.org/content_6002.cfm

Summary To introduce African American and other underrepresented minority undergraduate students to the world of graduate study and to encourage their eventual application to a Ph.D. program in political science.

Eligibility This program is open to African American, Latino(a), Native American, and Pacific Islander college students completing their junior year. Applicants must be interested in attending graduate school and working on a degree in a field related to political science. Along with their application, they must submit a 2-page personal statement on their reasons for wanting to participate in this program and their future academic and professional plans. U.S. citizenship is required.

Financial data Participants receive a stipend of $200 per week plus full support of tuition, transportation, room, board, books, and instructional materials.

Duration 5 weeks during the summer.

Additional information The institute includes 2 transferable credit courses (1 in quantitative analysis and the other on race and American politics). In addition, guest lecturers and recruiters from Ph.D. programs visit the students. Classes are held on the campus of Duke University. Most students who attend the institute excel in their senior year and go on to graduate school, many with full graduate fellowships and teaching assistantships. This program is funded by the National Science Foundation.

Number awarded 20 each year.

Deadline January of each year.

[457]
RAYMOND R. DAVIS SCHOLARSHIP

African Methodist Episcopal Church
Third Episcopal District Lay Organization
c/o Kimberley Gordon Brooks, Director of Lay Activities
904 South Main Street
Urbana, OH 43078
(937) 925-2299   E-mail: kimberlysaponi@yahoo.com
Web: www.thirddistrictame.org/raydavis.htm

Summary To provide financial assistance to members of African Methodist Episcopal (AME) churches in its Third Episcopal District who are interested in attending college in any state.

Eligibility This program is open to members of Third Episcopal District AME churches (in Ohio, western Pennsylvania, and West Virginia). Applicants must be high school seniors or students already enrolled in a bachelor's degree program in any field at an accredited college or university in any state. Along with their application, they must submit an essay of 500 to 700 words on how they have demonstrated leadership ability in the AME church, school, and community. Selection is based on that essay, academic achievement, quality and level of church participation, leadership, extracurricular activities, honors, and letters of recommendation.

Financial data Stipends range from $500 to $1,000.

Duration 1 year.

Number awarded 1 or more each year.

Deadline February of each year.

[458]
RDW GROUP, INC. MINORITY SCHOLARSHIP FOR COMMUNICATIONS

Rhode Island Foundation
Attn: Funds Administrator
One Union Station
Providence, RI 02903
(401) 427-4017   Fax: (401) 331-8085
E-mail: lmonahan@rifoundation.org
Web: www.rifoundation.org

Summary To provide financial assistance to African Americans and other Rhode Island undergraduate and graduate students of color who are interested in preparing for a career in communications at a school in any state.

Eligibility This program is open to undergraduate and graduate students at colleges and universities in any state who are Rhode Island residents of color. Applicants must intend to work on a degree in communications (including computer graphics, art, cinematography, or other fields that would prepare them for a career in advertising). They must be able to demonstrate financial need and a commitment to a career in communications. Along with their application, they must submit an essay (up to 300 words) on the impact they would like to have on the communications field.

Financial data The stipend ranges from $1,000 to $2,500 per year.

Duration 1 year; recipients may reapply.

Additional information This program is sponsored by the RDW Group, Inc.

Number awarded 1 each year.

Deadline April of each year.

[459]
REAR ADMIRAL BENJAMIN T. HACKER, USN MEMORIAL SCHOLARSHIP

National Naval Officers Association-Washington, D.C.
  Chapter
Attn: Scholarship Program
2701 Park Center Drive, A1108
Alexandria, VA 22302
(703) 566-3840   Fax: (703) 566-3813
E-mail: Stephen.Williams@Navy.mil
Web: dcnnoa.memberlodge.com

Summary To provide financial assistance to minority high school seniors from the Washington, D.C. area who are interested in attending an Historically Black College or University (HBCU) in any state and enrolling in the Navy Reserve Officers Training Corps (NROTC) program.

Eligibility This program is open to minority seniors graduating from high schools in the Washington, D.C. metropolitan area who plan to enroll full time at an HBCU in any state that has an NROTC program; they may enroll at another college or university that shares the NROTC unit located at an HBCU. Applicants must have a GPA of 2.5 or higher and be U.S. citizens or permanent residents. Selection is based on academic achievement, community involvement, and financial need.

Financial data The stipend is $1,500.

Duration 1 year; nonrenewable.

Additional information If the recipient fails to enroll in the NROTC unit, all scholarship funds must be returned.

Number awarded 1 each year.

Deadline March of each year.

[460]
REAR ADMIRAL MACK AND NANCY GASTON LEADERSHIP SCHOLARSHIP

National Naval Officers Association-Washington, D.C.
  Chapter
Attn: Scholarship Program
2701 Park Center Drive, A1108
Alexandria, VA 22302
(703) 566-3840   Fax: (703) 566-3813
E-mail: Stephen.Williams@Navy.mil
Web: dcnnoa.memberlodge.com

Summary To provide financial assistance to African American high school seniors from the Washington, D.C. area who are interested in attending college in any state.

Eligibility This program is open to African American seniors graduating from high schools in the Washington, D.C. metropolitan area who plan to enroll full time at an accredited 2- or 4-year college or university in any state. Applicants must have a GPA of 2.5 or higher. Selection is based on academic achievement, community involvement, and financial need.

Financial data The stipend is $1,000.

Duration 1 year; nonrenewable.

Additional information Recipients are not required to join or affiliate with the military in any way.

Number awarded 1 each year.

Deadline March of each year.

[461]
REAR ADMIRAL MICHELLE HOWARD SCHOLARSHIP

National Naval Officers Association-Washington, D.C.
  Chapter
Attn: Scholarship Program
2701 Park Center Drive, A1108
Alexandria, VA 22302
(703) 566-3840   Fax: (703) 566-3813
E-mail: Stephen.Williams@Navy.mil
Web: dcnnoa.memberlodge.com

Summary To provide financial assistance to African American high school seniors from the Washington, D.C. area who are interested in attending college in any state.

Eligibility This program is open to African American seniors graduating from high schools in the Washington, D.C. metropolitan area who plan to enroll full time at an accredited 2- or 4-year college or university in any state. Applicants must have a GPA of 2.5 or higher and be U.S. citizens or permanent residents. Selection is based on academic achievement, community involvement, and financial need.

Financial data The stipend is $1,000.

Duration 1 year; nonrenewable.

Additional information Recipients are not required to join or affiliate with the military in any way.

Number awarded 1 each year.

Deadline March of each year.

[462]
REJESTA V. PERRY SCHOLARSHIP

Sigma Gamma Rho Sorority, Inc.
Attn: National Education Fund
1000 Southhill Drive, Suite 200
Cary, NC 27513
(919) 678-9720   Toll Free: (888) SGR-1922
Fax: (919) 678-9721   E-mail: info@sgrho1922.org
Web: www.sgrho1922.org/service.htm

Summary To provide financial assistance to African American and other undergraduate students working on a degree in education.

Eligibility This program is open to undergraduates working on a degree in education. The sponsor is a traditionally African American sorority, but support is available to both males and females. Applicants must have a GPA of "C" or higher and be able to demonstrate financial need.

Financial data A stipend is awarded (amount not specified).

Duration 1 year.

Additional information A processing fee of $20 is required.

Number awarded 1 each year.

Deadline April of each year.

[463]
RESEARCH IN SCIENCE AND ENGINEERING PROGRAM

Rutgers University
Attn: Graduate School
25 Bishop Place
New Brunswick, NJ 08901-1181
(732) 932-7275   Fax: (732) 932-7407
E-mail: rise@rci.rutgers.edu
Web: rise.rutgers.edu

Summary To provide an opportunity for underrepresented minorities and other undergraduate students from any state to work on a summer research project in science, mathematics, or engineering at designated universities in New Jersey.

Eligibility This program is open to undergraduates majoring in science (especially the biomedical sciences), mathematics, or engineering at a college or university in any state. Applicants must be interested in participating in a summer research project under the guidance of a faculty member at the graduate school of Rutgers University in New Brunswick or the Graduate School of Biomedical Sciences of the University of Medicine and Dentistry of New Jersey (UMDNJ) in Piscataway. They should have completed at least the sophomore year and have a GPA of 3.0 or higher. Applications are especially encouraged from members of groups underrepresented in the sciences, mathematics, or engineering; students from economically or educationally disadvantaged backgrounds; members of the first generation in their family to attend college; undergraduates attending schools that do not offer opportunities for independent research or mentoring by research-active faculty; and nontraditional students.

Financial data The stipend is $400 per week. Reimbursements for housing and travel (up to $500) are also provided.

Duration 8 or 10 weeks during the summer.

Additional information This program is jointly administered by the Rutgers University Graduate School and the UMDNJ. Support is provided by many sponsors, including the National Science Foundation, the Federation of American Societies for Experimental Biology, Merck Research Laboratories, Public Service Electric and Gas, the New Jersey Space Grant Consortium, the New Jersey Commission on Cancer Research, and the McNair Scholars Program.

Number awarded 20 to 25 each year.

Deadline Applications are accepted on a rolling basis; selection begins in January and continues until all places are filled.

[464]
RESEARCH INTERNSHIPS IN SCIENCE OF THE ENVIRONMENT

Arkansas State University
Attn: Department of Chemistry and Physics
P.O. Box 419
State University, AR 72467
(870) 972-3298   Fax: (870) 972-3089
E-mail: jpratte@astate.edu
Web: www2.astate.edu

Summary To provide an opportunity for African American and other minority undergraduates to participate in a summer research activity at Arkansas State University in Jonesboro.

Eligibility This program is open to underrepresented minority undergraduate students who have completed at least 1 course sequence in environmental science (including biology, chemistry, or geology), have a GPA of 2.5 or higher in their major, and are U.S. citizens or permanent residents. Applicants must be interested in participating in a summer research experience centered on exploring the relationships between agricultural land use and ecosystem function. Along with their application, they must submit a brief essay on their career goals after completing their bachelor's degree, their interests related to environmental science, any specific research interests, and how a research internship will contribute to their career goals.

Financial data Interns receive a stipend of $4,000; housing and travel to the site are also provided.

Duration 10 weeks during the summer.

Additional information This program is funded by the National Science Foundation as part of its Research Experiences for Undergraduates program.

Number awarded Approximately 12 each year.

Deadline March of each year.

[465]
RESOURCES FOR THE FUTURE SUMMER INTERNSHIPS

Resources for the Future
Attn: Internship Coordinator
1616 P Street, N.W., Suite 600
Washington, DC 20036-1400
(202) 328-5008   Fax: (202) 939-3460
E-mail: IC@rff.org
Web: www.rff.org

Summary To provide internships to undergraduate and graduate students (particularly African Americans or other minorities and women) who are interested in working on research projects in public policy during the summer.

Eligibility This program is open to undergraduate and graduate students (with priority to graduate students) interested in an internship at Resources for the Future (RFF). Applicants must be working on a degree in the social and natural sciences and have training in economics and quantitative methods or an interest in public policy. They should display strong writing skills and a desire to analyze complex environmental policy problems amenable to interdisciplinary methods. The ability to work without supervision in a careful and conscientious manner is essential. Women and minority candidates are strongly encouraged to apply. Both U.S. and non-U.S. citizens are eligible, if the latter have proper work and residency documentation.

Financial data The stipend is $375 per week for graduate students or $350 per week for undergraduates. Housing assistance is not provided.

Duration 10 weeks during the summer; beginning and ending dates can be adjusted to meet particular student needs.

Deadline March of each year.

[466]
REV. CHARLES WILLIAMS MINORITY SCHOLARSHIP

Indiana Broadcasters Association
Attn: Scholarship Administrator
3003 East 98th Street, Suite 161
Indianapolis, IN 46280
(317) 573-0119   Toll Free: (800) 342-6276 (within IN)
Fax: (317) 573-0895   E-mail: INDBA@aol.com
Web: www.indianabroadcasters.org

Summary To provide financial assistance to African American college students in Indiana who are interested in preparing for a career in a field related to broadcasting.

Eligibility This program is open to African American residents of Indiana who are attending a college or university in the state that is a member of the Indiana Broadcasters Association (IBA) or that has a radio/TV facility on campus. Applicants must be majoring in telecommunications or broadcast journalism and have a GPA of 3.0 or higher. They must be actively participating at a college broadcast facility or working for a commercial broadcast facility while attending college. Along with their application, they must submit an essay on their interest in continuing an education in telecommunications or broadcast journalism. Financial need is not considered in the selection process.

Financial data The stipend is $2,000.

Duration 1 year.

Number awarded 1 each year.

Deadline March of each year.

[467]
REYNELDA MUSE TELEVISION JOURNALISM SCHOLARSHIP

Colorado Association of Black Journalists
Attn: Scholarship Committee
P.O. Box 48192
Denver, CO 80204
(303) 929-7299   E-mail: info@cabj-denver.org
Web: www.cabj-denver.org/awards.html

Summary To provide financial assistance to African American residents of Colorado who are majoring in television journalism at a college in any state.

Eligibility This program is open to African American residents of Colorado who are majoring in television journalism at an accredited institution of higher learning in any state. Applicants must submit a 2-page essay that covers why they chose their particular field of study; their career goals; their involvement in campus, community, or school activities that demonstrates their commitment to television journalism; how they imagine making a contribution to the African American community through a career in television journalism; any circumstances that have affected their GPA or decreased campus involvement (if any); and why they feel they should receive this scholarship.

Financial data A stipend is awarded (amount not specified).

Duration 1 year.

Number awarded 1 or more each year.

Deadline June of each year.

[468]
RICHARD HECKERT FELLOWSHIP

National Action Council for Minorities in Engineering
Attn: University Programs
440 Hamilton Avenue, Suite 302
White Plains, NY 10601-1813
(914) 539-4010   Fax: (914) 539-4032
E-mail: scholarships@nacme.org
Web: www.nacme.org/NACME_D.aspx?pageid=105

Summary   To provide financial assistance to African Americans and other underrepresented minority high school seniors interested in studying engineering or related fields in college.

Eligibility   This program is open to African American, Latino, and American Indian high school seniors who are in the top 10% of their graduating class, have a GPA of 3.0 or higher, and have demonstrated academic excellence, leadership skills, and a commitment to science and engineering as a career. Candidates must have been accepted as a full-time student at an ABET-accredited engineering program. They must be nominated by their school (each high school may nominate only 1 student). Fields of study include all areas of engineering as well as computer science, materials science, mathematics, operations research, or physics. Letters of nomination must be accompanied by a transcript, SAT or ACT report form, resume, and 100-word statement of why the student should receive this scholarship.

Financial data   The stipend is $5,000 per year. Funds are sent directly to the recipient's university.

Duration   4 years.

Number awarded   1 each year.

Deadline   April of each year.

[469]
RICHARD S. SMITH SCHOLARSHIP

United Methodist Church
Attn: General Board of Discipleship
Division on Ministries with Young People
P.O. Box 340003
Nashville, TN 37203-0003
(615) 340-7184   Toll Free: (877) 899-2780, ext. 7184
Fax: (615) 340-7063   E-mail: youngpeople@gbod.org
Web: www.gbod.org

Summary   To provide financial assistance to African American and other minority high school seniors who wish to prepare for a Methodist church-related career.

Eligibility   This program is open to graduating high school seniors who are members of racial/ethnic minority groups and have been active members of a United Methodist Church for at least 1 year. Applicants must have been admitted to an accredited college or university to prepare for a church-related career. They must have maintained at least a "C" average throughout high school and be able to demonstrate financial need. Along with their application, they must submit brief essays on their participation in church projects and activities, a leadership experience, the role their faith plays in their life, the church-related vocation to which God is calling them, and their extracurricular interests and activities. U.S. citizenship or permanent resident status is required.

Financial data   The stipend is $1,000.

Duration   1 year; nonrenewable.

Additional information   This scholarship was first awarded in 1997. Recipients must enroll full time in their first year of undergraduate study.

Number awarded   2 each year.

Deadline   May of each year.

[470]
ROBERT A. ELLIS SCHOLARSHIP IN PHYSICS

National Society of Black Physicists
Attn: Scholarship Committee Chair
1100 North Glebe Road, Suite 1010
Arlington, VA 22201
(703) 536-4207   Fax: (703) 536-4203
E-mail: scholarship@nsbp.org
Web: www.nsbp.org/scholarships

Summary   To provide financial assistance to African American students majoring in physics in college.

Eligibility   This program is open to African American students who are entering their junior or senior year of college and majoring in physics. Applicants must submit an essay on their academic and career objectives, information on their participation in extracurricular activities, a description of any awards and honors they have received, and 3 letters of recommendation. Financial need is not considered.

Financial data   A stipend is awarded (amount not specified).

Duration   1 year; nonrenewable.

Number awarded   1 each year.

Deadline   January of each year.

[471]
ROBERT D. LYNCH LEADERSHIP SCHOLARSHIP

Pennsylvania Black Conference on Higher Education
c/o Judith A.W. Thomas, Scholarship Committee Chair
Lincoln University, School of Social Sciences and
  Behavioral Studies
1570 Old Baltimore Pike
P.O. Box 179
Lincoln University, PA 19352
(484) 365-8159   E-mail: scholarships@pbcohe.org
Web: www.phcohe.org

Summary   To provide financial assistance to African American residents of any state who are enrolled as undergraduates at colleges in Pennsylvania and have demonstrated outstanding leadership skills.

Eligibility   This program is open to African Americans from any state who have completed at least the first semester as an undergraduate at a college or university in Pennsylvania. Applicants must have a GPA of 3.0 or higher. Along with their application, they must submit an essay, up to 5 pages in length, on why they should receive this scholarship. Selection is based on leadership skills and academic record.

Financial data   The stipend is $1,000.

Duration   1 year.

Number awarded   1 each year.

Deadline   January of each year.

[472]
ROBERT P. MADISON SCHOLARSHIP IN ARCHITECTURE

Cleveland Foundation
Attn: Scholarship Officer
1422 Euclid Avenue, Suite 1300
Cleveland, OH 44115-2001
(216) 861-3810   Fax: (216) 861-1729
E-mail: mbaker@clevefdn.org
Web: www.clevelandfoundation.org/Scholarships

Summary   To provide financial assistance to African American high school seniors and undergraduates from any state who are interested in studying architecture.

Eligibility   This program is open to African American high school seniors and current undergraduates. Applicants must be accepted or enrolled at an accredited college or university that has a degree-granting program in architecture. They must have a GPA of 3.0 or higher and be able to demonstrate financial need. Along with their application, they must submit a brief essay on why they want to be an architect. Selection is based on evidence of commitment to a career as an architect, academic performance, and special skill or talent related to excelling in architectural course work.

Financial data   The stipend is $1,000. Funds are paid directly to the recipient's institution to be used for tuition, fees, books, supplies, and/or equipment required for courses.

Duration   1 year; nonrenewable.

Additional information   This program was established in 2004 by the firm of Robert P. Madison International to honor its founder, the first African American registered to practice architecture in Ohio.

Number awarded   Varies each year.

Deadline   March of each year.

[473]
ROCHON/DAVIS SCHOLARSHIP

National Naval Officers Association-Washington, D.C.
  Chapter
Attn: Scholarship Program
2701 Park Center Drive, A1108
Alexandria, VA 22302
(703) 566-3840   Fax: (703) 566-3813
E-mail: Stephen.Williams@Navy.mil
Web: dcnnoa.memberlodge.com

Summary   To provide financial assistance to African American high school seniors from the Washington, D.C. area who are interested in attending an Historically Black College or University (HBCU) in any state.

Eligibility   This program is open to African American seniors graduating from high schools in the Washington, D.C. metropolitan area who plan to enroll full time at an HBCU in any state. Applicants must have a GPA of 3.0 or higher and be U.S. citizens or permanent residents. Selection is based on academic achievement, community involvement, and financial need.

Financial data   The stipend is $1,000.

Duration   1 year; nonrenewable.

Additional information   Recipients are not required to join or affiliate with the military in any way.

Number awarded   1 each year.

Deadline   March of each year.

[474]
ROCKWELL AUTOMATION SCHOLARSHIPS

Society of Women Engineers
Attn: Scholarship Selection Committee
120 South LaSalle Street, Suite 1515
Chicago, IL 60603-3572
(312) 596-5223   Toll Free: (877) SWE-INFO
Fax: (312) 644-8557
E-mail: scholarshipapplication@swe.org
Web: societyofwomenengineers.swe.org

Summary   To provide financial assistance to upper-division women (particularly African American and other minority women) majoring in computer science or selected engineering specialties.

Eligibility   This program is open to women who are entering their junior year at an ABET-accredited college or university. Applicants must be majoring in computer science or computer, electrical, industrial, manufacturing, mechanical, or software engineering and have a GPA of 3.0 or higher. Selection is based on merit and demonstrated leadership potential. Preference is given to students attending designated universities and to members of groups underrepresented in computer science and engineering.

Financial data   The stipend is $2,500.

Duration   1 year.

Additional information   This program, established in 1991, is supported by Rockwell Automation, Inc. For a list of the preferred universities, contact the sponsor.

Number awarded   2 each year.

Deadline   February of each year.

[475]
ROCKWELL COLLINS NSBE CORPORATE SCHOLARSHIPS

National Society of Black Engineers
Attn: Programs Department
205 Daingerfield Road
Alexandria, VA 22314
(703) 549-2207   Fax: (703) 683-5312
E-mail: scholarships@nsbe.org
Web: www.nsbe.org

Summary   To provide financial assistance and work experience to members of the National Society of Black Engineers (NSBE) who are majoring in computer science or designated engineering fields.

Eligibility   This program is open to members of the society who are enrolled as college sophomores or juniors and majoring in aerospace engineering, computer engineering, computer science (with an emphasis on software engineering), or electrical engineering. Applicants must have a GPA of 3.0 or higher and a demonstrated interest in employment with Rockwell Collins. They must be U.S. citizens or otherwise eligible to work in the United States.

Financial data   The stipend is $2,500.

Duration   1 year.

Additional information   This program is sponsored by Rockwell Collins, Inc. Recipients must be available to accept, if offered, an internship or co-op with Rockwell Collins prior to completion of their undergraduate program.

Number awarded 3 each year: 1 for a student in aerospace engineering, 1 for a student in electrical and/or computer engineering, and 1 for a student in computer science.

Deadline January of each year.

[476]
ROCKWELL COLLINS SWE SCHOLARSHIPS

Society of Women Engineers
Attn: Scholarship Selection Committee
120 South LaSalle Street, Suite 1515
Chicago, IL 60603-3572
(312) 596-5223   Toll Free: (877) SWE-INFO
Fax: (312) 644-8557
E-mail: scholarshipapplication@swe.org
Web: societyofwomenengineers.swe.org

Summary To provide financial assistance to undergraduate members of the Society of Women Engineers (SWE) (especially African Americans and other underrepresented minorities) who are majoring in computer science or selected engineering specialties.

Eligibility This program is open to members of the society who are entering their sophomore or junior year at a 4-year ABET-accredited college or university. Applicants must be majoring in computer science or computer, electrical, or software engineering and have a GPA of 3.0 or higher. Selection is based on merit. Preference is given to members of groups underrepresented in computer science and engineering.

Financial data The stipend is $2,250.

Duration 1 year.

Additional information This program, established in 1991, is supported by Rockwell Collins, Inc.

Number awarded 3 each year.

Deadline February of each year.

[477]
RONALD E. MCNAIR SCHOLARSHIP IN SPACE AND OPTICAL PHYSICS

National Society of Black Physicists
Attn: Scholarship Committee Chair
1100 North Glebe Road, Suite 1010
Arlington, VA 22201
(703) 536-4207   Fax: (703) 536-4203
E-mail: scholarship@nsbp.org
Web: www.nsbp.org/scholarships

Summary To provide financial assistance to African American students majoring in space or optical physics in college.

Eligibility This program is open to African American students who are entering their junior or senior year of college and majoring in space or optical physics. Applicants must submit an essay on their academic and career objectives, information on their participation in extracurricular activities, a description of any awards and honors they have received, and 3 letters of recommendation. Financial need is not considered.

Financial data The stipend is $1,000.

Duration 1 year; nonrenewable.

Additional information This program is offered in partnership with the American Astronomical Society.

Number awarded 1 each year.

Deadline January of each year.

[478]
RONALD E. MCNAIR SCIENTIFIC ACHIEVEMENT AWARD

Omega Psi Phi Fraternity
Attn: Charles R. Drew Memorial Scholarship Commission
3951 Snapfinger Parkway
Decatur, GA 30035-3203
(404) 284-5533   Fax: (404) 284-0333
E-mail: scholarshipchairman@oppf.org
Web: oppf.org/scholarship

Summary To provide financial assistance to undergraduate Omega Psi Phi Fraternity brothers who are majoring in the sciences.

Eligibility This program is open to fraternity brothers in good standing who are at least sophomores in college and are majoring in chemistry, physics, biology, engineering, or mathematics. Applicants must be enrolled full time and have a GPA of 3.5 or higher. Along with their application, they must submit a statement of 200 to 250 words on their purpose for applying for this scholarship, how they believe funds from the fraternity can assist them in achieving their career goals, and other circumstances (including financial need) that make it important for them to receive financial assistance.

Financial data The stipend is $7,500.

Duration 1 year.

Number awarded 1 or more each year.

Deadline May of each year.

[479]
ROSEWOOD FAMILY SCHOLARSHIP FUND

Florida Department of Education
Attn: Office of Student Financial Assistance
325 West Gaines Street
Tallahassee, FL 32399-0400
(850) 410-5160   Toll Free: (888) 827-2004
Fax: (850) 487-1809   E-mail: osfa@fldoe.org
Web: www.floridastudentfinancialaid.org

Summary To provide financial assistance for undergraduate education to needy African American and other minority students who wish to study in Florida.

Eligibility This program is open to residents of any state who wish to enroll full time at a state university, public community college, or public postsecondary vocational/technical school in Florida. Applicants must be a descendant of an African American Rosewood family (whose members were killed by a mob in January 1923). Other minority undergraduate students are considered if funds remain available after awarding Rosewood descendants. Financial need must be demonstrated.

Financial data Stipends depend on the need of the recipient; recently, they averaged $3,134 for students at public state universities and $2,407 for students at public community colleges.

Duration 1 year; may be renewed up to 3 additional years, provided the student maintains full-time enrollment and a GPA of 2.0 or higher.

Number awarded Varies each year; recently, this program presented 12 new and 10 renewal awards.

Deadline March of each year.

[480]
ROY WILKINS SCHOLARSHIP PROGRAM

National Association for the Advancement of Colored People
Attn: Education Department
4805 Mt. Hope Drive
Baltimore, MD 21215-3297
(410) 580-5760   Toll Free: (877) NAACP-98
E-mail: youth@naacpnet.org
Web: www.naacp.org/pages/naacp-scholarships

Summary To provide financial assistance for college to student members of the National Association for the Advancement of Colored People (NAACP).

Eligibility This program is open to graduating high school seniors who have a GPA of 2.5 or higher, Applicants must intend to enroll full time at an accredited college in the United States. Along with their application, they must submit a 1-page essay on their interest in their major and a career, their life's ambition, what they hope to accomplish in their lifetime, and what position they hope to attain. Membership and participation in the association are highly desirable. U.S. citizenship is required. Financial need is also considered in the selection process.

Financial data The stipend is $1,000.

Duration 1 year; nonrenewable.

Additional information This program was established in 1963.

Number awarded Varies each year; recently, 14 of these scholarships were awarded.

Deadline March of each year.

[481]
ROYCE R. WATTS SR. SCHOLARSHIP

Watts Charity Association, Inc.
6245 Bristol Parkway, Suite 224
Culver City, CA 90230
(323) 671-0394   Fax: (323) 778-2613
E-mail: wattscharity@aol.com
Web: 4watts.tripod.com/id5.html

Summary To provide financial assistance to upper-division African American college students interested in health, civil rights, or administration.

Eligibility This program is open to U.S. citizens of African American descent who are enrolled full time as a college or university junior. Applicants must have an interest in health and pre-medicine, community activities and civil rights, or administration. They must have a GPA of 3.0 or higher, be between 17 and 24 years of age, and be able to demonstrate that they intend to continue their education for at least 2 more years. Along with their application, they must submit 1) a 1-paragraph statement on why they should be awarded a Watts Foundation scholarship, and 2) a 1- to 2-page essay on a specific type of cancer, based either on how it has impacted their life or on researched information.

Financial data A stipend is awarded (amount not specified).

Duration 1 year.

Additional information Royce R. Watts, Sr. established the Watts Charity Association after he learned he had cancer in 2001.

Number awarded 1 each year.

Deadline May of each year.

[482]
RUTH M. BATSON SCHOLARSHIPS

Ruth M. Batson Educational Foundation
250 Cambridge Street, Suite 701
Boston, MA 02114
(617) 742-1070   E-mail: dao5753@aol.com

Summary To provide financial assistance to African American college students who face serious financial need.

Eligibility This program is open to African American college students who need aid as a supplement to other financial assistance. Emergency grants are also available to students who need assistance to remain in school. Selection is based on academic achievement, character, extracurricular activities, and financial need.

Financial data Assistance ranges from $500 to $1,500.

Duration 1 year.

Number awarded Varies each year.

Deadline June of each year.

[483]
SACHS FOUNDATION SCHOLARSHIPS

Sachs Foundation
90 South Cascade Avenue, Suite 1410
Colorado Springs, CO 80903-1691
(719) 633-2353
Web: www.sachsfoundation.org

Summary To provide financial assistance to Black high school seniors in Colorado who plan to attend college in any state.

Eligibility This program is open to Black graduating high school seniors who are U.S. citizens and have been residents of Colorado for at least 5 years. Applicants must be planning to attend a college or university in any state. Along with their application, they must submit a 1-page personal biography, transcripts, 3 references, and documentation of financial need. Once accepted as undergraduate scholars, students may later apply for support in graduate school.

Financial data The average annual stipend recently is $5,000 for undergraduates or $6,000 for graduate students. Funds are sent to the financial aid office of the recipient's school.

Duration Normally, undergraduate students receive 4 years of support, as long as they maintain full-time enrollment and a current GPA of 2.5 or higher per term. Graduate students receive up to an additional 4 years of support.

Additional information This foundation was established in 1931. Since its founding, it has provided more than 8,000 scholarships to African Americans in Colorado.

Number awarded Varies each year. Approximately 50 new undergraduate scholarships and 10 graduate fellowships are awarded annually.

Deadline March of each year.

[484]
SANDRA R. SPAULDING MEMORIAL SCHOLARSHIPS

California Nurses Association
Attn: Scholarship Fund
2000 Franklin Street, Suite 300
Oakland, CA 94612
(510) 273-2200, ext. 344   Fax: (510) 663-1625
E-mail: membershipbenefits@calnurses.org
Web: www.calnurses.org/membership

Summary   To provide financial assistance to African American and other students from diverse ethnic backgrounds who are enrolled in an associate degree in nursing (A.D.N.) program in California.

Eligibility   This program is open to students who have been admitted to a second-year accredited A.D.N. program in California and plan to complete the degree within 2 years. Along with their application, they must submit a 1-page essay describing their personal and professional goals. Selection is based on that essay, commitment and active participation in nursing and health-related organizations, professional vision and direction, and financial need. A goal of this scholarship program is to encourage ethnic and socioeconomic diversity in nursing.

Financial data   A stipend is awarded (amount not specified).

Duration   1 year; nonrenewable.

Additional information   This program was established in 1985.

Number awarded   1 or more each year.

Deadline   June of each year.

[485]
SCHOLARSHIP FOR DIVERSITY IN ENGINEERING

Association of Independent Colleges and Universities of Pennsylvania
101 North Front Street
Harrisburg, PA 17101-1405
(717) 232-8649   Fax: (717) 233-8574
E-mail: info@aicup.org
Web: www.aicup.org

Summary   To provide financial assistance to African Americans, other minorities, and women from any state who are enrolled at member institutions of the Association of Independent Colleges and Universities of Pennsylvania (AICUP) and majoring in designated fields of engineering.

Eligibility   This program is open to undergraduate students from any state enrolled full time at AICUP colleges and universities. Applicants must be women and/or members of the following minority groups: American Indians, Alaska Natives, Asians, Blacks/African Americans, Hispanics/Latinos, Native Hawaiians, or Pacific Islanders. They must be juniors majoring in chemical or mechanical engineering with a GPA of 2.7 or higher. Along with their application, they must submit an essay on their characteristics, accomplishments, primary interests, plans, goals, and uniqueness.

Financial data   The stipend is $7,500 per year.

Duration   1 year; may be renewed 1 additional year if the recipient maintains appropriate academic standards.

Additional information   This program, sponsored by Air Products and Chemicals, Inc., is available at the 83 private colleges and universities in Pennsylvania that comprise the AICUP.

Number awarded   1 each year.

Deadline   April of each year.

[486]
SCHOLARSHIP FOR DIVERSITY IN TEACHING

Mid-Atlantic Association for Employment in Education
c/o Kerri G. Gardi
Kutztown University
Director, Career Development Center
P.O. Box 730
Kutztown, PA 19530
(610) 683-4647   E-mail: gardi@kutztown.edu
Web: www.maeeonline.org/pages/scholarships_jump.aspx

Summary   To provide financial assistance to African American and other minority upper-division students at universities in the Mid-Atlantic region who are preparing for a career as a teacher.

Eligibility   This program is open to members of racial and ethnic minority groups who have completed between 48 and 90 credits at a college or university in Delaware, Maryland, New Jersey, New York, Pennsylvania, Virginia, Washington, D.C., or West Virginia. Applicants must be enrolled full time majoring in a field to prepare for a career in teaching. Along with their application, they must submit a 1-page essay on why they have chosen to become a teacher and what they hope to accomplish as an educator. Selection is based on academic success, service to college and/or community, and potential to achieve excellence as a teacher. U.S. citizenship is required.

Financial data   The stipend is $1,000.

Duration   1 year; nonrenewable.

Number awarded   1 each year.

Deadline   November of each year.

[487]
SCHOLARSHIPS FOR MINORITY ACCOUNTING STUDENTS

American Institute of Certified Public Accountants
Attn: Academic and Career Development Division
220 Leigh Farm Road
Durham, NC 27707-8110
(919) 402-4931   Fax: (919) 419-4705
E-mail: MIC_Programs@aicpa.org
Web: www.aicpa.org/members/div/career/mini/smas.htm

Summary   To provide financial assistance to African American and other minorities interested in studying accounting at the undergraduate or graduate school level.

Eligibility   This program is open to minority undergraduate and graduate students, enrolled full time, who have a GPA of 3.3 or higher (both cumulatively and in their major) and intend to pursue a C.P.A. credential. Undergraduates must have completed at least 30 semester hours, including at least 6 semester hours of a major in accounting. Graduate students must be working on a master's degree in accounting, finance, taxation, or a related program. Applicants must be U.S. citizens or permanent residents and student affiliate members of the American Institute of Certified Public Accountants

(AICPA). The program defines minority students as those whose heritage is Black or African American, Hispanic or Latino, Native American, or Asian American.

Financial data Stipends range from $1,500 to $3,000 per year. Funds are disbursed directly to the recipient's school.

Duration 1 year; may be renewed up to 3 additional years or until completion of a bachelor's or master's degree, whichever is earlier.

Additional information This program is administered by The Center for Scholarship Administration, E-mail: allison-lee@bellsouth.net. The most outstanding applicant for this program is awarded the Stuart A. Kessler Scholarship for Minority Students.

Number awarded Varies each year; recently, 94 students received funding through this program.

Deadline March of each year.

[488]
SCHOLARSHIPS FOR MINORITY UNDERGRADUATE PHYSICS MAJORS

American Physical Society
Attn: Committee on Minorities
One Physics Ellipse
College Park, MD 20740-3844
(301) 209-3232   Fax: (301) 209-0865
Web: www.aps.org

Summary To provide financial assistance to African Americans and other underrepresented minority students interested in studying physics on the undergraduate level.

Eligibility Any African American, Hispanic American, or Native American who plans to major in physics and who is a high school senior or college freshman or sophomore may apply. U.S. citizenship or permanent resident status is required. The selection committee especially encourages applications from students who are attending or planning to attend institutions with historically or predominantly Black, Hispanic, or Native American enrollment. Selection is based on commitment to the study of physics and plans to work on a physics baccalaureate degree.

Financial data Stipends are $2,000 per year in the first year or $3,000 in the second year; funds must be used for tuition, room, and board. In addition, $500 is awarded to the host department.

Duration 1 year; renewable for 1 additional year with the approval of the APS selection committee.

Additional information APS conducts this program, which began in 1980 as the Corporate-Sponsored Scholarships for Minority Undergraduate Students Who Major in Physics, in conjunction with the Corporate Associates of the American Institute of Physics. Each scholarship is sponsored by a corporation, which is normally designated as the sponsor. A corporation generally sponsors from 1 to 10 scholarships, depending upon its size and utilization of physics in the business.

Number awarded Varies each year; recently, 40 of these scholarships were awarded.

Deadline February of each year.

[489]
SCHOLARSHIPS FOR SOCIAL JUSTICE

Higher Education Consortium for Urban Affairs
Attn: Student Services
2233 University Avenue West, Suite 210
St. Paul, MN 55114-1698
(651) 646-8831   Toll Free: (800) 554-1089
Fax: (651) 659-9421   E-mail: hecua@hecua.org
Web: www.hecua.org/scholarships.php

Summary To provide financial assistance to African Americans and other students from targeted groups who are enrolled in programs of the Higher Education Consortium for Urban Affairs (HECUA) at participating colleges and universities.

Eligibility This program is open to students at member colleges and universities who are participating in HECUA programs. Applicants must be a first-generation college student, from a low-income family, or a student of color. Along with their application, they must submit a reflective essay, drawing on their life experiences and their personal and academic goals, on what they believe they can contribute to the mission of HECUA to equip students with the knowledge, experiences, tools, and passion to address issues of social justice and social change. The essay should also explain how the HECUA program will benefit them and the people, issues, and communities they care about.

Financial data The stipend is $1,500. Funds are applied as a credit to the student's HECUA program fees for the semester.

Duration 1 semester.

Additional information This program was established in 2006. Consortium members include Augsburg College (Minneapolis, Minnesota), Augustana College (Sioux Falls, South Dakota), Carleton College (Northfield, Minnesota), College of Saint Scholastica (Duluth, Minnesota), Colorado College (Colorado Springs, Colorado), Denison University (Granville, Ohio), Gustavus Adolphus College (St. Peter, Minnesota), Hamline University (St. Paul, Minnesota), Macalester College (St. Paul, Minnesota), Saint Mary's University (Winona, Minnesota), Saint Catherine University (St. Paul, Minnesota), Saint Olaf College (Northfield, Minnesota), Swarthmore College (Swarthmore, Pennsylvania), University of Minnesota (Minneapolis, Minnesota), University of Saint Thomas (St. Paul, Minnesota), and Viterbo University (La Crosse, Wisconsin).

Number awarded 2 each year.

Deadline April of each year for summer and fall programs; November of each year for January and spring programs.

[490]
SCIENCE AND MATHEMATICS SCHOLARSHIP

National Naval Officers Association-Washington, D.C. Chapter
Attn: Scholarship Program
2701 Park Center Drive, A1108
Alexandria, VA 22302
(703) 566-3840   Fax: (703) 566-3813
E-mail: Stephen.Williams@Navy.mil
Web: dcnnoa.memberlodge.com

Summary To provide financial assistance to African American and other minority high school seniors from the Washington, D.C. area who are interested in majoring in science or mathematics at a college in any state.

Eligibility This program is open to minority seniors graduating from high schools in the Washington, D.C. metropolitan area who plan to enroll full time at an accredited 2- or 4-year college or university in any state and major in science or mathematics. Applicants must have a GPA of 2.5 or higher and be U.S. citizens or permanent residents. Selection is based on academic achievement, community involvement, and financial need.

Financial data The stipend is $4,500.

Duration 1 year; nonrenewable.

Additional information Recipients are not required to join or affiliate with the military in any way. This program is sponsored by Science Applications International Corporation.

Number awarded 1 each year.

Deadline March of each year.

[491]
SCIENCE APPLICATIONS INTERNATIONAL CORPORATION ENGINEERING SCHOLARSHIP

National Naval Officers Association-Washington, D.C.
  Chapter
Attn: Scholarship Program
2701 Park Center Drive, A1108
Alexandria, VA 22302
(703) 566-3840   Fax: (703) 566-3813
E-mail: Stephen.Williams@Navy.mil
Web: dcnnoa.memberlodge.com

Summary To provide financial assistance to African American and other minority high school seniors from the Washington, D.C. area who are interested in majoring in engineering at a college in any state.

Eligibility This program is open to minority seniors graduating from high schools in the Washington, D.C. metropolitan area who plan to enroll full time in an engineering program at an accredited 2- or 4-year college or university in any state. Applicants must have a GPA of 2.5 or higher and be U.S. citizens or permanent residents. Selection is based on academic achievement, community involvement, and financial need.

Financial data The stipend is $4,500.

Duration 1 year; nonrenewable.

Additional information Recipients are not required to join or affiliate with the military in any way. This program is sponsored by Science Applications International Corporation.

Number awarded 1 each year.

Deadline March of each year.

[492]
SCIENCE TEACHER PREPARATION PROGRAM

Alabama Alliance for Science, Engineering, Mathematics,
  and Science Education
Attn: Project Director
University of Alabama at Birmingham
Campbell Hall, Room 401
1300 University Boulevard
Birmingham, AL 35294-1170
(205) 934-8762   Fax: (205) 934-1650
E-mail: LDale@uab.edu
Web: www.uab.edu/istp/alabama.html

Summary To provide financial assistance to African American and other underrepresented minority students at designated institutions in Alabama who are interested in preparing for a career as a science teacher.

Eligibility This program is open to members of underrepresented minority groups who have been unconditionally admitted to a participating Alabama college or university. Applicants must be interested in becoming certified to teach science and mathematics in K-12 schools. They may be 1) entering freshmen enrolling in a science education program leading to a bachelor's degree and certification; 2) students transferring from a community college and enrolling in a science education program leading to a bachelor's degree and certification; 3) students with a bachelor's degree in mathematics, science, or education and enrolling in a certification program; or 4) students with a bachelor's degree in mathematics, science, or education and enrolling in a fifth-year program leading to a master's degree and certification.

Financial data The stipend is $1,000 per year.

Duration 1 year; may be renewed.

Additional information Support for this program is provided by the National Science Foundation. The participating institutions are Alabama A&M University, Alabama State University, Auburn University, Miles College, Stillman College, Talladega College, Tuskegee University, University of Alabama at Birmingham, and University of Alabama in Huntsville.

Number awarded Varies each year.

Deadline Deadline not specified.

[493]
SCOTTS COMPANY SCHOLARS PROGRAM

Golf Course Superintendents Association of America
Attn: Environmental Institute for Golf
1421 Research Park Drive
Lawrence, KS 66049-3859
(785) 832-4445   Toll Free: (800) 472-7878, ext. 4445
Fax: (785) 832-4448   E-mail: mwright@gcsaa.org
Web: www.gcsaa.org/students/Scholarships.aspx

Summary To provide financial assistance and summer work experience to high school seniors and college students (particularly African Americans and those from diverse backgrounds) who are preparing for a career in golf management.

Eligibility This program is open to high school seniors and college students (freshmen, sophomores, and juniors) who are interested in preparing for a career in golf management (the "green industry"). Applicants should come from diverse ethnic, cultural, or socioeconomic backgrounds, defined to include women, minorities, and people with disabilities. Selection is based on cultural diversity, academic achievement, extracurricular activities, leadership, employment potential, essay responses, and letters of recommendation. Financial need is not considered. Finalists are selected for summer internships and then compete for scholarships.

Financial data The finalists receive a $500 award to supplement their summer internship income. Scholarship stipends are $2,500.

Duration 1 year.

Additional information The program is funded from a permanent endowment established by Scotts Company. Finalists are responsible for securing their own internships.

Number awarded 5 finalists, of whom 2 receive scholarships, are selected each year.

Deadline February of each year.

[494]
S.D. BECHTEL JR. FOUNDATION ENGINEERING SCHOLARSHIPS

National Society of Black Engineers
Attn: Programs Department
205 Daingerfield Road
Alexandria, VA 22314
(703) 549-2207   Fax: (703) 683-5312
E-mail: scholarships@nsbe.org
Web: www.nsbe.org

Summary To provide financial assistance to undergraduate members of the National Society of Black Engineers (NSBE) who are studying civil or mechanical engineering.

Eligibility This program is open to members of the society who are current college sophomores, juniors, or seniors. Applicants must be majoring in civil or mechanical engineering. They must have a GPA of 3.0 or higher. Along with their application, they must submit 3 essays of 300 words each on assigned topics. Selection is based on academic standing, leadership skills, focus on engineering in the work world, and financial need.

Financial data The stipend is $15,000 per year.

Duration 1 year; may be renewed, depending on academic performance and progress toward graduation.

Additional information This program is sponsored by the S.D. Bechtel, Jr. Foundation.

Number awarded 3 each year.

Deadline January of each year.

[495]
SEATTLE CHAPTER AWIS SCHOLARSHIPS

Association for Women in Science-Seattle Chapter
c/o Fran Solomon, Scholarship Committee Chair
5805 16th Avenue, N.E.
Seattle, WA 98105
(206) 522-6441   E-mail: scholarship@seattleawis.org
Web: www.seattleawis.org/programs/scholarship.html

Summary To provide financial assistance to women (especially African American and other minority women) who are undergraduates from any state majoring in science, mathematics, or engineering at colleges and universities in Washington.

Eligibility This program is open to women from any state entering their junior or senior year at a 4-year college or university in Washington. Applicants must have a declared major in science (e.g., biological sciences, environmental science, biochemistry, chemistry, pharmacy, geology, computer science, physics), mathematics, or engineering. Along with their application, they must submit essays on the events that led to their choice of a major, their current career plans and long-term goals, and their volunteer and community activities. Financial need is considered in the selection process. At least 1 scholarship is reserved for a woman from a group that is underrepresented in science, mathematics, and engineering careers, including Native American Indians and Alaska Natives, Black/African Americans, Mexican Americans/Chi-

canas/Latinas, Native Pacific Islanders (Polynesians, Melanesians, and Micronesians), and women with disabilities.

Financial data Stipends range from $1,000 to $1,500.

Duration 1 year.

Additional information This program includes the following named awards: the Virginia Badger Scholarship, the Angela Paez Memorial Scholarship, and the Fran Solomon Scholarship. Support for the program is provided by several sponsors, including the American Chemical Society, Iota Sigma Pi, Rosetta Inpharmatics, and ZymoGenetics, Inc.

Number awarded 5 to 8 each year.

Deadline April of each year.

[496]
SEATTLE CHAPTER NABA SCHOLARSHIPS

National Association of Black Accountants-Seattle Chapter
Attn: Scholarship Committee
P.O. Box 18105
Seattle, WA 98118
E-mail: info@nabaseattle.org
Web: www.nabaseattle.org/nabaseattle/scholarships.asp

Summary To provide financial assistance to members of the National Association of Black Accountants (NABA) from any state who are working on an undergraduate or graduate degree in a business-related field at colleges and universities in Washington.

Eligibility This program is open to full-time freshmen, sophomores, juniors, first-year seniors, and graduate students working on a degree in accounting, finance, or other business-related field at colleges and universities in Washington. Applicants must be ethnic minorities and active NABA members. They must have a GPA of 3.0 or higher. Along with their application, they must submit a 500-word essay on a topic that changes annually. Financial need is not considered in the selection process.

Financial data The stipend is $1,000.

Duration 1 year.

Number awarded 1 or more each year.

Deadline April of each year.

[497]
SELMO BRADLEY SCHOLARSHIP

African Methodist Episcopal Church
Attn: Eleventh Episcopal District Lay Organization
101 East Union Street, Suite 301
Jacksonville, FL 32202
(904) 355-8262   Fax: (904) 356-1617
E-mail: eedlo@eedlo.org
Web: www.eedlo.org/scholarships.html

Summary To provide financial assistance to members of African Methodist Episcopal (AME) churches in Florida who are interested in attending college in any state.

Eligibility This program is open to seniors graduating from public or private high schools in Florida who are members of AME churches. Applicants must be planning to enroll full time at an institution of higher learning in any state: an AME-supported college, a Predominantly Black College or University, or an accredited trade school. They must have a GPA of 2.5 or higher. Along with their application, they must submit a 1-

page essay on why a college education is important and a statement regarding their financial need.

Financial data A stipend is awarded (amount not specified).

Duration 1 year.

Number awarded 1 or more each year.

Deadline April of each year.

[498]
SEMESTER INTERNSHIPS IN GEOSCIENCE PUBLIC POLICY

American Geological Institute
Attn: Government Affairs Program
4220 King Street
Alexandria, VA 22302-1502
(703) 379-2480   Fax: (703) 379-7563
E-mail: govt@agiweb.org
Web: www.agiweb.org/gap/interns/index.html

Summary To provide work experience to geoscience students (especially African Americans and other minorities or women) who have a strong interest in federal science policy.

Eligibility This program is open to geoscience students who are interested in working with Congress and federal agencies to promote sound public policy in areas that affect geoscientists, including water, energy, and mineral resources; geologic hazards; environmental protection, and federal funding for geoscience research and education. Applicants must submit official copies of college transcripts, a resume with the names and contact information for 2 references, and a statement of their science and policy interests and what they feel they can contribute to the program. Women and minorities are especially encouraged to apply.

Financial data The stipend is $5,000.

Duration 14 weeks, during the fall or spring semester. A similar program is also offered by the sponsor for summer internships.

Additional information This program is jointly funded by the American Geological Institute (AGI) and the American Association of Petroleum Geologists (AAPG). Activities for the interns include monitoring and analyzing geoscience-related legislation in Congress, updating legislative and policy information on AGI's web site, attending House and Senate hearings and preparing summaries, responding to information requests from AGI's member societies, and attending meetings with policy-level staff members in Congress, federal agencies, and non-governmental organizations.

Number awarded 1 each semester.

Deadline April of each year for fall internships; October of each year for spring internships.

[499]
SEO CAREER PROGRAM

Sponsors for Educational Opportunity
Attn: Career Program
55 Exchange Place
New York, NY 10005
(212) 979-2040   Toll Free: (800) 462-2332
Fax: (646) 706-7113
E-mail: careerprogram@seo-usa.org
Web: www.seo-usa.org/Career/Career_Program_Overview

Summary To provide African American undergraduates and other students of color with an opportunity to gain summer work experience in selected fields.

Eligibility This program is open to sophomores, juniors, and seniors of color at colleges and universities in the United States. Applicants must be interested in a summer internship in 1 of the following fields: corporate financial leadership, banking and asset management (including accounting/ finance, asset management, information technology, investment banking, investment research, sales and trading, or transaction services), or nonprofit sector. They should be able to demonstrate analytical and quantitative skills, interpersonal and community skills, maturity, and a cumulative GPA of 3.0 or higher. Along with their application, they must submit 1) information on their extracurricular and employment experience; 2) an essay of 75 to 100 words on how the program area to which they are applying relates to their professional goals; and 3) an essay of 250 to 400 words on either an example of a time when they had to operate outside their "comfort zone" or their definition of success. Personal interviews are required.

Financial data Interns receive a competitive stipend.

Duration 10 weeks during the summer.

Additional information This program was established in 1980. Most banking and asset management internships are available in the New York City metropolitan area (including Connecticut and New Jersey), but corporate financial leadership and nonprofit sector placements are nationwide.

Number awarded Varies each year; recently, more than 300 internships were available at more than 40 firms.

Deadline October of each year for most programs; December of each year for sales and trading or nonprofit sector.

[500]
SHELL INCENTIVE FUND SCHOLARSHIPS

Shell Oil Company
Attn: Scholarship Administrator
910 Louisiana, Suite 4476C
Houston, TX 77002
(713) 241-0514
Web: www.shell.com.sg

Summary To provide financial assistance to African Americans and other underrepresented minority students majoring in specified engineering and geosciences fields at designated universities.

Eligibility This program is open to students enrolled full time as sophomores, juniors, or seniors at 21 participating universities. Applicants must be U.S. citizens or authorized to work in the United States and members of a race or ethnicity underrepresented in the technical and scientific academic areas (Black, Hispanic/Latino, American Indian, or Alaskan Native). They must have a GPA of 3.2 or higher with a major in engineering (chemical, civil, electrical, geological, geophysical, mechanical, or petroleum) or geosciences (geology, geophysics, or physics). Along with their application, they must submit a 100-word essay on the kind of work they plan to be doing in 10 years, both in their career and in their community. Financial need is not considered in the selection process.

Financial data The stipend is $5,000 per year.

Duration 1 year; may be renewed up to 3 additional years, provided the recipient remains qualified and accepts a Shell Oil Company internship (if offered).

Additional information This program is administered by Educational Testing Service's Scholarship and Recognition Programs. The participating institutions are Colorado School of Mines, Cornell University, Florida A&M University, Georgia Institute of Technology, Louisiana State University, Massachusetts Institute of Technology, Michigan State University, North Carolina A&T State University, Ohio State University, Pennsylvania State University, Prairie View A&M University, Purdue University, Rice University, Texas A&M University, University of Colorado at Boulder, University of Houston, University of Illinois at Urbana-Champaign, University of Michigan, University of Oklahoma, University of Texas at Austin, and University of Texas at El Paso.

Number awarded Approximately 20 each year.

Deadline February of each year.

[501]
SHELL MINORITY SCHOLARSHIP PROGRAM

Shell Oil Company
Attn: Scholarship Administrator
910 Louisiana, Suite 4476C
Houston, TX 77002
(713) 241-0514
Web: www.shell.com.sg

Summary To provide financial assistance to African Americans and other underrepresented minority high school seniors planning to major in specified engineering and geosciences fields at designated universities.

Eligibility This program is open to graduating high school seniors planning to enroll full time at 22 participating universities. Applicants must be U.S. citizens or authorized to work in the United States and members of a race or ethnicity underrepresented in the technical and scientific academic areas (Black, Hispanic/Latino, American Indian, or Alaskan Native). They must be planning to major in engineering (chemical, civil, electrical, geological, geophysical, mechanical, or petroleum) or geosciences (geology, geophysics, or physics). Along with their application, they must submit a 100-word essay on the kind of work they plan to be doing in 10 years, both in their career and in their community; they should comment specifically on how they could potentially contribute to the petrochemical industry. Financial need is not considered in the selection process.

Financial data The stipend is $2,500.

Duration 1 year; nonrenewable, although recipients may apply for a Shell Incentive Fund Scholarship to cover the remaining years of their undergraduate program.

Additional information This program is administered by Educational Testing Service's Scholarship and Recognition Programs. The participating institutions are Colorado School of Mines, Cornell University, Florida A&M University, Georgia Institute of Technology, Louisiana State University, Massachusetts Institute of Technology, Michigan State University, North Carolina A&T State University, Ohio State University, Pennsylvania State University, Prairie View A&M University, Purdue University, Rice University, Stanford University, Texas A&M University, University of Colorado at Boulder, University of Houston, University of Illinois at Urbana-Champaign, Uni-

versity of Michigan, University of Oklahoma, University of Texas at Austin, and University of Texas at El Paso.

Number awarded Approximately 20 each year.

Deadline February of each year.

[502]
SIEMENS TEACHER SCHOLARSHIPS

Thurgood Marshall College Fund
Attn: Scholarship Manager
80 Maiden Lane, Suite 2204
New York, NY 10038
(212) 573-8487   Toll Free: (877) 690-8673
Fax: (212) 573-8497   E-mail: srogers@tmcfund.org
Web: www.thurgoodmarshallfund.net

Summary To provide financial assistance to upper-division students at colleges and universities that are members of the Thurgood Marshall College Fund (TMCF) and who are preparing for a career as a science and mathematics teacher.

Eligibility This program is open to full-time students entering their junior or senior year at 1 of the 47 colleges and universities that are TMCF members. Applicants must be majoring in education or a field of science or mathematics and preparing for a career as a teacher of science or mathematics at the elementary or secondary level. They must have a GPA of 2.75 or higher and be able to demonstrate financial need. U.S. citizenship is required.

Financial data The stipend is $2,200 per semester ($4,400 per year).

Duration 1 year.

Additional information The Siemens Foundation established this program in 2005. The 47 participating TMCF institutions are Alabama A&M University, Alabama State University, Albany State University, Alcorn State University, Bluefield State College, Bowie State University, Central State University (Ohio), Charles R. Drew University of Medicine (California), Cheyney University of Pennsylvania, Chicago State University, Coppin State College, Delaware State University, Elizabeth City State University, Fayetteville State University, Florida A&M University, Fort Valley State University, Grambling State University, Harris-Stowe State College, Howard University, Jackson State University, Kentucky State University, Langston University, Lincoln University (Missouri), Lincoln University (Pennsylvania), Medgar Evers College (New York), Mississippi Valley State University, Morgan State University, Norfolk State University, North Carolina A&T State University, North Carolina Central University, Prairie View A&M University, Savannah State University, South Carolina State University, Southern University and A&M College, Southern University at New Orleans, Southern University at Shreveport-Bossier City, Tennessee State University, Texas Southern University, Tuskegee University, University of Arkansas at Pine Bluff, University of the District of Columbia, University of Maryland-Eastern Shore, University of the Virgin Islands, Virginia State University, West Virginia State College, Winston-Salem State University, and York College. Recipients are required to serve as a volunteer for a Siemens Science Day by speaking about mathematics, science, and engineering for about 2 hours at a local elementary school.

Number awarded 20 each year.

Deadline September of each year.

[503]
SIGMA GAMMA RHO SCHOLARSHIPS/ FELLOWSHIPS

Sigma Gamma Rho Sorority, Inc.
Attn: National Education Fund
1000 Southhill Drive, Suite 200
Cary, NC 27513
(919) 678-9720   Toll Free: (888) SGR-1922
Fax: (919) 678-9721   E-mail: info@sgrho1922.org
Web: www.sgrho1922.org/service.htm

Summary To provide financial assistance for undergraduate or graduate study to African American and other applicants who can demonstrate financial need.

Eligibility This program is open to high school seniors, undergraduates, and graduate students who can demonstrate financial need. The sponsor is a traditionally African American sorority, but support is available to both males and females. Applicants must have a GPA of "C" or higher.

Financial data A stipend is awarded (amount not specified).

Duration 1 year.

Additional information This program includes the following named awards: the Lorraine A. Williams Scholarship, the Philo Sallie A. Williams Scholarship, the Cleo W. Higgins Scholarship (limited to doctoral students), the Angela E. Randall Scholarship, the Inez Colson Memorial Scholarship (limited to students majoring in education or mathematics at Savannah State University), and the Philo Geneva Young Scholarship. A processing fee of $20 is required.

Number awarded Varies each year.

Deadline April of each year.

[504]
SISTER THEA BOWMAN FOUNDATION KNIGHTS OF COLUMBUS SCHOLARSHIPS

Knights of Columbus
Attn: Department of Scholarships
P.O. Box 1670
New Haven, CT 06507-0901
(203) 752-4332   Fax: (203) 772-2696
E-mail: info@kofc.org
Web: www.kofc.org/un/en/scholarships/bowman.html

Summary To provide financial assistance to African American high school seniors interested in attending a Catholic college.

Eligibility This program is open to African American seniors graduating from high schools in the United States. Applicants must be planning to attend a Catholic college or university. They are not required to be the children of members of the Knights of Columbus.

Financial data The stipend is $5,000 per year.

Duration 1 year; may be renewed up to 3 additional years.

Additional information This program was established in 1996.

Number awarded Scholarships are offered when funds are available.

Deadline February of the year when available.

[505]
SMITHSONIAN MINORITY STUDENT INTERNSHIP

Smithsonian Institution
Attn: Office of Fellowships
Victor Building, Suite 9300, MRC 902
P.O. Box 37012
Washington, DC 20013-7012
(202) 633-7070   Fax: (202) 633-7069
E-mail: siofg@si.edu
Web: www.si.edu/ofg/Applications/MIP/MIPapp.htm

Summary To provide African Americans and other minority undergraduate or graduate students with the opportunity to work on research or museum procedure projects in specific areas of history, art, or science at the Smithsonian Institution.

Eligibility Internships are offered to minority students who are actively engaged in graduate study at any level or in upper-division undergraduate study. An overall GPA of 3.0 or higher is generally expected. Applicants must be interested in conducting research in specified fields of interest to the Smithsonian.

Financial data The program provides a stipend of $550 per week; travel allowances may also be offered.

Duration 10 weeks during the summer or academic year.

Additional information Eligible fields of study currently include animal behavior, ecology, and environmental science (including an emphasis on the tropics); anthropology (including archaeology); astrophysics and astronomy; earth sciences and paleobiology; evolutionary and systematic biology; history of science and technology; history of art (especially American, contemporary, African, Asian, and 20th-century art); American crafts and decorative arts; social and cultural history of the United States; and folklife.

Number awarded Varies each year.

Deadline January of each year for summer or fall; September of each year for spring.

[506]
SOUTH CAROLINA ACCESS AND EQUITY UNDERGRADUATE SCHOLARS PROGRAM

South Carolina Commission on Higher Education
Attn: Director of Student Services
1333 Main Street, Suite 200
Columbia, SC 29201
(803) 737-2244   Toll Free: (877) 349-7183
Fax: (803) 737-2297   E-mail: kwoodfaulk@che.sc.gov
Web: www.che.sc.gov

Summary To provide financial assistance to African American and other underrepresented students at public colleges or universities in South Carolina.

Eligibility Eligible to apply are residents of South Carolina who are members of a traditionally underrepresented group at the senior institution, regional campuses of the University of South Carolina, or South Carolina technical college they are or will be attending. Full-time entering freshmen must have a high school GPA of at least 3.0 (or 2.5 for students entering a technical college); continuing full-time college students, continuing part-time college students, and those transferring to a 4-year institution must have a cumulative GPA of at least 2.0. Priority is given to full-time students. U.S. citizenship is required.

Financial data Stipends of up to $2,000 per year are provided, funding permitting.

Duration 1 year; may be renewed.

Number awarded Varies each year, but no more than 20% of the grant funds at each institution may be used for entering freshmen.

Deadline Deadline not specified.

[507]
SOUTH EASTERN REGION FELLOWSHIP FOR LIFE-LONG LEARNING

Alpha Kappa Alpha Sorority, Inc.
Attn: Educational Advancement Foundation
5656 South Stony Island Avenue
Chicago, IL 60637
(773) 947-0026   Toll Free: (800) 653-6528
Fax: (773) 947-0277   E-mail: akaeaf@akaeaf.net
Web: www.akaeaf.org/fellowships_endowments.htm

Summary To provide financial assistance to residents of southeastern states (especially African American women) who are engaged in a program of lifelong learning at a college in any state.

Eligibility This program is open to students who are enrolled full time as sophomores or higher in an accredited degree-granting institution and are planning to continue their program of education. Applicants must be residents of Alabama, Mississippi, or Tennessee and enrolled in a program of lifelong learning at a college or university in any state. Along with their application, they must submit 1) a list of honors, awards, and scholarships received; 2) a list of organizations in which they have memberships, especially minority organizations; and 3) a statement of their personal and career goals, including how this scholarship will enhance their ability to attain those goals. The sponsor is a traditionally African American women's sorority.

Financial data A stipend is awarded (amount not specified).

Duration 1 year.

Number awarded 1 or more each even-numbered year.

Deadline April of each even-numbered year.

[508]
SOUTH FLORIDA CHAPTER NBMBAA UNDERGRADUATE SCHOLARSHIP

National Black MBA Association-South Florida Chapter
Attn: Scholarship Program
P.O. Box 278872
Miramar, FL 33027
(786) 255-5775   E-mail: plw8620@aol.com
Web: www.nbmbaasfl.org/scholarship.htm

Summary To provide financial assistance to African American and other minority residents of Florida who are working on a bachelor's degree in business or management at a school in any state.

Eligibility This program is open to African American and other minority residents of Florida who are working full time on a bachelor's degree in business or management at an AACSB-accredited college or university in any state. Applicants must submit a 2-page essay on a topic that changes annually but relates to African Americans and business. Financial need is not considered in the selection process.

Financial data The stipend is $1,000.

Duration 1 year.

Number awarded 1 or more each year.

Deadline June of each year.

[509]
SPHINX COMPETITION AWARDS

Sphinx Organization
Attn: Screening Committee
400 Renaissance Center, Suite 2550
Detroit, MI 48243
(313) 877-9100   Fax: (313) 877-0164
E-mail: info@sphinxmusic.org
Web: www.sphinxmusic.org

Summary To recognize and reward outstanding junior high, high school, and college-age Black and Latino string instrumentalists.

Eligibility This competition is open to Black and Latino instrumentalists in 2 divisions: junior, for participants who are younger than 18 years of age, and senior, for participants who are between 18 and 27 years of age. All entrants must be current U.S. residents who can compete in the instrumental categories of violin, viola, cello, and double bass. Along with their applications, they must submit a preliminary audition tape that includes all of the required preliminary repertoire for their instrument category. Based on those tapes, qualifiers are invited to participate in the semifinals and finals competitions, held at sites in Detroit and Ann Arbor, Michigan.

Financial data In the senior division, the first-place winner receives a $10,000 cash prize, solo appearances with major orchestras, and a performance with the Sphinx Symphony; the second-place winner receives a $5,000 cash prize and a performance with the Sphinx Symphony; the third-place winner receives a $3,500 cash prize and a performance with the Sphinx Symphony. In the junior division, the first-place winner receives a $5,000 cash prize, solo appearances with major orchestras, a national radio debut, and 2 performances with the Sphinx Symphony; the second-place winner receives a $3,500 cash prize and a performance with the Sphinx Symphony; the third-place winner receives a $2,000 cash prize and a performance with the Sphinx Symphony. All semifinalists receive scholarships to attend designated summer programs. They also receive full tuition scholarships for their instrumental studies at selected colleges and universities from the Sphinx Music Assistance Fund (MAF) of the League of American Orchestras.

Duration The competition is held annually.

Additional information The sponsoring organization was incorporated in 1996 to hold this competition, first conducted in 1998. The Sphinx Symphony is an all African American and Latino orchestra that performs at Orchestra Hall in Detroit. The MAF program was established by the New York Philharmonic in 1965, transferred to the American Symphony Orchestra League in 1994, and to the League of American Orchestras in 2001. In 2002, it partnered with the Sphinx Organization to provide scholarships to all 18 semifinalists. Applications must be accompanied by a $35 fee. That fee may be waived if demonstrable need is shown.

Number awarded 18 semifinalists (from both divisions and all instrumental categories) are selected each year. Of those, 3 junior and 3 senior competitors win cash prizes.

Deadline November of each year.

[510]
SPORTS ILLUSTRATED SCHOLARSHIP

National Association of Black Journalists
Attn: Program Coordinator
8701-A Adelphi Road
Adelphi, MD 20783-1716
(301) 445-7100, ext. 108   Toll Free: (866) 479-NABJ
Fax: (301) 445-7101   E-mail: nabj@nabj.org
Web: www.nabj.org/programs/scholarships/si

Summary   To provide financial assistance to female student members of the National Association of Black Journalists (NABJ) who are preparing for a career in sports journalism.

Eligibility   This program is open to female African American students who are entering their senior year of college. Applicants must be preparing for a career in sports journalism. They must be NABJ members. Along with their application, they must submit samples of their work, an official college transcript, 2 letters of recommendation, a resume, and a 500- to 800-word essay describing their accomplishments as a student journalist, their career goals, and their financial need.

Financial data   The stipend is $5,000. Funds are paid directly to the recipient's college or university.

Duration   1 year; nonrenewable.

Additional information   This program is sponsored by Sports Illustrated.

Number awarded   1 each year.

Deadline   February of each year.

[511]
STANFORD SUMMER RESEARCH PROGRAM/ AMGEN SCHOLARS PROGRAM

Stanford University
School of Medicine
Attn: Office of Graduate Affairs
M.S.O.B. Second Floor
251 Campus Drive
Stanford, CA 94305-5421
(650) 725-8791   E-mail: ssrpmail@stanford.edu
Web: ssrp.stanford.edu

Summary   To provide African American and other underrepresented minority undergraduate students with a summer research experience at Stanford University in biological and biomedical sciences.

Eligibility   This program is open to sophomores, juniors, and non-graduating seniors at 4-year colleges and universities in the United States, Puerto Rico, and U.S. territories. Students from all ethnic backgrounds are eligible, but the program especially encourages applications from Black/African Americans, Latino/Chicano Americans, Native Americans, Pacific Islanders, and other undergraduates who, by reason of their culture, class, race, ethnicity, background, work and life experiences, skills, and interests would bring diversity to graduate study in the biological and biomedical sciences (biochemistry, bioengineering, biology, biomedical informatics, biophysics, cancer biology, chemistry, chemical and systems biology, chemical engineering, developmental biology, earth sciences, genetics, immunology, microbiology, molecular and cellular physiology, neurosciences, statistics, and structural biology). Applicants must have at least 1 year of undergraduate education remaining before graduation and should be planning to prepare for and enter a Ph.D. program in the biological or biomedical sciences. They must have a GPA of 3.2 or higher. U.S. citizenship or permanent resident status is required.

Financial data   The program provides a stipend of $3,400, housing, meals, and transportation to and from the San Francisco Bay area.

Duration   8 weeks during the summer.

Additional information   This program currently serves as the Stanford component of the Amgen Scholars Program, which operates at 9 other U.S. universities and is funded by the Amgen Foundation.

Number awarded   Up to 25 each year.

Deadline   January of each year.

[512]
STATE FARM COMMUNICATIONS INTERNSHIP PROGRAM

Congressional Black Caucus Foundation, Inc.
Attn: Internship Coordinator
1720 Massachusetts Avenue, N.W.
Washington, DC 20036
(202) 263-2800   Toll Free: (800) 784-2577
Fax: (202) 775-0773   E-mail: internships@cbcfinc.org
Web: www.cbcfinc.org

Summary   To provide African American and other undergraduate students with an opportunity to work during the fall with the press secretary or communications director in the office of a member of the Congressional Black Caucus (CBC).

Eligibility   This program is open to African American and other full-time undergraduate students majoring in public relations, journalism, or other media-related field. Applicants must be interested in working with the press secretary or communications director of a CBC member. They should have a demonstrated professional familiarity with public relations, journalism, or other media-related field. Selection is based on strength of a faculty nomination, evidence of leadership skills, writing skills, and work experience in communications fields.

Financial data   Interns receive housing accommodations and a stipend (amount not specified) to cover expenses related to travel, meals, and personal expenses.

Duration   13 weeks during the fall.

Additional information   This program is sponsored by State Farm. Interns research legislation, prepare press releases, write op-editorials, write arguments for a position, organize and help to prepare for briefings and forums, and perform various office tasks.

Number awarded   Varies each year.

Deadline   May of each year.

[513]
STUART BROTMAN STUDENT RESEARCH FELLOWSHIP AWARDS

American Gastroenterological Association
Attn: AGA Research Foundation
Research Awards Manager
4930 Del Ray Avenue
Bethesda, MD 20814-2512
(301) 222-4012   Fax: (301) 654-5920
E-mail: awards@gastro.org
Web: www.gastro.org/aga-foundation/grants

Summary To provide funding for research on digestive diseases or nutrition to high school and undergraduate students, especially Black Americans and other minorities.

Eligibility This program is open to high school and undergraduate students at accredited institutions in North America. Applicants must be interested in conducting research on digestive diseases or nutrition. They may not hold similar salary support awards from other agencies (e.g., American Liver Foundation, Crohn's and Colitis Foundation). Research must be conducted under the supervision of a preceptor who is a full-time faculty member at a North American institution, directing a research project in a gastroenterology-related area, and a member of the American Gastroenterological Association (AGA). The program includes awards reserved for underprivileged and underrepresented undergraduates, including (but not limited to) Black Americans, Hispanic or Latino Americans, Native Americans, and Pacific Islanders. Selection is based on novelty, feasibility, and significance of the proposal; attributes of the candidate; record of the preceptor; evidence of institutional commitment; and laboratory environment.

Financial data The grant is $2,500. No indirect costs are allowed. The award is paid directly to the student and is to be used as a stipend.

Duration At least 10 weeks. The work may take place at any time during the year.

Number awarded 11 high school students and 24 undergraduates (of whom 10 must be underprivileged or underrepresented students) are supported each year.

Deadline March of each year.

[514]
STUDENT OPPORTUNITY SCHOLARSHIPS FOR ETHNIC MINORITY GROUPS

Presbyterian Church (USA)
Attn: Office of Financial Aid for Studies
100 Witherspoon Street, Room M-052
Louisville, KY 40202-1396
(502) 569-5224   Toll Free: (888) 728-7228, ext. 5224
Fax: (502) 569-8766   E-mail: finaid@pcusa.org
Web: www.pcusa.org

Summary To provide financial assistance to African American and other upper-division college students who are Presbyterians and majoring in designated fields.

Eligibility This program is open to members of the Presbyterian Church (USA), especially those from racial/ethnic minority groups (Asian American, African American, Hispanic American, Native American, Alaska Native). Applicants must be able to demonstrate financial need, be entering their junior or senior year of college as full-time students, and have a GPA of 2.5 or higher. Preference is given to applicants who

are majoring in the following fields of interest to missions of the church: education, health services and sciences, religious studies, sacred music, social services, and social sciences.

Financial data Stipends range up to $3,000 per year, depending upon the financial need of the recipient.

Duration 1 year; may be renewed for up to 3 additional years if the recipient continues to need financial assistance and demonstrates satisfactory academic progress.

Number awarded Varies each year.

Deadline June of each year.

[515]
SUMMER CLINICAL AND TRANSLATIONAL RESEARCH PROGRAM

Harvard Medical School
Office for Diversity and Community Partnership
Attn: Minority Faculty Development Program
164 Longwood Avenue, Second Floor
Boston, MA 02115-5810
(617) 432-1892   Fax: (617) 432-3834
E-mail: pfdd_dcp@hms.harvard.edu
Web: www.mfdp.med.harvard.edu

Summary To provide an opportunity for undergraduate students, especially African Americans and other underrepresented minorities, to engage in research at Harvard Medical School during the summer.

Eligibility This program is open to undergraduate sophomores, juniors, and seniors who are preparing for a career in medical research. Priority is given to students at schools that receive funding from the Minority Biomedical Research Support (MBRS) or Minority Access to Research Careers (MARC) programs of the National Institute of Health (NIH), Historically Black Colleges and Universities (HBCUs), Hispanic Serving Institutions (HSIs), or Tribal Colleges and Universities (TCUs). Applicants must be interested in working on a summer research program at Harvard Medical School under the mentorship of a faculty advisor. They must be interested in a research and health-related career, especially in clinical or translational research or research that transforms scientific discoveries arising from laboratory, clinical, or population studies into clinical or population-based applications to improve health. U.S. citizenship, nationality, or permanent resident status is required.

Financial data Participants receive a stipend (amount not specified), housing, and limited reimbursement of transportation costs to Boston.

Duration 8 weeks during the summer.

Additional information This program, established in 2008, is funded by the National Center for Research Resources of the NIH. It is a joint enterprise of Harvard University, its 10 schools, its 17 Academic Healthcare Centers, Boston College School of Nursing, MIT, the Cambridge Health Alliance, and other community partners. Interns attend weekly seminars with Harvard faculty focusing on such topics as research methodology, health disparities, ethics, and career paths. They also have the opportunity to participate in offerings of other Harvard Medical School programs, such a career development seminars and networking dinners.

Number awarded Varies each year.

Deadline February of each year.

[516]
SUMMER DIVERSITY INTERNSHIP PROGRAM

Ad Club
Attn: Director of Content and Programming
9 Hamilton Place, Second Floor
Boston, MA 02108
(617) 262-1100, ext. 103   Fax: (617) 456-1772
E-mail: kate@adclub.org
Web: www.adclub.org/div_int

Summary   To provide summer work experience in advertising or a related industry at agencies in New England to upper-division students, especially African Americans and other members of minority groups.

Eligibility   This program is open to advertising and marketing students who have junior standing or above and a GPA of 3.0 or higher. Special consideration is given to students who are African American, Asian American, Indian American, Hispanic American, Native American, biracial, or multiracial. Applicants must be interested in a summer internship at an advertising agency in New England. Positions are available in account management, branding, creative, design, digital, and system operations/IT.

Financial data   The stipend is $3,500.

Duration   10 weeks during the summer.

Number awarded   12 each year.

Deadline   April of each year.

[517]
SUMMER MEDICAL AND DENTAL EDUCATION PROGRAM

Association of American Medical Colleges
Attn: Diversity Policy and Programs
2450 N Street, N.W.
Washington, DC 20037-1126
(202) 828-0400   Toll Free: (866) 58-SMDEP
Fax: (202) 828-1125   E-mail: smdep@aamc.org
Web: www.smdep.org

Summary   To provide college freshmen and sophomores (particularly African Americans and other minorities) with an opportunity to learn more about careers in medicine and dentistry in a summer academic enrichment program at designated universities.

Eligibility   This program is open to freshmen and sophomores currently enrolled at colleges and universities in the United States. Applicants must be U.S. citizens or permanent residents and have a GPA of 2.5 or higher. They must be interested in participating in a summer academic enrichment program at designated universities that includes: study in the basic sciences (organic chemistry, physics, biology) and calculus; career development; learning-skills seminar; limited clinical exposure; and a financial planning workshop. Priority is given to applicants who 1) identify with a group that is racially or ethnically underrepresented in medicine and/or dentistry; 2) comes from an economically or educationally disadvantaged background; or 3) has demonstrated interest in issues affecting underserved populations.

Financial data   Each participating university provides a stipend to students participating in its program. All of them include housing and at least some meals; most of them also provide a travel allowance.

Duration   6 weeks during the summer.

Additional information   This program is jointly administered by the Association of American Medical Colleges and the American Dental Education Association. Funding is provided by the Robert Wood Johnson Foundation. The designated institutions are Case Western Reserve University (Cleveland, Ohio), Columbia University (New York, New York), University of California at Los Angeles, Duke University (Durham, North Carolina), Howard University (Washington, D.C.), University of Texas Dental Branch and Medical School at Houston, University of Medicine and Dentistry of New Jersey (Newark), University of Louisville (Kentucky), University of Nebraska Medical Center (Omaha), University of Virginia (Charlottesville), University of Washington (Seattle), and Yale University (New Haven, Connecticut).

Number awarded   Varies each year.

Deadline   February of each year; admissions are made on a first-come, first-served basis.

[518]
SUMMER PROGRAM IN QUANTITATIVE SCIENCES FOR PUBLIC HEALTH RESEARCH

Harvard School of Public Health
Department of Biostatistics
Attn: Diversity Program Coordinator
655 Huntington Avenue, SPH2, Fourth Floor
Boston, MA 02115
(617) 432-3175   Fax: (617) 432-5619
E-mail: biostat_diversity@hsph.harvard.edu
Web: www.hsph.harvard.edu/biostats/diversity/summer

Summary   To enable underrepresented minority and other disadvantaged science undergraduates to participate in a summer research internship at Harvard School of Public Health that focuses on biostatistics, epidemiology, and health and social behavior.

Eligibility   This program is open to 1) members of ethnic groups underrepresented in the sciences (African Americans, Hispanics, Native American, Pacific Islanders, biracial/multiracial); 2) first-generation college students; 3) low-income students; or 4) individuals with a disability. Applicants must be current undergraduates interested in participating in a summer program on the use of quantitative methods for biological, environmental, and medical research as preparation for graduate studies in public health, biostatistics, or epidemiology. They must have a GPA of 3.0 or higher, including course work in calculus, but prior exposure to statistics is not required. U.S. citizenship or permanent resident status is required.

Financial data   Funding covers travel, housing, course materials, and a stipend to cover meals and incidental.

Duration   4 weeks, in June.

Additional information   Interns participate in seminars, led by faculty members from various departments at the Harvard School of Public Health and Harvard Medical School, that are designed to broaden a participant's understanding of the relationship of biostatistics to human health. They also attend non-credit classes in biostatistics, epidemiology, and health and social behavior.

Number awarded   Varies each year.

Deadline   February of each year.

[519]
SUMMER RESEARCH DIVERSITY FELLOWSHIPS IN LAW AND SOCIAL SCIENCE FOR UNDERGRADUATE STUDENTS

American Bar Foundation
Attn: Summer Research Diversity Fellowship
750 North Lake Shore Drive
Chicago, IL 60611-4403
(312) 988-6560   Fax: (312) 988-6579
E-mail: fellowships@abfn.org
Web: www.americanbarfoundation.org

Summary To provide an opportunity for African Americans and other undergraduate students from diverse backgrounds to work on a summer research project in the field of law and social science.

Eligibility This program is open to U.S. citizens and permanent residents who are African Americans, Hispanic/Latinos, Puerto Ricans, Native Americans, or other individuals who will add diversity to the field of law and social science. Applicants must be sophomores or juniors in college, have a GPA of 3.0 or higher, be majoring in the social sciences or humanities, and be willing to consider an academic or research career. Along with their application, they must submit a 200-word essay on their future plans and why this fellowship would contribute to them, another essay on an assigned topic, official transcripts, and a letter of recommendation from a faculty member familiar with their work.

Financial data Participants receive a stipend of $3,600.

Duration 35 hours per week for 8 weeks during the summer.

Additional information Students are assigned to an American Bar Foundation Research Professor who involves the student in the design and conduct of the professor's research project and who acts as mentor during the student's tenure.

Number awarded 4 each year.

Deadline February of each year.

[520]
SUMMER TRANSPORTATION INTERNSHIP PROGRAM FOR DIVERSE GROUPS

Department of Transportation
Attn: Summer Transportation Internship Program for
  Diverse Groups
HAHR-40, Room E63-433
1200 New Jersey Avenue, S.E.
Washington, DC 20590
(202) 366-2907   E-mail: lafayette.melton@dot.gov
Web: www.fhwa.dot.gov/education/stipdg.htm

Summary To enable African American and other undergraduate, graduate, and law students from diverse groups to gain work experience during the summer at facilities of the U.S. Department of Transportation (DOT).

Eligibility This program is open to all qualified applicants, but it is designed to provide women, persons with disabilities, and members of diverse social and ethnic groups with summer opportunities in transportation. Applicants must be U.S. citizens currently enrolled in a degree-granting program of study at an accredited institution of higher learning at the undergraduate (community or junior college, university, college, or Tribal College or University) or graduate level. Under-

graduates must be entering their junior or senior year; students attending a Tribal or community college must have completed their first year of school; law students must be entering their second or third year of school. Students who will graduate during the spring or summer are not eligible unless they have been accepted for enrollment in graduate school. The program accepts applications from students in all majors who are interested in working on transportation-related topics and issues. Preference is given to students with a GPA of 3.0 or higher. Undergraduates must submit a 1-page essay on their transportation interests and how participation in this program will enhance their educational and career plans and goals. Graduate students must submit a writing sample representing their educational and career plans and goals. Law students must submit a legal writing sample.

Financial data The stipend is $4,000 for undergraduates or $5,000 for graduate and law students. The program also provides housing and reimbursement of travel expenses from interns' homes to their assignment location.

Duration 10 weeks during the summer.

Additional information Assignments are at the DOT headquarters in Washington, D.C., a selected modal administration, or selected field offices around the country.

Number awarded 80 to 100 each year.

Deadline January of each year.

[521]
SUMMER UNDERGRADUATE RESEARCH FELLOWSHIP PROGRAM

Boston University
Attn: Undergraduate Research Opportunities Program
143 Bay State Road
Boston, MA 02215-1719
(617) 353-2020   Fax: (617) 353-2056
E-mail: urop@bu.edu
Web: www.bu.edu/urop/surf-program/about

Summary To provide an opportunity for undergraduates, especially African Americans and members of other underrepresented minority groups, to participate in scientific research projects during the summer at Boston University.

Eligibility This program is open to undergraduates who are entering their junior or senior year and have a GPA of 3.0 or higher. Applicants must be interested in working on a summer research project in biology, chemistry, computer science, engineering, or psychology under the mentorship of a Boston University professor. Along with their application, they must submit an essay of 400 to 1,000 words explaining why they wish to participate in the program. Preference is given to members of minority groups traditionally underrepresented in the sciences: African Americans, Hispanics, Native Americans and Native Alaskans, Pacific Islanders (including Native Hawaiians and Polynesians), and Asians (except Indians, Chinese, Japanese, Koreans, Filipinos, and Thais). U.S. citizenship or permanent resident status is required.

Financial data Participants receive a $4,500 stipend, a $600 supplies allowance, up to $550 in travel expenses, and housing in a Boston University dormitory.

Duration 10 weeks during the summer.

Additional information Support for this program is provided by the National Science Foundation (NSF) through its Research Experiences for Undergraduates (REU) program, the Department of Defense through its Awards to Stimulate and Support Undergraduate Research Experiences (ASSURE) program, and the Northeast Alliance for Graduate Education and the Professoriate.

Number awarded 10 to 20 each year, including 2 or 3 positions reserved for Boston University students who serve as peer mentors for the other participants.

Deadline February of each year.

[522]
SUMMER UNDERGRADUATE RESEARCH FELLOWSHIPS IN ORGANIC CHEMISTRY

American Chemical Society
Division of Organic Chemistry
1155 16th Street, N.W.
Washington, DC 20036
(202) 872-4401   Toll Free: (800) 227-5558, ext. 4401
E-mail: division@acs.org
Web: www.organicdivision.org/?nd=p_surf_program

Summary To provide an opportunity for college juniors (particularly African Americans and other minorities) to work on a research project in organic chemistry during the summer.

Eligibility This program is open to students who are currently enrolled as juniors at a college or university in the United States and are nominated by their school. Nominees must be interested in conducting a mentored research project in organic chemistry at the home institution during the following summer. Along with their application, they must submit brief statements on the project they propose to undertake, their background that has prepared them to do this work, their proposed methodology, and how a summer research project fits into their long-range plans. U.S. citizenship or permanent resident status is required. Selection is based on demonstrated interest and talent in organic chemistry, merit and feasibility of the research project, commitment of a faculty mentor to support the student, academic record (particularly in organic chemistry and related sciences), and importance of the award in facilitating the personal and career plans of the student. Applications from minorities are especially encouraged.

Financial data Grants range up to $5,000. Funding includes the costs of a trip by all participants to an industrial campus in the fall for a dinner, award session, scientific talks, a tour of the campus, and a poster session where the results of the summer research investigations are presented.

Duration Summer months.

Additional information Current corporate sponsors of this program include Pfizer, Roche, Cubist, Novartis, and Amgen.

Number awarded 16 each year.

Deadline January of each year.

[523]
SYLVIA C. EDGE ENDOWMENT SCHOLARSHIP

New Jersey State Nurses Association
Attn: Institute for Nursing
1479 Pennington Road
Trenton, NJ 08618-2661
(609) 883-5335   Toll Free: (888) UR-NJSNA
Fax: (609) 883-5343   E-mail: institute@njsna.org
Web: www.njsna.org/displaycommon.cfm?an=5

Summary To provide financial assistance to New Jersey residents of African descent who are preparing for a career as a nurse.

Eligibility Applicants must be New Jersey residents of African descent currently enrolled in a diploma, associate, baccalaureate nursing program located in the state. Selection is based on financial need, GPA, and leadership potential.

Financial data The stipend is $1,000.

Duration 1 year.

Number awarded 1 each year.

Deadline January of each year.

[524]
SYMANTEC SCHOLARSHIPS

Society of Women Engineers
Attn: Scholarship Selection Committee
120 South LaSalle Street, Suite 1515
Chicago, IL 60603-3572
(312) 596-5223   Toll Free: (877) SWE-INFO
Fax: (312) 644-8557
E-mail: scholarshipapplication@swe.org
Web: societyofwomenengineers.swe.org

Summary To provide financial assistance to undergraduate women (especially African American and other minority women) who are majoring in designated engineering specialties.

Eligibility This program is open to women who are entering their junior or senior year at a 4-year ABET-accredited college or university. Applicants must be majoring in computer science or computer or electrical engineering. They must have a GPA of 3.0 or higher. Preference is given to members of groups underrepresented in engineering or computer science. Selection is based on merit.

Financial data The stipend is $5,000.

Duration 1 year.

Additional information This program is sponsored by Symantec Corporation.

Number awarded 3 each year.

Deadline February of each year.

[525]
TARGETED OPPORTUNITY PROGRAM (TOPJOBS)

Wisconsin Office of State Employment Relations
Attn: Division of Affirmative Action Workforce Planning
101 East Wilson Street, Fourth Floor
P.O. Box 7855
Madison, WI 53707-7855
(608) 267-1005   Fax: (608) 267-1020
E-mail: Claire.Dehnert@wisconsin.gov
Web: oser.state.wi.us/category.asp?linkcatid=342

Summary To provide an opportunity for African Americans, other minorities, women, and persons with disabilities to gain summer work experience with agencies of the state of Wisconsin.

Eligibility This program is open to women, ethnic/racial minorities (Black or African American, Asian, Native Hawaiian or other Pacific Islander, American Indian or Alaska Native, or Hispanic or Latino), and persons with disabilities. Applicants must be juniors, seniors, or graduate students at an accredited 4-year college or university or second-year students in the second year of a 2-year technical or vocational school program. They must be 1) Wisconsin residents enrolled full time at a school in Wisconsin or any other state, or 2) residents of other states who are enrolled full time at a school in Wisconsin.

Financial data Most internships provide a competitive stipend.

Duration Summer months.

Additional information This program was established in 1974. Relevant fields of study include, but are not limited to, the liberal arts and sciences (e.g., history, mathematics, library science, political science, philosophy, physics, psychology, social services, social work, sociology, women's studies); agriculture and natural resources (e.g., animal and dairy science, biology, botany, chemistry, geography, entomology, environmental studies, horticulture, landscape architecture, microbiology, plant pathology, soil science, urban planning, water resources management, wildlife ecology); business (e.g., accounting, business management, economics, finance, human resources, marketing, public administration, real estate); criminal justice; education; health care (including nursing); engineering; information systems and computers; journalism and communications; and law.

Number awarded Varies each year. Since the program was established, it has placed more than 2,500 students with more than 30 different agencies and universities throughout the state.

Deadline February of each year.

[526]
TDC SCHOLARSHIP

National Association of Black Accountants
Attn: National Scholarship Program
7474 Greenway Center Drive, Suite 1120
Greenbelt, MD 20770
(301) 474-NABA, ext. 114   Fax: (301) 474-3114
E-mail: customerservice@nabainc.org
Web: www.nabainc.org

Summary To provide financial assistance to student members of the National Association of Black Accountants (NABA) who are working on an undergraduate or graduate degree in a field related to accounting.

Eligibility This program is open to NABA members enrolled full time as 1) an undergraduate freshman, sophomore, junior, or first-semester senior majoring in accounting, business, or finance at a 4-year college or university; or 2) a graduate student working on a master's degree in accounting. High school seniors are not eligible. Applicants must have a GPA of 2.0 or higher in their major and 2.5 or higher overall. Selection is based on grades, financial need, and a 500-word autobiography that discusses career objectives,

leadership abilities, community activities, and involvement in NABA.

Financial data The stipend is $1,000.

Duration 1 year.

Number awarded 1 each year.

Deadline January of each year.

[527]
TEACHER QUEST SCHOLARSHIP

Brown Foundation for Educational Equity, Excellence and Research
Attn: Scholarship Committee
1515 S.E. Monroe
Topeka, KS 66615
(785) 235-3939   Fax: (785) 235-1001
E-mail: brownfound@juno.com
Web: brownvboard.org

Summary To provide financial assistance to African Americans and other undergraduate and graduate students of color who are interested in preparing for a teaching career.

Eligibility This program is open to members of minority groups who are enrolled at least half time at an institution of higher education with an accredited teacher education program. Applicants must be enrolled at the undergraduate, graduate, or post-baccalaureate level and have a GPA of 3.0 or higher. Along with their application, they must submit brief essays on 1) their involvement in school, community, and/or other activities and how those activities have prepared them to be an educator; 2) why they aspire to a career in education, their goals, and the level at which they plan to teach; and 3) how they think *Brown v. Board of Education* has influenced their own life experiences. Selection is based on the essays; GPA; school, community, and leisure activities; career plans and goals in education; and recommendations.

Financial data The stipend is $1,000 per year.

Duration 2 years.

Additional information The first Brown Foundation Scholarships were awarded in 1989. The current program replaced the Brown Foundation Academic Scholarships in 2009.

Number awarded Varies each year; recently, 5 of these scholarships were awarded.

Deadline March of each year.

[528]
TECHNICAL RESEARCH EXHIBITION AWARDS

National Society of Black Engineers
Attn: Programs Department
205 Daingerfield Road
Alexandria, VA 22314
(703) 549-2207   Fax: (703) 683-5312
E-mail: programs@nsbe.org
Web: www.nsbe.org

Summary To recognize and reward outstanding technical papers by undergraduate and graduate student members of the National Society of Black Engineers (NSBE).

Eligibility This competition is open to undergraduate and graduate student members of the society. Candidates must submit technical papers that are between 10 and 20 pages in length and that follow a standard style for such work. All papers must include an abstract and a high degree of technical content. International members who are unable to attend the national convention may also apply through an online procedure. Undergraduate students (both domestic and international) are encouraged to submit results from project-based research as well as theoretical research with an academic or project-based focus. Graduate students (both domestic and international) are encouraged to submit topics demonstrating theoretical research with an academic focus. Domestic applicants must specify whether they wish to participate in a poster session, oral presentation (10 minutes, followed by a 10-minute question and answer session), or both at the NSBE national convention. Based on the abstracts, 50 members are selected to present their research at the convention. In addition, 20 international members (10 undergraduates and 10 graduate students) are selected to have their posters showcased on the NSBE web site. Winners are selected, either from presentations at the convention or from posts on the web site. Selection is based on format (15 points), organization (10 points), technical content (40 points), clarity (10 points), grammar (15 points), and use of visual aids (10 points).

Financial data   In the oral presentations category, first prize is $2,000, second $1,000, and third $500. In the posters category, first prize is $1,600, second $800, and third $400. In the international category, first prize is $1,200, second $800, and third $500.

Duration   The competition is held annually.

Number awarded   9 cash awards (3 for oral presentations, 3 for posters, and 3 for international submissions) are presented each year.

Deadline   January of each year.

[529]
TENNESSEE MINORITY TEACHING FELLOWS PROGRAM

Tennessee Student Assistance Corporation
Parkway Towers
404 James Robertson Parkway, Suite 1510
Nashville, TN 37243-0820
(615) 741-1346   Toll Free: (800) 342-1663
Fax: (615) 741-6101   E-mail: TSAC.Aidinfo@tn.gov
Web: www.tn.gov

Summary   To provide funding to African Americans and other minority residents of Tennessee who wish to attend college in the state to prepare for a career in the teaching field.

Eligibility   This program is open to minority residents of Tennessee who are either high school seniors planning to enroll full time at a college or university in the state or continuing college students at a Tennessee college or university. High school seniors must have a GPA of 2.75 or higher and an ACT score of at least 18, a combined mathematics and critical reading SAT score of at least 860, or a rank in the top 25% of their high school class. Continuing college students must have a college GPA of 2.5 or higher. All applicants must agree to teach at the K-12 level in a Tennessee public school following graduation from college. Along with their application, they must submit a 250-word essay on why they chose teaching as a profession. U.S. citizenship is required.

Financial data   The funding is $5,000 per year. Recipients incur an obligation to teach at the preK-12 level in a Tennessee public school 1 year for each year the award is received.

Duration   1 year; may be renewed for up to 3 additional years, provided the recipient maintains full-time enrollment and a cumulative GPA of 2.5 or higher.

Additional information   This program was established in 1989.

Number awarded   20 new awards are granted each year.

Deadline   April of each year.

[530]
THE DEVELOPMENT FUND FOR BLACK STUDENTS IN SCIENCE AND TECHNOLOGY SCHOLARSHIPS

The Development Fund for Black Students in Science and Technology
2705 Bladensburg Road, N.E.
Washington, DC 20018
(202) 635-3604   E-mail: DLHinson@earthlink.net
Web: dfbsst.dlhjr.com/dfb_sch.html

Summary   To provide scholarships to African American students who enroll in scientific or technical fields of study at designated Historically Black Colleges and Universities (HBCUs).

Eligibility   Deans and faculty members of engineering and science departments at selected HBCUs are invited to identify students to be considered for these scholarships. Nominees must be enrolled or planning to enroll at a predominantly Black college or university or already be enrolled at the school and planning to major in a technical field (e.g., engineering, mathematics, science). U.S. citizenship or permanent resident status is required. Selection is based on academic achievement (grades and SAT scores, especially in science and mathematics), a personal essay describing career goals and relevant extracurricular activities, recommendations, and financial need.

Financial data   Stipends range up to $2,000 per year.

Duration   1 year; may be renewed for up to 4 years, as long as the recipient remains in good academic standing and enrolled full time in a science or engineering curriculum.

Additional information   Prior to 1995, these scholarships were awarded solely or primarily through the National Merit Scholarship Corporation's National Achievement Scholarship Program. Scholarship applications are available only through the financial aid offices of prequalified schools. Currently, these are: Bennett College, Clark Atlanta University, Elizabeth City State University, Fisk University, Florida A&M University, Fort Valley State College, Hampton University, Howard University, Langston University, Lincoln University of Pennsylvania, Morehouse University, Morgan State University, North Carolina A&T State University, Prairie View A&M University, Southern University and A&M College, Spelman College, Tennessee State University, Tuskegee University, Wilberforce University, and Xavier University of Louisiana.

Number awarded   Several each year.

Deadline   June of each year.

[531]
THOMARA LATIMER CANCER FOUNDATION SCHOLARSHIPS

Thomara Latimer Cancer Foundation
Attn: Scholarship Committee
Franklin Plaza Center
29193 Northeastern Highway, Suite 528
Southfield, MI 48034-1006
(248) 557-2346   Fax: (248) 557-8063
E-mail: scholarships@thomlatimercares.org
Web: www.thomlatimercares.org

Summary To provide financial assistance to African American residents of Michigan, (especially those who have had cancer) who are interested in studying a medically-related field at a college in any state.

Eligibility This program is open to African American residents of Michigan between 17 and 30 years of age. Applicants must be 1) a high school senior accepted at an accredited college or university in any state in a medically-related program (e.g., medical technician, physician assistant); 2) a student admitted to a medically-related professional program (e.g., nursing, medicine, physical or occupational therapy) at a college or university in any state. They must have a GPA of 3.0 or higher. Along with their application, they must submit a brief essay on why they should be awarded this scholarship. Financial need is not considered in the selection process. Special consideration is given to students who are cancer survivors.

Financial data The stipend is $1,000.

Duration 1 year; may be renewed 1 additional year.

Number awarded 10 each year.

Deadline December of each year.

[532]
THOMAS G. NEUSOM SCHOLARSHIPS

Conference of Minority Transportation Officials
Attn: National Scholarship Program
818 18th Street, N.W., Suite 850
Washington, DC 20006
(202) 530-0551   Fax: (202) 530-0617
Web: www.comto.org/news-youth.php

Summary To provide financial assistance for college or graduate school to African American and other members of the Conference of Minority Transportation Officials (COMTO).

Eligibility This program is open to undergraduate and graduate students who have been members of COMTO for at least 1 year. Applicants must be working on a degree in a field related to transportation with a GPA of 2.5 or higher. Along with their application, they must submit a cover letter with a 500-word statement of career goals. Financial need is not considered in the selection process. U.S. citizenship is required.

Financial data The stipend is $5,500. Funds are paid directly to the recipient's college or university.

Duration 1 year.

Additional information COMTO was established in 1971 to promote, strengthen, and expand the roles of minorities in all aspects of transportation. Recipients are expected to attend the COMTO National Scholarship Luncheon.

Number awarded 2 each year.

Deadline April of each year.

[533]
THOMAS S. WATSON, JR. MEMORIAL SCHOLARSHIP

National Association of Black Accountants
Attn: National Scholarship Program
7474 Greenway Center Drive, Suite 1120
Greenbelt, MD 20770
(301) 474-NABA, ext. 114   Fax: (301) 474-3114
E-mail: customerservice@nabainc.org
Web: www.nabainc.org

Summary To provide financial assistance to student members of the National Association of Black Accountants (NABA) who are working on an undergraduate or graduate degree in a field related to accounting.

Eligibility This program is open to NABA members enrolled full time as 1) an undergraduate freshman, sophomore, junior, or first-semester senior majoring in accounting, business, or finance at a 4-year college or university; or 2) a graduate student working on a master's degree in accounting. High school seniors are not eligible. Applicants must have a GPA of 3.5 or higher in their major and 3.3 or higher overall. Selection is based on grades, financial need, and a 500-word autobiography that discusses career objectives, leadership abilities, community activities, and involvement in NABA.

Financial data The stipend ranges form $1,000 to $3,000.

Duration 1 year.

Number awarded 1 each year.

Deadline January of each year.

[534]
THURGOOD MARSHALL SCHOLARSHIPS

Thurgood Marshall College Fund
Attn: Scholarship Manager
80 Maiden Lane, Suite 2204
New York, NY 10038
(212) 573-8487   Toll Free: (877) 690-8673
Fax: (212) 573-8497   E-mail: srogers@tmcfund.org
Web: www.thurgoodmarshallfund.net

Summary To provide financial assistance to African American high school seniors or previous graduates who are or will be working on a degree at a college or university that is a member of the Thurgood Marshall College Fund (TMCF).

Eligibility This program is open to full-time students enrolled or accepted at 1 of 47 designated TMCF institutions, most of which are Historically Black Colleges and Universities (HBCUs) or other schools with large African American enrollments. Applicants must be African Americans who are U.S. citizens, have a high school GPA of 3.0 or higher, have scored at least 1650 on the SAT or 25 on the ACT, are recommended by their high school as academically exceptional or outstanding in the creative and performing arts, and can demonstrate financial need. They must apply through the TMCF school they attend, and the institutions select the recipients. Along with their application, they must submit an essay of 500 to 1,000 words on what made them choose to attend an HBCU, how they have made a difference on their college campus, and what legacy will they leave behind once they have graduated.

Financial data Stipends range up to $2,200 per semester, depending on the need of the recipient. Funds are awarded through the institution to be used for tuition, room, board, books, and fees.

Duration 1 year; may be renewed for up to 3 additional years if the recipient maintains a GPA of 3.0 or higher in college.

Additional information This program was founded in 1987 by the Miller Brewing Company (now MillerCoors) in cooperation with the American Association of State Colleges and Universities and the Office for the Advancement of Public Black Colleges of the National Association of State Universities and Land-Grant Colleges. Additional support is provided by the Bank of America Foundation, Costco, General Mills, HSBC, and USA Funds. The participating TMCF institutions are Alabama A&M University, Alabama State University, Albany State University, Alcorn State University, Bluefield State College, Bowie State University, Central State University (Ohio), Charles R. Drew University of Medicine (California), Cheyney University of Pennsylvania, Chicago State University, Coppin State College, Delaware State University, Elizabeth City State University, Fayetteville State University, Florida A&M University, Fort Valley State University, Grambling State University, Harris-Stowe State College, Howard University, Jackson State University, Kentucky State University, Langston University, Lincoln University (Missouri), Lincoln University (Pennsylvania), Medgar Evers College (New York), Mississippi Valley State University, Morgan State University, Norfolk State University, North Carolina A&T State University, North Carolina Central University, Prairie View A&M University, Savannah State University, South Carolina State University, Southern University and A&M College, Southern University at New Orleans, Southern University at Shreveport-Bossier City, Tennessee State University, Texas Southern University, Tuskegee University, University of Arkansas at Pine Bluff, University of the District of Columbia, University of Maryland-Eastern Shore, University of the Virgin Islands, Virginia State University, West Virginia State College, Winston-Salem State University, and York College.

Number awarded Varies each year; recently, nearly 1,000 students were receiving support from this program.

Deadline The online application process closes in August of each year.

[535]
TIGER PERSONNEL SERVICES SCHOLARSHIP

National Naval Officers Association-Washington, D.C.
   Chapter
Attn: Scholarship Program
2701 Park Center Drive, A1108
Alexandria, VA 22302
(703) 566-3840   Fax: (703) 566-3813
E-mail: Stephen.Williams@Navy.mil
Web: dcnnoa.memberlodge.com

Summary To provide financial assistance to male African American high school seniors from the Washington, D.C. area who are interested in attending college in any state.

Eligibility This program is open to male African American seniors graduating from high schools in the Washington, D.C. metropolitan area who plan to enroll full time at an accredited 2- or 4-year college or university in any state. Applicants must have a GPA of 2.5 or higher and be U.S. citizens or permanent residents. Selection is based on academic achievement, community involvement, and financial need.

Financial data The stipend is $1,000.

Duration 1 year; nonrenewable.

Additional information Recipients are not required to join or affiliate with the military in any way. This program is sponsored by Tiger Personnel Services, Inc.

Number awarded 1 each year.

Deadline March of each year.

[536]
TMCF COCA-COLA FOUNDATION SCHOLARSHIPS

Thurgood Marshall College Fund
Attn: Scholarship Manager
80 Maiden Lane, Suite 2204
New York, NY 10038
(212) 573-8487   Toll Free: (877) 690-8673
Fax: (212) 573-8497   E-mail: srogers@tmcfund.org
Web: www.thurgoodmarshallfund.net

Summary To provide financial assistance to students majoring in finance at colleges and universities that are members of the Thurgood Marshall College Fund (TMCF) and who are the first member of their family to attend college.

Eligibility This program is open to full-time students majoring in finance at 1 of the 47 colleges and universities that are TMCF members. Applicants must be the first member of their family to attend college. They must have a GPA of 3.0 or higher and be able to demonstrate financial need. U.S. citizenship is required.

Financial data The stipend is $1,100 per semester ($2,200 per year).

Duration 1 year.

Additional information This program is sponsored by the Coca-Cola Foundation. The 47 participating TMCF institutions are Alabama A&M University, Alabama State University, Albany State University, Alcorn State University, Bluefield State College, Bowie State University, Central State University (Ohio), Charles R. Drew University of Medicine (California), Cheyney University of Pennsylvania, Chicago State University, Coppin State College, Delaware State University, Elizabeth City State University, Fayetteville State University, Florida A&M University, Fort Valley State University, Grambling State University, Harris-Stowe State College, Howard University, Jackson State University, Kentucky State University, Langston University, Lincoln University (Missouri), Lincoln University (Pennsylvania), Medgar Evers College (New York), Mississippi Valley State University, Morgan State University, Norfolk State University, North Carolina A&T State University, North Carolina Central University, Prairie View A&M University, Savannah State University, South Carolina State University, Southern University and A&M College, Southern University at New Orleans, Southern University at Shreveport-Bossier City, Tennessee State University, Texas Southern University, Tuskegee University, University of Arkansas at Pine Bluff, University of the District of Columbia, University of Maryland-Eastern Shore, University of the Virgin Islands, Virginia State University, West Virginia State College, Winston-Salem State University, and York College.

Number awarded 47 each year: 1 at each participating institution.

Deadline July of each year.

[537]
TOYOTA NSBE CORPORATE SCHOLARSHIPS

National Society of Black Engineers
Attn: Programs Department
205 Daingerfield Road
Alexandria, VA 22314
(703) 549-2207   Fax: (703) 683-5312
E-mail: scholarships@nsbe.org
Web: www.nsbe.org

Summary To provide financial assistance to members of the National Society of Black Engineers (NSBE) who are majoring in designated engineering fields.

Eligibility This program is open to members of the society who are enrolled as college sophomores, juniors, or seniors and majoring in chemical, electrical, industrial, materials, or mechanical engineering. Applicants must have a GPA of 3.0 or higher and a demonstrated interest in employment with Toyota.

Financial data The stipend is $2,500.

Duration 1 year.

Additional information This program is sponsored by Toyota Motor Sales, U.S.A., Inc.

Number awarded 4 each year.

Deadline January of each year.

[538]
TRAILBLAZER SCHOLARSHIPS

Conference of Minority Transportation Officials
Attn: National Scholarship Program
818 18th Street, N.W., Suite 850
Washington, DC 20006
(202) 530-0551   Fax: (202) 530-0617
Web: www.comto.org/news-youth.php

Summary To provide financial assistance to African Americans and other undergraduate and graduate minority students working on a degree in a field related to transportation.

Eligibility This program is open to undergraduate and graduate students who are working on a degree in a field related to transportation with a GPA of 2.5 or higher. Along with their application, they must submit a cover letter with a 500-word statement of career goals. Financial need is not considered in the selection process. U.S. citizenship is required.

Financial data The stipend is $2,500. Funds are paid directly to the recipient's college or university.

Duration 1 year.

Additional information The Conference of Minority Transportation Officials (COMTO) was established in 1971 to promote, strengthen, and expand the roles of minorities in all aspects of transportation. Recipients are expected to attend the COMTO National Scholarship Luncheon.

Number awarded 2 each year.

Deadline April of each year.

[539]
TRAVIS C. TOMLIN MEMORIAL SCHOLARSHIP

National Association of Black Accountants
Attn: National Scholarship Program
7474 Greenway Center Drive, Suite 1120
Greenbelt, MD 20770
(301) 474-NABA, ext. 114   Fax: (301) 474-3114
E-mail: customerservice@nabainc.org
Web: www.nabainc.org

Summary To provide financial assistance to student members of the National Association of Black Accountants (NABA) who are working on an undergraduate or graduate degree in a field related to accounting.

Eligibility This program is open to NABA members enrolled full time as 1) an undergraduate freshman, sophomore, junior, or first-semester senior majoring in accounting, business, or finance at a 4-year college or university; or 2) a graduate student working on a master's degree in accounting. High school seniors are not eligible. Applicants must have a GPA of 3.5 or higher in their major and 3.3 or higher overall. Selection is based on grades, financial need, and a 500-word autobiography that discusses career objectives, leadership abilities, community activities, and involvement in NABA.

Financial data The stipend ranges from $1,500 to $2,000.

Duration 1 year.

Number awarded 1 each year.

Deadline January of each year.

[540]
TWIN CITIES CHAPTER NBMBAA
UNDERGRADUATE BUSINESS SCHOLARSHIPS

National Black MBA Association-Twin Cities Chapter
Attn: Scholarship Committee Chair
P.O. Box 2709
Minneapolis, MN 55402
(651) 734-0808   E-mail: scholarships@nbmbaatc.org
Web: www.nbmbaatc.org/education.htm

Summary To provide financial assistance to African American students from Minnesota who are interested in working on a bachelor's degree in business administration.

Eligibility This program is open to African and African American students enrolled full time in an undergraduate business or management program; this includes high school seniors who are about to enter college, preferably to work on a bachelor's degree in business or management. Applicants must be residents of and/or attending school in Minnesota. Along with their application, they must submit a 2-page essay on a topic that changes annually. Selection is based on the essay, career aspirations, GPA, activities, and a 150-word biography that covers their background, experiences, accomplishments, and career goals.

Financial data The stipend is $1,000.

Duration 1 year.

Number awarded 1 each year.

Deadline June of each year.

[541]
UNCF GEOGRAPHICALLY-BASED SCHOLARSHIPS

United Negro College Fund
Attn: Scholarships and Grants Department
8260 Willow Oaks Corporate Drive
P.O. Box 10444
Fairfax, VA 22031-8044
(703) 205-3466   Toll Free: (800) 331-2244
Fax: (703) 205-3574
Web: www.uncf.org/forstudents/scholarship.asp

Summary   To provide financial assistance to high school juniors or seniors from designated areas who are interested in attending a member institution of the United Negro College Fund (UNCF).

Eligibility   These programs are open to students from designated geographical areas. Applicants must be high school seniors or graduates with strong academic backgrounds (minimum GPA of 2.5). Students who have completed their junior year in high school with a record of distinction may also be considered. Financial need must be demonstrated. Applications should be submitted directly to the UNCF-member institution the student plans to attend.

Financial data   The awards are intended to cover tuition and range from a minimum of $500 to a maximum of $7,500 per year.

Duration   1 year; may be renewed.

Additional information   Recipients must attend a UNCF-member institution of higher learning. These are: Miles College, Oakwood College, Stillman College, Talladega College, and Tuskegee University in Alabama; Philander Smith College in Arkansas; Bethune-Cookman College, Edward Waters College, and Florida Memorial University in Florida; Clark Atlanta University, Interdenominational Theological Center, Morehouse College, Paine College, and Spelman College in Georgia; Dillard University and Xavier University in Louisiana; Rust College and Tougaloo College in Mississippi; Bennett College, Johnson C. Smith University, Livingstone College, Saint Augustine's College, and Shaw University in North Carolina; Wilberforce University in Ohio; Allen University, Benedict College, Claflin University, Morris College, and Voorhees College in South Carolina; Fisk University, Lane College, and LeMoyne-Owen College in Tennessee; Huston-Tillotson College, Jarvis Christian College, Paul Quinn College, Texas College, and Wiley College in Texas; and Saint Paul's College and Virginia Union University in Virginia.

Number awarded   A total of nearly 1,200 UNCF scholarships are awarded each year.

Deadline   Deadline dates vary, depending upon the individual institution's requirements.

[542]
UNCF/MERCK UNDERGRADUATE SCIENCE RESEARCH SCHOLARSHIPS

United Negro College Fund
Attn: Merck Science Initiative
8260 Willow Oaks Corporate Drive, Suite 110
P.O. Box 10444
Fairfax, VA 22031-4511
(703) 205-3503   Fax: (703) 205-3574
E-mail: uncfmerck@uncf.org
Web: umsi.uncf.org

Summary   To provide financial assistance and summer work experience to African American undergraduates who are interested in preparing for a career in biomedical research.

Eligibility   This program is open to African American students currently enrolled as full-time juniors and planning to graduate in the coming year. Applicants must be majoring in a life or physical science or engineering, be interested in biomedical research, and have a GPA of 3.3 or higher; physical science majors have completed 2 semesters of organic chemistry. All applicants must be interested in working at Merck as a summer intern. Candidates for professional (Pharm.D., D.V.M., D.D.S., etc.) degrees are ineligible. U.S. citizenship or permanent resident status is required. Selection is based on GPA, demonstrated interest in a scientific education and a career in scientific research, and interest in and ability to perform laboratory work.

Financial data   The total award is $30,000, including up to $25,000 for tuition, fees, room, and board, and at least $5,000 for a summer internship stipend. In addition, the department of the recipient may receive a grant of up to $10,000. The department grant may not be used to support salaries, travel, or indirect costs.

Duration   1 academic year plus an internship of 10 to 12 weeks during the summer.

Additional information   This program, established in 1995, is funded by the Merck Company Foundation.

Number awarded   At least 15 each year.

Deadline   December of each year.

[543]
UNDERGRADUATE STUDENT INDUSTRIAL FELLOWSHIPS/TRAINEESHIPS

National Science Foundation
Directorate for Engineering
Attn: Division of Industrial Innovation and Partnerships
4201 Wilson Boulevard, Room 550S
Arlington, VA 22230
(703) 292-7082   Fax: (703) 292-9056
TDD: (800) 281-8749   E-mail: dsenich@nsf.gov
Web: www.nsf.gov/funding/pgm_summ.jsp?pims_id=13706

Summary   To provide an opportunity for undergraduate students (especially African Americans or other underrepresented minorities and students with disabilities) to work in industry as part of the Grant Opportunities for Academic Liaison with Industry (GOALI) program of the National Science Foundation (NSF).

Eligibility   This program is open to undergraduate students in science, engineering, and mathematics fields of interest to NSF. Applicants must be U.S. citizens, nationals, or permanent residents. They must be proposing a program of full- or part-time work in industry in an area related to their academic program under the guidance of an academic adviser and an industrial mentor. The program encourages applications from underrepresented minorities and persons with disabilities.

Financial data   Undergraduate students may receive stipends from $500 to $800 per week; they may also receive some assistance with housing or travel expenses, or both. No indirect costs are allowed. The total award may be up to $10,000 for a fellowship for a single student.

Duration   Support may be provided for a summer project, or for 1 or 2 semesters of part- or full-time work.

Additional information This program is also offered by most other NSF directorates. Check the web site for a name and e-mail address of the contact person in each directorate.

Number awarded A total of 60 to 80 grants for all GOALI programs is awarded each year; total funding is approximately $5 million.

Deadline Applications may be submitted at any time.

[544]
UNITED METHODIST ETHNIC MINORITY SCHOLARSHIPS

United Methodist Church
Attn: General Board of Higher Education and Ministry
Office of Loans and Scholarships
1001 19th Avenue South
P.O. Box 340007
Nashville, TN 37203-0007
(615) 340-7344   Fax: (615) 340-7367
E-mail: umscholar@gbhem.org
Web: www.gbhem.org/loansandscholarships

Summary To provide financial assistance to African American or other minority undergraduate Methodist students.

Eligibility This program is open to full-time undergraduate students at accredited colleges and universities in the United States who have been active, full members of a United Methodist Church for at least 1 year prior to applying. Applicants must have at least 1 parent who is African American, Hispanic, Asian, Native American, or Pacific Islander. They must have a GPA of 2.5 or higher and be able to demonstrate financial need. U.S. citizenship, permanent resident status, or membership in a central conference of the United Methodist Church is required. Selection is based on church membership, involvement in church and community activities, GPA, and financial need.

Financial data A stipend is awarded (amount not specified).

Duration 1 year; recipients may reapply.

Number awarded Varies each year.

Deadline March of each year.

[545]
UNITED PARCEL SERVICE SCHOLARSHIP FOR MINORITY STUDENTS

Institute of Industrial Engineers
Attn: Scholarship Coordinator
3577 Parkway Lane, Suite 200
Norcross, GA 30092
(770) 449-0461, ext. 105   Toll Free: (800) 494-0460
Fax: (770) 441-3295   E-mail: bcameron@iienet.org
Web: www.iienet2.org/Details.aspx?id=857

Summary To provide financial assistance to African American and other minority undergraduates who are studying industrial engineering at a school in the United States, Canada, or Mexico.

Eligibility Eligible to be nominated are minority undergraduate students enrolled at any school in the United States and its territories, Canada, or Mexico, provided the school's engineering program is accredited by an agency recognized by the Institute of Industrial Engineers (IIE) and the student is pursuing a full-time course of study in industrial engineering with a GPA of at least 3.4. Nominees must have at least 5 full

quarters or 3 full semesters remaining until graduation. Students may not apply directly for these awards; they must be nominated by the head of their industrial engineering department. Nominees must be IIE members. Selection is based on scholastic ability, character, leadership, potential service to the industrial engineering profession, and need for financial assistance.

Financial data The stipend is $4,000.

Duration 1 year.

Additional information Funding for this program is provided by the UPS Foundation.

Number awarded 1 each year.

Deadline Schools must submit nominations by November of each year.

[546]
UNITED STATES STEEL NSBE ACADEMIC SCHOLARSHIPS

National Society of Black Engineers
Attn: Programs Department
205 Daingerfield Road
Alexandria, VA 22314
(703) 549-2207   Fax: (703) 683-5312
E-mail: scholarships@nsbe.org
Web: www.nsbe.org

Summary To provide financial assistance to members of the National Society of Black Engineers (NSBE) who are majoring in engineering or related fields.

Eligibility This program is open to members of the society who are entering the junior year of a 4-year program or the fifth year of a 5-year program. Applicants must be majoring in chemistry, computer science, engineering technology, materials science, mathematics, applied or engineering physics, or the following fields of engineering: chemical, civil, electrical, environmental, industrial, manufacturing, materials, or mechanical. They must have a GPA of 2.75 or higher. U.S. citizenship is required.

Financial data The stipend is $5,000.

Duration 1 year.

Additional information This program is supported by the United States Steel Foundation.

Number awarded 1 each year.

Deadline January of each year.

[547]
UNIVERSITY OF CALIFORNIA AT BERKELEY AMGEN SCHOLARS PROGRAM

University of California at Berkeley
Attn: Amgen Scholars Program
158 Barrows Hall
MC 2990
Berkeley, CA 94720-2990
(510) 642-0280   Fax: (510) 643-6762
E-mail: amgenscholars@berkeley.edu
Web: amgenscholars.berkeley.edu

Summary To provide undergraduate students (particularly African Americans and other minorities) with a summer research experience at the University of California at Berkeley in biological and biomedical sciences.

Eligibility This program is open to sophomores, juniors, and non-graduating seniors at 4-year colleges and universities in the United States, Puerto Rico, and U.S. territories. Applicants must be interested in a summer research experience at UC Berkeley in biochemistry, bioengineering, bioinformatics, biology (molecular, cell, and developmental), biopsychology, biotechnology, chemical and biomedical engineering, chemistry, immunology, medical pharmacology, microbiology, molecular genetics, molecular medicine, molecular pharmacology, neurobiology, neuroscience, pathology, physiological psychology, physiological science, statistics, or toxicology. They must have a GPA of 3.2 or higher and an interest in continuing on to a Ph.D. or M.D./Ph.D. (but not M.D.) program. Applications are especially encouraged from students from diverse populations and backgrounds. U.S. citizenship or permanent resident status is required.

Financial data Housing, travel to and from Berkeley, meals, and a stipend of $3,800 are provided.

Duration 10 weeks during the summer.

Additional information This program serves as the UC Berkeley component of the Amgen Scholars Program, which operates at 9 other U.S. universities and is funded by the Amgen Foundation.

Number awarded 25 each year.

Deadline January of each year.

[548]
UNIVERSITY OF CALIFORNIA AT SAN FRANCISCO SUMMER RESEARCH OPPORTUNITIES

University of California at San Francisco
Office of Graduate Outreach
Attn: Director of Recruitment and Retention Programs
1675 Owens Street, Room 310
Box 0523
San Francisco, CA 94143-0523
(415) 514-0840   Fax: (415) 514-0844
E-mail: strp@ucsf.edu
Web: graduate.ucsf.edu

Summary To provide undergraduate students (especially African Americans and other minorities) with a summer research experience at the University of California at San Francisco in biological and biomedical sciences.

Eligibility This activity consists of 3 separate programs, but they operate together and have a common application and requirements. The 3 programs are the Amgen Scholars Program, the Molecular Biosciences Research Experience for Undergraduates (REU), and the Summer Research Training Program (SRTP). The activity is open to sophomores, juniors, and non-graduating seniors at 4-year colleges and universities in the United States, Puerto Rico, and U.S. territories. Applicants must be interested in a summer research experience at UC San Francisco in biochemistry, bioengineering, bioinformatics, biology (molecular, cell, and developmental), biopsychology, biotechnology, chemical and biomedical engineering, chemistry, immunology, medical pharmacology, microbiology, molecular genetics, molecular medicine, molecular pharmacology, neurobiology, neuroscience, pathology, physiological psychology, physiological science, statistics, or toxicology. The Amgen Scholars Program requires a GPA of 3.2 or higher but the other 2 components have no minimum GPA requirement; all programs require an interest in continuing on to a Ph.D. or M.D./Ph.D. (but not

M.D.) program. Applications are especially encouraged from underrepresented minority, socioeconomically disadvantaged, and first generation college students and from students with limited access to research laboratories. U.S. citizenship or permanent resident status is required.

Financial data Housing, travel to and from San Francisco, a stipend of $4,500, and a subsistence allowance of $1,300 are provided.

Duration 10 weeks during the summer.

Additional information This program is comprised of 1) the UC San Francisco component of the Amgen Scholars Program, which operates at 9 other U.S. universities and is funded by the Amgen Foundation; 2) the REU program, funded by the National Science Foundation; and 3) the SRTP, which is a UCSF program with supplemental funding from Genentech and the Howard Hughes Medical Institute.

Number awarded Approximately 60 each year.

Deadline January of each year.

[549]
UNIVERSITY OF NORTH CAROLINA CAMPUS SCHOLARSHIPS

North Carolina State Education Assistance Authority
Attn: Scholarship and Grant Services
10 Alexander Drive
P.O. Box 14103
Research Triangle Park, NC 27709-4103
(919) 549-8614   Toll Free: (800) 700-1775
Fax: (919) 549-8481   E-mail: information@ncseaa.edu
Web: www.ncseaa.edu

Summary To provide financial assistance to African Americans and other students at University of North Carolina (UNC) constituent institutions whose enrollment contributes to the diversity of the undergraduate or graduate population.

Eligibility This program is open to undergraduate and doctoral students who are enrolled or planning to enroll full time at 1 of the 16 UNC institutions. Applicants must have graduated in the top 40% of their high school class, have a weighted GPA of 3.0 or higher, have an SAT score higher than the SAT score of the previous freshman class, and have a record of positive involvement in extracurricular activities. They must be able to demonstrate "exceptional financial need." Their enrollment must "contribute to the intellectual experiences and diversity of the undergraduate population." A portion of the funds are reserved specifically for American Indian students who can provide evidence of tribal affiliation.

Financial data The amount of the award depends upon the financial need of the recipient and the availability of funds; recently, stipends averaged more than $1,900.

Duration 1 year; may be renewed.

Additional information This program was established in 2002 as a replacement for the former North Carolina Minority Presence Grants, North Carolina Freshmen Scholars Program, North Carolina Incentive Scholarship Program, North Carolina Legislative College Opportunity Program, and North Carolina Incentive Scholarship and Grant Program for Native Americans. Students must submit applications to the constituent institution's financial aid office rather than directly to the North Carolina State Education Assistance Authority.

Number awarded Varies each year; recently, a total of 2,793 of these scholarships, with a total value of $5,435,826, were awarded.

Deadline Deadline dates vary; check with the appropriate constituent institution.

[550]
URBAN LEAGUE OF NEBRASKA SCHOLARSHIPS

Urban League of Nebraska
Attn: Courtney Eugene Carter
3040 Lake Street
Omaha, NE 68111
(402) 451-1066, ext. 30
E-mail: ccarter@urbanleagueneb.org
Web: www.urbanleagueneb.org

Summary To provide financial assistance to African American and other high school seniors in Nebraska who plan to attend college in any state.

Eligibility This program is open to seniors graduating from high schools in Nebraska who are planning to enroll at a college or university in any state. Applicants must have a GPA of 2.5 or higher and a record of at least 10 hours of documented community involvement. Along with their application, they must submit an essay of 250 to 500 words on their educational and career goals, ambitions, and reasons why they should receive this scholarship. Financial need is also considered in the selection process.

Financial data A stipend is awarded (amount not specified).

Duration 1 year.

Additional information The sponsor's historic mission has been to assist African Americans to improve their lives and careers.

Number awarded 1 or more each year.

Deadline March of each year.

[551]
USA FUNDS ACCESS TO EDUCATION SCHOLARSHIPS

Scholarship America
Attn: Scholarship Management Services
One Scholarship Way
P.O. Box 297
St. Peter, MN 56082
(507) 931-1682   Toll Free: (800) 537-4180
Fax: (507) 931-9168   E-mail: scholarship@usafunds.org
Web: www.usafunds.org

Summary To provide financial assistance to undergraduate and graduate students, especially those who are African Americans, members of other minority groups, and students with physical disabilities.

Eligibility This program is open to high school seniors and graduates who plan to enroll or are already enrolled in full- or half-time undergraduate or full-time graduate course work at an accredited 2- or 4-year college, university, or vocational/technical school. GED recipients are also eligible. Up to 50% of the awards are targeted at students who have a documented physical disability or are a member of an ethnic minority group, including but not limited to Native Hawaiian, Alaskan Native, Black/African American, Asian, Pacific Islander, American Indian, Hispanic/Latino, or multiracial.

Residents of all 50 states, the District of Columbia, Puerto Rico, Guam, the U.S. Virgin Islands, and all U.S. territories and commonwealths are eligible. Applicants must also be U.S. citizens or eligible noncitizens and come from a family with an annual adjusted gross income of $35,000 or less. In addition to financial need, selection is based on past academic performance and future potential, leadership and participation in school and community activities, work experience, career and educational aspirations and goals, and unusual personal or family circumstances.

Financial data The stipend is $1,500 per year for full-time undergraduate or graduate students or $750 per year for half-time undergraduate students. Funds are paid jointly to the student and the school.

Duration 1 year; may be renewed until the student receives a final degree or certificate or until the total award to a student reaches $6,000, whichever comes first. Renewal requires the recipient to maintain a GPA of 2.5 or higher.

Additional information This program, established in 2000, is sponsored by USA Funds.

Number awarded Varies each year; recently, a total of $3.2 million was available for this program.

Deadline February of each year.

[552]
USDA/1890 NATIONAL SCHOLARS PROGRAM

Department of Agriculture
Office of the Assistant Secretary for Civil Rights
Attn: 1890 National Scholars Program Manager
1400 Independence Avenue, S.W.
Mail Stop 9478
Washington, DC 20250
(202) 205-4307   E-mail: 1890init@usda.gov
Web: www.usda.gov

Summary To provide financial assistance to high school seniors and graduates interested in majoring in a field related to agriculture or agribusiness at 1 of the 18 Historically Black 1890 Land Grant Institutions.

Eligibility This program is open to U.S. citizens who have or will have a high school diploma or GED certificate with a GPA of 3.0 or higher and a combined critical reading and mathematics score of at least 1000 on the SAT or a composite score of at least 21 on the ACT. They must be planning to attend 1 of the 18 Historically Black 1890 Land Grant Institutions and study such fields as agriculture, agricultural business/management, agricultural economics, agricultural engineering/mechanics, agricultural production and technology, agronomy or crop science, animal sciences, botany, farm and range management, fish and game management, food sciences/technology, forestry and related services, home economics and human development, horticulture, natural resources management, nutrition, soil conservation/soil science, wildlife management, or other related disciplines. Currently-enrolled undergraduate students attending an 1890 institution are not eligible.

Financial data Each award provides annual tuition, employment, employee benefits, use of a laptop computer and software while receiving the scholarship, fees, books, and room and board. Following graduation, scholars are required to perform 1 year of service to the U.S. Department of Agriculture for each year of support received.

Duration 4 years, provided the scholar maintains normal progress toward the bachelor's degree and satisfactory performance.

Additional information The Historically Black Land Grant institutions are: Alabama A&M University, Alcorn State University, University of Arkansas at Pine Bluff, Delaware State University, Florida A&M University, Fort Valley State University, Kentucky State University, Lincoln University of Missouri, Langston University, University of Maryland-Eastern Shore, North Carolina A&T State University, Prairie View A&M University, South Carolina State University, Southern University and A&M College, Tennessee State University, Tuskegee University, Virginia State University, and West Virginia State University. Applications must be submitted to the Liaison Officer of the U.S. Department of Agriculture at a participating 1890 institution.

Number awarded 36 or more each year: at least 2 at each of the participating universities.

Deadline January of each year.

[553]
VADM SAMUEL L. GRAVELY, JR., USN (RET.) MEMORIAL SCHOLARSHIPS

Armed Forces Communications and Electronics Association
Attn: AFCEA Educational Foundation
4400 Fair Lakes Court
Fairfax, VA 22033-3899
(703) 631-6149   Toll Free: (800) 336-4583, ext. 6149
Fax: (703) 631-4693   E-mail: scholarship@afcea.org
Web: www.afcea.org

Summary To provide funding to students majoring in specified scientific fields at an Historically Black College or University (HBCU).

Eligibility This program is open to sophomores and juniors enrolled full or part time at an accredited 2- or 4-year HBCU or in a distance learning or online degree program affiliated with those institutions. They must be working toward a degree in engineering (aerospace, computer, electrical, or systems), computer science, computer engineering technology, computer information systems, mathematics, physics, information systems management, or other field directly related to the support of U.S. intelligence or homeland security enterprises. Special consideration is given to military enlisted personnel and veterans.

Financial data The stipend is $5,000.

Duration 1 year; may be renewed.

Additional information This program was established in 2009 with support from American Systems.

Number awarded At least 2 each year.

Deadline October of each year.

[554]
VAID FELLOWSHIPS

National Gay and Lesbian Task Force
Attn: The Task Force Policy Institute
80 Maiden Lane, Suite 1504
New York, NY 10038
(212) 604-9830   Fax: (212) 604-9831
E-mail: ngltf@ngltf.org
Web: www.thetaskforce.org

Summary To provide work experience to undergraduate and graduate students (particularly African Americans and other minorities) who are interested in participating in the leadership of people of color in the progressive movement for gay, lesbian, bisexual, and transgender (GLBT) equality.

Eligibility Applicants must be enrolled in a degree program at least half time as a law, graduate, or undergraduate student or have successfully completed a law, graduate, or undergraduate degree within the preceding 12 months. They should have 1) a desire to work in a multicultural environment where commitment to diversity based on race, ethnic origin, gender, age, sexual orientation, and physical ability is an important institutional value; 2) demonstrated leadership in progressive and/or GLBT communities; 3) extensive research, writing, and critical thinking skills; 4) knowledge of, and commitment to, GLBT issues; and 5) computer proficiency in word processing, database work, e-mail, and Internet research. The program supports and recognizes the leadership of people of color and other emerging leaders in public policy, legal, and social science research.

Financial data The stipend ranges from $200 to $400 per week ($10 per hour). Fellows are responsible for their own housing and living expenses.

Duration Summer fellowships are 40 hours per week and spring/fall fellowships are 20 hours per week.

Additional information The Policy Institute of the National Gay and Lesbian Task Force (NGLTF), founded in 1995, is the largest think tank in the United States engaged in research, policy analysis, and strategic action to advance equality and understanding of GLBT people. Its primary programs are the racial and economic justice initiative, the family policy program, and the aging initiative. In addition to their primary roles of providing research and analysis, all 3 programs work closely with NGLTF colleagues in Washington, D.C. and other allies on advocacy and legislative efforts to actively change laws and policies affecting GLBT people.

Number awarded 3 fellows are selected each session.

Deadline April for the summer, July for the fall, and November for the spring.

[555]
VANGUARD MINORITY SCHOLARSHIP PROGRAM

Scholarship America
Attn: Scholarship Management Services
One Scholarship Way
P.O. Box 297
St. Peter, MN 56082
(507) 931-1682   Toll Free: (800) 537-4180
Fax: (507) 931-9168
Web: sms.scholarshipamerica.org/vanguard

Summary To provide financial assistance to African American and other minority students working on an undergraduate degree in specified fields.

Eligibility This program is open to U.S. citizens and permanent residents who are members of racial or ethnic minorities. Applicants must be entering their junior or senior year as a full-time student at an accredited 4-year college or university in the United States and have a GPA of 3.0 or higher. They must be working on a degree in accounting, business, economics, or finance. Selection is based on academic record, demonstrated leadership and participation in school and community activities, honors, work experience, a statement of goals and aspirations, unusual personal or family circumstances, recommendations, and a resume; financial need is not considered. Students who attended a 2-year college while working on a bachelor's degree are not eligible.

Financial data The stipend ranges up to $10,000.

Duration 1 year; nonrenewable.

Additional information This program, established in 2004, is sponsored by Vanguard Group, Inc.

Number awarded Up to 10 each year.

Deadline November of each year.

[556]
VERIZON NSBE CORPORATE SCHOLARSHIPS

National Society of Black Engineers
Attn: Programs Department
205 Daingerfield Road
Alexandria, VA 22314
(703) 549-2207   Fax: (703) 683-5312
E-mail: scholarships@nsbe.org
Web: www.nsbe.org

Summary To provide financial assistance to members of the National Society of Black Engineers (NSBE) who are working on an undergraduate or graduate degree in specified fields of science, engineering, or business.

Eligibility This program is open to members of the society who are undergraduate or graduate students working on a degree in computer engineering, computer science, electric engineering, wireless communication, or business (M.B.A. degree only). Applicants must have a GPA of 3.0 or higher and a demonstrated interest in employment with Verizon and its affiliated companies in the fields of wireless, business, or telecommunications.

Financial data Stipends are $6,500 or $5,000.

Duration 1 year.

Additional information This program is supported by Verizon.

Number awarded 3 each year: 1 at $6,500 and 2 at $5,000.

Deadline January of each year.

[557]
VICE ADMIRAL SAMUEL L. GRAVELY, JR. MEMORIAL SCHOLARSHIP

National Naval Officers Association-Washington, D.C.
   Chapter
Attn: Scholarship Program
2701 Park Center Drive, A1108
Alexandria, VA 22302
(703) 566-3840   Fax: (703) 566-3813
E-mail: Stephen.Williams@Navy.mil
Web: dcnnoa.memberlodge.com

Summary To provide financial assistance to African American high school seniors from the Washington, D.C. area who plan to attend college in any state.

Eligibility This program is open to African American seniors graduating from high schools in the Washington, D.C. metropolitan area who plan to enroll full time at an accredited 2- or 4-year college or university in any state. Applicants must have a GPA of 2.5 or higher. Selection is based on academic achievement, community involvement, and financial need.

Financial data The stipend is $1,000.

Duration 1 year; nonrenewable.

Additional information Recipients are not required to join or affiliate with the military in any way.

Number awarded 1 each year.

Deadline March of each year.

[558]
VIRGINIA CITE TRADITIONAL SCHOLARSHIPS

Consortium of Information and Telecommunications
   Executives-Virginia Chapter
c/o Rhonda Stanford, Scholarship Committee
P.O. Box 950
Glen Allen, VA 23065-0950
(804) 756-5286
E-mail: Rhonda.s.stanford@citevirginia.org
Web: www.citevirginia.org/scholarship.html

Summary To provide financial assistance to African American high school seniors in Virginia who plan to attend college in any state and major in designated business- and engineering-related fields.

Eligibility This program is open to African American seniors graduating from high schools in Virginia with a GPA of 3.0 or higher. Applicants must have been accepted by an accredited college or university in any state as a full-time student. They must be planning to major in 1 of the following fields: accounting, advertising, business, computer science, electrical engineering, finance, industrial engineering, information technology, marketing, or mathematics. Their family income must be $75,000 per year or less. Along with their application, they must submit a 1-page essay on their educational and career goals. Employees and immediate family members of employees of the Verizon Corporation or an affiliated subsidiary are ineligible. U.S. citizenship is required.

Financial data The stipend is $1,000.

Duration 1 year.

Additional information The Consortium of Information and Telecommunications Executives (CITE) is an organization of African American employees of Verizon, founded in 1984 after the dissolution of the former Bell systems. Recipients must attend the sponsor's scholarship event in June.

Number awarded 1 or more each year.

Deadline April of each year.

[559]
VIRGINIA TEACHING SCHOLARSHIP LOAN PROGRAM

Virginia Department of Education
Division of Teacher Education and Licensure
Attn: Director of Teacher Education
P.O. Box 2120
Richmond, VA 23218-2120
(804) 371-2475   Toll Free: (800) 292-3820
Fax: (804) 786-6759
E-mail: JoAnne.Carver@doe.virginia.gov
Web: www.doe.virginia.gov

Summary To provide funding to upper-division and graduate students in Virginia (especially African Americans and other minorities) who are interested in a career in teaching.

Eligibility This program is open to Virginia residents who are enrolled full or part time as a sophomore, junior, senior, or graduate student in a state-approved teacher preparation program in Virginia with a GPA of 2.7 or higher. Applicants must agree to engage in full-time teaching following graduation in 1) designated teacher shortage areas within Virginia; 2) a school with a high concentration of students eligible for free or reduced lunch; 3) within a school division with a shortage of teachers; 4) in a rural or urban region of the state with a teacher shortage; or 5) in a career and technical education discipline. Males interested in teaching in the elementary grades and people of color in all teaching areas also qualify.

Financial data The scholarship/loan is $3,720 per year. Loans are forgiven at the rate of $1,000 for each semester the recipient teaches in designated teacher shortage areas. If the recipient fails to fulfill the teaching service requirement, the loan must be repaid with interest.

Duration 1 year; may be renewed 1 additional year.

Additional information Critical shortage teaching areas in Virginia are currently identified as all areas of special education (severe disturbances, hearing impairment, learning disabilities, mental retardation, severe disabilities, visual impairment, early childhood special education, emotional disturbance, and speech and language disorders), career and technical education (including technology education, trade and industrial education, business education, and family and consumer sciences), mathematics (6-12), foreign language (preK-12), English (6-12), middle school (6-8), elementary education (preK-6), science (6-12), health and physical education (preK-12), and school counselor (preK-12).

Number awarded Varies each year; recently, 265 of these scholarship/loans were granted, including 111 in elementary education, 14 in English, 8 in foreign languages, 2 in history and social science, 18 in mathematics, 22 in middle grades, 2 in science, 30 in special education, 20 for males in elementary grades, 4 for males in middle grades, and 34 for people of color.

Deadline Deadline not specified.

[560]
VISUAL TASK FORCE SCHOLARSHIPS

National Association of Black Journalists
Attn: Program Coordinator
8701-A Adelphi Road
Adelphi, MD 20783-1716
(301) 445-7100, ext. 108   Toll Free: (866) 479-NABJ
Fax: (301) 445-7101   E-mail: nabj@nabj.org
Web: www.nabj.org

Summary To provide financial assistance to undergraduate or graduate student members of the National Association of Black Journalists (NABJ) who are interested in a career in visual journalism.

Eligibility This program is open to African American undergraduate or graduate students who are currently attending an accredited 4-year college or university. Applicants must be majoring in visual journalism, have a GPA of 2.75 or higher, have experience working on their campus newspaper or TV studio, and have held an internship. They must be NABJ members. Along with their application, they must submit samples of their work, an official college transcript, 2 letters of recommendation, a resume, and a 500- to 800-word essay describing their accomplishments as a student journalist, their career goals, and their financial need.

Financial data The stipend is $1,250. Funds are paid directly to the recipient's college or university.

Duration 1 year; nonrenewable.

Number awarded 2 each year.

Deadline April of each year.

[561]
VIVIAN D. TILLMAN SCHOLARSHIP

Sigma Gamma Rho Sorority, Inc.
Attn: National Education Fund
1000 Southhill Drive, Suite 200
Cary, NC 27513
(919) 678-9720   Toll Free: (888) SGR-1922
Fax: (919) 678-9721   E-mail: info@sgrho1922.org
Web: www.sgrho1922.org/service.htm

Summary To provide financial assistance to African American and other undergraduate students working on a degree in journalism or communications.

Eligibility This program is open to undergraduates working on a degree in journalism or communications. Applicants must have a GPA of "C" or higher and be able to demonstrate financial need. Along with their application, they must submit a 500-word essay on how they will use their communication or journalism skills for the betterment of the country.

Financial data A stipend is awarded (amount not specified).

Duration 1 year.

Additional information The sponsor is a traditionally African American sorority. A processing fee of $20 is required.

Number awarded 1 each year.

Deadline April of each year.

[562]
WAL-MART EMERGING LEADERS INTERNSHIP PROGRAM

Congressional Black Caucus Foundation, Inc.
Attn: Internship Coordinator
1720 Massachusetts Avenue, N.W.
Washington, DC 20036
(202) 263-2800   Toll Free: (800) 784-2577
Fax: (202) 775-0773   E-mail: internships@cbcfinc.org
Web: www.cbcfinc.org

Summary To provide African American and other undergraduate students with an opportunity to work during the fall in a Congressional office or federal government agency.

Eligibility This program is open to African American and other full-time undergraduate students in good academic standing. Applicants must be interested in a legislative internship on the staff of an African American member of Congress or an assignment with a federal government agency. They should have a demonstrated interest in public service, governance, and the policy-making process. Selection is based on scholastic achievement, evidence of leadership skills, writing skills, and community service contributions.

Financial data Interns receive housing accommodations and a stipend (amount not specified) to cover expenses related to travel, meals, and personal expenses.

Duration 13 weeks during the fall.

Additional information This program, established in 2007, is sponsored by Wal-Mart. In addition to their work assignments, interns attend educational seminars that focus on domestic and international issues, participate in leadership training sessions, and visit cultural and historical sites in the Washington, D.C. area. As a team, they participate in a community service project.

Number awarded Varies each year; recently, 9 interns served in this program.

Deadline May of each year.

[563]
WAL-MART SCHOLARSHIPS OF THE THURGOOD MARSHALL COLLEGE FUND

Thurgood Marshall College Fund
Attn: Scholarship Manager
80 Maiden Lane, Suite 2204
New York, NY 10038
(212) 573-8487   Toll Free: (877) 690-8673
Fax: (212) 573-8497   E-mail: srogers@tmcfund.org
Web: www.thurgoodmarshallfund.net

Summary To provide financial assistance to African American males enrolled at colleges and universities that are members of the Thurgood Marshall College Fund (TMCF).

Eligibility This program is open to African American males currently enrolled full time at 1 of the 47 colleges and universities that are TMCF members. Applicants must have a GPA of 2.5 or higher and be able to demonstrate financial need. First-generation college students are strongly encouraged to apply. U.S. citizenship is required.

Financial data The stipend is $2,200 per semester ($4,400 per year).

Duration 1 year.

Additional information This program is sponsored by Wal-Mart Corporation. The 47 participating TMCF institutions are Alabama A&M University, Alabama State University, Albany State University, Alcorn State University, Bluefield State College, Bowie State University, Central State University (Ohio), Charles R. Drew University of Medicine (California), Cheyney University of Pennsylvania, Chicago State University, Coppin State College, Delaware State University, Elizabeth City State University, Fayetteville State University, Florida A&M University, Fort Valley State University, Grambling State University, Harris-Stowe State College, Howard University, Jackson State University, Kentucky State University, Langston University, Lincoln University (Missouri), Lincoln University (Pennsylvania), Medgar Evers College (New York), Mississippi Valley State University, Morgan State University, Norfolk State University, North Carolina A&T State University, North Carolina Central University, Prairie View A&M University, Savannah State University, South Carolina State University, Southern University and A&M College, Southern University at New Orleans, Southern University at Shreveport-Bossier City, Tennessee State University, Texas Southern University, Tuskegee University, University of Arkansas at Pine Bluff, University of the District of Columbia, University of Maryland-Eastern Shore, University of the Virgin Islands, Virginia State University, West Virginia State College, Winston-Salem State University, and York College.

Number awarded 66 each year.

Deadline July of each year.

[564]
WAL-MART STRIVE FOR EXCELLENCE SCHOLARSHIPS

Congressional Black Caucus Foundation, Inc.
Attn: Director, Educational Programs
1720 Massachusetts Avenue, N.W.
Washington, DC 20036
(202) 263-2800   Toll Free: (800) 784-2577
Fax: (202) 775-0773   E-mail: info@cbcfinc.org
Web: www.cbcfinc.org/scholarships.html

Summary To provide financial assistance to students who reside or attend school in a Congressional district represented by a member of the Congressional Black Caucus (CBC).

Eligibility This program is open to high school seniors and graduates and current full-time undergraduates. Applicants must reside or attend school in a Congressional District represented by a CBC member. They must be able to demonstrate academic achievement (GPA of 2.5 or higher), leadership ability, financial need, and participation in community service activities. Along with their application, they must submit a personal statement of 500 to 1,000 words on 1) their future goals, major field of study, and how that field of study will help them to achieve their future career goals; 2) involvement in school activities, community and public service, hobbies, and sports; 3) how receiving this award will affect their current and future plans; and 4) other experiences, skills, or qualifications. U.S. citizenship or permanent resident status is required.

Financial data The stipend is $5,000. Funds are paid directly to the student's institution.

Duration 1 year.

Additional information This program was established in 2006 by Wal-Mart Stores.

Number awarded 1 or more each year.

Deadline March of each year.

[565]
WALTER AND VICTORIA SMITH AWARD

National Association of Black Accountants
Attn: National Scholarship Program
7474 Greenway Center Drive, Suite 1120
Greenbelt, MD 20770
(301) 474-NABA, ext. 114   Fax: (301) 474-3114
E-mail: customerservice@nabainc.org
Web: www.nabainc.org

Summary To provide financial assistance to student members of the National Association of Black Accountants (NABA) who are working on an undergraduate or graduate degree in a field related to accounting.

Eligibility This program is open to NABA members enrolled full time as 1) an undergraduate freshman, sophomore, junior, or first-semester senior majoring in accounting, business, or finance at a 4-year college or university; or 2) a graduate student working on a master's degree in accounting. High school seniors are not eligible. Applicants must have a GPA of 3.5 or higher in their major and 3.3 or higher overall. Selection is based on grades, financial need, and a 500-word autobiography that discusses career objectives, leadership abilities, community activities, and involvement in NABA.

Financial data The stipend is $1,000.
Duration 1 year.
Number awarded 1 each year.
Deadline January of each year.

[566]
WALTER SAMUEL MCAFEE SCHOLARSHIP IN SPACE PHYSICS

National Society of Black Physicists
Attn: Scholarship Committee Chair
1100 North Glebe Road, Suite 1010
Arlington, VA 22201
(703) 536-4207   Fax: (703) 536-4203
E-mail: scholarship@nsbp.org
Web: www.nsbp.org/scholarships

Summary To provide financial assistance to African American students majoring in space physics in college.
Eligibility This program is open to African American students who are entering their junior or senior year of college and majoring in space physics. Applicants must submit an essay on their academic and career objectives, information on their participation in extracurricular activities, a description of any awards and honors they have received, and 3 letters of recommendation. Financial need is not considered.
Financial data The stipend is $1,000.
Duration 1 year; nonrenewable.
Additional information This program is offered in partnership with the American Astronomical Society.
Number awarded 1 each year.
Deadline January of each year.

[567]
WALTER VAUGHN EXCELLENCE IN HUMAN RESOURCES SCHOLARSHIP

National Forum for Black Public Administrators
Attn: Scholarship Program
777 North Capitol Street, N.E., Suite 807
Washington, DC 20002
(202) 408-9300, ext. 112   Fax: (202) 408-8558
E-mail: vreed@nfbpa.org
Web: www.nfbpa.org/i4a/pages/index.cfm?pageid=3630

Summary To provide financial assistance to African Americans working on an undergraduate or graduate degree in public administration with an emphasis on human resource management.
Eligibility This program is open to African American undergraduate and graduate students preparing for a career in public service. Applicants must be working full time on a degree in public administration, human resource management, or a related field. They must have a GPA of 3.0 or higher, a record of involvement in extracurricular activities (excluding athletics), excellent interpersonal and leadership abilities, and strong oral and written communication skills. Along with their application, they must submit a 3-page autobiographical essay that includes their academic and career goals and objectives. First consideration is given to applicants who are not currently receiving other financial aid.
Financial data The stipend is $2,500.
Duration 1 year.

Additional information This program is sponsored by CPS Human Resource Services. Recipients are required to attend the sponsor's annual conference to receive their scholarship; limited hotel and air accommodations are arranged and provided.
Number awarded 1 each year.
Deadline February of each year.

[568]
WARNER NORCROSS & JUDD PARALEGAL ASSISTANT SCHOLARSHIP

Grand Rapids Community Foundation
Attn: Education Program Officer
185 Oakes Street S.W.
Grand Rapids, MI 49503-4008
(616) 454-1751, ext. 103   Fax: (616) 454-6455
E-mail: rbishop@grfoundation.org
Web: www.grfoundation.org/scholarships

Summary To provide financial assistance to African Americans and other minority residents of Michigan who are interested in working on a paralegal studies degree at an institution in the state.
Eligibility This program is open to residents of Michigan who are students of color attending or planning to attend an accredited public or private 2- or 4-year college or university in the state. Applicants must have a declared major in paralegal/legal assistant studies. They must be U.S. citizens or permanent residents and have a GPA of 2.5 or higher. Financial need is considered in the selection process.
Financial data The stipend is $2,000. Funds are paid directly to the recipient's institution.
Duration 1 year.
Additional information Funding for this program is provided by the law firm Warner Norcross & Judd LLP.
Number awarded 1 each year.
Deadline March of each year.

[569]
WASHINGTON ADMIRAL'S FUND SCHOLARSHIP

National Naval Officers Association-Washington, D.C. Chapter
Attn: Scholarship Program
2701 Park Center Drive, A1108
Alexandria, VA 22302
(703) 566-3840   Fax: (703) 566-3813
E-mail: Stephen.Williams@Navy.mil
Web: dcnnoa.memberlodge.com

Summary To provide financial assistance to African American and other minority high school seniors from the Washington, D.C. area who are interested in attending a college or university in any state and enrolling in the Navy Reserve Officers Training Corps (NROTC) program.
Eligibility This program is open to minority seniors graduating from high schools in the Washington, D.C. metropolitan area who plan to enroll full time at an accredited 2- or 4-year college or university in any state. Applicants also must be planning to enroll in the NROTC program. They must have a GPA of 2.5 or higher and be U.S. citizens or permanent residents. Selection is based on academic achievement, community involvement, and financial need.
Financial data The stipend is $1,000.

Duration 1 year; nonrenewable.

Additional information If the recipient fails to enroll in the NROTC unit, all scholarship funds must be returned.

Number awarded 1 each year.

Deadline March of each year.

[570]
WASHINGTON ALUMNAE CHAPTER SCHOLARSHIPS

Delta Sigma Theta Sorority, Inc.-Washington DC Alumnae Chapter
Attn: Scholarship Committee
P.O. Box 90202
Washington, DC 20090-0202
Fax: (888) 259-4398 E-mail: scholarship@wdcac.org
Web: www.wdcac.org/scholar_standards.html

Summary To provide financial assistance to African American and other high school seniors in Washington, D.C. who plan to attend college in any state.

Eligibility This program is open to seniors graduating from public, charter, parochial, and private high schools in Washington, D.C. and planning to enroll full time at a 2- or 4-year college or university in any state. Applicants must submit an official high school transcript, a copy of their SAT or ACT scores, documentation of financial need, 2 letters of recommendation, and a 1-page autobiographical essay including their academic and career goals, public service involvement, why the scholarship is important, and its expected benefit.

Financial data Stipends range from $1,000 to $3,000 per year.

Duration 1 year; may be renewed.

Additional information The sponsor is the local alumnae chapter of a traditionally African American social sorority.

Number awarded Varies each year.

Deadline March of each year.

[571]
WASHINGTON CHAPTER CONCERNED BLACK MEN SCHOLARSHIP AWARDS

Concerned Black Men, Inc.-Washington DC Chapter
Thurgood Marshall Center
1816 12th Street, N.W., Suite 203
Washington, DC 20009-4422
(202) 797-7444 Fax: (202) 797-7447
E-mail: office@cbmdc.org
Web: www.cbmdc.org

Summary To provide financial assistance to African American and other high school seniors in Washington, D.C. who plan to attend college in any state.

Eligibility This program is open to seniors who are graduating from high schools in Washington, D.C. and planning to enroll at a college or university in any state. Applicants must have a GPA of 2.5 or higher. Along with their application, they must submit a 500-word essay on why they should be a recipient of this scholarship. Financial need may also be considered in the selection process.

Financial data A stipend is awarded (amount not specified).

Duration 1 year.

Additional information The sponsor is an organization of African American men, but both men and women are eligible for this scholarship.

Number awarded 1 or more each year.

Deadline May of each year.

[572]
WASHINGTON, D.C. CHAPTER SCHOLARSHIP PROGRAM

National Naval Officers Association-Washington, D.C. Chapter
Attn: Scholarship Program
2701 Park Center Drive, A1108
Alexandria, VA 22302
(703) 566-3840 Fax: (703) 566-3813
E-mail: Stephen.Williams@Navy.mil
Web: dcnnoa.memberlodge.com

Summary To provide financial assistance to African American and other minority high school seniors from the Washington, D.C. area who plan to attend college in any state.

Eligibility This program is open to minority seniors graduating from high schools in the Washington, D.C. metropolitan area who plan to enroll full time at an accredited 2- or 4-year college or university in any state. Applicants must have a GPA of 2.5 or higher (depending upon the specific scholarship). U.S. citizenship or permanent resident status is required. Selection is based on academic achievement, community involvement, and financial need.

Financial data The stipend is $1,000.

Duration 1 year; nonrenewable.

Additional information Recipients are not required to join or affiliate with the military in any way. A number of named scholarship are awarded, including the Capstone Corporation Scholarship Award, the Captain Willie Evans Scholarship, the Cochran/Greene Scholarship, the Ester Boone Memorial Scholarship, and the Madison/Kalathas/Davis Scholarship Award,.

Number awarded Several each year.

Deadline March of each year.

[573]
WASHINGTON POST URBAN JOURNALISM WORKSHOP

Washington Post
Attn: Young Journalists Development Program
1150 15th Street, N.W.
Washington, DC 20071
(202) 334-7132 Fax: (202) 496-3516
E-mail: knighta@washpost.com
Web: washpost.com/community/education/yjdp/urban.shtml

Summary To provide financial assistance to African American and other high school students in the Washington D.C. area who are interested in preparing for a career in journalism.

Eligibility This program is open to African American and other high school seniors in 19 designated public school systems in the Washington, D.C. area. Applicants must have an interest in a journalism career and strong writing skills. Along with their application, they must submit 1) an autobiography of 200 to 250 words, including what is important to them, why they want to participate in the program, and what they have to share with other students who will participate in the workshop; 2) a 1-page essay on the topic of what makes a good journalist; and 3) a news report based on a set of hypothetical facts. Students who are accepted to the program attend workshops on 8 consecutive Saturdays. They are assigned to 1 of 3 segments: newspaper, radio, or television. Scholarship recipients are selected on the basis of participation in those sessions and their application information.

Financial data The stipend is $2,500.

Duration 1 year; nonrenewable.

Additional information The eligible public school systems are those in Washington, D.C.; the counties of Anne Arundel, Calvert, Charles, Frederick, Howard, Montgomery, Prince George's, and St. Mary's in Maryland; the cities of Alexandria, Falls Church, Manassas, and Manassas Park in Virginia; and the counties of Arlington, Fairfax, Fauquier, Loudoun, Prince William, and Stafford in Virginia. This program, which began in 1986, is offered in collaboration with the Washington Association of Black Journalists (WABJ).

Number awarded Recently, 32 students were selected to participate in the workshop. From those, 3 were chosen to receive scholarships (1 each in the newspaper, radio, and television segments).

Deadline January of each year.

[574]
WASHINGTON UNIVERSITY AMGEN SCHOLARS PROGRAM

Washington University
Division of Biology and Biomedical Sciences
Attn: Summer Research Admissions
660 South Euclid Avenue
Campus Box 8226
St. Louis, MO 63110-1093
(314) 362-7963   Toll Free: (800) 852-9074
E-mail: DBBS-summerresearch@wusm.wustl.edu
Web: dbbssummerresearch.wustl.edu/amgen

Summary To provide undergraduate students (particularly African Americans and disadvantaged students) with a summer research experience at Washington University in St. Louis in biological and biomedical sciences.

Eligibility This program is open to sophomores, juniors, and non-graduating seniors at 4-year colleges and universities in the United States, Puerto Rico, and U.S. territories. Applicants must be interested in a summer research experience at Washington University in biochemistry, bioengineering, bioinformatics, biology (molecular, cell, and developmental), biopsychology, biotechnology, chemical and biomedical engineering, chemistry, immunology, medical pharmacology, microbiology, molecular genetics, molecular medicine, molecular pharmacology, neurobiology, neuroscience, pathology, physiological psychology, physiological science, statistics, or toxicology. They must have a GPA of 3.2 or higher and an interest in continuing on to a Ph.D. or M.D./Ph.D. (but not M.D.) program. Applications are especially encouraged from residents of rural and inner-city areas and from members of groups traditionally underrepresented in biomedical research (African Americans, Hispanic Americans, Native Americans, Pacific Islanders, women, and people with disabilities). U.S. citizenship or permanent resident status is required.

Financial data Housing, travel to and from St. Louis, meals, and a stipend of $4,000 are provided.

Duration 10 weeks during the summer.

Additional information This program serves as the Washington University component of the Amgen Scholars Program, which operates at 9 other U.S. universities and is funded by the Amgen Foundation.

Number awarded 25 each year.

Deadline January of each year.

[575]
WATSON MIDWIVES OF COLOR SCHOLARSHIP

American College of Nurse-Midwives
Attn: ACNM Foundation, Inc.
8403 Colesville Road, Suite 1550
Silver Spring, MD 20910-6374
(240) 485-1850   Fax: (240) 485-1818
Web: www.midwife.org/foundation_award.cfm

Summary To provide financial assistance for midwifery education to African Americans and other students of color who belong to the American College of Nurse-Midwives (ACNM).

Eligibility This program is open to ACNM members of color who are currently enrolled in an accredited basic midwife education program and have successfully completed 1 academic or clinical semester/quarter or clinical module. Applicants must submit a 150-word essay on their 5-year midwifery career plans and a 100-word essay on their intended future participation in the local, regional, and/or national activities of the ACNM. Selection is based on leadership potential, financial need, academic history, and potential for future professional contribution to the organization.

Financial data The stipend is $3,000.

Duration 1 year.

Number awarded Varies each year; recently, 3 of these scholarships were awarded.

Deadline March of each year.

[576]
WAYNE D. CORNILS SCHOLARSHIP

Idaho State Broadcasters Association
270 North 27th Street, Suite B
Boise, ID 83702-4741
(208) 345-3072   Fax: (208) 343-8946
E-mail: isba@qwestoffice.net
Web: www.idahobroadcasters.org/scholarships.aspx

Summary To provide financial assistance to students at Idaho colleges and universities (especially African Americans and disadvantaged students) who are preparing for a career in the broadcasting field and can demonstrate financial need.

Eligibility This program is open to full-time students at Idaho schools who are preparing for a career in broadcasting, including business administration, sales, journalism, or engineering. Applicants must have a GPA of at least 2.0 for the first 2 years of school or 2.5 for the last 2 years. Along with their application, they must submit a letter of recommendation from the general manager of a broadcasting station that is a member of the Idaho State Broadcasters Association and a 1-page essay describing their career plans and why they want the scholarship. Applications are encouraged from a wide and diverse student population. This scholarship is reserved for a less advantaged applicant.

Financial data The stipend depends on the need of the recipient.

Duration 1 year.

Number awarded 1 each year.

Deadline March of each year.

[577]
WEISMAN SCHOLARSHIPS

Connecticut Department of Higher Education
Attn: Office of Student Financial Aid
61 Woodland Street
Hartford, CT 06105-2326
(860) 947-1857   Fax: (860) 947-1838
E-mail: mtip@ctdhe.org
Web: www.ctdhe.org/SFA/default.htm

Summary To provide financial assistance to African American and other minority upper-division college students from any state who are enrolled at a college in Connecticut and interested in teaching mathematics or science at public middle and high schools in the state.

Eligibility This program is open to residents of any state who are enrolled full time as juniors or seniors at Connecticut colleges and universities and preparing to become a mathematics or science teacher at the middle or high school level. Applicants must be members of a minority group, defined as African American, Hispanic/Latino, Asian American, or Native American. They must be nominated by the education dean at their institution.

Financial data The maximum stipend is $5,000 per year. In addition, if recipients complete a credential and begin teaching at a public school in Connecticut within 16 months of graduation, they may receive up to $2,500 per year, for up to 4 years, to help pay off college loans.

Number awarded Varies each year.

Deadline September of each year.

[578]
WELLS FARGO SCHOLARSHIPS OF THE THURGOOD MARSHALL COLLEGE FUND

Thurgood Marshall College Fund
Attn: Scholarship Manager
80 Maiden Lane, Suite 2204
New York, NY 10038
(212) 573-8487   Toll Free: (877) 690-8673
Fax: (212) 573-8497   E-mail: srogers@tmcfund.org
Web: www.thurgoodmarshallfund.net

Summary To provide financial assistance to students (especially those majoring in business or finance) who are enrolled at colleges and universities that are members of the Thurgood Marshall College Fund (TMCF).

Eligibility This program is open to full-time students currently enrolled as sophomores at 1 of the 47 colleges and universities that are TMCF members. Applicants must have a GPA of 3.0 or higher and be able to demonstrate financial need. Special consideration is given to students majoring in business or finance. First-generation college students are strongly encouraged to apply. U.S. citizenship is required.

Financial data The stipend is $2,200 per semester ($4,400 per year).

Duration 1 year.

Additional information The 47 participating TMCF institutions are Alabama A&M University, Alabama State University, Albany State University, Alcorn State University, Bluefield State College, Bowie State University, Central State University (Ohio), Charles R. Drew University of Medicine (California), Cheyney University of Pennsylvania, Chicago State University, Coppin State College, Delaware State University, Elizabeth City State University, Fayetteville State University, Florida A&M University, Fort Valley State University, Grambling State University, Harris-Stowe State College, Howard University, Jackson State University, Kentucky State University, Langston University, Lincoln University (Missouri), Lincoln University (Pennsylvania), Medgar Evers College (New York), Mississippi Valley State University, Morgan State University, Norfolk State University, North Carolina A&T State University, North Carolina Central University, Prairie View A&M University, Savannah State University, South Carolina State University, Southern University and A&M College, Southern University at New Orleans, Southern University at Shreveport-Bossier City, Tennessee State University, Texas Southern University, Tuskegee University, University of Arkansas at Pine Bluff, University of the District of Columbia, University of Maryland-Eastern Shore, University of the Virgin Islands, Virginia State University, West Virginia State College, Winston-Salem State University, and York College. Formerly, this program was known as the Wachovia Scholarships of the Thurgood Marshall College Fund.

Number awarded 35 each year; approximately 25% of the scholarships are reserved for students majoring in business or finance and the other 75% are open to students with any major.

Deadline July of each year.

[579]
WESTERN STATES AHA AFFILIATE UNDERGRADUATE STUDENT RESEARCH PROGRAM

American Heart Association-Western States Affiliate
Attn: Research Department
1710 Gilbreth Road
Burlingame, CA 94010-1317
(650) 259-6700   Fax: (650) 259-6891
E-mail: research@heart.org
Web: www.americanheart.org

Summary To provide students from California (especially African American and other minority or women students) with an opportunity to work on a cardiovascular research project during the summer.

Eligibility This program is open to college students who are enrolled full time at an accredited academic institution at the junior or senior level and are interested in a career in heart or stroke research. Applicants must be residents of California, Nevada, or Utah (or attending a college or university in 1 of those states) and interested in a summer internship at a cardiovascular research laboratory in those states. They must be U.S. citizens or foreign nationals holding a student, exchange, or permanent resident visa. They must have completed the following (or equivalent) courses: 4 semesters (or 6 quarters) of biological sciences, physics, or chemistry; and 1 quarter of calculus, statistics, computational methods, or computer science. Selection is based on an assessment of the student's application, academic record (preference is given to students with superior academic standing), and faculty recommendations. Women and minorities are particularly encouraged to apply.

Financial data   Participants receive a $4,000 stipend.

Duration   10 weeks during the summer.

Additional information   Participants are assigned to laboratories in California, Nevada, or Utah to work under the direction and supervision of experienced scientists.

Deadline   December of each year.

[580]
WILLIAM A. BORDERS JR. JUSTICE SCHOLARSHIP

National Naval Officers Association-Washington, D.C.
  Chapter
Attn: Scholarship Program
2701 Park Center Drive, A1108
Alexandria, VA 22302
(703) 566-3840   Fax: (703) 566-3813
E-mail: Stephen.Williams@Navy.mil
Web: dcnnoa.memberlodge.com

Summary   To provide financial assistance to African American high school seniors from the Washington, D.C. area who are interested in attending college in any state.

Eligibility   This program is open to African American seniors graduating from high schools in the Washington, D.C. metropolitan area who plan to enroll full time at an accredited 2- or 4-year college or university in any state. Applicants must have a GPA of 2.5 or higher and be U.S. citizens or permanent residents. Selection is based on academic achievement, community involvement, and financial need.

Financial data   The stipend is $1,000.

Duration   1 year; nonrenewable.

Additional information   Recipients are not required to join or affiliate with the military in any way.

Number awarded   1 each year.

Deadline   March of each year.

[581]
WILLIAM K. SCHUBERT M.D. MINORITY NURSING SCHOLARSHIP PROGRAM

Cincinnati Children's Hospital Medical Center
Attn: Office of Diversity and Inclusion, MLC 9008
3333 Burnet Avenue
Cincinnati, OH 45229-3039
(513) 803-6416   Toll Free: (800) 344-2462
Fax: (513) 636-5643   TDD: (513) 636-4900
E-mail: owen.burke@cchmc.org
Web: www.cincinnatichildrens.org

Summary   To provide financial assistance to African Americans and members of other underrepresented groups who are interested in working on a bachelor's or master's degree in nursing to prepare for licensure in Ohio.

Eligibility   This program is open to members of groups underrepresented in the nursing profession (males, American Indians or Alaska Natives, Blacks or African Americans, Hawaiian Natives or other Pacific Islanders, Hispanics or Latinos, or Asians). Applicants must be enrolled or accepted in a professional bachelor's or master's registered nurse program at an accredited school of nursing to prepare for initial licen-

sure in Ohio. They must have a GPA of 2.75 or higher. Along with their application, they must submit a 750-word essay that covers 1) their long-range personal, educational, and professional goals and why they chose nursing as a profession; 2) any unique qualifications, experiences, or special talents that demonstrate their creativity; and 3) if they are able to pay any college expenses through work and how their work experience has contributed to their personal development.

Financial data   The stipend is $2,750 per year.

Duration   1 year. May be renewed up to 3 additional years for students working on a bachelor's degree or 1 additional year for students working on a master's degree; renewal requires that students maintain a GPA of 2.75 or higher.

Number awarded   1 or more each year.

Deadline   April of each year.

[582]
WILLIAM RANDOLPH HEARST ENDOWMENT SCHOLARSHIPS

National Action Council for Minorities in Engineering
Attn: University Programs
440 Hamilton Avenue, Suite 302
White Plains, NY 10601-1813
(914) 539-4010   Fax: (914) 539-4032
E-mail: scholarships@nacme.org
Web: www.nacme.org/NACME_D.aspx?pageid=105

Summary   To provide financial assistance to African Americans and other underrepresented minority college freshmen or sophomores majoring in engineering or related fields.

Eligibility   This program is open to African American, Latino, and American Indian college freshmen and sophomores who have a GPA of 2.8 or higher and have demonstrated academic excellence, leadership skills, and a commitment to science and engineering as a career. Applicants must be enrolled full time at an ABET-accredited engineering program. Fields of study include all areas of engineering as well as computer science, materials science, mathematics, operations research, or physics.

Financial data   The stipend is $2,500 per year. Funds are sent directly to the recipient's university.

Duration   Up to 4 years.

Additional information   This program was established by the William Randolph Hearst Foundation.

Number awarded   2 each year.

Deadline   April of each year.

[583]
WILLIAM RUCKER GREENWOOD SCHOLARSHIP

Association for Women Geoscientists
Attn: AWG Foundation
12000 North Washington Street, Suite 285
Thornton, CO 80241
(303) 412-6219   Fax: (303) 253-9220
E-mail: office@awg.org
Web: www.awg.org/EAS/scholarships.html

Summary   To provide financial assistance to African American and other minority women from any state working on an undergraduate or graduate degree in the geosciences at a college in the Potomac Bay region.

Eligibility   This program is open to minority women who are residents of any state and currently enrolled as full-time undergraduate or graduate geoscience majors at an accredited, degree-granting college or university in Delaware, the District of Columbia, Maryland, Virginia, or West Virginia. Selection is based on the applicant's 1) participation in geoscience or earth science educational activities, and 2) potential for leadership as a future geoscience professional.

Financial data The stipend is $1,000. The recipient also is granted a 1-year membership in the Association for Women Geoscientists (AWG).

Duration 1 year.

Additional information This program is sponsored by the AWG Potomac Area Chapter.

Number awarded 1 each year.

Deadline April of each year.

[584]
WILLIAM SAMBER SR. AVIATION/MATH AND SCIENCE SCHOLARSHIP

African-American/Caribbean Education Association, Inc.
P.O. Box 1224
Valley Stream, NY 11582-1224
(718) 949-6733   E-mail: aaceainc@yahoo.com
Web: www.aaceainc.com/Scholarships.html

Summary To provide financial assistance to high school seniors of African American or Caribbean heritage who plan to study a field related to aviation, mathematics, or science in college.

Eligibility This program is open to graduating high school seniors who are U.S. citizens of African American or Caribbean heritage. Applicants must be planning to attend a college or university and major in a field related to a career in aviation, mathematics, or science. They must have completed 4 years of specified college preparatory courses with a grade of 90 or higher and have an SAT score of at least 1790. They must also have completed at least 200 hours of community service during their 4 years of high school, preferably in the field that they plan to study in college. Financial need is not considered in the selection process. New York residency is not required, but applicants must be available for an interview in the Queens, New York area.

Financial data The stipend ranges from $1,000 to $2,500. Funds are paid directly to the recipient.

Duration 1 year.

Number awarded 2 each year.

Deadline April of each year.

[585]
WILLIAM ZEITLER SCHOLARSHIPS

National Action Council for Minorities in Engineering
Attn: University Programs
440 Hamilton Avenue, Suite 302
White Plains, NY 10601-1813
(914) 539-4010   Fax: (914) 539-4032
E-mail: scholarships@nacme.org
Web: www.nacme.org/NACME_D.aspx?pageid=105

Summary To provide financial assistance to African American and other underrepresented minority college sophomores majoring in engineering or related fields.

Eligibility This program is open to African American, Latino, and American Indian college sophomores who have a GPA of 3.0 or higher and have demonstrated academic excellence, leadership skills, and a commitment to science and engineering as a career. Applicants must be enrolled full time at an ABET-accredited engineering program. Fields of study include all areas of engineering as well as computer science, materials science, mathematics, operations research, and physics.

Financial data The stipend is $5,000 per year. Funds are sent directly to the recipient's university.

Duration Up to 4 years.

Number awarded 2 each year.

Deadline April of each year.

[586]
WILLIE HOBBS MOORE SCHOLARSHIP

National Society of Black Physicists
Attn: Scholarship Committee Chair
1100 North Glebe Road, Suite 1010
Arlington, VA 22201
(703) 536-4207   Fax: (703) 536-4203
E-mail: scholarship@nsbp.org
Web: www.nsbp.org/scholarships

Summary To provide financial assistance to African American students majoring in physics in college.

Eligibility This program is open to African American students who are entering their junior or senior year of college and majoring in physics. Applicants must submit an essay on their academic and career objectives, information on their participation in extracurricular activities, a description of any awards and honors they have received, and 3 letters of recommendation. Financial need is not considered.

Financial data The stipend is $1,000.

Duration 1 year; nonrenewable.

Number awarded 1 each year.

Deadline January of each year.

[587]
WILLIE J. WILLIAMS SCHOLARSHIP

African Methodist Episcopal Church
Attn: Eleventh Episcopal District Lay Organization
101 East Union Street, Suite 301
Jacksonville, FL 32202
(904) 355-8262   Fax: (904) 356-1617
E-mail: eedlo@eedlo.org
Web: www.eedlo.org/scholarships.html

Summary To provide financial assistance to members of African Methodist Episcopal (AME) churches in Florida who are interested in studying music at a college in any state.

Eligibility This program is open to seniors graduating from public or private high schools in Florida who are members of AME churches. Applicants must be planning to enroll full time at an institution of higher learning in any state: an AME-supported college, a Predominantly Black College or University, or an accredited trade school. They must have a GPA of 2.5 or higher and be planning to major in music. Along with their application, they must submit a 1-page essay on why a college education is important and a statement regarding their financial need.

Financial data A stipend is awarded (amount not specified).

Duration 1 year.

Number awarded 1 or more each year.

Deadline April of each year.

[588]
WILLIE T. LOUD-CH2M HILL SCHOLARSHIP

National Forum for Black Public Administrators
Attn: Scholarship Program
777 North Capitol Street, N.E., Suite 807
Washington, DC 20002
(202) 408-9300, ext. 112   Fax: (202) 408-8558
E-mail: vreed@nfbpa.org
Web: www.nfbpa.org/i4a/pages/index.cfm?pageid=3630

Summary To provide financial assistance to African Americans working on a bachelor's or master's degree in public administration.

Eligibility This program is open to African American graduate students preparing for a career in public service. Applicants must be working full time on a bachelor's or master's degree in public administration, urban affairs, or a related field. They must have a GPA of 3.0 or higher, strong interpersonal skills, and excellent writing, analytical, and oral communication abilities. Along with their application, they must submit a 3-page autobiographical essay that describes their academic and career goals and objectives. First consideration is given to applicants who are not currently receiving other financial aid.

Financial data The stipend is $5,000.

Duration 1 year.

Additional information This program, established in 1997, is sponsored by CH2M Hill. Recipients are required to attend the sponsor's annual conference to receive their scholarship; limited hotel and air accommodations are arranged and provided.

Number awarded 1 each year.

Deadline February of each year.

[589]
WINGS FINANCIAL SCHOLARSHIPS

Organization of Black Aerospace Professionals, Inc.
Attn: Scholarship Coordinator
1 Westbrook Corporate Center, Suite 300
Westchester, IL 60154
(708) 449-7755   Toll Free: (800) JET-OBAP
Fax: (708) 449-7754
E-mail: obapscholarship@gmail.com
Web: www.obap.org/scholarships

Summary To provide financial assistance to African American high school seniors who plan to work on an aerospace degree at a school in any state.

Eligibility This program is open to African American high school seniors who plan to enroll in an aerospace program at an accredited college or university. Applicants must have a GPA of 2.7 or higher. Along with their application, they must submit a 500-word essay describing how this scholarship would impact their career goals.

Financial data The stipend is $1,000.

Duration 1 year.

Additional information This program is sponsored by Wings Financial Credit Union.

Number awarded 1 each year.

Deadline Deadline not specified.

[590]
WISCONSIN MINORITY TEACHER LOANS

Wisconsin Higher Educational Aids Board
131 West Wilson Street, Suite 902
P.O. Box 7885
Madison, WI 53707-7885
(608) 267-2212   Fax: (608) 267-2808
E-mail: Mary.Kuzdas@wisconsin.gov
Web: heab.state.wi.us/programs.html

Summary To provide funding to African Americans and other minorities in Wisconsin who are interested in teaching in Wisconsin school districts with large minority enrollments.

Eligibility This program is open to residents of Wisconsin who are African Americans, Hispanic Americans, American Indians, or southeast Asians (students who were admitted to the United States after December 31, 1975 and who are a former citizen of Laos, Vietnam, or Cambodia or whose ancestor was a citizen of 1 of those countries). Applicants must be enrolled at least half time as juniors, seniors, or graduate students at an independent or public institution in the state in a program leading to teaching licensure and have a GPA of 2.5 or higher. They must agree to teach in a Wisconsin school district in which minority students constitute at least 29% of total enrollment or in a school district participating in the interdistrict pupil transfer program. Financial need is not considered in the selection process.

Financial data forgivable loans are provided up to $2,500 per year. For each year the student teaches in an eligible school district, 25% of the loan is forgiven; if the student does not teach in an eligible district, the loan must be repaid at an interest rate of 5%.

Duration 1 year; may be renewed 1 additional year.

Additional information Eligible students should apply through their school's financial aid office.

Number awarded Varies each year.

Deadline Deadline dates vary by institution; check with your school's financial aid office.

[591]
WISCONSIN MINORITY UNDERGRADUATE RETENTION GRANTS

Wisconsin Higher Educational Aids Board
131 West Wilson Street, Suite 902
P.O. Box 7885
Madison, WI 53707-7885
(608) 267-2212   Fax: (608) 267-2808
E-mail: Mary.Kuzdas@wisconsin.gov
Web: heab.state.wi.us/programs.html

Summary To provide financial assistance to African Americans and other minorities in Wisconsin who are currently enrolled at a college in the state.

Eligibility This program is open to residents of Wisconsin who are African Americans, Hispanic Americans, American Indians, or southeast Asians (students who were admitted to the United States after December 31, 1975 and who are a former citizen of Laos, Vietnam, or Cambodia or whose ancestor was a citizen of 1 of those countries). Applicants must be enrolled at least half time as sophomores, juniors, seniors, or fifth-year undergraduates at a Wisconsin technical college, tribal college, or independent college or university in the state. They must be nominated by their institution and be able to demonstrate financial need.

Financial data Stipends range from $250 to $2,500 per year, depending on the need of the recipient.

Duration Up to 4 years.

Additional information The Wisconsin Higher Educational Aids Board administers this program for students at private nonprofit institutions, technical colleges, and tribal colleges. The University of Wisconsin has a similar program for students attending any of the branches of that system. Eligible students should apply through their school's financial aid office.

Number awarded Varies each year.

Deadline Deadline dates vary by institution; check with your school's financial aid office.

[592]
WISCONSIN PUBLIC SERVICE FOUNDATION BUSINESS AND TECHNOLOGY SCHOLARSHIPS

Wisconsin Public Service Corporation
Attn: Wisconsin Public Service Foundation
c/o Scholarship Assessment Service
P.O. Box 997
Appleton, WI 54912-0997
(920) 832-8322
Web: www.wisconsinpublicservice.com

Summary To provide financial assistance to African Americans, other minorities, and women who are upper-division students and majoring in business or engineering at universities in selected states.

Eligibility This program is open to women and African American, Native American, Asian American, and Hispanic students from any state who are enrolled full time as a junior or senior with a GPA of 2.8 or higher. Applicants must be attending a college or university in Illinois, Indiana, Iowa, Michigan, Minnesota, or Wisconsin. They must be majoring in business or engineering (chemical, civil, computer, electrical, environmental, industrial, or mechanical). Along with their application, they must submit 250-word essays on 1) their educational goals and why they have chosen their major; and 2) how they have demonstrated their leadership skills.

Financial data The stipend is $1,500 per year.

Duration 1 year; may be renewed if the recipient remains in good academic standing.

Number awarded Varies each year; recently, 15 of these scholarships were awarded.

Deadline February of each year.

[593]
WISCONSIN TALENT INCENTIVE PROGRAM (TIP) GRANTS

Wisconsin Higher Educational Aids Board
131 West Wilson Street, Suite 902
P.O. Box 7885
Madison, WI 53707-7885
(608) 266-1665   Fax: (608) 267-2808
E-mail: colettem1.brown@wi.gov
Web: heab.state.wi.us/programs.html

Summary To provide financial assistance for college to African Americans and other needy or educationally disadvantaged students in Wisconsin.

Eligibility This program is open to residents of Wisconsin entering a college or university in the state who meet the requirements of both financial need and educational disadvantage. Financial need qualifications include 1) family contribution (a dependent student whose expected parent contribution is $200 or less, an independent student with dependents whose academic year contribution is $200 or less, or an independent student with no dependents whose maximum contribution is $200 or less); 2) Temporary Assistance to Needy Families (TANF) or Wisconsin Works (W2) benefits (a dependent student whose family is receiving TANF or W2 benefits or an independent student who is receiving TANF or W2 benefits); or 3) unemployment (a dependent student whose parents are ineligible for unemployment compensation and have no current income from employment, or an independent student and spouse, if married, who are ineligible for unemployment compensation and have no current income from employment). Educational disadvantage qualifications include students who are 1) minorities (African American, Native American, Hispanic, or southeast Asian); 2) enrolled in a special academic support program due to insufficient academic preparation; 3) a first-generation college student (neither parent graduated from a 4-year college or university); 4) disabled according to the Department of Workforce Development, the Division of Vocational Rehabilitation, or a Wisconsin college or university that uses the Americans with Disabilities Act definition; 5) currently or formerly incarcerated in a correctional institution; or 6) from an environmental and academic background that deters the pursuit of educational plans. Students already in college are not eligible.

Financial data Stipends range up to $1,800 per year.

Duration 1 year; may be renewed up to 4 additional years, provided the recipient continues to be a Wisconsin resident enrolled at least half time in a degree or certificate program, makes satisfactory academic progress, demonstrates financial need, and remains enrolled continuously from semester to semester and from year to year. If recipients withdraw from school or cease to attend classes for any reason (other than medical necessity), they may not reapply.

Number awarded Varies each year.

Deadline Deadline not specified.

[594]
WOODS HOLE OCEANOGRAPHIC INSTITUTION MINORITY FELLOWSHIPS

Woods Hole Oceanographic Institution
Attn: Academic Programs Office
Clark Laboratory 223, MS 31
360 Woods Hole Road
Woods Hole, MA 02543-1541
(508) 289-2219   Fax: (508) 457-2188
E-mail: education@whoi.edu
Web: www.whoi.edu/page.do?pid=36375

Summary To provide work experience to African Americans and other minorities who are interested in preparing for careers in the marine sciences, oceanographic engineering, or marine policy.

Eligibility This program is open to ethnic minority undergraduates enrolled in U.S. colleges or universities who have completed at least 2 semesters of study and who are interested in the physical or natural sciences, mathematics, engineering, or marine policy. Applicants must be U.S. citizens or permanent residents and African American or Black; Asian American; Chicano, Mexican American, Puerto Rican or other Hispanic; or Native American, Alaska Native, or Native Hawaiian. They must be interested in participating in a program of study and research at Woods Hole Oceanographic Institution.

Financial data   The stipend is $488 per week; trainees may also receive additional support for travel to Woods Hole.

Duration   10 to 12 weeks during the summer or 1 semester during the academic year; renewable.

Additional information   Trainees are assigned advisers who supervise their research programs and supplementary study activities. Some traineeships involve field work or research cruises. This program is conducted with support from and in cooperation with the Center for Marine and Coastal Geology of the U.S. Geological Survey.

Number awarded   4 to 5 each year.

Deadline   For a summer appointment, applications must be submitted in February of each year. For the remaining portion of the year, applications may be submitted at any time, but they must be received at least 2 months before the anticipated starting date.

[595]
XEROX TECHNICAL MINORITY SCHOLARSHIP PROGRAM

Xerox Corporation
Attn: Technical Minority Scholarship Program
150 State Street, Fourth Floor
Rochester, NY 14614
(585) 422-7689   E-mail: xtmsp@rballiance.com
Web: www.xeroxstudentcareers.com

Summary   To provide financial assistance to African Americans and other minorities interested in undergraduate or graduate education in the sciences and/or engineering.

Eligibility   This program is open to minorities (people of African American, Asian, Pacific Islander, Native American, Native Alaskan, or Hispanic descent) working full time on a bachelor's, master's, or doctoral degree in chemistry, computing and software systems, engineering (chemical, computer, electrical, imaging, manufacturing, mechanical, optical, or software), information management, laser optics, materials science, physics, or printing management science. Applicants must be U.S. citizens or permanent residents with a GPA of 3.0 or higher and attending a 4-year college or university.

Financial data   Stipends range from $1,000 to $10,000.

Duration   1 year.

Number awarded   Varies each year, recently, 125 of these scholarships were awarded.

Deadline   September of each year.

[596]
XI PSI OMEGA CHAPTER SCHOLARSHIPS

Alpha Kappa Alpha Sorority, Inc.-Xi Psi Omega Chapter
Attn: President
P.O. Box 140894
Anchorage, AK 99514
(907) 346-3998
Web: xipsiomega.com/scholarship.html

Summary   To provide financial assistance to high school seniors (especially African American women) from Alaska who plan to attend college in any state.

Eligibility   This program is open to African American and other seniors graduating from high schools in Alaska who are planning to attend a 2- or 4-year accredited college or university in any state. Applicants must have a GPA of 2.5 or higher and a record of active participation in school and community activities.

Financial data   A stipend is awarded (amount not specified).

Duration   1 year; nonrenewable.

Additional information   Alpha Kappa Alpha (AKA) is currently 1 of the largest social sororities whose membership is predominantly African American women. The Xi Psi Omega chapter of AKA serves alumnae members in Alaska.

Number awarded   1 or more each year.

Deadline   March of each year.

[597]
YOUNG VOCALISTS COLLEGE SCHOLARSHIP COMPETITION

Ebony Classical Music Society, Inc.
Attn: Auditions Chair
P.O. Box 2483
Columbia, MD 21045
(410) 456-1112

Summary   To recognize and reward, with college scholarships, African American and other students from the Baltimore-Washington metropolitan area who plan to study voice at a school in any state.

Eligibility   This program is open to African American and other students at high schools in the Baltimore-Washington metropolitan area. Applicants must have a GPA of 2.5 or higher and be planning to attend college in any state to major in voice. They must submit a letter of recommendation from a school music or voice teacher attesting to their talent. Selection is based on a tape or CD of the required repertoire: 2 Negro spirituals, an aria or oratorio sung in the original language, and a foreign language art song.

Financial data   First prize is a $2,000 college scholarship, second $1,000, and third $500.

Duration   The competition is held annually.

Additional information   Applications must be accompanied by a $25 entry fee.

Number awarded   3 scholarship prizes are awarded each year.

Deadline   February of each year.

[598]
YOUTH PARTNERS IN ACCESS TO CAPITAL PROGRAM

Alpha Kappa Alpha Sorority, Inc.
Attn: Educational Advancement Foundation
5656 South Stony Island Avenue
Chicago, IL 60637
(773) 947-0026   Toll Free: (800) 653-6528
Fax: (773) 947-0277   E-mail: akaeaf@akaeaf.net
Web: www.akaeaf.org/undergraduate_scholarships.htm

Summary To provide funding to undergraduate members of Alpha Kappa Alpha sorority interested in conducting a project to support the platform of the sorority.

Eligibility This program is open to members of the organization, a traditionally African American women's sorority, who are working at least as sophomores on an undergraduate degree at an accredited degree-granting institution. Applicants must have a GPA of 3.0 or higher and a record of demonstrated participation in leadership, volunteer, and civic services. They must be proposing to conduct a community service project that will implement 1 of the platforms of the sorority: emerging young leaders, health, global poverty, economic security, social justice and human rights, or internal leadership training for external service. Along with their application, they must submit a personal goal statement on how they promote healing, nurturing, learning, and uplifting of youth by assisting in developing lifelong learning skills.

Financial data Grants range from $500 to $1,000.

Duration 1 year; nonrenewable.

Additional information This program began in 1997.

Number awarded Varies each year; recently, 13 of these grants were awarded.

Deadline April of each year.

[599]
ZANNONI INDIVIDUAL SUMMER UNDERGRADUATE RESEARCH FELLOWSHIPS

American Society for Pharmacology and Experimental Therapeutics
9650 Rockville Pike
Bethesda, MD 20814-3995
(301) 634-7060   Fax: (301) 634-7061
E-mail: info@aspet.org
Web: www.aspet.org/awards/SURF

Summary To provide funding to undergraduate students (especially African Americans and other minorities or women) who are interested in participating in a summer research project at a laboratory affiliated with the American Society for Pharmacology and Experimental Therapeutics (ASPET).

Eligibility This program is open to undergraduate students interested in working during the summer in the laboratory of a society member who must agree to act as a sponsor. Applications must be submitted jointly by the student and the sponsor, and they must include 1) a letter from the sponsor with a brief description of the proposed research, a statement of the qualifications of the student, the degree of independence the student will have, a description of complementary activities available to the student, and a description of how the student will report on the research results; 2) a letter from the student indicating the nature of his or her interest in the project and a description of future plans; 3) a copy of the sponsor's updated curriculum vitae; and 4) copies of the student's undergraduate transcripts. Selection is based on the nature of the research opportunities provided, student and sponsor qualifications, and likelihood the student will prepare for a career in pharmacology. Applications from underrepresented minorities and women are particularly encouraged.

Financial data The stipend is $2,800. Funds are paid directly to the institution and may be used only for student stipends.

Duration 10 weeks during the summer.

Additional information Some of these awards are funded through the Glenn E. Ullyot Fund; those recipients are designated as the Ullyot Fellows.

Number awarded Varies each year; recently, 4 of these fellowships were awarded.

Deadline February of each year.

Graduate Students

Listed alphabetically by program title and described in detail here are 482 fellowships, fellowship/loans, grants, awards, internships, and other sources of "free money" set aside for African Americans who are incoming, continuing, or returning graduate students working on a master's, doctoral, or professional degree. This funding is available to support study, training, research, and/or creative activities in the United States.

[600]
A. GRACE LEE MIMS VOCAL SCHOLARSHIP

Cleveland Foundation
Attn: Scholarship Officer
1422 Euclid Avenue, Suite 1300
Cleveland, OH 44115-2001
(216) 861-3810   Fax: (216) 861-1729
E-mail: mbaker@clevefdn.org
Web: www.clevelandfoundation.org/Scholarships

Summary To provide financial assistance to African Americans who have a connection to Ohio and are interested in working on a master's degree in vocal music or education with an emphasis on Negro spirituals.

Eligibility This program is open to African American graduate students born, reared, or residing in Ohio. Applicants must be working on a master's degree at an institution (college, university, conservatory) in any state in vocal performance or music education with an emphasis on voice. Along with their application, they must submit 1) 3 letters of recommendation from voice teachers or music professors attesting to their musical talent, moral character, and dedication to the survival of the Negro spiritual; 2) a personal statement describing their commitment to ensure the preservation of the Negro spiritual through their performance or teaching career; 3) an audio tape or CD of a recent performance (concert or recital); 4) 3 music programs over at least a 2-year span including their performance of Negro spirituals; and 5) a detailed budget for their academic year's educational expenses. U.S. citizenship is required.

Financial data The stipend is $10,000 per year. Funds must be applied to tuition, fees, books, supplies, and equipment required for the program.

Duration 1 year; recipients may reapply.

Number awarded 1 or more each year.

Deadline April of each year.

[601]
ABSALOM JONES SCHOLARSHIP FUND

St. Philip's Episcopal Church
Attn: Absalom Jones Scholarship Selection Committee
522 Main Street
Laurel, MD 20707
(301) 776-5151   Fax: (301) 776-6337
E-mail: absalomjonesfund@stphilipslaurel.org
Web: www.stphilipslaurel.org

Summary To provide financial assistance to African American and other undergraduate and graduate students at schools in any state who have a tie to the Episcopal Diocese of Washington, D.C.

Eligibility This program is open to students who reside, work, attend school, or are members of a parish in the Episcopal Diocese of Washington. Applicants must be attending or planning to attend a college, seminary, or vocational/technical institute in any state as an undergraduate or graduate student. They must be able to demonstrate the qualities for which Absalom Jones, the first African American priest in the Episcopal Church, was noted: compassion, service, leadership, and an emphasis on education. Financial need is considered in the selection process.

Financial data The stipend is $1,000.

Duration 1 year.

Additional information The Episcopal Diocese of Washington serves the District of Columbia and the Maryland counties of Charles, St. Mary's, Prince George's, and Montgomery.

Number awarded 2 each year.

Deadline March of each year.

[602]
ACADEMIC LIBRARY ASSOCIATION OF OHIO DIVERSITY SCHOLARSHIP

Academic Library Association of Ohio
c/o Ken Burhanna, Diversity Committee Chair
Kent State University, Instructional Services
P.O. Box 5190
Kent, OH 44242-0001
(330) 672-1660   E-mail: kburhann@kent.edu
Web: www.alaoweb.org

Summary To provide financial assistance to African American and other residents of Ohio who are working on a master's degree in library science at a school in any state and will contribute to diversity in the profession.

Eligibility This program is open to residents of Ohio who are enrolled or entering an ALA-accredited program for a master's degree in library science, either on campus or via distance education. Applicants must be able to demonstrate how they will contribute to diversity in the profession, including (but not limited to) race or ethnicity, sexual orientation, life experience, physical ability, and a sense of commitment to those and other diversity issues. Along with their application, they must submit 1) a list of participation in honor societies or professional organizations, awards, scholarships, prizes, honors, or class offices; 2) a list of community, civic, organizational, or volunteer experiences; and 3) an essay on their understanding of and commitment to diversity in libraries, including how they, as library school students and future professionals, might address the issue.

Financial data The stipend is $1,500.

Duration 1 year.

Number awarded 1 each year.

Deadline March of each year.

[603]
ACOUSTICAL SOCIETY OF AMERICA MINORITY FELLOWSHIP

Acoustical Society of America
Attn: Office Manager
2 Huntington Quadrangle, Suite 1NO1
Melville, NY 11747-4502
(516) 576-2360   Fax: (516) 576-2377
E-mail: asa@aip.org
Web: asa.aip.org/fellowships.html

Summary To provide financial assistance to African Americans and other underrepresented minorities who are working on a graduate degree involving acoustics.

Eligibility This program is open to U.S. and Canadian citizens and permanent residents who are members of a minority group that is underrepresented in the sciences (Hispanic, African American, or Native American). Applicants must be enrolled in or accepted to a graduate degree program as a full-time student. Their program of study may be in any field of pure or applied science and engineering directly related to acoustics, including acoustical oceanography, architectural acoustics, animal bioacoustics, biomedical ultrasound and bioresponse to vibration, engineering acoustics, musical acoustics, noise, physical acoustics, psychological acoustics, physiological acoustics, signal processing in acoustics, speech communication, structural acoustics and vibration, and underwater acoustics. Along with their application, student must submit a statement on why they are enrolled in their present academic program, including how they intend to use their graduate education to develop a career and how the study of acoustics is relevant to their career objectives.

Financial data The stipend is $20,000 per year. The sponsor strongly encourages the host educational institution to waive all tuition costs and assessed fees. Fellows also receive $1,000 for travel to attend a national meeting of the sponsor.

Duration 1 year; may be renewed for 1 additional year if the recipient is making normal progress toward a degree and is enrolled full time.

Additional information This program was established in 1992.

Number awarded 1 each year.

Deadline April of each year.

[604]
ADLER POLLOCK & SHEEHAN DIVERSITY SCHOLARSHIP

Adler Pollock & Sheehan P.C.
Attn: Diversity Committee Chair
175 Federal Street
Boston, MA 02110-2210
(617) 482-0600   Fax: (617) 482-0604
E-mail: Diversitycomm@apslaw.com
Web: www.apslaw.com/firm-diversity.html

Summary To provide financial assistance to African Americans and other residents of Massachusetts and Rhode Island who are members of diverse groups and plan to attend law school in any state.

Eligibility This program is open to residents of Massachusetts and Rhode Island who are members of a diverse group, including African American, American Indian, Hispanic, Asian/Pacific Islander, gay/lesbian, or other minority group. Applicants must be entering their first year at an ABA-accredited law school anywhere in the United States. They must be able to demonstrate academic achievement, a desire to work and reside in Massachusetts or Rhode Island after graduation, a demonstrated commitment to the community, a vision of contributions to the profession and community after graduation, and financial need.

Financial data The stipend is $10,000.

Duration 1 year.

Number awarded 1 each year.

Deadline May of each year.

[605]
ADRIENNE M. AND CHARLES SHELBY ROOKS FELLOWSHIP FOR RACIAL AND ETHNIC THEOLOGICAL STUDENTS

United Church of Christ
Attn: Local Church Ministries
700 Prospect Avenue East
Cleveland, OH 44115-1100
(216) 736-3865   Toll Free: (866) 822-8224, ext. 3848
Fax: (216) 736-3783   E-mail: lcm@ucc.org
Web: www.ucc.org/seminarians/ucc-scholarships-for.html

Summary To provide financial assistance to African Americans and other minority students who are either enrolled at an accredited seminary preparing for a career of service in the United Church of Christ (UCC) or working on a doctoral degree in the field of religion.

Eligibility This program is open to members of underrepresented ethnic groups (African American, Hispanic American, Asian American, Native American Indian, or Pacific Islander) who have been a member of a UCC congregation for at least 1 year. Applicants must be either 1) enrolled in an accredited school of theology in the United States or Canada and working on an M.Div. degree with the intent of becoming a pastor or teacher within the UCC, or 2) doctoral (Ph.D., Th.D., or Ed.D.) students within a field related to religious studies. Seminary students must have a GPA in all postsecondary work of 3.0 or higher and must have begun the in-care process; preference is given to students who have demonstrated leadership (through a history of service to the church) and scholarship (through exceptional academic performance). For doctoral students, preference is given to applicants who have demonstrated academic excellence, teaching effectiveness, and commitment to the UCC and who intend to become professors in colleges, seminaries, or graduate schools.

Financial data Grants range from $500 to $5,000 per year.

Duration 1 year; may be renewed.

Number awarded Varies each year; recently, 11 of these scholarships, including 8 for M.Div. students and 3 for doctoral students, were awarded.

Deadline February of each year.

[606]
AERA DISSERTATION GRANTS PROGRAM

American Educational Research Association
1430 K Street, N.W., Suite 1200
Washington, DC 20005
(202) 238-3200   Fax: (202) 238-3250
Web: www.aera.net

Summary To provide funding to doctoral students (especially African Americans and other minorities) who are writing their dissertation on educational policy.

Eligibility This program is open to advanced graduate students who are writing their dissertations in such disciplines as (but not limited to) education, sociology, economics, psychology, demography, statistics, or psychometrics. Applicants may be U.S. citizens, U.S. permanent residents, or non-U.S. citizens working at a U.S. institution. Underrepresented minority researchers are strongly encouraged to apply. Dissertation topics may cover a wide range of policy-related issues, but priority is given to proposals that 1) develop or benefit from new quantitative measures or methodological approaches for addressing education issues; 2) incorporate subject matter expertise, especially when studying science, technology, engineering, or mathematics (STEM) learning; 3) analyze TIMSS, PISA, or other international data resources; or 4) include the integration and analysis of more than 1 data set. The research project must include the analysis of data from at least 1 of the large-scale nationally or internationally representative data sets, such as those of the National Science Foundation (NSF), National Center for Education Statistics (NCES), or National Institutes of Health (NIH). Selection is based on the importance of the proposed policy issue, strength of the methodological model and proposed statistical analysis of the study, and relevant experience or research record of the applicant.

Financial data The maximum grant is $20,000 per year. No support is provided for indirect costs to institutions. Funding is linked to approval of the recipient's progress report and final report. Grantees receive one-third of the total award at the beginning of the grant period, one-third upon acceptance of the progress report, and one-third upon acceptance of the final report. Funds can be sent either to the recipients or to their institutions.

Duration 1 year; nonrenewable.

Additional information Funding for this program is provided by the NSF and the NCES. Grantees must submit a brief (3 to 6 pages) progress report midway through the grant period. A final report must be submitted at the end of the grant period. The final report may be either an article suitable for publication in a scholarly journal or a copy of the dissertation.

Number awarded Approximately 15 each year.

Deadline January, March, or August of each year.

[607]
AFRICAN-AMERICAN LAW STUDENT FELLOWSHIP PROGRAM

National Bar Institute
1225 11th Street, N.W.
Washington, DC 20001-4217
(202) 842-3900   Fax: (202) 289-6170
Web: www.nationalbar.org/nbi/nbigrants.html

Summary To provide financial assistance to African American students working on a law degree.

Eligibility This program is open to African Americans who have completed at least 2 consecutive years of full-time study at a U.S. law school. Applicants must have demonstrated a commitment to creating equality and justice for African Americans through work in their law schools, neighborhoods, and community and must intend to return to a Black community to practice law once their legal training is completed. U.S. citizenship or permanent resident status and membership in the National Bar Association (NBA) are required. Selection is based on the applicant's academic qualifications, potential to make a significant contribution to the field, commitment to African American issues in the field of study and/or community, and financial need.

Financial data Stipends range from $1,000 to $10,000, but most are approximately $2,500.

Duration 1 year.

Additional information The National Bar Institute was established in 1982 as the philanthropic arm of the National Bar Association, an organization of African American lawyers.

Number awarded Up to 3 each year.

Deadline May of each year.

[608]
AFRICAN-AMERICAN PH.D./TH.D. SCHOLARS DISSERTATION AWARDS

The Fund for Theological Education, Inc.
Attn: Dissertation Fellows Program
825 Houston Mill Road, Suite 100
Atlanta, GA 30329-4211
(404) 727-1450   Fax: (404) 727-1490
Web: www.fteleaders.org/pages/dissertation-fellowships

Summary To provide funding to African Americans who are completing a dissertation on religion or theology and are preparing for a scholarly or research career.

Eligibility This program is open to African Americans who are U.S. citizens involved in the final writing of a doctoral dissertation (Ph.D. or Th.D. in religion, theological studies, or biblical studies at a university or school of theology. Applicants must be able to write full time during the fellowship year. Their dissertation committee must have approved the dissertation research proposal and writing plan. Along with their application, they must submit a 1-page essay that covers their specific area of scholarship (e.g., ethics, biblical studies, religion and culture), their plans to contribute to teaching and scholarship, and how their dissertation will contribute to theological education and the church. Students enrolled in Doctor of Ministry (D.Min.) programs are ineligible.

Financial data The stipend is $20,000.

Duration 1 year (to complete the final writing of their dissertation).

Additional information Fellows also receive reimbursement of expenses to attend the sponsor's doctoral conference that includes lectures, panels, and workshops. They have an opportunity to meet with religious and theological faculty, we well as peers, to discuss contemporary issues in religion and theology, scholarship, and teaching.

Number awarded Varies each year; recently, 10 of these fellowships were awarded.

Deadline January of each year.

[609]
AFRICAN-AMERICAN PH.D./TH.D. SCHOLARS DOCTORAL FELLOWSHIPS

The Fund for Theological Education, Inc.
Attn: Doctoral Fellows Program
825 Houston Mill Road, Suite 100
Atlanta, GA 30329
(404) 727-1450   Fax: (404) 727-1490
Web: www.fteleaders.org/pages/doctoral-fellowships

Summary To provide funding to African Americans who are entering graduate school to prepare for teaching and scholarly research careers in religion or theology.

Eligibility This program is open to African Americans who are U.S. citizens entering their first year of graduate school in religious or theological studies to work on a Ph.D. or Th.D. degree. Applicants must be committed to providing leadership within theological education and strongly considering a career in seminary teaching and research. Along with their application, they must submit an essay of 2 to 3 pages describing the discipline area (e.g., biblical studies, ethics, religious history) that is the focus of their graduate study and what they hope to explore in it, their academic goals and commitments to theological teaching and scholarship, and why they have chosen their first choice institution and their disciplinary area. Students who are currently enrolled in a graduate program or who are working on a Doctor of Ministry (D.Min.) degree are not eligible.

Financial data The stipend is $20,000 per year.

Duration 2 years (the first 2 years of a doctoral program).

Additional information Fellows also receive reimbursement of expenses to attend the sponsor's doctoral conference that includes lectures, panels, and workshops. They have an opportunity to meet with religious and theological faculty, we well as peers, to discuss contemporary issues in religion and theology, scholarship, and teaching.

Number awarded Varies each year; recently, 14 of these fellowships were awarded.

Deadline February of each year.

[610]
AFRICAN-AMERICAN STUDIES FELLOWSHIP

Massachusetts Historical Society
Attn: Short-Term Fellowships
1154 Boylston Street
Boston, MA 02215-3695
(617) 646-0568   Fax: (617) 859-0074
E-mail: fellowships@masshist.org
Web: www.masshist.org/fellowships/short_term.cfm

Summary To fund research visits to the Massachusetts Historical Society for graduate students and other scholars interested in African American history.

Eligibility This program is open to advanced graduate students, postdoctorates, and independent scholars who are conducting research in African American history and need to use the resources of the Massachusetts Historical Society. Applicants must be U.S. citizens or foreign nationals holding appropriate U.S. government documents. Along with their application, they must submit a curriculum vitae and a proposal describing the project and indicating collections at the society to be consulted. Graduate students must also arrange for a letter of recommendation from a faculty member familiar with their work and with the project being proposed. Preference is given to candidates who live 50 or more miles from Boston.

Financial data The grant is $1,500.

Duration 4 weeks.

Additional information This fellowship was first awarded in 1999.

Number awarded 1 each year.

Deadline February of each year.

[611]
AGING RESEARCH DISSERTATION AWARDS TO INCREASE DIVERSITY

National Institute on Aging
Attn: Office of Extramural Affairs
7201 Wisconsin Avenue, Suite 2C-218
Bethesda, MD 20814
(301) 402-7713   Fax: (301) 402-2945
TDD: (301) 451-0088
E-mail: michael-david.kerns@nih.hhs.gov
Web: www.nia.nih.gov

Summary To provide financial assistance to doctoral candidates (particularly African Americans, other minorities, and students with disabilities) who wish to conduct research on aging.

Eligibility This program is open to doctoral candidates conducting research on a dissertation with an aging-related focus, including the 4 extramural programs within the National Institute on Aging (NIA): the biology of aging program, the behavioral and social research on aging program, the neuroscience and neuropsychology of aging program, and the geriatrics and clinical gerontology program. Applicants must be 1) members of an ethnic or racial group underrepresented in biomedical or behavioral research; 2) individuals with disabilities; or 3) individuals from socially, culturally, economically, or educationally disadvantaged backgrounds that have inhibited their ability to prepare for a career in health-related research. They must be U.S. citizens, nationals, or permanent residents.

Financial data Grants provide $21,180 per year for stipend and up to $15,000 for additional expenses. No funds may be used to pay for tuition or fees associated with completion of doctoral studies. The institution may receive up to 8% of direct costs as facilities and administrative costs per year.

Duration Up to 2 years.

Number awarded Up to 5 each year.

Deadline Letters of intent must be submitted by February, June, or October of each year.

[612]
AGNES JONES JACKSON SCHOLARSHIPS

National Association for the Advancement of Colored People
Attn: Education Department
4805 Mt. Hope Drive
Baltimore, MD 21215-3297
(410) 580-5760   Toll Free: (877) NAACP-98
E-mail: youth@naacpnet.org
Web: www.naacp.org/pages/naacp-scholarships

Summary To provide financial assistance to members of the National Association for the Advancement of Colored People (NAACP) who are attending or planning to attend college or graduate school.

Eligibility This program is open to members of the NAACP who are younger than 25 years of age and full-time undergraduates or full- or part-time graduate students. The minimum GPA is 2.5 for graduating high school seniors and undergraduate students or 3.0 for graduate students. All applicants must be able to demonstrate financial need (family income must be less than $16,245 for a family of 1, ranging up to $49,905 for a family of 7) and U.S. citizenship. Along with their application, they must submit a 1-page essay on their interest in their major and a career, their life's ambition, what they hope to accomplish in their lifetime, and what position they hope to attain.

Financial data The stipend is $1,500 per year for undergraduate students or $2,500 per year for graduate students.

Duration 1 year; recipients may apply for renewal.

Number awarded Varies each year; recently, 5 of these scholarships were awarded.

Deadline March of each year.

[613]
AIR FORCE SUMMER FACULTY FELLOWSHIP PROGRAM

American Society for Engineering Education
Attn: Projects Department
1818 N Street, N.W., Suite 600
Washington, DC 20036-2479
(202) 331-5763   Fax: (202) 265-8504
E-mail: sffp@asee.org
Web: sffp.asee.org

Summary To provide funding to science and engineering faculty and graduate students (especially those at Historically Black Colleges and Universities and other Minority Serving Institutions) who are interested in conducting summer research at Air Force facilities.

Eligibility This program is open to U.S. citizens and permanent residents who have a full-time faculty appointment at a U.S. college or university in a field of engineering or science of interest to the Air Force. Applicants must be interested in conducting a research project, under the direction of an Air Force research adviser, at an Air Force Research Laboratory, the U.S. Air Force Academy, or the Air Force Institute of Technology. A graduate student may accompany the faculty member. Faculty and students at Historically Black Colleges and Universities ((HBCUs), Minority Institutions (MIs), American Indian Tribal Colleges and Universities (TCUs), and Hispanic Serving Institutions (HSIs) are especially encouraged to apply.

Financial data Stipends are $1,700 per week for full professors, $1,500 per week for associate professors, $1,300 per week for assistant professors, $884 per week for graduate students who have a bachelor's degree, or $1,037 per week for graduate students who have a master's degree. Relocation reimbursement and a daily expense allowance of $50 (for fellows with a commute distance greater than 50 miles) are also available.

Duration 8 to 12 weeks during the summer. May be renewed for a second and third summer, but recipients may not reapply for 2 years after completing a third summer.

Additional information This program first operated in 2005. Research must be conducted in residence at an Air Force facility.

Number awarded Varies each year; recently, 93 of these fellowships were awarded.

Deadline November of each year.

[614]
ALFRED M. GREENFIELD FOUNDATION FELLOWSHIPS IN AFRICAN AMERICAN HISTORY

Library Company of Philadelphia
Attn: Librarian
1314 Locust Street
Philadelphia, PA 19107-5698
(215) 546-3181   Fax: (215) 546-5167
E-mail: jgreen@librarycompany.org
Web: www.librarycompany.org/fellowships/american.htm

Summary To provide funding to pre- and postdoctorates interested in conducting research on African American history at designated libraries in Philadelphia.

Eligibility This program is open to candidates interested in conducting dissertation, postdoctoral, or advanced research in Philadelphia at the Library Company and/or the Historical Society of Pennsylvania. The proposed research must relate to African American history.

Financial data The stipend is $2,000.

Duration 1 month.

Number awarded 4 each year.

Deadline February of each year.

[615]
ALLISON E. FISHER SCHOLARSHIP

National Association of Black Journalists
Attn: Program Coordinator
8701-A Adelphi Road
Adelphi, MD 20783-1716
(301) 445-7100, ext. 108   Toll Free: (866) 479-NABJ
Fax: (301) 445-7101   E-mail: nabj@nabj.org
Web: www.nabj.org

Summary To provide financial assistance to undergraduate or graduate student members of the National Association of Black Journalists (NABJ) who are majoring in journalism.

Eligibility This program is open to African American undergraduate or graduate students who are currently attending an accredited 4-year college or university. Applicants must be majoring in print or broadcast journalism, have a GPA of 3.0 or higher, and be able to demonstrate community service. They must be NABJ members. Along with their application, they must submit samples of their work, an official college transcript, 2 letters of recommendation, a resume, and a 500- to 800-word essay describing their accomplishments as a student journalist, their career goals, and their financial need.

Financial data The stipend is $2,500. Funds are paid directly to the recipient's college or university.

Duration 1 year; nonrenewable.

Number awarded 1 each year.

Deadline April of each year.

[616]
ALPHA KAPPA ALPHA ENDOWMENT AWARDS

Alpha Kappa Alpha Sorority, Inc.
Attn: Educational Advancement Foundation
5656 South Stony Island Avenue
Chicago, IL 60637
(773) 947-0026   Toll Free: (800) 653-6528
Fax: (773) 947-0277   E-mail: akaeaf@akaeaf.net
Web: www.akaeaf.org/fellowships_endowments.htm

Summary To provide financial assistance to undergraduate and graduate students (especially African American women) who meet designated requirements.

Eligibility This program is open to undergraduate and graduate students who are enrolled full time as sophomores or higher in an accredited degree-granting institution and are planning to continue their program of education. Applicants may apply for scholarships that include specific requirements established by the donor of the endowment that supports it. Along with their application, they must submit 1) a list of honors, awards, and scholarships received; 2) a list of organizations in which they have memberships, especially minority organizations; and 3) a statement of their personal and career goals, including how this scholarship will enhance their ability to attain those goals. The sponsor is a traditionally African American women's sorority.

Financial data Award amounts are determined by the availability of funds from the particular endowment. Recently, stipends averaged more than $1,700 per year.

Duration 1 year or longer.

Additional information Each endowment establishes its own requirements. Examples of requirements include residence of the applicant, major field of study, minimum GPA, attendance at an Historically Black College or University (HBCU) or member institution of the United Negro College Fund (UNCF), or other personal feature. For further information on all endowments, contact the sponsor.

Number awarded Varies each year; recently, 30 of these scholarships, with a total value of $52,082, were awarded.

Deadline April of each year.

[617]
ALPHA KAPPA ALPHA GRADUATE SCHOLARSHIPS

Alpha Kappa Alpha Sorority, Inc.
Attn: Educational Advancement Foundation
5656 South Stony Island Avenue
Chicago, IL 60637
(773) 947-0026   Toll Free: (800) 653-6528
Fax: (773) 947-0277   E-mail: akaeaf@akaeaf.net
Web: www.akaeaf.org/graduate_scholarships.htm

Summary To provide financial assistance for study or research to graduate students (especially African American women).

Eligibility This program is open to students who are working full time on a graduate degree in any state. Applicants may apply either for a scholarship based on merit (requires a GPA of 3.0 or higher) or on financial need (requires a GPA of 2.5 or higher). Along with their application, they must submit 1) a list of honors, awards, and scholarships received; 2) a list of organizations in which they have memberships, especially minority organizations; 3) a description of the project or research on which they are currently working, or (if they are not involved in a project or research) the aspects of their field that interest them; and 4) a statement of their personal and career goals, including how this scholarship will enhance their ability to attain those goals. The sponsor is a traditionally African American women's sorority.

Financial data Stipends range from $750 to $1,500 per year.

Duration 1 year; nonrenewable.

Number awarded Varies each year; recently, 60 of these scholarships, with a total value of $47,550, were awarded.

Deadline August of each year.

[618]
ALPHA PHI ALPHA FRATERNITY SCHOLARSHIPS

Alpha Phi Alpha Fraternity, Inc.
Attn: Director of Educational Activities
2313 St. Paul Street
Baltimore, MD 21218-5234
(410) 554-0040   Fax: (410) 554-0054
E-mail: jjames@apa1906.net
Web: www.alpha-phi-alpha.com/Page.php?id=102

Summary To provide financial assistance for college or graduate school to brothers of Alpha Phi Alpha Fraternity.

Eligibility This program is open to brothers of the fraternity who either 1) are working full time on an undergraduate degree, or 2) have been admitted to a graduate or professional program. Applicants must have a GPA of 3.5 or higher. Along with their application, they must submit a resume, a list of their involvement in the fraternity's national programs and special projects, an official transcript, 3 letters of recommendation, and an essay on their career ambitions, goals, and why they should be awarded the scholarship.

Financial data The stipend is $1,500.

Duration 1 year.

Additional information Alpha Phi Alpha is the first collegiate fraternity established primarily for African American men.

Number awarded 15 each year: 3 in each of the fraternity's 5 geographic regions.

Deadline April of each year.

[619]
ALUMNI EXTENSION TECHNICAL SCHOLARSHIPS

National Society of Black Engineers
Attn: Programs Department
205 Daingerfield Road
Alexandria, VA 22314
(703) 549-2207   Fax: (703) 683-5312
E-mail: scholarships@nsbe.org
Web: www.nsbe.org/Programs/Scholarships/Alumni.aspx

Summary To provide financial assistance to members of the National Society of Black Engineers (NSBE) who are entering or enrolled in a graduate program in engineering or science.

Eligibility This program is open to members of the society who are either graduating college seniors planning to enter graduate school or current graduate students with at least 1 academic year remaining. All technical fields of engineering and science are eligible. Preference is given to members of the NSBE Alumni Extension (AE) or an NSBE Special Interest Group (SIG). Applicants must submit an essay of 200 to 250 words on a topic that changes annually; recently, they were invited to describe a technical design, process, or program that NSBE technical professionals (alumni) or specialists (graduate students) can implement via a new or existing SIG to improve the quality of life in the Black community.

Financial data The stipend is $2,000.

Duration 1 year.
Number awarded 3 each year.
Deadline January of each year.

[620]
AMA FOUNDATION MINORITY SCHOLARS AWARDS

American Medical Association
Attn: AMA Foundation
515 North State Street
Chicago, IL 60610
(312) 464-4193 Fax: (312) 464-4142
E-mail: amafoundation@ama-assn.org
Web: www.ama-assn.org

Summary To provide financial assistance to African American and other underrepresented minorities who are enrolled in medical school.

Eligibility This program is open to first- and second-year medical students who are members of the following minority groups: African American/Black, American Indian, Native Hawaiian, Alaska Native, or Hispanic/Latino. Only nominations are accepted. Each medical school is invited to submit 2 nominees. U.S. citizenship or permanent resident status is required.

Financial data The stipend is $10,000.

Duration 1 year.

Additional information This program is offered by the AMA Foundation of the American Medical Association in collaboration with the Minority Affairs Consortium (MAC) and with support from the Pfizer Medical Humanities Initiative.

Number awarded 12 each year.

Deadline April of each year.

[621]
AMERICAN BAR ASSOCIATION LEGAL OPPORTUNITY SCHOLARSHIP

American Bar Association
Attn: Fund for Justice and Education
321 North Clark Street
Chicago, IL 60654-7598
(312) 988-5415 Fax: (312) 988-6392
E-mail: legalosf@staff.abanet.org
Web: www.abanet.org/fje/losfpage.html

Summary To provide financial assistance to African Americans and other minority students who are interested in attending law school.

Eligibility This program is open to racial and ethnic minority college graduates who are interested in attending an ABA-accredited law school. Only students beginning law school may apply; students who have completed 1 or more semesters of law school are not eligible. Applicants must have a cumulative GPA of 2.5 or higher and be citizens or permanent residents of the United States. Along with their application, they must submit a 1,000-word statement describing their personal and family background, community service activities, and other connections to their racial and ethnic minority community. Financial need is also considered in the selection process.

Financial data The stipend is $5,000 per year.

Duration 1 year; may be renewed for 2 additional years if satisfactory performance in law school has been achieved.

Additional information This program began in the 2000-01 academic year.

Number awarded Approximately 20 each year.

Deadline February of each year.

[622]
AMERICAN DIETETIC ASSOCIATION GRADUATE SCHOLARSHIPS

American Dietetic Association
Attn: Commission on Accreditation for Dietetics Education
120 South Riverside Plaza, Suite 2000
Chicago, IL 60606-6995
(312) 899-0040 Toll Free: (800) 877-1600, ext. 5400
Fax: (312) 899-4817 E-mail: education@eatright.org
Web: www.eatright.org/CADE/content.aspx?id=7934

Summary To provide financial assistance to graduate student members of the American Dietetic Association (ADA), especially African American and other underrepresented minority members.

Eligibility This program is open to ADA members who are enrolled or planning to enroll in a master's or doctoral degree program in dietetics. Applicants who are currently completing a dietetic internship or preprofessional practice program that is combined with a graduate program may also apply. The graduate scholarships are available only to U.S. citizens and permanent residents. Applicants should intend to practice in the field of dietetics. Some scholarships require specific areas of study (e.g., public health nutrition, food service administration) and status as a registered dietitian. Others may require membership in a specific dietetic practice group, residency in a specific state, or underrepresented minority group status. The same application form can be used for all categories.

Financial data Stipends range from $500 to $3,000; most are for $1,000.

Duration 1 year.

Number awarded Varies each year, depending upon the funds available; recently, the sponsoring organization awarded 222 scholarships for all its programs.

Deadline February of each year.

[623]
AMERICAN POLITICAL SCIENCE ASSOCIATION MINORITY FELLOWS PROGRAM

American Political Science Association
Attn: APSA Minority Fellows Program
1527 New Hampshire Avenue, N.W.
Washington, DC 20036-1206
(202) 483-2512, ext. 123 Fax: (202) 483-2657
E-mail: apsa@apsanet.org
Web: www.apsanet.org/content_3284.cfm

Summary To provide financial assistance to African Americans and other underrepresented minorities interested in working on a doctoral degree in political science.

Eligibility This program is open to African Americans, Asian Pacific Americans, Latino(a)s, and Native Americans who are in their senior year at a college or university or currently enrolled in a master's degree program. Applicants must be planning to enroll in a doctoral program in political science to prepare for a career in teaching and research. They must be U.S. citizens and able to demonstrate financial need.

Along with their application, they must submit a 500-word personal statement that includes why they are interested in attending graduate school in political science, what specific fields within the discipline they plan to study, and how they intend to contribute to research within the discipline. Selection is based on interest in teaching and potential for research in political science.

Financial data The stipend is $2,000 per year.

Duration 2 years.

Additional information In addition to the fellows who receive stipends from this program, students who are selected as fellows without stipend are recommended for admission and financial support to every doctoral political science program in the country. This program was established in 1969.

Number awarded Up to 12 fellows receive stipends each year.

Deadline October of each year.

[624]
AMERICAN SPEECH-LANGUAGE-HEARING FOUNDATION SCHOLARSHIP FOR MINORITY STUDENTS

American Speech-Language-Hearing Foundation
Attn: Program Assistant
2200 Research Boulevard
Rockville, MD 20850-3289
(301) 296-8703   Toll Free: (800) 498-2071, ext. 8703
E-mail: foundationprograms@asha.org
Web: www.ashfoundation.org/grants/GraduateScholarships

Summary To provide financial assistance to graduate students (especially African American and other minority students) who are enrolled in communication sciences and disorders programs.

Eligibility This program is open to full-time graduate students who are enrolled in communication sciences and disorders programs, with preference given to U.S. citizens who are members of a racial or ethnic minority group. Applicants must submit an essay, up to 5 pages in length, on a topic that relates to the future of leadership in the discipline. Selection is based on academic promise and outstanding academic achievement.

Financial data The stipend ranges from $2,000 to $4,000. Funds must be used for educational support (e.g., tuition, books, school living expenses), not for personal or conference travel.

Duration 1 year.

Number awarded 1 each year.

Deadline June of each year.

[625]
ANAPATA DIVERSITY SCHOLARSHIP CONTEST

Ms. JD
Attn: Executive Director
1659 Lyman Place
Los Angeles, CA 90027
(917) 446-8991   E-mail: kornberg@ms-jd.org
Web: ms-jd.org/anapata-student-scholarship

Summary To provide financial assistance to law students who are African American or members of other groups traditionally underrepresented in the legal profession.

Eligibility This program is open to students currently enrolled at ABA-approved law schools in the United States. Members of groups traditionally underrepresented in the legal profession are especially encouraged to apply. They must submit a resume, transcript, personal introduction paragraph, 2 recommendations, and a 750-word essay demonstrating their personal philosophy regarding diversity in the legal profession. Selection is based on academic achievement, leadership ability, writing and interpersonal skills, and interest in promoting diversity in the legal profession.

Financial data The stipend is $1,000.

Duration 1 year.

Additional information This program is offered by Ms. JD in partnership with Anapata, Inc.

Number awarded 1 or more each year.

Deadline February of each year.

[626]
ANDREW W. MELLON FOUNDATION/ACLS DISSERTATION COMPLETION FELLOWSHIPS

American Council of Learned Societies
Attn: Office of Fellowships and Grants
633 Third Avenue
New York, NY 10017-6795
(212) 697-1505   Fax: (212) 949-8058
E-mail: fellowships@acls.org
Web: www.acls.org/programs/dcf

Summary To provide research funding to doctoral candidates (particularly African Americans and other minorities) in all disciplines of the humanities and the humanities-related social sciences who are ready to complete their dissertations.

Eligibility This program is open to doctoral candidates in a humanities or humanities-related social science discipline at a U.S. institution. Applicants must have completed all requirements for the Ph.D. except the dissertation. They may have completed no more than 6 years in the degree program. Research may be conducted at the home institution, abroad, or another appropriate site. Appropriate fields of specialization include, but are not limited to, American studies; anthropology; archaeology; art and architectural history; classics; economics; film; geography; history; languages and literatures; legal studies; linguistics; musicology; philosophy; political science; psychology; religious studies; rhetoric, communication, and media studies; sociology; and theater, dance, and performance studies. Proposals in the social sciences are eligible only if they employ predominantly humanistic approaches (e.g., economic history, law and literature, political philosophy). Proposals in interdisciplinary and cross-disciplinary studies are welcome, as are proposals focused on a geographic region or on a cultural or linguistic group. Applications are particularly invited from women and members of minority groups.

Financial data Grants provide a stipend of $25,000, funds for research costs up to $3,000, and payment of university fees up to $5,000.

Duration 1 academic year. Grantees may accept this fellowship no later than their seventh year.

Additional information This program, which began in 2006, is supported by funding from the Andrew W. Mellon Foundation and administered by the American Council of Learned Societies (ACLS).

Number awarded 65 each year.

Deadline November of each year.

[627]
ANNA M. WINSTON AWARD

National Association of Black Accountants
Attn: National Scholarship Program
7474 Greenway Center Drive, Suite 1120
Greenbelt, MD 20770
(301) 474-NABA, ext. 114   Fax: (301) 474-3114
E-mail: customerservice@nabainc.org
Web: www.nabainc.org

Summary To provide financial assistance to student members of the National Association of Black Accountants (NABA) who are attending an Historically Black College or University (HBCU) to work on an undergraduate or graduate degree in a field related to accounting.

Eligibility This program is open to NABA members enrolled full time as 1) an undergraduate freshman, sophomore, junior, or first-semester senior majoring in accounting, business, or finance at an HBCU; or 2) a graduate student working on a master's degree in accounting at an HBCU. High school seniors are not eligible. Applicants must have a GPA of 2.0 or higher in their major and 2.5 or higher overall. Selection is based on grades, financial need, and a 500-word autobiography that discusses career objectives, leadership abilities, community activities, and involvement in NABA.

Financial data The stipend ranges from $500 to $1,000.

Duration 1 year.

Additional information Applicants for this scholarship are required to sign a pledge form with a promise to fund it within 5 years of graduation from college.

Number awarded 1 each year.

Deadline January of each year.

[628]
AOS/NORMAN'S ORCHIDS MASTERS SCHOLARSHIP

American Orchid Society
16700 AOS Lane
Delray Beach, FL 33446-4351
(561) 404-2000   Fax: (561) 404-2045
E-mail: TheAOS@aos.org
Web: www.aos.org

Summary To provide funding for research to students (especially African Americans, other minorities, women, and students with disabilities) who are working on a master's degree in a field related to orchids.

Eligibility This program is open to students working on a master's degree at an accredited institution. Applicants must have a thesis project that deals with an aspect of orchid education, applied science, or orchid biology in the disciplines of physiology, molecular biology, structure, systematics, cytology, ecology, or evolution. They must submit a current curriculum vitae, transcripts of all college course work, a synopsis of the proposed project or research, a 1-page statement of the value of their project and importance to the future of orchid education or orchidology, and a letter of recommendation from their chairperson. Women, minorities, and persons with disabilities are especially encouraged to apply.

Financial data The grant is $5,000 per year. Funds are paid through the recipient's college or university, but institutional overhead is not allowed.

Duration 2 years.

Additional information This program, established in 2005, is supported by Norman's Orchids of Montclair, California.

Number awarded 1 each year.

Deadline February of each year.

[629]
APA MINORITY MEDICAL STUDENT SUMMER MENTORING PROGRAM

American Psychiatric Association
Attn: Department of Minority and National Affairs
1000 Wilson Boulevard, Suite 1825
Arlington, VA 22209-3901
(703) 907-8653   Toll Free: (888) 35-PSYCH
Fax: (703) 907-7852   E-mail: mking@psych.org
Web: www.psych.org/Resources/OMNA/MFP.aspx

Summary To provide funding to African Americans and other minority medical students who are interested in working on a summer project with a psychiatrist mentor.

Eligibility This program is open to minority medical students who are interested in psychiatric issues. Minorities include American Indians, Alaska Natives, Native Hawaiians, Asian Americans, Hispanic/Latinos, and African Americans. Applicants must be interested in working with a psychiatrist mentor, primarily on clinical work with underserved minority populations and mental health care disparities. Work settings may be in a research, academic, or clinical environment. Most of them are inner-city or rural and dealing with psychiatric subspecialties, particularly substance abuse and geriatrics. Selection is based on interest of the medical student and specialty of the mentor, practice setting, and geographic proximity of the mentor to the student. U.S. citizenship or permanent resident status is required.

Financial data Fellowships provide $1,500 for living and out-of-pocket expenses directly related to the conduct of the fellowship.

Duration Summer months.

Additional information This program is funded by the Substance Abuse and Mental Health Services Administration.

Number awarded Varies each year.

Deadline February of each year.

[630]
APA PLANNING FELLOWSHIPS

American Planning Association
Attn: Leadership Affairs Associate
205 North Michigan Avenue, Suite 1200
Chicago, IL 60601
(312) 431-9100   Fax: (312) 786-6700
E-mail: fellowship@planning.org
Web: www.planning.org/scholarships/apa

Summary To provide financial assistance to African American and other underrepresented minority students enrolled in master's degree programs at recognized planning schools.

Eligibility This program is open to first- and second-year graduate students in urban and regional planning who are members of the following minority groups: African American, Hispanic American, or Native American. Applicants must be citizens of the United States and able to document financial need. They must intend to work as practicing planners in the public sector. Along with their application, they must submit a 2- to 5-page personal statement describing how their graduate education will be applied to career goals and why they chose planning as a career path. Selection is based (in order of importance) on 1) commitment to planning as reflected in the personal statement and resume; 2) academic achievement and/or improvement during the past 2 years; 3) letters of recommendation; 4) financial need; and 5) professional presentation.

Financial data Stipends range from $1,000 to $5,000 per year. The money may be applied to tuition and living expenses only. Payment is made to the recipient's university and divided by terms in the school year.

Duration 1 year; recipients may reapply.

Additional information The fellowship program started in 1970 as a Ford Foundation Minority Fellowship Program.

Number awarded Varies each year; recently, 6 of these fellowships were awarded.

Deadline April of each year.

[631]
ARENT FOX DIVERSITY SCHOLARSHIPS

Arent Fox LLP
Attn: Attorney Recruitment and Professional Development
  Coordinator
1050 Connecticut Avenue, N.W.
Washington, DC 20036-5339
(202) 715-8503   Fax: (202) 857-6395
E-mail: lawrecruit@arentfox.com
Web: www.arentfox.com

Summary To provide financial assistance and work experience to African American and other minority law students.

Eligibility This program is open to first-year law students who are members of a diverse population that historically has been underrepresented in the legal profession. Applicants must be U.S. citizens or otherwise authorized to work in the United States. They must also be willing to work as a summer intern at the sponsoring law firm's offices in Los Angeles, New York City, or Washington, D.C. Along with their application, they must submit a resume, an undergraduate transcript and law school grades when available, a 5- to 10-page legal writing sample, 3 letters of recommendation, and an essay on how their background, skills, experience, and interest equip them to meet the sponsor's goal of commitment to diversity. Selection is based on academic performance during college and law school, oral and writing communication skills, leadership qualities, and community involvement.

Financial data The scholarship stipend is $15,000. The summer salary is $2,500 per week.

Duration 1 year.

Additional information These scholarships were first offered in 2006. Recipients are also offered summer internships with Arent Fox: 1 in Los Angeles, 1 in New York City, and 1 in Washington, D.C.

Number awarded 3 each year.

Deadline January of each year.

[632]
ARKANSAS CONFERENCE ETHNIC LOCAL CHURCH CONCERNS SCHOLARSHIPS

United Methodist Church-Arkansas Conference
Attn: Committee on Ethnic Local Church Concerns
800 Daisy Bates Drive
Little Rock, AR 72202
(501) 324-8045   Toll Free: (877) 646-1816
Fax: (501) 324-8018   E-mail: mallen@arumc.org
Web: www.arumc.org

Summary To provide financial assistance to African American and other minority Methodist students from Arkansas who are interested in attending college or graduate school in any state.

Eligibility This program is open to ethnic minority undergraduate and graduate students who are active members of local congregations affiliated with the Arkansas Conference of the United Methodist Church (UMC). Applicants must be currently enrolled in an accredited institution of higher education in any state. Along with their application, they must submit a transcript (GPA of 2.0 or higher) and documentation of participation in local church activities. Preference is given to students attending a UMC-affiliated college or university.

Financial data The stipend is $500 per semester ($1,000 per year) for undergraduates or $1,000 per semester ($2,000 per year) for graduate students.

Duration 1 year; may be renewed.

Number awarded 1 or more each year.

Deadline September of each year.

[633]
ARKANSAS MINORITY MASTERS FELLOWS PROGRAM

Arkansas Department of Higher Education
Attn: Financial Aid Division
114 East Capitol Avenue
Little Rock, AR 72201-3818
(501) 371-2050   Toll Free: (800) 54-STUDY
Fax: (501) 371-2001   E-mail: finaid@adhe.edu
Web: www.adhe.edu

Summary To provide funding to African Americans and other minority graduate students in Arkansas who want to become teachers in the state.

Eligibility This program is open to minority (African American, Hispanic, Native American, or Asian American) residents of Arkansas who are U.S. citizens or permanent residents and enrolled in a master's degree program in education (other than administration) at an Arkansas public or independent institution. Applicants must have a cumulative GPA of 2.75 or higher. They must be willing to teach in an Arkansas public school or public institution of higher education for at least 2 years after completion of their education. Preference is given to applicants who completed their baccalaureate degrees within the previous 2 years.

Financial data The loan is $1,250 per 3-credit course, to a maximum of $3,750 per semester or $7,500 over a lifetime. The loan will be forgiven if the recipient teaches full time in an Arkansas public school or public institution of higher education for 2 years. If the recipient withdraws from an approved teacher education program or does not fulfill the required teaching obligation, the loan must be repaid in full with 10% interest.

Duration 1 semester; may be renewed until the recipient completes 3 years of study, earns a master's degree, or reaches the maximum lifetime loan limit, whichever comes first. Renewal requires the recipient to maintain a GPA of 3.0 or higher.

Number awarded Varies each year; recently, 25 of these forgivable loans were approved.

Deadline May of each year.

[634]
ARL CAREER ENHANCEMENT PROGRAM

Association of Research Libraries
Attn: Director of Diversity Programs
21 Dupont Circle, N.W., Suite 800
Washington, DC 20036
(202) 296-2296   Fax: (202) 872-0884
E-mail: mpuente@arl.org
Web: www.arl.org/diversity/cep/index.shtml

Summary To provide financial assistance for further study and an opportunity for African Americans or other minorities to gain work experience at a library that is a member of the Association of Research Libraries (ARL).

Eligibility This program is open to members of racial and ethnic minority groups that are underrepresented as professionals in academic and research libraries (American Indian or Alaska Native, Asian, Black or African American, Native Hawaiian or other Pacific Islander, or Hispanic or Latino). Applicants must have completed at least 12 credit hours of an M.L.I.S. degree program at an ALA-accredited institution. They must be interested in an internship at 1 of 7 ARL member institutions. Along with their application, they must submit a 400-word essay on what attracts them to an internship opportunity in an ARL library, their professional interests as related to the internship, and their goals for the internship.

Financial data Fellows receive a stipend of $4,800 for the internship, an academic stipend of up to $2,500, a housing stipend of up to $2,000, a travel stipend of up to $1,000 for transportation expenses to and from the internship site, and financial support (approximately $1,000) to attend the annual ARL Leadership Institute.

Duration The internship lasts 6 to 12 weeks (or 240 hours). The academic stipend is for 1 year.

Additional information This program is funded by the Institute of Museum and Library Services. Recently, the 7 participating ARL institutions were the University of Arizona, University of California at San Diego, Columbia University, University of Kentucky, National Library of Medicine, North Carolina State University, and University of Washington.

Number awarded Varies each year; recently, 18 of these fellows were selected.

Deadline October of each year.

[635]
ARL INITIATIVE TO RECRUIT A DIVERSE WORKFORCE

Association of Research Libraries
Attn: Director of Diversity Programs
21 Dupont Circle, N.W., Suite 800
Washington, DC 20036
(202) 296-2296   Fax: (202) 872-0884
E-mail: mpuente@arl.org
Web: www.arl.org/diversity/init/index.shtml

Summary To provide financial assistance to African Americans and other minorities interested in preparing for a career as an academic or research librarian.

Eligibility This program is open to members of racial and ethnic minority groups that are underrepresented as professionals in academic and research libraries (American Indian or Alaska Native, Asian, Black or African American, Native Hawaiian or other Pacific Islander, or Hispanic or Latino). Applicants must be interested in working on an M.L.I.S. degree at an ALA-accredited program. Along with their application, they must submit a 350-word essay on what attracts them to a career in a research library. The essays are judged on clarity and content of form, clear goals and benefits, enthusiasm, potential growth perceived, and professional goals.

Financial data The stipend is $5,000 per year.

Duration 2 years.

Additional information This program began in 2000. Funding is currently provided by the Institute of Museum and Library Services and by the contributions of 52 libraries that are members of the Association of Research Libraries (ARL). Recipients must agree to work for at least 2 years in an ARL library after completing their degree.

Number awarded 20 each year.

Deadline August of each year.

[636]
ARMY JUDGE ADVOCATE GENERAL CORPS SUMMER INTERN PROGRAM

U.S. Army
Attn: Judge Advocate Recruiting Office
1777 North Kent Street, Suite 5200
Rosslyn, VA 22209-2194
(703) 696-2822   Toll Free: (866) ARMY-JAG
Fax: (703) 588-0100
Web: www.goarmy.com/jag/summer_intern_program.jsp

Summary To provide law students (especially African Americans, other minorities, and women) with an opportunity to gain work experience during the summer in Army legal offices throughout the United States and overseas.

Eligibility This program is open to full-time students enrolled in law schools accredited by the American Bar Association. Applications are accepted both from students who are completing the first year of law school and those completing the second year. Students must be interested in a summer internship with the Army Judge Advocate General's Corps (JAGC). U.S. citizenship is required. The program actively seeks applications from women and minority group members. Selection is based on academic ability and demonstrated leadership potential.

Financial data Interns who have completed the first year of law school are paid at the GS-5 scale, starting at $474 per week. Interns who have completed the second year of law school are paid at the GS-7 scale, starting at $588 per week.

Duration Approximately 60 days, beginning in May or June.

Additional information Interns work under the supervision of an attorney and perform legal research, write briefs and opinions, conduct investigations, interview witnesses, and otherwise assist in preparing civil or criminal cases. Positions are available at Department of the Army legal offices in Washington, D.C. and at Army installations throughout the United States and overseas. These are not military positions. No military obligation is incurred by participating in the summer intern program.

Number awarded 100 per year: 25 first-year students and 75 second-year students.

Deadline February of each year for first-year students; October of each year for second-year students.

[637]
ARMY MINORITY COLLEGE RELATIONS PROGRAM INTERNSHIPS

Vista Sciences Corporation
Attn: Intern Program Manager
7700 Alabama Street, Suite E
El Paso, TX 79904
(915) 757-3331   Fax: (915) 757-3371
E-mail: romy.ledesma@vistasciences.com
Web: www.vistasciences.com/services.asp?service=19

Summary To provide work experience at facilities of the U.S. Army to upper-division and graduate students at Historically Black Colleges and Universities and other minority institutions.

Eligibility This program is open to students working on an undergraduate or graduate degree at Historically Black Colleges and Universities (HBCUs), Hispanic Serving Institutions (HSIs), or Tribal Colleges and Universities (TCUs). Applicants must be U.S. citizens currently enrolled as a junior or above and have a GPA of 2.5 or higher; recent (within 6 months) graduates are also eligible. They must be interested in an internship at an Army facility in such fields as engineering (civil, computer, construction, electrical, environmental), sciences (agronomy, biology, environmental, natural resources, safety), business (accounting, finance, legal, management, marketing, operations), computer science and engineering (data management, information systems, information technology, languages, programming, trouble shooting, website/webpage design and management), or other (communications, English, history, human resources, journalism, library sciences, mathematics, public administration, public relations, quality control, risk management, statistics, training development and management). Along with their application, they must submit a resume and a transcript.

Financial data Interns are paid a stipend of $500 per week and are reimbursed for housing and transportation costs.

Duration 10 weeks in the summer or 15 weeks in spring.

Additional information This program, which began in 1997, is currently administered by Vista Sciences Corporation under a contract with the Army. Recently, assignments were available at the Crane Army Ammunition Activity (Crane, Indiana), Sierra Army Depot (Herlong, California),

McAlester Army Ammunition Plant (McAlester, Oklahoma), Blue Grass Army Depot (Richmond, Kentucky), Rock Island Arsenal (Rock Island, Illinois), Anniston Defense Munitions Center (Anniston, Alabama), Pine Bluff Arsenal (Pine Bluff, Arkansas), and Tooele Army Depot (Tooele, Utah).

Number awarded Varies each year.

Deadline May of each year for summer; November of each year for spring.

[638]
ASA MINORITY FELLOWSHIP PROGRAM GENERAL FELLOWSHIP

American Sociological Association
Attn: Minority Affairs Program
1430 K Street, N.W., Suite 600
Washington, DC 20005-2504
(202) 383-9005, ext. 322   Fax: (202) 638-0882
TDD: (202) 638-0981 E-mail: minority.affairs@asanet.org
Web: www.asanet.org/funding/mfp.cfm

Summary To provide financial assistance to African American and other minority doctoral students in sociology.

Eligibility This program is open to U.S. citizens, permanent residents, and non-citizen nationals who are Blacks/African Americans, Latinos (e.g., Mexican Americans, Puerto Ricans, Cubans), American Indians or Alaskan Natives, Asian Americans (e.g., southeast Asians, Japanese, Chinese, Koreans), or Pacific Islanders (e.g., Filipinos, Samoans, Hawaiians, Guamanians). Applicants must be entering or continuing students in sociology at the doctoral level. Along with their application, they must submit 3-page essays on 1) the reasons why they decided to undertake graduate study in sociology, their primary research interests, and why they hope to do with a Ph.D. in sociology; and 2) what led them to select the doctoral program they attend or hope to attend and how they see that doctoral program preparing them for a professional career in sociology. Selection is based on commitment to research, focus of research experience, academic achievement, writing ability, research potential, and financial need.

Financial data The stipend is $18,000 per year.

Duration 1 year; may be renewed up to 2 additional years.

Additional information This program, which began in 1974, is supported by individual members of the American Sociological Association (ASA) and by several affiliated organizations (Alpha Kappa Delta, Sociologists for Women in Society, the Association of Black Sociologists, and the Southwestern Sociological Association).

Number awarded Varies each year; since the program began, approximately 500 of these fellowships have been awarded.

Deadline January of each year.

[639]
ASCA FOUNDATION SCHOLARSHIPS

American School Counselor Association
Attn: ASCA Foundation
1101 King Street, Suite 625
Alexandria, VA 22314
(703) 683-ASCA   Toll Free: (800) 306-4722
Fax: (703) 683-1619   E-mail: asca@schoolcounselor.org
Web: www.schoolcounselor.org

Summary To provide financial assistance for graduate school to members of the American School Counselor Association (ASCA), especially African Americans, other minorities, and males.

Eligibility This program is open to ASCA members working full time on a master's degree in school counseling. Applicants must submit a 2-page essay on a topic that changes annually but relates to the role of counselors in schools. Males and minorities are especially encouraged to apply.

Financial data The stipend is $1,000.

Duration 1 year.

Additional information Support for this program is provided by Anheuser-Busch.

Number awarded Up to 10 each year.

Deadline October of each year.

[640]
ASCO MEDICAL STUDENT ROTATION

American Society of Clinical Oncology
Attn: Conquer Cancer Foundation of ASCO
2318 Mill Road, Suite 800
Alexandria, VA 22314
(571) 483-1700
E-mail: grants@conquercancerfoundation.org
Web: www.conquercancerfoundation.org

Summary To provide funding to African American and other minority medical students interested in a clinical research oncology rotation.

Eligibility This program is open to U.S. citizens, nationals, and permanent residents who are currently enrolled at a U.S. medical school. Applicants must be a member of a group currently underrepresented in medicine, defined as American Indian/Alaska Native, Black/African American, Hispanic/Latino, or Native Hawaiian/Pacific Islander. They must be interested in a rotation either in a patient cancer care setting or a clinical cancer research setting; the rotation may take place either at their own school or another institution but must have a faculty member who belongs to the American Society of Clinical Oncology (ASCO) and is willing to serve as a mentor. Selection is based on interest in preparing for a career in oncology and academic standing.

Financial data Students receive a stipend of $5,000 plus $1,500 for future travel to the annual meeting of the American Society of Clinical Oncology (ASCO). Their mentor receives a grant of $2,000.

Duration 8 to 10 weeks.

Additional information This program, which began in 2009, is sponsored by Susan G. Komen for the Cure.

Number awarded Varies each year; recently, 6 of these grants were awarded.

Deadline January of each year.

[641]
AT&T LABORATORIES FELLOWSHIP PROGRAM

AT&T Laboratories
Attn: Fellowship Administrator
180 Park Avenue, Room C103
P.O. Box 971
Florham Park, NJ 07932-0971
(973) 360-8109   Fax: (973) 360-8881
E-mail: recruiting@research.att.com
Web: www.research.att.com

Summary To provide financial assistance and work experience to African Americans, other underrepresented minorities, and women students who are working on a doctoral degree in computer and technology-related fields.

Eligibility This program is open to minorities underrepresented in the sciences (African Americans, Hispanics, and Native Americans) and to women. Applicants must be U.S. citizens or permanent residents who are graduating college seniors or graduate students enrolled in their first or second year. They must be working on or planning to work on a Ph.D. in a field of study relevant to the business of AT&T; currently, those include computer science, electrical engineering, industrial engineering, mathematics, operations research, systems engineering, statistics, and related fields. Along with their application, they must submit a personal statement on why they are enrolled in their present academic program and how they intend to use their technical training, official transcripts, 3 academic references, and GRE scores. Selection is based on potential for success in scientific research.

Financial data This program covers all educational expenses during the school year, including tuition, books, fees, and approved travel expenses; educational expenses for summer study or university research; a stipend for living expenses (recently, $2,380 per month); and support for attending approved scientific conferences.

Duration 1 year; may be renewed for up to 2 additional years, as long as the fellow continues making satisfactory progress toward the Ph.D.

Additional information The AT&T Laboratories Fellowship Program (ALFP) provides a mentor who is a staff member at AT&T Labs as well as a summer research internship with AT&T Labs during the first summer. The ALFP replaces the Graduate Research Program for Women (GRPW) and the Cooperative Research Fellowship Program (CRFP) run by the former AT&T Bell Laboratories. If recipients accept other support, the tuition payment and stipend received from that fellowship will replace the funds provided by this program. The other provisions of this fellowship will remain in force and the stipend will be replaced by an annual grant of $2,000.

Number awarded Approximately 8 each year.

Deadline January of each year.

[642]
BAKER & DANIELS DIVERSITY SCHOLARSHIPS

Baker & Daniels LLP
Attn: Diversity and Pro Bono Coordinator
300 North Meridian Street, Suite 2700
Indianapolis, IN 46204
(317) 237-8298   Fax: (317) 237-1000
E-mail: brita.horvath@bakerd.com
Web: www.bakerdaniels.com/AboutUs/recruitment.aspx

Summary To provide financial assistance and summer work experience to African American and other students from diverse backgrounds entering the second year of law school in Indiana.

Eligibility This program is open to residents of any state who are entering their second year at selected law schools in Indiana. Applicants must reflect diversity, defined to mean that they come from varied ethnic, racial, cultural, and lifestyle backgrounds, as well as those with disabilities or unique viewpoints. They must also be interested in a place in the sponsor's summer associate program. Along with their application, they must submit a personal statement that includes an explanation of how this scholarship would benefit them, an overview of their background and interests, an explanation of what diversity they would bring to the firm, and any other financial assistance they are receiving. Selection is based primarily on academic excellence.

Financial data The stipend is $10,000.

Duration 1 year.

Additional information The eligible law schools are those at Indiana University at Bloomington, Indiana University at Indianapolis, and the University of Notre Dame.

Number awarded 2 each year.

Deadline June of each year.

[643]
BAKER DONELSON DIVERSITY SCHOLARSHIPS

Baker, Donelson, Bearman, Caldwell & Berkowitz, P.C.
Attn: Director of Attorney Recruiting
3414 Peachtree Road N.E.
Atlanta, GA 30326
(404) 577-6000   Fax: (404) 221-6501
E-mail: lklein@bakerdonelson.com
Web: www.bakerdonelson.com

Summary To provide financial assistance to law students who are African Americans or members of other groups underrepresented at large law firms.

Eligibility This program is open to students who have completed the first year at an ABA-accredited law school. Applicants must be members of a group traditionally underrepresented at large law firms (American Indian or Alaskan Native, Native Hawaiian or Pacific Islander, Hispanic or Latino, Black, or Asian). Along with their application, they must submit a 10-page legal writing sample and a 1-page personal statement on challenges they have faced in pursuit of their legal career that have helped them to understand the value of diversity and its inclusion in the legal profession. Finalists are interviewed.

Financial data The stipend is $10,000.

Duration 1 year.

Additional information Recipients are also offered summer internships at Baker Donelson offices in Atlanta (Georgia), Baton Rouge (Louisiana), Birmingham (Alabama), Chattanooga (Tennessee), Jackson (Mississippi), Johnson City (Tennessee), Knoxville (Tennessee), Memphis (Tennessee), Nashville (Tennessee), and New Orleans (Louisiana).

Number awarded 3 each year.

Deadline June of each year.

[644]
BAKER HOSTETLER DIVERSITY FELLOWSHIP PROGRAM

Baker Hostetler LLP
Attn: Attorney Recruitment and Development Manager
PNC Center
1900 East Ninth Street, Suite 3200
Cleveland, OH 44114-3482
(216) 621-0200   Fax: (216) 696-0740
E-mail: ddriscole@bakerlaw.com
Web: www.bakerlaw.com/diversity/fellowshipprogram

Summary To provide summer work experience to African American and other minority law school students.

Eligibility This program is open to full-time second-year students at ABA-accredited law schools who are members of underrepresented groups (Black/African American, Hispanic, Asian American/Pacific Islander, American Indian/Alaskan Native, 2 or more races, or gay, lesbian, bisexual, transgender). Applicants must be interested in a summer associate position with Baker Hostetler and possible full-time employment following graduation. They must be U.S. citizens or otherwise authorized to work in the United States. Along with their application, they must submit a 500-word personal statement presenting their views of or experience with diversity, including why they are interested in Baker Hostetler and how they will be able to contribute to the diversity objectives of the firm. Selection is based on academic performance in college and law school, personal achievements, community involvement, oral and written communication skills, demonstrated leadership achievements, and a sincere interest and commitment to join Baker Hostetler.

Financial data The stipend is $25,000, of which $10,000 is paid within the first 30 days of starting a summer associate position with the firm and the remaining $15,000 is contingent upon receiving and accepting a full-time offer with the firm.

Duration Summer associate positions are for 8 weeks.

Additional information Summer associate positions may be performed at any of the firm's offices in Chicago, Cincinnati, Cleveland, Columbus, Costa Mesa, Denver, Houston, Los Angeles, New York, Orlando, or Washington, D.C.

Number awarded 1 or more each year.

Deadline October of each year.

[645]
BAKER HUGHES SCHOLARSHIPS

Society of Women Engineers
Attn: Scholarship Selection Committee
120 South LaSalle Street, Suite 1515
Chicago, IL 60603-3572
(312) 596-5223   Toll Free: (877) SWE-INFO
Fax: (312) 644-8557
E-mail: scholarshipapplication@swe.org
Web: societyofwomenengineers.swe.org

Summary To provide financial assistance to African Americans and other minorities or women who are working on an undergraduate or graduate degree in designated engineering specialties.

Eligibility This program is open to women who are sophomores, juniors, seniors, or graduate students at 4-year ABET-accredited colleges and universities. Applicants must be working on a degree in computer science or chemical, electrical, mechanical, or petroleum engineering and have a GPA of 3.0 or higher. Preference is given to members of groups underrepresented in engineering or computer science. Selection is based on merit.

Financial data The stipend is $5,000 per year.

Duration 1 year; may be renewed up to 2 additional years.

Additional information This program is sponsored by Baker Hughes Incorporated.

Number awarded 3 each year.

Deadline February of each year.

[646]
BALFOUR PHI DELTA PHI MINORITY SCHOLARSHIP PROGRAM

Phi Delta Phi International Legal Fraternity
1426 21st Street, N.W., First Floor
Washington, DC 20036
(202) 223-6801   Toll Free: (800) 368-5606
Fax: (202) 223-6808   E-mail: info@phideltaphi.org
Web: www.phideltaphi.org

Summary To provide financial assistance to African Americans and other minorities who are members of Phi Delta Phi International Legal Fraternity.

Eligibility All ethnic minority members of the legal fraternity are eligible to apply for this scholarship. Selection is based on participation, ethics, and scholastics.

Financial data The stipend is $3,000.

Duration 1 year.

Additional information This scholarship was established in 1997. Funding for this scholarship comes from the Lloyd G. Balfour Foundation.

Number awarded 1 each year.

Deadline October of each year.

[647]
BARBARA JORDAN MEMORIAL SCHOLARSHIPS

Association of Texas Professional Educators
Attn: ATPE Foundation
305 East Huntland Drive, Suite 300
Austin, TX 78752-3792
(512) 467-0071   Toll Free: (800) 777-ATPE
Fax: (512) 467-2203   E-mail: admin@atpefoundation.org
Web: www.atpefoundation.org/scholarships.asp

Summary To provide financial assistance to upper-division and graduate students from any state who are enrolled in educator preparation programs at Historically Black Colleges and Universities or other predominantly ethnic minority institutions in Texas.

Eligibility This program is open to juniors, seniors, and graduate students from any state who are enrolled in educator preparation programs at predominantly ethnic minority institutions in Texas. Applicants must submit a 2-page essay on their personal educational philosophy, why they want to become an educator, who influenced them the most in making their career decision, and why they are applying for the scholarship. Financial need is not considered in the selection process.

Financial data The stipend is $1,500.

Duration 1 year.

Additional information The qualifying institutions are Huston-Tillotson College, Jarvis Christian College, Our Lady of the Lake University, Paul Quinn College, Prairie View A&M University, St. Mary's University of San Antonio, Sul Ross State University, Sul Ross State University Rio Grande College, Texas A&M International University, Texas A&M University at Kingsville, Texas Southern University, University of Houston, University of Houston-Downtown, University of Texas at Brownsville and Texas Southmost College, University of Texas at El Paso, University of Texas at San Antonio, University of Texas-Pan American, University of the Incarnate Word, and Wiley College.

Number awarded Up to 6 each year.

Deadline May of each year.

[648]
BEHAVIORAL SCIENCES STUDENT FELLOWSHIPS IN EPILEPSY

Epilepsy Foundation
Attn: Research Department
8301 Professional Place
Landover, MD 20785-2237
(301) 459-3700   Toll Free: (800) EFA-1000
Fax: (301) 577-2684   TDD: (800) 332-2070
E-mail: grants@efa.org
Web: www.epilepsyfoundation.org

Summary To provide funding to undergraduate and graduate students (particularly African Americans or other minorities, women, and students with disabilities) who are interested in working on a summer research training project in a behavioral science field relevant to epilepsy.

Eligibility This program is open to undergraduate and graduate students in a behavioral science program relevant to epilepsy research or clinical care, including, but not limited to, sociology, social work, psychology, anthropology, nursing, economics, vocational rehabilitation, counseling, or political science. Applicants must be interested in working on an epilepsy research project under the supervision of a qualified mentor. Because the program is designed as a training opportunity, the quality of the training plans and environment are considered in the selection process. Other selection criteria include the quality of the proposed project, the relevance of the proposed work to epilepsy, the applicant's interest in the field of epilepsy, the applicant's qualifications, and the mentor's qualifications (including his or her commitment to the student and the project), and the quality of the training environment for research related to epilepsy. U.S. citizenship is not required, but the project must be conducted in the United States. Applications from women, members of minority groups, and people with disabilities are especially encouraged. The program is not intended for students working on a dissertation research project.

Financial data The grant is $3,000.

Duration 3 months during the summer.

Additional information This program is supported by the American Epilepsy Society, Abbott Laboratories, Ortho-McNeil Pharmaceutical Corporation, and Pfizer Inc.

Number awarded Varies each year.

Deadline March of each year.

[649]
BERNADINE JOHNSON MARSHALL-MARTHA BELLE SCHOLARSHIPS

Association of Black Women Lawyers of New Jersey, Inc.
P.O. Box 22524
Trenton, NJ 08607
E-mail: abwlnj@yahoo.com
Web: www.abwlnj.org

Summary To provide financial assistance to African American women from New Jersey attending law school in any state.

Eligibility This program is open to African American women who are 1) residents of New Jersey and currently enrolled in their first, second, or third year at an accredited law school in any state; or 2) residents of other states enrolled at a law school in New Jersey. Selection is based on a writing sample, community service, and financial need.

Financial data The stipend is $1,000.

Duration 1 year.

Number awarded At least 3 each year.

Deadline February of each year.

[650]
BESLA GENERAL SCHOLARSHIP FUND

Black Entertainment and Sports Lawyers Association
Attn: Scholarships
P.O. Box 441485
Fort Washington, MD 20749-1485
Toll Free: (301) 248-1818   Fax: (301) 248-0700
E-mail: info@besla.org
Web: www.besla.org/students.html

Summary To provide financial assistance to students at Historically Black Law Schools who are interested in the fields of entertainment and/or sports law.

Eligibility This program is open to students who have completed at least 1 year of full-time study at an Historically Black Law School (Howard University School of Law, North Carolina Central University School of Law, Southern University Law Center, Florida A&M University School of Law, and Texas Southern University Thurgood Marshall School of Law). Applicants must be able to demonstrate an interest in entertainment or sports law by 1 or more of the following: 1) completing an entertainment law or sports law related course; 2) internship or clerkship in the entertainment or sports law field; 3) current job in the field of entertainment or sports; 4) current membership in an entertainment or sports law society or association; or 5) attendance at an entertainment law or sports law seminar or conference since enrolling in law school. They must have a GPA of 2.5 or higher. Along with their application, they must submit an essay of 750 to 1,000 words or a digital video or slide show presentation up to 3 minutes on a legal issue facing the entertainment or sports industry.

Financial data The stipend is at least $1,500.

Duration 1 year.

Additional information This program, established in 1989, includes the Spencer Boyer Scholarship.

Number awarded Varies each year; recently, 8 of these scholarships were awarded.

Deadline September of each year.

[651]
BESLA LEGAL WRITING COMPETITION

Black Entertainment and Sports Lawyers Association
Attn: Scholarships
P.O. Box 441485
Fort Washington, MD 20749-1485
Toll Free: (301) 248-1818   Fax: (301) 248-0700
E-mail: BESLAmailbox@aol.com
Web: www.besla.org/students.html

Summary To recognize and reward African American and other law students who submit outstanding papers or digital responses on topics related to the fields of entertainment and/or sports law.

Eligibility This program is open to students who have completed at least 1 full year at a law school in any country. Applicants must submit a written essay or a digital response (in the form of a video or slide show presentation) on a legal issue facing the entertainment or sports industry. Recently, students were asked to write on either 1) how the continuing growth of social media (social networks, blogging, microblogging) is impacting the entertainment and sports industries, or 2) "greening" the entertainment and sports industries. Selection is based on focus, organization, critical legal analysis, conclusions and recommendations, originality, voice, and style and mechanics.

Financial data Awards range from $500 to $1,500.

Duration The competition is held annually.

Additional information This program was established in 2004.

Number awarded Varies each year; recently, 5 of these awards were granted: 2 at $1,500, 1 at $1,000, and 2 at $500.

Deadline September of each year.

[652]
BILL BERNBACH DIVERSITY SCHOLARSHIPS

American Association of Advertising Agencies
Attn: AAAA Foundation
405 Lexington Avenue, 18th Floor
New York, NY 10174-1801
(212) 682-2500   Toll Free: (800) 676-9333
Fax: (212) 682-2028   E-mail: ameadows@aaaa.org
Web: www2.aaaa.org

Summary To provide financial assistance to African Americans and other multicultural students interested in working on a graduate degree in advertising at designated schools.

Eligibility This program is open to African Americans, Asian Americans, Hispanic Americans, and Native Americans who are interested in studying the advertising creative arts at designated institutions. Applicants must have already received an undergraduate degree and be able to demonstrate creative talent and promise. Along with their application, they must submit 10 samples of creative work in their respective field of expertise. U.S. citizenship or permanent resident status is required.

Financial data The stipend is $5,000.

Duration 1 year.

Additional information This program, which began in 1998, is currently sponsored by DDB Worldwide. The participating schools are the AdCenter at Virginia Commonwealth University, the Creative Circus and the Portfolio Center in Atlanta, the Miami Ad School, the University of Texas at Austin, and the Art Center College of Design in Pasadena, California.

Number awarded 5 each year.

Deadline Deadline not specified.

[653]
BIOMEDICAL RESEARCH TRAINING PROGRAM FOR UNDERREPRESENTED GROUPS

National Heart, Lung, and Blood Institute
Attn: Office of Training and Minority Health
6701 Rockledge Drive, Suite 9180
Bethesda, MD 20892-7913
(301) 451-5081   Toll Free: (301) 451-0088
Fax: (301) 480-0862   E-mail: mishoeh@nhlbi.nih.gov
Web: www.nhlbi.nih.gov

Summary To provide training in fundamental biomedical sciences and clinical research disciplines to African Americans and other undergraduates, graduate students, and postbaccalaureates from underrepresented groups.

Eligibility This program is open to underrepresented undergraduate and graduate students (and postbaccalaureate individuals) interested in receiving training in fundamental biomedical sciences and clinical research disciplines of interest to the National Heart, Lung, and Blood Institute (NHLBI) of the National Institutes of Health (NIH). Underrepresented individuals include African Americans, Hispanic Americans, Native Americans, Alaskan Natives, Native Hawaiians and Pacific Islanders, individuals with disabilities, and individuals from disadvantaged backgrounds. Applicants must be U.S. citizens or permanent residents; have completed academic course work relevant to biomedical, behavioral, or statistical research; be enrolled full time or have recently completed baccalaureate work; and have a GPA of 3.3 or higher. Research experiences are available in the NHLBI Division of Intramural Research (in its cardiology, hematology, vascular medicine, or pulmonary critical care medicine branches) and its Division of Cardiovascular Sciences (which provides training in the basic principles of design, implementation, and analysis of epidemiology studies and clinical trials).

Financial data Stipends are paid at the annual rate of $24,000 for sophomores, $25,200 for juniors, $26,400 for seniors, $27,200 for postbaccalaureate individuals, $27,600 for first-year graduate students, $31,200 for second-year graduate students, or $34,900 for third-year graduate students.

Duration 6 to 24 months over a 2-year period; training must be completed in increments during consecutive academic years.

Additional information Training is conducted in the laboratories of the NHLBI in Bethesda, Maryland.

Number awarded Varies each year.

Deadline January of each year for placements beginning in June; March of each year for post-baccalaureate research internships beginning from June through September.

[654]
BISHOP THOMAS HOYT, JR. FELLOWSHIP

St. John's University
Attn: Collegeville Institute for Ecumenical and Cultural Research
14027 Fruit Farm Road
Box 2000
Collegeville, MN 56321-2000
(320) 363-3366   Fax: (320) 363-3313
E-mail: staff@CollegevilleInstitute.org
Web: collegevilleinstitute.org/res-fellowships

Summary To provide funding to African Americans and other students of color who wish to complete their doctoral dissertation while in residence at the Collegeville Institute for Ecumenical and Cultural Research of St. John's University in Collegeville, Minnesota.

Eligibility This program is open to people of color completing a doctoral dissertation in ecumenical and cultural research. Applicants must be interested in a residency at the Collegeville Institute for Ecumenical and Cultural Research of St. John's University. Along with their application, they must submit a 1,000-word description of the research project they plan to complete while in residence at the Institute.

Financial data The stipend covers the residency fee of $2,000, which includes housing and utilities.

Duration 1 year.

Additional information Residents at the Institute engage in study, research, and publication on the important intersections between faith and culture. They seek to discern and communicate the meaning of Christian identity and unity in a religiously and culturally diverse world.

Number awarded 1 each year.

Deadline October of each year.

[655]
BLACK WOMEN IN ENTERTAINMENT LAW STUDENT SCHOLARSHIP

Black Women in Entertainment Law
c/o Angela M. Rogers
James E. McMillan, P.C.
19 Fulton Street, Suite 400
New York, NY 10038-2110
(212) 986-6262
Web: www.bwelfoundation.org/scholarships.html

Summary To provide financial assistance to African American women or other women of color who are enrolled in law school and have an interest in entertainment law.

Eligibility This program is open to women of color who have completed at least 1 semester of law school as a full- or part-time student. Applicants must list the entertainment law courses they have taken and write a 1,500-word essay on a question related to entertainment law. They must have a GPA of 2.5 or higher. Financial need is considered in the selection process.

Financial data The stipend is $5,000.

Duration 1 year.

Number awarded 2 each year.

Deadline October of each year.

[656]
BLACK WOMEN LAWYERS ASSOCIATION OF LOS ANGELES SCHOLARSHIPS

Black Women Lawyers Association of Los Angeles, Inc.
Attn: BWL Foundation Scholarship Selection Committee
P.O. Box 8179
Los Angeles, CA 90008
(213) 488-4411
Web: www.bwlfoundation.org/scholarships.html

Summary   To provide financial assistance to African American and other law students from any state who intend to practice in southern California.

Eligibility   This program is open to law students entering their second or third year (or fourth year of a night program). Applicants may be attending an accredited law school in any state but they must intend to practice law in southern California. Selection is based on financial need, community service, academic achievement, and legal writing ability.

Financial data   The stipend is $1,000.

Duration   1 year.

Additional information   The sponsoring organization held its first scholarship event in 1975. Since then, the association and its foundation have awarded more than $230,000 in scholarships. The program includes the following named awards: the Dolores Randolph Bauer Memorial Scholarship, the Sheryl L. Meshack Memorial Scholarship, the Rachel Young Scholarship, the Lillie M. Stith Memorial Scholarship, and the Baxter Healthcare Corporation Scholarship.

Number awarded   Varies each year; recently, 4 of these scholarships were awarded.

Deadline   March of each year.

[657]
BOARD OF CORPORATE AFFILIATES SCHOLARS AWARDS

National Society of Black Engineers
Attn: Programs Department
205 Daingerfield Road
Alexandria, VA 22314
(703) 549-2207   Fax: (703) 683-5312
E-mail: scholarships@nsbe.org
Web: www.nsbe.org

Summary   To provide financial assistance to members of the National Society of Black Engineers (NSBE) who are working on a degree in engineering.

Eligibility   This program is open to members of the society who are undergraduate or graduate engineering students. Applicants must have a GPA of 3.0 or higher. Selection is based on an essay; academic achievement; service to the society at the chapter, regional, and/or national level; and other professional, campus, and community activities. Applicants for the National Society of Black Engineers Fellows Scholarship Program who rank in the highest of 3 tiers receive these awards.

Financial data   The stipend is $3,000. Travel, hotel accommodations, and registration to the national convention are also provided.

Duration   1 year.

Number awarded   Varies each year; recently, 37 of these scholarships were awarded.

Deadline   January of each year.

[658]
BREAKTHROUGH TO NURSING SCHOLARSHIPS

National Student Nurses' Association
Attn: Foundation
45 Main Street, Suite 606
Brooklyn, NY 11201
(718) 210-0705   Fax: (718) 797-1186
E-mail: nsna@nsna.org
Web: www.nsna.org

Summary   To provide financial assistance to African Americans and other minority undergraduate and graduate students who wish to prepare for careers in nursing.

Eligibility   This program is open to students currently enrolled in state-approved schools of nursing or pre-nursing associate degree, baccalaureate, diploma, generic master's, generic doctoral, R.N. to B.S.N., R.N. to M.S.N., or L.P.N./ L.V.N. to R.N. programs. Graduating high school seniors are not eligible. Support for graduate education is provided only for a first degree in nursing. Applicants must be members of a racial or ethnic minority underrepresented among registered nurses (American Indian or Alaska Native, Hispanic or Latino, Native Hawaiian or other Pacific Islander, Black or African American, or Asian). They must be committed to providing quality health care services to underserved populations. Along with their application, they must submit a 200-word description of their professional and educational goals and how this scholarship will help them achieve those goals. Selection is based on academic achievement, financial need, and involvement in student nursing organizations and community health activities. U.S. citizenship or permanent resident status is required.

Financial data   Stipends range from $1,000 to $2,500. A total of approximately $155,000 is awarded each year by the foundation for all its scholarship programs.

Duration   1 year.

Additional information   Applications must be accompanied by a $10 processing fee.

Number awarded   Varies each year; recently, 5 of these scholarships were awarded: 2 sponsored by the American Association of Critical-Care Nurses and 3 sponsored by the Mayo Clinic.

Deadline   January of each year.

[659]
BUILDING ACADEMIC GERIATRIC NURSING CAPACITY PROGRAM PREDOCTORAL SCHOLARSHIP PROGRAM

American Academy of Nursing
Attn: Building Academic Geriatric Nursing Capacity
   Program
888 17th Street, N.W., Suite 800
Washington, DC 20006
(202) 777-1170   Fax: (202) 777-0107
E-mail: bagnc@aannet.org
Web: www.geriatricnursing.org

Summary   To provide funding to nurses (particularly African American and other underrepresented minority nurses) who are interested in working on a doctoral degree in gerontological nursing.

Eligibility   This program is open to registered nurses who hold a degree in nursing and have been admitted to a doctoral program as a full-time student. Applicants must plan an academic career in geriatric nursing. They must identify a mentor/adviser with whom they will work and whose program of research in geriatric nursing is a good match with their own research interest area. Selection is based on potential for substantial long-term contributions to the knowledge base in geriatric nursing; leadership potential; evidence of commitment to a career in academic geriatric nursing; and evidence of involvement in educational, research, and professional activities. Members of underrepresented minority groups (American Indians, Alaska Natives, Asians, Blacks or African Americans, Hispanics or Latinos/Latinas, Native Hawaiians or other Pacific Islanders) are especially encouraged to apply. U.S. citizenship or permanent resident status is required.

Financial data The stipend is $50,000 per year. An additional stipend of $5,000 is available to fellows whose research includes the study of pain in the elderly.

Duration 2 years.

Additional information This program began in 2001 with funding from the John A. Hartford Foundation. In 2004, the Mayday Fund added support to scholars who focus on the study of pain in the elderly.

Number awarded Varies each year; recently, 12 of these scholarships were awarded.

Deadline January of each year.

[660]
BULLIVANT HOUSER BAILEY LAW STUDENT DIVERSITY FELLOWSHIP PROGRAM

Bullivant Houser Bailey PC
Attn: Recruitment and Diversity Manager
888 S.W. Fifth Avenue, Suite 300
Portland, OR 97204-2089
(503) 499-4558   Toll Free: (800) 654-8972
Fax: (503) 295-0915   E-mail: jill.valentine@bullivant.com
Web: www.bullivant.com/diversity

Summary To provide financial assistance and work experience to African American law students and others who come from a minority or disadvantaged background.

Eligibility This program is open to first-year law students who are members of a minority group (including any group underrepresented in the legal profession) and/or students coming from a disadvantaged educational or economic background. Applicants must have 1) a record of academic achievement and leadership in college and law school; 2) a willingness to complete a 12-week summer associateship at an office of the firm; and 3) a record of contributions to the community that promote diversity within society, the legal community, and/or law school.

Financial data The program provides a salaried associate position at an office of the firm during the summer following the first year of law school and a stipend of $7,500 for the second year.

Duration 1 year.

Number awarded 2 each year: 1 assigned to an associateship in the Sacramento office and 1 assigned to an associateship in the Portland office.

Deadline January of each year.

[661]
BUTLER RUBIN DIVERSITY SCHOLARSHIP

Butler Rubin Saltarelli & Boyd LLP
Attn: Diversity Partner
70 West Madison Street, Suite 1800
Chicago, IL 60602
(312) 242-4120   Fax: (312) 444-9843
E-mail: kborg@butlerrubin.com
Web: www.butlerrubin.com/web/br.nsf/diversity

Summary To provide financial assistance and summer work experience to African American and other minority law students who are interested in the area of business litigation.

Eligibility This program is open to law students of racial and ethnic backgrounds that will contribute to diversity in the legal profession. Applicants must be interested in the private practice of law in the area of business litigation and in a summer associateship in that field with Butler Rubin Saltarelli & Boyd in Chicago. Selection is based on academic performance and achievement, intention to remain in the Chicago area following graduation, and interpersonal and communication skills.

Financial data The stipend is $10,000 per year; funds are to be used for tuition and other expenses associated with law school. For the summer associateship, a stipend is paid.

Duration 1 year; may be renewed.

Additional information This program was established in 2006.

Number awarded 1 each year.

Deadline Deadline not specified.

[662]
C. CLYDE FERGUSON LAW SCHOLARSHIP

New Jersey Commission on Higher Education
Attn: Educational Opportunity Fund
20 West State Street, Fourth Floor
P.O. Box 542
Trenton, NJ 08625-0542
(609) 984-2709   Fax: (609) 292-7225
E-mail: nj_che@che.state.nj.us
Web: www.nj.gov

Summary To provide financial assistance to disadvantaged and minority students from New Jersey who want to study law in the state.

Eligibility This program is open to students who 1) fall within specified income guidelines (currently, less than $21,660 for a family of 1 rising to $74,020 for a family of 8); 2) minority or disadvantaged students with financial need; or 3) former or current recipients of a New Jersey Educational Opportunity Fund undergraduate or graduate grant, or who would have been eligible to receive the grant as an undergraduate. Applicants must have been New Jersey residents for at least 12 months before receiving the award and must plan to enroll full time in the Minority Student Program at law schools in New Jersey (Rutgers University School of Law at Newark, Rutgers University School of Law at Camden, or Seton Hall Law School).

Financial data Awards are based on financial need. In no case, however, can awards exceed the maximum amount of tuition, fees, room, and board charged at Rutgers University School of Law at Newark.

Duration 1 year; may be renewed.

Deadline Deadline not specified.

[663]
CALIFORNIA BAR FOUNDATION DIVERSITY SCHOLARSHIPS

State Bar of California
Attn: California Bar Foundation
180 Howard Street
San Francisco, CA 94105-1639
(415) 856-0780, ext. 302   Fax: (415) 856-0788
E-mail: jguillory@calbarfoundation.org
Web: www.calbarfoundation.org

Summary To provide financial assistance to law students from any state who are African Americans or members of other ethnic groups historically underrepresented in the legal profession and entering law school in California.

Eligibility This program to open to residents of any state who are entering their first year at a law school in California. Applicants must self-identify as being from a racial or ethnic group that historically has been underrepresented in the legal profession (Latino, African American, Asian and Pacific Islander, and Native American). They must be committed to making an impact in the community through leadership. Along with their application, they must submit a 500-word essay describing their commitment to serving the community and, if applicable, any significant obstacles or hurdles they have overcome to attend law school. Financial need is considered in the selection process.

Financial data Stipends for named awards are $7,500. Other stipends are $5,000 or $2,500.

Duration 1 year.

Additional information These scholarships were first awarded in 2008. Each year, the foundation grants awards named after sponsors that donate funding for the scholarships. Recipients are required to attend a reception in their honor in October of the year of their award and to submit a report on their progress at the end of that year.

Number awarded Varies each year; recently, the foundation awarded 28 of these scholarships: 20 named awards at $7,500, 4 awards at $5,000, and 4 awards at $2,500.

Deadline June of each year.

[664]
CALIFORNIA DIVERSITY FELLOWSHIPS IN ENVIRONMENTAL LAW

American Bar Association
Attn: Section of Environment, Energy, and Resources
321 North Clark Street
Chicago, IL 60654-7598
(312) 988-5602   Fax: (312) 988-5572
E-mail: jonusaid@staff.abanet.org
Web: www.abanet.org

Summary To provide funding to African American law students and those from other underrepresented or underserved groups who are interested in working on a summer project in environmental, energy, or resources law in California.

Eligibility This program is open to first- and second-year law students and third-year night students who are members of underrepresented and underserved groups, such as minority or low-income populations. Students may be resi-

dents of any state and attending school in any state; preference is given to residents of California and to students who are enrolled at law schools in California or who have a strong interest in the state. Applicants must be interested in working during the summer at a government agency or public interest organization on a project in California, with an emphasis on air quality issues in the Los Angeles basin and the Central Valley. Selection is based on interest in environmental issues, academic record, personal qualities, and leadership abilities.

Financial data The stipend is $5,000.

Duration 8 to 10 weeks during the summer.

Additional information This program is cosponsored by the State Bar of California's Environmental Law Section and the William and Flora Hewlett Foundation.

Number awarded Varies each year; recently, 13 of these fellowships were awarded.

Deadline April of each year.

[665]
CALIFORNIA PLANNING FOUNDATION OUTSTANDING DIVERSITY AWARD

American Planning Association-California Chapter
Attn: California Planning Foundation
c/o Paul Wack
P.O. Box 1086
Morro Bay, CA 93443-1086
(805) 756-6331   Fax: (805) 756-1340
E-mail: pwack@calpoly.edu
Web: www.californiaplanningfoundation.org

Summary To provide financial assistance to African Americans and other undergraduate and graduate students in accredited planning programs at California universities who will increase diversity in the profession.

Eligibility This program is open to students entering their final year for an undergraduate or master's degree in an accredited planning program at a university in California. Applicants must be students who will increase diversity in the planning profession. Selection is based on academic performance, professional promise, and financial need.

Financial data The stipend is $3,000. The award includes a 1-year student membership in the American Planning Association (APA) and payment of registration for the APA California Conference.

Duration 1 year.

Additional information The accredited planning programs are at 3 campuses of the California State University system (California State Polytechnic University at Pomona, California Polytechnic State University at San Luis Obispo, and San Jose State University), 3 campuses of the University of California (Berkeley, Irvine, and Los Angeles), and the University of Southern California.

Number awarded 1 each year.

Deadline March of each year.

[666]
CANFIT PROGRAM GRADUATE SCHOLARSHIPS

California Adolescent Nutrition and Fitness Program
Attn: Scholarship Program
2140 Shattuck Avenue, Suite 610
Berkeley, CA 94704
(510) 644-1533   Toll Free: (800) 200-3131
Fax: (510) 644-1535   E-mail: info@canfit.org
Web: canfit.org/scholarships

Summary To provide financial assistance to African American and other minority graduate students who are working on a degree in nutrition, physical education, or public health in California.

Eligibility This program is open to American Indians, Alaska Natives, African Americans, Asian Americans, Pacific Islanders, and Latinos/Hispanics from California who are enrolled in 1) an approved master's or doctoral program in nutrition, public health, or physical education in the state, or 2) a preprofessional practice program approved by the American Dietetic Association at an accredited university in the state. Applicants must have completed 12 to 15 units of graduate course work and have a cumulative GPA of 3.0 or higher. Along with their application, they must submit 1) documentation of financial need; 2) letters of recommendation from 2 individuals; 3) a 1-to 2-page letter describing their academic goals and involvement in community nutrition and/or physical education activities; and 4) an essay of 500 to 1,000 words on a topic related to healthy foods for youth from low-income communities of color.

Financial data A stipend is awarded (amount not specified).

Number awarded 1 or more each year.

Deadline March of each year.

[667]
CAREER DEVELOPMENT GRANTS

American Association of University Women
Attn: AAUW Educational Foundation
301 ACT Drive, Department 60
P.O. Box 4030
Iowa City, IA 52243-4030
(319) 337-1716, ext. 60   Fax: (319) 337-1204
E-mail: aauw@act.org
Web: www.aauw.org

Summary To provide financial assistance to African American and other women who are seeking career advancement, career change, or reentry into the workforce.

Eligibility This program is open to women who are U.S. citizens or permanent residents, have earned a bachelor's degree, received their most recent degree more than 4 years ago, and are making career changes, seeking to advance in current careers, or reentering the work force. Applicants must be interested in working toward a master's degree, second bachelor's or associate degree, professional degree (e.g., M.D., J.D.), certification program, or technical school certificate. They must be planning to undertake course work at an accredited 2- or 4-year college or university (or a technical school that is licensed, accredited, or approved by the U.S. Department of Education). Special consideration is given to women of color and women pursuing credentials in nontraditional fields. Support is not provided for prerequisite course work or for Ph.D. course work or dissertations. Selection is based on demonstrated commitment to education and equity for women and girls, reason for seeking higher education or technical training, degree to which study plan is consistent with career objectives, potential for success in chosen field, documentation of opportunities in chosen field, feasibility of study plans and proposed time schedule, validity of proposed budget and budget narrative (including sufficient outside support), and quality of written proposal.

Financial data Grants range from $2,000 to $12,000. Funds may be used for tuition, fees, books, supplies, local transportation, dependent child care, or purchase of a computer required for the study program.

Duration 1 year, beginning in July; nonrenewable.

Additional information The filing fee is $35.

Number awarded Varies each year; recently, 47 of these grants, with a value of $500,000, were awarded.

Deadline December of each year.

[668]
CARMEN E. TURNER SCHOLARSHIPS

Conference of Minority Transportation Officials
Attn: National Scholarship Program
818 18th Street, N.W., Suite 850
Washington, DC 20006
(202) 530-0551   Fax: (202) 530-0617
Web: www.comto.org/news-youth.php

Summary To provide financial assistance for college or graduate school to African American and other members of the Conference of Minority Transportation Officials (COMTO).

Eligibility This program is open to undergraduate and graduate students who have been members of COMTO for at least 1 year. Applicants must be working on a degree in a field related to transportation with a GPA of 2.5 or higher. Along with their application, they must submit a cover letter with a 500-word statement of career goals. Financial need is not considered in the selection process. U.S. citizenship is required.

Financial data The stipend is $3,500. Funds are paid directly to the recipient's college or university.

Duration 1 year.

Additional information COMTO was established in 1971 to promote, strengthen, and expand the roles of minorities in all aspects of transportation. Recipients are expected to attend the COMTO National Scholarship Luncheon.

Number awarded 2 each year.

Deadline April of each year.

[669]
CAROLE SIMPSON NABJ SCHOLARSHIP

National Association of Black Journalists
Attn: Program Coordinator
8701-A Adelphi Road
Adelphi, MD 20783-1716
(301) 445-7100, ext. 108   Toll Free: (866) 479-NABJ
Fax: (301) 445-7101   E-mail: nabj@nabj.org
Web: www.nabj.org

Summary To provide financial assistance to undergraduate or graduate student members of the National Association of Black Journalists (NABJ) who are majoring in broadcast journalism.

Eligibility This program is open to African American undergraduate or graduate students who are currently attending an accredited 4-year college or university. Applicants must be majoring in broadcast journalism and have a GPA of 2.5 or higher. They must be NABJ members. Along with their application, they must submit samples of their work, an official college transcript, 2 letters of recommendation, a resume, and a 500- to 800-word essay describing their accomplishments as a student journalist, their career goals, and their financial need.

Financial data The stipend is $2,500. Funds are paid directly to the recipient's college or university.

Duration 1 year; nonrenewable.

Number awarded 1 each year.

Deadline April of each year.

[670]
CARTER G. WOODSON INSTITUTE PREDOCTORAL RESIDENTIAL RESEARCH FELLOWSHIP

University of Virginia
Carter G. Woodson Institute for African-American and
 African Studies
Attn: Associate Director for Research
108 Minor Hall
P.O. Box 400162
Charlottesville, VA 22904-4162
Charlottesville, VA 22903
(804) 924-3109   Fax: (804) 924-8820
E-mail: woodson@virginia.edu
Web: artsandsciences.virginia.edu

Summary To provide funding to doctoral candidates interested in conducting research at the University of Virginia's Woodson Institute in those disciplines of the humanities and social sciences concerned with African American and African studies.

Eligibility This program is open to doctoral candidates who have completed all requirements for the Ph.D. except the dissertation prior to August of the fellowship year. There are no citizenship or residence requirements. Applicants must be working in a field of the humanities or social sciences that focuses on Africa and/or the African Diaspora. Along with their application, they must submit a description of a research project to be conducted during the fellowship period at the Woodson Institute. Selection is based on the significance of the proposed work, the qualifications of the applicant, familiarity with existing relevant research literature, the research design of the project, and the promise of completion within the award period.

Financial data The stipend is $20,000 per year. Health insurance is also provided.

Duration 2 years; nonrenewable.

Additional information Fellows must be in residence at the University of Virginia for the duration of the award period. They are expected to contribute to the intellectual life of the university.

Number awarded 4 each year.

Deadline November of each year.

[671]
CATHY L. BROCK MEMORIAL SCHOLARSHIP

Institute for Diversity in Health Management
Attn: Executive Assistant
One North Franklin Street, 30th Floor
Chicago, IL 60606
(312) 422-2630   Toll Free: (800) 233-0996
Fax: (312) 895-4511   E-mail: ejohnson@aha.org
Web: www.applicantsoft.com

Summary To provide financial assistance to African American and other minority graduate students in health care management, especially those focusing on financial operations.

Eligibility This program is open to members of ethnic minority groups who are accepted or enrolled in an accredited graduate program in health care administration. Applicants must have a GPA of 3.0 or higher. They must demonstrate commitment to a career in health care administration. Along with their application, they must submit a personal statement of 300 to 500 words on their interest in health care management and their career goals. Selection is based on academic achievement, leadership potential, financial need, community involvement, commitment to health care administration, and overall professional maturity. Preference is given to applicants studying financial operations. U.S. citizenship is required.

Financial data The stipend ranges from $500 to $1,000.

Duration 1 year.

Number awarded 1 or more each year, depending on the availability of funds.

Deadline December of each year.

[672]
CBC SPOUSES VISUAL ARTS SCHOLARSHIP

Congressional Black Caucus Foundation, Inc.
Attn: Director, Educational Programs
1720 Massachusetts Avenue, N.W.
Washington, DC 20036
(202) 263-2800   Toll Free: (800) 784-2577
Fax: (202) 775-0773   E-mail: info@cbcfinc.org
Web: www.cbcfinc.org/scholarships.html

Summary To provide financial assistance to Black Americans and other undergraduate and graduate students who are interested in studying the visual arts.

Eligibility This program is open to 1) minority and other graduating high school seniors planning to attend an accredited institution of higher education; and 2) currently-enrolled full-time undergraduate, graduate, and doctoral students in good academic standing with a GPA of 2.5 or higher. Applicants must be interested in preparing for a career in the visual arts. Along with their application, they must submit a CD of 5 original pieces of their artwork and a personal statement of 500 to 1,000 words on 1) their future goals, major field of study, and how that field of study will help them to achieve their future career goals; 2) involvement in school activities, community and public service, hobbies, and sports; 3) how receiving this award will affect their current and future plans; and 4) other experiences, skills, or qualifications. They must also be able to demonstrate financial need, leadership ability, and participation in community service activities.

Financial data The stipend is $3,000.

Duration 1 year.

Additional information This program was established in 2006.

Number awarded 5 each year.

Deadline April of each year.

[673]
CDC/PRC MINORITY FELLOWSHIPS

Association of Schools of Public Health
Attn: Senior Manager, Graduate Training Programs
1101 15th Street, N.W., Suite 910
Washington, DC 20005
(202) 296-1099   Fax: (202) 296-1252
E-mail: TrainingPrograms@asph.org
Web: www.asph.org

Summary To provide an opportunity for African American and other minority doctoral students to conduct research at Prevention Research Centers (PRCs) funded by the U.S. Centers for Disease Control and Prevention (CDC).

Eligibility This program is open to minority (African American/Black American, Hispanic/Latino, American Indian/Alaska Native, and Asian/Pacific Islander) students working on a doctoral degree at a school of public health with a CDC-funded PRC. Applicants must be proposing to conduct a research project that is related to the PRC activities and is endorsed by the PRC director. Along with their application, they must submit a personal statement (2 pages or less) on why they are interested in this fellowship, including specifics regarding their interest in the opportunity, benefits they expect to receive from the fellowship experience, how the experience will shape their future career plans, and how the proposed project will advance the field of public health prevention research. Selection is based on the personal statement (30 points), curriculum vitae and transcripts (20 points), and project proposal (50 points). U.S. citizenship or permanent resident status is required.

Financial data The stipend is $22,500 per year. Fellows are also reimbursed up to $3,000 per year for health-related expenses, project-related travel, tuition, journal subscriptions, and association dues.

Duration 2 years.

Number awarded Varies each year; recently, 11 of these fellowships were awarded.

Deadline March of each year.

[674]
CDM SCHOLARSHIP

National Forum for Black Public Administrators
Attn: Scholarship Program
777 North Capitol Street, N.E., Suite 807
Washington, DC 20002
(202) 408-9300, ext. 112   Fax: (202) 408-8558
E-mail: vreed@nfbpa.org
Web: www.nfbpa.org/i4a/pages/index.cfm?pageid=3630

Summary To provide financial assistance to African Americans working on a undergraduate or graduate degree in public administration or a related field.

Eligibility This program is open to African American undergraduate and graduate students preparing for a career in public service. Applicants must be working full time on a degree in public administration, political science, urban affairs, public policy, or a related field. They must have a GPA

of 3.0 or higher, excellent interpersonal and analytical abilities, and strong oral and written communication skills. Along with their application, they must submit a 3-page autobiographical essay that includes their academic and career goals and objectives. Although this is not a need-based program, first consideration is given to applicants who are not currently receiving other financial aid.

Financial data The stipend is $5,000.

Duration 1 year.

Additional information This program is sponsored by the consulting, engineering, construction, and operations firm CDM. Recipients are required to attend the sponsor's annual conference to receive their scholarship; limited hotel and air accommodations are arranged and provided.

Number awarded 1 each year.

Deadline February of each year.

[675]
CENIE JOMO WILLIAMS TUITION SCHOLARSHIP

National Association of Black Social Workers
Attn: Office of Student Affairs
2305 Martin Luther King Avenue, S.E.
Washington, DC 20020
(202) 678-4570   Fax: (202) 678-4572
E-mail: nabsw.Harambee@verizon.net
Web: www.nabsw.org/mserver/StudentAffairs.aspx

Summary To provide financial assistance for college or graduate school to members of the National Association of Black Social Workers (NABSW).

Eligibility This program is open to African American members of NABSW who are enrolled full time in an accredited social work or social welfare program and have a GPA of 2.5 or higher. Applicants must be able to demonstrate community service and a research interest in the Black community. Along with their application, they must submit an essay of 2 to 3 pages on their professional interests, future social work aspirations, previous social work experiences (volunteer and professional), honors and achievements (academic and community service), and research interests within the Black community (for master's and doctoral students). Financial need is considered in the selection process.

Financial data The stipend is $2,000. Funds are sent directly to the recipient's school.

Duration 1 year.

Number awarded 2 each year.

Deadline December of each year.

[676]
CENTER ON BUDGET AND POLICY PRIORITIES INTERNSHIPS

Center on Budget and Policy Priorities
Attn: Internship Coordinator
820 First Street, N.E., Suite 510
Washington, DC 20002
(202) 408-1080   Fax: (202) 408-1056
E-mail: internship@cbpp.org
Web: www.cbpp.org/jobs/index.cfm?fa=internships

Summary To provide work experience at the Center on Budget and Policy Priorities (CBPP) in Washington, D.C. to African Americans and other undergraduates, graduate students, and recent college graduates.

Eligibility This program is open to undergraduates, graduate students, and recent college graduates who are interested in public policy issues affecting low-income families and individuals. Applicants must be interested in working at CBPP in the following areas: media, federal legislation, health policy, housing policy, international budget project, Food Stamps, national budget and tax policy, outreach campaigns, state budget and tax policy, welfare reform, and income support. They should have research, fact-gathering, writing, analytic, and computer skills and a willingness to do administrative as well as substantive tasks. Women, international students, and minorities are encouraged to apply.

Financial data Hourly stipends are $8.50 for undergraduates, $9.50 for interns with a bachelor's degree, $10.50 for graduate students, $12.50 for interns with a master's or law degree, and $12.50 to $15.50 for doctoral students (depending on progress towards completion of degree requirements, relevant course work, and research).

Duration 1 semester; may be renewed.

Additional information The center specializes in research and analysis oriented toward practical policy decisions and produces analytic reports that are accessible to public officials at national, state, and local levels, to nonprofit organizations, and to the media.

Number awarded Varies each semester; recently, 5 interns were appointed for a fall semester.

Deadline February of each year for summer internships; June of each year for fall internships; October of each year for spring internships.

[677]
CENTRAL FLORIDA CHAPTER NBMBAA GRADUATE SCHOLARSHIP

National Black MBA Association-Central Florida Chapter
Attn: Scholarship Committee Chair
P.O. Box 692696
Orlando, FL 32869-2696
E-mail: scholarships@cflblackmba.org
Web: www.cflblackmba.org/30801.html

Summary To provide financial assistance to African American and other minority residents of any state who are working on a graduate degree in business at a university in Florida.

Eligibility This program is open to members of the following groups from any state: African American/Black, American Indian/Alaska Native, Asian American/Pacific Islander, or Hispanic/Latino. Applicants must be enrolled in a graduate business program at an AACSB-accredited college or university in Florida. They must have a GPA of 3.0 or higher. Along with their application, they must submit a 2-page essay on a topic that changes annually but relates to minorities and business. Selection is based on that essay, transcripts, a resume, and extracurricular activities.

Financial data Recently, stipends were $1,500.

Duration 1 year.

Number awarded 2 each year.

Deadline September of each year.

[678]
CHARLES HOUSTON BAR ASSOCIATION ANNUAL SCHOLARSHIP

Charles Houston Bar Association
P.O. Box 1474
Oakland, CA 94604
Toll Free: (866) 712-7974
Web: www.charleshoustonbar.org/lawstudents.html

Summary To provide financial assistance to law students who are members of the Charles Houston Bar Association (CHBA).

Eligibility This program is open to CHBA members who are enrolled in the second or third year of law school. Applicants must submit a 500-word essay on their professional plans for the future and how they will assist the African American community with their law degree.

Financial data The stipend is $1,000.

Duration 1 year.

Additional information The CHBA was established in 1955 by a group of African American lawyers in northern California.

Number awarded 1 or more each year.

Deadline November of each year.

[679]
CHARLES S. BROWN SCHOLARSHIP IN PHYSICS

National Society of Black Physicists
Attn: Scholarship Committee Chair
1100 North Glebe Road, Suite 1010
Arlington, VA 22201
(703) 536-4207   Fax: (703) 536-4203
E-mail: scholarship@nsbp.org
Web: www.nsbp.org/scholarships

Summary To provide financial assistance to African American students working on an undergraduate or graduate degree in physics.

Eligibility This program is open to African American students who are working on an undergraduate or graduate degree in physics. Applicants must submit an essay on their academic and career objectives, information on their participation in extracurricular activities, a description of any awards and honors they have received, and 3 letters of recommendation. Financial need is not considered.

Financial data A stipend is awarded (amount not specified).

Duration 1 year; nonrenewable.

Number awarded 1 each year.

Deadline January of each year.

[680]
CIGNA HEALTHCARE GRADUATE SCHOLARSHIPS

National Forum for Black Public Administrators
Attn: Scholarship Program
777 North Capitol Street, N.E., Suite 807
Washington, DC 20002
(202) 408-9300, ext. 112   Fax: (202) 408-8558
E-mail: vreed@nfbpa.org
Web: www.nfbpa.org/i4a/pages/index.cfm?pageid=3630

Summary To provide financial assistance to African Americans working on a graduate degree in public administration at an Historically Black College or University (HBCU).

Eligibility This program is open to African American graduate students preparing for a career in public administration. Applicants must be working on a degree in public administration, political science, urban affairs, public policy, or a related field at an HBCU. They must have a GPA of 3.0 or higher, excellent interpersonal and analytical abilities, and strong oral and written communication skills. Along with their application, they must submit a 3-page autobiographical essay that includes their academic and career goals and objectives. Although this is not a need-based program, first consideration is given to applicants who are not currently receiving other financial aid.

Financial data The stipend is $5,000.

Duration 1 year.

Additional information This program is sponsored by CIGNA Healthcare. Recipients are required to attend the sponsor's annual conference to receive their scholarship; limited hotel and air accommodations are arranged and provided.

Number awarded 2 each year.

Deadline February of each year.

[681]
CNA NSBE CORPORATE SCHOLARSHIP PROGRAM

National Society of Black Engineers
Attn: Programs Department
205 Daingerfield Road
Alexandria, VA 22314
(703) 549-2207   Fax: (703) 683-5312
E-mail: scholarships@nsbe.org
Web: www.nsbe.org

Summary To provide financial assistance to members of the National Society of Black Engineers (NSBE) who are working on a graduate degree in designated fields.

Eligibility This program is open to members of the society who are graduate students working on a degree in chemistry, economics, engineering, mathematics, physics, political science, statistics, or other scientific and professional fields. Applicants must have a GPA of 3.0 or higher. Along with their application, they must submit a 250-word essay describing how they will use their education to make a positive impact on the African American community and how this scholarship will advance their career goals and benefit CNA. U.S. citizenship is required.

Financial data The stipend is $4,500.

Duration 1 year.

Additional information This program is sponsored by the CNA Foundation.

Number awarded 1 each year.

Deadline January of each year.

[682]
COLLEGE SCHOLARSHIPS FOUNDATION MINORITY STUDENT SCHOLARSHIP

College Scholarships Foundation
5506 Red Robin Road
Raleigh, NC 27613
(919) 630-4895   Toll Free: (888) 501-9050
E-mail: info@collegescholarships.org
Web: www.collegescholarships.org

Summary To provide financial assistance to African Americans and other minority undergraduate and graduate students.

Eligibility This program is open to full-time undergraduate and graduate students who are Black, Hispanic, Native American, or Pacific Islander. Applicants must have a GPA of 3.0 or higher. Along with their application, they must submit a 300-word essay on how being a minority affected their pre-college education, how being a minority has positively affected their character, and where they see themselves in 10 years. U.S. citizenship is required.

Financial data The stipend is $1,000.

Duration 1 year.

Additional information This scholarship was first awarded in 2006. The sponsor was formerly known as the Daniel Kovach Scholarship Foundation.

Number awarded 1 each year.

Deadline December of each year.

[683]
COMMERCIAL AND FEDERAL LITIGATION SECTION MINORITY FELLOWSHIP

The New York Bar Foundation
One Elk Street
Albany, NY 12207
(518) 487-5651   Fax: (518) 487-5699
E-mail: foundation@tnybf.org
Web: www.tnybf.org/restrictedfunds.htm

Summary To provide an opportunity for African American and other minority residents of any state attending law school in New York to gain summer work experience in a litigation position in the public sector in the state.

Eligibility This program is open to minority students from any state who are enrolled in the first year at a law school in New York state. Applicants must have demonstrated an interest in commercial and federal litigation. They must be interested in working in a litigation position during the summer in the public sector in New York.

Financial data The stipend is $5,000.

Duration 10 weeks during the summer.

Additional information This program was established in 2007 by the Commercial and Federal Litigation Section of the New York State Bar Association. It is administered by The New York Bar Foundation.

Number awarded 1 each year.

Deadline January of each year.

[684]
COMMITTEE ON ETHNIC MINORITY RECRUITMENT SCHOLARSHIP

United Methodist Church-California-Pacific Annual
　Conference
Attn: Board of Ordained Ministry
1720 East Linfield Street
Glendora, CA 91740
(626) 335-6629　　　　　　　　　Fax: (626) 335-5750
E-mail: cathy.adminbom@gmail.com
Web: www.calpacordainedministry.org/523451

Summary To provide financial assistance to African Americans and other minorities in the California-Pacific Annual Conference of the United Methodist Church (UMC) who are attending a seminary in any state to qualify for ordination as an elder or deacon.

Eligibility This program is open to members of ethnic minority groups in the UMC California-Pacific Annual Conference who are enrolled at a seminary in any state approved by the UMC University Senate. Applicants must have been approved as certified candidates by their district committee and be seeking Probationary Deacon or Elder's Orders. They may apply for 1 or more types of assistance: tuition scholarships, grants for books and school supplies (including computers), or emergency living expense grants.

Financial data Tuition stipends are $1,000 per year; books and supplies grants range up to $1,000 per year; emergency living expense grants depend on need and the availability of funds.

Duration 1 year; may be renewed up to 2 additional years.

Additional information The California-Pacific Annual Conference includes churches in southern California, Hawaii, Guam, and Saipan.

Number awarded Varies each year.

Deadline August of each year for fall term; December of each year for spring term.

[685]
COMTO ROSA L. PARKS SCHOLARSHIPS

Conference of Minority Transportation Officials
Attn: National Scholarship Program
818 18th Street, N.W., Suite 850
Washington, DC 20006
(202) 530-0551　　　　　　　　　Fax: (202) 530-0617
Web: www.comto.org/news-youth.php

Summary To provide financial assistance for college to 1) children of African American and other members of the Conference of Minority Transportation Officials (COMTO) and 2) other students working on a bachelor's or master's degree in transportation.

Eligibility This program is open to 1) college-bound high school seniors whose parent has been a COMTO member for at least 1 year; 2) undergraduates who have completed at least 60 semester credit hours in a transportation discipline; and 3) students working on a master's degree in transportation who have completed at least 15 credits. Applicants must have a GPA of 3.0 or higher. Along with their application, they must submit a cover letter with a 500-word statement of career goals. Financial need is not considered in the selection process. U.S. citizenship is required.

Financial data The stipend is $4,500. Funds are paid directly to the recipient's college or university.

Duration 1 year.

Additional information COMTO was established in 1971 to promote, strengthen, and expand the roles of minorities in all aspects of transportation. Recipients are expected to attend the COMTO National Scholarship Luncheon.

Number awarded 2 each year.

Deadline April of each year.

[686]
CONGRESSIONAL BLACK CAUCUS SPOUSES EDUCATION SCHOLARSHIP

Congressional Black Caucus Foundation, Inc.
Attn: Director, Educational Programs
1720 Massachusetts Avenue, N.W.
Washington, DC 20036
(202) 263-2800　　　　　　Toll Free: (800) 784-2577
Fax: (202) 775-0773　　　　　E-mail: info@cbcfinc.org
Web: www.cbcfinc.org/scholarships.html

Summary To provide financial assistance to African American and other undergraduate and graduate students who reside in a Congressional district represented by an African American.

Eligibility This program is open to 1) African American and other graduating high school seniors planning to attend an accredited institution of higher education; and 2) currently-enrolled full-time undergraduate, graduate, and doctoral students in good academic standing with a GPA of 2.5 or higher. Applicants must reside or attend school in a Congressional district represented by a member of the Congressional Black Caucus. Along with their application, they must a personal statement of 500 to 1,000 words on 1) their future goals, major field of study, and how that field of study will help them to achieve their future career goals; 2) involvement in school activities, community and public service, hobbies, and sports; 3) how receiving this award will affect their current and future plans; and 4) other experiences, skills, or qualifications. They must also be able to demonstrate financial need, leadership ability, and participation in community service activities.

Financial data A stipend is awarded (amount not specified).

Duration 1 year.

Additional information The program was established in 1988.

Number awarded Varies each year.

Deadline May of each year.

[687]
CONNECTICUT COMMUNITY COLLEGE MINORITY FELLOWSHIP PROGRAM

Connecticut Community College System
Attn: System Officer for Diversity Awareness
61 Woodland Street
Hartford, CT 06105-9949
(860) 244-7606　　　　　　　　　Fax: (860) 566-6624
E-mail: karmstrong@commnet.edu
Web: www.commnet.edu/minority_fellowship.asp

Summary To provide financial assistance and work experience to graduate students in Connecticut, especially African Americans and other minorities, who are interested in preparing for a career in community college teaching or administration.

Eligibility This program is open to graduate students who have completed at least 6 credits of graduate work and have indicated an interest in a career in community colleges. Current employees of the Connecticut Community Colleges are also eligible. Applicants must be willing to commit to at least 1 year of employment in the Connecticut Community College System. Although all qualified graduate students are eligible, the program encourages applicants to register who strengthen the racial and cultural diversity of the minority fellow registry. That includes, in particular, making all possible efforts to recruit from historically underrepresented groups.

Financial data Non-employee fellows receive a stipend of $3,500 per semester. Fellows who are current employees are reassigned time from their responsibilities.

Duration 1 year; may be renewed.

Additional information Teaching fellows are expected to spend 6 hours per week in teaching-related activities under the supervision of the mentor; those activities may include assisting the mentor. Administrative fellows spend at least 6 hours per week in structured administrative activity. In addition, all fellows are expected to spend at least 3 hours per week in additional assigned activities, including (but not limited to) attendance at Minority Fellowship Program and campus orientation activities, attendance at relevant faculty and staff meetings, participation in other system and college meetings or professional development activities, and evaluation of the fellowship experience at the end of the academic year.

Number awarded Up to 13 each year: 1 at each of the 12 colleges in the system and 1 in the chancellor's office.

Deadline July of each year.

[688]
CONSORTIUM FOR GRADUATE STUDY IN MANAGEMENT FELLOWSHIPS

Consortium for Graduate Study in Management
5585 Pershing Avenue, Suite 240
St. Louis, MO 63112-1795
(314) 877-5500   Toll Free: (888) 658-6814
Fax: (314) 877-5505   E-mail: recruiting@cgsm.org
Web: www.cgsm.org

Summary To provide financial assistance and work experience to African Americans and other underrepresented minorities interested in preparing for a management career in business.

Eligibility This program is open to African Americans, Hispanic Americans (Chicanos, Cubans, Dominicans, and Puerto Ricans), and Native Americans who have graduated from college and are interested in preparing for a career in business. Other U.S. citizens and permanent residents who can demonstrate a commitment to the sponsor's mission of enhancing diversity in business education are also eligible. An undergraduate degree in business or economics is not required. Applicants must be planning to work on an M.B.A. degree at 1 of the consortium's 17 schools. Preference is given to applicants under 31 years of age.

Financial data The fellowship pays full tuition and required fees. Summer internships with the consortium's cooperative sponsors, providing paid practical experience, are also offered.

Duration Up to 4 semesters.

Additional information This program was established in 1966. The participating schools are Carnegie Mellon University, Cornell University, Dartmouth College, Emory University, Indiana University, University of Michigan, New York University, University of California at Berkeley, University of California at Los Angeles, University of North Carolina at Chapel Hill, University of Rochester, University of Southern California, University of Texas at Austin, University of Virginia, Washington University, University of Wisconsin at Madison, and Yale. Fellowships are tenable at member schools only. Application fees are $150 for students applying to 1 or 2 schools, $200 for 3 schools, $240 for 4 schools, $275 for 5 schools, or $300 for 6 schools.

Number awarded Varies each year; recently, more than 330 of these fellowships were awarded.

Deadline March of each year.

[689]
CONSTANGY, BROOKS & SMITH DIVERSITY SCHOLARS AWARD

Constangy, Brooks & Smith LLC
Attn: Chair, Diversity Council
200 West Forsyth Street, Suite 1700
Jacksonville, FL 32202-4317
(904) 356-8900   Fax: (904) 356-8200
E-mail: mzabijaka@constangy.com
Web: www.constangy.com/f-4.html

Summary To provide financial assistance to students (especially African American and other minority students) who are enrolled in law schools in selected states.

Eligibility This program is open to second-year students enrolled in accredited law schools located in 1 of 3 regions: South (Alabama, Florida, Georgia, Tennessee), Midwest/West Coast (California, Illinois, Missouri, Texas, Wisconsin), or East (Massachusetts, New Jersey, North Carolina, South Carolina, Virginia/Washington, D.C.). Applicants must submit a personal statement on why diversity is important to them personally and in the legal profession. They must have a GPA of 2.7 or higher. Selection is based on academic achievement, commitment to diversity, and personal achievement in overcoming obstacles.

Financial data The stipend is $3,000.

Duration 1 year.

Number awarded 3 each year: 1 in each region.

Deadline November of each year.

[690]
CORPORATE PARTNER SCHOLARSHIPS

National Association of Black Accountants
Attn: National Scholarship Program
7474 Greenway Center Drive, Suite 1120
Greenbelt, MD 20770
(301) 474-NABA, ext. 114   Fax: (301) 474-3114
E-mail: customerservice@nabainc.org
Web: www.nabainc.org

Summary To provide financial assistance to student members of the National Association of Black Accountants (NABA) who are working on an undergraduate or graduate degree in a field related to accounting.

Eligibility This program is open to NABA members who are enrolled full time as 1) an undergraduate freshman, sophomore, junior, or first-semester senior majoring in accounting, business, or finance at a 4-year college or university; or 2) a graduate student working on a master's degree in accounting. High school seniors are not eligible. Applicants must have a GPA of 3.5 or higher in their major and 3.3 or higher overall. Selection is based on grades, financial need, and a 500-word autobiography that discusses career objectives, leadership abilities, community activities, and involvement in NABA.

Financial data Stipends range from $1,000 to $10,000.

Duration 1 year.

Number awarded Varies each year.

Deadline January of each year.

[691]
CROWELL & MORING DIVERSITY IN THE LEGAL PROFESSION SCHOLARSHIP

Crowell & Moring LLP
Attn: Diversity in the Legal Profession Scholarship
1001 Pennsylvania Avenue, N.W.
Washington, DC 20004-2595
(202) 624-2500   Fax: (202) 628-5116
E-mail: scholarship@crowell.com
Web: www.crowell.com/Careers/DiversityScholarship.aspx

Summary To provide financial assistance to African American and minorities underrepresented in the legal profession who are attending law school in the District of Columbia.

Eligibility This program is open to underrepresented racial and ethnic minorities (American Indians/Alaskan Natives, Blacks/African Americans or Africans, Hispanics/Latinos, or Asians/Pacific Islanders) from any state currently working on a J.D. degree and enrolled in their second year at an accredited law school in the District of Columbia. Applicants must have overcome significant obstacles, disadvantages, or challenges in their pursuit of a legal education. Selection is based on academic performance, demonstrated leadership skills, relevant work experience, community service, special accomplishments and honors, and financial need. Finalists are interviewed.

Financial data Stipends are $10,000 or $7,500.

Duration 1 year; nonrenewable.

Number awarded 3 each year: 1 at $10,000 and 2 at $7,500.

Deadline December of each year.

[692]
CSLA LEADERSHIP FOR DIVERSITY SCHOLARSHIP

California School Library Association
Attn: Executive Director
950 Glenn Drive, Suite 150
Folsom, CA 95630
(916) 447-2684   Fax: (916) 447-2695
E-mail: info@csla.net
Web: www.csla.net/awa/scholarships.htm

Summary To provide financial assistance to African Americans and other students who reflect the diversity of California's population and are interested in earning a credential as a library media teacher in the state.

Eligibility This program is open to students who are members of a traditionally underrepresented group enrolled in a college or university library media teacher credential program in California. Applicants must intend to work as a library media teacher in a California school library media center for a minimum of 3 years. Along with their application, they must submit a 250-word statement on their school library media career interests and goals, why they should be considered, what they can contribute, their commitment to serving the needs of multicultural and multilingual students, and their financial situation.

Financial data The stipend is $1,500.

Duration 1 year.

Number awarded 1 each year.

Deadline April of each year.

[693]
CSPI PUBLIC INTEREST INTERNSHIP PROGRAM

Center for Science in the Public Interest
Attn: Internships
1875 Connecticut Avenue, N.W., Suite 300
Washington, DC 20009-5728
(202) 332-9110   Fax: (202) 265-4954
E-mail: hr@cspinet.org
Web: www.cspinet.org/about/jobs/200801042.html

Summary To provide summer work experience to minority and other students who are interested in working on health and nutritional issues at the Center for Science in the Public Interest (CSPI).

Eligibility This program is open to undergraduate, graduate, law, and medical students who are interested in working at the center, which is concerned with evaluating the effects of science and technology on society and promoting national policies responsive to consumers' interests. CSPI focuses primarily on health and nutritional issues, disclosing deceptive marketing practices, dangerous food additives or contaminants, and flawed science propagated by profits. Applicants must submit a cover letter indicating issues of interest, future plans, and dates of availability; a resume; writing samples; 2 letters of recommendation from instructors or employers; and an official transcript of courses and grades. Minorities, women, and persons with disabilities are especially encouraged to apply.

Financial data Undergraduate interns earn $8.25 per hour; graduate student interns earn $9.25 per hour.

Duration 10 weeks during the summer.

Number awarded A small number each year.

Deadline January of each year.

[694]
CULTURAL RESOURCES DIVERSITY INTERNSHIP PROGRAM

Student Conservation Association, Inc.
Attn: Diversity Internships
1800 North Kent Street, Suite 102
Arlington, VA 22209
(703) 524-2441   Fax: (703) 524-2451
E-mail: jchow@thesca.org
Web: www.thesca.org/partners/special-initiatives

Summary To provide summer work experience to African Americans, other ethnically diverse undergraduate and graduate students, and students with disabilities at facilities of the U.S. National Park Service (NPS).

Eligibility This program is open to currently-enrolled students at the sophomore or higher level. Applicants must be U.S. citizens or permanent residents with a GPA of 3.0 or higher. Although all students may apply, the program is designed to give ethnically diverse students and students with disabilities the opportunity to experience the diversity of careers in the federal sector. Applicants are assigned to a position within the NPS. Possible projects include editing publications, planning exhibits, participating in archaeological excavations, preparing research reports, cataloguing park and museum collections, providing interpretive programs on historical topics, developing community outreach, and writing lesson plans based on historical themes.

Financial data Interns receive a salary of $225 per week, basic medical insurance coverage, a housing stipend of up to $800 per month, a $100 uniform allowance, travel expenses up to $630, and eligibility for an Americorps Educational Award of $1,000.

Duration 10 weeks in the summer (beginning in June).

Additional information While participating in the internship, students engage in tri-weekly evening career and professional development events, ongoing career counseling, mentoring, and personal and career development services.

Number awarded Approximately 15 each year.

Deadline February of each year.

[695]
CUMMINS SCHOLARSHIPS

Society of Women Engineers
Attn: Scholarship Selection Committee
120 South LaSalle Street, Suite 1515
Chicago, IL 60603-3572
(312) 596-5223 Toll Free: (877) SWE-INFO
Fax: (312) 644-8557
E-mail: scholarshipapplication@swe.org
Web: societyofwomenengineers.swe.org

Summary To provide financial assistance to minority and other women working on an undergraduate or graduate degree in designated engineering specialties.

Eligibility This program is open to women who are sophomores, juniors, seniors, or graduate students at 4-year ABET-accredited colleges and universities. Applicants must be working on a degree in computer science or automotive, chemical, computer, electrical, industrial, manufacturing, materials, or mechanical engineering and have a GPA of 3.5 or higher. Preference is given to members of groups underrepresented in engineering or computer science. Selection is based on merit. U.S. citizenship is required.

Financial data The stipend is $1,000.

Duration 1 year.

Additional information This program is sponsored by Cummins, Inc.

Number awarded 2 each year.

Deadline February of each year.

[696]
CUTLER-DEKNIGHT NATIONAL GRADUATE FELLOWSHIP

American Association of Family and Consumer Sciences
Attn: Manager of Awards and Grants
400 North Columbus Street, Suite 202
Alexandria, VA 22314
(703) 706-4600 Toll Free: (800) 424-8080, ext. 119
Fax: (703) 706-4663 E-mail: staff@aafcs.org
Web: www.aafcs.org/Recognition/Fellowships.asp

Summary To provide financial assistance to African American graduate students who are working on a degree in family and consumer sciences, especially as related to communications or cooperative extension.

Eligibility This program is open to African American graduate students who are working full time on a degree in family and consumer sciences. Preference is given to qualified applicants who plan a career in family and consumer sciences communications or cooperative extension. Applicants must have completed at least 1 year as a student assistant, trainee, or intern. Selection is based on ability to pursue graduate study (10 points); experience in relation to preparation for study in proposed field (15 points); special recognition and awards (5 points); voluntary participation in professional and community organizations and activities (10 points); evidence (or degree) of professional commitment and leadership (10 points); significance of proposed study or research interests to families and individuals (15 points); professional goals (15 points); written communication (10 points); and recommendations (10 points). Special consideration is given to applicants who have been members of the American Association of Family and Consumer Sciences (AAFCS) for up to 2 years (2 points) or for 2 or more years (5 points) or who have AAFCS credentials in family and consumer sciences (5 points). U.S. citizenship or permanent residence status is required.

Financial data The award provides a stipend of $5,000 and financial support of up to $1,000 for 1 year of AAFCS membership and participation in its annual conference and exposition.

Duration 1 year.

Additional information The Virginia F. Cutler Fellowship in Consumer Studies was first awarded for the 1976-77 academic year. The Freda A. DeKnight National Fellowship was established in 1975 in memory of the late food and home service editor of *Ebony* magazine, a creator of the "Ebony Fashion Fair" (an annual charitable event presented in over 100 American cities). Those 2 programs have been combined to produce this fellowship.

Number awarded 1 each year.

Deadline January of each year.

[697]
D. AUGUSTUS STRAKER SCHOLARSHIP

D. Augustus Straker Bar Association
Attn: Foundation Board
19785 West 12 Mile Road, Suite 176
Southfield, MI 48076
E-mail: info@strakerlaw.org
Web: www.strakerlaw.org/index-2.html

Summary To provide financial assistance to African Americans and other minority students from any state who are enrolled at law schools in Michigan.

Eligibility This program is open to minority students from any state who are entering their second or third year at a certified law school program within the state of Michigan. Applicants must demonstrate scholarly dedication, involvement in school and community activities, and the ability to articulate a vision that indicates prospects for long-term success in the practice of law, especially as it relates to representing minority viewpoints within the system of jurisprudence.

Financial data The stipend is $2,500.

Duration 1 year.

Additional information The D. Augustus Straker Bar Association was founded in 1990 as a proactive organization for African American attorneys. It was named in honor of the first African American attorney to argue a case before the Michigan Supreme Court (in 1890).

Number awarded 2 each year.

Deadline April of each year.

[698]
DAN BRADLEY FELLOWSHIP PROGRAM

Legal Aid Association of California
c/o Public Interest Clearinghouse
433 California Street, Suite 815
San Francisco, CA 94104
(415) 834-0100, ext. 306   Fax: (415) 834-0202
E-mail: scopeland@pic.org
Web: www.calegaladvocates.org/search/item.339371aw

Summary To provide financial assistance to students from any state (particularly African Americans and other students of color) who are interested in a summer internship with legal services programs that are members of the Legal Aid Association of California (LAAC).

Eligibility This program is open to law students who have a strong interest in working to defend and expand the legal rights of the poor and the disadvantaged. Applicants must be interested in a summer internship with a legal aid services agency that is an LAAC member and that agrees to supervise the student on a major litigation or "impact" advocacy project. Applications must be submitted jointly by the student and a representative of an eligible legal services program. Students must include a personal statement describing how their experience relates to the goals of the program, the nature of the work they will perform if awarded a fellowship, their current career objectives, and how they envision their project playing a role in moving toward their objectives. People of color and students from low-income or working class backgrounds are particularly encouraged to apply. At least 1 fellowship is reserved for a student who works in a rural program or on a rural issue.

Financial data The stipend is up to $3,500. The LAAC contributes $3,000 and the program selected to receive the fellow is expected to provide up to an additional $500.

Duration 10 weeks during the summer.

Additional information This program began in 1991.

Number awarded Varies each year; recently, 3 of these fellowships were awarded.

Deadline April of each year.

[699]
DAVID HILLIARD EATON SCHOLARSHIP

Unitarian Universalist Association
Attn: Ministerial Credentialing Office
25 Beacon Street
Boston, MA 02108-2800
(617) 948-6403   Fax: (617) 742-2875
E-mail: mco@uua.org
Web: www.uua.org

Summary To provide financial assistance to African American and other minority women preparing for the Unitarian Universalist (UU) ministry.

Eligibility This program is open to women from historically marginalized groups who are currently enrolled or planning to enroll full or at least half time in a UU ministerial training program with aspirant or candidate status. Applicants must be citizens of the United States or Canada. Priority is given first to those who have demonstrated outstanding ministerial ability and secondarily to students with the greatest financial need (especially persons of color).

Financial data The stipend ranges from $1,000 to $11,000 per year.

Duration 1 year.

Number awarded Varies each year; recently, 2 of these scholarships were awarded.

Deadline April of each year.

[700]
DAVID SANKEY MINORITY SCHOLARSHIP IN METEOROLOGY

National Weather Association
Attn: Executive Director
228 West Millbrook Road
Raleigh, NC 27609-4304
(919) 845-1546   Fax: (919) 845-2956
E-mail: exdir@nwas.org
Web: www.nwas.org

Summary To provide financial assistance to African Americans and other minorities working on an undergraduate or graduate degree in meteorology.

Eligibility This program is open to members of minority groups who are either entering their sophomore or higher year of undergraduate study or enrolled as graduate students. Applicants must be working on a degree in meteorology. Along with their application, they must submit a 1-page statement explaining why they are applying for this scholarship. Selection is based on that statement, academic achievement, and 2 letters of recommendation.

Financial data The stipend is $1,000.

Duration 1 year.

Additional information This program was established in 2002.

Number awarded 1 each year.

Deadline April of each year.

[701]
DAVIS WRIGHT TREMAINE 1L DIVERSITY SCHOLARSHIP PROGRAM

Davis Wright Tremaine LLP
Attn: Diversity Scholarship Program
1201 Third Avenue, Suite 2200
Seattle, WA 98101-3045
(206) 622-3150   Toll Free: (877) 398-8416
Fax: (206) 757-7700   E-mail: carolyuly@dwt.com
Web: www.dwt.com

Summary To provide financial assistance and summer work experience to African American and other law students of color.

Eligibility This program is open to first-year law students of color and others of diverse backgrounds. Applicants must have a record of academic achievement as an undergraduate and in the first year of law school that demonstrates promise for a successful career in law, a commitment to civic involvement that promotes diversity and will continue after entering the legal profession, and a willingness to become an associate in the sponsor's Seattle or Portland office during the summer between their first and second year of law school. They must submit a current resume, a complete undergraduate transcript, grades from the first semester of law school, a 1-page essay describing their eligibility for and interest in the scholarship, a legal writing sample, and 2 or 3 references. Although demonstrated need may be taken into account, applicants need not disclose their financial circumstances.

Financial data The award consists of a $7,500 stipend for second-year tuition and expenses and a paid summer clerkship.

Duration 1 academic year and summer.

Number awarded 2 each year: 1 in the Seattle office and 1 in the Portland office.

Deadline January of each year.

[702]
DCBMBAA CHAPTER GRADUATE SCHOLARSHIP PROGRAM

National Black MBA Association-Washington, DC Chapter
Attn: Scholarship Program
P.O. Box 14042
Washington, DC 20044
(202) 628-0138   E-mail: info@dcbmbaa.org
Web: www.dcbmbaa.org/scholarships.htm

Summary To provide financial assistance to African American and other minority students from Washington, D.C., Maryland, or Virginia who are working on a graduate degree in business or management at a school in any state.

Eligibility This program is open to minority students who are enrolled full or part time in a graduate business or management program in any state and working on an M.B.A. degree. Applicants must currently reside in Washington, D.C., Maryland, or Virginia, either permanently or as a student. Along with their application, they must submit an essay (from 2 to 5 pages) on 1 of 2 assigned topics that change annually but focus on minorities in business. Selection is based on the essay, transcripts, and a list of extracurricular activities and awards.

Financial data The stipend is $2,500 or $1,500.

Duration 1 year.

Additional information This program began in 2000.

Number awarded Varies each year; recently, 2 of these scholarships were awarded: 1 at $2,500 and 1 at $1,500.

Deadline June of each year.

[703]
DELL THURMOND WOODARD FELLOWSHIP

The Fund for American Studies
Attn: Fellowships
1706 New Hampshire Avenue, N.W.
Washington, DC 20009
(202) 986-0384   Toll Free: (800) 741-6964
Fax: (202) 986-8930   E-mail: jtilley@tfas.org
Web: www.tfas.org/Page.aspx?pid=1511

Summary To provide an opportunity for upper-division and graduate students (especially African Americans and others with an interest in diversity and ethics issues) to learn about high technology public policy issues during a summer internship in Washington, D.C.

Eligibility This program is open to juniors, seniors, and graduate students who have an interest and background in issues regarding diversity and ethics and are currently enrolled at a 4-year college or university in the United States. Applicants must be interested in working in the government relations office of a high technology company or association in Washington while they also attend weekly seminar lunches hosted by the program's sponsors. They must have an interest in public policy and the high technology industry; a background in computer science or other high technology fields is helpful but not required. International students are eligible. Selection is based on evidence of a strong interest in a career in high technology public policy, civic mindedness and participation in community activities or organizations, academic achievements, and recommendations.

Financial data Fellows receive a grant of $5,000.

Duration 8 weeks during the summer.

Additional information This program was established in 2007 with support from the Congressional Black Caucus Foundation (CBCF), the Congressional Hispanic Caucus Institute (CHCI), and the Asian Pacific Institute for Congressional Studies (APAICS). Those 3 sponsors select the fellow on a rotational basis.

Number awarded 1 each year.

Deadline February of each year.

[704]
DELPHI NSBE CORPORATE SCHOLARSHIPS

National Society of Black Engineers
Attn: Programs Department
205 Daingerfield Road
Alexandria, VA 22314
(703) 549-2207   Fax: (703) 683-5312
E-mail: scholarships@nsbe.org
Web: www.nsbe.org

Summary To provide financial assistance to undergraduate and graduate student members of the National Society of Black Engineers (NSBE) who are working on a degree in designated fields of engineering.

Eligibility This program is open to members of the society who are enrolled as college sophomores, juniors, or seniors or as full-time graduate students, Applicants must be working on a degree in electrical, industrial, or mechanical engineering. They must have a GPA of 3.0 or higher and a demonstrated interest in employment (summer or full time) with Delphi. Along with their application, they must submit a 250-word essay on how they, Delphi, and their community will benefit from this support.

Financial data The stipend is $2,500.

Duration 1 year.

Additional information This program is sponsored by Delphi Corporation.

Number awarded 1 each year.

Deadline January of each year.

[705]
DELTA SIGMA THETA SORORITY GENERAL SCHOLARSHIPS

Delta Sigma Theta Sorority, Inc.
Attn: Scholarship and Standards Committee Chair
1707 New Hampshire Avenue, N.W.
Washington, DC 20009
(202) 986-2400   Fax: (202) 986-2513
E-mail: dstemail@deltasigmatheta.org
Web: www.deltasigmatheta.org

Summary To provide financial assistance to members of Delta Sigma Theta who are working on an undergraduate or graduate degree in any field.

Eligibility This program is open to active, dues-paying members of Delta Sigma Theta who are currently enrolled in college or graduate school. Applicants must submit an essay on their major goals and educational objectives, including realistic steps they foresee as necessary for the fulfillment of their plans. Financial need is considered in the selection process.

Financial data The stipends range from $1,000 to $2,000. The funds may be used to cover tuition, fees, and living expenses.

Duration 1 year; may be renewed for 1 additional year.

Additional information This sponsor is a traditionally African American social sorority. The application fee is $20.

Deadline April of each year.

[706]
DEPARTMENT OF HOMELAND SECURITY SUMMER FACULTY AND STUDENT RESEARCH TEAM PROGRAM

Oak Ridge Institute for Science and Education
Attn: Science and Engineering Education
P.O. Box 117
Oak Ridge, TN 37831-0117
(865) 574-1447   Fax: (865) 241-5219
E-mail: Patti.Obenour@orau.gov
Web: see.orau.org

Summary To provide an opportunity for teams of students and faculty from Historically Black Colleges and Universities (HBCUs) and other minority serving educational institutions to conduct summer research in areas of interest to the Department of Homeland Security (DHS).

Eligibility This program is open to teams of up to 2 students (undergraduate and/or graduate) and 1 faculty from Historically Black Colleges and Universities (HBCUs), Hispanic Serving Institutions (HSIs), Tribal Colleges and Univer-

sities (TCUs), Alaska Native Serving Institutions (ANSIs), and Native Hawaiian Serving Institutions (NHSIs). Applicants must be interested in conducting research at designated DHS Centers of Excellence in science, technology, engineering, or mathematics related to homeland security (HS-STEM), including explosives detection, mitigation, and response; social, behavioral, and economic sciences; risk and decision sciences; human factors aspects of technology; chemical threats and countermeasures; biological threats and countermeasures; community, commerce, and infrastructure resilience; food and agricultural security; transportation security; border security; immigration studies; maritime and port security; infrastructure protection; natural disasters and related geophysical studies; emergency preparedness and response; communications and interoperability; or advanced data analysis and visualization. Faculty must have a full-time appointment at an eligible institution and have received a Ph.D. in an HS-STEM discipline no more than 7 years previously; at least 2 years of full-time research and/or teaching experience is preferred. Students must have a GPA of 3.0 or higher and be enrolled full time. Undergraduates must be entering their junior or senior year. U.S. citizenship is required. Selection is based on relevance and intrinsic merit of the research (40%), faculty applicant qualifications (30%), academic benefit to the faculty applicant and his/her institution (10%), and student applicant qualifications (20%).

Financial data Stipends are $1,200 per week for faculty, $600 per week for graduate students, and $500 per week for undergraduates. Faculty members who live more than 50 miles from their assigned site may receive a relocation allowance of $1,500 and travel expenses up to an additional $500. Limited travel expenses for 1 round trip are reimbursed for undergraduate and graduate students living more than 50 miles from their assigned site.

Duration 12 weeks during the summer.

Additional information This program is funded by DHS and administered by Oak Ridge Institute for Science and Education (ORISE). Recently, the available DHS Centers of Excellence were the Center for Advancing Microbial Risk Assessment (led by Michigan State University and Drexel University); the Center for Risk and Economic Analysis of Terrorism Events (led by University of Southern California); the National Center for Food Protection and Defense (led by University of Minnesota); the Center of Excellence for Foreign Animal and Zoonotic Disease Defense (led by Texas A&M University and Kansas State University); the National Center for the Study of Preparedness and Catastrophic Event Response (led by Johns Hopkins University); the National Consortium for the Study of Terrorism and Responses to Terrorism (led by University of Maryland); the Center of Excellence for Awareness and Location of Explosives-Related Threats (led by Northeastern University and University of Rhode Island); the National Center for Border Security and Immigration (led by the University of Arizona and the University of Texas at El Paso); the Center for Maritime, Island and Remote and Extreme Environment Security (led by the University of Hawaii and Stevens Institute of Technology); the Center for Natural Disasters, Coastal Infrastructure, and Emergency Management (led by the University of North Carolina at Chapel Hill and Jackson State University); the National Transportation Security Center of Excellence (consisting of 7 institutions); and the Center of Excellence in Command, Control, and Interoperability (led by Purdue University and Rutgers University).

Number awarded Approximately 12 teams are selected each year.

Deadline January of each year.

[707]
DEPARTMENT OF STATE STUDENT INTERN PROGRAM

Department of State
Attn: HR/REE
2401 E Street, N.W., Suite 518 H
Washington, DC 20522-0108
(202) 261-8888   Toll Free: (800) JOB-OVERSEAS
Fax: (301) 562-8968   E-mail: Careers@state.gov
Web: www.careers.state.gov/students/programs

Summary To provide a work/study opportunity to undergraduate and graduate students (especially African Americans, other minorities, and women) who are interested in foreign service.

Eligibility This program is open to full- and part-time continuing college and university juniors, seniors, and graduate students. Applications are encouraged from students with a broad range of majors, such as business or public administration, social work, economics, information management, journalism, and the biological, engineering, and physical sciences, as well as those majors more traditionally identified with international affairs. U.S. citizenship is required. The State Department particularly encourages eligible women and minority students with an interest in foreign affairs to apply.

Financial data Most internships are unpaid. A few paid internships are granted to applicants who can demonstrate financial need. If they qualify for a paid internship, they are placed at the GS-4 step 5 level (currently with an annual rate of $27,786). Interns placed abroad may also receive housing, medical insurance, a travel allowance, and a dependents' allowance.

Duration Paid internships are available only for 10 weeks during the summer. Unpaid internships are available for 1 semester or quarter during the academic year, or for 10 weeks during the summer.

Additional information About half of all internships are in Washington, D.C., or occasionally in other large cities in the United States. The remaining internships are at embassies and consulates abroad. Depending upon the needs of the department, interns are assigned junior-level professional duties, which may include research, preparing reports, drafting replies to correspondence, working in computer science, analyzing international issues, financial management, intelligence, security, or assisting in cases related to domestic and international law. Interns must agree to return to their schooling immediately upon completion of their internship.

Number awarded Approximately 800 internships are offered each year, but only about 5% of those are paid positions.

Deadline February of each year for fall internships; June of each year for spring internships; October of each year for summer internships.

[708]
DEPARTMENT OF THE INTERIOR DIVERSITY INTERN PROGRAM

Department of the Interior
Attn: Office of Educational Partnerships
1849 C Street, N.W., MS 5221 MIB
Washington, DC 20240
(202) 208-6403   Toll Free: (888) 447-4392
Fax: (202) 208-3620   TDD: (202) 208-5069
E-mail: ed_partners@ios.doi.gov
Web: www.doi.gov/hrm/dipfact.html

Summary To provide work experience to 1) African American and other minority college and graduate students and 2) students with disabilities at federal agencies involved with natural and cultural resources.

Eligibility This program is open to currently-enrolled students at the sophomore or higher level at Historically Black Colleges and Universities (HBCUs), Hispanic-Serving Institutions (HSIs), Tribal Colleges and Universities (TCUs), and some other major institutions. Applicants must be U.S. citizens or permanent residents with a GPA of 3.0 or higher. Although all students may apply, the program is designed to give ethnically diverse students and students with disabilities the opportunity to experience the diversity of careers in the federal sector. Applicants are assigned to a position within the U.S. Department of the Interior (DOI). Possible placements include archaeology and anthropology; wildlife and fisheries biology; business administration, accounting, and finance; civil and environmental engineering; computer science, especially GIS applications; human resources; mining and petroleum engineering; communications and public relations; web site and database design; environmental and realty law; geology, hydrology, and geography; Native American studies; interpretation and environmental education; natural resource and range management; public policy and administration; and surveying and mapping.

Financial data The weekly stipend is $420 for sophomores and juniors, $450 for seniors, or $520 for law and graduate students. Other benefits include a pre-term orientation, transportation to the orientation and the work site, worker's compensation, and accident insurance.

Duration 10 weeks in the summer (beginning in June) or 15 weeks in the fall (beginning in September) or spring (beginning in January).

Additional information This program, which began in 1994, is administered through 5 nonprofit organizations: Hispanic Association of Colleges and Universities, Minority Access, Inc., Student Conservation Association, and National Association for Equal Opportunity in Higher Education. While participating in the internship, students engage in tri-weekly evening career and professional development events, ongoing career counseling, mentoring, and personal and career development services.

Number awarded Varies each year; since the program began, more than 700 interns have participated.

Deadline February of each year for summer; June of each year for fall; November of each year for spring.

[709]
DETROIT CHAPTER NBMBAA GRADUATE SCHOLARSHIP

National Black MBA Association-Detroit Chapter
Attn: Scholarship Awards
P.O. Box 02398
Detroit, MI 48202
(313) 237-0089   Fax: (313) 237-0093
Web: www.nbmbaa.org

Summary To provide financial assistance to African American and other minority graduate students from any state working on a graduate degree in business at a college or university in the Detroit area of Michigan.

Eligibility This program is open to African American and other minority residents of any state enrolled as full-time students at a college or university in the Detroit area. Applicants must be working on an graduate degree in business or management. Along with their application, they must submit a 2-page essay on their choice of 2 topics that change annually but relate to African Americans and business. Selection is based on that essay, transcripts, and extracurricular activities.

Financial data The stipend is $2,000.

Duration 1 year.

Number awarded 1 each year.

Deadline April of each year.

[710]
DICKSTEIN SHAPIRO DIVERSITY SCHOLARSHIP

Dickstein Shapiro LLP
Attn: Director of Professional Development and Attorney Recruiting
1825 Eye Street, N.W.
Washington, DC 20006-5403
(202) 420-4880   Fax: (202) 420-2201
E-mail: careers@docksteinshapiro.com
Web: www.docksteinshapiro.com/careers/diversity

Summary To provide financial assistance and summer work experience at Dickstein Shapiro in Washington, D.C. or New York City to African American and other diverse law students from any state.

Eligibility This program is open to second-year diverse law students, including 1) members of the lesbian, gay, bisexual, and transgender (LGBT) community; 2) members of minority ethnic and racial groups (Blacks, Hispanics and Latinos, Asians, American Indians and Native Alaskans, and Native Hawaiians and Pacific Islanders); and 3) students with disabilities. Applicants must be interested in a summer associateship with Dickstein Shapiro in Washington, D.C. or New York City. Selection is based on academic and professional experience as well as the extent to which they reflect the core values of the firm: excellence, loyalty, respect, initiative, and integrity.

Financial data The stipend is $25,000, including $15,000 upon completion of the summer associate program and $10,000 upon acceptance of a full-time offer of employment following graduation.

Duration The associateship takes place during the summer following the second year of law school and the stipend covers the third year of law school.

Additional information This program was established in 2006.

Number awarded 1 or more each year.

Deadline September of each year.

[711]
DIETETIC INTERNSHIP SCHOLARSHIPS

American Dietetic Association
Attn: Commission on Accreditation for Dietetics Education
120 South Riverside Plaza, Suite 2000
Chicago, IL 60606-6995
(312) 899-0040   Toll Free: (800) 877-1600, ext. 5400
Fax: (312) 899-4817   E-mail: education@eatright.org
Web: www.eatright.org/CADE/content.aspx?id=7934

Summary To provide financial assistance to student members of the American Dietetic Association (ADA), especially African Americans and other underrepresented minorities who have applied for a dietetic internship.

Eligibility This program is open to student members who have applied for a CADE-accredited dietetic internship. Applicants must be participating in the computer-matching process, be U.S. citizens or permanent residents, and show promise of being a valuable, contributing member of the profession. Some scholarships require membership in a specific dietetic practice group, residency in a specific state, or underrepresented minority group status. The same application form can be used for all categories. Students who are currently completing the internship component of a combined graduate/dietetic internship should apply for the American Dietetic Association's Graduate Scholarship.

Financial data Stipends range from $500 to $3,000; most are for $1,000.

Duration 1 year.

Number awarded Varies each year, depending upon the funds available; recently, the sponsoring organization awarded 222 scholarships for all its programs.

Deadline February of each year.

[712]
DINSMORE & SHOHL LLP DIVERSITY SCHOLARSHIP PROGRAM

Dinsmore & Shohl LLP
Attn: Manager of Legal Recruiting
255 East Fifth Street, Suite 1900
Cincinnati, OH 45202
(513) 977-8488   Fax: (513) 977-8141
E-mail: dinsmore.legalrecruiting@dinslaw.com
Web: www.dinslaw.com/careers/diversityscholarship

Summary To provide financial assistance and summer work experience to African American and other law students from groups traditionally underrepresented in the legal profession.

Eligibility This program is open to first- and second-year law students who are members of groups traditionally underrepresented in the legal profession. Applicants must have a demonstrated record of academic or professional achievement and leadership qualities. They must also be interested in a summer associateship with Dinsmore & Shohl LLP. Along with their application, they must submit a 500-word personal statement explaining their interest in the scholarship program and how diversity has impacted their life.

Financial data The program provides an academic scholarship of $10,000 and a paid associateship at the firm.

Duration The academic scholarship is for 1 year. The summer associateship is for 12 weeks.

Additional information Associateships are available at firm offices in Charleston (West Virginia), Cincinnati (Ohio), Columbus (Ohio), Lexington (Kentucky), or Louisville (Kentucky). The program includes 1 associateship in which the student spends 6 weeks as a clerk in the legal department of the Procter & Gamble Company's worldwide headquarters in Cincinnati and 6 weeks at Dinsmore & Shohl's Cincinnati office. All associates are assigned to an attorney with the firm who serves as a mentor.

Number awarded Varies each year.

Deadline September of each year for second-year students; December of each year for first-year students.

[713]
DISSERTATION FELLOWSHIPS IN EAST EUROPEAN STUDIES

American Council of Learned Societies
Attn: Office of Fellowships and Grants
633 Third Avenue
New York, NY 10017-6795
(212) 697-1505   Fax: (212) 949-8058
E-mail: fellowships@acls.org
Web: www.acls.org/grants/Default.aspx?id=532

Summary To provide funding to doctoral candidates (particularly African Americans, other minorities, and women) who are interested in conducting dissertation research in the social sciences and humanities relating to eastern Europe.

Eligibility This program is open to U.S. citizens or permanent residents who are working on a dissertation in the humanities or social sciences as related to eastern Europe, including Albania, Bosnia and Herzegovina, Bulgaria, Croatia, Czech Republic, Estonia, Hungary, Latvia, Lithuania, Former Yugoslav Republic of Macedonia, Kosovo, Montenegro, Poland, Romania, Serbia, Slovakia, and Slovenia. Applicants may be proposing projects comparing more than 1 country of eastern Europe or relating eastern European societies to those of other parts of the world. They may be seeking support for research fellowships (for use in eastern Europe to conduct fieldwork or archival investigations) or writing fellowships (for use in the United States, after all research is complete, to write the dissertation). Selection is based on the scholarly potential of the applicant, the quality and scholarly importance of the proposed work, and its importance to the development of scholarship on eastern Europe. Applications are particularly invited from women and members of minority groups.

Financial data The maximum stipend is $18,000. Recipients' home universities are required (consistent with their policies and regulations) to provide or to waive normal academic year tuition payments or to provide alternative cost-sharing support.

Duration 1 year. Students may apply for 1-year research and writing fellowships in sequence, but they may not apply for a second year of funding in either category.

Additional information This program is sponsored jointly by the American Council of Learned Societies, (ACLS) and the Social Science Research Council, funded by the U.S. Department of State under the Research and Training for Eastern Europe and the Independent States of the Former Soviet Union Act of 1983 (Title VIII) but administered by ACLS.

Number awarded Varies each year; recently, 8 of these fellowships were awarded.

Deadline November of each year.

[714]
DISSERTATION FELLOWSHIPS OF THE FORD FOUNDATION DIVERSITY FELLOWSHIP PROGRAM

National Research Council
Attn: Fellowships Office, Keck 576
500 Fifth Street, N.W.
Washington, DC 20001
(202) 334-2872   Fax: (202) 334-3419
E-mail: infofell@nas.edu
Web: www.nationalacademies.org

Summary To provide funding for dissertation research to African American and other graduate students whose success will increase the racial and ethnic diversity of U.S. colleges and universities.

Eligibility This program is open to citizens and nationals of the United States who are Ph.D. or Sc.D. degree candidates committed to a career in teaching and research at the college or university level. Applicants must be completing a degree in fields of the arts, sciences, humanities, and social sciences, but not for most practice-oriented areas, terminal master's degrees, other doctoral degrees (e.g., Ed.D., D.F.A., Psy.D.), professional degrees (e.g., medicine, law, public health), or joint degrees (e.g., M.D./Ph.D., J.D./Ph.D., M.F.A./Ph.D). The following are considered as positive factors in the selection process: evidence of superior academic achievement; promise of continuing achievement as scholars and teachers; membership in a group whose underrepresentation in the American professoriate has been severe and longstanding, including Black/African Americans, Puerto Ricans, Mexican Americans/Chicanos/Chicanas, Native American Indians, Alaska Natives (Eskimos, Aleuts, and other indigenous people of Alaska), and Native Pacific Islanders (Hawaiians, Micronesians, or Polynesians); capacity to respond in pedagogically productive ways to the learning needs of students from diverse backgrounds; sustained personal engagement with communities that are underrepresented in the academy and an ability to bring this asset to learning, teaching, and scholarship at the college and university level; and likelihood of using the diversity of human experience as an educational resource in teaching and scholarship.

Financial data The stipend is $21,000 per year; stipend payments are made through fellowship institutions.

Duration 9 to 12 months.

Additional information The competition for this program is conducted by the National Research Council on behalf of the Ford Foundation. Fellows may not accept remuneration from another fellowship or similar external award while supported by this program; however, supplementation from institutional funds, educational benefits from the Department of Veterans Affairs, or educational incentive funds may be received concurrently with Ford Foundation support. Dissertation fellows are required to submit an interim progress report 6 months after the start of the fellowship and a final report at the end of the 12 month tenure.

Number awarded   Approximately 35 each year.

Deadline   November of each year.

[715]
DISSERTATION FELLOWSHIPS OF THE MINORITY SCHOLAR-IN-RESIDENCE PROGRAM

Consortium for Faculty Diversity at Liberal Arts Colleges
c/o DePauw University
Academic Affairs Office
305 Harrison Hall
7 East Larabee Street
Greencastle, IN 46135
(765) 658-6595   E-mail: jgriswold@depauw.edu
Web: www.depauw.edu

Summary   To provide an opportunity for African Americans and other minority students to work on their dissertation while in residence at selected liberal arts colleges.

Eligibility   This program is open to African American, Asian American, Hispanic American, and Native American doctoral candidates who have completed all the requirements for the Ph.D. or M.F.A. except the dissertation. Applicants must be interested in a residency at a member institution of the Consortium for Faculty Diversity at Liberal Arts Colleges during which they will complete their dissertation. They must be U.S. citizens or permanent residents.

Financial data   Dissertation fellows receive a stipend based on the average salary paid to instructors at the participating college. Modest funds are made available to finance the fellow's proposed research, subject to the usual institutional procedures.

Duration   1 year.

Additional information   The following schools are participating in the program: Agnes Scott College, Bard College at Simon's Rock, Bowdoin College, Bryn Mawr College, Carleton College, Centre College, College of Wooster, Colorado College, Denison University, DePauw University, Dickinson College, Gettysburg College, Goucher College, Grinnell College, Hamilton College, Harvey Mudd College, Haverford College, Hobart and William Smith Colleges, Kalamazoo College, Lafayette College, Lawrence University, Luther College, Macalester College, Mount Holyoke College, Muhlenberg College, New College of Florida, Oberlin College, Pomona College, Reed College, Rhodes College, University of Richmond, Scripps College, St. Olaf College, Sewanee: The University of the South, Skidmore College, Smith College, Southwestern University, Swarthmore College, Trinity College, Vassar College, Wellesley College, Whitman College, and Willamette University. Fellows are expected to teach at least 1 course, participate in departmental seminars, and interact with students.

Number awarded   Varies each year.

Deadline   October of each year.

[716]
DISSERTATION PROPOSAL DEVELOPMENT FELLOWSHIP PROGRAM

Social Science Research Council
Attn: DPDF Program
One Pierrepont Plaza, 15th Floor
Brooklyn, NY 11201
(212) 377-2700   Fax: (212) 377-2727
E-mail: dpdf@ssrc.org
Web: www.ssrc.org/fellowships/dpdf-fellowship

Summary   To provide an opportunity for doctoral students in the social sciences and humanities (especially African Americans, other minorities, and women) to formulate their dissertation proposals and conduct predissertation research.

Eligibility   This program is open to full-time graduate students in the second or third year of a doctoral program who have not yet had their dissertation proposals accepted by their thesis directors and their home institutions. Each year, the program selects 6 subdisciplinary and interdisciplinary fields within the social sciences and humanities, and students apply to participate in 1 of those fields. They must be able to attend a workshop in the spring to prepare to undertake predissertation research, spend the summer conducting that research, and then attend another workshop in the fall to synthesize their summer research and draft proposals for dissertation funding. Workshop participants are selected on the basis of the originality and appropriateness of their dissertation topic, the preparation of the student, and the quality of the summer predissertation research plan. Minorities and women are particularly encouraged to apply.

Financial data   For all fellows, expenses to attend the workshops (airfare, hotel, meals, ground transport) are paid. Those fellows who are selected for summer predissertation research receive $5,000 grants.

Duration   The program extends over 1 calendar year.

Additional information   Funding for this program is provided by the Andrew W. Mellon Foundation. Recently, the designated research fields were: new approaches to religion and modernity; discrimination studies; interdisciplinary approaches to the study of contentious politics; multiculturalism, immigration, and identity in western Europe and the United States; spaces of inquiry; and virtual worlds.

Number awarded   Each research field accepts 10 to 12 graduate students.

Deadline   January of each year.

[717]
DISSERTATION YEAR VISITING DIVERSITY FELLOWSHIPS FOR ADVANCED GRADUATE STUDENTS

Northeast Consortium for Faculty Diversity
Attn: JoAnn Moody
13345 Benchley Road
San Diego, CA 92130-1247
E-mail: joann.moody@earthlink.net
Web: www.diversityoncampus.com/id15.html

Summary   To provide an opportunity for African American and other doctoral candidates from underrepresented minority groups to complete their dissertation while in residence at participating colleges and universities in the Northeast.

Eligibility This program is open to members of underrepresented minority groups who are at the dissertation writing stage of their doctoral program in any field. Applicants may be working at a university anywhere in the country, but they must be interested in completing their dissertation at a college or university in the Northeast. They must be able to demonstrate that they can complete the dissertation while at the host campus. There is no application form; interested students must submit a curriculum vitae, a statement of scholarship and teaching goals, 3 letters of recommendation (including 1 from the dissertation advisor at their home campus), a copy of the dissertation prospectus, and a graduate school transcript. U.S. citizenship is required.

Financial data The stipend ranges from $25,000 to $33,000. The host campus will provide computer and library privileges, office space, and health insurance.

Duration 12 months.

Additional information This program began in 2001. Recently, the host campuses were Northeastern University, Colgate University, Allegheny College, and the University of Rochester. Although the scholars have no formal teaching assignment, they are expected to present their work-in-progress at 2 or 3 campus-wide or department-wide forums during the year and to teach or co-teach a course.

Number awarded Varies each year. Each participating college or university hosts 1 or more dissertation scholars.

Deadline February of each year.

[718]
DISTRICT OF COLUMBIA-ELI DIVERSITY FELLOWSHIPS IN ENVIRONMENTAL LAW

American Bar Association
Attn: Section of Environment, Energy, and Resources
321 North Clark Street
Chicago, IL 60654-7598
(312) 988-5602   Fax: (312) 988-5572
E-mail: jonusaid@staff.abanet.org
Web: www.abanet.org

Summary To provide funding to African American and other law students from traditionally underrepresented groups who are interested in working on a summer project at the Environmental Law Institute (ELI) in Washington, D.C.

Eligibility This program is open to first- and second-year law students and third-year night students who come from minority or other disadvantaged households. Students may be residents of any state and attending school in any state; preference is given to residents of the District of Columbia and to students who are enrolled at law schools in the District or who have a strong interest in the District. Applicants must be interested in a summer internship at ELI, where they work on projects involving domestic and international environmental law. Subject areas include wetlands and watershed policy, sustainable land use, biodiversity, environmental enforcement, long-term management of hazardous sites, public participation, and international environmental policy. Selection is based on research and writing skills, academic performance, and communication skills.

Financial data The stipend is $5,000.

Duration 8 to 10 weeks during the summer.

Additional information This program is cosponsored by ELI. Additional support is provided by Pfizer Inc. and Beveridge & Diamond PC.

Number awarded 2 each year.

Deadline November of each year.

[719]
DIVERSIFIED INVESTMENT ADVISORS LEADERS IN HEALTHCARE SCHOLARSHIP

Institute for Diversity in Health Management
Attn: Executive Assistant
One North Franklin Street, 30th Floor
Chicago, IL 60606
(312) 422-2630   Toll Free: (800) 233-0996
Fax: (312) 895-4511   E-mail: ejohnson@aha.org
Web: www.applicantsoft.com

Summary To provide financial assistance to African Americans and other minority graduate students in health services management.

Eligibility This program is open to members of ethnic minority groups who are accepted or enrolled in a graduate program in health care administration. Applicants must have a GPA of 3.0 or higher. They must demonstrate commitment to a career in health care administration. Along with their application, they must submit a personal statement of 300 to 500 words on their interest in health care management and their career goals. Selection is based on academic achievement, leadership potential, financial need, community involvement, commitment to health care administration, and overall professional maturity. U.S. citizenship is required.

Financial data The stipend is $5,000.

Duration 1 year.

Additional information This program was established in 2007 by Diversified Investment Advisors.

Number awarded 2 each year.

Deadline December of each year.

[720]
DIVERSITY COMMITTEE SCHOLARSHIP

American Society of Safety Engineers
Attn: ASSE Foundation
1800 East Oakton Street
Des Plaines, IL 60018
(847) 768-3435   Fax: (847) 768-3434
E-mail: agabanski@asse.org
Web: www.asse.org

Summary To provide financial assistance to upper-division and graduate student members of the American Society of Safety Engineers (ASSE) who are African American or come from other diverse groups.

Eligibility This program is open to ASSE student members who are working on an undergraduate or graduate degree in occupational safety, health, and environment or a closely-related field (e.g., industrial or environmental engineering, environmental science, industrial hygiene, occupational health nursing). Applicants must be full-time students who have completed at least 60 semester hours with a GPA of 3.0 or higher as undergraduates or at least 9 semester hours with a GPA of 3.5 or higher as graduate students. Along with their application, they must submit 2 essays of 300 words or less: 1) why they are seeking a degree in occupational safety and health or a closely-related field, a brief description of their current activities, and how those relate to their career goals and objectives; and 2) why they should be awarded this scholarship (including career goals and financial need). A goal of this program is to support individuals regardless of race, ethnicity, gender, religion, personal beliefs, age, sexual orientation, physical challenges, geographic location, university, or specific area of study. U.S. citizenship is not required.

Financial data   The stipend is $1,000 per year.

Duration   1 year; recipients may reapply.

Number awarded   1 each year.

Deadline   November of each year.

[721]
DOCTORAL DISSERTATION IMPROVEMENT GRANTS IN THE DIRECTORATE FOR BIOLOGICAL SCIENCES

National Science Foundation
Directorate for Biological Sciences
Attn: Division of Environmental Biology
4201 Wilson Boulevard
Arlington, VA 22230
(703) 292-8480   TDD: (800) 281-8749
E-mail: ddig-deb@nsf.gov
Web: www.nsf.gov/funding/pgm_summ.jsp?pims_id=5234

Summary   To provide partial support to students (especially African Americans, other minorities, and students with disabilities) for dissertation research in selected areas supported by the National Science Foundation (NSF) Directorate for Biological Sciences (DBS).

Eligibility   Applications may be submitted through regular university channels by dissertation advisers on behalf of graduate students who have advanced to candidacy and have begun or are about to begin dissertation research. Students must be enrolled at U.S. institutions but need not be U.S. citizens. Proposals should focus on the ecology, ecosystems, systematics, or population biology programs in the DBS Division of Environmental Biology, or the animal behavior or ecological and evolutionary physiology programs in the DBS Division of Integrative Organismal Systems. The program encourages applications from underrepresented minorities and persons with disabilities.

Financial data   Grants range up to $15,000; funds may be used for travel to specialized facilities or field research locations, specialized research equipment, purchase of supplies and services not otherwise available, fees for computerized or other forms of data, and rental of environmental chambers or other research facilities. Funding is not provided for stipends, tuition, textbooks, journals, allowances for dependents, travel to scientific meetings, publication costs, dissertation preparation or reproduction, or indirect costs.

Duration   Normally 2 years.

Number awarded   100 to 120 each year; approximately $1,600,000 is available for this program each year.

Deadline   November of each year.

[722]
DOCTORAL FELLOWSHIPS IN ARCHIVAL STUDIES

UCLA Center for Information as Evidence
c/o Department of Information Studies
GSEIS Building 208A
P.O. Box 951520
Los Angeles, CA 90095-1520
(310) 825-7310   Fax: (310) 206-4460
E-mail: aeri@gseis.ucla.edu
Web: aeri.gseis.ucla.edu/fellowships.htm

Summary   To provide financial assistance to students (especially African American and other minority students) who are entering a doctoral program in archival studies at designated universities.

Eligibility   This program is open to students entering a doctoral program in archival studies at the University of California at Los Angeles, University of Michigan, University of Pittsburgh, University of North Carolina at Chapel Hill, Simmons College, University of Maryland, University of Texas at Austin, or University of Wisconsin at Madison. Applicants are not required to have received a master's degree in archival studies, library and information studies, or a related field, but they must be able to exhibit evidence of the ability to excel as a scholar and educator in the field. Selection is based on commitment to archival studies education, potential to make a strong scholarly contribution to the field of archival studies, and commitment to diversity within archival studies education and scholarship. Applications are particularly encouraged from students of American Indian/Alaska Native, Asian, Black/African American, Hispanic/Latino, or Native Hawaiian/other Pacific Islander heritage. U.S. citizenship or permanent resident status is required.

Financial data   The program provides payment of full tuition and a stipend of $20,000 per year.

Duration   2 years; the partner universities provide full tuition and stipends to their fellows for 2 additional years of study.

Additional information   These fellowships were first awarded in 2010. Funding for the program is provided by a grant from the Laura Bush 21st Century Librarian Program of the Institute of Museum and Library Services.

Number awarded   At least 2 each year.

Deadline   January of each year.

[723]
DOCTORAL FELLOWSHIPS IN LAW AND SOCIAL SCIENCE

American Bar Foundation
Attn: Administrative Assistant for Academic Affairs and
   Research Administration
750 North Lake Shore Drive
Chicago, IL 60611-4403
(312) 988-6548   Fax: (312) 988-6579
E-mail: alynch@abfn.org
Web: www.americanbarfoundation.org

Summary   To provide research funding to scholars (especially African Americans and other minorities) who are completing or have completed doctoral degrees in fields related to law, the legal profession, and legal institutions.

Eligibility This program is open to Ph.D. candidates in the social sciences who have completed all doctoral requirements except the dissertation. Applicants who have completed the dissertation are also eligible. Doctoral and proposed research must be in the general area of sociolegal studies or in social scientific approaches to law, the legal profession, or legal institutions and legal processes. Applications must include 1) a dissertation abstract or proposal with an outline of the substance and methods of the research; 2) 2 letters of recommendation; and 3) a curriculum vitae. Minority candidates are especially encouraged to apply.

Financial data The stipend is $27,000. Fellows may request up to $1,500 to reimburse expenses associated with research, travel to meet with advisers, or travel to conferences at which papers are presented. Relocation expenses of up to $2,500 may be reimbursed on application.

Duration 12 months, beginning in September.

Additional information Fellows are offered access to the computing and word processing facilities of the American Bar Foundation and the libraries of Northwestern University and the University of Chicago. This program was established in 1996. Fellowships must be held in residence at the American Bar Foundation. Appointments to the fellowship are full time; fellows are not permitted to undertake other work.

Number awarded 1 or more each year.

Deadline December of each year.

[724]
DOLORES NYHUS GRADUATE FELLOWSHIP

California Dietetic Association
Attn: CDA Foundation
7740 Manchester Avenue, Suite 102
Playa del Rey, CA 90293-8499
(310) 822-0177   Fax: (310) 823-0264
E-mail: patsmith@dietitian.org
Web: www.dietitian.org/cdaf_scholarships.htm

Summary To provide financial assistance to members (especially African Americans or other minorities and members with disabilities) of the American Dietetic Association (ADA) who live in California and are interested in working on a graduate degree in dietetics or a related field at a school in any state.

Eligibility This program is open to California residents who are ADA members and have a bachelor's degree with 3 to 5 years of professional experience. Applicants must be a registered dietitian (R.D.), be a registered dietetic technician (D.T.R.), or have a credential earned at least 6 months previously. They must be enrolled in or admitted to a graduate school in any state in the areas of public health, gerontology, or a community-related program with the intention of practicing in the field of dietetics. Along with their application, they must submit a letter of application that includes a discussion of their career goals. Selection is based on that letter (15%), academic ability (25%), work or volunteer experience (15%), letters of recommendation (15%), extracurricular activities (5%), and financial need (25%). Applications are especially encouraged from ethnic minorities, men, and people with physical disabilities.

Financial data The stipend is normally $1,000.

Duration 1 year.

Number awarded 1 each year.

Deadline February of each year.

[725]
DONALD W. BANNER DIVERSITY SCHOLARSHIP

Banner & Witcoff, Ltd.
Attn: Christopher Hummel
1100 13th Street, N.W., Suite 1200
Washington, DC 20005-4051
(202) 824-3000   Fax: (202) 824-3001
E-mail: chummel@bannerwitcoff.com
Web: www.bannerwitcoff.com

Summary To provide financial assistance to African Americans and other law students who come from groups historically underrepresented in intellectual property law.

Eligibility This program is open to students enrolled in the first or second year of a J.D. program at an ABA-accredited law school in the United States. Applicants must come from a group historically underrepresented in intellectual property law; that underrepresentation may be the result of race, sex, ethnicity, sexual orientation, or disability. Selection is based on academic merit, commitment to the pursuit of a career in intellectual property law, written communication skills, oral communication skills (determined through an interview), leadership qualities, and community involvement.

Financial data The stipend is $5,000 per year.

Duration 1 year (the second or third year of law school); students who accept and successfully complete the firm's summer associate program may receive an additional $5,000 for a subsequent semester of law school.

Number awarded 2 each year.

Deadline October of each year.

[726]
DOROTHY ATKINSON LEGAL EDUCATION SCHOLARSHIP

National Association of Bench and Bar Spouses, Inc.
Attn: NABBS, Inc. Foundation
c/o Maris DesChamps Cannon
203 Rose Creek Court
Columbia, SC 29229-0243
(803) 360-1054
Web: www.nabbsinc.org/NABBS_Foundation_7UN4.html

Summary To provide financial assistance to African American law students.

Eligibility This program is open to students enrolled full time in a legal education program at an ABA-accredited law school. Applicants must have a GPA of 2.0 or higher and be able to demonstrate financial need. They must be sponsored by a local chapter of the National Association of Bench and Bar Spouses (NABBS), an organization with historic roots in the African American legal community.

Financial data A stipend is awarded (amount not specified).

Duration 1 year; may be renewed if the recipient maintains a GPA of 2.0 or higher and continues to demonstrate financial need.

Additional information NABBS was founded in 1951 as the National Barristers' Wives, affiliated with the National Bar Association for African American attorneys. In 1987, it adopted its current name, and in 1994 it organized the NABBS, Inc. Foundation.

Number awarded 1 or more each year.

Deadline July of each year.

[727]
DOROTHY E. GENERAL SCHOLARSHIP

Seattle Foundation
Attn: African American Scholarship Program
1200 Fifth Avenue, Suite 1300
Seattle, WA 98101-3151
(206) 622-2294   Fax: (206) 622-7673
E-mail: scholarships@seattlefoundation.org
Web: www.seattlefoundation.org

Summary To provide financial assistance to African Americans from any state working on an undergraduate or graduate degree in a field related to health care.

Eligibility This program is open to African American undergraduate and graduate students who are preparing for a career in a health care profession, including public health, medicine, nursing, or dentistry; pre-professional school students are also eligible. Applicants must be able to demonstrate financial need, academic competence, and leadership of African American students. They may be residents of any state attending school in any state. Along with their application, they must submit a 2-page essay describing their future aspirations, including their career goals and how their study of health care will help them achieve those goals and contribute to the African American community.

Financial data The stipend is $1,000 per year. Payments are made directly to the recipient's educational institution.

Duration 1 year; may be renewed.

Number awarded 1 or more each year.

Deadline February of each year.

[728]
DORSEY & WHITNEY DIVERSITY FELLOWSHIPS

Dorsey & Whitney LLP
Attn: Recruiting Manager
50 South Sixth Street, Suite 1500
Minneapolis, MN 55402-1498
(612) 340-2600   Toll Free: (800) 759-4929
Fax: (612) 340-2868 E-mail: forsmark.claire@dorsey.com
Web: www.dorsey.com/diversity_fellowship_12111

Summary To provide financial assistance for law school to African Americans and other students from diverse backgrounds who are interested in working during the summer at offices of the sponsoring law firm.

Eligibility This program is open to first-year students at ABA-accredited law schools who have accepted a summer associate position at an office of the sponsor in Denver, Minneapolis, or Seattle. Applicants must be able to demonstrate academic achievement and a commitment to promoting diversity in the legal community. Along with their application, they must submit a personal statement on the ways in which they have promoted and will continue to promote diversity in the legal community, what diversity means to them, and why they are interested in the sponsoring law firm.

Financial data Fellows receive a stipend of $7,500 for the second year of law school and, if they complete a summer associate position in the following summer, another stipend of

$7,500 for the third year of law school. If they join the firm following graduation, they receive an additional $5,000.

Duration 1 year; may be renewed for 1 additional year.

Additional information This program was established in 2006.

Number awarded 1 or more each year.

Deadline January of each year.

[729]
DR. DORRI PHIPPS FELLOWSHIPS

Alpha Kappa Alpha Sorority, Inc.
Attn: Educational Advancement Foundation
5656 South Stony Island Avenue
Chicago, IL 60637
(773) 947-0026   Toll Free: (800) 653-6528
Fax: (773) 947-0277   E-mail: akaeaf@akaeaf.net
Web: www.akaeaf.org/fellowships_endowments.htm

Summary To provide financial assistance to students (especially African American women) working on a degree in medicine or conducting research related to lupus.

Eligibility This program is open to students currently enrolled in a medical or related program in any state. Applicants must be working on a degree in medicine or conducting research related to lupus. Along with their application, they must submit 1) a list of honors, awards, and scholarships received; 2) a list of organizations in which they have memberships, especially minority organizations; 3) a description of the project or research on which they are currently working, of (if they are not involved in a project or research) the aspects of their field that interest them; and 4) a statement of their personal and career goals, including how this scholarship will enhance their ability to attain those goals. The sponsor is a traditionally African American women's sorority.

Financial data A stipend is awarded (amount not specified).

Duration 1 year.

Number awarded 1 each even-numbered year.

Deadline April of each even-numbered year.

[730]
DR. JOYCE BECKETT SCHOLARSHIP

National Association of Black Social Workers
Attn: Office of Student Affairs
2305 Martin Luther King Avenue, S.E.
Washington, DC 20020
(202) 678-4570   Fax: (202) 678-4572
E-mail: nabsw.Harambee@verizon.net
Web: www.nabsw.org/mserver/StudentAffairs.aspx

Summary To provide financial assistance to members of the National Association of Black Social Workers (NABSW) who are working on a graduate degree.

Eligibility This program is open to African American members of NABSW working full time on a graduate degree at an accredited U.S. social work or social welfare program with a GPA of 2.5 or higher. Applicants must be able to demonstrate community service and a research interest in the Black community. Along with their application, they must submit an essay of 2 to 3 pages on their professional interests, future social work aspirations, previous social work experiences (volunteer and professional), honors and achievements (academic and community service), and research interests within the Black community. Financial need is considered in the selection process.

Financial data The stipend is $1,000. Funds are sent directly to the recipient's school.

Duration 1 year.

Number awarded 1 each year.

Deadline December of each year.

[731]
DR. LENDON N. PRIDGEN GRADUATE FELLOWSHIP AWARD

National Organization for the Professional Advancement of Black Chemists and Chemical Engineers
Attn: Awards Committee Chair
P.O. Box 77040
Washington, DC 20013
Toll Free: (800) 776-1419   Fax: (202) 667-1705
E-mail: nobccheawards@gmail.com
Web: www.nobcche.org

Summary To provide funding to African American doctoral students interested in conducting research in synthetic organic chemistry.

Eligibility This program is open to African American candidates in the third or fourth year of a Ph.D. program for synthetic organic chemistry. Applicants must submit 3 letters of recommendation, a resume, official transcripts for undergraduate and graduate study, a description of their proposed research, and a statement of their career objective. U.S. citizenship is required.

Financial data The grant is $25,000.

Duration 1 year.

Additional information This program is sponsored by GlaxoSmithKline.

Number awarded 1 each year.

Deadline November of each year.

[732]
DRI LAW STUDENT DIVERSITY SCHOLARSHIP

DRI-The Voice of the Defense Bar
Attn: Deputy Executive Director
55 West Monroe Street, Suite 2000
Chicago, IL 60603
(312) 795-1101   Fax: (312) 795-0747
E-mail: dri@dri.org
Web: www.dri.org/open/About.aspx

Summary To provide financial assistance to African Americans, other minorities, and women law students.

Eligibility This program is open to students entering their second or third year of law school who are African American, Hispanic, Asian, Pan Asian, Native American, or female. Applicants must submit an essay, up to 1,000 words, on a topic that changes annually but relates to the work of defense attorneys. Selection is based on that essay, demonstrated academic excellence, service to the profession, service to the community, and service to the cause of diversity. Students affiliated with the American Association for Justice as members, student members, or employees are not eligible. Finalists are invited to participate in personal interviews.

Financial data The stipend is $10,000.

Duration 1 year.

Additional information This program was established in 2004.

Number awarded 2 each year.

Deadline May of each year.

[733]
DWIGHT DAVID EISENHOWER HISTORICALLY BLACK COLLEGES AND UNIVERSITIES TRANSPORTATION FELLOWSHIP PROGRAM

Department of Transportation
Federal Highway Administration
Attn: Office of PCD, HPC-32
4600 North Fairfax Drive, Suite 800
Arlington, VA 22203-1553
(703) 235-0538   Toll Free: (877) 558-6873
Fax: (703) 235-0593   E-mail: transportationedu@dot.gov
Web: www.fhwa.dot.gov/ugp/index.htm

Summary To provide financial assistance to undergraduate and graduate students working on a degree in a transportation-related field at an Historically Black College or University (HBCU).

Eligibility This program is open to students working on a bachelor's, master's, or doctoral degree at a federally-designated 4-year HBCU. Applicants must be working on a degree in a transportation-related field (i.e., engineering, accounting, business, architecture, environmental sciences). They must be U.S. citizens or have an I-20 (foreign student) or I-551 (permanent resident) identification card. Undergraduates must be entering at least their junior year and have a GPA of 3.0 or higher. Graduate students must have a GPA of at least 3.25. Selection is based on their proposed plan of study, academic achievement (based on class standing, GPA, and transcripts), transportation work experience, and letters of recommendation.

Financial data Fellows receive payment of full tuition and fees (to a maximum of $10,000) and a monthly stipend of $1,450 for undergraduates, $1,700 for master's students, or $2,000 for doctoral students. They are also provided with a 1-time allowance of up to $1,500 to attend the annual Transportation Research Board (TRB) meeting.

Duration 1 year.

Additional information This program is administered by the participating HBCUs.

Number awarded Varies each year.

Deadline January of each year.

[734]
EARL G. GRAVES SCHOLARSHIP

National Association for the Advancement of Colored People
Attn: Education Department
4805 Mt. Hope Drive
Baltimore, MD 21215-3297
(410) 580-5760   Toll Free: (877) NAACP-98
E-mail: youth@naacpnet.org
Web: www.naacp.org/pages/naacp-scholarships

Summary To provide financial assistance to African American and other upper-division and graduate students majoring in business.

Eligibility This program is open to full-time juniors, seniors, and graduate students working on a degree in business.

Applicants must be currently in good academic standing, making satisfactory progress toward an undergraduate or graduate degree, and in the top 20% of their class. Along with their application, they must submit a 1-page essay on their interest in their major and a career, their life's ambition, what they hope to accomplish in their lifetime, and what position they hope to attain. Financial need is not considered in the selection process.

Financial data The stipend is $5,000.

Duration 1 year.

Number awarded Varies each year; recently, 12 of these scholarships were awarded.

Deadline March of each year.

[735]
EARL WARREN LEGAL TRAINING PROGRAM

NAACP Legal Defense and Educational Fund
Attn: Director of Scholarship Programs
99 Hudson Street, Suite 1600
New York, NY 10013-2897
(212) 965-2265   Fax: (212) 219-1595
E-mail: scholarships@naacpldf.org
Web: www.naacpldf.org/scholarships

Summary To provide financial assistance to students, especially African Americans, who are entering law school.

Eligibility This program is open to students entering their first year at an accredited law school; it was originally established to enable African American law students to attend the newly desegregated colleges, public universities, and law schools of the South. Applicants must be dedicated to earning a law degree so they can protect and defend civil rights and liberties. Selection is based on academic achievement, leadership, commitment to public service (through volunteer or other activities), and financial need.

Financial data Stipends range from $3,000 to $5,000 per year.

Duration 1 year; may be renewed for up to 2 additional years if satisfactory academic performance is maintained.

Additional information This program was established in 1972. Recipients must attend law school on a full-time basis and must graduate within the normally prescribed time of 3 years.

Number awarded 15 to 20 each year.

Deadline April of each year.

[736]
EARTH AND SPACE SCIENCE FELLOWSHIP PROGRAM

National Aeronautics and Space Administration
Attn: Science Mission Directorate
NASA Headquarters
300 E Street, S.W., Suite 200
Washington, DC 20546-0001
(202) 358-0734   E-mail: hq-nessf-Space@nasa.gov
Web: science.nasa.gov/researchers/sara/student-programs

Summary To provide financial assistance to graduate students (especially African Americans and other students of color) who are working on degree in earth and space system sciences.

Eligibility This program is open to students accepted or enrolled in a full-time M.Sc. and/or Ph.D. program at accred-

ited U.S. universities. Applicants must be interested in conducting interdisciplinary research relevant to the 4 science divisions of the Science Mission Directorate of the U.S. National Aeronautics and Space Administration (NASA): earth science (climate variability and change, atmospheric composition, carbon cycle and ecosystems, water and energy cycle, weather and earth surface and interior), heliophysics (the scientific analysis of phenomena or the variable, magnetic Sun, its effects on the Earth and the other planets of the solar system, and its interaction with the interstellar medium), planetary science (research that enables, and is enabled by, the robotic exploration of the solar system), and astrophysics (the study of the universe beyond our solar system). U.S. citizens and permanent residents are given preference, although the program is not restricted to them. Students with disabilities and from underrepresented minority groups (African Americans, Native Americans, Alaskan Natives, Mexican Americans, Puerto Ricans, and Native Pacific Islanders) are especially urged to apply. Selection is based on quality of the proposed research, relevance of the proposed research to NASA's objectives in earth or space science, and academic excellence)based on transcripts and a letter of reference from the student's academic adviser).

Financial data The grant is $30,000 per year, including the recipient's stipend (comparable with the stipend rate on the student's campus), a student allowance of up to $3,000, and a university allowance of up to $3,000.

Duration 1 year; may be renewed for up to 2 additional years.

Additional information This program was established in 1990.

Number awarded Approximately 66 to 75 each year: 50 in earth science, 3 to 5 in heliophysics, 10 in planetary science, and 3 to 10 in astrophysics.

Deadline January of each year for new applications; March of each year for renewal applications.

[737]
EAST EUROPEAN LANGUAGE GRANTS TO INDIVIDUALS FOR SUMMER STUDY

American Council of Learned Societies
Attn: Office of Fellowships and Grants
633 Third Avenue
New York, NY 10017-6795
(212) 697-1505   Fax: (212) 949-8058
E-mail: fellowships@acls.org
Web: www.acls.org/grants/Default.aspx?id=540

Summary To provide financial support to graduate students, professionals, and postdoctorates (especially African Americans or other minorities and women) who are interested in studying eastern European languages during the summer.

Eligibility Applicants must have completed at least a 4-year college degree. They must be interested in a program of training in the languages of eastern Europe, including Albanian, Bosnian-Croatian-Serbian, Bulgarian, Czech, Estonian, Hungarian, Latvian, Lithuanian, Macedonian, Polish, Romanian, Slovak, or Slovene. The language course may be at the beginning, intermediate, or advanced level. Normally, requests for beginning and intermediate level training should be for attendance at intensive courses offered by institutions in the United States; proposals for study at the advanced level are ordinarily for courses in eastern Europe. Applications are particularly encouraged from women and members of minority groups.

Financial data Grants up to $2,500 are available.

Duration Summer months.

Additional information This program, reinstituted in 2002, is supported by the U.S. Department of State under the Research and Training for Eastern Europe and the Independent States of the Former Soviet Union Act of 1983 (Title VIII).

Number awarded Approximately 15 each year.

Deadline January of each year.

[738]
EDITH M. ALLEN SCHOLARSHIPS

United Methodist Church
Attn: General Board of Higher Education and Ministry
Office of Loans and Scholarships
1001 19th Avenue South
P.O. Box 340007
Nashville, TN 37203-0007
(615) 340-7344   Fax: (615) 340-7367
E-mail: umscholar@gbhem.org
Web: www.gbhem.org/loansandscholarships

Summary To provide financial assistance to Methodist students who are African American and working on an undergraduate or graduate degree in specified fields.

Eligibility This program is open to full-time undergraduate and graduate students at Methodist colleges and universities (preferably Historically Black United Methodist colleges) who have been active, full members of a United Methodist Church for at least 3 years prior to applying. Applicants must be African Americans working on a degree in education, social work, medicine, and/or other health professions. They must have at least a "B+" average and be recognized as a person whose academic and vocational contributions will help improve the quality of life for others.

Financial data A stipend is awarded (amount not specified).

Duration 1 year; recipients may reapply.

Number awarded Varies each year.

Deadline March of each year.

[739]
EDUCATIONAL TESTING SERVICE SUMMER INTERNSHIP PROGRAM FOR GRADUATE STUDENTS

Educational Testing Service
Attn: Fellowships
660 Rosedale Road
MS 19-T
Princeton, NJ 08541-0001
(609) 734-5543   Fax: (609) 734-5410
E-mail: internfellowships@ets.org
Web: www.ets.org/research/fellowships/summer

Summary To provide an internship opportunity to doctoral students (particularly African Americans and students from other diverse backgrounds) who are interested in conducting summer research under the guidance of senior staff at the Educational Testing Service (ETS).

Eligibility This program is open to doctoral students interested in working on a research project at ETS in 1 of the following areas: measurement theory, validity, natural language processing and computational linguistics, cognitive psychology, learning theory, linguistics, speech recognition and processing, teaching and classroom research, statistics, or international large scale assessments. Applicants must have completed at least 2 years of full-time study for a Ph.D. or Ed.D. Selection is based on the scholarship of the applicant, match of applicant interests with participating ETS researchers, and the ETS affirmative action objectives. An explicit goal of the program is to increase the number of scholars and students from diverse backgrounds, especially such traditionally underrepresented groups as African Americans, Hispanic/ Latino Americans, and American Indians, who are interested in conducting research during the summer in educational measurement and related fields.

Financial data The award includes a stipend of $5,000, up to $1,000 as round-trip travel reimbursement, and a $1,500 housing allowance for interns residing outside a 50-mile radius of the ETS campus.

Duration 8 weeks in the summer.

Additional information Fellows work with senior staff at ETS in Princeton, New Jersey.

Number awarded Up to 16 each year.

Deadline January of each year.

[740]
EDWARD S. ROTH MANUFACTURING ENGINEERING SCHOLARSHIP

Society of Manufacturing Engineers
Attn: SME Education Foundation
One SME Drive
P.O. Box 930
Dearborn, MI 48121-0930
(313) 425-3300   Toll Free: (800) 733-4763, ext. 3300
Fax: (313) 425-3411   E-mail: foundation@sme.org
Web: www.smeef.org

Summary To provide financial assistance to students (especially African Americans and other minorities) who are enrolled or planning to work on a bachelor's or master's degree in manufacturing engineering at selected universities.

Eligibility This program is open to U.S. citizens who are graduating high school seniors or currently-enrolled undergraduate or graduate students. Applicants must be enrolled or planning to enroll as a full-time student at 1 of 13 selected 4-year universities to work on a bachelor's or master's degree in manufacturing engineering. They must have a GPA of 3.0 or higher. Preference is given to 1) students demonstrating financial need, 2) minority students, and 3) students participating in a co-op program. Some preference may also be given to graduating high school seniors and graduate students. Along with their application, they must submit a 300-word essay that covers their career and educational objectives, how this scholarship will help them attain those objectives, and why they want to enter this field.

Financial data Stipend amounts vary; recently, the value of all scholarships provided by this foundation annually averages approximately $2,700.

Duration 1 year; may be renewed.

Additional information The eligible institutions are California Polytechnic State University at San Luis Obispo, California State Polytechnic State University at Pomona, University of Miami (Florida), Bradley University (Illinois), Central State University (Ohio), Miami University (Ohio), Boston University, Worcester Polytechnic Institute (Massachusetts), University of Massachusetts, St. Cloud State University (Minnesota), University of Texas-Pan American, Brigham Young University (Utah), and Utah State University.

Number awarded 2 each year.

Deadline January of each year.

[741]
EISENHOWER GRADUATE TRANSPORTATION FELLOWSHIPS

Department of Transportation
Federal Highway Administration
Attn: Office of PCD, HPC-32
4600 North Fairfax Drive, Suite 800
Arlington, VA 22203-1553
(703) 235-0538   Toll Free: (877) 558-6873
Fax: (703) 235-0593   E-mail: transportationedu@dot.gov
Web: www.fhwa.dot.gov/ugp/index.htm

Summary To provide financial assistance to graduate students (especially students at Historically Black Colleges and Universities and other minority serving institutions) who are working on a master's or doctoral degree in transportation-related fields.

Eligibility This program is open to students enrolled or planning to enroll full time to work on a master's or doctoral degree in a field of study directly related to transportation. Applicants must be planning to enter the transportation profession after completing their higher level education. They must be U.S. citizens or have an I-20 (foreign student) or I-551 (permanent resident) identification card. Selection is based on the proposed plan of study, academic records (class standing, GPA, and official transcripts), transportation work experience (including employer's endorsement), and recommendations. Students at Historically Black Colleges and Universities (HBCUs), Hispanic Serving Institutions (HSIs), and Tribal Colleges and Universities (TCUs) are especially encouraged to apply.

Financial data Fellows receive tuition and fees (to a maximum of $10,000 per year), monthly stipends of $1,700 for master's degree students or $2,000 for doctoral students, and a 1-time allowance of up to $1,500 for travel to an annual meeting of the Transportation Research Board.

Duration For master's degree students, 24 months, and the degree must be completed within 3 years; for doctoral students, 36 months, and the degree must be completed within 5 years.

Number awarded Approximately 100 to 150 each year.

Deadline March of each year.

[742]
EISENHOWER GRANTS FOR RESEARCH AND INTERN FELLOWSHIPS

Department of Transportation
Federal Highway Administration
Attn: Office of PCD, HPC-32
4600 North Fairfax Drive, Suite 800
Arlington, VA 22203-1553
(703) 235-0538   Toll Free: (877) 558-6873
Fax: (703) 235-0593   E-mail: transportationedu@dot.gov
Web: www.fhwa.dot.gov/ugp/grf_ann.htm

Summary To offer students (particularly African Americans and other minorities) an opportunity to participate in transportation-related research activities either at facilities of the U.S. Department of Transportation (DOT) Federal Highway Administration in the Washington, D.C. area or private organizations.

Eligibility This program is open to 1) students in their junior year of a baccalaureate program who will complete their junior year before being awarded a fellowship; 2) students in their senior year of a baccalaureate program; and 3) students who have completed their baccalaureate degree and are enrolled in a program leading to a master's, Ph.D., or equivalent degree. Applicants must be enrolled full time at an accredited U.S institution of higher education and planning to enter the transportation profession after completing their higher education. They must be U.S. citizens or have an I-20 (foreign student) or I-551 (permanent resident) identification card. For research fellowships, they select 1 or more projects from a current list of research activities underway at various DOT facilities; the research is conducted with academic supervision provided by a faculty adviser from their home university (which grants academic credit for the research project) and with technical direction provided by the DOT staff. Intern fellowships provide students with opportunities to perform transportation-related research, development, technology transfer, and other activities at public and private sector organizations. Specific requirements for the target projects vary; most require engineering backgrounds, but others involve transportation planning, information management, public administration, physics, materials science, statistical analysis, operations research, chemistry, economics, technology transfer, urban studies, geography, and urban and regional planning. The DOT encourages students at Historically Black Colleges and Universities (HBCUs), Hispanic Serving Institutions (HSIs), and Tribal Colleges and Universities (TCUs) to apply for these grants. Selection is based on match of the student's qualifications with the proposed research project (including the student's ability to accomplish the project in the available time), recommendation letters regarding the nominee's qualifications to conduct the research, academic records (including class standing, GPA, and transcripts), and transportation work experience (if any), including the employer's endorsement.

Financial data Fellows receive full tuition and fees that relate to the academic credits for the approved research project (to a maximum of $10,000) and a monthly stipend of $1,450 for undergraduates, $1,700 for master's students, or $2,000 for doctoral students. An allowance for travel to and from the DOT facility where the research is conducted is also provided, but selectees are responsible for their own housing accommodations. Recipients are also provided with a 1-time allowance of up to $1,500 to attend the annual Transportation Research Board (TRB) meeting.

Duration Projects normally range from 3 to 12 months.

Number awarded Varies each year; recently, 9 students participated in this program.

Deadline Applications remain open until each project is filled.

[743]
E.J. JOSEY SCHOLARSHIP AWARD

Black Caucus of the American Library Association
c/o Billy C. Beal, Scholarship Committee Chair
Meridian Community College
Dean of Learning Resources
910 Highway 19 North
Meridian, MS 39307
(601) 483-8241   Toll Free: (800) MCC-THE1
E-mail: bbeal@mcc.cc.ms.us
Web: www.bcala.org/awards/joseyapps.htm

Summary To provide financial assistance to African Americans interested in working on a graduate degree in librarianship.

Eligibility This program is open to African American citizens of the United States or Canada who are enrolled as graduate students in an accredited library or information science program. Applicants must submit an essay of 1,000 to 1,200 words on a topic that changes annually; recently, applicants were asked to present their opinions on whether or not there is still a need for ethnic library associations. Selection is based on the essay's argument development, critical analysis, clear language, conciseness, and creativity.

Financial data The stipend is $2,000.

Duration 1 year.

Number awarded 2 each year.

Deadline October of each year.

[744]
ELLA TACKWOOD FUND

United Methodist Higher Education Foundation
Attn: Scholarships Administrator
1001 19th Avenue South
P.O. Box 340005
Nashville, TN 37203-0005
(615) 340-7385   Toll Free: (800) 811-8110
Fax: (615) 340-7330
E-mail: umhefscholarships@gbhem.org
Web: www.umhef.org/receive.php?id=endowed_funds

Summary To provide financial assistance to Methodist undergraduate and graduate students at Historically Black Colleges and Universities (HBCUs) of the United Methodist Church.

Eligibility This program is open to students enrolling as full-time undergraduate and graduate students at HBCUs of the United Methodist Church. Applicants must have been active, full members of a United Methodist Church for at least 1 year prior to applying. They must have a GPA of 2.5 or higher and be able to demonstrate financial need. Along with their application, they must submit a 200-word essay on their involvement and/or leadership responsibilities in their church, school, and community within the last 3 years. U.S. citizenship or permanent resident status is required.

Financial data The stipend is at least $1,000 per year.

Duration 1 year; nonrenewable.

Additional information This program was established in 1985. The qualifying schools are Bennett College for Women, Bethune-Cookman College, Claflin University, Clark Atlanta University, Dillard University, Huston-Tillotson College, Meharry Medical College, Paine College, Philander Smith College, Rust College, and Wiley College.

Number awarded Varies each year; recently, 3 of these scholarships were awarded.

Deadline May of each year.

[745]
ELLIOTT C. ROBERTS, SR. SCHOLARSHIP

Institute for Diversity in Health Management
Attn: Executive Assistant
One North Franklin Street, 30th Floor
Chicago, IL 60606
(312) 422-2630   Toll Free: (800) 233-0996
Fax: (312) 895-4511   E-mail: ejohnson@aha.org
Web: www.applicantsoft.com

Summary To provide financial assistance to African Americans and other minority graduate students in health services management.

Eligibility This program is open to members of ethnic minority groups who are accepted or enrolled in a graduate program in health care administration. Applicants must have a GPA of 3.0 or higher. They must demonstrate commitment to a career in health care administration. Along with their application, they must submit a personal statement of 300 to 500 words on their interest in health care management and their career goals. Selection is based on academic achievement, leadership potential, financial need, community involvement, commitment to health care administration, and overall professional maturity. U.S. citizenship is required.

Financial data The stipend ranges from $500 to $1,000.

Duration 1 year.

Number awarded 1 or more each year, depending on the availability of funds.

Deadline December of each year.

[746]
ELLIOTT G. HEARD JR. MEMORIAL SCHOLARSHIP

Elliott G. Heard Jr. Memorial Scholarship Committee
P.O. Box 214
Mullica Hill, NJ 08062
(609) 202-0061   Fax: (856) 223-0888
E-mail: yhbautista@yahoo.com

Summary To provide financial assistance to African American and other students enrolled or planning to enroll at an accredited law school.

Eligibility This program is open to college seniors who have been accepted to an accredited law school and students currently enrolled in law school who are not in their final semester. Applicants must be U.S. citizens. Along with their application, they must submit a 500-word essay describing why they should be considered for this scholarship and why they decided on a career in the law. Minorities, women, and the physically challenged are especially encouraged to apply. Finalists are invited to an interview. Selection is based on academic achievement, community service, leadership, citizenship, and financial need.

Financial data The stipend is $1,000.

Duration 1 year; nonrenewable.

Additional information This program is named after the first African American jurist in Gloucester County, New Jersey.

Number awarded 1 or more each year.

Deadline October of each year.

[747]
ENVIRONMENTAL PROTECTION AGENCY STUDENT DIVERSITY INTERNSHIP PROGRAM

United Negro College Fund Special Programs
  Corporation
Attn: NASA Science and Technology Institute
6402 Arlington Boulevard, Suite 600
Falls Church, VA 22042
(703) 677-3400   Toll Free: (800) 530-6232
Fax: (703) 205-7645   E-mail: portal@uncfsp.org
Web: www.uncfsp.org

Summary To provide an opportunity for African Americans and other underrepresented undergraduate and graduate students to work on a summer research project at research sites of the U.S. Environmental Protection Agency (EPA).

Eligibility This program is open to rising college sophomores, juniors, and seniors and to full-time graduate students at accredited institutions who are members of underrepresented groups, including ethnic minorities (African Americans, Hispanic/Latinos, Native Americans, Asians, Alaskan Natives, and Native Hawaiians/Pacific Islanders) and persons with disabilities. Applicants must have a GPA of 2.8 or higher and be working on a degree in business, communications, economics, engineering, environmental science/management, finance, information technology, law, marketing, or science. They must be interested in working on a research project during the summer at their choice of 23 EPA research sites (for a list, contact EPA). U.S. citizenship is required.

Financial data The stipend is $5,000 for undergraduates or $6,000 for graduate students. Interns also receive a travel and housing allowance, but they are responsible for covering their local transportation, meals, and miscellaneous expenses.

Duration 10 weeks during the summer.

Additional information This program is funded by EPA and administered by the United Negro College Fund Special Programs Corporation.

Number awarded Varies each year.

Deadline May of each year.

[748]
ERSKINE A. PETERS FELLOWSHIPS

University of Notre Dame
Attn: Department of Africana Studies
327 O'Shaughnessy Hall
Notre Dame, IN 46556
(574) 631-0452   Fax: (574) 631-3587
E-mail: mmckenn9@nd.edu
Web: africana.nd.edu/erskine-a-peters-fellows

Summary To provide an opportunity for African American doctoral candidates in the humanities and social sciences to complete their dissertations while in residence at the University of Notre Dame.

Eligibility This program is open to African American doctoral candidates in the humanities and social sciences who have completed all requirements for the degree except the dissertation. Applicants must be interested in completing their dissertations while in residence at the University of Notre Dame. Along with their application, they must submit a cover letter, their curriculum vitae, a dissertation abstract, and a writing sample of 20 to 30 pages.

Financial data The stipend is $30,000. Fellows also receive a $2,000 research budget, office space and use of a personal computer, a faculty mentor in their department of specialization, and an opportunity to participate in forum discussions on professional development.

Duration 1 academic year.

Number awarded Varies each year; recently, 3 of these fellowships were awarded.

Deadline November of each year.

[749]
ESTELLE MASSEY OSBORNE SCHOLARSHIP

Nurses Educational Funds, Inc.
Attn: Scholarship Coordinator
304 Park Avenue South, 11th Floor
New York, NY 10010
(212) 590-2443   Fax: (212) 590-2446
E-mail: info@n-e-f.org
Web: www.n-e-f.org

Summary To provide financial assistance to African Americans working as nurses who are interested in earning a master's degree in nursing.

Eligibility This program is open to African American registered nurses who are members of a national professional nursing organization and enrolled full or part time in an accredited master's degree program in nursing. Applicants must have completed at least 12 credits and have a cumulative GPA of 3.6 or higher. They must be U.S. citizens or have declared their official intention of becoming a citizen. Along with their application, they must submit an 800-word essay on their professional goals and potential for making a contribution to the nursing profession. Selection is based on academic excellence and the essay's content and clarity.

Financial data Stipends range from $2,500 to $10,000, depending on the availability of funds.

Duration 1 year; nonrenewable.

Additional information There is a $20 application fee.

Number awarded 1 each year.

Deadline February of each year.

[750]
ESTHER MAYO SHERARD SCHOLARSHIP

American Health Information Management Association
Attn: AHIMA Foundation
233 North Michigan Avenue, 21st Floor
Chicago, IL 60601-5809
(312) 233-1175   Fax: (312) 233-1475
E-mail: info@ahimafoundation.org
Web: www.ahimafoundation.org

Summary To provide financial assistance to credentialed professionals who are African American, members of the

American Health Information Management Association (AHIMA), and interested in working on a graduate degree in a field related to health information management.

Eligibility This program is open to credentialed professionals in health information management (HIM) who are African American members of AHIMA. Applicants must be enrolled at least half time in a master's or doctoral degree program in an area related to HIM practice (e.g., computer science, business management, education, public health, informatics, health policy). They must have a GPA of 3.0 or higher and at least 1 full semester remaining after the date of the award. Financial need is not considered in the selection process.

Financial data The stipend is $2,500.

Duration 1 year.

Additional information This program was established in 2000 by the Esther Mayo Sherard Foundation.

Number awarded 1 each year.

Deadline April or October of each year.

[751]
ESTHER NGAN-LING CHOW AND MAREYJOYCE GREEN SCHOLARSHIP

Sociologists for Women in Society
Attn: Executive Officer
University of Rhode Island
Department of Sociology
10 Chafee Road
Kingston, RI 02881
(401) 874-9510   Fax: (401) 874-2588
E-mail: swseo@socwomen.org
Web: www.socwomen.org/page.php?sss=115

Summary To provide funding to African Americans and other women of color who are conducting dissertation research in sociology.

Eligibility This program is open to women from a racial/ethnic group that faces racial discrimination in the United States. Applicants must be in the early stages of writing a doctoral dissertation in sociology on a topic relating to the concerns that women of color face domestically and/or internationally. They must be able to demonstrate financial need. Both domestic and international students are eligible to apply. Along with their application, they must submit a personal statement that details their short- and long-term career and research goals; a resume or curriculum vitae; 2 letters of recommendation; and a 5-page dissertation proposal that includes the purpose of the research, the work to be accomplished through support from this scholarship, and a time line for completion.

Financial data The stipend is $15,000. An additional grant of $500 is provided to enable the recipient to attend the winter meeting of Sociologists for Women in Society (SWS), and travel expenses to attend the summer meeting are reimbursed.

Duration 1 year.

Additional information This program was established in 2007 and originally named the Women of Color Dissertation Scholarship.

Number awarded 1 each year.

Deadline March of each year.

[752]
ETHEL BOLDEN MINORITY SCHOLARSHIP

Richland County Public Library Foundation
Attn: Development Manager
1431 Assembly Street
Columbia, SC 29201
(803) 929-3424   E-mail: tgills@myrcpl.com
Web: www.myrcpl.com/foundation/bolden

Summary To provide financial assistance to African American and other minority residents of South Carolina who are interested in working on a master's degree in library and information science at a school in any state.

Eligibility This program is open to residents of South Carolina who are members of ethnic and racial groups underrepresented in the field of library and information science (American Indians, African Americans, Asian Americans, or Hispanic Americans). Applicants must have been admitted to an ALA-accredited school of library and information science in any state. Along with their application, they must submit a 300-word essay describing their interest and any work in the field of librarianship and the specific competencies or characteristics they believe they can contribute to the library profession. Selection is based on academic performance and demonstrated leadership abilities through participation in community service or other activities.

Financial data The stipend is $2,500.

Duration 1 year.

Additional information This program was established in 2010.

Number awarded 1 each year.

Deadline March of each year.

[753]
ETHNIC MINORITY ADMINISTRATOR IN TRAINING INTERNSHIP

Indiana Health Care Association
Attn: Executive Director
One North Capitol, Suite 100
Indianapolis, IN 46204
(317) 636-6406   Toll Free: (800) 466-IHCA
Fax: (877) 298-3749   E-mail: dhenry@ihca.org
Web: www.ihca.org

Summary To provide work experience to African Americans and other minority residents of Indiana interested in gaining work experience at the Indiana Health Care Association (IHCA).

Eligibility This program is open to residents of Indiana who are members of ethnic minority groups (African Americans, Hispanics, American Indians, Asian Americans). Applicants must have a bachelor's degree or higher and an employment history that reflects management or leadership skills. They must be interested in preparing for a career in long-term care as a health facility administrator by working under a preceptor at IHCA. Preference is given to applicants interested in working with elderly or disabled populations. An interview at IHCA headquarters is required.

Financial data This is a paid internship (stipend not specified).

Duration 6 months.

Number awarded 1 each year.

Deadline July of each year.

[754]
ETHNIC MINORITY POSTGRADUATE SCHOLARSHIP FOR CAREERS IN ATHLETICS

Black Coaches Association
Attn: Director of Operations and Administration
Pan American Plaza
201 South Capitol Avenue, Suite 495
Indianapolis, IN 46225-1089
(317) 829-5619   Toll Free: (877) 789-1222
Fax: (317) 829-5601
Web: bcasports.cstv.com

Summary   To provide financial assistance to African Americans and other minorities who participated in college athletics and are interested in working on a graduate degree in athletic administration.

Eligibility   This program is open to former student-athletes on the college level who are of ethnic minority origin. Applicants must be entering or enrolled full time in a graduate program in sports administration or a related field to prepare for a career in athletics. They must have performed with distinction as student body members at their undergraduate institution and have a GPA of 2.5 or higher. U.S. citizenship is required. Selection is based on academic course work, extracurricular activities, commitment to preparing for a career in athletics, and promise of success in their career.

Financial data   The stipend is $2,500. Funds are paid to the college or university of the recipient's choice.

Duration   1 year; nonrenewable.

Additional information   This program was established in 1995.

Number awarded   Varies each year; recently, 6 of these scholarships were awarded.

Deadline   April of each year.

[755]
EURASIA DISSERTATION SUPPORT FELLOWSHIPS

Social Science Research Council
Attn: Eurasia Program
One Pierrepont Plaza, 15th Floor
Brooklyn, NY 11201
(212) 377-2700   Fax: (212) 377-2727
E-mail: eurasia@ssrc.org
Web: www.ssrc.org/fellowships/Eurasia-fellowship

Summary   To provide funding to graduate students (particularly African Americans, other minorities, and women) who are completing a dissertation dealing with Eurasia.

Eligibility   This program is open to students who have completed field research for their doctoral dissertation and who plan to work on writing it during the next academic year. Applicants must have been conducting research in a discipline of the social sciences or humanities that deals with the Russian Empire, the Soviet Union, or the New States of Eurasia. Research related to the non-Russian states, regions, and peoples is particularly encouraged. Regions and countries currently supported by the program include Armenia, Azerbaijan, Belarus, Georgia, Kazakhstan, Kyrgyzstan, Moldova, Russian Federation, Tajikistan, Turkmenistan, Ukraine, and Uzbekistan; funding is not presently available for research on the Baltic states. U.S. citizenship or permanent

resident status is required. Minorities and women are particularly encouraged to apply.

Financial data   Grants up to $25,000 are available.

Duration   Up to 1 year.

Additional information   Funding for this program is provided by the U.S. Department of State under the Program for Research and Training on Eastern Europe and the Independent States of the Former Soviet Union (Title VIII).

Number awarded   Varies each year; recently, 7 of these fellowships were awarded.

Deadline   December of each year.

[756]
EVA LOIS EVANS MATHEMATICS AND SCIENCE FELLOWSHIPS

Alpha Kappa Alpha Sorority, Inc.
Attn: Educational Advancement Foundation
5656 South Stony Island Avenue
Chicago, IL 60637
(773) 947-0026   Toll Free: (800) 653-6528
Fax: (773) 947-0277   E-mail: akaeaf@akaeaf.net
Web: www.akaeaf.org/fellowships_endowments.htm

Summary   To provide funding to pre- and postdoctoral scholars (especially African American women) engaged in research in mathematics, science, or technology.

Eligibility   This program is open to graduate students and more advanced scholars who are interested in conducting research in the area of mathematics, science, or technology. Applicants must submit 1) a list of honors, awards, and scholarships received; 2) a list of organizations in which they have memberships, especially minority organizations; 3) a description of the project or research on which they are currently working, or (if they are not involved in a project or research) the aspects of their field that interest them; and 4) a statement of their personal and career goals, including how this scholarship will enhance their ability to attain those goals. The sponsor is a traditionally African American women's sorority.

Financial data   A stipend is awarded (amount not specified).

Duration   These fellowships are awarded biennially, in even-numbered years.

Number awarded   Varies; recently, 2 of these fellowships were awarded.

Deadline   April of even-numbered years.

[757]
EXCELLENCE IN CARDIOVASCULAR SCIENCES SUMMER RESEARCH PROGRAM

Wake Forest University School of Medicine
Attn: Hypertension and Vascular Research Center
Medical Center Boulevard
Winston-Salem, NC 27157-1032
(336) 716-1080   Fax: (336) 716-2456
E-mail: nsarver@wfubmc.edu
Web: www.wfubmc.edu

Summary   To provide African Americans and other underrepresented students with an opportunity to engage in a summer research project in cardiovascular science at Wake Forest University in Winston-Salem, North Carolina.

Eligibility This program is open to undergraduates and master's degree students who are members of underrepresented minority groups (African Americans, Alaskan Natives, Asian Americans, Native Americans, Pacific Islanders, and Hispanics) or who come from disadvantaged backgrounds (e.g., rural areas, first generation college students). Applicants must be interested in participating in a program of summer research in the cardiovascular sciences that includes "hands-on" laboratory research, a lecture series by faculty and guest speakers, and a research symposium at which students present their research findings. U.S. citizenship or permanent resident status is required.

Financial data The stipend is $1,731 per month, housing in a university dormitory, and round-trip transportation expense.

Duration 2 months during the summer.

Additional information This program is sponsored by the National Heart, Lung, and Blood Institute (NHLBI) of the National Institutes of Health (NIH).

Number awarded Approximately 10 each year.

Deadline February of each year.

[758]
FACSE GRADUATE FELLOWSHIPS

National Association of Teacher Educators for Family and
  Consumer Sciences
c/o Lela G. Goar, Fellowship Committee Chair
225 CR 207A
Burnet, TX 78611
(512) 715-8249   Fax: (512) 585-7606
E-mail: lkgoar@earthlink.net
Web: www.natefacs.org/scholarship.html

Summary To provide financial assistance to African American and other graduate students in family and consumer science education.

Eligibility This program is open to graduate students working on a master's or doctoral degree in family and consumer sciences education. Applicants must submit an autobiographical sketch (up to 3 pages in length) presenting their professional goals, including information on the institution where they are studying or planning to study, areas or emphases of study, possible research topic, and other pertinent information regarding their plans. Selection is based on likelihood of completing the degree, likelihood of contribution to family and consumer sciences education, previous academic work, professional association involvement, professional experience (including scholarly work), and references. At least 1 fellowship is reserved for a minority (African American, Hispanic American, Native American, or Asian American) candidate.

Financial data Stipends range from $2,000 to $4,000.

Duration 1 year.

Additional information The sponsor is an affiliate of the Family and Consumer Sciences (FACS) Division of the Association for Career and Technical Education.

Number awarded Varies each year.

Deadline November of each year.

[759]
FAEGRE & BENSON DIVERSITY SCHOLARSHIP

Faegre & Benson LLP
Attn: Manager of Junior Legal Talent Recruitment
2200 Wells Fargo Center
90 South Seventh Street
Minneapolis, MN 55402-3901
(612) 766-8952   Toll Free: (800) 328-4393
Fax: (612) 766-1600   E-mail: tselden@faegre.com
Web: www.faegre.com/12399

Summary To provide financial assistance and work experience to African American and other law students who will contribute to diversity in the legal profession.

Eligibility This program is open to students enrolled in the first year at an accredited law school in the United States. Applicants must submit a 500-word personal statement explaining their interest in the scholarship program, how diversity has influenced their life, and how it impacts the legal profession. Selection is based on that statement, a resume, undergraduate transcripts, a legal writing sample, and 2 professional recommendations.

Financial data The stipend is $6,000 per year.

Duration 2 years: the second and third year of law school.

Additional information Recipients are also offered an associateship during the summer between the first and second year at an office of the firm in Minneapolis, Denver, Boulder, or Des Moines. An attorney from the firm is assigned as a mentor to help them adjust to the firm and to the legal profession.

Number awarded 2 each year.

Deadline January of each year.

[760]
FARM CREDIT EAST SCHOLARSHIPS

Farm Credit East
Attn: Scholarship Program
240 South Road
Enfield, CT 06082
(860) 741-4380   Toll Free: (800) 562-2235
Fax: (860) 741-4389
Web: www.farmcrediteast.com

Summary To provide financial assistance to residents of designated northeastern states (especially African Americans and other minorities) who plan to attend school in any state to work on an undergraduate or graduate degree in a field related to agriculture, forestry, or fishing.

Eligibility This program is open to residents of Massachusetts, Connecticut, Rhode Island, New Jersey, and portions of New York and New Hampshire. Applicants must be working on or planning to work on an associate, bachelor's, or graduate degree in production agriculture, agribusiness, the forest products industry, or commercial fishing at a college or university in any state. They must submit a 200-word essay on why they wish to prepare for a career in agriculture, forestry, or fishing. Selection is based on the essay, extracurricular activities (especially farm work experience and activities indicative of an interest in preparing for a career in agriculture or agribusiness), and interest in agriculture. The program includes scholarships reserved for members of minority (Black or African American, American Indian or Alaska

Native, Asian, Native Hawaiian or other Pacific Islander, or Hispanic or Latino) groups.

Financial data The stipend is $1,500. Funds are paid directly to the student to be used for tuition, room and board, books, and other academic charges.

Duration 1 year; nonrenewable.

Additional information Recipients are given priority for an internship with the sponsor in the summer following their junior year. Farm Credit East was formerly named First Pioneer Farm Credit.

Number awarded Up to 28 each year, including several reserved for members of minority groups.

Deadline April of each year.

[761]
FASSE/CUFA INQUIRY GRANT

National Council for the Social Studies
Attn: Program Manager, External Relations
8555 16th Street, Suite 500
Silver Spring, MD 20910-2844
(301) 588-1800, ext. 106   Fax: (301) 588-2049
E-mail: excellence@ncss.org
Web: www.socialstudies.org/getinvolved/awards/fasse-cufa

Summary To provide funding to faculty and graduate student members of the National Council for the Social Studies (NCSS), especially African Americans and others from diverse backgrounds) who are interested in conducting research projects in "citizenship education."

Eligibility This program is open to members of the council who are assistant, associate, or full professors or graduate students with the demonstrated support of a university mentor/adviser. Graduate student applicants must have a mentor/adviser who is also an NCSS member. Researchers from all groups, including underrepresented groups, are encouraged to apply. They must be interested in a project in "citizenship education" that affirms social, cultural, and racial diversity and that addresses issues of equality, equity, and social justice. Proposals that address aims for citizen action are preferred. All proposals should be relevant to school, university, or community-based educational settings. They should either 1) serve student bodies that are socially, culturally, and racially diverse; or 2) involve teachers or prospective teachers who work or will work with diverse student populations. They can address a range of educational levels and settings, from K-12 to collegiate levels, and from school to community settings.

Financial data Grants up to $10,000 are available.

Duration Funded projects must be completed within 1 academic year.

Additional information This program is sponsored by the College and University Faculty Assembly (CUFA) and the Fund for the Advancement of Social Studies Education (FASSE), established by the NCAA in 1984.

Number awarded 1 every 2 or 3 years.

Deadline June of the years in which grants are offered.

[762]
FAYE AND ROBERT LETT SCHOLARSHIP

American Baptist Churches of Ohio
Attn: Ohio Baptist Education Society
136 Galway Drive North
P.O. Box 288
Granville, OH 43023-0288
(740) 587-0804   Fax: (740) 587-0807
E-mail: pastorchris@neo.rr.com
Web: www.abc-ohio.org

Summary To provide funding to African American upper-division and graduate students from Ohio who are interested in preparing for the Baptist ministry at a college or seminary in any state.

Eligibility This program is open to African American residents of Ohio who have completed at least 2 years of study at an accredited college or university in any state and are interested in continuing their education as an upper-division or seminary student. Applicants must 1) hold active membership in a church affiliated with the American Baptist Churches of Ohio or a church dually-aligned with the American Baptist Churches of Ohio; 2) be in the process of preparing for a professional career in Christian ministry (such as a local church pastor, church education, youth or young adult ministries, church music, specialized ministry, chaplaincy, ministry in higher education, or missionary service); 3) be committed to working professionally within the framework of the American Baptist Churches USA; and 4) acknowledge a personal commitment to the Gospel of Jesus Christ, an understanding of the Christian faith, and a definite call to professional Christian ministry as a life work. Financial need must be demonstrated.

Financial data Stipends generally range from $1,000 to $1,500 a year.

Duration 1 year.

Additional information This program was established in 1990.

Number awarded 1 or more each year.

Deadline March of each year.

[763]
FEDERAL EMPLOYEE EDUCATION AND ASSISTANCE FUND-BLACKS IN GOVERNMENT SCHOLARSHIP PROGRAM

Blacks in Government
c/o Federal Employee Education and Assistance Fund
Attn: Scholarship Program
3333 South Wadsworth Boulevard, Suite 300
Lakewood, CO 80227
(303) 933-7580   Toll Free: (800) 323-4140
Fax: (303) 933-7587   E-mail: admin@feea.org
Web: www.feea.org

Summary To provide financial assistance for college or graduate school to members of Blacks in Government (BIG) and their dependents.

Eligibility This program is open to BIG members and their children, stepchildren, and grandchildren. Applicants or their sponsoring BIG member must have at least 3 years of federal, state, or local government employment and 2 years of membership in BIG. They must be entering or enrolled full time in an accredited 2- or 4-year postsecondary, graduate, or postgraduate program with a GPA of 3.0 or higher. Along with their application, they must submit a 2-page essay on a topic related to a career in public service with the government, a letter of recommendation, a transcript, a list of extracurricular and community service activities, and verification of government employment; high school seniors must also submit a copy of their ACT, SAT, or other examination scores. Financial need is not considered in the selection process.

Financial data The stipend is $1,000 per year.

Duration 1 year; may be renewed.

Additional information This program, established in 2007, is jointly administered by BIG and the Federal Employee Education and Assistance Fund (FEEA).

Number awarded 22 each year: 2 in each BIG region.

Deadline March of each year.

[764]
FELLOWSHIPS FOR MINORITY DOCTORAL STUDENTS

American Institute of Certified Public Accountants
Attn: Academic and Career Development Division
220 Leigh Farm Road
Durham, NC 27707-8110
(919) 402-4931   Fax: (919) 419-4705
E-mail: MIC_Programs@aicpa.org
Web: www.aicpa.org/members/div/career/mini/fmds.htm

Summary To provide financial assistance to African American and other underrepresented minority doctoral students who wish to prepare for a career teaching accounting at the college level.

Eligibility This program is open to underrepresented minority students who have applied to and/or been accepted into a doctoral program with a concentration in accounting. Applicants must have earned a master's degree or completed a minimum of 3 years of full-time work in accounting. They must be attending or planning to attend school full time and agree not to work full time in a paid position, teach more than 1 course as a teaching assistant, or work more than 25% as a research assistant. U.S. citizenship or permanent resident status is required. Preference is given to applicants who have attained a C.P.A. designation and/or are members of the American Institute of Certified Public Accountants (AICPA) and those who perform AICPA committee service. For purposes of this program, the AICPA defines minority students as those whose heritage is Black or African American, Hispanic or Latino, or Native American. Selection is based on academic and professional achievement, commitment to earning an accounting doctoral degree, and financial need.

Financial data The stipend is $12,000 per year.

Duration 1 year; may be renewed up to 4 additional years.

Number awarded Varies each year; recently, 21 of these fellowships were awarded.

Deadline March of each year.

[765]
FELLOWSHIPS IN SCIENCE AND INTERNATIONAL AFFAIRS

Harvard University
John F. Kennedy School of Government
Belfer Center for Science and International Affairs
Attn: Fellowship Coordinator
79 John F. Kennedy Street
Cambridge, MA 02138
(617) 495-8806   Fax: (617) 495-8963
E-mail: bcsia_fellowships@ksg.harvard.edu
Web: belfercenter.ksg.harvard.edu/fellowships

Summary To provide funding to professionals, postdoctorates, and doctoral students (particularly African Americans, other minorities, and women) who are interested in conducting research in areas of concern to the Belfer Center for Science and International Affairs at Harvard University in Cambridge, Massachusetts.

Eligibility The postdoctoral fellowship is open to recent recipients of the Ph.D. or equivalent degree, university faculty members, and employees of government, military, international, humanitarian, and private research institutions who have appropriate professional experience. Applicants for predoctoral fellowships must have passed their general examinations. Lawyers, economists, political scientists, those in the natural sciences, and others of diverse disciplinary backgrounds are also welcome to apply. The program especially encourages applications from women, minorities, and citizens of all countries. All applicants must be interested in conducting research in 1 of the 3 major program areas of the center: 1) the International Security Program (ISP), including Religion in International Affairs; 2) the Science, Technology, and Public Policy Program (STPP), including information and communications technology, energy and water policy, managing the atom project, and the energy technology innovation policy research group; 3) and the Dubai initiative.

Financial data The stipend is $34,000 for postdoctoral research fellows or $20,000 for predoctoral research fellows. Health insurance is also provided.

Duration 10 months.

Number awarded A limited number each year.

Deadline January of each year.

[766]
FINNEGAN HENDERSON DIVERSITY SCHOLARSHIP

Finnegan, Henderson, Farabow, Garrett & Dunner, LLP
Attn: Attorney Recruitment Manager
901 New York Avenue, N.W.
Washington, DC 20001-4413
(202) 408-4034   Fax: (202) 408-4400
E-mail: diversityscholarship@finnegan.com
Web: www.finnegan.com/careers/summerprogram/overview

Summary To provide financial assistance and work experience to African American and other underrepresented minority law students interested in a career in intellectual property law.

Eligibility This program is open to law students from underrepresented minority groups who have demonstrated a commitment to a career in intellectual property law and are currently enrolled either as a first-year full-time student or second-year part-time student. The sponsor defines underrepresented minorities to include American Indians/Alaskan Natives, Blacks/African Americans, Asian Americans, Native Hawaiians or other Pacific Islanders, and Hispanics/Latinos. Applicants must have earned an undergraduate degree in life sciences, engineering, or computer science, or have substantial prior trademark experience. Selection is based on academic performance at the undergraduate, graduate (if applicable), and law school level; relevant work experience; community service; leadership skills; and special accomplishments.

Financial data The stipend is $15,000 per year.

Duration 1 year; may be renewed 1 additional year as long as the recipient completes a summer associateship with the sponsor and maintains of GPA of 3.0 or higher.

Additional information The sponsor, the world's largest intellectual property law firm, established this scholarship in 2003. Summer associateships are available at its offices in Washington, D.C.; Atlanta, Georgia; Cambridge, Massachusetts; Palo Alto, California; or Reston, Virginia.

Number awarded 1 each year.

Deadline February of each year.

[767]
FIRST-YEAR INTERNSHIP PROGRAM OF THE OREGON STATE BAR

Oregon State Bar
Attn: Affirmative Action Program
16037 S.W. Upper Boones Ferry Road
P.O. Box 231935
Tigard, OR 97281-1935
(503) 431-6338
Toll Free: (800) 452-8260, ext. 338 (within OR)
Fax: (503) 598-6938   E-mail: eyip@osbar.org
Web: www.osbar.org/aap

Summary To provide work experience to African American and other minority law students in Oregon.

Eligibility This program is open to ethnic minority students from any state who are completing the first year of law school in Oregon. Applicants must be interested in a summer internship at a law firm in the state. Along with their application, they must submit 1) a resume that includes their community activities; 2) up to 10 pages of a first-semester legal writing assignment; and 3) a 2-page personal statement that covers their past and present ties to ethnic minority communities in Oregon and elsewhere, diversity issues that inspired them to become a lawyer, and their expectations of this internship experience. Participating employers receive a catalog with all application packets; they select students whom they wish to interview and make the final hiring decisions.

Financial data Employers who hire interns through this program pay competitive stipends.

Duration Summer months.

Number awarded Varies each year.

Deadline January of each year.

[768]
FISH & RICHARDSON DIVERSITY FELLOWSHIP PROGRAM

Fish & Richardson P.C.
Attn: Recruiting Department
One Marina Park Drive
Boston, MA 02110
(617) 542-5070   Fax: (617) 542-8906
E-mail: Kiley@fr.com
Web: www.fr.com/careers/diversity

Summary To provide financial assistance for law school to African American and other students who will contribute to diversity in the legal profession.

Eligibility This program is open to students enrolled in the first year at a law school anywhere in the country. Applicants must be African American/Black, American Indian/Alaskan, Hispanic/Latino, Native Hawaiian/Pacific Islander, Asian, 2 or more races, disabled, or openly homosexual, bisexual, and/or transgender. Along with their application, they must submit a 500-word essay describing their background, what led them to the legal field, their interest in the sponsoring law firm, and what they could contribute to its practice and the profession. They must also indicate their first 3 choices of an office of the firm where they are interested in a summer associate clerkship.

Financial data The stipend is $5,000.

Duration 1 year: the second year of law school.

Additional information Recipients are also offered a paid associate clerkship during the summer following their first year of law school at an office of the firm in the location of their choice in Atlanta, Boston, Dallas, Delaware, Houston, New York, San Diego, Silicon Valley, Twin Cities, or Washington, D.C. This program began in 2005.

Number awarded 1 or more each year.

Deadline January of each year.

[769]
FIVE COLLEGE FELLOWSHIP PROGRAM

Five Colleges, Incorporated
Attn: Five Colleges Fellowship Program Committee
97 Spring Street
Amherst, MA 01002-2324
(413) 256-8316   Fax: (413) 256-0249
E-mail: neckert@fivecolleges.edu
Web: www.fivecolleges.edu

Summary To provide funding to African American and other graduate students from underrepresented groups who have completed all the requirements for the Ph.D. except the dissertation and are interested in teaching at selected colleges in Massachusetts.

Eligibility Fellows are chosen by the host department in each of the 5 participating campuses (Amherst, Hampshire, Mount Holyoke, Smith, and the University of Massachusetts). Applicants must be graduate students at an accredited school who have completed all doctoral requirements except the dissertation and are interested in devoting full time to the completion of the dissertation. The chief goal of the program is to support scholars from underrepresented groups and/or scholars "with unique interests and histories whose engagement in the Academy will enrich scholarship and teaching."

Financial data The program provides a stipend of $30,000, a research grant, fringe benefits, office space, library privileges, and housing assistance.

Duration 1 academic year; nonrenewable.

Additional information Although the primary goal is completion of the dissertation, each fellow also has many opportunities to experience working with students and faculty colleagues on the host campus as well as with those at the other colleges. The fellows are also given an opportunity to teach (generally as a team teacher, in a section of a core course, or in a component within a course). Fellows meet monthly with each other to share their experiences. At Smith College, this program is named Mendenhall Fellowships.

Number awarded 4 each year.

Deadline January of each year.

[770]
FLETCHER MAE HOWELL SCHOLARSHIP

Woman's Missionary Union of Virginia
2828 Emerywood Parkway
Richmond, VA 23294
(804) 915-5000, ext. 8267
Toll Free: (800) 255-2428 (within VA)
Fax: (804) 672-8008   E-mail: wmuv@wmuv.org
Web: wmuv.org/developing-future-leaders/scholarships

Summary To provide financial assistance to African American women from Virginia who are working on a graduate degree in Christian education.

Eligibility This program is open to African American women from Virginia who are interested in full-time graduate study in Christian education. An interview is required.

Financial data The stipend is $1,000.

Duration 1 year.

Number awarded Up to 2 each year.

Deadline January of each year.

[771]
FLORIDA BAR FOUNDATION LEGAL AID SUMMER FELLOWSHIP PROGRAM

Florida Bar Foundation
Attn: Grants Coordinator
250 South Orange Avenue, Suite 600P
P.O. Box 1553
Orlando, FL 32802-1553
(407) 843-0045, ext. 105
Toll Free: (800) 541-2195 (within FL)
Fax: (407) 839-0287   E-mail: cbevington@flabarfndn.org
Web: www.flabarfndn.org/grant-programs/lsa

Summary To provide summer work experience at Florida legal assistance providers to students from law schools in any state (particularly African American and other minority students).

Eligibility This program is open to first- and second-year students at accredited law schools in any state. Applicants must be interested in working during the summer at a legal aid and legal services provider funded by Florida's Interest on Trust Accounts (IOTA) program. Minority students are specifically encouraged to apply. Selection is based on experience in working with the low-income community, academic achievement, writing skills, and previous contact with and

long-term commitment and interest in public service/pro bono work.

Financial data The stipend is $5,500 for first-year students or $7,000 for second-year students.

Duration 11 weeks during the summer.

Additional information This program was initiated in 1995.

Number awarded Approximately 20 each year. Since the program began, more than 200 students have participated.

Deadline January of each year.

[772]
FLORIDA DIVERSITY FELLOWSHIPS IN ENVIRONMENTAL LAW

American Bar Association
Attn: Section of Environment, Energy, and Resources
321 North Clark Street
Chicago, IL 60654-7598
(312) 988-5602   Fax: (312) 988-5572
E-mail: jonusaid@staff.abanet.org
Web: www.abanet.org

Summary To provide funding to African American and other law students from underrepresented and underserved groups who are interested in working on a summer project in environmental, energy, or natural resources law in Florida.

Eligibility This program is open to first- and second-year law students and third-year night students who are members of underrepresented and underserved groups, such as minority or low-income populations. Students may be residents of any state and attending school in any state; preference is given to residents of Florida and to students who are enrolled at law schools in Florida or who have a strong interest in the state. Applicants must be interested in working during the summer at a government agency or public interest organization on a project in Florida in the areas of environmental, energy, or natural resources law. Selection is based on interest in environmental issues, academic record, personal qualities, and leadership abilities.

Financial data The stipend is $5,000.

Duration 8 to 10 weeks during the summer.

Additional information This program is cosponsored by the Florida Department of Environmental Protection and the Florida Bar Association's Environmental and Land Use Law Section.

Number awarded 2 each year.

Deadline March of each year.

[773]
FLORIDA LIBRARY ASSOCIATION MINORITY SCHOLARSHIPS

Florida Library Association
164 N.W. Madison Street, Suite 104
P.O. Box 1571
Lake City, FL 32056-1571
(336) 438-5795   Fax: (336) 438-5796
Web: www.flalib.org/scholarships.php

Summary To provide financial assistance to African American and other minority students working on a graduate degree in library and information science in Florida.

Eligibility This program is open to residents of Florida who are working on a graduate degree in library and information science at schools in the state. Applicants must be members of a minority group: Black/African American, American Indian/Alaska Native, Asian/Pacific Islander, or Hispanic/ Latino. They must have some experience in a Florida library, must be a member of the Florida Library Association, and must commit to working in a Florida library for at least 1 year after graduation. Along with their application, they must submit 1) a list of activities, honors, awards, and/or offices held during college and outside college; and 2) a statement of their reasons for entering librarianship and their career goals with respect to Florida libraries. Financial need is considered in the selection process.

Financial data The stipend is $2,000.

Duration 1 year.

Number awarded 1 each year.

Deadline February of each year.

[774]
FOCUS PROFESSIONS GROUP FELLOWSHIPS

American Association of University Women
Attn: AAUW Educational Foundation
301 ACT Drive, Department 60
P.O. Box 4030
Iowa City, IA 52243-4030
(319) 337-1716, ext. 60   Fax: (319) 337-1204
E-mail: aauw@act.org
Web: www.aauw.org/learn/fellowships_grants/selected.cfm

Summary To aid African American and other women of color who are in their final year of graduate training in the fields of business administration, law, or medicine.

Eligibility This program is open to women who are working full time on a degree in fields in which women of color have been historically underrepresented: business administration (M.B.A.), law (J.D.), or medicine (M.D., D.O.). They must be African Americans, Mexican Americans, Puerto Ricans and other Hispanics, Native Americans, Alaska Natives, Asian Americans, or Pacific Islanders. U.S. citizenship or permanent resident status is required. Applicants in business administration must be entering their second year of study; applicants in law must be entering their third year of study; applicants in medicine may be entering their third or fourth year of study. Special consideration is given to applicants who 1) demonstrate their intent to enter professional practice in disciplines in which women are underrepresented, to serve underserved populations and communities, or to pursue public interest areas; and 2) are nontraditional students. Selection is based on professional promise and personal attributes (50%), academic excellence and related academic success indicators (40%), and financial need (10%).

Financial data Stipends range from $5,000 to $18,000.

Duration 1 academic year, beginning in September.

Additional information The filing fee is $35.

Number awarded Varies each year.

Deadline January of each year.

[775]
FOLEY & LARDNER DIVERSITY SCHOLARSHIP

Foley & Lardner LLP
Attn: Diversity Outreach Coordinator
777 East Wisconsin Avenue
Milwaukee, WI 53202-5367
(414) 297-5452   Fax: (414) 297-4900
E-mail: alois@foley.com
Web: apps.foley.com

Summary To provide scholarships to African Americans and other first-year students who are attending selected law schools and will contribute to diversity in the legal profession.

Eligibility This program is open to students in the first year at the following law schools: Berkeley, Duke, Florida, Georgetown, Michigan, Northwestern, UCLA, or Wisconsin. Applicants must 1) be a member of a racial or ethnic group defined as minority (American Indian/Alaska Native, Asian/Pacific Islander, Black, or Hispanic); or 2) self-identify as lesbian, gay, bisexual, or transgender. Selection is based on involvement in diversity-related student organizations, involvement in community activities, undergraduate and law school academic achievement, and work or personal achievements. Financial need is not a consideration.

Financial data The stipend is $5,000; funds are paid at the beginning of the recipient's second semester in law school and must be applied to tuition, books, fees, and other expenses incidental to law school attendance.

Duration 1 semester (the second semester of the first year in law school).

Additional information This program was established in 1998.

Number awarded 8 each year (1 at each of the participating schools).

Deadline February of each year.

[776]
FOURTH DISTRICT MOSAIC SCHOLARSHIP

American Advertising Federation-District 4
c/o Tami L. Grimes, Education Chair
4712 Southwood Lane
Lakeland, FL 33813
(863) 648-5392   E-mail: tamilgrimes@yahoo.com
Web: www.4aaf.com/scholarships.cfm

Summary To provide financial assistance to African American and other minority undergraduate and graduate students from any state who are enrolled at colleges and universities in Florida and interested in entering the field of advertising.

Eligibility This program is open to undergraduate and graduate students from any state enrolled at accredited colleges and universities in Florida who are U.S. citizens or permanent residents of African, African American, Hispanic, Hispanic American, Indian, Native American, Asian, Asian American, or Pacific Islander descent. Applicants must be working on a bachelor's or master's degree in advertising, marketing, communications, public relations, art, graphic arts, or a related field. They must have an overall GPA of 3.0 or higher. Along with their application, they must submit a 250-word essay on why multiculturalism, diversity, and inclusion are important in the advertising, marketing, and communications industry today. Preference is given to members of the American Advertising Federation.

Financial data The stipend is $1,000.

Duration 1 year.

Number awarded 1 or more each year.

Deadline May of each year.

[777]
FRANCHISE LAW DIVERSITY SCHOLARSHIP AWARD

International Franchise Association
Attn: President, Educational Foundation
1501 K Street, N.W., Suite 350
Washington, DC 20005
(202) 662-0764   Fax: (202) 628-0812
E-mail: jreynolds@franchise.org
Web: www.franchise.org/files/Scholarships.aspx

Summary To provide financial assistance to African Americans and other students who will contribute to diversity in the field of franchise law.

Eligibility This program is open to second- and third-year students who are enrolled at ABA-accredited law schools and a member of a diverse group (defined as African Americans, American Indians, Hispanic Americans, Asian Americans, or gays/lesbians). Applicants must be enrolled in at least 1 course oriented toward franchise law (e.g., torts, unfair trade practices, trade secrets, antitrust, trademarks, contracts, agency, or securities). Along with their application, they must submit current transcript, an essay explaining their interest in franchise law, and 2 letters of recommendation.

Financial data The stipend is $4,000. Funds are paid to the recipient's law school and are to be used for tuition.

Duration 1 year.

Additional information This award is cosponsored by the IFA Educational Foundation and DLA Piper US LLP. It may not be used by the recipient's law school to reduce the amount of any institutionally-awarded financial aid.

Number awarded 1 or more each year.

Deadline October of each year.

[778]
FRANK/NORRELL SCHOLARSHIP PROGRAM

Southwestern Athletic Conference
A.G. Gaston Building, Third Floor
1527 Fifth Avenue, North
Birmingham, AL 35203
(205) 251-7573
Web: www.swac.org/ot/swac-scholarship-program.html

Summary To provide financial assistance to African American and other graduate students at member institutions of the Southwestern Athletic Conference (SWAC) who are interested in working on a degree in a field related to physical education.

Eligibility This program is open to students who have been accepted in a graduate program at an SWAC university in health, physical education, recreation, sports administration and management, or a related field. Applicants must have a GPA of 3.0 or higher, a commitment to working full time on a postbaccalaureate professional degree, and a record of participation in athletics that has been a positive influence on their personal and intellectual development.

Financial data The stipend is $3,000.

Duration 1 year.

Additional information This program was established in 1998 with funding from Dr. Gwen Norrell, former professor and faculty athletics representative at Michigan State University, in honor of Dr. James Frank, long-time commissioner of the SWAC. The members of the SWAC include the following Historically Black Colleges and Universities (HBCUs): Alabama A&M University (Normal), Alabama State University (Montgomery), Alcorn State University (Alcorn State, Mississippi), University of Arkansas at Pine Bluff, Grambling State University (Grambling, Louisiana), Jackson State University (Jackson, Mississippi), Mississippi Valley State University (Itta Bena, Mississippi), Prairie View A&M University (Prairie View, Texas), Southern University and A&M College (Baton Rouge, Louisiana), and Texas Southern University (Houston).

Number awarded 1 each year.

Deadline June of each year.

[779]
FRANKLIN WILLIAMS INTERNSHIP

Council on Foreign Relations
Attn: Human Resources Office
58 East 68th Street
New York, NY 10021
(212) 434-9489   Fax: (212) 434-9893
E-mail: humanresources@cfr.org
Web: www.cfr.org

Summary To provide undergraduate and graduate students (particularly African Americans and other minorities) with an opportunity to gain work experience in international affairs at the Council on Foreign Relations in New York.

Eligibility Applicants should be currently enrolled in either their senior year of an undergraduate program or in a graduate program in the area of international relations or a related field. They should have a record of high academic achievement, proven leadership ability, and previous related internship or work experience. Minority students are strongly encouraged to apply.

Financial data The stipend is $10 per hour.

Duration 1 academic term (fall, spring, or summer). Fall and spring interns are required to make a commitment of at least 12 hours per week. Summer interns may choose to make a full-time commitment.

Additional information Interns work closely with a program director or fellow in either the studies or meetings program and are involved with program coordination, substantive and business writing, research, and budget management. In addition, they are encouraged to attend the council's programs and participate in informal training designed to enhance management and leadership skills.

Number awarded 3 each year: 1 each academic term.

Deadline Applications may be submitted at any time.

[780]
FREDERICK DOUGLASS INSTITUTE FOR AFRICAN AND AFRICAN-AMERICAN STUDIES PREDOCTORAL DISSERTATION FELLOWSHIP

University of Rochester
Frederick Douglass Institute for African and African-
  American Studies
Attn: Director for Research Fellowships
302 Morey Hall
RC Box 270440
Rochester, NY 14627-0440
(585) 275-7235   Fax: (585) 256-2594
E-mail: fdi@mail.rochester.edu
Web: www.rochester.edu

Summary   To support doctoral research at the University of Rochester on Africa and its Diaspora.

Eligibility   Graduate students at any university in the United States who are conducting dissertation research on aspects of the African or African American experience are invited to apply if they are interested in spending a year in residence, working on their research, at the University of Rochester. Applicants must have completed their preliminary course work, qualifying exams, and field work.

Financial data   The stipend is $23,000.

Duration   1 academic year.

Additional information   Fellows are given office space within the institute, full access to the facilities of the university, and opportunities for collaboration and discussion. Predoctoral fellows are expected to organize a colloquium, prepare a lecture, and make other contributions to the institute's program. They are expected to be in full-time residence at the institute during the tenure of their award.

Number awarded   1 each year.

Deadline   January of each year.

[781]
FREDRIKSON & BYRON FOUNDATION MINORITY SCHOLARSHIP

Fredrikson & Byron Foundation
Attn: Attorney Recruiting Administrator
200 South Sixth Street, Suite 4000
Minneapolis, MN 55402-1425
(612) 492-7141   Fax: (612) 492-7077
E-mail: glarson@fredlaw.com
Web: www.fredlaw.com/firm/scholarship.htm

Summary   To provide financial assistance and summer work experience to African Americans and other minority law students from any state who are interested in practicing in the Twin Cities area of Minnesota.

Eligibility   This program is open to African American, Asian American, Pacific Islander, Hispanic, Native American, and Alaska Native students enrolled in their first year of law school. Applicants must be interested in practicing law in the Minneapolis-St. Paul area. Along with their application, they must submit brief statement on their expectations and objectives in applying for this scholarship; the factors they will use to measure success in their legal career; what they see as potential issues, obstacles, and opportunities facing new lawyers in a large private practice firm; and their interest in a summer associate position in private practice, including their interest in practicing law in the Minneapolis-St. Paul area. Financial need is not considered.

Financial data   The fellowship stipend is $10,000. The internship portion of the program provides a $1,000 weekly stipend.

Duration   1 year.

Additional information   Fellows are also eligible to participate in an internship at the firm's offices in Minneapolis.

Number awarded   1 each year.

Deadline   March of each year.

[782]
FULFILLING THE LEGACY SCHOLARSHIPS

National Society of Black Engineers
Attn: Programs Department
205 Daingerfield Road
Alexandria, VA 22314
(703) 549-2207   Fax: (703) 683-5312
E-mail: scholarships@nsbe.org
Web: www.nsbe.org

Summary   To provide financial assistance to members of the National Society of Black Engineers (NSBE) who are working on an undergraduate or graduate degree in engineering.

Eligibility   This program is open to members of the society who are undergraduate or graduate engineering students. High school seniors are also eligible. Applicants must epitomize the society's mission of producing culturally responsible Black engineers who excel academically, succeed professionally, and positively impact the community. Selection is based on an essay; academic achievement; service to the society at the chapter, regional, and/or national level; and other professional, campus, and community activities.

Financial data   The stipend is $1,000.

Duration   1 year; may be renewed.

Number awarded   Varies each year, depending on the availability of funds; recently, 10 of these scholarships were awarded to undergraduate and graduate students and 5 to high school seniors.

Deadline   January of each year.

[783]
FURNISS FOUNDATION/AOS GRADUATE FELLOWSHIP

American Orchid Society
16700 AOS Lane
Delray Beach, FL 33446-4351
(561) 404-2000   Fax: (561) 404-2045
E-mail: TheAOS@aos.org
Web: www.aos.org

Summary   To provide funding to doctoral candidates (particularly African Americans, other minorities, women, and students with disabilities) who are conducting dissertation research related to orchids.

Eligibility   This program is open to graduate students whose doctoral dissertation relates to orchids within the disciplines of physiology, molecular biology, structure, systematics, cytology, ecology, and/or evolution. Applicants must submit an outline of their project, their college transcript, a letter of recommendation from their chair, and a 1-page statement on why their project should be considered and the impact it will have on the future of orchidology. Women, minorities, and persons with disabilities are especially encouraged to apply.

Financial data The grant is $9,000 per year. Funds are paid directly to the recipient's college or university, but indirect overhead is not allowed.

Duration Up to a maximum of 3 years.

Additional information This fellowship was first awarded in 1990.

Number awarded 1 each year.

Deadline February of each year.

[784]
FUTURE ENGINEERING FACULTY FELLOWSHIP PROGRAM

Office of Naval Research
c/o North Carolina A&T State University
Department of Electrical and Computer Engineering
1601 East Market Street
Greensboro, NC 27411
(336) 334-7589, ext. 120   Fax: (336) 334-7540
E-mail: lrlittle@ncat.edu
Web: onrfellowship.ncat.edu

Summary To provide financial assistance for graduate education to students interested in becoming faculty members in engineering at Historically Black Engineering Colleges (HBECs).

Eligibility This program is open to U.S. citizens who intend to work on a Ph.D. in designated fields of engineering and, in return for the support, agree to join the engineering faculty of an HBEC. Applicants should be at or near the beginning of doctoral study. They must have a GPA of 3.3 or higher. The designated fields of study include the following specialties within engineering: aerospace, bio-environmental, chemical, civil, computer, electrical, environmental, industrial, manufacturing, mechanical, and ocean. Selection is based on academic achievement, area of study, a personal statement, and letters of recommendation.

Financial data The program provides full payment of tuition and required fees and a competitive stipend that varies each year; recently, stipends were $32,400 for the first year, $33,600 for the second year, and $34,800 for the third year. Allowances of $1,300 for health insurance and $3,000 for travel to attend conferences or meetings are also provided.

Duration Up to 3 years.

Additional information This program is administered by North Carolina A&T State University on behalf of the Office of Naval Research (ONR). HBEC university members include Alabama A&M University, Florida A&M University, Hampton University, Howard University, Jackson State University, Morgan State University, North Carolina A&T State University, Prairie View University, Southern University, Tennessee State University, and Tuskegee University.

Number awarded Approximately 3 each year.

Deadline March of each year.

[785]
GABWA FOUNDATION SCHOLARSHIPS

Georgia Association of Black Women Attorneys
Attn: GABWA Foundation
P.O. Box 4381
Atlanta, GA 30302
(404) 292-3567   E-mail: contact@gabwa.org
Web: www.gabwa.org/foundation.php

Summary To provide financial assistance to Black women from any state enrolled at law schools in Georgia.

Eligibility This program is open to Black women from any state enrolled in the second or third year at a law school in Georgia. Applicants must be able to demonstrate academic achievement, leadership, and commitment to the profession and their community. Along with their application, they must submit a 300-word personal statement that discusses their experience as a Black woman law student, how they expect their legal career to benefit the community at large, and how this scholarship will benefit their quest for a legal education and future career goals. Financial need is considered in the selection process, but it is not required.

Financial data Stipend amounts vary, depending on the availability of funds; recently, they averaged $5,000.

Duration 1 year.

Additional information This program was established in 2002.

Number awarded Varies each year. Since the program was established, it has awarded $80,000 to 21 African American women law students.

Deadline October of each year.

[786]
GAIUS CHARLES BOLIN DISSERTATION AND POST-MFA FELLOWSHIPS

Williams College
Attn: Dean of the Faculty
Hopkins Hall, Third Floor
P.O. Box 141
Williamstown, MA 01267
(413) 597-4351   Fax: (413) 597-3553
E-mail: gburda@williams.edu
Web: dean-faculty.williams.edu/graduate-fellowships

Summary To provide financial assistance to African Americans and members of other underrepresented groups who are interested in teaching courses at Williams College while working on their doctoral dissertation or building their post-M.F.A. professional portfolio.

Eligibility This program is open to members of underrepresented groups, including ethnic minorities, first-generation college students, women in predominantly male fields, and scholars with disabilities. Applicants must be 1) doctoral candidates in any field who have completed all work for a Ph.D. except for the dissertation; or 2) artists who completed an M.F.A. degree within the past 2 years and are building their professional portfolio. They must be willing to teach a course at Williams College. Along with their application, they must submit a full curriculum vitae, a graduate school transcript, 3 letters of recommendation, a copy of their dissertation prospectus or samples of their artistic work, and a description of their teaching interests within a department or program at

Williams College. U.S. citizenship or permanent resident status is required.

Financial data Fellows receive $33,000 for the academic year, plus housing assistance, office space, computer and library privileges, and a research allowance of up to $4,000.

Duration 2 years.

Additional information Bolin fellows are assigned a faculty advisor in the appropriate department. This program was established in 1985. Fellows are expected to teach a 1-semester course each year. They must be in residence at Williams College for the duration of the fellowship.

Number awarded 3 each year.

Deadline November of each year.

[787]
GE LLOYD TROTTER AFRICAN AMERICAN FORUM SCHOLARSHIP

National Society of Black Engineers
Attn: Programs Department
205 Daingerfield Road
Alexandria, VA 22314
(703) 549-2207   Fax: (703) 683-5312
E-mail: scholarships@nsbe.org
Web: www.nsbe.org

Summary To provide financial assistance to members of the National Society of Black Engineers (NSBE) who are working on an undergraduate or graduate degree in engineering.

Eligibility This program is open to members of the society who are U.S. citizens or authorized to work in the United States and rising sophomores, juniors, seniors, or graduate students. Applicants must be working on a degree in computer science, physics, or the engineering specialties of aeronautical/aerospace, biomechanical, chemical, computer, electrical, industrial, materials, mechanical, nuclear, or systems. They must have a GPA of 3.0 or higher. Selection is based on an essay; academic achievement; service to the society at the chapter, regional, and/or national level; and other professional, campus, and community activities.

Financial data The stipend is $2,500.

Duration 1 year.

Additional information This program is supported by General Electric employees with matching contributions from the GE Fund. Recipients must be willing to accept a paid internship at a GE location for 10 weeks during the summer.

Number awarded Varies each year, depending on the availability of funds; recently, 2 of these scholarships were awarded.

Deadline October of each year.

[788]
GEM M.S. ENGINEERING FELLOWSHIP PROGRAM

National Consortium for Graduate Degrees for Minorities
  in Engineering and Science (GEM)
Attn: Manager, Fellowships Administration
1430 Duke Street
Alexandria, VA 22314
(703) 562-3639   Fax: (202) 207-3518
E-mail: info@gemfellowship.org
Web: www.gemfellowship.org/gem-fellowship

Summary To provide financial assistance and summer work experience to African American and other underrepresented minority students interested in working on a master's degree in engineering or computer science.

Eligibility This program is open to U.S. citizens and permanent residents who are members of ethnic groups underrepresented in engineering: American Indians/Native Americans, Blacks/African Americans, or Latinos/Hispanic Americans. Applicants must be a junior, senior, or graduate of an ABET-accredited engineering or computer science program and have an academic record that indicates the ability to pursue graduate studies in engineering (including a GPA of 2.8 or higher). They must agree to apply to at least 3 of the 104 GEM member universities that offer a master's degree and to intern during summers with a sponsoring GEM employer.

Financial data The fellowship pays tuition, fees, and a stipend of $10,000 over its lifetime. In addition, each participant receives a salary during the summer work assignment as a GEM summer intern. Employer members reimburse GEM participants for travel expenses to and from the summer work site.

Duration Up to 3 semesters or 4 quarters, plus summer work internships lasting 10 to 14 weeks for up to 3 summers, depending on whether the student applies as a junior, senior, or college graduate; recipients begin their internship upon acceptance into the program and work each summer until completion of their master's degree.

Additional information During the summer internship, each fellow is assigned an engineering project in a research setting. Each project is based on the fellow's interest and background and is carried out under the supervision of an experienced engineer. At the conclusion of the internship, each fellow writes a project report. Recipients must work on a master's degree in the same engineering discipline as their baccalaureate degree.

Number awarded Approximately 300 each year.

Deadline November of each year.

[789]
GEM PH.D. ENGINEERING FELLOWSHIP PROGRAM

National Consortium for Graduate Degrees for Minorities
  in Engineering and Science (GEM)
Attn: Manager, Fellowships Administration
1430 Duke Street
Alexandria, VA 22314
(703) 562-3639   Fax: (202) 207-3518
E-mail: info@gemfellowship.org
Web: www.gemfellowship.org/gem-fellowship

Summary To provide financial assistance and summer work experience to African American and other underrepresented minority students interested in obtaining a Ph.D. degree in engineering.

Eligibility This program is open to U.S. citizens and permanent residents who are members of ethnic groups underrepresented in engineering: American Indians/Native Americans, Blacks/African Americans, and Latinos/Hispanic Americans. Applicants must be college seniors, master's degree students, or graduates of an ABET-accredited program in engineering and have an academic record that indicates the ability to work on a doctoral degree in engineering (including a GPA of 3.0 or higher). They must agree to apply to at least

3 of the 100 GEM member universities that offer a doctoral degree in engineering and to intern during summer with a sponsoring GEM employer.

Financial data The stipend is $14,000 for the first year; in subsequent years, fellows receive full payment of tuition and fees plus a stipend and assistantship from their university that is equivalent to funding received by other doctoral students in their department.

Duration 3 to 5 years for the fellowship; 12 weeks during the summer immediately after sponsorship for the internship.

Additional information This program is valid only at 1 of the 105 participating GEM member universities; write to GEM for a list. The fellowship award is designed to support the student in the first year of the doctoral program without working. Subsequent years are subsidized by the respective universities and will usually include either a teaching or research assistantship. Recipients must participate in the GEM summer internship; failure to agree to accept the internship cancels the fellowship.

Number awarded Approximately 50 each year.

Deadline November of each year.

[790]
GEM PH.D. SCIENCE FELLOWSHIP PROGRAM

National Consortium for Graduate Degrees for Minorities in Engineering and Science (GEM)
Attn: Manager, Fellowships Administration
1430 Duke Street
Alexandria, VA 22314
(703) 562-3639   Fax: (202) 207-3518
E-mail: info@gemfellowship.org
Web: www.gemfellowship.org/gem-fellowship

Summary To provide financial assistance and summer work experience to African American and other underrepresented minority students interested in working on a Ph.D. degree in the life sciences, mathematics, or physical sciences.

Eligibility This program is open to U.S. citizens and permanent residents who are members of ethnic groups underrepresented in the natural sciences: American Indians/Native Americans, Blacks/African Americans, and Latinos/Hispanic Americans. Applicants must be college seniors, master's degree students, or recent graduates in the biological sciences, mathematics, or physical sciences (chemistry, computer science, earth sciences, and physics) with an academic record that indicates the ability to pursue doctoral studies (including a GPA of 3.0 or higher). They must agree to apply to at least 3 of the 100 GEM member universities that offer a doctoral degree in science and to intern during summer with a sponsoring GEM employer.

Financial data The stipend is $14,000 for the first year; in subsequent years, fellows receive full payment of tuition and fees plus a stipend and assistantship from their university that is equivalent to funding received by other doctoral students in their department.

Duration 3 to 5 years for the fellowship; 12 weeks during the summer immediately after sponsorship for the internship.

Additional information This program is valid only at 1 of 105 participating GEM member universities; write to GEM for a list. The fellowship award is designed to support the student in the first year of the doctoral program without working. Subsequent years are subsidized by the respective university and

will usually include either a teaching or research assistantship. Recipients must participate in the GEM summer internship; failure to agree to accept the internship cancels the fellowship. Recipients must enroll in the same scientific discipline as their undergraduate major.

Number awarded Approximately 40 each year.

Deadline November of each year.

[791]
GEOCORPS AMERICA DIVERSITY INTERNSHIPS

Geological Society of America
Attn: Program Officer, GeoCorps America
3300 Penrose Place
P.O. Box 9140
Boulder, CO 80301-9140
(303) 357-1025   Toll Free: (800) 472-1988, ext. 1025
Fax: (303) 357-1070   E-mail: mdawson@geosociety.org
Web: rock.geosociety.org/g.corps/index

Summary To provide work experience at national parks to student members of the Geological Society of America (GSA) who are African American or come from other underrepresented groups.

Eligibility This program is open to all GSA members, but applications are especially encouraged from groups historically underrepresented in the sciences (African Americans, American Indians, Alaska Natives, Hispanics, Native Hawaiians, other Pacific Islanders, and persons with disabilities). Applicants must be interested in a summer work experience in facilities of the U.S. government, currently limited to the National Park Service but planned for expansion to the Forest Service and the Bureau of Land Management. Geoscience knowledge and skills are a significant requirement for most positions, but students from diverse disciplines (e.g., chemistry, physics, engineering, mathematics, computer science, ecology, hydrology, meteorology, the social sciences, and the humanities) are also invited to apply. Activities involve research; interpretation and education; inventory and monitoring; or mapping, surveying, and GIS. Prior interns are not eligible. U.S. citizenship or possession of a proper visa is required.

Financial data Each internship provides a $2,750 stipend. Also provided are free housing or a housing allowance of $1,500 to $2,000.

Duration 10 to 12 weeks during the summer.

Number awarded Varies each year.

Deadline Deadline not specified.

[792]
GEORGE A. LOTTIER GOLF FOUNDATION INTERNSHIP AND SCHOLARSHIP AWARD

Atlanta Tribune: The Magazine
Attn: Editor
875 Old Roswell Road, Suite C-100
Roswell, GA 30076-1660
(770) 587-0501, ext. 202   Fax: (770) 642-6501
E-mail: scholarships@atlantatribune.com
Web: www.atlantatribune.com

Summary To provide financial assistance and summer work experience at the *Atlanta Tribune: The Magazine* to African American and other minority upper-division and graduate students from any state.

Eligibility This program is open to African American and other minority college students from any state entering their junior or senior year of college or enrolled in a graduate program with a GPA of 3.0 or higher. Applicants must be majoring in a field related to print media, including communications, English, graphic design (with an emphasis on publication layout and design), journalism, marketing, or sales. Along with their application, they must submit a 500-word personal essay.

Financial data The program provides a paid internship and a scholarship stipend of $2,500.

Duration 1 year, including 10 weeks during the summer for the internship.

Number awarded Varies each year; recently, 4 of these scholarships and internships were awarded.

Deadline April of each year.

[793]
GEORGE A. STRAIT MINORITY SCHOLARSHIP ENDOWMENT

American Association of Law Libraries
Attn: Chair, Scholarships Committee
105 West Adams Street, Suite 3300
Chicago, IL 60603
(312) 939-4764   Fax: (312) 431-1097
E-mail: scholarships@aall.org
Web: www.aallnet.org/services/sch_strait.asp

Summary To provide financial assistance to African American and other minority college seniors or college graduates who are interested in becoming law librarians.

Eligibility This program is open to college graduates with meaningful law library experience who are members of minority groups and intend to have a career in law librarianship. Applicants must be degree candidates at an ALA-accredited library school or an ABA-accredited law school. Along with their application, they must submit a personal statement that discusses their interest in law librarianship, reason for applying for this scholarship, career goals as a law librarian, etc.

Financial data The stipend is $3,500.

Duration 1 year.

Additional information This program, established in 1990, is currently supported by Thomson West.

Number awarded Varies each year; recently, 5 of these scholarships were awarded.

Deadline March of each year.

[794]
GEORGE E. MEARES MEMORIAL SCHOLARSHIP

Omega Psi Phi Fraternity
Attn: Charles R. Drew Memorial Scholarship Commission
3951 Snapfinger Parkway
Decatur, GA 30035-3203
(404) 284-5533   Fax: (404) 284-0333
E-mail: scholarshipchairman@oppf.org
Web: oppf.org/scholarship

Summary To provide financial assistance to African American and other graduate students in selected social science fields.

Eligibility This program is open to U.S. citizens who are interested in working on a graduate degree in social work,

criminal justice, or social sciences. Applicants must include a statement of 200 to 250 words on their purpose for applying for this scholarship, how they believe funds from the fraternity can assist them in achieving their career goals, and other circumstances (including financial need) that make it important for them to receive financial assistance.

Financial data The stipend is $5,000.

Duration 1 year.

Additional information This program, established in 1977, is named for George E. Meares, who served as Grand Basileus of Omega Psi Phi (an historically Black fraternity) from 1964 to 1967.

Number awarded 1 or more each year.

Deadline May of each year.

[795]
GEORGE V. POWELL DIVERSITY SCHOLARSHIP

Lane Powell Spears Lubersky LLP
Attn: Manager of Attorney Recruiting
1420 Fifth Avenue, Suite 4100
Seattle, WA 98101-2338
(206) 223-6123   Fax: (206) 223-7107
E-mail: rodenl@lanepowell.com
Web: www.lanepowell.com/422/diversity-scholarship

Summary To provide financial assistance and work experience to African American and other law students who will contribute to the diversity of the legal community.

Eligibility This program is open to second-year students in good standing at an ABA-accredited law school. Applicants must be able to contribute meaningfully to the diversity of the legal community and have a demonstrated desire to work, live, and eventually practice law in Seattle or Portland. They must submit a cover letter that includes a statement indicating eligibility to participate in the program, a resume, a current copy of law school transcript, a legal writing sample, and a list of 2 or 3 professional or academic references. Selection is based on academic achievement and record of leadership abilities, community service, and involvement in community issues.

Financial data The program provides a stipend of $7,500 for the third year of law school and a paid summer associate clerkship.

Duration 1 year, including the summer.

Additional information This program was established in 2005. Clerkships are provided at the offices of the sponsor in Seattle or Portland.

Number awarded 1 each year.

Deadline September of each year.

[796]
GERALD BOYD/ROBIN STONE SCHOLARSHIP

National Association of Black Journalists
Attn: Program Coordinator
8701-A Adelphi Road
Adelphi, MD 20783-1716
(301) 445-7100, ext. 108   Toll Free: (866) 479-NABJ
Fax: (301) 445-7101   E-mail: nabj@nabj.org
Web: www.nabj.org

Summary To provide financial assistance to undergraduate or graduate student members of the National Association of Black Journalists (NABJ) who are majoring in print journalism.

Eligibility This program is open to African American undergraduate or graduate students who are currently attending an accredited 4-year college or university. Applicants must be majoring in print journalism and have a GPA of 2.5 or higher. They must be NABJ members. Along with their application, they submit samples of their work, an official college transcript, 2 letters of recommendation, a resume, and a 500- to 800-word essay describing their accomplishments as a student journalist, their career goals, and their financial need.

Financial data The stipend is $2,500. Funds are paid directly to the recipient's college or university.

Duration 1 year; nonrenewable.

Number awarded 1 each year.

Deadline April of each year.

[797]
GLOBAL CHANGE GRADUATE RESEARCH ENVIRONMENTAL FELLOWSHIPS (GREF)

Oak Ridge Institute for Science and Education
Attn: Global Change Education Program
120 Badger Avenue, M.S. 36
P.O. Box 117
Oak Ridge, TN 37831-0117
(865) 576-7009   Fax: (865) 241-9445
E-mail: gcep@orau.gov
Web: www.atmos.anl.gov/GCEP/GREF/index.html

Summary To provide doctoral students (particularly African Americans or other minorities and women) with an opportunity to conduct research on global change.

Eligibility This program is open to students who have completed their first year of graduate school, unless they previously participated in the Global Change Summer Undergraduate Research Experience (SURE). Applicants must be proposing to conduct research at a national laboratory in a program area within the Department of Energy's Office of Biological and Environmental Research (DOE-BER): the atmospheric science program, the environmental meteorology program, the atmospheric radiation measurement program, the terrestrial carbon processes effort, the program for ecosystem research, and studies carried out under the direction of the National Institute for Global Environmental Change. Minority and female students are particularly encouraged to apply. U.S. citizenship is required.

Financial data Participants receive an annual stipend of $19,500 ($1,500 per month plus a $600 research education supplement in March and October); reimbursement of tuition and fees at the college or university they attend; and transportation, per diem, and lodging for summer activities.

Duration Up to 3 years.

Additional information This program, funded by DOE-BER, began in 1999. Fellows are encouraged to participate in the Summer Undergraduate Research Experience (SURE) orientation and focus sessions at a participating university.

Number awarded 10 to 15 each year.

Deadline December of each year.

[798]
GOLDMAN SACHS MBA FELLOWSHIP

Goldman Sachs
Attn: Human Capital Management
30 Hudson Street, 34th Floor
Jersey City, NJ 07302
(212) 902-1000   E-mail: holly.jackson@gs.com
Web: www2.goldmansachs.com

Summary To provide financial assistance and work experience to African American and other underrepresented minority students interested in working on an M.B.A. degree.

Eligibility This program is open to graduate students of Black, Latino, or Native American descent who are interested in working on an M.B.A. degree. Applicants must be preparing for a career in the financial services industry. Along with their application, they must submit 2 essays of 500 words or less on the following topics: 1) why they are preparing for a career in the financial services industry; and 2) their current involvement with a community-based organization. Selection is based on analytical skills and the ability to identify significant problems, gather facts, and analyze situations in depth; interpersonal skills, including, but not limited to, poise, confidence, and professionalism; academic record; evidence of hard work and commitment; ability to work well with others; and commitment to community involvement.

Financial data Fellows receive $15,000 toward payment of tuition and living expenses for the first year of business school; an internship at a domestic office of Goldman Sachs during the summer after the first year of business school; and (after successful completion of the summer internship and acceptance of an offer to return to the firm after graduation as a full-time regular employee) either payment of tuition costs for the second year of business school or an additional $15,000 toward tuition and living costs.

Duration Up to 2 years.

Additional information This program was initiated in 1997.

Number awarded 1 or more each year.

Deadline December of each year.

[799]
GOODWIN PUBLIC INTEREST FELLOWSHIPS FOR LAW STUDENTS OF COLOR

Goodwin Procter LLP
Attn: Recruiting Manager
53 State Street
Boston, MA 02109
(617) 570-8156 E-mail: fellowships@goodwinprocter.com
Web: www.goodwinprocter.com

Summary To provide financial assistance to African American and other minority students who are interested in public interest law.

Eligibility This program is open to students of color entering their second year at a law school in any state. Applicants must actively express an interest in working in the sponsoring firm's summer program in public interest law. If they are applying for the Goodwin MassMutual Diversity, they must express an interest in working with MassMutual's legal department in Springfield, Massachusetts for 2 weeks as part of the summer program and specializing in the investment or insurance business or in a legal focus to advance business objectives. Selection is based on academic performance, leadership abilities, involvement in minority student organizations, commitment to community service, interpersonal skills, other special achievements and honors, and interest in working with the firm during the summer.

Financial data   The stipend is $7,500.

Duration   1 year; nonrenewable.

Additional information   This program was established in 2005. In 2007, it added the Goodwin MassMutual Diversity Fellowship, created in conjunction with its long-standing client, Massachusetts Mutual Life Insurance Company (MassMutual). Summer positions are available at the firm's offices in Boston, Los Angeles, New York, Palo Alto, San Diego, San Francisco, and Washington, D.C.

Number awarded   3 each year, including 1 Goodwin MassMutual Diversity Fellowship.

Deadline   October of each year.

[800]
GRADUATE FELLOWSHIP IN THE HISTORY OF SCIENCE

American Meteorological Society
Attn: Fellowship/Scholarship Program
45 Beacon Street
Boston, MA 02108-3693
(617) 227-2426, ext. 246   Fax: (617) 742-8718
E-mail: scholar@ametsoc.org
Web: www.ametsoc.org

Summary   To provide funding to African Americans and other underrepresented graduate student members of the American Meteorological Society (AMS) who are interested in conducting dissertation research on the history of meteorology.

Eligibility   This program is open to AMS members and student members who are planning to complete a doctoral dissertation on the history of the atmospheric or related oceanic or hydrologic sciences. Applicants must be U.S. citizens or permanent residents and working on a degree at a U.S. institution. Fellowships may be used to support research at a location away from the student's institution, provided the plan is approved by the student's thesis adviser. In such an instance, an effort is made to place the student into a mentoring relationship with a member of the society at an appropriate institution. The sponsor specifically encourages applications from women, minorities, and students with disabilities who are traditionally underrepresented in the atmospheric and related oceanic sciences.

Financial data   The stipend is $15,000.

Duration   1 year.

Number awarded   1 each year.

Deadline   February of each year.

[801]
GRADUATE RESEARCH FELLOWSHIP PROGRAM OF THE NATIONAL SCIENCE FOUNDATION

National Science Foundation
Directorate for Education and Human Resources
Attn: Division of Graduate Education
4201 Wilson Boulevard, Room 875S
Arlington, VA 22230
(703) 292-8694   Toll Free: (866) NSF-GRFP
Fax: (703) 292-9048   E-mail: grfp@nsf.gov
Web: www.nsf.gov/funding/pgm_summ.jsp?pims_id=6201

Summary   To provide financial assistance to graduate students (especially African Americans or other minorities, women, and students with disabilities) who are interested in working on a master's or doctoral degree in fields supported by the National Science Foundation (NSF).

Eligibility   This program is open to U.S. citizens, nationals, and permanent residents who wish to work on research-based master's or doctoral degrees in a field of science (including social science), technology, engineering, or mathematics (STEM) supported by NSF. Other work in medical, dental, law, public health, or practice-oriented professional degree programs, or in joint science-professional degree programs, such as M.D./Ph.D. and J.D./Ph.D. programs, is not eligible. Other categories of ineligible support include 1) clinical, counseling, business, or management fields; 2) education (except science and engineering education); 3) history (except the history of science); 4) social work; 5) medical sciences or research with disease-related goals, including work on the etiology, diagnosis, or treatment of physical or mental disease, abnormality, or malfunction in human beings or animals; 6) research involving animal models with disease-related goals; and 7) testing of drugs or other procedures for disease-related goals. Applications normally should be submitted during the senior year in college or in the first year of graduate study; eligibility is limited to those who have completed no more than 12 months of graduate study since completion of a baccalaureate degree. Applicants who have already earned an advanced degree in science, engineering, or medicine (including an M.D., D.D.S., or D.V.M.) are ineligible. Selection is based on 1) intellectual merit of the proposed activity (strength of the academic record, proposed plan of research, previous research experience, references, appropriateness of the choice of institution); and 2) broader impacts of the proposed activity (how well does the activity advance discovery and understanding, how well does it broaden the participation of underrepresented groups (e.g., gender, ethnicity, disability, geographic), to what extent will it enhance the infrastructure for research and education, will the results be disseminated broadly to enhance scientific and technological understanding, what may be the benefits of the proposed activity to society).

Financial data   The stipend is $30,000 per year; an additional $10,500 cost-of-education allowance is provided to the recipient's institution. If a fellow affiliates with a foreign institution, tuition and fees are reimbursed to the fellow up to a maximum of $10,500 per tenure year and an additional international research travel allowance of $1,000 is provided.

Duration   Up to 3 years, usable over a 5-year period.

Additional information Fellows may choose as their fellowship institution any appropriate nonprofit U.S. or foreign institution of higher education.

Number awarded Approximately 2,000 each year.

Deadline November of each year.

[802]
GRADUATE STUDENT INDUSTRIAL FELLOWSHIPS/TRAINEESHIPS

National Science Foundation
Directorate for Engineering
Attn: Division of Industrial Innovation and Partnerships
4201 Wilson Boulevard, Room 550S
Arlington, VA 22230
(703) 292-7082　　　　　　Fax: (703) 292-9056
TDD: (800) 281-8749　　　　E-mail: dsenich@nsf.gov
Web: www.nsf.gov/funding/pgm_summ.jsp?pims_id=13706

Summary To provide an opportunity for graduate students (particularly African Americans and other underrepresented minorities or students with disabilities) to work in industry as part of the Grant Opportunities for Academic Liaison with Industry (GOALI) program of the National Science Foundation (NSF).

Eligibility This program is open to graduate students (preferably Ph.D. students) in science, engineering, and mathematics fields of interest to NSF. Applicants must be U.S. citizens, nationals, or permanent residents. They must be proposing a program of full- or part-time work in industry in an area related to their research under the guidance of an academic adviser and an industrial mentor. The program encourages applications from underrepresented minorities and persons with disabilities.

Financial data Graduate students may receive stipends from $1,500 to $1,800 per month, plus transportation expenses. The faculty adviser may receive 10% of the total award for research-related expenses, excluding equipment. No indirect costs are allowed. The total award may be up to $30,000 for a fellowship for a single student.

Duration Up to 1 year.

Additional information This program is also offered by most other NSF directorates. Check the web site for a name and e-mail address of the contact person in each directorate.

Number awarded A total of 60 to 80 grants for all GOALI programs is awarded each year; total funding is approximately $5 million.

Deadline Applications may be submitted at any time.

[803]
GRAND BASILEUS AWARD

Omega Psi Phi Fraternity
Attn: Charles R. Drew Memorial Scholarship Commission
3951 Snapfinger Parkway
Decatur, GA 30035-3203
(404) 284-5533　　　　　　Fax: (404) 284-0333
E-mail: scholarshipchairman@oppf.org
Web: oppf.org/scholarship

Summary To provide financial assistance for graduate or professional education to members of Omega Psi Phi who have an outstanding academic record.

Eligibility This program is open to members of the fraternity who are graduating college seniors planning to continue

on to graduate or professional school. Applicants must be enrolled full time at a 4-year college or university and have a GPA of 3.3 or higher. Along with their application, they must submit a statement of 200 to 250 words on their purpose for applying for this scholarship, how they believe funds from the fraternity can assist them in achieving their career goals, and other circumstances (including financial need) that make it important for them to receive financial assistance.

Financial data The stipend is $6,500.

Duration 1 year.

Number awarded 1 or more each year.

Deadline May of each year.

[804]
GRANTS FOR HEALTH SERVICES RESEARCH DISSERTATIONS

Agency for Healthcare Research and Quality
Attn: Office of Extramural Research, Education, and
　Priority Populations
540 Gaither Road
Rockville, MD 20850
(301) 427-1527　　　　　　Fax: (301) 427-1562
TDD: (301) 451-0088
E-mail: Brenda.harding@ahrq.hhs.gov
Web: www.ahrq.gov/fund/grantix.htm

Summary To provide funding to African American and other doctoral candidates engaged in research for a dissertation that examines an aspect of the health care system.

Eligibility This program is open to students enrolled full time in an accredited research doctoral degree program in such fields as the social or behavioral sciences, health services, epidemiology, biostatistics, health policy, or health informatics. Applicants must have completed all requirements for the doctoral degree except for the dissertation. Their proposed dissertation topic must relate to the strategic goals of the Agency for Healthcare Research and Quality (AHRQ): 1) reducing the risk of harm from health care services by promoting the delivery of appropriate care that achieves the best quality outcomes; 2) achieving wider access to effective health care services and reducing health care costs; and 3) assuring that providers and consumers/patients use beneficial and timely health care information to make informed decisions. Priority is given to proposals that address health services research issues critical to such priority population as individuals living in inner city and rural (including frontier) areas; low-income and minority groups; women, children, and the elderly; and individuals with special health care needs, including those with disabilities and those who need chronic or end-of-life health care. U.S. citizenship or permanent resident status is required. Members of underrepresented racial and ethnic groups and individuals with disabilities are especially encouraged to apply.

Financial data Up to $40,000 is awarded for the investigator's salary, direct project expenses (travel, data purchasing, data processing, and supplies), and matriculation fees. The institution will receive facilities and administrative costs of 8% of total allowable direct costs, exclusive of tuition and related fees, health insurance, and expenditures for equipment.

Duration 9 to 17 months.

Number awarded Up to 30 each year.

Deadline February, June, or October of each year.

[805]
GREATER HARTFORD CHAPTER NBMBAA GRADUATE SCHOLARSHIP

National Black MBA Association-Greater Hartford
  Chapter
Attn: Scholarship Committee
P.O. Box 2332
Hartford, CT 06146
(860) 586-7002
Web: 111.blackmbahartford.com

Summary To provide financial assistance to African Americans and other minorities from any state who are working on a master's degree in business or management at a school in Connecticut or the Springfield area of Massachusetts.

Eligibility This program is open to minority students who may be residents of any state but must be enrolled full or part time at a university in Connecticut or the greater Springfield, Massachusetts area. Applicants must have completed at least 1 semester of a master's degree program in business or management. Along with their application, they must submit a 2-page essay on their choice of 4 topics that change annually but relate to African Americans and business. Selection is based on that essay, transcripts, a resume, and extracurricular activities.

Financial data Stipends range from $1,000 to $5,000.

Duration 1 year.

Number awarded 4 each year: 1 each at $5,000, $2,500, $2,000, and $1,000.

Deadline October.

[806]
HAMPTON ROADS BLACK MEDIA PROFESSIONALS SCHOLARSHIPS

Hampton Roads Black Media Professionals
P.O. Box 2622
Norfolk, VA 23501-2622
(757) 222-5857   E-mail: hrbmpinc@aim.com
Web: www.hrbmp.us

Summary To provide financial assistance to outstanding African American undergraduate and graduate students in Virginia who are preparing for a career in journalism.

Eligibility This program is open to 1) African American undergraduate and graduate students pursuing media-related degrees at a Virginia college or university, and 2) African American students who are residents of Hampton Roads and pursuing media-related degrees at a college or university anywhere in the country. Undergraduates must be freshmen, sophomores, or juniors taking at least 12 credit hours per semester; graduate students must be taking at least 9 credit hours. Applicants must submit an official college transcript, a resume, 2 letters of recommendation, and a 500-word essay that is judged on clarity, presentation, and originality.

Financial data The stipend is $1,000.

Duration 1 year; may be renewed.

Number awarded Varies; generally 5 to 6 each year. Since 1989, when the award was initiated, more than $70,000 in scholarships has been awarded.

Deadline December of each year.

[807]
HARRIETT G. JENKINS PRE-DOCTORAL FELLOWSHIP PROGRAM

United Negro College Fund Special Programs
  Corporation
6402 Arlington Boulevard, Suite 600
Falls Church, VA 22042
(703) 677-3400   Toll Free: (800) 530-6232
Fax: (703) 205-7645   E-mail: portal@uncfsp.org
Web: www.uncfsp.org

Summary To provide financial assistance and work experience to students (especially African Americans or other minorities, women, and students with disabilities) who are working on a graduate degree in a field of interest to the National Aeronautics and Space Administration (NASA).

Eligibility This program is open to members of groups underrepresented in science, technology, engineering, or mathematics (STEM), including women, minorities, and people with disabilities. Applicants must be full-time graduate students in a program leading to a master's or doctoral degree in a NASA-related discipline (aeronautics, aerospace engineering, astronomy, atmospheric science, bioengineering, biology, chemistry, computer science, earth sciences, engineering, environmental sciences, life sciences, materials sciences, mathematics, meteorology, neuroscience, physics, or robotics). They must be U.S. citizens and have a GPA of 3.0 or higher. Doctoral students who have advanced to candidacy are ineligible.

Financial data The stipend is $22,000 per year for doctoral fellows or $16,000 per year for master's degree students. The tuition offset is at least $8,500. Fellows who are also selected for a mini research award at a NASA Center or the Jet Propulsion Laboratory receive an additional grant of $7,000.

Duration 3 years.

Additional information This program, established in 2001, is funded by NASA and administered by the United Negro College Fund Special Programs Corporation. Fellows may also compete for a mini research award to engage in a NASA research experience that is closely aligned with the research conducted at the fellow's institution. The participating NASA facilities are Ames Research Center (Moffett Field, California), Jet Propulsion Laboratory (Pasadena, California), Dryden Flight Research Center (Edwards, California), Johnson Space Center (Houston, Texas), Stennis Space Center (Stennis Space Center, Mississippi), Marshall Space Flight Center (Marshall Space Flight Center, Alabama), Glenn Research Center (Cleveland, Ohio), Kennedy Space Center (Kennedy Space Center, Florida), Langley Research Center (Hampton, Virginia), and Goddard Space Flight Center (Greenbelt, Maryland).

Number awarded Approximately 20 each year.

Deadline April of each year.

[808]
HARRY R. KENDALL LEADERSHIP DEVELOPMENT SCHOLARSHIPS

United Methodist Church
General Board of Global Ministries
Attn: United Methodist Committee on Relief
475 Riverside Drive, Room 1522
New York, NY 10115
(212) 870-3871   Toll Free: (800) UMC-GBGM
E-mail: jyoung@gbgm-umc.org
Web: new.gbgm-umc.org/umcor/work/health/scholarships

Summary   To provide financial assistance to African Americans who are Methodists or other Christians and preparing for a career in a health-related field.

Eligibility   This program is open to undergraduate and graduate students who are U.S. citizens or permanent residents of African American descent. Applicants must be professed Christians, preferably United Methodists. They must be planning to enter a health care field or already be a practitioner in such a field. Financial need is considered in the selection process.

Financial data   The stipend is $2,000.

Duration   1 year.

Additional information   This program was established in 1980.

Number awarded   Varies each year.

Deadline   June of each year.

[809]
HAWAII DIVERSITY FELLOWSHIPS IN ENVIRONMENTAL LAW

American Bar Association
Attn: Section of Environment, Energy, and Resources
321 North Clark Street
Chicago, IL 60654-7598
(312) 988-5602   Fax: (312) 988-5572
E-mail: jonusaid@staff.abanet.org
Web: www.abanet.org

Summary   To provide funding to African American and other law students from underrepresented and underserved groups who are interested in working on a summer project in environmental, energy, or natural resources law in Hawaii.

Eligibility   This program is open to first- and second-year law students and third-year night students who 1) are either enrolled at a law school in Hawaii or residents of Hawaii enrolled at a law school in another state; and 2) will contribute to increasing diversity in the Hawaii environmental bar. Applicants must be interested in working during the summer at a government agency or public interest organization in Hawaii in the field of environmental, energy, or natural resources law. Selection is based on interest in environmental issues, academic record, personal qualities, leadership abilities, and ability to contribute to diversity in the Hawaii environmental bar.

Financial data   The stipend is $5,000.

Duration   8 to 10 weeks during the summer.

Additional information   This program is cosponsored by the Hawai'i State Bar Association's Natural Resources Section.

Number awarded   1 each year.

Deadline   April of each year.

[810]
HAYNES/HETTING AWARD

Philanthrofund Foundation
Attn: Scholarship Committee
1409 Willow Street, Suite 210
Minneapolis, MN 55403-3251
(612) 870-1806   Toll Free: (800) 435-1402
Fax: (612) 871-6587   E-mail: info@PfundOnline.org
Web: www.pfundonline.org/scholarships.html

Summary   To provide funds to African American and Native American Minnesota students who are associated with gay, lesbian, bisexual, and transgender (GLBT) activities.

Eligibility   This program is open to residents of Minnesota and students attending a Minnesota educational institution who are African American or Native American. Applicants must be self-identified as GLBT or from a GLBT family. They may be attending or planning to attend trade school, technical college, college, or university (as an undergraduate or graduate student). Selection is based on the applicant's 1) affirmation of GLBT identity or commitment to GLBT communities; 2) evidence of experience and skills in service and leadership; and 3) evidence of service and leadership in GLBT communities, including serving as a role model, mentor, and/or adviser.

Financial data   The stipend ranges up to $2,000. Funds must be used for tuition, books, fees, or dissertation expenses.

Duration   1 year.

Number awarded   1 or more each year.

Deadline   January of each year.

[811]
HEALTH RESEARCH AND EDUCATIONAL TRUST SCHOLARSHIPS

New Jersey Hospital Association
Attn: Health Research and Educational Trust
760 Alexander Road
P.O. Box 1
Princeton, NJ 08543-0001
(609) 275-4224   Fax: (609) 452-8097
Web: www.njha.com/hret/scholarship.aspx

Summary   To provide financial assistance to New Jersey residents (particularly African Americans, other minorities, and women) who are working on an undergraduate or graduate degree in a field related to health care administration at a school in any state.

Eligibility   This program is open to residents of New Jersey enrolled in an upper-division or graduate program in hospital or health care administration, public administration, nursing, or other allied health profession at a school in any state. Graduate students working on an advanced degree to prepare to teach nursing are also eligible. Applicants must have a GPA of 3.0 or higher and be able to demonstrate financial need. Along with their application, they must submit a 2-page essay (on which 50% of the selection is based) describing their academic plans for the future. Minorities and women are especially encouraged to apply.

Financial data   The stipend is $2,000.

Duration   1 year.

Additional information   This program began in 1983.

Number awarded Varies each year; recently, 3 of these scholarships were awarded.

Deadline July of each year.

[812]
HEALTH SCIENCES STUDENT FELLOWSHIPS IN EPILEPSY

Epilepsy Foundation
Attn: Research Department
8301 Professional Place
Landover, MD 20785-2237
(301) 459-3700   Toll Free: (800) EFA-1000
Fax: (301) 577-2684   TDD: (800) 332-2070
E-mail: grants@efa.org
Web: www.epilepsyfoundation.org

Summary To provide financial assistance to medical and health science graduate students (especially those who are African Americans or from other minority groups, women, and students with disabilities) who are interested in working on an epilepsy project during the summer.

Eligibility This program is open to students enrolled, or accepted for enrollment, in a medical school, a doctoral program, or other graduate program. Applicants must have a defined epilepsy-related study or research plan to be carried out under the supervision of a qualified mentor. Because the program is designed as a training opportunity, the quality of the training plans and environment are considered in the selection process. Other selection criteria include the quality of the proposed project, the relevance of the proposed work to epilepsy, the applicant's interest in the field of epilepsy, the applicant's qualifications, the mentor's qualifications (including his or her commitment to the student and the project), and the quality of the training environment for research related to epilepsy. U.S. citizenship is not required, but the project must be conducted in the United States. Applications from women, members of minority groups, and people with disabilities are especially encouraged. The program is not intended for students working on a dissertation research project.

Financial data Stipends are $3,000.

Duration 3 months during the summer.

Additional information Support for this program is provided by many individuals, families, and corporations, especially the American Epilepsy Society, Abbott Laboratories, Ortho-McNeil Pharmaceutical, and Pfizer Inc.

Number awarded Varies each year; recently, 3 of these fellowships were awarded.

Deadline March of each year.

[813]
HEINEKEN USA PERFORMING ARTS SCHOLARSHIP

Congressional Black Caucus Foundation, Inc.
Attn: Director, Educational Programs
1720 Massachusetts Avenue, N.W.
Washington, DC 20036
(202) 263-2800   Toll Free: (800) 784-2577
Fax: (202) 775-0773   E-mail: info@cbcfinc.org
Web: www.cbcfinc.org/scholarships.html

Summary To provide financial assistance to African American and other undergraduate and graduate students who are interested in studying the performing arts.

Eligibility This program is open to 1) minority and other graduating high school seniors planning to attend an accredited institution of higher education; and 2) currently-enrolled full-time undergraduate, graduate, and doctoral students in good academic standing with a GPA of 2.5 or higher. Applicants be interested in preparing for a career in the performing arts, including theater, motion pictures, drama, comedy, music, dance, opera, marching bands, and other musical ensembles. Along with their application, they must submit a 2-minute CD or DVD of their performance and a personal statement of 500 to 1,000 words on 1) their future goals, major field of study, and how that field of study will help them to achieve their future career goals; 2) involvement in school activities, community and public service, hobbies, and sports; 3) how receiving this award will affect their current and future plans; and 4) other experiences, skills, or qualifications. They must also be able to demonstrate financial need, leadership ability, and participation in community service activities.

Financial data The stipend is $3,000.

Duration 1 year.

Additional information This program, established in 2000, is sponsored by Heineken USA.

Number awarded 10 each year.

Deadline April of each year.

[814]
HELEN T. CARR FELLOWSHIPS

American Society for Engineering Education
Attn: Projects Department
1818 N Street, N.W., Suite 600
Washington, DC 20036-2479
(202) 331-3525   Fax: (202) 265-8504
E-mail: projects@asee.org
Web: www.asee.org/fellowships/hbecc.cfm

Summary To provide financial assistance to African American engineering faculty and graduate students at Historically Black Engineering Colleges (HBEC) who are interested in earning a doctoral degree.

Eligibility This program is open to African American engineering faculty and graduate students at any of the following HBECs: Alabama A&M University (Normal, Alabama), Hampton University (Hampton, Virginia), Howard University (Washington, D.C.), Morgan State University (Baltimore, Maryland), North Carolina A&T State University (Greensboro, North Carolina), Prairie View A&M University (Prairie View, Texas), Southern University and A&M College (Baton Rouge, Louisiana), Tennessee State University (Nashville, Tennessee), and Tuskegee University (Tuskegee, Alabama). Applicants may not have completed their doctorates, but they must be interested in doing so. Upon completion of the doctoral degree requirements, a fellow must agree to return to 1 of the HBEC institutions.

Financial data Up to $10,000 a year is provided through this program.

Duration 1 year; may be renewed.

Additional information Support for this program is provided by the GE Fund and the U.S. National Aeronautics and Space Administration.

Number awarded Varies each year.

Deadline Applications may be submitted at any time.

[815]
HENRY LUCE FOUNDATION/ACLS
DISSERTATION FELLOWSHIPS IN AMERICAN
ART

American Council of Learned Societies
Attn: Office of Fellowships and Grants
633 Third Avenue
New York, NY 10017-6795
(212) 697-1505   Fax: (212) 949-8058
E-mail: fellowships@acls.org
Web: www.acls.org/programs/American-art

Summary   To provide funding to doctoral students (particularly African Americans or other minorities and women) who are interested in conducting dissertation research anywhere in the world on the history of American art.

Eligibility   This program is open to Ph.D. candidates in departments of art history whose dissertations are focused on the history of the visual arts in the United States and are object-oriented. Applicants may be proposing to conduct research at their home institution, abroad, or at another appropriate site. U.S. citizenship or permanent resident status is required. Students preparing theses for a Master of Fine Arts degree are not eligible. Applications are particularly invited from women and members of minority groups.

Financial data   The grant is $25,000. Fellowship funds may not be used to pay tuition costs.

Duration   1 year; nonrenewable.

Additional information   This program is funded by the Henry Luce Foundation and administered by the American Council of Learned Societies (ACLS).

Number awarded   10 each year.

Deadline   November of each year.

[816]
HILLIS CLARK MARTIN & PETERSON DIVERSITY
FELLOWSHIP

Hillis Clark Martin & Peterson P.S.
Attn: Recruiting and Marketing Coordinator
1221 Second Avenue, Suite 500
Seattle, WA 98101-2925
(206) 623-1745   Fax: (206) 623-7789
E-mail: abt@hcmp.com
Web: www.hcmp.com

Summary   To provide financial assistance to African American and other law students who have diversity in their background and life experiences.

Eligibility   This program is open to students enrolled in the first year at an ABA-accredited law school. Applicants must have a diverse background and life experiences and demonstrate the capacity to contribute meaningfully to the diversity of the legal community. Along with their application, they must submit a resume, transcripts, a personal statement of 1 to 2 pages describing their background and addressing the selection criteria, a legal writing sample, and a list of 3 references. Selection is based on distinction in academic performance, accomplishments and activities, commitment to community service, leadership ability, and financial need.

Financial data   The stipend is $7,500.

Duration   1 year.

Additional information   The program includes a salaried summer associate position following the first year of law school.

Number awarded   1 or more each year.

Deadline   January of each year.

[817]
HUBERTUS W.V. WILLEMS SCHOLARSHIP FOR
MALE STUDENTS

National Association for the Advancement of Colored
   People
Attn: Education Department
4805 Mt. Hope Drive
Baltimore, MD 21215-3297
(410) 580-5760   Toll Free: (877) NAACP-98
E-mail: youth@naacpnet.org
Web: www.naacp.org/pages/naacp-scholarships

Summary   To provide funding to males, particularly male members of the National Association for the Advancement of Colored People (NAACP), who are interested in undergraduate or graduate education in selected scientific fields.

Eligibility   This program is open to males who are high school seniors, college students, or graduate students. Applicants must be majoring (or planning to major) in 1 of the following fields: engineering, chemistry, physics, or mathematics. Membership and participation in the NAACP are highly desirable. The required minimum GPA is 2.5 for graduating high school seniors and undergraduate students or 3.0 for graduate students. Applicants must be able to demonstrate financial need, defined as a family income of less than $16,245 for a family of 1 ranging to less than $49,905 for a family of 7. Along with their application, they must submit a 1-page essay on their interest in their major and a career, their life's ambition, what they hope to accomplish in their lifetime, and what position they hope to attain. Full-time enrollment is required for undergraduate students, although graduate students may be enrolled full or part time. U.S. citizenship is required.

Financial data   The stipend is $2,000 per year for undergraduate students or $3,000 per year for graduate students.

Duration   1 year; may be renewed.

Number awarded   Varies each year; recently, 7 of these scholarships were awarded.

Deadline   March of each year.

[818]
HUGGINS-QUARLES AWARD

Organization of American Historians
Attn: Award and Committee Coordinator
112 North Bryan Street
Bloomington, IN 47408-4141
(812) 855-7311   Fax: (812) 855-0696
E-mail: khamm@oah.org
Web: www.oah.org

Summary   To provide funding to African American and other minority graduate students who are completing dissertations in American history.

Eligibility   This program is open to graduate students of color at the dissertation research stage of their Ph.D. programs. Their dissertation must deal with a topic related to American history.

Financial data   The award is $1,200 (if 1 is presented) or $600 (if 2 are presented).

Additional information   This award was established in honor of Benjamin Quarles and the late Nathan Huggins, both outstanding historians of the African American past.

Number awarded   1 or 2 each year.

Deadline   November of each year.

[819]
HUGH J. ANDERSEN MEMORIAL SCHOLARSHIPS

National Medical Fellowships, Inc.
Attn: Scholarship Program
347 Fifth Avenue, Suite 510
New York, NY 10016
(212) 483-8880   Toll Free: (877) NMF-1DOC
Fax: (212) 483-8897   E-mail: info@nmfonline.org
Web: www.nmfonline.org

Summary   To provide financial assistance to African American and other underrepresented minority medical students who reside or attend school in Minnesota.

Eligibility   This program is open to African Americans, Mexican Americans, Native Hawaiians, Alaska Natives, American Indians, Vietnamese, Cambodians, and mainland Puerto Ricans who have completed at least 1 year of medical school. Applicants must be Minnesota residents enrolled in an accredited U.S. medical school or residents of other states attending medical school in Minnesota. Selection is based on leadership, community service, and financial need. Direct applications are not accepted; candidates must be nominated by medical school deans.

Financial data   The award is $2,500.

Duration   1 year.

Additional information   This award was established in 1982.

Number awarded   Up to 5 each year.

Deadline   Nominations must be submitted by March of each year.

[820]
HURSTON/WRIGHT AWARD FOR COLLEGE WRITERS

Zora Neale Hurston/Richard Wright Foundation
Attn: Hurston/Wright Awards
12138 Central Avenue, Suite 209
Bowie, MD 20721
(301) 459-2108   E-mail: info@hurstonwright.org
Web: www.hurstonwright.org

Summary   To recognize and reward the best fiction written by undergraduate or graduate students of African descent.

Eligibility   This program is open to students of African descent who are enrolled full time as undergraduate or graduate students at a college or university in the United States. Applicants should submit a manuscript of a short story (up to 25 pages) or novel excerpt (up to 15 pages). They should indicate whether it is a short story or novel excerpt. Only 1 entry may be submitted per applicant. Writers who have already published a book (in any genre) are ineligible.

Financial data   The first-place award is $1,000; finalist awards are $500.

Duration   The prizes are awarded annually.

Additional information   There is a $10 processing fee.

Number awarded   3 awards are presented each year: 1 first-place award and 2 finalist awards.

Deadline   January of each year.

[821]
IBM PHD FELLOWSHIP PROGRAM

IBM Corporation
Attn: University Relations
1133 Westchester Avenue
White Plains, NY 10604
Toll Free: (800) IBM-4YOU   TDD: (800) IBM-3383
E-mail: phdfellow@us.ibm.com
Web: www.ibm.com

Summary   To provide funding and work experience to students (especially African American and other minorities or women) who are working on a Ph.D. in a research area of broad interest to IBM.

Eligibility   Students nominated for this fellowship should be enrolled full time at an accredited college or university in any country and should have completed at least 1 year of graduate study in the following fields: business sciences (including financial services, risk management, marketing, communication, and learning/knowledge management); computer science and engineering; electrical and mechanical engineering; management; mathematical sciences (including analytics, statistics, operations research, and optimization); physical sciences (including chemistry, materials sciences, and physics); or service science, management, and engineering (SSME). They should be planning a career in research. Nominations must be made by a faculty member and endorsed by the department head. The program values diversity, and encourages nominations of women, minorities, and others who contribute to that diversity. Selection is based on the applicants' potential for research excellence, the degree to which their technical interests align with those of IBM, and academic progress to date. Preference is given to students who have had an IBM internship or have closely collaborated with technical or services people from IBM.

Financial data   Fellowships pay tuition, fees, and a stipend of $17,500 per year.

Duration   1 year; may be renewed up to 2 additional years, provided the recipient is renominated, interacts with IBM's technical community, and demonstrates continued progress and achievement.

Additional information   Recipients are offered an internship at 1 of the IBM Research Division laboratories and are given an IBM computer.

Number awarded   Varies each year; recently, 57 of these scholarships were awarded.

Deadline   October of each year.

[822]
ILLINOIS JUDICIAL COUNCIL FOUNDATION LAW SCHOOL SCHOLARSHIP

Illinois Judicial Council Foundation, Inc.
Attn: Foundation
20 South Clark Street, Suite 900
Chicago, IL 60603
(312) 726-8775   E-mail: info@illinoisjudicialcouncil.org
Web: www.illinoisjudicialcouncil.org

Summary To provide financial assistance to African American and other minority students from any state who are enrolled at law schools in Illinois.

Eligibility This program is open to minorities from any state who are enrolled full time at law schools in Illinois. Selection is based on academic achievement, community and extracurricular activities, honors and awards, an interview, a personal statement, recommendations, and financial need.

Financial data The stipend is $1,500.

Duration 1 year.

Additional information The Illinois Judicial Council was founded in 1983 as an organization of state and federal judges, administrative law judges, and judicial hearing officers of predominantly African American descent.

Number awarded 1 or more each year.

Deadline April of each year.

[823]
ILLINOIS NURSES ASSOCIATION CENTENNIAL SCHOLARSHIP

Illinois Nurses Association
Attn: Illinois Nurses Foundation
105 West Adams Street, Suite 2101
Chicago, IL 60603
(312) 419-2900   Fax: (312) 419-2920
E-mail: info@illinoisnurses.com
Web: www.illinoisnurses.com

Summary To provide financial assistance to nursing undergraduate and graduate students who are African American or members of other underrepresented groups.

Eligibility This program is open to students working on an associate, bachelor's, or master's degree at an accredited NLNAC or CCNE school of nursing. Applicants must be members of a group underrepresented in nursing (African Americans, Hispanics, American Indians, Asians, and males). Undergraduates must have earned a passing grade in all nursing courses taken to date and have a GPA of 2.85 or higher. Graduate students must have completed at least 12 semester hours of graduate work and have a GPA of 3.0 or higher. All applicants must be willing to 1) act as a spokesperson to other student groups on the value of the scholarship to continuing their nursing education, and 2) be profiled in any media or marketing materials developed by the Illinois Nurses Foundation. Along with their application, they must submit a narrative of 250 to 500 words on how they, nurses, plan to affect policy at either the state or national level that impacts on nursing or health care generally, or how they believe they will impact the nursing profession in general.

Financial data A stipend is awarded (amount not specified).

Duration 1 year.

Number awarded 1 or more each year.

Deadline March of each year.

[824]
INDIANA CLEO FELLOWSHIPS

Indiana Supreme Court
Attn: Division of State Court Administration
115 West Washington Street, Suite 1080
Indianapolis, IN 46204-3417
(317) 232-2542   Toll Free: (800) 452-9963
Fax: (317) 233-6586
Web: www.in.gov/judiciary/cleo

Summary To provide financial assistance to African Americans or other disadvantaged college seniors from any state interested in attending law school in Indiana.

Eligibility This program is open to graduating college seniors who have applied to a law school in Indiana. Selected applicants are invited to participate in the Indiana Conference for Legal Education Opportunity (Indiana CLEO) Summer Institute, held at a law school in the state. Admission to that program is based on GPA, LSAT scores, 3 letters of recommendation, a resume, a personal statement, and financial need. Students who successfully complete the Institute and become certified graduates of the program may be eligible to receive a fellowship.

Financial data All expenses for the Indiana CLEO Summer Institute are paid. The fellowship stipend is $6,500 per year for students who attend a public law school or $9,000 per year for students who attend a private law school.

Duration The Indiana CLEO Summer Institute lasts 6 weeks. Fellowships are for 1 year and may be renewed up to 2 additional years.

Additional information The first Summer Institute was held in 1997.

Number awarded 30 students are invited to participate in the summer institute; the number of those selected to receive a fellowship varies each year.

Deadline March of each year.

[825]
INDIANAPOLIS CHAPTER NBMBAA GRADUATE SCHOLARSHIP PROGRAM

National Black MBA Association-Indianapolis Chapter
Attn: Scholarship Program
P.O. Box 2325
Indianapolis, IN 46206-2325
(317) 308-6447   E-mail: scholarship@nbmbaa-indy.org
Web: www.nbmbaa-indy.org/nbmbaa_education.htm

Summary To provide financial assistance to African American students from Indiana working on an M.B.A. degree.

Eligibility This program is open to African American students enrolled full time in a graduate business or management program and working on an M.B.A. degree. Applicants must be Indiana residents or enrolled at an Indiana college or university and have a GPA of 2.0 or higher. They must submit essays on 3 topics that change annually but relate to African Americans and business. U.S. citizenship or permanent resident status is required.

Financial data The stipend is $2,000. A 1-year membership in the National Black MBA Association (NBMBAA) is also provided.

Duration 1 year.

Number awarded 2 each year.

Deadline October of each year.

[826]
INDUSTRY/GOVERNMENT GRADUATE FELLOWSHIPS

American Meteorological Society
Attn: Fellowship/Scholarship Coordinator
45 Beacon Street
Boston, MA 02108-3693
(617) 227-2426, ext. 246   Fax: (617) 742-8718
E-mail: scholar@ametsoc.org
Web: www.ametsoc.org

Summary   To encourage African American and other underrepresented students entering their first year of graduate school to work on an advanced degree in the atmospheric and related oceanic and hydrologic sciences.

Eligibility   This program is open to students entering their first year of graduate study who wish to pursue advanced degrees in the atmospheric or related oceanic or hydrologic sciences. Applicants must be U.S. citizens or permanent residents and have a GPA of 3.25 or higher. Along with their application, they must submit 200-word essays on 1) their most important achievements that qualify them for this scholarship, and 2) their career goals in the atmospheric or related sciences. Selection is based on academic record as an undergraduate. The sponsor specifically encourages applications from women, minorities, and students with disabilities who are traditionally underrepresented in the atmospheric and related oceanic sciences.

Financial data   The stipend is $24,000 per academic year.

Duration   9 months.

Additional information   This program was initiated in 1991. It is funded by high-technology firms and government agencies.

Number awarded   Varies each year; recently, 13 of these scholarships were awarded.

Deadline   February of each year.

[827]
INSTITUTE FOR INTERNATIONAL PUBLIC POLICY FELLOWSHIPS

United Negro College Fund Special Programs
  Corporation
Attn: Institute for International Public Policy
6402 Arlington Boulevard, Suite 600
Falls Church, VA 22042
(703) 677-3400   Toll Free: (800) 530-6232
Fax: (703) 205-7645   E-mail: iippl@uncfsp.org
Web: www.uncfsp.org

Summary   To provide financial assistance and work experience to African Americans and other minority students who are interested in preparing for a career in international affairs.

Eligibility   This program is open to full-time sophomores at 4-year institutions who have a GPA of 3.2 or higher and are nominated by the president of their institution. Applicants must be African American, Hispanic/Latino American, Asian American, American Indian, Alaskan Native, Native Hawaiian, or Pacific Islander. They must be interested in participating in policy institutes, study abroad, language training, internships, and graduate education that will prepare them for a career in international service. U.S. citizenship or permanent resident status is required.

Financial data   For the sophomore summer policy institute, fellows receive student housing and meals in a university facility, books and materials, all field trips and excursions, and a $1,050 stipend. For the junior year study abroad component, half the expenses for 1 semester, to a maximum of $8,000, is provided. For the junior summer policy institute, fellows receive student housing and meals in a university facility, books and materials, travel to and from the institute, and a $1,000 stipend. For the summer language institute, fellows receive tuition and fees, books and materials, room and board, travel to and from the institute, and a $1,000 stipend. During the internship, a stipend of up to $3,500 is paid. During the graduate school period, fellowships are funded jointly by this program and the participating graduate school. The program provides $15,000 toward a master's degree in international affairs with the expectation that the graduate school will provide $15,000 in matching funds.

Duration   2 years of undergraduate work and 2 years of graduate work, as well as the intervening summers.

Additional information   This program consists of 6 components: 1) a sophomore year summer policy institute based at Howard University that introduces fellows to international policy development, foreign affairs, cultural competence, careers in those fields, and options for graduate study; 2) a junior year study abroad program at an accredited overseas institution; 3) a 7-week junior year summer institute at the University of Maryland's School of Public Policy; 4) for students without established foreign language competency, a summer language institute at Middlebury College Language Schools in Middlebury, Vermont following the senior year; 5) fellows with previously established foreign language competence participate in a post-baccalaureate internship to provide the practical experience needed for successful graduate studies in international affairs; and 6) a master's degree in international affairs (for students who are admitted to such a program). This program is administered by the United Negro College Fund Special Programs Corporation with funding provided by a grant from the U.S. Department of Education.

Number awarded   30 each year.

Deadline   February of each year.

[828]
INTEL SCHOLARSHIP

Society of Women Engineers
Attn: Scholarship Selection Committee
120 South LaSalle Street, Suite 1515
Chicago, IL 60603-3572
(312) 596-5223   Toll Free: (877) SWE-INFO
Fax: (312) 644-8557
E-mail: scholarshipapplication@swe.org
Web: societyofwomenengineers.swe.org

Summary   To provide financial assistance to women (particularly African American and other minority women) working on a graduate degree in computer science or specified fields of engineering.

Eligibility   This program is open to women working on a graduate degree in computer science or chemical, computer, electrical, industrial, manufacturing, materials, or mechanical engineering. Applicants must have a GPA of 3.5 or higher. Selection is based on merit and financial need. Preference is given to members of groups underrepresented in computer science and engineering.

Financial data The stipend is $1,000.

Duration 1 year.

Additional information This program is sponsored by Intel Corporation.

Number awarded 3 each year.

Deadline February of each year.

[829]
INTELLECTUAL PROPERTY LAW SECTION WOMEN AND MINORITY SCHOLARSHIP

State Bar of Texas
Attn: Intellectual Property Law Section
c/o Bhaveeni D. Parmar, Scholarship Selection
  Committee
Klemchuk Kubasta LLP
Campbell Centre II
9150 North Central Expressway, Suite 1150
Dallas, TX 75206
(214) 367-6000   E-mail: bhaveeni@kk-llp.com
Web: www.texasbariplaw.org/index.htm

Summary To provide financial assistance to African Americans, other minorities, and females at law schools in Texas who plan to practice intellectual property law.

Eligibility This program is open to women and members of minority groups (African Americans, Hispanics, Asian Americans, and Native Americans) from any state who are currently enrolled at an ABA-accredited law school in Texas. Applicants must be planning to practice intellectual property law in Texas. Along with their application, they must submit a 2-page essay explaining why they plan to prepare for a career in intellectual property law in Texas, any qualifications they believe are relevant for their consideration for this scholarship, and (optionally) any issues of financial need they wish to have considered.

Financial data The stipend is $2,500.

Duration 1 year.

Number awarded 2 each year: 1 to a women and 1 to a minority.

Deadline April of each year.

[830]
INTERMOUNTAIN SECTION AWWA DIVERSITY SCHOLARSHIP

American Water Works Association-Intermountain
  Section
3430 East Danish Road
Sandy, UT 94093
(801) 712-1619   Fax: (801) 487-6699
E-mail: nicoleb@ims-awwa.org
Web: www.ims-awwa.org

Summary To provide financial assistance to African American and other underrepresented undergraduate and graduate students working on a degree in the field of water quality, supply, and treatment at a university in Idaho or Utah.

Eligibility This program is open to women and students who identify as Hispanic or Latino, Black or African American, Native Hawaiian or other Pacific Islander, Asian, or American Indian or Alaska Native. Applicants must be entering or enrolled in an undergraduate or graduate program at a college or university in Idaho or Utah that relates to water quality, supply, or treatment. Along with their application, they must

submit a 2-page essay on their academic interests and career goals and how those relate to water quality, supply, or treatment. Selection is based on that essay, letters of recommendation, and potential to contribute to the field of water quality, supply, and treatment in the Intermountain West.

Financial data The stipend is $1,000. The winner also receives a 1-year student membership in the Intermountain Section of the American Water Works Association (AWWA) and a 1-year subscription to *Journal AWWA*.

Duration 1 year; nonrenewable.

Number awarded 1 each year.

Deadline October of each year.

[831]
INTERNATIONAL ASSOCIATION OF BLACK ACTUARIES SCHOLARSHIPS

International Association of Black Actuaries
Attn: IABA Foundation Scholarship Committee
P.O. Box 369
Windsor, CT 06095
(860) 219-9534   Fax: (215) 219-9546
E-mail: iaba@blackactuaries.org
Web: www.blackactuaries.org/scholarships

Summary To provide financial assistance to Black upper-division and graduate students preparing for an actuarial career.

Eligibility This program is open to full-time juniors, seniors, and graduate students who are of African descent, originating from the United States, Canada, the Caribbean, or African nations. Applicants must have been admitted to a college or university offering either a program in actuarial science or courses that will prepare them for an actuarial career. They must be citizens or permanent residents of the United States or Canada or eligible to study in those countries under a U.S. student visa or Canadian student authorization. Other requirements include a GPA of 3.0 or higher, a mathematics SAT score of at least 600 or a mathematics ACT score of at least 28, completion of probability and calculus courses, attempting or passing an actuarial examination, completion of Validation by Educational Experience (VEE) requirements, and familiarity with actuarial profession demands. Selection is based on merit and financial need.

Financial data Stipends range from $500 to $4,000 per year.

Duration 1 year; may be renewed.

Number awarded 1 or more each year.

Deadline May of each year.

[832]
INTERNATIONAL COMMUNICATIONS INDUSTRIES FOUNDATION AV SCHOLARSHIPS

InfoComm International
International Communications Industries Foundation
11242 Waples Mill Road, Suite 200
Fairfax, VA 22030
(703) 273-7200   Toll Free: (800) 659-7469
Fax: (703) 278-8082   E-mail: srieger@infocomm.org
Web: www.infocomm.org

Summary To provide financial assistance to high school seniors and college students (especially African Americans, other minorities, and women) who are interested in preparing for a career in the audiovisual (AV) industry.

Eligibility This program is open to high school seniors, undergraduates, and graduate students already enrolled in college. Applicants must have a GPA of 2.75 or higher and be majoring or planning to major in audiovisual subjects or related fields, including audio, video, electronics, telecommunications, technical aspects of the theater, data networking, software development, or information technology. Students in other programs, such as journalism, may be eligible if they can demonstrate a relationship to career goals in the AV industry. Along with their application, they must submit 1) an essay of 150 to 200 words on the career path they plan to pursue in the audiovisual industry in the next 5 years, and 2) an essay of 250 to 300 words on the experience or person influencing them the most in selecting the audiovisual industry as their career of choice. Minority and women candidates are especially encouraged to apply. Selection is based on the essays, presentation of the application, GPA, AV-related experience, work experience, and letters of recommendation.

Financial data The stipend is $1,200 per year. Funds are sent directly to the school.

Duration 1 year; recipients may reapply.

Additional information InfoComm International, formerly the International Communications Industries Association, established the International Communications Industries Foundation (ICIF) to manage its charitable and educational activities.

Number awarded Varies each year; recently, 29 of these scholarships were awarded.

Deadline May of each year.

[833]
IRTS BROADCAST SALES ASSOCIATE PROGRAM

International Radio and Television Society Foundation
Attn: Director, Special Projects
420 Lexington Avenue, Suite 1601
New York, NY 10170-0101
(212) 867-6650   Toll Free: (888) 627-1266
Fax: (212) 867-6653   E-mail: apply@irts.org
Web: irts.org/broadcast-sales-associate-program.html

Summary To provide summer work experience to African American and other minority graduate students interested in working in broadcast sales in the New York City area.

Eligibility This program is open to graduate students at 4-year colleges and universities who are members of a minority (Black, Hispanic, Asian/Pacific Islander, American Indian/Alaskan Native) group. Applicants must be interested in working during the summer in a sales training program traditionally reserved for actual station group employees. They must be a communications major or have demonstrated a strong interest in the field through extracurricular activities or other practical experience, but they are not required to have experience in broadcast sales.

Financial data Travel, housing, and a living allowance are provided.

Duration 9 weeks during the summer.

Additional information The program consists of a 1-week orientation to the media and entertainment business,

followed by an 8-week internship experience in the sales division of a network stations group.

Number awarded Varies each year.

Deadline February of each year.

[834]
IRTS SUMMER FELLOWSHIP PROGRAM

International Radio and Television Society Foundation
Attn: Director, Special Projects
420 Lexington Avenue, Suite 1601
New York, NY 10170-0101
(212) 867-6650   Toll Free: (888) 627-1266
Fax: (212) 867-6653   E-mail: apply@irts.org
Web: irts.org/summerfellowshipprogram.html

Summary To provide summer work experience to upper-division and graduate students (particularly African Americans and other minorities) who are interested in working during the summer in broadcasting and related fields in the New York City area.

Eligibility This program is open to juniors, seniors, and graduate students at 4-year colleges and universities. Applicants must either be a communications major or have demonstrated a strong interest in the field through extracurricular activities or other practical experience. Minority (Black, Hispanic, Asian/Pacific Islander, American Indian/Alaskan Native) students are especially encouraged to apply.

Financial data Travel, housing, and a living allowance are provided.

Duration 9 weeks during the summer.

Additional information The first week consists of a comprehensive orientation to broadcasting, cable, advertising, and new media. Then, the participants are assigned an 8-week fellowship. This full-time "real world" experience in a New York-based corporation allows them to reinforce or redefine specific career goals before settling into a permanent job. Fellows have worked at all 4 major networks, at local New York City radio and television stations, and at national rep firms, advertising agencies, and cable operations. This program includes fellowships reserved for students at designated universities (Notre Dame, Pennsylvania State University, Boston College, Holy Cross College) and the following named awards: the Thomas S. Murphy Fellowship (sponsored by ABC National Television Sales), the Helen Karas Memorial Fellowship, the Leslie Moonves Fellowship (sponsored by CBS Television Station Sales), and the Sumner Redstone Fellowship (sponsored by CBS Television Station Sales).

Number awarded Varies; recently, 23 of these fellowships were awarded.

Deadline November of each year.

[835]
ISAAC J. "IKE" CRUMBLY MINORITIES IN ENERGY GRANT

American Association of Petroleum Geologists
  Foundation
Attn: Grants-in-Aid Program
1444 South Boulder Avenue
P.O. Box 979
Tulsa, OK 74101-0979
(918) 560-2644   Toll Free: (888) 945-2274, ext. 644
Fax: (918) 560-2642   E-mail: tcampbell@aapg.org
Web: foundation.aapg.org/gia/crumbly.cfm

Summary To provide funding to African Americans, other minorities, and female graduate students who are interested in conducting research related to earth science aspects of the petroleum industry.

Eligibility This program is open to women and ethnic minorities (Black, Hispanic, Asian, or Native American, including American Indian, Eskimo, Hawaiian, or Samoan) who are working on a master's or doctoral degree. Applicants must be interested in conducting research related to the search for and development of petroleum and energy-minerals resources and to related environmental geology issues. Selection is based on merit and, in part, on financial need. Factors weighed in selecting the successful applicants include: the applicant's past academic performance, originality and imagination of the proposed project, departmental support, and significance of the project to petroleum, energy minerals, and related environmental geology.

Financial data Grants range from $500 to $3,000. Funds are to be applied to research-related expenses (e.g., a summer of field work). They may not be used to purchase capital equipment or to pay salaries, tuition, room, or board.

Duration 1 year. Doctoral candidates may receive a 1-year renewal.

Number awarded 1 each year.

Deadline January of each year.

[836]
JACOBS ENGINEERING SCHOLARSHIP

Conference of Minority Transportation Officials
Attn: National Scholarship Program
818 18th Street, N.W., Suite 850
Washington, DC 20006
(202) 530-0551   Fax: (202) 530-0617
Web: www.comto.org/news-youth.php

Summary To provide financial assistance to African American and other minority upper-division and graduate students in a field related to transportation.

Eligibility This program is open to minority juniors, seniors, and graduate students in fields related to transportation (e.g., civil engineering, construction engineering, environmental engineering, safety, transportation, urban planning). Undergraduates must have a GPA of 3.0 or higher; graduate students must have a GPA of at least 3.5. Applicants must submit a cover letter with a 500-word statement of career goals. Financial need is not considered in the selection process. U.S. citizenship is required.

Financial data The stipend is $4,000. Funds are paid directly to the recipient's college or university.

Duration 1 year.

Additional information The Conference of Minority Transportation Officials (COMTO) was established in 1971 to promote, strengthen, and expand the roles of minorities in all aspects of transportation. This program is sponsored by Jacobs Engineering Group Inc. Recipients are required to become members of COMTO and attend the COMTO National Scholarship Luncheon.

Number awarded 1 or more each year.

Deadline April of each year.

[837]
JAMES B. MORRIS SCHOLARSHIP

James B. Morris Scholarship Fund
Attn: Scholarship Selection Committee
525 S.W. Fifth Street, Suite A
Des Moines, IA 50309-4501
(515) 282-8192   Fax: (515) 282-9117
E-mail: morris@assoc-mgmt.com
Web: www.morrisscholarship.org

Summary To provide financial assistance to African American and other minority undergraduate, graduate, and law students in Iowa.

Eligibility This program is open to minority students (African Americans, Asian/Pacific Islanders, Hispanics, or Native Americans) who are interested in studying at a college, graduate school, or law school. Applicants must be either Iowa residents and high school graduates who are attending a college or university anywhere in the United States or non-Iowa residents who are attending a college or university in Iowa; preference is given to native Iowans who are attending an Iowa college or university. Along with their application, they must submit an essay of 250 to 500 words on why they are applying for this scholarship, activities or organizations in which they are involved, and their future plans. Selection is based on the essay, academic achievement (GPA of 2.5 or higher), community service, and financial need. U.S. citizenship is required.

Financial data The stipend is $2,300 per year.

Duration 1 year; may be renewed.

Additional information This fund was established in 1978 in honor of the J.B. Morris family, who founded the Iowa branch of the National Association for the Advancement of Colored People and published the *Iowa Bystander* newspaper.

Number awarded Varies each year; recently, 24 of these scholarships were awarded.

Deadline March of each year.

[838]
JAMES CARLSON MEMORIAL SCHOLARSHIP

Oregon Student Assistance Commission
Attn: Grants and Scholarships Division
1500 Valley River Drive, Suite 100
Eugene, OR 97401-2146
(541) 687-7395   Toll Free: (800) 452-8807, ext. 7395
Fax: (541) 687-7414   TDD: (800) 735-2900
E-mail: awardinfo@osac.state.or.us
Web: www.osac.state.or.us/osac_programs.html

Summary To provide financial assistance to students from diverse environments (including African Americans) and other Oregon residents who are majoring in education on the undergraduate or graduate school level at a school in any state.

Eligibility This program is open to residents of Oregon who are U.S. citizens or permanent residents and enrolled at a college or university in any state. Applicants must be either 1) college seniors or fifth-year students majoring in elementary or secondary education or 2) graduate students working on an elementary or secondary certificate. Full-time enrollment and financial need are required. Priority is given to 1) students who come from diverse environments and submit an essay of 250 to 350 words on their experience living or working in diverse environments; 2) dependents of members of the Oregon Education Association; and 3) applicants committed to teaching autistic children.

Financial data Stipend amounts vary; recently, they were at least $1,300.

Duration 1 year.

Additional information This program is administered by the Oregon Student Assistance Commission (OSAC) with funds provided by the Oregon Community Foundation.

Number awarded Varies each year; recently, 3 of these scholarships were awarded.

Deadline February of each year.

[839]
JAMES E. WEBB INTERNSHIPS

Smithsonian Institution
Attn: Office of Fellowships
470 L'Enfant Plaza, Suite 7102
P.O. Box 37012, MRC 902
Washington, DC 20013-7012
(202) 633-7070   Fax: (202) 633-7069
E-mail: siofg@si.edu
Web: www.si.edu/ofg/Applications/WEBB/WEBBapp.htm

Summary To provide internship opportunities throughout the Smithsonian Institution to African American and other minority upper-division or graduate students in business or public administration.

Eligibility This program is open to minorities who are juniors, seniors, or graduate students majoring in areas of business or public administration (finance, human resource management, accounting, or general business administration). Applicants must have a GPA of 3.0 or higher. They must seek placement in offices, museums, and research institutes within the Smithsonian Institution.

Financial data Interns receive a stipend of $550 per week and a travel allowance.

Duration 10 weeks during the summer, fall, or spring.

Number awarded Varies each year; recently, 8 of these internships were awarded.

Deadline January of each year for summer or fall; September of each year for spring.

[840]
JAMES W. STOUDT SCHOLARSHIPS

Pennsylvania Bar Association
Attn: Foundation
100 South Street
P.O. Box 186
Harrisburg, PA 17108-0186
(717) 213-2501   Toll Free: (888) 238-3036
E-mail: info@pabarfoundation.org
Web: www.pabarfoundation.org

Summary To provide financial assistance to African Americans and other residents of Pennsylvania who are attending law school in the state.

Eligibility This program is open to residents of Pennsylvania who are currently enrolled in the second year (or third year of a 4- or 5-year law school program) at a law school in the state. Applicants must be or become student members of the Pennsylvania Bar Association. Some of the awards are reserved for students who are members of groups historically underrepresented in the legal profession (African Americans, Hispanic Americans, and Native Americans). Along with their application, they must submit a 500-word essay explaining how they plan to demonstrate their potential for making a contribution to society and the legal profession. Selection is based on that essay, academic achievement, and financial need.

Financial data The stipend is $3,000.

Duration 1 year.

Number awarded 8 each year: 1 at each accredited law school in Pennsylvania plus 4 reserved for underrepresented minority students.

Deadline November of each year.

[841]
JEANNE SPURLOCK MINORITY MEDICAL STUDENT CLINICAL FELLOWSHIP IN CHILD AND ADOLESCENT PSYCHIATRY

American Academy of Child and Adolescent Psychiatry
Attn: Department of Research, Training, and Education
3615 Wisconsin Avenue, N.W.
Washington, DC 20016-3007
(202) 966-7300, ext. 117   Fax: (202) 364-5925
E-mail: training@aacap.org
Web: www.aacap.org/cs/awards

Summary To provide funding to African American and other minority medical students who are interested in working with a child and adolescent psychiatrist during the summer.

Eligibility This program is open to African American, Asian American, Native American, Alaska Native, Mexican American, Hispanic, and Pacific Islander students in accredited U.S. medical schools. Applicants must present a plan for a clinical training experience that involves significant contact between the student and a mentor. The plan should include program planning discussions, instruction in treatment planning and implementation, regular meetings with the mentor and other treatment providers, and assigned readings. Clinical assignments may include responsibility for part of the observation or evaluation, conducting interviews or tests, using rating scales, and psychological or cognitive testing of patients. The training plan should also include discussion of ethical issues in treatment. U.S. citizenship or permanent resident status is required.

Financial data The stipend is $3,500. Fellows also receive reimbursement of travel expenses to attend the annual meeting of the American Academy of Child and Adolescent Psychiatry.

Duration 12 weeks during the summer.

Additional information Upon completion of the training program, the student is required to submit a brief paper summarizing the clinical experience. The fellowship pays expenses for the fellow to attend the academy's annual meeting and present this paper. This program is supported by the Center for Mental Health Services of the Substance Abuse and Mental Health Services Administration.

Number awarded Up to 14 each year.

Deadline February of each year.

[842]
JEANNE SPURLOCK RESEARCH FELLOWSHIP IN SUBSTANCE ABUSE AND ADDICTION FOR MINORITY MEDICAL STUDENTS

American Academy of Child and Adolescent Psychiatry
Attn: Department of Research, Training, and Education
3615 Wisconsin Avenue, N.W.
Washington, DC 20016-3007
(202) 966-7300, ext. 117   Fax: (202) 364-5925
E-mail: training@aacap.org
Web: www.aacap.org/cs/awards

Summary To provide funding to African American and other minority medical students who are interested in working on the topics of drug abuse and addiction with a child and adolescent psychiatrist researcher-mentor during the summer.

Eligibility This program is open to African American, Asian American, Native American, Alaska Native, Mexican American, Hispanic, and Pacific Islander students in accredited U.S. medical schools. Applicants must present a plan for a program of research training in drug abuse and addiction that involves significant contact with a mentor who is an experienced child and adolescent psychiatrist researcher. The plan should include program planning discussions; instruction in research planning and implementation; regular meetings with the mentor, laboratory director, and the research group; and assigned readings. The mentor must be a member of the American Academy of Child and Adolescent Psychiatry (AACAP). Research assignments may include responsibility for part of the observation or evaluation, developing specific aspects of the research mechanisms, conducting interviews or tests, using rating scales, and psychological or cognitive testing of subjects. The training plan also should include discussion of ethical issues in research, such as protocol development, informed consent, collection and storage of raw data, safeguarding data, bias in analyzing data, plagiarism, protection of patients, and ethical treatment of animals. U.S. citizenship or permanent resident status is required.

Financial data The stipend is $3,500. Fellows also receive reimbursement of travel expenses to attend the annual meeting of the American Academy of Child and Adolescent Psychiatry.

Duration 12 weeks during the summer.

Additional information Upon completion of the training program, the student is required to submit a brief paper summarizing the research experience. The fellowship pays expenses for the fellow to attend the academy's annual meeting and present this paper. This program is co-sponsored by the National Institute on Drug Abuse.

Number awarded Up to 5 each year.

Deadline February of each year.

[843]
JEFFREY CAMPBELL GRADUATE FELLOWS PROGRAM

St. Lawrence University
Attn: Human Resources/Office of Equity Programs
Jeffrey Campbell Graduate Fellowship Program
23 Romoda Drive
Canton, NY 13617
(315) 229-5509   E-mail: humanresources@stlawu.edu
Web: www.stlawu.edu

Summary To provide funding to African American and other minority graduate students who have completed their course work and are interested in conducting research at St. Lawrence University in New York.

Eligibility This program is open to graduate students who are members of racial or ethnic groups historically underrepresented at the university and in American higher education. Applicants must have completed their course work and preliminary examinations for the Ph.D. They must be interested in working on their dissertations or terminal degree projects while in residence at the University.

Financial data The stipend is $28,500 per academic year. Additional funds may be available to support travel to conferences and professional meetings. Office space and a personal computer are provided.

Duration 1 academic year.

Additional information This program is named for 1 of the university's early African American graduates. Recipients must teach 1 course a semester in a department or program at St. Lawrence University related to their research interests. In addition, they must present a research-based paper in the fellows' lecture series each semester.

Deadline January of each year.

[844]
JOHN AND MURIEL LANDIS SCHOLARSHIPS

American Nuclear Society
Attn: Scholarship Coordinator
555 North Kensington Avenue
La Grange Park, IL 60526-5592
(708) 352-6611   Toll Free: (800) 323-3044
Fax: (708) 352-0499   E-mail: outreach@ans.org
Web: www.ans.org/honors/scholarships

Summary To provide financial assistance to undergraduate or graduate students (especially African Americans, other minorities, and women) who are interested in preparing for a career in nuclear-related fields.

Eligibility This program is open to undergraduate and graduate students at colleges or universities located in the United States who are preparing for, or planning to prepare for, a career in nuclear science, nuclear engineering, or a nuclear-related field. Qualified high school seniors are also eligible. Applicants must have greater than average financial need and have experienced circumstances that render them disadvantaged. They must be sponsored by an organization (e.g., plant branch, local section, student section) within the American Nuclear Society (ANS). Along with their application, they must submit an essay on their academic and professional goals, experiences that have affected those goals, etc. Selection is based on that essay, academic achievement, letters of recommendation, and financial need. Women and members of minority groups are especially urged to apply. U.S. citizenship is not required.

Financial data The stipend is $5,000, to be used to cover tuition, books, fees, room, and board.

Duration 1 year; nonrenewable.

Number awarded Up to 8 each year.

Deadline January of each year.

[845]
JOHN HOPE FRANKLIN DISSERTATION FELLOWSHIP

American Philosophical Society
Attn: Committee on Research
104 South Fifth Street
Philadelphia, PA 19106-3387
(215) 440-3429   Fax: (215) 440-3436
E-mail: LMusumeci@amphilsoc.org
Web: www.amphilsoc.org/grants/johnhopefranklin

Summary To provide funding to African Americans and other underrepresented minority graduate students conducting research for a doctoral dissertation.

Eligibility This program is open to African American, Hispanic American, and Native American graduate students working on a degree at a Ph.D. granting institution in the United States. Other talented students who have a demonstrated commitment to eradicating racial disparities and enlarging minority representation in academia are also eligible. Applicants must have completed all course work and examinations preliminary to the doctoral dissertation and be able to devote full-time effort, with no teaching obligations, to researching or writing their dissertation. The proposed research should relate to a topic in which the holdings of the Library of the American Philosophical Society (APS) are particularly strong: quantum mechanics, nuclear physics, computer development, the history of genetics and eugenics, the history of medicine, Early American political and cultural history, natural history in the 18th and 19th centuries, the development of cultural anthropology, or American Indian culture and linguistics.

Financial data The grant is $25,000; an additional grant of $5,000 is provided to support the cost of residency in Philadelphia.

Duration 12 months, to begin at the discretion of the grantee.

Additional information This program was established in 2005. Recipients are expected to spend a significant amount of time in residence at the APS Library.

Number awarded 1 each year.

Deadline March of each year.

[846]
JOHN M. LANGSTON BAR ASSOCIATION SCHOLARSHIPS

John M. Langston Bar Association
c/o Zakiya N. Glass, Scholarship Committee
Harrington, Foxx, Dubrow & Canter
1055 West Seventh Street, 29th Floor
Los Angeles, CA 90017
(213) 489-3222   E-mail: info@langstonbar.org
Web: www.langstonbar.org

Summary To provide financial assistance to African American students from any state who are attending law schools in California.

Eligibility This program is open to African Americans from any state who are currently enrolled in the first year of a law school in California. Applicants must be able to demonstrate financial need. Along with their application, they must submit essays on 1) what "diversity" means to them and why they think it might be important to have a diverse bar; and 2) a current and prevalent civil rights issue of our time.

Financial data A stipend is awarded (amount not specified).

Duration 1 year.

Additional information The John M. Langston Bar Association, originally named the Langston Law Club, was founded in 1943 by African American attorneys in Los Angeles who were denied membership in other bar associations.

Number awarded 1 or more each year.

Deadline October of each year.

[847]
JOHN S. SHROPSHIRE GRADUATE SCHOLARSHIP

Pennsylvania Black Conference on Higher Education
c/o Judith A.W. Thomas, Scholarship Committee Chair
Lincoln University, School of Social Sciences and
  Behavioral Studies
1570 Old Baltimore Pike
P.O. Box 179
Lincoln University, PA 19352
(484) 365-8159   E-mail: scholarships@pbcohe.org
Web: www.phcohe.org

Summary To provide financial assistance to African American residents of any state who are enrolled as graduate students at universities in Pennsylvania.

Eligibility This program is open to African Americans from any state who have earned at least 6 hours of graduate study at a college or university in Pennsylvania. Applicants must have a GPA of 3.0 or higher. Along with their application, they must submit an essay, up to 5 pages in length, on why they should receive this scholarship. Selection is based on that essay, academics, extracurricular activity participation, leadership qualities, and interpersonal qualities.

Financial data The stipend is $1,000.

Duration 1 year.

Number awarded 1 each year.

Deadline January of each year.

[848]
JOHN STANFORD MEMORIAL WLMA SCHOLARSHIP

Washington Library Media Association
c/o Jeanne Staley
711 Scenic Bluff
Yakima, WA 98908
(509) 972-5899　　　E-mail: scholarships@wlma.org
Web: www.wlma.org/scholarships

Summary　To provide financial assistance to African Americans and other ethnic minorities in Washington who are interested in preparing for a library media career.

Eligibility　This program is open to residents of Washington who are working toward a library media endorsement or graduate degree in the field. Applicants must be members of an ethnic minority group. They must be working or planning to work in a school library. Along with their application, they must submit a brief description of their reasons for applying, goals as a teacher librarian, plans for the future, interest in librarianship, plans for further education, and interest in this award. Financial need is considered in the selection process.

Financial data　The stipend is $1,000.

Duration　1 year.

Number awarded　1 each year.

Deadline　March of each year.

[849]
JOHN W. WORK III MEMORIAL FOUNDATION SCHOLARSHIP

Community Foundation of Middle Tennessee
Attn: Scholarship Committee
3833 Cleghorn Avenue, Suite 400
Nashville, TN 37215-2519
(615) 321-4939　　　Toll Free: (888) 540-5200
Fax: (615) 327-2746　　　E-mail: mail@cfmt.org
Web: www.cfmt.org/scholarships

Summary　To provide financial assistance to upper-division and graduate students from Tennessee, especially African Americans who are working on a degree in music at a school in any state.

Eligibility　This program is open to residents of Tennessee, especially African Americans, enrolled as juniors, seniors, or graduate students at an accredited college, university, or institute in any state. Applicants must be working on a degree in music and have a GPA of 3.0 or higher. Selection is based on demonstrated potential for excellence in music, academic record, standardized test scores, extracurricular activities, work experience, community involvement, recommendations, and financial need.

Financial data　Stipends range from $500 to $2,500 per year. Funds are paid to the recipient's school and must be used for tuition, fees, books, supplies, room, board, or miscellaneous expenses.

Duration　1 year.

Number awarded　1 or more each year.

Deadline　March of each year.

[850]
JOHNNIE L. COCHRAN, JR./MWH SCHOLARSHIP

National Forum for Black Public Administrators
Attn: Scholarship Program
777 North Capitol Street, N.E., Suite 807
Washington, DC 20002
(202) 408-9300, ext. 112　　　Fax: (202) 408-8558
E-mail: vreed@nfbpa.org
Web: www.nfbpa.org/i4a/pages/index.cfm?pageid=3630

Summary　To provide financial assistance to African Americans working on a undergraduate or graduate degree in public administration.

Eligibility　This program is open to African American undergraduate and graduate students preparing for a career in public service. Applicants must be working full time on a degree in public administration, political science, urban affairs, public policy, or a related field. They must have a GPA of 3.0 or higher, excellent interpersonal and analytical abilities, and strong oral and written communication skills. Along with their application, they must submit a 3-page autobiographical essay that includes their academic and career goals and objectives. First consideration is given to applicants who are not currently receiving other financial aid.

Financial data　The stipend is $5,000.

Duration　1 year.

Additional information　This program is sponsored by the engineering and financial consulting firm MWH. Recipients are required to attend the sponsor's annual conference to receive their scholarship; limited hotel and air accommodations are arranged and provided.

Number awarded　1 each year.

Deadline　February of each year.

[851]
JOHNSON & JOHNSON CAMPAIGN FOR NURSING'S FUTURE-AMERICAN ASSOCIATION OF COLLEGES OF NURSING MINORITY NURSE FACULTY SCHOLARS PROGRAM

American Association of Colleges of Nursing
One Dupont Circle, N.W., Suite 530
Washington, DC 20036
(202) 463-6930　　　Fax: (202) 785-8320
E-mail: scholarship@aacn.nche.edu
Web: www.aacn.nche.edu/Education/financialaid.htm

Summary　To provide funding to African Americans and other minority students who are working on a graduate degree in nursing to prepare for a career as a faculty member.

Eligibility　This program is open to members of racial and ethnic minority groups (Alaska Native, American Indian, Black or African American, Native Hawaiian or other, Pacific Islander, Hispanic or Latino, or Asian American) who are enrolled full time at a school of nursing. Applicants must be working on 1) a doctoral nursing degree (e.g., Ph.D., D.N.P.), or 2) a clinically-focused master's degree in nursing (e.g., M.S.N., M.S.). They must commit to 1) serve in a teaching capacity at a nursing school for a minimum of 1 year for each year of support they receive; 2) provide 6-month progress reports to the American Association of Colleges of Nursing (AACN) throughout the entire funding process and during the payback period; 3) agree to work with an assigned mentor throughout the period of the scholarship grant; and 4) attend an annual leadership training conference to connect with their mentor, fellow scholars, and colleagues. Selection is based on ability to contribute to nursing education; leadership potential; development of goals reflecting education, research, and professional involvement; ability to work with a mentor/adviser throughout the award period; proposed research and/or practice projects that are significant and show commitment to improving nursing education and clinical nursing practice in the United States; and evidence of commitment to a career in nursing education and to recruiting, mentoring, and retaining future underrepresented minority nurses. Preference is given to students enrolled in doctoral nursing programs. Applicants must be U.S. citizens, permanent residents, refugees, or qualified immigrants.

Financial data The stipend is $18,000 per year. The award includes $1,500 that is held in escrow to cover the costs for the recipient to attend the leadership training conference. Recipients are required to sign a letter of commitment that they will provide 1 year of service in a teaching capacity at a nursing school in the United States for each year of support received; if they fail to complete that service requirement, they must repay all funds received.

Duration 1 year; may be renewed 1 additional year.

Additional information This program, established in 2007, is sponsored by the Johnson & Johnson Campaign for Nursing's Future.

Number awarded 5 each year.

Deadline May of each year.

[852]
JOSEPH L. FISHER DOCTORAL DISSERTATION FELLOWSHIPS

Resources for the Future
Attn: Coordinator for Academic Programs
1616 P Street, N.W., Suite 600
Washington, DC 20036-1400
(202) 328-5008   Fax: (202) 939-3460
E-mail: fisher-award@rff.org
Web: www.rff.org/About_RFF/Pages/default.aspx

Summary To provide funding to doctoral candidates in economics (particularly African Americans or other minorities and women) who are interested in conducting dissertation research on issues related to the environment, natural resources, or energy.

Eligibility This program is open to graduate students in their final year of research on a dissertation related to the environment, natural resources, or energy. Applicants must submit a brief letter of application and a curriculum vitae, a graduate transcript, a 1-page abstract of the dissertation, a technical summary of the dissertation (up to 2,500 words), a letter from the student's department chair, and 2 letters of recommendation from faculty members on the student's dissertation committee. The technical summary should describe clearly the aim of the dissertation, its significance in relation to the existing literature, and the research methods to be used. Women and minority candidates are strongly encouraged to apply.

Financial data The stipend is $18,000.

Duration 1 academic year.

Additional information It is expected that recipients will not hold other employment during the fellowship period. Recipients must notify Resources for the Future of any financial assistance they receive from any other source for support of doctoral work.

Number awarded 2 or 3 each year.

Deadline February of each year.

[853]
JOSEPHINE FORMAN SCHOLARSHIP

Society of American Archivists
Attn: Chair, Awards Committee
17 North State Street, Suite 1425
Chicago, IL 60602-3315
(312) 606-0722   Toll Free: (866) 722-7858
Fax: (312) 606-0728   E-mail: info@archivists.org
Web: www2.archivists.org

Summary To provide financial assistance to African Americans and other minority graduate students working on a degree in archival science.

Eligibility This program is open to members of minority groups (American Indian/Alaska Native, Asian, Black/African American, Hispanic/Latino, or Native Hawaiian/other Pacific Islander) currently enrolled in or accepted to a graduate program or a multi-course program in archival administration. The program must offer at least 3 courses in archival science and students may have completed no more than half of the credit requirements toward their graduate degree. Selection is based on potential for scholastic and personal achievement and commitment both to the archives profession and to advancing diversity concerns within it. U.S. citizenship or permanent resident status is required.

Financial data The stipend is $10,000.

Duration 1 year.

Additional information Funding for this program, established in 2011, is provided by the General Commission on Archives and History of the United Methodist Church.

Number awarded 1 each year.

Deadline February of each year.

[854]
JTBF JUDICIAL EXTERNSHIP PROGRAM

Just the Beginning Foundation
c/o Paula Lucas, Executive Director
Schiff Hardin LLP
233 South Wacker Drive, Suite 6600
Chicago, IL 60606
(312) 258-5930   E-mail: plucas@jtbf.org
Web: www.jtbf.org

Summary To provide work experience to African American and other underrepresented law students who plan to seek judicial clerkships after graduation.

Eligibility This program is open to students currently enrolled in their second or third year of law school who are members of minority or economically disadvantaged groups. Applicants must intend to work as a clerk in the federal or state judiciary upon graduation or within 5 years of graduation.

Financial data Program externs receive a quarterly or summer stipend in an amount determined by the sponsor.

Duration The academic year externships require a 1- or 2-year commitment, beginning each September and ending in May or June. During the academic year, participants are expected to work a minimum of 10 hours per week on externship assignments. The summer externships require students to perform at least 35 hours per week of work for at least 8 weeks during the summer.

Additional information This program began in 2005. Law students are matched with federal and state judges across the country who provide assignments to the participants that will enhance their legal research, writing, and analytical skills (e.g., drafting memoranda). Students are expected to complete at least 1 memorandum of law or other key legal document each semester of the externship. Course credit may be offered, but students may not receive academic credit and a stipend simultaneously.

Number awarded Varies each year.

Deadline February of each year for summer and fall appointments.

[855]
JUDICIAL INTERN OPPORTUNITY PROGRAM

American Bar Association
Attn: Section of Litigation
321 North Clark Street
Chicago, IL 60654-7598
(312) 988-6348   Fax: (312) 988-6234
E-mail: howardg@staff.abanet.org
Web: www.abanet.org/litigation/jiop

Summary To provide an opportunity for African American and other minority or economically disadvantaged law students to gain experience as judicial interns in selected courts during the summer.

Eligibility This program is open to first- and second-year students at ABA-accredited law schools who are 1) members racial or ethnic groups that are traditionally underrepresented in the legal profession (African Americans, Asians, Hispanics/Latinos, Native Americans); 2) students with disabilities; 3) students who are economically disadvantaged; or 4) students who identify themselves as lesbian, gay, bisexual, or transgender. Applicants must be interested in a judicial internship at courts in selected areas and communities. They may indicate a preference for the area in which they wish to work, but they may not specify a court or a judge. Along with their application, they must submit a current resume, a 10-page legal writing sample, and a 2-page statement of interest that outlines their qualifications for the internship. Screening interviews are conducted by staff of the American Bar Association, either in person or by telephone. Final interviews are conducted by the judges with whom the interns will work. Some spots are reserved for students with an interest in intellectual property law.

Financial data The stipend is $1,500.

Duration 6 weeks during the summer.

Additional information Recently, internships were available in the following locations: Chicago and surrounding suburbs; central and southern Illinois; Houston, Dallas, southern, and eastern Texas; Miami, Florida; Phoenix, Arizona; Los Angeles, California; Philadelphia, Pennsylvania; San Francisco, California; and Washington, D.C. Some internships in Chicago, Los Angeles, Texas, and Washington, D.C. are reserved for students with an interest in intellectual property law.

Number awarded Varies each year; recently, 171 of these internships were awarded, including 9 at courts in Arizona, 36 in California, 12 in Florida, 51 in Illinois, 17 in Pennsylvania, 33 in Texas, and 13 in Washington, D.C.

Deadline January of each year.

[856]
JUDITH MCMANUS PRICE SCHOLARSHIPS

American Planning Association
Attn: Leadership Affairs Associate
205 North Michigan Avenue, Suite 1200
Chicago, IL 60601
(312) 431-9100   Fax: (312) 786-6700
E-mail: fellowship@planning.org
Web: www.planning.org/scholarships/apa

Summary To provide financial assistance to African Americans and other underrepresented students enrolled in undergraduate or graduate degree programs at recognized planning schools.

Eligibility This program is open to undergraduate and graduate students in urban and regional planning who are women or members of the following minority groups: African American, Hispanic American, or Native American. Applicants must be citizens of the United States and able to document financial need. They must intend to work as practicing planners in the public sector. Along with their application, they must submit a 2-page personal and background statement describing how their education will be applied to career goals and why they chose planning as a career path. Selection is based (in order of importance), on: 1) commitment to planning as reflected in their personal statement and on their resume; 2) academic achievement and/or improvement during the past 2 years; 3) letters of recommendation; 4) financial need; and 5) professional presentation.

Financial data Stipends range from $2,000 to $4,000 per year. The money may be applied to tuition and living expenses only. Payment is made to the recipient's university and divided by terms in the school year.

Duration 1 year; recipients may reapply.

Additional information This program was established in 2002.

Number awarded Varies each year; recently, 3 of these scholarships were awarded.

Deadline April of each year.

[857]
JULIA BUMRY JONES SCHOLARSHIP PROGRAM

Delta Sigma Theta Sorority, Inc.
Attn: Scholarship and Standards Committee Chair
1707 New Hampshire Avenue, N.W.
Washington, DC 20009
(202) 986-2400   Fax: (202) 986-2513
E-mail: dstemail@deltasigmatheta.org
Web: www.deltasigmatheta.org

Summary To provide financial assistance to members of Delta Sigma Theta who are interested in working on a graduate degree in journalism or another area of communications.

Eligibility This program is open to graduating college seniors and graduate students who are interested in preparing for a career in journalism or another area of communications. Applicants must be active, dues-paying members of Delta Sigma Theta. Selection is based on meritorious achievement.

Financial data The stipends range from $1,000 to $2,000. The funds may be used to cover tuition, fees, and living expenses.

Duration 1 year; may be renewed for 1 additional year.

Additional information This sponsor is a traditionally African American social sorority. The application fee is $20.

Deadline April of each year.

[858]
JULIETTE DERRICOTTE SCHOLARSHIP

Delta Sigma Theta Sorority, Inc.
Attn: Scholarship and Standards Committee Chair
1707 New Hampshire Avenue, N.W.
Washington, DC 20009
(202) 986-2400   Fax: (202) 986-2513
E-mail: dstemail@deltasigmatheta.org
Web: www.deltasigmatheta.org

Summary To provide financial assistance to members of Delta Sigma Theta who are interested in preparing for a career in social work.

Eligibility This program is open to graduating college seniors or graduate students who are interested in preparing for a career in social work. Applicants must be active, dues-paying members of Delta Sigma Theta. Selection is based on meritorious achievement.

Financial data The stipends range from $1,000 to $2,000 per year. The funds may be used to cover tuition, school, and living expenses.

Duration 1 year; may be renewed for 1 additional year.

Additional information This sponsor is a traditionally African American social sorority. The application fee is $20.

Deadline April of each year.

[859]
JULIUS S., JR. AND IANTHIA H. SCOTT ENDOWED SCHOLARSHIP

United Methodist Higher Education Foundation
Attn: Scholarships Administrator
1001 19th Avenue South
P.O. Box 340005
Nashville, TN 37203-0005
(615) 340-7385   Toll Free: (800) 811-8110
Fax: (615) 340-7330
E-mail: umhefscholarships@gbhem.org
Web: www.umhef.org/receive.php?id=endowed_funds

Summary To provide financial assistance to Methodist undergraduate students at designated Historically Black Colleges and Universities of the United Methodist Church.

Eligibility This program is open to students entering their sophomore year at the following Historically Black Colleges and Universities of the United Methodist Church: Wiley College, Paine College, or Philander Smith College. Applicants must have been active, full members of a United Methodist Church for at least 1 year prior to applying. They must have a GPA of 3.0 or higher and be able to demonstrate financial need. Along with their application, they must submit a 200-word essay on their involvement and/or leadership responsi-

bilities in their church, school, and community within the last 3 years. U.S. citizenship or permanent resident status is required.

Financial data The stipend is at least $1,000 per year.

Duration 1 year; nonrenewable.

Additional information This program was established in 1999.

Number awarded 1 scholarship is awarded each year on a rotational basis among the 3 participating institutions.

Deadline May of each year.

[860]
KAISER PERMANENTE COLORADO DIVERSITY SCHOLARSHIP PROGRAM

Kaiser Permanente
Attn: Multicultural Associations/Employee Resource
  Groups
P.O. Box 378066
Denver, CO 80247-8066
E-mail: co-diversitydevelopment@kp.org
Web: physiciancareers.kp.org

Summary To provide financial assistance to Colorado residents who are African American or come from another diverse background and are interested in working on an undergraduate or graduate degree in a health care field at a school in any state.

Eligibility This program is open to all residents of Colorado, including those who identify as 1 or more of the following: African American, Asian Pacific, Latino, lesbian, gay, bisexual, transgender, intersex, Native American, and/or a person with a disability. Applicants must be 1) a graduating high school senior with a GPA of 2.7 or higher and planning to enroll full time at a college or technical school in any state; 2) a GED recipient with a GED score of 520 or higher and planning to enroll full time at a college or technical school in any state; 3) a full-time undergraduate student at a college or technical school in any state; or 4) a full-time graduate or doctoral student at a school in any state. They must be preparing for a career in health care (e.g., doctor, nurse, surgeon, physician assistant, dentist), mental health, public health, or health policy. Along with their application, they must submit 300-word essays on 1) a personal setback in their life and how they responded and learned from it; 2) how they give back to their community; and 3) why they have chosen health care and/or public health for their educational and career path. Selection is based on academic achievement, character qualities, community outreach and volunteering, and financial need.

Financial data Stipends range from $1,400 to $2,600.

Duration 1 year.

Number awarded Varies each year; recently, 17 of these scholarships were awarded.

Deadline January of each year.

[861]
KANSAS AFRICAN AMERICAN MONUMENTAL LIFE SETTLEMENT SCHOLARSHIPS

Kansas Insurance Department
Attn: Scholarship Fund
420 S.W. Ninth Street
Topeka, KS 66612-1678
(785) 296-3071   Toll Free: (800) 432-2484 (within KS)
Fax: (785) 296-7805
E-mail: commissioner@ksinsurance.org
Web: www.ksinsurance.org/gpa/scholarship.htm

Summary To provide financial assistance to African American upper-division and graduate students who are majoring in business, computer science, or mathematics at a college or university in Kansas.

Eligibility This program is open to African American students enrolled as juniors, seniors, or graduate students at accredited institutions of higher education in Kansas. Applicants must be majoring in business (with an emphasis on accounting, economics, finance, or investments), computer science, or mathematics. They must have a GPA of 3.0 or higher. Along with their application, they must submit a 1-page essay describing their career goals and how this scholarship would help them achieve those goals.

Financial data The stipend is $1,000.

Duration 1 year.

Additional information These scholarships were first awarded in 2005 with funds received in a settlement with Monumental Life as a result of the firm's race-based pricing of life insurance policies.

Number awarded 12 each year.

Deadline April of each year for fall semester; September of each year for spring semester.

[862]
KATTEN MUCHIN ROSENMAN MINORITY SCHOLARSHIPS

Katten Muchin Rosenman LLP
Attn: Legal Recruiting Coordinator
525 West Monroe Street
Chicago, IL 60661-3693
(312) 577-8406   Fax: (312) 577-4572
E-mail: grace.johnson@kattenlaw.com
Web: www.kattenlaw.com

Summary To provide financial assistance and summer work experience in Chicago or New York City to African American and other minority law students from any state.

Eligibility This program is open to minority students from any state who have completed their first year of law school. Applicants must have applied for and been accepted as a summer associate at the sponsoring law firm's Chicago or New York office. Along with their application, they must submit 250-word statements on 1) their strongest qualifications for this award; 2) their reasons for preparing for law as a profession; and 3) their views on diversity and how their personal experience and philosophy will be an asset to the firm. Selection is based on academic achievement, leadership experience, and personal qualities that reflect the potential for outstanding contributions to the firm and the legal profession.

Financial data Participants receive the standard salary for the summer internship and a stipend of $15,000 for the academic year.

Duration 1 year.

Number awarded 1 each year.

Deadline October of each year.

[863]
KAY LONGCOPE SCHOLARSHIP AWARD

National Lesbian & Gay Journalists Association
2120 L Street, N.W., Suite 850
Washington, DC 20037
(202) 588-9888   Fax: (202) 588-1818
E-mail: info@nlgfa.org
Web: www.nlgja.org/students/longcope.htm

Summary To provide financial assistance to African American and other lesbian, gay, bisexual, and transgender (LGBT) undergraduate and graduate students of color who are interested in preparing for a career in journalism.

Eligibility This program is open to LGBT students of color who are 1) high school seniors accepted to a U.S. community college or 4-year university and planning to enroll full time; 2) full-time undergraduate students at U.S. community colleges and 4-year universities; or 3) undergraduate students who have been accepted for their first year at a U.S. graduate school. Applicants must be planning a career in journalism and be committed to furthering the sponsoring organization's mission of fair and accurate coverage of the LGBT community. They must demonstrate an awareness of the issues facing the LGBT community and the importance of fair and accurate news coverage. For undergraduates, a declared major in journalism and/or communications is desirable but not required; non-journalism majors may demonstrate their commitment to a journalism career through work samples, internships, and work on a school news publication, online news service, or broadcast affiliate. Graduate students must be enrolled in a journalism program. Along with their application, they must submit a 1-page resume, 5 work samples, official transcripts, 3 letters of recommendation, and a 1,000-word autobiography written in the third person as a news story, describing the applicant's commitment and passion for journalism and career goals. U.S. citizenship or permanent resident status is required. Selection is based on journalistic and scholastic ability.

Financial data The stipend is $5,000.

Duration 1 year.

Additional information This program was established in 2008.

Number awarded 1 each year.

Deadline January of each year.

[864]
KEGLER, BROWN, HILL & RITTER MINORITY MERIT SCHOLARSHIP

Kegler, Brown, Hill & Ritter
Attn: Human Resources Manager
Capitol Square, Suite 1800
65 East State Street
Columbus, OH 43215
(614) 462-5467   Fax: (614) 464-2634
E-mail: ctammaro@keglerbrown.com
Web: www.keglerbrown.com

Summary To provide financial assistance and summer work experience at Kegler, Brown, Hill & Ritter in Columbus, Ohio to African American and other minority students at law schools in any state.

Eligibility This program is open to first-year students of minority descent at law schools in any state. Applicants must be interested in a summer clerkship with the firm following their first year of law school. Along with their application, they must submit brief essays on 1) a major accomplishment that has shaped their life, how it influenced their decision to prepare for a career in law, and how it prepared them for a future as a lawyer; 2) what diversity means to them; 3) why they have applied for the scholarship; and 4) any training and/or experience they believe to be relevant to the clerkship. Selection is based on academic performance, accomplishments, activities, and potential contributions to the legal community.

Financial data The program provides a $5,000 stipend for law school tuition and a paid summer clerkship position.

Duration 1 year.

Additional information This program began in 2004.

Number awarded 1 each year.

Deadline January of each year.

[865]
KING & SPALDING DIVERSITY FELLOWSHIP PROGRAM

King & Spalding
Attn: Diversity Fellowship Program
1180 Peachtree Street
Atlanta, GA 30309
(404) 572-4643   Fax: (404) 572-5100
E-mail: fellowship@kslaw.com
Web: www.kslaw.com

Summary To provide financial assistance and summer work experience to African American and other law students who will contribute to the diversity of the legal community.

Eligibility This program is open to second-year law students who 1) come from a minority ethnic or racial group (American Indian/Alaskan Native, Asian American/Pacific Islander, Black/African American, Hispanic, or multi-racial); 2) are a member of the gay, lesbian, bisexual, or transgender (GLBT) community; or 3) have a disability. Applicants must receive an offer of a clerkship at a U.S. office of King & Spalding during their second-year summer. Along with their application, they must submit a 500-word personal statement that describes their talents, qualities, and experiences and how they would contribute to the diversity of the firm.

Financial data Fellows receive a stipend of $10,000 for their second year of law school and a paid summer associate

clerkship at a U.S. office of the firm during the following summer.

Duration 1 year.

Additional information The firm's U.S. offices are located in Atlanta, Charlotte, Houston, New York, San Francisco, Silicon Valley, and Washington.

Number awarded Up to 4 each year.

Deadline August of each year.

[866]
KIRKLAND & ELLIS LLP DIVERSITY FELLOWSHIP PROGRAM

Kirkland & Ellis LLP
Attn: Attorney Recruiting Manager
333 South Hope Street
Los Angeles, CA 90071
(213) 680-8436   Fax: (213) 680-8500
E-mail: cherie.conrad@kirkland.com
Web: www.kirkland.com

Summary To provide financial assistance and summer work experience at an office of Kirkland & Ellis to African Americans and other minority law students from any state.

Eligibility This program is open to second-year students at ABA-accredited law schools who meet the racial and ethnic categories established by the Equal Employment Opportunity Commission. Applicants must have been accepted as summer associates at a domestic office of the sponsoring law firm (Chicago, Los Angeles, New York, Palo Alto, San Francisco, Washington, D.C.) and be likely to practice at 1 of those offices after graduation. Along with their application, they must submit a 1-page personal statement that describes ways in which they have promoted and will continue to promote diversity in the legal community, along with their interest in the firm. Selection is based on merit.

Financial data Fellows receive a salary during their summer associateship and a $15,000 stipend at the conclusion of the summer. Stipend funds are to be used for payment of educational expenses during the third year of law school.

Duration 1 year.

Additional information This program, which replaced the Kirkland & Ellis Minority Fellowship Program, was established at 14 law schools in 2004. In 2006, it began accepting a limited number of applications from students at all ABA-accredited law schools.

Number awarded Varies each year; recently, 14 of these fellowships were awarded.

Deadline September of each year.

[867]
K&L GATES DIVERSITY FELLOWSHIP

Kirkpatrick & Lockhart Preston Gates Ellis LLP
Attn: Regional Recruiting Manager
925 Fourth Avenue, Suite 2900
Seattle, WA 98104
(206) 370-5744   E-mail: dana.mills@klgates.com
Web: www.klgates.com/lawstudents/studentsdiversity

Summary To provide financial assistance and summer work experience in Seattle to African American and other law students from diverse racial and ethnic backgrounds.

Eligibility This program is open to first-year students at ABA-accredited law schools in the United States. Applicants must be members of minority racial and ethnic groups. Along with their application, they must submit a 500-word personal statement describing the contribution they would make to the legal profession and the sponsoring firm in particular.

Financial data Fellows receive a paid associateship with the Seattle office of the sponsoring firm during the summer following their first year of law school and an academic scholarship of $10,000 for their second year of law school.

Duration 1 year.

Number awarded 1 each year.

Deadline January of each year.

[868]
LAGRANT FOUNDATION GRADUATE SCHOLARSHIPS

Lagrant Foundation
Attn: Programs Manager
626 Wilshire Boulevard, Suite 700
Los Angeles, CA 90071-2920
(323) 469-8680   Fax: (323) 469-8683
E-mail: erickaavila@lagrant.com
Web: www.lagrantfoundation.org/site/?page_id=3

Summary To provide financial assistance to African Americans and other minority graduate students who are working on a degree in advertising, public relations, or marketing.

Eligibility This program is open to African Americans, Asian Pacific Americans, Hispanics/Latinos, and Native Americans/Alaska Natives who are full-time graduate students at an accredited institution. Applicants must have a GPA of 3.2 or higher and be working on a master's degree in advertising, marketing, or public relations. They must have at least 2 academic semesters remaining to complete their degree. Along with their application, they must submit 1) a 1- to 2-page essay outlining their career goals; why it is important to increase ethnic representation in the fields of advertising, marketing, and public relations; and the role of an advertising, marketing, or public relations practitioner; 2) a paragraph describing the graduate school and/or community activities in which they are involved; 3) a brief paragraph describing any honors and awards they have received; 4) a letter of reference; 5) a resume; and 6) an official transcript. U.S. citizenship or permanent resident status is required.

Financial data The stipend is $10,000 per year.

Duration 1 year.

Number awarded 5 each year.

Deadline February of each year.

[869]
LAND-USE PLANNING SCHOLARSHIP

National Forum for Black Public Administrators
Attn: Scholarship Program
777 North Capitol Street, N.E., Suite 807
Washington, DC 20002
(202) 408-9300, ext. 112   Fax: (202) 408-8558
E-mail: vreed@nfbpa.org
Web: www.nfbpa.org/i4a/pages/index.cfm?pageid=3630

Summary To provide financial assistance to African Americans from Maryland working on a graduate degree in a field related to land-use planning.

Eligibility This program is open to African American graduate students who are either residents of Maryland or attend-

ing a university in that state and preparing for a career in land-use planning. Applicants must be working full time on a master's or doctoral degree in urban planning or a related field (e.g., transportation engineering, landscape architecture, environmental planning). They must have a GPA of 3.0 or higher, excellent interpersonal and analytical abilities, and strong oral and written communication skills. Along with their application, they must submit a 3-page autobiographical essay that includes their academic and career goals and objectives. First consideration is given to applicants who are not currently receiving other financial aid.

Financial data The stipend is $3,000.

Duration 1 year.

Additional information This program is sponsored by the Maryland-National Capital Park and Planning Commission. Recipients are required to attend the sponsor's annual conference to receive their scholarship; limited hotel and air accommodations are arranged and provided.

Number awarded 1 each year.

Deadline February of each year.

[870]
LARRY W. CARTER SCHOLARSHIP

Greater Des Moines Community Foundation
Finkbine Mansion
1915 Grand Avenue
Des Moines, IA 50309
(515) 883-2626   Fax: (515) 883-2630
E-mail: info@desmoinesfoundation.org
Web: www.desmoinesfoundation.org/page32888.cfm

Summary To provide financial assistance to African American undergraduate and graduate students in Iowa.

Eligibility Eligible to apply are African Americans who reside in Iowa and are enrolled in college or graduate school on a full- or part-time basis. Applicants must submit a personal statement that includes their personal and educational goals, motivations, and reasons for pursuing higher education.

Financial data The stipend is $3,000.

Duration 1 year.

Number awarded Varies each year; recently, 3 of these scholarships were awarded.

Deadline May of each year.

[871]
LARRY WHITESIDE SCHOLARSHIP

National Association of Black Journalists
Attn: Program Coordinator
8701-A Adelphi Road
Adelphi, MD 20783-1716
(301) 445-7100, ext. 108   Toll Free: (866) 479-NABJ
Fax: (301) 445-7101   E-mail: nabj@nabj.org
Web: www.nabj.org

Summary To provide financial assistance to undergraduate or graduate student members of the National Association of Black Journalists (NABJ) who are preparing for a career in sports journalism.

Eligibility This program is open to African American juniors, seniors, and graduate students who are currently attending an accredited 4-year college or university. Applicants must be majoring in journalism or communications or have a demonstrated commitment to the field (e.g., long-term work on the school paper, internships at professional news gathering organizations). They must have a GPA of 2.5 or higher in their major and 2.0 overall, be NABJ members, and be preparing for a career in sports journalism. Along with their application, they must submit 3 samples of their work, an official college transcript, 3 letters of recommendation, a resume, and a 700- to 800-word profile of a sports journalist.

Financial data   The stipend is $2,500. Funds are paid directly to the recipient's college or university.

Duration   1 year; nonrenewable.

Number awarded   1 each year.

Deadline   May of each year.

[872]
LATHAM & WATKINS DIVERSITY SCHOLARS PROGRAM

Latham & Watkins LLP
Attn: Diversity Scholars Program Selection Panel
12636 High Bluff Drive, Suite 400
San Diego, CA 92130
(858) 523-5459   Fax: (858) 523-5450
E-mail: heather.sardinha@lw.com
Web: www.lw.com/AboutLatham.aspx?page=Diversity

Summary   To provide financial assistance to African American and other minority law students interested in working for a global law firm.

Eligibility   Applicants must be second-year law students at an ABA-accredited law school and plan to practice law in a major city in the United States. Students who have received a similar scholarship from another sponsor are not eligible to apply. Applicants must submit a 500-word personal statement that describes their ability to contribute to the diversity objects of global law firms; the life experiences that have shaped their values and that provide them with a unique perspective, including any obstacles or challenges they have overcome; their academic and/or leadership achievements; and their intent to practice in a global law firm environment.

Financial data   The stipend is $10,000.

Duration   1 year; nonrenewable.

Additional information   This program was established in 2005. Recipients are not required to work for Latham & Watkins after graduation.

Number awarded   4 each year.

Deadline   September of each year.

[873]
LAUNCHING LEADERS MBA SCHOLARSHIP

JPMorgan Chase
Campus Recruiting
Attn: Launching Leaders
277 Park Avenue, Second Floor
New York, NY 10172
(212) 270-6000
E-mail: bronwen.x.baumgardner@jpmorgan.com
Web: www.jpmorgan.com

Summary   To provide financial assistance and work experience to African American and other underrepresented minority students enrolled in the first year of an M.B.A. program.

Eligibility   This program is open to Black, Hispanic, and Native American students enrolled in the first year of an

M.B.A. program. Applicants must have a demonstrated commitment to working in financial services. Along with their application, they must submit essays on 1) a hypothetical proposal on how to use $50 million from a donor to their school to benefit all of its students; and 2) the special background and attributes they would contribute to the sponsor's diversity agenda and their motivation for applying to this scholarship program. They must be interested in a summer associate position in the sponsor's investment banking, sales and trading, or research divisions.

Financial data   The stipend is $40,000 for the first year of study; a paid summer associate position is also provided.

Duration   1 year; may be renewed 1 additional year if the recipient successfully completes the 10-week summer associate program.

Number awarded   Varies each year.

Deadline   October of each year.

[874]
LAURENCE R. FOSTER MEMORIAL GRADUATE SCHOLARSHIP

Oregon Student Assistance Commission
Attn: Grants and Scholarships Division
1500 Valley River Drive, Suite 100
Eugene, OR 97401-2146
(541) 687-7395   Toll Free: (800) 452-8807, ext. 7395
Fax: (541) 687-7414   TDD: (800) 735-2900
E-mail: awardinfo@osac.state.or.us
Web: www.osac.state.or.us/osac_programs.html

Summary   To provide financial assistance to residents of Oregon (especially African Americans and other residents from diverse environments) who are interested in enrolling in graduate school in any state to prepare for a public health career.

Eligibility   This program is open to residents of Oregon who are enrolled at least half time at a college or university in any state to prepare for a career in public health (not private practice). Applicants must be either working in public health or enrolled as graduate students in that field. Preference is given to applicants from diverse environments. Along with their application, they must submit brief essays on 1) what public health means to them; 2) the public health aspect they intend to practice and the health and population issues impacted by that aspect; and 3) their experience living or working in diverse environments.

Financial data   Stipend amounts vary; recently, they were at least $4,167.

Duration   1 year.

Additional information   This program is administered by the Oregon Student Assistance Commission (OSAC) with funds provided by the Oregon Community Foundation.

Number awarded   Varies each year; recently, 6 undergraduate and graduate scholarships were awarded.

Deadline   February of each year.

[875]
LEIGH COOK FELLOWSHIP

New Jersey Department of Health and Senior Services
Attn: Office of Minority and Multicultural Health
P.O. Box 360 Suite 501
Trenton, NJ 08625-0360
(609) 292-6962   Fax: (609) 292-8713
E-mail: Jose.Gonzalez@doh.state.nj.us
Web: www.state.nj.us/health/omh/index.shtml

Summary To provide financial support for a summer research internship to law, public health, and medical students in New Jersey, especially those who are African American or from a diverse environment.

Eligibility This program is open to students in medical science, law, or master's of public health programs who are 1) residents of New Jersey attending school in the state or elsewhere, or 2) residents of other states attending a college or university in New Jersey. Applicants must be interested in working on a supervised project at the New Jersey Department of Health and Senior Services in Trenton in the areas of minority health, senior services, HIV/AIDS, substance abuse, health insurance, environmental or occupational health, public health, or family health. Minority students are encouraged to apply. Selection is based on commitment to minority and/or public health, as demonstrated by community-based service, volunteer work, public health service advocacy, coalition building, and involvement in student organizations that address minority and public health issues.

Financial data The stipend is $6,000.

Duration 10 to 12 weeks during the summer.

Number awarded 1 each year.

Deadline April of each year.

[876]
LIBRARY OF CONGRESS JUNIOR FELLOWS PROGRAM

Library of Congress
Library Services
Attn: Junior Fellows Program Coordinator
101 Independence Avenue, S.E., Room LM-642
Washington, DC 20540-4600
(202) 707-0901   Fax: (202) 707-6269
E-mail: jrfell@loc.gov
Web: www.loc.gov/hr/jrfellows/index.html

Summary To provide summer work experience at the Library of Congress (LC) to African American and other 1) upper-division or graduate students and 2) recent graduates.

Eligibility This program is open to U.S. citizens with subject expertise in the following areas: American history, including veterans and military history; American popular culture; area studies (African, Asian, European, Hispanic, Middle Eastern); bibliographic description and access; film, television, and radio; folklife; geography and maps; history of photography; history of popular and applied graphic arts, architecture, and design; manuscript collections processing; music; preservation and conservation; rare books and manuscripts; science, technology, and business; serials and government publications and newspapers; or sound recordings. Applicants must 1) be juniors or seniors at an accredited college or university, 2) be graduate students, or 3) have completed their degree in the past year. Applications from women, minorities, and persons with disabilities are particularly encouraged. Selection is based on academic achievement, letters of recommendation, and an interview.

Financial data Fellows are paid a taxable stipend of $300 per week.

Duration 3 months, beginning in either May or June. Fellows work a 40-hour week.

Additional information Fellows work with primary source materials and assist selected divisions at LC in the organization and documentation of archival collections, production of finding aids and bibliographic records, preparation of materials for preservation and service, completion of bibliographical research, and digitization of LC's historical collections.

Number awarded Varies each year; recently, 6 of these internships were awarded.

Deadline March of each year.

[877]
LILLIAN AND SAMUEL SUTTON EDUCATION SCHOLARSHIPS

National Association for the Advancement of Colored
  People
Attn: Education Department
4805 Mt. Hope Drive
Baltimore, MD 21215-3297
(410) 580-5760   Toll Free: (877) NAACP-98
E-mail: youth@naacpnet.org
Web: www.naacp.org/pages/naacp-scholarships

Summary To provide financial assistance to members of the National Association for the Advancement of Colored People (NAACP) and others who are working on a degree in education on the undergraduate or graduate level.

Eligibility This program is open to full-time undergraduates and full- and part-time graduate students majoring in the field of education. The required minimum GPA is 2.5 for graduating high school seniors and current undergraduates or 3.0 for graduate students. Membership and participation in the association are highly desirable. Applicants must be able to demonstrate financial need and be U.S. citizens. Along with their application, they must submit a 1-page essay on their interest in their major and a career, their life's ambition, what they hope to accomplish in their lifetime, and what position they hope to attain.

Financial data The stipend is $1,000 per year for undergraduate students or $2,000 per year for graduate students.

Duration 1 year; may be renewed as long as the recipient maintains a GPA of 2.5 or higher as an undergraduate or 3.0 or higher as a graduate student.

Number awarded Varies each year; recently, 9 of these scholarships were awarded.

Deadline March of each year.

[878]
LIONEL C. BARROW MINORITY DOCTORAL STUDENT SCHOLARSHIP

Association for Education in Journalism and Mass
   Communication
Attn: Communication Theory and Methodology Division
234 Outlet Pointe Boulevard, Suite A
Columbia, SC 29210-5667
(803) 798-0271　　　　　　　　Fax: (803) 772-3509
E-mail: aejmc@aejmc.org
Web: aejmcctm.blogspot.com

Summary　To provide financial assistance to African Americans and other minorities who are interested in working on a doctorate in mass communication.

Eligibility　This program is open to minority students enrolled in a Ph.D. program in journalism and/or mass communication. Applicants must submit 2 letters of recommendation, a resume, and a brief letter outlining their research interests and career plans. Membership in the association is not required, but applicants must be U.S. citizens or permanent residents. Selection is based on the likelihood that the applicant's work will contribute to communication theory and/or methodology.

Financial data　The stipend is $1,400.

Duration　1 year.

Additional information　This program began in 1972.

Number awarded　1 each year.

Deadline　May of each year.

[879]
LLOYD M. JOHNSON, JR. SCHOLARSHIP PROGRAM

United Negro College Fund
Attn: Scholarships and Grants Department
8260 Willow Oaks Corporate Drive
P.O. Box 10444
Fairfax, VA 22031-8044
(703) 205-3466　　　　　　　Toll Free: (800) 331-2244
Fax: (703) 205-3574
Web: www.uncf.org

Summary　To provide financial assistance to African Americans and other law students who come from a disadvantaged background and will contribute to diversity in the legal profession.

Eligibility　Applicants must be U.S. citizens, have a strong academic record (at least a 3.2 GPA), have been accepted to an ABA-accredited law school, be able to demonstrate community service and leadership qualities, have an interest in diversity, be financially disadvantaged, plan to study on a full-time basis, and have an interest in corporate law, including working in a corporate law department and/or law firm. Applicants must submit a current transcript, a resume, 2 letters of recommendation, a personal statement, and a diversity essay (1 page). All students are eligible, but the sponsor expects that most recipients will be students of color.

Financial data　The stipend is $10,000 per year.

Duration　1 year. Full scholarships may be renewed for up to 2 additional years, provided the recipient maintains a GPA of 3.2 or higher. Other scholarships are for 1 year only.

Additional information　The Minority Corporate Counsel Association first began this program in 2005 and now cospon-

sors it with the United Negro College Fund. Mentoring and internship experiences are also offered to the winners.

Number awarded　Varies each year; recently, 17 of these scholarships were awarded.

Deadline　May of each year.

[880]
LOS ANGELES CHAPTER NBMBAA GRADUATE SCHOLARSHIPS

National Black MBA Association-Los Angeles Chapter
Attn: Education Committee Chair
P.O. Box 83731
Los Angeles, CA 90083
(310) 437-1033　　　　　　　E-mail: education@labmba.org
Web: www.labmba.org/categories/programs-1.html

Summary　To provide financial assistance to African Americans from any state working on a graduate business degree at a college in Nevada or central or southern California.

Eligibility　This program is open to African American residents of any state currently enrolled full time at an accredited college or university in Nevada or central or southern California. Applicants must be working on an M.B.A., Ph.D., or D.B.A. degree in business, management, organizational behavior, or other business-related field. Along with their application, they must submit 1) a resume of professional, community, and/or extracurricular activities; 2) a 1-paragraph statement of career objectives; and 3) a 3-page essay on a topic that changes annually but relates to African Americans and business. Students who submit outstanding essays are considered for sponsor awards.

Financial data　The stipend is $1,500. Sponsor awards, if available, range from $2,500 to $5,000.

Duration　1 year.

Additional information　Winners also receive a 2-year membership in the National Black MBA Association (NBMBAA); membership fees are deducted from the award.

Number awarded　1 or more each year.

Deadline　November of each year.

[881]
LOUISE JANE MOSES/AGNES DAVIS MEMORIAL SCHOLARSHIP

California Librarians Black Caucus-Greater Los Angeles
   Chapter
Attn: Scholarship Committee
P.O. Box 882276
Los Angeles, CA 90009
E-mail: scholarship@clbc.org
Web: www.clbc.org/home/scholarship

Summary　To provide financial assistance to African Americans in California who are interested in becoming librarians or library paraprofessionals.

Eligibility　This program is open to African American residents of California who are working on a degree from an accredited library/information science program or an accredited library/information science paraprofessional program in the state. Applicants must submit an essay of 300 to 500 words on their professional goals and their interest in a library or information-related career. Selection is based on demonstrated financial need, scholastic achievement, and commitment to the goals of encouraging and supporting African

American library professionals and improving library service to the African American community. Interviews are required.

Financial data Stipends range from $750 to $1,500.

Duration 1 year.

Number awarded 2 to 3 each year.

Deadline October of each year.

[882]
LOUISIANA WMU SCHOLARSHIP FOR AFRICAN-AMERICAN MISSION PASTORS

Louisiana Baptist Convention
Attn: Woman's Missionary Union
P.O. Box 311
Alexandria, LA 71309
(318) 448-3402   Toll Free: (800) 622-6549
E-mail: wmu@lbc.org
Web: www.lbc.org

Summary To provide financial assistance to African American Southern Baptists from Louisiana who are enrolled at a seminary in any state to prepare for a career as a missions pastor.

Eligibility This program is open to African Americans who are endorsed by the director of missions and the pastor of a sponsoring Southern Baptist church in Louisiana. Applicants must be enrolled full time at a seminary or a satellite campus to prepare for a career as a missions pastor and have a GPA of 2.5 or higher. They must be participating in a missions education organization of the church or on campus and must contribute to offerings of the church and other programs. Along with their application, they must submit a brief summary of their Christian walk in their life, including what they believe the Lord has called them to do in a church-related vocation.

Financial data The stipend is $1,200 per year.

Duration Up to 3 years.

Number awarded 1 or more each year.

Deadline June of each year.

[883]
LTK SCHOLARSHIP

Conference of Minority Transportation Officials
Attn: National Scholarship Program
818 18th Street, N.W., Suite 850
Washington, DC 20006
(202) 530-0551   Fax: (202) 530-0617
Web: www.comto.org/news-youth.php

Summary To provide financial assistance to African American and other minority upper-division and graduate students in engineering or other field related to transportation.

Eligibility This program is open to full-time minority juniors, seniors, and graduate students in engineering of other technical transportation-related disciplines. Applicants must have a GPA of 3.0 or higher. Along with their application, they must submit a cover letter with a 500-word statement of career goals. Financial need is not considered in the selection process. U.S. citizenship is required.

Financial data The stipend is $6,000. Funds are paid directly to the recipient's college or university.

Duration 1 year.

Additional information The Conference of Minority Transportation Officials (COMTO) was established in 1971 to promote, strengthen, and expand the roles of minorities in all aspects of transportation. This program is sponsored by LTK Engineering Services. Recipients are required to become members of COMTO if they are not already members and attend the COMTO National Scholarship Luncheon.

Number awarded 1 or more each year.

Deadline April of each year.

[884]
M. ELIZABETH CARNEGIE SCHOLARSHIP

Nurses Educational Funds, Inc.
Attn: Scholarship Coordinator
304 Park Avenue South, 11th Floor
New York, NY 10010
(212) 590-2443   Fax: (212) 590-2446
E-mail: info@n-e-f.org
Web: www.n-e-f.org

Summary To provide financial assistance to African American nurses who wish to work on a doctoral degree in nursing.

Eligibility This program is open to African American registered nurses who are members of a national professional nursing organization and enrolled in a nursing or nursing-related program at the doctoral level. Applicants must have a GPA of 3.6 or higher. They must be U.S. citizens or have declared their official intention of becoming a citizen. Along with their application, they must submit an 800-word essay on their professional goals and potential for making a contribution to the nursing profession. Selection is based on academic excellence and the essay's content and clarity.

Financial data Stipends range from $2,500 to $10,000, depending on the availability of funds.

Duration 1 year; nonrenewable.

Additional information There is a $20 application fee.

Number awarded 1 each year.

Deadline February of each year.

[885]
MABEL D. RUSSELL BLACK COLLEGE FUND

United Methodist Higher Education Foundation
Attn: Scholarships Administrator
1001 19th Avenue South
P.O. Box 340005
Nashville, TN 37203-0005
(615) 340-7385   Toll Free: (800) 811-8110
Fax: (615) 340-7330
E-mail: umhefscholarships@gbhem.org
Web: www.umhef.org/receive.php?id=endowed_funds

Summary To provide financial assistance to Methodist undergraduate and graduate students at Historically Black Colleges and Universities of the United Methodist Church.

Eligibility This program is open to students enrolling as full-time undergraduate and graduate students at the Historically Black Colleges and Universities of the United Methodist Church. Applicants must have been active, full members of a United Methodist Church for at least 1 year prior to applying. They must have a GPA of 3.0 or higher and be able to demonstrate financial need. Along with their application, they must submit a 200-word essay on their involvement and/or leadership responsibilities in their church, school, and community within the last 3 years. U.S. citizenship or permanent resident status is required.

Financial data   The stipend is at least $1,000 per year.

Duration   1 year; nonrenewable.

Additional information   This program was established in 1978. The qualifying schools are Bennett College for Women, Bethune-Cookman College, Claflin University, Clark Atlanta University, Dillard University, Huston-Tillotson College, Meharry Medical College, Paine College, Philander Smith College, Rust College, and Wiley College.

Number awarded   1 each year.

Deadline   May of each year.

[886]
MABEL G. YOUNG SCHOLARSHIP

National Forum for Black Public Administrators
Attn: Scholarship Program
777 North Capitol Street, N.E., Suite 807
Washington, DC 20002
(202) 408-9300, ext. 112   Fax: (202) 408-8558
E-mail: vreed@nfbpa.org
Web: www.nfbpa.org/i4a/pages/index.cfm?pageid=3630

Summary   To provide financial assistance to African Americans working on an undergraduate or graduate degree in public administration with an emphasis on public finance.

Eligibility   This program is open to African American undergraduate and graduate students preparing for a career in public service. Applicants must be working full time on a degree in public administration, public finance, accounting, political science, urban affairs, public policy, or a related field. They must have a GPA of 3.0 or higher, a record of involvement in extracurricular activities (excluding athletics), excellent interpersonal and leadership abilities, and strong oral and written communication skills. Along with their application, they must submit a 3-page autobiographical essay that includes their academic and career goals and objectives. First consideration is given to applicants who are not currently receiving other financial aid.

Financial data   The stipend is $5,000.

Duration   1 year.

Additional information   This program is sponsored by the Grant Capital Management Corporation. Recipients are required to attend the sponsor's annual conference to receive their scholarship; limited hotel and air accommodations are arranged and provided.

Number awarded   1 each year.

Deadline   February of each year.

[887]
MAJOR SPONSORS SCHOLARS AWARDS

National Society of Black Engineers
Attn: Programs Department
205 Daingerfield Road
Alexandria, VA 22314
(703) 549-2207   Fax: (703) 683-5312
E-mail: scholarships@nsbe.org
Web: www.nsbe.org

Summary   To provide financial assistance to members of the National Society of Black Engineers (NSBE) who are working on a degree in engineering.

Eligibility   This program is open to members of the society who are undergraduate or graduate engineering students. Applicants must have a GPA of 3.0 or higher. Selection is based on an essay; academic achievement; service to the society at the chapter, regional, and/or national level; and other professional, campus, and community activities. Applicants for the National Society of Black Engineers Fellows Scholarship Program who rank in the second of 3 tiers receive these awards.

Financial data   The stipend is $1,500. Travel, hotel accommodations, and registration to the national convention are also provided.

Duration   1 year.

Number awarded   Varies each year; recently, 10 of these scholarships were awarded.

Deadline   January of each year.

[888]
MARATHON OIL CORPORATION COLLEGE SCHOLARSHIP PROGRAM OF THE HISPANIC SCHOLARSHIP FUND

Hispanic Scholarship Fund
Attn: Selection Committee
55 Second Street, Suite 1500
San Francisco, CA 94105
(415) 808-2365   Toll Free: (877) HSF-INFO
Fax: (415) 808-2302   E-mail: scholar1@hsf.net
Web: www.hsf.net/Scholarships.aspx?id=464

Summary   To provide financial assistance to African American and other minority upper-division and graduate students working on a degree in a field related to the oil and gas industry.

Eligibility   This program is open to U.S. citizens and permanent residents (must have a permanent resident card or a passport stamped I-551) who are of Hispanic American, African American, Asian Pacific Islander American, or American Indian/Alaskan Native heritage. Applicants must be currently enrolled full time at an accredited 4-year college or university in the United States, Puerto Rico, Guam, or the U.S. Virgin Islands with a GPA of 3.0 or higher. They must be 1) sophomores majoring in accounting, chemical engineering, civil engineering, computer engineering, computer science, electrical engineering, energy management or petroleum land management, environmental engineering, environmental health and safety, finance, geology, geophysics, geotechnical engineering, global procurement or supply chain management, information technology/management information systems, marketing, mechanical engineering, petroleum engineering, or transportation and logistics,; or 2) seniors planning to work on a master's degree in geology or geophysics. Selection is based on academic achievement, personal strengths, interest and commitment to a career in the oil and gas industry, leadership, and financial need.

Financial data   The stipend is $15,000 per year.

Duration   2 years (the junior and senior undergraduate years or the first 2 years of a master's degree program).

Additional information   This program is jointly sponsored by Marathon Oil Corporation and the Hispanic Scholarship Fund (HSF). Recipients may be offered a paid 8- to 10-week summer internship at various Marathon Oil Corporation locations.

Number awarded   1 or more each year.

Deadline   November of each year.

[889]
MARK MILLER AWARD

National Association of Black Accountants
Attn: National Scholarship Program
7474 Greenway Center Drive, Suite 1120
Greenbelt, MD 20770
(301) 474-NABA, ext. 114   Fax: (301) 474-3114
E-mail: customerservice@nabainc.org
Web: www.nabainc.org

Summary To provide financial assistance to student members of the National Association of Black Accountants (NABA) who are working on an undergraduate or graduate degree in a field related to accounting.

Eligibility This program is open to NABA members who are ethnic minorities enrolled full time as 1) an undergraduate freshman, sophomore, junior, or first-semester senior majoring in accounting, business, or finance at a 4-year college or university; or 2) a graduate student working on a master's degree in accounting. High school seniors are not eligible. Applicants must have a GPA of 2.0 or higher in their major and 2.5 or higher overall. Along with their application, they must submit 1) a 500-word autobiography that discusses career objectives, leadership abilities, community activities, and involvement in NABA; and 2) a 500-word statement on a personal, family, or financial hardship they have overcome, the circumstances involved, and how the obstacles were overcome.

Financial data The stipend is $2,500.

Duration 1 year.

Number awarded 1 each year.

Deadline January of each year.

[890]
MARK T. BANNER SCHOLARSHIP FOR LAW STUDENTS

Richard Linn American Inn of Court
c/o Cynthia M. Ho, Programs Chair
Loyola University School of Law
25 East Pearson Street, Room 1324
Chicago, IL 60611
(312) 915-7148
Web: www.linninn.org/marktbanner.htm

Summary To provide financial assistance to law students who are African Americans or members of another group historically underrepresented in intellectual property law.

Eligibility This program is open to students at ABA-accredited law schools in the United States who are members of groups historically underrepresented (by race, sex, ethnicity, sexual orientation, or disability) in intellectual property law. Applicants must submit a 1-page statement on how they have focused on ethics, civility, and professionalism and how diversity has impacted them; transcripts; a writing sample; and contact information for 3 references. Selection is based on academic merit, written and oral communication skills (determined in part through a telephone interview), leadership qualities, community involvement, and commitment to the pursuit of a career in intellectual property law.

Financial data The stipend is $5,000.

Duration 1 year.

Number awarded 1 each year.

Deadline November of each year.

[891]
MARTHA AND ROBERT ATHERTON MINISTERIAL SCHOLARSHIP

Unitarian Universalist Association
Attn: Ministerial Credentialing Office
25 Beacon Street
Boston, MA 02108-2800
(617) 948-6403   Fax: (617) 742-2875
E-mail: mco@uua.org
Web: www.uua.org

Summary To provide financial assistance to seminary students (particularly African Americans and other students of color) who are preparing for the Unitarian Universalist (UU) ministry.

Eligibility This program is open to second- or third-year seminary students currently enrolled full or at least half time in a UU ministerial training program with aspirant or candidate status. Applicants must respect hard work as a foundation of a full life and appreciate the freedom, political system, and philosophical underpinnings of our country. They should be citizens of the United States or Canada. Preference is given to applicants who have demonstrated outstanding ministerial ability and to those with the greatest financial need, especially persons of color.

Financial data The stipend ranges from $1,000 to $11,000 per year.

Duration 1 year.

Additional information This program was established in 1997.

Number awarded 1 or 2 each year.

Deadline April of each year.

[892]
MARTIN LUTHER KING, JR. MEMORIAL SCHOLARSHIP FUND

California Teachers Association
Attn: Human Rights Department
1705 Murchison Drive
P.O. Box 921
Burlingame, CA 94011-0921
(650) 552-5446   Fax: (650) 552-5002
E-mail: scholarships@cta.org
Web: www.cta.org

Summary To provide financial assistance for college or graduate school to African American and other racial and ethnic minorities who are members of the California Teachers Association (CTA), children of members, or members of the Student CTA.

Eligibility This program is open to members of racial or ethnic minority groups (African Americans, American Indians/Alaska Natives, Asians/Pacific Islanders, and Hispanics) who are 1) active CTA members; 2) dependent children of active, retired, or deceased CTA members; or 3) members of Student CTA. Applicants must be interested in preparing for a teaching career in public education or already engaged in such a career.

Financial data Stipends vary each year; recently, they ranged from $1,000 to $4,000.

Duration 1 year.

Number awarded Varies each year; recently, 12 of these scholarships were awarded: 4 to CTA members, 6 to children of CTA members, and 2 to Student CTA members.
Deadline March of each year.

[893]
MARY ELIZABETH CARNEGIE AMERICAN NURSES FOUNDATION SCHOLAR AWARD

American Nurses Foundation
Attn: Nursing Research Grants Program
8515 Georgia Avenue, Suite 400
Silver Spring, MD 20910-3492
(301) 628-5227   Fax: (301) 628-5354
E-mail: anf@ana.org
Web: www.anfonline.org

Summary To provide funding to nurses, especially members of the National Black Nurses' Association (NBNA), who are interested in conducting research.
Eligibility This program is open to registered nurses who have earned a baccalaureate or higher degree. Preference is given to NBNA members. Applicants may be either beginning or experienced researchers. They must be interested in conducting research on a topic related to nursing. Proposed research may be for a master's thesis or doctoral dissertation if the project has been approved by the principal investigator's thesis or dissertation committee.
Financial data The grant is $8,500. Funds may not be used as a salary for the principal investigator.
Duration 1 year.
Additional information This award was first presented in 2007. There is a $100 application fee.
Number awarded 1 each year.
Deadline April of each year.

[894]
MARY WOLFSKILL TRUST FUND INTERNSHIP

Library of Congress
Library Services
Attn: Junior Fellows Program Coordinator
101 Independence Avenue, S.E., Room LM-642
Washington, DC 20540-4600
(202) 707-3301   Fax: (202) 707-6269
E-mail: jrfell@loc.gov
Web: www.loc.gov/hr/jrfellows/index.html

Summary To provide summer work experience in the Manuscript Division of the Library of Congress (LC) to upper-division and graduate students (especially African American and other minority students).
Eligibility This program is open to undergraduate and graduate students who have expertise in library science or collections conservation and preservation. Applicants must be interested in gaining an introductory knowledge of the principles, concepts, and techniques of archival management through a summer internship in the LC Manuscript Division. They should be able to demonstrate an ability to communicate effectively in writing and have knowledge of integrated library systems, basic library applications, and other information technologies. Knowledge of American history is beneficial. Applications from minorities and students at smaller and lesser-known schools are particularly encouraged. U.S. citizenship is required.

Financial data The stipend is $3,000.
Duration 10 weeks during the summer. Fellows work a 40-hour week.
Number awarded 1 each year.
Deadline March of each year.

[895]
MCANDREWS DIVERSITY IN PATENT LAW FELLOWSHIP

McAndrews, Held & Malloy, Ltd.
Attn: Diversity Fellowship
500 West Madison Street, 34th Floor
Chicago, IL 60661
(312) 775-8000   Fax: (312) 775-8100
E-mail: info@mcandrews-ip.com
Web: www.mcandrews-ip.com/diversity_fellowship.html

Summary To provide financial assistance to African American and other law students who come from a diverse background and are interested in patent law.
Eligibility This program is open to first-year students at ABA-accredited law schools who come from a diverse background. Applicants must have a degree in science or engineering and be planning to practice patent law in the Chicago area. Along with their application, they must submit a 500-word personal statement on why they wish to prepare for a career in patent law, why they are interested in the sponsoring firm as a place to work, and how their background and/or life experiences would improved diversity in the field of intellectual property law. Selection is based on that statement, a resume (including their science or engineering educational credentials), a legal writing sample, undergraduate transcript, and at least 1 letter of recommendation.
Financial data The stipend is $5,000.
Duration 1 year (the second year of law school).
Additional information This fellowship was first awarded in 2008. It includes a paid clerkship position at McAndrews, Held & Malloy during the summer after the first year of law school and possibly another clerkship during the summer after the second year.
Number awarded 1 each year.
Deadline January of each year.

[896]
MCDERMOTT MINORITY SCHOLARSHIP

McDermott Will & Emery
Attn: Recruiting Coordinator
227 West Monroe Street
Chicago, IL 60606
(312) 984-6470   Fax: (312) 984-7700
E-mail: mcdermottscholarship@mwe.com
Web: www.mwe.com

Summary To provide financial assistance and work experience to African American and other minority law students.
Eligibility This program is open to second-year minority (African American, Asian, Hispanic, Middle Eastern, Native American) law students at ABA-accredited U.S. law schools. Applicants must be able to demonstrate leadership, community involvement, and a commitment to improving diversity in the legal community. They must be interested in participating in the sponsor's summer program and be able to meet its hiring criteria. Along with their application, they must submit an

essay of 1 to 2 pages that provides ideas they have on how the number of minority students in law schools can be increased and how they have improved and intend to help improve diversity in the legal profession throughout their law school and legal career.

Financial data The stipend is $15,000.

Duration 1 year.

Additional information Recipients also participate in a summer program at the sponsor's offices in Boston, Chicago, Houston, Los Angeles, Miami, New York, Orange County, San Diego, Silicon Valley, or Washington, D.C.

Number awarded 2 each year.

Deadline October of each year.

[897]
MCKINLEY FINANCIAL SERVICES SCHOLARSHIP

National Forum for Black Public Administrators
Attn: Scholarship Program
777 North Capitol Street, N.E., Suite 807
Washington, DC 20002
(202) 408-9300, ext. 112　　　Fax: (202) 408-8558
E-mail: vreed@nfbpa.org
Web: www.nfbpa.org/i4a/pages/index.cfm?pageid=3630

Summary To provide financial assistance to African Americans working on an undergraduate or graduate degree in public administration.

Eligibility This program is open to African American undergraduate and graduate students preparing for a career in public service. Applicants must be working full time on a degree in public administration, political science, urban affairs, public policy, or a related field. They must have a GPA of 3.0 or higher, excellent interpersonal and analytical abilities, and strong oral and written communication skills. Along with their application, they must submit a 3-page autobiographical essay that includes their academic and career goals and objectives. First consideration is given to applicants who are not currently receiving other financial aid.

Financial data The stipend is $1,000.

Duration 1 year.

Additional information This program is sponsored by McKinley Financial Services, Inc. Recipients are required to attend the sponsor's annual conference to receive their scholarship; limited hotel and air accommodations are arranged and provided.

Number awarded 1 each year.

Deadline February of each year.

[898]
MCKNIGHT DOCTORAL FELLOWSHIP PROGRAM

Florida Education Fund
201 East Kennedy Boulevard, Suite 1525
Tampa, FL 33602
(813) 272-2772　　　Fax: (813) 272-2784
E-mail: mdf@fefonline.org
Web: www.fefonline.org/mdf.html

Summary To provide financial assistance to African American and Hispanic doctoral students from any state who are working on a degree in designated fields at selected universi-

ties in Florida and preparing for an academic career in that state.

Eligibility This program is open to African Americans and Hispanics from any state who are working on a Ph.D. degree at 1 of 9 universities in Florida. Fellowships may be given in any discipline in the arts and sciences, business, engineering, health sciences, nursing, or the visual and performing arts; preference is given to the following fields of study: agriculture, biology, business administration, chemistry, computer science, engineering, marine biology, mathematics, physics, or psychology. Academic programs that lead to professional degrees (such as the M.D., D.B.A., D.D.S., J.D., or D.V.M.) are not covered by the fellowship. Graduate study in education, whether leading to an Ed.D. or a Ph.D., is generally not supported. U.S. citizenship is required. Because this program is intended to increase African American graduate enrollment at the 9 participating universities, currently-enrolled doctoral students at those universities are not eligible to apply.

Financial data Each award provides annual tuition up to $5,000 and an annual stipend of $12,000. Recipients are also eligible for the Fellows Travel Fund, which supports recipients who wish to attend and present papers at professional conferences.

Duration 3 years; an additional 2 years of support may be provided by the university if the recipient maintains satisfactory performance and normal progress toward the Ph.D. degree.

Additional information This program was established in 1984. The participating universities are Florida Agricultural and Mechanical University, Florida Atlantic University, Florida Institute of Technology, Florida International University, Florida State University, University of Central Florida, University of Florida, University of Miami, and University of South Florida.

Number awarded Up to 50 each year.

Deadline January of each year.

[899]
MENTAL HEALTH DISSERTATION RESEARCH GRANT TO INCREASE DIVERSITY

National Institute of Mental Health
Attn: Division of Extramural Activities
6001 Executive Boulevard, Room 6138
Bethesda, MD 20892-9609
(301) 443-3534　　　Fax: (301) 443-4720
TDD: (301) 451-0088　　E-mail: armstrda@mail.nih.gov
Web: www.nimh.nih.gov

Summary To provide research funding to African American and other doctoral candidates from underrepresented groups planning to prepare for a research career in any area relevant to mental health and/or mental disorders.

Eligibility This program is open to doctoral candidates conducting dissertation research in a field related to mental health and/or mental disorders at a university, college, or professional school with an accredited doctoral degree granting program. Applicants must be 1) members of an ethnic or racial group that has been determined by their institution to be underrepresented in biomedical or behavioral research; 2) individuals with disabilities; or 3) individuals from socially, culturally, economically, or educationally disadvantaged backgrounds that have inhibited their ability to prepare for a career in health-related research. They must be U.S. citizens, nationals, or permanent residents.

Financial data The stipend is $21,180. An additional grant up to $15,000 is provided for additional research expenses, fringe benefits (including health insurance), travel to scientific meetings, and research costs of the dissertation. Facilities and administrative costs are limited to 8% of modified total direct costs.

Duration Up to 2 years; nonrenewable.

Number awarded Varies each year.

Deadline April, August, or December of each year.

[900]
METROPOLITAN LIFE FOUNDATION AWARDS PROGRAM FOR ACADEMIC EXCELLENCE IN MEDICINE

National Medical Fellowships, Inc.
Attn: Scholarship Program
347 Fifth Avenue, Suite 510
New York, NY 10016
(212) 483-8880   Toll Free: (877) NMF-1DOC
Fax: (212) 483-8897   E-mail: info@nmfonline.org
Web: www.nmfonline.org

Summary To provide financial assistance to African American and other underrepresented minority medical students who reside or attend school in designated cities throughout the country.

Eligibility This program is open to African American, mainland Puerto Rican, Mexican American, Native Hawaiian, Alaska Native, Vietnamese, Cambodian, or American Indian medical students in their second through fourth year who are nominated by their dean. Nominees must be enrolled in medical schools located in (or be residents of) designated cities that change annually. Selection is based on demonstrated financial need, outstanding academic achievement, leadership, and potential for distinguished contributions to medicine.

Financial data The stipend is $4,000.

Duration 1 year; nonrenewable.

Additional information Funding for this program, established in 1987, is provided by the Metropolitan Life Foundation of New York, New York.

Number awarded 17 each year.

Deadline March of each year.

[901]
MICKEY LELAND ENERGY FELLOWSHIPS

Department of Energy
Attn: Office of Fossil Energy
19901 Germantown Road, FE-6
Germantown, MD 20874
(301) 903-4293   E-mail: MLEF@hq.doe.gov
Web: fossil.energy.gov

Summary To provide summer work experience at fossil energy sites of the Department of Energy (DOE) to African American and other underrepresented students.

Eligibility This program is open to U.S. citizens currently enrolled full time at an accredited college or university. Applicants must be undergraduate, graduate, or postdoctoral students in mathematics, physical sciences, technology, or engineering and have a GPA of 3.0 or higher. They must be inter-

ested in a summer work experience at a DOE fossil energy research facility. Along with their application, they must submit a 100-word statement on why they want to participate in this program. A goal of the program is to recruit women and underrepresented minorities into careers related to fossil energy.

Financial data Weekly stipends are $500 for undergraduates, $650 for master's degree students, or $750 for doctoral and postdoctoral students. Travel costs for a round trip to and from the site and for a trip to a designated place for technical presentations are also paid.

Duration 10 weeks during the summer.

Additional information This program began as 3 separate activities: the Historically Black Colleges and Universities Internship Program, established in 1995; the Hispanic Internship Program, established in 1998; and the Tribal Colleges and Universities Internship Program, established in 2000. Those 3 programs were merged into the Fossil Energy Minority Education Initiative, renamed the Mickey Leland Energy Fellowship Program in 2000. Sites to which interns may be assigned include the Albany Research Center (Albany, Oregon), the National Energy Technology Laboratory (Morgantown, West Virginia and Pittsburgh, Pennsylvania), Pacific Northwest National Laboratory (Richland, Washington), Rocky Mountain Oilfield Testing Center (Casper, Wyoming), Strategic Petroleum Reserve Project Management Office (New Orleans, Louisiana), or U.S. Department of Energy Headquarters (Washington, D.C.).

Number awarded Varies each year; recently, 30 students participated in this program.

Deadline January of each year.

[902]
MIKE SHINN DISTINGUISHED MEMBER OF THE YEAR AWARDS

National Society of Black Engineers
Attn: Programs Department
205 Daingerfield Road
Alexandria, VA 22314
(703) 549-2207   Fax: (703) 683-5312
E-mail: scholarships@nsbe.org
Web: www.nsbe.org

Summary To provide financial assistance to male and female members of the National Society of Black Engineers (NSBE) who are working on a degree in engineering.

Eligibility This program is open to members of the society who are undergraduate or graduate engineering students. Applicants must have a GPA of 3.2 or higher. Selection is based on an essay; NSBE and university academic achievement; professional development; service to the society at the chapter, regional, and/or national level; and campus and community activities. The male and female applicants for the NSBE Fellows Scholarship Program who are judged most outstanding receive these awards.

Financial data The stipend is $7,500. Travel, hotel accommodations, and registration to the national convention are also provided.

Duration 1 year.

Number awarded 2 each year: 1 male and 1 female.

Deadline November of each year.

[903]
MILBANK DIVERSITY SCHOLARS PROGRAM

Milbank, Tweed, Hadley & McCloy LLP
Attn: Manager of Law School Recruiting
One Chase Manhattan Plaza
New York, NY 10005
(212) 530-5757   Fax: (212) 822-5757
E-mail: alevitt@milbank.com
Web: www.milbank.com/careers

Summary   To provide financial assistance and work experience to law students, especially those who are African American or members of other groups underrepresented at large law firms.

Eligibility   This program is open to students who have completed their first year of a full-time J.D. program at an ABA-accredited law school. Joint degree candidates must have successfully completed 2 years of a J.D. program. Applications are particularly encouraged from members of groups traditionally underrepresented at large law firms. Applicants must submit a 500-word essay on 1) the challenges they have faced in pursuit of a legal career that have helped them understand the value of diversity and inclusion in the legal profession; and 2) the personal contributions they would make to furthering the diversity objectives of the sponsoring law firm. Selection is based on academic achievement, demonstrated leadership ability, writing and interpersonal skills, and interest in the firm's practice.

Financial data   The stipend is $25,000. A paid associate position during the summer after the second year of law school is also provided. If the student is offered and accepts a permanent position with the firm after graduation, an additional $25,000 scholarship stipend is also awarded.

Duration   1 year (the third year of law school).

Additional information   Scholars may be offered a permanent position with the firm, but there is no guarantee of such an offer.

Number awarded   At least 2 each year.

Deadline   August of each year.

[904]
MILLER JOHNSON WEST MICHIGAN DIVERSITY LAW SCHOOL SCHOLARSHIP

Grand Rapids Community Foundation
Attn: Education Program Officer
185 Oakes Street S.W.
Grand Rapids, MI 49503-4008
(616) 454-1751, ext. 103   Fax: (616) 454-6455
E-mail: rbishop@grfoundation.org
Web: www.grfoundation.org/scholarships

Summary   To provide financial assistance to African Americans and other minorities from Michigan who are attending law school in any state.

Eligibility   This program is open to U.S. citizens and permanent residents who are students of color and residents of Michigan. Preference is given to residents of western Michigan. Applicants must be attending an accredited law school in any state. They must have a GPA of 3.0 or higher and be able to demonstrate financial need.

Financial data   The stipend is $5,000. Funds are paid directly to the recipient's institution.

Duration   1 year.

Number awarded   1 each year.
Deadline   March of each year.

[905]
MILLER NASH LAW STUDENT DIVERSITY FELLOWSHIP PROGRAM

Miller Nash LLP
Attn: Director of Recruiting and Professional Development
3400 U.S. Bancorp Tower
111 S.W. Fifth Avenue
Portland, OR 97204-3699
(503) 224-5858   Fax: (503) 224-0155
E-mail: michelle.baird-johnson@millernash.com
Web: www.millernash.com/fellowship.aspx

Summary   To provide financial assistance and work experience to African American and other law students who contribute to diversity and are interested in living and working in the Pacific Northwest following graduation from law school.

Eligibility   This program is open to first- and second-year students at ABA-accredited law schools in any state. Applicants must be able to demonstrate academic excellence, interpersonal skills, leadership qualities, contributions to diversity, and meaningful contributions to the community. They must intend to work, live, and practice law in the Pacific Northwest. Along with their application, they must submit a personal statement of 2 to 4 pages that includes a description of organizations or projects in which they currently participate or have participated that address diversity issues or support diversity in their legal, business, or local communities.

Financial data   Fellows receive a paid summer clerk position and a stipend of $7,500 for law school.

Duration   1 year (including 12 weeks for the summer clerk position); nonrenewable.

Additional information   Summer clerk positions may be offered (depending on availability) at the sponsoring law firm's offices in Portland (Oregon), Seattle (Washington), or Vancouver (Washington).

Number awarded   Up to 2 each year.

Deadline   September of each year for second-year students; January of each year for first-year students.

[906]
MINORITY ACCESS INTERNSHIP

Minority Access, Inc.
Attn: Directory of Internship Program
5214 Baltimore Avenue
Hyattsville, MD 20781
(301) 779-7100   Fax: (301) 779-9812
Web: www.minorityaccess.org

Summary   To provide work experience to African American and other minority undergraduate and graduate students interested in internships at participating entities in Washington, D.C. and throughout the United States.

Eligibility   This program is open to full-time undergraduate and graduate students who have a GPA of 3.0 or higher. Applicants must be U.S. citizens for most positions. All academic majors are eligible. Interns are selected by participating federal government and other agencies. Most of these are located in Washington, D.C., but placements may be made anywhere in the United States.

Financial data The weekly stipend is $450 for sophomores and juniors, $500 for seniors, or $550 for graduate and professional students. In addition, most internships include paid round-trip travel between home and the internship location.

Duration Spring internships are 5 months, starting in January; summer internships are 3 months, starting in August; fall internships are 4 months, starting in September.

Additional information Minority Access, Inc. is committed to the diversification of institutions, federal agencies, and corporations of all kinds and to improving their recruitment, retention, and enhancement of minorities. The majority of interns are placed in the Washington, D.C. metropolitan area. Both full-time and part-time internships are awarded. Students may receive academic credit for full-time internships. Students are expected to pay all housing costs. They are required to attend a pre-employment session in Washington, D.C., all seminars and workshops hosted by Minority Access, and any mandatory activities sponsored by the host agency.

Number awarded Varies each year.

Deadline February of each year for summer internships; June of each year for fall internships; and November of each year for spring internships.

[907]
MINORITY FACULTY DEVELOPMENT SCHOLARSHIP AWARD IN PHYSICAL THERAPY

American Physical Therapy Association
Attn: Honors and Awards Program
1111 North Fairfax Street
Alexandria, VA 22314-1488
(703) 684-APTA   Toll Free: (800) 999-APTA
Fax: (703) 684-7343   TDD: (703) 683-6748
E-mail: executivedept@apta.org
Web: www.apta.org

Summary To provide financial assistance to African American and other minority faculty members in physical therapy who are interested in working on a doctoral degree.

Eligibility This program is open to U.S. citizens and permanent residents who are members of the following minority groups: African American or Black, Asian, Native Hawaiian or other Pacific Islander, American Indian or Alaska Native, or Hispanic/Latino. Applicants must be full-time faculty members, teaching in an accredited or developing professional physical therapist education program, who will have completed the equivalent of 2 full semesters of post-professional doctoral course work. They must possess a license to practice physical therapy in a U.S. jurisdiction and be enrolled as a student in an accredited post-professional doctoral program whose content has a demonstrated relationship to physical therapy. Along with their application, they must submit a personal essay on their professional goals, including their plans to contribute to the profession and minority services. Selection is based on 1) commitment to minority affairs and services; 2) commitment to further the physical therapy profession through teaching and research; and 3) scholastic achievement.

Financial data A stipend is awarded (amount not specified).

Duration 1 year.

Additional information This program was established in 1999.

Number awarded 1 or more each year.

Deadline November of each year.

[908]
MINORITY FELLOWSHIPS IN EDUCATION RESEARCH

American Educational Research Association
1430 K Street, N.W., Suite 1200
Washington, DC 20005
(202) 238-3200   Fax: (202) 238-3250
E-mail: fellowships@aera.net
Web: www.aera.net

Summary To provide funding to African American and other minority doctoral students writing their dissertation on educational research.

Eligibility This program is open to U.S. citizens and permanent residents who have advanced to candidacy and successfully defended their Ph.D./Ed.D. dissertation research proposal. Applicants must plan to work full time on their dissertation in educational research. This program is targeted for members of groups historically underrepresented in higher education (African Americans, American Indians, Alaskan Natives, Asian Americans, Native Hawaiian or Pacific Islanders, and Hispanics or Latinos). Selection is based on scholarly achievements and publications, letters of recommendation, quality and significance of the proposed research, and commitment of the applicant's faculty mentor to the goals of the program.

Financial data The grant is $12,000. Up to $1,000 is provided to pay for travel to the sponsor's annual conference.

Duration 1 year; nonrenewable.

Additional information This program was established in 1991.

Number awarded Up to 3 each year.

Deadline December of each year.

[909]
MINORITY GEOSCIENCE STUDENT SCHOLARSHIPS

American Geological Institute
Attn: Minority Participation Program
4220 King Street
Alexandria, VA 22302-1502
(703) 379-2480, ext. 227   Fax: (703) 379-7563
E-mail: mpp@agiweb.org
Web: www.agiweb.org/mpp/index.html

Summary To provide financial assistance to African American and other underrepresented minority undergraduate or graduate students interested in working on a degree in the geosciences.

Eligibility This program is open to members of ethnic minority groups underrepresented in the geosciences (Blacks, Hispanics, American Indians, Eskimos, Hawaiians, and Samoans). U.S. citizenship is required. Applicants must be full-time students enrolled in an accredited institution working on an undergraduate or graduate degree in the geosciences, including geology, geochemistry, geophysics, hydrology, meteorology, physical oceanography, planetary geology, or earth science education; students in other natural sciences, mathematics, or engineering are not eligible. Selection is based on a 250-word essay on career goals and why the applicant has chosen a geoscience as a major, work experience, recommendations, honors and awards, extracurricular activities, and financial need.

Financial data Stipends range from $500 to $3,000 per year.

Duration 1 academic year; renewable if the recipient maintains satisfactory performance.

Additional information Funding for this program is provided by ExxonMobil Corporation, ConocoPhillips, Chevron-Texaco Corporation, Marathon Corporation, and the Seismological Society of America.

Number awarded Varies each year; recently, 18 of these scholarships were awarded.

Deadline March of each year.

[910]
MINORITY MEDICAL STUDENT ELECTIVE IN HIV PSYCHIATRY

American Psychiatric Association
Attn: Office of HIV Psychiatry
1000 Wilson Boulevard, Suite 1825
Arlington, VA 22209-3901
(703) 907-8668   Toll Free: (888) 357-7849
Fax: (703) 907-1089   E-mail: dpennessi@psych.org
Web: www.psych.org/Resources/OMNA/MFP.aspx

Summary To provide an opportunity for African American and other minority medical students to spend an elective residency learning about HIV psychiatry.

Eligibility This program is open to medical students entering their fourth year at an accredited M.D. or D.O. degree-granting institution. Preference is given to minority candidates and those who have primary interests in services related to HIV/AIDS and substance abuse and its relationship to the mental health or the psychological well being of ethnic minorities. Applicants should be interested in a psychiatry, internal medicine, pediatrics, or research career. They must be interested in participating in a program that includes intense training in HIV mental health (including neuropsychiatry), a clinical and/or research experience working with a mentor, and participation in the Committee on AIDS of the American Psychiatric Association (APA). U.S. citizenship is required.

Financial data A stipend is provided (amount not specified).

Duration 1 year.

Additional information The heart of the program is in establishing a mentor relationship at 1 of 5 sites, becoming involved with a cohort of medical students interested in HIV medicine/psychiatry, participating in an interactive didactic/ experimental learning program, and developing expertise in areas related to ethnic minority mental health research or psychiatric services. Students selected for the program who are not APA members automatically receive membership.

Number awarded Varies each year.

Deadline March of each year.

[911]
MINORITY MEDICAL STUDENT SUMMER EXTERNSHIP IN ADDICTION PSYCHIATRY

American Psychiatric Association
Attn: Department of Minority and National Affairs
1000 Wilson Boulevard, Suite 1825
Arlington, VA 22209-3901
(703) 907-8653   Toll Free: (888) 35-PSYCH
Fax: (703) 907-7852   E-mail: mking@psych.org
Web: www.psych.org/Resources/OMNA/MFP.aspx

Summary To provide funding to African American and other minority medical students who are interested in working on a research externship during the summer with a mentor who specializes in addiction psychiatry.

Eligibility This program is open to minority medical students who have a specific interest in services related to substance abuse treatment and prevention. Minorities include American Indians, Alaska Natives, Native Hawaiians, Asian Americans, Hispanic/Latinos, and African Americans. Applicants must be interested in working with a mentor who specializes in addiction psychiatry. Work settings provide an emphasis on working clinically with or studying underserved minority populations and issues of co-occurring disorders, substance abuse treatment, and mental health disparity. Most of them are in inner-city or rural settings.

Financial data Externships provide $1,500 for travel expenses to go to the work setting of the mentor and up to another $1,500 for out-of-pocket expenses directly related to the conduct of the externship.

Duration 1 month during the summer.

Additional information Funding for this program is provided by the Substance Abuse and Mental Health Services Administration (SAMHSA).

Number awarded 10 each year.

Deadline February of each year.

[912]
MINORITY PRE-DOCTORAL FELLOWSHIP IN CLINICAL PHARMACEUTICAL SCIENCE

American Foundation for Pharmaceutical Education
Attn: Grants Manager
One Church Street, Suite 400
Rockville, MD 20850-4158
(301) 738-2160   Fax: (301) 738-2161
E-mail: info@afpenet.org
Web: www.afpenet.org

Summary To provide funding for dissertation research to African American and Hispanic graduate students working on a Ph.D. in clinical pharmaceutical science.

Eligibility This program is open to African American/Black and Hispanic/Latino students who have completed at least 3 semesters of graduate study and have no more than 3 and a half years remaining to complete a Ph.D. in clinical pharmaceutical science at a U.S. school or college of pharmacy. Students enrolled in joint Pharm.D./Ph.D. programs are eligible if they have completed 3 full semesters of graduate credit toward the Ph.D. and if the Ph.D. degree will be awarded within 3 additional years. Applicants must be U.S. citizens or permanent residents. Along with their application, they must submit 1) a brief statement on their objective in pursuing graduate study; 2) a brief statement on their future career plans; and 3) a description of their dissertation research project that includes its nature and scope, area of research, hypothesis to be tested, plan of investigation, and methodologies to be employed. Students with the following majors are encouraged to apply: clinical pharmaceutical sciences, medicinal/pharmaceutical chemistry, pharmaceutics, pharmacology/toxicology, pharmacognosy, pharmacoeconomics and health outcomes, pharmacokinetics/metabolism, pharmacotherapy and experimental therapeutics, or social and administrative science.

Financial data The grant is $6,000 per year. Funds must be used to enable the students to make progress on their Ph.D. (e.g., student stipend, laboratory supplies, books, materials, travel) but not for indirect costs for the institution.

Duration 1 year; may be renewed 1 additional year.

Number awarded Up to 5 each year.

Deadline February of each year.

[913]
MINORITY PRE-DOCTORAL FELLOWSHIP IN PHARMACEUTICAL SCIENCE

American Foundation for Pharmaceutical Education
Attn: Grants Manager
One Church Street, Suite 400
Rockville, MD 20850-4158
(301) 738-2160   Fax: (301) 738-2161
E-mail: info@afpenet.org
Web: www.afpenet.org

Summary To provide funding for dissertation research to African American and Hispanic graduate students working on a Ph.D. in pharmaceutical science.

Eligibility This program is open to African American/Black and Hispanic/Latino students who have completed at least 3 semesters of graduate study and have no more than 3 and a half years remaining to complete a Ph.D. in pharmaceutical science at a U.S. school or college of pharmacy. Students enrolled in joint Pharm.D./Ph.D. programs are eligible if they have completed 3 full semesters of graduate credit toward the Ph.D. and if the Ph.D. degree will be awarded within 3 additional years. Applicants must be U.S. citizens or permanent residents. Along with their application, they must submit 1) a brief statement on their objective in pursuing graduate study; 2) a brief statement on their future career plans; and 3) a description of their dissertation research project that includes its nature and scope, area of research, hypothesis to be tested, plan of investigation, and methodologies to be employed. Students with the following majors are encouraged to apply: pharmaceutical sciences, medicinal/pharmaceutical chemistry, pharmaceutics, pharmacology/toxicology, pharmacognosy, pharmacoeconomics and health outcomes, pharmacokinetics/metabolism, pharmacotherapy and experimental therapeutics, or social and administrative science.

Financial data The grant is $6,000 per year. Funds must be used to enable the students to make progress on their Ph.D. (e.g., student stipend, laboratory supplies, books, materials, travel) but not for indirect costs for the institution.

Duration 1 year; may be renewed 1 additional year.

Number awarded Up to 5 each year.

Deadline February of each year.

[914]
MINORITY VISITING STUDENT AWARDS PROGRAM

Smithsonian Institution
Attn: Office of Fellowships
470 L'Enfant Plaza, Suite 7102
P.O. Box 37012, MRC 902
Washington, DC 20013-7012
(202) 633-7070   Fax: (202) 633-7069
E-mail: siofg@si.edu
Web: www.si.edu/ofg/Applications/MIP/MIPapp.htm

Summary To provide funding to African American and other minority graduate students interested in conducting research at the Smithsonian Institution.

Eligibility This program is open to members of U.S. minority groups underrepresented in the Smithsonian's scholarly programs. Applicants must be advanced graduate students interested in conducting research in the Institution's disciplines and in the museum field.

Financial data Students receive a grant of $550 per week.

Duration Up to 10 weeks.

Additional information Recipients must carry out independent research projects in association with the Smithsonian's research staff. Eligible fields of study currently include animal behavior, ecology, and environmental science (including an emphasis on the tropics); anthropology (including archaeology); astrophysics and astronomy; earth sciences and paleobiology; evolutionary and systematic biology; history of science and technology; history of art (especially American, contemporary, African, Asian, and 20th-century art); American crafts and decorative arts; social and cultural history of the United States; and folklife. Students are required to be in residence at the Smithsonian for the duration of the fellowship.

Number awarded Varies each year.

Deadline January of each year for summer and fall residency; September of each year for spring residency.

[915]
MIRIAM WEINSTEIN PEACE AND JUSTICE EDUCATION AWARD

Philanthrofund Foundation
Attn: Scholarship Committee
1409 Willow Street, Suite 210
Minneapolis, MN 55403-3251
(612) 870-1806   Toll Free: (800) 435-1402
Fax: (612) 871-6587   E-mail: info@PfundOnline.org
Web: www.pfundonline.org/scholarships.html

Summary To provide financial assistance to African Americans and other minority students from Minnesota who are associated with gay, lesbian, bisexual, and transgender (GLBT) activities and interested in working on a degree in education.

Eligibility This program is open to residents of Minnesota and students attending a Minnesota educational institution who are members of a religious, racial, or ethnic minority. Applicants must be self-identified as GLBT or from a GLBT family and have demonstrated a commitment to peace and justice issues. They may be attending or planning to attend trade school, technical college, college, or university (as an undergraduate or graduate student). Preference is given to students who have completed at least 2 years of college and are working on a degree in education. Selection is based on the applicant's 1) affirmation of GLBT identity or commitment to GLBT communities; 2) participation and leadership in community and/or GLBT activities; and 3) service as role model, mentor, and/or adviser for the GLBT community.

Financial data The stipend is $3,000. Funds must be used for tuition, books, fees, or dissertation expenses.

Duration 1 year.

Number awarded 1 each year.

Deadline January of each year.

[916]
MLA/NLM SPECTRUM SCHOLARSHIPS

Medical Library Association
Attn: Awards, Grants, and Scholarships
65 East Wacker Place, Suite 1900
Chicago, IL 60601-7246
(312) 419-9094   Fax: (312) 419-8950
E-mail: info@mlahq.org
Web: www.mlanet.org

Summary To provide financial assistance to African Americans and members of other minority groups interested in preparing for a career as a medical librarian.

Eligibility This program is open to members of minority groups (African Americans, Hispanics, Asian, Native Americans, and Pacific Islanders) who are attending library schools accredited by the American Library Association (ALA). Applicants must be interested in preparing for a career as a health sciences information professional.

Financial data The stipend is $3,250.

Duration 1 year.

Additional information This program, established in 2001, is jointly sponsored by the Medical Library Association (MLA) and the National Library of Medicine (NLM) of the U.S. National Institutes of Health (NIH). It operates as a component of the Spectrum Initiative Scholarship program of the ALA.

Number awarded 2 each year.

Deadline February of each year.

[917]
MLA SCHOLARSHIP FOR MINORITY STUDENTS

Medical Library Association
Attn: Professional Development Department
65 East Wacker Place, Suite 1900
Chicago, IL 60601-7246
(312) 419-9094, ext. 28   Fax: (312) 419-8950
E-mail: mlapd2@mlahq.org
Web: www.mlanet.org/awards/grants/minstud.html

Summary To assist African American and other minority students interested in preparing for a career in medical librarianship.

Eligibility This program is open to racial minority students (Asians, African Americans, Hispanics, Native Americans, or Pacific Islander Americans) who are entering an ALA-accredited graduate program in librarianship or who have completed less than half of their academic requirements for the master's degree in library science. They must be interested in preparing for a career in medical librarianship. Selection is based on academic record, letters of reference, professional potential,

and the applicant's statement of career objectives. U.S. or Canadian citizenship or permanent resident status is required.

Financial data The stipend is $5,000.

Duration 1 year.

Additional information This scholarship was first awarded in 1973.

Number awarded 1 each year.

Deadline November of each year.

[918]
MULTICULTURAL ADVERTISING INTERN PROGRAM

American Association of Advertising Agencies
Attn: Manager of Diversity Programs
405 Lexington Avenue, 18th Floor
New York, NY 10174-1801
(212) 850-0732   Toll Free: (800) 676-9333
Fax: (212) 682-2028   E-mail: maip@aaaa.org
Web: www2.aaaa.org

Summary To provide African American and other minority students with summer work experience in advertising agencies and to present them with an overview of the agency business.

Eligibility This program is open to U.S. citizens and permanent residents who are Black/African American, Asian/Asian American, Pacific Islander, Hispanic, North American Indian/Native American, or multiracial and either 1) college juniors, seniors, or graduate students at an accredited college or university, or 2) students at any academic level attending a portfolio school of the sponsor. Applicants may be majoring in any field, but they must be able to demonstrate a serious commitment to preparing for a career in advertising. They must have a GPA of 3.0 or higher. Students with a cumulative GPA of 2.7 to 2.9 are encouraged to apply, but they must complete an additional essay question.

Financial data Interns are paid a salary of at least $70 per day. If they do not live in the area of their host agencies, they may stay in housing arranged by the sponsor. They are responsible for a percentage of the cost of housing and materials.

Duration 10 weeks during the summer.

Additional information Interns may be assigned duties in the following departments: account management, broadcast production, media buying/planning, creative (art direction or copywriting), digital/interactive technologies, print production, strategic/account planning, or traffic. The portfolio schools are the AdCenter at Virginia Commonwealth University, the Creative Circus and the Portfolio Center in Atlanta, the Miami Ad School, the University of Texas at Austin, Pratt Institute, the Minneapolis College of Art and Design, and the Art Center College of Design in Pasadena, California.

Number awarded 70 to 100 each year.

Deadline December of each year.

[919]
MYRA DAVIS HEMMINGS SCHOLARSHIP

Delta Sigma Theta Sorority, Inc.
Attn: Scholarship and Standards Committee Chair
1707 New Hampshire Avenue, N.W.
Washington, DC 20009
(202) 986-2400   Fax: (202) 986-2513
E-mail: dstemail@deltasigmatheta.org
Web: www.deltasigmatheta.org

Summary To provide financial assistance to members of Delta Sigma Theta who are interested in working on a graduate degree in the performing or creative arts.

Eligibility This program is open to graduating college seniors and graduate students who are interested in preparing for a career in the performing or creative arts. Applicants must be active, dues-paying members of Delta Sigma Theta. Selection is based on meritorious achievement.

Financial data The stipends range from $1,000 to $2,000 per year. The funds may be used to cover tuition and living expenses.

Duration 1 year; may be renewed for 1 additional year.

Additional information This sponsor is a traditionally African American social sorority. The application fee is $20.

Number awarded 1 each year.

Deadline April of each year.

[920]
NABA 20 PEARLS SCHOLARSHIP

National Association of Black Accountants
Attn: National Scholarship Program
7474 Greenway Center Drive, Suite 1120
Greenbelt, MD 20770
(301) 474-NABA, ext. 114   Fax: (301) 474-3114
E-mail: customerservice@nabainc.org
Web: www.nabainc.org

Summary To provide financial assistance to student members of the National Association of Black Accountants (NABA) who are also members of Alpha Kappa Alpha sorority and working on an undergraduate or graduate degree in a field related to accounting.

Eligibility This program is open to NABA members who are also Alpha Kappa Alpha members and enrolled full time as 1) an undergraduate freshman, sophomore, junior, or first-semester senior majoring in accounting, business, or finance at a 4-year college or university; or 2) a graduate student working on a master's degree in accounting. High school seniors are not eligible. Applicants must have a GPA of 3.5 or higher in their major and 3.3 or higher overall. Selection is based on grades, financial need, and a 500-word autobiography that discusses career objectives, leadership abilities, community activities, and involvement in NABA.

Financial data The stipend is $1,500.

Duration 1 year.

Number awarded 1 each year.

Deadline January of each year.

[921]
NABJ SCHOLARSHIPS

National Association of Black Journalists
Attn: Program Coordinator
8701-A Adelphi Road
Adelphi, MD 20783-1716
(301) 445-7100, ext. 108   Toll Free: (866) 479-NABJ
Fax: (301) 445-7101   E-mail: nabj@nabj.org
Web: www.nabj.org

Summary To provide financial assistance to undergraduate or graduate student members of the National Association of Black Journalists (NABJ) who are majoring in a field related to journalism.

Eligibility This program is open to African American undergraduate or graduate students who are currently attending an accredited 4-year college or university. Applicants must be majoring in broadcast (radio or television), print, or online journalism and have a GPA of 2.5 or higher. They must be NABJ members. Along with their application, they must submit samples of their work, an official college transcript, 2 letters of recommendation, a resume, and a 500- to 800-word essay describing their accomplishments as a student journalist, their career goals, and their financial need.

Financial data The stipend is $2,500. Funds are paid directly to the recipient's college or university.

Duration 1 year; nonrenewable.

Number awarded Varies each year; recently, 10 of these scholarships were awarded.

Deadline April of each year.

[922]
NABNA-FEEA SCHOLARSHIP PROGRAM

National Association of Black Narcotic Agents
c/o Federal Employee Education and Assistance Fund
Attn: Scholarship Program
3333 South Wadsworth Boulevard, Suite 300
Lakewood, CO 80227
(303) 933-7580   Toll Free: (800) 323-4140
Fax: (303) 933-7587   E-mail: admin@feea.org
Web: www.feea.org

Summary To provide financial assistance for college or graduate school to members of the National Association of Black Narcotic Agents (NABNA) and their dependents.

Eligibility This program is open to federal employees who are NABNA members and their dependent spouses and children entering or enrolled in an accredited 2- or 4-year undergraduate, graduate, or postgraduate program. Dependents must be full-time students; federal employees may be part-time students. Applicants or their sponsoring federal employee must have at least 3 years of civilian federal service. Along with their application, they must submit a 2-page essay on a topic related to a career in public service with the federal government, a letter of recommendation, a transcript with a GPA of 3.0 or higher, and a copy of their federal "Notice of Personnel Action;" high school seniors must also submit a copy of their ACT, SAT, or other examination scores. Financial need is not considered in the selection process.

Financial data The stipend is $1,000 per year.

Duration 1 year; may be renewed.

Additional information This program is jointly administered by NABNA and the Federal Employee Education and Assistance Fund (FEEA).

Number awarded 1 or more each year.

Deadline March of each year.

[923]
NASA GRADUATE STUDENT RESEARCHERS PROGRAM

National Aeronautics and Space Administration
Attn: Acting National GSRP Project Manager
Jet Propulsion Laboratory
4800 Oak Grove Drive
Pasadena, CA 91109-8099
(818) 354-3274   Fax: (818) 393-4977
E-mail: Linda.L.Rodgers@jpl.nasa.gov
Web: fellowships.nasaprs.com/gsrp/nav

Summary To provide funding to graduate students (particularly African Americans, other minorities, women, and students with disabilities) who are interested in conducting research in fields of interest to the U.S. National Aeronautics and Space Administration (NASA).

Eligibility This program is open to full-time students enrolled or planning to enroll in an accredited graduate program at a U.S. college or university. Applicants must be citizens of the United States, sponsored by a faculty adviser or department chair, and interested in conducting research in a field of science, mathematics, or engineering related to NASA research and development. Students who are interested in becoming teaching or education administrators are also eligible. Selection is based on academic qualifications, quality of the proposed research and its relevance to NASA's program, proposed utilization of center research facilities (except for NASA headquarters), and ability of the student to accomplish the defined research. Individuals from underrepresented groups in science, technology, engineering, or mathematics (STEM) fields (African Americans, Native Americans, Alaskan Natives, Mexican Americans, Puerto Ricans, Native Pacific Islanders, women, and persons with disabilities) are strongly urged to apply.

Financial data The program provides a $20,000 student stipend, a $6,000 student travel allowance, up to $1,000 for health insurance, and a $3,000 university allowance. The student stipend may cover tuition, room and board, books, software, meal plans, school and laboratory supplies, and other related expenses. The student travel allowance may be used for national and international conferences and data collection. The university allowance is a discretionary award that typically goes to the research adviser. If the student already has health insurance, that $1,000 grant may be added to the student stipend or student travel allowance.

Duration 1 year; may be renewed for up to 1 additional year for master's degree students or 2 additional years for doctoral students.

Additional information This program was established in 1980. Students are required to participate in a 10-week research experience at NASA headquarters in Washington, D.C. or at 1 of 10 NASA centers.

Number awarded This program supports approximately 180 graduate students each year.

Deadline February of each year.

[924]
NASP MINORITY SCHOLARSHIP

National Association of School Psychologists
Attn: Education and Research Trust
4340 East-West Highway, Suite 402
Bethesda, MD 20814
(301) 657-0270, ext. 234   Toll Free: (866) 331-NASP
Fax: (301) 657-0275   TDD: (301) 657-4155
E-mail: kbritton@naspweb.org
Web: www.nasponline.org/about_nasp/minority.aspx

Summary To provide financial assistance to African American and other minority graduate students who are members of the National Association of School Psychologists (NASP) and enrolled in a school psychology program.

Eligibility This program is open to minority students who are NASP members enrolled in a regionally-accredited school psychology program in the United States. Applicants must have a GPA of 3.0 or higher. Doctoral candidates are not eligible. Applications must be accompanied by 1) a resume that includes undergraduate and/or graduate schools attended, awards and honors, student and professional activities, work and volunteer experiences, research and publications, workshops or other presentations, and any special skills, training, or experience, such as bilingualism, teaching experience, or mental health experience; 2) a statement, up to 1,000 words, of professional goals; 3) at least 2 letters of recommendation, including at least 1 from a faculty member from their undergraduate or graduate studies (if a first-year student) or at least 1 from a faculty member of their school psychology program (if a second- or third-year student); 4) a completed financial statement; 5) an official transcript of all graduate course work (first-year students may submit an official undergraduate transcript); 6) other personal accomplishments that the applicant wishes to be considered; and 7) a letter of acceptance from a school psychology program for first-year applicants. U.S. citizenship is required.

Financial data The stipend is $5,000 per year.

Duration 1 year; may be renewed up to 2 additional years.

Number awarded Varies each year; recently, 4 of these scholarships were awarded.

Deadline October of each year.

[925]
NATIONAL ASSOCIATION FOR EQUAL OPPORTUNITY INTERNSHIP PROGRAM

National Association for Equal Opportunity in Higher Education
Attn: Internship Program
209 Third Street, S.E.
Washington, DC 20003
(202) 552-3300   Fax: (202) 552-3330
E-mail: internships@nafeo.org
Web: www.nafeointernships.net/home.php

Summary To provide summer work experience in Washington, D.C. to undergraduate and graduate students enrolled at an Historically Black College or University (HBCU) or Predominantly Black Institute (PBI).

Eligibility This program is open undergraduate and graduate students currently enrolled at an HBCU or PBI. Applicants must be interested in a summer internship, mostly with federal agencies, in Washington, D.C. They must have a GPA of 3.0 or higher. Some positions require U.S. citizenship.

Financial data The stipend is $400 per week for undergraduates or $500 per week for graduate students. Other benefits include a housing stipend and a travel allowance of $200.

Duration 10 weeks during the summer.

Number awarded 1 or more each year.

Deadline March of each year.

[926]
NATIONAL ASSOCIATION OF BLACK ACCOUNTANTS NATIONAL SCHOLARSHIP

National Association of Black Accountants
Attn: National Scholarship Program
7474 Greenway Center Drive, Suite 1120
Greenbelt, MD 20770
(301) 474-NABA, ext. 114   Fax: (301) 474-3114
E-mail: customerservice@nabainc.org
Web: www.nabainc.org

Summary To provide financial assistance to student members of the National Association of Black Accountants (NABA) who are working on an undergraduate or graduate degree in a field related to accounting.

Eligibility This program is open to NABA members enrolled full time as 1) an undergraduate freshman, sophomore, junior, or first-semester senior majoring in accounting, business, or finance at a 4-year college or university; or 2) a graduate student working on a master's degree in accounting. High school seniors are not eligible. Applicants must have a GPA of 3.5 or higher in their major and 3.3 or higher overall. Selection is based on grades, financial need, and a 500-word autobiography that discusses career objectives, leadership abilities, community activities, and involvement in NABA.

Financial data The stipend is $3,000.

Duration 1 year.

Number awarded 1 each year.

Deadline January of each year.

[927]
NATIONAL ASSOCIATION OF BOND LAWYERS GOVERNMENTAL AFFAIRS SUMMER ASSOCIATE PROGRAM

National Association of Bond Lawyers
Attn: Governmental Affairs Office
601 13th Street, N.W., Suite 800 South
Washington, DC 20005-3875
(202) 682-1498   Fax: (202) 637-0217
E-mail: internship@nabl.org
Web: www.nabl.org/about/Governmental-Affairs.html

Summary To provide an opportunity for law students, especially African Americans and others from diverse backgrounds, to learn about municipal bond law during a summer internship at the Governmental Affairs Office of the National Association of Bond Lawyers (NABL) in Washington, D.C.

Eligibility This program is open to students currently enrolled in law school and interested in municipal bond law; diverse candidates are especially encouraged to apply. Applicants must be interested in a summer internship at the NABL Governmental Affairs Office in Washington, D.C. They should

be able to demonstrate a high regard for honesty, integrity, and professional ethics; excellent organization, time management, and coordination skills and judgment; strong interpersonal skills; ability to communicate effectively, both orally and in writing; strong personal computer and data processing skills; proven attention to detail; a basic knowledge of the structure of government; and an ability to work effectively in member-driven associations.

Financial data The stipend is $4,000.

Duration 3 months during the summer.

Number awarded 1 each year.

Deadline May of each year.

[928]
NATIONAL BLACK ASSOCIATION FOR SPEECH-LANGUAGE AND HEARING STUDENT RESEARCH AWARD

National Black Association for Speech-Language and Hearing
Attn: Awards and Scholarship Committee
700 McKnight Park Drive, Suite 708
Pittsburgh, PA 15237
(412) 366-1177   Fax: (412) 366-8804
E-mail: NBASLH@nbaslh.org
Web: www.nbaslh.org/scholarships.htm

Summary To recognize and reward outstanding research papers on communication sciences or disorders written by graduate student members of the National Black Association for Speech-Language and Hearing (NBASLH).

Eligibility This competition is open to African American students who are NBASLH members and enrolled full time in an ASHA-accredited master's degree program in speech-language pathology, audiology, or the speech-language-hearing sciences. Applicants must submit a paper of scientific or scholarly merit that deals with issues relevant to communication sciences and disorders. It is not required that the paper focus on African American populations or multicultural issues. It may address 1 of the following: 1) an empirical investigation that requires data gathering and analysis; 2) an issue paper that aims to redefine, evaluate, and synthesize existing knowledge in ways that offer a new conceptual framework or approach for conducting research or engaging in clinical practice; or 3) a description of a clinical case study that has implications for future research and/or clinical practice. The manuscript should not exceed 8 typed pages (2,000 words). Selection is based on completeness, appropriateness, manuscript quality, and significance.

Financial data The award is $1,000. In addition, the winner receives a travel allowance to attend the association's convention (and read the paper there).

Duration The award is presented annually.

Number awarded 1 each year.

Deadline January of each year.

[929]
NATIONAL BLACK MBA ASSOCIATION COLLEGIATE CHAPTER SCHOLARSHIP PROGRAM

National Black MBA Association
180 North Michigan Avenue, Suite 1400
Chicago, IL 60601
(312) 236-BMBA, ext. 8086   Fax: (312) 236-0390
E-mail: Scholarship@nbmbaa.org
Web: www.nbmbaa.org/index.aspx?pageID=792

Summary   To provide financial assistance to members of collegiate chapters of the National Black MBA Association (NBMBAA).

Eligibility   This program is open to minority students enrolled full time in their first, second, third, or fourth year of a bachelor's or master's business degree program at a college or university that has a collegiate chapter of the NBMBAA. Applicants must be chapter members actively involved in its activities and local communities through service to others. Along with their application, they must submit a 300-word essay on a topic that changes annually; recently, students were asked to explain how working on a graduate business degree would serve as a catalyst for change for the Black community. Selection is based on that essay, academic excellence, leadership potential, community involvement, and a recommendation from the faculty adviser.

Financial data   The stipend is $5,000. Recipients are also provided with complimentary registration, round-trip airfare, and housing to attend the NBMBAA annual conference and exposition.

Duration   1 year.

Number awarded   Varies each year; recently, 4 of these scholarships were awarded.

Deadline   May of each year.

[930]
NATIONAL BLACK MBA ASSOCIATION GRADUATE SCHOLARSHIP PROGRAM

National Black MBA Association
Attn: Scholarship Program
180 North Michigan Avenue, Suite 1400
Chicago, IL 60601
(312) 236-BMBA, ext. 8086   Fax: (312) 236-0390
E-mail: Scholarship@nbmbaa.org
Web: www.nbmbaa.org/index.aspx?pageID=790

Summary   To provide financial assistance to students interested in working on an M.B.A. degree and becoming involved in activities of the National Black MBA Association (NBMBAA).

Eligibility   This program is open to students enrolled full time in a graduate business program in the United States or Canada. Applicants must submit a 300-word essay on 1 of 2 topics that change annually but relate to African Americans in business. Selection is based on the essay, academic excellence, leadership potential, communication skills, and community involvement.

Financial data   Stipends range from $1,000 to $15,000. Recipients are also provided with membership in the NBMBAA and with complimentary registration, round-trip airfare, and housing to attend the NBMBAA annual conference and exposition.

Duration   1 year.

Additional information   Recipients must agree to become a member of the NBMBAA Scholarship Advisory Team and Scholarship Alumni Club, become an active member of their local NBMBAA chapter, and participate in limited public relations activities at the convention.

Number awarded   Varies each year; recently, 18 of these scholarships were awarded.

Deadline   May of each year.

[931]
NATIONAL BLACK MBA ASSOCIATION PHD FELLOWSHIP PROGRAM

National Black MBA Association
180 North Michigan Avenue, Suite 1400
Chicago, IL 60601
(312) 236-BMBA, ext. 8086   Fax: (312) 236-0390
E-mail: Scholarship@nbmbaa.org
Web: www.nbmbaa.org/index.aspx?pageID=791

Summary   To provide financial assistance to students interested in working on a doctoral degree in a field related to business and becoming involved in activities of the National Black MBA Association (NBMBAA).

Eligibility   This program is open to students who are enrolled full time in an accredited business, management, or related doctoral program in the United States or Canada. Applicants must submit an original 5-page research paper on the most pressing issue facing African American, Hispanic, and Native American academicians in their field of study. Selection is based on the quality of the paper, academic excellence, leadership potential, communication skills, and involvement in local communities through service to others.

Financial data   Stipends range from $2,500 to $10,000. Membership in the NBMBAA is also included. Some recipients are provided with complimentary registration, round-trip airfare, housing, and special VIP access to receptions and events at the NBMBAA annual conference and exposition.

Duration   1 year.

Additional information   Recipients must agree to become a member of the NBMBAA Scholarship Advisory Team and Scholarship Alumni Club, become an active member of their local NBMBAA chapter, and participate in limited public relations activities at the convention.

Number awarded   Varies each year; recently, 3 of these fellowships were awarded.

Deadline   May of each year.

[932]
NATIONAL DEFENSE SCIENCE AND ENGINEERING GRADUATE FELLOWSHIP PROGRAM

American Society for Engineering Education
Attn: NDSEG Fellowship Program
1818 N Street, N.W., Suite 600
Washington, DC 20036-2479
(202) 331-3516   Fax: (202) 265-8504
E-mail: ndseg@asee.org
Web: ndseg.asee.org

Summary   To provide financial assistance to doctoral students (particularly African Americans, other students of color, and students with disabilities) who are studying in areas of science and engineering that are of military importance.

Eligibility This program is open to U.S. citizens and nationals entering or enrolled in the early stages of a doctoral program in aeronautical and astronautical engineering; biosciences, including toxicology; chemical engineering; chemistry; civil engineering; cognitive, neural, and behavioral sciences; computer and computational sciences; electrical engineering; geosciences, including terrain, water, and air; materials science and engineering; mathematics; mechanical engineering; naval architecture and ocean engineering; oceanography; or physics, including optics. Applications are particularly encouraged from women, members of ethnic minority groups (American Indians, African Americans, Hispanics or Latinos, Native Hawaiians, Alaska Natives, Asians, and Pacific Islanders), and persons with disabilities. Selection is based on all available evidence of ability, including academic records, letters of recommendation, and GRE scores.

Financial data The annual stipend is $30,500 for the first year, $31,000 for the second year; and $31,500 for the third year; the program also pays the recipient's institution full tuition and required fees (not to include room and board). Medical insurance is covered up to $1,000 per year. An additional allowance may be considered for a student with a disability.

Duration 3 years, as long as satisfactory academic progress is maintained.

Additional information This program is sponsored by the Army Research Office, the Air Force Office of Scientific Research, and the Office of Naval Research. Recipients do not incur any military or other service obligation. They must attend school on a full-time basis.

Number awarded Approximately 200 each year.

Deadline January of each year.

[933]
NATIONAL MEDICAL FELLOWSHIPS EMERGENCY SCHOLARSHIP FUND

National Medical Fellowships, Inc.
Attn: Scholarship Program
347 Fifth Avenue, Suite 510
New York, NY 10016
(212) 483-8880   Toll Free: (877) NMF-1DOC
Fax: (212) 483-8897   E-mail: info@nmfonline.org
Web: www.nmfonline.org/programs.php

Summary To provide financial assistance to African American and other minority medical students who are facing financial emergencies.

Eligibility This program is open to U.S. citizens who are enrolled in the third or fourth year of an accredited M.D. or D.O. degree-granting program in the United States and are facing extreme financial difficulties because of unforeseen training-related expenses. Applicants must be African Americans, Mexican Americans, Native Hawaiians, Alaska Natives, American Indians, Vietnamese, Cambodians, or mainland Puerto Ricans who permanently reside in the United States. They must be interested in primary care practice in underserved communities.

Financial data Assistance ranges up to $20,000.

Duration Awards are available semi-annually.

Additional information This program was established in 2008, with support from the Kellogg Foundation.

Number awarded Varies each year; recently, 3 of these scholarships were awarded.

Deadline August of each year.

[934]
NATIONAL MEDICAL FELLOWSHIPS NEED-BASED SCHOLARSHIP PROGRAM

National Medical Fellowships, Inc.
Attn: Scholarship Program
347 Fifth Avenue, Suite 510
New York, NY 10016
(212) 483-8880   Toll Free: (877) NMF-1DOC
Fax: (212) 483-8897   E-mail: info@nmfonline.org
Web: www.nmfonline.org/programs.php

Summary To provide financial assistance to African American and other underrepresented minority medical students who demonstrate financial need.

Eligibility This program is open to U.S. citizens enrolled in the first or second year of an accredited M.D. or D.O. degree-granting program in the United States. Applicants must be African Americans, Mexican Americans, Native Hawaiians, Alaska Natives, American Indians, Vietnamese, Cambodians, or mainland Puerto Ricans who permanently reside in the United States. Along with their application, they must submit a 600-word essay on their motivation for a career in medicine and their personal and professional goals over the next 10 years. Selection is based primarily on financial need.

Financial data The amount of the award depends on the student's total resources (including parental and spousal support), cost of education, and receipt of additional scholarships; recently, individual awards ranged from $1,000 to $10,000 per year.

Duration 1 year for first-year students; may be renewed for the second year only.

Number awarded Varies each year; recently, 70 of these scholarships were awarded.

Deadline August of each year.

[935]
NATIONAL MINORITY STEM FELLOWSHIPS

Educational Advancement Alliance, Inc.
Attn: National Minority STEM Fellowship Program
4548 Market Street, Suite LL-04
Philadelphia, PA 19139
(215) 895-4003   E-mail: info@nmsfp.org
Web: www.nmsfp.org

Summary To provide financial assistance to African Americans and other residents of designated states who are working on a master's degree in fields of science, technology, engineering, or mathematics (STEM) at colleges in those states.

Eligibility This program is open to U.S. citizens who are residents of Delaware, Maryland, New Jersey, Pennsylvania, or Washington, D.C. Members of cultural, racial, geographic, and socioeconomic backgrounds that are currently underrepresented in graduate education are especially encouraged to apply; those are defined to include Hispanics or Latinos, American Indians or Alaska Natives, Asians, Native Hawaiians or other Pacific Islanders, or Blacks. Applicants must be enrolled full time at colleges or universities in those states and working on a master's degree in a field of STEM, including physics, chemistry, non-medical biology, mathematics, computer science, or environmental science. Their degree requirements must include a research thesis. Students working on other graduate degrees (e.g., joint B.S./M.S., M.B.A., D.V.M., M.D., joint M.D./Ph.D., J.D., joint J.D./Ph.D.) are not eligible. Along with their application, they must submit a 1,000-word essay on their qualifications for the fellowship and their career goals, college transcripts, information on extracurricular activities, a copy of their GRE scores, 3 letters of recommendation, and information on their financial situation.

Financial data The program provides a stipend of $18,000 per year and up to $20,500 per year as tuition support.

Duration 2 years.

Additional information This program is funded by the U.S. Department of Energy Office of Science and administered by the Educational Advancement Alliance, Inc.

Number awarded Up to 40 each year.

Deadline March of each year.

[936]
NATIONAL PHYSICAL SCIENCE CONSORTIUM DISSERTATION SUPPORT PROGRAM

National Physical Science Consortium
c/o University of Southern California
3716 South Hope Street, Suite 348
Los Angeles, CA 90007-4344
(213) 743-2409   Toll Free: (800) 854-NPSC
Fax: (213) 743-2407   E-mail: npschq@npsc.org
Web: www.npsc.org

Summary To provide funding to African Americans and other underrepresented minorities and women conducting dissertation research in designated science and engineering fields.

Eligibility This program is open to U.S. citizens who are enrolled in a doctoral program and about to begin dissertation research. Eligible fields of study are generally limited to astronomy, chemistry, computer science, geology, materials science, mathematical sciences, physics, their subdisciplines, and related engineering fields (chemical, computer, electrical, environmental, and mechanical). The program welcomes applications from all qualified students and continues to emphasize the recruitment of underrepresented minority (African American, Hispanic, Native American Indian, Eskimo, Aleut, and Pacific Islander) and women physical science and engineering students. Fellowships are provided to students at the 119 universities that are members of the consortium. Selection is based on academic standing (GPA), undergraduate and graduate course work and grades, university and/or industry research experience, letters of recommendation, and GRE scores.

Financial data The fellowship pays tuition and fees plus an annual stipend of $20,000.

Duration Up to 4 years.

Number awarded Varies each year.

Deadline November of each year.

[937]
NATIONAL PHYSICAL SCIENCE CONSORTIUM GRADUATE FELLOWSHIPS

National Physical Science Consortium
c/o University of Southern California
3716 South Hope Street, Suite 348
Los Angeles, CA 90007-4344
(213) 743-2409   Toll Free: (800) 854-NPSC
Fax: (213) 743-2407   E-mail: npschq@npsc.org
Web: www.npsc.org/students/info.html

Summary To provide financial assistance and summer work experience to African Americans and other underrepresented minorities and women interested in working on a Ph.D. in designated science and engineering fields.

Eligibility This program is open to U.S. citizens who are seniors graduating from college with a GPA of 3.0 or higher, enrolled in the first year of a doctoral program, completing a terminal master's degree, or returning from the workforce and holding no more than a master's degree. Students currently in the third or subsequent year of a Ph.D. program or who already have a doctoral degree in any field (Ph.D., M.D., J.D., Ed.D.) are ineligible. Applicants must be interested in working on a Ph.D. in the physical sciences or related fields of science or engineering. The program welcomes applications from all qualified students and continues to emphasize the recruitment of underrepresented minority (African American, Hispanic, Native American Indian, Eskimo, Aleut, and Pacific Islander) and women physical science and engineering students. Fellowships are provided to students at the 119 universities that are members of the consortium. Selection is based on academic standing (GPA), course work taken in preparation for graduate school, university and/or industry research experience, letters of recommendation, and GRE scores.

Financial data The fellowship pays tuition and fees plus an annual stipend of $20,000. It also provides on-site paid summer employment to enhance technical experience. The exact value of the fellowship depends on academic standing, summer employment, and graduate school attended; the total amount generally exceeds $200,000.

Duration Support is initially provided for 2 or 3 years, depending on the employer-sponsor. If the fellow makes satisfactory progress and continues to meet the conditions of the award, support may continue for a total of up to 6 years or completion of the Ph.D., whichever comes first.

Additional information This program began in 1989. Tuition and fees are provided by the participating universities. Stipends and summer internships are provided by sponsoring organizations. Students must submit separate applications for internships, which may have additional eligibility requirements. Internships are currently available at Lawrence Livermore National Laboratory in Livermore, California (astronomy, chemistry, computer science, geology, materials science, mathematics, and physics); National Security Agency in Fort Meade, Maryland (astronomy, chemistry, computer science, geology, materials science, mathematics, and physics); Sandia National Laboratory in Livermore, California (biology, chemistry, computer science, environmental science, geology, materials science, mathematics, and physics); and Sandia National Laboratory in Albuquerque, New Mexico (chemical engineering, chemistry, computer science, materials science, mathematics, mechanical engineering, and physics). Fellows must submit a separate application for dissertation support in the year prior to the beginning of their dissertation research program, but not until they can describe their intended research in general terms.

Number awarded Varies each year; recently, 11 of these fellowships were awarded.

Deadline November of each year.

[938]
NATIONAL SOCIETY OF BLACK ENGINEERS FELLOWS SCHOLARSHIP PROGRAM

National Society of Black Engineers
Attn: Programs Department
205 Daingerfield Road
Alexandria, VA 22314
(703) 549-2207   Fax: (703) 683-5312
E-mail: scholarships@nsbe.org
Web: www.nsbe.org

Summary To provide financial assistance to members of the National Society of Black Engineers (NSBE) who are working on a degree in engineering.

Eligibility This program is open to members of the society who are undergraduate or graduate engineering students. Applicants must have a GPA of 2.7 or higher. Selection is based on an essay; academic achievement; service to the society at the chapter, regional, and/or national level; and other professional, campus, and community activities.

Financial data The stipend is $1,000.

Duration 1 year.

Number awarded Varies each year; recently, 10 of these scholarships were awarded.

Deadline January of each year.

[939]
NATIONAL SPACE GRANT COLLEGE AND FELLOWSHIP PROGRAM

National Aeronautics and Space Administration
Attn: Office of Education
300 E Street, S.W.
Mail Suite 6M35
Washington, DC 20546-0001
(202) 358-1069   Fax: (202) 358-7097
E-mail: Diane.D.DeTroye@nasa.gov
Web: www.nasa.gov

Summary To provide financial assistance to African Americans and other undergraduate and graduate students interested in preparing for a career in a space-related field.

Eligibility This program is open to undergraduate and graduate students at colleges and universities that participate in the National Space Grant program of the U.S. National Aeronautics and Space Administration (NASA) through their state consortium. Applicants must be interested in a program of study and/or research in a field of science, technology, engineering, or mathematics (STEM) related to space. A specific goal of the program is to increase preparation by members of underrepresented groups (minorities, women, and persons with disabilities) for STEM space-related careers. Financial need is not considered in the selection process.

Financial data Each consortium establishes the terms of the fellowship program in its state.

Additional information NASA established the Space Grant program in 1989. It operates through 52 consortia in

each state, the District of Columbia, and Puerto Rico. Each consortium includes selected colleges and universities in that state as well as other affiliates from industry, museums, science centers, and state and local agencies.

Number awarded Varies each year.

Deadline Each consortium sets its own deadlines.

[940]
NCAA ETHNIC MINORITY POSTGRADUATE SCHOLARSHIP PROGRAM

National Collegiate Athletic Association
Attn: Office for Diversity and Inclusion
1802 Alonzo Watford Sr. Drive
P.O. Box 6222
Indianapolis, IN 46206-6222
(317) 917-6222   Fax: (317) 917-6888
E-mail: tstrum@ncaa.org
Web: www.ncaa.org

Summary To provide funding to African Americans and other minority graduate students who are interested in preparing for a career in intercollegiate athletics.

Eligibility This program is open to members of minority groups who have been accepted into a program at a National Collegiate Athletic Association (NCAA) member institution that will prepare them for a career in intercollegiate athletics (athletics administrator, coach, athletic trainer, or other career that provides a direct service to intercollegiate athletics). Applicants must be U.S. citizens, have performed with distinction as a student body member at their respective undergraduate institution, and be entering the first semester or term of full-time postgraduate study. Selection is based on the applicant's involvement in extracurricular activities, course work, commitment to preparing for a career in intercollegiate athletics, and promise for success in that career. Financial need is not considered.

Financial data The stipend is $6,000; funds are paid to the college or university of the recipient's choice.

Duration 1 year; nonrenewable.

Number awarded 13 each year.

Deadline November of each year.

[941]
NELSON MANDELA SCHOLARSHIPS

National Black Law Students Association
Attn: Director of Education and Career Development
1225 11th Street, N.W.
Washington, DC 20001-4217
(202) 618-2572   E-mail: educationcareer@nblsa.org
Web: www.nblsa.org/index.php?pID=57

Summary To provide financial assistance to members of the National Black Law Students Association (NBLSA) entering or completing their first year of law school.

Eligibility This program is open to NBLSA College Student Division members who plan to enter law school in the following fall or are currently enrolled in their first year of law school. Applicants must submit a 500-word essay on a topic that changes annually; recently, students were asked to identify a major social issue facing the African American community and describe how the law and public policy can interact to address that problem.

Financial data The stipend is $1,000.

Duration 1 year.
Number awarded 6 each year: 1 in each of the sponsor's regions.
Deadline February of each year.

[942]
NELSON URBAN SCHOLARSHIP FUND
James B. Morris Scholarship Fund
Attn: Scholarship Selection Committee
525 S.W. Fifth Street, Suite A
Des Moines, IA 50309-4501
(515) 282-8192　　　　　Fax: (515) 282-9117
E-mail: morris@assoc-mgmt.com
Web: www.morrisscholarship.org
Summary To provide financial assistance to African American teachers and graduate students from Iowa interested in preparing to work with "at risk" students.
Eligibility This program is open to African American teachers and graduate students who are Iowa residents and interested in working with "at risk" minority students in the elementary or secondary schools. Applicants must be enrolled full or part time at a graduate school in any state. Along with their application, they must submit a 250-word essay describing the "at risk" students emphasized in their course of study and how they plan to use their training. U.S. citizenship is required.
Financial data The awards generally range from $2,500 to $5,000.
Duration 1 year.
Number awarded At least 2 each year.
Deadline March of each year.

[943]
NEW MEXICO DIVERSITY FELLOWSHIPS IN ENVIRONMENTAL LAW
American Bar Association
Attn: Section of Environment, Energy, and Resources
321 North Clark Street
Chicago, IL 60654-7598
(312) 988-5602　　　　　Fax: (312) 988-5572
E-mail: jonusaid@staff.abanet.org
Web: www.abanet.org
Summary To provide funding to African American and other law students from traditionally underrepresented groups who are interested in working on a summer project in environmental, energy, or natural resources law in New Mexico.
Eligibility This program is open to first- and second-year law students and third-year night students who are residents of New Mexico or residents of other states with a demonstrated interest in practicing law in New Mexico. Preference is given to students at law schools in New Mexico. Applicants must be members of minority and traditionally underrepresented groups preparing for a career in environmental, energy, or natural resources law. They must be interested in working during the summer at a government agency or public interest organization in New Mexico. Selection is based on interest in environmental and natural resource issues, academic record, personal qualities, and leadership abilities.
Financial data The stipend is $5,000.
Duration 8 to 10 weeks during the summer.

Additional information This program is supported by the New Mexico Environment Department.
Number awarded 1 each year.
Deadline February of each year.

[944]
NEW MEXICO MINORITY DOCTORAL LOAN-FOR-SERVICE PROGRAM
New Mexico Higher Education Department
Attn: Financial Aid Division
2048 Galisteo Street
Santa Fe, NM 87505-2100
(505) 476-8411　　　　　Toll Free: (800) 279-9777
Fax: (505) 476-8454　E-mail: Theresa.acker@state.nm.us
Web: hed.state.nm.us
Summary To provide funding to African Americans, other underrepresented minorities, and women who reside in New Mexico and are interested in working on a doctoral degree in selected fields.
Eligibility This program is open to ethnic minorities and women who are residents of New Mexico and have received a baccalaureate degree from a public 4-year college or university in the state in mathematics, engineering, the physical or life sciences, or any other academic discipline in which ethnic minorities and women are demonstrably underrepresented in New Mexico academic institutions. Applicants must have been admitted as a full-time doctoral student at an approved university in any state. They must be sponsored by a New Mexico institution of higher education which has agreed to employ them in a tenure-track faculty position after they obtain their degree. U.S. citizenship is required.
Financial data Students can receive $25,000 per year, but the average is $15,000. This is a loan-for-service program; for every year of service as a college faculty member in New Mexico, a portion of the loan is forgiven. If the entire service agreement is fulfilled, 100% of the loan is eligible for forgiveness. Penalties may be assessed if the service agreement is not satisfied.
Duration 1 year; may be renewed up to 3 additional years.
Number awarded Up to 12 each year.
Deadline March of each year.

[945]
NEW YORK MINORITY FELLOWSHIP IN ENVIRONMENTAL LAW
American Bar Association
Attn: Section of Environment, Energy, and Resources
321 North Clark Street
Chicago, IL 60654-7598
(312) 988-5602　　　　　Fax: (312) 988-5572
E-mail: jonusaid@staff.abanet.org
Web: www.abanet.org
Summary To provide funding to African American and other law students from traditionally underrepresented groups who are interested in working on a summer project related to environmental, energy, or natural resources law in New York.
Eligibility This program is open to first- and second-year law students and third-year night students who are African American, Latino, Native American, Alaskan Native, Asian, or Pacific Islander. Applicants may be enrolled at a law school in

New York or be residents of New York and enrolled at a law school in another state. They must be interested in a summer internship at a government agency or public interest organization in New York in the field of environmental, energy, or natural resources law. Selection is based on interest in environmental issues, academic record, personal qualities, financial need, and leadership abilities.

Financial data The stipend is $6,000.

Duration At least 10 weeks during the summer.

Additional information This program is cosponsored by the Environmental Law Section of the New York State Bar Association and the Committee on Environmental Law of the New York City Bar Association.

Number awarded 1 or more each year.

Deadline November of each year.

[946]
NEXSEN PRUET DIVERSITY SCHOLARSHIPS

Nexsen Pruet
Attn: Diversity Scholarship
1230 Main Street, Suite 700
P.O. Drawer 2426
Columbia, SC 29202-2426
(803) 771-8900   Fax: (803) 727-1469
E-mail: diversity@nexsenpruet.com
Web: www.nexsenpruet.com/firm-diversity.html

Summary To provide financial assistance to African Americans and other minorities attending designated law schools in North and South Carolina.

Eligibility This program is open to minority students currently enrolled in the first year at the University of North Carolina School of Law, University of South Carolina School of Law, Wake Forest University School of Law, North Carolina Central University School of Law, Charleston School of Law, or Charlotte School of Law. Applicants must be interested in practicing law in North or South Carolina after graduation. Along with their application, they must submit information on their academic achievements; their contributions to promoting diversity in their community, school, or work environment; and their ability to overcome challenges in the pursuit of their goals. They must also submit essays of 250 words each on 1) their reasons for preparing for a legal career; 2) their interest in the private practice of law in North Carolina and/or South Carolina; 3) any obstacles, including but not limited to financial obstacles, that the scholarship will help them overcome; and 4) what they see as potential obstacles, issues, and opportunities facing new minority lawyers.

Financial data The stipend is $3,000 per year.

Duration 1 year; recipients may reapply.

Additional information Recipients are considered for summer employment in an office of the firm after completion of their first year of law school.

Number awarded Varies each year; recently, 3 of these scholarships were awarded.

Deadline October of each year.

[947]
NINA C. LEIBMAN FELLOWSHIP

California Women's Law Center
5700 Wilshire Boulevard, Suite 460
Los Angeles, CA 90036
(323) 951-1041   Fax: (323) 951-9870
E-mail: info@cwlc.org
Web: www.cwlc.org

Summary To provide summer work experience at the California Women's Law Center (CWLC) in Los Angeles to graduate students (especially African Americans, other students of color, and students with disabilities) who are working on a degree in a media-related field.

Eligibility This program is open to students who are currently working on a graduate degree in film studies, television studies, or communications. Applicants must have a record of interest in media issues affecting the civil rights of women and girls. They must be able to demonstrate strong research, writing, and problem-solving skills; excellent communication skills; and the ability to work independently, take direction, and follow through on assignments. Along with their application, they must submit a proposal for a summer research project on representation of women and/or girls in various media, representation of gender roles in various media, or treatment of women in either the creative or business side of media employment. Projects can focus on a single medium or compare 2 or more media. They must include the development of concrete advocacy strategies that can be implemented by the fellow over the summer and/or continued by CWLC following the fellowship. Men, persons with disabilities, the elderly, and people of color are encouraged to apply.

Financial data The stipend is $4,500; an additional $500 is available for purchase of project materials and supplies.

Duration 10 weeks during the summer.

Additional information This program was established in 2006.

Number awarded 1 each year.

Deadline May of each year.

[948]
NJLA DIVERSITY SCHOLARSHIP

New Jersey Library Association
4 Lafayette Street
P.O. Box 1534
Trenton, NJ 08607
(609) 394-8032   Fax: (609) 394-8164
E-mail: ptumulty@njla.org
Web: www.njla.org/honorsawards/scholarship

Summary To provide financial assistance to African Americans or other New Jersey minorities who are interested in working on a graduate or postgraduate degree in public librarianship at a school in any state.

Eligibility This program is open to residents of New Jersey and individuals who have worked in a New Jersey library for at least 12 months. Applicants must be members of a minority group (African American, Asian/Pacific Islander, Latino/Hispanic, or Native American/Native Alaskan). They must be enrolled or planning to enroll at an ALA-accredited school of library science in any state to work on a graduate or postgraduate degree in librarianship. Along with their application, they must submit an essay of 150 to 250 words explaining their choice of librarianship as a profession. An interview is required. Selection is based on academic ability and financial need.

Financial data The stipend is $1,300.

Duration 1 year.

Number awarded 1 each year.

Deadline February of each year.

[949]
NORTH AMERICAN DOCTORAL FELLOWSHIPS

The Fund for Theological Education, Inc.
Attn: North American Doctoral Fellows Program
825 Houston Mill Road, Suite 100
Atlanta, GA 30329
(404) 727-1450   Fax: (404) 727-1490
Web: www.fteleaders.org/pages/NAD-fellowships

Summary To provide financial assistance to African American and other underrepresented racial and ethnic minority students enrolled in a doctoral program in religious or theological studies.

Eligibility This program is open to continuing students enrolled full time in a Ph.D. or Th.D. program in religious or theological studies. Applicants must be citizens or permanent residents of the United States or Canada who are racial or ethnic minority students traditionally underrepresented in graduate education (e.g., African Americans, Asian Americans, Native Hawaiians, Native Americans, Alaska Natives, Hispanics). D.Min. students are ineligible. Preference is given to students nearing completion of their degree. Selection is based on commitment to teaching and scholarship, academic achievement, capacity for leadership in theological scholarship, and financial need.

Financial data Stipends range from $5,000 to $10,000 per year, depending on financial need.

Duration 1 year; may be renewed up to 2 additional years.

Additional information Funding for this program is provided by the National Council of Churches, proceeds from the book *Stony the Road We Trod: African American Biblical Interpretation,* an endowment from the Hearst Foundation, and the previously established FTE Black Doctoral Program supported by Lilly Endowment, Inc.

Number awarded Varies each year; recently, 12 of these fellowships were awarded.

Deadline February of each year.

[950]
NORTH CAROLINA DIVERSITY FELLOWSHIPS IN ENVIRONMENTAL LAW

American Bar Association
Attn: Section of Environment, Energy, and Resources
321 North Clark Street
Chicago, IL 60654-7598
(312) 988-5602   Fax: (312) 988-5572
E-mail: jonusaid@staff.abanet.org
Web: www.abanet.org

Summary To provide funding to African American and other law students from traditionally underrepresented groups who are interested in working on a summer project related to environmental, energy, or natural resources law in North Carolina.

Eligibility This program is open to first- and second-year law students and third-year night students who are members of underrepresented and underserved groups, such as minority or low-income populations. Students may be residents of any state and attending school in any state; preference is given to residents of North Carolina and to students who are enrolled at law schools in North Carolina or who have a strong interest in the state. Applicants must be interested in a summer internship at a government agency or public interest organization in North Carolina and working on an environmental project. Selection is based on interest in environmental issues, academic record, personal qualities, and leadership abilities.

Financial data The stipend is $5,000.

Duration 8 to 10 weeks during the summer.

Additional information This program is cosponsored by the Environment, Energy and Natural Resources Law Section of the North Carolina Bar Association.

Number awarded 2 each year.

Deadline February of each year.

[951]
NUCLEAR REGULATORY COMMISSION HISTORICALLY BLACK COLLEGES AND UNIVERSITIES STUDENT RESEARCH PARTICIPATION PROGRAM

Oak Ridge Institute for Science and Education
Attn: Science and Engineering Education
P.O. Box 117
Oak Ridge, TN 37831-0117
(865) 576-3937   Fax: (865) 241-5220
E-mail: michael.hubbard@orau.gov
Web: see.orau.org

Summary To provide funding to students at Historically Black Colleges and Universities (HBCUs) who wish to participate in research at various facilities of the U.S. Nuclear Regulatory Commission (NRC).

Eligibility This program is open to undergraduate and graduate students at HBCUs who are U.S. citizens or permanent residents. Applicants must be studying computer science, engineering, earth or geosciences, health physics, materials science, mathematics, molecular/radiation biology, performance and risk assessments, physical sciences, or statistics-related nuclear material control and accounting. They must be interested in participating in a research project at a laboratory where NRC research is being conducted, on an HBCU campus, or at a host university under the guidance of a principal investigator who has an NRC research grants.

Financial data The stipend is $600 per week for graduate students or $500 per week for undergraduates. Also provided is limited travel reimbursement for round-trip transportation between the facility and home or campus.

Duration 10 to 12 weeks during the summer. Some 1-year appointments at participating facilities or on campus are also available.

Additional information This program is funded by the NRC and administered by Oak Ridge Institute for Science and Education (ORISE).

Number awarded Varies each year.

Deadline Applications may be submitted at any time.

[952]
OLIVER GOLDSMITH, M.D. SCHOLARSHIP

Kaiser Permanente Southern California
Attn: Resident Recruitment and Outreach
393 East Walnut Street
Pasadena, CA 91188
Toll Free: (877) 574-0002   Fax: (626) 405-6581
E-mail: socal.residency@kp.org
Web: residency.kp.org

Summary   To provide financial assistance to African American and other medical students who will help bring diversity to the profession.

Eligibility   This program is open to students entering their third or fourth year of allopathic or osteopathic medical school. Applicants must have demonstrated their commitment to diversity through community service, clinical volunteering, or research. They may be attending medical school in any state, but they must intend to practice in southern California and they must be available to participate in a mentoring program and a clinical rotation at a Kaiser Permanente facility in that region.

Financial data   The stipend is $5,000.

Duration   1 year.

Additional information   These scholarships were first awarded in 2004.

Number awarded   12 each year.

Deadline   February of each year.

[953]
OLIVER W. HILL SCHOLARSHIP

LeClairRyan
Attn: Director, Recruiting and Diversity
Riverfront Plaza, East Tower
951 East Byrd Street, Eighth Floor
Richmond, VA 23219
(804) 783-7597   Fax: (804) 783-2294
E-mail: george.braxton@leclairryan.com
Web: www.leclairryan.com

Summary   To provide financial assistance to African Americans and other students of color at law schools in Virginia and Washington, D.C.

Eligibility   This program is open to students of color who have completed at least 1 semester at a law school in Virginia or Washington, D.C. Applicants must be planning to practice in Virginia after graduation. They must have a GPA of 2.5 or higher. Along with their application, they must submit a 2,000-word essay presenting their ideas of pursuing social justice through the law.

Financial data   The stipend is $5,000.

Duration   1 year.

Additional information   This program was established in 2009.

Number awarded   1 each year.

Deadline   March of each year.

[954]
OLYMPIA BROWN AND MAX KAPP AWARD

Unitarian Universalist Association
Attn: Ministerial Credentialing Office
25 Beacon Street
Boston, MA 02108-2800
(617) 948-6403   Fax: (617) 742-2875
E-mail: mco@uua.org
Web: www.uua.org/giving/awardsscholarships/57793.shtml

Summary   To provide financial assistance to minority and other Unitarian Universalist (UU) candidates for the ministry (especially African Americans and other students of color) who submit a project on an aspect of Universalism.

Eligibility   This program is open to students currently enrolled full or at least half time in a UU ministerial training program with aspirant or candidate status. Applicants are primarily citizens of the United States or Canada. Along with their application, they may submit a paper, sermon, or a special project on an aspect of Unitarian Universalism. Priority is given first to those who have demonstrated outstanding ministerial ability and secondarily to students with the greatest financial need (especially persons of color).

Financial data   The stipend is $2,500.

Duration   1 year.

Number awarded   1 each year.

Deadline   April of each year.

[955]
OMEGA PSI PHI FOUNDERS' MEMORIAL SCHOLARSHIPS

Omega Psi Phi Fraternity
Attn: Charles R. Drew Memorial Scholarship Commission
3951 Snapfinger Parkway
Decatur, GA 30035-3203
(404) 284-5533   Fax: (404) 284-0333
E-mail: scholarshipchairman@oppf.org
Web: oppf.org/scholarship

Summary   To provide financial assistance to outstanding undergraduate and graduate members of Omega Psi Phi fraternity.

Eligibility   This program is open to members of the fraternity who are enrolled full time as sophomores, juniors, or graduate students and have a GPA of 3.0 or higher. Each chapter may nominate 1 undergraduate and 1 graduate member to the district. Candidates must submit a statement of 200 to 250 words on their purpose for applying for this scholarship, how they believe funds from the fraternity can assist them in achieving their career goals, and other circumstances (including financial need) that make it important for them to receive financial assistance. Selection is based on academic achievement, extracurricular activities, and community and campus involvement.

Financial data   The stipend is $5,000.

Duration   The scholarships are offered annually.

Number awarded   4 each year: 3 to undergraduates and 1 to a graduate student.

Deadline   Applications must be submitted to the district scholarship committee chair by January of each year.

[956]
OMEGA PSI PHI UNDERGRADUATE AND GRADUATE SCHOLARSHIPS

Omega Psi Phi Fraternity
Attn: Charles R. Drew Memorial Scholarship Commission
3951 Snapfinger Parkway
Decatur, GA 30035-3203
(404) 284-5533   Fax: (404) 284-0333
E-mail: scholarshipchairman@oppf.org
Web: oppf.org/scholarship

Summary To provide financial assistance for undergraduate, graduate, or professional education to members of Omega Psi Phi who have an outstanding academic record.

Eligibility This program is open to members of the fraternity who are either 1) a sophomore, junior, or senior planning to continue on to graduate or professional school, or 2) currently attending graduate or professional school. Applicants must be enrolled full time at a 4-year college or university and have a GPA of 3.0 or higher. Along with their application, they must submit a statement of 200 to 250 words on their purpose for applying for this scholarship, how they believe funds from the fraternity can assist them in achieving their career goals, and other circumstances (including financial need) that make it important for them to receive financial assistance.

Financial data The stipend is $5,000.

Duration 1 year.

Number awarded 2 each year: 1 to an undergraduate and 1 to a graduate student.

Deadline May of each year.

[957]
OPERATION JUMP START III SCHOLARSHIPS

American Association of Advertising Agencies
Attn: AAAA Foundation
405 Lexington Avenue, 18th Floor
New York, NY 10174-1801
(212) 682-2500   Toll Free: (800) 676-9333
Fax: (212) 682-2028   E-mail: ameadows@aaaa.org
Web: www2.aaaa.org

Summary To provide financial assistance to African American and other minority art directors and copywriters interested in working on an undergraduate or graduate degree in advertising.

Eligibility This program is open to African Americans, Asian Americans, Hispanic Americans, and Native Americans who are U.S. citizens or permanent residents. Applicants must be incoming graduate students at 1 of 6 designated portfolio schools or full-time juniors at 1 of 2 designated colleges. They must be able to demonstrate extreme financial need, creative talent, and promise. Along with their application, they must submit 10 samples of creative work in their respective field of expertise.

Financial data The stipend is $5,000 per year.

Duration Most awards are for 2 years.

Additional information Operation Jump Start began in 1997 and was followed by Operation Jump Start II in 2002. The current program began in 2006. The 6 designated portfolio schools are the AdCenter at Virginia Commonwealth University, the Creative Circus in Atlanta, the Portfolio Center in Atlanta, the Miami Ad School, the University of Texas at Austin, and Pratt Institute. The 2 designated colleges are the Min-

neapolis College of Art and Design and the Art Center College of Design at Pasadena, California.

Number awarded 20 each year.

Deadline Deadline not specified.

[958]
OREGON DEPARTMENT OF TRANSPORTATION SCHOLARSHIPS

National Society of Black Engineers
Attn: Programs Department
205 Daingerfield Road
Alexandria, VA 22314
(703) 549-2207   Fax: (703) 683-5312
E-mail: scholarships@nsbe.org
Web: www.nsbe.org

Summary To provide financial assistance to members of the National Society of Black Engineers (NSBE) in designated regions who are working on an undergraduate or graduate degree in a field related to transportation.

Eligibility This program is open to members of the society who have completed at least their freshman year at a college or university in its Region 2 (which covers the central Atlantic states), Region 3 (which covers the Southeast), or Region 6 (which covers western states). Applicants must be working on an undergraduate or graduate degree in civil engineering, construction engineering, or other field related to transportation. They must have a GPA of 2.5 or higher. Along with their application, they must submit a 2-page concept paper for a research project on a topic related to the work of the Oregon Department of Transportation (which sponsors the program). U.S. citizenship or permanent resident status is required.

Financial data Stipends are $1,000 or $500.

Duration 1 year.

Number awarded 2 each year: 1 at $1,000 and 1 at $500.

Deadline October of each year.

[959]
OREGON DIVERSITY FELLOWSHIPS IN ENVIRONMENTAL LAW

American Bar Association
Attn: Section of Environment, Energy, and Resources
321 North Clark Street
Chicago, IL 60654-7598
(312) 988-5602   Fax: (312) 988-5572
E-mail: jonusaid@staff.abanet.org
Web: www.abanet.org

Summary To provide funding to African American and other law students from traditionally underrepresented groups who are interested in working on a summer project related to environmental, energy, or natural resources law in Oregon.

Eligibility This program is open to first- and second-year law students and third-year night students who are members of underrepresented and underserved groups, such as minority or low-income populations. Students may be residents of any state and attending school in any state; preference is given to residents of Oregon and to students who are enrolled at law schools in Oregon or who have a strong interest in the state. Applicants must be interested in a summer internship at a government agency or public interest organization in Oregon and working on a project in the fields of environmental, energy, or natural resources law. Selection is based on interest in environmental issues, academic record, personal qualities, and leadership abilities.

Financial data The stipend is $5,000.

Duration 8 to 10 weeks during the summer.

Additional information This program is cosponsored by the Affirmative Action Program of the Oregon State Bar.

Number awarded 1 each year.

Deadline January of each year.

[960]
OREGON STATE BAR CLERKSHIP STIPENDS

Oregon State Bar
Attn: Affirmative Action Program
16037 S.W. Upper Boones Ferry Road
P.O. Box 231935
Tigard, OR 97281-1935
(503) 431-6338
Toll Free: (800) 452-8260, ext. 338 (within OR)
Fax: (503) 598-6938   E-mail: eyip@osbar.org
Web: www.osbar.org/aap

Summary To provide summer job opportunities for African American and other law students in Oregon, especially those who will help the Oregon State Bar achieve its Affirmative Action objectives.

Eligibility This program is open to students currently enrolled in the first or second year of law school (or third year of a 4-year program). Applicants are not required to be enrolled at a law school in Oregon, but they must demonstrate a commitment to practice in the state. Preference is given to students who will contribute to the Oregon State Bar's Affirmative Action Program and "increase the diversity of the Oregon bench and bar to reflect the diversity of the people of Oregon." They must be interested in working in a law office during the summer; the employment should be in Oregon, although exceptions will be made if the job offers the student special experience not available within the state. Along with their application, they must submit 1) a personal statement on their history of disadvantage or barriers to educational advancement, personal experiences of discrimination, extraordinary financial obligations, composition of immediate family, extraordinary health or medical needs, and languages in which they are fluent as well as barriers they have experienced because English is a second language; and 2) a state bar statement on why they chose to attend an Oregon law school (if relevant); if they are not committed but are considering practicing in Oregon, what would help them to decide to practice in the state; and how they will improve the quality of legal service or increase access to justice in Oregon. Selection is based on financial need (30%), the personal statement (25%), the state bar statement (25%), community activities (10%), and employment history (10%).

Financial data This program pays a stipend of $7.00 per hour; the employer must then at least match that stipend.

Duration 12 weeks during the summer.

Additional information The selected students are responsible for finding work under this program.

Number awarded Approximately 20 each year.

Deadline January of each year.

[961]
OREGON STATE BAR SCHOLARSHIPS

Oregon State Bar
Attn: Affirmative Action Program
16037 S.W. Upper Boones Ferry Road
P.O. Box 231935
Tigard, OR 97281-1935
(503) 431-6338
Toll Free: (800) 452-8260, ext. 338 (within OR)
Fax: (503) 598-6938   E-mail: eyip@osbar.org
Web: www.osbar.org/aap

Summary To provide financial assistance to African American and other entering and continuing students from any state enrolled at law schools in Oregon, especially those who will help the Oregon State Bar achieve its Affirmative Action objectives.

Eligibility This program is open to students entering or continuing at 1 of the law schools in Oregon (Willamette, University of Oregon, and Lewis and Clark). Preference is given to students who will contribute to the Oregon State Bar's Affirmative Action Program to "increase the diversity of the Oregon bench and bar to reflect the diversity of the people of Oregon." Applicants must submit 1) a personal statement on their history of disadvantage or barriers to educational advancement, personal experiences of discrimination, extraordinary financial obligations, composition of immediate family, extraordinary health or medical needs, and languages in which they are fluent as well as barriers they have experienced because English is a second language; and 2) a state bar statement on why they chose to attend an Oregon law school; if they are not committed but are considering practicing in Oregon, what would help them to decide to practice in the state; and how they will improve the quality of legal service or increase access to justice in Oregon. Selection is based on financial need (30%), the personal statement (25%), the state bar statement (25%), community activities (10%), and employment history (10%).

Financial data The stipend is $2,000 per year. Funds are credited to the recipient's law school tuition account.

Duration 1 year; recipients may reapply.

Number awarded 10 each year.

Deadline March of each year.

[962]
ORGANIC CHEMISTRY GRADUATE STUDENT FELLOWSHIPS

American Chemical Society
Division of Organic Chemistry
1155 16th Street, N.W.
Washington, DC 20036
(202) 872-4401   Toll Free: (800) 227-5558, ext. 4401
E-mail: division@acs.org
Web: www.organicdivision.org/?nd=graduate_fellowship

Summary To provide funding for research to members of the Division of Organic Chemistry of the American Chemical Society (ACS), particularly African Americans or other minorities and women, who are working on a doctoral degree in organic chemistry.

Eligibility This program is open to members of the division who are entering the third or fourth year of a Ph.D. program in organic chemistry. Applicants must submit 3 letters of recommendation, a resume, and a short essay on a research area of their choice. U.S. citizenship or permanent resident status is required. Selection is based primarily on evidence of research accomplishment. Applications from women and minorities are especially encouraged.

Financial data The stipend is $26,000; that includes $750 for travel support to present a poster of their work at the National Organic Symposium.

Duration 1 year.

Additional information This program was established in 1982. It includes the Emmanuil Troyansky Fellowship. Current corporate sponsors include Eli Lilly, Pfizer, Roche, GlaxoSmithKline, Genentech, Organic Reactions, Organic Syntheses, Boehringer Ingelheim, and Amgen.

Number awarded Varies each year; recently, 10 of these fellowships were awarded.

Deadline May of each year.

[963]
PATRICK D. MCJULIEN MINORITY GRADUATE SCHOLARSHIP

Association for Educational Communications and
 Technology
Attn: ECT Foundation
1800 North Stonelake Drive, Suite 2
Bloomington, IN 47408
(812) 335-7675   Toll Free: (877) 677-AECT
Fax: (812) 335-7678
Web: www.aect.org/Foundation/Awards/McJulien.asp

Summary To provide financial assistance to African Americans and other minority members of the Association for Educational Communications and Technology (AECT) working on a graduate degree in the field of educational communications and technology.

Eligibility This program is open to AECT members who are members of minority groups. Applicants must be full-time graduate students enrolled in a degree-granting program in educational technology at the master's (M.S.), specialist (Ed.S.), or doctoral (Ph.D., Ed.D.) levels. They must have a GPA of 3.0 or higher.

Financial data A stipend is awarded (amount not specified).

Duration 1 year.

Number awarded 1 each year.

Deadline July of each year.

[964]
PAUL D. WHITE SCHOLARSHIP

Baker Hostetler LLP
Attn: Attorney Recruitment and Development Manager
PNC Center
1900 East Ninth Street, Suite 3200
Cleveland, OH 44114-3482
(216) 621-0200   Fax: (216) 696-0740
E-mail: ddriscole@bakerlaw.com
Web: www.bakerlaw.com/firmdiversity/scholarship

Summary To provide financial assistance and summer work experience to African American and other minority law school students.

Eligibility This program is open to first- and second-year law students of African American, Hispanic, Asian American,

or American Indian descent. Selection is based on law school performance, demonstrated leadership abilities (as evidenced by community and collegiate involvement), collegiate academic record, extracurricular activities, work experience, and a written personal statement.

Financial data The program provides a stipend of $7,500 for the scholarship and a paid summer clerkship with the sponsoring firm. To date, the firm has expended nearly $2.0 million in scholarships and clerkships.

Duration 1 year, including the following summer.

Additional information This program was established in 1997. Clerkships may be performed at any of the firm's offices in Chicago, Cincinnati, Cleveland, Columbus, Costa Mesa, Denver, Houston, Los Angeles, New York, Orlando, or Washington, D.C.

Number awarded 1 or more each year.

Deadline January of each year.

[965]
PAULA J. CARTER GRADUATE SCHOLARSHIP

Missouri Legislative Black Caucus Foundation
c/o Senator Yvonne Wilson
4609 Paseo Boulevard, Suite 102
Kansas City, MO 64110
Toll Free: (877) 63-MLBCF   E-mail: mlbcf@aol.com
Web: www.mlbcf.com

Summary To provide financial assistance to African American and other residents of Missouri who come from a disadvantaged background and are interested in working on a graduate degree in any field at a school in any state.

Eligibility This program is open to graduate students from Missouri who come from a disadvantaged background. Applicants may be attending or planning to attend a college or university in any state. They must have a GPA of 3.0 or higher. Along with their application, they must submit a 250-word personal statement on how their education will assist them in achieving their goals. Selection is based on academic excellence, community service, leadership skills, and financial need.

Financial data A stipend is awarded (amount not specified).

Duration 1 year; recipients may reapply for up to 3 years of support.

Number awarded 1 or more each year.

Deadline April of each year.

[966]
PBS&J ACHIEVEMENT SCHOLARSHIP

Conference of Minority Transportation Officials
Attn: National Scholarship Program
818 18th Street, N.W., Suite 850
Washington, DC 20006
(202) 530-0551   Fax: (202) 530-0617
Web: www.comto.org/news-youth.php

Summary To provide financial assistance to African American and other minority high school seniors, undergraduates, and graduate students interested in studying the field of transportation.

Eligibility This program is open to minority graduating high school seniors, current undergraduates, and graduate students interested in the field of transportation. Applicants must be enrolled or planning to enroll full time at an accredited college, university, or vocational/technical institution. They must have a GPA of 2.0 or higher. Along with their application, they must submit a cover letter with a 500-word statement of career goals. Financial need is not considered in the selection process. U.S. citizenship is required.

Financial data The stipend is $4,000. Funds are paid directly to the recipient's college or university.

Duration 1 year.

Additional information The Conference of Minority Transportation Officials (COMTO) was established in 1971 to promote, strengthen, and expand the roles of minorities in all aspects of transportation. This program is sponsored by the engineering, architecture, and sciences company PBS&J. Recipients are expected to attend the COMTO National Scholarship Luncheon.

Number awarded 1 or more each year.

Deadline April of each year.

[967]
PERKINS COIE DIVERSITY STUDENT FELLOWSHIPS

Perkins Coie LLP
Attn: Chief Diversity Officer
131 South Dearborn Street, Suite 1700
Chicago, IL 60603-5559
(312) 324-8593　　　　　　　　Fax: (312) 324-9400
E-mail: TCropper@perkinscoie.com
Web: www.perkinscoie.com/diversity/Diversity.aspx

Summary To provide financial assistance and work experience to African American and other law students who reflect the diversity of communities in the country.

Eligibility This program is open to students enrolled in the first year of a J.D. program at an ABA-accredited law school. Applicants must contribute meaningfully to the diversity of the law school student body and the legal profession. Diversity is defined broadly to include members of racial, ethnic, disabled, and sexual orientation minority groups, as well as those who may be the first person in their family to pursue higher education. Applicants must submit a 1-page personal statement that describes their unique personal history, a legal writing sample, a current resume, and undergraduate and law school transcripts. They are not required to disclose their financial circumstances, but a demonstrated need for financial assistance may be taken into consideration.

Financial data The stipend is $7,500.

Duration 1 year.

Additional information Fellows are also offered a summer associateship at their choice of the firm's offices in Anchorage, Bellevue, Boise, Chicago, Dallas, Los Angeles, Madison, Palo Alto, Phoenix, Portland, San Diego, San Francisco, Seattle, or Washington, D.C.

Number awarded Varies each year; recently, 7 of these fellowships were awarded.

Deadline January of each year.

[968]
PGA TOUR DIVERSITY INTERNSHIP PROGRAM

PGA Tour, Inc.
Attn: Minority Internship Program
100 PGA Tour Boulevard
Ponte Vedra Beach, FL 32082
(904) 285-3700
Web: www.pgatour.com/company/internships.html

Summary To provide summer work experience to African American and other undergraduate or graduate students who are interested in learning about the business side of golf and will contribute to diversity in the profession.

Eligibility This program is open to students who either have completed at least their sophomore year at an accredited 4-year college or university or are enrolled in graduate school. Applicants should be able to enrich the PGA Tour and its partnering organizations through diversity. They must have a GPA of 2.8 or higher. International students are eligible if they are legally permitted to work in the United States. Although all interns work in the business side of golf, the ability to play golf or knowledge of the game is not required for many positions.

Financial data Interns receive competitive wages and up to $500 for travel expenses to orientation in Ponte Vedra Beach, Florida or their initial work location. Depending on position and location, other benefits include subsidized housing, discounts on company merchandise, access to company training seminars, and possible golf privileges.

Duration Most assignments are for 10 to 12 weeks during the summer.

Additional information This program was established in 1992. Positions are available in accounting, corporate marketing, business development, international TV, information systems, event management, tournament services, tournament operations, retail licensing, sales, human resources, new media, and other areas within the PGA Tour. Most assignments are in Ponte Vedra Beach, Florida.

Number awarded Approximately 30 each year.

Deadline February of each year.

[969]
PHIL B. CURLS, SR. SCHOLARSHIP

Missouri Legislative Black Caucus Foundation
c/o Senator Yvonne Wilson
4609 Paseo Boulevard, Suite 102
Kansas City, MO 64110
Toll Free: (877) 63-MLBCF　　　　E-mail: mlbcf@aol.com
Web: www.mlbcf.com

Summary To provide financial assistance to African Americans and other residents of Missouri who come from a disadvantaged background and are interested in working on an undergraduate or graduate degree in a health-related field at a school in any state.

Eligibility This program is open to undergraduate and graduate students from Missouri who are preparing for a career as a physician, nurse, dentist, health researcher, hospital administrator, or other health-related professional. Applicants must come from a disadvantaged background and have a GPA of 2.5 or higher. They may be attending a college or university in any state. Along with their application, they must submit a 250-word personal statement on how their education will assist them in achieving their goals. Selection is based on academic excellence, community service, leadership skills, and financial need.

Financial data A stipend is awarded (amount not specified).

Duration 1 year; recipients may reapply for up to 5 years of support.

Additional information This foundation was established in 1989 to provide scholarships and other assistance to disadvantaged youths in Missouri. Its motto is, "Building a Brighter Future for African American families."

Number awarded 1 or more each year.

Deadline April of each year.

[970]
PHYSICAL AND LIFE SCIENCES DIRECTORATE INTERNSHIPS

Lawrence Livermore National Laboratory
Physical and Life Sciences Directorate
Attn: Education Coordinator
7000 East Avenue, L-418
Livermore, CA 94550
(925) 422-0455   E-mail: hutcheon3@llnl.gov
Web: www-pls.llnl.gov

Summary To provide an opportunity for undergraduate and graduate students (particularly African Americans, other minorities, and women) to work on summer research projects within the Physical and Life Sciences Directorate (PLS) of Lawrence Livermore National Laboratory (LLNL).

Eligibility This program is open to full-time undergraduate and graduate students who are interested in working on research projects within the PLS Directorate of LLNL. Openings are currently available in chemistry (organic, inorganic, synthetic, analytical, computational, nuclear, and environmental) and materials science (theory, simulation and modeling, synthesis and processing, materials under extreme conditions, dynamic materials science, metallurgy, nuclear fuels, optical materials, and surface science). Applicants must have a GPA of 3.0 or higher. Selection is based on academic record, aptitude, research interests, and recommendations of instructors. Women and minorities are encouraged to apply.

Financial data The stipend is $14 to $20 per hour for undergraduates or $4,100 to $4,900 per month for graduate students. Living accommodations and arrangements are the responsibility of the intern.

Duration 2 or 3 months, during the summer.

Number awarded Varies each year.

Deadline February of each year.

[971]
PORTER PHYSIOLOGY DEVELOPMENT AWARDS

American Physiological Society
Attn: Education Office
9650 Rockville Pike, Room 3111
Bethesda, MD 20814-3991
(301) 634-7132   Fax: (301) 634-7098
E-mail: education@the-aps.org
Web: www.the-aps.org

Summary To provide research funding to African Americans and other minorities who are members of the American

Physiological Society (APS) and interested in working on a doctoral degree in physiology.

Eligibility This program is open to U.S. citizens and permanent residents who are members of racial or ethnic minority groups (Hispanic or Latino, American Indian or Alaska Native, Asian, Black or African American, or Native Hawaiian or other Pacific Islander). Applicants must be currently enrolled in or accepted to a doctoral program in physiology at a university as full-time students. They must be APS members. Selection is based on the applicant's potential for success (academic record, statement of interest, previous awards and experiences, letters of recommendation); applicant's proposed training environment (including quality of preceptor); and applicant's research and training plan (clarity and quality).

Financial data The stipend is $28,300. No provision is made for a dependency allowance or tuition and fees.

Duration 1 year; may be renewed for 1 additional year and, in exceptional cases, for a third year.

Additional information This program is supported by the William Townsend Porter Foundation (formerly the Harvard Apparatus Foundation). The first Porter Fellowship was awarded in 1920. In 1966 and 1967, the American Physiological Society established the Porter Physiology Development Committee to award fellowships to minority students engaged in graduate study in physiology.

Number awarded Varies each year; recently, 8 of these fellowships were awarded.

Deadline January of each year.

[972]
POST-BACCALAUREATE TRAINING IN DISPARITIES RESEARCH GRANTS

Susan G. Komen Breast Cancer Foundation
Attn: Grants Department
5005 LBJ Freeway, Suite 250
Dallas, TX 75244
(972) 855-1616   Toll Free: (866) 921-9678
Fax: (972) 855-1640
E-mail: helpdesk@komengrantsaccess.org
Web: ww5.komen.org

Summary To provide funding to graduate students (especially African Americans and other disadvantaged students) who are interested in conducting research related to disparities in breast cancer outcomes.

Eligibility This program provides support to students enrolled in a master's, combined master's/doctoral, or doctoral degree program. Applications must be submitted by a full-time faculty member at their institution who is currently conducting research on disparities in breast cancer outcomes. Neither the students nor the faculty mentors are required to be U.S. citizens or residents. The application must describe a training program that combines didactic course work and hands-on laboratory, clinical, and/or public health research. The training program must ensure that all students at all levels will develop the analytic, research, scientific, clinical, and public health skills critical for them to effectively explore the basis for differences in breast cancer outcomes and to develop and translate research discoveries into clinical and public health practice to eliminate those disparities. Strong preference is given to involving trainees from populations adversely affected by disparities in breast cancer outcomes.

Financial data The grant is $45,000 per student per year for direct costs only.

Duration 2 years; a third year may be approved, based on an assessment of first-year progress.

Number awarded Varies each year; recently, 5 of these grants were awarded.

Deadline Pre-applications must be submitted by the end of September of each year; full applications are due in November.

[973]
PREDOCTORAL FELLOWSHIP IN MENTAL HEALTH AND SUBSTANCE ABUSE SERVICES

American Psychological Association
Attn: Minority Fellowship Program
750 First Street, N.E.
Washington, DC 20002-4242
(202) 336-6127   Fax: (202) 336-6012
TDD: (202) 336-6123   E-mail: mfp@apa.org
Web: www.apa.org

Summary To provide financial assistance to doctoral students (especially African Americans and other minorities) who are committed to providing mental health and substance abuse services to ethnic minority populations.

Eligibility Applicants must be U.S. citizens or permanent residents, enrolled full time in an accredited doctoral program, and committed to a career in psychology related to ethnic minority mental health and substance abuse services. Members of ethnic minority groups (African Americans, Hispanics/Latinos, American Indians, Alaskan Natives, Asian Americans, Native Hawaiians, and other Pacific Islanders) are especially encouraged to apply. Preference is given to students specializing in clinical, school, and counseling psychology. Students of any other specialty will be considered if they plan careers in which their training will lead to delivery of mental health or substance abuse services to ethnic minority populations. Selection is based on commitment to ethnic minority health and substance abuse services, knowledge of ethnic minority psychology or mental health issues, the fit between career goals and training environment selected, potential to become a culturally competent mental health service provider as demonstrated through accomplishments and goals, scholarship and grades, and letters of recommendation.

Financial data The stipend varies but is based on the amount established by the National Institutes of Health for predoctoral students; recently that was $21,600 per year.

Duration 1 academic or calendar year; may be renewed for up to 2 additional years.

Additional information Funding is provided by the U.S. Substance Abuse and Mental Health Services Administration.

Number awarded Varies each year.

Deadline January of each year.

[974]
PREDOCTORAL FELLOWSHIPS OF THE FORD FOUNDATION DIVERSITY FELLOWSHIP PROGRAM

National Research Council
Attn: Fellowships Office, Keck 576
500 Fifth Street, N.W.
Washington, DC 20001
(202) 334-2872   Fax: (202) 334-3419
E-mail: infofell@nas.edu
Web: www.nationalacademies.org

Summary To provide financial assistance for graduate school to African American and other students whose success will increase the racial and ethnic diversity of U.S. colleges and universities.

Eligibility This program is open to citizens and nationals of the United States who are enrolled or planning to enroll full time in a Ph.D. or Sc.D. degree program and are committed to a career in teaching and research at the college or university level. Applicants may be undergraduates in their senior year, individuals who have completed undergraduate study or some graduate study, or current Ph.D. or Sc.D. students who can demonstrate that they can fully utilize a 3-year fellowship award. They must be working on or planning to work on a degree in most areas of the arts, sciences, humanities, and social sciences or in interdisciplinary ethnic or area studies. Support is not provided to students working on a degree in most practice-oriented areas, terminal master's degrees, other doctoral degrees (e.g., Ed.D., D.F.A., Psy.D.), professional degrees (e.g., medicine, law, public health), or joint degrees (e.g., M.D./Ph.D., J.D./Ph.D., M.F.A./Ph.D). The following are considered as positive factors in the selection process: evidence of superior academic achievement; promise of continuing achievement as scholars and teachers; membership in a group whose underrepresentation in the American professoriate has been severe and longstanding, including Black/African Americans, Puerto Ricans, Mexican Americans/Chicanos/Chicanas, Native American Indians, Alaska Natives (Eskimos, Aleuts, and other indigenous people of Alaska), and Native Pacific Islanders (Hawaiians, Micronesians, or Polynesians); capacity to respond in pedagogically productive ways to the learning needs of students from diverse backgrounds; sustained personal engagement with communities that are underrepresented in the academy and an ability to bring this asset to learning, teaching, and scholarship at the college and university level; and likelihood of using the diversity of human experience as an educational resource in teaching and scholarship.

Financial data The program provides a stipend to the student of $20,000 per year and an award to the host institution of $2,000 per year in lieu of tuition and fees.

Duration 3 years of support is provided, to be used within a 5-year period.

Additional information The competition for this program is conducted by the National Research Council on behalf of the Ford Foundation. Applicants who merit receiving the fellowship but to whom awards cannot be made because of insufficient funds are given Honorable Mentions; this recognition does not carry with it a monetary award but honors applicants who have demonstrated substantial academic achievement. The National Research Council publishes a list of those Honorable Mentions who wish their names publicized. Fellows may not accept remuneration from another fellowship or similar external award while on this program; however, supplementation from institutional funds, educational benefits from the Department of Veterans Affairs, or educational incentive funds may be received concurrently with Ford Foundation support. Predoctoral fellows are required to submit an interim progress report 6 months after the start of the fellowship and a final report at the end of the 12 month tenure.

Number awarded Approximately 60 each year.

Deadline November of each year.

[975]
PREDOCTORAL RESEARCH TRAINING FELLOWSHIPS IN EPILEPSY

Epilepsy Foundation
Attn: Research Department
8301 Professional Place
Landover, MD 20785-2237
(301) 459-3700   Toll Free: (800) EFA-1000
Fax: (301) 577-2684   TDD: (800) 332-2070
E-mail: grants@efa.org
Web: www.epilepsyfoundation.org

Summary To provide funding to doctoral candidates (especially African Americans, other minorities, women, and students with disabilities) who are conducting dissertation research on a topic related to epilepsy.

Eligibility This program is open to full-time graduate students working on a Ph.D. in biochemistry, genetics, neuroscience, nursing, pharmacology, pharmacy, physiology, or psychology. Applicants must be conducting dissertation research on a topic relevant to epilepsy under the guidance of a mentor with expertise in the area of epilepsy investigation. Applications from women, members of minority groups, and people with disabilities are especially encouraged. U.S. citizenship is not required, but the project must be conducted in the United States. Selection is based on the relevance of the proposed work to epilepsy, the applicant's qualifications, the mentor's qualifications, the scientific quality of the proposed dissertation research, the quality of the training environment for research related to epilepsy, and the adequacy of the facility.

Financial data The grant is $20,000, consisting of $19,000 for a stipend and $1,000 to support travel to attend the annual meeting of the American Epilepsy Society.

Duration 1 year.

Additional information Support for this program, which began in 1998, is provided by many individuals, families, and corporations, especially the American Epilepsy Society, Abbott Laboratories, Ortho-McNeil Pharmaceutical, and Pfizer Inc.

Number awarded Varies each year.

Deadline August of each year.

[976]
PROGRESSUS THERAPY SCHOLARSHIP

National Black Association for Speech-Language and Hearing
Attn: Awards and Scholarship Committee
700 McKnight Park Drive, Suite 708
Pittsburgh, PA 15237
(412) 366-1177   Fax: (412) 366-8804
E-mail: NBASLH@nbaslh.org
Web: www.nbaslh.org/scholarships.htm

Summary To provide financial assistance to African American and other students who are working on a master's degree in speech-language pathology and who demonstrate an interest in mentoring.

Eligibility This program is open to students who are enrolled in an ASHA-accredited master's degree program in communication sciences and disorders (speech-language pathology). Applicants must indicate a primary career interest in providing speech-language services to children in school or early intervention settings. Along with their application, they must submit 500-word essays on 1) how a mentor has influenced their decision to prepare for a career in early intervention or school-based services; 2) the type of support they have received from a mentor when they experienced a challenging situation; and 3) their personal vision of their professional career as a school-based speech-language pathologist.

Financial data The stipend is $3,000. Funds are to be used for educational and clinical expenses (e.g., books, clinical materials or equipment, tuition, or other expenses related to an educational program.

Duration 1 year.

Additional information This scholarship, first awarded in 2010, is supported by Progressus Therapy and administered by the National Black Association for Speech-Language and Hearing (NBASLH).

Number awarded 1 each year.

Deadline February of each year.

[977]
PUBLIC HONORS FELLOWSHIPS OF THE OREGON STATE BAR

Oregon State Bar
Attn: Affirmative Action Program
16037 S.W. Upper Boones Ferry Road
P.O. Box 231935
Tigard, OR 97281-1935
(503) 431-6338
Toll Free: (800) 452-8260, ext. 338 (within OR)
Fax: (503) 598-6938   E-mail: eyip@osbar.org
Web: www.osbar.org/aap

Summary To provide African American and other law students in Oregon with summer work experience in public interest law, especially those who will help the Oregon State Bar achieve its Affirmative Action objectives.

Eligibility This program is open to students at Oregon's law schools (Willamette, University of Oregon, and Lewis and Clark) who are not in the first or final year of study. Each school may nominate up to 5 students. Nominees must have demonstrated a career goal in public interest or public sector law. Preference is given to students who will contribute to the

Oregon State Bar's Affirmative Action Program and "increase the diversity of the Oregon bench and bar to reflect the diversity of the people of Oregon." They must be interested in working in a law office during the summer; the employment should be in Oregon, although exceptions will be made if the job offers the student special experience not available within the state. Along with their application, they must submit 1) a personal statement on their history of disadvantage or barriers to educational advancement, personal experiences of discrimination, extraordinary financial obligations, composition of immediate family, extraordinary health or medical needs, and languages in which they are fluent as well as barriers they have experienced because English is a second language; and 2) a state bar statement on why they chose to attend an Oregon law school; if they are not committed but are considering practicing in Oregon, what would help them to decide to practice in the state; and how they will improve the quality of legal service or increase access to justice in Oregon. From the nominees of each school, 2 students are selected on the basis of financial need (30%), the personal statement (25%), the state bar statement (25%), and public service (20%). The information on those students is forwarded to prospective employers in Oregon and they arrange to interview the selectees.

Financial data   Fellows receive a stipend of $4,800.

Duration   3 months during the summer.

Additional information   There is no guarantee that all students selected by the sponsoring organization will receive fellowships at Oregon law firms.

Number awarded   6 each year: 2 from each of the law schools.

Deadline   Each law school sets its own deadline.

[978]
PUBLIC INTEREST LAW INITIATIVE SUMMER INTERNSHIPS

Public Interest Law Initiative
c/o Foley & Lardner
321 North Clark Street, 28th Floor
Chicago, IL 60610-4764
(312) 832-5127   Fax: (312) 467-6367
E-mail: pili@pili-law.org
Web: www.pili-law.org/internships.htm

Summary   To provide an opportunity for minority and other law students to gain summer work experience at public interest law agencies in the Chicago area.

Eligibility   This program is open to students in their first or second year at law schools across the country. Applicants must be interested in working at a public interest law agency in the Chicago area during the summer. The program is especially interested in recruiting a diverse group of interns; applicants should provide information about their minority status and foreign language fluency.

Financial data   The stipend is $5,000.

Duration   10 weeks during the summer.

Additional information   The Public Interest Law Initiative (PILI) established this program in 1977. Some of the 50 agencies where interns are assigned include the AIDS Legal Council of Chicago, Environmental Law and Policy Center of the Midwest, Lawyers' Committee for Better Housing, and National Immigrant Justice Center. PILI recruits applicants,

funds stipends, and acts as a clearinghouse, but the agencies select the interns.

Number awarded   Varies each year.

Deadline   March of each year.

[979]
RA CONSULTING SERVICE MARIA RILEY SCHOLARSHIP

National Forum for Black Public Administrators
Attn: Scholarship Program
777 North Capitol Street, N.E., Suite 807
Washington, DC 20002
(202) 408-9300, ext. 112   Fax: (202) 408-8558
E-mail: vreed@nfbpa.org
Web: www.nfbpa.org/i4a/pages/index.cfm?pageid=3630

Summary   To provide financial assistance to African Americans working on a undergraduate or graduate degree in engineering technology.

Eligibility   This program is open to African American undergraduate and graduate students preparing for a career as a public administrator serving the engineering and information technology fields. Applicants must be working full time on a degree in engineering or information technology. They must have a GPA of 3.0 or higher, excellent interpersonal and analytical abilities, and strong oral and written communication skills. Along with their application, they must submit a 3-page autobiographical essay that includes their academic and career goals and objectives. First consideration is given to applicants who are not currently receiving other financial aid.

Financial data   The stipend is $2,500.

Duration   1 year.

Additional information   This program is sponsored by RA Consulting Service. Recipients are required to attend the sponsor's annual conference to receive their scholarship; limited hotel and air accommodations are arranged and provided.

Number awarded   1 each year.

Deadline   February of each year.

[980]
RACE RELATIONS MULTIRACIAL STUDENT SCHOLARSHIP

Christian Reformed Church
Attn: Office of Race Relations
2850 Kalamazoo Avenue, S.E.
Grand Rapids, MI 49560-0200
(616) 241-1691   Toll Free: (877) 279-9994
Fax: (616) 224-0803   E-mail: crcna@crcna.org
Web: www.crcna.org/pages/racerelations_scholar.cfm

Summary   To provide financial assistance to African American and other undergraduate and graduate minority students interested in attending colleges related to the Christian Reformed Church in North America (CRCNA).

Eligibility   Students of color in the United States and Canada are eligible to apply. Normally, applicants are expected to be members of CRCNA congregations who plan to pursue their educational goals at Calvin Theological Seminary or any of the colleges affiliated with the CRCNA. Students who have no prior history with the CRCNA must attend a CRCNA-related college or seminary for a full academic year before they are eligible to apply for this program. Students entering their sophomore year must have earned a GPA of 2.0 or higher as freshmen; students entering their junior year must have earned a GPA of 2.3 or higher as sophomores; students entering their senior year must have earned a GPA of 2.6 or higher as juniors.

Financial data First-year students receive $500 per semester. Other levels of students may receive up to $2,000 per academic year.

Duration 1 year.

Additional information This program was first established in 1971 and revised in 1991. Recipients are expected to train to engage actively in the ministry of racial reconciliation in church and in society. They must be able to work in the United States or Canada upon graduating and must consider working for 1 of the agencies of the CRCNA.

Number awarded Varies each year; recently, 31 students received a total of $21,000 in support.

Deadline March of each year.

[981]
RACIAL ETHNIC SUPPLEMENTAL GRANTS

Presbyterian Church (USA)
Attn: Office of Financial Aid for Studies
100 Witherspoon Street, Room M-052
Louisville, KY 40202-1396
(502) 569-5224   Toll Free: (888) 728-7228, ext. 5224
Fax: (502) 569-8766   E-mail: finaid@pcusa.org
Web: www.pcusa.org/financialaid/programs/grant.htm

Summary To provide financial assistance to African American and other minority graduate students who are Presbyterian Church (USA) members interested in preparing for church occupations.

Eligibility This program is open to racial/ethnic graduate students (Asian American, African American, Hispanic American, Native American, or Alaska Native) who are enrolled full time at a PCUSA seminary or accredited theological institution approved by their Committee on Preparation for Ministry. Applicants must be working on 1) an M.Div. degree and enrolled as an inquirer or candidate by a PCUSA presbytery, or 2) an M.A.C.E. degree and preparing for a church occupation. They must be PCUSA members, U.S. citizens or permanent residents, able to demonstrate financial need, and recommended by the financial aid officer at their theological institution. Along with their application, they must submit a 1,000-word essay on what they believe God is calling them to do in ministry.

Financial data Stipends range from $500 to $1,000 per year. Funds are intended as supplements to students who have been awarded a Presbyterian Study Grant but still demonstrate remaining financial need.

Duration 1 year; may be renewed up to 2 additional years.

Number awarded Varies each year.

Deadline June of each year.

[982]
RALEIGH-DURHAM CHAPTER NBMBAA GRADUATE SCHOLARSHIPS

National Black MBA Association-Raleigh-Durham Chapter
Attn: Scholarship Program
P.O. Box 13614
Research Triangle Park, NC 27709
(919) 990-2351   E-mail: rdumba@gmail.com
Web: www.rdumba.org/?page_id=25

Summary To provide financial assistance to African American and other minority students who have ties to North Carolina and are working on a graduate degree in business.

Eligibility This program is open to African American and other minority students who are enrolled full time in a business or management graduate degree program at a college or university in any state. Applicants must have some ties to North Carolina, either through residence or college attendance there. Along with their application, they must submit a 2-page essay on a topic that changes annually but relates to African Americans and business. Selection is based on that essay, transcripts, a resume, and extracurricular activities.

Financial data The stipend is $1,000.

Duration 1 year.

Additional information Recipients must be available attend the sponsor's scholarship reception in October.

Number awarded 1 or more each year.

Deadline October of each year.

[983]
RALPH AND VALERIE THOMAS SCHOLARSHIP

National Association of Black Accountants
Attn: National Scholarship Program
7474 Greenway Center Drive, Suite 1120
Greenbelt, MD 20770
(301) 474-NABA, ext. 114   Fax: (301) 474-3114
E-mail: customerservice@nabainc.org
Web: www.nabainc.org

Summary To provide financial assistance to student members of the National Association of Black Accountants (NABA) who are working on an undergraduate or graduate degree in a field related to accounting.

Eligibility This program is open to NABA members enrolled full time as 1) an undergraduate freshman, sophomore, junior, or first-semester senior majoring in accounting, business, or finance at a 4-year college or university; or 2) a graduate student working on a master's degree in accounting. High school seniors are not eligible. Applicants must have a GPA of 3.5 or higher in their major and 3.3 or higher overall. Selection is based on grades, financial need, and a 500-word autobiography that discusses career objectives, leadership abilities, community activities, and involvement in NABA.

Financial data The stipend is $1,000.

Duration 1 year.

Number awarded 1 each year.

Deadline January of each year.

[984]
RALPH K. FRASIER SCHOLARSHIP

Porter Wright Morris & Arthur LLP
Huntington Center
41 South High Street
Columbus, OH 43215
(614) 227-2000   Toll Free: (800) 533-2794
Fax: (614) 227-2100
Web: www.porterwright.com/diversity_statement

Summary To provide financial assistance and summer work experience to African American and other minority students from any state who are enrolled at designated law schools in Ohio.

Eligibility This program is open to minority students enrolled in the first year at the following law schools: Ohio State University Moritz College of Law, Capital University Law School, Case Western Reserve University School of Law, Cleveland-Marshall College of Law, University of Cincinnati College of Law, University of Dayton School of Law, and University of Toledo College of Law. Applicants must submit undergraduate and law school transcripts, a resume, and an essay in the form of a legal memorandum on a hypothetical law case. They must also indicate their choice of the sponsoring firm's offices in Cleveland and Columbus for a summer clerkship.

Financial data The program provides a competitive salary for the summer clerkship and a stipend of $5,000 for the second year of law school.

Duration 1 year.

Additional information This program was established in 2005.

Number awarded 2 each year: 1 for a clerkship in Cleveland and 1 for a clerkship in Columbus.

Deadline January of each year.

[985]
RALPH W. SHRADER DIVERSITY SCHOLARSHIPS

Armed Forces Communications and Electronics
  Association
Attn: AFCEA Educational Foundation
4400 Fair Lakes Court
Fairfax, VA 22033-3899
(703) 631-6149   Toll Free: (800) 336-4583, ext. 6149
Fax: (703) 631-4693   E-mail: scholarship@afcea.org
Web: www.afcea.org

Summary To provide financial assistance to master's degree students (especially African Americans or other minorities and women) who are working on a degree in a field related to communications and electronics.

Eligibility This program is open to U.S. citizens working on a master's degree at an accredited college or university in the United States. Applicants must be enrolled full time and studying computer science, computer technology, engineering (chemical, electrical, electronic, communications, or systems), mathematics, physics, management information systems, or a field directly related to the support of U.S. national security or intelligence enterprises. At least 1 of these scholarships is set aside for a woman or a minority. Selection is based primarily on academic excellence.

Financial data The stipend is $3,000. Funds are paid directly to the recipient.

Duration 1 year.

Additional information This program is sponsored by Booz Allen Hamilton.

Number awarded Up to 5 each year, at least 1 of which is for a woman or minority candidate.

Deadline February of each year.

[986]
RDW GROUP, INC. MINORITY SCHOLARSHIP FOR COMMUNICATIONS

Rhode Island Foundation
Attn: Funds Administrator
One Union Station
Providence, RI 02903
(401) 427-4017   Fax: (401) 331-8085
E-mail: lmonahan@rifoundation.org
Web: www.rifoundation.org

Summary To provide financial assistance to African Americans and other Rhode Island undergraduate and graduate students of color who are interested in preparing for a career in communications at a school in any state.

Eligibility This program is open to undergraduate and graduate students at colleges and universities in any state who are Rhode Island residents of color. Applicants must intend to work on a degree in communications (including computer graphics, art, cinematography, or other fields that would prepare them for a career in advertising). They must be able to demonstrate financial need and a commitment to a career in communications. Along with their application, they must submit an essay (up to 300 words) on the impact they would like to have on the communications field.

Financial data The stipend ranges from $1,000 to $2,500 per year.

Duration 1 year; recipients may reapply.

Additional information This program is sponsored by the RDW Group, Inc.

Number awarded 1 each year.

Deadline April of each year.

[987]
REAL PROPERTY LAW SECTION MINORITY FELLOWSHIP

The New York Bar Foundation
One Elk Street
Albany, NY 12207
(518) 487-5651   Fax: (518) 487-5699
E-mail: foundation@tnybf.org
Web: www.tnybf.org/restrictedfunds.htm

Summary To provide an opportunity for African American and other minority residents of any state attending law school in New York to gain summer work experience at a public interest organization that represents tenants in local landlord/tenant cases.

Eligibility This program is open to minority students from any state who are enrolled at a law school in New York state. Students must be interested in working during the summer for a public interest legal organization in the state that represents tenants in local landlord/tenant cases. Applications must be submitted by the organization, which must be located in New York City or on Long Island.

Financial data The stipend is $3,333.

Duration 8 weeks during the summer.

Additional information This program was established in 2007 by the Real Property Law Section of the New York State Bar Association. It is administered by The New York Bar Foundation.

Number awarded 1 or more each year.

Deadline October of each year.

[988]
RECRUITMENT, TRAINING AND DEVELOPMENT GRANTS

Episcopal Church Center
Attn: Office of Black Ministries
815 Second Avenue, Eighth Floor
New York, NY 10017-4594
(212) 922-5343   Toll Free: (800) 334-7626
Fax: (212) 867-7652   E-mail: aifill@episcopalchurch.org
Web: www.episcopalchurch.org

Summary To provide financial assistance and work experience to African Americans interested in theological education within the Episcopal Church in the United States of America (ECUSA).

Eligibility Applicants must be African Americans who are postulants and candidates for holy orders, canonically resident in 1 of the 9 provinces of the ECUSA, and attending 1 of the Episcopal Church's accredited seminaries. Selection is based on participation in the Organization of Black Seminarians Conference (OBES), academic achievement, involvement in the Retention, Training and Deployment (RT&D) programs, and service to the Black community. Financial need is also considered.

Financial data The maximum scholarship stipend is $3,000.

Duration Seminarians may apply a maximum of 3 times: in their junior, middler, and senior year.

Additional information These scholarships are offered as part of the RT&D program, which involves 3 components: 1) recruitment, which helps to identify Black Episcopalians as aspirants for Holy Orders and advise them of the availability of these scholarships; 2) training, which is comprised of the OBES, a mentoring program, and the Black Seminarian Summer Internship; and 3) deployment, which assists the newly ordained persons in fulfilling their call to employ ministry.

Number awarded Varies each year; recently, 17 of these scholarships were awarded.

Deadline March of each year for fall term; September of each year for spring term.

[989]
REED SMITH DIVERSE SCHOLARS PROGRAM

Reed Smith LLP
Attn: U.S. Director of Legal Recruiting
2500 One Liberty Place
1650 Market Street
Philadelphia, PA 19103
(215) 851-8100   E-mail: dlevin@reedsmith.com
Web: diversity.reedsmith.com

Summary To provide financial assistance and summer work experience to African American and other law students who are committed to diversity.

Eligibility This program is open to students completing their first year of law school. Applicants must be able to demonstrate a record of academic excellence and a commitment to diversity, inclusion, and community. Along with their application, they must submit 500-word statements on 1) the goals of diversity and inclusion in the legal profession and how their life experiences will enable them to contribute to those goals; and 2) their community involvement and/or volunteer efforts.

Financial data The stipend is $10,000. Recipients are also offered a summer associate position at their choice of 8 of the firm's U.S. offices after completion of their second year of law school.

Duration 1 year (the second year of law school).

Additional information The firm established this program in 2008 as part of its commitment to promote diversity in the legal profession.

Number awarded Several each year.

Deadline July of each year.

[990]
RESOURCES FOR THE FUTURE SUMMER INTERNSHIPS

Resources for the Future
Attn: Internship Coordinator
1616 P Street, N.W., Suite 600
Washington, DC 20036-1400
(202) 328-5008   Fax: (202) 939-3460
E-mail: IC@rff.org
Web: www.rff.org

Summary To provide internships to undergraduate and graduate students (particularly African Americans or other minorities and women) who are interested in working on research projects in public policy during the summer.

Eligibility This program is open to undergraduate and graduate students (with priority to graduate students) interested in an internship at Resources for the Future (RFF). Applicants must be working on a degree in the social and natural sciences and have training in economics and quantitative methods or an interest in public policy. They should display strong writing skills and a desire to analyze complex environmental policy problems amenable to interdisciplinary methods. The ability to work without supervision in a careful and conscientious manner is essential. Women and minority candidates are strongly encouraged to apply. Both U.S. and non-U.S. citizens are eligible, if the latter have proper work and residency documentation.

Financial data The stipend is $375 per week for graduate students or $350 per week for undergraduates. Housing assistance is not provided.

Duration 10 weeks during the summer; beginning and ending dates can be adjusted to meet particular student needs.

Deadline March of each year.

[991]
RICHARD AND HELEN BROWN COREM SCHOLARSHIPS

United Church of Christ
Parish Life and Leadership Ministry Team
Attn: COREM Administrator
700 Prospect Avenue East
Cleveland, OH 44115-1100
(216) 736-2113   Toll Free: (866) 822-8224, ext. 2113
Fax: (216) 736-3783
Web: www.ucc.org/seminarians/ucc-scholarships-for.html

Summary To provide financial assistance to African American and other minority seminary students who are interested in becoming a pastor in the United Church of Christ (UCC).

Eligibility This program is open to students at accredited seminaries who have been members of a UCC congregation for at least 1 year. Applicants must work through 1 of the member bodies of the Council for Racial and Ethnic Ministries (COREM): United Black Christians (UBC), Ministers for Racial, Social and Economic Justice (MRSEJ), Council for Hispanic Ministries (CHM), Pacific Islander and Asian American Ministries (PAAM), or Council for American Indian Ministries (CAIM). They must 1) have a GPA of 3.0 or higher, 2) be enrolled in a course of study leading to ordained ministry, 3) be in care of an association or conference at the time of application, and 4) demonstrate leadership ability through participation in their local church, association, conference, or academic environment.

Financial data Stipends are approximately $10,000 per year.

Duration 1 year.

Number awarded Varies each year; recently, 4 scholarships were awarded by UBC, 3 by MRSEJ, and 2 by CHM.

Deadline Deadline not specified.

[992]
RICHARD D. HAILEY AAJ LAW STUDENT SCHOLARSHIPS

American Association for Justice
Attn: Minority Caucus
777 Sixth Street, N.W., Suite 200
Washington, DC 20001
(202) 965-3500, ext. 8302
Toll Free: (800) 424-2725, ext. 8302
Fax: (202) 965-0355
E-mail: brandon.grubesky@justice.org
Web: www.justice.org/cps/rde/xchg/justice/hs.xsl/1737.htm

Summary To provide financial assistance for law school to African American and other minority student members of the American Association for Justice (AAJ).

Eligibility This program is open to African American, Hispanic, Asian American, Native American, and biracial members of the association who are entering the first, second, or third year of law school. Applicants must submit a 500-word essay on how they meet the selection criteria: commitment to the association, involvement in student chapter and minority caucus activities, desire to represent victims, interest and proficiency of skills in trial advocacy, and financial need.

Financial data The stipend is $1,000.

Duration 1 year.

Additional information The American Association for Justice was formerly the Association of Trial Lawyers of America.

Number awarded Up to 6 each year.

Deadline May of each year.

[993]
ROBERT A. CATLIN/DAVID W. LONG MEMORIAL SCHOLARSHIP

American Planning Association
Attn: Planning and the Black Community Division
205 North Michigan Avenue, Suite 1200
Chicago, IL 60601
(312) 431-9100   Fax: (312) 786-6700
E-mail: pbcd.policy@gmail.com
Web: www.planning.org

Summary To provide financial assistance to African Americans interested in working on a graduate degree in planning or a related field.

Eligibility This program is open to African Americans who are 1) undergraduate students applying to or accepted into an urban planning program for graduate students; or 2) graduate students already working on a degree in urban planning or a related field (e.g., geography, environmental studies, urban studies, urban policy). Along with their application, they must submit 1) a 1-page personal statement on what interests them about the field of planning and their professional goals; and 2) a 3-page essay explaining the positive role that planning could play in developing and supporting Black communities. Financial need is not considered in the selection process.

Financial data The stipend is $2,500.

Duration 1 year; nonrenewable.

Number awarded 1 each year.

Deadline February of each year.

[994]
ROBERT D. WATKINS GRADUATE RESEARCH FELLOWSHIP

American Society for Microbiology
Attn: Education Board
1752 N Street, N.W.
Washington, DC 20036-2904
(202) 942-9283   Fax: (202) 942-9329
E-mail: fellowships@asmusa.org
Web: www.asm.org

Summary To provide funding for research in microbiology to African Americans and other underrepresented minority doctoral students who are members of the American Society for Microbiology (ASM).

Eligibility This program is open to African Americans, Hispanics, Native Americans, Alaskan Natives, and Pacific Islanders enrolled as full-time graduate students who have completed their first year of doctoral study and who are members of the society. Applicants must propose a joint research plan in collaboration with a society member scientist. They must have completed all graduate course work requirements for the doctoral degree by the date of the activation of the fellowship. U.S. citizenship or permanent resident status is required. Selection is based on academic achievement, evidence of a successful research plan developed in collaboration with a research adviser/mentor, relevant career goals in the microbiological sciences, and involvement in activities that serve the needs of underrepresented groups.

Financial data Students receive $21,000 per year as a stipend; funds may not be used for tuition or fees.

Duration 3 years.

Number awarded Varies each year.

Deadline April of each year.

[995]
ROBIN GAINES MEMORIAL SCHOLARSHIP

New England Regional Black Nurses Association, Inc.
P.O. Box 190690
Boston, MA 02119
(617) 524-1951
Web: www.nerbna.org/org/scholarships.html

Summary To provide financial assistance to registered nurses (R.N.s) from New England who are working on a master's degree and have contributed to the African American community.

Eligibility The program is open to residents of the New England states who are R.N.s and currently working on a master's degree (nursing, advanced nursing practice, or public health) at a school in any state. Applicants must have at least 1 full year of school remaining. Along with their application, they must submit a 3-page essay that covers their career aspirations in the nursing profession; how they have contributed to the African American or other communities of color in such areas as work, volunteering, church, or community outreach; an experience that has enhanced their personal and/or professional growth; and any financial hardships that may hinder them from completing their education.

Financial data A stipend is awarded (amount not specified).

Duration 1 year.

Number awarded 1 or more each year.

Deadline March of each year.

[996]
RONALD M. DAVIS SCHOLARSHIP

American Medical Association
Attn: AMA Foundation
515 North State Street
Chicago, IL 60610
(312) 464-4193   Fax: (312) 464-4142
E-mail: amafoundation@ama-assn.org
Web: www.ama-assn.org

Summary To provide financial assistance to African American and other underrepresented minority medical school students who are planning to become a primary care physician.

Eligibility This program is open to first- and second-year medical students who are members of the following minority groups: African American/Black, American Indian, Native Hawaiian, Alaska Native, or Hispanic/Latino. Candidates must have an interest in becoming a primary care physician. Only nominations are accepted. Each medical school is invited to submit 2 nominees. U.S. citizenship or permanent resident status is required.

Financial data The stipend is $10,000.

Duration 1 year.

Additional information This program is offered by the AMA Foundation of the American Medical Association in collaboration with the National Business Group on Health.

Number awarded 12 each year.

Deadline April of each year.

[997]
ROY H. POLLACK SCHOLARSHIP

Unitarian Universalist Association
Attn: Ministerial Credentialing Office
25 Beacon Street
Boston, MA 02108-2800
(617) 948-6403   Fax: (617) 742-2875
E-mail: mco@uua.org
Web: www.uua.org

Summary To provide financial assistance to seminary students (especially African Americans and other students of color) who are preparing for the Unitarian Universalist (UU) ministry.

Eligibility This program is open to seminary students who are enrolled full or at least half time in their second or third year in a UU ministerial training program with aspirant or candidate status. Applicants are generally citizens of the United States or Canada. Priority is given first to those who have demonstrated outstanding ministerial ability and secondarily to students with the greatest financial need (especially persons of color).

Financial data The stipend ranges from $1,000 to $11,000 per year.

Duration 1 year.

Number awarded Varies each year; recently, 2 of these scholarships were awarded.

Deadline April of each year.

[998]
RUDEN MCCLOSKY DIVERSITY SCHOLARSHIP PROGRAM

Community Foundation of Sarasota County
Attn: Scholarship Manager
2635 Fruitville Road
P.O. Box 49587
Sarasota, FL 34230-6587
(941) 556-7156   Fax: (941) 556-7157
E-mail: mimi@cfsarasota.org
Web: www.cfsarasota.org/Default.aspx?tabid=263

Summary To provide financial assistance to African American and other minority students from any state attending designated law schools (most of which are in Florida).

Eligibility This program is open to racial and ethnic minority students from any state who are members of groups traditionally underrepresented in the legal profession. Applicants must be entering their second year of full-time study at the University of Florida Levin College of Law, Florida State University College of Law, Stetson University College of Law, Nova Southeastern University Shepard Broad Law Center, St. Thomas University School of Law, Florida A&M University College of Law, Howard University College of Law, Texas Southern University Thurgood Marshall School of Law, Florida Coastal School of Law, Florida International University College of Law, or Barry University Dwayne O. Andreas School of Law. They must have a GPA of 2.6 or higher. Along with their application, they must submit a 1,000-word personal statement that describes their personal strengths, their contributions through community service, any special or unusual circumstances that may have affected their academic performance, or their personal and family history of educational or socioeconomic disadvantage; it must include their plans for practicing law in Florida after graduation. Applicants may also include information about their financial circumstances if they wish to have those considered in the selection process. U.S. citizenship or permanent resident status is required.

Financial data   The stipend is $2,500 per semester.

Duration   1 semester (the spring semester of the second year of law school); may be renewed 1 additional semester (the fall semester of the third year).

Additional information   This program is sponsored by the Florida law firm Ruden McClosky, which makes the final selection of recipients, and administered by the Community Foundation of Sarasota County.

Number awarded   1 or more each year.

Deadline   July of each year.

[999]
RUTH L. KIRSCHSTEIN NATIONAL RESEARCH SERVICE AWARDS FOR INDIVIDUAL PREDOCTORAL FELLOWSHIPS TO PROMOTE DIVERSITY IN HEALTH-RELATED RESEARCH

National Institutes of Health
Office of Extramural Research
Attn: Grants Information
6705 Rockledge Drive, Suite 4090
Bethesda, MD 20892-7983
(301) 435-0714   Fax: (301) 480-0525
TDD: (301) 451-5936   E-mail: GrantsInfo@nih.gov
Web: grants.nih.gov/grants/guide/pa-files/PA-11-112.html

Summary   To provide financial assistance to African Americans and other students from underrepresented groups interested in working on a doctoral degree and preparing for a career in biomedical and behavioral research.

Eligibility   This program is open to students enrolled or accepted for enrollment in a Ph.D. or equivalent research degree program; a formally combined M.D./Ph.D. program; or other combined professional doctoral/research Ph.D. program in the biomedical, behavioral, health, or clinical sciences. Students in health professional degree programs (e.g., M.D., D.O., D.D.S., D.V.M.) are not eligible. Applicants must be 1) members of an ethnic or racial group underrepresented in biomedical or behavioral research; 2) individuals with disabilities; or 3) individuals from socially, culturally, economically, or educationally disadvantaged backgrounds that have inhibited their ability to prepare for a career in health-related research. They must be U.S. citizens, nationals, or permanent residents.

Financial data   The fellowship provides an annual stipend of $21,180, a tuition and fee allowance (60% of costs up to $16,000 or 60% of costs up to $21,000 for dual degrees), and an institutional allowance of $4,200 ($3,100 at for-profit and federal institutions) for travel to scientific meetings, health insurance, and laboratory and other training expenses.

Duration   Up to 5 years.

Additional information   These fellowships are offered by most components of the National Institutes of Health (NIH). Check with the sponsor for a list of names and telephone numbers of responsible officers at each component.

Number awarded   Varies each year.

Deadline   April, August, or December of each year.

[1000]
RUTH WHITEHEAD WHALEY SCHOLARSHIP

Association of Black Women Attorneys, Inc.
Attn: Scholarship Committee Chair
255 West 36th Street, Suite 800
New York, NY 10018
(212) 300-2193   E-mail: abwagroup@yahoo.com
Web: www.abwanewyork.org

Summary   To provide financial assistance to African American and other minority students at law schools in Connecticut, New Jersey, and New York who are interested in public interest or civil rights law.

Eligibility   This program is open to African American and other minority students from any state who are currently enrolled at accredited law schools in Connecticut, New Jersey, or New York. Applicants must be able to demonstrate financial need and an interest in public interest or civil rights law. Along with their application, they must submit a 200-word essay on their professional goals, especially community service activities or events in areas where they have been employed or volunteered. In the selection process, academic performance is not the deciding factor.

Financial data   A stipend is awarded (amount not specified).

Duration   1 year.

Additional information   This program was established in 1995 to honor the first African American woman admitted to the North Carolina Bar.

Number awarded   Varies each year; since the program was established, it has awarded more than $35,000 in scholarships.

Deadline   April of each year.

[1001]
SADIE T.M. ALEXANDER SCHOLARSHIP

Delta Sigma Theta Sorority, Inc.
Attn: Scholarship and Standards Committee Chair
1707 New Hampshire Avenue, N.W.
Washington, DC 20009
(202) 986-2400   Fax: (202) 986-2513
E-mail: dstemail@deltasigmatheta.org
Web: www.deltasigmatheta.org

Summary   To provide financial assistance to members of Delta Sigma Theta who are interested in preparing for a career in law.

Eligibility   This program is open to graduating college seniors and students who are currently enrolled in law school. Applicants must be active, dues-paying members of Delta Sigma Theta. Selection is based on meritorious achievement.

Financial data   The stipends range from $1,000 to $2,000 per year. The funds may be used to cover tuition and living expenses.

Duration   1 year; may be renewed for 1 additional year.

Additional information This sponsor is a traditionally African American social sorority. The application fee is $20.
Deadline April of each year.

[1002]
SANDIA MASTER'S FELLOWSHIP PROGRAM

Sandia National Laboratories
Attn: Staffing Department 3535
MS-1023
P.O. Box 5800
Albuquerque, NM 87185-1023
(505) 844-3441   Fax: (505) 844-6636
E-mail: empsite@sandia.gov
Web: www.sandia.gov/careers/fellowships.html

Summary To enable African American and other minority students to obtain a master's degree in engineering or computer science and also work at Sandia National Laboratories.

Eligibility This program is open to minority (American Indian, Asian, Black, or Hispanic) students who have a bachelor's degree in engineering or computer science and a GPA of 3.2 or higher. Participants must apply to 3 schools jointly selected by the program and themselves. They must be prepared to obtain a master's degree within 1 year. The fields of study (not all fields are available at all participating universities) include computer science, electrical engineering, mechanical engineering, civil engineering, chemical engineering, nuclear engineering, materials sciences, and petroleum engineering. Applicants must be interested in working at the sponsor's laboratories during the summer between graduation from college and the beginning of their graduate program, and then following completion of their master's degree. U.S. citizenship is required.

Financial data Participants receive a competitive salary while working at the laboratories on a full-time basis and a stipend while attending school.

Duration 1 year.

Additional information During their summer assignment, participants work at the laboratories, either in Albuquerque, New Mexico or in Livermore, California. Upon successful completion of the program, they return to Sandia's hiring organization as a full-time member of the technical staff. This program began in 1968. Application to schools where students received their undergraduate degree is not recommended. After the schools accept an applicant, the choice of a school is made jointly by the laboratories and the participant.

Number awarded Varies each year; since the program began, more than 350 engineers and computer scientists have gone to work at Sandia with master's degrees.

Deadline Deadline not specified.

[1003]
SBE DOCTORAL DISSERTATION RESEARCH IMPROVEMENT GRANTS

National Science Foundation
Attn: Directorate for Social, Behavioral, and Economic Sciences
4201 Wilson Boulevard, Room 905N
Arlington, VA 22230
(703) 292-8700   Fax: (703) 292-9083
TDD: (800) 281-8749
Web: www.nsf.gov/funding/pgm_summ.jsp?pims_id=13453

Summary To provide partial support to doctoral candidates (particularly African Americans, other minorities, women, and students with disabilities) who are conducting dissertation research in areas of interest to the Directorate for Social, Behavioral, and Economic Sciences (SBE) of the National Science Foundation (NSF).

Eligibility Applications may be submitted through regular university channels by dissertation advisers on behalf of graduate students who have advanced to candidacy and have begun or are about to begin dissertation research. Students must be enrolled at U.S. institutions, but they need not be U.S. citizens. The proposed research must relate to SBE's Division of Behavioral and Cognitive Sciences (archaeology, cultural anthropology, geography and spatial sciences, linguistics, or physical anthropology); Division of Social and Economic Sciences (decision, risk, and management science; economics; law and social science; methodology, measurement, and statistics; political science; sociology; or science, technology, and society); Division of Science Resources Statistics (research on science and technology surveys and statistics); or Office of Multidisciplinary Activities (science and innovation policy). Women, minorities, and persons with disabilities are strongly encouraged to apply.

Financial data Grants have the limited purpose of providing funds to enhance the quality of dissertation research. They are to be used exclusively for necessary expenses incurred in the actual conduct of the dissertation research, including (but not limited to) conducting field research in settings away from campus that would not otherwise be possible, data collection and sample survey costs, payments to subjects or informants, specialized research equipment, analysis and services not otherwise available, supplies, travel to archives, travel to specialized facilities or field research locations, and partial living expenses for conducting necessary research away from the student's U.S. academic institution. Funding is not provided for stipends, tuition, textbooks, journals, allowances for dependents, travel to scientific meetings, publication costs, dissertation preparation or reproduction, or indirect costs.

Duration Up to 2 years.

Number awarded 200 to 300 each year. Approximately $2.5 million is available for this program annually.

Deadline Deadline dates for the submission of dissertation improvement grant proposals differ by program within the divisions of the SBE Directorate; applicants should obtain information regarding target dates for proposals from the relevant program.

[1004]
SCHOLARSHIPS FOR MINORITY ACCOUNTING STUDENTS

American Institute of Certified Public Accountants
Attn: Academic and Career Development Division
220 Leigh Farm Road
Durham, NC 27707-8110
(919) 402-4931   Fax: (919) 419-4705
E-mail: MIC_Programs@aicpa.org
Web: www.aicpa.org/members/div/career/mini/smas.htm

Summary   To provide financial assistance to African American and other minorities interested in studying accounting at the undergraduate or graduate school level.

Eligibility   This program is open to minority undergraduate and graduate students, enrolled full time, who have a GPA of 3.3 or higher (both cumulatively and in their major) and intend to pursue a C.P.A. credential. Undergraduates must have completed at least 30 semester hours, including at least 6 semester hours of a major in accounting. Graduate students must be working on a master's degree in accounting, finance, taxation, or a related program. Applicants must be U.S. citizens or permanent residents and student affiliate members of the American Institute of Certified Public Accountants (AICPA). The program defines minority students as those whose heritage is Black or African American, Hispanic or Latino, Native American, or Asian American.

Financial data   Stipends range from $1,500 to $3,000 per year. Funds are disbursed directly to the recipient's school.

Duration   1 year; may be renewed up to 3 additional years or until completion of a bachelor's or master's degree, whichever is earlier.

Additional information   This program is administered by The Center for Scholarship Administration, E-mail: allison-lee@bellsouth.net. The most outstanding applicant for this program is awarded the Stuart A. Kessler Scholarship for Minority Students.

Number awarded   Varies each year; recently, 94 students received funding through this program.

Deadline   March of each year.

[1005]
SCHWABE, WILLIAMSON & WYATT SUMMER ASSOCIATE DIVERSITY SCHOLARSHIP

Schwabe, Williamson & Wyatt, Attorneys at Law
Attn: Attorney Recruiting Administrator
1211 S.W. Fifth Avenue, Suite 1500-2000
Portland, OR 97204
(503) 796-2889   Fax: (503) 796-2900
E-mail: dcphillips@schwabe.com
Web: www.schwabe.com/recruitdiversity.aspx

Summary   To provide financial assistance and summer work experience in Portland, Oregon to African American and other law students who will contribute to the diversity of the legal profession.

Eligibility   This program is open to first-year students working on a J.D. degree at an ABA-accredited law school. Applicants must 1) contribute to the diversity of the law school student body and the legal community; 2) possess a record of academic achievement, capacity, and leadership as an undergraduate and in law school that indicates promise for a successful career in the legal profession; and 3) demonstrate a commitment to practice law in the Pacific Northwest upon completion of law school. They must be interested in a paid summer associateship at the sponsoring law firm's office in Portland, Oregon. Along with their application, they must submit a resume, undergraduate and law school transcripts, a legal writing sample, and a 1- to 2-page personal statement explaining their interest in the scholarship and how they will contribute to diversity in the legal community.

Financial data   The program provides a paid summer associateship during the summer following completion of the first year of law school and an academic scholarship of $7,500 to help pay tuition and other expenses during the recipient's second year of law school.

Duration   1 year.

Number awarded   1 each year.

Deadline   January of each year.

[1006]
SCIENCE TEACHER PREPARATION PROGRAM

Alabama Alliance for Science, Engineering, Mathematics, and Science Education
Attn: Project Director
University of Alabama at Birmingham
Campbell Hall, Room 401
1300 University Boulevard
Birmingham, AL 35294-1170
(205) 934-8762   Fax: (205) 934-1650
E-mail: LDale@uab.edu
Web: www.uab.edu/istp/alabama.html

Summary   To provide financial assistance to African American and other underrepresented minority students at designated institutions in Alabama who are interested in preparing for a career as a science teacher.

Eligibility   This program is open to members of underrepresented minority groups who have been unconditionally admitted to a participating Alabama college or university. Applicants must be interested in becoming certified to teach science and mathematics in K-12 schools. They may be 1) entering freshmen enrolling in a science education program leading to a bachelor's degree and certification; 2) students transferring from a community college and enrolling in a science education program leading to a bachelor's degree and certification; 3) students with a bachelor's degree in mathematics, science, or education and enrolling in a certification program; or 4) students with a bachelor's degree in mathematics, science, or education and enrolling in a fifth-year program leading to a master's degree and certification.

Financial data   The stipend is $1,000 per year.

Duration   1 year; may be renewed.

Additional information   Support for this program is provided by the National Science Foundation. The participating institutions are Alabama A&M University, Alabama State University, Auburn University, Miles College, Stillman College, Talladega College, Tuskegee University, University of Alabama at Birmingham, and University of Alabama in Huntsville.

Number awarded   Varies each year.

Deadline   Deadline not specified.

[1007]
SCOVEL RICHARDSON SCHOLARSHIP

Mound City Bar Association
Attn: Scholarship Committee
P.O. Box 1543
St. Louis, MO 63188
E-mail: moundcitybar@att.net
Web: www.moundcitybar.com/scholarship.html

Summary To provide financial assistance to African American and other minority law students who have limited financial resources.

Eligibility This program is open to minority students entering the second or third year of law school. Applicants must be able to demonstrate financial need and a record of community service and leadership. Along with their application, they must submit a short autobiographical sketch, including the individuals and/or events that have helped to shape your life, their short- and long-term career goals, and the contributions they would like to make to create a better community. Special consideration is given to students who plan to live and work in the greater St. Louis metropolitan area.

Financial data The stipend ranges from $2,500 to $3,000.

Duration 1 year.

Additional information The Mound City Bar Association was established in 1922 as the St. Louis Negro Bar Association. It established this program is help create a judiciary that is more responsive and accountable to African Americans and other minorities.

Number awarded 1 or more each year.

Deadline April of each year.

[1008]
SEATTLE CHAPTER NABA SCHOLARSHIPS

National Association of Black Accountants-Seattle
  Chapter
Attn: Scholarship Committee
P.O. Box 18105
Seattle, WA 98118
E-mail: info@nabaseattle.org
Web: www.nabaseattle.org/nabaseattle/scholarships.asp

Summary To provide financial assistance to members of the National Association of Black Accountants (NABA) from any state who are working on an undergraduate or graduate degree in a business-related field at colleges and universities in Washington.

Eligibility This program is open to full-time freshmen, sophomores, juniors, first-year seniors, and graduate students working on a degree in accounting, finance, or other business-related field at colleges and universities in Washington. Applicants must be ethnic minorities and active NABA members. They must have a GPA of 3.0 or higher. Along with their application, they must submit a 500-word essay on a topic that changes annually. Financial need is not considered in the selection process.

Financial data The stipend is $1,000.

Duration 1 year.

Number awarded 1 or more each year.

Deadline April of each year.

[1009]
SECTION OF BUSINESS LAW DIVERSITY CLERKSHIP PROGRAM

American Bar Association
Attn: Section of Business Law
321 North Clark Street
Chicago, IL 60654-7598
(312) 988-5588   Fax: (312) 988-5578
E-mail: businesslaw@abanet.org
Web: www.abanet.org/buslaw/students/clerkship.shtml

Summary To provide summer work experience in business law to African American and other student members of the American Bar Association (ABA) and its Section of Business Law who will help the section to fulfill its goal of promoting diversity.

Eligibility This program is open to first- and second-year students at ABA-accredited law schools who are interested in a summer business court clerkship. Applicants must 1) be a member of an underrepresented group (student of color, woman, student with disabilities, gay, lesbian, bisexual, or transgender); or 2) have overcome social or economic disadvantages, such as a physical disability, financial constraints, or cultural impediments to becoming a law student. They must be able to demonstrate financial need. Along with their application, they must submit a 500-word essay that covers why they are interested in this clerkship program, what they would gain from the program, how it would positively influence their future professional goals as a business lawyer, and how they meet the program's criteria. Membership in the ABA and its Section of Business Law are required.

Financial data The stipend is $6,000.

Duration Summer months.

Additional information This program began in 2008. Assignments vary, but have included the Philadelphia Commerce Court, the Prince George's District Court in Upper Marlboro, Maryland, and the Delaware Court of Chancery.

Number awarded 9 each year.

Deadline January of each year.

[1010]
SEMESTER INTERNSHIPS IN GEOSCIENCE PUBLIC POLICY

American Geological Institute
Attn: Government Affairs Program
4220 King Street
Alexandria, VA 22302-1502
(703) 379-2480   Fax: (703) 379-7563
E-mail: govt@agiweb.org
Web: www.agiweb.org/gap/interns/index.html

Summary To provide work experience to geoscience students (especially African Americans and other minorities or women) who have a strong interest in federal science policy.

Eligibility This program is open to geoscience students who are interested in working with Congress and federal agencies to promote sound public policy in areas that affect geoscientists, including water, energy, and mineral resources; geologic hazards; environmental protection, and federal funding for geoscience research and education. Applicants must submit official copies of college transcripts, a resume with the names and contact information for 2 references, and a statement of their science and policy interests and what they feel they can contribute to the program. Women and minorities are especially encouraged to apply.

Financial data The stipend is $5,000.

Duration 14 weeks, during the fall or spring semester. A similar program is also offered by the sponsor for summer internships.

Additional information This program is jointly funded by the American Geological Institute (AGI) and the American Association of Petroleum Geologists (AAPG). Activities for the interns include monitoring and analyzing geoscience-related legislation in Congress, updating legislative and policy information on AGI's web site, attending House and Senate hearings and preparing summaries, responding to information requests from AGI's member societies, and attending meetings with policy-level staff members in Congress, federal agencies, and non-governmental organizations.

Number awarded 1 each semester.

Deadline April of each year for fall internships; October of each year for spring internships.

[1011]
SEMICONDUCTOR RESEARCH CORPORATION MASTER'S SCHOLARSHIP PROGRAM

Semiconductor Research Corporation
Attn: Global Research Collaboration
1101 Slater Road, Suite 120
P.O. Box 12053
Research Triangle Park, NC 27709-2053
(919) 941-9400   Fax: (919) 941-9450
E-mail: apply@src.org
Web: www.src.org/student-center/fellowship

Summary To provide financial assistance to students (especially African Americans or other minorities and women) who are interested in working on a master's degree in a field of microelectronics relevant to the interests of the Semiconductor Research Corporation (SRC).

Eligibility This program is open to women and members of underrepresented minority groups (African Americans, Hispanics, and Native Americans). Applicants must be U.S. citizens or have permanent resident, refugee, or political asylum status in the United States. They must be admitted to an SRC participating university to work on a master's degree in a field relevant to microelectronics under the guidance of an SRC-sponsored faculty member and under an SRC-funded contract. Selection is based on academic achievement.

Financial data The fellowship provides full tuition and fee support, a monthly stipend of $2,186, an annual grant of $2,000 to the university department with which the student recipient is associated, and travel expenses to the Graduate Fellowship Program Annual Conference.

Duration Up to 2 years.

Additional information This program was established in 1997 for underrepresented minorities and expanded to include women in 1999.

Number awarded Up to 30 each year.

Deadline February of each year.

[1012]
SEO CORPORATE LAW PROGRAM

Sponsors for Educational Opportunity
Attn: Career Program
55 Exchange Place
New York, NY 10005
(212) 979-2040   Toll Free: (800) 462-2332
Fax: (646) 706-7113
E-mail: careerprogram@seo-usa.org
Web: www.seo-usa.org/Career/Corporate_Law

Summary To provide summer work experience to African Americans and other students of color interested in studying corporate law.

Eligibility This program is open to students of color who are college seniors or recent graduates planning to attend law school in the United States. Applicants must be interested in a summer internship at a participating law firm that specializes in corporate law. They should be able to demonstrate analytical and quantitative skills, interpersonal and community skills, maturity, and a cumulative GPA of 3.0 or higher. Along with their application, they must submit 1) information on their extracurricular and employment experience; 2) an essay of 75 to 100 words on how the program area to which they are applying related to their professional goals; and 3) an essay of 250 to 400 words on either an example of a time when they had to operate outside their "comfort zone" or their definition of success. Personal interviews are required.

Financial data Interns receive a competitive stipend.

Duration 10 weeks during the summer.

Additional information This program was established in 1980. Most internships are available in New York City or Washington, D.C.

Number awarded Varies each year.

Deadline December of each year.

[1013]
SHERRY R. ARNSTEIN MINORITY STUDENT SCHOLARSHIP

American Association of Colleges of Osteopathic
   Medicine
Attn: Office of Government Relations
5550 Friendship Boulevard, Suite 310
Chevy Chase, MD 20815-7231
(301) 968-4142   Fax: (301) 968-4101
Web: www.aacom.org

Summary To provide financial assistance to African Americans and other underrepresented minority students already enrolled in osteopathic medical school.

Eligibility This program is open to African American, mainland Puerto Rican, Hispanic, Native American, Native Hawaiian, and Alaska Native students currently enrolled in good standing in their first, second, or third year of osteopathic medical school. Applicants must submit a 750-word essay on what osteopathic medical schools can do to recruit and retain more underrepresented minority students, what they personally plan to do as a student and as a future D.O. to help increase minority student enrollment at a college of osteopathic medicine, and how and why they were drawn to osteopathic medicine.

Financial data The stipend is $2,500.

Duration 1 year; nonrenewable.

Number awarded 1 each year.
Deadline March of each year.

[1014]
SHERRY R. ARNSTEIN NEW STUDENT MINORITY STUDENT SCHOLARSHIP

American Association of Colleges of Osteopathic
Medicine
Attn: Office of Government Relations
5550 Friendship Boulevard, Suite 310
Chevy Chase, MD 20815-7231
(301) 968-4142   Fax: (301) 968-4101
Web: www.aacom.org

Summary To provide financial assistance to African Americans and other underrepresented minority students planning to enroll at an osteopathic medical school.

Eligibility This program is open to African American, mainland Puerto Rican, Hispanic, Native American, Native Hawaiian, and Alaska Native students who have been accepted and are planning to enroll as a first-time student at any of the 20 colleges of osteopathic medicine that are members of the American Association of Colleges of Osteopathic Medicine (AACOM). Applicants must submit a 750-word essay on what osteopathic medical schools can do to recruit and retain more underrepresented minority students, what they personally plan to do as a student and as a future D.O. to help increase minority student enrollment at a college of osteopathic medicine, and how and why they were drawn to osteopathic medicine.

Financial data The stipend is $2,500.
Duration 1 year; nonrenewable.
Number awarded 1 each year.
Deadline March of each year.

[1015]
SIDLEY DIVERSITY AND INCLUSION SCHOLARSHIP

Sidley Austin LLP
Attn: Scholarships
One South Dearborn
Chicago, IL 60603
(312) 853-7000   Fax: (312) 853-7036
E-mail: scholarship@sidley.com
Web: www.sidley.com

Summary To provide financial assistance and work experience to African American and other law students who come from a diverse background.

Eligibility The program is open to students entering their second year of law school; preference is given to students at schools where the sponsor conducts on-campus interviews or participates in a resume collection. Applicants must have a demonstrated ability to contribute meaningfully to the diversity of the law school and/or legal profession. Along with their application, they must submit a 500-word essay that includes their thoughts on and efforts to improve diversity, how they might contribute to the sponsor's commitment to improving diversity, and their interest in practicing law at a global firm and specifically the sponsor. Selection is based on academic achievement and leadership qualities.

Financial data The stipend is $15,000.
Duration 1 year.

Additional information These scholarships were first offered in 2011. Recipients are expected to participate in the sponsor's summer associate program following their second year of law school. They must apply separately for the associate position. The firm has offices in Chicago, Dallas, Los Angeles, New York, Palo Alto, San Francisco, and Washington, D.C.

Number awarded A limited number are awarded each year.
Deadline Applications are accepted throughout the fall recruiting season.

[1016]
SIDNEY B. WILLIAMS, JR. INTELLECTUAL PROPERTY LAW SCHOOL SCHOLARSHIPS

American Intellectual Property Law Education Foundation
485 Kinderkamack Road
Oradell, NJ 07649
(201) 634-1870   Fax: (201) 634-1871
E-mail: admin@aiplef.org
Web: www.aiplef.org/scholarships/sidney_b_williams

Summary To provide financial assistance to African American and other minority law students who are interested in preparing for a career in intellectual property law.

Eligibility This program is open to members of minority groups currently enrolled in or accepted to an ABA-accredited law school. Applicants must be U.S. citizens with a demonstrated intent to engage in the full-time practice of intellectual property law. Along with their application, they must submit a 250-word essay on how this scholarship will make a difference to them in meeting their goal of engaging in the full-time practice of intellectual property law and why they intend to do so. Selection is based on 1) demonstrated commitment to developing a career in intellectual property law; 2) academic performance at the undergraduate, graduate, and law school levels (as applicable); 3) general factors, such as leadership skills, community activities, or special accomplishments; and 4) financial need.

Financial data The stipend is $10,000 per year. Funds may be used for tuition, fees, books, supplies, room, board, and a patent bar review course.

Duration 1 year; may be renewed if the recipient maintains a GPA of 2.0 or higher.

Additional information This program, which began in 2002, is administered by the Thurgood Marshall Scholarship Fund, 80 Maiden Lane, Suite 2204, New York, NY 10038, (212) 573-8487, Fax: (212) 573-8497, E-mail: srogers@tmcfund.org. Additional funding is provided by the American Intellectual Property Law Association, the American Bar Association's Section of Intellectual Property Law, and the Minority Corporate Counsel Association. Recipients are required to join and maintain membership in the American Intellectual Property Law Association.

Number awarded Varies each year; recently, 12 of these scholarships were awarded.
Deadline March of each year.

[1017]
SIGMA GAMMA RHO SCHOLARSHIPS/ FELLOWSHIPS

Sigma Gamma Rho Sorority, Inc.
Attn: National Education Fund
1000 Southhill Drive, Suite 200
Cary, NC 27513
(919) 678-9720   Toll Free: (888) SGR-1922
Fax: (919) 678-9721   E-mail: info@sgrho1922.org
Web: www.sgrho1922.org/service.htm

Summary To provide financial assistance for undergraduate or graduate study to African American and other applicants who can demonstrate financial need.

Eligibility This program is open to high school seniors, undergraduates, and graduate students who can demonstrate financial need. The sponsor is a traditionally African American sorority, but support is available to both males and females. Applicants must have a GPA of "C" or higher.

Financial data A stipend is awarded (amount not specified).

Duration 1 year.

Additional information This program includes the following named awards: the Lorraine A. Williams Scholarship, the Philo Sallie A. Williams Scholarship, the Cleo W. Higgins Scholarship (limited to doctoral students), the Angela E. Randall Scholarship, the Inez Colson Memorial Scholarship (limited to students majoring in education or mathematics at Savannah State University), and the Philo Geneva Young Scholarship. A processing fee of $20 is required.

Number awarded Varies each year.

Deadline April of each year.

[1018]
SMITHSONIAN MINORITY STUDENT INTERNSHIP

Smithsonian Institution
Attn: Office of Fellowships
Victor Building, Suite 9300, MRC 902
P.O. Box 37012
Washington, DC 20013-7012
(202) 633-7070   Fax: (202) 633-7069
E-mail: siofg@si.edu
Web: www.si.edu/ofg/Applications/MIP/MIPapp.htm

Summary To provide African Americans and other minority undergraduate or graduate students with the opportunity to work on research or museum procedure projects in specific areas of history, art, or science at the Smithsonian Institution.

Eligibility Internships are offered to minority students who are actively engaged in graduate study at any level or in upper-division undergraduate study. An overall GPA of 3.0 or higher is generally expected. Applicants must be interested in conducting research in specified fields of interest to the Smithsonian.

Financial data The program provides a stipend of $550 per week; travel allowances may also be offered.

Duration 10 weeks during the summer or academic year.

Additional information Eligible fields of study currently include animal behavior, ecology, and environmental science (including an emphasis on the tropics); anthropology (including archaeology); astrophysics and astronomy; earth sciences and paleobiology; evolutionary and systematic biology; history of science and technology; history of art (especially American, contemporary, African, Asian, and 20th-century art); American crafts and decorative arts; social and cultural history of the United States; and folklife.

Number awarded Varies each year.

Deadline January of each year for summer or fall; September of each year for spring.

[1019]
SOCIETY FOR THE STUDY OF SOCIAL PROBLEMS RACIAL/ETHNIC MINORITY GRADUATE SCHOLARSHIP

Society for the Study of Social Problems
Attn: Executive Officer
University of Tennessee
901 McClung Tower
Knoxville, TN 37996-0490
(865) 689-1531   Fax: (865) 689-1534
E-mail: sssp@utk.edu
Web: www.sssp1.org/index.cfm/m/261

Summary To provide funding to African American and other minority members of the Society for the Study of Social Problems (SSSP) who are interested in conducting research for their doctoral dissertation.

Eligibility This program is open to SSSP members who are Black or African American, Hispanic or Latino, Asian or Asian American, Native Hawaiian or other Pacific Islander, or American Indian or Alaska Native. Applicants must have completed all requirements for a Ph.D. (course work, examinations, and approval of a dissertation prospectus) except the dissertation. They must have a GPA of 3.25 or higher and be able to demonstrate financial need. Their field of study may be any of the social and/or behavioral sciences that will enable them to expand their perspectives in the investigation into social problems. U.S. citizenship or permanent resident status is required.

Financial data The stipend is $12,000. Additional grants provide $500 for the recipient to 1) attend the SSSP annual meeting prior to the year of the work to receive the award, and 2) attend the meeting after the year of the award to present a report on the work completed.

Duration 1 year.

Number awarded 1 each year.

Deadline January of each year.

[1020]
SOCIETY OF AMERICAN ARCHIVISTS MOSAIC SCHOLARSHIPS

Society of American Archivists
Attn: Chair, Awards Committee
17 North State Street, Suite 1425
Chicago, IL 60602-3315
(312) 606-0722   Toll Free: (866) 722-7858
Fax: (312) 606-0728   E-mail: info@archivists.org
Web: www2.archivists.org

Summary To provide financial assistance to African American and other minority students who are working on a graduate degree in archival science.

Eligibility This program is open to minority graduate students, defined as those of American Indian/Alaska Native, Asian, Black/African American, Hispanic/Latino, or Native

Hawaiian/other Pacific Islander descent. Applicants must be enrolled or planning to enroll in a graduate program or a multi-course program in archival administration. They may have completed no more than half of the credit requirements for a degree. Along with their application, they must submit a 500-word essay outlining their interests and future goals in the archives profession. U.S. or Canadian citizenship or permanent resident status is required.

Financial data The stipend is $5,000.

Duration 1 year.

Additional information This scholarship was first awarded in 2009.

Number awarded 2 each year.

Deadline February of each year.

[1021]
SOCIETY OF PEDIATRIC PSYCHOLOGY DIVERSITY RESEARCH GRANT

American Psychological Association
Attn: Division 54 (Society of Pediatric Psychology)
c/o John M. Chaney
Oklahoma State University
Department of Psychology
407 North Murray
Stillwater, OK 74078
(405) 744-5703   E-mail: john.chaney@okstate.edu
Web: www.societyofpediatricpsychology.org

Summary To provide funding to graduate student and postdoctoral members of the Society of Pediatric Psychology (especially African Americans and other minorities or women) who are interested in conducting research on diversity aspects of pediatric psychology.

Eligibility This program is open to current members of the society who are graduate students, fellows, or early-career (within 3 years of appointment) faculty. Applicants must be interested in conducting pediatric psychology research that features diversity-related variables, such as race or ethnicity, gender, culture, sexual orientation, language differences, socioeconomic status, and/or religiosity. Along with their application, they must submit a 2,000-word description of the project, including its purpose, methodology, predictions, and implications; a detailed budget; a current curriculum vitae, and (for students) a curriculum vitae of the faculty research mentor and a letter of support from that mentor. Selection is based on relevance to diversity in child health (5 points), significance of the study (5 points), study methods and procedures (10 points), and investigator qualifications (10 points).

Financial data Grants up to $1,000 are available. Funds may not be used for convention or meeting travel, indirect costs, stipends of principal investigators, or costs associated with manuscript preparation.

Duration The grant is presented annually.

Additional information The Society of Pediatric Psychology is Division 54 of the American Psychological Association (APA). This grant was first presented in 2008.

Number awarded 1 each year.

Deadline September of each year.

[1022]
SOUTH CAROLINA GRADUATE INCENTIVE SCHOLARSHIP PROGRAM

South Carolina Commission on Higher Education
Attn: Director of Student Services
1333 Main Street, Suite 200
Columbia, SC 29201
(803) 737-2144   Toll Free: (877) 349-7183
Fax: (803) 737-2297   E-mail: mbrown@che.sc.gov
Web: www.che.sc.gov/AccessEquity/GISInfoCtr.htm

Summary To provide funding to graduate students from African American and other historically underrepresented groups who are preparing for careers as college teachers in South Carolina.

Eligibility This program is open to historically underrepresented students, defined as African Americans at traditionally white public institutions in South Carolina and whites at traditionally Black public institutions in the state. Applicants must be U.S. citizens and accepted for admission or enrolled in a doctoral program, a terminal degree program in the fine or applied arts, a first professional level degree program, or a master's degree program. Students in master's and professional degree programs must also be South Carolina residents; students in doctoral and terminal arts degree programs may be residents of any state, but preference is given to South Carolina residents. All applicants must be studying or planning to study in designated academic or professional areas in which overall shortages exist in South Carolina or areas in which Black residents are underrepresented.

Financial data The stipend is $7,500 per year for full-time master's degree students or $15,000 per year for full-time doctoral and certain first-year professional students. Stipends for part-time students are prorated accordingly. This is a forgivable loan program; for each year of full-time employment in South Carolina in the designated shortage area following graduation, up to $5,000 of the total amount borrowed will be forgiven. Requests for forgiveness must be submitted to the respective institution within 6 months following the recipient's graduation. Otherwise, the full amount of the loan must be repaid within 5 years at 8% interest.

Duration 1 year; may be renewed if the recipient maintains satisfactory academic standing and continued enrollment in an eligible program.

Additional information The participating institutions are Clemson University, Medical University of South Carolina, University of South Carolina, University of South Carolina School of Medicine, College of Charleston, The Citadel, Winthrop University, South Carolina State University, and Francis Marion University. Information on the program and applications are available from the financial aid office of the institution.

Number awarded Varies each year.

Deadline Each participating institution sets its own deadline.

[1023]
SOUTH FLORIDA CHAPTER NBMBAA GRADUATE SCHOLARSHIP

National Black MBA Association-South Florida Chapter
Attn: Scholarship Program
P.O. Box 278872
Miramar, FL 33027
(786) 255-5775   E-mail: plw8620@aol.com
Web: www.nbmbaasfl.org/scholarship.htm

Summary   To provide financial assistance to African Americans and other minority residents of Florida who are working on a graduate degree in business or management at a school in any state.

Eligibility   This program is open to African American and other minority residents of Florida who are working full time on a graduate business or management degree at an AACSB-accredited college or university in any state. Applicants must submit a 2-page essay on 1 of 3 assigned topics that change annually but relate to African Americans and business. Selection is based on the essay, academic excellence, leadership potential, and community involvement.

Financial data   The stipend is at least $1,500.

Duration   1 year.

Additional information   Recipients must agree to participate in the scholarship reception of the South Florida Chapter of the National Black MBA Association (NBMBAA) and to become a member.

Number awarded   1 or more each year.

Deadline   June of each year.

[1024]
SOUTHERN REGIONAL EDUCATION BOARD DISSERTATION AWARDS

Southern Regional Education Board
Attn: Coordinator, Program and Scholar Services
592 Tenth Street N.W.
Atlanta, GA 30318-5776
(404) 879-5569   Fax: (404) 872-1477
E-mail: doctoral.scholars@sreb.org
Web: www.sreb.org/page/1113/types_of_awards.html

Summary   To provide funding to African Americans and other minority students who wish to complete a Ph.D. dissertation, especially in fields of science, technology, engineering, or mathematics (STEM), while in residence at a university in the southern states.

Eligibility   This program is open to U.S. citizens and permanent residents who are members of racial/ethnic minority groups (Native Americans, Hispanic Americans, Asian Americans, and African Americans) and have completed all requirements for a Ph.D. except the dissertation. Preference is given to students in STEM disciplines with particularly low minority representation, although all academic fields are eligible. Applicants must be in a position to write full time and must expect to complete their dissertation within the year of the fellowship. Eligibility is limited to individuals who plan to become full-time faculty members at a southern institution upon completion of their doctoral degree. The program does not include students working on other doctoral degrees (e.g., M.D., D.B.A., D.D.S., J.D., D.V.M., Ed.D., Pharm.D., D.N.P., D.P.T.).

Financial data   Fellows receive waiver of tuition and fees (in or out of state), a stipend of $20,000, a $500 research allowance, and reimbursement of expenses for attending the Compact for Faculty Diversity's annual Institute on Teaching and Mentoring.

Duration   1 year; nonrenewable.

Additional information   This program was established in 1993 as part of the Compact for Faculty Diversity, supported by the Pew Charitable Trusts and the Ford Foundation.

Number awarded   Varies each year.

Deadline   February of each year.

[1025]
SPECTRUM SCHOLARSHIP PROGRAM

American Library Association
Attn: Office for Diversity
50 East Huron Street
Chicago, IL 60611-2795
(312) 280-5048   Toll Free: (800) 545-2433, ext. 5048
Fax: (312) 280-3256   TDD: (888) 814-7692
E-mail: spectrum@ala.org
Web: www.ala.org

Summary   To provide financial assistance to African American and other minority students interested in working on a degree in librarianship.

Eligibility   This program is open to ethnic minority students (African American or Black, Asian, Native Hawaiian or other Pacific Islander, Latino or Hispanic, and American Indian or Alaska Native). Applicants must be U.S. or Canadian citizens or permanent residents who have completed no more than a third of the requirements for a master's or school library media degree. They must be enrolled full or part time at an ALA-accredited school of library and information studies or an ALA-recognized NCATE school library media program. Selection is based on academic leadership, outstanding service, commitment to a career in librarianship, statements indicating the nature of the applicant's library and other work experience, letters of reference, and personal presentation.

Financial data   The stipend is $5,000.

Duration   1 year; nonrenewable.

Additional information   This program began in 1998. It is administered by a joint committee of the American Library Association (ALA). Units with ALA sponsor a number of other programs aimed at minority recipients, including the LITA/OCLC Minority Scholarship and the LITA/LSSI Minority Scholarship, both offered by ALA's Library and Information Technology Association.

Number awarded   Varies each year; recently, 69 of these scholarships were awarded.

Deadline   February of each year.

[1026]
SREB DOCTORAL AWARDS

Southern Regional Education Board
Attn: Coordinator, Program and Scholar Services
592 Tenth Street N.W.
Atlanta, GA 30318-5776
(404) 879-5569   Fax: (404) 872-1477
E-mail: doctoral.scholars@sreb.org
Web: www.sreb.org/page/1113/types_of_awards.html

Summary To provide financial assistance to African American and other minority students who wish to work on a doctoral degree, especially in fields of science, technology, engineering, or mathematics (STEM), at designated universities in the southern states.

Eligibility This program is open to U.S. citizens and permanent residents who are members of racial/ethnic minority groups (Native Americans, Hispanic Americans, Asian Americans, and African Americans) and have or will receive a bachelor's or master's degree. Applicants must be entering or enrolled in the first year of a Ph.D. program at an accredited college or university. They must indicate an interest in becoming a college professor at an institution in the South. The program does not support students working on other doctoral degrees (e.g., M.D., D.B.A., D.D.S., J.D., D.V.M., Ed.D., Pharm.D., D.N.P., D.P.T.). Preference is given to applicants in STEM disciplines with particularly low minority representation, although all academic fields are eligible.

Financial data Scholars receive a waiver of tuition and fees (in or out of state) for up to 5 years, an annual stipend of $20,000 for 3 years, an annual allowance for professional development activities, and reimbursement of travel expenses to attend the Company for Faculty Diversity's annual Institute on Teaching and Mentoring.

Duration Up to 5 years.

Additional information This program was established in 1993 as part of the Compact for Faculty Diversity, supported by the Pew Charitable Trusts and the Ford Foundation.

Number awarded Varies each year; recently, the program was supporting more than 300 scholars. Since its founding, it has supported more than 900 scholars at 83 institutions in 29 states.

Deadline February of each year.

[1027]
STANLEY J. TARVER MEMORIAL SCHOLARSHIP FUND

Community Foundation of Dutchess County
Attn: Scholarship Committee
80 Washington Street, Suite 201
Poughkeepsie, NY 12601
(845) 452-3077   Fax: (845) 452-3083
E-mail: cfdc@cfdcny.org
Web: www.cfdcny.org/page30020.cfm

Summary To provide financial assistance to students of African descent who are working on a graduate degree in African history and/or culture.

Eligibility This program is open to graduate students of African descent, including African Americans and Black people of other nationalities. Applicants must be working on a master's or doctorate degree in African history and/or culture and have completed at least 1 year of graduate study at a college or university in the United States. Along with their application, they must submit a 500-word essay on their interest, project, and activities in African history and/or culture.

Financial data The stipend is $2,000.

Duration 1 year; nonrenewable.

Additional information This program was established in 1994.

Number awarded 1 or more each year.

Deadline March of each year.

[1028]
STOEL RIVES FIRST-YEAR DIVERSITY FELLOWSHIPS

Stoel Rives LLP
Attn: Professional Development and Diversity Manager
900 S.W. Fifth Avenue, Suite 2600
Portland, OR 97204
(503) 294-9496   Fax: (503) 220-2480
E-mail: lddecker@stoel.com
Web: www.stoel.com/diversity.aspx?Show=2805

Summary To provide financial assistance and work experience to African American and other law students who bring diversity to the profession and are interested in a summer associate position with Stoel Rives.

Eligibility This program is open to first-year law students who contribute to the diversity of the student body at their law school and who will contribute to the diversity of the legal community. Applicants must be willing to accept a summer associate position at Stoel Rives offices in Boise, Portland, and Seattle. Selection is based on academic excellence, leadership, community service, interest in practicing in the Pacific Northwest, and financial need.

Financial data The program provides a stipend of $7,500 to help defray expenses of law school and a salaried summer associate position.

Duration 1 year.

Additional information This program began in 2004.

Number awarded 3 each year: 1 each in Boise, Portland, and Seattle.

Deadline January of each year.

[1029]
SUMMER TRANSPORTATION INTERNSHIP PROGRAM FOR DIVERSE GROUPS

Department of Transportation
Attn: Summer Transportation Internship Program for
    Diverse Groups
HAHR-40, Room E63-433
1200 New Jersey Avenue, S.E.
Washington, DC 20590
(202) 366-2907   E-mail: lafayette.melton@dot.gov
Web: www.fhwa.dot.gov/education/stipdg.htm

Summary To enable African American and other undergraduate, graduate, and law students from diverse groups to gain work experience during the summer at facilities of the U.S. Department of Transportation (DOT).

Eligibility This program is open to all qualified applicants, but it is designed to provide women, persons with disabilities, and members of diverse social and ethnic groups with summer opportunities in transportation. Applicants must be U.S. citizens currently enrolled in a degree-granting program of study at an accredited institution of higher learning at the undergraduate (community or junior college, university, college, or Tribal College or University) or graduate level. Undergraduates must be entering their junior or senior year; students attending a Tribal or community college must have completed their first year of school; law students must be entering their second or third year of school. Students who will graduate during the spring or summer are not eligible unless they have been accepted for enrollment in graduate school. The program accepts applications from students in all majors who are interested in working on transportation-related topics and issues. Preference is given to students with a GPA of 3.0 or higher. Undergraduates must submit a 1-page essay on their transportation interests and how participation in this program will enhance their educational and career plans and goals. Graduate students must submit a writing sample representing their educational and career plans and goals. Law students must submit a legal writing sample.

Financial data The stipend is $4,000 for undergraduates or $5,000 for graduate and law students. The program also provides housing and reimbursement of travel expenses from interns' homes to their assignment location.

Duration 10 weeks during the summer.

Additional information Assignments are at the DOT headquarters in Washington, D.C., a selected modal administration, or selected field offices around the country.

Number awarded 80 to 100 each year.

Deadline January of each year.

[1030]
SYNOD OF LAKES AND PRAIRIES RACIAL ETHNIC SCHOLARSHIPS

Synod of Lakes and Prairies
Attn: Committee on Racial Ethnic Ministry
2115 Cliff Drive
Eagen, MN 55122-3327
(651) 357-1140   Toll Free: (800) 328-1880
Fax: (651) 357-1141 E-mail: mkes@lakesandprairies.org
Web: www.lakesandprairies.org

Summary To provide financial assistance to African Americans and other minority residents of the Presbyterian Church (USA) Synod of Lakes and Prairies who are studying for the ministry at a seminary in any state.

Eligibility This program is open to members of Presbyterian churches who reside within the Synod of Lakes and Prairies (Iowa, Minnesota, Nebraska, North Dakota, South Dakota, and Wisconsin). Applicants must be members of ethnic minority groups studying for the ministry in the Presbyterian Church (USA) or a related ecumenical organization. They must be in good academic standing, making progress toward a degree, and able to demonstrate financial need. Along with their application, they must submit essays of 200 to 500 words each on 1) their vision for the church, and either 2) how their school experience will prepare them to work in the church, or 3) the person who most influenced their commitment to Christ.

Financial data Stipends range from $850 to $3,500.

Duration 1 year.

Number awarded Varies each year; recently, 9 of these scholarships were awarded.

Deadline September of each year.

[1031]
SYNOD OF THE COVENANT ETHNIC THEOLOGICAL SCHOLARSHIPS

Synod of the Covenant
Attn: Ministries in Higher Education
1911 Indianwood Circle, Suite B
Maumee, OH 43537-4063
(419) 754-4050
Toll Free: (800) 848-1030 (within MI and OH)
Fax: (419) 754-4051
Web: www.synodofthecovenant.org

Summary To provide financial assistance to African American and other minority students working on a master's degree at an approved Presbyterian theological institution (with priority given to Presbyterian applicants from Ohio and Michigan).

Eligibility This program is open to ethnic individuals enrolled full time in church vocations programs at approved Presbyterian theological institutions. Priority is given to Presbyterian applicants from the states of Michigan and Ohio. Financial need is considered in the selection process.

Financial data Students may be awarded a maximum of $1,500 on initial application. They may receive up to $2,000 on subsequent applications, with evidence of continuing progress. Funds are made payable to the session for distribution.

Duration Students are eligible to receive scholarships 1 time per year, up to a maximum of 5 years.

Number awarded Varies each year.

Deadline August of each year for fall semester; January of each year for spring semester.

[1032]
TARGETED OPPORTUNITY PROGRAM (TOPJOBS)

Wisconsin Office of State Employment Relations
Attn: Division of Affirmative Action Workforce Planning
101 East Wilson Street, Fourth Floor
P.O. Box 7855
Madison, WI 53707-7855
(608) 267-1005   Fax: (608) 267-1020
E-mail: Claire.Dehnert@wisconsin.gov
Web: oser.state.wi.us/category.asp?linkcatid=342

Summary To provide an opportunity for African Americans, other minorities, women, and persons with disabilities to gain summer work experience with agencies of the state of Wisconsin.

Eligibility This program is open to women, ethnic/racial minorities (Black or African American, Asian, Native Hawaiian or other Pacific Islander, American Indian or Alaska Native, or Hispanic or Latino), and persons with disabilities. Applicants must be juniors, seniors, or graduate students at an accredited 4-year college or university or second-year students in the second year of a 2-year technical or vocational school program. They must be 1) Wisconsin residents enrolled full time at a school in Wisconsin or any other state, or 2) residents of other states who are enrolled full time at a school in Wisconsin.

Financial data Most internships provide a competitive stipend.

Duration Summer months.

Additional information This program was established in 1974. Relevant fields of study include, but are not limited to, the liberal arts and sciences (e.g., history, mathematics, library science, political science, philosophy, physics, psychology, social services, social work, sociology, women's studies); agriculture and natural resources (e.g., animal and dairy science, biology, botany, chemistry, geography, entomology, environmental studies, horticulture, landscape architecture, microbiology, plant pathology, soil science, urban planning, water resources management, wildlife ecology); business (e.g., accounting, business management, economics, finance, human resources, marketing, public administration, real estate); criminal justice; education; health care (including nursing); engineering; information systems and computers; journalism and communications; and law.

Number awarded Varies each year. Since the program was established, it has placed more than 2,500 students with more than 30 different agencies and universities throughout the state.

Deadline February of each year.

[1033]
TDC SCHOLARSHIP

National Association of Black Accountants
Attn: National Scholarship Program
7474 Greenway Center Drive, Suite 1120
Greenbelt, MD 20770
(301) 474-NABA, ext. 114   Fax: (301) 474-3114
E-mail: customerservice@nabainc.org
Web: www.nabainc.org

Summary To provide financial assistance to student members of the National Association of Black Accountants (NABA) who are working on an undergraduate or graduate degree in a field related to accounting.

Eligibility This program is open to NABA members enrolled full time as 1) an undergraduate freshman, sophomore, junior, or first-semester senior majoring in accounting, business, or finance at a 4-year college or university; or 2) a graduate student working on a master's degree in accounting. High school seniors are not eligible. Applicants must have a GPA of 2.0 or higher in their major and 2.5 or higher overall. Selection is based on grades, financial need, and a 500-word autobiography that discusses career objectives, leadership abilities, community activities, and involvement in NABA.

Financial data The stipend is $1,000.

Duration 1 year.

Number awarded 1 each year.

Deadline January of each year.

[1034]
TEACHER QUEST SCHOLARSHIP

Brown Foundation for Educational Equity, Excellence and Research
Attn: Scholarship Committee
1515 S.E. Monroe
Topeka, KS 66615
(785) 235-3939   Fax: (785) 235-1001
E-mail: brownfound@juno.com
Web: brownvboard.org

Summary To provide financial assistance to African Americans and other undergraduate and graduate students of color who are interested in preparing for a teaching career.

Eligibility This program is open to members of minority groups who are enrolled at least half time at an institution of higher education with an accredited teacher education program. Applicants must be enrolled at the undergraduate, graduate, or post-baccalaureate level and have a GPA of 3.0 or higher. Along with their application, they must submit brief essays on 1) their involvement in school, community, and/or other activities and how those activities have prepared them to be an educator; 2) why they aspire to a career in education, their goals, and the level at which they plan to teach; and 3) how they think *Brown v. Board of Education* has influenced their own life experiences. Selection is based on the essays; GPA; school, community, and leisure activities; career plans and goals in education; and recommendations.

Financial data The stipend is $1,000 per year.

Duration 2 years.

Additional information The first Brown Foundation Scholarships were awarded in 1989. The current program replaced the Brown Foundation Academic Scholarships in 2009.

Number awarded Varies each year; recently, 5 of these scholarships were awarded.

Deadline March of each year.

[1035]
TECHNICAL RESEARCH EXHIBITION AWARDS

National Society of Black Engineers
Attn: Programs Department
205 Daingerfield Road
Alexandria, VA 22314
(703) 549-2207   Fax: (703) 683-5312
E-mail: programs@nsbe.org
Web: www.nsbe.org

Summary To recognize and reward outstanding technical papers by undergraduate and graduate student members of the National Society of Black Engineers (NSBE).

Eligibility This competition is open to undergraduate and graduate student members of the society. Candidates must submit technical papers that are between 10 and 20 pages in length and that follow a standard style for such work. All papers must include an abstract and a high degree of technical content. International members who are unable to attend the national convention may also apply through an online procedure. Undergraduate students (both domestic and international) are encouraged to submit results from project-based research as well as theoretical research with an academic or project-based focus. Graduate students (both domestic and international) are encouraged to submit topics demonstrating theoretical research with an academic focus. Domestic applicants must specify whether they wish to participate in a poster session, oral presentation (10 minutes, followed by a 10-minute question and answer session), or both at the NSBE national convention. Based on the abstracts, 50 members are selected to present their research at the convention. In addition, 20 international members (10 undergraduates and 10 graduate students) are selected to have their posters showcased on the NSBE web site. Winners are selected, either from presentations at the convention or from posts on the web site. Selection is based on format (15 points), organization (10 points), technical content (40 points), clarity (10 points), grammar (15 points), and use of visual aids (10 points).

Financial data In the oral presentations category, first prize is $2,000, second $1,000, and third $500. In the posters category, first prize is $1,600, second $800, and third $400. In the international category, first prize is $1,200, second $800, and third $500.

Duration The competition is held annually.

Number awarded 9 cash awards (3 for oral presentations, 3 for posters, and 3 for international submissions) are presented each year.

Deadline January of each year.

[1036]
TEXAS MEDICAL ASSOCIATION MINORITY SCHOLARSHIP PROGRAM

Texas Medical Association
Attn: Educational Loans, Scholarships and Awards
401 West 15th Street
Austin, TX 78701-1680
(512) 370-1300   Toll Free: (800) 880-1300, ext. 1600
Fax: (512) 370-1630   E-mail: info@tmaloanfunds.com
Web: www.tmaloanfunds.com/Content/Template.aspx?id=9

Summary To provide financial assistance to African Americans and members of other underrepresented minority groups from any state who are entering medical school in Texas.

Eligibility This program is open to members of minority groups that are underrepresented in the medical profession (African American, Mexican American, Native American). Applicants must have been accepted at a medical school in Texas; students currently enrolled are not eligible. Along with their application, they must submit a 750-word essay on how they, as a physician, would improve the health of all Texans.

Financial data The stipend is $5,000.

Duration 1 year; renewable.

Additional information This program began in 1999.

Number awarded 1 to 8 each year.

Deadline April of each year.

[1037]
TEXAS YOUNG LAWYERS ASSOCIATION MINORITY SCHOLARSHIP PROGRAM

Texas Young Lawyers Association
Attn: Minority Involvement Committee
1414 Colorado, Suite 502
P.O. Box 12487
Austin, TX 78711-2487
(512) 427-1529   Toll Free: (800) 204-2222, ext. 1529
Fax: (512) 427-4117   E-mail: btrevino@texasbar.com
Web: www.tyla.org

Summary To provide financial assistance to African Americans and other minorities or women residents of any state who are attending law school in Texas.

Eligibility This program is open to members of recognized minority groups, including but not limited to women, African Americans, Hispanic Americans, Asian Americans, and Native Americans. Applicants must be attending an ABA-accredited law school in Texas. Along with their application, they must submit a 2-page essay on either 1) the role the

minority attorney should play in the community and profession, or 2) how attorneys, specifically minority attorneys, can improve the image of the legal profession. Selection is based on academic performance, merit, participation in extracurricular activities inside and outside law school, and financial need.

Financial data The stipend is $1,000.

Duration 1 year.

Number awarded 9 each year: 1 at each accredited law school in Texas.

Deadline October of each year.

[1038]
THOMAS G. NEUSOM SCHOLARSHIPS

Conference of Minority Transportation Officials
Attn: National Scholarship Program
818 18th Street, N.W., Suite 850
Washington, DC 20006
(202) 530-0551   Fax: (202) 530-0617
Web: www.comto.org/news-youth.php

Summary To provide financial assistance for college or graduate school to African American and other members of the Conference of Minority Transportation Officials (COMTO).

Eligibility This program is open to undergraduate and graduate students who have been members of COMTO for at least 1 year. Applicants must be working on a degree in a field related to transportation with a GPA of 2.5 or higher. Along with their application, they must submit a cover letter with a 500-word statement of career goals. Financial need is not considered in the selection process. U.S. citizenship is required.

Financial data The stipend is $5,500. Funds are paid directly to the recipient's college or university.

Duration 1 year.

Additional information COMTO was established in 1971 to promote, strengthen, and expand the roles of minorities in all aspects of transportation. Recipients are expected to attend the COMTO National Scholarship Luncheon.

Number awarded 2 each year.

Deadline April of each year.

[1039]
THOMAS S. WATSON, JR. MEMORIAL SCHOLARSHIP

National Association of Black Accountants
Attn: National Scholarship Program
7474 Greenway Center Drive, Suite 1120
Greenbelt, MD 20770
(301) 474-NABA, ext. 114   Fax: (301) 474-3114
E-mail: customerservice@nabainc.org
Web: www.nabainc.org

Summary To provide financial assistance to student members of the National Association of Black Accountants (NABA) who are working on an undergraduate or graduate degree in a field related to accounting.

Eligibility This program is open to NABA members enrolled full time as 1) an undergraduate freshman, sophomore, junior, or first-semester senior majoring in accounting, business, or finance at a 4-year college or university; or 2) a graduate student working on a master's degree in accounting. High school seniors are not eligible. Applicants must have a GPA of 3.5 or higher in their major and 3.3 or higher overall. Selection is based on grades, financial need, and a 500-word autobiography that discusses career objectives, leadership abilities, community activities, and involvement in NABA.

Financial data The stipend ranges form $1,000 to $3,000.

Duration 1 year.

Number awarded 1 each year.

Deadline January of each year.

[1040]
THOMPSON HINE DIVERSITY SCHOLARSHIP PROGRAM

Thompson Hine LLP
Attn: Manager of New Lawyer Recruiting
3900 Key Center
127 Public Square
Cleveland, OH 44114-1291
(216) 566-5500   Fax: (216) 566-5800
E-mail: info@thompsonhine.com
Web: www.thompsonhine.com

Summary To provide financial assistance and work experience to African American and other minority law students from any state who have been accepted as a summer associate with the law firm of Thompson Hine.

Eligibility This program is open to second-year law students who are members of minority groups as defined by the Equal Employment Opportunity Commission (Native American or Alaskan Native, Asian or Pacific Islander African American or Black, or Hispanic). Applicants must first be offered a summer associateship at an office of Thompson Hine in Atlanta, Cincinnati, Cleveland, Columbus, Dayton, New York, or Washington, D.C. Along with their application, they must submit a writing sample (a legal brief or memorandum prepared for their first-year legal writing course or a prior employer), law school and undergraduate transcripts, a current resume, and a list of at least 2 references.

Financial data The stipend is $10,000. Funds are paid to the student after completing the summer associateship and may be used for tuition and other law school expenses during the third year.

Duration 1 year.

Number awarded 1 each year.

Deadline August of each year.

[1041]
THURGOOD MARSHALL DISSERTATION FELLOWSHIP FOR AFRICAN-AMERICAN SCHOLARS

Dartmouth College
Attn: Office of Graduate Studies
6062 Wentworth Hall, Room 304
Hanover, NH 03755-3526
(603) 646-2106   Fax: (603) 646-8762
Web: graduate.dartmouth.edu

Summary To provide funding to African American and other doctoral students who are interested in working on their dissertation at Dartmouth College.

Eligibility This program is open to doctoral candidates who have completed all requirements for the Ph.D. except the dissertation and are planning a career in higher education.

Applicants must be African Americans or other graduate students with a demonstrated commitment and ability to advance educational diversity. They must be interested in working on their dissertation at Dartmouth College. All academic fields that are taught in the Dartmouth undergraduate Arts and Sciences curriculum are eligible. Selection is based on academic achievement and promise; demonstrated commitment to increasing opportunities for underrepresented minorities and increasing cross-racial understanding; and potential for serving as an advocate and mentor for minority undergraduate and graduate students.

Financial data The stipend is $25,000. In addition, fellows receive office space, library privileges, and a $2,500 research allowance.

Duration 1 year, beginning in September.

Additional information The fellows are affiliated with a department or program at Dartmouth College. Fellows are expected to be in residence at Dartmouth College for the duration of the program and to complete their dissertation during that time. They are also expected to teach a course, either as the primary instructor or as part of a team.

Number awarded 1 each year.

Deadline January of each year.

[1042]
TONKON TORP FIRST-YEAR DIVERSITY FELLOWSHIP PROGRAM

Tonkon Torp LLP
Attn: Director of Attorney Recruiting
1600 Pioneer Tower
888 S.W. Fifth Avenue
Portland, OR 97204
(503) 221-1440   Fax: (503) 972-3760
E-mail: Loree.Devery@tonkon.com
Web: www.tonkon.com/Careers/-1LDiversityFellowship.html

Summary To provide financial assistance and summer work experience in Portland, Oregon to African American and other first-year minority law students from any state.

Eligibility This program is open to members of racial and ethnic minority groups who are currently enrolled in their first year at an ABA-accredited law school. Applicants must be able to demonstrate 1) a record of academic achievement that indicates a strong likelihood of a successful career during the remainder of law school and in the legal profession; 2) a commitment to practice law in Portland, Oregon following graduation from law school; and 3) an ability to contribute meaningfully to the diversity of the law school student body and, after entering the legal profession, the legal community. They are not required to disclose their financial circumstances, but a demonstrated need for financial assistance may be taken into consideration.

Financial data The recipient is offered a paid summer associateship at Tonkon Torp in Portland, Oregon for the summer following the first year of law school and, depending on the outcome of that experience, may be invited for a second summer following the second year of law school. Following the successful completion of that second associateship, the recipient is awarded an academic scholarship of $7,500 for the third year of law school.

Duration The program covers 2 summers and 1 academic year.

Additional information For 2 weeks during the summer, the fellow works in the legal department of Portland General Electric Company, Oregon's largest electric utility and a client of the sponsoring firm.

Number awarded 1 each year.

Deadline January of each year.

[1043]
TOWNSEND AND TOWNSEND AND CREW DIVERSITY SCHOLARSHIP

Townsend and Townsend and Crew LLP
Attn: Diversity Committee
Two Embarcadero Center, Eighth Floor
San Francisco, CA 94111-3834
(415) 576-0200   Fax: (415) 576-0300
Web: www.townsend.com/Who/Who-Diversity

Summary To provide financial assistance to women and African American or minority students attending law school to prepare for a career in patent law.

Eligibility This program is open to students enrolled at ABA-accredited law schools who are women or members of minority groups that have historically been underrepresented in the field of patent law (American Indians/Alaskan Natives, Blacks/African Americans, Hispanics/Latinos, and Asian Americans/Pacific Islanders). Applicants must have an undergraduate or graduate degree in a field that will help prepare them for a career in patent law (e.g., life sciences, engineering). They must have a demonstrated commitment to preparing for a career in patent law in a city in which the sponsoring law firm has an office. Selection is based on academic performance; work experience related to science, engineering, or patent law; community service; and demonstrated leadership ability.

Financial data The stipend is $2,000 per year.

Duration 1 year; recipients may reapply.

Additional information This program was established in 2005. Townsend and Townsend and Crew has offices in San Francisco, Palo Alto (California), Denver, Walnut Creek (California), San Diego, Seattle, Tokyo, and Washington, D.C.

Number awarded Varies each year; recently, 11 of these scholarships were awarded.

Deadline April of each year.

[1044]
TRAILBLAZER SCHOLARSHIPS

Conference of Minority Transportation Officials
Attn: National Scholarship Program
818 18th Street, N.W., Suite 850
Washington, DC 20006
(202) 530-0551   Fax: (202) 530-0617
Web: www.comto.org/news-youth.php

Summary To provide financial assistance to African Americans and other undergraduate and graduate minority students working on a degree in a field related to transportation.

Eligibility This program is open to undergraduate and graduate students who are working on a degree in a field related to transportation with a GPA of 2.5 or higher. Along with their application, they must submit a cover letter with a 500-word statement of career goals. Financial need is not considered in the selection process. U.S. citizenship is required.

Financial data The stipend is $2,500. Funds are paid directly to the recipient's college or university.

Duration 1 year.

Additional information The Conference of Minority Transportation Officials (COMTO) was established in 1971 to promote, strengthen, and expand the roles of minorities in all aspects of transportation. Recipients are expected to attend the COMTO National Scholarship Luncheon.

Number awarded 2 each year.

Deadline April of each year.

[1045]
TRAVIS C. TOMLIN MEMORIAL SCHOLARSHIP

National Association of Black Accountants
Attn: National Scholarship Program
7474 Greenway Center Drive, Suite 1120
Greenbelt, MD 20770
(301) 474-NABA, ext. 114   Fax: (301) 474-3114
E-mail: customerservice@nabainc.org
Web: www.nabainc.org

Summary To provide financial assistance to student members of the National Association of Black Accountants (NABA) who are working on an undergraduate or graduate degree in a field related to accounting.

Eligibility This program is open to NABA members enrolled full time as 1) an undergraduate freshman, sophomore, junior, or first-semester senior majoring in accounting, business, or finance at a 4-year college or university; or 2) a graduate student working on a master's degree in accounting. High school seniors are not eligible. Applicants must have a GPA of 3.5 or higher in their major and 3.3 or higher overall. Selection is based on grades, financial need, and a 500-word autobiography that discusses career objectives, leadership abilities, community activities, and involvement in NABA.

Financial data The stipend ranges from $1,500 to $2,000.

Duration 1 year.

Number awarded 1 each year.

Deadline January of each year.

[1046]
TWIN CITIES CHAPTER NBMBAA GRADUATE MANAGEMENT SCHOLARSHIPS

National Black MBA Association-Twin Cities Chapter
Attn: Scholarship Committee Chair
P.O. Box 2709
Minneapolis, MN 55402
(651) 734-0808   E-mail: scholarships@nbmbaatc.org
Web: www.nbmbaatc.org/education.htm

Summary To provide financial assistance to African American students from Minnesota who are interested in working on a master's degree in business administration.

Eligibility This program is open to African and African American students enrolled in a graduate business or management program; this includes undergraduate seniors who are about to enter graduate school. Applicants must be residents of and/or attending school in Minnesota. Along with their application, they must submit a 2-page essay on a topic that changes annually but relates to African Americans and business. Selection is based on the essay, career aspirations, GPA, activities, and a 150-word biography that covers their background, experiences, accomplishments, and career goals.

Financial data Stipends range from $1,000 to $5,000.
Duration 1 year.
Number awarded 3 to 5 each year.
Deadline July of each year.

[1047]
TWIN CITIES CHAPTER NBMBAA PHD GRADUATE SCHOLARSHIP

National Black MBA Association-Twin Cities Chapter
Attn: Scholarship Committee Chair
P.O. Box 2709
Minneapolis, MN 55402
(651) 734-0808   E-mail: scholarships@nbmbaatc.org
Web: www.nbmbaatc.org/education.htm

Summary To provide financial assistance to African American students from Minnesota who are interested in working on a Ph.D. degree in business administration.

Eligibility This program is open to African and African American students enrolled full time in a doctoral business or management program; this includes students who have accepted admission to a Ph.D. program. Applicants must be residents of and/or attending school in Minnesota. Along with their application, they must submit a 3-page essay on a topic that changes annually but relates to African Americans and business. Selection is based on the essay, career aspirations, GPA, activities, and a 150-word biography that covers their background, experiences, accomplishments, and career goals.

Financial data The stipend is $2,000.
Duration 1 year.
Number awarded 1 each year.
Deadline July of each year.

[1048]
UCSB BLACK STUDIES DISSERTATION FELLOWSHIPS

University of California at Santa Barbara
Attn: Department of Black Studies
South Hall, Room 3631
Santa Barbara, CA 93106-3150
(805) 893-3800   Fax: (805) 893-3597
E-mail: dnash@blackstudies.ucsb.edu
Web: www.blackstudies.ucsb.edu

Summary To enable doctoral candidates in African, Caribbean, and African American studies to complete their dissertations while teaching at the University of California at Santa Barbara (UCSB).

Eligibility This program is open to students currently enrolled in a doctoral program at an accredited university who have completed all requirements for the Ph.D. except the dissertation. Applicants should be conducting research that focuses on intersections of race, class, gender, and sexuality in African, Caribbean, African American, or Diasporic studies. They must be interested in working on their dissertation at UCSB.

Financial data The fellowship provides a stipend of $22,000, office space, and library privileges.
Duration 9 months.

Additional information Fellows are expected to work on their dissertation, teach 1 undergraduate course in their specified area of research, and present 1 public lecture during the fellowship period. Recipients must be in residence at UCSB for the entire fellowship period.

Number awarded 2 each year.
Deadline February of each year.

[1049]
UNCF/MERCK GRADUATE SCIENCE RESEARCH DISSERTATION FELLOWSHIPS

United Negro College Fund
Attn: Merck Science Initiative
8260 Willow Oaks Corporate Drive, Suite 110
P.O. Box 10444
Fairfax, VA 22031-4511
(703) 205-3503   Fax: (703) 205-3574
E-mail: uncfmerck@uncf.org
Web: umsi.uncf.org

Summary To provide financial assistance to African American graduate students who are interested in pursuing biomedical study and research.

Eligibility This program is open to African American graduate students currently enrolled full time in a Ph.D. or equivalent doctoral program in the life or physical sciences or in engineering. Candidates for an M.D./Ph.D. degree are also eligible. Applicants must be U.S. citizens or permanent residents within 1 to 3 years of completing their dissertation. Selection is based on 1) the applicant's academic ability and record of accomplishment, and 2) the soundness of the proposed doctoral research.

Financial data The total award is $53,500, including up to $43,500 as a stipend for the student (the maximum stipend is $30,000 for any 12-month period) and a research grant up to $10,000. Funds must be used for completing course work, conducting research, and preparing the dissertation. Fringe benefits up to $5,350 are also allowed.

Duration 12 to 24 months.

Additional information This program, established in 1995, is funded by the Merck Company Foundation.

Number awarded At least 12 each year.
Deadline December of each year.

[1050]
UNDERREPRESENTED MINORITY DENTAL STUDENT SCHOLARSHIP

American Dental Association
Attn: ADA Foundation
211 East Chicago Avenue
Chicago, IL 60611
(312) 440-2547   Fax: (312) 440-3526
E-mail: adaf@ada.org
Web: www.ada.org/ada/adaf/grants/scholarships.asp

Summary To provide financial assistance to African Americans and other underrepresented minorities who wish to enter the field of dentistry.

Eligibility This program is open to U.S. citizens from a minority group that is currently underrepresented in the dental profession: Native American, African American, or Hispanic. Applicants must have a GPA of 3.0 or higher and be entering their second year of study at a dental school in the

United States accredited by the Commission on Dental Accreditation. Selection is based upon academic achievement, a written summary of personal and professional goals, letters of reference, and demonstrated financial need.

Financial data The maximum stipend is $2,500. Funds are sent directly to the student's financial aid office to be used to cover tuition, fees, books, supplies, and living expenses.

Duration 1 year.

Additional information This program, established in 1991, is supported by the Harry J. Bosworth Company, Colgate-Palmolive, Sunstar Americas, and Procter & Gamble Company. Students receiving a full scholarship from any other source are ineligible to receive this scholarship.

Number awarded At least 10 each year.

Deadline October of each year.

[1051]
UNITARIAN UNIVERSALIST ASSOCIATION INCENTIVE GRANTS

Unitarian Universalist Association
Attn: Ministerial Credentialing Office
25 Beacon Street
Boston, MA 02108-2800
(617) 948-6403   Fax: (617) 742-2875
E-mail: mco@uua.org
Web: www.uua.org

Summary To provide financial aid to African Americans and other persons of color who the Unitarian Universalist Association is interested in attracting to the ministry.

Eligibility These grants are offered to persons of color who the association is particularly interested in attracting to Unitarian Universalist ministry to promote racial, cultural, or class diversity. Applicants must be in their first year of study. Decisions regarding potential recipients are made in consultation with the schools. Selection is based on merit.

Financial data A stipend is awarded (amount not specified).

Duration 1 year; nonrenewable.

Additional information In subsequent years, recipients may apply for the association's General Financial Aid Grants.

Number awarded Varies each year.

Deadline April of each year.

[1052]
UNITED METHODIST WOMEN OF COLOR SCHOLARS PROGRAM

United Methodist Church
Attn: General Board of Higher Education and Ministry
Office of Loans and Scholarships
1001 19th Avenue South
P.O. Box 340007
Nashville, TN 37203-0007
(615) 340-7344   Fax: (615) 340-7367
E-mail: umscholar@gbhem.org
Web: www.gbhem.org/loansandscholarships

Summary To provide financial assistance to African American Methodist women, and other women of color, who are working on a doctoral degree to prepare for a career as an educator at a United Methodist seminary.

Eligibility This program is open to women of color (have at least 1 parent who is African American, African, Hispanic, Asian, Native American, Alaska Native, or Pacific Islander) who have an M.Div. degree. Applicants must have been active, full members of a United Methodist Church for at least 3 years prior to applying. They must be enrolled full time in a degree program at the Ph.D. or Th.D. level to prepare for a career teaching at a United Methodist seminary.

Financial data The maximum stipend is $10,000 per year.

Duration 1 year; may be renewed up to 3 additional years.

Number awarded Varies each year; recently, 10 of these scholarships were awarded.

Deadline January of each year.

[1053]
UNIVERSITY OF NORTH CAROLINA CAMPUS SCHOLARSHIPS

North Carolina State Education Assistance Authority
Attn: Scholarship and Grant Services
10 Alexander Drive
P.O. Box 14103
Research Triangle Park, NC 27709-4103
(919) 549-8614   Toll Free: (800) 700-1775
Fax: (919) 549-8481   E-mail: information@ncseaa.edu
Web: www.ncseaa.edu

Summary To provide financial assistance to African Americans and other students at University of North Carolina (UNC) constituent institutions whose enrollment contributes to the diversity of the undergraduate or graduate population.

Eligibility This program is open to undergraduate and doctoral students who are enrolled or planning to enroll full time at 1 of the 16 UNC institutions. Applicants must have graduated in the top 40% of their high school class, have a weighted GPA of 3.0 or higher, have an SAT score higher than the SAT score of the previous freshman class, and have a record of positive involvement in extracurricular activities. They must be able to demonstrate "exceptional financial need." Their enrollment must "contribute to the intellectual experiences and diversity of the undergraduate population." A portion of the funds are reserved specifically for American Indian students who can provide evidence of tribal affiliation.

Financial data The amount of the award depends upon the financial need of the recipient and the availability of funds; recently, stipends averaged more than $1,900.

Duration 1 year; may be renewed.

Additional information This program was established in 2002 as a replacement for the former North Carolina Minority Presence Grants, North Carolina Freshmen Scholars Program, North Carolina Incentive Scholarship Program, North Carolina Legislative College Opportunity Program, and North Carolina Incentive Scholarship and Grant Program for Native Americans. Students must submit applications to the constituent institution's financial aid office rather than directly to the North Carolina State Education Assistance Authority.

Number awarded Varies each year; recently, a total of 2,793 of these scholarships, with a total value of $5,435,826, were awarded.

Deadline Deadline dates vary; check with the appropriate constituent institution.

[1054]
USA FUNDS ACCESS TO EDUCATION SCHOLARSHIPS

Scholarship America
Attn: Scholarship Management Services
One Scholarship Way
P.O. Box 297
St. Peter, MN 56082
(507) 931-1682   Toll Free: (800) 537-4180
Fax: (507) 931-9168   E-mail: scholarship@usafunds.org
Web: www.usafunds.org

Summary To provide financial assistance to undergraduate and graduate students, especially those who are African Americans, members of other minority groups, and students with physical disabilities.

Eligibility This program is open to high school seniors and graduates who plan to enroll or are already enrolled in full- or half-time undergraduate or full-time graduate course work at an accredited 2- or 4-year college, university, or vocational/technical school. GED recipients are also eligible. Up to 50% of the awards are targeted at students who have a documented physical disability or are a member of an ethnic minority group, including but not limited to Native Hawaiian, Alaskan Native, Black/African American, Asian, Pacific Islander, American Indian, Hispanic/Latino, or multiracial. Residents of all 50 states, the District of Columbia, Puerto Rico, Guam, the U.S. Virgin Islands, and all U.S. territories and commonwealths are eligible. Applicants must also be U.S. citizens or eligible noncitizens and come from a family with an annual adjusted gross income of $35,000 or less. In addition to financial need, selection is based on past academic performance and future potential, leadership and participation in school and community activities, work experience, career and educational aspirations and goals, and unusual personal or family circumstances.

Financial data The stipend is $1,500 per year for full-time undergraduate or graduate students or $750 per year for half-time undergraduate students. Funds are paid jointly to the student and the school.

Duration 1 year; may be renewed until the student receives a final degree or certificate or until the total award to a student reaches $6,000, whichever comes first. Renewal requires the recipient to maintain a GPA of 2.5 or higher.

Additional information This program, established in 2000, is sponsored by USA Funds.

Number awarded Varies each year; recently, a total of $3.2 million was available for this program.

Deadline February of each year.

[1055]
UUA/DAVID POHL SCHOLARSHIP

Unitarian Universalist Association
Attn: Ministerial Credentialing Office
25 Beacon Street
Boston, MA 02108-2800
(617) 948-6403   Fax: (617) 742-2875
E-mail: mco@uua.org
Web: www.uua.org

Summary To provide financial assistance to seminary students (especially African Americans and other students of color) who are preparing for the Unitarian Universalist (UU) ministry.

Eligibility This program is open to seminary students who are enrolled full or at least half time in a UU ministerial training program with aspirant or candidate status. Applicants must be citizens of the United States or Canada. Priority is given first to those who have demonstrated outstanding ministerial ability and secondarily to students with the greatest financial need (especially persons of color).

Financial data The stipend ranges from $1,000 to $11,000 per year.

Duration 1 year.

Number awarded 1 each year.

Deadline April of each year.

[1056]
VAID FELLOWSHIPS

National Gay and Lesbian Task Force
Attn: The Task Force Policy Institute
80 Maiden Lane, Suite 1504
New York, NY 10038
(212) 604-9830   Fax: (212) 604-9831
E-mail: ngltf@ngltf.org
Web: www.thetaskforce.org

Summary To provide work experience to undergraduate and graduate students (particularly African Americans and other minorities) who are interested in participating in the leadership of people of color in the progressive movement for gay, lesbian, bisexual, and transgender (GLBT) equality.

Eligibility Applicants must be enrolled in a degree program at least half time as a law, graduate, or undergraduate student or have successfully completed a law, graduate, or undergraduate degree within the preceding 12 months. They should have 1) a desire to work in a multicultural environment where commitment to diversity based on race, ethnic origin, gender, age, sexual orientation, and physical ability is an important institutional value; 2) demonstrated leadership in progressive and/or GLBT communities; 3) extensive research, writing, and critical thinking skills; 4) knowledge of, and commitment to, GLBT issues; and 5) computer proficiency in word processing, database work, e-mail, and Internet research. The program supports and recognizes the leadership of people of color and other emerging leaders in public policy, legal, and social science research.

Financial data The stipend ranges from $200 to $400 per week ($10 per hour). Fellows are responsible for their own housing and living expenses.

Duration Summer fellowships are 40 hours per week and spring/fall fellowships are 20 hours per week.

Additional information The Policy Institute of the National Gay and Lesbian Task Force (NGLTF), founded in 1995, is the largest think tank in the United States engaged in research, policy analysis, and strategic action to advance equality and understanding of GLBT people. Its primary programs are the racial and economic justice initiative, the family policy program, and the aging initiative. In addition to their primary roles of providing research and analysis, all 3 programs work closely with NGLTF colleagues in Washington, D.C. and other allies on advocacy and legislative efforts to actively change laws and policies affecting GLBT people.

Number awarded 3 fellows are selected each session.

Deadline April for the summer, July for the fall, and November for the spring.

[1057]
VARNUM DIVERSITY AND INCLUSION SCHOLARSHIPS FOR LAW STUDENTS

Varnum LLP
Attn: Scholarships
333 Bridge Street N.W.
P.O. Box 352
Grand Rapids, MI 49501-0352
(616) 336-6620   Fax: (616) 336-7000
E-mail: ewskaggs@varnumlaw.com
Web: www.varnumlaw.com

Summary   To provide financial assistance to African American and other law students from Michigan who will contribute to diversity in the legal profession.

Eligibility   This program is open to Michigan residents accepted or currently enrolled at an accredited law school in any state or residents of other states attending an accredited Michigan law school. Applicants must be members of an ethnic or racial minority or demonstrate a significant commitment to issues of diversity and inclusion. They must have a GPA of 3.0 or higher. Along with their application, they must submit a 750-word statement on their efforts to promote greater ethnic or racial diversity and inclusion within the legal profession and/or their community.

Financial data   The stipend is $4,000.

Duration   1 year.

Number awarded   2 each year.

Deadline   January of each year.

[1058]
VASHTI TURLEY MURPHY SCHOLARSHIP PROGRAM

Delta Sigma Theta Sorority, Inc.
Attn: Scholarship and Standards Committee Chair
1707 New Hampshire Avenue, N.W.
Washington, DC 20009
(202) 986-2400   Fax: (202) 986-2513
E-mail: dstemail@deltasigmatheta.org
Web: www.deltasigmatheta.org

Summary   To provide financial assistance to members of Delta Sigma Theta who are interested in working on a graduate degree to prepare for a career in ministry.

Eligibility   This program is open to graduating college seniors and graduate students who are interested in working on a master's or doctoral degree to prepare for a career in ministry. Applicants must be active, dues-paying members of Delta Sigma Theta. Selection is based on meritorious achievement.

Financial data   The stipends range from $1,000 to $2,000. The funds may be used to cover tuition, fees, and living expenses.

Duration   1 year; may be renewed for 1 additional year.

Additional information   This sponsor is a traditionally African American social sorority. The application fee is $20.

Deadline   April of each year.

[1059]
VERIZON NSBE CORPORATE SCHOLARSHIPS

National Society of Black Engineers
Attn: Programs Department
205 Daingerfield Road
Alexandria, VA 22314
(703) 549-2207   Fax: (703) 683-5312
E-mail: scholarships@nsbe.org
Web: www.nsbe.org

Summary   To provide financial assistance to members of the National Society of Black Engineers (NSBE) who are working on an undergraduate or graduate degree in specified fields of science, engineering, or business.

Eligibility   This program is open to members of the society who are undergraduate or graduate students working on a degree in computer engineering, computer science, electric engineering, wireless communication, or business (M.B.A. degree only). Applicants must have a GPA of 3.0 or higher and a demonstrated interest in employment with Verizon and its affiliated companies in the fields of wireless, business, or telecommunications.

Financial data   Stipends are $6,500 or $5,000.

Duration   1 year.

Additional information   This program is supported by Verizon.

Number awarded   3 each year: 1 at $6,500 and 2 at $5,000.

Deadline   January of each year.

[1060]
VERNE LAMARR LYONS MEMORIAL SCHOLARSHIP

National Association of Social Workers
Attn: NASW Foundation
750 First Street, N.E., Suite 700
Washington, DC 20002-4241
(202) 408-8600, ext. 504   Fax: (202) 336-8292
E-mail: naswfoundation@naswdc.org
Web: www.naswfoundation.org/lyons.asp

Summary   To provide financial assistance to African American and other students interested in working on a master's degree in social work.

Eligibility   This program is open to members of the National Association of Social Workers (NASW) who have applied to or been accepted into an accredited M.S.W. program. Applicants must have demonstrated a commitment to working with African American communities and have an interest and/or demonstrated ability in health/mental health practice. They must have the potential for completing an M.S.W. program and have a GPA of 3.0 or higher.

Financial data   The stipend is $1,000 per year.

Duration   Up to 1 year; may be renewed for 1 additional year.

Number awarded   1 each year.

Deadline   March of each year.

[1061]
VICTORIA NAMAN GRADUATE SCHOOL SCHOLARSHIP

Delta Sigma Theta Sorority, Inc.-Denver Alumnae
  Chapter
Attn: Scholarship Committee
P.O. Box 7330
Denver, CO 80207
(303) 371-7112   E-mail: info@milehighdst.com
Web: www.milehighdst.com/EducationalDevelopment.aspx

Summary   To provide financial assistance to female African American residents of Colorado who are interested in attending graduate school in any state.

Eligibility   This program is open to African American women who are residents of Colorado and enrolled or planning to enroll at a graduate school in any state. Applicants must have a GPA of 3.0 or higher. They must submit an essay of at least 200 words on their personal goals, academic achievements, and plans for making a difference in their community. Selection is based on the essay, financial need, scholastic record, 2 letters of recommendation, and an interview.

Financial data   Stipends range from $1,000 to $3,000.

Duration   1 year.

Number awarded   1 or more each year.

Deadline   March of each year.

[1062]
VINSON & ELKINS DIVERSITY FELLOWSHIPS

Vinson & Elkins L.L.P.
Attn: Attorney Initiatives Assistant
1001 Fannin Street, Suite 2500
Houston, TX 77002-6760
(713) 758-2222   Fax: (713) 758-2346
Web: www.velaw.com/careers/law_students.aspx?id=602

Summary   To provide financial assistance to African American and other minority law students who are interested in working in a law firm setting.

Eligibility   This program is open to students who are entering the second year at an ABA-accredited law school and are members of a racial or ethnic group that has been historically underrepresented in the legal profession (Asian, American Indian/Alaskan Native, Black/African American, Hispanic/Latino, multiracial, or Native Hawaiian or other Pacific Islander). Applicants must be able to demonstrate a strong undergraduate and law school record, excellent writing skills, and an interest in working in a law firm setting.

Financial data   The stipend is $3,500 per year.

Duration   2 years (the second and third year of law school).

Additional information   Fellows are also considered for summer associate positions at the sponsor's offices in Austin, Dallas, or Houston following their first year of law school.

Number awarded   4 each year.

Deadline   January of each year.

[1063]
VIRGINIA TEACHING SCHOLARSHIP LOAN PROGRAM

Virginia Department of Education
Division of Teacher Education and Licensure
Attn: Director of Teacher Education
P.O. Box 2120
Richmond, VA 23218-2120
(804) 371-2475   Toll Free: (800) 292-3820
Fax: (804) 786-6759
E-mail: JoAnne.Carver@doe.virginia.gov
Web: www.doe.virginia.gov

Summary   To provide funding to upper-division and graduate students in Virginia (especially African Americans and other minorities) who are interested in a career in teaching.

Eligibility   This program is open to Virginia residents who are enrolled full or part time as a sophomore, junior, senior, or graduate student in a state-approved teacher preparation program in Virginia with a GPA of 2.7 or higher. Applicants must agree to engage in full-time teaching following graduation in 1) designated teacher shortage areas within Virginia; 2) a school with a high concentration of students eligible for free or reduced lunch; 3) within a school division with a shortage of teachers; 4) in a rural or urban region of the state with a teacher shortage; or 5) in a career and technical education discipline. Males interested in teaching in the elementary grades and people of color in all teaching areas also qualify.

Financial data   The scholarship/loan is $3,720 per year. Loans are forgiven at the rate of $1,000 for each semester the recipient teaches in designated teacher shortage areas. If the recipient fails to fulfill the teaching service requirement, the loan must be repaid with interest.

Duration   1 year; may be renewed 1 additional year.

Additional information   Critical shortage teaching areas in Virginia are currently identified as all areas of special education (severe disturbances, hearing impairment, learning disabilities, mental retardation, severe disabilities, visual impairment, early childhood special education, emotional disturbance, and speech and language disorders), career and technical education (including technology education, trade and industrial education, business education, and family and consumer sciences), mathematics (6-12), foreign language (preK-12), English (6-12), middle school (6-8), elementary education (preK-6), science (6-12), health and physical education (preK-12), and school counselor (preK-12).

Number awarded   Varies each year; recently, 265 of these scholarship/loans were granted, including 111 in elementary education, 14 in English, 8 in foreign languages, 2 in history and social science, 18 in mathematics, 22 in middle grades, 2 in science, 30 in special education, 20 for males in elementary grades, 4 for males in middle grades, and 34 for people of color.

Deadline   Deadline not specified.

[1064]
VISITING RESEARCH INTERNSHIP PROGRAM

Harvard Medical School
Office for Diversity and Community Partnership
Attn: Minority Faculty Development Program
164 Longwood Avenue, Second Floor
Boston, MA 02115-5810
(617) 432-1892   Fax: (617) 432-3834
E-mail: pfdd_dcp@hms.harvard.edu
Web: www.mfdp.med.harvard.edu

Summary   To provide an opportunity for medical students, especially African Americans and other underrepresented minorities, to conduct a mentored research internship at Harvard Medical School during the summer.

Eligibility   This program is open to first- and second-year medical students, particularly underrepresented minority and/or disadvantaged individuals, in good standing at accredited U.S. medical schools. Applicants must be interested in conducting a summer research project at Harvard Medical School under the mentorship of a faculty advisor. They must be interested in a research and health-related career, especially in clinical or translational research or research that transforms scientific discoveries arising from laboratory, clinical, or population studies into clinical or population-based applications to improve health. U.S. citizenship, nationality, or permanent resident status is required.

Financial data   Participants receive a stipend (amount not specified), housing, and limited reimbursement of transportation costs to Boston.

Duration   8 weeks during the summer.

Additional information   This program, established in 2008, is funded by the National Center for Research Resources of the National Institutes of Health NIH). It is a joint enterprise of Harvard University, its 10 schools, its 17 Academic Healthcare Centers, Boston College School of Nursing, MIT, the Cambridge Health Alliance, and other community partners. Interns attend weekly seminars with Harvard faculty focusing on such topics as research methodology, health disparities, ethics, and career paths. They also have the opportunity to participate in offerings of other Harvard Medical School programs, such a career development seminars and networking dinners.

Number awarded   Varies each year.

Deadline   February of each year.

[1065]
VISUAL TASK FORCE SCHOLARSHIPS

National Association of Black Journalists
Attn: Program Coordinator
8701-A Adelphi Road
Adelphi, MD 20783-1716
(301) 445-7100, ext. 108   Toll Free: (866) 479-NABJ
Fax: (301) 445-7101   E-mail: nabj@nabj.org
Web: www.nabj.org

Summary   To provide financial assistance to undergraduate or graduate student members of the National Association of Black Journalists (NABJ) who are interested in a career in visual journalism.

Eligibility   This program is open to African American undergraduate or graduate students who are currently attending an accredited 4-year college or university. Applicants must be majoring in visual journalism, have a GPA of 2.75 or higher,

have experience working on their campus newspaper or TV studio, and have held an internship. They must be NABJ members. Along with their application, they must submit samples of their work, an official college transcript, 2 letters of recommendation, a resume, and a 500- to 800-word essay describing their accomplishments as a student journalist, their career goals, and their financial need.

Financial data   The stipend is $1,250. Funds are paid directly to the recipient's college or university.

Duration   1 year; nonrenewable.

Number awarded   2 each year.

Deadline   April of each year.

[1066]
WALTER AND VICTORIA SMITH AWARD

National Association of Black Accountants
Attn: National Scholarship Program
7474 Greenway Center Drive, Suite 1120
Greenbelt, MD 20770
(301) 474-NABA, ext. 114   Fax: (301) 474-3114
E-mail: customerservice@nabainc.org
Web: www.nabainc.org

Summary   To provide financial assistance to student members of the National Association of Black Accountants (NABA) who are working on an undergraduate or graduate degree in a field related to accounting.

Eligibility   This program is open to NABA members enrolled full time as 1) an undergraduate freshman, sophomore, junior, or first-semester senior majoring in accounting, business, or finance at a 4-year college or university; or 2) a graduate student working on a master's degree in accounting. High school seniors are not eligible. Applicants must have a GPA of 3.5 or higher in their major and 3.3 or higher overall. Selection is based on grades, financial need, and a 500-word autobiography that discusses career objectives, leadership abilities, community activities, and involvement in NABA.

Financial data   The stipend is $1,000.

Duration   1 year.

Number awarded   1 each year.

Deadline   January of each year.

[1067]
WALTER VAUGHN EXCELLENCE IN HUMAN RESOURCES SCHOLARSHIP

National Forum for Black Public Administrators
Attn: Scholarship Program
777 North Capitol Street, N.E., Suite 807
Washington, DC 20002
(202) 408-9300, ext. 112   Fax: (202) 408-8558
E-mail: vreed@nfbpa.org
Web: www.nfbpa.org/i4a/pages/index.cfm?pageid=3630

Summary   To provide financial assistance to African Americans working on an undergraduate or graduate degree in public administration with an emphasis on human resource management.

Eligibility   This program is open to African American undergraduate and graduate students preparing for a career in public service. Applicants must be working full time on a degree in public administration, human resource management, or a related field. They must have a GPA of 3.0 or higher, a record of involvement in extracurricular activities (excluding athletics), excellent interpersonal and leadership abilities, and strong oral and written communication skills. Along with their application, they must submit a 3-page autobiographical essay that includes their academic and career goals and objectives. First consideration is given to applicants who are not currently receiving other financial aid.

Financial data   The stipend is $2,500.

Duration   1 year.

Additional information   This program is sponsored by CPS Human Resource Services. Recipients are required to attend the sponsor's annual conference to receive their scholarship; limited hotel and air accommodations are arranged and provided.

Number awarded   1 each year.

Deadline   February of each year.

[1068]
WARNER NORCROSS & JUDD LAW SCHOOL SCHOLARSHIP

Grand Rapids Community Foundation
Attn: Education Program Officer
185 Oakes Street S.W.
Grand Rapids, MI 49503-4008
(616) 454-1751, ext. 103   Fax: (616) 454-6455
E-mail: rbishop@grfoundation.org
Web: www.grfoundation.org/scholarships

Summary   To provide financial assistance to African Americans and other minorities from Michigan who are attending law school.

Eligibility   This program is open to students of color who are attending or planning to attend an accredited law school. Applicants must be residents of Michigan or attending law school in the state. They must be U.S. citizens or permanent residents and have a GPA of 2.5 or higher. Financial need is considered in the selection process.

Financial data   The stipend is $5,000. Funds are paid directly to the recipient's institution.

Duration   1 year.

Additional information   Funding for this program is provided by the law firm Warner Norcross & Judd LLP.

Number awarded   1 each year.

Deadline   March of each year.

[1069]
WASHINGTON DIVERSITY FELLOWSHIPS IN ENVIRONMENTAL LAW

American Bar Association
Attn: Section of Environment, Energy, and Resources
321 North Clark Street
Chicago, IL 60654-7598
(312) 988-5602   Fax: (312) 988-5572
E-mail: jonusaid@staff.abanet.org
Web: www.abanet.org

Summary   To provide funding to African American and other law students from underrepresented groups who are interested in working on a summer project in environmental, energy, or resources law in Washington.

Eligibility   This program is open to first- and second-year law students and third-year night students who are members of underrepresented and underserved groups, such as

minority or low-income populations. Students may be residents of any state and attending school in any state; preference is given to residents of Washington and to students who are enrolled at law schools in Washington or who have a strong interest in the state. Applicants must be interested in working during the summer at a government agency or public interest organization on a project in Washington in the fields of environmental, energy, or resources law. Selection is based on interest in environmental issues, academic record, personal qualities, and leadership abilities.

Financial data   The stipend is $5,000.

Duration   8 to 10 weeks during the summer.

Number awarded   1 each year.

Deadline   February of each year.

[1070]
WATSON MIDWIVES OF COLOR SCHOLARSHIP

American College of Nurse-Midwives
Attn: ACNM Foundation, Inc.
8403 Colesville Road, Suite 1550
Silver Spring, MD 20910-6374
(240) 485-1850   Fax: (240) 485-1818
Web: www.midwife.org/foundation_award.cfm

Summary   To provide financial assistance for midwifery education to African Americans and other students of color who belong to the American College of Nurse-Midwives (ACNM).

Eligibility   This program is open to ACNM members of color who are currently enrolled in an accredited basic midwife education program and have successfully completed 1 academic or clinical semester/quarter or clinical module. Applicants must submit a 150-word essay on their 5-year midwifery career plans and a 100-word essay on their intended future participation in the local, regional, and/or national activities of the ACNM. Selection is based on leadership potential, financial need, academic history, and potential for future professional contribution to the organization.

Financial data   The stipend is $3,000.

Duration   1 year.

Number awarded   Varies each year; recently, 3 of these scholarships were awarded.

Deadline   March of each year.

[1071]
WILLIAM K. SCHUBERT M.D. MINORITY NURSING SCHOLARSHIP PROGRAM

Cincinnati Children's Hospital Medical Center
Attn: Office of Diversity and Inclusion, MLC 9008
3333 Burnet Avenue
Cincinnati, OH 45229-3039
(513) 803-6416   Toll Free: (800) 344-2462
Fax: (513) 636-5643   TDD: (513) 636-4900
E-mail: owen.burke@cchmc.org
Web: www.cincinnatichildrens.org

Summary   To provide financial assistance to African Americans and members of other underrepresented groups who are interested in working on a bachelor's or master's degree in nursing to prepare for licensure in Ohio.

Eligibility   This program is open to members of groups underrepresented in the nursing profession (males, American Indians or Alaska Natives, Blacks or African Americans,

Hawaiian Natives or other Pacific Islanders, Hispanics or Latinos, or Asians). Applicants must be enrolled or accepted in a professional bachelor's or master's registered nurse program at an accredited school of nursing to prepare for initial licensure in Ohio. They must have a GPA of 2.75 or higher. Along with their application, they must submit a 750-word essay that covers 1) their long-range personal, educational, and professional goals and why they chose nursing as a profession; 2) any unique qualifications, experiences, or special talents that demonstrate their creativity; and 3) if they are able to pay any college expenses through work and how their work experience has contributed to their personal development.

Financial data The stipend is $2,750 per year.

Duration 1 year. May be renewed up to 3 additional years for students working on a bachelor's degree or 1 additional year for students working on a master's degree; renewal requires that students maintain a GPA of 2.75 or higher.

Number awarded 1 or more each year.

Deadline April of each year.

[1072]
WILLIAM RUCKER GREENWOOD SCHOLARSHIP

Association for Women Geoscientists
Attn: AWG Foundation
12000 North Washington Street, Suite 285
Thornton, CO 80241
(303) 412-6219   Fax: (303) 253-9220
E-mail: office@awg.org
Web: www.awg.org/EAS/scholarships.html

Summary To provide financial assistance to African American and other minority women from any state working on an undergraduate or graduate degree in the geosciences at a college in the Potomac Bay region.

Eligibility This program is open to minority women who are residents of any state and currently enrolled as full-time undergraduate or graduate geoscience majors at an accredited, degree-granting college or university in Delaware, the District of Columbia, Maryland, Virginia, or West Virginia. Selection is based on the applicant's 1) participation in geoscience or earth science educational activities, and 2) potential for leadership as a future geoscience professional.

Financial data The stipend is $1,000. The recipient also is granted a 1-year membership in the Association for Women Geoscientists (AWG).

Duration 1 year.

Additional information This program is sponsored by the AWG Potomac Area Chapter.

Number awarded 1 each year.

Deadline April of each year.

[1073]
WILLIAM TOWNSEND PORTER FELLOWSHIP FOR MINORITY INVESTIGATORS

Woods Hole Marine Biological Laboratory
Attn: Research Award Coordinator
7 MBL Street
Woods Hole, MA 02543-1015
(508) 289-7171   Fax: (508) 457-1924
E-mail: researchawards@mbl.edu
Web: www.mbl.edu/research/summer/awards_general.html

Summary To support African American and other underrepresented minority scientists who wish to conduct research during the summer at the Woods Hole Marine Biological Laboratory (MBL).

Eligibility This program is open to young scientists (senior graduate students and postdoctoral trainees) who are from an underrepresented minority group (African American, Hispanic American, or Native American), are U.S. citizens or permanent residents, and are interested in conducting research with senior investigators at MBL. Fields of study include, but are not limited to, cell biology, developmental biology, ecology, evolution, microbiology, neurobiology, physiology, and tissue engineering.

Financial data Participants receive a stipend and a travel allowance. Recently, grants averaged approximately $1,500.

Duration At least 6 weeks during the summer.

Additional information This fellowship was first awarded in 1921. Funding is provided by the Harvard Apparatus Foundation.

Number awarded 1 or more each year.

Deadline December of each year.

[1074]
WILLIE T. LOUD-CH2M HILL SCHOLARSHIP

National Forum for Black Public Administrators
Attn: Scholarship Program
777 North Capitol Street, N.E., Suite 807
Washington, DC 20002
(202) 408-9300, ext. 112   Fax: (202) 408-8558
E-mail: vreed@nfbpa.org
Web: www.nfbpa.org/i4a/pages/index.cfm?pageid=3630

Summary To provide financial assistance to African Americans working on a bachelor's or master's degree in public administration.

Eligibility This program is open to African American graduate students preparing for a career in public service. Applicants must be working full time on a bachelor's or master's degree in public administration, urban affairs, or a related field. They must have a GPA of 3.0 or higher, strong interpersonal skills, and excellent writing, analytical, and oral communication abilities. Along with their application, they must submit a 3-page autobiographical essay that describes their academic and career goals and objectives. First consideration is given to applicants who are not currently receiving other financial aid.

Financial data The stipend is $5,000.

Duration 1 year.

Additional information This program, established in 1997, is sponsored by CH2M Hill. Recipients are required to attend the sponsor's annual conference to receive their scholarship; limited hotel and air accommodations are arranged and provided.

Number awarded 1 each year.

Deadline February of each year.

[1075]
WINSTON & STRAWN DIVERSITY SCHOLARSHIP PROGRAM

Winston & Strawn LLP
Attn: Attorney Recruitment Assistant
35 West Wacker Drive
Chicago, IL 60601-9703
(312) 558-5600   Fax: (312) 558-5700
E-mail: diversityscholarship@winston.com
Web: www.winston.com

Summary To provide financial assistance to African American and other underrepresented law students who are interested in practicing in a city in which Winston & Strawn LLP has an office.

Eligibility This program is open to second-year law students who self-identify as a member of 1 of the following groups: American Indian or Alaska Native, Asian or Pacific Islander, Black or African American, or Hispanic or Latino. Applicants must submit a resume, law school transcript, and 500-word personal statement. Selection is based on 1) interest in practicing law after graduation in a large law firm in a city in which Winston & Strawn has an office (currently, Charlotte, Chicago, Los Angeles, New York, San Francisco, and Washington, D.C.); 2) law school and undergraduate record, including academic achievements and involvement in extracurricular activities; 3) demonstrated leadership skills; 4) and interpersonal skills.

Financial data The stipend is $10,000.

Duration 1 year (the third year of law school).

Additional information This program began in 2001.

Number awarded 3 each year.

Deadline October of each year.

[1076]
WISCONSIN MINORITY TEACHER LOANS

Wisconsin Higher Educational Aids Board
131 West Wilson Street, Suite 902
P.O. Box 7885
Madison, WI 53707-7885
(608) 267-2212   Fax: (608) 267-2808
E-mail: Mary.Kuzdas@wisconsin.gov
Web: heab.state.wi.us/programs.html

Summary To provide funding to African Americans and other minorities in Wisconsin who are interested in teaching in Wisconsin school districts with large minority enrollments.

Eligibility This program is open to residents of Wisconsin who are African Americans, Hispanic Americans, American Indians, or southeast Asians (students who were admitted to the United States after December 31, 1975 and who are a former citizen of Laos, Vietnam, or Cambodia or whose ancestor was a citizen of 1 of those countries). Applicants must be enrolled at least half time as juniors, seniors, or graduate students at an independent or public institution in the state in a program leading to teaching licensure and have a GPA of 2.5 or higher. They must agree to teach in a Wisconsin school district in which minority students constitute at least 29% of total enrollment or in a school district participating in the interdistrict pupil transfer program. Financial need is not considered in the selection process.

Financial data forgivable loans are provided up to $2,500 per year. For each year the student teaches in an eligible

school district, 25% of the loan is forgiven; if the student does not teach in an eligible district, the loan must be repaid at an interest rate of 5%.

Duration 1 year; may be renewed 1 additional year.

Additional information Eligible students should apply through their school's financial aid office.

Number awarded Varies each year.

Deadline Deadline dates vary by institution; check with your school's financial aid office.

[1077]
WMACCA CORPORATE SCHOLARS PROGRAM

Washington Metropolitan Area Corporate Counsel
    Association, Inc.
Attn: Executive Director
P.O. Box 2147
Rockville, MD 20847-2147
(301) 881-3018   E-mail: Ilene.Reid@wmacca.com
Web: www.wmacca.org

Summary To provide a summer internship in the metropolitan Washington, D.C. area to African Americans and other students at law schools in the area who will contribute to the diversity of the profession.

Eligibility This program is open to students entering their second or third year of part- or full-time study at law schools in the Washington, D.C. metropolitan area (including suburban Maryland and all of Virginia). Applicants must be able to demonstrate how they contribute to diversity in the legal profession, based not only on ideas about gender, race, and ethnicity, but also on concepts of socioeconomic background and their individual educational and career path. They must be interested in working during the summer at a sponsoring private corporation and nonprofit organizations in the Washington, D.C. area. Along with their application, they must submit a personal statement of 250 to 500 words explaining why they qualify for this program, a writing sample, their law school transcript, and a resume.

Financial data The stipend is at least $9,000.

Duration 10 weeks during the summer.

Additional information The Washington Metropolitan Area Corporate Counsel Association (WMACCA) is the local chapter of the Association of Corporate Counsel (ACC). It established this program in 2004 with support from the Minority Corporate Counsel Association (MCCA).

Number awarded Varies each year; recently, 11 of these internships were awarded.

Deadline January of each year.

[1078]
WOLVERINE BAR FOUNDATION SCHOLARSHIP

Wolverine Bar Association
Attn: Wolverine Bar Foundation
645 Griswold, Suite 961
Detroit, MI 48226-4017
(313) 962-0250   Fax: (313) 962-5906
E-mail: wbaoffice@ameritech.net
Web: www.wbadirect.org

Summary To provide financial assistance for law school to African Americans and other minorities in Michigan.

Eligibility This program is open to minority law students who are either currently enrolled in a Michigan law school or are Michigan residents enrolled in an out-of-state law school. Applicants must be in at least their second year of law school. Selection is based on financial need, merit, and an interview.

Financial data The stipend is at least $1,000.

Duration 1 year; nonrenewable.

Additional information The Wolverine Bar Association was established by a number of African American attorneys during the 1930s. It was the successor to the Harlan Law Club, founded in 1919 by attorneys in the Detroit area who were excluded from other local bar associations in Michigan.

Number awarded 1 or more each year.

Deadline April of each year.

[1079]
WOMBLE CARLYLE SCHOLARS PROGRAM

Womble Carlyle Sandridge & Rice, PLLC
Attn: Director of Entry-Level Recruiting and Development
301 South College Street, Suite 3500
Charlotte, NC 28202-6037
(704) 331-4900   Fax: (704) 331-4955
E-mail: wcsrscholars@wcsr.com
Web: www.wcsr.com/firm/diversity

Summary To provide financial assistance and summer work experience to African Americans and other diverse students at designated law schools.

Eligibility This program is open to students at designated law schools who are members of underrepresented groups. Applicants must be able to demonstrate solid academic credentials, personal or professional achievement outside the classroom, and significant participation in community service. Along with their application, they must submit a 300-word essay on their choice of 2 topics that change annually but relate to the legal profession. They must also submit a brief statement explaining how they would contribute to the goal of creating a more diverse legal community.

Financial data The stipend is $4,000. Recipients are also offered summer employment at an office of the sponsoring law firm. Salaries are the same as the firm's other summer associates in each office.

Duration 1 year (the second year of law school); may be renewed 1 additional year.

Additional information This program was established in 2004. The eligible law schools are North Carolina Central University School of Law (Durham, North Carolina), University of North Carolina at Chapel Hill School of Law (Chapel Hill, North Carolina), Duke University School of Law (Durham, North Carolina), Wake Forest University School of Law (Winston-Salem, North Carolina), University of South Carolina School of Law (Columbia, South Carolina), Howard University School of Law (Washington, D.C.), University of Virginia School of Law (Charlottesville, Virginia), University of Georgia School of Law (Athens, Georgia), Georgia Washington University Law School (Washington, D.C.), Emory University School of Law (Atlanta, Georgia), and University of Maryland School of Law (Baltimore, Maryland). The sponsoring law firm has offices in Atlanta (Georgia), Baltimore (Maryland), Charlotte (North Carolina), Greensboro (North Carolina), Greenville (South Carolina), Raleigh (North Carolina), Research Triangle Park (North Carolina), Tysons Corner (Virginia), Washington (D.C.), Wilmington (Delaware), and Winston-Salem (North Carolina).

Number awarded Varies each year; recently, 9 of these scholarships were awarded.

Deadline May of each year.

[1080]
WORLD COMMUNION SCHOLARSHIPS

United Methodist Church
General Board of Global Ministries
Attn: Scholarship Office
475 Riverside Drive, Room 1351
New York, NY 10115
(212) 870-3787   Toll Free: (800) UMC-GBGM
E-mail: scholars@gbgm-umc.org
Web: new.gbgm-umc.org

Summary To provide financial assistance to African Americans, other minorities, and foreign students who are interested in attending graduate school to prepare for leadership in promoting the goals of the United Methodist Church.

Eligibility This program is open to 1) students from Methodist churches in nations other than the United States, and 2) members of ethnic and racial minorities in the United States. Applicants must have applied to or been admitted to a master's, doctoral, or professional program at a university or seminary in the United States. They should be planning to return to their communities to work in furthering Christian mission, whether that be in the local church, the neighborhood clinic, the state rural development office, or the national office on education. Financial need must be demonstrated.

Financial data The stipend ranges from $250 to $12,500, depending on the recipient's related needs and school expenses.

Duration 1 year.

Additional information These awards are funded by the World Communion Offering received in United Methodist Churches on the first Sunday in October.

Number awarded 5 to 10 each year.

Deadline November of each year.

[1081]
XEROX TECHNICAL MINORITY SCHOLARSHIP PROGRAM

Xerox Corporation
Attn: Technical Minority Scholarship Program
150 State Street, Fourth Floor
Rochester, NY 14614
(585) 422-7689   E-mail: xtmsp@rballiance.com
Web: www.xeroxstudentcareers.com

Summary To provide financial assistance to African Americans and other minorities interested in undergraduate or graduate education in the sciences and/or engineering.

Eligibility This program is open to minorities (people of African American, Asian, Pacific Islander, Native American, Native Alaskan, or Hispanic descent) working full time on a bachelor's, master's, or doctoral degree in chemistry, computing and software systems, engineering (chemical, computer, electrical, imaging, manufacturing, mechanical, optical, or software), information management, laser optics, materials science, physics, or printing management science. Applicants must be U.S. citizens or permanent residents with a GPA of 3.0 or higher and attending a 4-year college or university.

Financial data Stipends range from $1,000 to $10,000.
Duration 1 year.
Number awarded Varies each year, recently, 125 of these scholarships were awarded.
Deadline September of each year.

Professionals/ Postdoctorates

Listed alphabetically by program title and described in detail here are 211 grants, awards, educational support programs, residencies, and other sources of "free money" available to African American professionals and postdoctorates. This funding is available to support research, creative activities, formal academic classes, training courses, and/or residencies in the United States.

[1082]
AACAP-NIDA CAREER DEVELOPMENT AWARD

American Academy of Child and Adolescent Psychiatry
Attn: Department of Research, Training, and Education
3615 Wisconsin Avenue, N.W.
Washington, DC 20016-3007
(202) 966-7300   Fax: (202) 966-2891
E-mail: research@aacap.org
Web: www.aacap.org/cs/awards

Summary To provide funding to child and adolescent psychiatrists (especially African Americans, other minorities, and women) who are interested in a program of mentored training in addiction-related research focused on children and adolescents.

Eligibility This program is open to qualified child and adolescent psychiatrists who intend to established careers as independent investigators in mental health and addiction research. Applicants must design a career development and research training program in collaboration with a research mentor. The program may include prevention; early intervention or treatment research; epidemiology; etiology; genetics, gene-environment interactions, or pharmacogenetics; developmental risk factors; psychiatric comorbidity; medical comorbidity including HIV, Hepatitis C, and STD risk reduction; pathophysiology; services research; special populations (minorities, pregnancy, juvenile justice); health disparities; or imaging studies. U.S. citizenship, nationality, or permanent resident status is required. Women and minority candidates are especially encouraged to apply.

Financial data Grants provide salary support for 75% of the recipient's salary (up to $90,000 plus fringe benefits) and $50,000 per year to cover research and training costs.

Duration Up to 5 years.

Additional information This program is co-sponsored by the American Academy of Child and Adolescent Psychiatry (AACAP) and the National Institute on Drug Abuse (NIDA) as a K12 program of the National Institutes of Health (NIH).

Number awarded 1 or more each year.

Deadline Letters of intent must be submitted in early January of each year; completed applications are due the following March.

[1083]
ADVANCED POSTDOCTORAL FELLOWSHIPS IN DIABETES RESEARCH

Juvenile Diabetes Research Foundation International
Attn: Grant Administrator
26 Broadway, 14th Floor
New York, NY 10004
(212) 479-7572   Toll Free: (800) 533-CURE
Fax: (212) 785-9595   E-mail: info@jdrf.org
Web: www.jdrf.org/index.cfm?page_id=111715

Summary To provide advanced research training to scientists (particularly African Americans, other minorities, women, and individuals with disabilities) who are beginning their professional careers and are interested in conducting research on the causes, treatment, prevention, or cure of diabetes or its complications.

Eligibility This program is open to postdoctorates who show extraordinary promise for a career in diabetes research. Applicants must have received their first doctoral degree (M.D., Ph.D., D.M.D., or D.V.M.) within the past 5 years and should have completed 1 to 3 years of postdoctoral training. They may not have a faculty appointment. There are no citizenship requirements. Applications are encouraged from women, members of minority groups underrepresented in the sciences, and people with disabilities. The proposed research training may be conducted at foreign and domestic, for-profit and nonprofit, and public and private institutions, including universities, colleges, hospitals, laboratories, units of state and local government, and eligible agencies of the federal government. Selection is based on the applicant's previous experience and academic record; the caliber of the proposed research; the quality of the mentor, training program, and environment; and the applicant's potential to obtain an independent research position in the future. Fellows who obtain a faculty position at any time during the term of the fellowship may apply for a transition award for support during their first year as a faculty member.

Financial data The total award is $90,000 per year, including salary that depends on number of years of experience, ranging from $37,740 for zero up to $52,068 for 7 or more years of experience. In the first year only, funds in excess of the grant may be used for travel to scientific meetings (up to $2,000), journal subscriptions, books, training courses, laboratory supplies, equipment, or purchase of a personal computer (up to $2,000). Indirect costs are not allowed. Fellows who receive a faculty position are granted a transition award of up to $110,000 for 1 year, including up to 10% in indirect costs.

Duration Up to 3 years.

Deadline January or July of each year.

[1084]
AFRICAN AMERICAN STUDIES PROGRAM VISITING SCHOLARS

University of Houston
African American Studies Program
Attn: Visiting Scholars Program
629 Agnes Arnold Hall
Houston, TX 77204-3047
(713) 743-2811   Fax: (713) 743-2818
E-mail: jconyers@uh.edu
Web: www.class.uh.edu/aas

Summary To provide support to junior scholars who are interested in conducting research on the African American community while affiliated with the University of Houston's African American Studies Program.

Eligibility Applications are sought from junior scholars in social sciences, humanities, or African American studies who completed their Ph.D. within the past 6 years. They must be interested in conducting research on the African American community while affiliated with the University of Houston's African American Studies Program and in assuming a tenured or tenure-track position there after their residency as a Visiting Scholar is completed. They must be available for consultation with students and professional colleagues, make at least 2 formal presentations based on their research project, and contribute generally to the intellectual discourse in the discipline of African Studies/Africology. Along with their application, they must submit a current curriculum vitae, a 2-page description of the proposed research, 3 letters of recommendation, and a syllabus of the undergraduate course to be taught. Minorities, women, veterans, and persons with disabilities are specifically encouraged to apply.

Financial data Visiting Scholars receive a salary appropriate to their rank.

Duration 1 academic year.

Additional information Visiting Scholars are assigned a research assistant, if needed, and are provided administrative support. Recipients must teach 1 class related to African American studies. They are required to be in residence at the university for the entire academic year and must make 2 presentations on their research. In addition, they must acknowledge the sponsor's support in any publication that results from their tenure at the university.

Number awarded At least 2 each year.

Deadline February of each year.

[1085]
AFRICAN AMERICAN STUDIES VISITING SCHOLAR AND VISITING RESEARCHER PROGRAM

University of California at Los Angeles
Institute of American Cultures
Attn: Bunche Center for African American Studies
160 Haines Hall
P.O. Box 951545
Los Angeles, CA 90095-1545
(310) 825-7403   Fax: (310) 206-3421
Web: www.gdnet.ucla.edu/iacweb/pstweber.htm

Summary To provide funding to scholars interested in conducting research in African American studies at UCLA's Bunche Center for African American Studies.

Eligibility Applicants must have completed a doctoral degree in African American or related studies. They must be interested in teaching or conducting research at UCLA's Bunche Center for African American Studies. Visiting Scholar appointments are available to people who currently hold permanent academic appointments; Visiting Researcher appointments are available to newly-degree scholars. UCLA faculty, students, and staff are not eligible. U.S. citizenship or permanent resident status is required.

Financial data Fellows receive a stipend of $32,000 to $35,000 (depending on rank, experience, and date of completion of the Ph.D.), health benefits, and up to $4,000 in research support. Visiting Scholars are paid through their home institution; Visiting Researchers receive their funds directly from UCLA.

Duration 9 months, beginning in October.

Additional information Fellows must teach or do research in the programs of the center. The award is offered in conjunction with UCLA's Institute of American Cultures (IAC).

Number awarded 1 each year.

Deadline January of each year.

[1086]
AFRICAN-AMERICAN STUDIES FELLOWSHIP

Massachusetts Historical Society
Attn: Short-Term Fellowships
1154 Boylston Street
Boston, MA 02215-3695
(617) 646-0568   Fax: (617) 859-0074
E-mail: fellowships@masshist.org
Web: www.masshist.org/fellowships/short_term.cfm

Summary To fund research visits to the Massachusetts Historical Society for graduate students and other scholars interested in African American history.

Eligibility This program is open to advanced graduate students, postdoctorates, and independent scholars who are conducting research in African American history and need to use the resources of the Massachusetts Historical Society. Applicants must be U.S. citizens or foreign nationals holding appropriate U.S. government documents. Along with their application, they must submit a curriculum vitae and a proposal describing the project and indicating collections at the society to be consulted. Graduate students must also arrange for a letter of recommendation from a faculty member familiar with their work and with the project being proposed. Preference is given to candidates who live 50 or more miles from Boston.

Financial data The grant is $1,500.

Duration 4 weeks.

Additional information This fellowship was first awarded in 1999.

Number awarded 1 each year.

Deadline February of each year.

[1087]
AHRQ INDIVIDUAL AWARDS FOR POSTDOCTORAL FELLOWS

Agency for Healthcare Research and Quality
Attn: Office of Extramural Research, Education, and
  Priority Populations
540 Gaither Road
Rockville, MD 20850
(301) 427-1528   Fax: (301) 427-1562
TDD: (301) 451-0088
E-mail: Shelley.Benjamin@ahrq.hhs.gov
Web: www.ahrq.gov/fund/grantix.htm

Summary To provide funding to postdoctoral scholars (especially African Americans, other minorities and individuals with disabilities) who are interested in academic training and supervised experience in applying quantitative research methods to the systematic analysis and evaluation of health services.

Eligibility Applicants must be U.S. citizens or permanent residents who have received a Ph.D., M.D., D.O., D.C., D.D.S., D.M.D., O.D., D.P.M., D.N.S., N.D., Dr.P.H., Pharm.D., D.S.W., Psych.D., or equivalent doctoral degree from an accredited domestic or foreign institution. They must be proposing to pursue postdoctoral training at an appropriate institution under the guidance of a sponsor who is an established investigator active in health services research. The proposed training should help promote the sponsoring agency's strategic research goals of 1) reducing the risk of harm from health care services by promoting the delivery of appropriate care that achieves the best quality outcomes; 2) achieving wider access to effective health care services and reducing health care costs; and 3) assuring that providers and consumers/patients use beneficial and timely health care information to make informed decisions. Priority is given to proposals that address health services research issues critical to such priority populations as individuals living in inner city and rural (including frontier) areas; low-income and minority groups; women, children, and the elderly; and individuals with special health care needs, including those with disabilities and those who need chronic or end-of-life health care. Members of underrepresented ethnic and racial groups and individuals with disabilities are especially encouraged to apply.

Financial data The award provides an annual stipend based on the number of years of postdoctoral experience, ranging from $37,740 for less than 1 year to $52,068 for 7 or more years. For fellows sponsored by domestic nonfederal institutions, the stipend is paid through the sponsoring institution; for fellows sponsored by federal or foreign institutions, the monthly stipend is paid directly to the fellow. Institutions also receive an allowance to help defray such awardee expenses as self-only health insurance, research supplies, equipment, travel to scientific meetings, and related items; the allowance is $7,850 per 12-month period for fellows at nonfederal, nonprofit, and foreign institutions and $6,750 per 12-month period at federal laboratories and for-profit institutions. In addition, tuition and fees are reimbursed at a rate of 60%, up to $4,500; if the fellow's program supports postdoctoral individuals in formal degree-granting training, tuition is supported at the rate of 60%, up to $16,000 for an additional degree. The initial 12 months of National Research Service Award postdoctoral support carries a service payback requirement, which can be fulfilled by continued training under the award or by engaging in other health-related research training, health-related research, or health-related teaching. Fellows who fail to fulfill the payback requirement of 1 month of acceptable service for each month of the initial 12 months of support received must repay all funds received with interest.

Duration 1 to 3 years.

Number awarded Varies each year.

Deadline April, August, or December of each year.

[1088]
AIR FELLOWS PROGRAM

American Educational Research Association
1430 K Street, N.W., Suite 1200
Washington, DC 20005
(202) 238-3200   Fax: (202) 238-3250
E-mail: fellowships@aera.net
Web: www.aera.net

Summary To provide an opportunity for junior scholars in the field of education (especially African Americans and other underrepresented minorities) to engage in a program of research and advanced training while in residence in Washington, D.C.

Eligibility This program is open to early scholars who received a Ph.D. or Ed.D. degree within the past 3 years in a field related to education and educational processes. Applicants must be proposing a program of intensive research and training in Washington, D.C. Selection is based on past academic record, writing sample, goal statement, range and

quality of research experiences, other relevant work or professional experiences, potential contributions to education research, and references. A particular goal of the program is to increase the number of underrepresented minority professionals conducting advanced research or providing technical assistance. U.S. citizenship or permanent resident status is required.

Financial data Stipends range from $45,000 to $50,000 per year.

Duration Up to 2 years.

Additional information This program, jointly sponsored by the American Educational Research Association (AERA) and the American Institutes for Research (AIR), was first offered for 2006. Fellows rotate between the 2 organizations and receive mentoring from recognized researchers and practitioners in a variety of substantive areas in education.

Number awarded Up to 3 each year.

Deadline December of each year.

[1089]
AIR FORCE OFFICE OF SCIENTIFIC RESEARCH BROAD AGENCY ANNOUNCEMENT

Air Force Office of Scientific Research
Attn: Directorate of Academic and International Affairs
875 North Randolph Street, Room 3112
Arlington, VA 22203-1954
(703) 696-9738   Fax: (703) 696-9733
E-mail: afosr.baa@afosr.af.mil
Web: www.wpafb.mil/afrl/afosr

Summary To provide funding to investigators (particularly investigators from Historically Black Colleges and Universities and other minority institutions) who are interested in conducting scientific research of interest to the U.S. Air Force.

Eligibility This program is open to investigators who are qualified to conduct research in designated scientific and technical areas. The general fields of interest include 1) aerospace, chemical, and materials sciences; 2) physics and electronics; 3) mathematics, information, and life sciences; 4) discovery challenge thrusts; and 5) other innovative research concepts. Assistance includes grants to university scientists, support for academic institutions, contracts for industry research, cooperative agreements, and support for basic research in Air Force laboratories. Because the Air Force encourages the sharing and transfer of technology, it welcomes proposals that envision cooperation among 2 or more partners from academia, industry, and Air Force organizations. It particularly encourages proposals from small businesses, Historically Black Colleges and Universities (HBCUs), other Minority Institutions (MIs), and minority researchers.

Financial data The amounts of the awards depend on the nature of the proposals and the availability of funds. Recently, grants averaged approximately $150,000 per year.

Duration Grants range up to 5 years.

Additional information Contact the Air Force Office of Scientific Research for details on particular program areas of interest. Outstanding principal investigators on grants issued through this program are nominated to receive Presidential Early Career Awards for Scientists and Engineers.

Number awarded Varies each year; recently, this program awarded approximately 1,650 grants and contracts to applicants at about 450 academic institutions and industrial firms.

Deadline Each program area specifies deadline dates.

[1090]
AIR FORCE SUMMER FACULTY FELLOWSHIP PROGRAM

American Society for Engineering Education
Attn: Projects Department
1818 N Street, N.W., Suite 600
Washington, DC 20036-2479
(202) 331-5763   Fax: (202) 265-8504
E-mail: sffp@asee.org
Web: sffp.asee.org

Summary To provide funding to science and engineering faculty and graduate students (especially those at Historically Black Colleges and Universities and other Minority Serving Institutions) who are interested in conducting summer research at Air Force facilities.

Eligibility This program is open to U.S. citizens and permanent residents who have a full-time faculty appointment at a U.S. college or university in a field of engineering or science of interest to the Air Force. Applicants must be interested in conducting a research project, under the direction of an Air Force research adviser, at an Air Force Research Laboratory, the U.S. Air Force Academy, or the Air Force Institute of Technology. A graduate student may accompany the faculty member. Faculty and students at Historically Black Colleges and Universities ((HBCUs), Minority Institutions (MIs), American Indian Tribal Colleges and Universities (TCUs), and Hispanic Serving Institutions (HSIs) are especially encouraged to apply.

Financial data Stipends are $1,700 per week for full professors, $1,500 per week for associate professors, $1,300 per week for assistant professors, $884 per week for graduate students who have a bachelor's degree, or $1,037 per week for graduate students who have a master's degree. Relocation reimbursement and a daily expense allowance of $50 (for fellows with a commute distance greater than 50 miles) are also available.

Duration 8 to 12 weeks during the summer. May be renewed for a second and third summer, but recipients may not reapply for 2 years after completing a third summer.

Additional information This program first operated in 2005. Research must be conducted in residence at an Air Force facility.

Number awarded Varies each year; recently, 93 of these fellowships were awarded.

Deadline November of each year.

[1091]
ALFRED M. GREENFIELD FOUNDATION FELLOWSHIPS IN AFRICAN AMERICAN HISTORY

Library Company of Philadelphia
Attn: Librarian
1314 Locust Street
Philadelphia, PA 19107-5698
(215) 546-3181   Fax: (215) 546-5167
E-mail: jgreen@librarycompany.org
Web: www.librarycompany.org/fellowships/american.htm

Summary To provide funding to pre- and postdoctorates interested in conducting research on African American history at designated libraries in Philadelphia.

Eligibility This program is open to candidates interested in conducting dissertation, postdoctoral, or advanced research in Philadelphia at the Library Company and/or the Historical Society of Pennsylvania. The proposed research must relate to African American history.

Financial data The stipend is $2,000.

Duration 1 month.

Number awarded 4 each year.

Deadline February of each year.

[1092]
ALFRED P. SLOAN FOUNDATION RESEARCH FELLOWSHIPS

Alfred P. Sloan Foundation
630 Fifth Avenue, Suite 2550
New York, NY 10111-0242
(212) 649-1649   Fax: (212) 757-5117
E-mail: researchfellows@sloan.org
Web: www.sloan.org/fellowships

Summary To provide funding for research in selected fields of science to recent doctorates (especially African Americans, other minorities, and women).

Eligibility This program is open to scholars who are no more than 6 years from completion of the most recent Ph.D. or equivalent in computational and evolutionary molecular biology, chemistry, physics, mathematics, computer science, economics, neuroscience, or a related interdisciplinary field. Direct applications are not accepted; candidates must be nominated by department heads or other senior scholars. Although fellows must be at an early stage of their research careers, they should give strong evidence of independent research accomplishments and creativity. The sponsor strongly encourages the participation of women and members of underrepresented minority groups.

Financial data The stipend is $25,000 per year. Funds are paid directly to the fellow's institution to be used by the fellow for equipment, technical assistance, professional travel, trainee support, or any other research-related expense; they may not be used to augment an existing full-time salary.

Duration 2 years; may be extended if unexpended funds still remain.

Additional information This program began in 1955, when it awarded $235,000 to 22 chemists, physicists, and pure mathematicians. Neuroscience was added in 1972, economics and applied mathematics in 1980, computer science in 1993, and computational and evolutionary molecular biology in 2002. Currently, the program awards $5.22 million in grants annually.

Number awarded 118 each year: 23 in chemistry, 12 in computational and evolutionary molecular biology, 16 in computer science, 8 in economics, 20 in mathematics, 16 in neuroscience, and 23 in physics.

Deadline September of each year.

[1093]
ALZHEIMER'S ASSOCIATION INVESTIGATOR-INITIATED RESEARCH GRANTS

Alzheimer's Association
Attn: Medical and Scientific Affairs
225 North Michigan Avenue, 17th Floor
Chicago, IL 60601-7633
(312) 335-5747   Toll Free: (800) 272-3900
Fax: (866) 699-1246   TDD: (312) 335-5886
E-mail: grantsapp@alz.org
Web: www.alz.org

Summary To provide funding to scientists (particularly African Americans and other underrepresented minorities) who are interested in conducting research on Alzheimer's Disease.

Eligibility This program is open to postdoctoral investigators at public, private, domestic, and foreign research laboratories, medical centers, hospitals, and universities. Applicants must be proposing to conduct research with focus areas that change annually but are related to Alzheimer's Disease. They must have a full-time staff or faculty appointment. Scientists from underrepresented groups are especially encouraged to apply.

Financial data Grants up to $100,000 per year, including direct expenses and up to 10% for overhead costs, are available. The total award for the life of the grant may not exceed $240,000.

Duration Up to 3 years.

Number awarded Up to 30 each year.

Deadline Letters of intent must be submitted by the end of December of each year. Final applications are due in February.

[1094]
ALZHEIMER'S ASSOCIATION NEW INVESTIGATOR RESEARCH GRANTS

Alzheimer's Association
Attn: Medical and Scientific Affairs
225 North Michigan Avenue, 17th Floor
Chicago, IL 60601-7633
(312) 335-5747   Toll Free: (800) 272-3900
Fax: (866) 699-1246   TDD: (312) 335-5886
E-mail: grantsapp@alz.org
Web: www.alz.org

Summary To provide funding for research on Alzheimer's Disease to junior and postdoctoral investigators, especially African American and underrepresented minority investigators.

Eligibility This program is open to investigators, including postdoctoral fellows, at public, private, domestic, and foreign research laboratories, medical centers, hospitals, and universities. Applicants must be proposing to conduct research with focus areas that change annually but are related to

Alzheimer's Disease. Eligibility is restricted to investigators who have less than 10 years of research experience, including postdoctoral fellowships or residencies. Scientists from underrepresented groups are especially encouraged to apply.

Financial data Grants up to $60,000 per year, including direct expenses and up to 10% for overhead costs, are available. The total award for the life of the grant may not exceed $100,000.

Duration Up to 2 years.

Number awarded Up to 45 each year.

Deadline Letters of intent must be submitted by the end of December of each year. Final applications are due in February.

[1095]
AMERICAN ASSOCIATION OF OBSTETRICIANS AND GYNECOLOGISTS FOUNDATION SCHOLARSHIPS

American Gynecological and Obstetrical Society
Attn: American Association of Obstetricians and
  Gynecologists Foundation
409 12th Street, S.W.
Washington, DC 20024-2188
(202) 863-1649   Fax: (202) 554-0453
E-mail: clarkins@acog.org
Web: www.agosonline.org/aaogf/index.asp

Summary To provide funding to physicians (particularly African Americans or other minorities and women) who are interested in a program of research training in obstetrics and gynecology.

Eligibility Applicants must have an M.D. degree and be eligible for the certification process of the American Board of Obstetrics and Gynecology (ABOG). They must be interested in participating in research training conducted by 1 or more faculty mentors at an academic department of obstetrics and gynecology in the United States or Canada. the research training may be either laboratory-based or clinical, and should focus on fundamental biology, disease mechanisms, interventions or diagnostics, epidemiology, or translational research. There is no formal application form, but departments must supply a description of the candidate's qualifications, including a curriculum vitae, bibliography, prior training, past research experience, and evidence of completion of residency training in obstetrics and gynecology; a comprehensive description of the proposed training program; a description of departmental resources appropriate to the training; a detailed mentoring plan; a list of other research grants, training grants, or scholarships previously or currently held by the applicant; and a budget. Applicants for the scholarship co-sponsored by the Society for Maternal-Fetal Medicine (SMFM) must also be members or associate members of the SMFM. Women and minority candidates are strongly encouraged to apply. Selection is based on the scholarly, clinical, and research qualifications of the candidate; evidence of the candidate's commitment to an investigative career in academic obstetrics and gynecology in the United States or Canada; qualifications of the sponsoring department and mentor; overall quality of the mentoring plan, and quality of the research project. Preference may be given to applications from candidates training in areas currently underrepresented in academic obstetrics and gynecology (e.g., urogynecology, family planning).

Financial data   The grant is $100,000 per year, of which at least $5,000 but not more than $15,000 must be used for employee benefits. In addition, sufficient funds to support travel to the annual fellows' retreat must be set aside. The balance of the funds may be used for salary, technical support, and supplies. The grant co-sponsored by the SMFM must be matched by an institutional commitment of at least $30,000 per year.

Duration   1 year; may be renewed for 2 additional years, based on satisfactory progress of the scholar.

Additional information   Scholars must devote at least 75% of their effort to the program of research training.

Number awarded   2 each year: 1 co-sponsored by ABOG and 1 co-sponsored by SMFM.

Deadline   June of each year.

[1096]
AMERICAN COUNCIL OF LEARNED SOCIETIES FELLOWSHIPS

American Council of Learned Societies
Attn: Office of Fellowships and Grants
633 Third Avenue
New York, NY 10017-6795
(212) 697-1505   Fax: (212) 949-8058
E-mail: fellowships@acls.org
Web: www.acls.org/programs/acls

Summary   To provide research funding to minority and other scholars in all disciplines of the humanities and the humanities-related social sciences.

Eligibility   This program is open to scholars at all stages of their careers who received a Ph.D. degree at least 2 years previously. Established scholars who can demonstrate the equivalent of the Ph.D. in publications and professional experience may also qualify. Applicants must be U.S. citizens or permanent residents who have not had supported leave time for at least 2 years prior to the start of the proposed research. Appropriate fields of specialization include, but are not limited to, American studies; anthropology; archaeology; art and architectural history; classics; economics; film; geography; history; languages and literatures; legal studies; linguistics; musicology; philosophy; political science; psychology; religious studies; rhetoric, communication, and media studies; sociology; and theater, dance, and performance studies. Proposals in those fields of the social sciences are eligible only if they employ predominantly humanistic approaches (e.g., economic history, law and literature, political philosophy). Proposals in interdisciplinary and cross-disciplinary studies are welcome, as are proposals focused on a geographic region or on a cultural or linguistic group. Awards are available at 3 academic levels: full professor, associate professor, and assistant professor. Applications are particularly invited from women and members of minority groups.

Financial data   The maximum grant is $60,000 for full professors and equivalent, $40,000 for associate professors and equivalent, or $35,000 for assistant professors and equivalent. Normally, fellowships are intended as salary replacement and may be held concurrently with other fellowships, grants, and sabbatical pay, up to an amount equal to the candidate's current academic year salary.

Duration   6 to 12 months.

Additional information   This program is supported in part by funding from the Ford Foundation, the Andrew W. Mellon Foundation, the National Endowment for the Humanities, the William and Flora Hewlett Foundation, and the Rockefeller Foundation.

Number awarded   Approximately 57 each year: 17 at the full professor level, 18 at the association professor level, and 22 at the assistant professor level.

Deadline   September of each year.

[1097]
AMERICAN EDUCATIONAL RESEARCH ASSOCIATION GRANTS PROGRAM

American Educational Research Association
1430 K Street, N.W., Suite 1200
Washington, DC 20005
(202) 238-3200   Fax: (202) 238-3250
Web: www.aera.net

Summary   To provide funding to faculty members and post-doctorates (particularly African Americans and other underrepresented minorities) who are interested in conducting research on educational policy.

Eligibility   This program is open to scholars who have completed a doctoral degree in such disciplines as (but not limited to) education, sociology, economics, psychology, demography, statistics, or psychometrics. Applicants may be U.S. citizens, U.S. permanent residents, or non-U.S. citizens working at a U.S. institution. Underrepresented minority researchers are strongly encouraged to apply. Research topics may cover a wide range of policy-related issues, but priority is given to proposals that 1) develop or benefit from new quantitative measures or methodological approaches for addressing education issues; 2) include interdisciplinary teams with subject matter expertise, especially when studying science, technology, engineering, or mathematics (STEM) learning; 3) analyze TIMSS, PISA, or other international data resources; or 4) include the integration and analysis of more than 1 data set. Research projects must include the analysis of data from at least 1 of the large-scale, nationally or internationally representative data sets, such as those of the National Science Foundation (NSF), National Center for Education Statistics (NCES), or National Institutes of Health (NIH). Selection is based on the importance of the proposed policy issue, the strength of the methodological model and proposed statistical analysis of the study, and relevant experience or research record.

Financial data   Grants up to $20,000 for 1 year or $35,000 for 2 years are available. Funding is linked to the approval of the recipient's progress report and final report. Grantees receive one-third of the total award at the beginning of the grant period, one-third upon acceptance of the progress report, and one-third upon acceptance of the final report.

Duration   1 or 2 years.

Additional information   Funding for this program is provided by the NSF and the NCES. Grantees must submit a brief (3 to 6 pages) progress report midway through the grant period. A final report must be submitted at the end of the grant period.

Number awarded   Approximately 15 each year.

Deadline   January, March, or August of each year.

[1098]
AMERICAN GASTROENTEROLOGICAL ASSOCIATION RESEARCH SCHOLAR AWARDS

American Gastroenterological Association
Attn: AGA Research Foundation
Research Awards Manager
4930 Del Ray Avenue
Bethesda, MD 20814-2512
(301) 222-4012 Fax: (301) 654-5920
E-mail: awards@gastro.org
Web: www.gastro.org/aga-foundation/grants

Summary To provide research funding to young investigators (particularly African Americans or other minorities and women) who are interested in developing an independent career in an area of gastroenterology, hepatology, or related fields.

Eligibility Applicants must hold full-time faculty positions at North American universities or professional institutes at the time of application. They should be early in their careers (fellows and established investigators are not appropriate candidates). Candidates with an M.D. degree must have completed clinical training within the past 5 years and those with a Ph.D. must have completed their degree within the past 5 years. Membership in the American Gastroenterological Association (AGA) is required. Selection is based on significance, investigator, innovation, approach, environment, relevance to AGA mission, and evidence of institutional commitment. Women, minorities, and physician/scientist investigators are strongly encouraged to apply.

Financial data The grant is $60,000 per year. Funds are to be used for project costs, including salary, supplies, and equipment but excluding travel. Indirect costs are not allowed.

Duration 2 years; a third year of support may be available, contingent upon availability of funds and a competitive review.

Additional information At least 70% of the recipient's research effort should relate to the gastrointestinal tract or liver.

Number awarded 1 or more each year.

Deadline September of each year.

[1099]
AMERICAN SOCIETY FOR CELL BIOLOGY MINORITIES AFFAIRS COMMITTEE VISITING PROFESSOR AWARDS

American Society for Cell Biology
Attn: Minority Affairs Committee
8120 Woodmont Avenue, Suite 750
Bethesda, MD 20814-2762
(301) 347-9323 Fax: (301) 347-9310
E-mail: dmccall@ascb.org
Web: www.ascb.org

Summary To provide funding for research during the summer to 1) African American and other minority faculty and 2) faculty members at primarily teaching institutions that serve minority students and scientists.

Eligibility Eligible to apply for this support are professors at primarily teaching institutions. They must be interested in working in the laboratories of members of the American Society for Cell Biology during the summer. Hosts and visitor scientists are asked to submit their applications together as a proposed team. Minority professors and professors in col-

leges and universities with a high minority enrollment are especially encouraged to apply for this award. Minorities are defined as U.S. citizens of Black, Native American, Chicano/Hispanic, or Pacific Islands background.

Financial data The stipend for the summer is $13,500 plus $700 for travel expenses and $4,000 to the host institution for supplies.

Duration From 8 to 10 weeks during the summer.

Additional information Funds for this program, established in 1997, are provided by the Minorities Access to Research Careers (MARC) program of the National Institutes of Health.

Number awarded Varies each year; recently, 3 of these grants were awarded.

Deadline March of each year.

[1100]
ANDREW W. MELLON FOUNDATION/ACLS RECENT DOCTORAL RECIPIENTS FELLOWSHIPS

American Council of Learned Societies
Attn: Office of Fellowships and Grants
633 Third Avenue
New York, NY 10017-6795
(212) 697-1505 Fax: (212) 949-8058
E-mail: fellowships@acls.org
Web: www.acls.org/programs/rdr

Summary To provide funding to recent doctoral recipients (particularly African Americans and other underrepresented minorities) who received their degree in any discipline of the humanities and the humanities-related social sciences who need funding to advance their scholarly career.

Eligibility This program is open to recent recipients of a doctoral degree in a humanities or humanities-related social science discipline. Applicants must have been 1) a recipient of an Andrew W. Mellon Foundation/ACLS Dissertation Completion Fellowship in the previous year; 2) designated as an alternate in that fellowship program; or 3) a recipient of a dissertation completion fellowship in another program of national stature (e.g., Whiting, AAUW, Newcombe). They must be seeking funding to position themselves for further scholarly advancement, whether or not they hold academic positions. Appropriate fields of specialization include, but are not limited to, American studies; anthropology; archaeology; art and architectural history; classics; economics; film; geography; history; languages and literatures; legal studies; linguistics; musicology; philosophy; political science; psychology; religious studies; rhetoric, communication, and media studies; sociology; and theater, dance, and performance studies. Proposals in those fields of the social sciences are eligible only if they employ predominantly humanistic approaches (e.g., economic history, law and literature, political philosophy). Proposals in interdisciplinary and cross-disciplinary studies are welcome, as are proposals focused on any geographic region or on any cultural or linguistic group. Applications are particularly invited from women and members of minority groups.

Financial data The stipend is $30,000.

Duration 1 academic year. Grantees may accept this fellowship during the 2 years following the date of the award.

Additional information This program, which began in 2007, is supported by funding from the Andrew W. Mellon Foundation and administered by the American Council of Learned Societies (ACLS). Fellows may not teach during the tenure of the fellowship. If they have a faculty position, they may use the fellowship to take research leave. Fellows who do not have a full-time position may choose to affiliate with a humanities research center or conduct research independently.

Number awarded 25 each year.

Deadline November of each year.

[1101]
ANTARCTIC RESEARCH PROGRAM

National Science Foundation
Office of Polar Programs
Attn: Division of Antarctic Sciences
4201 Wilson Boulevard, Room 755S
Arlington, VA 22230
(703) 292-7457   Fax: (703) 292-9080
TDD: (800) 281-8749   E-mail: jlcrain@nsf.gov
Web: www.nsf.gov/funding/pgm_summ.jsp?pims_id=5519

Summary To provide funding to scientists (especially African Americans, other minorities, and individuals with disabilities) who are interested in conducting research related to Antarctica.

Eligibility This program is open to investigators at U.S. institutions, primarily universities and, to a lesser extent, federal agencies and other organizations. Applicants must be proposing to conduct Antarctic-related research in the following major areas: aeronomy and astrophysics, organisms and ecosystems, earth sciences, ocean and atmospheric sciences, glaciology, and integrated system science. The program encourages applications from underrepresented minorities and persons with disabilities.

Financial data The amounts of the awards depend on the nature of the proposal and the availability of funds.

Additional information The NSF operates 3 year-round research stations in Antarctica, additional research facilities and camps, airplanes, helicopters, various types of surface vehicles, and ships.

Number awarded Varies each year; recently, the program planned to make 50 awards with a total budget of $22 million for new awards and $30 million for continuing awards.

Deadline May of each year.

[1102]
APA/SAMHSA MINORITY FELLOWSHIP PROGRAM

American Psychiatric Association
Attn: Department of Minority and National Affairs
1000 Wilson Boulevard, Suite 1825
Arlington, VA 22209-3901
(703) 907-8653   Toll Free: (888) 35-PSYCH
Fax: (703) 907-7852   E-mail: mking@psych.org
Web: www.psych.org/Resources/OMNA/MFP.aspx

Summary To provide educational enrichment to African American and other minority psychiatrists-in-training and stimulate interested in providing quality and effective services to minorities and the underserved.

Eligibility This program is open to residents who are in at least their second year of psychiatric training, members of the American Psychiatric Association (APA), and U.S. citizens or permanent residents. A goal of the program is to develop leadership to improve the quality of mental health care for members of ethnic minority groups (American Indians, Native Alaskans, Asian Americans, Native Hawaiians, Native Pacific Islanders, African Americans, and Hispanics/Latinos). Applicants must be interested in working with a component of the APA that is of interest to them and relevant to their career goals. Along with their application, they must submit a 2-page essay on how the fellowship would be utilized to alter their present training and ultimately assist them in achieving their career goals. Selection is based on commitment to serve ethnic minority populations, demonstrated leadership abilities, awareness of the importance of culture in mental health, and interest in the interrelationship between mental health/illness and transcultural factors.

Financial data Fellows receive a monthly stipend (amount not specified) and reimbursement of transportation, lodging, meals, and incidentals in connection with attendance at program-related activities. They are expected to use the funds to enhance their own professional development, improve training in cultural competence at their training institution, improve awareness of culturally relevant issues in psychiatry at their institution, expand research in areas relevant to minorities and underserved populations, enhance the current treatment modalities for minority patients and underserved individuals at their institution, and improve awareness in the surrounding community about mental health issues (particularly with regard to minority populations).

Duration 1 year; may be renewed 1 additional year.

Additional information Funding for this program is provided by the Substance Abuse and Mental Health Services Administration (SAMHSA). As part of their assignment to an APA component, fellows must attend the fall component meetings in September and the APA annual meeting in May. At those meeting, they can share their experiences as residents and minorities and discuss issues that impact on minority populations. This program is an outgrowth of the fellowships that were established in 1974 under a grant from the National Institute of Mental Health in answer to concerns about the underrepresentation of minorities in psychiatry.

Number awarded Varies each year; recently, 16 of these fellowships were awarded.

Deadline January of each year.

[1103]
ARCTIC RESEARCH OPPORTUNITIES

National Science Foundation
Office of Polar Programs
Attn: Division of Arctic Sciences
4201 Wilson Boulevard, Suite 755S
Arlington, VA 22230
(703) 292-8577   Fax: (703) 292-9082
TDD: (800) 281-8749   E-mail: phaggert@nsf.gov
Web: www.nsf.gov/funding/pgm_summ.jsp?pims_id=5521

Summary To provide funding to scientists (particularly African Americans, other minorities, and individuals with disabilities) who are interested in conducting research related to the Arctic.

Eligibility This program is open to investigators affiliated with U.S. universities, research institutions, or other organizations, including local or state governments. Applicants must be proposing to conduct research in the 4 program areas of Arctic science: 1) Arctic Natural Sciences, with areas of special interest in marine and terrestrial ecosystems, Arctic atmospheric and oceanic dynamics and climatology, Arctic geological and glaciological processes, and their connectivity to lower latitudes; 2) Arctic Social Sciences, including (but not limited to) anthropology, archaeology, economics, geography, linguistics, political science, psychology, science and technology studies, sociology, traditional knowledge, and related subjects; 3) Arctic System Science, for research focused on a system understanding of the Arctic, understanding the behavior of the Arctic system (past, present, and future), understanding the role of the Arctic as a component of the global system, and society as an integral part of the Arctic system; 4) Arctic Observing Networks, for work related to a pan-Arctic, science-driven, observing system; or 5) Cyberinfrastructure, for projects using high-performance computing for direct and sustainable advances in current Arctic research. The program encourages proposals from underrepresented minorities and persons with disabilities.

Financial data The amounts of the awards depend on the nature of the proposal and the availability of funds.

Number awarded Approximately 75 each year; recently, this program awarded approximately $25 million in grants.

Deadline October of each year.

[1104]
ARMY RESEARCH LABORATORY BROAD AGENCY ANNOUNCEMENT

Army Research Office
Attn: AMSRL-RO-RI
4300 South Miami Boulevard
P.O. Box 12211
Research Triangle Park, NC 27709-2211
(919) 549-4375   Fax: (919) 549-4388
Web: www.arl.army.mil/www/default.cfm?Action=6&Page=8

Summary To provide funding to investigators (especially those at Historically Black Colleges and Universities and individuals with disabilities) who are interested in conducting scientific research of interest to the U.S. Army.

Eligibility This program is open to investigators qualified to perform research in designated scientific and technical areas. Included within the program are several sites within the Army Research Laboratory (ARL): 1) the Army Research Office (ARO), which supports research in the areas of chemistry, computing and information sciences, electronics, environmental sciences, life sciences, materials sciences, mathematics, mechanical sciences, and physics; 2) the Computational and Information Sciences Directorate; 3) the Human Research and Engineering Directorate; 4) the Sensors and Electron Devices Directorate; 5) the Survivability/Lethality Analysis Directorate; 6) the Vehicle Technology Directorate; and 7) the Weapons and Materials Research Directorate. Applications are especially encouraged from Historically Black Colleges and Universities (HBCUs) and Minority Institutions (MIs).

Financial data The amounts of the awards depend on the nature of the proposal and the availability of funds.

Duration 3 years.

Additional information Although the Army Research Office intends to award a fair proportion of its acquisitions to HBCUs and MIs, it does not set aside a specified percentage.

Number awarded Varies each year.

Deadline Applications may be submitted at any time.

[1105]
ASH-AMFDP RESEARCH GRANTS

American Society of Hematology
Attn: Awards Manager
2021 L Street, N.W., Suite 900
Washington, DC 20036
(202) 776-0544   Fax: (202) 776-0545
E-mail: awards@hematology.org
Web: www.hematology.org

Summary To provide an opportunity for African Americans and other historically disadvantaged postdoctoral physicians to conduct a research project in hematology.

Eligibility This program is open to postdoctoral physicians who are members of historically disadvantaged groups, defined as individuals who face challenges because of their race, ethnicity, socioeconomic status, or other similar factors. Applicants must be committed to a career in academic medicine in hematology and to serving as a role model for students and faculty of similar backgrounds. They must identify a mentor at their institution to work with them and give them research and career guidance. Selection is based on excellence in educational career; willingness to devote 4 consecutive years to research; and commitment to an academic career, improving the health status of the underserved, and decreasing health disparities. U.S. citizenship or permanent resident status is required.

Financial data The grant includes a stipend of up to $75,000 per year, a grant of $30,000 per year for support of research activities, complimentary membership in the American Society of Hematology (ASH), and travel support to attend the ASH annual meeting.

Duration 4 years.

Additional information This program, first offered in 2006, is a partnership between the ASH and the Robert Wood Johnson Foundation, whose Minority Medical Faculty Development Program (MMFDP) was renamed the Harold Amos Medical Faculty Development Program (AMFDP) in honor of the first African American to chair a department at the Harvard Medical School. Scholars must spend at least 70% of their time in research activities.

Number awarded At least 1 each year.

Deadline March of each year.

[1106]
ASTRONOMY AND ASTROPHYSICS POSTDOCTORAL FELLOWSHIPS

National Science Foundation
Directorate for Mathematical and Physical Sciences
Attn: Division of Astronomical Sciences
4201 Wilson Boulevard, Room 1030S
Arlington, VA 22230
(703) 292-7456   Fax: (703) 292-9034
TDD: (800) 281-8749   E-mail: dlehr@nsf.gov
Web: www.nsf.gov/funding/pgm_summ.jsp?pims_id=5291

Summary To provide funding to recent doctoral recipients in astronomy or astrophysics (particularly African Americans, other underrepresented minorities, and individuals with disabilities) who are interested in pursuing a program of research and education.

Eligibility This program is open to U.S. citizens, nationals, and permanent residents who completed a Ph.D. in astronomy or astrophysics during the previous 5 years. Applicants must be interested in a program of research of an observational, instrumental, or theoretical nature, especially research that is facilitated or enabled by new ground-based capability in radio, optical/IR, or solar astrophysics. Research may be conducted at a U.S. institution of higher education; a national center, facility, or institute funded by the National Science Foundation (NSF), such as the Kavli Institute for Theoretical Physics; a U.S. nonprofit organization with research and educational missions; and/or an international site operated by a U.S. organization eligible for NSF funding, such as Cerro Tololo InterAmerican Observatory. The proposal must include a coherent program of educational activities, such as teaching a course each year at the host institution or an academic institution with ties to the host institution, developing educational materials, or engaging in a significant program of outreach or general education. The program encourages applications from underrepresented minorities and persons with disabilities.

Financial data Grants up to $83,000 per year are available, including stipends of $58,000 per year, a research allowance of $12,000 per year, an institutional allowance of $3,000 per year, and a benefits allowance of $10,000 per year, paid either to the fellow or the host institution in support of fringe benefits.

Duration Up to 3 years.

Number awarded 8 to 9 each year.

Deadline October of each year.

[1107]
ATMOSPHERIC AND GEOSPACE SCIENCES POSTDOCTORAL RESEARCH FELLOWSHIPS

National Science Foundation
Directorate for Geosciences
Attn: Division of Atmospheric and Geospace Sciences
4201 Wilson Boulevard, Room 775S
Arlington, VA 22230
(703) 292-4708   Fax: (703) 292-9022
TDD: (800) 281-8749   E-mail: cweiler@nsf.gov
Web: www.nsf.gov/funding/pgm_summ.jsp?pims_id=12779

Summary To provide funding to postdoctoral scientists (particularly African Americans, other minorities, and individuals with disabilities) who are interested in conducting research related to activities of the National Science Foundation (NSF) Division of Atmospheric and Geospace Sciences.

Eligibility This program is open to U.S. citizens, nationals, and permanent residents who received a Ph.D. within the past 3 years. Applicants must be interested in conducting a research project that is relevant to the activities of NSF Division of Atmospheric and Geospace Sciences: studies of the physics, chemistry, and dynamics of Earth's upper and lower atmosphere and its space environment; research on climate processes and variations; or studies to understand the natural global cycles of gases and particles in Earth's atmosphere. The project should be conducted at an institution (college or university, private nonprofit institute or museum, government installation, or laboratory) in the United States or abroad other than the applicant's Ph.D.-granting institution. Applications are encouraged from underrepresented minorities and persons with disabilities.

Financial data Grants are $86,000 per year, including a stipend of $58,000 per year, a research allowance of $19,000 per year, and a fringe benefit allowance of $9,000 per year.

Duration 2 years.

Number awarded 10 each year.

Deadline January of each year.

[1108]
AWARDS FOR FACULTY AT HISTORICALLY BLACK COLLEGES AND UNIVERSITIES

National Endowment for the Humanities
Attn: Division of Research Programs
1100 Pennsylvania Avenue, N.W., Room 318
Washington, DC 20506
(202) 606-8200   Toll Free: (800) NEH-1121
Fax: (202) 606-8204   TDD: (866) 372-2930
E-mail: FacultyAwards@neh.gov
Web: www.neh.gov/grants/guidelines/AF_HBCU.html

Summary To provide funding to faculty members at Historically Black Colleges and Universities (HBCUs) who are interested in working on a research project in the humanities.

Eligibility This program is open to current and retired faculty members affiliated with an HBCU. Applicants must be U.S. citizens or foreign nationals who have resided in the United States or its jurisdictions for at least 3 years. Eligible projects include conducting research in primary and secondary materials; producing articles, monographs, books, digital materials, archaeological site reports, translations, editions, or other scholarly resources; or conducting basic research leading to the improvement of an existing undergraduate course or the achievement of institutional or community research goals. Support is not provided for graduate course work, but the proposed project may contribute to the completion of a doctoral dissertation. Grants are not provided for curricular or pedagogical methods, theories, or surveys; preparation or revision of textbooks; research leading to the improvement of graduate courses; works in the creative or performing arts; projects that seek to promote a particular political, philosophical, religious, or ideological point of view; or projects that advocate a particular program of social action. Selection is based on: 1) the intellectual significance of the proposed project, including its value to scholars and general audiences in the humanities; 2) the quality or promise of quality of the applicant as a humanities teacher and researcher; 3) the quality of the conception, definition, organization, and description of the project; 4) the feasibility of the proposed plan of work; and 5) the likelihood that the applicant will complete the project.

Financial data The grant is $4,200 per month of full-time work, to a maximum of $50,400 for 12 months.

Duration 2 to 12 months.

Number awarded Varies each year.

Deadline April of each year.

[1109]
BEHAVIORAL SCIENCES POSTDOCTORAL FELLOWSHIPS IN EPILEPSY

Epilepsy Foundation
Attn: Research Department
8301 Professional Place
Landover, MD 20785-2237
(301) 459-3700   Toll Free: (800) EFA-1000
Fax: (301) 577-2684   TDD: (800) 332-2070
E-mail: grants@efa.org
Web: www.epilepsyfoundation.org

Summary To provide funding to postdoctorates in the behavioral sciences (particularly African Americans, other minorities, women, and individuals with disabilities) who wish to pursue research training in an area related to epilepsy.

Eligibility Applicants must have received a Ph.D. or equivalent degree in a field of social science, including (but not limited to) sociology, social work, anthropology, nursing, or economics. They must be interested in receiving additional research training to prepare for a career in clinical behavioral aspects of epilepsy. Academic faculty holding the rank of instructor or above are not eligible, nor are graduate or medical students, medical residents, permanent government employees, or employees in private industry. Because these fellowships are designed as training opportunities, the quality of the training plans and environment are considered in the selection process. Other selection criteria include the scientific quality of the proposed research, a statement regarding the relevance of the research to epilepsy, the applicant's qualifications, the preceptor's qualifications, adequacy of the facility, and related epilepsy programs at the institution. Applications from women, members of minority groups, and people with disabilities are especially encouraged. U.S. citizenship is not required, but the research must be conducted in the United States.

Financial data Grants up to $40,000 are available.

Duration 1 year.

Number awarded Varies each year.

Deadline March of each year.

[1110]
BEYOND MARGINS AWARD

PEN American Center
Attn: Beyond Margins Coordinator
588 Broadway, Suite 303
New York, NY 10012
(212) 334-1660, ext. 108   Fax: (212) 334-2181
E-mail: nick@pen.org
Web: www.pen.org/page.php/prmID/280

Summary To recognize and reward African Americans and other outstanding authors of color from any country.

Eligibility This award is presented to an author of color (African, Arab, Asian, Caribbean, Latino, and Native American) whose book-length writings were published in the United States during the current calendar year. Works of fiction, literary nonfiction, biography/memoir, and other works of literary character are strongly preferred. U.S. citizenship or residency is not required. Nominations must be submitted by publishers or agents.

Financial data The prize is $1,000.

Duration The prizes are awarded annually.

Number awarded 5 each year.

Deadline December of each year.

[1111]
BLACK FILMMAKER SHOWCASE

Showtime Networks Inc.
Attn: Nicki Lamirault
10880 Wilshire Boulevard, Suite 1600
Los Angeles, CA 90024
(310) 234-5241   Toll Free: (800) SHOWTIME
Web: www.sho.com

Summary To provide funding to filmmakers who submit outstanding work to the Black Filmmaker Showcase series on Showtime network.

Eligibility Filmmakers over 18 years of age who are legal U.S. residents may submit films for consideration in the Showtime Black Filmmaker Showcase. Entries must be videocassette copies of a 15- to 30-minute film created and produced by the entrant, preferably originally shot on 16mm or 35mm film. Judges select 3 to 5 finalists whose films are featured on Showtime during Black History Month. The film judged most outstanding receives this grant.

Financial data That grant is $30,000. Funds must be used to produce an original short film that will premiere exclusively on Showtime.

Duration The competition is held annually.

Additional information This program was established in 1992 as part of Showtime's ongoing effort to support up-and-coming talent in the African American community.

Number awarded 1 each year.

Deadline February of each year.

[1112]
BYRD FELLOWSHIP PROGRAM

Ohio State University
Byrd Polar Research Center
Attn: Fellowship Committee
Scott Hall Room 108
1090 Carmack Road
Columbus, OH 43210-1002
(614) 292-6531   Fax: (614) 292-4697
Web: bprc.osu.edu/byrdfellow

Summary To provide funding to postdoctorates (particularly African Americans and others from underrepresented groups) who are interested in conducting research on the Arctic or Antarctic areas at Ohio State University.

Eligibility This program is open to postdoctorates of superior academic background who are interested in conducting advanced research on either Arctic or Antarctic problems at the Byrd Polar Research Center at Ohio State University. Applicants must have received their doctorates within the past 5 years. Each application should include a statement of general research interest, a description of the specific research to be conducted during the fellowship, and a curriculum vitae. Women, minorities, Vietnam-era veterans, disabled veterans, and individuals with disabilities are particularly encouraged to apply.

Financial data The stipend is $40,000 per year; an allowance of $3,000 for research and travel is also provided.

Duration 18 months.

Additional information This program was established by a major gift from the Byrd Foundation in memory of Rear Admiral Richard Evelyn Byrd and Marie Ames Byrd, his wife. Except for field work or other research activities requiring absence from campus, fellows are expected to be in residence at the university for the duration of the program.

Deadline October of each year.

[1113]
CAREER AWARDS FOR MEDICAL SCIENTISTS

Burroughs Wellcome Fund
21 T.W. Alexander Drive, Suite 100
P.O. Box 13901
Research Triangle Park, NC 27709-3901
(919) 991-5100   Fax: (919) 991-5160
E-mail: info@bwfund.org
Web: www.bwfund.org

Summary To provide funding to biomedical scientists in the United States and Canada (especially African Americans or other minorities and women) who require assistance to make the transition from postdoctoral training to faculty appointment.

Eligibility This program is open to citizens and permanent residents of the United States and Canada who have an M.D., D.D.S., D.V.M., Pharm.D., or equivalent clinical degree. Applicants must be interested in a program of research training in the area of basic biomedical, disease-oriented, translational, or molecular, genetic, or pharmacological epidemiology research. Training must take place at a degree-granting medical school, graduate school, hospital, or research institute in the United States or Canada. Each U.S. and Canadian institution may nominate up to 5 candidates. The sponsor encourages institutions to nominate women and underrepresented minorities (African Americans, Hispanics, or Native Americans); if a woman or underrepresented minority is among the initial 5 candidates, the institution may nominate a sixth candidate who is a woman or underrepresented minority. Following their postdoctoral training, awardees may accept a faculty position at a U.S. or Canadian institution.

Financial data For each year of postdoctoral support, the stipend is $65,000, the research allowance is $20,500, and the administrative fee is $9,500. For each year of faculty support, the stipend is $150,000, the research allowance is $3,000, and the administrative fee is $17,000. The maximum portion of the award that can be used during the postdoctoral period is $190,000 or $95,000 per year. The faculty portion of the award is $700,000 minus the portion used during the postdoctoral years.

Duration The awards provide up to 2 years of postdoctoral support and up to 3 years of support during the faculty appointment.

Additional information This program began in 1995 as Career Awards in the Biomedical Sciences (CABS). It was revised to its current format in 2006 as a result of the NIH K99/R00 Pathway to Independence program. As the CABS, the program provided more than $100 million in support to 241 U.S. and Canadian scientists. Awardees are required to devote at least 75% of their time to research-related activities.

Number awarded Varies each year: recently, 5 of these awards were granted.

Deadline September of each year.

[1114]
CAREER DEVELOPMENT AWARD TO PROMOTE DIVERSITY IN NEUROSCIENCE RESEARCH

National Institute of Neurological Disorders and Stroke
Attn: Office of Minority Health and Research
6001 Executive Boulevard, Suite 2150
Bethesda, MD 20892-9527
(301) 496-3102   Fax: (301) 594-5929
TDD: (301) 451-0088 E-mail: jonesmiche@ninds.nih.gov
Web: www.ninds.nih.gov

Summary To provide funding to neurological research scientists who are African Americans or members of other underrepresented groups interested in making a transition to a career as an independent investigator.

Eligibility This program is open to full-time faculty members at domestic, for-profit and nonprofit, public and private institutions, such as universities, colleges, hospitals, and laboratories. Applicants must be junior neuroscience investigators making the transition to an independent scientific career at the senior postdoctoral and junior faculty stages under the supervision of a qualified mentor. They must qualify as 1) a member of an ethnic or racial group shown to be underrepresented in health-related sciences on a national basis; 2) an individual with a disability; or 3) an individual from a disadvantaged background, including those from a low-income family and those from a social, cultural, and/or educational environment that has inhibited them from preparation for a research career. Selection is based on qualifications of the applicant, soundness of the proposed career development plan, training in the responsible conduct of research, nature and scientific/technical merit of the proposed research plan, qualifications and appropriateness of the mentor, environment and institutional commitment to the applicant's career, and strength of the description of how this particular award will promote diversity within the institution or in science nationally. Only U.S. citizens, nationals, and permanent residents are eligible.

Financial data Grants provide an annual award of up to $85,000 for salary and fringe benefits and an annual research allowance of up to $50,000 for direct research costs. The institution may apply for up to 8% of direct costs for facilities and administrative costs.

Duration 3 to 5 years; nonrenewable.

Additional information Recipients must devote 75% of full-time professional effort to conducting health-related research.

Number awarded Varies each year.

Deadline February, June, or October of each year.

[1115]
CAREER DEVELOPMENT AWARDS IN DIABETES RESEARCH

Juvenile Diabetes Research Foundation International
Attn: Grant Administrator
26 Broadway, 14th Floor
New York, NY 10004
(212) 479-7572   Toll Free: (800) 533-CURE
Fax: (212) 785-9595   E-mail: info@jdrf.org
Web: www.jdrf.org/index.cfm?page_id=111715

Summary To provide assistance to young scientists (especially African American and other underrepresented scientists) who are interested in developing into independent investigators in diabetes-related research.

Eligibility This program is open to postdoctorates early in their faculty careers who show promise as diabetes researchers. Applicants must have received their first doctoral (M.D., Ph.D., D.M.D., D.V.M., or equivalent) degree at least 3 but not more than 7 years previously. They may not have an academic position at the associate professor, professor, or equivalent level, but they must be a faculty member (instructor or assistant professor) at a university, health science center, or comparable institution with strong, well-established research and training programs. The proposed research must relate to Type 1 diabetes, but it may be basic or clinical. There are no citizenship requirements. Applications are encouraged from women, members of minority groups underrepresented in the sciences, and people with disabilities. The proposed research may be conducted at foreign and domestic, for-profit and non-profit, and public and private institutions, including universities, colleges, hospitals, laboratories, units of state and local government, and eligible agencies of the federal government. Selection is based on the applicant's perceived ability and potential for a career in Type 1 diabetes research, the caliber of the proposed research, and the quality and commitment of the host institution.

Financial data The total award may be up to $150,000 each year. Indirect costs cannot exceed 10%.

Duration Up to 5 years.

Additional information Fellows must spend up to 75% of their time in research.

Deadline January or July of each year.

[1116]
CAREER DEVELOPMENT GRANTS
American Association of University Women
Attn: AAUW Educational Foundation
301 ACT Drive, Department 60
P.O. Box 4030
Iowa City, IA 52243-4030
(319) 337-1716, ext. 60   Fax: (319) 337-1204
E-mail: aauw@act.org
Web: www.aauw.org

Summary To provide financial assistance to African American and other women who are seeking career advancement, career change, or reentry into the workforce.

Eligibility This program is open to women who are U.S. citizens or permanent residents, have earned a bachelor's degree, received their most recent degree more than 4 years ago, and are making career changes, seeking to advance in current careers, or reentering the work force. Applicants must be interested in working toward a master's degree, second bachelor's or associate degree, professional degree (e.g., M.D., J.D.), certification program, or technical school certificate. They must be planning to undertake course work at an accredited 2- or 4-year college or university (or a technical school that is licensed, accredited, or approved by the U.S. Department of Education). Special consideration is given to women of color and women pursuing credentials in nontraditional fields. Support is not provided for prerequisite course work or for Ph.D. course work or dissertations. Selection is based on demonstrated commitment to education and equity for women and girls, reason for seeking higher education or technical training, degree to which study plan is consistent with career objectives, potential for success in chosen field, documentation of opportunities in chosen field, feasibility of

study plans and proposed time schedule, validity of proposed budget and budget narrative (including sufficient outside support), and quality of written proposal.

Financial data Grants range from $2,000 to $12,000. Funds may be used for tuition, fees, books, supplies, local transportation, dependent child care, or purchase of a computer required for the study program.

Duration 1 year, beginning in July; nonrenewable.

Additional information The filing fee is $35.

Number awarded Varies each year; recently, 47 of these grants, with a value of $500,000, were awarded.

Deadline December of each year.

[1117]
CAROLINA POSTDOCTORAL PROGRAM FOR FACULTY DIVERSITY
University of North Carolina at Chapel Hill
Attn: Office of the Vice Chancellor for Research
312 South Building, CB #4000
Chapel Hill, NC 27599-4000
(919) 962-4041   Fax: (919) 962-1476
E-mail: susan_walters@.unc.edu
Web: research.unc.edu

Summary To support African American and other minority scholars who are interested in teaching and conducting research at the University of North Carolina (UNC).

Eligibility This program is open to scholars from underrepresented groups who have completed their doctoral degree within the past 4 years. Applicants must be interested in teaching and conducting research at UNC. Preference is given to U.S. citizens and permanent residents. Selection is based on the evidence of scholarship potential and ability to compete for tenure-track appointments at UNC and other research universities.

Financial data Fellows receive $36,282 per year, plus an allowance for research and travel. Health benefits are also available.

Duration Up to 2 years.

Additional information Fellows must be in residence at the Chapel Hill campus for the duration of the program. They teach 1 course per year and spend the rest of the time in research. This program began in 1983.

Number awarded 5 or 6 each year.

Deadline January of each year.

[1118]
CARTER G. WOODSON INSTITUTE POSTDOCTORAL RESIDENTIAL RESEARCH AND TEACHING FELLOWSHIP
University of Virginia
Carter G. Woodson Institute for African-American and African Studies
Attn: Associate Director for Research
108 Minor Hall
P.O. Box 400162
Charlottesville, VA 22904-4162
(804) 924-3109   Fax: (804) 924-8820
E-mail: woodson@virginia.edu
Web: artsandsciences.virginia.edu

Summary To support postdoctoral research at the University of Virginia's Woodson Institute in those disciplines of the humanities and social sciences concerned with African American and African studies.

Eligibility Applicants for postdoctoral fellowships must have completed their Ph.D. by the time of application or furnish proof of its receipt before July of the fellowship year. They must be interested in conducting research in the fields of African American studies, African studies, or Afro-Caribbean studies, and in those disciplines within the humanities and social sciences traditionally related to those fields. Preference is given to applicants whose work 1) elucidates the trans-continental experiences and discourses related to the social, historical, and cultural construction of people of African descent through both traditional and recent approaches (Pan-Africanism, Afrocentrism, Trans-Atlantic Studies, African Diaspora Studies, critical race theory, or cultural studies); 2) advances theories on the construction of race and race in relation to other social identities (class, gender, sexuality, nationality, disability) as well as that which focuses on refining methods of interdisciplinary scholarship on race; 3) engages the professions (law, medicine, social work, public policy, education, architecture, planning) in innovative ways; or 4) can be readily adapted for the creation of courses and pedagogies directly related to the institute's curriculum in African American and Diasporic Studies. Selection is based on the significance of the proposed work, the qualifications of the applicant, familiarity with existing relevant research literature, the research design of the project, and the promise of completion within the award period. Awards are granted without restriction on citizenship or current residence.

Financial data The grant is $45,000 per year.

Duration 2 years.

Additional information Fellows must be in residence at the University of Virginia for the duration of the award period. They are expected to contribute to the intellectual life of the university.

Number awarded 1 or 2 each year.

Deadline November of each year.

[1119]
CAVE CANEM FELLOWSHIP

Vermont Studio Center
80 Pearl Street
P.O. Box 613
Johnson, VT 05656
(802) 635-2727   Fax: (802) 635-2730
E-mail: info@vermontstudiocenter.org
Web: www.vermontstudiocenter.org

Summary To provide funding to African American poets who are interested in a residency at the Vermont Studio Center in Johnson, Vermont.

Eligibility This program is open to African American poets who are interested in a residency at the center in Johnson, Vermont. Applicants must submit up to 10 pages of their work. Selection is based on artistic merit.

Financial data The award pays $3,750, which covers all residency fees.

Duration 4 weeks.

Additional information This fellowship, first awarded in 2009, is sponsored by Cave Canem, an organization of African American poets founded in 1996. The application fee is $25.

Number awarded 1 each year.

Deadline June of each year.

[1120]
CENTER FOR ADVANCED STUDY IN THE BEHAVIORAL SCIENCES RESIDENTIAL POSTDOCTORAL FELLOWSHIPS

Center for Advanced Study in the Behavioral Sciences
Attn: Secretary and Program Coordinator
75 Alta Road
Stanford, CA 94305-8090
(650) 321-2052   Fax: (650) 321-1192
E-mail: secretary@casbs.org
Web: www.casbs.org

Summary To provide funding to behavioral scientists (especially African Americans and other underrepresented scientists) who are interested in conducting research at the Center for Advanced Study in the Behavioral Sciences in Stanford, California.

Eligibility Eligible to be nominated for this fellowship are scientists and scholars from this country or abroad who show exceptional accomplishment or promise in the core social and behavioral disciplines: anthropology, economics, political science, psychology, or sociology; applications are also accepted from scholars in a wide range of humanistic disciplines, education, linguistics, and the biological sciences. Selection is based on standing in the field rather than on the merit of a particular project under way at a given time. A special effort is made to promote diversity among the scholars by encouraging participation from groups that often have been overlooked in academia: younger scholars, women, minorities, international scholars, and scholars whose home universities are not research-oriented.

Financial data The stipend is based on the fellow's regular salary for the preceding year, with a cap of $60,000. In most cases, the fellow contributes to the cost of the stipend with support from sabbatical or other funding source.

Duration From 9 to 11 months.

Additional information Fellows must be in residence in a community within 10 miles of the center for the duration of the program.

Number awarded Approximately 45 each year.

Deadline February of each year.

[1121]
CENTER ON BUDGET AND POLICY PRIORITIES INTERNSHIPS

Center on Budget and Policy Priorities
Attn: Internship Coordinator
820 First Street, N.E., Suite 510
Washington, DC 20002
(202) 408-1080   Fax: (202) 408-1056
E-mail: internship@cbpp.org
Web: www.cbpp.org/jobs/index.cfm?fa=internships

Summary To provide work experience at the Center on Budget and Policy Priorities (CBPP) in Washington, D.C. to African Americans and other undergraduates, graduate students, and recent college graduates.

Eligibility This program is open to undergraduates, graduate students, and recent college graduates who are interested in public policy issues affecting low-income families and individuals. Applicants must be interested in working at CBPP in the following areas: media, federal legislation, health policy, housing policy, international budget project, Food Stamps, national budget and tax policy, outreach campaigns, state budget and tax policy, welfare reform, and income support. They should have research, fact-gathering, writing, analytic, and computer skills and a willingness to do administrative as well as substantive tasks. Women, international students, and minorities are encouraged to apply.

Financial data Hourly stipends are $8.50 for undergraduates, $9.50 for interns with a bachelor's degree, $10.50 for graduate students, $12.50 for interns with a master's or law degree, and $12.50 to $15.50 for doctoral students (depending on progress towards completion of degree requirements, relevant course work, and research).

Duration 1 semester; may be renewed.

Additional information The center specializes in research and analysis oriented toward practical policy decisions and produces analytic reports that are accessible to public officials at national, state, and local levels, to nonprofit organizations, and to the media.

Number awarded Varies each semester; recently, 5 interns were appointed for a fall semester.

Deadline February of each year for summer internships; June of each year for fall internships; October of each year for spring internships.

[1122]
CHANCELLOR'S POSTDOCTORAL FELLOWSHIPS FOR ACADEMIC DIVERSITY

University of California at Berkeley
Attn: Office for Faculty Equity
200 California Hall
Berkeley, CA 94720-1500
(510) 642-1935   E-mail: admin.ofe@berkeley.edu
Web: vcei.berkeley.edu/ChancPostdocFellowship

Summary To provide an opportunity for African American and other recent postdoctorates who will increase diversity at the University of California at Berkeley to conduct research on the campus.

Eligibility This program is open to U.S. citizens and permanent residents who received a doctorate within 3 years of the start of the fellowship. The program particularly solicits applications from individuals who are members of groups that are underrepresented in American universities (e.g., women, ethnic minorities, religious minorities, differently-abled, lesbian/gay/bisexual/transgender). Special consideration is given to applicants committed to careers in university research and teaching and whose life experience, research, or employment background will contribute significantly to academic diversity and excellence at the Berkeley campus.

Financial data The stipend is $41,496 per year (11 months, plus 1 month vacation). The award also includes health insurance, vision and dental benefits, and up to $4,000 for research-related and program travel expenses.

Duration 1 year; may be renewed 1 additional year.

Additional information Research opportunities, mentoring, and guidance are provided as part of the program.

Number awarded Varies each year; recently, 5 of these fellowships were awarded.

Deadline November of each year.

[1123]
CHARLES A. RYSKAMP RESEARCH FELLOWSHIPS

American Council of Learned Societies
Attn: Office of Fellowships and Grants
633 Third Avenue
New York, NY 10017-6795
(212) 697-1505   Fax: (212) 949-8058
E-mail: fellowships@acls.org
Web: www.acls.org/programs/ryskamp

Summary To provide research funding to African American and other advanced assistant professors in all disciplines of the humanities and the humanities-related social sciences.

Eligibility This program is open to advanced assistant and untenured associate professors in the humanities and related social sciences. Applicants must have successfully completed their institution's last reappointment review before tenure review. They must have a Ph.D. or equivalent degree and be employed at an academic institution in the United States. Appropriate fields of specialization include, but are not limited to, American studies; anthropology; archaeology; art and architectural history; classics; economics; film; geography; history; languages and literatures; legal studies; linguistics; musicology; philosophy; political science; psychology; religious studies; rhetoric, communication, and media studies; sociology; and theater, dance, and performance studies. Proposals in those fields of the social sciences are eligible only if they employ predominantly humanistic approaches (e.g., economic history, law and literature, political philosophy). Proposals in interdisciplinary and cross-disciplinary studies are welcome, as are proposals focused on any geographic region or on any cultural or linguistic group. Applicants are encouraged to spend substantial periods of their leaves in residential interdisciplinary centers, research libraries, or other scholarly archives in the United States or abroad. Applications are particularly invited from women and members of minority groups.

Financial data Fellows receive a stipend of $64,000, a grant of $2,500 for research and travel, and the possibility of an additional summer's support, if justified by a persuasive case.

Duration 1 academic year (9 months) plus an additional summer's research (2 months) if justified.

Additional information This program, first available for the 2002-03 academic year, is supported by funding from the Andrew W. Mellon Foundation.

Number awarded Up to 12 each year.

Deadline September of each year.

[1124]
CHIPS QUINN SCHOLARS PROGRAM

Freedom Forum
Attn: Chips Quinn Scholars Program
555 Pennsylvania Avenue, N.W.
Washington, DC 20001
(202) 292-6271   Fax: (202) 292-6275
E-mail: kcatone@freedomforum.org
Web: www.chipsquinn.org

Summary To provide work experience to African American and other minority college students or recent graduates who are majoring in journalism.

Eligibility This program is open to students of color who are college juniors, seniors, or recent graduates with journalism majors or career goals in newspapers. Candidates must be nominated or endorsed by journalism faculty, campus media advisers, editors of newspapers, or leaders of minority journalism associations. Along with their application, they must submit a resume, transcripts, 2 letters of recommendation, and an essay of 200 to 500 words on why they want to be a Chips Quinn Scholar. Reporters must also submit 6 samples of published articles they have written; photographers must submit 10 to 20 photographs on a CD. Applicants must have a car and be available to work as a full-time intern during the spring or summer. U.S. citizenship or permanent resident status is required. Campus newspaper experience is strongly encouraged.

Financial data Students chosen for this program receive a travel stipend to attend a Multimedia training program in Nashville, Tennessee prior to reporting for their internship, a $500 housing allowance from the Freedom Forum, and a competitive salary during their internship.

Duration Internships are for 10 to 12 weeks, in spring or summer.

Additional information This program was established in 1991 in memory of the late John D. Quinn Jr., managing editor of the *Poughkeepsie Journal.* Funding is provided by the Freedom Forum, formerly the Gannett Foundation. After graduating from college and obtaining employment with a newspaper, alumni of this program are eligible to apply for fellowship support to attend professional journalism development activities.

Number awarded Approximately 70 each year. Since the program began, more than 1,200 scholars have been selected.

Deadline October of each year.

[1125]
CLAIRE M. FAGIN FELLOWSHIP

American Academy of Nursing
Attn: Geriatric Nursing Capacity Program
888 17th Street, N.W., Suite 800
Washington, DC 20006
(202) 777-1170   Fax: (202) 777-0107
E-mail: bagnc@aannet.org
Web: www.geriatricnursing.org

Summary To provide funding to nurses (particularly African American and other underrepresented nurses) who are interested in a program of postdoctoral research training in geriatric nursing.

Eligibility This program is open to registered nurses who hold a doctoral degree in nursing and have a faculty position as an assistant or associate professor at a school of nursing. Recent doctorates in nursing are also eligible. Priority is given to those who received a Ph.D. within the past 7 years. Applicants must demonstrate evidence of commitment to a career in geriatric nursing and education and the potential to develop into independent investigators. They must submit 1) a professional development plan that identifies activities intended to prepare the applicant in research, teaching, and leadership; and 2) a geriatric nursing research project consistent with their interests and previous research or clinical experience, including a mentor who is a geriatric nurse scientist and with whom they will work. Selection is based on potential for sub-

stantial long-term contributions to the knowledge base in geriatric nursing; leadership potential; evidence of commitment to a career in academic geriatric nursing; and evidence of involvement in educational, research, and professional activities. U.S citizenship or permanent resident status is required. Members of underrepresented minority groups (American Indians, Alaska Natives, Asians, Blacks or African Americans, Hispanics or Latinos/Latinas, Native Hawaiians or other Pacific Islanders) are especially encouraged to apply.

Financial data The stipend is $60,000 per year. An additional $5,000 is available to fellows whose research includes the study of pain in the elderly.

Duration 2 years.

Additional information This program began in 2001 with funding from the John A. Hartford Foundation. In 2004, the Atlantic Philanthropies of New York City provided additional support and the Mayday Fund added funding for scholars who focus on the study of pain in the elderly.

Number awarded Varies each year; recently, 9 of these fellowships were awarded.

Deadline January of each year.

[1126]
CMS HISTORICALLY BLACK COLLEGES AND UNIVERSITIES HEALTH SERVICES RESEARCH GRANT PROGRAM

Centers for Medicare & Medicaid Services
Attn: Office of Research, Development, and Information
C3-19-07
7500 Security Boulevard
Baltimore, MD 21244-1850
(410) 786-7250   Toll Free: (877) 267-2323
TDD: (877) 486-2048
E-mail: Richard.Bragg@cms.hhs.gov
Web: www.cms.gov/ResearchDemoGrantsOpt

Summary To provide funding to faculty at Historically Black Colleges and Universities (HBCUs) interested in carrying out health services research activities.

Eligibility This program is open to faculty at HBCUs that meet 1 of the following requirements: 1) offers a Ph.D. or master's degree in 1 or more of these disciplines: allied health, economics, gerontology, health services administration, health care administration, health education, health management, human services and consumer sciences, nursing, nutrition, pharmacology, psychology, public health, public policy, or social work; 2) has a school of medicine; or 3) is a member of the National HBCU Network for Health Services and Health Disparities. Applicants must be interested in conducting small research projects that relate to health care deliver and health financing issues affecting African American communities, including issues of access to health care, utilization of health care services, health outcomes, quality of services, cost of care, health and racial disparities, socio-economic differences, cultural barriers, managed care systems, and activities related to health screening, prevention, outreach, and education.

Financial data Grants range up to $100,000 per year.

Duration Up to 2 years.

Additional information This program began in 1997. Until 2001, the Centers for Medicare & Medicaid Services was known as the Health Care Financing Administration.

Number awarded Up to 5 each year.

Deadline Letters of intent must be submitted in May of each year. Final applications are due in June.

[1127]
COLLABORATIVE RESEARCH FELLOWSHIPS

American Council of Learned Societies
Attn: Office of Fellowships and Grants
633 Third Avenue
New York, NY 10017-6795
(212) 697-1505   Fax: (212) 949-8058
E-mail: fellowships@acls.org
Web: www.acls.org

Summary To provide funding for collaborative research to scholars in any discipline of the humanities and the humanities-related social sciences, especially African Americans, other minorities, and women.

Eligibility This program is open to teams of 2 or more scholars interested in collaborating on a single, substantive project. The project coordinator must have an appointment at a U.S.-based institution of higher education; other project members may be at institutions outside the United States or may be independent scholars. Appropriate fields of specialization include, but are not limited to, American studies; anthropology; archaeology; art and architectural history; classics; economics; film; geography; history; languages and literatures; legal studies; linguistics; musicology; philosophy; political science; psychology; religious studies; rhetoric, communication, and media studies; sociology; and theater, dance, and performance studies. Proposals in those fields of the social sciences are eligible only if they employ predominantly humanistic approaches (e.g., economic history, law and literature, political philosophy). Proposals in interdisciplinary and cross-disciplinary studies are welcome, as are proposals focused on a geographic region or on a cultural or linguistic group. Applications are particularly invited from women and members of minority groups.

Financial data The amount of the grant depends on the number of collaborators, their academic rank, and the duration of research leaves. Funding for salaries is provided at the rate of $60,000 for full professors, $40,000 for associate professors, or $35,000 for assistant professors. An additional $20,000 may be provided for collaboration funds (e.g., travel, materials, research assistance). The maximum amount for any single project is $140,000.

Duration Up to 24 months.

Additional information This program, established in 2008, is supported by funding from the Andrew W. Mellon Foundation.

Number awarded Up to 7 each year.

Deadline September of each year.

[1128]
CONGRESSIONAL BLACK CAUCUS FOUNDATION CONGRESSIONAL FELLOWS PROGRAM

Congressional Black Caucus Foundation, Inc.
Attn: Director, Educational Programs
1720 Massachusetts Avenue, N.W.
Washington, DC 20036
(202) 263-2800   Toll Free: (800) 784-2577
Fax: (202) 775-0773   E-mail: info@cbcfinc.org
Web: www.cbcfinc.org

Summary To provide African Americans with the opportunity to work directly with members of Congress on their committees or as personal staff.

Eligibility This program is open to African Americans who have a master's or professional degree and familiarity with the federal legislative process, Congress, the Congressional Black Caucus (CBC), and its members. Applicants must be interested in working in Washington, D.C. on the staff or committee of a member of the CBC. They must be able to demonstrate an interest in public policy, a commitment to creating and implementing policy to improve the living conditions for underserved and underrepresented minorities, a record of academic and professional achievement, evidence of leadership skills, and the potential for further growth. Preference is given to applicants with expertise in areas that support policy agendas of CBC members.

Financial data The stipend is $40,000; fellows are responsible for their own travel, housing, and other expenses.

Duration 9 months, beginning in September. An optional summer placement is also available.

Additional information This program began in 1976 as a graduate intern program and was expanded to its present form in 1982.

Number awarded 6 to 9 each year.

Deadline March of each year.

[1129]
CONGRESSIONAL FELLOWSHIPS OF THE AMERICAN ASSOCIATION FOR THE ADVANCEMENT OF SCIENCE

American Association for the Advancement of Science
Attn: Science and Technology Policy Fellowships
1200 New York Avenue, N.W.
Washington, DC 20005-3920
(202) 326-6700   Fax: (202) 289-4950
E-mail: fellowships@aaas.org
Web: fellowships.aaas.org

Summary To provide postdoctoral scientists and engineers (especially African Americans, other minorities, and individuals with disabilities) with an opportunity to work as special legislative assistants on the staffs of members of Congress or Congressional committees.

Eligibility This program is open to doctoral-level scientists (Ph.D., M.D., D.V.M., D.Sc., and other terminal degrees) in any physical, biological, medical, or social science; any field of engineering; or any relevant interdisciplinary field. Engineers with a master's degree and at least 3 years of professional experience are also eligible. Applicants must demonstrate exceptional competence in some area of science or engineering; have a good scientific and technical background; be cognizant of many matters in nonscientific areas; demonstrate sensitivity toward political and social issues; have a strong interest and some experience in applying personal knowledge toward the solution of societal problems; and be interested in working as special legislative assistants for Congress. U.S. citizenship is required; federal employees are not eligible. Members of underrepresented minority groups and persons with disabilities are encouraged to apply.

Financial data The stipend is $74,872. Also provided are a $4,000 relocation allowance for fellows from outside the Washington, D.C. area, reimbursement for health insurance, and a $4,000 travel allowance.

Duration 1 year, beginning in September.

Additional information The program includes an orientation on Congressional and executive branch operations and a year-long seminar program on issues involving science and public policy. Approximately 30 other national science and engineering societies sponsor fellows in collaboration with this program; for a list of all of those, contact the sponsor.

Number awarded 2 each year.

Deadline December of each year.

[1130]
CORETTA SCOTT KING BOOK AWARD

American Library Association
Ethnic and Multicultural Material Information Exchange
  Round Table
c/o Office for Literacy and Outreach Services
50 East Huron Street
Chicago, IL 60611-2795
(312) 280-4295   Toll Free: (800) 545-2433, ext. 4295
Fax: (312) 280-3256   TDD: (888) 814-7692
E-mail: olos@ala.org
Web: www.ala.org

Summary To recognize and reward African American authors and illustrators of published works for youth on the African American experience.

Eligibility This award is available to African American authors and illustrators who have written or illustrated work for a young audience. Entries must be original work that portrays an aspect of the African American experience, including biographical, social, historical, and social history treatments. Work by authors must meet established standards of quality writing for youth, including clear plot, well-drawn characters that portray growth and development during the course of the story, writing style that is consistent with and suitable to the audience, and accuracy. Work by illustrators should lead to an appreciation of beauty, be neither coy nor condescending, enlarge upon the story elements that were suggested in the text, and include details that will awaken and strengthen the imagination of readers and permit them to interpret the words and pictures in a manner unique to them. Particular attention is given to titles that seek to motivate readers to develop their own attitudes and behaviors as well as comprehend their personal duty and responsibility as citizens in a pluralistic society. Authors and illustrators must live in the United States or maintain dual residency/citizenship.

Financial data The awards, presented at the annual conference of the American Library Association, consist of a plaque, $1,000, and a set of encyclopedias (*World Book* to the illustrator and *Britannica* to the author).

Duration The award is presented annually.

Additional information These awards, presented since 1969, are sponsored by the Coretta Scott King Book Award Committee (for the author's award) and Demco, Inc. (for the illustrator's award).

Number awarded 2 each year: 1 to an author and 1 to an illustrator.

Deadline November of each year.

[1131]
CORETTA SCOTT KING-VIRGINIA HAMILTON AWARD FOR LIFETIME ACHIEVEMENT/ AUTHOR-ILLUSTRATOR CATEGORY

American Library Association
Ethnic and Multicultural Material Information Exchange
  Round Table
c/o Office for Literacy and Outreach Services
50 East Huron Street
Chicago, IL 60611-2795
(312) 280-4295   Toll Free: (800) 545-2433, ext. 4295
Fax: (312) 280-3256   TDD: (888) 814-7692
E-mail: olos@ala.org
Web: www.ala.org

Summary To recognize and reward African American authors and illustrators who have made outstanding contributions to literature for children and/or young adults.

Eligibility This award is available to African American authors and illustrators whose published books for children and/or young adults has made a significant and lasting contribution. Nominees' work must represent distinguished writing and/or illustrations by and about the African American experience. In the selection process, special consideration is given to bodies of work 1) whose interpretation consistently motivates youth readers to stretch their imagination and thinking; 2) which denote exceptional examples of specific types of literature; and 3) the represent trend-setters, innovations, or fresh explorations of themes, topics, or perspectives in African American literature for children and/or young adults.

Financial data The award includes an honorarium of $1,500 and a plaque.

Duration The award is presented biennially, in even-numbered years.

Additional information This award was first presented in 2010.

Number awarded 1 each year.

Deadline December of each odd-numbered year.

[1132]
CORETTA SCOTT KING-VIRGINIA HAMILTON AWARD FOR LIFETIME ACHIEVEMENT/ PRACTITIONER CATEGORY

American Library Association
Ethnic and Multicultural Material Information Exchange
  Round Table
c/o Office for Literacy and Outreach Services
50 East Huron Street
Chicago, IL 60611-2795
(312) 280-4295   Toll Free: (800) 545-2433, ext. 4295
Fax: (312) 280-3256   TDD: (888) 814-7692
E-mail: olos@ala.org
Web: www.ala.org

Summary To recognize and reward youth advocates who have contributed to the promotion and use of African American literature.

Eligibility This award is available to youth advocates, including public librarians, academic librarians, school librarians (public or private), educators (preK-12 or higher education), or youth literature practitioners. Nominees must have made a significant contribution to champion youth reading and engagement with award-winning African American literature. Their vocation, work, volunteer service, or ongoing promotion of books with and/or on behalf of youth must have been significant and sustained. Preference is given to nominees whose service has been significant over at least 10 years. Selection is based on level of dedication to the promotion of reading and implementation of various reading and reading-related programs, depth of involvement, impact of work, and overall amount of time committed to such service.

Financial data The award includes an honorarium of $1,500 and a plaque.

Duration The award is presented biennially, in odd-numbered years.

Additional information This award was first presented in 2011.

Number awarded 1 each year.

Deadline December of each even-numbered year.

[1133]
CURRICULUM DEVELOPMENT, IMPLEMENTATION, AND SUSTAINABILITY GRANTS

United Negro College Fund Special Programs Corporation
Attn: Institute for International Public Policy
6402 Arlington Boulevard, Suite 600
Falls Church, VA 22042
(703) 677-3400   Toll Free: (800) 530-6232
Fax: (703) 205-7645   E-mail: iippl@uncfsp.org
Web: www.uncfsp.org

Summary To provide funding to faculty at Historically Black Colleges and Universities (HBCUs) or other Minority Serving Institutions (MSIs) who are interested in developing new courses or enhancing existing courses focusing on international affairs, international relations, area studies, or Less Commonly Taught Languages (LCTLs).

Eligibility This program is open to full-time and adjunct faculty at Alaska Native Serving Institutions, Hispanic Serving Institutions, Historically Black Colleges and Universities, Native Hawaiian Serving Institutions, and Tribal Colleges or University/Tribally Controlled Colleges and Universities. Applicants must be proposing to conduct a project involving 1) development of new courses focusing on international affairs, international relations, area studies, or LCTLs; 2) enhancement of existing course curricula; 3) development and enhancement of strategic plans; 4) program development assessment; and/or 5) staff development. They may be instructors of international relations, foreign policy, foreign languages (especially LCTLs), political science, sociology, economics, statistics, journalism, world geography, or other relevant disciplines. Selection is based on significance of the project (15 points), quality of project design (15 points), quality of project personnel (10 points), quality of management

plan (15 points), adequacy of resources (15 points), quality of project evaluation (15 points), and project budget (15 points).

Financial data The grant is $5,000 per year.

Duration 2 years.

Number awarded 3 each year.

Deadline January of each year.

[1134]
DANIEL H. EFRON RESEARCH AWARD

American College of Neuropsychopharmacology
Attn: Executive Office
5034-A Thoroughbred Lane
Brentwood, TN 37027
(615) 324-2360   Fax: (615) 523-1715
E-mail: acnp@acnp.org
Web: www.acnp.org/programs/awards.aspx

Summary To recognize and reward young scientists (particularly African Americans, other minorities, and women) who have conducted outstanding basic or translational research in neuropsychopharmacology.

Eligibility This award is available to scientists who are younger than 50 years of age. Nominees must have made an outstanding basic or translational contribution to neuropsychopharmacology. The contribution may be preclinical or work that emphasizes the relationship between basic and clinical research. Selection is based on the quality of the contribution and its impact on advancing neuropsychopharmacology. Membership in the American College of Neuropsychopharmacology (ACNP) is not required. Nomination of women and minorities is highly encouraged.

Financial data The award consists of an expense-paid trip to the ACNP annual meeting, a monetary honorarium, and a plaque.

Duration The award is presented annually.

Additional information This award was first presented in 1974.

Number awarded 1 each year.

Deadline Nominations must be submitted by June of each year.

[1135]
DARLENE CLARK HINE AWARD

Organization of American Historians
Attn: Award and Committee Coordinator
112 North Bryan Street
Bloomington, IN 47408-4141
(812) 855-7311   Fax: (812) 855-0696
E-mail: khamm@oah.org
Web: www.oah.org/awards/awards.hine.index.html

Summary To recognize and reward authors of outstanding books dealing with African American women's and gender history.

Eligibility This award is presented to the author of the outstanding book on African American women's and gender history. Entries must have been published during the current calendar year.

Financial data The award is $1,000.

Duration The award is presented annually.

Additional information This award was first presented in 2010.

Number awarded 1 each year.

Deadline September of each year.

[1136]
DEFENSE UNIVERSITY RESEARCH INSTRUMENTATION PROGRAM

Army Research Office
Attn: AMSRD-ARL-RO-SG-SI(DURIP)
4300 South Miami Boulevard
P.O. Box 12211
Research Triangle Park, NC 27709-2211
(919) 549-4207   Fax: (919) 549-4248
Web: www.arl.army.mil/www/default.cfm?Action=6&Page=8

Summary To provide funding to researchers at colleges and universities in designated states, especially those at Historically Black Colleges and Universities (HBCUs) and other Minority Institutions (MIs), for the purchase of equipment.

Eligibility This program is open to researchers at colleges and universities in the United States with degree-granting programs in science, mathematics, and/or engineering. Applicants must be seeking funding for the acquisition of major equipment to augment current or to develop new research capabilities to support research in technical areas of interest to the Department of Defense. Proposals are encouraged from researchers at HBCUs and MIs.

Financial data Grants range from $50,000 to $1,000,000; recently, they averaged $235,000.

Duration Grants are typically 1 year in length.

Number awarded Varies each year; recently, 222 of these grants, worth $52.5 million, were awarded.

Deadline September of each year.

[1137]
DEPARTMENT OF DEFENSE EXPERIMENTAL PROGRAM TO STIMULATE COMPETITIVE RESEARCH

Army Research Office
Attn: AMSRL-RO-RI
4300 South Miami Boulevard
P.O. Box 12211
Research Triangle Park, NC 27709-2211
(919) 549-4234   Fax: (919) 549-4248
Web: www.arl.army.mil/www/default.cfm?Action=6&Page=8

Summary To provide funding to researchers at colleges and universities in designated states, especially those at Historically Black Colleges and Universities (HBCUs) and other Minority Institutions (MIs).

Eligibility This program is open to researchers at colleges and universities in states and territories that traditionally have not received a large number of research awards (Alaska, Arkansas, Delaware, Idaho, Kansas, Kentucky, Louisiana, Maine, Montana, Nebraska, Nevada, New Hampshire, North Dakota, Oklahoma, Puerto Rico, Rhode Island, South Carolina, South Dakota, Tennessee, Vermont, U.S. Virgin Islands, West Virginia, and Wyoming). Special consideration is given to applications from scholars at MIs. All applying institutions must have an accredited, degree-granting program in science, engineering, or mathematics and a history of graduating students in those fields. Applicants must be proposing a program of research in a science, engineering, or mathematics field of interest to the Department of Defense.

Financial data Grants range from $300,000 to $600,000.

Duration Up to 3 years.

Number awarded Varies; a total of approximately $13 million in new awards is available through the participating Department of Defense agencies each year.

Deadline May of each year.

[1138]
DEPARTMENT OF HOMELAND SECURITY SMALL BUSINESS INNOVATION RESEARCH GRANTS

Department of Homeland Security
Homeland Security Advanced Research Projects Agency
Attn: SBIR Program Manager
Washington, DC 20528
(202) 254-6768   Toll Free: (800) 754-3043
Fax: (202) 254-7170   E-mail: elissa.sobolewski@dhs.gov
Web: www.dhs.gov/files/grants/gc_1247254058883.shtm

Summary To support small businesses (especially those owned by African Americans, other minorities, disabled veterans, and women) that have the technological expertise to contribute to the research and development mission of the Department of Homeland Security (DHS).

Eligibility For the purposes of this program, a "small business" is defined as a firm that is organized for profit with a location in the United States; is in the legal form of an individual proprietorship, partnership, limited liability company, corporation, joint venture, association, trust, or cooperative; is at least 51% owned and controlled by 1 or more individuals who are citizens or permanent residents of the United States; and has (including its affiliates) fewer than 500 employees. The primary employment of the principal investigator must be with the firm at the time of award and during the conduct of the proposed project. Preference is given to women-owned small business concerns, service-disabled veteran small business concerns, veteran small business concerns, and socially and economically disadvantaged small business concerns. Women-owned small business concerns are those that are at least 51% owned by a woman or women who also control and operate them. Service-disabled veteran small business concerns are those that are at least 51% owned by a service-disabled veteran and controlled by such a veteran or (for veterans with permanent and severe disability) the spouse or permanent caregiver of such a veteran. Veteran small business concerns are those that are at least 51% owned by a veteran or veterans who also control and manage them. Socially and economically disadvantaged small business concerns are at least 51% owned by an Indian tribe, a Native Hawaiian organization, a Community Development Corporation, or 1 or more socially and economically disadvantaged individuals (African Americans, Hispanic Americans, Native Americans, Asian Pacific Americans, or subcontinent Asian Americans). The project must be performed in the United States. Currently, DHS has 7 research priorities: explosives; border and maritime security; command, control, and interoperability; human factors; infrastructure and geophysical; chemical and biological; and domestic nuclear detection. Selection is based on the soundness, technical merit, and innovation of the proposed approach and its incremental progress toward topic or subtopic solution; the qualifications of the proposed principal investigators, supporting staff, and consultants; and the potential for commercial application and the benefits expected to accrue from this commercialization.

Financial data Grants are offered in 2 phases. In phase 1, awards normally range up to $100,000 (or $150,000 for domestic nuclear detection); in phase 2, awards normally range up to $750,000 (or $1,000,000 for domestic nuclear detection).

Duration Phase 1 awards may extend up to 6 months; phase 2 awards may extend up to 2 years.

Number awarded Varies each year; recently, 61 Phase 1 awards were granted.

Deadline February of each year.

[1139]
DEPARTMENT OF HOMELAND SECURITY SUMMER FACULTY AND STUDENT RESEARCH TEAM PROGRAM

Oak Ridge Institute for Science and Education
Attn: Science and Engineering Education
P.O. Box 117
Oak Ridge, TN 37831-0117
(865) 574-1447   Fax: (865) 241-5219
E-mail: Patti.Obenour@orau.gov
Web: see.orau.org

Summary To provide an opportunity for teams of students and faculty from Historically Black Colleges and Universities (HBCUs) and other minority serving educational institutions to conduct summer research in areas of interest to the Department of Homeland Security (DHS).

Eligibility This program is open to teams of up to 2 students (undergraduate and/or graduate) and 1 faculty from Historically Black Colleges and Universities (HBCUs), Hispanic Serving Institutions (HSIs), Tribal Colleges and Universities (TCUs), Alaska Native Serving Institutions (ANSIs), and Native Hawaiian Serving Institutions (NHSIs). Applicants must be interested in conducting research at designated DHS Centers of Excellence in science, technology, engineering, or mathematics related to homeland security (HS-STEM), including explosives detection, mitigation, and response; social, behavioral, and economic sciences; risk and decision sciences; human factors aspects of technology; chemical threats and countermeasures; biological threats and countermeasures; community, commerce, and infrastructure resilience; food and agricultural security; transportation security; border security; immigration studies; maritime and port security; infrastructure protection; natural disasters and related geophysical studies; emergency preparedness and response; communications and interoperability; or advanced data analysis and visualization. Faculty must have a full-time appointment at an eligible institution and have received a Ph.D. in an HS-STEM discipline no more than 7 years previously; at least 2 years of full-time research and/or teaching experience is preferred. Students must have a GPA of 3.0 or higher and be enrolled full time. Undergraduates must be entering their junior or senior year. U.S. citizenship is required. Selection is based on relevance and intrinsic merit of the research (40%), faculty applicant qualifications (30%), academic benefit to the faculty applicant and his/her institution (10%), and student applicant qualifications (20%).

Financial data Stipends are $1,200 per week for faculty, $600 per week for graduate students, and $500 per week for undergraduates. Faculty members who live more than 50

miles from their assigned site may receive a relocation allowance of $1,500 and travel expenses up to an additional $500. Limited travel expenses for 1 round trip are reimbursed for undergraduate and graduate students living more than 50 miles from their assigned site.

Duration 12 weeks during the summer.

Additional information This program is funded by DHS and administered by Oak Ridge Institute for Science and Education (ORISE). Recently, the available DHS Centers of Excellence were the Center for Advancing Microbial Risk Assessment (led by Michigan State University and Drexel University); the Center for Risk and Economic Analysis of Terrorism Events (led by University of Southern California); the National Center for Food Protection and Defense (led by University of Minnesota); the Center of Excellence for Foreign Animal and Zoonotic Disease Defense (led by Texas A&M University and Kansas State University); the National Center for the Study of Preparedness and Catastrophic Event Response (led by Johns Hopkins University); the National Consortium for the Study of Terrorism and Responses to Terrorism (led by University of Maryland); the Center of Excellence for Awareness and Location of Explosives-Related Threats (led by Northeastern University and University of Rhode Island); the National Center for Border Security and Immigration (led by the University of Arizona and the University of Texas at El Paso); the Center for Maritime, Island and Remote and Extreme Environment Security (led by the University of Hawaii and Stevens Institute of Technology); the Center for Natural Disasters, Coastal Infrastructure, and Emergency Management (led by the University of North Carolina at Chapel Hill and Jackson State University); the National Transportation Security Center of Excellence (consisting of 7 institutions); and the Center of Excellence in Command, Control, and Interoperability (led by Purdue University and Rutgers University).

Number awarded Approximately 12 teams are selected each year.

Deadline January of each year.

[1140]
DEPARTMENT OF TRANSPORTATION SMALL BUSINESS INNOVATION RESEARCH GRANTS

Department of Transportation
Attn: Research and Innovative Technology Administration
John A. Volpe National Transportation Systems Center
55 Broadway, Kendall Square
Cambridge, MA 02142-1093
(617) 494-2051   Fax: (617) 494-2370
E-mail: leisa.moniz@dot.gov
Web: www.volpe.dot.gov/sbir/index.html

Summary To support small businesses (especially those owned by African Americans, other minorities, veterans, and women) that have the technological expertise to contribute to the research and development mission of the Department of Transportation.

Eligibility For the purposes of this program, a "small business" is defined as a firm that is organized for profit with a location in the United States; is in the legal form of an individual proprietorship, partnership, limited liability company, corporation, joint venture, association, trust, or cooperative; is at least 51% owned and controlled by 1 or more individuals who are citizens or permanent residents of the United States; and has (including its affiliates) fewer than 500 employees. The primary employment of the principal investigator must be with the firm at the time of award and during the conduct of the proposed project. Preference is given to 1) women-owned small business concerns; 2) veteran-owned small businesses; and 3) socially and economically disadvantaged small business concerns. Women-owned small business concerns are those that are at least 51% owned by a woman or women who also control and operate them. Veteran-owned small businesses are those that are at least 51% owned and controlled by 1 or more veterans. Socially and economically disadvantaged small business concerns are at least 51% owned by an Indian tribe, a Native Hawaiian organization, or 1 or more socially and economically disadvantaged individuals (African Americans, Hispanic Americans, Native Americans, Asian Pacific Americans, or subcontinent Asian Americans). The project must be performed in the United States. Selection is based on scientific and technical merit, the feasibility of the proposal's commercial potential, the adequacy of the work plan, qualifications of the principal investigator, and adequacy of supporting staff and facilities, equipment, and data.

Financial data Support is offered in 2 phases. In phase 1, awards normally do not exceed $100,000 (for both direct and indirect costs); in phase 2, awards normally do not exceed $750,000 (including both direct and indirect costs).

Duration Phase 1 awards may extend up to 6 months; phase 2 awards may extend up to 2 years.

Number awarded Varies each year; recently, DOT planned to award 16 of these grants: 1 to the Federal Aviation Administration, 3 to the Federal Highway Administration, 1 to the Pipeline and Hazardous Materials Safety Administration, 2 to the National Highway and Traffic Safety Administration, 3 to the Federal Transit Administration, and 6 to the Federal Railroad Administration.

Deadline November of each year.

[1141]
DIETETIC INTERNSHIP SCHOLARSHIPS

American Dietetic Association
Attn: Commission on Accreditation for Dietetics Education
120 South Riverside Plaza, Suite 2000
Chicago, IL 60606-6995
(312) 899-0040   Toll Free: (800) 877-1600, ext. 5400
Fax: (312) 899-4817   E-mail: education@eatright.org
Web: www.eatright.org/CADE/content.aspx?id=7934

Summary To provide financial assistance to student members of the American Dietetic Association (ADA), especially African Americans and other underrepresented minorities who have applied for a dietetic internship.

Eligibility This program is open to student members who have applied for a CADE-accredited dietetic internship. Applicants must be participating in the computer-matching process, be U.S. citizens or permanent residents, and show promise of being a valuable, contributing member of the profession. Some scholarships require membership in a specific dietetic practice group, residency in a specific state, or underrepresented minority group status. The same application form can be used for all categories. Students who are currently completing the internship component of a combined graduate/dietetic internship should apply for the American Dietetic Association's Graduate Scholarship.

Financial data Stipends range from $500 to $3,000; most are for $1,000.

Duration 1 year.

Number awarded Varies each year, depending upon the funds available; recently, the sponsoring organization awarded 222 scholarships for all its programs.

Deadline February of each year.

[1142]
DIGITAL INNOVATION FELLOWSHIPS

American Council of Learned Societies
Attn: Office of Fellowships and Grants
633 Third Avenue
New York, NY 10017-6795
(212) 697-1505   Fax: (212) 949-8058
E-mail: fellowships@acls.org
Web: www.acls.org/programs/digital

Summary To provide funding to scholars (especially African Americans, other minorities, and women) who are interested in conducting digitally-based research in the humanities and the humanities-related social sciences.

Eligibility This program is open to scholars who have a Ph.D. in any field of the humanities or the humanistic social sciences. Applicants must be interested in conducting research projects that utilize digital technologies intensively and innovatively. Projects might include, but are not limited to, new digital tools that further humanistic research (such as digital research archives or innovative databases), research that depends on or is greatly enhanced by the use of such tools, the representation of research that depends on or is greatly enhanced by the use of such tools, or some combination of those features. The program does not support creative works (e.g., novels or films), textbooks, straightforward translations, or purely pedagogical projects. U.S. citizenship or permanent resident status is required. Applications are particularly invited from women and members of minority groups. Selection is based on scholarly excellence (the project's intellectual ambitions and technological underpinnings), the project's likely contribution as a digital scholarly work to humanistic study, satisfaction of technical requirements for completing a successful research project, degree and significance of preliminary work already completed, extent to which the proposed project would promote teamwork and collaboration, and the project's articulation with local infrastructure.

Financial data Fellows receive a stipend of $60,000 and up to $25,000 for project costs.

Duration 1 academic year.

Additional information This program, first available for the 2006-07 academic year, is supported by funding from the Andrew W. Mellon Foundation.

Number awarded Up to 6 each year.

Deadline September of each year.

[1143]
DOCTORAL FELLOWSHIPS IN LAW AND SOCIAL SCIENCE

American Bar Foundation
Attn: Administrative Assistant for Academic Affairs and
   Research Administration
750 North Lake Shore Drive
Chicago, IL 60611-4403
(312) 988-6548   Fax: (312) 988-6579
E-mail: alynch@abfn.org
Web: www.americanbarfoundation.org

Summary To provide research funding to scholars (especially African Americans and other minorities) who are completing or have completed doctoral degrees in fields related to law, the legal profession, and legal institutions.

Eligibility This program is open to Ph.D. candidates in the social sciences who have completed all doctoral requirements except the dissertation. Applicants who have completed the dissertation are also eligible. Doctoral and proposed research must be in the general area of sociolegal studies or in social scientific approaches to law, the legal profession, or legal institutions and legal processes. Applications must include 1) a dissertation abstract or proposal with an outline of the substance and methods of the research; 2) 2 letters of recommendation; and 3) a curriculum vitae. Minority candidates are especially encouraged to apply.

Financial data The stipend is $27,000. Fellows may request up to $1,500 to reimburse expenses associated with research, travel to meet with advisers, or travel to conferences at which papers are presented. Relocation expenses of up to $2,500 may be reimbursed on application.

Duration 12 months, beginning in September.

Additional information Fellows are offered access to the computing and word processing facilities of the American Bar Foundation and the libraries of Northwestern University and the University of Chicago. This program was established in 1996. Fellowships must be held in residence at the American Bar Foundation. Appointments to the fellowship are full time; fellows are not permitted to undertake other work.

Number awarded 1 or more each year.

Deadline December of each year.

[1144]
DUBOIS-MANDELA-RODNEY FELLOWSHIP PROGRAM

University of Michigan
Attn: Center for Afroamerican and African Studies
4700 Haven Hall
505 South State Street
Ann Arbor, MI 48109-1045
(734) 764-5513   Fax: (734) 763-0543
E-mail: gricer@umich.edu
Web: www.lsa.umich.edu/caas/fellowships

Summary To provide funding to scholars who are interested in conducting research on African American, African, and Caribbean experiences at the University of Michigan's Center for Afroamerican and African Studies.

Eligibility Applicants must have a Ph.D. in hand but be no more than 5 years beyond completion of their degree. They should be interested in conducting research on Africa or the African Diaspora at the center. Consideration is given to all disciplines, including, but not limited to, the humanities, social sciences, physical sciences, and professional schools. Scholars from or who study the Gullah speaking Sea islands, Cape Verde islands, the Anglophone Caribbean, the Canary islands, Madagascar, and/or other less studied areas are especially encouraged to apply.

Financial data The stipend is $42,000. Health insurance plus $1,000 for research and up to $2,000 for travel expenses are also included.

Duration 1 year.

Additional information Fellows must spend their fellowship year at the University of Michigan's Center for Afroamerican and African Studies. They must conduct at least 1 seminar.

Deadline November of each year.

[1145]
DUPONT MINORITIES IN ENGINEERING AWARD

American Society for Engineering Education
Attn: Manager, Administrative Services
1818 N Street, N.W., Suite 600
Washington, DC 20036-2479
(202) 331-3500   Fax: (202) 265-8504
Web: www.asee.org/activities/awards/special.cfm

Summary To recognize and reward outstanding achievements by African Americans and other engineering educators who have worked to increase diversity by ethnicity and gender in science, engineering, and technology.

Eligibility Eligible for nomination are engineering or engineering technology educators who, as part of their educational activity, either assume or are charged with the responsibility of motivating underrepresented students to enter and continue in engineering or engineering technology curricula at the college or university level, graduate or undergraduate. Nominees must demonstrate leadership in the conception, organization, and operation of pre-college and college activities designed to increase participation by underrepresented students in engineering and engineering technology.

Financial data The award consists of $1,500, a certificate, and a grant of $500 for travel expenses to the ASEE annual conference.

Duration The award is granted annually.

Additional information Funding for this award is provided by DuPont. It was originally established in 1956 as the Vincent Bendix Minorities in Engineering Award.

Number awarded 1 each year.

Deadline January of each year.

[1146]
EARLY CAREER PATIENT-ORIENTED DIABETES RESEARCH AWARD

Juvenile Diabetes Research Foundation International
Attn: Grant Administrator
26 Broadway, 14th Floor
New York, NY 10004
(212) 479-7572   Toll Free: (800) 533-CURE
Fax: (212) 785-9595   E-mail: info@jdrf.org
Web: www.jdrf.org/index.cfm?page_id=111715

Summary To provide funding to physician scientists (particularly African Americans, other minorities, women, and persons with disabilities) who are interested in pursuing a program of clinical diabetes-related research training.

Eligibility This program is open to investigators in diabetes-related research who have an M.D. or M.D./Ph.D. degree and a faculty appointment at the late training or assistant professor level. Applicants must be sponsored by an investigator who is affiliated full time with an accredited institution, who pursues patient-oriented clinical research, and who agrees to supervise the applicant's training. There are no citizenship requirements. Applications are encouraged from women, members of minority groups underrepresented in the sciences, and people with disabilities. Areas of relevant research can include: mechanisms of human disease, therapeutic interventions, clinical trials, and the development of new technologies. The proposed research may be conducted at foreign and domestic, for-profit and nonprofit, and public and private institutions, including universities, colleges, hospitals, laboratories, units of state and local government, and eligible agencies of the federal government.

Financial data The total award may be up to $150,000 each year, up to $75,000 of which may be requested for research (including a technician, supplies, equipment, and travel). The salary request must be consistent with the established salary structure of the applicant's institution. Equipment purchases in years other than the first must be strongly justified. Indirect costs may not exceed 10%.

Duration The award is for 5 years.

Deadline January or July of each year.

[1147]
EARLY CAREER POSTDOCTORAL FELLOWSHIPS IN EAST EUROPEAN STUDIES

American Council of Learned Societies
Attn: Office of Fellowships and Grants
633 Third Avenue
New York, NY 10017-6795
(212) 697-1505   Fax: (212) 949-8058
E-mail: fellowships@acls.org
Web: www.acls.org/grants/Default.aspx?id=534

Summary To provide funding to postdoctorates (particularly African Americans, other minorities, and women) who are interested in conducting original research in the social sciences and humanities relating to eastern Europe.

Eligibility This program is open to U.S. citizens and permanent residents who hold a Ph.D. degree or equivalent as demonstrated by professional experience and publications. Priority is given to scholars in the early part of their careers; tenured faculty are not eligible. Applicants must be interested in conducting research in the social sciences or humanities relating to Albania, Bosnia and Herzegovina, Bulgaria, Croatia, Czech Republic, Estonia, Hungary, Former Yugoslav Republic of Macedonia, Kosovo, Latvia, Lithuania, Montenegro, Poland, Romania, Serbia, Slovakia, or Slovenia. Projects comparing more than 1 country in eastern Europe or relating eastern European societies to those of other parts of the world are also supported. Selection is based on the scholarly merit of the proposal, its importance to the development of eastern European studies, and the scholarly potential and accomplishments of the applicant. Applications are particularly invited from women and members of minority groups.

Financial data Up to $25,000 is provided as a stipend. Funds are intended primarily as salary replacement, but they

may be used to supplement sabbatical salaries or awards from other sources.

Duration 6 to 12 consecutive months.

Additional information This program is sponsored jointly by the American Council of Learned Societies, (ACLS) and the Social Science Research Council, funded by the U.S. Department of State under the Research and Training for Eastern Europe and the Independent States of the Former Soviet Union Act of 1983 (Title VIII) but administered by ACLS. Funds may not be used in western Europe.

Number awarded Varies each year; recently, 3 of these fellowships were awarded.

Deadline November of each year.

[1148]
EARTH SCIENCES POSTDOCTORAL FELLOWSHIPS

National Science Foundation
Directorate for Geosciences
Attn: Division of Earth Sciences
4201 Wilson Boulevard, Room 785S
Arlington, VA 22230
(703) 292-5047   Fax: (703) 292-9025
TDD: (800) 281-8749   E-mail: lpatino@nsf.gov
Web: www.nsf.gov

Summary To provide funding to postdoctoral scientists (particularly African Americans, other underrepresented minorities, and individuals with disabilities) who are interested in participating in a program of research training and education, in the United States or abroad, in a field relevant to the work of the Division of Earth Sciences of the National Science Foundation (NSF).

Eligibility This program is open to U.S. citizens, nationals, and permanent residents who received a Ph.D. within the past 3 years. Applicants must be interested in a program of research training in any of the disciplines supported by the NSF Division of Earth Sciences: improving our understanding of the Earth's structure, composition, evolution, and the interaction with the Earth's biosphere, atmosphere, and hydrosphere. The project should be conducted at an institution (college or university, private nonprofit institute or museum, government installation, or laboratory), in the United States or abroad other than the applicant's Ph.D.-granting institution. Part of the project should include such educational activities as teaching a course each year at the host institution or an academic institution with ties to the host institution, developing educational materials for formal or informal education venues, or engaging in a significant program of outreach or public education. Applicants must select a sponsoring scientist at the host institution to provide mentoring and guidance with the research and education activities. Applications are encouraged from underrepresented minorities and persons with disabilities.

Financial data Grants are $85,000 per year, including a stipend of $58,000 per year, a research allowance of $15,000 per year, a host institutional allowance of $3,000 per year, and a fringe benefit allowance of $9,000 per year.

Duration 2 years.

Number awarded 10 each year.

Deadline June of each year.

[1149]
EAST EUROPEAN LANGUAGE GRANTS TO INDIVIDUALS FOR SUMMER STUDY

American Council of Learned Societies
Attn: Office of Fellowships and Grants
633 Third Avenue
New York, NY 10017-6795
(212) 697-1505   Fax: (212) 949-8058
E-mail: fellowships@acls.org
Web: www.acls.org/grants/Default.aspx?id=540

Summary To provide financial support to graduate students, professionals, and postdoctorates (especially African Americans or other minorities and women) who are interested in studying eastern European languages during the summer.

Eligibility Applicants must have completed at least a 4-year college degree. They must be interested in a program of training in the languages of eastern Europe, including Albanian, Bosnian-Croatian-Serbian, Bulgarian, Czech, Estonian, Hungarian, Latvian, Lithuanian, Macedonian, Polish, Romanian, Slovak, or Slovene. The language course may be at the beginning, intermediate, or advanced level. Normally, requests for beginning and intermediate level training should be for attendance at intensive courses offered by institutions in the United States; proposals for study at the advanced level are ordinarily for courses in eastern Europe. Applications are particularly encouraged from women and members of minority groups.

Financial data Grants up to $2,500 are available.

Duration Summer months.

Additional information This program, reinstituted in 2002, is supported by the U.S. Department of State under the Research and Training for Eastern Europe and the Independent States of the Former Soviet Union Act of 1983 (Title VIII).

Number awarded Approximately 15 each year.

Deadline January of each year.

[1150]
EDUCATIONAL TESTING SERVICE POSTDOCTORAL FELLOWSHIP AWARD PROGRAM

Educational Testing Service
Attn: Fellowships
660 Rosedale Road
MS 19-T
Princeton, NJ 08541-0001
(609) 734-5543   Fax: (609) 734-5410
E-mail: internfellowships@ets.org
Web: www.ets.org/research/fellowships/postdoctoral

Summary To provide funding to postdoctorates (particularly African Americans and other minorities) who wish to conduct independent research at the Educational Testing Service (ETS).

Eligibility Applicants must have a doctorate in a relevant discipline and be able to provide evidence of prior research. They must be interested in conducting research at ETS in 1 of the following areas: measurement theory, validity, natural language processing and computational linguistics, cognitive psychology, learning theory, linguistics, speech recognition and processing, teaching and classroom research, or statis-

tics. Selection is based on the scholarly and technical strength of the proposed research, the relationship between the objective of the research and ETS goals and priorities, and the ETS affirmative action objectives. An explicit goal of the program is to increase the number of scholars and students from diverse backgrounds, especially such traditionally underrepresented groups as African Americans, Hispanic/Latino Americans, and American Indians, who are conducting research in educational measurement and related fields.

Financial data The stipend is $55,000 per year; fellows and their families also receive limited reimbursement for relocation expenses.

Duration Up to 2 years.

Additional information Fellows work with senior staff at ETS in Princeton, New Jersey.

Number awarded Up to 3 each year.

Deadline January of each year.

[1151]
EDWARD A. BOUCHET AWARD

American Physical Society
Attn: Honors Program
One Physics Ellipse
College Park, MD 20740-3844
(301) 209-3268   Fax: (301) 209-0865
E-mail: honors@aps.org
Web: www.aps.org/programs/honors/awards/bouchet.cfm

Summary To recognize and reward outstanding research in physics by African Americans or members of other underrepresented minority groups.

Eligibility Nominees for this award must be African Americans, Hispanic Americans, or Native Americans who have made significant contributions to physics research and are effective communicators.

Financial data The award consists of a grant of $3,500 to the recipient, a travel allowance for the recipient to visit 3 academic institutions to deliver lectures, and an allowance for travel expenses to the meeting of the American Physical Society (APS) at which the prize is presented.

Duration The award is presented annually.

Additional information This award was established in 1994 and is currently funded by a grant from the Research Corporation. As part of the award, the recipient visits 3 academic institutions where the impact of the visit on minority students will be significant. The purpose of those visits is to deliver technical lectures on the recipient's field of specialization, to visit classrooms where appropriate, to assist the institution with precollege outreach efforts where appropriate, and to talk informally with faculty and students about research and teaching careers in physics.

Number awarded 1 each year.

Deadline June of each year.

[1152]
E.E. JUST ENDOWED RESEARCH FELLOWSHIP FUND

Woods Hole Marine Biological Laboratory
Attn: Research Award Coordinator
7 MBL Street
Woods Hole, MA 02543-1015
(508) 289-7173   Fax: (508) 457-1924
E-mail: researchawards@mbl.edu
Web: www.mbl.edu/research/summer/awards_general.html

Summary To provide funding to African Americans and other minority scientists who wish to conduct summer research at the Woods Hole Marine Biological Laboratory (MBL).

Eligibility This program is open to minority faculty members who are interested in conducting summer research at the MBL. Applicants must submit a statement of the potential impact of this award on their career development. Fields of study include, but are not limited to, cell biology, developmental biology, ecology, evolution, microbiology, neurobiology, physiology, regenerative biology, and tissue engineering.

Financial data The fellowship supports a minority scientist's participation in research at MBL. Recently, grants averaged $1,500.

Duration At least 6 weeks during the summer.

Number awarded 1 each year.

Deadline December of each year.

[1153]
EINSTEIN POSTDOCTORAL FELLOWSHIP PROGRAM

Smithsonian Astrophysical Observatory
Attn: Chandra X-Ray Center
Einstein Fellowship Program Office
60 Garden Street, MS4
Cambridge, MA 02138
(617) 496-7941   Fax: (617) 495-7356
E-mail: fellows@head.cfa.harvard.edu
Web: cxc.harvard.edu/fellows

Summary To provide funding to recent postdoctoral scientists (especially African Americans, other minorities, and women) who are interested in conducting research related to high energy astrophysics missions of the National Aeronautics and Space Administration (NASA).

Eligibility This program is open to postdoctoral scientists who completed their Ph.D., Sc.D., or equivalent doctoral degree within the past 3 years in astronomy, physics, or related disciplines. Applicants must be interested in conducting research related to NASA Physics of the Cosmos program missions: Chandra, Fermi, XMM-Newton and International X-Ray Observatory, cosmological investigations relevant to the Planck and JDEM missions, and gravitational astrophysics relevant to the LISA mission. They must be citizens of the United States or English-speaking citizens of other countries who have valid visas. Women and minorities are strongly encouraged to apply.

Financial data Stipends are approximately $64,500 per year. Fellows may also receive health insurance, relocation costs, and moderate support (up to $16,000 per year) for research-related travel, computing services, publications, and other direct costs.

Duration 3 years (depending on a review of scientific activity).

Additional information This program, which began in 2009 with funding from NASA, incorporates the former Chandra and GLAST Fellowship programs.

Number awarded Up to 10 each year.

Deadline November of each year.

[1154]
ELSEVIER PILOT RESEARCH AWARDS

American Gastroenterological Association
Attn: AGA Research Foundation
Research Awards Manager
4930 Del Ray Avenue
Bethesda, MD 20814-2512
(301) 222-4012   Fax: (301) 654-5920
E-mail: awards@gastro.org
Web: www.gastro.org/aga-foundation/grants

Summary To provide funding to new or established investigators (particularly African Americans, other minorities, and women) for pilot research projects in areas related to gastroenterology or hepatology.

Eligibility Applicants must have an M.D., Ph.D., or equivalent degree and a full-time faculty position at an accredited North American institution. They may not hold grants for projects on a similar topic from other agencies. Individual membership in the American Gastroenterology Association (AGA) is required. The proposal must involve obtaining new data that can ultimately provide the basis for subsequent grant applications for more substantial funding and duration in gastroenterology- or hepatology-related areas. Women and minority investigators are strongly encouraged to apply. Selection is based on novelty, importance, feasibility, environment, commitment of the institution, and overall likelihood that the project will lead to more substantial grant applications.

Financial data The grant is $25,000 per year. Funds may be used for salary, supplies, or equipment. Indirect costs are not allowed.

Duration 1 year.

Additional information This award is sponsored by Elsevier Science.

Number awarded 1 each year.

Deadline January of each year.

[1155]
EPILEPSY FOUNDATION RESEARCH GRANTS PROGRAM

Epilepsy Foundation
Attn: Research Department
8301 Professional Place
Landover, MD 20785-2237
(301) 459-3700   Toll Free: (800) EFA-1000
Fax: (301) 577-2684   TDD: (800) 332-2070
E-mail: grants@efa.org
Web: www.epilepsyfoundation.org

Summary To provide funding to junior investigators (particularly African Americans, other minorities, women, and individuals with disabilities) who are interested in conducting research that will advance the understanding, treatment, and prevention of epilepsy.

Eligibility Applicants must have a doctoral degree and an academic appointment at the level of assistant professor in a university or medical school (or equivalent standing at a research institution or medical center). They must be interested in conducting basic or clinical research in the biological, behavioral, or social sciences related to the causes of epilepsy. Faculty with appointments at the level of associate professor or higher are not eligible. Applications from women, members of minority groups, and people with disabilities are especially encouraged. U.S. citizenship is not required, but the research must be conducted in the United States. Selection is based on the scientific quality of the research plan, the relevance of the proposed research to epilepsy, the applicant's qualifications, and the adequacy of the institution and facility where research will be conducted.

Financial data The grant is $50,000 per year.

Duration 1 year; recipients may reapply for 1 additional year of funding.

Additional information Support for this program is provided by many individuals, families, and corporations, especially the American Epilepsy Society, Abbott Laboratories, Ortho-McNeil Pharmaceutical, and Pfizer Inc.

Number awarded Varies each year.

Deadline August of each year.

[1156]
EPILEPSY RESEARCH RECOGNITION AWARDS PROGRAM

American Epilepsy Society
342 North Main Street
West Hartford, CT 06117-2507
(860) 586-7505   Fax: (860) 586-7550
E-mail: ctubby@aesnet.org
Web: www.aesnet.org/research/research-awards

Summary To provide funding to investigators (especially African Americans, other minorities, and individuals with disabilities) who are interested in conducting research related to epilepsy.

Eligibility This program is open to active scientists and clinicians working in any aspect of epilepsy. Candidates must be nominated by their home institution and be at the level of associate professor or professor. There are no geographic restrictions; nominations from outside the United States and North America are welcome. Nominations of women and members of minority groups are especially encouraged. Selection is based on pioneering research, originality of research, quality of publications, research productivity, relationship of the candidate's work to problems in epilepsy, training activities, other contributions in epilepsy, and productivity over the next decade; all criteria are weighted equally.

Financial data The grant is $10,000. No institutional overhead is allowed.

Additional information This program was established in 1991.

Number awarded 2 each year.

Deadline August of each year.

[1157]
EQUAL JUSTICE WORKS FELLOWSHIPS

Equal Justice Works
2120 L Street, N.W., Suite 450
Washington, DC 20037-1541
(202) 466-3686   Fax: (202) 429-9766
E-mail: fellowships@equaljusticeworks.org
Web: www.equaljusticeworks.org

Summary To provide funding to graduating law students and recent law school graduates (particularly African Americans and others from diverse cultural and experiential backgrounds) who are committed to public interest law and interested in working on projects at selected nonprofit legal services organizations.

Eligibility This program is open to third-year law students and recent law graduates. Third-year law students must be able to graduate and begin the fellowship by September following the application. Candidates must 1) be graduating or have graduated from a law school that is an Equal Justice Works member, and 2) be interested in working at a nonprofit host legal services organization that has been selected to participate in this program. Host organizations must have been approved to offer a project that involves legal advocacy on behalf of disenfranchised individuals or groups or issues that are not adequately represented by some aspect of our legal system. Advocacy may entail a wide range of approaches, including, but not limited to, community legal education and training, organizing, direct services, litigation, transactional work, and administrative efforts. The project must address the legal needs of individuals or communities in the United States or its territories. Preference is given to projects that are designed to impact a large number of people, create programs that can be replicated in other communities, and create lasting institutions or programs. The organizations where the applicants propose to conduct their projects are evaluated on the basis of their history of accomplishments; how the project fits into their priorities; their commitment and ability to provide training, support, and supervision throughout the fellowship; and their commitment and ability to provide health insurance and other standard employee fringe benefits to the fellow during the fellowship. Candidates are evaluated on the basis of their demonstrated or stated commitment to public interest law generally and specifically to the community in which they are planning to work; their professional, volunteer, and/or subject matter expertise; and their commitment and ability to fulfill the full term of the program. Preference is given to candidates who will bring a diverse perspective to their project and the legal profession; applications are strongly encouraged from people who 1) are from diverse cultural and experiential backgrounds; 2) have disabilities; 3) are from diverse ethnic, racial, religious, and socioeconomic backgrounds, work experiences, national origins, sexual orientations, and ages.

Financial data Fellows receive the normal salary paid by their host organization. This program provides a grant of $39,000 per year as a contribution to the stipend, and the host organization is expected to pay the difference if its normal salary is higher. They are also expected to provide health insurance and standard fringe benefits. Fellows are eligible to apply to the Equal Justice Works Loan Repayment Assistance Program (LRAP), which repays a portion of their educational debts.

Duration 2 years.

Additional information This program began in 1992. Additional funding provided by the Open Society Institute permitted its expansion in 1997.

Number awarded Varies each year. At any given time, approximately 100 fellows are receiving support from this program.

Deadline September of each year.

[1158]
ESTELLE MASSEY OSBORNE SCHOLARSHIP

Nurses Educational Funds, Inc.
Attn: Scholarship Coordinator
304 Park Avenue South, 11th Floor
New York, NY 10010
(212) 590-2443   Fax: (212) 590-2446
E-mail: info@n-e-f.org
Web: www.n-e-f.org

Summary To provide financial assistance to African Americans working as nurses who are interested in earning a master's degree in nursing.

Eligibility This program is open to African American registered nurses who are members of a national professional nursing organization and enrolled full or part time in an accredited master's degree program in nursing. Applicants must have completed at least 12 credits and have a cumulative GPA of 3.6 or higher. They must be U.S. citizens or have declared their official intention of becoming a citizen. Along with their application, they must submit an 800-word essay on their professional goals and potential for making a contribution to the nursing profession. Selection is based on academic excellence and the essay's content and clarity.

Financial data Stipends range from $2,500 to $10,000, depending on the availability of funds.

Duration 1 year; nonrenewable.

Additional information There is a $20 application fee.

Number awarded 1 each year.

Deadline February of each year.

[1159]
ESTHER MAYO SHERARD SCHOLARSHIP

American Health Information Management Association
Attn: AHIMA Foundation
233 North Michigan Avenue, 21st Floor
Chicago, IL 60601-5809
(312) 233-1175   Fax: (312) 233-1475
E-mail: info@ahimafoundation.org
Web: www.ahimafoundation.org

Summary To provide financial assistance to credentialed professionals who are African American, members of the American Health Information Management Association (AHIMA), and interested in working on a graduate degree in a field related to health information management.

Eligibility This program is open to credentialed professionals in health information management (HIM) who are African American members of AHIMA. Applicants must be enrolled at least half time in a master's or doctoral degree program in an area related to HIM practice (e.g., computer science, business management, education, public health, informatics, health policy). They must have a GPA of 3.0 or higher and at least 1 full semester remaining after the date of the award. Financial need is not considered in the selection process.

Financial data The stipend is $2,500.

Duration 1 year.

Additional information This program was established in 2000 by the Esther Mayo Sherard Foundation.

Number awarded 1 each year.

Deadline April or October of each year.

[1160]
EVA LOIS EVANS MATHEMATICS AND SCIENCE FELLOWSHIPS

Alpha Kappa Alpha Sorority, Inc.
Attn: Educational Advancement Foundation
5656 South Stony Island Avenue
Chicago, IL 60637
(773) 947-0026   Toll Free: (800) 653-6528
Fax: (773) 947-0277   E-mail: akaeaf@akaeaf.net
Web: www.akaeaf.org/fellowships_endowments.htm

Summary To provide funding to pre- and postdoctoral scholars (especially African American women) engaged in research in mathematics, science, or technology.

Eligibility This program is open to graduate students and more advanced scholars who are interested in conducting research in the area of mathematics, science, or technology. Applicants must submit 1) a list of honors, awards, and scholarships received; 2) a list of organizations in which they have memberships, especially minority organizations; 3) a description of the project or research on which they are currently working, or (if they are not involved in a project or research) the aspects of their field that interest them; and 4) a statement of their personal and career goals, including how this scholarship will enhance their ability to attain those goals. The sponsor is a traditionally African American women's sorority.

Financial data A stipend is awarded (amount not specified).

Duration These fellowships are awarded biennially, in even-numbered years.

Number awarded Varies; recently, 2 of these fellowships were awarded.

Deadline April of even-numbered years.

[1161]
EVERYDAY TECHNOLOGIES FOR ALZHEIMER CARE (ETAC) GRANTS

Alzheimer's Association
Attn: Medical and Scientific Affairs
225 North Michigan Avenue, 17th Floor
Chicago, IL 60601-7633
(312) 335-5747   Toll Free: (800) 272-3900
Fax: (866) 699-1246   TDD: (312) 335-5886
E-mail: grantsapp@alz.org
Web: www.alz.org

Summary To provide funding to investigators (especially African Americans and other underrepresented minorities) who are interested in developing technology for uses related to Alzheimer's Disease.

Eligibility This program is open to investigators who are full-time staff or faculty at public, private, domestic, and foreign research laboratories, medical centers, hospitals, and universities. Applicants must be interested in conducting research on personalized diagnostics, preventive tools, and interventions for adults coping with the spectrum of cognitive aging and neurodegenerative disease, particularly Alzheimer's Disease. Priority is given to groundbreaking studies on emerging information and communication technologies as well as their clinical and social implications. Research topics may include, but are not limited to, behavioral assessment for early detection, prevention, safety monitoring and support for caregivers, supporting independent function in daily life, social support through face or audio recognition, detecting moments and patterns of lucidity, and privacy and security concerns of Alzheimer's families. Scientists from underrepresented groups are especially encouraged to apply.

Financial data Grants up to $90,000 per year, including direct expenses and up to 10% for overhead costs, are available. The total award for the life of the grant may not exceed $200,000.

Duration Up to 3 years.

Additional information This program is jointly supported by the Alzheimer's Association and Intel Corporation.

Number awarded Up to 4 each year.

Deadline Letters of intent must be submitted by the end of December of each year. Final applications are due in February.

[1162]
FACULTY EARLY CAREER DEVELOPMENT PROGRAM

National Science Foundation
Directorate for Education and Human Resources
Senior Staff Associate for Cross Directorate Programs
4201 Wilson Boulevard, Room 805
Arlington, VA 22230
(703) 292-8600   TDD: (800) 281-8749
Web: www.nsf.gov

Summary To provide funding to outstanding new faculty in science and engineering fields of interest to the National Science Foundation (especially African Americans, other minorities, women, and persons with disabilities) who intend to develop academic careers involving both research and education.

Eligibility This program, identified as the CAREER program, is open to faculty members who meet all of the following requirements: 1) be employed in a tenure-track (or equivalent) position at an institution in the United States, its territories or possessions, or the Commonwealth of Puerto Rico that awards degrees in a field supported by the National Science Foundation (NSF) or that is a nonprofit, non-degree granting organization, such as a museum, observatory, or research laboratory; 2) have a doctoral degree in a field of science or engineering supported by NSF: 3) not have competed more than 3 times in this program; 4) be untenured; and 5) not be a current or former recipient of a Presidential Early Career Award for Scientists and Engineers (PECASE) or CAREER award. Applicants are not required to be U.S. citizens or permanent residents. They must submit a career development plan that indicates a description of the proposed research project, including preliminary supporting data if appropriate, specific objectives, methods, and procedures to be used; expected significance of the results; a description of the proposed educational activities, including plans to evaluate their impact; a description of how the research and educational activities are integrated with each other; and results

of prior NSF support, if applicable. Proposals from women, underrepresented minorities, and persons with disabilities are especially encouraged.

Financial data The grant is at least $80,000 per year (or $100,000 per year for the Directorate of Biological Sciences), including indirect costs or overhead.

Duration 5 years.

Additional information This program is operated by various disciplinary divisions within the NSF; for a list of the participating divisions and their telephone numbers, contact the sponsor. Outstanding recipients of these grants are nominated for the NSF component of the PECASE awards, which are awarded to 20 recipients of these grants as an honorary award.

Number awarded Approximately 425 each year.

Deadline July of each year.

[1163]
FACULTY IN INDUSTRY AWARDS

National Science Foundation
Directorate for Engineering
Attn: Division of Industrial Innovation and Partnerships
4201 Wilson Boulevard, Room 550S
Arlington, VA 22230
(703) 292-7082   Fax: (703) 292-9056
TDD: (800) 281-8749   E-mail: dsenich@nsf.gov
Web: www.nsf.gov/funding/pgm_summ.jsp?pims_id=13706

Summary To provide funding to faculty members in science, engineering, and mathematics (particularly African Americans, other minorities, and individuals with disabilities) who wish to conduct research in an industrial setting as part of the Grant Opportunities for Academic Liaison with Industry (GOALI) program of the National Science Foundation (NSF).

Eligibility This program is open to full-time faculty members at U.S. colleges and universities in science, engineering, and mathematics fields of interest to NSF. Applicants must be U.S. citizens, nationals, or permanent residents. They must present a plan for collaboration between their institution and industry, with a description of the facilities and resources that will be available at the industrial site to support the proposed research. The program encourages applications from underrepresented minorities and persons with disabilities.

Financial data Grants range from $30,000 to $75,000, including 50% of the faculty member's salary and fringe benefits during the industrial residency period. Up to 20% of the total requested amount may be used for travel and research expenses for the faculty and his/her students, including materials but excluding equipment. The industrial partner must commit to support the other 50% of the faculty salary and fringe benefits.

Duration 3 to 12 months.

Additional information This program is also offered by most other NSF directorates. Check the web site for a name and e-mail address of the contact person in each directorate.

Number awarded A total of 60 to 80 grants for all GOALI programs is awarded each year; total funding is approximately $5 million.

Deadline Applications may be submitted at any time.

[1164]
FASEB POSTDOCTORAL PROFESSIONAL DEVELOPMENT AND ENRICHMENT AWARD

Federation of American Societies for Experimental
  Biology
Attn: MARC Section
9650 Rockville Pike
Bethesda, MD 20814-3998
(301) 634-7000   Fax: (301) 634-7001
E-mail: info@faseb.org
Web: www1.faseb.org/postdocprofdevaward

Summary To recognize and reward African American and other underrepresented minority members of component societies of the Federation of American Societies for Experimental Biology (FASEB).

Eligibility This program is open to postdoctoral members of minority groups underrepresented in the biomedical and behavioral sciences (African Americans, Alaskan Natives, Hispanic Americans, Natives of the U.S. Pacific Islands, and American Indians/Native Americans). Applicants must be U.S. citizens, nationals, or permanent residents and members of a FASEB component society. They must be seeking funding to gain knowledge, skills, and training to assist in becoming competitive for publication in top tier journals and for faculty positions in prestigious research intensive settings. Selection is based on demonstrated research productivity, including publication of first-author papers in scientific journals, mentoring of underrepresented minority undergraduate and graduate students, and service leading to improving and expanding opportunities for minorities in the scientific work force and academia.

Financial data The award consists of a $3,000 career development grant, a certificate of recognition, and a $2,500 travel grant.

Duration This award is presented annually.

Additional information Funding for this award is provided by the Minority Access to Research Careers (MARC) program of the National Institute of General Medical Sciences of the National Institutes of Health (NIH). Member societies of FASEB include the American Physiological Society (APS), American Society for Biochemistry and Molecular Biology (ASBMB), American Society for Pharmacology and Experimental Therapeutics (ASPET), American Society for Investigative Pathology (ASIP), American Society for Nutrition(ASN), American Association of Immunologists (AAI), American Association of Anatomists (AAA), The Protein Society, American Society for Bone and Mineral Research (ASBMR), American Society for Clinical Investigation (ASCI), The Endocrine Society, American Society of Human Genetics (ASHG), Society for Developmental Biology (SDB), American Peptide Society (APEPS), Association of Biomolecular Resource Facilities (ABRF), Society for the Study of Reproduction (SSR), Teratology Society, Environmental Mutagen Society (EMS), International Society for Computational Biology (ISCB), American College of Sports Medicine (ACSM), Biomedical Engineering Society (BMES), Genetics Society of America, American Federation for Medical Research (AFMR), and The Histochemical Society (HCS).

Number awarded 6 each year.

Deadline May of each year.

[1165]
FASSE/CUFA INQUIRY GRANT

National Council for the Social Studies
Attn: Program Manager, External Relations
8555 16th Street, Suite 500
Silver Spring, MD 20910-2844
(301) 588-1800, ext. 106   Fax: (301) 588-2049
E-mail: excellence@ncss.org
Web: www.socialstudies.org/getinvolved/awards/fasse-cufa

Summary To provide funding to faculty and graduate student members of the National Council for the Social Studies (NCSS), especially African Americans and others from diverse backgrounds) who are interested in conducting research projects in "citizenship education."

Eligibility This program is open to members of the council who are assistant, associate, or full professors or graduate students with the demonstrated support of a university mentor/adviser. Graduate student applicants must have a mentor/adviser who is also an NCSS member. Researchers from all groups, including underrepresented groups, are encouraged to apply. They must be interested in a project in "citizenship education" that affirms social, cultural, and racial diversity and that addresses issues of equality, equity, and social justice. Proposals that address aims for citizen action are preferred. All proposals should be relevant to school, university, or community-based educational settings. They should either 1) serve student bodies that are socially, culturally, and racially diverse; or 2) involve teachers or prospective teachers who work or will work with diverse student populations. They can address a range of educational levels and settings, from K-12 to collegiate levels, and from school to community settings.

Financial data Grants up to $10,000 are available.

Duration Funded projects must be completed within 1 academic year.

Additional information This program is sponsored by the College and University Faculty Assembly (CUFA) and the Fund for the Advancement of Social Studies Education (FASSE), established by the NCAA in 1984.

Number awarded 1 every 2 or 3 years.

Deadline June of the years in which grants are offered.

[1166]
FDA FACULTY GRANTS

National Science Foundation
Directorate for Engineering
Attn: Division of Chemical, Bioengineering,
  Environmental, and Transport Systems
4201 Wilson Boulevard, Room 565S
Arlington, VA 22230
(703) 292-7942   Fax: (703) 292-9098
TDD: (800) 281-8749   E-mail: lesterow@nsf.gov
Web: www.nsf.gov/funding/pgm_summ.jsp?pims_id=5605

Summary To provide an opportunity for faculty members (particularly African Americans, other underrepresented minorities, and individuals with disabilities) to conduct research at an intramural laboratory of the U.S. Food and Drug Administration (FDA).

Eligibility This program is open to full-time faculty members at U.S. colleges and universities in science, engineering, and mathematics fields of interest to the National Science Foundation (NSF). Applicants must be U.S. citizens, nationals, or permanent residents. They must present a plan for collaboration between their institution and the FDA, with a description of the facilities and resources that will be available at an FDA laboratory to support the proposed research. The program encourages applications from underrepresented minorities and persons with disabilities.

Financial data Grants range from $25,000 to $150,000, including 85% of the faculty member's salary and fringe benefits during the industrial residency period. Up to 20% of the total requested amount may be used for travel and research expenses for the faculty and his/her students, including materials but excluding equipment. In lieu of indirect costs, up to 15% of the total cost may be allocated for administrative expenses. The fellow's home institution must commit to support the other 15% of the faculty salary and fringe benefits. FDA provides office space, research facilities, research costs in the form of expendable and minor equipment purchases in the host laboratory, and the time of its research staff.

Duration 3 to 12 months.

Additional information This program is also offered by the NSF Directorate for Computer and Information Science and Engineering.

Number awarded A total of 3 to 10 grants for all FDA programs is awarded each year; total funding is approximately $500,000.

Deadline March of each year.

[1167]
FELLOWSHIP PROGRAM IN MEASUREMENT

American Educational Research Association
1430 K Street, N.W., Suite 1200
Washington, DC 20005
(202) 238-3200   Fax: (202) 238-3250
E-mail: fellowships@aera.net
Web: www.aera.net

Summary To provide an opportunity for junior scholars in the field of education (particularly African Americans, other minorities, and women) to engage in a program of research and advanced training while in residence at Educational Testing Service (ETS) in Princeton, New Jersey.

Eligibility This program is open to junior scholars and early career research scientists in fields and disciplines related to education research. Applicants must have completed their Ph.D. or Ed.D. degree within the past 3 years. They must be proposing a program of intensive research and training at the ETS campus in Princeton, New Jersey in such areas as educational measurement, assessment design, psychometrics, statistical analyses, large-scale evaluations, and other studies directed to explaining student progress and achievement. A particular goal of the program is to increase the involvement of women and underrepresented minority professionals in measurement, psychometrics, assessment, and related fields. U.S. citizenship or permanent resident status is required.

Financial data The stipend is $50,000 per year. Fellows also receive relocation expenses and ETS employee benefits.

Duration Up to 2 years.

Additional information This program is jointly sponsored by the American Educational Research Association (AERA) and ETS.

Number awarded Up to 2 each year.

Deadline December of each year.

[1168]
FELLOWSHIP TO FACULTY TRANSITION AWARDS

American Gastroenterological Association
Attn: AGA Research Foundation
Research Awards Manager
4930 Del Ray Avenue
Bethesda, MD 20814-2512
(301) 222-4012   Fax: (301) 654-5920
E-mail: awards@gastro.org
Web: www.gastro.org/aga-foundation/grants

Summary To provide funding to physicians (especially African Americans, other minorities, and women) who are interested in research training in an area of gastrointestinal, liver function, or related diseases.

Eligibility This program is open to trainee members of the American Gastroenterological Association (AGA) who have an M.D. or equivalent degree and a gastroenterology-related fellowship at an accredited institution. Applicants must be committed to an academic career; have completed at least 1 year of research training at their current institution; have a commitment from their home institution for a full-time faculty position; and have a preceptor who will supervise their research activities and serve as a mentor. Women and minority investigators are strongly encouraged to apply. Selection is based on the candidate's promise for future success, feasibility and significance of the proposal, attributes of the candidate, record and commitment of the sponsors, and institutional and laboratory environment.

Financial data The grant is $40,000 per year. Funds are to be used as salary support for the recipient. Indirect costs are not allowed.

Duration 2 years.

Additional information Fellows must devote 70% effort to research related to the gastrointestinal tract or liver.

Number awarded 2 each year.

Deadline August of each year.

[1169]
FELLOWSHIPS FOR TRANSFORMATIVE COMPUTATIONAL SCIENCE USING CYBERINFRASTRUCTURE

National Science Foundation
Attn: Office of Cyberinfrastructure
4201 Wilson Boulevard, Room 1145S
Arlington, VA 22230
(703) 292-4766   Fax: (703) 292-9060
TDD: (800) 281-8749   E-mail: citracs@nsf.gov
Web: www.nsf.gov

Summary To provide funding for research training to postdoctoral scientists (particularly African Americans, other minorities, and individuals with disabilities) who are interested in working in areas of interest to the Office of Cyberinfrastructure of the National Science Foundation (NSF).

Eligibility This program is open to citizens, nationals, and permanent residents of the United States who are graduate students completing a Ph.D. or have earned the degree no earlier than 2 years preceding the deadline date. Applicants must be interested in a program of research and training in the use of computational concepts, methodologies, and technologies in all sciences (including physical, biological, geological, mathematical, social, behavioral, economic, computer, information, and data). They must identify a host research organization (college, university, privately-sponsored nonprofit institute, government agency, or laboratory) that has agreed to support the applicant's proposed research and educational activities and has identified a mentor to work with the applicant. Selection is based on the applicant's ability to contribute to computational research and educational efforts that integrate distinct theoretical models and computational methodologies to achieve overall goals and lead to a new generation of applications and technologies for solving important real-world problems using cyberinfrastructure (CI). The program encourages applications from underrepresented minorities and persons with disabilities.

Financial data Stipends are $60,000 for the first year, $65,000 for the second year, and $70,000 for the third year. Also provided are a research allowance supplement of $10,000 per year and an institutional allowance of $5,000 per year. Fellows who complete this program and move on to a tenure-track faculty position may apple for a research starter supplement of up to $50,000 to support the setup of their research environment.

Duration Up to 3 years.

Number awarded 6 to 8 each year. Approximately $2.0 million is available for this program annually.

Deadline January of each year.

[1170]
FELLOWSHIPS IN SCIENCE AND INTERNATIONAL AFFAIRS

Harvard University
John F. Kennedy School of Government
Belfer Center for Science and International Affairs
Attn: Fellowship Coordinator
79 John F. Kennedy Street
Cambridge, MA 02138
(617) 495-8806   Fax: (617) 495-8963
E-mail: bcsia_fellowships@ksg.harvard.edu
Web: belfercenter.ksg.harvard.edu/fellowships

Summary To provide funding to professionals, postdoctorates, and doctoral students (particularly African Americans, other minorities, and women) who are interested in conducting research in areas of concern to the Belfer Center for Science and International Affairs at Harvard University in Cambridge, Massachusetts.

Eligibility The postdoctoral fellowship is open to recent recipients of the Ph.D. or equivalent degree, university faculty members, and employees of government, military, international, humanitarian, and private research institutions who have appropriate professional experience. Applicants for predoctoral fellowships must have passed their general examinations. Lawyers, economists, political scientists, those in the natural sciences, and others of diverse disciplinary backgrounds are also welcome to apply. The program especially encourages applications from women, minorities, and citizens of all countries. All applicants must be interested in conducting research in 1 of the 3 major program areas of the center: 1) the International Security Program (ISP), including Religion in International Affairs; 2) the Science, Technology,

and Public Policy Program (STPP), including information and communications technology, energy and water policy, managing the atom project, and the energy technology innovation policy research group; 3) and the Dubai initiative.

Financial data The stipend is $34,000 for postdoctoral research fellows or $20,000 for predoctoral research fellows. Health insurance is also provided.

Duration 10 months.

Number awarded A limited number each year.

Deadline January of each year.

[1171]
FIRST BOOK GRANT PROGRAM FOR MINORITY SCHOLARS

Louisville Institute
Attn: Executive Director
1044 Alta Vista Road
Louisville, KY 40205-1798
(502) 992-5432   Fax: (502) 894-2286
E-mail: info@louisville-institute.org
Web: www.louisville-institute.org/Grants/programs.aspx

Summary To provide funding to African American and other scholars of color interested in completing a major research and book project that focuses on an aspect of Christianity in North America.

Eligibility This program is open to members of racial/ethnic minority groups (African Americans, Hispanics, Native Americans, Asian Americans, Arab Americans, and Pacific Islanders) who have an earned doctoral degree (normally the Ph.D. or Th.D.). Applicants must be a pre-tenured faculty member in a full-time, tenure-track position at an accredited institution of higher education (college, university, or seminary) in North America. They must be able to negotiate a full academic year free from teaching and committee responsibilities in order to engage in a scholarly research project leading to the publication of their first (or second) book focusing on an aspect of Christianity in North America. Selection is based on the intellectual quality of the research and writing project, its potential to contribute to scholarship in religion, and the potential contribution of the research to the vitality of North American Christianity.

Financial data The grant is $40,000. Awards are intended to make possible a full academic year of sabbatical research and writing by providing up to half of the grantee's salary and benefits for that year. Funds are paid directly to the grantee's institution, but no indirect costs are allowed.

Duration 1 academic year; nonrenewable.

Additional information The Louisville Institute is located at Louisville Presbyterian Theological Seminary and is supported by the Lilly Endowment. These grants were first awarded in 2003. Grantees may not accept other awards that provide a stipend during the tenure of this award, and they must be released from all teaching and committee responsibilities during the award year.

Number awarded Varies each year; recently, 4 of these grants were awarded.

Deadline January of each year.

[1172]
FREDERICK BURKHARDT RESIDENTIAL FELLOWSHIPS FOR RECENTLY TENURED SCHOLARS

American Council of Learned Societies
Attn: Office of Fellowships and Grants
633 Third Avenue
New York, NY 10017-6795
(212) 697-1505   Fax: (212) 949-8058
E-mail: fellowships@acls.org
Web: www.acls.org/programs/burkhardt

Summary To provide funding to African American and other scholars in all disciplines of the humanities and the humanities-related social sciences who are interested in conducting research at designated residential centers.

Eligibility This program is open to citizens and permanent residents of the United States who achieved tenure in a humanities or humanities-related social science discipline at a U.S. institution within the past 4 years. Applicants must be interested in conducting research at 1 of 12 participating residential centers in the United States or abroad. Appropriate fields of specialization include, but are not limited to, American studies; anthropology; archaeology; art and architectural history; classics; economics; film; geography; history; languages and literatures; legal studies; linguistics; musicology; philosophy; political science; psychology; religious studies; rhetoric, communication, and media studies; sociology; and theater, dance, and performance studies. Proposals in those fields of the social sciences are eligible only if they employ predominantly humanistic approaches (e.g., economic history, law and literature, political philosophy). Proposals in interdisciplinary and cross-disciplinary studies are welcome, as are proposals focused on a geographic region or on a cultural or linguistic group. Applications are particularly invited from women and members of minority groups.

Financial data The stipend is $75,000. If that stipend exceeds the fellow's normal academic year salary, the excess is available for research and travel expenses.

Duration 1 academic year.

Additional information This program, which began in 1999, is supported by funding from the Andrew W. Mellon Foundation. The participating residential research centers are the National Humanities Center (Research Triangle Park, North Carolina), the Center for Advanced Study in the Behavioral Sciences (Stanford, California), the Institute for Advanced Study, Schools of Historical Studies and Social Science (Princeton, New Jersey), the Radcliffe Institute for Advanced Study at Harvard University (Cambridge, Massachusetts), the American Antiquarian Society (Worcester, Massachusetts), the John W. Kluge Center at the Library of Congress (Washington, D.C.), the Folger Shakespeare Library (Washington, D.C.), the Newberry Library (Chicago, Illinois), the Huntington Library, Art Collections, and Botanical Gardens (San Marino, California), the American Academy in Rome, Collegium Budapest, and Villa I Tatti (Florence, Italy).

Number awarded Up to 9 each year.

Deadline September of each year.

[1173]
FREDERICK DOUGLASS INSTITUTE FOR AFRICAN AND AFRICAN-AMERICAN STUDIES POSTDOCTORAL FELLOWSHIP

University of Rochester
Frederick Douglass Institute for African and African-American Studies
Attn: Director for Research Fellowships
302 Morey Hall
RC Box 270440
Rochester, NY 14627-0440
(585) 275-7235   Fax: (585) 256-2594
E-mail: fdi@mail.rochester.edu
Web: www.rochester.edu

Summary To support postdoctoral research on African and African American studies at the University of Rochester.

Eligibility This program is open to scholars who have a Ph.D. degree in a field related to the African and African American experience. Applicants must be interested in completing a research project at the Frederick Douglass Institute at the University of Rochester. Along with their application, they must submit a curriculum vitae, a 3- to 5-page description of the project, a sample of published or unpublished writing on a topic related to the proposal, and 3 letters of recommendation.

Financial data The stipend is $35,000.

Duration 1 year; nonrenewable.

Additional information This is a residential fellowship. All fellows are given office space within the institute, full access to the facilities of the university, and opportunities for collaboration and discussion there. Fellows are expected to teach 2 courses (1 each semester) during the fellowship year. Fellows must be in full-time residence at the institution during the tenure of the award.

Number awarded 1 each year.

Deadline January of each year.

[1174]
FRONTIERS IN PHYSIOLOGY RESEARCH TEACHER FELLOWSHIPS

American Physiological Society
Attn: Education Office
9650 Rockville Pike, Room 3111
Bethesda, MD 20814-3991
(301) 634-7132   Fax: (301) 634-7098
E-mail: education@the-aps.org
Web: www.frontiersinphys.org

Summary To provide an opportunity for African American and other middle/high school life science teachers to participate in a summer research project in physiology.

Eligibility This program is open to science teachers at middle schools (grades 6-9) and high schools (grades 9-12) who do not have recent (within 10 years) laboratory experience in physiology or the life sciences, do not have an advanced degree in laboratory science, and are not a candidate for an advanced degree in a laboratory science. Applicants do not need to have extensive mathematics skills, but they must be able to demonstrate a commitment to excellence in teaching, strong observation skills, and a desire to learn about research first-hand. Teachers who are members of minority groups underrepresented in science (African Americans, Hispanics,

Native Americans, and Pacific Islanders) or who teach in schools with a predominance of underrepresented minority students are especially encouraged to apply. Teachers must apply jointly with a member of the American Physiological Society (APS) at a research institution in the same geographic area as their home and school. Selection is based on the quality of the summer research experience and potential long-term impact on teaching and on students.

Financial data For the summer research experience, teachers receive a stipend of $500 per week (to a maximum of $4,000), a grant of $1,000 for completion of online and live professional development, a grant of $600 for development and field testing of inquiry-based lessons and materials, and $100 for completion of project evaluation activities. For the remainder of the year, they receive $2,500 for reimbursement of travel costs to attend the Science Teaching Forum, $1,200 for reimbursement of travel costs to attend the Experimental Biology meeting, $300 for materials to field-test a new inquiry-based laboratory or lesson, and $60 for a 1-year affiliate membership with the APS. The maximum total value of the fellowship is $9,760.

Duration 1 year, including 7 to 8 weeks during the summer for participation in the research experience.

Additional information This program enables teachers to work on a summer research project in the laboratory of their APS sponsor, use the Internet to expand their repertory of teaching methods and their network of colleagues, and develop an inquiry-based classroom activity or laboratory, along with a corresponding web page. They also take a break from their summer research to attend a 1-week Science Teaching Forum in Washington D.C. where they work with APS staff, physiologists, and mentors to explore and practice effective teaching methods focused on how to integrate inquiry, equity, and the Internet into their classrooms. This program is supported by the National Center for Research Resources (NCRR) and the National Institute of Diabetes and Digestive and Kidney Diseases (NIDDK). both components of the National Institutes of Health (NIH).

Number awarded Varies each year; recently 17 of these fellowships were awarded.

Deadline January of each year.

[1175]
GAIUS CHARLES BOLIN DISSERTATION AND POST-MFA FELLOWSHIPS

Williams College
Attn: Dean of the Faculty
Hopkins Hall, Third Floor
P.O. Box 141
Williamstown, MA 01267
(413) 597-4351   Fax: (413) 597-3553
E-mail: gburda@williams.edu
Web: dean-faculty.williams.edu/graduate-fellowships

Summary To provide financial assistance to African Americans and members of other underrepresented groups who are interested in teaching courses at Williams College while working on their doctoral dissertation or building their post-M.F.A. professional portfolio.

Eligibility This program is open to members of underrepresented groups, including ethnic minorities, first-generation college students, women in predominantly male fields, and scholars with disabilities. Applicants must be 1) doctoral candidates in any field who have completed all work for a Ph.D. except for the dissertation; or 2) artists who completed an M.F.A. degree within the past 2 years and are building their professional portfolio. They must be willing to teach a course at Williams College. Along with their application, they must submit a full curriculum vitae, a graduate school transcript, 3 letters of recommendation, a copy of their dissertation prospectus or samples of their artistic work, and a description of their teaching interests within a department or program at Williams College. U.S. citizenship or permanent resident status is required.

Financial data Fellows receive $33,000 for the academic year, plus housing assistance, office space, computer and library privileges, and a research allowance of up to $4,000.

Duration 2 years.

Additional information Bolin fellows are assigned a faculty advisor in the appropriate department. This program was established in 1985. Fellows are expected to teach a 1-semester course each year. They must be in residence at Williams College for the duration of the fellowship.

Number awarded 3 each year.

Deadline November of each year.

[1176]
GEORGE A. STRAIT MINORITY SCHOLARSHIP ENDOWMENT

American Association of Law Libraries
Attn: Chair, Scholarships Committee
105 West Adams Street, Suite 3300
Chicago, IL 60603
(312) 939-4764   Fax: (312) 431-1097
E-mail: scholarships@aall.org
Web: www.aallnet.org/services/sch_strait.asp

Summary To provide financial assistance to African American and other minority college seniors or college graduates who are interested in becoming law librarians.

Eligibility This program is open to college graduates with meaningful law library experience who are members of minority groups and intend to have a career in law librarianship. Applicants must be degree candidates at an ALA-accredited library school or an ABA-accredited law school. Along with their application, they must submit a personal statement that discusses their interest in law librarianship, reason for applying for this scholarship, career goals as a law librarian, etc.

Financial data The stipend is $3,500.

Duration 1 year.

Additional information This program, established in 1990, is currently supported by Thomson West.

Number awarded Varies each year; recently, 5 of these scholarships were awarded.

Deadline March of each year.

[1177]
GERTRUDE AND MAURICE GOLDHABER DISTINGUISHED FELLOWSHIPS

Brookhaven National Laboratory
Attn: Dr. Kathleen Barkigia
Building 460
P.O. Box 5000
Upton, NY 11973-5000
(631) 344-4467   E-mail: Barkigia@bnl.gov
Web: www.bnl.gov/hr/goldhaber.asp

Summary To provide funding to postdoctoral scientists (especially African Americans, other minorities, and women) who are interested in conducting research at Brookhaven National Laboratory (BNL).

Eligibility This program is open to scholars who are no more than 3 years past receipt of the Ph.D. and are interested in working at BNL. Candidates must be interested in working in close collaboration with a member of the BNL scientific staff and qualifying for a scientific staff position at BNL upon completion of the appointment. The sponsoring scientist must have an opening and be able to support the candidate at the standard starting salary for postdoctoral research associates. The program especially encourages applications from minorities and women.

Financial data The program provides additional funds to bring the salary to $75,000 per year.

Duration 3 years.

Additional information This program is funded by Battelle Memorial Institute and the State University of New York at Stony Brook.

Number awarded Up to 8 each year.

Deadline August of each year.

[1178]
GILBERT F. WHITE POSTDOCTORAL FELLOWSHIP PROGRAM

Resources for the Future
Attn: Coordinator for Academic Programs
1616 P Street, N.W., Suite 600
Washington, DC 20036-1400
(202) 328-5008   Fax: (202) 939-3460
E-mail: white-award@rff.org
Web: www.rff.org/About_RFF/Pages/default.aspx

Summary To provide funding to African American and other postdoctoral researchers who wish to devote a year to scholarly work at Resources for the Future (RFF) in Washington, D.C.

Eligibility This program is open to individuals in any discipline who have completed their doctoral requirements and are interested in conducting scholarly research at RFF in social or policy science areas that relate to natural resources, energy, or the environment. Teaching and/or research experience at the postdoctoral level is preferred but not essential. Individuals holding positions in government as well as at academic institutions are eligible. Women and minority candidates are strongly encouraged to apply.

Financial data Fellows receive an annual stipend (based on their academic salary) plus research support, office facilities at RFF, and an allowance of up to $1,000 for moving or living expenses. Fellowships do not provide medical insurance or other RFF fringe benefits.

Duration 11 months.

Additional information Fellows are assigned to an RFF research division: the Energy and Natural Resources division, the Quality of the Environment division, or the Center for Risk, Resource, and Environmental Management. Fellows are expected to be in residence at Resources for the Future for the duration of the program.

Number awarded 1 each year.

Deadline February of each year.

[1179]
GLORIA E. ANZALDUA BOOK PRIZE

National Women's Studies Association
Attn: Book Prizes
7100 Baltimore Avenue, Suite 203
College Park, MD 20740
(301) 403-0407   Fax: (301) 403-4137
E-mail: nwsaoffice@nwsa.org
Web: www.nwsa.org/awards/index.php

Summary To recognize and reward African American and other members of the National Women's Studies Association (NWSA) who have written outstanding books on women of color and transnational issues.

Eligibility This award is available to NWSA members who submit a book that was published during the preceding year. Entries must present groundbreaking scholarship in women's studies that makes a significant multicultural feminist contribution to women of color and/or transnational studies.

Financial data The award provides an honorarium of $1,000 and lifetime membership in NWSA.

Duration The award is presented annually.

Additional information This award was first presented in 2008.

Number awarded 1 each year.

Deadline April of each year.

[1180]
HARRY R. KENDALL LEADERSHIP DEVELOPMENT SCHOLARSHIPS

United Methodist Church
General Board of Global Ministries
Attn: United Methodist Committee on Relief
475 Riverside Drive, Room 1522
New York, NY 10115
(212) 870-3871   Toll Free: (800) UMC-GBGM
E-mail: jyoung@gbgm-umc.org
Web: new.gbgm-umc.org/umcor/work/health/scholarships

Summary To provide financial assistance to African Americans who are Methodists or other Christians and preparing for a career in a health-related field.

Eligibility This program is open to undergraduate and graduate students who are U.S. citizens or permanent residents of African American descent. Applicants must be professed Christians, preferably United Methodists. They must be planning to enter a health care field or already be a practitioner in such a field. Financial need is considered in the selection process.

Financial data The stipend is $2,000.

Duration 1 year.

Additional information This program was established in 1980.

Number awarded Varies each year.
Deadline June of each year.

[1181]
HEALTH AND AGING POLICY FELLOWSHIPS

Columbia University College of Physicians and Surgeons
Attn: Department of Psychiatry
Deputy Director, Health and Aging Policy Fellows
1051 Riverside Drive, Unit 9
New York, NY 10032
(212) 543-6213 Fax: (212) 543-6021
E-mail: healthandagingpolicy@columbia.edu
Web: www.healthandagingpolicy.org

Summary To provide an opportunity for health professionals (particularly African Americans and members of other underrepresented groups) with an interest in aging and policy issues to work as legislative assistants in Congress or at other sites.

Eligibility This program is open to physicians, nurses, and social workers who have a demonstrated commitment to health and aging issues and a desire to be involved in health policy at the federal, state, or local levels. Other professionals with clinical backgrounds (e.g., pharmacists, dentists, clinical psychologists) working in the field of health and aging are also eligible. Preference is given to professionals early or midway through their careers. Applicants must be interested serving as residential fellows by participating in the policy-making process on either the federal or state level as legislative assistants in Congress or as professional staff members in executive agencies or policy organizations. A non-residential track is also available to applicants who wish to work on a policy project throughout the year at relevant sites. The program seeks to achieve racial, ethnic, gender, and discipline diversity; members of groups that historically have been underrepresented are strongly encouraged to apply. Selection is based on commitment to health and aging issues and improving the health and well being of older Americans, potential for leadership in health policy, professional qualifications and achievements, impact of the fellowship experience on the applicant's career, and interpersonal and communication skills. U.S. citizenship or permanent resident status is required.

Financial data For residential fellows, the stipend depends on their current base salary, to a maximum of $120,000 per year; other benefits include a travel allowance for pre-fellowship arrangements and to fellowship-related meetings, a relocation grant of up to $3,500, and up to $400 per month for health insurance. For non-residential fellows, grants provide up to $30,000 to cover related fellowship and travel costs.

Duration 9 to 12 months; fellows may apply for a second year of participation.

Additional information This program, which began in 2009, operates in collaboration with the American Political Science Association Congressional Fellowship Program. Funding is provided by The Atlantic Philanthropies. The John Heinz Senate Fellowship Program, an activity of the Teresa and H. John Heinz III Foundation, supports 1 fellow to work in the Senate. In addition, the Centers for Disease Control and Prevention Health Aging Program sponsors 1 non-residential fellow to work with its staff in Atlanta, Georgia.

Number awarded Varies each year; recently, 4 residential and 5 non-residential fellowships were awarded.
Deadline May of each year.

[1182]
HELEN T. CARR FELLOWSHIPS

American Society for Engineering Education
Attn: Projects Department
1818 N Street, N.W., Suite 600
Washington, DC 20036-2479
(202) 331-3525 Fax: (202) 265-8504
E-mail: projects@asee.org
Web: www.asee.org/fellowships/hbecc.cfm

Summary To provide financial assistance to African American engineering faculty and graduate students at Historically Black Engineering Colleges (HBEC) who are interested in earning a doctoral degree.

Eligibility This program is open to African American engineering faculty and graduate students at any of the following HBECs: Alabama A&M University (Normal, Alabama), Hampton University (Hampton, Virginia), Howard University (Washington, D.C.), Morgan State University (Baltimore, Maryland), North Carolina A&T State University (Greensboro, North Carolina), Prairie View A&M University (Prairie View, Texas), Southern University and A&M College (Baton Rouge, Louisiana), Tennessee State University (Nashville, Tennessee), and Tuskegee University (Tuskegee, Alabama). Applicants may not have completed their doctorates, but they must be interested in doing so. Upon completion of the doctoral degree requirements, a fellow must agree to return to 1 of the HBEC institutions.

Financial data Up to $10,000 a year is provided through this program.

Duration 1 year; may be renewed.

Additional information Support for this program is provided by the GE Fund and the U.S. National Aeronautics and Space Administration.

Number awarded Varies each year.

Deadline Applications may be submitted at any time.

[1183]
HIGH PRIORITY, SHORT-TERM BRIDGE AWARDS IN DIABETES RESEARCH

Juvenile Diabetes Research Foundation International
Attn: Grant Administrator
26 Broadway, 14th Floor
New York, NY 10004
(212) 479-7572 Toll Free: (800) 533-CURE
Fax: (212) 785-9595 E-mail: info@jdrf.org
Web: www.jdrf.org/index.cfm?page_id=111715

Summary To provide funding to scientists (particularly African Americans, other underrepresented minorities, and individuals with disabilities) who are interested in conducting diabetes-related research but have not yet received any support.

Eligibility Applicants must have an M.D., D.M.D., D.V.M., Ph.D., or equivalent degree and have a full-time faculty position or equivalent at a college, university, medical school, or other research facility. They must have applied for grants previously and scored within 10% of the funding payline of a research funding agency but failed to receive support. Awards must be used to obtain new data to support the feasibility or validity of the research, address reviewers' concerns, or revise approaches to the research. There are no citizenship requirements. Applications are encouraged from women, members of minority groups underrepresented in the sciences, and people with disabilities. The proposed research may be conducted at foreign or domestic, for-profit or nonprofit, or public or private institutions, including universities, colleges, hospitals, laboratories, units of state or local government, or eligible agencies of the federal government.

Financial data Awards are limited to $50,000 plus 10% indirect costs.

Duration 1 year; may be renewed 1 additional year.

Deadline February, June, or November of each year.

[1184]
HIGH RISK RESEARCH IN ANTHROPOLOGY GRANTS

National Science Foundation
Social, Behavioral, and Economic Sciences
Attn: Division of Behavioral and Cognitive Sciences
4201 Wilson Boulevard, Room 995 N
Arlington, VA 22230
(703) 292-8759   Fax: (703) 292-9068
TDD: (800) 281-8749   E-mail: jyellen@nsf.gov
Web: www.nsf.gov/funding/pgm_summ.jsp?pims_id=5319

Summary To provide funding to scholars (especially African Americans, other underrepresented minorities, and individuals with disabilities) who are interested in conducting high-risk research in anthropology.

Eligibility This program is open to scholars interested in conducting research projects in cultural anthropology, archaeology, or physical anthropology that might be considered too risky for normal review procedures. A project is considered risky if the data may not be obtainable in spite of all reasonable preparation on the researcher's part. Proposals for extremely urgent research where access to the data may not be available in the normal review schedule, even with all reasonable preparation by the researcher, are also appropriate for this program. Graduate students are not eligible. Applications are encouraged from underrepresented minorities and persons with disabilities.

Financial data Grants up to $25,000, including indirect costs, are available.

Duration 1 year.

Number awarded Generally, 5 of these grants are awarded each year.

Deadline Applications may be submitted at any time.

[1185]
HIVMA MINORITY CLINICAL FELLOWSHIPS

Infectious Diseases Society of America
Attn: HIV Medicine Association
1300 Wilson Boulevard, Suite 300
Arlington, VA 22209
(703) 299-1215   Toll Free: (888) 844-4372
Fax: (703) 299-8766   E-mail: info@hivma.org
Web: www.hivma.org/Content.aspx?id=1482

Summary To provide an opportunity for African American and Latino physicians to participate in a clinical training program related to HIV.

Eligibility This program is open to physicians (M.D. or D.O.) who are of African American or Latino descent and have a demonstrated interest in HIV medicine. Applicants must be legal residents of the United States and have an intent to establish their practice in areas of the country with large minority populations. They must have completed their residencies (or be within the first 5 years of clinical practice) and be board eligible. Their proposed clinical training program must have a link to an academic institution where the majority of their time will be spent engaged in HIV clinical care and where they will have the opportunity to manage continuously at least 30 HIV patients in both inpatient and outpatient settings. Clinical settings with large minority patient populations are required. Applicants must identify a mentor to oversee their clinical experience; mentors must be members of the HIV Medicine Association (HIVMA).

Financial data The stipend is $60,000. Fellows also receive fringe benefits equivalent to those enjoyed by staff of similar rank at the sponsoring institution, 1 year membership in HIVMA, and free registration and travel support for the annual meeting of the Infectious Diseases Society of America (IDSA).

Duration 1 year.

Additional information Fellows may elect to spend up to 2 months of their fellowship at another approved institution, clinic, or practice to supplement their clinical experience. Support for this program is provided by Pfizer, Gilead Sciences, Bristol-Myers Squibb, and Tibotec. Fellows currently in clinical practice are expected to spend at least 50% of their time on clinical care and clinical education associated with the fellowship.

Number awarded 2 each year: 1 African American and 1 Latino.

Deadline March of each year.

[1186]
HUBBLE FELLOWSHIPS

Space Telescope Science Institute
Attn: Hubble Fellowship Program Office
3700 San Martin Drive
Baltimore, MD 21218
(410) 338-4574   Fax: (410) 338-4211
E-mail: rjallen@stsci.edu
Web: www.stsci.edu

Summary To provide funding to recent postdoctoral scientists (particularly African Americans, other minorities, and women) who are interested in conducting research related to the Hubble Space Telescope or related missions of the National Aeronautics and Space Administration (NASA).

Eligibility This program is open to postdoctoral scientists who completed their doctoral degree within the past 3 years in astronomy, physics, or related disciplines. Applicants must be interested in conducting research related to NASA Cosmic Origins missions: the Hubble Space Telescope, Herschel Space Observatory, James Webb Space Telescope, Stratospheric Observatory for Infrared Astronomy, or the Spitzer Space Telescope. They may be of any nationality, provided that all research is conducted at U.S. institutions and that non-U.S. nationals have valid visas. Research may be theoretical, observational, or instrumental. Women and members of minority groups are strongly encouraged to apply.

Financial data Stipends are $58,500 for the first year, $59,500 for the second year, and $60,500 for the third year. Other benefits may include health insurance, relocation costs, and support for travel, equipment, and other direct costs of research.

Duration 3 years: an initial 1-year appointment and 2 annual renewals, contingent on satisfactory performance and availability of funds.

Additional information This program, funded by NASA, began in 1990 and was limited to work with the Hubble Space Telescope. A parallel program, called the Spitzer Fellowship, began in 2002 and was limited to work with the Spitzer Space Telescope. In 2009, those programs were combined into this single program, which was also broadened to include the other NASA Cosmic Origins missions. Fellows are required to be in residence at their host institution engaged in full-time research for the duration of the grant.

Number awarded Varies each year; recently, 17 of these fellowships were awarded.

Deadline June of each year.

[1187]
HURSTON/WRIGHT LEGACY AWARD

Zora Neale Hurston/Richard Wright Foundation
Attn: Hurston/Wright Awards
12138 Central Avenue, Suite 209
Bowie, MD 20721
(301) 459-2108   E-mail: info@hurstonwright.org
Web: www.hurstonwright.org/ProgramsAwards/legacy.html

Summary To recognize and reward the best fiction, nonfiction, and poetry written by authors of African descent.

Eligibility This award is available to writers of African descent from any area of the Diaspora. Publishers may submit (with permission of the author) full-length books of fiction and nonfiction, collections of short stories, or collections of essays in 4 categories: debut fiction (debut book-length novel, novella, or short story collection); fiction (novel, novella, or short story collection); nonfiction (autobiography, memoir, biography, history, social issues, or literary criticism); or poetry (books in verse, prose poetry, formal verse, experimental verse). Paperback originals, self-published authors, and English translations of books originally written in another language are eligible, but reprints of a book published in a previous year and anthologies containing works written by multiple authors are not considered. Entries must have been published in the preceding calendar year in the United States or be U.S. editions of foreign books published for the first time in the United States.

Financial data Cash prizes are awarded.

Duration The prizes are awarded annually.

Additional information This program, established in 2002, is sponsored by Busboys and Poets restaurants in the Washington, D.C. area. There is a $25 entry fee for each title.

Number awarded 12 awards are presented each year: 1 first-place award and 2 finalist awards in each of the 4 categories.

Deadline December of each year.

[1188]
INNOVATIONS IN CLINICAL RESEARCH AWARDS

Doris Duke Charitable Foundation
Attn: Grantmaking Programs
650 Fifth Avenue, 19th Floor
New York, NY 10019
(212) 974-7000   Fax: (212) 974-7590
E-mail: ddcf@aibs.org
Web: www.ddcf.org

Summary To provide funding to investigators (especially African Americans, other minorities, and women) who are interested in conducting clinical research that may develop innovations in specified disease areas.

Eligibility This program is open to investigators who have received an M.D., Ph.D., M.D./Ph.D., or foreign equivalent and have a faculty appointment at a U.S. degree-granting institution (although U.S. citizenship is not required). Applicants must be interested in conducting innovative clinical research on a topic that changes annually but recently was limited to sickle cell disease; in other years, research was restricted to cardiovascular disease, stroke, blood disorders, or the development of diagnostics and therapeutic monitoring of AIDS in resource-poor countries. Preference is given to applicants who 1) work in other research areas, in an effort to bring new thinking to the field of sickle cell disease research; 2) are women or underrepresented minorities in medicine (Blacks or African Americans, Hispanics or Latinos, American Indians, Alaskan Natives or Native Hawaiians); or 3) propose the following types of sickle cell disease research: drug discovery, genetic and genomic approaches to study variability in the severity of sickle cell disease, early phase corrective approaches such as gene therapy and transplantation of blood-forming cells, identification of new risks for disease complication, or development of new treatments drawing from innovations in other fields such as cancer research. Selection is based on originality and inventiveness of the concept and approach, relevance of the question posed to the field of sickle cell disease, potential for clinical application, and evidence of the investigator's potential to drive innovation in sickle cell disease clinical research.

Financial data Grants provide $150,000 per year for direct costs and $12,000 per year for indirect costs.

Duration 3 years.

Additional information This program began in 2000.

Number awarded Up to 9 each year. Since this program was established, it has awarded 49 grants worth approximately $12 million.

Deadline Letters of intent must be submitted by June of each year.

[1189]
INTERNATIONAL AND AREA STUDIES FELLOWSHIPS

American Council of Learned Societies
Attn: Office of Fellowships and Grants
633 Third Avenue
New York, NY 10017-6795
(212) 697-1505   Fax: (212) 949-8058
E-mail: fellowships@acls.org
Web: www.acls.org/programs/acls

Summary To provide funding to postdoctoral scholars (especially African Americans, other minorities, and women) who are interested in conducting humanities-related research on the societies and cultures of Asia, Africa, the Middle East, Latin America and the Caribbean, eastern Europe, and the former Soviet Union.

Eligibility This program is open to U.S. citizens and residents who have lived in the United States for at least 3 years. Applicants must have a Ph.D. degree and not have received supported research leave time for at least 3 years prior to the start of the proposed research. They must be interested in conducting humanities and humanities-related social science research on the societies and cultures of Asia, Africa, the Middle East, Latin America and the Caribbean, eastern Europe, or the former Soviet Union. Selection is based on the intellectual merit of the proposed research and the likelihood that it will produce significant and innovative scholarship. Applications are particularly invited from women and members of minority groups.

Financial data The maximum grant is $60,000 for full professors and equivalent, $40,000 for associate professors and equivalent, or $35,000 for assistant professors and equivalent. These fellowships may not be held concurrently with another major fellowship.

Duration 6 to 12 months.

Additional information This program is jointly supported by the American Council of Learned Societies (ACLS) and the Social Science Research Council (SSRC), with funding provided by the National Endowment for the Humanities (NEH).

Number awarded Up to 10 each year.

Deadline September of each year.

[1190]
INVESTIGATORS IN PATHOGENESIS OF INFECTIOUS DISEASE

Burroughs Wellcome Fund
21 T.W. Alexander Drive, Suite 100
P.O. Box 13901
Research Triangle Park, NC 27709-3901
(919) 991-5100   Fax: (919) 991-5160
E-mail: info@bwfund.org
Web: www.bwfund.org

Summary To provide funding to physician/scientists in the United States and Canada especially African Americans, other underrepresented minorities, and women) who wish to conduct research on pathogenesis, with a focus on the intersection of human and pathogen biology.

Eligibility This program is open to established independent physician/scientists who are citizens or permanent residents of the United States or Canada and affiliated with accredited degree-granting U.S. or Canadian medical schools. Applicants must be interested in conducting research projects that hold potential for advancing significantly the biochemical, pharmacological, immunological, and molecular biological understanding of how infectious agents and the human body interact. Although work on AIDS, malaria, and tuberculosis is not excluded, preference is given to research shedding new light on unexplored pathogenesis. Research on understudied infectious diseases, including pathogenic fungi, protozoan and metazoan diseases, and emerging infections, is of especial interest. Candidates must have an M.D., D.V.M., or Ph.D. degree and be tenure-track investigators as an assistant professor or equivalent at a

degree-granting institution. Each institution (including its medical school, graduate schools, and all affiliated hospitals and research institutes) may nominate up to 2 candidates. Institutions that nominate a researcher who has a D.V.M. are allowed 3 nominations. The sponsor also encourages institutions to nominate underrepresented minorities and women. Selection is based on qualifications of the candidate and potential to conduct innovative research; demonstration of an established record of independent research; and quality and originality of the proposed research and its potential to advance understanding of fundamental issues of how infectious agents and human hosts interact.

Financial data The grant provides $100,000 per year.

Duration 5 years.

Additional information This program was established in 2001 as a replacement for several former programs: New Investigator and Scholar Awards in Molecular Pathogenic Mycology, New Investigator and Scholar Awards in Molecular Parasitology, and New Initiatives in Malaria Awards. Awardees are required to devote at least 75% of their time to research-related activities.

Number awarded Varies each year; recently, 6 of these grants were awarded.

Deadline October of each year.

[1191]
JAMES A. RAWLEY PRIZE

Organization of American Historians
Attn: Award and Committee Coordinator
112 North Bryan Street
Bloomington, IN 47408-4141
(812) 855-7311   Fax: (812) 855-0696
E-mail: khamm@oah.org
Web: www.oah.org/awards/awards.rawley.index.html

Summary To recognize and reward African American and other authors of outstanding books dealing with race relations in the United States.

Eligibility This award is presented to the author of the outstanding book on the history of race relations in America. Entries must have been published during the current calendar year.

Financial data The award is $1,000 and a certificate.

Duration The award is presented annually.

Additional information This award was established in 1990.

Number awarded 1 each year.

Deadline September of each year.

[1192]
JAMES H. DUNN, JR. MEMORIAL FELLOWSHIP PROGRAM

Office of the Governor
Attn: Department of Central Management Services
503 William G. Stratton Building
Springfield, IL 62706
(217) 524-1381   Fax: (217) 558-4497
TDD: (217) 785-3979
Web: www.ilga.gov/commission/lru/internships.html

Summary To provide recent college graduates (particularly African Americans, other minorities, women, and persons with disabilities) with work experience in the Illinois Governor's office.

Eligibility This program in open to residents of any state who have completed a bachelor's degree and are interested in working in the Illinois Governor's office or in various agencies under the Governor's jurisdiction. Applicants may have majored in any field, but they must be able to demonstrate a substantial commitment to excellence as evidenced by academic honors, leadership ability, extracurricular activities, and involvement in community or public service. Along with their application, they must submit 1) a 500-word personal statement on the qualities or attributes they will bring to the program, their career goals or plans, how their selection for this program would assist them in achieving those goals, and what they expect to gain from the program; and 2) a 1,000-word essay in which they identify and analyze a public issue that they feel has great impact on state government. A particular goal of the program is to achieve affirmative action through the nomination of qualified minorities, women, and persons with disabilities.

Financial data The stipend is $2,611 per month.

Duration 1 year, beginning in August.

Additional information Assignments are in Springfield and, to a limited extent, in Chicago or Washington, D.C.

Number awarded Varies each year.

Deadline February of each year.

[1193]
JAMES WELDON JOHNSON FELLOW IN AFRICAN AMERICAN STUDIES

Yale University
Attn: Beinecke Rare Book and Manuscript Library
P.O. Box 208240
New Haven, CT 06520-8240
(203) 432-2956   Fax: (203) 432-4047
E-mail: beinecke.fellowships@yale.edu
Web: www.library.yale.edu

Summary To provide long-term funding to scholars interested in conducting research in African American studies using the resources of the James Weldon Johnson Collection at the Beinecke Rare Book and Manuscript Library at Yale University.

Eligibility This program is open to scholars who have a distinguished scholarly record. Applicants must be interested in conducting research in African American studies at the Beinecke Library. Selection is based on scholarly qualifications and promise, merits and significance of the research, and relevance of the Beinecke collections to the proposed project.

Financial data A stipend is awarded (amount not specified); postdoctoral fellowships at Yale are generally in the range of $45,000.

Duration 10 months, beginning in August.

Additional information This fellowship was first awarded in 2008. Fellows are provided with an office in the Yale African American studies department and are invited to participate in its scholarly activities.

Number awarded 1 each year.

Deadline December of each year.

[1194]
JDRF SCHOLAR AWARDS

Juvenile Diabetes Research Foundation International
Attn: Grant Administrator
26 Broadway, 14th Floor
New York, NY 10004
(212) 479-7572   Toll Free: (800) 533-CURE
Fax: (212) 785-9595   E-mail: info@jdrf.org
Web: www.jdrf.org/index.cfm?page_id=111715

Summary To provide funding to established independent physician scientists (particularly African Americans, other minorities, women, and individuals with disabilities) who are interested in conducting basic or clinical diabetes-related research.

Eligibility This program is open to established investigators in diabetes-related research who have an M.D., D.M.D., D.O., Ph.D., D.V.M., or equivalent degree and an independent investigator position at a university, health science center, or comparable institution. Normally, applicants should have at least 7 years of relevant experience since receiving their doctoral degree. They must be willing to take risks and attempt new approaches to accelerate Type 1 diabetes research. This program is not intended to expand the funding of scientists already well supported for exploring this concept. There are no citizenship requirements. Applications are encouraged from women, members of minority groups underrepresented in the sciences, and people with disabilities. The proposed research may be conducted at foreign or domestic, for-profit or nonprofit, or public or private institutions, including universities, colleges, hospitals, laboratories, units of state or local government, or eligible agencies of the federal government. Selection is based on relevance of the research to and impact on the mission of the Juvenile Diabetes Research Foundation (JDRF); innovation, creativity, and the potential for future innovation relative to the applicant's career stage; and the applicant's motivation, enthusiasm, and intellectual energy to pursue a challenging problem.

Financial data The total award may be up to $250,000 each year, including indirect costs.

Duration Up to 5 years.

Number awarded Up to 4 each year.

Deadline An intent to submit must be received by August of each year. Completed applications are due in September.

[1195]
JESSICA M. BLANDING MEMORIAL SCHOLARSHIP

New England Regional Black Nurses Association, Inc.
P.O. Box 190690
Boston, MA 02119
(617) 524-1951
Web: www.nerbna.org/org/scholarships.html

Summary To provide financial assistance to licensed practical nurses from New England who are working on a degree and have contributed to the African American community.

Eligibility The program is open to residents of the New England states who are licensed practical nurses working on an associate or bachelor's degree in nursing at a school in any state. Applicants must have at least 1 full year of school remaining. Along with their application, they must submit a 3-page essay that covers their career aspirations in the nursing profession; how they have contributed to the African American or other communities of color in such areas as work, volunteering, church, or community outreach; an experience that has enhanced their personal and/or professional growth; and any financial hardships that may hinder them from completing their education.

Financial data A stipend is awarded (amount not specified).

Duration 1 year.

Number awarded 1 or more each year.

Deadline March of each year.

[1196]
JOEL ELKES RESEARCH AWARD

American College of Neuropsychopharmacology
Attn: Executive Office
5034-A Thoroughbred Lane
Brentwood, TN 37027
(615) 324-2360   Fax: (615) 523-1715
E-mail: acnp@acnp.org
Web: www.acnp.org/programs/awards.aspx

Summary To recognize and reward young scientists (especially African Americans, other minorities, and women) who have contributed outstanding clinical or translational research to neuropsychopharmacology.

Eligibility This award is available to scientists who are younger than 50 years of age. Nominees must have made an outstanding clinical or translational contribution to neuropsychopharmacology. The contribution may be based on a single discovery or a cumulative body of work. Emphasis is placed on contributions that further understanding of self-regulatory processes as they affect mental function and behavior in disease and well-being. Membership in the American College of Neuropsychopharmacology (ACNP) is not required. Nomination of women and minorities is highly encouraged.

Financial data The award consists of an expense-paid trip to the ACNP annual meeting, a monetary honorarium, and a plaque.

Duration The award is presented annually.

Additional information This award was first presented in 1986.

Number awarded 1 each year.

Deadline Nominations must be submitted by June of each year.

[1197]
JOHN PAVLIS FELLOWSHIP AWARD

Vermont Studio Center
80 Pearl Street
P.O. Box 613
Johnson, VT 05656
(802) 635-2727   Fax: (802) 635-2730
E-mail: info@vermontstudiocenter.org
Web: www.vermontstudiocenter.org

Summary To provide funding to African American artists and writers who are interested in a residency at the Vermont Studio Center in Johnson, Vermont.

Eligibility This program is open to African American painters, sculptors, printmakers, new and mixed-media artists, photographers, poets, and other writers of fiction and creative nonfiction. Applicants must be interested in a residency at the

center in Johnson, Vermont. Visual artists must submit up to 20 slides or visual images of their work, poets must submit up to 10 pages, and other writers must submit 10 to 15 pages. Selection is based on artistic merit. Preference is given to students and graduates from Spelman College, Morehouse College, and Fisk University.

Financial data The award pays $3,750, which covers all residency fees.

Duration 4 weeks.

Additional information The application fee is $25.

Number awarded 3 each year: 2 visual artists and 1 writer.

Deadline February of each year.

[1198]
JOHN V. KRUTILLA RESEARCH STIPEND

Resources for the Future
Attn: Coordinator for Academic Programs
1616 P Street, N.W., Suite 600
Washington, DC 20036-1400
(202) 328-5088   Fax: (202) 939-3460
E-mail: krutilla-award@rff.org
Web: www.rff.org/About_RFF/Pages/default.aspx

Summary To provide funding for research related to environmental and resource economics to African American and other young scholars.

Eligibility This program is open to scholars who received their doctoral degree within the past 5 years. Applicants must be interested in conducting research related to environmental and resource economics. They must submit a short description of the proposed research, a curriculum vitae, and a letter of recommendation. Women and minority candidates are strongly encouraged to apply.

Financial data The grant is $9,000.

Duration 1 year.

Additional information This award was first presented in 2006.

Number awarded 1 each year.

Deadline February of each year.

[1199]
JOHN W. BLASSINGAME AWARD

Southern Historical Association
c/o John C. Inscoe, Secretary-Treasurer
University of Georgia
Department of History
LeConte Hall, Room 111
Athens, GA 30602-1602
(706) 542-8848   E-mail: jinscoe@uga.edu
Web: www.uga.edu/sha/awards/blassingame.htm

Summary To recognize and reward faculty members who have contributed outstanding scholarship and mentorship in African American studies.

Eligibility This award is available to members of all areas of the academic community, including community and junior colleges, Historically Black Colleges and Universities, and large research universities. Nominations may be submitted by members of the Southern Historical Association, based on distinguished careers as mentors of African American students, personal scholarly accomplishments, or some combination of both. For nominations involving a primary role in mentoring African American students, letters from students (undergraduate or graduate) are particularly welcome.

Financial data   The award is $1,000.

Duration   The award is presented biennially.

Additional information   This award was first presented in 2004.

Number awarded   1 every even-numbered year.

Deadline   Deadline not specified.

[1200]
JUDITH L. WEIDMAN RACIAL ETHNIC MINORITY FELLOWSHIP

United Methodist Communications
Attn: Communications Resourcing Team
810 12th Avenue South
P.O. Box 320
Nashville, TN 37202-0320
(615) 742-5481   Toll Free: (888) CRT-4UMC
Fax: (615) 742-5485   E-mail: scholarships@umcom.org
Web: crt.umc.org/interior.asp?ptid=1&mid=6891

Summary   To provide work experience to African Americans and other minorities who are Methodists and interested in a communications career.

Eligibility   This program is open to United Methodists of racial ethnic minority heritage who are interested in preparing for a career in communications with the United Methodist Church. Applicants must be recent college or seminary graduates who have broad communications training, including work in journalism, mass communications, marketing, public relations, and electronic media. They must be able to understand and speak English proficiently and to relocate for a year. Selection is based on Christian commitment and involvement in the life of the United Methodist Church; achievement as revealed by transcripts, GPA, letters of reference, and work samples; study, experience, and evidence of talent in the field of communications; clarity of purpose and goals for the future; desire to learn how to be a successful United Methodist conference communicator; and potential leadership ability as a professional religion communicator for the United Methodist Church.

Financial data   The stipend is $30,000 per year. Benefits and expenses for moving and professional travel are also provided.

Duration   1 year, starting in July.

Additional information   This program was established in 1998. Recipients are assigned to 1 of the 63 United Methodist Annual Conferences, the headquarters of local churches within a geographic area. At the Annual Conference, the fellow will be assigned an experienced communicator as a mentor and will work closely with that mentor and with United Methodist Communications in Nashville, Tennessee. Following the successful completion of the fellowship, United Methodist Communications and the participating Annual Conference will assist in a search for permanent employment within the United Methodist Church but cannot guarantee a position.

Number awarded   1 each year.

Deadline   March of each year.

[1201]
JULIUS AXELROD MENTORSHIP AWARD

American College of Neuropsychopharmacology
Attn: Executive Office
5034-A Thoroughbred Lane
Brentwood, TN 37027
(615) 324-2360   Fax: (615) 523-1715
E-mail: acnp@acnp.org
Web: www.acnp.org/programs/awards.aspx

Summary   To recognize and reward members of the American College of Neuropsychopharmacology (particularly African Americans, other minorities, and women) who have demonstrated outstanding mentoring of young scientists.

Eligibility   This award is available to ACNP members who have made an outstanding contribution to neuropsychopharmacology by mentoring and developing young scientists into leaders in the field. Nominations must be accompanied by letters of support from up to 3 people who have been mentored by the candidate. Nomination of women and minorities is highly encouraged.

Financial data   The award consists of a monetary honorarium and a plaque.

Duration   The award is presented annually.

Additional information   This award was first presented in 2004.

Number awarded   1 each year.

Deadline   Nominations must be submitted by June of each year.

[1202]
JUVENILE DIABETES RESEARCH FOUNDATION INNOVATIVE GRANTS

Juvenile Diabetes Research Foundation International
Attn: Grant Administrator
26 Broadway, 14th Floor
New York, NY 10004
(212) 479-7572   Toll Free: (800) 533-CURE
Fax: (212) 785-9595   E-mail: info@jdrf.org
Web: www.jdrf.org/index.cfm?page_id=111715

Summary   To provide funding to scientists (especially African Americans, other underrepresented scientists, women, and individuals with disabilities) who are interested in conducting innovative diabetes-related research.

Eligibility   Applicants must have an M.D., D.M.D., D.V.M., Ph.D., or equivalent degree and have a full-time faculty position or equivalent at a college, university, medical school, or other research facility. They must be seeking "seed" money for investigative work based on a sound hypothesis for which preliminary data are insufficient for a regular research grant but that are likely to lead to important results for the treatment of diabetes and its complications. Applicants must specifically explain how the proposal is innovative. Selection is based on whether 1) the proposed research is innovative; 2) the underlying premise, goal, or hypothesis is plausible; 3) the proposed research can be completed in 1 year; and 4) the proposed research is relevant to the mission of the Juvenile Diabetes Research Foundation and its potential impact. Applications are encouraged from women, members of minority groups underrepresented in the sciences, and people with disabilities. The proposed research may be conducted at foreign or domestic, for-profit or nonprofit, or public or private institutions, including universities, colleges, hospitals, laboratories, units of state or local government, or eligible agencies of the federal government.

Financial data Awards are limited to $100,000 plus 10% indirect costs.

Duration 1 year; nonrenewable.

Deadline January or July of each year.

[1203]
JUVENILE DIABETES RESEARCH FOUNDATION PRIORITY RESEARCH GRANTS

Juvenile Diabetes Research Foundation International
Attn: Grant Administrator
26 Broadway, 14th Floor
New York, NY 10004
(212) 479-7572   Toll Free: (800) 533-CURE
Fax: (212) 785-9595   E-mail: info@jdrf.org
Web: www.jdrf.org/index.cfm?page_id=111715

Summary To provide funding to scientists (especially African Americans, other underrepresented scientists, women, and individuals with disabilities) who are interested in conducting research on diabetes and its related complications.

Eligibility Applicants must have an M.D., D.M.D., D.V.M., Ph.D., or equivalent degree and have a full-time faculty position or equivalent at a college, university, medical school, or other research facility. They must be interested in conducting research related to the priorities of the Juvenile Diabetes Research Foundation (JDRF), which currently include 1) restoration and maintenance of normal glucose regulation in Type 1 diabetes, including restoration of beta cell function, immunoregulation, and metabolic control; 2) prevention and treatment of complications of diabetes; 3) improvements in glucose control; and 4) prevention of Type 1 diabetes. Applications are encouraged from women, members of minority groups underrepresented in the sciences, and people with disabilities. The proposed research may be conducted at foreign or domestic, for-profit or nonprofit, or public or private institutions, including universities, colleges, hospitals, laboratories, units of state or local government, or eligible agencies of the federal government. Selection is based on potential to generate new approaches to unsolved scientific problems related to Type 1 diabetes; relevance to the objectives of JDRF: scientific, technical, or medical significance of the research proposal; innovativeness; appropriateness and adequacy of the experimental approach and methodology; qualifications and research experience of the principal investigator and collaborators; availability of resources and facilities necessary for the project; and appropriateness of the proposed budget in relation to the proposed research.

Financial data Grants up to $165,000 (plus 10% for indirect costs) per year are available.

Duration 3 years.

Deadline Letters of intent must be submitted by November of each year.

[1204]
LAURENCE R. FOSTER MEMORIAL GRADUATE SCHOLARSHIP

Oregon Student Assistance Commission
Attn: Grants and Scholarships Division
1500 Valley River Drive, Suite 100
Eugene, OR 97401-2146
(541) 687-7395   Toll Free: (800) 452-8807, ext. 7395
Fax: (541) 687-7414   TDD: (800) 735-2900
E-mail: awardinfo@osac.state.or.us
Web: www.osac.state.or.us/osac_programs.html

Summary To provide financial assistance to residents of Oregon (especially African Americans and other residents from diverse environments) who are interested in enrolling in graduate school in any state to prepare for a public health career.

Eligibility This program is open to residents of Oregon who are enrolled at least half time at a college or university in any state to prepare for a career in public health (not private practice). Applicants must be either working in public health or enrolled as graduate students in that field. Preference is given to applicants from diverse environments. Along with their application, they must submit brief essays on 1) what public health means to them; 2) the public health aspect they intend to practice and the health and population issues impacted by that aspect; and 3) their experience living or working in diverse environments.

Financial data Stipend amounts vary; recently, they were at least $4,167.

Duration 1 year.

Additional information This program is administered by the Oregon Student Assistance Commission (OSAC) with funds provided by the Oregon Community Foundation.

Number awarded Varies each year; recently, 6 undergraduate and graduate scholarships were awarded.

Deadline February of each year.

[1205]
LEE & LOW BOOKS NEW VOICES AWARD

Lee & Low Books
95 Madison Avenue, Suite 1205
New York, NY 10016
(212) 779-4400   Fax: (212) 683-1894
E-mail: general@leeandlow.com
Web: www.leeandlow.com/p/new_voices_award.mhtml

Summary To recognize and reward outstanding unpublished children's picture books by African Americans and other writers of color.

Eligibility The contest is open to writers of color who are residents of the United States and who have not previously published a children's picture book. Writers who have published in other venues, (e.g., children's magazines, young adult fiction and nonfiction) are eligible. Manuscripts previously submitted to the sponsor are not eligible. Submissions should be no more than 1,500 words and must address the needs of children of color by providing stories with which they can identify and relate and that promote a greater understanding of each other. Submissions may be fiction or nonfiction for children between the ages of 5 and 12. Folklore and animal stories are not considered. Up to 2 submissions may be submitted per entrant.

Financial data The award is a $1,000 cash grant plus the standard publication contract, including the standard advance and royalties. The Honor Award winner receives a cash grant of $500.

Duration The competition is held annually.

Additional information This program was established in 2000. Manuscripts may not be sent to any other publishers while under consideration for this award.

Number awarded 2 each year.

Deadline October of each year.

[1206]
LIBRARY OF CONGRESS JUNIOR FELLOWS PROGRAM

Library of Congress
Library Services
Attn: Junior Fellows Program Coordinator
101 Independence Avenue, S.E., Room LM-642
Washington, DC 20540-4600
(202) 707-0901   Fax: (202) 707-6269
E-mail: jrfell@loc.gov
Web: www.loc.gov/hr/jrfellows/index.html

Summary To provide summer work experience at the Library of Congress (LC) to African American and other 1) upper-division or graduate students and 2) recent graduates.

Eligibility This program is open to U.S. citizens with subject expertise in the following areas: American history, including veterans and military history; American popular culture; area studies (African, Asian, European, Hispanic, Middle Eastern); bibliographic description and access; film, television, and radio; folklife; geography and maps; history of photography; history of popular and applied graphic arts, architecture, and design; manuscript collections processing; music; preservation and conservation; rare books and manuscripts; science, technology, and business; serials and government publications and newspapers; or sound recordings. Applicants must 1) be juniors or seniors at an accredited college or university, 2) be graduate students, or 3) have completed their degree in the past year. Applications from women, minorities, and persons with disabilities are particularly encouraged. Selection is based on academic achievement, letters of recommendation, and an interview.

Financial data Fellows are paid a taxable stipend of $300 per week.

Duration 3 months, beginning in either May or June. Fellows work a 40-hour week.

Additional information Fellows work with primary source materials and assist selected divisions at LC in the organization and documentation of archival collections, production of finding aids and bibliographic records, preparation of materials for preservation and service, completion of bibliographical research, and digitization of LC's historical collections.

Number awarded Varies each year; recently, 6 of these internships were awarded.

Deadline March of each year.

[1207]
LONG RANGE ANNUAL FUNDING OPPORTUNITY ANNOUNCEMENT FOR NAVY AND MARINE CORPS SCIENCE, TECHNOLOGY, ENGINEERING & MATHEMATICS (STEM) PROGRAMS

Office of Naval Research
Attn: Code 03R
875 North Randolph Street, Suite 1410
Arlington, VA 22203-1995
(703) 696-4111   E-mail: kam.ng1@navy.mil
Web: www.onr.navy.mil

Summary To provide financial support to investigators (particularly those from Historically Black Colleges and Universities and other minority institutions) who are interested in conducting long-range science, technology, engineering, or mathematics (STEM) projects on topics of interest to the U.S. Navy.

Eligibility This program is open to faculty and staff from academia (colleges and universities), middle and high schools, nonprofit organizations, and industry. Applicants must be interested in conducting long-range projects in STEM fields that offer potential for advancement and improvement of Navy and Marine Corps operations. The projects should help fulfill the mission of the program to foster an interest in, knowledge of, and study in STEM to ensure an educated and well-prepared work force that meets naval and national competitive needs. Applicants at Historically Black Colleges and Universities (HBCUs) and Minority Institutions (MIs) are encouraged to submit proposals and join others in submitting proposals.

Financial data Grants range up to $200,000 per year.

Duration 12 to 36 months.

Number awarded Varies each year; recently, a total of $10 million was available for this program.

Deadline Full proposals must be submitted by September of each year.

[1208]
LONG RANGE BROAD AGENCY ANNOUNCEMENT FOR NAVY AND MARINE CORPS SCIENCE AND TECHNOLOGY

Office of Naval Research
Attn: Acquisition Department, Code BD255
875 North Randolph Street
Arlington, VA 22203-1995
(703) 696-2570   Fax: (703) 696-3365
E-mail: misale.abdi@navy.mil
Web: www.onr.navy.mil

Summary To provide financial support to investigators (especially those from Historically Black Colleges and Universities and minority institutions) who are interested in conducting long-range science and technology research on topics of interest to the U.S. Navy and Marine Corps.

Eligibility This program is open to researchers from academia (colleges and universities) and industry. Applicants must be interested in conducting long-range projects in fields of science and technology that offer potential for advancement and improvement of Navy and Marine Corps operations. The proposed research must relate to 1 of the following topic areas: 1) expeditionary maneuver warfare and combating terrorism; 2) command, control communications, computers, intelligence, surveillance, and reconnaissance; 3) ocean battlespace sensing; 4) sea warfare and weapons; 5) warfighter performance; and 6) naval air warfare and weapons. Researchers at Historically Black Colleges and Universities (HBCUs) and Minority Institutions (MIs) are encouraged to submit proposals and join others in submitting proposals.

Financial data Grant amounts depend on the nature of the proposal.

Number awarded Varies each year.

Deadline White papers must be submitted in November of each year.

[1209]
LOUIS STOKES URBAN HEALTH POLICY FELLOWS PROGRAM

Congressional Black Caucus Foundation, Inc.
Attn: Director, Educational Programs
1720 Massachusetts Avenue, N.W.
Washington, DC 20036
(202) 263-2800   Toll Free: (800) 784-2577
Fax: (202) 775-0773   E-mail: info@cbcfinc.org
Web: www.cbcfinc.org/internships.html

Summary To provide an opportunity for health policy professionals to work on a program of original research, advanced legislative training, and health policy analysis in collaboration with the Congressional Black Caucus (CBC).

Eligibility This program is open to professionals who have a graduate or professional degree in a health-related field (behavioral sciences, social sciences, biological sciences, and health professions). Applicants must be interested in working in Washington, D.C. on health-related issues as a member of the staff or committee of a member of the CBC. They must be able to demonstrate an interest in public health policy, a commitment to creating and implementing policy to improve the living conditions for underserved and underrepresented minorities, an interest in how health policies affect African Americans and minorities, a record of academic and professional achievement, evidence of leadership skills, the potential for further growth, and familiarity with the federal legislative process, Congress, and the CBC.

Financial data Fellows receive a stipend of $40,000 and benefits.

Duration 1 year, beginning in September.

Additional information This program was established in 2003. Fellows are assigned to Congressional offices or committees and work on issues related to minority health.

Number awarded 2 each year.

Deadline March of each year.

[1210]
M. ELIZABETH CARNEGIE SCHOLARSHIP

Nurses Educational Funds, Inc.
Attn: Scholarship Coordinator
304 Park Avenue South, 11th Floor
New York, NY 10010
(212) 590-2443   Fax: (212) 590-2446
E-mail: info@n-e-f.org
Web: www.n-e-f.org

Summary To provide financial assistance to African American nurses who wish to work on a doctoral degree in nursing.

Eligibility This program is open to African American registered nurses who are members of a national professional nursing organization and enrolled in a nursing or nursing-related program at the doctoral level. Applicants must have a GPA of 3.6 or higher. They must be U.S. citizens or have declared their official intention of becoming a citizen. Along with their application, they must submit an 800-word essay on their professional goals and potential for making a contribution to the nursing profession. Selection is based on academic excellence and the essay's content and clarity.

Financial data Stipends range from $2,500 to $10,000, depending on the availability of funds.

Duration 1 year; nonrenewable.

Additional information There is a $20 application fee.

Number awarded 1 each year.

Deadline February of each year.

[1211]
MANY VOICES RESIDENCIES

Playwrights' Center
2301 East Franklin Avenue
Minneapolis, MN 55406-1024
(612) 332-7481   Fax: (612) 332-6037
E-mail: info@pwcenter.org
Web: www.pwcenter.org/fellows_voices.php

Summary To provide funding to Minnesota playwrights of color so they can spend a year at the Playwrights' Center in Minneapolis.

Eligibility This program is open to playwrights of color who are citizens or permanent residents of the United States and have been residents of Minnesota for at least 1 year. Applicants must be interested in playwriting and creating theater in a supportive artist community at the Playwrights' Center. They may be beginning playwrights (with little or no previous playwriting experience) or emerging playwrights (with previous playwriting experience and/or training). Selection is based on the applicant's commitment, proven talent, and artistic potential.

Financial data Beginning playwrights receive a $1,000 stipend, $250 in play development funds, and a structured curriculum of playwriting instruction and dramaturgical support. Emerging playwrights receive a $3,600 stipend, $1,000 in play development funds, and dramaturgical support.

Duration 9 months, beginning in October.

Additional information This program, which began in 1994, is funded by the Jerome Foundation. Fellows must be in residence at the Playwrights' Center for the duration of the program.

Number awarded 5 each year: 2 beginning playwrights and 3 emerging playwrights.

Deadline February of each year.

[1212]
MARTIN LUTHER KING, JR. MEMORIAL SCHOLARSHIP FUND

California Teachers Association
Attn: Human Rights Department
1705 Murchison Drive
P.O. Box 921
Burlingame, CA 94011-0921
(650) 552-5446   Fax: (650) 552-5002
E-mail: scholarships@cta.org
Web: www.cta.org

Summary   To provide financial assistance for college or graduate school to African American and other racial and ethnic minorities who are members of the California Teachers Association (CTA), children of members, or members of the Student CTA.

Eligibility   This program is open to members of racial or ethnic minority groups (African Americans, American Indians/Alaska Natives, Asians/Pacific Islanders, and Hispanics) who are 1) active CTA members; 2) dependent children of active, retired, or deceased CTA members; or 3) members of Student CTA. Applicants must be interested in preparing for a teaching career in public education or already engaged in such a career.

Financial data   Stipends vary each year; recently, they ranged from $1,000 to $4,000.

Duration   1 year.

Number awarded   Varies each year; recently, 12 of these scholarships were awarded: 4 to CTA members, 6 to children of CTA members, and 2 to Student CTA members.

Deadline   March of each year.

[1213]
MARY ELIZABETH CARNEGIE AMERICAN NURSES FOUNDATION SCHOLAR AWARD

American Nurses Foundation
Attn: Nursing Research Grants Program
8515 Georgia Avenue, Suite 400
Silver Spring, MD 20910-3492
(301) 628-5227   Fax: (301) 628-5354
E-mail: anf@ana.org
Web: www.anfonline.org

Summary   To provide funding to nurses, especially members of the National Black Nurses' Association (NBNA), who are interested in conducting research.

Eligibility   This program is open to registered nurses who have earned a baccalaureate or higher degree. Preference is given to NBNA members. Applicants may be either beginning or experienced researchers. They must be interested in conducting research on a topic related to nursing. Proposed research may be for a master's thesis or doctoral dissertation if the project has been approved by the principal investigator's thesis or dissertation committee.

Financial data   The grant is $8,500. Funds may not be used as a salary for the principal investigator.

Duration   1 year.

Additional information   This award was first presented in 2007. There is a $100 application fee.

Number awarded   1 each year.

Deadline   April of each year.

[1214]
MATHEMATICAL SCIENCES POSTDOCTORAL RESEARCH FELLOWSHIPS

National Science Foundation
Directorate for Mathematical and Physical Sciences
Attn: Division of Mathematical Sciences
4201 Wilson Boulevard, Room 1025N
Arlington, VA 22230
(703) 292-8132   Fax: (703) 292-9032
TDD: (800) 281-8749   E-mail: devasius@nsf.gov
Web: www.nsf.gov/funding/pgm_summ.jsp?pims_id=5301

Summary   To provide financial assistance to underrepresented minorities and other postdoctorates interested in pursuing research training in mathematics.

Eligibility   Applicants for these fellowships must 1) be U.S. citizens, nationals, or permanent residents; 2) have earned a Ph.D. in a mathematical science or have had equivalent research training and experience; 3) have held the Ph.D. for no more than 2 years; and 4) have not previously held any other postdoctoral fellowship from the National Science Foundation (NSF) or been offered an award from this program. They must be proposing to conduct a program of postdoctoral research training at an appropriate nonprofit U.S. institution, including government laboratories, national laboratories, and privately sponsored nonprofit institutes, as well as institutions of higher education. A senior scientist at the institution must indicate availability for consultation and agreement to work with the fellow. Applications are encouraged from underrepresented minorities and persons with disabilities.

Financial data   The total award is $135,000, consisting of 3 components: 1) a monthly stipend of $5,000 for full-time support or $2,500 for half-time support, paid directly to the fellow; 2) a research allowance of $10,000, also paid directly to the fellow; and 3) an institutional allowance of $5,000, paid to the host institution for fringe benefits (including health insurance payments for the fellow) and expenses incurred in support of the fellow, such as space, equipment, and general purpose supplies.

Duration   Fellows may select either of 2 options: the research fellowship option provides full-time support for any 18 academic-year months in a 3-year period, in intervals not shorter than 3 consecutive months; the research instructorship option provides a combination of full-time and half-time support over a period of 3 academic years, usually 1 academic year full time and 2 academic years part time. Under both options, the award includes 6 summer months, but no more than 2 summer months of support may be received in any calendar year. The stipend support for 24 months (18 academic year months plus 6 summer months) is provided within a 48-month period.

Additional information   Under certain circumstances, it may be desirable for portions of the work to be done at foreign institutions. Approval to do so must be obtained in advance from both the sponsoring senior scientist and the NSF.

Number awarded   30 to 35 each year. A total of $4.8 million is available for this program annually.

Deadline   October of each year.

[1215]
MAXINE V. FENNELL MEMORIAL SCHOLARSHIP

New England Regional Black Nurses Association, Inc.
P.O. Box 190690
Boston, MA 02119
(617) 524-1951
Web: www.nerbna.org/org/scholarships.html

Summary To provide financial assistance to licensed practical nurses from New England who are studying to become a registered nurse (R.N.) and have contributed to the African American community.

Eligibility The program is open to residents of the New England states who are licensed practical nurses and currently enrolled in an NLN-accredited R.N. program (diploma, associate, baccalaureate) at a school in any state. Applicants must have at least 1 full year of school remaining. Along with their application, they must submit a 3-page essay that covers their career aspirations in the nursing profession; how they have contributed to the African American or other communities of color in such areas as work, volunteering, church, or community outreach; an experience that has enhanced their personal and/or professional growth; and any financial hardships that may hinder them from completing their education.

Financial data A stipend is awarded (amount not specified).

Duration 1 year.

Number awarded 1 or more each year.

Deadline March of each year.

[1216]
MENTOR-BASED MINORITY POSTDOCTORAL FELLOWSHIPS IN DIABETES

American Diabetes Association
Attn: Senior Manager, Research Programs
1701 North Beauregard Street
Alexandria, VA 22311
(703) 549-1500, ext. 2362   Toll Free: (800) DIABETES
Fax: (703) 549-1715
E-mail: grantquestions@diabetes.org
Web: professional.diabetes.org

Summary To provide financial assistance to African American and other minority postdoctoral fellows working with established diabetes investigators.

Eligibility Applications for these fellowships may be submitted by established and active investigators in diabetes research who wish to supervise the work of a postdoctoral fellow, whom they will select. They must currently hold a grant from the American Diabetes Association. The fellow selected by the investigator must be a member of an underrepresented minority group (African American; Spanish, Hispanic, or Latino; American Indian or Alaskan Native; Native Hawaiian or Pacific Islander); must have an M.D., Ph.D., D.O., D.P.M., or Pharm.D. degree; must not be serving an internship or residency during the fellowship period; and must not have more than 3 years of postdoctoral research experience in the field of diabetes/endocrinology. Applicant investigators and fellows must be U.S. citizens or permanent residents. The applicant investigator must also hold an appointment at a U.S. research institution and have sufficient research support to provide an appropriate training environment for the fellow. The applicant investigator must be a member of the Professional Section of the American Diabetes Association; the fel-

low must also be, or agree to become, a member. Selection is based on the quality and activity of the applicant investigator's diabetes research program, the likelihood that the fellow trained by the mentor will actively pursue a career in diabetes research, the applicant investigator's past training record, and evidence of sufficient research support and adequate facilities to provide an appropriate training environment for a postdoctoral fellow.

Financial data The grant is $45,000 per year. Within that total, the applicant investigator may determine the salary of the fellow; up to $3,000 per year of the total may be used for laboratory supply costs, up to $1,000 may be used for travel by the fellow to attend diabetes-related scientific meetings, and up to $500 may be used for book purchases.

Duration 2 to 3 years.

Number awarded Varies each year.

Deadline January of each year.

[1217]
MENTORED NEW INVESTIGATOR RESEARCH GRANTS TO PROMOTE DIVERSITY OF THE ALZHEIMER'S ASSOCIATION

Alzheimer's Association
Attn: Medical and Scientific Affairs
225 North Michigan Avenue, 17th Floor
Chicago, IL 60601-7633
(312) 335-5747   Toll Free: (800) 272-3900
Fax: (866) 699-1246   TDD: (312) 335-5886
E-mail: grantsapp@alz.org
Web: www.alz.org

Summary To provide funding for mentored research on Alzheimer's Disease to African Americans and other junior investigators who will contribute to diversity in the field.

Eligibility This program is open to investigators who have less than 10 years of research experience after receipt of their terminal degree. Applicants must be proposing to conduct research with focus areas that change annually but are related to Alzheimer's Disease. They must identify a mentor who is experienced in conducting Alzheimer's and related dementia research and in mentoring investigators. Eligibility is restricted to investigators who will contribute to diversity in the field of biomedical research, including members of underrepresented racial and ethnic minority groups (African Americans, Hispanic Americans, American Indians/Alaska Natives, Native Hawaiians, and Pacific Islanders) and individuals with disabilities.

Financial data Grants up to $60,000 per year, including direct expenses and up to 10% for overhead costs, are available. The total award for the life of the grant may not exceed $170,000, including $150,000 for costs related to the proposed research, $10,000 to the fellow upon successful completion of the program, and $10,000 to the mentor upon successful completion of the program.

Duration Up to 3 years.

Number awarded Up to 4 of these and parallel grants are awarded each year.

Deadline Letters of intent must be submitted by the end of December of each year. Final applications are due in February.

[1218]
MICKEY LELAND ENERGY FELLOWSHIPS

Department of Energy
Attn: Office of Fossil Energy
19901 Germantown Road, FE-6
Germantown, MD 20874
(301) 903-4293   E-mail: MLEF@hq.doe.gov
Web: fossil.energy.gov

Summary   To provide summer work experience at fossil energy sites of the Department of Energy (DOE) to African American and other underrepresented students.

Eligibility   This program is open to U.S. citizens currently enrolled full time at an accredited college or university. Applicants must be undergraduate, graduate, or postdoctoral students in mathematics, physical sciences, technology, or engineering and have a GPA of 3.0 or higher. They must be interested in a summer work experience at a DOE fossil energy research facility. Along with their application, they must submit a 100-word statement on why they want to participate in this program. A goal of the program is to recruit women and underrepresented minorities into careers related to fossil energy.

Financial data   Weekly stipends are $500 for undergraduates, $650 for master's degree students, or $750 for doctoral and postdoctoral students. Travel costs for a round trip to and from the site and for a trip to a designated place for technical presentations are also paid.

Duration   10 weeks during the summer.

Additional information   This program began as 3 separate activities: the Historically Black Colleges and Universities Internship Program, established in 1995; the Hispanic Internship Program, established in 1998; and the Tribal Colleges and Universities Internship Program, established in 2000. Those 3 programs were merged into the Fossil Energy Minority Education Initiative, renamed the Mickey Leland Energy Fellowship Program in 2000. Sites to which interns may be assigned include the Albany Research Center (Albany, Oregon), the National Energy Technology Laboratory (Morgantown, West Virginia and Pittsburgh, Pennsylvania), Pacific Northwest National Laboratory (Richland, Washington), Rocky Mountain Oilfield Testing Center (Casper, Wyoming), Strategic Petroleum Reserve Project Management Office (New Orleans, Louisiana), or U.S. Department of Energy Headquarters (Washington, D.C.).

Number awarded   Varies each year; recently, 30 students participated in this program.

Deadline   January of each year.

[1219]
MILDRED BARRY GARVIN PRIZE

New Jersey Historical Commission
Attn: Grants and Prizes
225 West State Street
P.O. Box 305
Trenton, NJ 08625-0305
(609) 292-6062   Fax: (609) 633-8168
E-mail: Feedback@sos.state.nj.us
Web: www.state.nj.us/state/historical/dos_his_grants.html

Summary   To recognize and reward New Jersey educators for outstanding teaching of Black American history.

Eligibility   This program is open to teachers, guidance counselors, and school librarians in New Jersey. Nominees must have demonstrated outstanding teaching of Black American history in kindergarten through high school or outstanding performance in a related activity, such as developing curriculum materials. Self-nominations are accepted.

Financial data   The award is $1,500.

Duration   The award is presented annually.

Number awarded   1 each year.

Deadline   October of each year.

[1220]
MINORITY ENTREPRENEURS SCHOLARSHIP PROGRAM

International Franchise Association
Attn: IFA Educational Foundation
1501 K Street, N.W., Suite 350
Washington, DC 20005
(202) 662-0784   Fax: (202) 628-0812
E-mail: mbrewer@franchise.org
Web: www.franchise.org/Scholarships.aspx

Summary   To provide financial assistance to African Americans, other minority students, and adult entrepreneurs enrolled in academic or professional development programs related to franchising.

Eligibility   This program is open to 1) college students enrolled at an accredited college or university, and 2) adult entrepreneurs who have at least 5 years of business ownership or managerial experience. Applicants must be U.S. citizens and members of a minority group (defined as African Americans, American Indians, Hispanic Americans, and Asian Americans). Students should be enrolled in courses or programs relating to business, finance, marketing, hospitality, franchising, or entrepreneurship. Adult entrepreneurs should be enrolled in professional development courses related to franchising, such as those recognized by the Institute of Certified Franchise Executives (ICFE). All applicants must submit a 500-word essay on why they want the scholarship and their career goals. Financial need is not considered in the selection process.

Financial data   The stipend is $3,000.

Duration   1 year.

Additional information   This program is cosponsored by the IFA Educational Foundation and Marriott International.

Number awarded   5 each year.

Deadline   June of each year.

[1221]
MINORITY FACULTY DEVELOPMENT SCHOLARSHIP AWARD IN PHYSICAL THERAPY

American Physical Therapy Association
Attn: Honors and Awards Program
1111 North Fairfax Street
Alexandria, VA 22314-1488
(703) 684-APTA   Toll Free: (800) 999-APTA
Fax: (703) 684-7343   TDD: (703) 683-6748
E-mail: executivedept@apta.org
Web: www.apta.org

Summary   To provide financial assistance to African American and other minority faculty members in physical therapy who are interested in working on a doctoral degree.

Eligibility   This program is open to U.S. citizens and permanent residents who are members of the following minority groups: African American or Black, Asian, Native Hawaiian or other Pacific Islander, American Indian or Alaska Native, or Hispanic/Latino. Applicants must be full-time faculty members, teaching in an accredited or developing professional physical therapist education program, who will have completed the equivalent of 2 full semesters of post-professional doctoral course work. They must possess a license to practice physical therapy in a U.S. jurisdiction and be enrolled as a student in an accredited post-professional doctoral program whose content has a demonstrated relationship to physical therapy. Along with their application, they must submit a personal essay on their professional goals, including their plans to contribute to the profession and minority services. Selection is based on 1) commitment to minority affairs and services; 2) commitment to further the physical therapy profession through teaching and research; and 3) scholastic achievement.

Financial data A stipend is awarded (amount not specified).

Duration 1 year.

Additional information This program was established in 1999.

Number awarded 1 or more each year.

Deadline November of each year.

[1222]
MOREHOUSE PHYSICS PRIZE

National Society of Black Physicists
1100 North Glebe Road, Suite 1010
Arlington, VA 22201
(703) 536-4207   Fax: (703) 536-4203
E-mail: headquarters@nsbp.org
Web: www.nsbp.org/morehouse_prize

Summary To recognize and reward graduates of Historically Black Colleges and Universities (HBCUs) who demonstrate promise as a physics researcher.

Eligibility This award is available to anyone who has 1) received an earned degree from an HBCU, 2) earned a doctorate in physics, and 3) demonstrated promise as a physics researcher. Applicants must submit a full curriculum vitae, representative publications, a research plan, a teaching plan, and 3 letters of reference.

Financial data The awardee receives a cash award and a travel stipend to give a colloquium at Morehouse College.

Duration The prize is awarded annually.

Additional information This prize was first awarded in 2007.

Number awarded 1 each year.

Deadline November of each year.

[1223]
NASA ASTROBIOLOGY PROGRAM MINORITY INSTITUTION RESEARCH SUPPORT

United Negro College Fund Special Programs
  Corporation
Attn: NASA Astrobiology Program
6402 Arlington Boulevard, Suite 600
Falls Church, VA 22042
(703) 205-7641   Toll Free: (800) 530-6232
Fax: (703) 205-7645   E-mail: portal@uncfsp.org
Web: www.uncfsp.org

Summary To provide an opportunity for faculty at Historically Black Colleges and Universities (HBCUs) and other Minority Serving Institutions (MSIs) to work on a summer research project in partnership with an established astrobiology investigator.

Eligibility This program is open to full-time tenured or tenure-track faculty members at MSIs who have a Ph.D., Sc.D., or equivalent degree in a field of STEM (science, technology, engineering, or mathematics). Applicants must be interested in conducting a summer research project on a topic related to astrobiology. They must identify an established investigator of the National Aeronautics and Space Administration (NASA) Astrobiology Program who has agreed to serve as host researcher. Eligible fields of study include biology, microbiology, astronomy, planetary science, astrochemistry, astrophysics, geology, geochemistry, or geobiochemistry. U.S. citizenship or permanent resident status is required.

Financial data Fellows receive a stipend of $10,000 and an additional grant of $5,000 to cover travel, lodging, and living expenses.

Duration 10 weeks during the summer.

Additional information This program is funded by NASA and administered by the United Negro College Fund Special Programs Corporation.

Number awarded Varies each year.

Deadline March of each year.

[1224]
NATIONAL ASSOCIATION OF BLACK ACCOUNTANTS MICROSOFT INNOVATION AWARD

National Association of Black Accountants
Attn: National Scholarship Program
7474 Greenway Center Drive, Suite 1120
Greenbelt, MD 20770
(301) 474-NABA, ext. 114   Fax: (301) 474-3114
E-mail: customerservice@nabainc.org
Web: www.nabainc.org

Summary To recognize and reward members of the National Association of Black Accountants (NABA) who submit outstanding essays on topics related to innovation in business.

Eligibility This competition is open to undergraduate student and professional members of NABA who are 18 years of age or older and U.S. citizens or equivalent. Applicants must submit a paper following an online template that addresses their choice from among 3 categories. Recently, those were 1) the recession challenge, on how they would, as CFO of Microsoft, respond to the financial challenges arising from the recession; 2) the green challenge, on how they would, as CFO of Microsoft, propose decreasing the firm's carbon footprint; or 3) the business challenger, in which they assess a change that would enable Microsoft to achieve majority market share. Based on those papers, 2 students and 2 professionals are invited to the NABA national convention, where they make an oral presentation of their ideas. The winner and runner-up are selected at the convention on the basis of quality, clarity, and overall creativity of recommendations; innovative incorporation of technology into the solution; feasibility of the recommendations; and presentation style and persuasiveness.

Financial data The award is $10,000 for each winner and $2,500 for each runner-up.

Duration The competition is held annually.

Additional information This competition, first held in 2009, is sponsored by Microsoft.

Number awarded 2 winners (1 student and 1 professional) and 2 runners-up (1 student and 1 professional) are selected each year.

Deadline May of each year.

[1225]
NATIONAL CANCER INSTITUTE MENTORED CLINICAL SCIENTIST RESEARCH CAREER DEVELOPMENT AWARD TO PROMOTE DIVERSITY

National Cancer Institute
Attn: Center to Reduce Cancer Health Disparities
6116 Executive Boulevard, Suite 602
Bethesda, MD 20852-8341
(301) 496-7344						Fax: (301) 435-9225
TDD: (301) 451-0088			E-mail: ojeifojo@mail.nih.gov
Web: www.cancer.gov/researchandfunding

Summary To provide funding to African Americans and members of other underrepresented groups who are interested in a program of training in cancer research under the supervision of an experienced mentor.

Eligibility This program is open to U.S. citizens, nationals, and permanent residents who have a clinical doctoral degree; individuals with a Ph.D. or other doctoral degree in clinical disciplines (such as clinical psychology, nursing, clinical genetics, speech-language pathology, audiology, or rehabilitation) are also eligible. Candidates must be nominated by an eligible institution (e.g., a domestic, nonprofit or for-profit public or private institution, such as a university, college, hospital, or laboratory; a unit of state or local government; or an eligible agency of the federal government) on the basis of their intent to conduct a research project highly relevant to cancer biology, cancer health disparities, etiology, pathogenesis, prevention, diagnosis, and treatment that has the potential for establishing an independent research program. They must qualify as 1) members of an ethnic or racial group shown to be underrepresented in health-related sciences on a national basis; 2) individuals with a disability; or 3) individuals from a disadvantaged background, including those from a low-income family and those from a social, cultural, and/or educational environment that has inhibited them from preparation for a research career. The mentor must be a senior or mid-level faculty member with research competence and an appreciation of the cultural, socioeconomic, and research background of the individual candidate. Selection is based on the applicant's qualifications, interests, accomplishments, motivation, and potential for a career in laboratory or field-based cancer research.

Financial data The award provides salary up to $100,000 per year plus related fringe benefits. In addition, up to $30,000 per year is provided for research development support. Facilities and administrative costs are reimbursed at 8% of modified total direct costs.

Duration Up to 5 years.

Additional information This program was originally established in 2002 as the successor of a program designated the Minorities in Clinical Oncology Program Grants.

Recipients must devote at least 75% of their full-time professional effort to cancer-related research and training activities.

Number awarded Varies each year, depending on the availability of funds.

Deadline February, June, or October of each year.

[1226]
NATIONAL CANCER INSTITUTE TRANSITION CAREER DEVELOPMENT AWARD TO PROMOTE DIVERSITY

National Cancer Institute
Attn: Center to Reduce Cancer Health Disparities
6116 Executive Boulevard, Suite 602
Bethesda, MD 20852-8341
(301) 496-8589						Fax: (301) 435-9225
TDD: (301) 451-0088			E-mail: walia@mail.nih.gov
Web: www.cancer.gov/researchandfunding

Summary To provide funding to African American and other underrepresented scientists who are establishing an independent research and academic career in cancer research.

Eligibility This program is open to U.S. citizens, nationals, and permanent residents who have earned a terminal clinical or research doctorate and intend to conduct a research project highly relevant to cancer biology, cancer health disparities, etiology, pathogenesis, prevention, diagnosis, and treatment that has the potential for establishing an independent research program. Candidates must be sponsored by a domestic nonprofit or for-profit organization, public or private (such as a university, college, hospital, laboratory, unit of state or local government, or eligible agency of the federal government), that can demonstrate a commitment to the promotion of diversity in their student and faculty populations. They must qualify as a member of a group underrepresented in biomedical research, defined as members of a particular ethnic, racial, or other group determined by their institution to be underrepresented in biomedical, behavioral, clinical, or social sciences, e.g., first-generation college students or graduates, socio-economically disadvantaged persons, or persons with disabilities.

Financial data The award provides salary up to $100,000 per year plus related fringe benefits. In addition, up to $50,000 per year is provided for research support costs. Facilities and administrative costs are reimbursed at 8% of modified total direct costs.

Duration Up to 3 years.

Additional information Recipients must devote at least 75% of their full-time professional effort to cancer-related research and peer review activities. The remaining 25% can be divided among other activities only if they are consistent with the program goals, i.e., the candidate's development into an independent investigator.

Number awarded Approximately 10 each year.

Deadline February, June, or October of each year.

[1227]
NATIONAL HEART, LUNG, AND BLOOD INSTITUTE MENTORED CAREER AWARD FOR FACULTY AT MINORITY SERVING INSTITUTIONS

National Heart, Lung, and Blood Institute
Attn: Division of Blood Diseases and Resources
6701 Rockledge Drive, Room 10135
Bethesda, MD 20892-7950
(301) 435-0052   Fax: (301) 480-1060
TDD: (301) 451-0088   E-mail: mondorot@nhlbi.nih.gov
Web: www.nhlbi.nih.gov/funding/inits/index.htm

Summary To provide funding to faculty investigators at Historically Black Colleges and Universities (HBCUs) and other minority serving institutions interested in receiving further research training in areas relevant to the mission of the National Heart, Lung, and Blood Institute (NHLBI) of the National Institutes of Health (NIH).

Eligibility This program is open to full-time faculty members at colleges and universities with student enrollment drawn substantially from minority ethnic groups (including African Americans/Blacks, Hispanics, American Indians, Alaska Native, and non-Asian Pacific Islanders). Candidates must have received a doctoral degree at least 2 years previously and be able to demonstrate a commitment to develop into an independent biomedical investigator in research areas related to cardiovascular, pulmonary, hematologic, and sleep disorders of interest to NHLBI. They must identify and complete arrangements with a mentor (at the same institution or at a collaborating research center) who is recognized as an accomplished investigator in the research area proposed and who will provide guidance for their development and research plans. They must also be U.S. citizens, nationals, or permanent residents.

Financial data The awardee receives salary support of up to $75,000 per year plus fringe benefits. In addition, up to $36,000 per year may be provided for research project requirements and related support (e.g., technical personnel costs, supplies, equipment, candidate travel, telephone charges, publication costs, and tuition for necessary courses). Facilities and administrative costs may be reimbursed at the rate of 8% of total direct costs.

Duration 3 to 5 years.

Additional information Awardees must commit 75% of their effort to the proposed project.

Number awarded 2 to 3 each year; a total of approximately $300,000 is available for this program annually.

Deadline Letters of intent must be submitted by July of each year; final applications are due in August.

[1228]
NAVAL RESEARCH LABORATORY BROAD AGENCY ANNOUNCEMENT

Naval Research Laboratory
Attn: Contracting Division
4555 Overlook Avenue, S.W.
Washington, DC 20375-5320
(202) 767-5227   Fax: (202) 767-0494
Web: heron.nrl.navy.mil/contracts/home.htm

Summary To provide funding to investigators (especially African Americans and other minorities) who are interested in conducting scientific research of interest to the U.S. Navy.

Eligibility This program is open to investigators qualified to perform research in designated scientific and technical areas. Topics cover a wide range of technical and scientific areas; recent programs included radar technology, information technology, optical sciences, tactical electronic warfare, materials science and component technology, chemistry, computational physics and fluid dynamics, plasma physics, electronics science and technology, biomolecular science and engineering, ocean and atmospheric science and technology, acoustics, remote sensing, oceanography, marine geosciences, marine meteorology, and space science. Proposals may be submitted by any non-governmental entity, including commercial firms, institutions of higher education with degree-granting programs in science or engineering, or by consortia led by such concerns. The Naval Research Laboratory (NRL) encourages participation by small businesses, small disadvantaged business concerns, women-owned small businesses, veteran-owned small businesses, service-disabled veteran-owned small businesses, HUBZone small businesses, Historically Black Colleges and Universities, and Minority Institutions. Selection is based on the degree to which new and creative solutions to technical issues important to NRL programs are proposed and the feasibility of the proposed approach and technical objectives; the offeror's ability to implement the proposed approach; the degree to which technical data and/or computer software developed under the proposed contract are to be delivered to the NRL with rights compatible with NRL research and development objectives; and proposed cost and cost realism.

Financial data The typical range of funding is from $100,000 to $2,000,000.

Duration 1 year.

Additional information The Naval Research Laboratory conducts most of its research in its own facilities in Washington, D.C., Stennis Space Center, Mississippi, and Monterey, California, but it also funds some related research.

Number awarded Varies each year.

Deadline Each program establishes its own application deadline; for a complete list of all the programs, including their deadlines, contact the NRL.

[1229]
NCI MENTORED PATIENT-ORIENTED RESEARCH CAREER DEVELOPMENT AWARD TO PROMOTE DIVERSITY

National Cancer Institute
Attn: Comprehensive Minority Biomedical Branch
6116 Executive Boulevard, Suite 7031
Bethesda, MD 20892-8350
(301) 496-7344   Fax: (301) 402-4551
TDD: (301) 451-0088   E-mail: lockeb@mail.nih.gov
Web: www.cancer.gov/researchandfunding

Summary To provide funding to African Americans and members of other underrepresented groups who are interested in a program of research training in patient-oriented oncology under the supervision of an experienced mentor.

Eligibility This program is open to U.S. citizens, nationals, and permanent residents who have a health professional doctoral degree or a doctoral degree in nursing research or practice; individuals with a Ph.D. degree in clinical disciplines (such as clinical psychology, clinical genetics, social work, speech-language pathology, audiology, or rehabilitation) are also eligible. Candidates must be nominated by a domestic nonprofit or for-profit organization, public or private (such as a university, college, hospital, laboratory, unit of state or local government, or eligible agency of the federal government), that can demonstrate a commitment to diversification of their student and faculty populations. Institutions must certify that the candidate qualifies as 1) a member of an ethnic or racial group shown to be underrepresented in health-related sciences on a national basis; 2) an individual with a disability; or 3) an individual from a disadvantaged background, including those from a low-income family and those from a social, cultural, and/or educational environment that have inhibited them from preparation for a research career. At least 2 mentors are required: 1 who is recognized as an accomplished clinical investigator and at least 1 additional mentor or adviser who is recognized as an accomplished independent basic science investigator in the proposed research area.

Financial data The award provides salary up to $100,000 per year plus related fringe benefits. In addition, up to $30,000 per year is provided for research development support. Facilities and administrative costs are reimbursed at 8% of modified total direct costs.

Duration Up to 5 years.

Additional information Recipients must devote at least 75% of their full-time professional effort to cancer-related research and training activities.

Number awarded Varies each year.

Deadline February, June, or October of each year.

[1230]
NCI MENTORED RESEARCH SCIENTIST DEVELOPMENT AWARD TO PROMOTE DIVERSITY

National Cancer Institute
Attn: Center to Reduce Cancer Health Disparities
6116 Executive Boulevard, Suite 602
Bethesda, MD 20852-8341
(301) 496-7344   Fax: (301) 435-9225
TDD: (301) 451-0088   E-mail: ojeifojo@mail.nih.gov
Web: www.cancer.gov/researchandfunding

Summary To provide funding to African Americans and members of other underrepresented groups who need a period of "protected time" for intensive cancer research career development under the guidance of an experienced mentor.

Eligibility This program is open to U.S. citizens, nationals, and permanent residents who have a research or health professional doctorate and have completed a mentored research training experience. Candidates must be proposing to conduct a research project to prepare for an independent research career related to cancer biology, cancer health disparities, etiology, pathogenesis, prevention, diagnosis, and/or treatment. They must be nominated by a domestic nonprofit or for-profit organization, public or private (such as a university, college, hospital, or laboratory), that can demonstrate a commitment to the promotion of diversity of their student and faculty populations. Institutions must certify that the candidate qualifies as 1) a member of an ethnic or racial group shown to be underrepresented in health-related sciences on a national basis; 2) an individual with a disability; or 3) an individual from a disadvantaged background, including those from a low-income family and those from a social, cultural,

and/or educational environment that have inhibited them from preparation for a research career. The mentor must have extensive research experience and an appreciation of the cultural, socioeconomic, and research background of the candidate.

Financial data The award provides salary up to $100,000 per year plus related fringe benefits. In addition, up to $30,000 per year is provided for research development support. Facilities and administrative costs are reimbursed at 8% of modified total direct costs.

Duration 3, 4, or 5 years.

Additional information Recipients must devote at least 75% of their full-time professional effort to cancer-related research and training activities.

Number awarded Varies each year.

Deadline February, June, or October of each year.

[1231]
NELSON URBAN SCHOLARSHIP FUND

James B. Morris Scholarship Fund
Attn: Scholarship Selection Committee
525 S.W. Fifth Street, Suite A
Des Moines, IA 50309-4501
(515) 282-8192   Fax: (515) 282-9117
E-mail: morris@assoc-mgmt.com
Web: www.morrisscholarship.org

Summary To provide financial assistance to African American teachers and graduate students from Iowa interested in preparing to work with "at risk" students.

Eligibility This program is open to African American teachers and graduate students who are Iowa residents and interested in working with "at risk" minority students in the elementary or secondary schools. Applicants must be enrolled full or part time at a graduate school in any state. Along with their application, they must submit a 250-word essay describing the "at risk" students emphasized in their course of study and how they plan to use their training. U.S. citizenship is required.

Financial data The awards generally range from $2,500 to $5,000.

Duration 1 year.

Number awarded At least 2 each year.

Deadline March of each year.

[1232]
NEW INVESTIGATOR RESEARCH GRANTS TO PROMOTE DIVERSITY OF THE ALZHEIMER'S ASSOCIATION

Alzheimer's Association
Attn: Medical and Scientific Affairs
225 North Michigan Avenue, 17th Floor
Chicago, IL 60601-7633
(312) 335-5747   Toll Free: (800) 272-3900
Fax: (866) 699-1246   TDD: (312) 335-5886
E-mail: grantsapp@alz.org
Web: www.alz.org

Summary To provide funding for research on Alzheimer's Disease to African Americans and other junior investigators who will contribute to diversity in the field.

Eligibility This program is open to investigators who have less than 10 years of research experience after receipt of their terminal degree. Applicants must be proposing to conduct research with focus areas that change annually but are related to Alzheimer's Disease. Eligibility is restricted to investigators who will contribute to diversity in the field of biomedical research, including members of underrepresented racial and ethnic minority groups (African Americans, Hispanic Americans, American Indians/Alaska Natives, Native Hawaiians, and Pacific Islanders) and individuals with disabilities.

Financial data Grants up to $60,000 per year, including direct expenses and up to 10% for overhead costs, are available. The total award for the life of the grant may not exceed $100,000.

Duration Up to 2 years.

Number awarded Up to 4 of these and parallel grants are awarded each year.

Deadline Letters of intent must be submitted by the end of December of each year. Final applications are due in February.

[1233]
NEW YORK PUBLIC LIBRARY FELLOWSHIPS

American Council of Learned Societies
Attn: Office of Fellowships and Grants
633 Third Avenue
New York, NY 10017-6795
(212) 697-1505   Fax: (212) 949-8058
E-mail: fellowships@acls.org
Web: www.acls.org/programs/acls

Summary To provide funding to postdoctorates (particularly African Americans, other minorities, and women) who are interested in conducting research at the Dorothy and Lewis B. Cullman Center for Scholars and Writers of the New York Public Library.

Eligibility This program is open to scholars at all stages of their careers who received a Ph.D. degree at least 2 years previously. Established scholars who can demonstrate the equivalent of the Ph.D. in publications and professional experience may also qualify. Applicants must be U.S. citizens or permanent residents who have not had supported leave time for at least 2 years prior to the start of the proposed research. Appropriate fields of specialization include, but are not limited to, American studies; anthropology; archaeology; art and architectural history; classics; economics; film; geography; history; languages and literatures; legal studies; linguistics; musicology; philosophy; political science; psychology; religious studies; rhetoric, communication, and media studies; sociology; and theater, dance, and performance studies. Proposals in the fields social science fields are eligible only if they employ predominantly humanistic approaches (e.g., economic history, law and literature, political philosophy). Proposals in interdisciplinary and cross-disciplinary studies are welcome, as are proposals focused on any geographic region or on any cultural or linguistic group. Applicants must be interested in conducting research at the New York Public Library's Dorothy and Lewis B. Cullman Center for Scholars and Writers. Women and members of minority groups are particularly invited to apply.

Financial data The stipend is $60,000.

Duration 9 months, beginning in September.

Additional information This program was first offered for 1999-2000, the inaugural year of the center. Candidates must also submit a separate application that is available from the New York Public Library, Humanities and Social Sciences Library, Dorothy and Lewis B. Cullman Center for Scholars and Writers, Fifth Avenue and 42nd Street, New York, NY 10018-2788, E-mail: csw@nypl.org. Fellows are required to be in continuous residence at the center and participate actively in its activities and programs.

Number awarded Up to 5 each year.

Deadline September of each year.

[1234]
NHLBI MENTORED CAREER DEVELOPMENT AWARD TO PROMOTE FACULTY DIVERSITY/RE-ENTRY IN BIOMEDICAL RESEARCH

National Heart, Lung, and Blood Institute
Attn: Division of Cardiovascular Sciences
6701 Rockledge Drive
Bethesda, MD 20892-7936
(301) 435-0709   Fax: (301) 480-1455
E-mail: silsbeeL@nhlbi.nih.gov
Web: www.nhlbi.nih.gov/funding/inits/index.htm

Summary To provide funding to African Americans and members of other underrepresented groups interested in developing into independent biomedical investigators in research areas relevant to the mission of the National Heart, Lung, and Blood Institute (NHLBI).

Eligibility This program is open to U.S. citizens, nationals, and permanent residents who are full-time non-tenured faculty members at U.S. domestic institutions of higher education and eligible agencies of the federal government; applications are especially encouraged from faculty at Historically Black Colleges and Universities (HBCUs), Tribally Controlled Colleges and Universities (TCCUs), Hispanic-Serving Institutions (HSIs), and Alaska Native and Native Hawaiian Serving Institutions. Candidates must have received, at least 2 years previously, a doctoral degree or equivalent in a basic or clinical area related to cardiovascular, pulmonary, or hematologic diseases. Applications are especially encouraged from members of a group that will promote greater diversity in scientific research, including 1) members of underrepresented racial and ethnic groups (African Americans, Hispanic Americans, Alaska Natives, American Indians, Native Hawaiians, non-Asian Pacific Islanders); 2) individuals with disabilities; and 3) individuals from disadvantaged backgrounds. Candidates who have experienced an interruption in their research careers for a period of at least 3 but no more than 8 years (e.g., starting and/or raising a family, an incapacitating illness or injury, caring for an ill immediate family member, performing military service) are also eligible. The proposed research development plan must enable the candidate to become an independent investigator in cardiovascular, pulmonary, hematologic, and sleep disorders research with either a clinical or basic science emphasis.

Financial data The grant provides salary support of up to $75,000 per year plus fringe benefits. In addition, up to $30,000 per year may be provided for research project requirements and related support (e.g., technical personnel costs, supplies, equipment, candidate travel, telephone charges, publication costs, and tuition for necessary courses). Facilities and administrative costs may be reimbursed at the rate of 8% of total direct costs.

Duration 3 to 5 years.

Additional information   At least 75% of the awardee's effort must be devoted to the research program. The remainder may be devoted to other clinical and teaching pursuits that are consistent with the program goals of developing the awardee into an independent biomedical scientist or the maintenance of the teaching and/or clinical skills needed for an academic research career.

Number awarded   Varies each year; recently, 8 to 10 awards were available through this program.

Deadline   Letters of intent must be submitted by August of each year; completed applications are due in September.

[1235]
NHLBI SHORT-TERM RESEARCH EDUCATION PROGRAM TO INCREASE DIVERSITY IN HEALTH-RELATED RESEARCH

National Heart, Lung, and Blood Institute
Attn: Division of Cardiovascular Diseases
6701 Rockledge Drive
Bethesda, MD 20892-7940
(301) 435-0535   Fax: (301) 480-1454
TDD: (301) 451-0088   E-mail: Commaram@nhlbi.nih.gov
Web: www.nhlbi.nih.gov/funding/inits/index.htm

Summary   To provide funding to African Americans and members of other underrepresented groups interested in conducting a research education program relevant to the mission of the National Heart, Lung, and Blood Institute (NHLBI).

Eligibility   This program is open to principal investigators at U.S. domestic institutions (universities, colleges, hospitals, laboratories, units of state and local governments, and eligible agencies of the federal government) who are interested in conducting a research education program related to activities of NHLBI. Applications are especially encouraged from principal investigators who qualify as underrepresented: 1) a member of an ethnic or racial group shown to be underrepresented in health-related sciences on a national basis; 2) an individual with a disability; or 3) an individual from a disadvantaged background, including those from a low-income family and those from a social, cultural, and/or educational environment that has inhibited them from preparation for a research career. The proposed education program must encourage the participation of undergraduate and health professional students who are also currently underrepresented in the biomedical, clinical, and behavioral sciences. Students participating in the program are not required to be enrolled at the sponsoring institution.

Financial data   Grants depend on the nature of the project and the number of student participants. Maximum total direct costs should not exceed $311,088. Compensation to participating students must conform to the established salary and wage policies of the institution. Facilities and administrative costs may be reimbursed at the rate of 8% of total direct costs.

Duration   Up to 5 years.

Number awarded   Up to 8 each year; a total of $900,000 is available for this program annually.

Deadline   Letters of intent must be submitted by August of each year; final applications are due in September.

[1236]
NICKELODEON WRITING FELLOWSHIP PROGRAM

Nickelodeon Animation Studios
Attn: Nick Writing Fellowship
231 West Olive Avenue
Burbank, CA 91502
(818) 736-3663   E-mail: info.writing@nick.com
Web: www.nickwriting.com

Summary   To provide an opportunity for young writers and animators (especially African Americans and other minorities) to gain experience working at Nickelodeon Animation Studio in Burbank, California.

Eligibility   This program is open to writers, whether experienced or not, who are at least 18 years of age. Applicants must submit a spec script, 1-page resume, and half-page biography. The spec script may be either live action (half hour television script based on a current television series) or animation (11- or 30-minute script based on a current animated television series). Scripts should focus on comedy. The program encourages applications from culturally and ethnically diverse writing talent.

Financial data   This is a salaried position.

Duration   Up to 1 year, divided into 3 phases: a 6-week audition phase in which the fellows write 1 spec script and their talent and progress are evaluated to determine if they are qualified to remain in the program; a 10-week development phase in which they write 1 spec script and are integrated into the activities of the production and development department; and a 34-week placement phase in which they write another spec script and pitch 1 original idea.

Number awarded   Up to 4 each year.

Deadline   February of each year.

[1237]
NIDDK SMALL GRANTS FOR CLINICAL SCIENTISTS TO PROMOTE DIVERSITY IN HEALTH-RELATED RESEARCH

National Institute of Diabetes and Digestive and Kidney Diseases
Attn: Office of Minority Health Research Coordination
6707 Democracy Boulevard, Room 653
Bethesda, MD 20892-5454
(301) 594-1932   Fax: (301) 594-9358
TDD: (301) 451-0088   E-mail: la21i@nih.gov
Web: www2.niddk.nih.gov/Funding

Summary   To provide funding to African American and other underrepresented physicians who are interested in conducting a research project in fields of interest to the National Institute of Diabetes and Digestive and Kidney Diseases (NIDDK) of the National Institutes of Health.

Eligibility   This program is open to investigators who 1) have a health professional doctoral degree (e.g., M.D., D.D.S., D.O., D.V.M., O.D., Psy.D., Dr.P.H.); 2) have at least 2 to 4 years of postdoctoral research experience; 3) qualify as new investigators; and 4) belong to a population group nationally underrepresented in biomedical or behavioral research, including members of designated racial and ethnic groups (e.g., African Americans, Hispanics, Native Americans, Alaska Natives, Hawaiian Natives, and non-Asian Pacific Islanders), individual with disabilities, or individuals from a disadvantaged background (defined to include those who come from a low-income family and those who come from a social, cultural, and/or educational environment that has inhibited them from obtaining the knowledge, skills, and abilities necessary to develop and participate in a research career). Applicants must be interested in conducting a research project in the area of diabetes, endocrinology, metabolism, digestive diseases, hepatology, obesity, nutrition, kidney, urology, or hematology. They must be sponsored by a domestic for-profit or nonprofit public or private institution, such as a university, college, hospital, or laboratory.

Financial data Direct costs are limited to $125,000 per year. Facilities and administrative costs are reimbursed at 8% of modified total direct costs.

Duration 3 years; nonrenewable.

Additional information This program is also supported by the Office of Dietary Supplements within NIH.

Number awarded Varies each year.

Deadline February, June, or October of each year.

[1238]
NINR MENTORED RESEARCH SCIENTIST DEVELOPMENT AWARD FOR UNDERREPRESENTED OR DISADVANTAGED INVESTIGATORS

National Institute of Nursing Research
Attn: Office of Extramural Programs
6701 Democracy Boulevard, Suite 710
Bethesda, MD 20892-4870
(301) 496-9558   Fax: (301) 480-8260
TDD: (301) 451-0088   E-mail: banksd@mail.nih.gov
Web: www.ninr.nih.gov

Summary To provide funding for research career development to postdoctoral nursing investigators who are African Americans or members of other underrepresented or disadvantaged groups.

Eligibility This program is open to nurses who have a research or health-professional doctoral degree and are employed full time at an institution that conducts research. Applicants must qualify as an individual whose participation in scientific research will increase diversity, including 1) individuals from racial and ethnic groups that have been shown to be underrepresented in health-related science on a national basis; 2) individuals with disabilities; and 3) individuals from disadvantaged backgrounds, including those from a family with an annual income below established levels and those from a social, cultural, or educational environment that has demonstrably and recently directly inhibited the individual from obtaining the knowledge, skills, and abilities necessary to develop and participate in a research career. They must secured the commitment of an appropriate research mentor actively involved in research relevant to the mission of the National Institute of Nursing Research (NINR). Only U.S. citizens, nationals, and permanent residents are eligible.

Financial data The grant provides up to $50,000 per year for salary and fringe benefits plus an additional $20,000 per year for research development support. Facilities and administrative costs are allowed at 8% of total direct costs.

Duration Up to 3 years.

Additional information These grants have been awarded annually since 1998. Grantees are expected to spend at least

75% of their professional time to the program and the other 25% to other research-related and/or teaching or clinical pursuits consistent with the objectives of the award.

Number awarded 3 to 4 new grants are awarded each year.

Deadline February, June, or October of each year.

[1239]
NJLA DIVERSITY SCHOLARSHIP

New Jersey Library Association
4 Lafayette Street
P.O. Box 1534
Trenton, NJ 08607
(609) 394-8032   Fax: (609) 394-8164
E-mail: ptumulty@njla.org
Web: www.njla.org/honorsawards/scholarship

Summary To provide financial assistance to African Americans or other New Jersey minorities who are interested in working on a graduate or postgraduate degree in public librarianship at a school in any state.

Eligibility This program is open to residents of New Jersey and individuals who have worked in a New Jersey library for at least 12 months. Applicants must be members of a minority group (African American, Asian/Pacific Islander, Latino/Hispanic, or Native American/Native Alaskan). They must be enrolled or planning to enroll at an ALA-accredited school of library science in any state to work on a graduate or postgraduate degree in librarianship. Along with their application, they must submit an essay of 150 to 250 words explaining their choice of librarianship as a profession. An interview is required. Selection is based on academic ability and financial need.

Financial data The stipend is $1,300.

Duration 1 year.

Number awarded 1 each year.

Deadline February of each year.

[1240]
NON-PHARMACOLOGICAL STRATEGIES TO AMELIORATE SYMPTOMS OF ALZHEIMER'S DISEASE

Alzheimer's Association
Attn: Medical and Scientific Affairs
225 North Michigan Avenue, 17th Floor
Chicago, IL 60601-7633
(312) 335-5747   Toll Free: (800) 272-3900
Fax: (866) 699-1246   TDD: (312) 335-5886
E-mail: grantsapp@alz.org
Web: www.alz.org

Summary To provide funding to scientists (particularly African Americans and other minorities) who are interested in conducting research on developing non-pharmacological strategies to improve the care of persons with Alzheimer's Disease and related disorders (ADRD).

Eligibility This program is open to postdoctoral investigators at public, private, domestic, and foreign research laboratories, medical centers, hospitals, and universities. Applicants must be proposing to conduct research aimed at the identification, validation, and investigation of non-pharmacological approaches to improve the care of older adults with ADRD. They must have full-time staff or faculty appointments. Proposed research topics may include (but are not limited to) non-pharmacological intervention studies that incorporate state-of-the-science methodologies to investigate outcomes; research on improving methodologies to be employed in non-pharmacological trials; evaluation of new non-pharmacological approaches that have a conceptual and/or empirical basis for potential to impact patient outcomes; or research that moves promising non-pharmacological interventions for treatment of ADRD into the field. Scientists from underrepresented groups are especially encouraged to apply.

Financial data Grants up to $200,000 per year, including direct expenses and up to 10% for overhead costs, are available. The total award for the life of the grant may not exceed $400,000.

Duration Up to 2 years.

Additional information This program began in 2009.

Number awarded Up to 2 each year.

Deadline Letters of intent must be submitted by the end of December of each year. Final applications are due in February.

[1241]
NOVEL PHARMACOLOGICAL STRATEGIES TO PREVENT ALZHEIMER'S DISEASE

Alzheimer's Association
Attn: Medical and Scientific Affairs
225 North Michigan Avenue, 17th Floor
Chicago, IL 60601-7633
(312) 335-5747   Toll Free: (800) 272-3900
Fax: (866) 699-1246   TDD: (312) 335-5886
E-mail: grantsapp@alz.org
Web: www.alz.org

Summary To provide funding to scientists (particularly African American and other scientists from underrepresented groups) who are interested in conducting research on developing new pharmacological strategies to prevent or treat Alzheimer's Disease.

Eligibility This program is open to postdoctoral investigators at public, private, domestic, and foreign research laboratories, medical centers, hospitals, and universities. Applicants must be proposing to conduct research aimed at the identification and validation of novel drug targets for prevention or treatment of Alzheimer's Disease, the screening and development of drugs for such targets, and the evaluation of drug safety and efficacy. They must have full-time staff or faculty appointments. Scientists from underrepresented groups are especially encouraged to apply.

Financial data Grants up to $200,000 per year, including direct expenses and up to 10% for overhead costs, are available. The total award for the life of the grant may not exceed $400,000.

Duration Up to 2 years.

Additional information This program began in 2009.

Number awarded Up to 2 each year.

Deadline Letters of intent must be submitted by the end of December of each year. Final applications are due in February.

[1242]
NSF DIRECTOR'S AWARD FOR DISTINGUISHED TEACHING SCHOLARS

National Science Foundation
Directorate for Education and Human Resources
Attn: Division of Undergraduate Education
4201 Wilson Boulevard, Room 835N
Arlington, VA 22230
(703) 292-4627   Fax: (703) 292-9015
TDD: (800) 281-8749   E-mail: npruitt@nsf.gov
Web: www.nsf.gov/funding/pgm_summ.jsp?pims_id=8170

Summary To recognize and reward, with funding for additional research, African American and other scholars affiliated with institutions of higher education who have contributed to the teaching of science, technology, engineering, or mathematics (STEM) at the K-12 and undergraduate level.

Eligibility This program is open to teaching-scholars affiliated with institutions of higher education who are nominated by their president, chief academic officer, or other independent researcher. Nominees should have integrated research and education and approached both education and research in a scholarly manner. They should have demonstrated leadership in their respective fields as well as innovativeness and effectiveness in facilitating K-12 and undergraduate student learning in STEM disciplines. Consideration is given to faculty who have a history of substantial impact on 1) research in a STEM discipline or on STEM educational research; or 2) the STEM education of K-16 students who have diverse interests and aspirations, including future K-12 teachers of science and mathematics, students who plan to pursue STEM careers, and those who need to understand science and mathematics in a society increasingly dependent on science and technology. Based on letters of nomination, selected scholars are invited to submit applications for support of their continuing efforts to integrate education and research. Nominations of all citizens, including women and men, underrepresented minorities, and persons with disabilities are especially encouraged.

Financial data The maximum grant is $300,000 for the life of the project.

Duration 4 years.

Number awarded Approximately 6 each year.

Deadline Letters of intent are due in September of each year; full applications must be submitted in October.

[1243]
NSF STANDARD AND CONTINUING GRANTS

National Science Foundation
4201 Wilson Boulevard
Arlington, VA 22230
(703) 292-5111   TDD: (800) 281-8749
E-mail: info@nsf.gov
Web: www.nsf.gov

Summary To provide financial support to scientists, engineers, and educators (particularly African Americans and those from other underrepresented groups) for research in broad areas of science and engineering.

Eligibility The National Science Foundation (NSF) supports research through its Directorates of Biological Sciences; Computer and Information Science and Engineering; Education and Human Resources; Engineering; Geosciences; Mathematical and Physical Sciences; and Social,

Behavioral, and Economic Sciences. Within those general areas of science and engineering, NSF awards 2 types of grants: 1) standard grants, in which NSF agrees to provide a specific level of support for a specified period of time with no statement of NSF intent to provide additional future support without submission of another proposal; and 2) continuing grants, in which NSF agrees to provide a specific level of support for an initial specified period of time with a statement of intent to provide additional support of the project for additional periods, provided funds are available and the results achieved warrant further support. Although NSF often solicits proposals for support of targeted areas through issuance of specific program solicitations, it also accepts unsolicited proposals. Scientists, engineers, and educators usually act as the principal investigator and initiate proposals that are officially submitted by their employing organization. Most employing organizations are universities, colleges, and non-profit nonacademic organizations (such as museums, observatories, research laboratories, and professional societies). Certain programs are open to for-profit organizations, state and local governments, or unaffiliated individuals. Principal investigators usually must be U.S. citizens, nationals, or permanent residents. NSF particularly encourages applications from underrepresented minorities and persons with disabilities.

Financial data Funding levels vary, depending on the nature of the project and the availability of funds. Awards resulting from unsolicited research proposals are subject to statutory cost-sharing.

Duration Standard grants specify the period of time, usually up to 1 year; continuing grants normally specify 1 year as the initial period of time, with support to continue for additional periods.

Additional information Researchers interested in support from NSF should contact the address above to obtain further information on areas of support and programs operating within the respective directorates. They should consult with a program officer before submitting an application. Information on programs is available on the NSF home page. NSF does not normally support technical assistance, pilot plant efforts, research requiring security classification, the development of products for commercial marketing, or market research for a particular project or invention. Bioscience research with disease-related goals, including work on the etiology, diagnosis, or treatment of physical or mental disease, abnormality, or malfunction in human beings or animals, is normally not supported.

Number awarded Approximately 11,000 new grants are awarded each year.

Deadline Many programs accept proposals at any time. Other programs establish target dates or deadlines; those target dates and deadlines are published in the *NSF Bulletin* and in specific program announcements/solicitations.

[1244]
OFFICE OF NAVAL RESEARCH SABBATICAL LEAVE PROGRAM

American Society for Engineering Education
Attn: Projects Department
1818 N Street, N.W., Suite 600
Washington, DC 20036-2479
(202) 331-3558   Fax: (202) 265-8504
E-mail: onrsummer@asee.org
Web: onr.asee.org/about_the_sabbatical_leave_program

Summary To provide support to faculty members in engineering and science (particularly those from Historically Black Colleges and Universities or other Minority Serving Institutions) who wish to conduct research at selected Navy facilities while on sabbatical leave.

Eligibility This program is open to U.S. citizens with teaching or research appointments in engineering and science at U.S. universities or colleges. Applicants must intend to conduct research while in residence at selected facilities of the U.S. Navy. Faculty from Historically Black Colleges and Universities, Hispanic Serving Institutions, and Tribal Colleges and Universities are especially encouraged to apply.

Financial data Fellows receive a stipend equivalent to the difference between their regular salary and the sabbatical leave pay from their home institution. Fellows who must relocate their residence receive a relocation allowance and all fellows receive a travel allowance.

Duration Appointments are for a minimum of 1 semester and a maximum of 1 year.

Additional information Participating facilities include the Naval Air Warfare Center, Aircraft Division (Patuxent River, Maryland); Naval Air Warfare Center, Naval Training Systems Division (Orlando, Florida); Naval Air Warfare Center, Weapons Division (China Lake, California); Space and Naval Warfare Systems Center (San Diego, California); Naval Facilities Engineering Service Center (Port Hueneme, California); Naval Research Laboratories (Washington, D.C.; Stennis Space Center, Mississippi; and Monterey, California); Naval Surface Warfare Centers (Bethesda, Maryland; Indian Head, Maryland; Dahlgren, Virginia; and Panama City, Florida); Naval Undersea Warfare Center (Newport, Rhode Island and New London, Connecticut); Defense Equal Opportunity Management Institute (Cocoa Beach, Florida); Navy Personnel Research, Studies & Technology Department (Millington, Tennessee); Naval Aerospace Medical Research Laboratory (Pensacola, Florida); Naval Health Research Center (San Diego, California); Naval Medical Research Center (Silver Spring, Maryland); and Naval Submarine Medical Research Laboratory (Groton, Connecticut). This program is funded by the U.S. Navy's Office of Naval Research and administered by the American Society for Engineering Education.

Number awarded Varies each year.

Deadline Applications may be submitted at any time, but they must be received at least 6 months prior to the proposed sabbatical leave starting date.

[1245]
OFFICE OF NAVAL RESEARCH SUMMER FACULTY RESEARCH PROGRAM

American Society for Engineering Education
Attn: Projects Department
1818 N Street, N.W., Suite 600
Washington, DC 20036-2479
(202) 331-3558   Fax: (202) 265-8504
E-mail: a.hicks@asee.org
Web: 0nr.asee.org/about_the_summer_faculty_program

Summary   To provide support to faculty members in engineering and science (especially faculty at Historically Black Colleges and Universities or other Minority Serving Institutions) who wish to conduct summer research at selected Navy facilities.

Eligibility   This program is open to U.S. citizens and permanent residents who have teaching or research appointments in engineering and science at U.S. universities or colleges. In addition to appointments as Summer Faculty Fellows, positions as Senior Summer Faculty Fellows are available to applicants who have at least 6 years of research experience in their field of expertise since earning a Ph.D. or equivalent degree and a substantial, significant record of research accomplishments and publications. A limited number of appointments are also available as Distinguished Summer Faculty Fellows to faculty members who are preeminent in their field of research, have a senior appointment at a leading research university, and are internationally recognized for their research accomplishments. Faculty from Historically Black Colleges and Universities, Hispanic Serving Institutions, and Tribal Colleges and Universities are especially encouraged to apply.

Financial data   The weekly stipend is $1,400 at the Summer Faculty Fellow level, $1,650 at the Senior Summer Faculty Fellow level, and $1,900 at the Distinguished Summer Faculty Fellow level. Fellows who must relocate their residence receive a relocation allowance and all fellows receive a travel allowance.

Duration   10 weeks during the summer; fellows may reapply in subsequent years.

Additional information   Participating facilities include the Naval Air Warfare Center, Aircraft Division (Patuxent River, Maryland); Naval Air Warfare Center, Naval Training Systems Division (Orlando, Florida); Naval Air Warfare Center, Weapons Division (China Lake, California); Space and Naval Warfare Systems Center (San Diego, California); Naval Facilities Engineering Service Center (Port Hueneme, California); Naval Research Laboratories (Washington, D.C.; Stennis Space Center, Mississippi; and Monterey, California); Naval Surface Warfare Centers (Bethesda, Maryland; Indian Head, Maryland; Dahlgren, Virginia; and Panama City, Florida); Naval Undersea Warfare Center (Newport, Rhode Island and New London, Connecticut); Defense Equal Opportunity Management Institute (Cocoa Beach, Florida); Navy Personnel Research, Studies & Technology Department (Millington, Tennessee); Naval Aerospace Medical Research Laboratory (Pensacola, Florida); Naval Health Research Center (San Diego, California); Naval Medical Research Center (Silver Spring, Maryland); and Naval Submarine Medical Research Laboratory (Groton, Connecticut). This program is funded by the U.S. Navy's Office of Naval Research and administered by the American Society for Engineering Education.

Number awarded   Varies each year.
Deadline   December of each year.

[1246]
OFFICE OF NAVAL RESEARCH YOUNG INVESTIGATOR PROGRAM

Office of Naval Research
Attn: Code 03R
875 North Randolph Street, Suite 1409
Arlington, VA 22203-1995
(703) 696-4111   E-mail: William.lukens1@navy.mil
Web: www.onr.navy.mil/Education-Outreach.aspx

Summary   To provide funding to academic scientists and engineers (especially those at Historically Black Colleges and Universities and other Minority Serving Institutions) who are interested in conducting research on topics of interest to the U.S. Navy.

Eligibility   This program is open to U.S. citizens, nationals, and permanent residents holding tenure-track faculty positions at U.S. universities who received their graduate degrees (Ph.D. or equivalent) within the preceding 5 years. Applicants must be proposing to conduct research relevant to 1 of the divisions within the Office of Naval Research: expeditionary warfare and combating terrorism; command, control communications, computers, intelligence, surveillance, and reconnaissance; ocean battlespace sensing; sea warfare and weapons; warfighter performance; and naval air warfare and weapons. Selection is based on 1) past performance, demonstrated by the significance and impact of previous research, publications, professional activities, awards, and other recognition; 2) a creative proposal, demonstrating the potential for making progress in a listed priority research area; and 3) a long-term commitment by the university to the applicant and the research. Researchers at Historically Black Colleges and Universities (HBCUs) and Minority Institutions (MIs) are encouraged to submit proposals and join others in submitting proposals.

Financial data   Awards up to $170,000 per year are available.

Duration   3 years.

Additional information   Approximately 2 recipients of these awards are also nominated to receive Presidential Early Career Awards for Scientists and Engineers to provide an additional 2 years of funding.

Number awarded   Approximately 18 each year.

Deadline   December of each year.

[1247]
ONLINE BIBLIOGRAPHIC SERVICES/ TECHNICAL SERVICES JOINT RESEARCH GRANT

American Association of Law Libraries
Attn: Online Bibliographic Services Special Interest
    Section
105 West Adams Street, Suite 3300
Chicago, IL 60603
(312) 939-4764   Fax: (312) 431-1097
E-mail: aallhq@aall.org
Web: www.aallnet.org/sis/obssis/research/funding.htm

Summary   To provide funding to members of the American Association of Law Libraries (AALL), especially African Americans or other minorities and women, who are interested in conducting a research project related to technical services.

Eligibility This program is open to AALL members who are technical services law librarians. Preference is given to members of the Online Bibliographic Services and Technical Services Special Interest Sections, although members of other special interest sections are eligible if their work relates to technical services law librarianship. Applicants must be interested in conducting research that will enhance law librarianship. Women and minorities are especially encouraged to apply. Preference is given to projects that can be completed in the United States or Canada, although foreign research projects are given consideration.

Financial data Grants range up to $1,000.

Duration 1 year.

Number awarded 1 or more each year.

Deadline June of each year.

[1248]
ORGANIZATION OF BLACK AEROSPACE PROFESSIONALS GENERAL SCHOLARSHIP

Organization of Black Aerospace Professionals, Inc.
Attn: Scholarship Coordinator
1 Westbrook Corporate Center, Suite 300
Westchester, IL 60154
(708) 449-7755   Toll Free: (800) JET-OBAP
Fax: (708) 449-7754
E-mail: obapscholarship@gmail.com
Web: www.obap.org/scholarships

Summary To provide financial assistance to members of the Organization of Black Aerospace Professionals (OBAP) who are interested in further training to advance their career in the aviation industry.

Eligibility This program is open to OBAP members who have participated in at least 1 of its events and have at least a private pilot's license. Applicants must be interested in participating in further training that will advance their career in the aviation industry. Along with their application, they must submit an essay on their greatest life challenge and how it has enriched their and/or someone else's life, a current resume, 2 letters of recommendation, a copy of their medical permit, and a 2-page autobiography.

Financial data The stipend is $7,000.

Duration 1 year.

Additional information The OBAP was originally established in 1976 as the Organization of Black Airline Pilots to make certain Blacks and other minorities had a group that would keep them informed about opportunities for advancement within commercial aviation.

Number awarded 1 each year.

Deadline Applications must be submitted at least 30 days prior to the OBAP convention.

[1249]
PAUL HOCH DISTINGUISHED SERVICE AWARD

American College of Neuropsychopharmacology
Attn: Executive Office
5034-A Thoroughbred Lane
Brentwood, TN 37027
(615) 324-2360   Fax: (615) 523-1715
E-mail: acnp@acnp.org
Web: www.acnp.org/programs/awards.aspx

Summary To recognize and reward members of the American College of Neuropsychopharmacology (ACNP), especially African Americans or other minorities and women, who have contributed outstanding service to the organization.

Eligibility This award is available to ACNP members who have made unusually significant contributions to the College. The emphasis of the award is on service to the organization, not on teaching, clinical, or research accomplishments. Any member or fellow of ACNP may nominate another member. Nomination of women and minorities is highly encouraged.

Financial data The award consists of an expense-paid trip to the ACNP annual meeting, a monetary honorarium, and a plaque.

Duration The award is presented annually.

Additional information This award was first presented in 1965.

Number awarded 1 each year.

Deadline Nominations must be submitted by June of each year.

[1250]
PAUL TOBENKIN MEMORIAL AWARD

Columbia University
Attn: Graduate School of Journalism
Mail Code 3809
2950 Broadway
New York, NY 10027-7004
(212) 854-5377   Fax: (212) 854-7837
E-mail: am494@columbia.edu
Web: www.journalism.columbia.edu

Summary To recognize and reward outstanding newspaper writing that reflects the spirit of Paul Tobenkin, who fought all his life against racial and religious hatred, bigotry, bias, intolerance, and discrimination.

Eligibility Materials reflecting the spirit of Paul Tobenkin may be submitted by newspaper reporters in the United States, editors of their publications, or interested third parties. The items submitted must have been published during the previous calendar year in a weekly or daily newspaper.

Financial data The award is $1,000 plus a plaque.

Duration The award is presented annually.

Additional information This award was first presented in 1961,.

Number awarded 1 each year.

Deadline February of each year.

[1251]
PAULA DE MERIEUX RHEUMATOLOGY FELLOWSHIP AWARD

American College of Rheumatology
Attn: Research and Education Foundation
2200 Lake Boulevard N.E.
Atlanta, GA 30319
(404) 633-3777   Fax: (404) 633-1870
E-mail: ref@rheumatology.org
Web: www.rheumatology.org/ref/awards/index.asp

Summary   To provide funding to African Americans, other underrepresented minorities, and women who are interested in a program of training for a career providing clinical care to people affected by rheumatic diseases.

Eligibility   This program is open to trainees at ACGME-accredited institutions. Applications must be submitted by the training program director at the institution who is responsible for selection and appointment of trainees. The program must train and prepare fellows to provide clinical care to those affected by rheumatic diseases. Trainees must be women or members of underrepresented minority groups, defined as Black Americans, Hispanics, and Native Americans (Native Hawaiians, Alaska Natives, and American Indians). They must be U.S. citizens, nationals, or permanent residents. Selection is based on the institution's pass rate of rheumatology fellows, publication history of staff and previous fellows, current positions of previous fellows, and status of clinical faculty.

Financial data   The grant is $25,000 per year, to be used as salary for the trainee. Other trainee costs (e.g., fees, health insurance, travel, attendance at scientific meetings) are to be incurred by the recipient's institutional program. Supplemental or additional support to offset the cost of living may be provided by the grantee institution.

Duration   Up to 1 year.

Additional information   This fellowship was first awarded in 2005.

Number awarded   1 each year.

Deadline   July of each year.

[1252]
PEGGY VATTER MEMORIAL SCHOLARSHIPS

Washington Science Teachers Association
c/o Patricia MacGowan, Washington MESA
University of Washington
P.O. Box 352181
Seattle, WA 98195-2181
(206) 543-0562   Fax: (206) 685-0666
E-mail: macgowan@engr.washington.edu
Web: www.wsta.net

Summary   To provide financial assistance to upper-division students and teachers in Washington (especially African Americans, other underrepresented minorities, and women)interested in training in science education.

Eligibility   This program is open to 1) juniors and seniors at colleges and universities in Washington who are working on certification in science education or in elementary education with an emphasis on science; and 2) certified teachers in Washington interested in improving their skills in providing equitable science education through professional development. In the student category, preference is given to African

Americans, Hispanics, Native Americans, and women. Applicants must submit a 1-page essay on why they are applying for this scholarship.

Financial data   The stipend is $1,500.

Duration   1 year; nonrenewable.

Additional information   This program was established in 2003.

Number awarded   1 or more each year.

Deadline   April of each year.

[1253]
POSTDOCTORAL FELLOWSHIP IN MENTAL HEALTH AND SUBSTANCE ABUSE SERVICES

American Psychological Association
Attn: Minority Fellowship Program
750 First Street, N.E.
Washington, DC 20002-4242
(202) 336-6127   Fax: (202) 336-6012
TDD: (202) 336-6123   E-mail: mfp@apa.org
Web: www.apa.org/pi/mfp/psychology/postdoc/index.aspx

Summary   To provide financial assistance to postdoctoral scholars (especially African American and other minority scholars) who are interested in a program of research training related to providing mental health and substance abuse services to ethnic minority populations.

Eligibility   This program is open to U.S. citizens and permanent residents who received a doctoral degree in psychology in the last 5 years. Applicants must be interested in participating in a program of training under a qualified sponsor for research, delivery of services, or policy related to substance abuse and its relationship to the mental health or psychological well-being of ethnic minorities. Members of ethnic minority groups (African Americans, Hispanics/Latinos, American Indians, Alaskan Natives, Asian Americans, Native Hawaiians, and other Pacific Islanders) are especially encouraged to apply. Selection is based on commitment to a career in ethnic minority mental health service delivery, research, or policy; qualifications of the sponsor; the fit between career goals and training environment selected; merit of the training proposal; potential demonstrated through accomplishments and goals; appropriateness to goals of the program; and letters of recommendation.

Financial data   The stipend depends on the number of years of research experience and is equivalent to the standard postdoctoral stipend level of the National Institutes of Health (recently ranging from $38,496 for no years of experience to $53,112 for 7 or more years of experience).

Duration   1 academic or calendar year; may be renewed for 1 additional year.

Additional information   Funding is provided by the U.S. Substance Abuse and Mental Health Services Administration.

Number awarded   Varies each year.

Deadline   January of each year.

[1254]
POSTDOCTORAL FELLOWSHIPS IN DIABETES RESEARCH

Juvenile Diabetes Research Foundation International
Attn: Grant Administrator
26 Broadway, 14th Floor
New York, NY 10004
(212) 479-7572   Toll Free: (800) 533-CURE
Fax: (212) 785-9595   E-mail: info@jdrf.org
Web: www.jdrf.org/index.cfm?page_id=111715

Summary To provide research training to scientists (particularly African Americans, other minorities, women, and individuals with disabilities) who are beginning their professional careers and are interested in participating in research training on the causes, treatment, prevention, or cure of diabetes or its complications.

Eligibility This program is open to postdoctorates who are interested in a career in Type 1 diabetes-relevant research. Applicants must have received their first doctoral degree (M.D., Ph.D., D.M.D., or D.V.M.) within the past 5 years and may not have a faculty appointment. There are no citizenship requirements. Applications are encouraged from women, members of minority groups underrepresented in the sciences, and people with disabilities. The proposed research training may be conducted at foreign or domestic, for-profit or nonprofit, or public or private institutions, including universities, colleges, hospitals, laboratories, units of state or local government, or eligible agencies of the federal government. Applicants must be sponsored by an investigator who is affiliated full time with an accredited institution and who agrees to supervise the applicant's training. Selection is based on the applicant's previous experience and academic record; the caliber of the proposed research; and the quality of the mentor, training program, and environment.

Financial data Stipends range from $37,740 to $47,940 (depending upon years of experience). In any case, the award may not exceed the salary the recipient is currently earning. Fellows also receive a research allowance of $5,500 per year.

Duration 1 year; may be renewed for up to 1 additional year.

Additional information Fellows must devote at least 80% of their effort to the fellowship project.

Deadline January or July of each year.

[1255]
POSTDOCTORAL FELLOWSHIPS IN POLAR REGIONS RESEARCH

National Science Foundation
Attn: Office of Polar Programs
4201 Wilson Boulevard, Suite 755S
Arlington, VA 22230
(703) 292-8029   Fax: (703) 292-9079
TDD: (800) 281-8749   E-mail: OPPfellow@nsf.gov
Web: www.nsf.gov/funding/pgm_summ.jsp?pims_id=5650

Summary To provide funding to recent postdoctorates (particularly African Americans, other underrepresented minorities, and individuals with disabilities) who are interested in a program of research training related to the polar regions.

Eligibility This program is open to U.S. citizens and permanent residents in appropriate scientific fields who either completed a doctoral degree within the previous 4 years or will complete the degree within 1 year of the proposal deadline. Applicants may be proposing 1) a fellowship, for which they must identify a sponsoring scientist and a U.S. host organization that have agreed to provide a program of research training for fellows, or 2) a travel grant, for travel and per diem expenses to meet prospective sponsoring scientists in their host organizations before submitting a fellowship proposal. The host organization may be a college or university, government or national laboratory or facility, nonprofit institute, museum, or for-profit organization. The proposed or prospective research training should relate to an aspect of scientific study of the Antarctic or Arctic. The program encourages proposals from underrepresented minorities and persons with disabilities.

Financial data The maximum fellowship is $75,000 per year (including $50,000 as a stipend for the fellow, an annual research allowance of up to $11,000, an annual institutional allowance of $5,000, and an annual health insurance allowance of up to $3,600 for a single fellow, up to $6,000 for a fellow with 1 dependent, or up to $9,000 for a fellow with 2 or more dependents). The maximum travel grant is $3,000 for visits to 1 or 2 prospective host organizations. Indirect costs are not allowed for either fellowships or travel grants.

Duration Fellowships are typically 1 to 2 years long; 3-year fellowships may be justified for research and training plans that include field research.

Number awarded 5 fellowships and up to 10 travel grants may be awarded each year; recently, this program awarded approximately $1,000,000 in fellowships and travel grants.

Deadline Applications for fellowships must be submitted by October of each year. Applications for travel grants may be submitted at any time.

[1256]
POSTDOCTORAL FELLOWSHIPS OF THE FORD FOUNDATION DIVERSITY FELLOWSHIP PROGRAM

National Research Council
Attn: Fellowships Office, Keck 576
500 Fifth Street, N.W.
Washington, DC 20001
(202) 334-2872   Fax: (202) 334-3419
E-mail: infofell@nas.edu
Web: www.nationalacademies.org

Summary To provide funding for postdoctoral research to African American scholars and others whose success will increase the racial and ethnic diversity of U.S. colleges and universities.

Eligibility This program is open to U.S. citizens and nationals who earned a Ph.D. or Sc.D. degree within the past 7 years and are committed to a career in teaching and research at the college or university level. The following are considered as positive factors in the selection process: evidence of superior academic achievement; promise of continuing achievement as scholars and teachers; membership in a group whose underrepresentation in the American professoriate has been severe and longstanding, including Black/African Americans, Puerto Ricans, Mexican Americans/Chicanos/Chicanas, Native American Indians, Alaska Natives (Eskimos, Aleuts, and other indigenous people of Alaska), and Native Pacific Islanders (Hawaiians, Micronesians, or Polynesians); capacity to respond in pedagogically productive ways to the learning needs of students from diverse backgrounds; sustained personal engagement with communities that are underrepresented in the academy and an ability to bring this asset to learning, teaching, and scholarship at the college and university level; and likelihood of using the diversity of human experience as an educational resource in teaching and scholarship. Eligible areas of study include most fields of the arts, sciences, humanities, or social sciences or many interdisciplinary ethnic or area studies, but not for most practice-oriented areas. Research may be conducted at an appropriate institution of higher education in the United States (normally) or abroad, including universities, museums, libraries, government or national laboratories, privately sponsored nonprofit institutes, government chartered nonprofit research organizations, or centers for advanced study. Applicants should designate a faculty member or other scholar to serve as host at the proposed fellowship institution. They are encouraged to choose a host institution other than that where they are affiliated at the time of application.

Financial data The stipend is $40,000. Funds may be supplemented by sabbatical leave pay or other sources of support that do not carry with them teaching or other responsibilities. The employing institution receives an allowance of $1,500, paid after fellowship tenure is completed; the employing institution is expected to match the grant and to use the allowance and the match to assist with the fellow's continuing research expenditures.

Duration 9 to 12 months.

Additional information Fellows may not accept another major fellowship while they are being supported by this program.

Number awarded Approximately 20 each year.

Deadline November of each year.

[1257]
POSTDOCTORAL FELLOWSHIPS OF THE MINORITY SCHOLAR-IN-RESIDENCE PROGRAM

Consortium for Faculty Diversity at Liberal Arts Colleges
c/o DePauw University
Academic Affairs Office
305 Harrison Hall
7 East Larabee Street
Greencastle, IN 46135
(765) 658-6595   E-mail: jgriswold@depauw.edu
Web: www.depauw.edu

Summary To make available the facilities of liberal arts colleges to African American and other minority scholars who recently received their doctoral/advanced degree.

Eligibility This program is open to African American, Asian American, Hispanic American, and Native American scholars in the liberal arts and engineering who received the Ph.D. or M.F.A. degree within the past 5 years. Applicants must be interested in a residency at a participating institution that is part of the Consortium for a Strong Minority Presence at Liberal Arts Colleges. They must be U.S. citizens or permanent residents.

Financial data Fellows receive a stipend equivalent to the average salary paid by the host college to beginning assistant professors. Modest funds are made available to finance the fellow's proposed research, subject to the usual institutional procedures.

Duration 1 year.

Additional information The following schools are participating in the program: Agnes Scott College, Bard College at Simon's Rock, Bowdoin College, Bryn Mawr College, Carleton College, Centre College, College of Wooster, Colorado College, Denison University, DePauw University, Dickinson College, Gettysburg College, Goucher College, Grinnell College, Hamilton College, Harvey Mudd College, Haverford College, Hobart and William Smith Colleges, Kalamazoo College, Lafayette College, Lawrence University, Luther College, Macalester College, Mount Holyoke College, Muhlenberg College, New College of Florida, Oberlin College, Pomona College, Reed College, Rhodes College, University of Richmond, Scripps College, St. Olaf College, Sewanee: The University of the South, Skidmore College, Smith College, Southwestern University, Swarthmore College, Trinity College, Vassar College, Wellesley College, Whitman College, and Willamette University. Fellows are expected to teach at least 1 course in each academic term of residency, participate in departmental seminars, and interact with students.

Number awarded Varies each year.

Deadline November of each year.

[1258]
POSTDOCTORAL INDUSTRIAL FELLOWSHIPS

National Science Foundation
Directorate for Engineering
Attn: Division of Industrial Innovation and Partnerships
4201 Wilson Boulevard, Room 550S
Arlington, VA 22230
(703) 292-7082   Fax: (703) 292-9056
TDD: (800) 281-8749   E-mail: dsenich@nsf.gov
Web: www.nsf.gov/funding/pgm_summ.jsp?pims_id=13706

Summary To provide an opportunity for recent postdoctorates (particularly African Americans, other minorities, and individuals with disabilities) to work in industry as part of the Grant Opportunities for Academic Liaison with Industry (GOALI) program of the National Science Foundation (NSF).

Eligibility Applicants for these fellowships must have held a Ph.D. degree in a science, engineering, or mathematics field of interest to NSF for no more than 3 years. They must be U.S. citizens, nationals, or permanent residents. Along with their application, they must submit a plan for full-time work in industry under the guidance of an academic adviser and an industrial mentor. The program encourages applications from underrepresented minorities and persons with disabilities.

Financial data Grants range up to $75,000 per year. Funding, up to $4,000, may also be provided for transportation and moving expenses. Indirect costs are not allowed, but an institutional allowance of $5,000 is provided.

Duration 1 or 2 years.

Additional information This program is also offered by most other NSF directorates. Check the web site for a name and e-mail address of the contact person in each directorate.

Number awarded A total of 60 to 80 grants for all GOALI programs is awarded each year; total funding is approximately $5 million.

Deadline Applications may be submitted at any time.

[1259]
POSTDOCTORAL RESEARCH FELLOWSHIPS IN BIOLOGY

National Science Foundation
Directorate for Biological Sciences
Attn: Division of Biological Infrastructure
4201 Wilson Boulevard, Room 615N
Arlington, VA 22230
(703) 292-8470　　　　　　　Fax: (703) 292-9063
TDD: (800) 281-8749　　　　E-mail: ckimsey@nsf.gov
Web: www.nsf.gov

Summary　To provide funding for research and training in specified areas related to biology to African Americans and other junior doctoral-level scientists at sites in the United States or abroad.

Eligibility　This program is open to citizens, nationals, and permanent residents of the United States who are graduate students completing a Ph.D. or who have earned the degree no earlier than 12 months preceding the deadline date. Applicants must be interested in a program of research and training in either of 2 competitive areas: 1) Broadening Participation in Biology, designed to increase the diversity of scientists by providing support for research and training to biologists with disabilities and underrepresented minority (Native American, Native Pacific Islander, Alaskan Native, African American, and Hispanic) biologists; or 2) Intersections of Biology and Mathematical and Physical Sciences, for junior researchers who have conducted doctoral research in biology or physical and mathematical sciences and who present a research and training plan at the intersection of biology with mathematical and physical sciences. They may not have been a principal investigator or co-principal investigator on a federal research grant of more than $20,000. Fellowships are available to postdoctorates who are proposing a research and training plan at an appropriate nonprofit U.S. or foreign host institution (colleges and universities, government and national laboratories and facilities, and privately-sponsored nonprofit institutes and museums).

Financial data　The fellowship grant is $60,000 for the first year, $63,000 for the second year, and $66,000 for the third year; that includes 1) an annual stipend of $45,000 for the first year, $48,000 for the second year, and $51,000 for the third year; 2) a research allowance of $10,000 per year paid to the fellow for materials and supplies, subscription fees, and recovery costs for databases, travel, and publication expenses; and 3) an institutional allowance of $5,000 per year for fringe benefits and expenses incurred in support of the fellow.

Duration　Fellowships in the area of Broadening Participation in Biology are normally for 36 continuous months; those in the area of Intersections of Biology and Mathematical and Physical Sciences are normally for 24 months (unless the fellow spends more than 1 year at a foreign institution, in which case a third year of support at a U.S. institution may be requested).

Number awarded　Approximately 15 fellowships are awarded each year.

Deadline　October of each year.

[1260]
POSTDOCTORAL RESEARCH TRAINING FELLOWSHIPS IN EPILEPSY

Epilepsy Foundation
Attn: Research Department
8301 Professional Place
Landover, MD 20785-2237
(301) 459-3700　　　　　　Toll Free: (800) EFA-1000
Fax: (301) 577-2684　　　　TDD: (800) 332-2070
E-mail: grants@efa.org
Web: www.epilepsyfoundation.org

Summary　To provide funding for a program of postdoctoral training to academic physicians and scientists (particularly African Americans, other minorities, women, and individuals with disabilities) who are committed to epilepsy research.

Eligibility　Applicants must have a doctoral degree (M.D., Sc.D., Ph.D., or equivalent) and be a clinical or postdoctoral fellow at a university, medical school, research institution, or medical center. They must be interested in participating in a training experience and research project that has potential significance for understanding the causes, treatment, or consequences of epilepsy. The program is geared toward applicants who will be trained in research in epilepsy rather than those who use epilepsy as a tool for research in other fields. Equal consideration is given to applicants interested in acquiring experience either in basic laboratory research or in the conduct of human clinical studies. Academic faculty holding the rank of instructor or higher are not eligible, nor are graduate or medical students, medical residents, permanent government employees, or employees of private industry. Applications from women, members of minority groups, and people with disabilities are especially encouraged. U.S. citizenship is not required, but the project must be conducted in the United States. Selection is based on scientific quality of the proposed research, a statement regarding its relevance to epilepsy, the applicant's qualifications, the preceptor's qualifications, and the adequacy of facility and related epilepsy programs at the institution.

Financial data　The grant is $45,000. No indirect costs are covered.

Duration　1 year.

Additional information　Support for this program is provided by many individuals, families, and corporations, especially the American Epilepsy Society, Abbott Laboratories, Ortho-McNeil Pharmaceutical, and Pfizer Inc. The fellowship must be carried out at a facility in the United States where there is an ongoing epilepsy research program.

Number awarded　Varies each year.

Deadline　August of each year.

[1261]
PRESIDENTIAL EARLY CAREER AWARDS FOR SCIENTISTS AND ENGINEERS

National Science and Technology Council
Executive Office of the President
Attn: Office of Science and Technology Policy
725 17th Street, Room 5228
Washington, DC 20502
(202) 456-7116　　　　　　Fax: (202) 456-6021
Web: www.ostp.gov

Summary　To recognize and reward the nation's most outstanding young science and engineering faculty members (especially African Americans and other minorities) by providing them with additional research funding.

Eligibility Eligible for these awards are U.S. citizens, nationals, and permanent residents who have been selected to receive research grants from other departments of the U.S. government. Recipients of designated research grant programs are automatically considered for these Presidential Early Career Awards for Scientists and Engineers (PECASE). Most of the participating programs encourage applications from racial/ethnic minority individuals, women, and persons with disabilities.

Financial data Awards carry a grant of at least $80,000 per year.

Duration 5 years.

Additional information The departments with research programs that nominate candidates for the PECASE program are: 1) the National Aeronautics and Space Administration, which selects recipients of Early Career Awards based on exceptionally meritorious proposals funded through the traditional research grant process or the unsolicited proposal process; 2) the Department of Veterans Affairs, which nominates the most meritorious recipients of Veterans Health Administration Research Awards in the categories in medical research, rehabilitation research, and health services research; 3) the National Institutes of Health, which nominates the most meritorious investigators funded through its First Independent Research Support and Transition (FIRST) Awards and NIH Individual Research Project Grants (R01) programs; 4) the Department of Energy, which nominates staff members of the national laboratories and the most meritorious recipients of the DOE–Energy Research Young Scientist Awards and DOE–Defense Programs Early Career Scientist and Engineer Awards; 5) the Department of Defense, which nominates outstanding recipients of the Office of Naval Research Young Investigator Program, the Air Force Office of Scientific Research Broad Agency Program, and the Army Research Office Young Investigator Program; 6) the Department of Agriculture, which nominates staff scientists from the Agricultural Research Service, the most meritorious investigators funded through the National Research Initiative Competitive Grants Program (NRICGP) New Investigator Awards, and staff scientists of the Forest Service; 7) the Department of Commerce, which nominates outstanding staff members of the National Oceanic and Atmospheric Administration and the National Institute of Standards and Technology; 8) the Department of Transportation, which nominates the most qualified and innovative researchers in its University Transportation Centers and University Research Institutes programs; and 9) the National Science Foundation, which selects its nominees from the most meritorious investigators funded through the Faculty Early Career Development (CAREER) Program. For a list of the names, addresses, and telephone numbers of contact persons at each of the participating agencies, contact the Office of Science and Technology Policy.

Number awarded Varies each year; recently, 85 of these awards were granted.

Deadline Deadline not specified.

[1262]
R. ROBERT & SALLY D. FUNDERBURG RESEARCH AWARD IN GASTRIC CANCER

American Gastroenterological Association
Attn: AGA Research Foundation
Research Awards Manager
4930 Del Ray Avenue
Bethesda, MD 20814-2512
(301) 222-4012   Fax: (301) 654-5920
E-mail: awards@gastro.org
Web: www.gastro.org/aga-foundation/grants

Summary To provide funding to African American and other established investigators who are working on research that enhances fundamental understanding of gastric cancer pathobiology.

Eligibility This program is open to faculty at accredited North American institutions who have established themselves as independent investigators in the field of gastric biology, pursuing novel approaches to gastric mucosal cell biology, including the fields of gastric mucosal cell biology, regeneration and regulation of cell growth, inflammation as precancerous lesions, genetics of gastric carcinoma, oncogenes in gastric epithelial malignancies, epidemiology of gastric cancer, etiology of gastric epithelial malignancies, or clinical research in diagnosis or treatment of gastric carcinoma. Applicants must be individual members of the American Gastroenterological Association (AGA). Women and minority investigators are strongly encouraged to apply. Selection is based on the novelty, feasibility, and significance of the proposal. Preference is given to novel approaches.

Financial data The grant is $50,000 per year. Funds are to be used for the salary of the investigator. Indirect costs are not allowed.

Duration 2 years.

Number awarded 1 each year.

Deadline September of each year.

[1263]
RALPH J. BUNCHE AWARD

American Political Science Association
1527 New Hampshire Avenue, N.W.
Washington, DC 20036-1206
(202) 483-2512   Fax: (202) 483-2657
E-mail: apsa@apsanet.org
Web: www.apsanet.org/content_4129.cfm

Summary To recognize and reward outstanding scholarly books on ethnic/cultural pluralism.

Eligibility Eligible to be nominated (by publishers or individuals) are scholarly political science books issued the previous year that explore issues of ethnic and/or cultural pluralism.

Financial data The award is $1,000.

Duration The award is presented annually.

Additional information This award was first presented in 1978.

Number awarded 1 each year.

Deadline January of each year for nominations from individuals; February of each year for nominations from publishers.

[1264]
RESEARCH AND TRAINING FELLOWSHIPS IN EPILEPSY FOR CLINICIANS

Epilepsy Foundation
Attn: Research Department
8301 Professional Place
Landover, MD 20785-2237
(301) 459-3700   Toll Free: (800) EFA-1000
Fax: (301) 577-2684   TDD: (800) 332-2070
E-mail: clinical_postdocs@efa.org
Web: www.epilepsyfoundation.org

Summary To provide funding to African American, women, and other clinically-trained professionals interested in gaining additional training in order to develop an epilepsy research program.

Eligibility Applicants must have an M.D., D.O., Ph.D., D.S., or equivalent degree and be a clinical or postdoctoral fellow at a university, medical school, or other appropriate research institution. Holders of other doctoral-level degrees (e.g., Pharm.D., D.S.N.) may also be eligible. Candidates must be interested in a program of research training that may include mechanisms of epilepsy, novel therapeutic approaches, clinical trials, development of new technologies, or behavioral and psychosocial impact of epilepsy. The training program may consist of both didactic training and a supervised research experience that is designed to develop the necessary knowledge and skills in the chosen area of research and foster the career goals of the candidate. Academic faculty holding the rank of instructor or higher are not eligible, nor are graduate or medical students, medical residents, permanent government employees, or employees of private industry. Applications from women, members of minority groups, and people with disabilities are especially encouraged. U.S. citizenship is not required, but the project must be conducted in the United States. Selection is based on the quality of the proposed research training program, the applicant's qualifications, the preceptor's qualifications, and the adequacy of clinical training, research facilities, and other epilepsy-related programs at the institution.

Financial data The grant is $50,000 per year. No indirect costs are provided.

Duration Up to 2 years.

Additional information Support for this program is provided by many individuals, families, and corporations, especially the American Epilepsy Society, Abbott Laboratories, Ortho-McNeil Pharmaceutical, and Pfizer Inc. Grantees are expected to dedicate at least 50% of their time to research training and conducting research.

Number awarded Varies each year.

Deadline September of each year.

[1265]
RESEARCH INITIATION GRANTS TO BROADEN PARTICIPATION IN BIOLOGY

National Science Foundation
Directorate for Biological Sciences
Attn: Division of Biological Infrastructure
4201 Wilson Boulevard, Room 615N
Arlington, VA 22230
(703) 292-8470   Fax: (703) 292-9063
TDD: (800) 281-8749   E-mail: amaglia@nsf.gov
Web: www.nsf.gov/funding/pgm_summ.jsp?pims_id=10676

Summary To provide funding for research to African American and other scientists underrepresented in the field of biological science.

Eligibility This program is open to U.S. citizens, nationals, and permanent residents who have a doctoral degree or equivalent experience in a field of biology supported by the National Science Foundation (NSF). Applicants must be able to show how their proposal will increase the participation of scientists from underrepresented groups (African Americans, Hispanics, Native Americans, Native Hawaiians, and Alaska Natives) in biological research and the numbers of such individuals that serve as role models for the scientific workforce of the future. They must be in their first academic appointment as a faculty member or research-related position. Proposers affiliated with Minority Serving Institutions (MSIs), including Historically Black Colleges and Universities (HBCUs), Hispanic-Serving Institutions (HSIs), and Tribal Colleges and Universities (TCUs), are especially encouraged to apply. Selection is based on the scientific merit of the proposed research and the extent to which the proposed activities will broaden participation of individuals from underrepresented groups in the areas of the biological sciences supported by NSF.

Financial data Grants provide up to $175,000 over the life of the award, including both direct and indirect costs. An additional $25,000 may be provided for equipment.

Duration 24 months.

Number awarded 10 to 15 each year.

Deadline January of each year.

[1266]
RIDGE 2000 POSTDOCTORAL FELLOWSHIP PROGRAM

National Science Foundation
Directorate for Geosciences
Attn: Division of Ocean Sciences
4201 Wilson Boulevard, Room 725N
Arlington, VA 22230
(703) 292-7588   Fax: (703) 292-9085
TDD: (800) 281-8749   E-mail: dgarriso@nsf.gov
Web: www.nsf.gov/funding/pgm_summ.jsp?pims_id=5513

Summary To provide opportunities for young scientists (particularly American Americans or other underrepresented minorities and individuals with disabilities) to conduct geological research on the mid-ocean ridge system as part of the Ridge Inter-Disciplinary Global Experiments (RIDGE) 2000 Initiative.

Eligibility Eligible are U.S. citizens, nationals, or permanent residents who will have earned a doctoral degree within 2 years of taking up the award and who have arranged to conduct research under a senior scientist at an appropriate U.S. nonprofit institution (government laboratory, privately-sponsored nonprofit institution, national laboratory, or institution of higher education). Applicants must be proposing to conduct research that attempts to understand the geological processes of planetary renewal occurring along the mid-oceanic plate boundary and the chemical and biological processes that sustain life, in the absence of sunlight, in the deep ocean. Currently, the program has identified 3 sites as the focus of research: 9-10 degrees North segment of the East Pacific Rise, the East Lau Spreading Center in the western Pacific, and the Endeavor segment of the Juan de Fuca Ridge in the northwestern Pacific. Selection is based on ability as evidenced by past research work; suitability and availability of the sponsoring senior scientist and other associated colleagues; suitability of the host institution for the proposed research; likely impact on the future scientific development of the applicant; scientific quality of the research likely to emerge; and the potential impact of the research on the RIDGE 2000 Initiative. The program encourages applications from underrepresented minorities and persons with disabilities.

Financial data Grants range from $100,000 to $150,000. Funding includes a research allowance of $5,000 per year and an institutional allowance (in lieu of indirect costs) of $300 per month.

Duration 2 years; may be renewed for 1 additional year.

Number awarded 10 each year.

Deadline April of each year.

[1267]
ROBERT WOOD JOHNSON HEALTH POLICY FELLOWSHIPS

Institute of Medicine
Attn: Health Policy Fellowships Program
500 Fifth Street, N.W.
Washington, DC 20001
(202) 334-1506   Fax: (202) 334-3862
E-mail: mmichnich@nas.edu
Web: www.healthpolicyfellows.org

Summary To provide an opportunity to African American and other health professionals and behavioral and social scientists with an interest in health to participate in the formulation of national health policies while in residence at the Institute of Medicine (IOM) in Washington, D.C.

Eligibility This program is open to mid-career professionals from academic faculties and nonprofit health care organizations who are interested in experiencing health policy processes at the federal level. Applicants must have a background in allied health professions, biomedical sciences, dentistry, economics or other social sciences, health services organization and administration, medicine, nursing, public health, or social and behavioral health. They must be sponsored by the chief executive office of an eligible nonprofit health care organization or academic institution. Selection is based on potential for leadership in health policy, potential for future growth and career advancement, professional achievements, interpersonal and communication skills, and individual plans for incorporating the fellowship experience into specific career goals. U.S. citizenship or permanent resident status is required. Applications are especially encouraged from candidates with diverse backgrounds.

Financial data Total support for the Washington stay and continuing activities may not exceed $165,000. Grant funds may cover salary support at a level of up to $94,000 plus fringe benefits. Fellows are reimbursed for relocation expenses to and from Washington, D.C. No indirect costs are paid.

Duration The program begins in September with an orientation that includes meeting with key executive branch officials responsible for health activities, members of Congress and their staffs, and representatives of health interest groups; also included in the orientation period are seminars on health economics, major federal health and health research programs, the Congressional budget process, background on the major current issues in federal health policy, and the politics and process of federal decision-making. In November, the fellows join the American Political Science Association Congressional Fellowship Program for sessions with members of Congress, journalists, policy analysts, and other experts on the national political and governmental process. During that stage, fellows make contact with Congressional or executive branch offices involved in health issues and negotiate their working assignments. Those assignments begin in January and end in August, with an option for extending through the legislative term (which normally ends in October or early November). Fellows then return to their home institutions, but they receive up to 2 years of continued support for further development of health policy leadership skills.

Additional information This program, initiated in 1973, is funded by the Robert Wood Johnson Foundation.

Number awarded Up to 6 each year.

Deadline November of each year.

[1268]
ROBIN GAINES MEMORIAL SCHOLARSHIP

New England Regional Black Nurses Association, Inc.
P.O. Box 190690
Boston, MA 02119
(617) 524-1951
Web: www.nerbna.org/org/scholarships.html

Summary To provide financial assistance to registered nurses (R.N.s) from New England who are working on a master's degree and have contributed to the African American community.

Eligibility The program is open to residents of the New England states who are R.N.s and currently working on a master's degree (nursing, advanced nursing practice, or public health) at a school in any state. Applicants must have at least 1 full year of school remaining. Along with their application, they must submit a 3-page essay that covers their career aspirations in the nursing profession; how they have contributed to the African American or other communities of color in such areas as work, volunteering, church, or community outreach; an experience that has enhanced their personal and/or professional growth; and any financial hardships that may hinder them from completing their education.

Financial data A stipend is awarded (amount not specified).

Duration 1 year.

Number awarded 1 or more each year.

Deadline March of each year.

[1269]
RUTH L. KIRSCHSTEIN NATIONAL RESEARCH SERVICE AWARDS FOR INDIVIDUAL SENIOR FELLOWS

National Institutes of Health
Office of Extramural Research
Attn: Grants Information
6705 Rockledge Drive, Suite 4090
Bethesda, MD 20892-7983
(301) 435-0714   Fax: (301) 480-0525
TDD: (301) 451-5936   E-mail: GrantsInfo@nih.gov
Web: grants.nih.gov/grants/guide/index.html

Summary To provide funding for mentored research training to experienced scientists (especially African Americans, other minorities, and individuals with disabilities) who wish to make major changes in the direction of their research careers.

Eligibility This program is open to U.S. citizens, nationals, and permanent residents who have a doctoral degree and at least 7 subsequent years of relevant research or professional experience. Applications may be submitted on behalf of the candidates by a sponsoring institution, which may be a domestic or foreign, for-profit or nonprofit, public or private institution (such as a university, college, hospital, laboratory, agency or laboratory of the federal government, or intramural laboratory of the National Institutes of Health). Individuals requesting foreign-site training must justify the particular suitability of the foreign site, based on the nature of the facilities and/or training opportunity, rather than a domestic institution. In cases where there are clear scientific advantages, foreign training will be supported. Candidates must have received a Ph.D., M.D., D.O., D.C., D.D.S., D.V.M., O.D., D.P.M., Sc.D., Eng.D., Dr.P.H., D.N.Sc., N.D., Pharm.D., D.S.W., Psy.D., or equivalent degree from an accredited domestic or foreign institution. Members of diverse racial and ethnic groups, individuals with disabilities, and individuals from disadvantaged backgrounds are especially encouraged to apply.

Financial data The award provides an annual stipend based on the number of years of postdoctoral experience, ranging from $37,368 for less than 1 year to $51,552 for 7 or more years. For fellows sponsored by domestic nonfederal institutions, the stipend is paid through the sponsoring institution; for fellows sponsored by federal or foreign institutions, the monthly stipend is paid directly to the fellow. Institutions also receive an allowance to help defray such awardee expenses as self-only health insurance, research supplies, equipment, travel to scientific meetings, and related items; the allowance is $7,850 per 12-month period for fellows at nonfederal, nonprofit, and foreign institutions and $6,750 per 12-month period at federal laboratories and for-profit institutions. In addition, tuition and fees are reimbursed at a rate of 60%, up to $4,500; if the fellow's program supports postdoctoral individuals in formal degree-granting training, tuition is supported at the rate of 60%, up to $16,000 for an additional degree. The initial 12 months of National Research Service Award postdoctoral support carries a service payback requirement, which can be fulfilled by continued training under the award or by engaging in other health-related research training, health-related research, or health-related teaching. Fellows who fail to fulfill the payback requirement of 1 month of acceptable service for each month of the initial 12 months of support received must repay all funds received with interest.

Duration Up to 2 years.

Additional information This program is offered by 16 components of the National Institutes of Health: the National Institute on Aging, the National Institute on Alcohol Abuse and Alcoholism, the National Institute of Allergy and Infectious Diseases, the National Institute of Arthritis and Musculoskeletal and Skin Diseases, the National Cancer Institute, the National Institute of Child Health and Human Development, the National Institute on Deafness and Other Communication Disorders, the National Institute of Dental and Craniofacial Research, the National Institute of Environmental Health Sciences, the National Eye Institute, the National Institute of General Medical Sciences, the National Institute of Neurological Disorders and Stroke, the National Institute of Nursing Research, and the Office of Dietary Supplements.

Number awarded Varies each year.

Deadline April, August, or December of each year.

[1270]
SARA WHALEY BOOK PRIZE

National Women's Studies Association
Attn: Book Prizes
7100 Baltimore Avenue, Suite 203
College Park, MD 20740
(301) 403-0407   Fax: (301) 403-4137
E-mail: nwsaoffice@nwsa.org
Web: www.nwsa.org/awards/index.php

Summary To recognize and reward members of the National Women's Studies Association (NWSA), particularly African American and other women of color, who have written outstanding books on topics related to women and labor.

Eligibility This award is available to NWSA members who submit a book manuscript that relates to women and labor, including migration and women's paid jobs, illegal immigration and women's work, impact of AIDS on women's employment, trafficking of women and women's employment, women and domestic work, or impact of race on women's work. Both senior scholars (who have a record of publication of at least 2 books and published the entry within the past year) and junior scholars (who have a publication contract or a book in production) are eligible. Women of color of American or international origin are encouraged to apply.

Financial data The award is $2,000.

Duration The awards are presented annually.

Additional information This award was first presented in 2008.

Number awarded 2 each year: 1 to a senior scholar and 1 to a junior scholar.

Deadline April of each year.

[1271]
SBE MINORITY POSTDOCTORAL RESEARCH FELLOWSHIPS AND FOLLOW-UP RESEARCH STARTER GRANTS

National Science Foundation
Directorate for Social, Behavioral, and Economic
  Sciences
Attn: Office of Multidisciplinary Activities
4201 Wilson Boulevard, Room 907.09
Arlington, VA 22230
(703) 292-4672   Fax: (703) 292-9083
TDD: (800) 281-8749   E-mail: fchowdhu@nsf.gov
Web: www.nsf.gov

Summary To provide financial assistance for postdoctoral research training in the United States or abroad to African American and other underrepresented minority scientists in fields of interest to the Directorate for Social, Behavioral, and Economic Sciences (SBE) of the National Science Foundation (NSF).

Eligibility This program is open to U.S. citizens, nationals, and permanent residents who will complete their doctorate within a year or have completed it within the previous 30 months but have not completed more than 12 months in a postdoctoral research position. Applicants must be a member of an ethnic group that is significantly underrepresented at advanced levels of science and engineering in the United States, including Native Americans (Alaska Natives and American Indians), African Americans, Hispanics, and Native Pacific Islanders. They must be seeking fellowship funding for research training that falls within the program areas of the SBE to be conducted at any appropriate nonprofit U.S. or foreign institution (government laboratory, institution of higher education, national laboratory, or public or private research institute), but not at the same institution where the doctorate was obtained. Fellows who accept a tenure-track position at a U.S. academic institution may apply for a follow-up research starter grant.

Financial data The fellowship grant is $60,000 per year, including an annual stipend of $45,000, a research allowance of $10,000 per year, and an institutional allowance of $5,000 per year for partial reimbursement of indirect research costs (space, equipment, general purpose supplies, and fringe benefits). Follow-up research starter grants are $50,000.

Duration Fellowships are for 2 years; applicants who propose to spend their 2-year tenure at a foreign institution may apply for a third year of support at an appropriate U.S. institution. Follow-up research starter grants are for 1 year.

Number awarded Up to 12 each year.

Deadline October of each year.

[1272]
SCHOMBURG CENTER SCHOLARS-IN-RESIDENCE PROGRAM

New York Public Library
Attn: Schomburg Center for Research in Black Culture
515 Malcolm X Boulevard
New York, NY 10037-1801
(212) 491-2218   Fax: (212) 491-6760
Web: www.nypl.org/locations/tid/64/node/131

Summary To provide financial support for research and writing on the history, literature, and cultures of the peoples of Africa and the African Diaspora at the Schomburg Center of the New York Public Library.

Eligibility This program is open to 1) scholars studying the history, literature, and culture of the peoples of African descent from a humanistic perspective, and 2) professionals in fields related to the sponsor's collections and program activities. Projects in the social sciences, psychology, science and technology, education, and religion are eligible if they utilize a humanistic approach and contribute to humanistic knowledge. Applicants must be U.S. citizens or foreign nationals who have resided in the United States for at least 3 years. Selection is based on qualifications of the applicant, quality and feasibility of the project plan, importance of the proposed project to the applicant's field and to the humanities, relationship of the project to the humanities, relationship of the project to the resources of the Schomburg Center, likelihood that the project will be completed successfully, and provisions for making the results of the project available to scholars and to the public at large.

Financial data The stipend is $30,000 for 6 months or $60,000 for 1 year.

Duration From 6 months to 1 year.

Additional information This program is made possible by grants from the National Endowment for the Humanities, the

Andrew W. Mellon Foundation, the Ford Foundation, and the Samuel I. Newhouse Foundation. Participants in the program must be in residence at the Schomburg Center of the New York Public Library on a full-time basis. They may not hold other major fellowships/grants or be employed during the residency. No support is available to students conducting research leading to a degree.

Number awarded Up to 6 each year.

Deadline November of each year.

[1273]
SOCIETY OF PEDIATRIC PSYCHOLOGY DIVERSITY RESEARCH GRANT

American Psychological Association
Attn: Division 54 (Society of Pediatric Psychology)
c/o John M. Chaney
Oklahoma State University
Department of Psychology
407 North Murray
Stillwater, OK 74078
(405) 744-5703   E-mail: john.chaney@okstate.edu
Web: www.societyofpediatricpsychology.org

Summary To provide funding to graduate student and postdoctoral members of the Society of Pediatric Psychology (especially African Americans and other minorities or women) who are interested in conducting research on diversity aspects of pediatric psychology.

Eligibility This program is open to current members of the society who are graduate students, fellows, or early-career (within 3 years of appointment) faculty. Applicants must be interested in conducting pediatric psychology research that features diversity-related variables, such as race or ethnicity, gender, culture, sexual orientation, language differences, socioeconomic status, and/or religiosity. Along with their application, they must submit a 2,000-word description of the project, including its purpose, methodology, predictions, and implications; a detailed budget; a current curriculum vitae, and (for students) a curriculum vitae of the faculty research mentor and a letter of support from that mentor. Selection is based on relevance to diversity in child health (5 points), significance of the study (5 points), study methods and procedures (10 points), and investigator qualifications (10 points).

Financial data Grants up to $1,000 are available. Funds may not be used for convention or meeting travel, indirect costs, stipends of principal investigators, or costs associated with manuscript preparation.

Duration The grant is presented annually.

Additional information The Society of Pediatric Psychology is Division 54 of the American Psychological Association (APA). This grant was first presented in 2008.

Number awarded 1 each year.

Deadline September of each year.

[1274]
SONIA KOVALEVSKY HIGH SCHOOL MATHEMATICS DAYS GRANTS

Association for Women in Mathematics
11240 Waples Mill Road, Suite 200
Fairfax, VA 22030
(703) 934-0163   Fax: (703) 359-7562
E-mail: awm@awm-math.org
Web: sites.google.com

Summary To provide funding to African American and other faculty at colleges and universities who wish to conduct Sonia Kovalevsky High School and Middle School Mathematics Days.

Eligibility Faculty and staff at universities and colleges may apply for these grants to support Sonia Kovalevsky High School and Middle School Mathematics Days; staff at Historically Black Colleges and Universities are particularly encouraged to apply. Programs targeted towards inner-city or rural high schools are especially welcomed. The proposed activity should consist of workshops, talks, and problem-solving competitions for female high school or middle school students and their teachers (both women and men).

Financial data The maximum grant is $3,000; most range from $1,500 to $2,200. Funds must be used for direct costs for the activity. Stipends and personnel costs are not permitted for organizers. Reimbursement for indirect costs or fringe benefits is not allowed.

Duration The grants are awarded annually.

Additional information This program is supported by grants from the National Security Agency and Elizabeth City State University.

Number awarded 12 to 20 each year.

Deadline August or February of each year.

[1275]
SUBSTANCE ABUSE FELLOWSHIP PROGRAM

American Psychiatric Association
Attn: Department of Minority and National Affairs
1000 Wilson Boulevard, Suite 1825
Arlington, VA 22209-3901
(703) 907-8653   Toll Free: (888) 35-PSYCH
Fax: (703) 907-7852   E-mail: mking@psych.org
Web: www.psych.org/Resources/OMNA/MFP.aspx

Summary To provide educational enrichment to African American and other minority psychiatrists-in-training and stimulate their interest in providing quality and effective services related to substance abuse to minorities and the underserved.

Eligibility This program is open to psychiatric residents who are members of the American Psychiatric Association (APA) and U.S. citizens or permanent residents. A goal of the program is to develop leadership to improve the quality of mental health care for members of ethnic minority groups (American Indians, Native Alaskans, Asian Americans, Native Hawaiians, Native Pacific Islanders, African Americans, and Hispanics/Latinos). Applicants must be in at least their fifth year of a substance abuse training program approved by an affiliated medical school or agency where a significant number of substance abuse patients are from minority and underserved groups. They must also be interested in working with a component of the APA that is of interest to them and relevant to their career goals. Along with their application, they must submit a 2-page essay on how the fellowship would be utilized to alter their present training and ultimately assist them in achieving their career goals. Selection is based on commitment to serve ethnic minority populations, demonstrated leadership abilities, awareness of the importance of culture in mental health, and interest in the interrelationship between mental health/illness and transcultural factors.

Financial data Fellows receive a monthly stipend (amount not specified) and reimbursement of transportation, lodging, meals, and incidentals in connection with attendance at program-related activities. They are expected to use the funds to enhance their own professional development, improve training in cultural competence at their training institution, improve awareness of culturally relevant issues in psychiatry at their institution, expand research in areas relevant to minorities and underserved populations, enhance the current treatment modalities for minority patients and underserved individuals at their institution, and improve awareness in the surrounding community about mental health issues (particularly with regard to minority populations).

Duration 1 year; may be renewed 1 additional year.

Additional information Funding for this program is provided by the Substance Abuse and Mental Health Services Administration (SAMHSA). As part of their assignment to an APA component, fellows must attend the fall component meetings in September and the APA annual meeting in May. At those meeting, they can share their experiences as residents and minorities and discuss issues that impact minority populations. This program is an outgrowth of the fellowships that were established in 1974 under a grant from the National Institute of Mental Health in answer to concerns about the underrepresentation of minorities in psychiatry.

Number awarded Varies each year; recently, 3 of these fellowships were awarded.

Deadline January of each year.

[1276]
SUSAN G. KOMEN BREAST CANCER FOUNDATION POSTDOCTORAL FELLOWSHIP

Susan G. Komen Breast Cancer Foundation
Attn: Grants Department
5005 LBJ Freeway, Suite 250
Dallas, TX 75244
(972) 855-1616   Toll Free: (866) 921-9678
Fax: (972) 855-1640
E-mail: helpdesk@komengrantsaccess.org
Web: ww5.komen.org

Summary To provide funding to postdoctoral fellows (particularly African Americans and other minorities) who are interested in pursuing research training related to breast cancer.

Eligibility This program is open to postdoctorates who are no more than 5 years past completion of their Ph.D. or, if an M.D., no more than 3 years past completion of clinical fellowship or 5 years past completion of residency. Applicants may not hold any current faculty appointments and may not currently be or have been a fellow for the same sponsor. They are not required to be U.S. citizens or residents. A principal investigator who is a full-time faculty member at the same institution must sponsor the applicant. Currently, proposals must focus on 4 types of research training activities: 1) basic research that substantially advances progress in breast cancer research and will lead to future reductions in breast cancer incidence and/or mortality; 2) translational research that expands skills and expertise in the application of laboratory, clinical, and applied disciplines to research that translates laboratory, clinical, and/or population discoveries into new clinical tools and applications leading to reductions of breast cancer incidence and/or mortality; 3) clinical research for physicians who wish to pursue a career path that blends patient care with high impact, clinical, and/or translational breast cancer research; expands their skills; positions them for independent careers as physician scientists; and supports high quality research concepts; or 4) disparities research that expands skills and expertise in research exploring the basis for differences in breast cancer outcomes and the translation of this research into clinical and public health practice interventions, particularly among junior scientists from populations affected by breast cancer disparities. The program is especially interested in providing training support for minority scientists; a portion of available funds are designated for minority fellows.

Financial data The grant is $60,000 per year for direct costs only.

Duration 2 years; a third year may be approved, based on an assessment of first-year progress.

Number awarded Varies each year; recently, 56 of these fellowships were awarded.

Deadline Pre-applications must be submitted in September of each year; full applications are due in January.

[1277]
SYLVIA TAYLOR JOHNSON MINORITY FELLOWSHIP IN EDUCATIONAL MEASUREMENT

Educational Testing Service
Attn: Fellowships
660 Rosedale Road
MS 19-T
Princeton, NJ 08541-0001
(609) 734-5543   Fax: (609) 734-5410
E-mail: internfellowships@ets.org
Web: www.ets.org/research/fellowships/johnson

Summary To provide funding to African American and other minority scholars who are interested in conducting independent research under the mentorship of senior researchers at the Educational Testing Service (ETS).

Eligibility This program is open to scholars from diverse backgrounds (especially members of traditionally underrepresented groups such as African Americans, Hispanic/Latino Americans, and American Indians) who have earned a doctorate within the past 10 years and are U.S. citizens or permanent residents. Applicants must be prepared to conduct independent research at ETS under the mentorship of a senior researcher. They should have a commitment to education and an independent body of scholarship that signals the promise of continuing contributions to educational measurement. Projects should relate to issues involved in measurement theory, validity, natural language processing and computational linguistics, cognitive psychology, learning theory, linguistics, speech recognition and processing, teaching and classroom research, or statistics. Studies focused on issues concerning the education of minority students are especially

encouraged. Selection is based on the scholar's record of accomplishment, proposed topic of research, commitment to education, and promise of continuing contributions to educational measurement.

Financial data The stipend is set in relation to compensation at the home institution. Scholars and their families also receive reimbursement for relocation expenses.

Duration Up to 2 years.

Number awarded 1 each year.

Deadline January of each year.

[1278]
TRAINEESHIPS IN AIDS PREVENTION STUDIES (TAPS) PROGRAM POSTDOCTORAL FELLOWSHIPS

University of California at San Francisco
Attn: Center for AIDS Prevention Studies
50 Beale Street, Suite 1300
San Francisco, CA 94105
(415) 597-9260   Fax: (415) 597-9213
E-mail: Rochelle.Blanco@ucsf.edu
Web: www.caps.ucsf.edu

Summary To provide funding to scientists (especially African Americans and other minorities) who are interested in conducting HIV prevention research.

Eligibility This program is open to U.S. citizens, nationals, and permanent residents who have a Ph.D., M.D., or equivalent degree. Applicants must be interested in a program of research training at CAPS in the following areas of special emphasis in AIDS research: epidemiological research, studies of AIDS risk behaviors, substance abuse and HIV, primary prevention interventions, research addressing minority populations, studies of HIV-positive individuals, policy and ethics, international research, and other public health and clinical aspects of AIDS. Recent postdoctorates who have just completed their training as well as those who are already faculty members in academic or clinical departments are eligible. Members of minority ethnic groups are strongly encouraged to apply.

Financial data Stipends depend on years of relevant postdoctoral experience, based on the NIH stipend scale for Institutional Research Training Grants (currently ranging from $37,740 for fellows with no relevant postdoctoral experience to $52,068 to those with 7 or more years of experience). Other benefits include a computer, travel to at least 1 annual professional meeting, health insurance, and other required support. The costs of the M.P.H. degree, if required, are covered.

Duration 2 or 3 years.

Additional information The TAPS program is designed to ensure that at the end of the training each fellow will have: 1) completed the M.P.H. degree or its equivalent; 2) taken advanced courses in research methods, statistics, and other topics relevant to a major field of interest; 3) participated in and led numerous seminars on research topics within CAPS, as well as in the formal teaching programs of the university; 4) designed several research protocols and completed at least 1 significant research project under the direction of a faculty mentor; and 5) made presentations at national or international meetings and submitted several papers for publication.

Number awarded Varies each year.

Deadline November of each year.

[1279]
TRAINING PROGRAM FOR SCIENTISTS CONDUCTING RESEARCH TO REDUCE HIV/STI HEALTH DISPARITIES

University of California at San Francisco
Attn: Center for AIDS Prevention Studies
50 Beale Street, Suite 1300
San Francisco, CA 94105
(415) 597-4976   Fax: (415) 597-9213
E-mail: jackie.ramos@ucsf.edu
Web: www.caps.ucsf.edu

Summary To provide funding to scientists (especially African Americans and other minorities) who are interested in obtaining additional training at the University of California at San Francisco (UCSF) Center for AIDS Prevention Studies (CAPS) for HIV prevention research in minority communities.

Eligibility This program is open to scientists in tenure-track positions or investigators in research institutes who have not yet obtained research funding from the U.S. National Institutes of Health (NIH) or equivalent. Applicants must be interested in a program of activity at CAPS to improve their programs of HIV-prevention research targeting vulnerable ethnic minority populations. They must be eligible to serve as principal investigators at their home institutions. Selection is based on commitment to HIV social and behavioral research, prior HIV prevention research with communities and community-based organizations targeting communities with high levels of health disparities (e.g., communities with a high proportion of disadvantaged or disabled persons, racial and ethnic minority communities), creativity and innovativeness for a pilot research project to serve as a preliminary study for a subsequent larger R01 grant proposal to NIH or other suitable funding agency, past experience conducting research and writing papers, quality of letters of recommendation from colleagues and mentors, and support from the home institution (e.g., time off for research, seed money). A goal of the program is to increase the number of minority group members among principal investigators funded by NIH and other agencies.

Financial data Participants receive 1) a monthly stipend for living expenses and round-trip airfare to San Francisco for each summer, and 2) a grant of $25,000 to conduct preliminary research before the second summer to strengthen their R01 application.

Duration 6 weeks during each of 3 consecutive summers.

Additional information This program is funded by the NIH National Institute of Child Health and Human Development (NICHHD) and National Institute on Drug Abuse (NIDA).

Number awarded Approximately 4 each year.

Deadline January of each year.

[1280]
UCSB LIBRARY FELLOWSHIP PROGRAM

University of California at Santa Barbara
Attn: Associate University Librarian, Human Resources
Davidson Library
Santa Barbara, CA 93106-9010
(805) 893-3841   Fax: (805) 893-7010
E-mail: bankhead@library.ucsb.edu
Web: www.library.ucsb.edu/hr/fellowship.html

Summary To provide an opportunity for recent library school graduates, especially African Americans and members of other underrepresented groups, to serve in the library system at the University of California at Santa Barbara (UCSB).

Eligibility This program is open to recent graduates of library schools accredited by the American Library Association. Applicants must be interested in a postgraduate appointment at UCSB. They must have a knowledge of and interest in academic librarianship and a strong desire for professional growth. Members of underrepresented groups are encouraged to apply.

Financial data Fellows are regular (but temporary) employees of the university and receive the same salary and benefits as other librarians at the assistant librarian level ($46,164 to $48,029 per year).

Duration 2 years.

Additional information The program began in 1985. Fellows spend time in at least 2 different departments in the library, serve on library committees, attend professional meetings, receive travel support for 2 major conferences, and participate in the Librarians' Association of the University of California.

Number awarded 1 each year.

Deadline January of each year.

[1281]
UNCF/MERCK POSTDOCTORAL SCIENCE RESEARCH FELLOWSHIPS

United Negro College Fund
Attn: Merck Science Initiative
8260 Willow Oaks Corporate Drive, Suite 110
P.O. Box 10444
Fairfax, VA 22031-4511
(703) 205-3503   Fax: (703) 205-3574
E-mail: uncfmerck@uncf.org
Web: umsi.uncf.org

Summary To provide financial assistance to African American postdoctoral fellows who are interested in pursuing research in the life or physical sciences.

Eligibility This program is open to African Americans who have been appointed as a postdoctoral fellow at an academic or non-academic research institution (private industrial laboratories are excluded). Applicants must be U.S. citizens or permanent residents interested in preparing for a career in the life or physical sciences. Selection is based on the record of accomplishments and soundness of the proposed postdoctoral research.

Financial data The total award is $92,000, including up to $77,000 as a stipend for the fellow (the maximum stipend is $55,000 for any 12-month period) and a research grant up to

$15,000. Fringe benefits up to $9,200 are also allowed, but no provision is made for indirect costs.

Duration 12 to 24 months.

Additional information This program, established in 1995, is funded by the Merck Company Foundation.

Number awarded At least 10 each year.

Deadline December of each year.

[1282]
UNIVERSITY OF CALIFORNIA PRESIDENT'S POSTDOCTORAL FELLOWSHIP PROGRAM FOR ACADEMIC DIVERSITY

University of California at Berkeley
Attn: Office of Equity and Inclusion
102 California Hall
Berkeley, CA 94720-1508
(510) 643-6566   E-mail: kadkinson@berkeley.edu
Web: www.ucop.edu/acadadv/ppfp

Summary To provide an opportunity to conduct research at campuses of the University of California to African American and other recent postdoctorates who are committed to careers in university teaching and research and who will contribute to diversity.

Eligibility This program is open to U.S. citizens or permanent residents who have a Ph.D. from an accredited university. Applicants must be proposing to conduct research at a branch of the university under the mentorship of a faculty or laboratory sponsor. Preference is given to applicants 1) with the potential to bring to their academic careers the critical perspective that comes from their nontraditional educational background or their understanding of the experiences of groups historically underrepresented in higher education; 2) who have the communications skill and cross-cultural abilities to maximize effective collaboration with a diverse cross-section of the academic community; 3) who have demonstrated significant academic achievement by overcoming barriers such as economic, social, or educational disadvantage; and 4) who have the potential to contribute to higher education through their understanding of the barriers facing women, domestic minorities, students with disabilities, and other members of groups underrepresented in higher education careers, as evidenced by life experiences and educational background.

Financial data The stipend ranges from $40,000 to $50,000, depending on the field and level of experience. The program also offers health benefits and up to $4,000 for supplemental and research-related expenses.

Duration Appointments are for 1 academic year, with possible renewal for a second year.

Additional information Research may be conducted at any of the University of California's 10 campuses (Berkeley, Davis, Irvine, Los Angeles, Merced, Riverside, San Diego, San Francisco, Santa Barbara, or Santa Cruz). The program provides mentoring and guidance in preparing for an academic career. This program was established in 1984 to encourage applications from minority and women scholars in fields where they were severely underrepresented; it is now open to all qualified candidates who are committed to university careers in research, teaching, and service that will enhance the diversity of the academic community at the university.

Number awarded 15 to 20 each year.

Deadline November of each year.

[1283]
VAID FELLOWSHIPS

National Gay and Lesbian Task Force
Attn: The Task Force Policy Institute
80 Maiden Lane, Suite 1504
New York, NY 10038
(212) 604-9830   Fax: (212) 604-9831
E-mail: ngltf@ngltf.org
Web: www.thetaskforce.org

Summary To provide work experience to undergraduate and graduate students (particularly African Americans and other minorities) who are interested in participating in the leadership of people of color in the progressive movement for gay, lesbian, bisexual, and transgender (GLBT) equality.

Eligibility Applicants must be enrolled in a degree program at least half time as a law, graduate, or undergraduate student or have successfully completed a law, graduate, or undergraduate degree within the preceding 12 months. They should have 1) a desire to work in a multicultural environment where commitment to diversity based on race, ethnic origin, gender, age, sexual orientation, and physical ability is an important institutional value; 2) demonstrated leadership in progressive and/or GLBT communities; 3) extensive research, writing, and critical thinking skills; 4) knowledge of, and commitment to, GLBT issues; and 5) computer proficiency in word processing, database work, e-mail, and Internet research. The program supports and recognizes the leadership of people of color and other emerging leaders in public policy, legal, and social science research.

Financial data The stipend ranges from $200 to $400 per week ($10 per hour). Fellows are responsible for their own housing and living expenses.

Duration Summer fellowships are 40 hours per week and spring/fall fellowships are 20 hours per week.

Additional information The Policy Institute of the National Gay and Lesbian Task Force (NGLTF), founded in 1995, is the largest think tank in the United States engaged in research, policy analysis, and strategic action to advance equality and understanding of GLBT people. Its primary programs are the racial and economic justice initiative, the family policy program, and the aging initiative. In addition to their primary roles of providing research and analysis, all 3 programs work closely with NGLTF colleagues in Washington, D.C. and other allies on advocacy and legislative efforts to actively change laws and policies affecting GLBT people.

Number awarded 3 fellows are selected each session.

Deadline April for the summer, July for the fall, and November for the spring.

[1284]
VITO MARZULLO INTERNSHIP PROGRAM

Office of the Governor
Attn: Department of Central Management Services
503 William G. Stratton Building
Springfield, IL 62706
(217) 524-1381   Fax: (217) 558-4497
TDD: (217) 785-3979
Web: www.ilga.gov/commission/lru/internships.html

Summary To provide African Americans and other recent college graduates with work experience in the Illinois Governor's office.

Eligibility This program is open to residents of Illinois who have completed a bachelor's degree and are interested in working in the Illinois Governor's office or in various agencies under the Governor's jurisdiction. Applicants may have majored in any field, but they must be able to demonstrate a substantial commitment to excellence as evidenced by academic honors, leadership ability, extracurricular activities, and involvement in community or public service. Along with their application, they must submit 1) a 500-word personal statement on the qualities or attributes they will bring to the program, their career goals or plans, how their selection for this program would assist them in achieving those goals, and what they expect to gain from the program; and 2) a 1,000-word essay in which they identify and analyze a public issue that they feel has great impact on state government. A particular goal of the program is to achieve affirmative action through the nomination of qualified minorities, women, and persons with disabilities.

Financial data The stipend is $2,611 per month.

Duration 1 year, beginning in August.

Additional information Assignments are in Springfield and, to a limited extent, in Chicago or Washington, D.C.

Number awarded Varies each year.

Deadline February of each year.

[1285]
WASHINGTON UNIVERSITY POST DOCTORAL FELLOWSHIP FOR AFRICAN-AMERICAN SCHOLARS

Washington University
African and African American Studies Program
Attn: Director
Campus Box 1109
One Brookings Drive
St. Louis, MO 63130-4899
(314) 935-5631   Fax: (314) 935-9390
E-mail: afas@artsci.wustl.edu
Web: afas.wustl.edu/~afas/AFAS/Post-Doc.html

Summary To offer African American scholars a residency at Washington University (in St. Louis, Missouri).

Eligibility This program is open to African American scholars who specialize in either the African or African American aspect of their field. Applicants must have completed their doctorate no more than 3 years ago and must be interested in an appointment at Washington University. They must submit a letter of interest, a detailed statement of proposed research, a curriculum vitae, a writing sample, and an official graduate transcript.

Financial data The fellowship stipend is $36,000 plus a $2,000 travel fund to be used to attend academic conferences and a $1,500 moving allowance.

Duration 1 year.

Additional information This program was started in 1995. Scholars are provided with office space and computer equipment. They are asked to teach courses in their area of scholarly specialty, but they are given a reduced teaching load.

Number awarded 2 each year.

Deadline January of each year.

[1286]
W.E.B. DUBOIS FELLOWSHIP PROGRAM

Department of Justice
National Institute of Justice
Attn: W.E.B. DuBois Fellowship Program
810 Seventh Street, N.W.
Washington, DC 20531
(202) 514-6205   E-mail: Marilyn.Moses@usdoj.gov
Web: www.nij.gov

Summary To provide funding to junior investigators (especially African Americans and other minorities) who are interested in conducting research on "crime, violence and the administration of justice in diverse cultural contexts."

Eligibility This program is open to investigators who have a Ph.D. or other doctoral-level degree (including a legal degree of J.D. or higher). Applicants should be early in their careers. They must be interested in conducting research that relates to specific areas that change annually but relate to criminal justice policy and practice in the United States. The sponsor strongly encourages applications from diverse racial and ethnic backgrounds. Selection is based on quality and technical merit; impact of the proposed project; capabilities, demonstrated productivity, and experience of the applicant; budget; dissemination strategy; and relevance of the project for policy and practice.

Financial data Grants range up to $100,000. Funds may be used for salary, fringe benefits, reasonable costs of relocation, travel essential to the project, and office expenses not provided by the sponsor. Indirect costs are limited to 20%.

Duration 6 to 12 months; fellows are required to be in residence at the National Institute of Justice (NIJ) for the first 2 months and may elect to spend all or part of the remainder of the fellowship period either in residence at NIJ or at their home institution.

Number awarded 1 each year.

Deadline January of each year.

[1287]
WESLEY-LOGAN PRIZE IN AFRICAN DIASPORA HISTORY

American Historical Association
Attn: Book Prize Administrator
400 A Street, S.E.
Washington, DC 20003-3889
(202) 544-2422   Fax: (202) 544-8307
E-mail: info@historians.org
Web: www.historians.org

Summary To recognize and reward outstanding publications dealing with African Diaspora history.

Eligibility The prize is awarded to the best book on some aspect of the history of the dispersion, settlement, adjustment, or return of peoples originally from Africa. Books in any chronological period and any geographical location are eligible. Only works of high scholarly and literary merit are considered.

Financial data The prize is $1,000.

Duration The award is granted annually.

Additional information This prize was established in 1992 to honor 2 early pioneers in the field, Charles H. Wesley and Rayford W. Logan. It is jointly sponsored by the American Historical Association and the Association for the Study of African American Life and History.

Number awarded 1 each year.

Deadline May of each year.

[1288]
WILLIAM SANDERS SCARBOROUGH PRIZE

Modern Language Association of America
Attn: Committee on Honors and Awards
26 Broadway, Third Floor
New York, NY 10004-1789
(646) 576-5141   Fax: (646) 458-0030
E-mail: awards@mla.org
Web: www.mla.org

Summary To recognize and reward authors of outstanding books on African American literature.

Eligibility This award is presented to authors of outstanding scholarly studies of African American literature or culture published the previous year. Books that are primarily translations are not eligible. Authors need not be members of the Modern Language Association.

Financial data The prize is $1,000 and a certificate.

Duration The prize is awarded annually.

Additional information This prize was first awarded in 2001.

Number awarded 1 each year.

Deadline April of each year.

[1289]
WILLIAM TOWNSEND PORTER FELLOWSHIP
FOR MINORITY INVESTIGATORS

Woods Hole Marine Biological Laboratory
Attn: Research Award Coordinator
7 MBL Street
Woods Hole, MA 02543-1015
(508) 289-7171   Fax: (508) 457-1924
E-mail: researchawards@mbl.edu
Web: www.mbl.edu/research/summer/awards_general.html

Summary To support African American and other underrepresented minority scientists who wish to conduct research during the summer at the Woods Hole Marine Biological Laboratory (MBL).

Eligibility This program is open to young scientists (senior graduate students and postdoctoral trainees) who are from an underrepresented minority group (African American, Hispanic American, or Native American), are U.S. citizens or permanent residents, and are interested in conducting research with senior investigators at MBL. Fields of study include, but are not limited to, cell biology, developmental biology, ecology, evolution, microbiology, neurobiology, physiology, and tissue engineering.

Financial data Participants receive a stipend and a travel allowance. Recently, grants averaged approximately $1,500.

Duration At least 6 weeks during the summer.

Additional information This fellowship was first awarded in 1921. Funding is provided by the Harvard Apparatus Foundation.

Number awarded 1 or more each year.

Deadline December of each year.

[1290]
WILLIAM W. GRIMES AWARD FOR EXCELLENCE
IN CHEMICAL ENGINEERING

American Institute of Chemical Engineers
Attn: Minority Affairs Committee
Three Park Avenue
New York, NY 10016-5991
(646) 495-1348   Fax: (646) 495-1504
E-mail: awards@aiche.org
Web: www.aiche.org

Summary To recognize and reward chemical engineers who serve as a role model for African American students.

Eligibility Members of the American Institute of Chemical Engineers (AIChE) may nominate any individual who serves as a role model for African Americans in chemical engineering. Nominees must be chemical engineers who have demonstrated outstanding technical, business, or related achievements and have voluntarily given time and effort to help increase the interest and/or performance of members of underrepresented minority groups in science, mathematics, engineering, and related areas in either an educational or business environment.

Financial data The award consists of a plaque and $1,000, plus a $500 travel allowance to attend the AIChE annual meeting where the award is presented.

Duration The award is presented annually.

Additional information The Minority Affairs Committee has presented this award in honor of William W. Grimes, the first African American Fellow of AIChE, since 1995.

Number awarded 1 each year.

Deadline Nominations must be submitted by June of each year.

[1291]
YERBY POSTDOCTORAL FELLOWSHIP
PROGRAM

Harvard School of Public Health
Attn: Office of Faculty Affairs
635 Huntington Avenue, Second Floor
Boston, MA 02115
(617) 432-1047   Fax: (617) 432-4711
E-mail: facultyaffairs@hsph.harvard.edu
Web: www.hsph.harvard.edu

Summary To provide an opportunity for African American and other minority or disadvantaged postdoctorates to pursue a program of research training at Harvard School of Public Health.

Eligibility This program is open to 1) members of minority groups underrepresented in public health (American Indians or Alaska Natives, Blacks or African Americans, Hispanics or Latinos, and Native Hawaiians or other Pacific Islanders); 2) individuals from socioeconomically disadvantaged backgrounds; and 3) others whose background will contribute to academic diversity. Applicants must have a doctoral degree and be interested in preparing for a career in public health. They must submit 3 letters of recommendation; a curriculum vitae; a proposal for research to be undertaken during the fellowship; a statement of professional objectives in academic public health, including how those objectives would be advanced by research opportunities at HSPH; and a sample publication.

Financial data Fellows receive a competitive salary.

Duration 1 year; may be renewed 1 additional year.

Additional information Fellows are associated with a faculty mentor who assists in the transition to an academic career. With the help of the faculty mentor, fellows develop their research agendas, gain experience in publishing papers in peer-reviewed journals and in obtaining grant support, participate in a variety of professional development workshops, and increase their teaching expertise.

Number awarded Up to 5 each year.

Deadline October of each year.

[1292]
ZENITH FELLOWS AWARD PROGRAM

Alzheimer's Association
Attn: Medical and Scientific Affairs
225 North Michigan Avenue, 17th Floor
Chicago, IL 60601-7633
(312) 335-5747   Toll Free: (800) 272-3900
Fax: (866) 699-1246   TDD: (312) 335-5886
E-mail: grantsapp@alz.org
Web: www.alz.org

Summary To provide funding to established investigators (particularly African Americans and other minorities) who are interested in conducting advanced research on Alzheimer's Disease.

Eligibility Eligible are scientists who have already contributed significantly to the field of Alzheimer's Disease research and are likely to continue to make significant contributions for many years to come. The proposed research must be "on the cutting edge" of basic, biomedical research and may not fit current conventional scientific wisdom or may challenge the prevailing orthodoxy. It should address fundamental problems related to early detection, etiology, pathogenesis, treatment, and/or prevention of Alzheimer's Disease. Scientists from underrepresented groups are especially encouraged to apply.

Financial data Grants up to $250,000 per year, including direct expenses and up to 10% for overhead costs, are available. The total award for the life of the grant may not exceed $450,000.

Duration 2 or 3 years.

Additional information This program was established in 1991.

Number awarded Up to 4 each year.

Deadline Letters of intent must be submitted by the end of December of each year. Final applications are due in February.

Indexes

Program Title Index ●

Sponsoring Organization Index ●

Residency Index ●

Tenability Index ●

Subject Index ●

Calendar Index ●

Program Title Index

If you know the name of a particular funding program open to African Americans and want to find out where it is covered in the directory, use the Program Title Index. Here, program titles are arranged alphabetically, word by word. To assist you in your search, every program is listed by all its known names or abbreviations. In addition, we've used an alphabetical code (within parentheses) to help you determine if the program is aimed at you: U = Undergraduates;   G = Graduate Students;   P = Professionals/Postdoctorates. Here's how the code works: if a program is followed by (U) 241, the program is described in the Undergraduates section, in entry 241. If the same program title is followed by another entry number—for example, (P) 1101—the program is also described in the Professionals/Postdoctorates section, in entry 1101. Remember: the numbers cited here refer to program entry numbers, not to page numbers in the book.

Alfred M. Greenfield Foundation Fellowships in African American History, (G) 614, (P) 1091

Alfred P. Sloan Foundation Research Fellowships, (P) 1092

Algood Scholarship. *See* Emma and Meloid Algood Scholarship, entry (U) 172

Allan Murphy Endowed Memorial Scholarship. *See* Ethan and Allan Murphy Endowed Memorial Scholarship, entry (U) 176

Allen Scholarships. *See* Edith M. Allen Scholarships, entries (U) 163, (G) 738

Allison E. Fisher Scholarship, (U) 14, (G) 615

Alma Exley Scholarship, (U) 15

Alpha Kappa Alpha Endowment Awards, (U) 16, (G) 616

Alpha Kappa Alpha Graduate Scholarships, (G) 617

Alpha Kappa Alpha Undergraduate Scholarships, (U) 17

Alpha Phi Alpha Fraternity Scholarships, (U) 18, (G) 618

Alphonso Deal Scholarship Award, (U) 19

Altria Scholarships of the Thurgood Marshall College Fund, (U) 20

Alumni Extension Technical Scholarships, (G) 619

Alzheimer's Association Investigator-Initiated Research Grants, (P) 1093

Alzheimer's Association New Investigator Research Grants, (P) 1094

AMA Foundation Minority Scholars Awards, (G) 620

AME Church Preacher's Kid Scholarship, (U) 21

American Academy of Child and Adolescent Psychiatry-National Institute on Drug Abuse Career Development Award. *See* AACAP-NIDA Career Development Award, entry (P) 1082

American Advertising Federation Lincoln Cultural Diversity Scholarship. *See* Lincoln Cultural Diversity Scholarship, entry (U) 314

American Association for the Advancement of Science Minority Science Writers Internship. *See* Minority Science Writers Internship, entry (U) 368

American Association of Blacks in Energy National Scholarships, (U) 22

American Association of Obstetricians and Gynecologists Foundation Scholarships, (P) 1095

American Association of University Women Career Development Grants. *See* Career Development Grants, entries (U) 75, (G) 667, (P) 1116

American Bar Association Judicial Intern Opportunity Program. *See* Judicial Intern Opportunity Program, entry (G) 855

American Bar Association Legal Opportunity Scholarship, (G) 621

American Chemical Society Scholars Program, (U) 23

American Council of Learned Societies Collaborative Research Fellowships. *See* Collaborative Research Fellowships, entry (P) 1127

American Council of Learned Societies Digital Innovation Fellowships. *See* Digital Innovation Fellowships, entry (P) 1142

American Council of Learned Societies Dissertation Completion Fellowships. *See* Andrew W. Mellon Foundation/ACLS Dissertation Completion Fellowships, entry (G) 626

American Council of Learned Societies Dissertation Fellowships in American Art. *See* Henry Luce Foundation/ACLS Dissertation Fellowships in American Art, entry (G) 815

American Council of Learned Societies Fellowships, (P) 1096

American Council of Learned Societies Recent Doctoral Recipients Fellowships. *See* Andrew W. Mellon Foundation/ACLS Recent Doctoral Recipients Fellowships, entry (P) 1100

American Council of Learned Societies/SSRC/NEH International and Area Studies Fellowships. *See* International and Area Studies Fellowships, entry (P) 1189

American Dietetic Association Graduate Scholarships, (G) 622

American Educational Research Association Dissertation Grants Program<GX>Foreign countries. *See* AERA Dissertation Grants Program, entry (G) 606

American Educational Research Association Grants Program, (P) 1097

American Educational Research Association-American Institutes for Research Fellows Program. *See* AIR Fellows Program, entry (P) 1088

American Educational Research Association-Educational Testing Service Fellowship Program in Measurement. *See* Fellowship Program in Measurement, entry (P) 1167

American Gastroenterological Association Research Scholar Awards, (P) 1098

American Health Information Management Association Foundation Diversity Scholarships. *See* AHIMA Foundation Diversity Scholarships, entry (U) 10

American Institute of Certified Public Accountants Fellowships for Minority Doctoral Students. *See* Fellowships for Minority Doctoral Students, entry (G) 764

American Institutes for Research Fellows Program. *See* AIR Fellows Program, entry (P) 1088

American Medical Association Foundation Minority Scholars Awards. *See* AMA Foundation Minority Scholars Awards, entry (G) 620

American Meteorological Society Undergraduate Named Scholarships, (U) 24

American Nuclear Society Accelerator Applications Division Scholarship. *See* ANS Accelerator Applications Division Scholarship, entry (U) 28

American Orchid Society Graduate Fellowship. *See* Furniss Foundation/AOS Graduate Fellowship, entry (G) 783

American Orchid Society/Norman's Orchids Masters Scholarship. *See* AOS/Norman's Orchids Masters Scholarship, entry (G) 628

American Planning Association Planning Fellowships. *See* APA Planning Fellowships, entry (G) 630

American Political Science Association Minority Fellows Program, (G) 623

American Psychiatric Association Minority Medical Student Summer Mentoring Program. *See* APA Minority Medical Student Summer Mentoring Program, entry (G) 629

American Psychiatric Association/SAMSHA Minority Fellowship Program. *See* APA/SAMHSA Minority Fellowship Program, entry (P) 1102

American School Counselor Association Foundation Scholarships. *See* ASCA Foundation Scholarships, entry (G) 639

American Society for Cell Biology Minorities Affairs Committee Visiting Professor Awards, (P) 1099

American Society for Microbiology Minority Undergraduate Research Fellowship. *See* Microbiology Undergraduate Research Fellowship, entry (U) 353

American Society of Civil Engineers Maine Section Scholarship. *See* Maine Section Scholarship, entry (U) 329

American Society of Clinical Oncology Medical Student Rotation. *See* ASCO Medical Student Rotation, entry (G) 640

American Society of Hematology-Amos Medical Faculty Development Program Research Grants. *See* ASH-AMFDP Research Grants, entry (P) 1105

American Society of Landscape Architecture Council of Fellows Scholarships. *See* ASLA Council of Fellows Scholarships, entry (U) 34

American Society of Safety Engineers Diversity Committee Scholarship. *See* Diversity Committee Scholarship, entries (U) 150, (G) 720

American Society of Safety Engineers UPS Diversity Scholarships. *See* ASSE UPS Diversity Scholarships, entry (U) 35

American Sociological Association Minority Fellowship Program General Fellowship. *See* ASA Minority Fellowship Program General Fellowship, entry (G) 638

American Speech-Language-Hearing Foundation Scholarship for Minority Students, (G) 624

ANA Multicultural Excellence Scholarship, (U) 25

Anapata Diversity Scholarship Contest, (G) 625

Andersen Memorial Scholarships. *See* Hugh J. Andersen Memorial Scholarships, entry (G) 819

Anderson Scholarship Award. *See* Irlet Anderson Scholarship Award, entry (U) 259

Anderson Scholarship in Space Science. *See* Michael P. Anderson Scholarship in Space Science, entry (U) 350

Andrew W. Mellon Foundation/ACLS Dissertation Completion Fellowships, (G) 626

Andrew W. Mellon Foundation/ACLS Recent Doctoral Recipients Fellowships, (P) 1100

Angela E. Randall Scholarship. *See* Sigma Gamma Rho Scholarships/Fellowships, entries (U) 503, (G) 1017

Angela Paez Memorial Scholarship. *See* Seattle Chapter AWIS Scholarships, entry (U) 495

Anna Johnson Scholarships. *See* Clanseer and Anna Johnson Scholarships, entry (U) 103

Anna M. Winston Award, (U) 26, (G) 627

Annie B. and L. Essex Moseley Scholarship Fund, (U) 27

ANS Accelerator Applications Division Scholarship, (U) 28

ANSP Research Experiences for Undergraduates Fellowships, (U) 29

Antarctic Research Program, (P) 1101

Anzaldúa Book Prize. *See* Gloria E. Anzaldúa Book Prize, entry (P) 1179

AOS Graduate Fellowship. *See* Furniss Foundation/AOS Graduate Fellowship, entry (G) 783

AOS/Norman's Orchids Masters Scholarship, (G) 628

APA Minority Medical Student Summer Mentoring Program, (G) 629

APA Planning Fellowships, (G) 630

APA/SAMHSA Minority Fellowship Program, (P) 1102

Arctic Research Opportunities, (P) 1103

Arent Fox Diversity Scholarships, (G) 631

Arkansas Conference Ethnic Local Church Concerns Scholarships, (U) 30, (G) 632

Arkansas Minority Masters Fellows Program, (G) 633

Arkansas Minority Teachers Scholarships, (U) 31

ARL Career Enhancement Program, (G) 634

ARL Initiative to Recruit a Diverse Workforce, (G) 635

Armstrong Scholars Award. *See* Byron K. Armstrong Scholars Award, entry (U) 69

Army Judge Advocate General Corps Summer Intern Program, (G) 636

Army Minority College Relations Program Internships, (U) 32, (G) 637

Army Research Laboratory Broad Agency Announcement, (P) 1104

Arnstein Minority Student Scholarship. *See* Sherry R. Arnstein Minority Student Scholarship, entry (G) 1013

Arnstein New Student Minority Student Scholarship. *See* Sherry R. Arnstein New Student Minority Student Scholarship, entry (G) 1014

Arthur B.C. Walker Scholarship, (U) 33

ASA Minority Fellowship Program General Fellowship, (G) 638

ASCA Foundation Scholarships, (G) 639

ASCO Medical Student Rotation, (G) 640

ASH-AMFDP Research Grants, (P) 1105

ASLA Council of Fellows Scholarships, (U) 34

ASSE UPS Diversity Scholarships, (U) 35

Associated Food and Petroleum Dealers Minority Scholarships, (U) 36

Association for Women Geoscientists Minority Scholarship. *See* AWG Minority Scholarship, entry (U) 38

Association for Women in Science Internships. *See* AWIS Internships, entry (U) 39

Association for Women in Science Seattle Scholarships. *See* Seattle Chapter AWIS Scholarships, entry (U) 495

Association of National Advertisers Multicultural Excellence Scholarship. *See* ANA Multicultural Excellence Scholarship, entry (U) 25

Association of Research Libraries Career Enhancement Program. *See* ARL Career Enhancement Program, entry (G) 634

Association of Research Libraries Initiative to Recruit a Diverse Workforce. *See* ARL Initiative to Recruit a Diverse Workforce, entry (G) 635

Astronomy and Astrophysics Postdoctoral Fellowships, (P) 1106

Atherton Ministerial Scholarship. *See* Martha and Robert Atherton Ministerial Scholarship, entry (G) 891

Atkinson Legal Education Scholarship. *See* Dorothy Atkinson Legal Education Scholarship, entry (G) 726

Atmospheric and Geospace Sciences Postdoctoral Research Fellowships, (P) 1107

AT&T Laboratories Fellowship Program, (G) 641

Award for Excellence in Business Commentary, (U) 37

Awards for Faculty at Historically Black Colleges and Universities, (P) 1108

AWG Minority Scholarship, (U) 38

AWIS Internships, (U) 39

Axelrod Mentorship Award. *See* Julius Axelrod Mentorship Award, entry (P) 1201

B

Baker Corporation Scholarship Program for Diversity in Engineering. *See* Michael Baker Corporation Scholarship Program for Diversity in Engineering, entry (U) 349

Baker & Daniels Diversity Scholarships, (G) 642

Baker Donelson Diversity Scholarships, (G) 643

Baker Hostetler Diversity Fellowship Program, (G) 644

Baker Hughes Scholarships, (U) 40, (G) 645

Balfour Phi Delta Phi Minority Scholarship Program, (G) 646

Banks Scholarship in Astronomy. *See* Harvey Washington Banks Scholarship in Astronomy, entry (U) 219

Banner Diversity Scholarship. *See* Donald W. Banner Diversity Scholarship, entry (G) 725

Banner Scholarship for Law Students. *See* Mark T. Banner Scholarship for Law Students, entry (G) 890

Barbara Jordan Historical Essay Competition, (U) 41

Barbara Jordan Memorial Scholarships, (U) 42, (G) 647

Barrow Minority Doctoral Student Scholarship. *See* Lionel C. Barrow Minority Doctoral Student Scholarship, entry (G) 878

Batson Scholarships. *See* Ruth M. Batson Scholarships, entry (U) 482

Battelle Collegiate Scholarships, (U) 43

Battelle High School Scholarship Program, (U) 44

Bauer Memorial Scholarship. *See* Black Women Lawyers Association of Los Angeles Scholarships, entry (G) 656

Baxter Healthcare Corporation Scholarship. *See* Black Women Lawyers Association of Los Angeles Scholarships, entry (G) 656

BB&T Charitable Foundation Scholarship Program of the Hispanic Scholarship Fund, (U) 45

BDPA Oracle Scholarship, (U) 46

Bechtel Undergraduate Fellowship Award, (U) 47

Beckett Scholarship. *See* Dr. Joyce Beckett Scholarship, entry (G) 730

Behavioral Sciences Postdoctoral Fellowships in Epilepsy, (P) 1109

Behavioral Sciences Student Fellowships in Epilepsy, (U) 48, (G) 648

Belle Scholarships. *See* Bernadine Johnson Marshall-Martha Belle Scholarships, entry (G) 649

Bemley Scholarship. *See* Dr. Jesse Bemley Scholarship, entry (U) 155

Bendix Minorities in Engineering Award. *See* DuPont Minorities in Engineering Award, entry (P) 1145

Benjamin Banneker Chapter Scholarship, (U) 49

Benjamin T. Hacker, USN Memorial Scholarship. *See* Rear Admiral Benjamin T. Hacker, USN Memorial Scholarship, entry (U) 459

Bernadine Johnson Marshall-Martha Belle Scholarships, (G) 649

Bernard Harris Math and Science Scholarships, (U) 50

Bernbach Diversity Scholarships. *See* Bill Bernbach Diversity Scholarships, entry (G) 652

Bertha Pitts Campbell Scholarship Program, (U) 51

BESLA General Scholarship Fund, (G) 650

BESLA Legal Writing Competition, (G) 651

Bethea Scholarships. *See* Bishop Joseph B. Bethea Scholarships, entry (U) 54

Bethune Scholarships. *See* Mary McLeod Bethune Scholarships, entry (U) 339

Beyond Margins Award, (P) 1110

Bill Bernbach Diversity Scholarships, (G) 652

Biomedical Research Training Program for Underrepresented Groups, (U) 52, (G) 653

Birmingham Chapter AABE Scholarships, (U) 53

Bishop Joseph B. Bethea Scholarships, (U) 54

Bishop T. Larry Kirkland Scholarship of Excellence, (U) 55

Bishop Thomas Hoyt, Jr. Fellowship, (G) 654

Black Data Processing Associates Oracle Scholarship. *See* BDPA Oracle Scholarship, entry (U) 46

Black Entertainment and Sports Lawyers Association General Scholarship Fund. *See* BESLA General Scholarship Fund, entry (G) 650

Black Entertainment and Sports Lawyers Association Legal Writing Competition. *See* BESLA Legal Writing Competition, entry (G) 651

Black Filmmaker Showcase, (P) 1111

Black Women in Entertainment Law Student Scholarship, (G) 655

Black Women Lawyers Association of Los Angeles Scholarships, (G) 656

Blacks at Microsoft Scholarships, (U) 56

Blacks in Safety Engineering Scholarship, (U) 57

Blanca Moore-Velez Woman of Substance Scholarship. *See* Dr. Blanca Moore-Velez Woman of Substance Scholarship, entry (U) 154

Blanding Memorial Scholarship. *See* Jessica M. Blanding Memorial Scholarship, entries (U) 274, (P) 1195

Blassingame Award. *See* John W. Blassingame Award, entry (P) 1199

Blitman, P.E. Scholarship to Promote Diversity in Engineering. *See* Maureen L. and Howard N. Blitman, P.E. Scholarship to Promote Diversity in Engineering, entry (U) 343

Board of Corporate Affiliates Scholars Awards, (U) 58, (G) 657

Bob Glahn Scholarship in Statistical Meteorology, (U) 59

Bob Stanley Minority and International Scholarship. *See* Alan Compton and Bob Stanley Minority and International Scholarship, entry (U) 13

Bolden Minority Scholarship. *See* Ethel Bolden Minority Scholarship, entry (G) 752

Bolin Dissertation and Post-MFA Fellowships. *See* Gaius Charles Bolin Dissertation and Post-MFA Fellowships, entries (G) 786, (P) 1175

Booker T. Washington Scholarships, (U) 60

Boone Memorial Scholarship. *See* Washington, D.C. Chapter Scholarship Program, entry (U) 572

Boone Memorial Scholarships. *See* Ester Boone Memorial Scholarships, entry (U) 175

Borders Jr. Justice Scholarship. *See* William A. Borders Jr. Justice Scholarship, entry (U) 580

Boston Alumnae Chapter Scholarships, (U) 61

Boston University Research Experience for Undergraduates in Biophotonics, (U) 62

Bouchet Award. *See* Edward A. Bouchet Award, entry (P) 1151

Bouchet Scholarships. *See* Promising Scholars Fund Edward A. Bouchet Scholarships, entry (U) 445

Bowman Foundation Knights of Columbus Scholarships. *See* Sister Thea Bowman Foundation Knights of Columbus Scholarships, entry (U) 504

Boyd/Robin Stone Scholarship. *See* Gerald Boyd/Robin Stone Scholarship, entries (U) 202, (G) 796

Boyer Scholarship. *See* BESLA General Scholarship Fund, entry (G) 650

BP NSBE Corporate Scholarship Program, (U) 63

Bradley Fellowship Program. *See* Dan Bradley Fellowship Program, entry (G) 698

Bradley Scholarship. *See* Ed Bradley Scholarship, entry (U) 162, 497

Breakthrough to Nursing Scholarships, (U) 64, (G) 658

Bro. Dr. Frank T. Simpson Scholarships, (U) 65

Brock Memorial Scholarship. *See* Cathy L. Brock Memorial Scholarship, entry (G) 671

Brookhaven National Laboratory Science and Engineering Programs for Women and Minorities, (U) 66

Brotman Student Research Fellowship Awards. *See* Stuart Brotman Student Research Fellowship Awards, entry (U) 513

Brown and Caldwell Minority Scholarship, (U) 67

Brown and Max Kapp Award. *See* Olympia Brown and Max Kapp Award, entry (G) 954

Brown COREM Scholarships. *See* Richard and Helen Brown COREM Scholarships, entry (G) 991

Brown Scholarship in Physics. *See* Charles S. Brown Scholarship in Physics, entries (U) 93, (G) 679

Brown Scholarships. *See* Hallie Q. Brown Scholarships, entry (U) 210

Buick Achievers Scholarship Program, (U) 68

Crumbly Minorities in Energy Grant. *See* Isaac J. "Ike" Crumbly Minorities in Energy Grant, entry (G) 835

CSLA Leadership for Diversity Scholarship, (U) 126, (G) 692

CSPI Public Interest Internship Program, (U) 127, (G) 693

CUFA Inquiry Grant. *See* FASSE/CUFA Inquiry Grant, entries (G) 761, (P) 1165

Cultural Resources Diversity Internship Program, (U) 128, (G) 694

Cummins NSBE Corporate Scholarship Program, (U) 129

Cummins Scholarships, (U) 130, (G) 695

Curls, Sr. Scholarship. *See* Phil B. Curls, Sr. Scholarship, entries (U) 435, (G) 969

Current, Sr. Scholarship. *See* Gloster B. Current, Sr. Scholarship, entry (U) 205

Curriculum Development, Implementation, and Sustainability Grants, (P) 1133

Cutler Fellowship in Consumer Studies. *See* Cutler-DeKnight National Graduate Fellowship, entry (G) 696

Cutler-DeKnight National Graduate Fellowship, (G) 696

Cynthia J. Hickman "Pay It Forward" Scholarship. *See* National Black Nurses Association Scholarships, entry (U) 398

D

D. Augustus Straker Scholarship, (G) 697

Damon P. Moore Scholarship, (U) 131

Dan Bradley Fellowship Program, (G) 698

Daniel H. Efron Research Award, (P) 1134

Daniel Kovach Foundation Minority Student Scholarship. *See* College Scholarships Foundation Minority Student Scholarship, entries (U) 110, (G) 682

Dargan Scholarship. *See* KATU Thomas R. Dargan Scholarship, entry (U) 294

Darlene Clark Hine Award, (P) 1135

David A. DeBolt Teacher Shortage Scholarship Program. *See* Illinois Future Teacher Corps Program, entry (U) 245

David and Sheila Garnett Leadership Scholarship, (U) 132

David Hilliard Eaton Scholarship, (G) 699

David Pohl Scholarship. *See* UUA/David Pohl Scholarship, entry (G) 1055

David Sankey Minority Scholarship in Meteorology, (U) 133, (G) 700

David W. Long Memorial Scholarship. *See* Robert A. Catlin/David W. Long Memorial Scholarship, entry (G) 993

Davis & Davis Scholarship, (U) 134

Davis/McKinney Scholarship. *See* Maude Davis/Joseph C. McKinney Scholarship, entry (U) 342

Davis Memorial Scholarship. *See* Louise Jane Moses/Agnes Davis Memorial Scholarship, entries (U) 319, (G) 881

Davis Scholarship. *See* Raymond R. Davis Scholarship, entry (U) 457, (G) 996

Davis Scholarship Award. *See* Washington, D.C. Chapter Scholarship Program, entry (U) 572

Davis Wright Tremaine 1L Diversity Scholarship Program, (G) 701

Dawson Genesis Scholarship. *See* National Black Nurses Association Scholarships, entry (U) 398

DCBMBAA Chapter Graduate Scholarship Program, (G) 702

DCBMBAA Chapter Undergraduate Scholarship Program, (U) 135

DCNNOA/General Dynamics Scholarship, (U) 136

de Merieux Rheumatology Fellowship Award. *See* Paula de Merieux Rheumatology Fellowship Award, entry (P) 1251

Deal Scholarship Award. *See* Alphonso Deal Scholarship Award, entry (U) 19

DeBolt Teacher Shortage Scholarship Program. *See* Illinois Future Teacher Corps Program, entry (U) 245

Defense Intelligence Agency Undergraduate Training Assistance Program, (U) 137

Defense University Research Instrumentation Program, (P) 1136

DeKnight National Fellowship. *See* Cutler-DeKnight National Graduate Fellowship, entry (G) 696

Dell Thurmond Woodard Fellowship, (U) 138, (G) 703

Delphi NSBE Corporate Scholarships, (U) 139, (G) 704

Delta Sigma Theta Sorority General Scholarships, (U) 140, (G) 705

Department of Agriculture 1890 National Scholars Program. *See* USDA/1890 National Scholars Program, entry (U) 552

Department of Defense Experimental Program to Stimulate Competitive Research, (P) 1137

Department of Energy Thurgood Marshall College Fund Scholarships, (U) 141

Department of Homeland Security Small Business Innovation Research Grants, (P) 1138

Department of Homeland Security Summer Faculty and Student Research Team Program, (U) 142, (G) 706, (P) 1139

Department of State Student Intern Program, (U) 143, (G) 707

Department of the Interior Diversity Intern Program, (U) 144, (G) 708

Department of Transportation Small Business Innovation Research Grants, (P) 1140

Derricotte Scholarship. *See* Juliette Derricotte Scholarship, entry (G) 858

Detroit Chapter NBMBAA Graduate Scholarship, (G) 709

Detroit Chapter NBMBAA Undergraduate Scholarship, (U) 145

The Development Fund for Black Students in Science and Technology Scholarships, (U) 530

DeVerne Calloway Scholarship, (U) 146

Dickstein Shapiro Diversity Scholarship, (G) 710

Dietetic Internship Scholarships, (G) 711, (P) 1141

Dietetic Technician Program Scholarships, (U) 147

Digital Innovation Fellowships, (P) 1142

Dinsmore & Shohl LLP Diversity Scholarship Program, (G) 712

Dissertation Fellowship for African-American Scholars. *See* Thurgood Marshall Dissertation Fellowship for African-American Scholars, entry (G) 1041

Dissertation Fellowships in East European Studies, (G) 713

Dissertation Fellowships of the Ford Foundation Diversity Fellowship Program, (G) 714

Dissertation Fellowships of the Minority Scholar-in-Residence Program, (G) 715

Dissertation Proposal Development Fellowship Program, (G) 716

Dissertation Year Visiting Diversity Fellowships for Advanced Graduate Students, (G) 717

District and International Scholar of the Year Awards, (U) 148

District of Columbia Black MBA Association Chapter Graduate Scholarship Program. *See* DCBMBAA Chapter Graduate Scholarship Program, entry (G) 702

District of Columbia Black MBA Association Chapter Undergraduate Scholarship Program. *See* DCBMBAA Chapter Undergraduate Scholarship Program, entry (U) 135

District of Columbia Chapter AABE Scholarships, (U) 149

District of Columbia National Naval Officers Association/General Dynamics Scholarship. *See* DCNNOA/General Dynamics Scholarship, entry (U) 136

District of Columbia-ELI Diversity Fellowships in Environmental Law, (G) 718

Diversified Investment Advisors Leaders in Healthcare Scholarship, (G) 719

Graves Scholarship. *See* Earl G. Graves Scholarship, entries (U) 161, (G) 734

Greater Hartford Chapter NBMBAA Graduate Scholarship, (G) 805

Green Scholarship. *See* Esther Ngan-ling Chow and Mareyjoyce Green Scholarship, entry (G) 751

Greene Scholarship. *See* Washington, D.C. Chapter Scholarship Program, entry (U) 572

Greenwood Scholarship. *See* William Rucker Greenwood Scholarship, entries (U) 583, (G) 1072

H

Hacker, USN Memorial Scholarship. *See* Rear Admiral Benjamin T. Hacker, USN Memorial Scholarship, entry (U) 459

Hailey AAJ Law Student Scholarships. *See* Richard D. Hailey AAJ Law Student Scholarships, entry (G) 992

Haitian American Nurses Association Scholarships, (U) 209

Hallie Q. Brown Scholarships, (U) 210

Hamilton Award for Lifetime Achievement/Author-Illustrator Category. *See* Coretta Scott King-Virginia Hamilton Award for Lifetime Achievement/Author-Illustrator Category, entry (P) 1131

Hamilton Award for Lifetime Achievement/Practitioner Category. *See* Coretta Scott King-Virginia Hamilton Award for Lifetime Achievement/Practitioner Category, entry (P) 1132

Hampton Roads Black Media Professionals Scholarships, (U) 211, (G) 806

Handy Simmons Scholarship, (U) 212

Harold Hayden Memorial Scholarship, (U) 213

Harriett G. Jenkins Pre-doctoral Fellowship Program, (G) 807

Harris Math and Science Scholarships. *See* Bernard Harris Math and Science Scholarships, entry (U) 50

Harris Scholarship. *See* Frances W. Harris Scholarship, entry (U) 188

Harry L. Morrison Scholarship, (U) 214

Harry R. Kendall Leadership Development Scholarships, (U) 215, (G) 808, (P) 1180

Harvard Medical School Summer Honors Undergraduate Research Program, (U) 216

Harvard School of Public Health Summer Program in Biological Sciences in Public Health, (U) 217

Harvard-Smithsonian Center for Astrophysics Solar REU Program, (U) 218

Harvey Washington Banks Scholarship in Astronomy, (U) 219

Hawaii Diversity Fellowships in Environmental Law, (G) 809

Hayden Memorial Scholarship. *See* Harold Hayden Memorial Scholarship, entry (U) 213

Haynes/Hetting Award, (U) 220, (G) 810

HBCU Scholarships, (U) 221

HBCUConnect Member Scholarships, (U) 222

HDR Engineering Scholarship for Diversity in Engineering, (U) 223

Health and Aging Policy Fellowships, (P) 1181

Health Research and Educational Trust Scholarships, (U) 224, (G) 811

Health Sciences Student Fellowships in Epilepsy, (G) 812

Heard Jr. Memorial Scholarship. *See* Elliott G. Heard Jr. Memorial Scholarship, entry (G) 746

Hearst Endowment Scholarships. *See* William Randolph Hearst Endowment Scholarships, entry (U) 582

Heckert Fellowship. *See* Richard Heckert Fellowship, entry (U) 468

Heineken USA Performing Arts Scholarship, (U) 225, (G) 813

Helen Brown COREM Scholarships. *See* Richard and Helen Brown COREM Scholarships, entry (G) 991

Helen Karas Memorial Fellowship. *See* IRTS Summer Fellowship Program, entries (U) 260, (G) 834

Helen T. Carr Fellowships, (G) 814, (P) 1182

Hemmings Scholarship. *See* Myra Davis Hemmings Scholarship, entry (G) 919

Henry Arthur Callis Scholarship Fund, (U) 226

Henry Luce Foundation/ACLS Dissertation Fellowships in American Art, (G) 815

Herbert Lehman Education Fund, (U) 227

Herman S. Dreer Scholarship/Leadership Award, (U) 228

Hickman "Pay It Forward" Scholarship. *See* National Black Nurses Association Scholarships, entry (U) 398

Higgins Scholarship. *See* Sigma Gamma Rho Scholarships/Fellowships, entries (U) 503, (G) 1017

High Priority, Short-Term Bridge Awards in Diabetes Research, (P) 1183

High Risk Research in Anthropology Grants, (P) 1184

Hilda Richards Scholarship. *See* National Black Nurses Association Scholarships, entry (U) 398

Hill Scholarship. *See* Oliver W. Hill Scholarship, entry (G) 953

Hillis Clark Martin & Peterson Diversity Fellowship, (G) 816

Hilton Worldwide NSBE Corporate Scholarship Program, (U) 229

Hine Award. *See* Darlene Clark Hine Award, entry (P) 1135

Historically Black College Scholarships, (U) 230

Historically Black Colleges and Universities Scholarships. *See* HBCU Scholarships, entry (U) 221

HIV Medicine Association Minority Clinical Fellowships. *See* HIVMA Minority Clinical Fellowships, entry (P) 1185

HIVMA Minority Clinical Fellowships, (P) 1185

Hoch Distinguished Service Award. *See* Paul Hoch Distinguished Service Award, entry (P) 1249

Holy Family Memorial Scholarship Program, (U) 231

Honeywell International Scholarships, (U) 232

Honorable Ernestine Washington Library Science/English Language Arts Scholarship, (U) 233

Hood Jr. Scholarship. *See* LoVette Hood Jr. Scholarship, entry (U) 321

Horace and Susie Revels Cayton Scholarship, (U) 234

Houston Bar Association Annual Scholarship. *See* Charles Houston Bar Association Annual Scholarship, entry (G) 678

Houston Memorial Scholarship. *See* Jerry Morris and Summer Houston Memorial Scholarship, entry (U) 273

Houston Sun Scholarship, (U) 235

Howard N. Blitman, P.E. Scholarship to Promote Diversity in Engineering. *See* Maureen L. and Howard N. Blitman, P.E. Scholarship to Promote Diversity in Engineering, entry (U) 343

Howard Scholarship. *See* Rear Admiral Michelle Howard Scholarship, entry (U) 461

Howell Scholarship. *See* Fletcher Mae Howell Scholarship, entry (G) 770

Hoyt, Jr. Fellowship. *See* Bishop Thomas Hoyt, Jr. Fellowship, entry (G) 654

Hubble Fellowships, (P) 1186

Hubertus W.V. Willems Scholarship for Male Students, (U) 236, (G) 817

Huggins-Quarles Award, (G) 818

Hugh J. Andersen Memorial Scholarships, (G) 819

Hurston/Wright Award for College Writers, (U) 237, (G) 820

Hurston/Wright Legacy Award, (P) 1187

Mendenhall Fellowships. *See* Five College Fellowship Program, entry (G) 769

Mental Health Dissertation Research Grant to Increase Diversity, (G) 899

Mentor-Based Minority Postdoctoral Fellowships in Diabetes, (P) 1216

Mentored New Investigator Research Grants to Promote Diversity of the Alzheimer's Association, (P) 1217

Mentorship for Environmental Scholars, (U) 348

Mercer Scholarship. *See* Carmen Mercer Scholarship, entry (U) 78

Merck Graduate Science Research Dissertation Fellowships. *See* UNCF/Merck Graduate Science Research Dissertation Fellowships, entry (G) 1049

Merck Postdoctoral Science Research Fellowships. *See* UNCF/Merck Postdoctoral Science Research Fellowships, entry (P) 1281

Merck Undergraduate Science Research Scholarships. *See* UNCF/Merck Undergraduate Science Research Scholarships, entry (U) 542

Meshack Memorial Scholarship. *See* Black Women Lawyers Association of Los Angeles Scholarships, entry (G) 656

Metropolitan Life Foundation Awards Program for Academic Excellence in Medicine, (G) 900

Michael Baker Corporation Scholarship Program for Diversity in Engineering, (U) 349

Michael P. Anderson Scholarship in Space Science, (U) 350

Michelle Howard Scholarship. *See* Rear Admiral Michelle Howard Scholarship, entry (U) 461

Michigan Chapter AABE Scholarships, (U) 351

Mickey Leland Energy Fellowships, (U) 352, (G) 901, (P) 1218

Microbiology Undergraduate Research Fellowship, (U) 353

Midwest Conference Women's Missionary Society Youth Education Scholarship Award, (U) 354

Mike Shinn Distinguished Member of the Year Awards, (U) 355, (G) 902

Milbank Diversity Scholars Program, (G) 903

Mildred Barry Garvin Prize, (P) 1219

Mildred Collins Nursing/Health Science/Medicine Scholarship, (U) 356

Mildred Towle Scholarship for African Americans, (U) 357

Miller Award. *See* Mark Miller Award, entries (U) 333, (G) 889

Miller Brewing Company Scholarship. *See* N. Joyce Payne/Miller Brewing Company Scholarship, entry (U) 380

Miller/Curry/Jackson Leadership and Excellence Scholarship, (U) 358

Miller Johnson West Michigan Diversity Law School Scholarship, (G) 904

Miller Nash Law Student Diversity Fellowship Program, (G) 905

Miller Scholarship. *See* National Black Nurses Association Scholarships, entry (U) 398

Milly Woodward Memorial Scholarship. *See* Northwest Journalists of Color Scholarship Awards, entry (U) 418

Mims Vocal Scholarship. *See* A. Grace Lee Mims Vocal Scholarship, entry (G) 600

Minorities in Clinical Oncology Program Grants. *See* National Cancer Institute Mentored Clinical Scientist Research Career Development Award to Promote Diversity, entry (P) 1225

Minorities in Hospitality Scholars Program, (U) 359

Minorities in Leadership Scholarship. *See* George Geng On Lee Minorities in Leadership Scholarship, entry (U) 201

Minorities in Marine and Environmental Sciences Internship Program, (U) 360

Minority Access Internship, (U) 361, (G) 906

Minority Affairs Committee Award for Outstanding Scholastic Achievement, (U) 362

Minority Entrepreneurs Scholarship Program, (U) 363, (P) 1220

Minority Faculty Development Scholarship Award in Physical Therapy, (G) 907, (P) 1221

Minority Fellowships in Education Research, (G) 908

Minority Geoscience Student Scholarships, (U) 364, (G) 909

Minority Medical Student Clinical Fellowship in Child and Adolescent Psychiatry. *See* Jeanne Spurlock Minority Medical Student Clinical Fellowship in Child and Adolescent Psychiatry, entry (G) 841

Minority Medical Student Elective in HIV Psychiatry, (G) 910

Minority Medical Student Summer Externship in Addiction Psychiatry, (G) 911

Minority Pre-Doctoral Fellowship in Clinical Pharmaceutical Science, (G) 912

Minority Pre-Doctoral Fellowship in Pharmaceutical Science, (G) 913

Minority Scholarship Award for Academic Excellence in Physical Therapy, (U) 365

Minority Scholarship Awards for College Students in Chemical Engineering, (U) 366

Minority Scholarship Awards for Incoming College Freshmen in Chemical Engineering, (U) 367

Minority Science Writers Internship, (U) 368

Minority Teachers of Illinois Scholarship Program, (U) 369

Minority Visiting Student Awards Program, (G) 914

Miriam Weinstein Peace and Justice Education Award, (U) 370, (G) 915

Miss Black America, (U) 371

Mississippi Chapter AABE Scholarships, (U) 372

Missouri Minority Teacher Education Scholarship Program, (U) 373

MLA/NLM Spectrum Scholarships, (G) 916

MLA Scholarship for Minority Students, (G) 917

Moonves Fellowship. *See* IRTS Summer Fellowship Program, entries (U) 260, (G) 834

Moore Scholarship. *See* Damon P. Moore Scholarship, entry (U) 131, 586

Moorer Scholarship. *See* Duane Moorer Scholarship, entry (U) 158

Moore-Velez Woman of Substance Scholarship. *See* Dr. Blanca Moore-Velez Woman of Substance Scholarship, entry (U) 154

Morehouse Physics Prize, (P) 1222

Morris and Summer Houston Memorial Scholarship. *See* Jerry Morris and Summer Houston Memorial Scholarship, entry (U) 273

Morris Scholarship. *See* LaRona J. Morris Scholarship, entry (U) 303

Morrison Scholarship. *See* Harry L. Morrison Scholarship, entry (U) 214

Mosaic Scholarships. *See* Society of American Archivists Mosaic Scholarships, entry (G) 1020

Moseley Scholarship Fund. *See* Annie B. and L. Essex Moseley Scholarship Fund, entry (U) 27

Moses/Agnes Davis Memorial Scholarship. *See* Louise Jane Moses/Agnes Davis Memorial Scholarship, entries (U) 319, (G) 881

Mosley Scholarship. *See* J. Paris Mosley Scholarship, entry (U) 263

Mr. Collegiate African American Scholarship Program, (U) 374

Mrs. Patricia Thompson Scholarship, (U) 375

Multicultural Advertising Intern Program, (U) 376, (G) 918

U–Undergraduates   **G–Graduate Students**   **P–Professionals/Postdoctorates**

Semester Internships in Geoscience Public Policy, (U) 498, (G) 1010

Semiconductor Research Corporation Master's Scholarship Program, (G) 1011

SEO Career Program, (U) 499

SEO Corporate Law Program, (G) 1012

Sheila Garnett Leadership Scholarship. *See* David and Sheila Garnett Leadership Scholarship, entry (U) 132

Shell Incentive Fund Scholarships, (U) 500

Shell Minority Scholarship Program, (U) 501

Sherard Scholarship. *See* Esther Mayo Sherard Scholarship, entries (G) 750, (P) 1159

Sherry R. Arnstein Minority Student Scholarship, (G) 1013

Sherry R. Arnstein New Student Minority Student Scholarship, (G) 1014

Sheryl L. Meshack Memorial Scholarship. *See* Black Women Lawyers Association of Los Angeles Scholarships, entry (G) 656

Shinn Distinguished Member of the Year Awards. *See* Mike Shinn Distinguished Member of the Year Awards, entries (U) 355, (G) 902

Shrader Diversity Scholarships. *See* Ralph W. Shrader Diversity Scholarships, entry (G) 985

Shropshire Graduate Scholarship. *See* John S. Shropshire Graduate Scholarship, entry (G) 847

Sidley Diversity and Inclusion Scholarship, (G) 1015

Sidney B. Williams, Jr. Intellectual Property Law School Scholarships, (G) 1016

Siemens Teacher Scholarships, (U) 502

Sigma Gamma Rho Scholarships/Fellowships, (U) 503, (G) 1017

Simpson NABJ Scholarship. *See* Carole Simpson NABJ Scholarship, entries (U) 80, (G) 669

Simpson RTDNF Scholarship. *See* Carole Simpson RTDNF Scholarship, entry (U) 81

Simpson Scholarships. *See* Bro. Dr. Frank T. Simpson Scholarships, entry (U) 65

Sister Thea Bowman Foundation Knights of Columbus Scholarships, (U) 504

Sloan Foundation Research Fellowships. *See* Alfred P. Sloan Foundation Research Fellowships, entry (P) 1092

Smith Award. *See* Walter and Victoria Smith Award, entries (U) 565, (G) 1066

Smith Memorial Scholarship. *See* Catheryn Smith Memorial Scholarship, entry (U) 85, 326

Smith Scholarship. *See* Richard S. Smith Scholarship, entry (U) 469

Smithsonian Minority Student Internship, (U) 505, (G) 1018

Social, Behavioral, and Economic Sciences Doctoral Dissertation Research Improvement Grants. *See* SBE Doctoral Dissertation Research Improvement Grants, entry (G) 1003

Social Science Research Council/NEH International and Area Studies Fellowships. *See* International and Area Studies Fellowships, entry (P) 1189

Society for the Study of Social Problems Racial/Ethnic Minority Graduate Scholarship, (G) 1019

Society of American Archivists Mosaic Scholarships, (G) 1020

Society of Pediatric Psychology Diversity Research Grant, (G) 1021, (P) 1273

Sonia Kovalevsky High School Mathematics Days Grants, (P) 1274

South Carolina Access and Equity Undergraduate Scholars Program, (U) 506

South Carolina Graduate Incentive Scholarship Program, (G) 1022

South Eastern Region Fellowship for Life-Long Learning, (U) 507

South Florida Chapter NBMBAA Graduate Scholarship, (G) 1023

South Florida Chapter NBMBAA Undergraduate Scholarship, (U) 508

Southern Regional Education Board Dissertation Awards, (G) 1024

Southern Regional Education Board Doctoral Awards. *See* SREB Doctoral Awards, entry (G) 1026

Spaulding Memorial Scholarships. *See* Sandra R. Spaulding Memorial Scholarships, entry (U) 484

Spectrum Scholarship Program, (G) 1025

Spencer Boyer Scholarship. *See* BESLA General Scholarship Fund, entry (G) 650

Sphinx Competition. *See* Sphinx Competition Awards, entry (U) 509

Sphinx Competition Awards, (U) 509

Spitzer Fellowship. *See* Hubble Fellowships, entry (P) 1186

Sponsors for Educational Opportunity Career Program. *See* SEO Career Program, entry (U) 499

Sponsors for Educational Opportunity Corporate Law Program. *See* SEO Corporate Law Program, entry (G) 1012

Sports Illustrated Scholarship, (U) 510

Spurlock Minority Medical Student Clinical Fellowship in Child and Adolescent Psychiatry. *See* Jeanne Spurlock Minority Medical Student Clinical Fellowship in Child and Adolescent Psychiatry, entry (G) 841

Spurlock Research Fellowship in Substance Abuse and Addiction for Minority Medical Students. *See* Jeanne Spurlock Research Fellowship in Substance Abuse and Addiction for Minority Medical Students, entry (G) 842

SREB Doctoral Awards, (G) 1026

SSRC/NEH International and Area Studies Fellowships. *See* International and Area Studies Fellowships, entry (P) 1189

Stanford Memorial WLMA Scholarship. *See* John Stanford Memorial WLMA Scholarship, entry (G) 848

Stanford Summer Research Program/Amgen Scholars Program, (U) 511

Stanley J. Tarver Memorial Scholarship Fund, (G) 1027

Stanley Minority and International Scholarship. *See* Alan Compton and Bob Stanley Minority and International Scholarship, entry (U) 13

State Farm Communications Internship Program, (U) 512

Stith Memorial Scholarship. *See* Black Women Lawyers Association of Los Angeles Scholarships, entry (G) 656

Stoel Rives First-Year Diversity Fellowships, (G) 1028

Stokes Health Scholars Program. *See* Louis Stokes Health Scholars Program, entry (U) 318

Stokes Urban Health Policy Fellows Program. *See* Louis Stokes Urban Health Policy Fellows Program, entry (P) 1209

Stone Scholarship. *See* Gerald Boyd/Robin Stone Scholarship, entries (U) 202, (G) 796

Stoudt Scholarships. *See* James W. Stoudt Scholarships, entry (G) 840

Stout Scholarship Program. *See* Juanita Kidd Stout Scholarship Program, entry (U) 284

Strait Minority Scholarship Endowment. *See* George A. Strait Minority Scholarship Endowment, entries (G) 793, (P) 1176

Straker Scholarship. *See* D. Augustus Straker Scholarship, entry (G) 697

Stuart A. Kessler Scholarship for Minority Students. *See* Scholarships for Minority Accounting Students, entries (U) 487, (G) 1004

Stuart Brotman Student Research Fellowship Awards, (U) 513

U–Undergraduates **G–Graduate Students** **P–Professionals/Postdoctorates**

Sponsoring Organization Index

The Sponsoring Organization Index makes it easy to identify agencies that offer financial aid to African Americans. In this index, the sponsoring organizations are listed alphabetically, word by word. In addition, we've used an alphabetical code (within parentheses) to help you identify the intended recipients of the funding offered by the organizations: U = Undergraduates; G = Graduate Students; P = Professionals/Postdoctorates. For example, if the name of a sponsoring organization is followed by (U) 241, a program sponsored by that organization is described in the Undergraduate section, in entry 241. If that sponsoring organization's name is followed by another entry number—for example, (P) 1101—the same or a different program sponsored by that organization is described in the Professionals/Postdoctorates section, in entry 1101. Remember: the numbers cited here refer to program entry numbers, not to page numbers in the book.

American Association of Critical-Care Nurses, (U) 64, (G) 658

American Association of Family and Consumer Sciences, (G) 696

American Association of Law Libraries, (G) 793, (P) 1176, 1247

American Association of Petroleum Geologists, (U) 498, (G) 1010

American Association of Petroleum Geologists Foundation, (G) 835

American Association of State Colleges and Universities, (U) 534

American Association of University Women, (U) 75, (G) 667, 774, (P) 1116

American Astronomical Society, (U) 219, 350, 477, 566

American Baptist Churches of Ohio, (U) 181, (G) 762

American Bar Association, (G) 1069

American Bar Association. Fund for Justice and Education, (G) 621

American Bar Association. Section of Business Law, (G) 1009

American Bar Association. Section of Environment, Energy, and Resources, (G) 664, 718, 772, 809, 943, 945, 950, 959

American Bar Association. Section of Intellectual Property Law, (G) 1016

American Bar Association. Section of Litigation, (G) 855

American Bar Foundation, (U) 519, (G) 723, (P) 1143

American Board of Obstetrics and Gynecology, (P) 1095

American Chemical Society, (U) 444, 495

American Chemical Society. Department of Diversity Programs, (U) 23

American Chemical Society. Division of Organic Chemistry, (U) 522, (G) 962

American College of Neuropsychopharmacology, (P) 1134, 1196, 1201, 1249

American College of Nurse-Midwives, (U) 575, (G) 1070

American College of Rheumatology, (P) 1251

American Council of Learned Societies, (G) 626, 713, 737, 815, (P) 1096, 1100, 1123, 1127, 1142, 1147, 1149, 1172, 1189, 1233

American Dental Association, (G) 1050

American Dental Education Association, (U) 517

American Dental Hygienists' Association, (U) 108

American Diabetes Association, (P) 1216

American Dietetic Association, (U) 147, (G) 622, 711, (P) 1141

American Educational Research Association, (G) 606, 908, (P) 1088, 1097, 1167

American Epilepsy Society, (U) 48, (G) 648, 812, 975, (P) 1155-1156, 1260, 1264

American Foundation for Pharmaceutical Education, (G) 912-913

American Gastroenterological Association, (U) 513, (P) 1098, 1154, 1168, 1262

American Geological Institute, (U) 364, 498, (G) 909, 1010

American Gynecological and Obstetrical Society, (P) 1095

American Health Information Management Association, (U) 10, (G) 750, (P) 1159

American Heart Association. Western States Affiliate, (U) 579

American Historical Association, (P) 1287

American Hotel & Lodging Educational Foundation, (U) 238

American Indian Graduate Center, (U) 195

American Institute of Certified Public Accountants, (U) 487, (G) 764, 1004

American Institute of Chemical Engineers, (U) 362, 366-367, (P) 1290

American Institutes for Research, (P) 1088

American Intellectual Property Law Association, (G) 1016

American Library Association. Black Caucus, (G) 743

American Library Association. Ethnic and Multicultural Material Information Exchange Round Table, (P) 1130-1132

American Library Association. Library and Information Technology Association, (G) 1025

American Library Association. Office for Diversity, (G) 1025

American Medical Association, (G) 620, 996

American Meteorological Society, (U) 24, 59, 176, 251, 316, 344, (G) 800, 826

American Nuclear Society, (U) 28, 277, (G) 844

American Nurses Foundation, (G) 893, (P) 1213

American Orchid Society, (G) 628, 783

American Philosophical Society, (G) 845

American Physical Society, (U) 488, (P) 1151

American Physical Therapy Association, (U) 365, (G) 907, (P) 1221

American Physiological Society, (G) 971, (P) 1174

American Planning Association, (U) 285, (G) 630, 856, 993

American Planning Association. California Chapter, (U) 71, (G) 665

American Political Science Association, (U) 456, (G) 623, (P) 1181, 1263

American Psychiatric Association, (G) 629, 910-911, (P) 1102, 1275

American Psychological Association. Division 54, (G) 1021, (P) 1273

American Psychological Association. Minority Fellowship Program, (G) 973, (P) 1253

American School Counselor Association, (G) 639

American Society for Cell Biology, (P) 1099

American Society for Engineering Education, (G) 613, 814, 932, (P) 1090, 1145, 1182, 1244-1245

American Society for Microbiology, (U) 353, (G) 994

American Society for Pharmacology and Experimental Therapeutics, (U) 599

American Society of Civil Engineers. Maine Section, (U) 329

American Society of Clinical Oncology, (G) 640

American Society of Hematology, (P) 1105

American Society of Landscape Architecture, (U) 34

American Society of Safety Engineers, (U) 35, 57, 150, (G) 720

American Sociological Association, (G) 638

American Speech-Language-Hearing Foundation, (G) 624

American Systems, (U) 553

American Water Works Association. Intermountain Section, (U) 254, (G) 830

Amgen Foundation, (U) 511, 547-548, 574

Amgen Inc., (U) 522, (G) 962

Andrew W. Mellon Foundation, (G) 626, 716, (P) 1096, 1100, 1123, 1127, 1142, 1172, 1272

Anheuser-Busch Companies, Inc., (G) 639

Arent Fox LLP, (G) 631

Arkansas Department of Higher Education, (U) 31, 328, (G) 633

Arkansas State University, (U) 464

Armed Forces Communications and Electronics Association, (U) 553, (G) 985

Asian American Journalists Association. Seattle Chapter, (U) 418

Asian Pacific American Institute for Congressional Studies, (U) 138, (G) 703

Asian & Pacific Islander American Scholarship Fund, (U) 195

Associated Food and Petroleum Dealers, (U) 36

Association for Computing Machinery, (U) 439

Association for Education in Journalism and Mass Communication, (G) 878

Association for Educational Communications and Technology, (G) 963

Association for the Study of African American Life and History, (P) 1287

U–Undergraduates   **G–Graduate Students**   **P–Professionals/Postdoctorates**

U–Undergraduates   **G–Graduate Students**   **P–Professionals/Postdoctorates**

Organic Syntheses, Inc., (G) 962
Organization of American Historians, (G) 818, (P) 1135, 1191
Organization of Black Aerospace Professionals, Inc., (U) 158, 426, 589, (P) 1248
Ortho-McNeil Pharmaceutical Corporation, (U) 48, (G) 648, 812, 975, (P) 1155, 1260, 1264

P
Pacific Northwest National Laboratory, (U) 43
Page Education Foundation, (U) 427
Parsons Brinckerhoff, Inc., (U) 428-429
PBS&J, (U) 431, (G) 966
PEN American Center, (P) 1110
Pennsylvania Bar Association, (G) 840
Pennsylvania Black Conference on Higher Education, (U) 288, 471, (G) 847
Pennsylvania Dietetic Association, (U) 433
Perkins Coie LLP, (G) 967
Pew Charitable Trusts, (G) 1024, 1026
Pfizer Inc., (U) 48, 522, (G) 620, 648, 718, 812, 962, 975, (P) 1155, 1185, 1260, 1264
PGA Tour, Inc., (U) 434, (G) 968
Phi Delta Kappa International, (U) 156
Phi Delta Phi International Legal Fraternity, (G) 646
Philanthrofund Foundation, (U) 220, 370, (G) 810, 915
Playwrights' Center, (P) 1211
Porter Wright Morris & Arthur LLP, (G) 984
Portland General Electric Company, (G) 1042
Presbyterian Church (USA), (U) 514, (G) 981
Presbyterian Church (USA). Synod of Lakes and Prairies, (G) 1030
Presbyterian Church (USA). Synod of the Covenant, (G) 1031
Presbyterian Church (USA). Synod of the Mid-Atlantic, (U) 27
Presbyterian Church (USA). Synod of the Trinity, (U) 453
PricewaterhouseCoopers LLP, (U) 450
Princeton University. Graduate School, (U) 441
Princeton University. Institute for Advanced Study, (P) 1172
Procter & Gamble Company, (G) 1050
Professional Golfers' Association of America, (U) 443
Progressus Therapy, (G) 976
Public Interest Law Initiative, (G) 978
Public Relations Society of America. Puget Sound Chapter, (U) 234
Public Relations Student Society of America, (U) 449
Public Service Electric and Gas, (U) 463

R
RA Consulting Service, (U) 451, (G) 979
Radcliffe Institute for Advanced Study at Harvard University, (P) 1172
Radio Television Digital News Foundation, (U) 81, 162, 297
RDW Group, Inc., (U) 458, (G) 986
Reed Smith LLP, (G) 989
Research Corporation, (P) 1151
Resources for the Future, (U) 465, (G) 852, 990, (P) 1178, 1198
Rhode Island Foundation, (U) 458, (G) 986
Richard Linn American Inn of Court, (G) 890
Richland County Public Library Foundation, (G) 752
Robert Wood Johnson Foundation, (U) 517, (P) 1105, 1267
Roche Pharmaceuticals, (U) 522, (G) 962
Rockefeller Foundation, (P) 1096
Rockefeller University, (U) 196

Rockwell Automation, Inc., (U) 474
Rockwell Collins, Inc., (U) 475-476
Ronald McDonald House Charities, (U) 7
Rosetta Inpharmatics, (U) 495
Ruden McClosky, (G) 998
Rutgers University. Graduate School, (U) 463
Ruth M. Batson Educational Foundation, (U) 482

S
Sachs Foundation, (U) 483
St. John's University. Collegeville Institute for Ecumenical and Cultural Research, (G) 654
St. Lawrence University, (G) 843
St. Philip's Episcopal Church, (U) 2, (G) 601
Samuel I. Newhouse Foundation, (U) 410, (P) 1272
Sandia National Laboratories, (G) 937, 1002
Scholarship Administrative Services, Inc., (U) 6
Scholarship America, (U) 68, 445, 551, 555, (G) 1054
Schwabe, Williamson & Wyatt, Attorneys at Law, (G) 1005
Science Applications International Corporation, (U) 490-491
Scotts Company, (U) 493
Scripps Howard Foundation, (U) 276
S.D. Bechtel, Jr. Foundation, (U) 494
Seattle Foundation, (U) 153, (G) 727
Seismological Society of America, (U) 364, (G) 909
Semiconductor Research Corporation, (G) 1011
ServiceMaster Company, (U) 117
Shell Oil Company, (U) 500-501
Showtime Networks Inc., (P) 1111
Sickle Cell Disease Association of America, (U) 298
Sickle Cell Disease Association of America. Connecticut Chapter, (U) 243
Sidley Austin LLP, (G) 1015
Siemens Foundation, (U) 502
Sigma Gamma Rho Sorority, Inc., (U) 303, 321, 462, 503, 561, (G) 1017
Sigma Pi Phi Fraternity. Beta Tau Boulé, (U) 445
Sloan-Kettering Institute, (U) 196
Smithsonian Astrophysical Observatory, (P) 1153
Smithsonian Institution. Office of Fellowships, (U) 269, 505, (G) 839, 914, 1018
Social Science Research Council, (G) 713, 716, 755, (P) 1147, 1189
Society for Maternal-Fetal Medicine, (P) 1095
Society for the Study of Social Problems, (G) 1019
Society of American Archivists, (G) 853, 1020
Society of Manufacturing Engineers, (U) 84, 165, (G) 740
Society of Professional Journalists. Kansas Professional Chapter, (U) 292
Society of Professional Journalists. Western Washington Chapter, (U) 418
Society of Women Engineers, (U) 40, 96, 130, 232, 240, 261, 474, 476, 524, (G) 645, 695, 828
Sociologists for Women in Society, (G) 638, 751
South Carolina Commission on Higher Education, (U) 506, (G) 1022
South Carolina Department of Natural Resources, (U) 360
Southern Historical Association, (P) 1199
Southern Regional Education Board, (G) 1024, 1026
Southwestern Athletic Conference, (G) 778
Southwestern Sociological Association, (G) 638

U–Undergraduates   G–Graduate Students   P–Professionals/Postdoctorates

Residency Index

Some programs listed in this book are set aside for African Americans who are residents of a particular state or region. Others are open to applicants wherever they may live. The Residency Index will help you pinpoint programs available in your area as well as programs that have no residency restrictions at all (these are listed under the term "United States"). To use this index, look up the geographic areas that apply to you (always check the listings under "United States"), jot down the entry numbers listed for the educational level that applies to you (Undergraduates, Graduate Students, or Professionals/Postdoctorates), and use those numbers to find the program descriptions in the directory. To help you in your search, we've provided some "see" and "see also" references in the index entries. Remember: the numbers cited here refer to program entry numbers, not to page numbers in the book.

A

Alabama: **Undergraduates,** 45, 53-54, 158, 177, 203, 208, 507. *See also* Southern states; United States

Alaska: **Undergraduates,** 55, 191, 596; **Professionals/ Postdoctorates,** 1137. *See also* United States

Alexandria, Virginia: **Undergraduates,** 573. *See also* Virginia

Anne Arundel County, Maryland: **Undergraduates,** 573. *See also* Maryland

Arizona: **Undergraduates,** 55, 191. *See also* United States

Arkansas: **Undergraduates,** 30-31, 158, 203, 208, 235; **Graduate Students,** 632-633; **Professionals/Postdoctorates,** 1137. *See also* Southern states; United States

Arlington County, Virginia: **Undergraduates,** 573. *See also* Virginia

B

Belmont County, Ohio: **Undergraduates,** 453. *See also* Ohio

Burnett County, Wisconsin: **Undergraduates,** 173. *See also* Wisconsin

C

California: **Undergraduates,** 55, 71, 73-74, 79, 98, 126, 184, 191, 319, 334, 484, 579; **Graduate Students,** 664-666, 678, 692, 724, 881, 892; **Professionals/Postdoctorates,** 1212. *See also* United States

California, southern: **Graduate Students,** 684. *See also* California

Calvert County, Maryland: **Undergraduates,** 573. *See also* Maryland

Charles County, Maryland: **Undergraduates,** 2, 573; **Graduate Students,** 601. *See also* Maryland

Colorado: **Undergraduates,** 55, 70, 91, 104, 113, 191, 289, 467, 483; **Graduate Students,** 860, 1061. *See also* United States

Columbiana County, Ohio: **Undergraduates,** 453. *See also* Ohio

Connecticut: **Undergraduates,** 15, 65, 119, 180, 208, 243, 257, 332, 445; **Graduate Students,** 760. *See also* New England states; United States

D

Delaware: **Undergraduates,** 208, 302, 436; **Graduate Students,** 935; **Professionals/Postdoctorates,** 1137. *See also* Southern states; United States

District of Columbia. *See* Washington, D.C.

F

Fairfax County, Virginia: **Undergraduates,** 573. *See also* Virginia

Falls Church, Virginia: **Undergraduates,** 573. *See also* Virginia

Fauquier County, Virginia: **Undergraduates,** 573. *See also* Virginia

Florida: **Undergraduates,** 45, 54, 125, 177, 185-186, 208, 296, 339, 497, 508, 587; **Graduate Students,** 772-773, 1023. *See also* Southern states; United States

Florida, northwestern: **Undergraduates,** 158. *See also* Florida

Frederick County, Maryland: **Undergraduates,** 573. *See also* Maryland

G

Georgia: **Undergraduates,** 45, 54, 177, 208, 296. *See also* Southern states; United States

Georgia, western: **Undergraduates,** 158. *See also* Georgia

Guam: **Undergraduates,** 111, 331, 551; **Graduate Students,** 684, 888, 1054. *See also* United States

H

Hampton Roads, Virginia: **Undergraduates,** 211; **Graduate Students,** 806. *See also* Virginia

Harrison County, Ohio: **Undergraduates,** 453. *See also* Ohio

Hawaii: **Graduate Students,** 684, 809. *See also* United States

Howard County, Maryland: **Undergraduates,** 573. *See also* Maryland

Tenability Index

Some programs listed in this book can be used only in specific cities, counties, states, or regions. Others may be used anywhere in the United States (or even abroad). The Tenability Index will help you locate funding that is restricted to a specific area as well as funding that has no tenability restrictions (these are listed under the term "United States"). To use this index, look up the geographic areas where you'd like to go (always check the listings under "United States"), jot down the entry numbers listed for the recipient group that represents you (Undergraduates, Graduate Students, Professionals/Postdoctorates), and use those numbers to find the program descriptions in the directory. To help you in your search, we've provided some "see" and "see also" references in the index entries. Remember: the numbers cited here refer to program entry numbers, not to page numbers in the book.

A

Alabama: **Undergraduates,** 3, 45, 492, 541; **Graduate Students,** 689, 1006. *See also* Southern states; United States; names of specific cities and counties

Alaska: **Professionals/Postdoctorates,** 1137. *See also* United States; names of specific cities

Albany, Oregon: **Undergraduates,** 352; **Graduate Students,** 901; **Professionals/Postdoctorates,** 1218. *See also* Oregon

Albuquerque, New Mexico: **Graduate Students,** 937, 1002. *See also* New Mexico

Alcorn State, Mississippi: **Graduate Students,** 778. *See also* Mississippi

Allentown, Pennsylvania: **Graduate Students,** 715; **Professionals/Postdoctorates,** 1257. *See also* Pennsylvania

Amherst, Massachusetts: **Undergraduates,** 165; **Graduate Students,** 740, 769. *See also* Massachusetts

Ann Arbor, Michigan: **Graduate Students,** 688, 722, 775; **Professionals/Postdoctorates,** 1144. *See also* Michigan

Anniston, Alabama: **Undergraduates,** 32; **Graduate Students,** 637. *See also* Alabama

Appleton, Wisconsin: **Graduate Students,** 715; **Professionals/Postdoctorates,** 1257. *See also* Wisconsin

Arkansas: **Undergraduates,** 3, 31, 328, 541; **Graduate Students,** 633; **Professionals/Postdoctorates,** 1137. *See also* Southern states; United States; names of specific cities and counties

Athens, Georgia: **Graduate Students,** 1079. *See also* Georgia

Atlanta, Georgia: **Undergraduates,** 76, 199, 230, 423, 530; **Graduate Students,** 652, 688, 766, 792, 865, 957, 1040, 1079. *See also* Georgia

Augusta, Georgia: **Undergraduates,** 286; **Graduate Students,** 859. *See also* Georgia

Austin, Texas: **Undergraduates,** 76, 230, 423; **Graduate Students,** 652, 688, 722, 957, 1062. *See also* Texas

B

Baltimore, Maryland: **Undergraduates,** 142, 530; **Graduate Students,** 706, 715, 814, 1079; **Professionals/Postdoctorates,** 1139, 1182, 1257. *See also* Maryland

Baton Rouge, Louisiana: **Undergraduates,** 230, 530, 552; **Graduate Students,** 650, 778, 814; **Professionals/Postdoctorates,** 1182. *See also* Louisiana

Berkeley, California: **Undergraduates,** 547; **Graduate Students,** 688, 775; **Professionals/Postdoctorates,** 1122, 1282. *See also* California

Bethesda, Maryland: **Undergraduates,** 52, 412; **Graduate Students,** 653; **Professionals/Postdoctorates,** 1244-1245. *See also* Maryland

Big Rapids, Michigan: **Undergraduates,** 443. *See also* Michigan

Bloomington, Indiana: **Graduate Students,** 642, 688. *See also* Indiana

Boise, Idaho: **Graduate Students,** 1028. *See also* Idaho

Boston, Massachusetts: **Undergraduates,** 62, 142, 165, 216-217, 515, 518, 521; **Graduate Students,** 610, 706, 722, 740, 896, 1064; **Professionals/Postdoctorates,** 1086, 1139, 1291. *See also* Massachusetts

Brunswick, Maine: **Graduate Students,** 715; **Professionals/Postdoctorates,** 1257. *See also* Maine

Bryn Mawr, Pennsylvania: **Graduate Students,** 715; **Professionals/Postdoctorates,** 1257. *See also* Pennsylvania

Buies Creek, North Carolina: **Undergraduates,** 443. *See also* North Carolina

Burbank, California: **Professionals/Postdoctorates,** 1236. *See also* California

C

California: **Undergraduates,** 71, 73-74, 98, 126, 184, 319, 334, 484, 579; **Graduate Students,** 656, 663-666, 678, 689, 692, 698, 846, 881, 892; **Professionals/Postdoctorates,** 1212. *See also* United States; Western states; names of specific cities and counties

California, central: **Graduate Students,** 880. *See also* California

Subject Index

There are hundreds of specific subject fields covered in this directory. Use the Subject Index to identify this focus, as well as the recipient level supported (Undergraduates, Graduate Students, or Professionals/Postdoctorates) by the available funding programs. To help you pinpoint your search, we've included many "see" and "see also" references. Since a large number of programs are not restricted by subject, be sure to check the references listed under the "General programs" heading in the subject index (in addition to the specific terms that directly relate to your interest areas); hundreds of funding opportunities are listed there that can be used to support activities in any subject area—although the programs may be restricted in other ways. Remember: the numbers cited in this index refer to program entry numbers, not to page numbers in the book.

A

A.V. *See* Audiovisual materials and equipment

Academic librarianship. *See* Libraries and librarianship, academic

Accounting: **Undergraduates,** 4, 20, 26, 32, 68, 101-102, 122, 144, 160, 269, 290, 325, 331, 333, 382, 394, 409, 434, 450, 455, 487, 496, 499, 525-526, 533, 539, 555, 558, 565; **Graduate Students,** 627, 637, 690, 708, 733, 764, 839, 861, 886, 888-889, 920, 926, 968, 983, 1004, 1008, 1032-1033, 1039, 1045, 1066. *See also* Finance; General programs

Acoustical engineering. *See* Engineering, acoustical

Acoustics: **Graduate Students,** 603. *See also* General programs; Physics

Acquired Immunodeficiency Syndrome. *See* AIDS

Acting. *See* Performing arts

Actuarial sciences: **Undergraduates,** 255, 379, 450; **Graduate Students,** 831. *See also* General programs; Statistics

Addiction. *See* Alcohol use and abuse; Drug use and abuse

Administration. *See* Business administration; Education, administration; Management; Personnel administration; Public administration

Adolescents: **Graduate Students,** 841-842; **Professionals/Postdoctorates,** 1082. *See also* Child development; General programs

Advertising: **Undergraduates,** 25, 70, 101-102, 114, 187, 257, 301, 314, 376, 409, 423, 458, 516, 558; **Graduate Students,** 652, 776, 868, 918, 957, 986. *See also* Communications; General programs; Marketing; Public relations

Aeronautical engineering. *See* Engineering, aeronautical

Aeronautics: **Undergraduates,** 158, 589; **Graduate Students,** 807, 923. *See also* Aviation; Engineering, aeronautical; General programs; Physical sciences

Aerospace engineering. *See* Engineering, aerospace

Aerospace sciences. *See* Space sciences

Affirmative action: **Undergraduates,** 248. *See also* Equal opportunity; General programs

African American affairs: **Undergraduates,** 186; **Professionals/Postdoctorates,** 1130-1131. *See also* General programs; Minority affairs

African American studies: **Graduate Students,** 610, 614, 670, 780, 818, 1048; **Professionals/Postdoctorates,** 1084-1086, 1091, 1118, 1135, 1144, 1173, 1193, 1199, 1219, 1272, 1285, 1287-1288. *See also* African American affairs; General programs; Minority studies

African history. *See* History, African

African studies: **Undergraduates,** 311; **Graduate Students,** 670, 780, 876, 1027, 1048; **Professionals/Postdoctorates,** 1118, 1144, 1173, 1189, 1206, 1272, 1285, 1287. *See also* General programs; Humanities

Aged and aging: **Graduate Students,** 611, 724, 875; **Professionals/Postdoctorates,** 1126, 1181. *See also* General programs; Social sciences

Agribusiness: **Undergraduates,** 180, 400, 552; **Graduate Students,** 760. *See also* Agriculture and agricultural sciences; Business administration; General programs

Agricultural economics. *See* Economics, agricultural

Agricultural engineering. *See* Engineering, agricultural

Agricultural technology: **Undergraduates,** 552. *See also* Agriculture and agricultural sciences; General programs; Technology

Agriculture and agricultural sciences: **Undergraduates,** 60, 142, 180, 400, 464, 525, 552; **Graduate Students,** 706, 760, 898, 1032; **Professionals/Postdoctorates,** 1139. *See also* Biological sciences; General programs

Agrimarketing and sales. *See* Agribusiness

Agronomy: **Undergraduates,** 32, 400, 552; **Graduate Students,** 637. *See also* Agriculture and agricultural sciences; General programs

AIDS: **Undergraduates,** 217; **Graduate Students,** 875; **Professionals/Postdoctorates,** 1185, 1278-1279. *See also* Disabilities; General programs; Immunology; Medical sciences

Albanian language. *See* Language, Albanian

Lung disease: **Undergraduates,** 52, 217; **Graduate Students,** 653; **Professionals/Postdoctorates,** 1227, 1234-1235. *See also* Disabilities; General programs; Health and health care; Medical sciences

M

Macedonian language. *See* Language, Macedonian

Magazines. *See* Journalism; Literature

Malacology: **Undergraduates,** 29. *See also* General programs; Zoology

Management: **Undergraduates,** 32, 68, 94, 135, 145, 250, 252, 454, 499, 508, 540; **Graduate Students,** 637, 702, 709, 805, 821, 825, 880, 930-931, 982, 1003, 1023, 1046-1047. *See also* General programs; Social sciences

Manufacturing engineering. *See* Engineering, manufacturing

Marine sciences: **Undergraduates,** 341, 360, 594; **Graduate Students,** 898; **Professionals/Postdoctorates,** 1101. *See also* General programs; Sciences; names of specific marine sciences

Marketing: **Undergraduates,** 32, 56, 68, 101-102, 174, 184, 187, 199, 252, 301, 313-314, 331, 363, 409, 429, 434, 516, 525, 558; **Graduate Students,** 637, 747, 776, 792, 821, 868, 888, 968, 1032; **Professionals/Postdoctorates,** 1200, 1220. *See also* Advertising; General programs; Public relations; Sales

Marketing education. *See* Education, business

Mass communications. *See* Communications

Materials engineering. *See* Engineering, materials

Materials sciences: **Undergraduates,** 23, 28, 43, 83, 109, 166, 200, 386, 419, 437-438, 444, 468, 546, 582, 585, 595; **Graduate Students,** 742, 807, 821, 932, 936-937, 951, 970, 1002, 1081; **Professionals/Postdoctorates,** 1089, 1104. *See also* General programs; Physical sciences

Mathematics: **Undergraduates,** 8, 22, 32, 39, 43-44, 46, 50, 53, 62, 66, 68, 101-102, 104, 119, 141-142, 149, 195, 198, 200, 206, 236, 247, 282, 290, 315, 341, 348, 351-352, 372-373, 379, 386-388, 404, 409, 413, 416-417, 419, 424, 436-437, 463, 468, 478, 490, 495, 525, 530, 543, 546, 553, 558-559, 582, 584-585, 594; **Graduate Students,** 637, 641, 681, 706, 756, 790-791, 801-802, 807, 817, 821, 861, 898, 901, 932, 935-937, 939, 944, 951, 985, 1024, 1026, 1032, 1063; **Professionals/Postdoctorates,** 1089, 1092, 1104, 1136-1137, 1139, 1160, 1163, 1166, 1207, 1214, 1218, 1242, 1258-1259, 1261, 1274. *See also* Computer sciences; General programs; Physical sciences; Statistics

Measurement. *See* Testing

Mechanical engineering. *See* Engineering, mechanical

Media. *See* Broadcasting; Communications

Media specialists. *See* Libraries and librarianship, school; Library and information services, general

Medical journalism. *See* Science reporting

Medical librarianship. *See* Libraries and librarianship, medical

Medical malpractice. *See* Personal injury law

Medical sciences: **Undergraduates,** 8, 66, 95, 151, 153, 163, 178, 196, 289, 356, 435, 440, 481, 515, 517-518, 531; **Graduate Students,** 620, 727, 729, 738, 757, 774, 812, 819, 860, 875, 900, 910, 933-934, 952, 969, 996, 1036, 1064; **Professionals/Postdoctorates,** 1101, 1129, 1181, 1185, 1188, 1190, 1267, 1269. *See also* General programs; Health and health care; Sciences; names of medical specialties; names of specific diseases

Medical technology: **Undergraduates,** 231, 308, 531. *See also* General programs; Medical sciences; Technology

Mental health: **Undergraduates,** 289; **Graduate Students,** 860, 899, 973; **Professionals/Postdoctorates,** 1102, 1253, 1275. *See also* General programs; Health and health care; Psychiatry

Merchandising. *See* Sales

Metallurgical engineering. *See* Engineering, metallurgical

Metallurgy: **Undergraduates,** 438; **Graduate Students,** 970. *See also* Engineering, metallurgical; General programs; Sciences

Meteorology: **Undergraduates,** 24, 38, 59, 133, 176, 198, 251, 282, 316, 344, 364, 372, 436; **Graduate Students,** 700, 791, 800, 807, 826, 909. *See also* Atmospheric sciences; General programs

Microbiology: **Undergraduates,** 8, 137, 159, 353, 360, 511, 525, 547-548, 574; **Graduate Students,** 994, 1032, 1073; **Professionals/Postdoctorates,** 1152, 1223, 1289. *See also* Biological sciences; General programs

Microcomputers. *See* Computer sciences

Microscopy. *See* Medical technology

Middle Eastern studies: **Undergraduates,** 311; **Graduate Students,** 765, 876; **Professionals/Postdoctorates,** 1170, 1189, 1206. *See also* General programs; Humanities

Midwifery. *See* Nurses and nursing, midwifery

Military history. *See* History, military

Military law: **Graduate Students,** 636. *See also* General programs; Law, general

Mineral law. *See* Environmental law

Mining engineering. *See* Engineering, mining

Mining industry: **Undergraduates,** 193. *See also* General programs

Minority affairs: **Graduate Students,** 875, 973; **Professionals/Postdoctorates,** 1205, 1253, 1263, 1277. *See also* General programs; names of specific ethnic minority groups

Minority studies: **Professionals/Postdoctorates,** 1179. *See also* General programs; names of specific ethnic minority studies

Missionary work. *See* Religion and religious activities

Molecular biology: **Undergraduates,** 159, 419, 547-548, 574; **Graduate Students,** 628, 783, 951; **Professionals/Postdoctorates,** 1092. *See also* Biological sciences; General programs

Motel industry. *See* Hotel and motel industry

Municipal law. *See* Government law

Museum studies: **Undergraduates,** 128, 377, 505; **Graduate Students,** 694, 914, 1018. *See also* Archives; General programs; Library and information services, general; Preservation

Music: **Undergraduates,** 8, 225, 279, 311, 378, 587; **Graduate Students,** 603, 813, 849, 876; **Professionals/Postdoctorates,** 1206. *See also* Education, music; Fine arts; General programs; Humanities; Performing arts

Music, church: **Undergraduates,** 514. *See also* General programs; Music; Performing arts; Religion and religious activities

Music, classical: **Undergraduates,** 8, 310. *See also* General programs; Music

Music education. *See* Education, music

Music, strings: **Undergraduates,** 509. *See also* General programs; Music

Musicology: **Graduate Students,** 626; **Professionals/Postdoctorates,** 1096, 1100, 1123, 1127, 1172, 1233. *See also* General programs; Music

N

Narcotics. *See* Drug use and abuse

National security. *See* Security, national

Native American language. *See* Language, Native American

Native American studies: **Undergraduates,** 144; **Graduate Students,** 708, 845. *See also* General programs; Minority studies

Natural history. *See* History, natural

Natural resources: **Undergraduates,** 32, 144, 360, 400, 465, 552; **Graduate Students,** 637, 708, 852, 990; **Professionals/ Postdoctorates,** 1178, 1198. *See also* General programs; names of specific resources

Natural resources law. *See* Environmental law

Natural sciences: **Undergraduates,** 62, 465, 594; **Graduate Students,** 765, 790, 990; **Professionals/Postdoctorates,** 1170. *See also* General programs; Sciences; names of specific sciences

Naval architecture: **Undergraduates,** 416-417; **Graduate Students,** 932. *See also* Architecture; General programs; Naval science

Naval science: **Undergraduates,** 230; **Professionals/ Postdoctorates,** 1228, 1244-1245. *See also* General programs

Nephrology. *See* Kidney disease

Neuroscience: **Undergraduates,** 511, 547-548, 574; **Graduate Students,** 975, 1073; **Professionals/Postdoctorates,** 1092, 1114, 1134, 1152, 1196, 1201, 1249, 1289. *See also* General programs; Medical sciences

Neuroscience nurses and nursing. *See* Nurses and nursing, neuroscience

Newspapers. *See* Journalism

Nonprofit sector: **Undergraduates,** 90, 499; **Graduate Students,** 676; **Professionals/Postdoctorates,** 1121. *See also* General programs; Public administration

Nuclear engineering. *See* Engineering, nuclear

Nuclear science: **Undergraduates,** 28, 277, 438; **Graduate Students,** 844, 970. *See also* General programs; Physical sciences

Nurses and nursing, educator: **Undergraduates,** 224; **Graduate Students,** 811. *See also* General programs; Nurses and nursing, general

Nurses and nursing, general: **Undergraduates,** 64, 95, 153, 188, 209, 224, 231, 246, 274, 287, 308, 337, 345, 356, 398, 435, 484, 523, 525, 531, 581; **Graduate Students,** 658, 727, 749, 811, 823, 851, 884, 893, 898, 969, 995, 1032, 1071; **Professionals/ Postdoctorates,** 1126, 1158, 1181, 1191, 1195, 1210, 1213, 1215, 1238, 1267-1268. *See also* General programs; Health and health care; Medical sciences; names of specific nursing specialties

Nurses and nursing, geriatrics: **Graduate Students,** 659; **Professionals/Postdoctorates,** 1125. *See also* Aged and aging; General programs; Nurses and nursing, general

Nurses and nursing, midwifery: **Undergraduates,** 575; **Graduate Students,** 1070. *See also* General programs; Nurses and nursing, general

Nurses and nursing, neuroscience: **Undergraduates,** 48; **Graduate Students,** 648, 975; **Professionals/ Postdoctorates,** 1109. *See also* General programs; Neuroscience; Nurses and nursing, general

Nurses and nursing, occupational health: **Undergraduates,** 35, 57, 150; **Graduate Students,** 720. *See also* General programs; Nurses and nursing, general

Nurses and nursing, oncology: **Professionals/Postdoctorates,** 1225, 1229. *See also* Cancer; General programs; Nurses and nursing, general

Nurses and nursing, public health: **Graduate Students,** 995; **Professionals/Postdoctorates,** 1268. *See also* General programs; Nurses and nursing, general; Public health

Nutrition: **Undergraduates,** 74, 79, 95, 127, 147, 217, 433, 513, 552; **Graduate Students,** 622, 666, 693, 711, 724; **Professionals/Postdoctorates,** 1126, 1141, 1237. *See also* General programs; Home economics; Medical sciences

O

Obstetrics: **Professionals/Postdoctorates,** 1095. *See also* General programs; Gynecology; Medical sciences

Occupational health nurses and nursing. *See* Nurses and nursing, occupational health

Occupational safety: **Undergraduates,** 35, 57, 68, 150; **Graduate Students,** 720. *See also* General programs; Health and health care

Occupational safety and health law. *See* Health care law

Occupational therapy: **Undergraduates,** 231, 249, 531. *See also* Counseling; General programs

Ocean engineering. *See* Engineering, ocean

Oceanography: **Undergraduates,** 24, 38, 59, 176, 251, 316, 344, 364; **Graduate Students,** 603, 736, 800, 826, 909, 932; **Professionals/Postdoctorates,** 1101, 1103, 1266. *See also* General programs; Marine sciences

Oncology. *See* Cancer

Oncology nurses and nursing. *See* Nurses and nursing, oncology

Online journalism. *See* Journalism, online

Opera. *See* Music; Voice

Operations research: **Undergraduates,** 32, 166, 200, 386, 437, 468, 582, 585; **Graduate Students,** 637, 641, 742. *See also* General programs; Mathematics; Sciences

Optical engineering. *See* Engineering, optical

Optics: **Undergraduates,** 477, 595; **Graduate Students,** 932, 1081. *See also* General programs; Physics

Oratory: **Undergraduates,** 8. *See also* General programs

Osteopathy: **Graduate Students,** 774, 952, 1013-1014. *See also* General programs; Medical sciences

P

Painting: **Undergraduates,** 8; **Professionals/Postdoctorates,** 1197. *See also* Art; General programs

Paleontology: **Undergraduates,** 29. *See also* Archaeology; General programs; Geology

Paralegal studies: **Undergraduates,** 568. *See also* General programs; Social sciences

Patent law. *See* Intellectual property law

Pathology: **Undergraduates,** 159, 547-548, 574. *See also* General programs; Medical sciences

Pay equity. *See* Equal opportunity

Peace studies: **Graduate Students,** 765; **Professionals/ Postdoctorates,** 1170. *See also* General programs; Political science and politics

Pediatrics: **Graduate Students,** 910, 1021; **Professionals/ Postdoctorates,** 1273. *See also* General programs; Medical sciences

Calendar Index

Since most funding programs have specific deadline dates, some may have already closed by the time you begin to look for money. You can use the Calendar Index to identify which programs are still open. To do that, go to the recipient category (Undergraduates, Graduate Students, or Professionals/ Postdoctorates) that interests you, think about when you'll be able to complete your application forms, go to the appropriate months, jot down the entry numbers listed there, and use those numbers to find the program descriptions in the directory. Keep in mind that the numbers cited here refer to program entry numbers, not to page numbers in the book.

Undergraduates:

January: 26, 28, 33, 41, 43-44, 49, 58, 63-64, 78, 83-84, 93, 108, 114, 122, 127, 129, 139, 142, 148, 156, 160, 165, 171, 179, 194-196, 203, 206, 212, 214, 216-217, 219-220, 229-230, 237, 257, 269, 277, 288-289, 295, 315, 329-330, 333, 335, 350, 352-353, 359, 370, 382, 387-388, 394, 400, 402-403, 416, 421, 424, 439-441, 455-456, 463, 470-471, 475, 477, 494, 505, 511, 520, 522-523, 526, 528, 533, 537, 539, 546-548, 552, 556, 565-566, 573-574, 586

February: 1, 7, 23-24, 27, 29, 34, 40, 52, 59-60, 62, 67, 79, 87, 90, 96, 99, 111, 116, 128, 130-131, 138, 143, 147, 149, 151-154, 157, 159, 164, 176-178, 182, 186, 193, 218, 221, 226, 232, 235, 240, 245, 251, 253, 261, 268, 276, 280, 282, 300-301, 305, 308, 316-317, 325, 341, 343-344, 346-348, 357, 361, 368-369, 373-374, 377, 396, 401, 411-412, 430, 434, 438, 446-448, 451, 457, 474, 476, 488, 493, 500-501, 504, 510, 515, 517-519, 521, 524-525, 551, 567, 588, 592, 597, 599

March: 2, 9, 22, 36, 39, 48, 53-54, 56, 65, 68, 71, 73-74, 91-92, 101-107, 113, 117, 132, 134, 136, 161, 163, 168, 170, 175, 181, 183, 188, 192, 209-210, 227, 236, 242, 246-248, 252, 259, 263-265, 267, 273-274, 279, 287, 293, 309, 311-313, 318, 327, 334, 337, 340, 345, 351, 358, 360, 364, 372, 375, 381, 385, 391-392, 399, 405, 407-409, 413, 417, 420, 433, 436, 442, 444-445, 452, 459-461, 464-466, 472-473, 479-480, 483, 487, 490-491, 513, 527, 535, 544, 550, 557, 564, 568-570, 572, 575-576, 580, 596

April: 6, 10, 14, 16-18, 21, 47, 51, 61, 66, 76-77, 80, 86, 115, 119, 126, 133, 140, 145-146, 180, 199-200, 202, 205, 223, 225, 233-234, 238-239, 243, 258, 262, 266, 281, 284-285, 290-292, 294, 296, 303, 321-322, 338, 349, 356, 378, 383-384, 386, 398, 410, 418, 427-429, 431-432, 435, 437, 449, 453, 458, 462, 468, 485, 495-498, 503, 507, 516, 529, 532, 538, 554, 558, 560-561, 581-585, 587, 598

May: 19, 31-32, 37, 42, 50, 55, 81, 89, 95, 98, 118, 162, 169, 173-174, 184, 187, 189, 191, 222, 228, 255-256, 271-272, 283, 286, 297-298, 304, 306, 310, 324, 326, 336, 362, 393, 397, 406, 422, 469, 478, 481, 512, 562, 571

June: 38, 70, 135, 213, 215, 270, 320, 332, 342, 354, 363, 366-367, 467, 482, 484, 508, 514, 530, 540

July: 8, 125, 141, 167, 185, 201, 224, 299, 380, 536, 563, 578

August: 94, 100, 534

September: 30, 120, 389, 502, 577, 595

October: 5, 15, 85, 97, 109, 112, 123, 197, 250, 254, 307, 314, 319, 328, 379, 390, 415, 425, 454, 553

November: 35, 46, 57, 137, 144, 150, 260, 331, 355, 365, 486, 489, 509, 545, 555

December: 13, 45, 75, 88, 110, 121, 172, 204, 207-208, 211, 302, 371, 376, 395, 450, 499, 531, 542, 579

Any time: 4, 11-12, 190, 419, 543, 594

Deadline not specified: 3, 20, 25, 69, 72, 82, 124, 155, 158, 166, 198, 231, 241, 244, 249, 275, 278, 323, 339, 404, 414, 423, 426, 443, 492, 506, 541, 549, 559, 589-591, 593

Graduate Students:

January: 608, 619, 627, 631, 638, 640-641, 657-660, 679, 681, 683, 690, 693, 696, 701, 704, 706, 716, 722, 728, 733, 736-737, 739-740, 759, 765, 767-771, 774, 780, 782, 810, 816, 820, 835, 839, 843-844, 847, 855, 860, 863-864, 867, 887, 889, 895, 898, 901, 905, 914-915, 920, 926, 928, 932, 938, 955, 959-960, 964, 967, 971, 973, 983-984, 1005, 1009, 1018-1019, 1028-1029, 1033, 1035, 1039, 1041-1042, 1045, 1052, 1057, 1059, 1062, 1066, 1077

February: 605, 609-611, 614, 621-622, 625, 628-629, 645, 649, 653, 674, 676, 680, 694-695, 703, 707, 711, 717, 724, 727, 749, 757, 766, 773, 775, 783, 800, 826-828, 833, 838, 841-842, 850, 852-854, 868-869, 874, 884, 886, 897, 906, 911-913, 916, 923, 941, 943, 948-950, 952, 968, 970, 976, 979, 985, 993, 1011, 1020, 1024-1026, 1032, 1048, 1054, 1064, 1067, 1069, 1074

March: 601-602, 606, 612, 648, 656, 665-666, 673, 688, 734, 738, 741, 751-752, 762-764, 772, 781, 784, 793, 812, 817, 819, 823-824, 837, 845, 848-849, 876-877, 892, 894, 900, 904, 909-910, 922, 925, 935, 942, 944, 953, 961, 978, 980, 988, 990, 995, 1004, 1013-1014, 1016, 1027, 1034, 1060-1061, 1068, 1070

April: 600, 603, 615-616, 618, 620, 630, 664, 668-669, 672, 685, 692, 697-700, 705, 709, 729, 735, 754, 756, 760, 792, 796, 807, 809, 813, 822, 829, 836, 856-858, 861, 875, 883, 891, 893, 919, 921, 954, 965-966, 969, 986, 994, 996-997, 999-1001, 1007-1008, 1010, 1017, 1036, 1038, 1043-1044, 1051, 1055-1056, 1058, 1065, 1071-1072, 1078

May: 604, 607, 633, 637, 647, 686, 732, 744, 747, 776, 794, 803, 831-832, 851, 859, 870-871, 878-879, 885, 927, 929-931, 947, 956, 962, 992, 1079

13/12

FOR REFERENCE
Do Not Take From This Room